# Ken Akamatsu

TRANSLATED & ADAPTED BY
Alethea Nibley & Athena Nibley


LETTERING AND RETOUCH BY
Steve Palmer

KC
KODANSHA
COMICS

A Kodansha Comics Trade Paperback Original.

Published in the United States by Kodansha Comics, an imprint of Kodansha USA Publishing, LLC, New York.

Publication rights for this English edition arranged through Kodansha Ltd., Tokyo.

First published in Japan in 2008 by Kodansha Ltd., Tokyo, as *Maho sensei Negima!* volumes 22, 23 and 24.

ISBN 978-1-61262-272-9

Printed in the United States of America.

www.kodanshacomics.com

9 8 7 6 5 4 3 2 1

Translator & Adaptor: Alethea Nibley & Athena Nibley
Lettering: Steve Palmer

# CONTENTS

# A Word from the Author

I bring you *Negima!* volume 22. There was kind of a lot of eros in the last volume (^^;). But I've repented of that, so this time we're focusing on *battles*!

In order to defeat his arch-nemesis, Fate, Negi decides to train under a new master. Will he really be able to master such a powerful finishing move!?

And what is dark magic, really!?

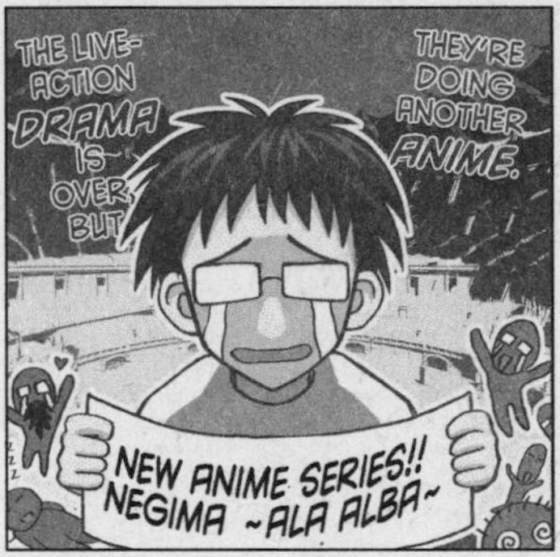
THEY'RE DOING ANOTHER ANIME.
THE LIVE-ACTION DRAMA IS OVER, BUT
NEW ANIME SERIES!! NEGIMA ~ALA ALBA~

Now, another new anime is about to begin!

First, the next three volumes, starting with volume 23, will have limited editions that come with DVDs! (*For preorder only)

This time, they're staying true to the original and animating the manga's summer vacation arc. The theme song will be *that* song. Please look forward to it!

Ken Akamatsu
www.ailove.net

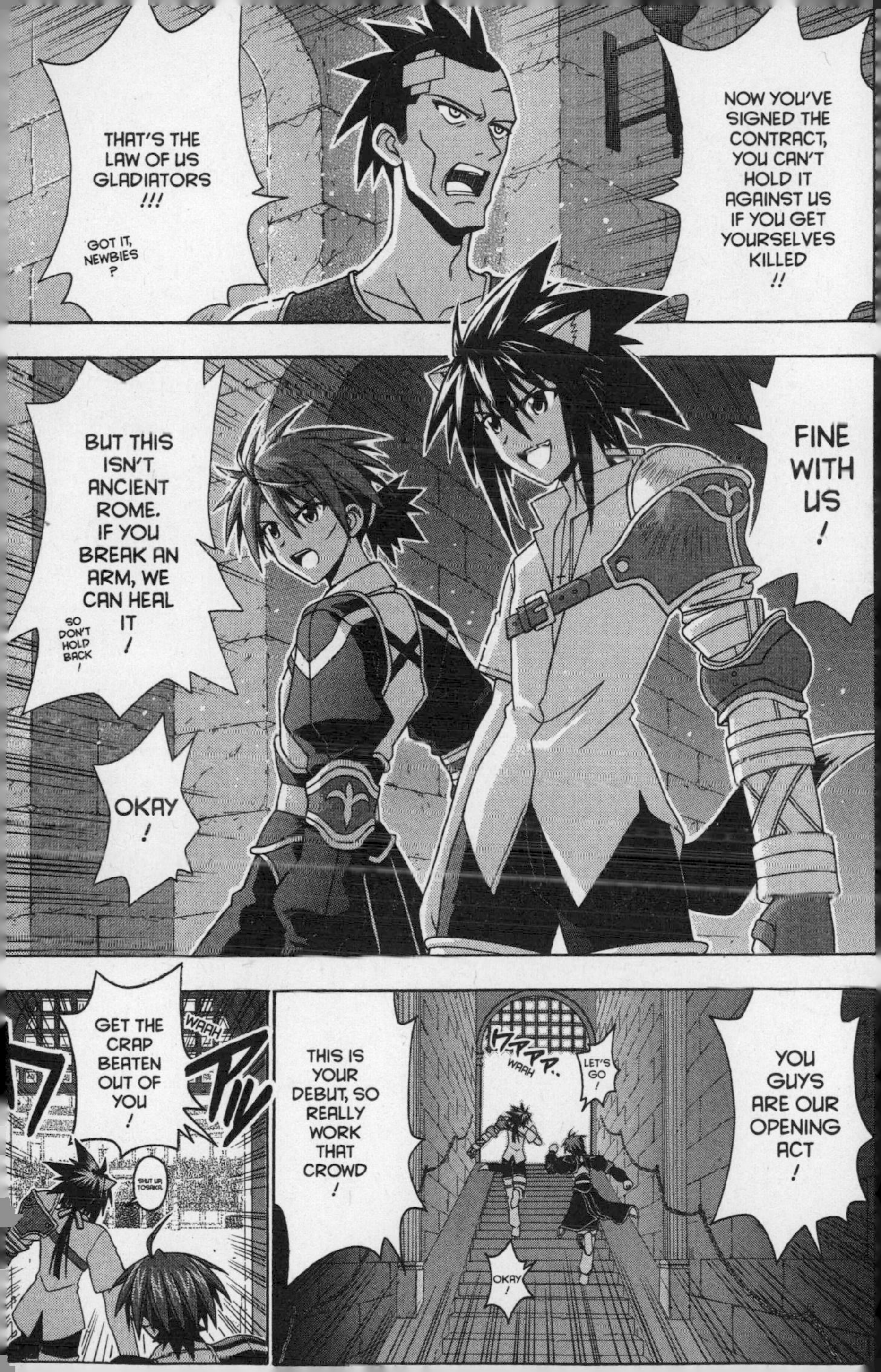
NOW YOU'VE SIGNED THE CONTRACT, YOU CAN'T HOLD IT AGAINST US IF YOU GET YOURSELVES KILLED!!
THAT'S THE LAW OF US GLADIATORS!!!
GOT IT, NEWBIES?
FINE WITH US!
BUT THIS ISN'T ANCIENT ROME. IF YOU BREAK AN ARM, WE CAN HEAL IT!
SO DON'T HOLD BACK!
OKAY!
YOU GUYS ARE OUR OPENING ACT!
WAAH
LET'S GO!
THIS IS YOUR DEBUT, SO REALLY WORK THAT CROWD!
OKAY!
WAAH
GET THE CRAP BEATEN OUT OF YOU!
SHUT UP, TOSAKA.

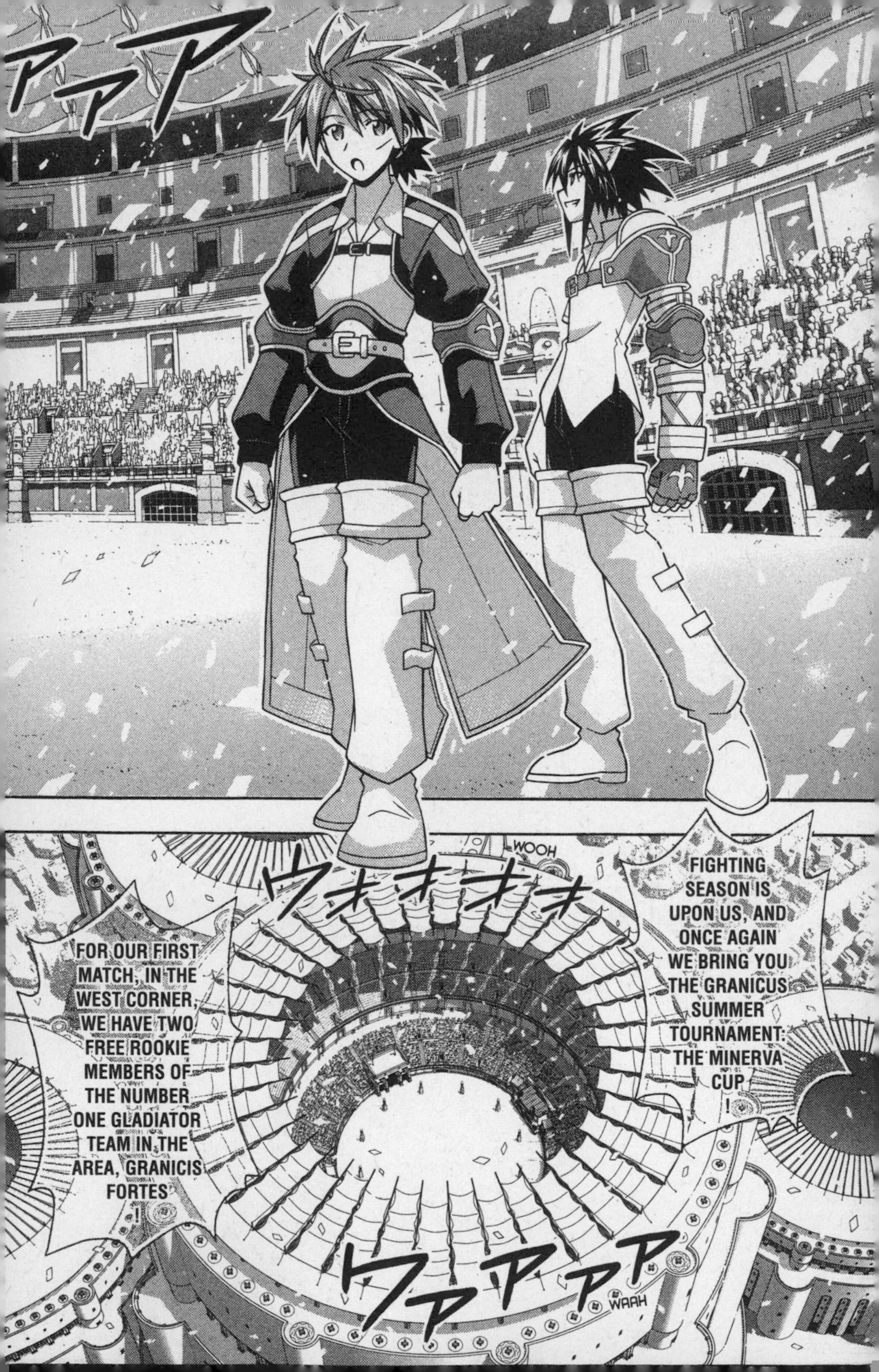
アァア
ウォォォォ
WOOH
FIGHTING SEASON IS UPON US, AND ONCE AGAIN WE BRING YOU THE GRANICUS SUMMER TOURNAMENT: THE MINERVA CUP!
FOR OUR FIRST MATCH, IN THE WEST CORNER, WE HAVE TWO FREE ROOKIE MEMBERS OF THE NUMBER ONE GLADIATOR TEAM IN THE AREA, GRANICIS FORTES!
ワァァァ
WAAH

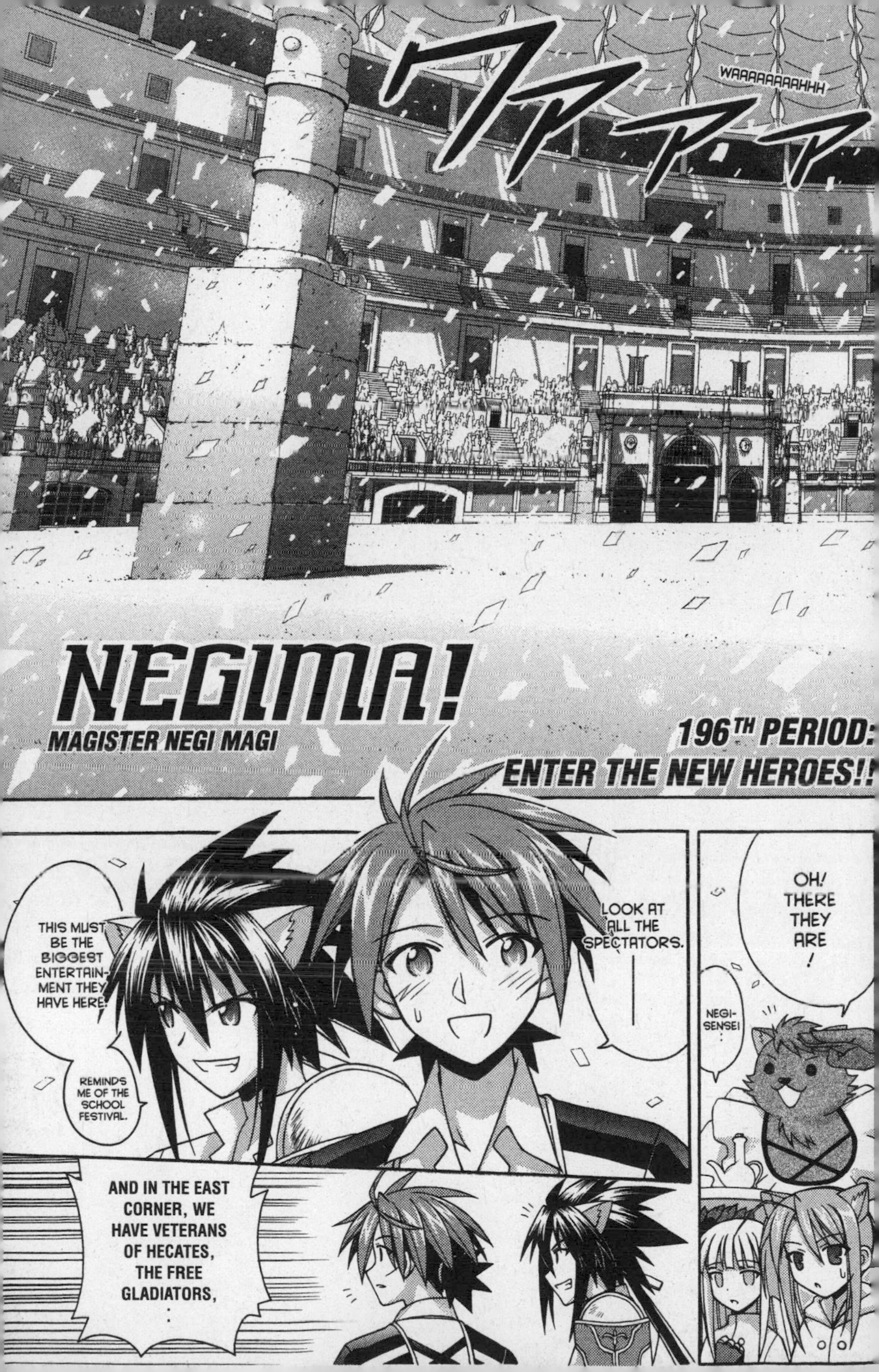
WAAAAAAAAHHH
NEGIMA!
MAGISTER NEGI MAGI
196TH PERIOD: ENTER THE NEW HEROES!!
OH! THERE THEY ARE!
NEGI-SENSEI...
LOOK AT ALL THE SPECTATORS.
THIS MUST BE THE BIGGEST ENTERTAINMENT THEY HAVE HERE.
REMINDS ME OF THE SCHOOL FESTIVAL.
AND IN THE EAST CORNER, WE HAVE VETERANS OF HECATES, THE FREE GLADIATORS, ...

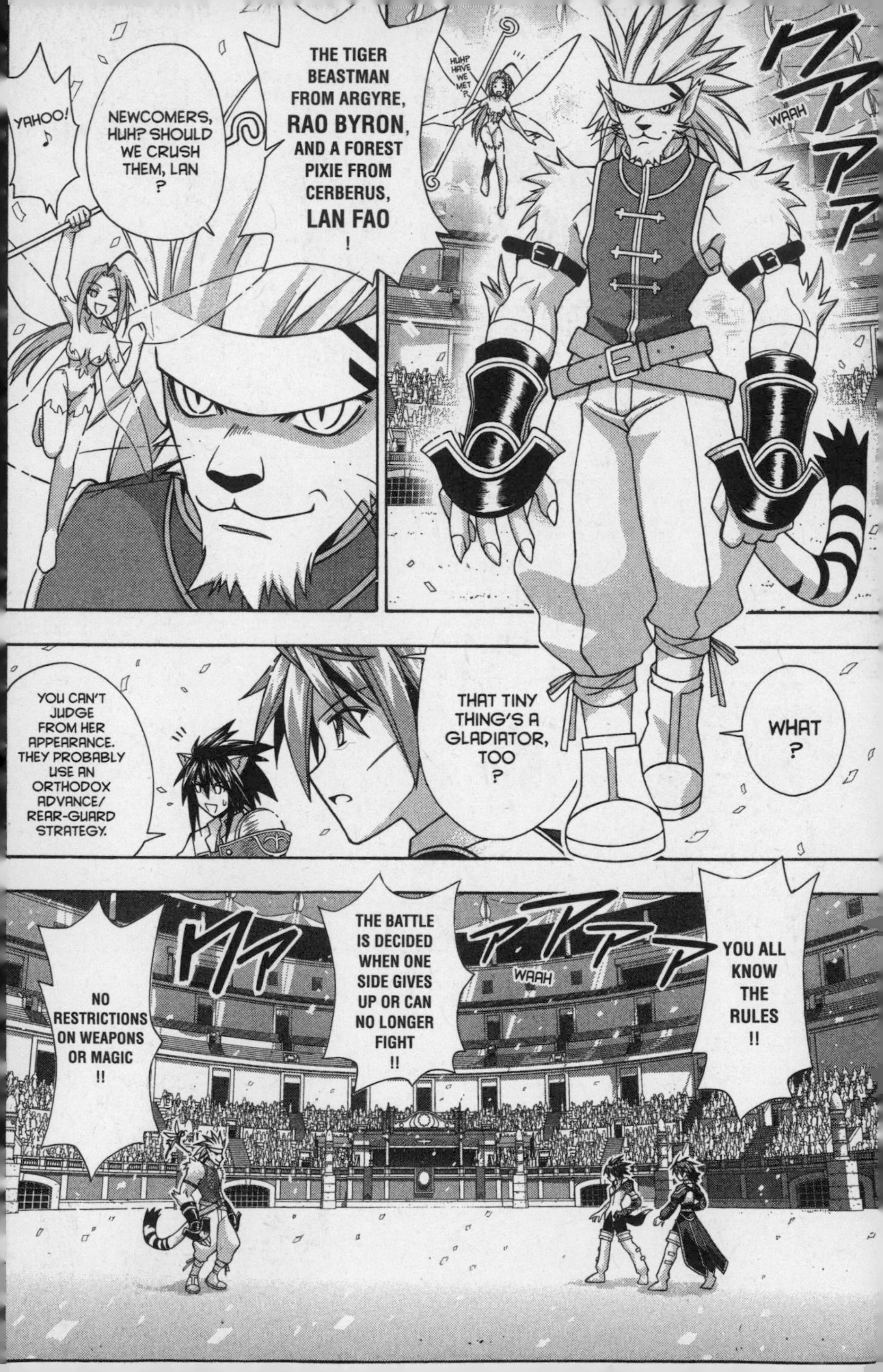
WAAH
THE TIGER BEASTMAN FROM ARGYRE, RAO BYRON, AND A FOREST PIXIE FROM CERBERUS, LAN FAO!
HUHP HAVE WE MET?
NEWCOMERS, HUH? SHOULD WE CRUSH THEM, LAN?
YAHOO! ♪
WHAT?
THAT TINY THING'S A GLADIATOR, TOO?
YOU CAN'T JUDGE FROM HER APPEARANCE. THEY PROBABLY USE AN ORTHODOX ADVANCE/REAR-GUARD STRATEGY.
YOU ALL KNOW THE RULES!!
WAAH
THE BATTLE IS DECIDED WHEN ONE SIDE GIVES UP OR CAN NO LONGER FIGHT!!
NO RESTRICTIONS ON WEAPONS OR MAGIC!!

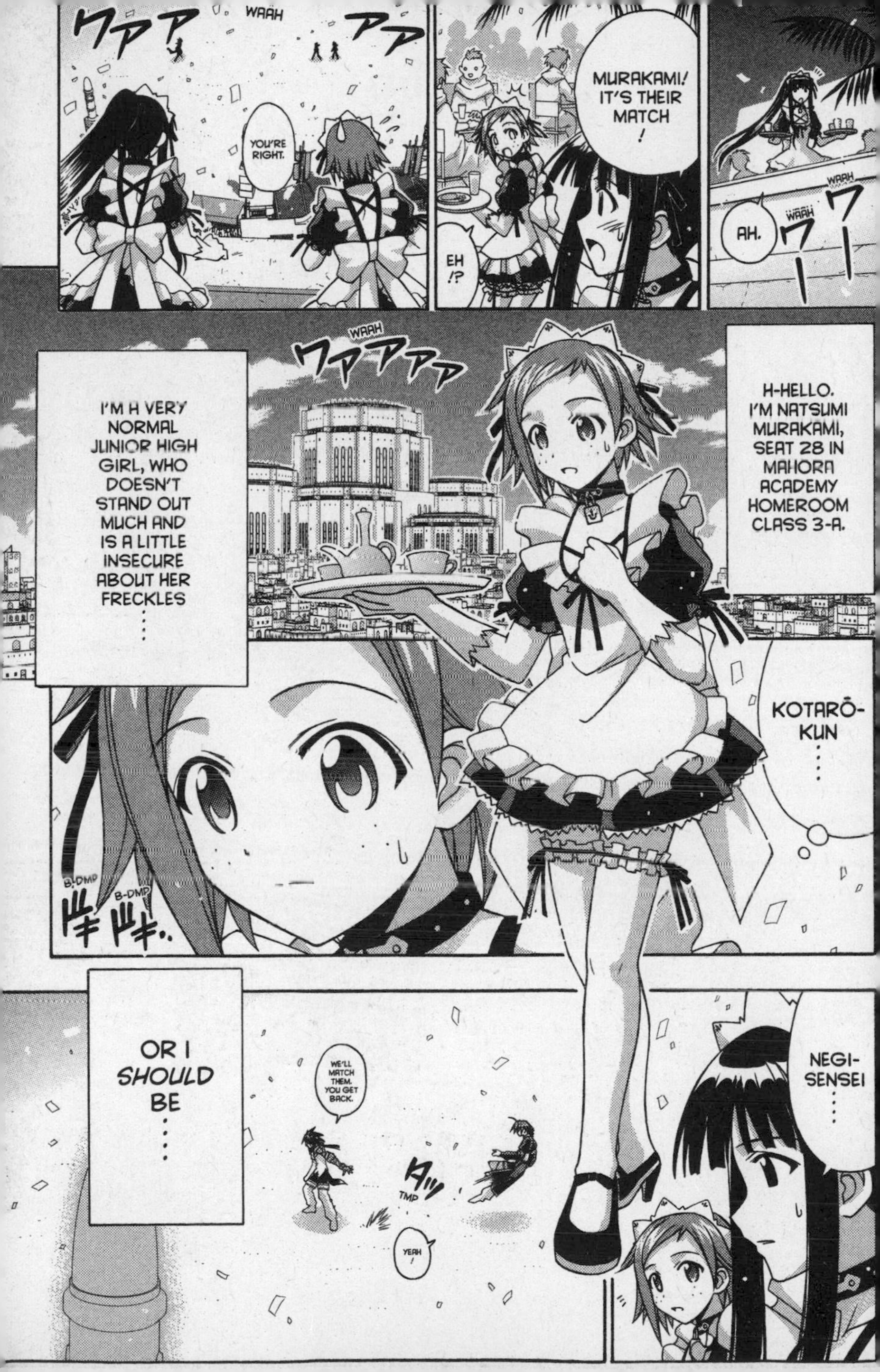
WAAH
WAAH
AH.
MURAKAMI! IT'S THEIR MATCH!
EH!?
WAAH
YOU'RE RIGHT.
H-HELLO. I'M NATSUMI MURAKAMI, SEAT 28 IN MAHORA ACADEMY HOMEROOM CLASS 3-A.
WAAH
I'M A VERY NORMAL JUNIOR HIGH GIRL, WHO DOESN'T STAND OUT MUCH AND IS A LITTLE INSECURE ABOUT HER FRECKLES ...
KOTARŌ-KUN ...
B-DMP
B-DMP
NEGI-SENSEI ...
WE'LL MATCH THEM. YOU GET BACK.
TMP
YEAH!
OR I SHOULD BE ...

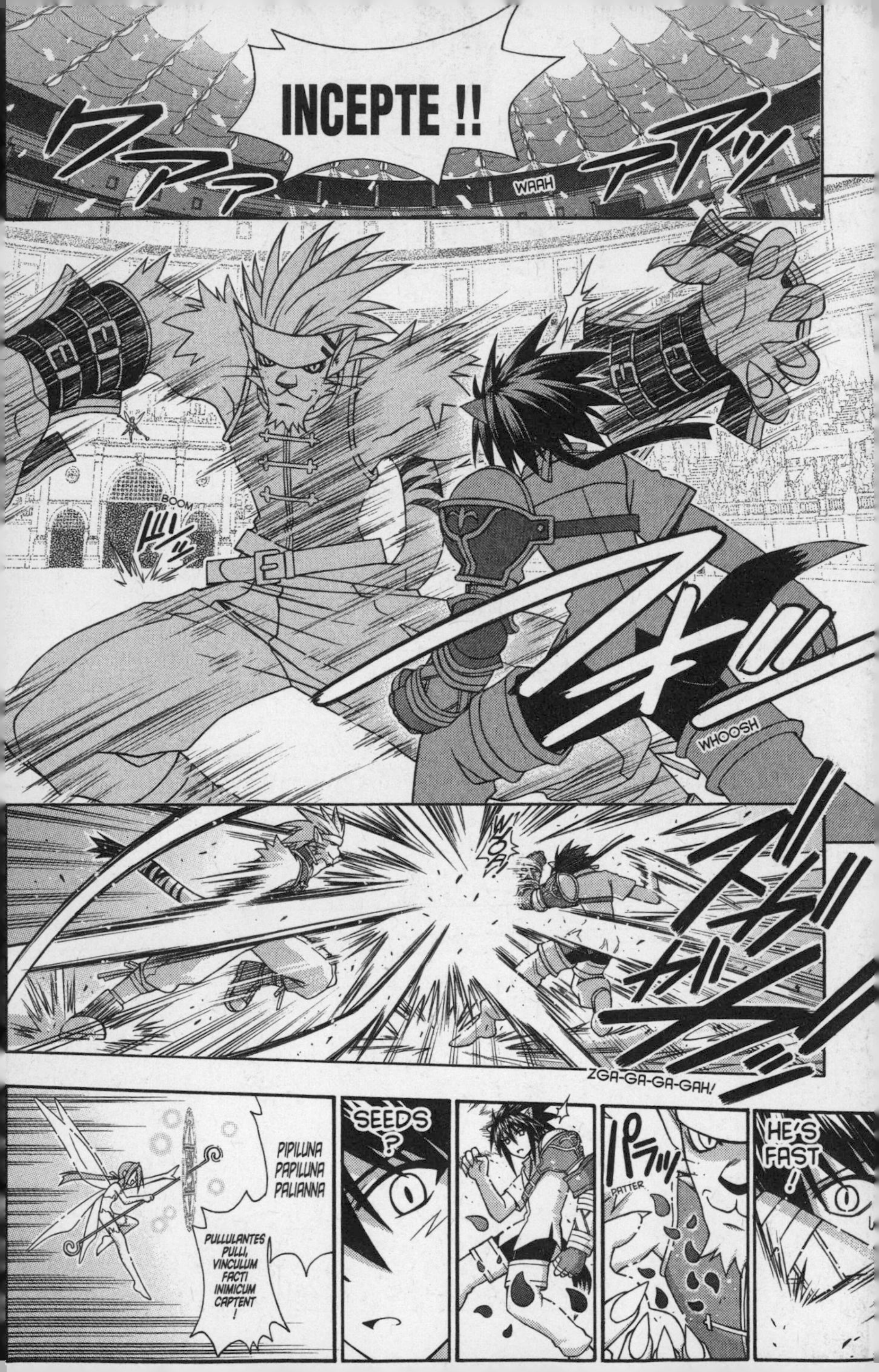
INCEPTE !!
WAAH
BOOM
WHOOSH
WOA!
ZGA-GA-GA-GAH!
HE'S FAST!
PATTER
SEEDS?
PIPILUNA PAPILUNA PALIANNA
PULLULANTES PULLI, VINCULUM FACTI INIMICUM CAPTENT!

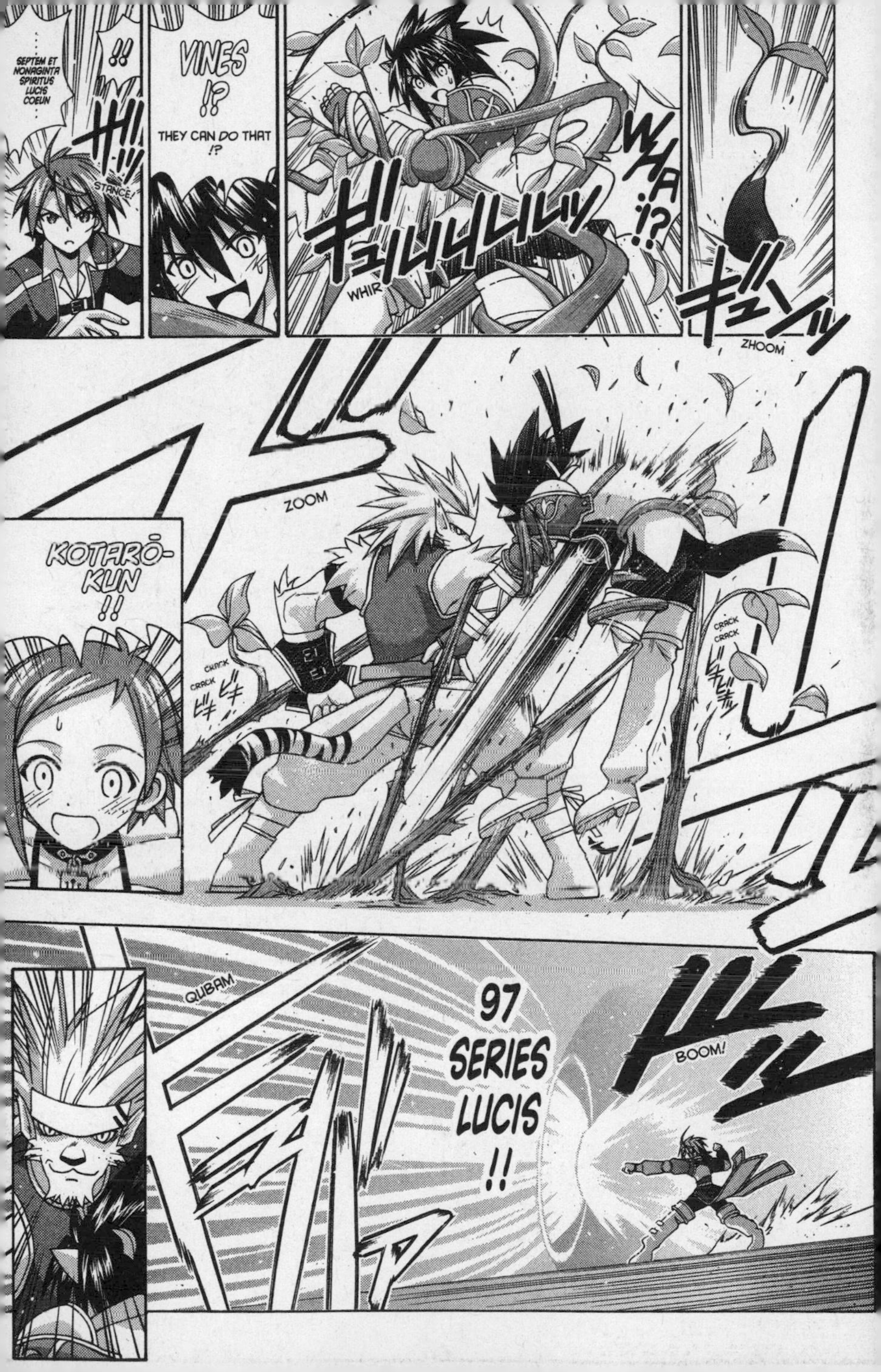
ZHOOM
WHA !?
WHIR
VINES !?
THEY CAN DO THAT !?
!!
SEPTEM ET NONAGINTA SPIRITUS LUCIS COEUN
STANCE!
ZOOM
CRACK CRACK
CRACK CRACK
KOTARŌ-KUN !!
BOOM!
97 SERIES LUCIS !!
QUBAM

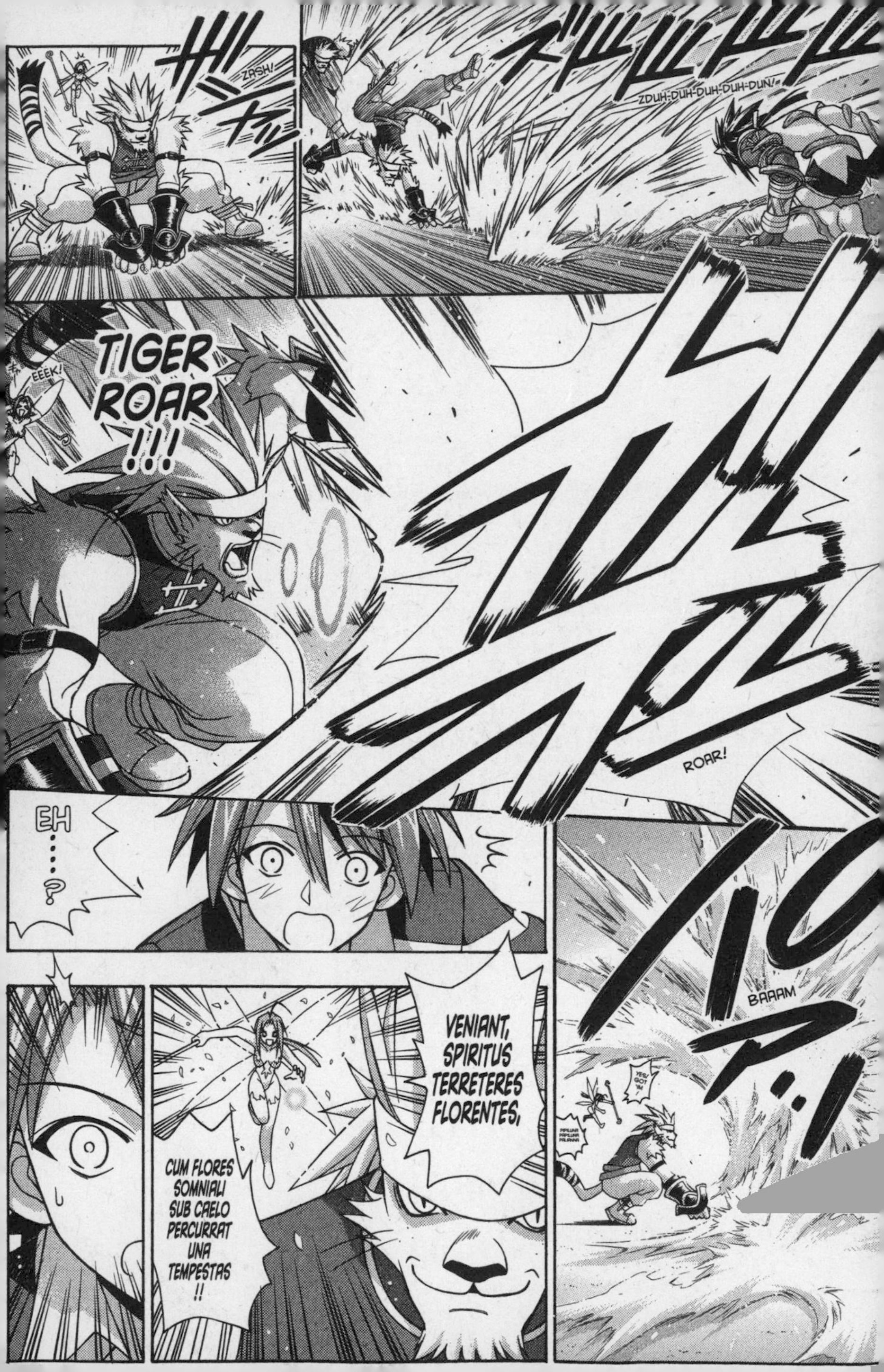
ZDUH-DUH-DUH-DUH-DUN!
ZASH!
TIGER ROAR !!!
EEEK!
ROAR!
BAAAM
YES! GOT 'EM!
EH....?
VENIANT, SPIRITUS TERRETERES FLORENTES,
CUM FLORES SOMNIALI SUB CAELO PERCURRAT UNA TEMPESTAS !!

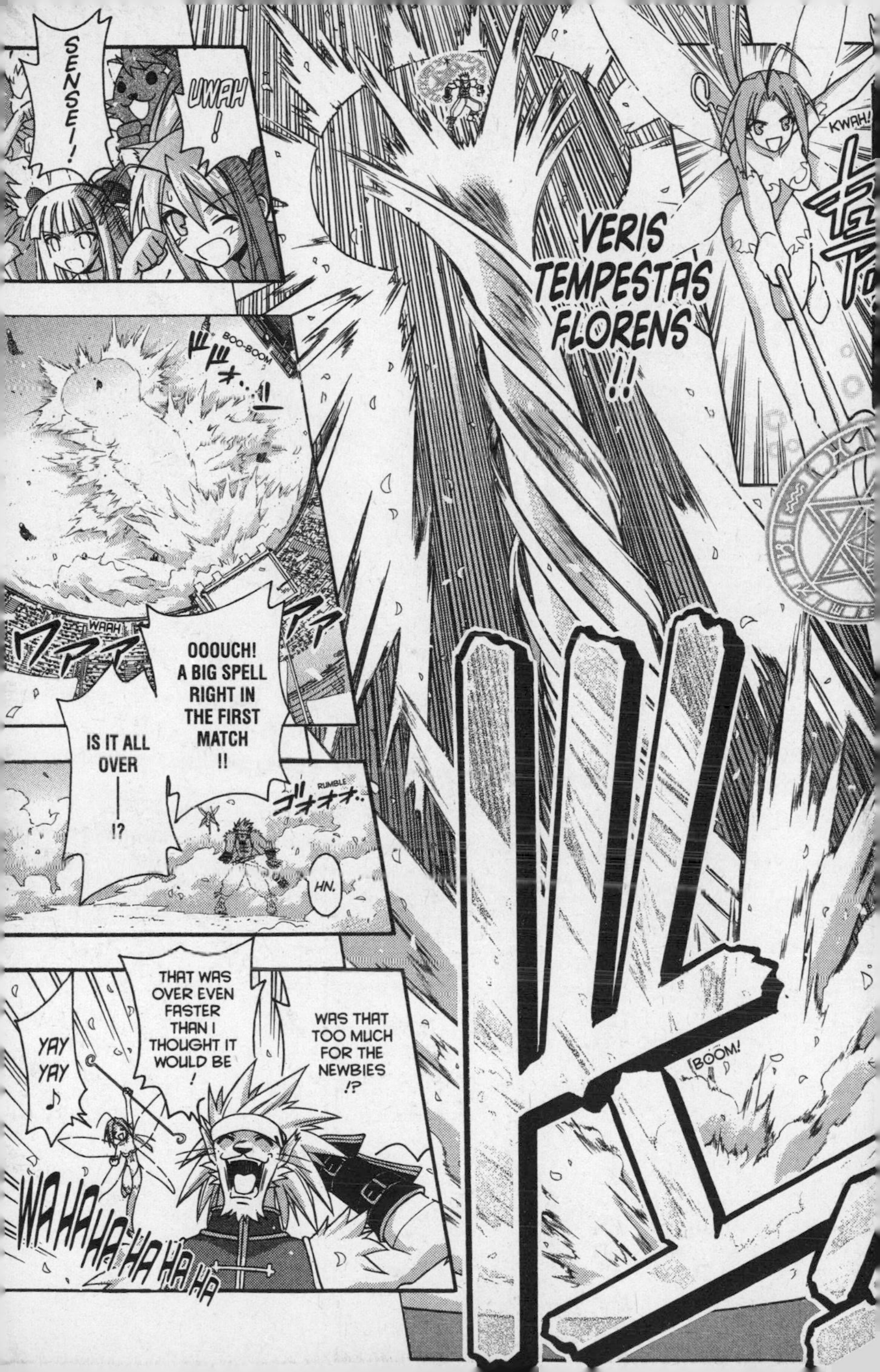
KWAH!
VERIS TEMPESTAS FLORENS !!
BOOM!
UWAH !
SENSEI!!
BOO-BOOM
WAAH
OOOUCH! A BIG SPELL RIGHT IN THE FIRST MATCH !!
IS IT ALL OVER —— !?
RUMBLE
HN.
WAS THAT TOO MUCH FOR THE NEWBIES !?
THAT WAS OVER EVEN FASTER THAN I THOUGHT IT WOULD BE !
YAY YAY ♪
WA HA HA HA HA HA HA

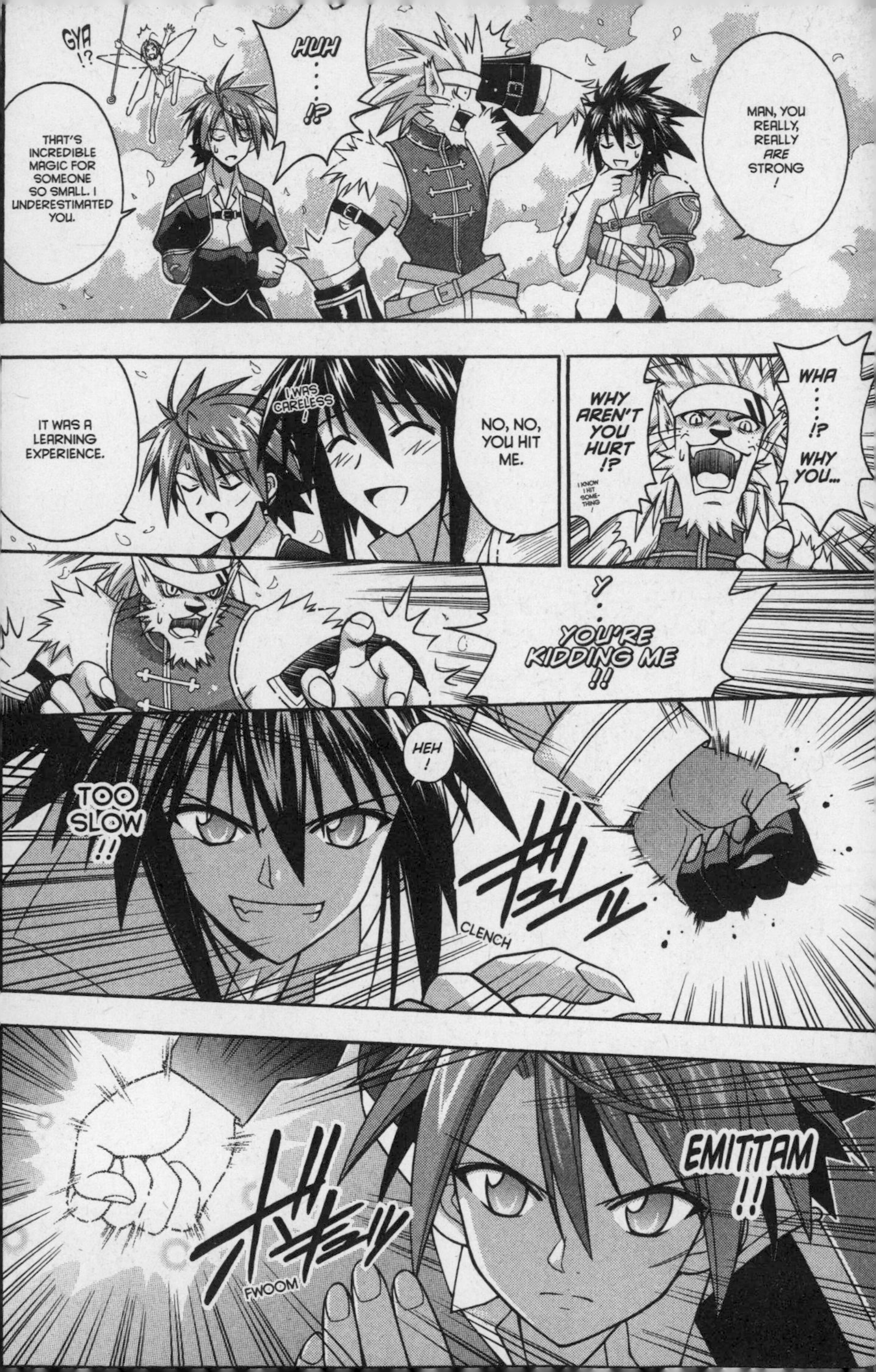
MAN, YOU REALLY, REALLY ARE STRONG!
HUH...!?
GYA!?
THAT'S INCREDIBLE MAGIC FOR SOMEONE SO SMALL. I UNDERESTIMATED YOU.
WHA...!? WHY YOU...
WHY AREN'T YOU HURT!?
I KNOW I HIT SOMETHING!
NO, NO, YOU HIT ME.
I WAS CARELESS!
IT WAS A LEARNING EXPERIENCE.
Y... YOU'RE KIDDING ME!!
HEH!
CLENCH
TOO SLOW!!
EMITTAM!!
FWOOM

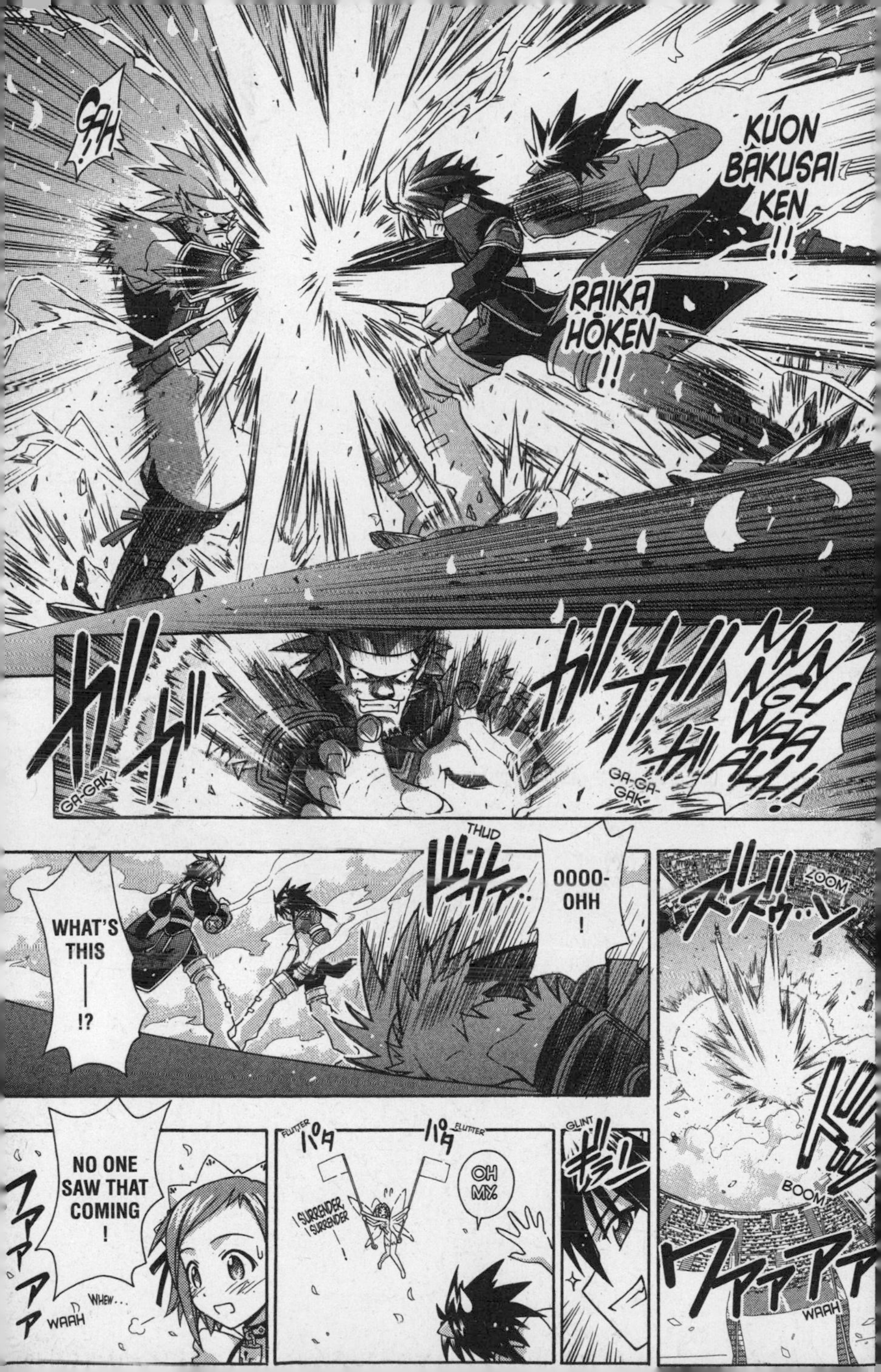

KUON BAKUSAI KEN!!
RAIKA HÖKEN!!
GAH!?
NNNNGH WAAAHH!!
GA-GA-GAK
GA-GAK
ZOOM
BOOM
WAAH
THUD
OOOO-OHH!
WHAT'S THIS —!?
GLINT
OH MY.
FLUTTER
FLUTTER
I SURRENDER, I SURRENDER!
NO ONE SAW THAT COMING!
WHEW...
WAAH

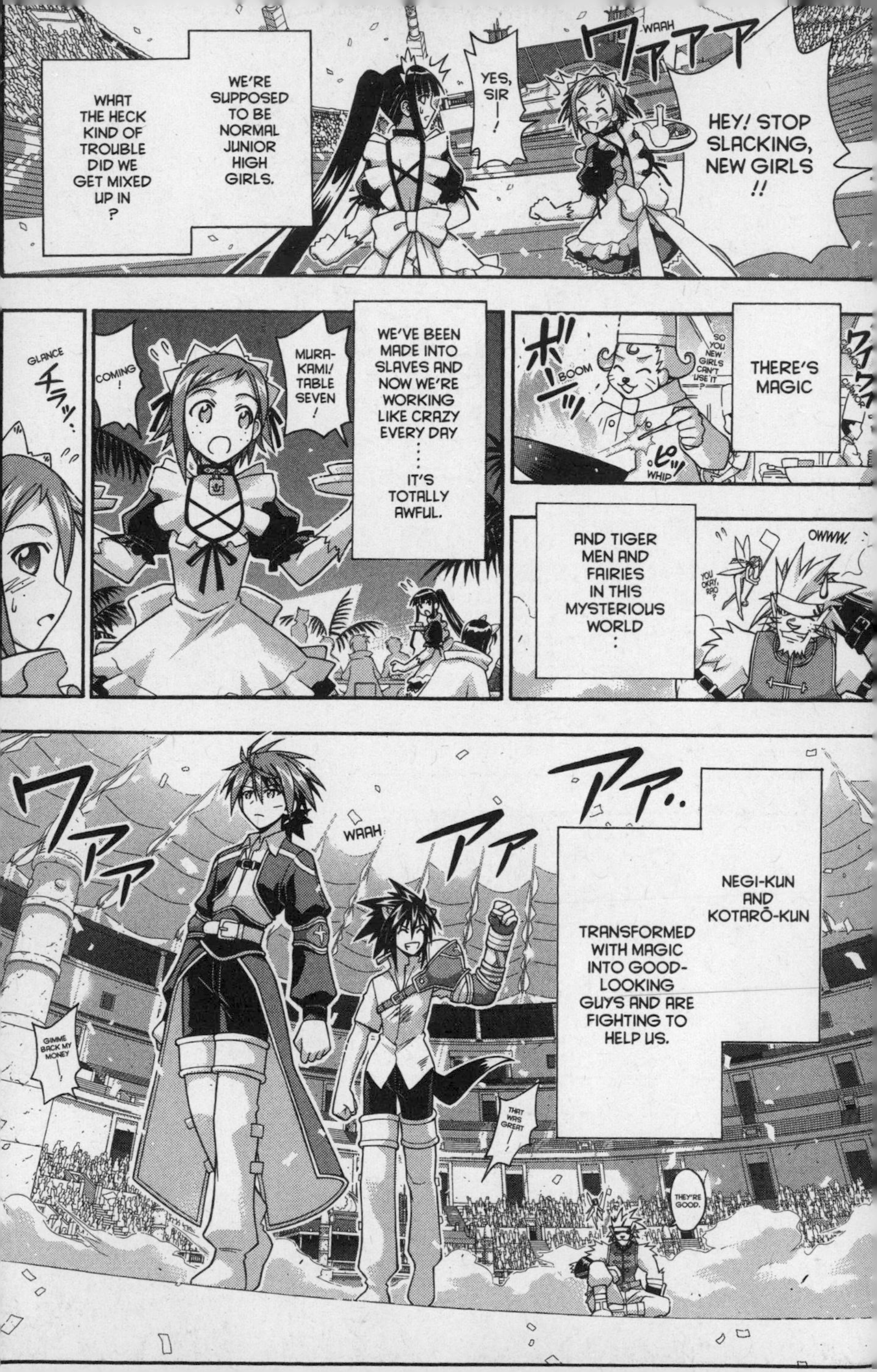
ワァアア
WAAH
HEY! STOP SLACKING, NEW GIRLS!!
YES, SIR!
WE'RE SUPPOSED TO BE NORMAL JUNIOR HIGH GIRLS.
WHAT THE HECK KIND OF TROUBLE DID WE GET MIXED UP IN?
CLAMOR CLAMOR
THERE'S MAGIC
SO YOU NEW GIRLS CAN'T USE IT?
BOOM
WHIP
OWWW.
YOU OKAY, RAO?
AND TIGER MEN AND FAIRIES IN THIS MYSTERIOUS WORLD...
WE'VE BEEN MADE INTO SLAVES AND NOW WE'RE WORKING LIKE CRAZY EVERY DAY.... IT'S TOTALLY AWFUL.
MURA-KAMI! TABLE SEVEN!
COMING!
GLANCE
NEGI-KUN AND KOTARŌ-KUN
TRANSFORMED WITH MAGIC INTO GOOD-LOOKING GUYS AND ARE FIGHTING TO HELP US.
WAAH
THEY'RE GOOD.
THAT WAS GREAT!
GIMME BACK MY MONEY!

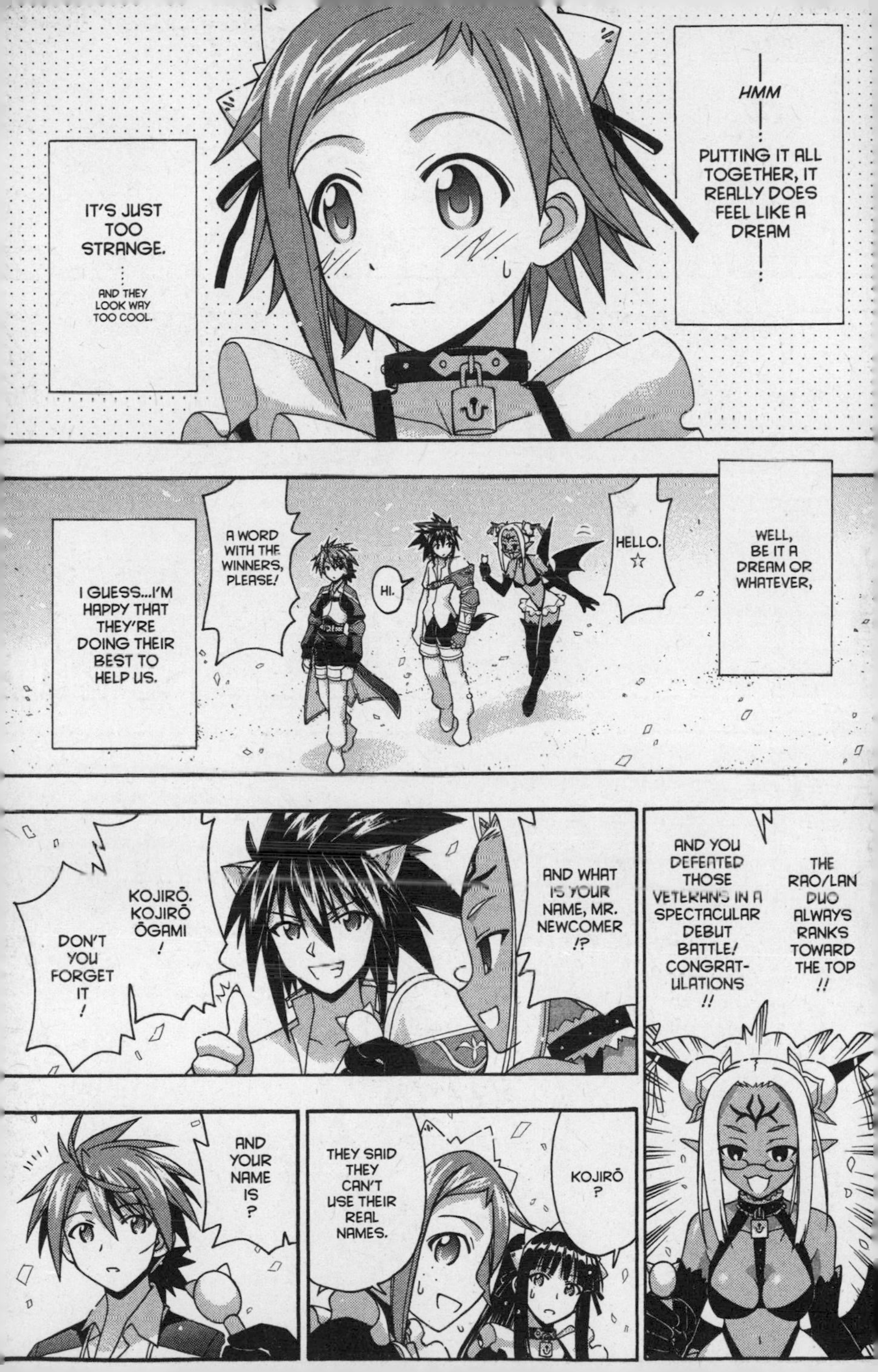
HMM
PUTTING IT ALL TOGETHER, IT REALLY DOES FEEL LIKE A DREAM
IT'S JUST TOO STRANGE.
AND THEY LOOK WAY TOO COOL.
WELL, BE IT A DREAM OR WHATEVER,
HELLO. ☆
A WORD WITH THE WINNERS, PLEASE!
HI.
I GUESS...I'M HAPPY THAT THEY'RE DOING THEIR BEST TO HELP US.
THE RAO/LAN DUO ALWAYS RANKS TOWARD THE TOP!!
AND YOU DEFEATED THOSE VETERANS IN A SPECTACULAR DEBUT BATTLE! CONGRATULATIONS!!
AND WHAT IS YOUR NAME, MR. NEWCOMER!?
KOJIRŌ. KOJIRŌ ŌGAMI!
DON'T YOU FORGET IT!
KOJIRŌ?
THEY SAID THEY CAN'T USE THEIR REAL NAMES.
AND YOUR NAME IS?

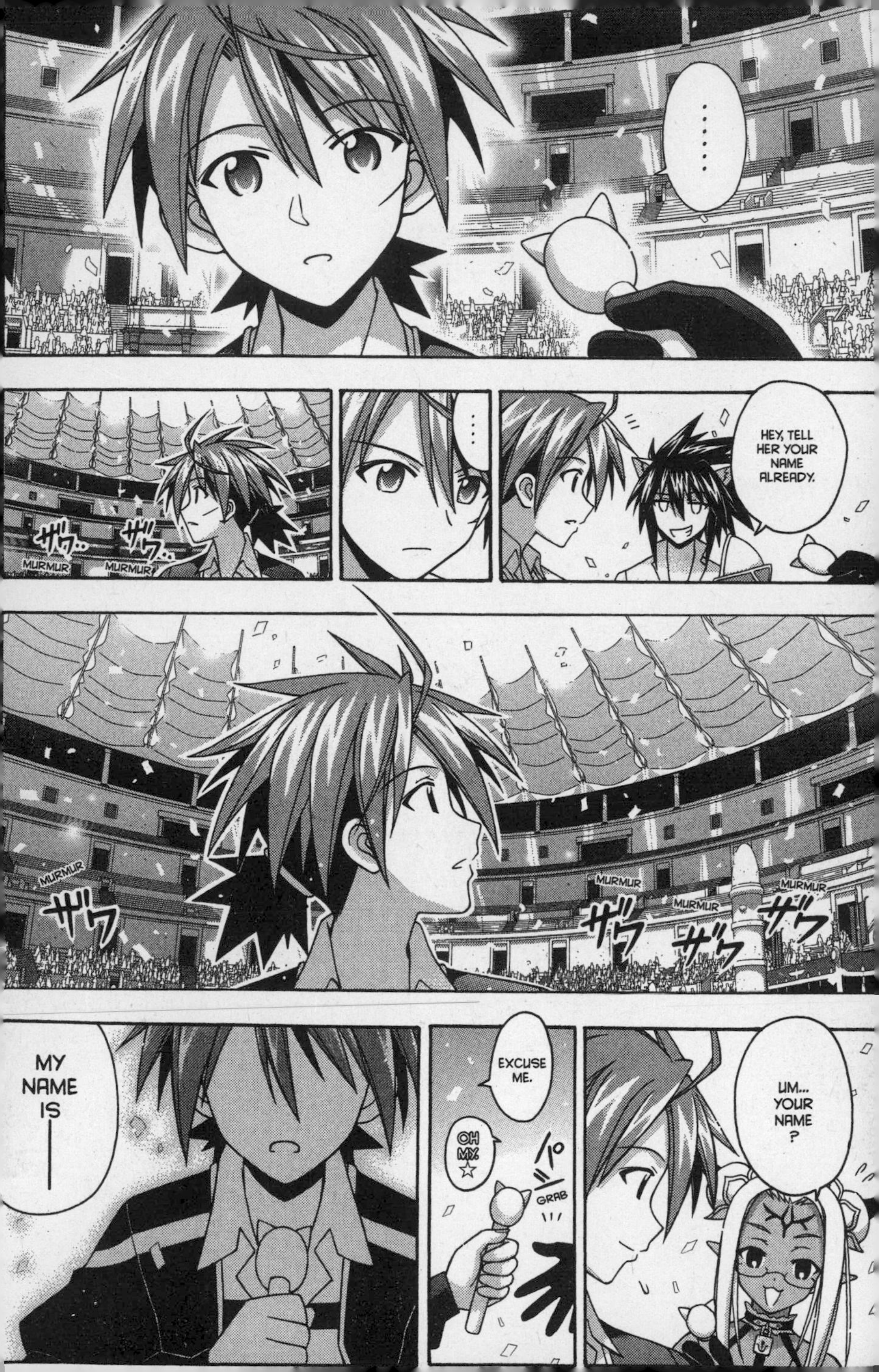
......
HEY, TELL HER YOUR NAME ALREADY.
....
ザワ MURMUR
ザワ MURMUR
MURMUR ザワ
MURMUR ザワ
MURMUR ザワ
MURMUR ザワ
UM... YOUR NAME?
EXCUSE ME.
OH MY. ☆
GRAB
MY NAME IS—

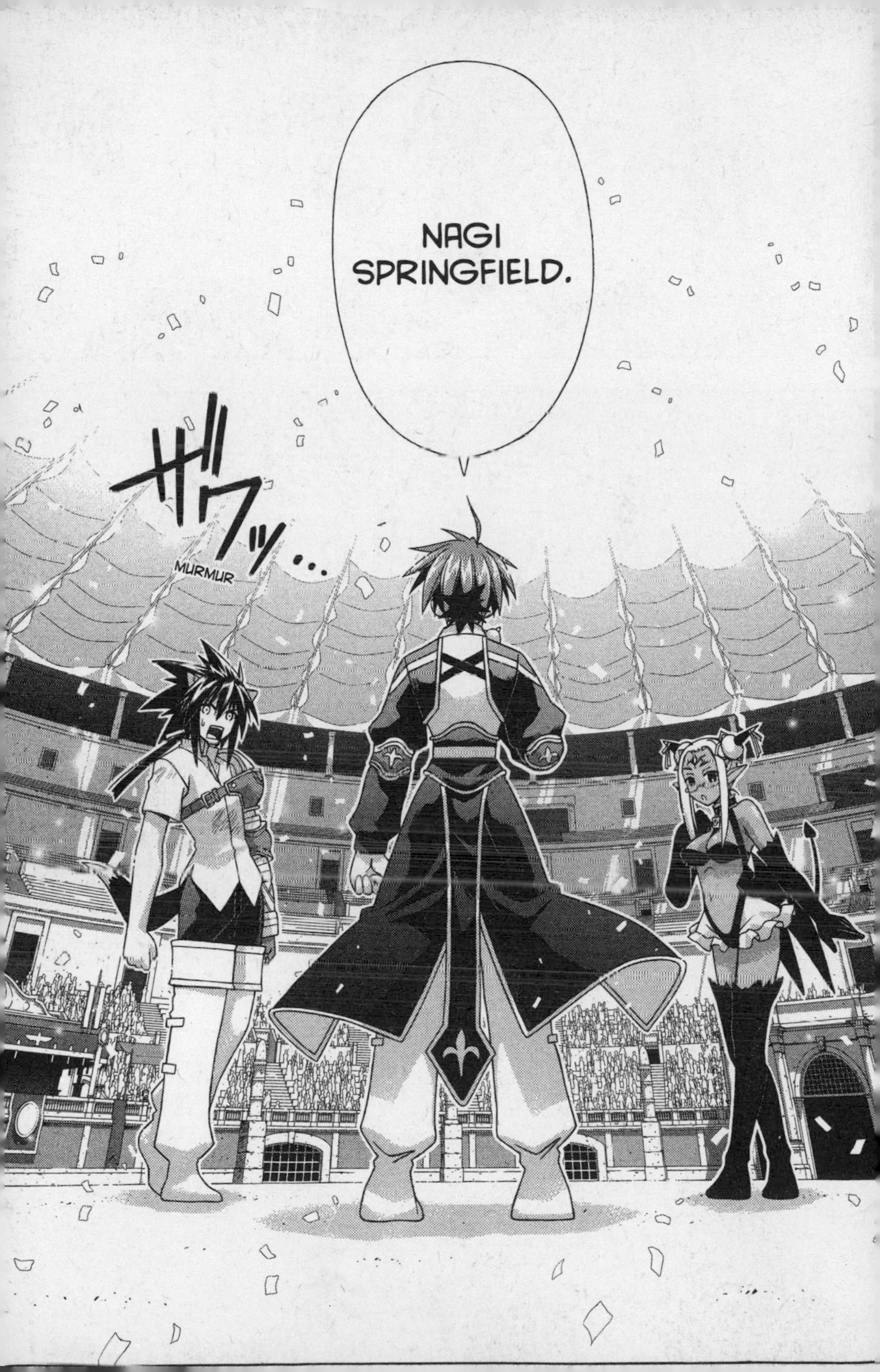
NAGI SPRINGFIELD.
ザワッ...
MURMUR

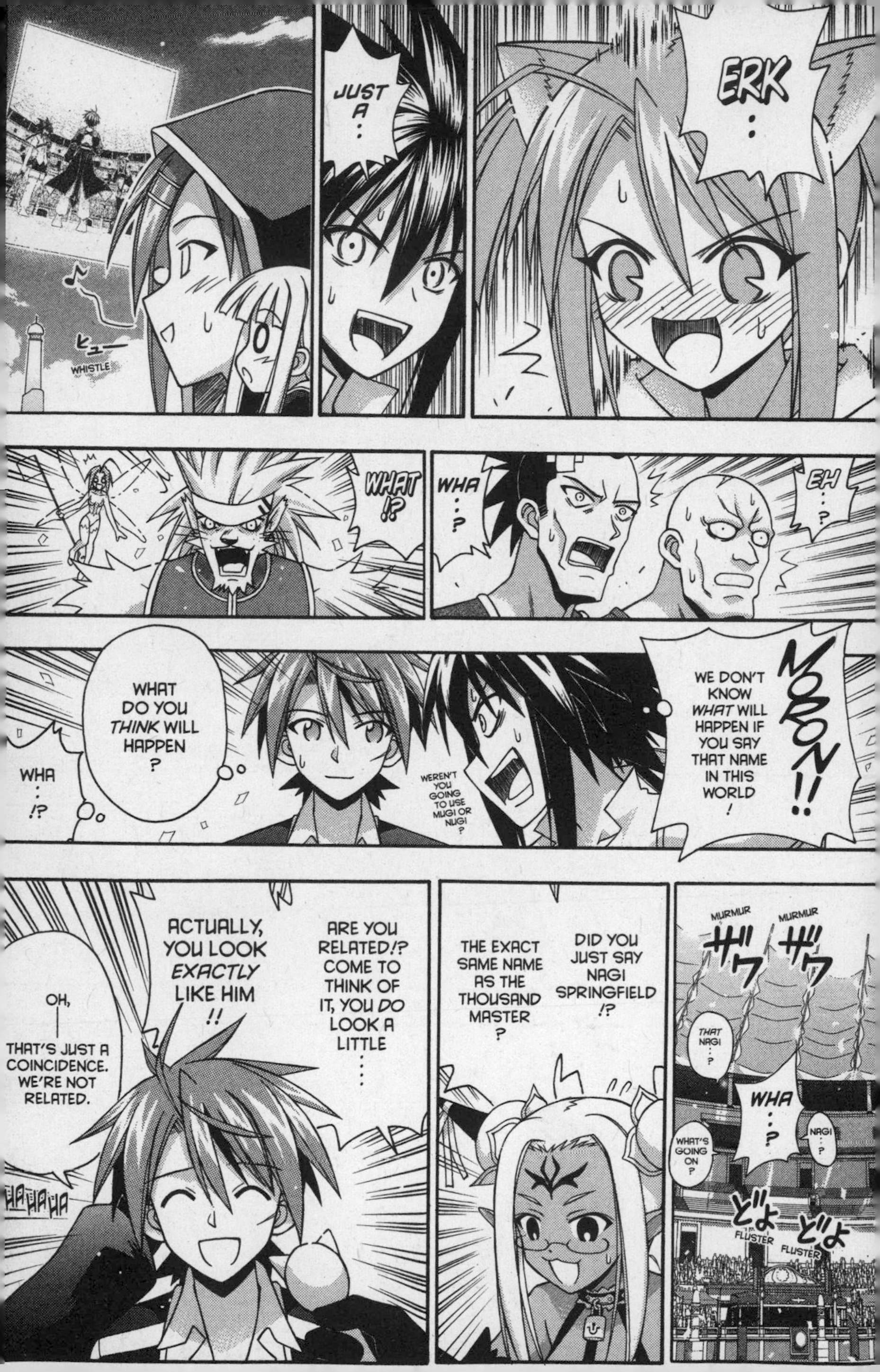
ERK...
JUST A...
ヒュー
WHISTLE
EH...?
WHA...?
WHAT!?
MORON!!
WE DON'T KNOW *WHAT* WILL HAPPEN IF YOU SAY THAT NAME IN THIS WORLD!
WEREN'T YOU GOING TO USE MUGI OR NUGI?
WHAT DO YOU *THINK* WILL HAPPEN?
WHA...!?
ザワ
MURMUR
ザワ
MURMUR
THAT NAGI...?
WHA...?
NAGI...?
WHAT'S GOING ON?
どよ
FLUSTER
どよ
FLUSTER
DID YOU JUST SAY NAGI SPRINGFIELD!?
THE EXACT SAME NAME AS THE THOUSAND MASTER?
ARE YOU RELATED!? COME TO THINK OF IT, YOU *DO* LOOK A LITTLE...
ACTUALLY, YOU LOOK *EXACTLY* LIKE HIM!!
OH, THAT'S JUST A COINCIDENCE. WE'RE NOT RELATED.
HA HA HA

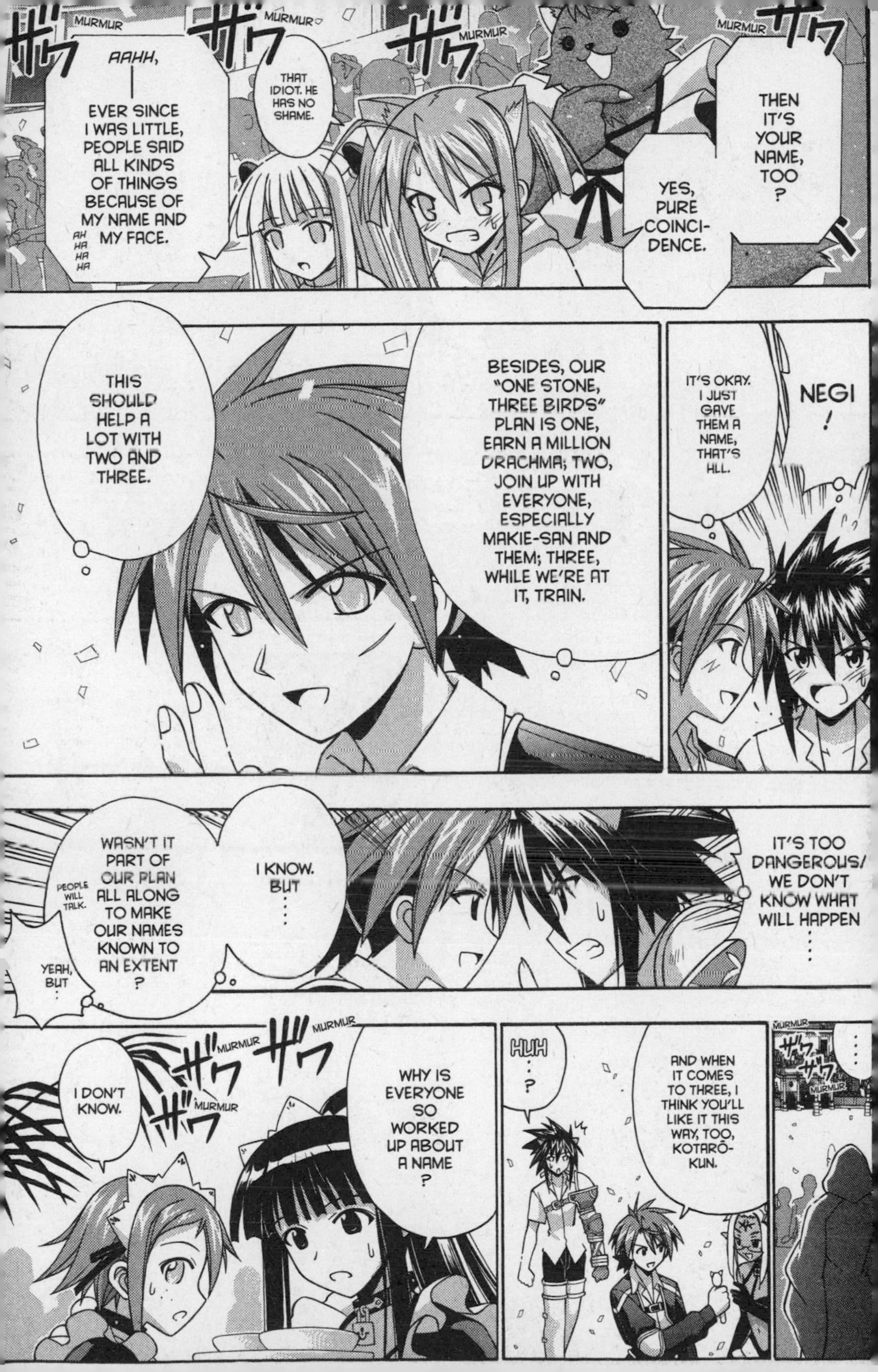
ザワ
MURMUR
THEN IT'S YOUR NAME, TOO?
YES, PURE COINCIDENCE.
ザワ
MURMUR
THAT IDIOT. HE HAS NO SHAME.
ザワ
MURMUR
AAHH, — EVER SINCE I WAS LITTLE, PEOPLE SAID ALL KINDS OF THINGS BECAUSE OF MY NAME AND MY FACE.
AH HA HA HA
NEGI!
IT'S OKAY. I JUST GAVE THEM A NAME, THAT'S ALL.
BESIDES, OUR "ONE STONE, THREE BIRDS" PLAN IS ONE, EARN A MILLION DRACHMA; TWO, JOIN UP WITH EVERYONE, ESPECIALLY MAKIE-SAN AND THEM; THREE, WHILE WE'RE AT IT, TRAIN.
THIS SHOULD HELP A LOT WITH TWO AND THREE.
IT'S TOO DANGEROUS/ WE DON'T KNOW WHAT WILL HAPPEN...
I KNOW. BUT...
WASN'T IT PART OF OUR PLAN ALL ALONG TO MAKE OUR NAMES KNOWN TO AN EXTENT?
PEOPLE WILL TALK.
YEAH, BUT...
MURMUR
...
ザワザワ
MURMUR
AND WHEN IT COMES TO THREE, I THINK YOU'LL LIKE IT THIS WAY, TOO, KOTARŌ-KUN.
HUH...?
MURMUR
ザワ
WHY IS EVERYONE SO WORKED UP ABOUT A NAME?
MURMUR
ザワ
MURMUR
ザワ
I DON'T KNOW.

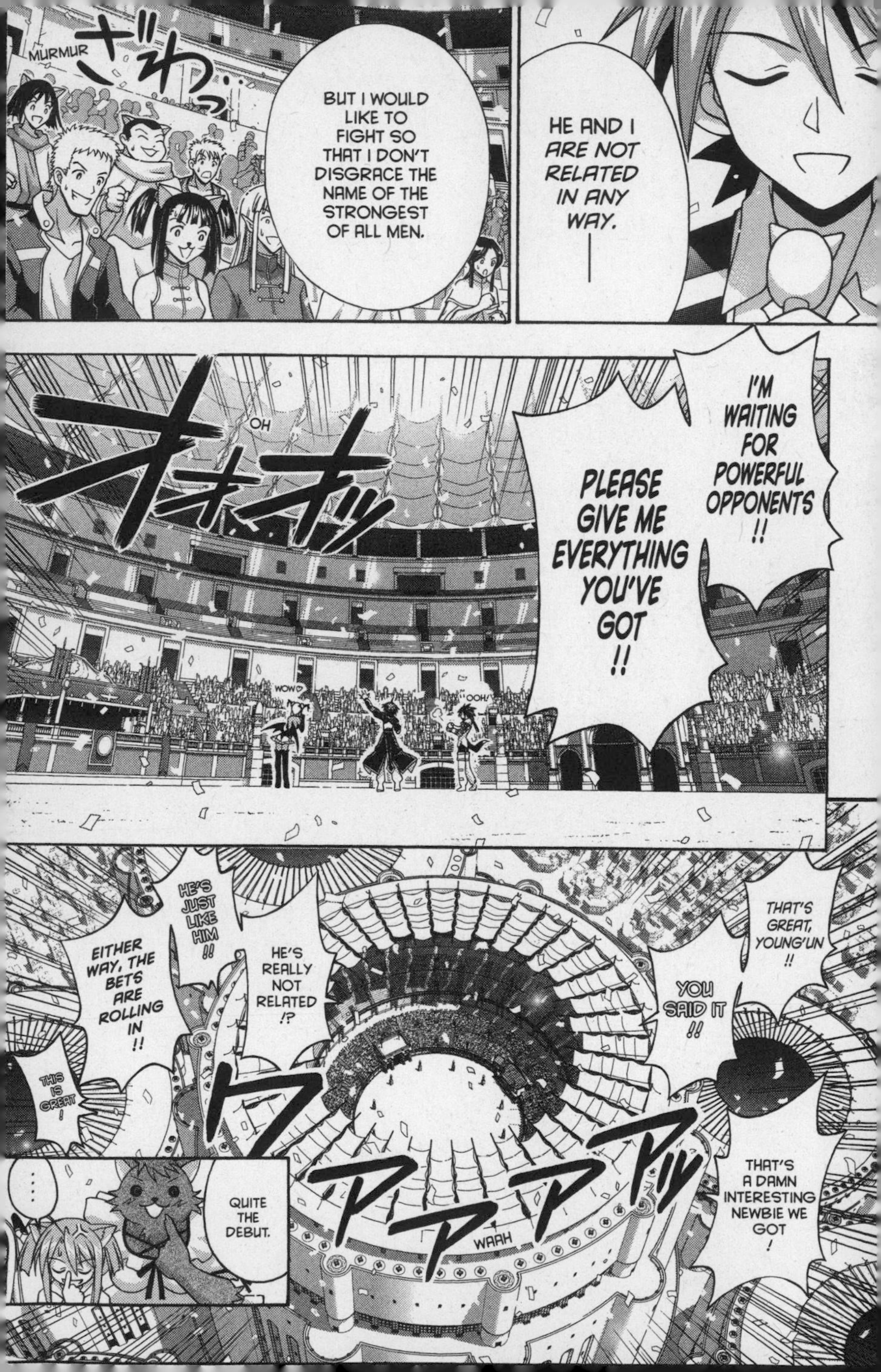
HE AND I ARE NOT RELATED IN ANY WAY.
MURMUR
BUT I WOULD LIKE TO FIGHT SO THAT I DON'T DISGRACE THE NAME OF THE STRONGEST OF ALL MEN.
I'M WAITING FOR POWERFUL OPPONENTS!!
PLEASE GIVE ME EVERYTHING YOU'VE GOT!!
OH
OOH!
WOW♡
THAT'S GREAT, YOUNG'UN!!
YOU SAID IT!!
HE'S JUST LIKE HIM!!
HE'S REALLY NOT RELATED!?
EITHER WAY, THE BETS ARE ROLLING IN!!
THIS IS GREAT!
THAT'S A DAMN INTERESTING NEWBIE WE GOT!
WAAH
QUITE THE DEBUT.
......

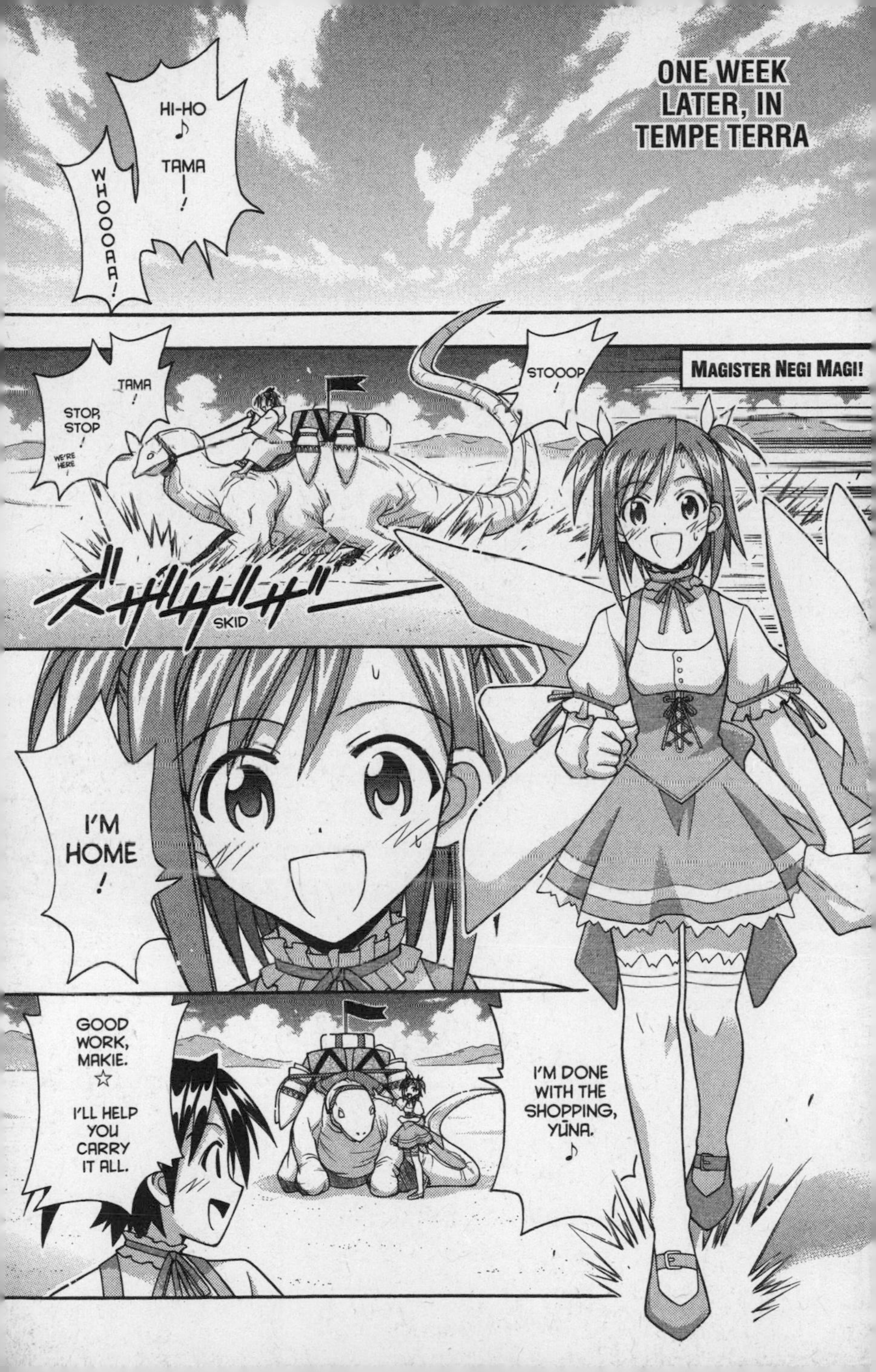
ONE WEEK LATER, IN TEMPE TERRA
HI-HO ♪ TAMA—!
WHOOOAAA!
Magister Negi Magi!
STOOOP!
TAMA! STOP, STOP! WE'RE HERE!
SKID
I'M HOME!
I'M DONE WITH THE SHOPPING, YŪNA. ♪
GOOD WORK, MAKIE. ☆
I'LL HELP YOU CARRY IT ALL.

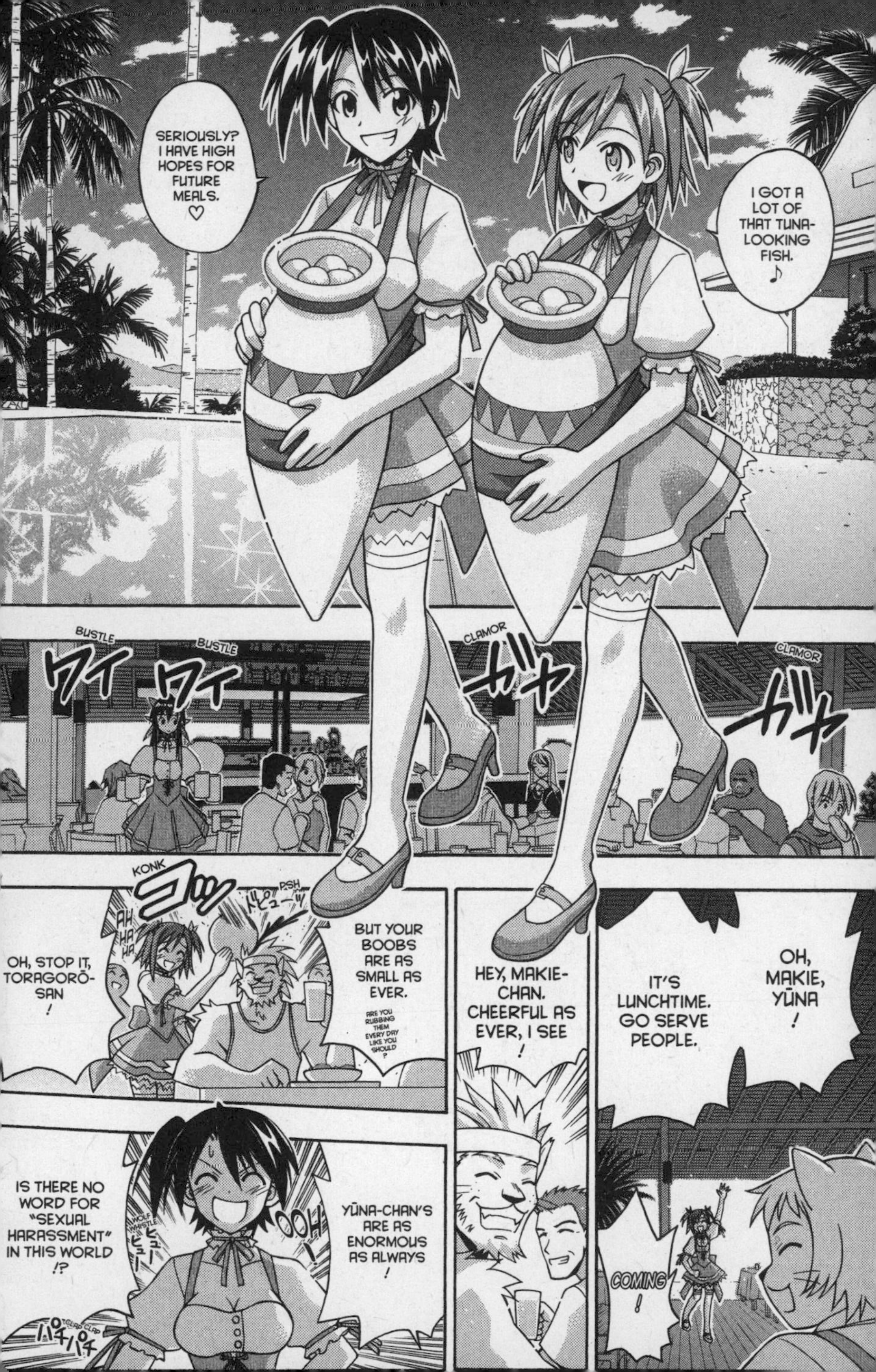
I GOT A LOT OF THAT TUNA-LOOKING FISH. ♪
SERIOUSLY? I HAVE HIGH HOPES FOR FUTURE MEALS. ♡
CLAMOR
CLAMOR
BUSTLE
BUSTLE
OH, MAKIE, YŪNA!
IT'S LUNCHTIME. GO SERVE PEOPLE.
COMING!
HEY, MAKIE-CHAN. CHEERFUL AS EVER, I SEE!
PSH
KONK
BUT YOUR BOOBS ARE AS SMALL AS EVER.
ARE YOU RUBBING THEM EVERY DAY LIKE YOU SHOULD?
AH HA HA
OH, STOP IT, TORAGORŌ-SAN!
OOH!
YŪNA-CHAN'S ARE AS ENORMOUS AS ALWAYS!
WOLF WHISTLE
IS THERE NO WORD FOR "SEXUAL HARASSMENT" IN THIS WORLD!?
CLAP CLAP

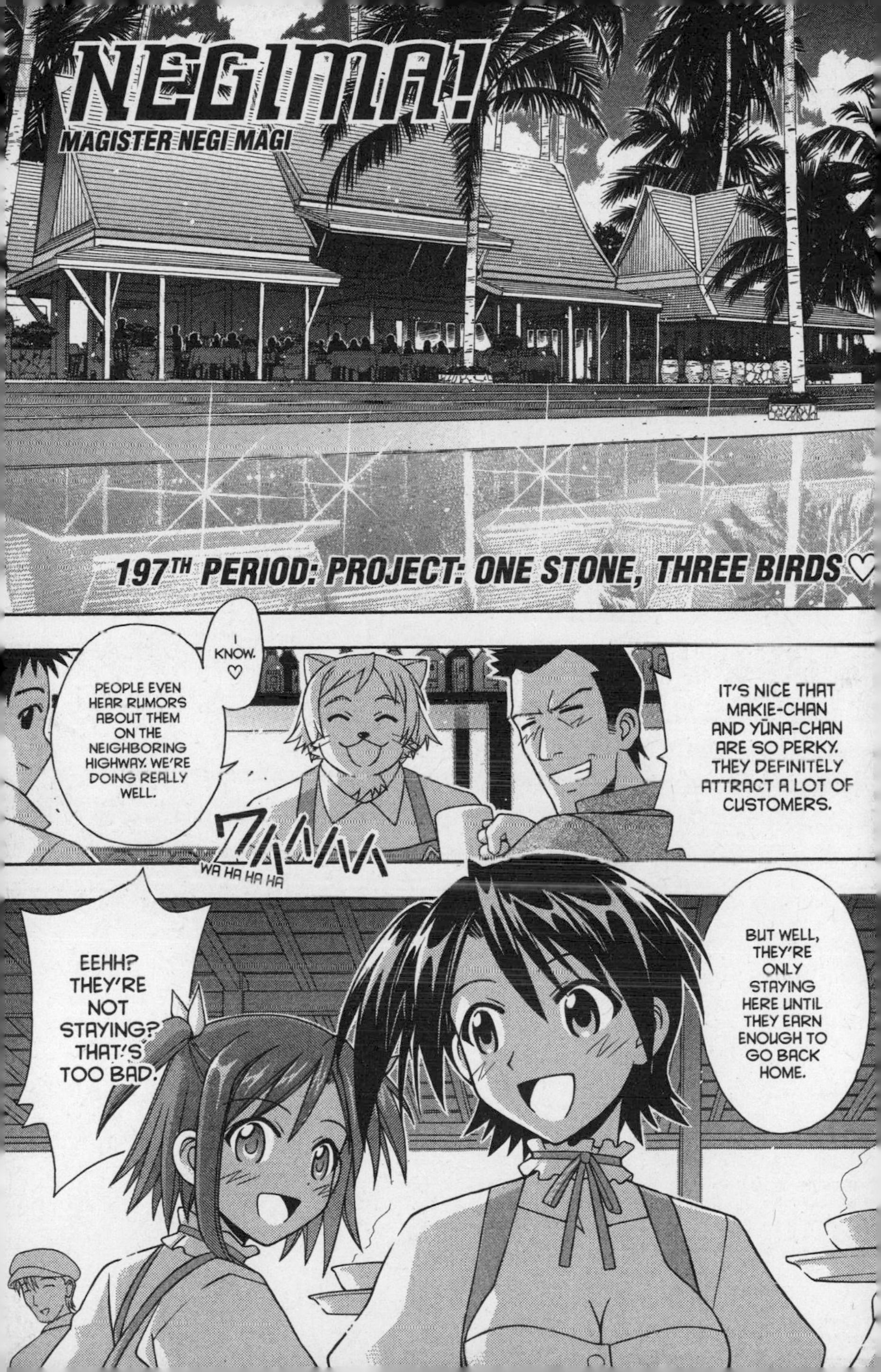
NEGIMA!
MAGISTER NEGI MAGI
197TH PERIOD: PROJECT: ONE STONE, THREE BIRDS ♡
IT'S NICE THAT MAKIE-CHAN AND YŪNA-CHAN ARE SO PERKY. THEY DEFINITELY ATTRACT A LOT OF CUSTOMERS.
I KNOW. ♡
PEOPLE EVEN HEAR RUMORS ABOUT THEM ON THE NEIGHBORING HIGHWAY. WE'RE DOING REALLY WELL.
WA HA HA HA
BUT WELL, THEY'RE ONLY STAYING HERE UNTIL THEY EARN ENOUGH TO GO BACK HOME.
EEHH? THEY'RE NOT STAYING? THAT'S TOO BAD.

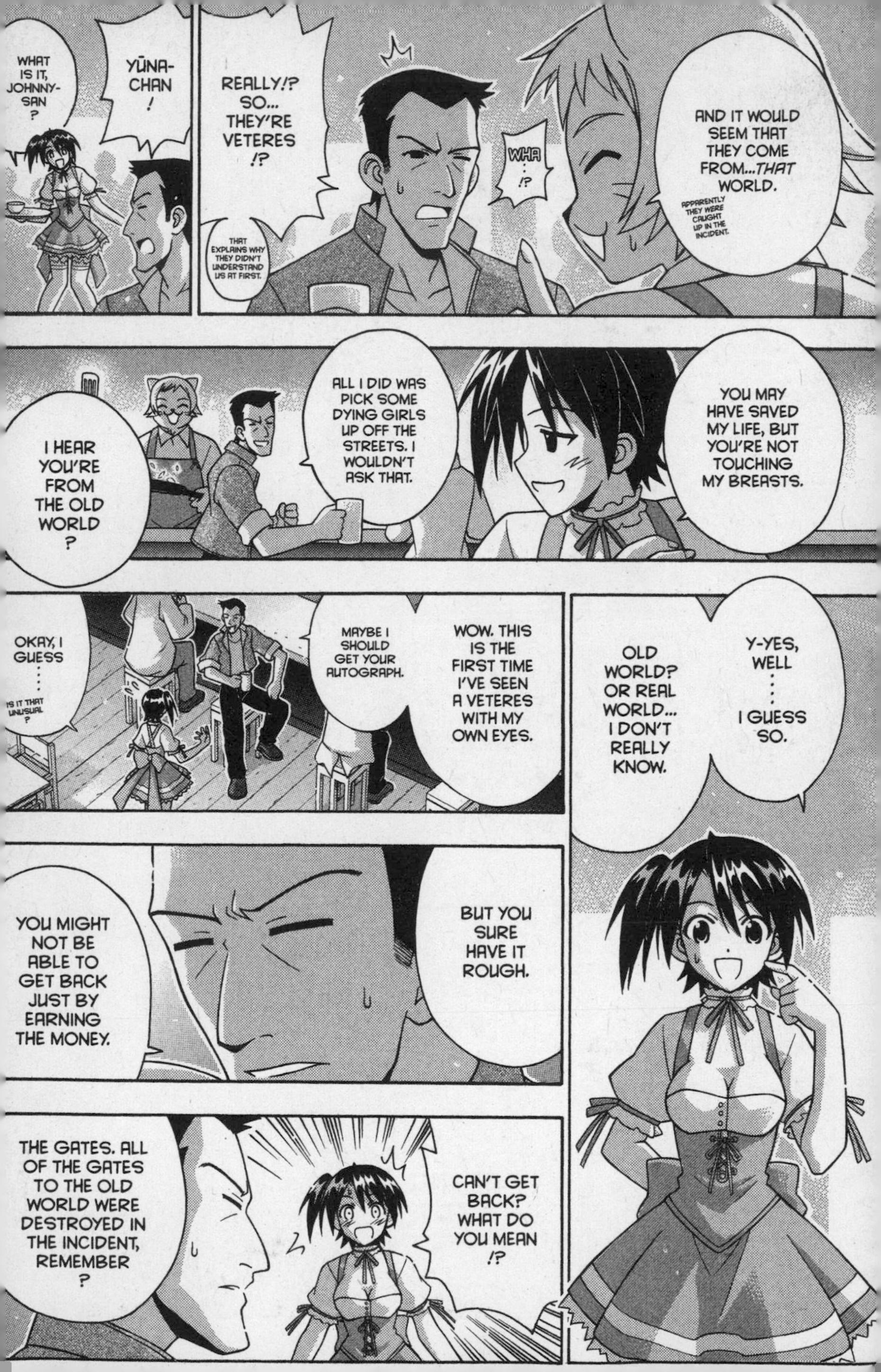
AND IT WOULD SEEM THAT THEY COME FROM...*THAT* WORLD.
APPARENTLY THEY WERE CAUGHT UP IN THE INCIDENT.
WHA...!?
REALLY!? SO... THEY'RE VETERES!?
THAT EXPLAINS WHY THEY DIDN'T UNDERSTAND US AT FIRST.
YŪNA-CHAN!
WHAT IS IT, JOHNNY-SAN?
YOU MAY HAVE SAVED MY LIFE, BUT YOU'RE NOT TOUCHING MY BREASTS.
ALL I DID WAS PICK SOME DYING GIRLS UP OFF THE STREETS. I WOULDN'T ASK THAT.
I HEAR YOU'RE FROM THE OLD WORLD?
Y-YES, WELL... I GUESS SO.
OLD WORLD? OR REAL WORLD... I DON'T REALLY KNOW.
WOW. THIS IS THE FIRST TIME I'VE SEEN A VETERES WITH MY OWN EYES.
MAYBE I SHOULD GET YOUR AUTOGRAPH.
OKAY, I GUESS...
IS IT THAT UNUSUAL?
BUT YOU SURE HAVE IT ROUGH.
YOU MIGHT NOT BE ABLE TO GET BACK JUST BY EARNING THE MONEY.
CAN'T GET BACK? WHAT DO YOU MEAN!?
THE GATES. ALL OF THE GATES TO THE OLD WORLD WERE DESTROYED IN THE INCIDENT, REMEMBER?

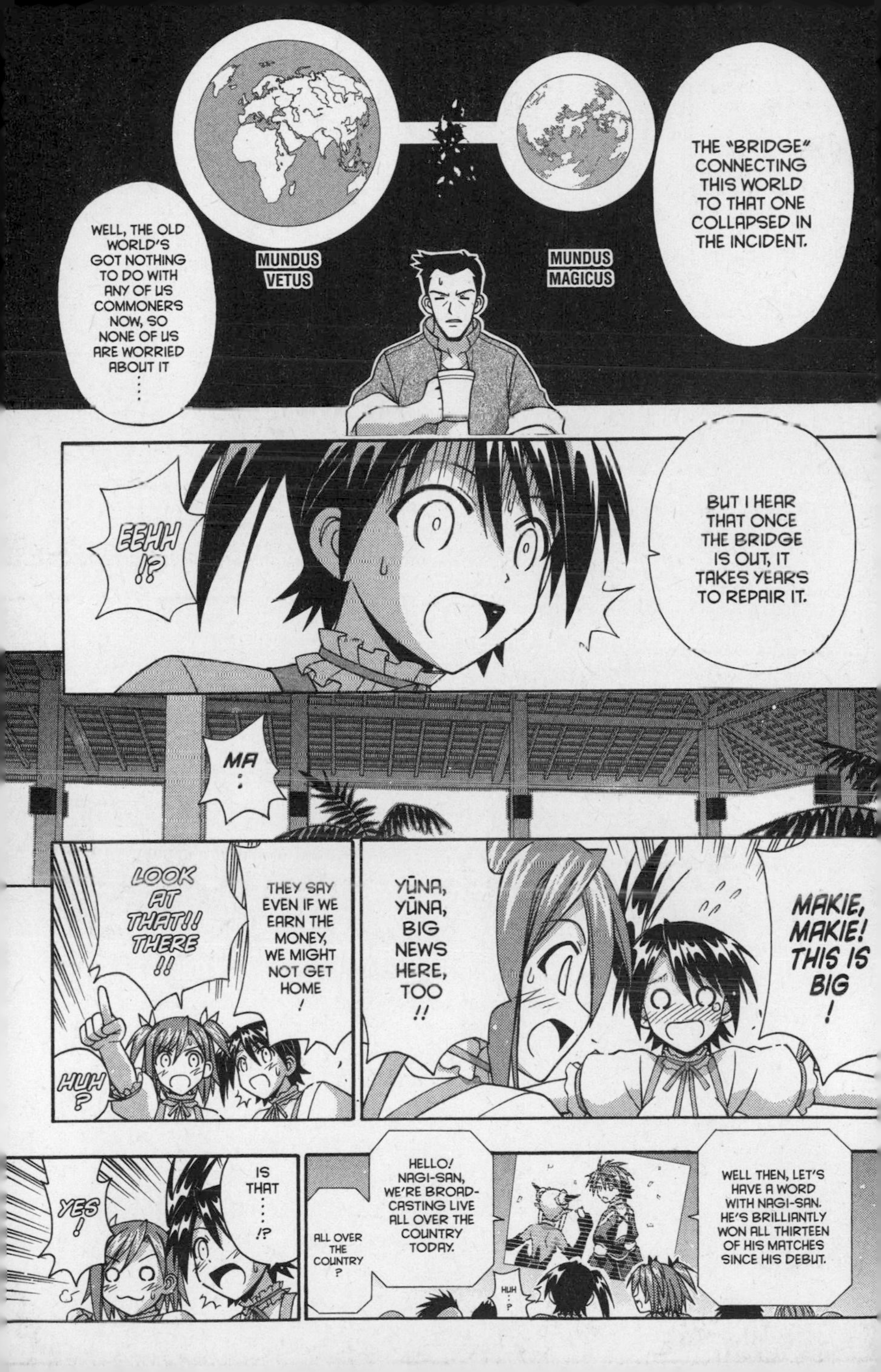
THE "BRIDGE" CONNECTING THIS WORLD TO THAT ONE COLLAPSED IN THE INCIDENT.
MUNDUS MAGICUS
MUNDUS VETUS
WELL, THE OLD WORLD'S GOT NOTHING TO DO WITH ANY OF US COMMONERS NOW, SO NONE OF US ARE WORRIED ABOUT IT ......
BUT I HEAR THAT ONCE THE BRIDGE IS OUT, IT TAKES YEARS TO REPAIR IT.
EEHH !?
MA ..
MAKIE, MAKIE! THIS IS BIG !
YŪNA, YŪNA, BIG NEWS HERE, TOO !!
THEY SAY EVEN IF WE EARN THE MONEY, WE MIGHT NOT GET HOME !
LOOK AT THAT!! THERE !!
HUH ?
WELL THEN, LET'S HAVE A WORD WITH NAGI-SAN. HE'S BRILLIANTLY WON ALL THIRTEEN OF HIS MATCHES SINCE HIS DEBUT.
HELLO! NAGI-SAN, WE'RE BROAD-CASTING LIVE ALL OVER THE COUNTRY TODAY.
ALL OVER THE COUNTRY ?
HUH .. ?
IS THAT ..... !?
YES !

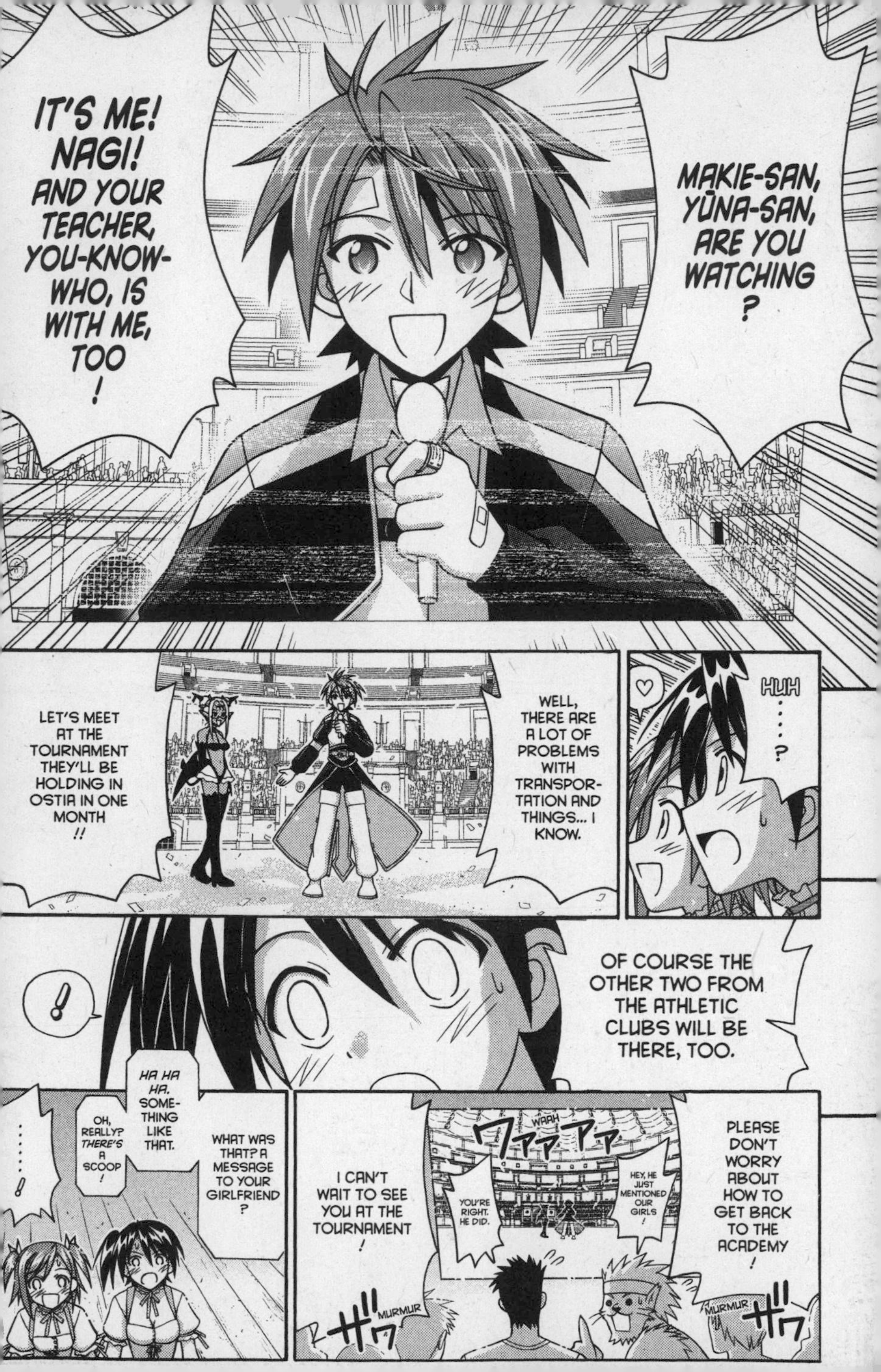
MAKIE-SAN, YŪNA-SAN, ARE YOU WATCHING?
IT'S ME! NAGI! AND YOUR TEACHER, YOU-KNOW-WHO, IS WITH ME, TOO!
HUH...?
WELL, THERE ARE A LOT OF PROBLEMS WITH TRANSPORTATION AND THINGS... I KNOW.
LET'S MEET AT THE TOURNAMENT THEY'LL BE HOLDING IN OSTIA IN ONE MONTH!!
OF COURSE THE OTHER TWO FROM THE ATHLETIC CLUBS WILL BE THERE, TOO.
!
PLEASE DON'T WORRY ABOUT HOW TO GET BACK TO THE ACADEMY!
HEY, HE JUST MENTIONED OUR GIRLS!
WAAH
YOU'RE RIGHT. HE DID.
I CAN'T WAIT TO SEE YOU AT THE TOURNAMENT!
MURMUR
MURMUR
WHAT WAS THAT? A MESSAGE TO YOUR GIRLFRIEND?
HA HA HA. SOMETHING LIKE THAT.
OH, REALLY? THERE'S A SCOOP!
......!

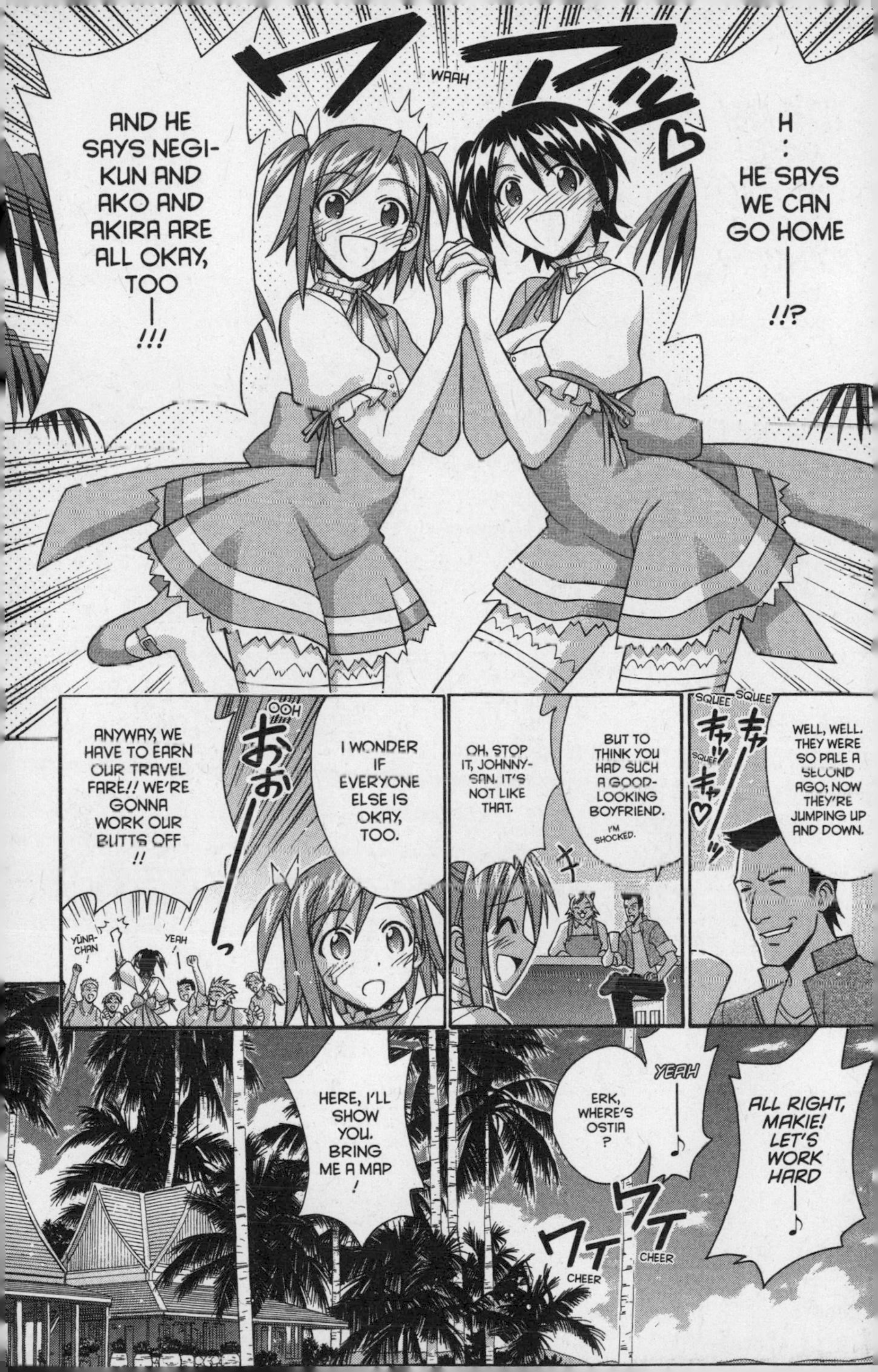
WAAH
H... HE SAYS WE CAN GO HOME—!!?
AND HE SAYS NEGI-KUN AND AKO AND AKIRA ARE ALL OKAY, TOO—!!!
SQUEE SQUEE SQUEE
WELL, WELL. THEY WERE SO PALE A SECOND AGO; NOW THEY'RE JUMPING UP AND DOWN.
BUT TO THINK YOU HAD SUCH A GOOD-LOOKING BOYFRIEND.
I'M SHOCKED.
OH, STOP IT, JOHNNY-SAN. IT'S NOT LIKE THAT.
I WONDER IF EVERYONE ELSE IS OKAY, TOO.
OOH
ANYWAY, WE HAVE TO EARN OUR TRAVEL FARE!! WE'RE GONNA WORK OUR BUTTS OFF!!
YEAH!
YŪNA-CHAN!
ALL RIGHT, MAKIE! LET'S WORK HARD—♪
YEAH—♪
CHEER
CHEER
ERK, WHERE'S OSTIA?
HERE, I'LL SHOW YOU. BRING ME A MAP!

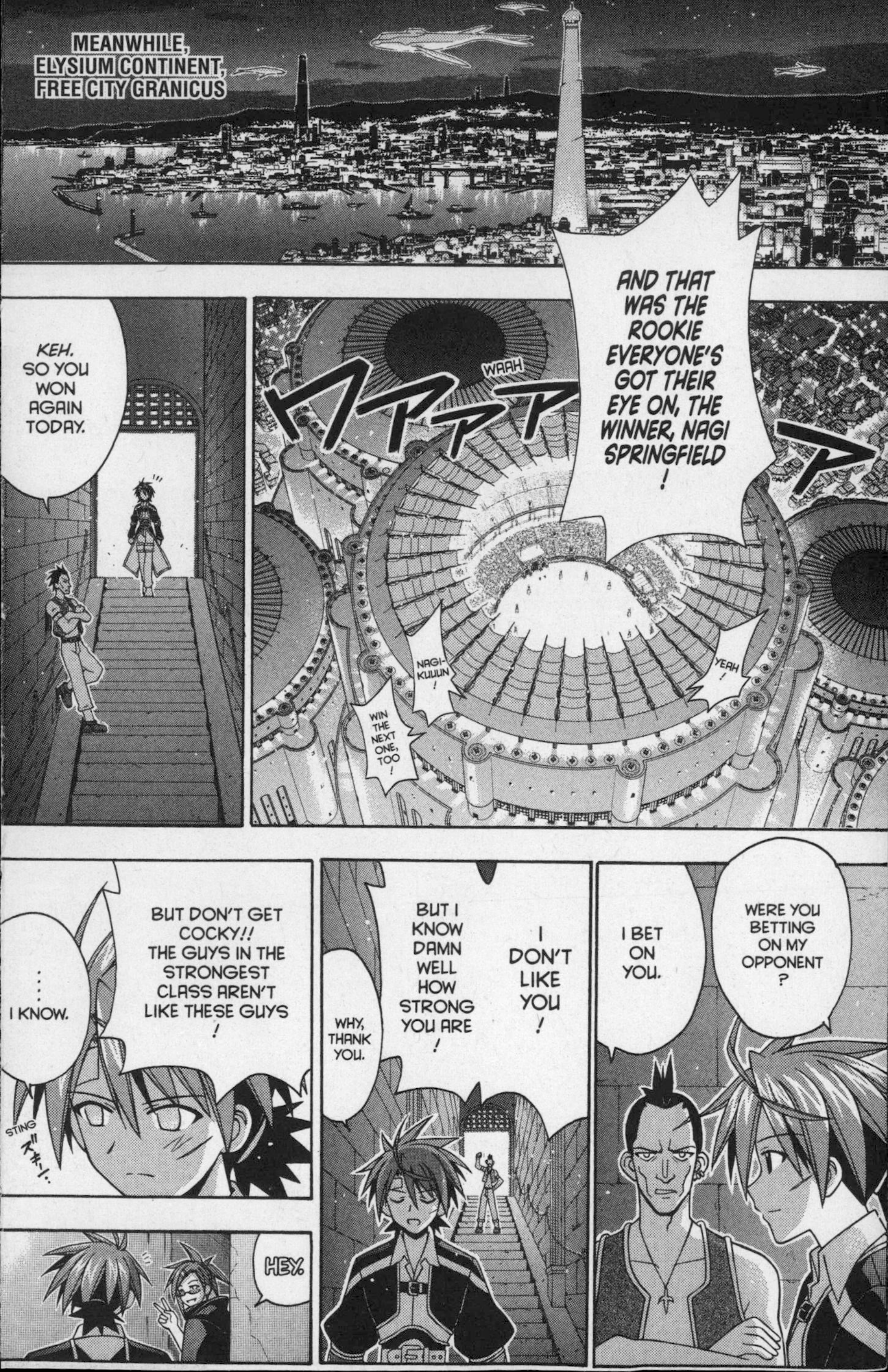
MEANWHILE, ELYSIUM CONTINENT, FREE CITY GRANICUS
WAAH
AND THAT WAS THE ROOKIE EVERYONE'S GOT THEIR EYE ON, THE WINNER, NAGI SPRINGFIELD!
YEAH!
NAGI-KUUUN!
WIN THE NEXT ONE, TOO!
KEH. SO YOU WON AGAIN TODAY.
WERE YOU BETTING ON MY OPPONENT?
I BET ON YOU.
I DON'T LIKE YOU!
BUT I KNOW DAMN WELL HOW STRONG YOU ARE!
WHY, THANK YOU.
BUT DON'T GET COCKY!! THE GUYS IN THE STRONGEST CLASS AREN'T LIKE THESE GUYS!
...I KNOW.
STING
HEY.

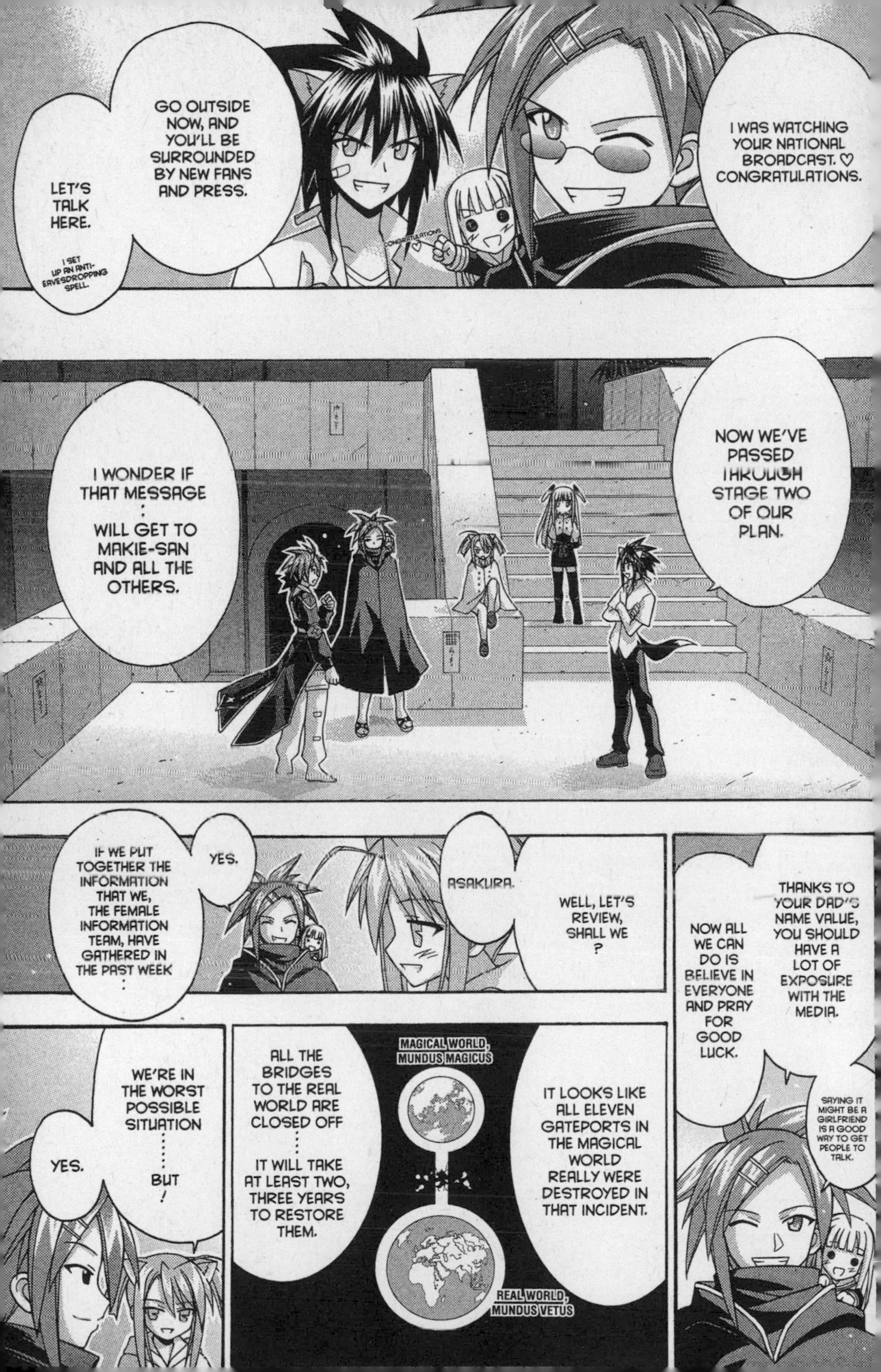
I WAS WATCHING YOUR NATIONAL BROADCAST. ♡ CONGRATULATIONS.
CONGRATULATIONS ♡
GO OUTSIDE NOW, AND YOU'LL BE SURROUNDED BY NEW FANS AND PRESS.
LET'S TALK HERE.
I SET UP AN ANTI-EAVESDROPPING SPELL.
NOW WE'VE PASSED THROUGH STAGE TWO OF OUR PLAN.
I WONDER IF THAT MESSAGE : WILL GET TO MAKIE-SAN AND ALL THE OTHERS.
THANKS TO YOUR DAD'S NAME VALUE, YOU SHOULD HAVE A LOT OF EXPOSURE WITH THE MEDIA.
NOW ALL WE CAN DO IS BELIEVE IN EVERYONE AND PRAY FOR GOOD LUCK.
SAYING IT MIGHT BE A GIRLFRIEND IS A GOOD WAY TO GET PEOPLE TO TALK.
WELL, LET'S REVIEW, SHALL WE ?
ASAKURA.
YES.
IF WE PUT TOGETHER THE INFORMATION THAT WE, THE FEMALE INFORMATION TEAM, HAVE GATHERED IN THE PAST WEEK :
IT LOOKS LIKE ALL ELEVEN GATEPORTS IN THE MAGICAL WORLD REALLY WERE DESTROYED IN THAT INCIDENT.
MAGICAL WORLD, MUNDUS MAGICUS
REAL WORLD, MUNDUS VETUS
ALL THE BRIDGES TO THE REAL WORLD ARE CLOSED OFF ⁝ IT WILL TAKE AT LEAST TWO, THREE YEARS TO RESTORE THEM.
WE'RE IN THE WORST POSSIBLE SITUATION ...... BUT !
YES.

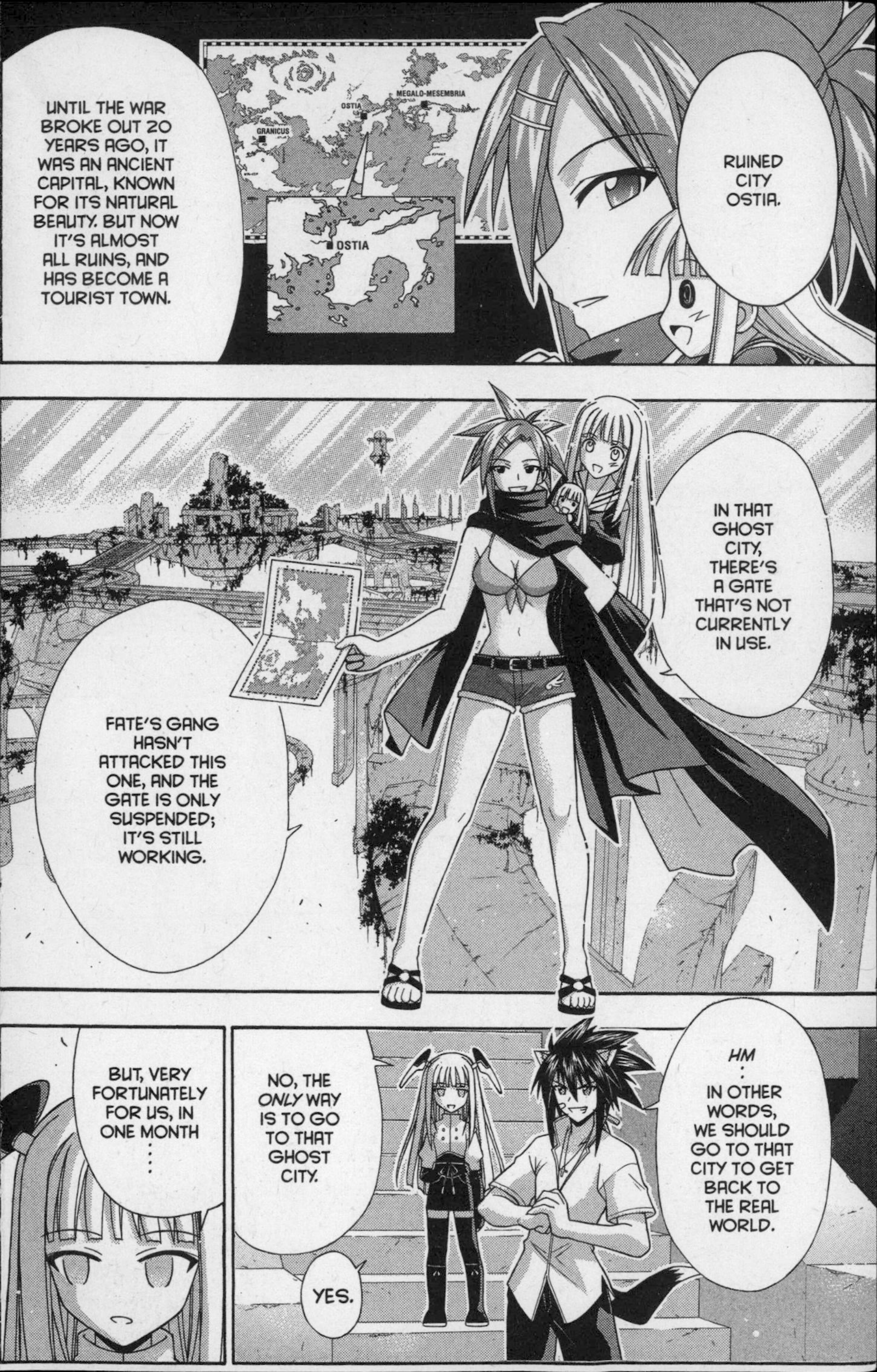
RUINED CITY OSTIA.
MEGALO-MESEMBRIA
OSTIA
GRANICUS
OSTIA
UNTIL THE WAR BROKE OUT 20 YEARS AGO, IT WAS AN ANCIENT CAPITAL, KNOWN FOR ITS NATURAL BEAUTY. BUT NOW IT'S ALMOST ALL RUINS, AND HAS BECOME A TOURIST TOWN.
IN THAT GHOST CITY, THERE'S A GATE THAT'S NOT CURRENTLY IN USE.
FATE'S GANG HASN'T ATTACKED THIS ONE, AND THE GATE IS ONLY SUSPENDED; IT'S STILL WORKING.
*HM* : IN OTHER WORDS, WE SHOULD GO TO THAT CITY TO GET BACK TO THE REAL WORLD.
NO, THE *ONLY* WAY IS TO GO TO THAT GHOST CITY.
YES.
BUT, VERY FORTUNATELY FOR US, IN ONE MONTH . . .

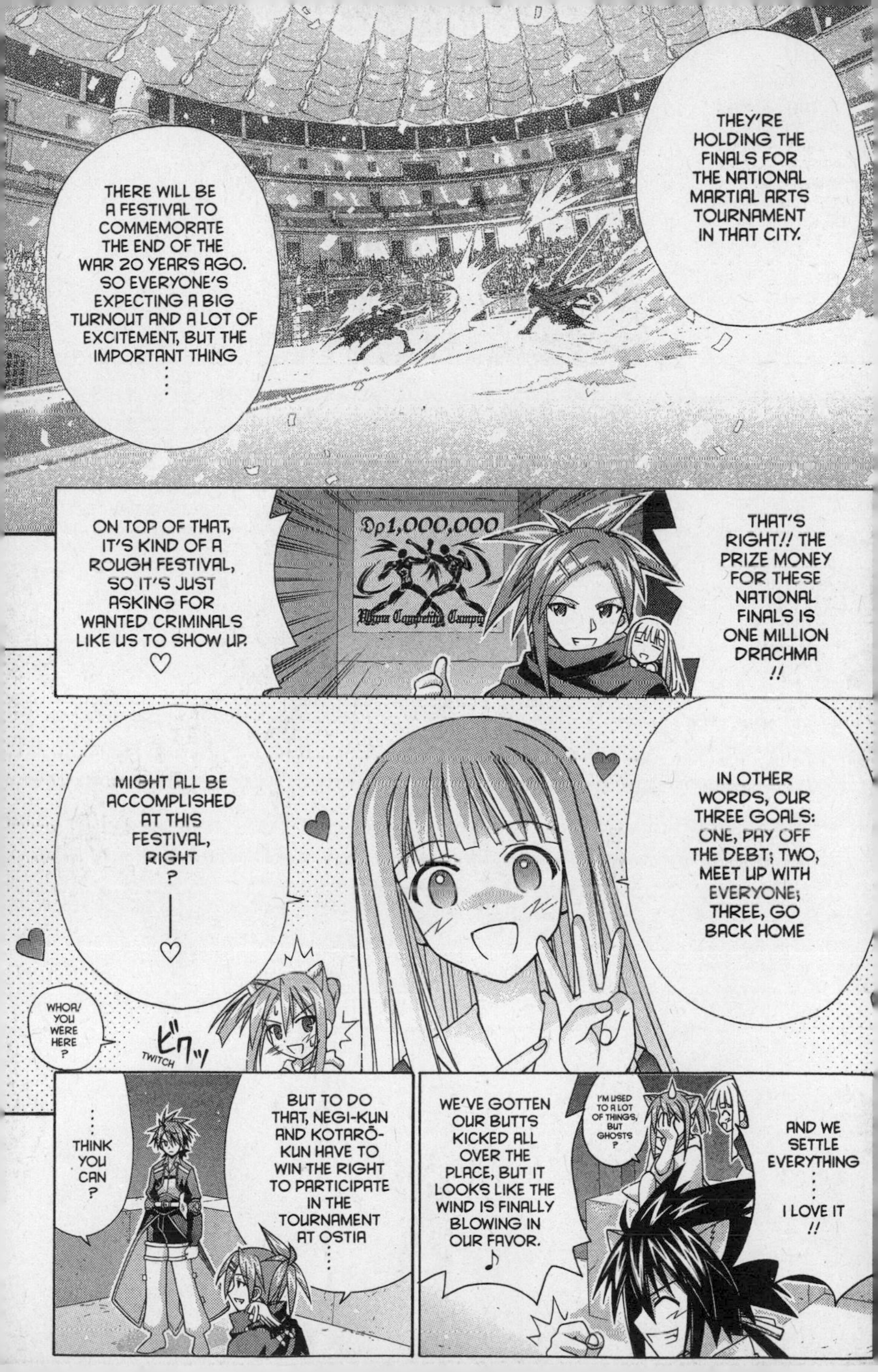
THEY'RE HOLDING THE FINALS FOR THE NATIONAL MARTIAL ARTS TOURNAMENT IN THAT CITY.
THERE WILL BE A FESTIVAL TO COMMEMORATE THE END OF THE WAR 20 YEARS AGO. SO EVERYONE'S EXPECTING A BIG TURNOUT AND A LOT OF EXCITEMENT, BUT THE IMPORTANT THING ...
THAT'S RIGHT!! THE PRIZE MONEY FOR THESE NATIONAL FINALS IS ONE MILLION DRACHMA!!
Dp1,000,000
ON TOP OF THAT, IT'S KIND OF A ROUGH FESTIVAL, SO IT'S JUST ASKING FOR WANTED CRIMINALS LIKE US TO SHOW UP. ♡
IN OTHER WORDS, OUR THREE GOALS: ONE, PAY OFF THE DEBT; TWO, MEET UP WITH EVERYONE; THREE, GO BACK HOME
MIGHT ALL BE ACCOMPLISHED AT THIS FESTIVAL, RIGHT? ♡
WHOA! YOU WERE HERE?
ビクッ
TWITCH
AND WE SETTLE EVERYTHING ... I LOVE IT!!
I'M USED TO A LOT OF THINGS, BUT GHOSTS?
WE'VE GOTTEN OUR BUTTS KICKED ALL OVER THE PLACE, BUT IT LOOKS LIKE THE WIND IS FINALLY BLOWING IN OUR FAVOR. ♪
BUT TO DO THAT, NEGI-KUN AND KOTARŌ-KUN HAVE TO WIN THE RIGHT TO PARTICIPATE IN THE TOURNAMENT AT OSTIA ...
... THINK YOU CAN?

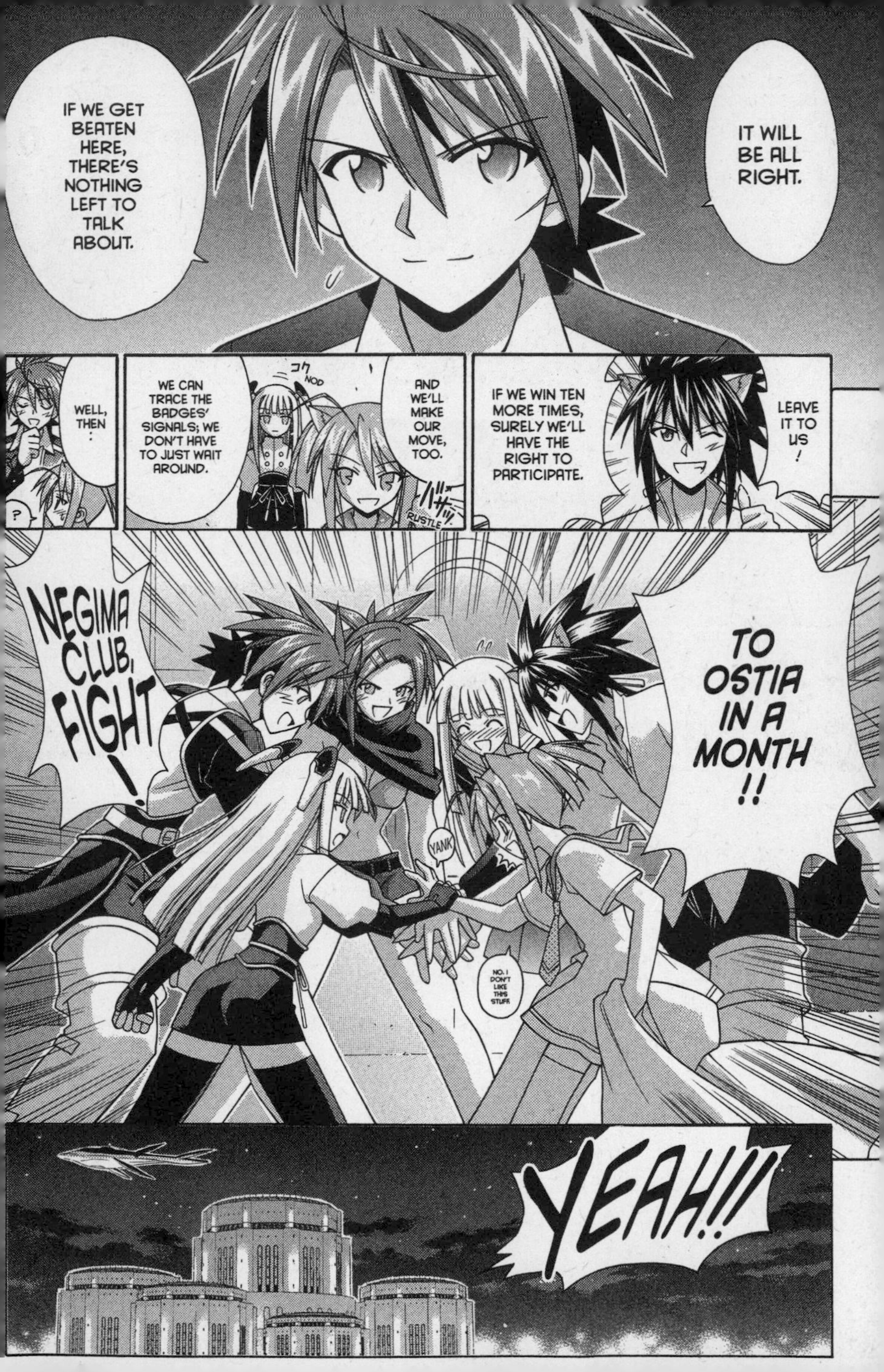
IT WILL BE ALL RIGHT.
IF WE GET BEATEN HERE, THERE'S NOTHING LEFT TO TALK ABOUT.
LEAVE IT TO US!
IF WE WIN TEN MORE TIMES, SURELY WE'LL HAVE THE RIGHT TO PARTICIPATE.
AND WE'LL MAKE OUR MOVE, TOO.
RUSTLE
コク NOD
WE CAN TRACE THE BADGES' SIGNALS; WE DON'T HAVE TO JUST WAIT AROUND.
WELL, THEN...
?
TO OSTIA IN A MONTH!!
NEGIMA CLUB, FIGHT!
YANK
NO, I DON'T LIKE THIS STUFF.
YEAH!!

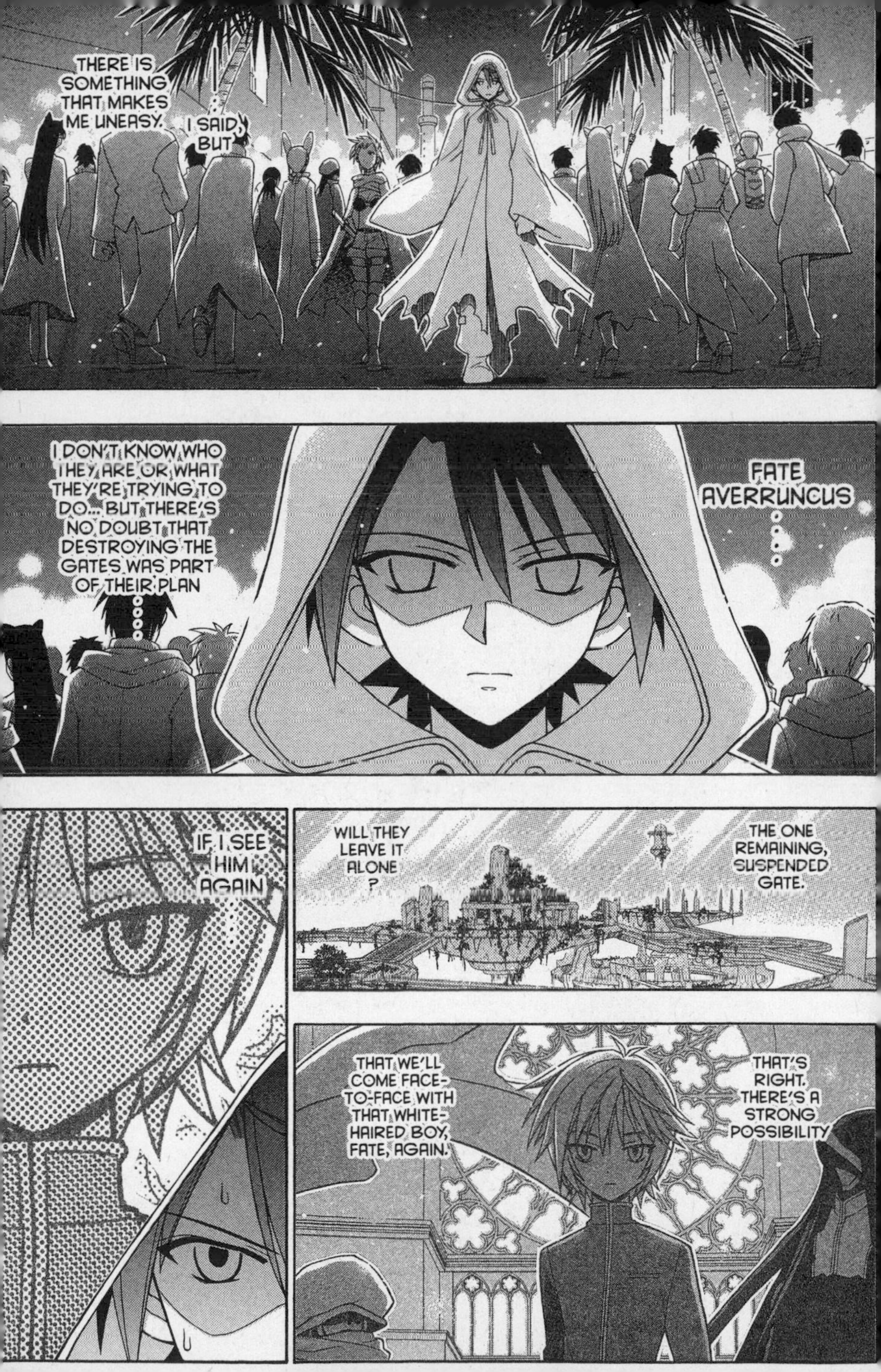
THERE IS SOMETHING THAT MAKES ME UNEASY.
I SAID, BUT
FATE AVERRUNCUS . . . .
I DON'T KNOW WHO THEY ARE OR WHAT THEY'RE TRYING TO DO... BUT THERE'S NO DOUBT THAT DESTROYING THE GATES WAS PART OF THEIR PLAN
THE ONE REMAINING, SUSPENDED GATE.
WILL THEY LEAVE IT ALONE ?
THAT'S RIGHT. THERE'S A STRONG POSSIBILITY
THAT WE'LL COME FACE-TO-FACE WITH THAT WHITE-HAIRED BOY, FATE, AGAIN.
IF I SEE HIM AGAIN

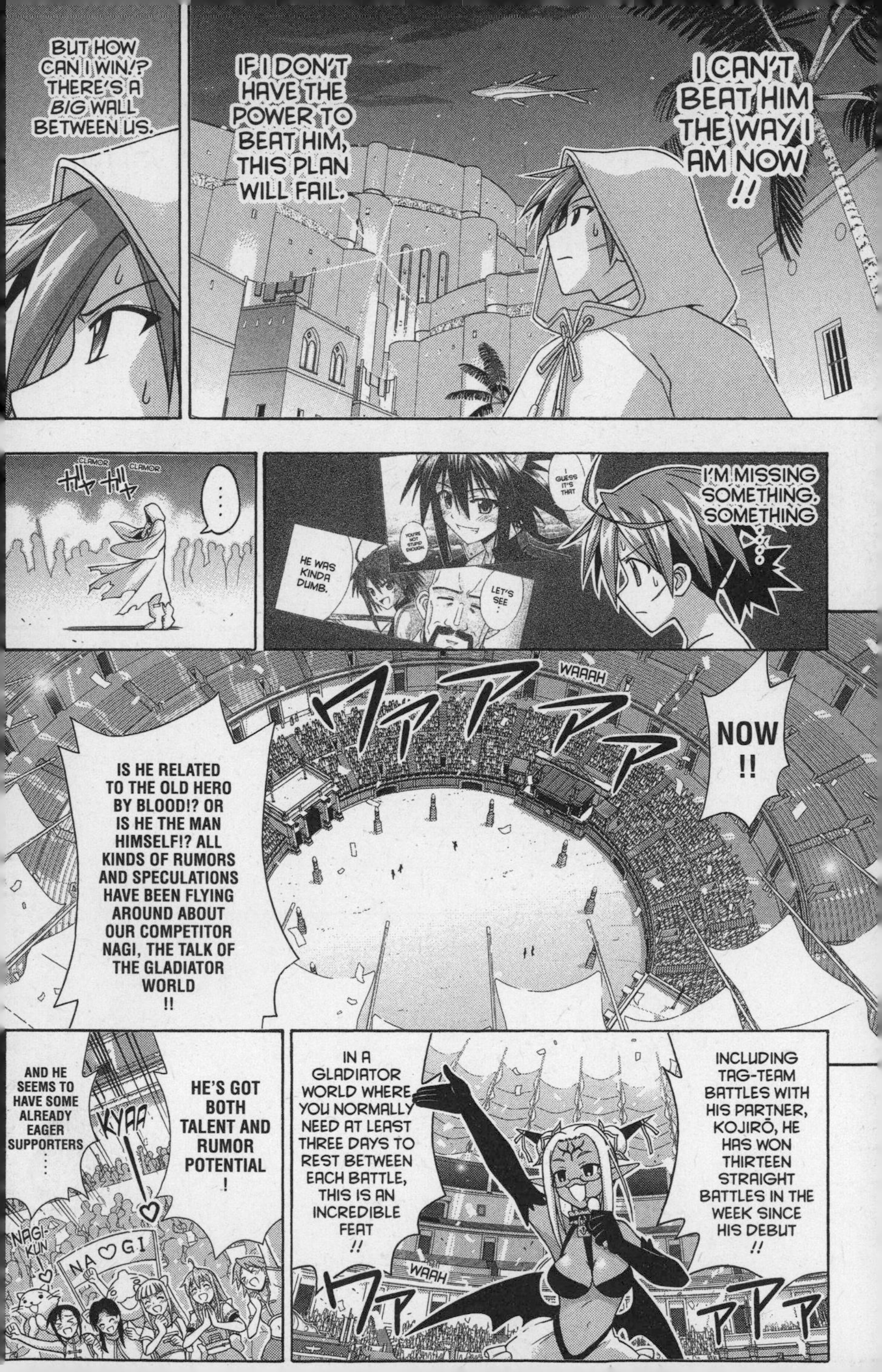
I CAN'T BEAT HIM THE WAY I AM NOW !!
IF I DON'T HAVE THE POWER TO BEAT HIM, THIS PLAN WILL FAIL.
BUT HOW CAN I WIN!? THERE'S A BIG WALL BETWEEN US.
I'M MISSING SOMETHING. SOMETHING ...
I GUESS IT'S THAT
YOU'RE NOT STUPID ENOUGH.
LET'S SEE ...
HE WAS KINDA DUMB.
CLAMOR
CLAMOR
...
WAAAH
NOW !!
IS HE RELATED TO THE OLD HERO BY BLOOD!? OR IS HE THE MAN HIMSELF!? ALL KINDS OF RUMORS AND SPECULATIONS HAVE BEEN FLYING AROUND ABOUT OUR COMPETITOR NAGI, THE TALK OF THE GLADIATOR WORLD !!
INCLUDING TAG-TEAM BATTLES WITH HIS PARTNER, KOJIRŌ, HE HAS WON THIRTEEN STRAIGHT BATTLES IN THE WEEK SINCE HIS DEBUT !!
IN A GLADIATOR WORLD WHERE YOU NORMALLY NEED AT LEAST THREE DAYS TO REST BETWEEN EACH BATTLE, THIS IS AN INCREDIBLE FEAT !!
WAAH
HE'S GOT BOTH TALENT AND RUMOR POTENTIAL !
AND HE SEEMS TO HAVE SOME ALREADY EAGER SUPPORTERS ...
KYAA !
NAGI-KUN
NA♡GI

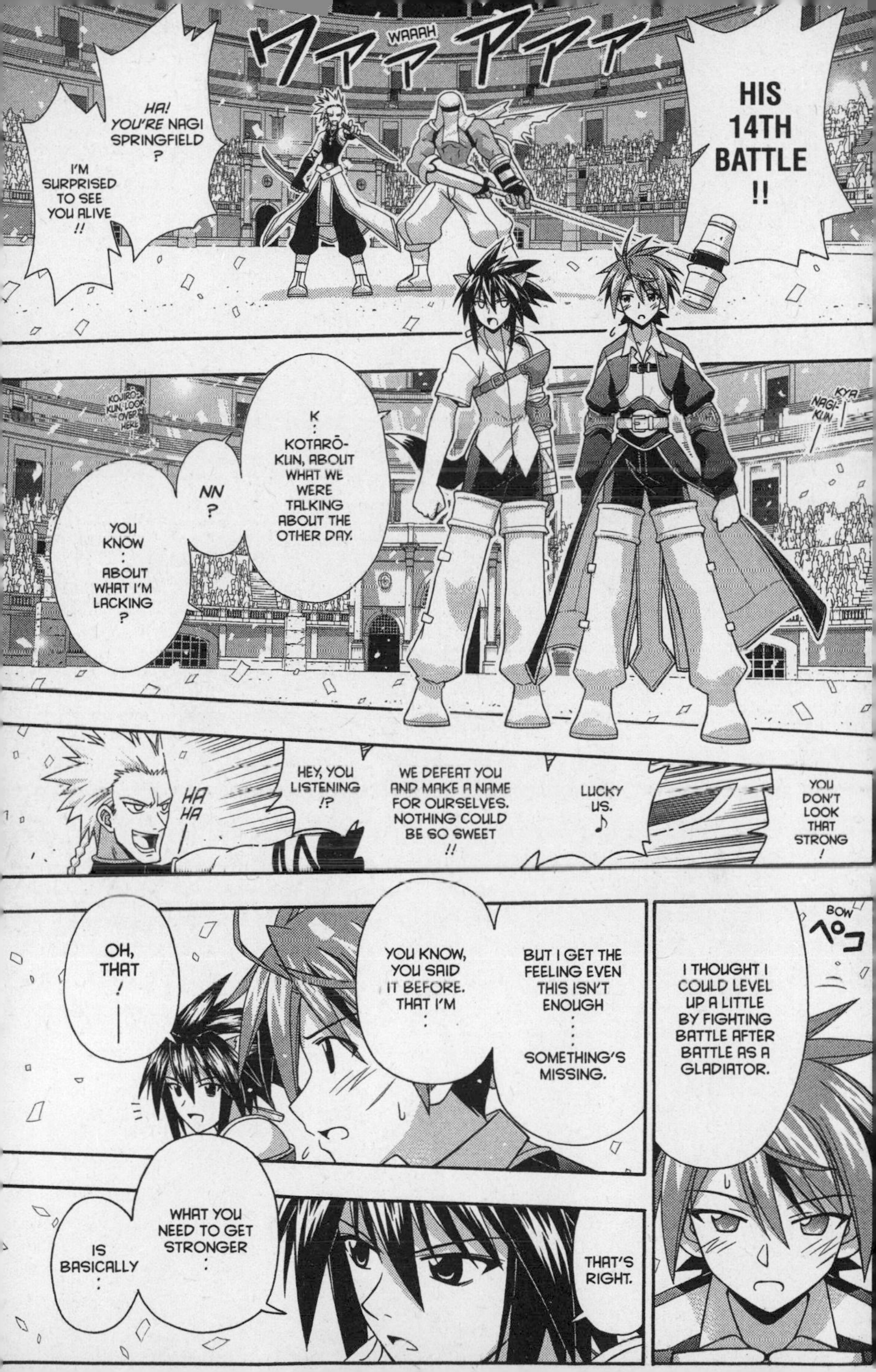
WAAAH
HIS 14TH BATTLE !!
HA! YOU'RE NAGI SPRINGFIELD ?
I'M SURPRISED TO SEE YOU ALIVE !!
KYA NAGI-KUN
K: KOTARŌ-KUN, ABOUT WHAT WE WERE TALKING ABOUT THE OTHER DAY.
NN ?
YOU KNOW: ABOUT WHAT I'M LACKING ?
KOJIRO-KUN, LOOK OVER HERE !
YOU DON'T LOOK THAT STRONG !
LUCKY US. ♪
WE DEFEAT YOU AND MAKE A NAME FOR OURSELVES. NOTHING COULD BE SO SWEET !!
HEY, YOU LISTENING !?
HA HA
BOW
I THOUGHT I COULD LEVEL UP A LITTLE BY FIGHTING BATTLE AFTER BATTLE AS A GLADIATOR.
BUT I GET THE FEELING EVEN THIS ISN'T ENOUGH... SOMETHING'S MISSING.
YOU KNOW, YOU SAID IT BEFORE. THAT I'M :
OH, THAT !
THAT'S RIGHT.
WHAT YOU NEED TO GET STRONGER :
IS BASICALLY :

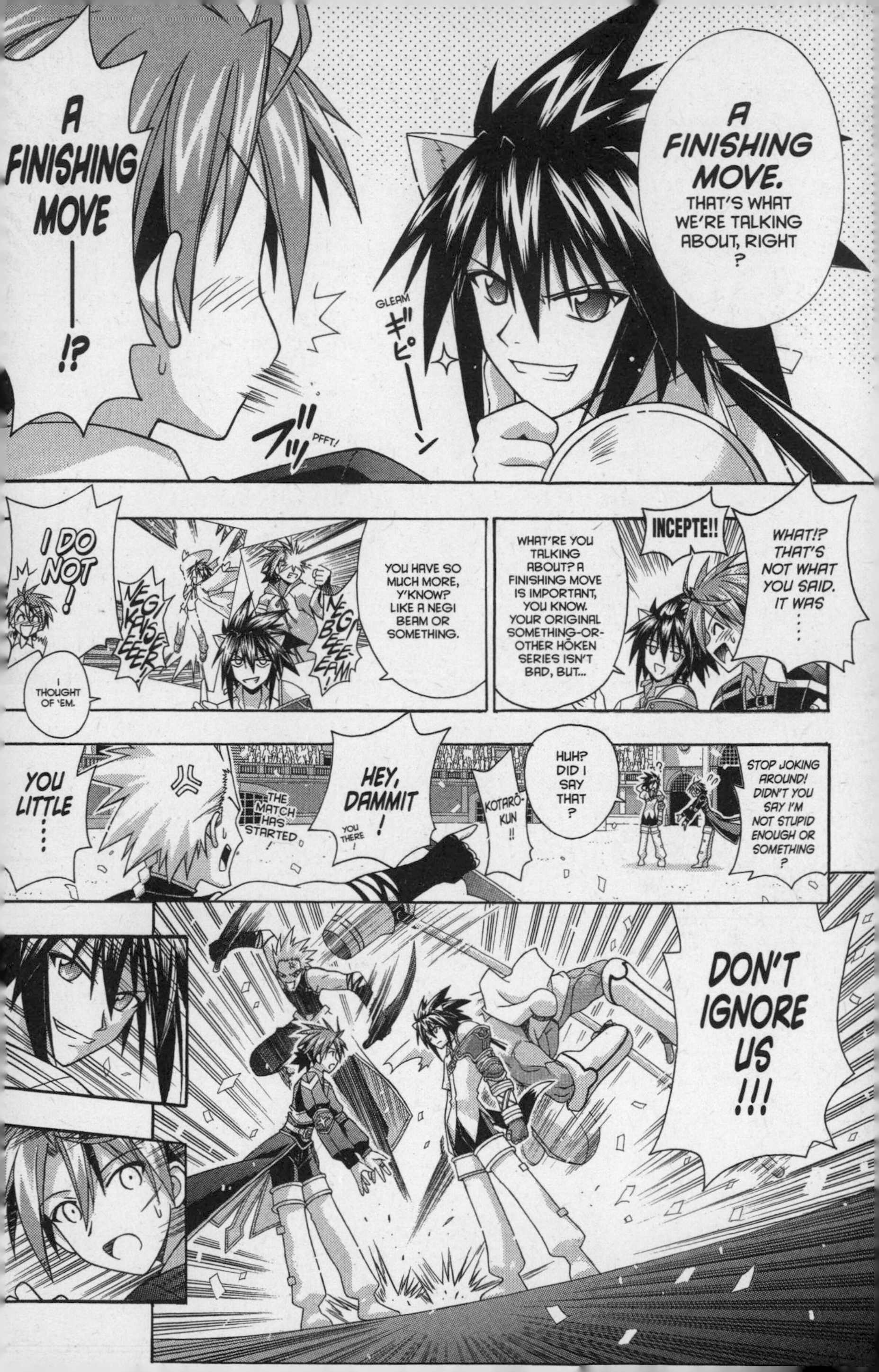
A FINISHING MOVE. THAT'S WHAT WE'RE TALKING ABOUT, RIGHT?
GLEAM
ギピーン
PFFT!
ブッ
A FINISHING MOVE——!?
WHAT!? THAT'S NOT WHAT YOU SAID. IT WAS......
INCEPTE!!
WHAT'RE YOU TALKING ABOUT? A FINISHING MOVE IS IMPORTANT, YOU KNOW. YOUR ORIGINAL SOMETHING-OR-OTHER HŌKEN SERIES ISN'T BAD, BUT...
YOU HAVE SO MUCH MORE, Y'KNOW? LIKE A NEGI BEAM OR SOMETHING.
NEGI BEEEEAM!
NEGI KAISEEEER!
I DO NOT!
I THOUGHT OF 'EM.
STOP JOKING AROUND! DIDN'T YOU SAY I'M NOT STUPID ENOUGH OR SOMETHING?
HUH? DID I SAY THAT?
KOTARŌ-KUN!!
HEY, DAMMIT!
YOU THERE!
THE MATCH HAS STARTED!
YOU LITTLE......
DON'T IGNORE US!!!

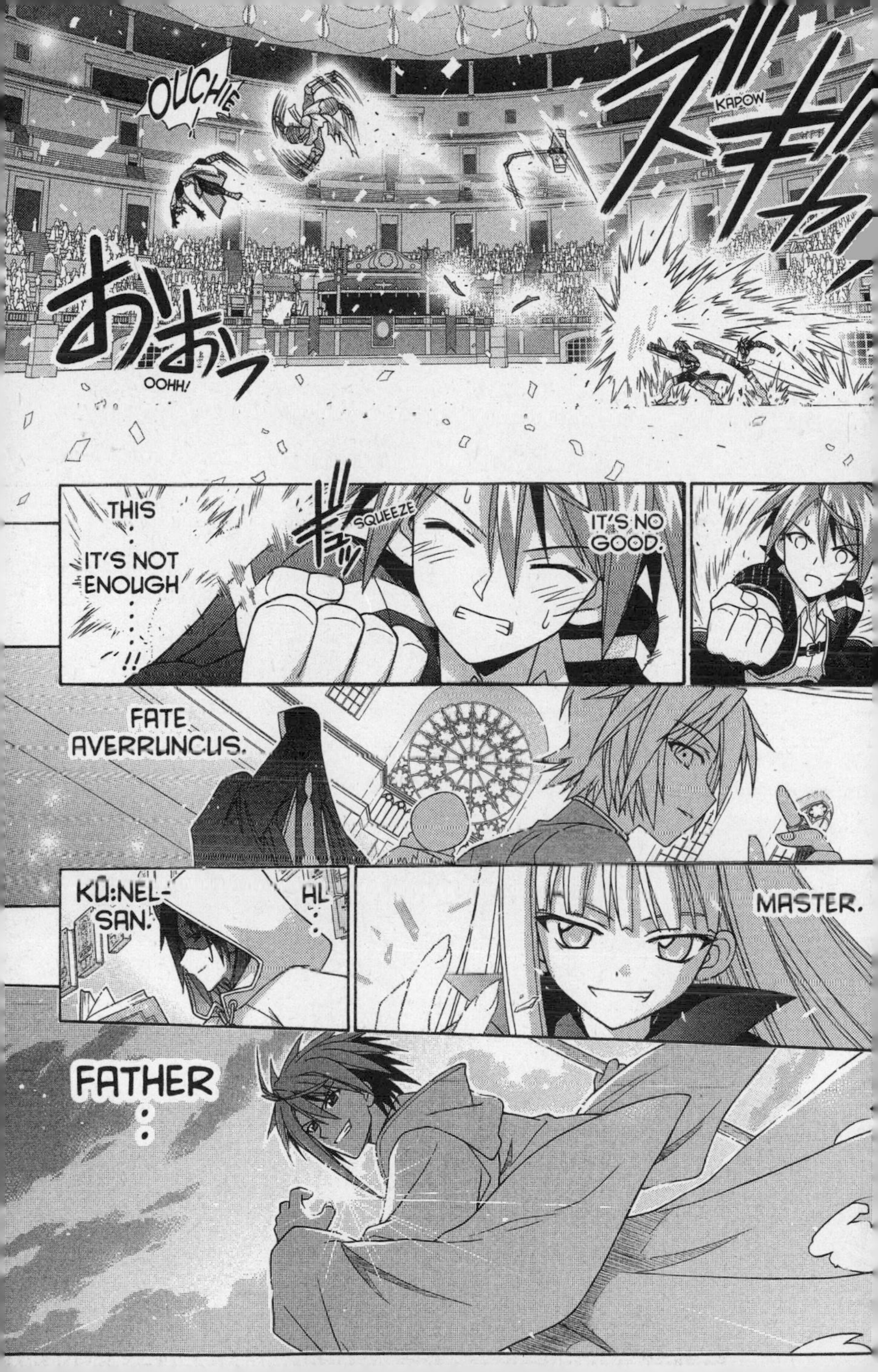
KAPOW
OUCHIE!
おおっ
OOHH!
IT'S NO GOOD.
SQUEEZE
THIS... IT'S NOT ENOUGH......!!
FATE AVERRUNCUS.
MASTER.
HI...
KŪ:NEL-SAN.
FATHER...

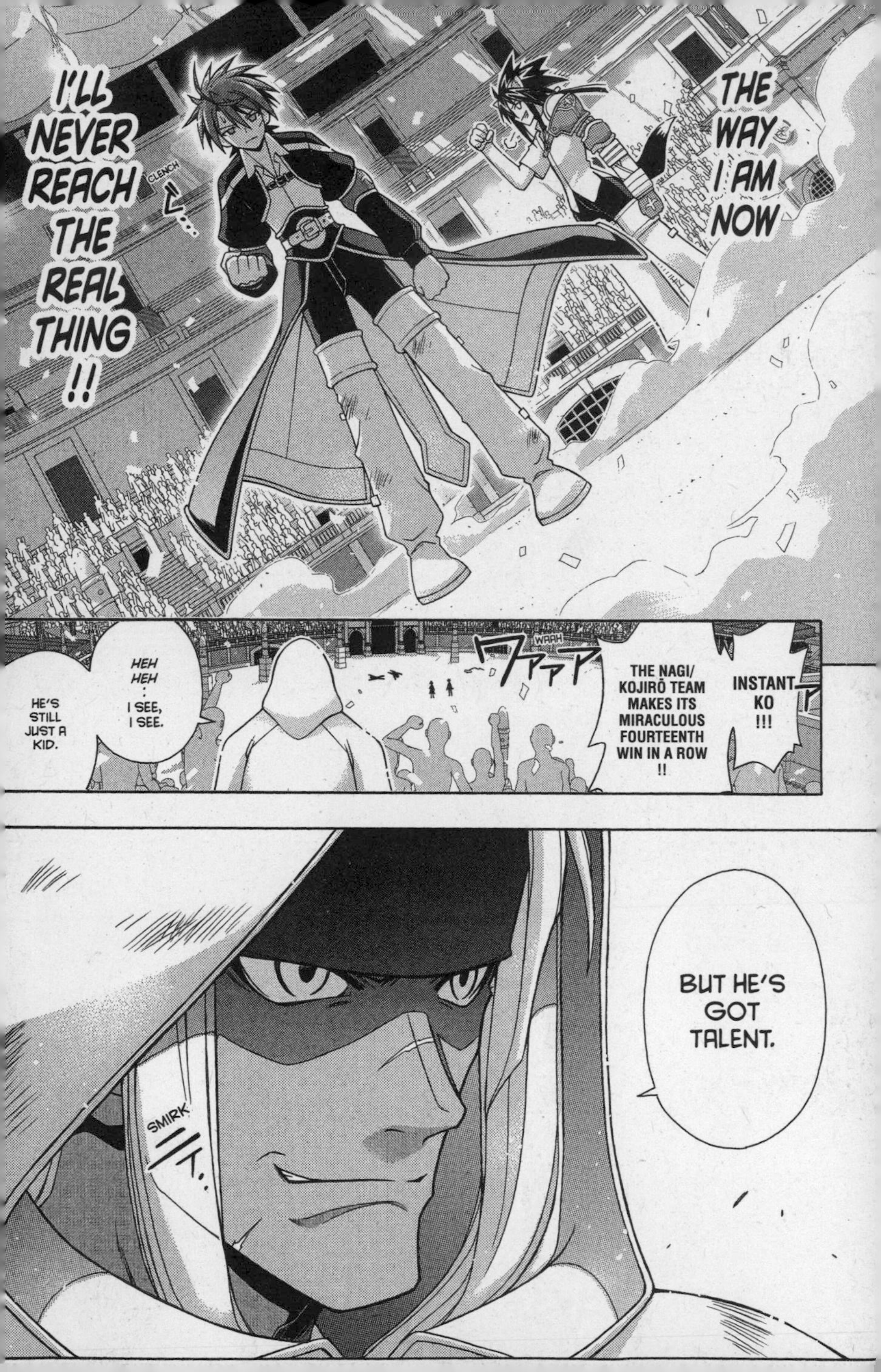
THE WAY I AM NOW
CLENCH
I'LL NEVER REACH THE REAL THING !!
INSTANT KO !!!
THE NAGI/ KOJIRŌ TEAM MAKES ITS MIRACULOUS FOURTEENTH WIN IN A ROW !!
WAAH
HEH HEH : I SEE, I SEE.
HE'S STILL JUST A KID.
BUT HE'S GOT TALENT.
SMIRK

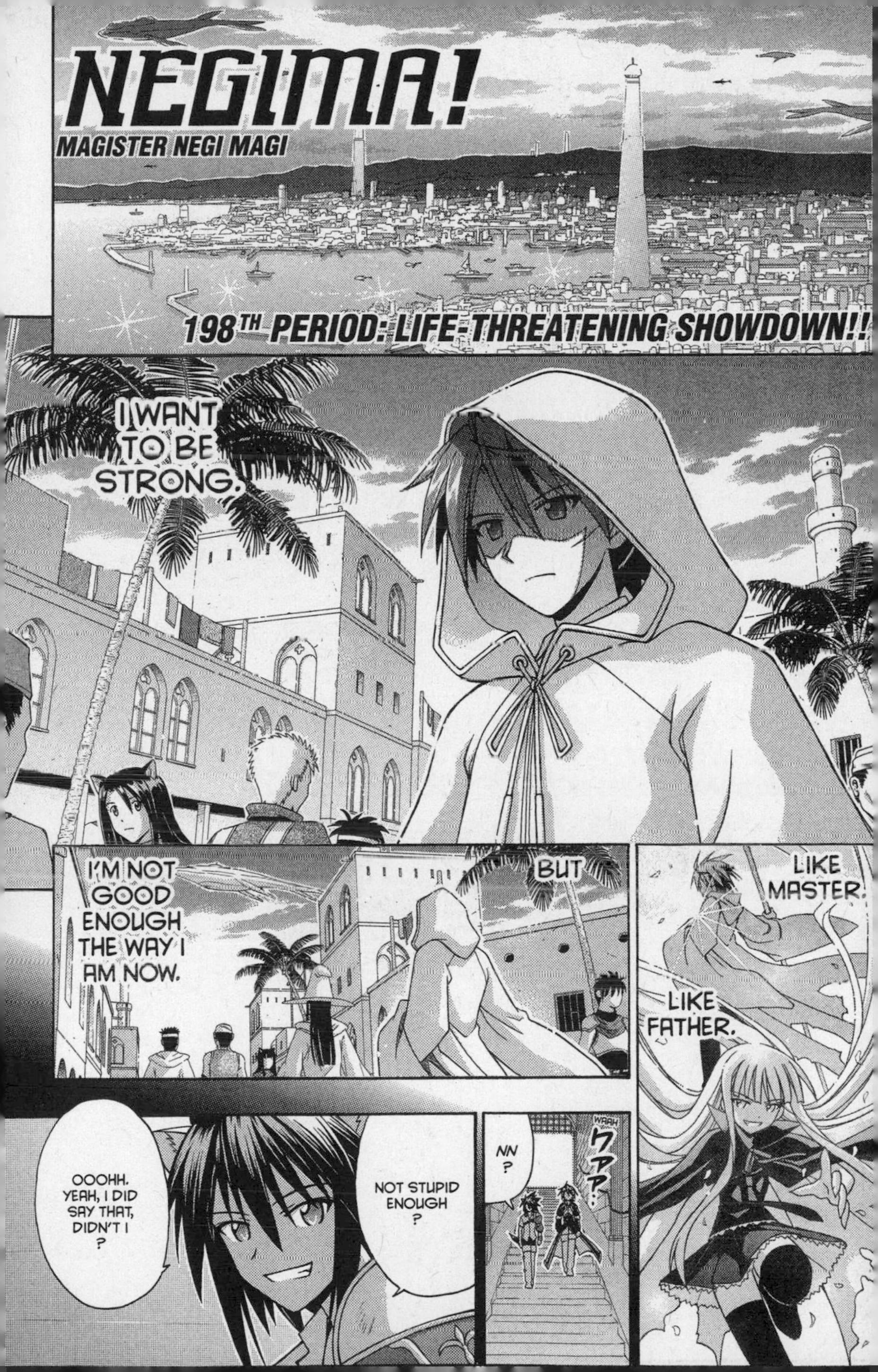
NEGIMA!
MAGISTER NEGI MAGI
198TH PERIOD: LIFE-THREATENING SHOWDOWN!!
I WANT TO BE STRONG.
LIKE MASTER.
LIKE FATHER.
BUT
I'M NOT GOOD ENOUGH THE WAY I AM NOW.
WAAH ワァ
NN?
NOT STUPID ENOUGH?
OOOHH. YEAH, I DID SAY THAT, DIDN'T I?

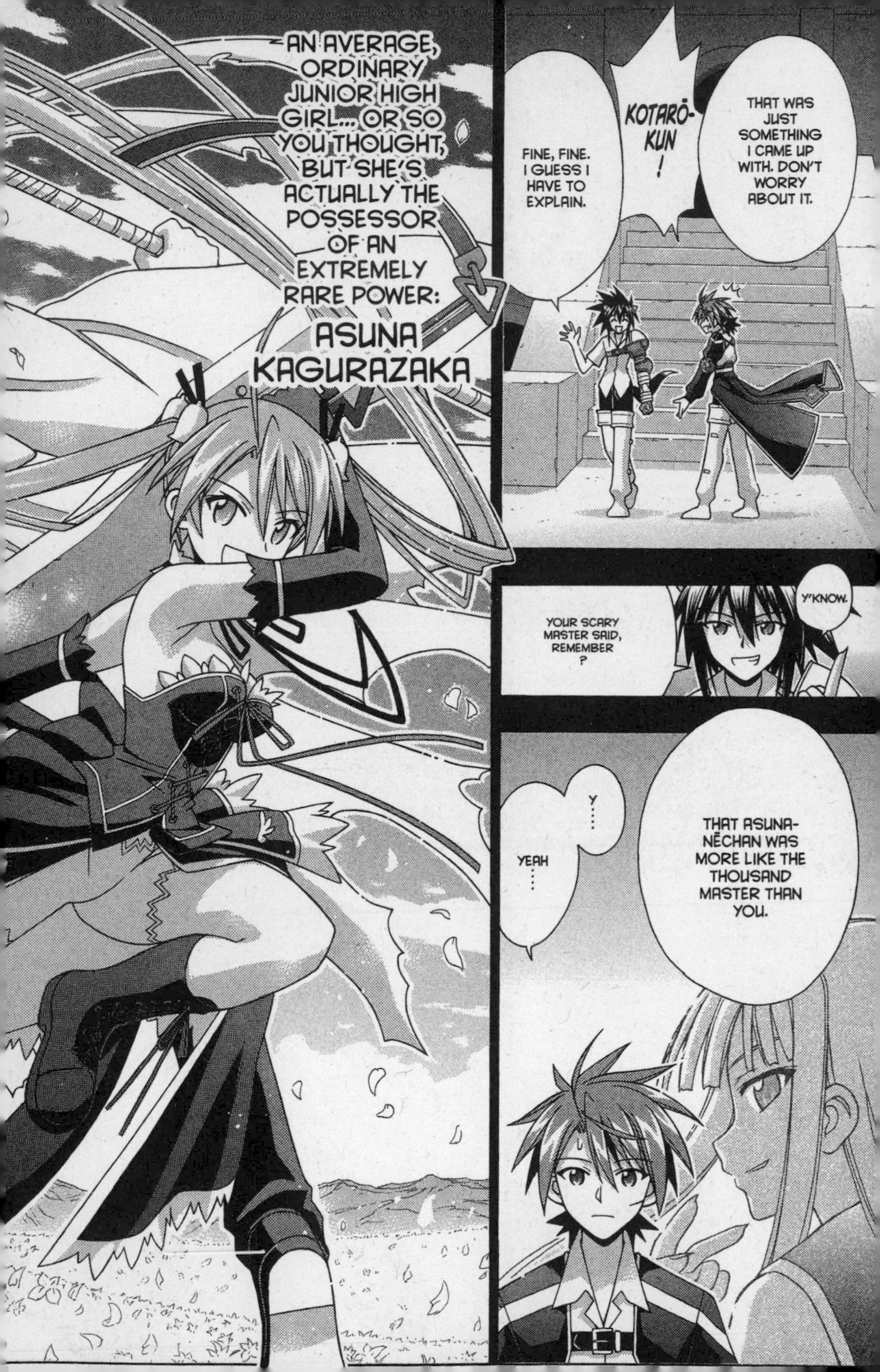
THAT WAS JUST SOMETHING I CAME UP WITH. DON'T WORRY ABOUT IT.
KOTARŌ-KUN!
FINE, FINE. I GUESS I HAVE TO EXPLAIN.
Y'KNOW.
YOUR SCARY MASTER SAID, REMEMBER?
THAT ASUNA-NĒCHAN WAS MORE LIKE THE THOUSAND MASTER THAN YOU.
Y.... YEAH....
AN AVERAGE, ORDINARY JUNIOR HIGH GIRL... OR SO YOU THOUGHT, BUT SHE'S ACTUALLY THE POSSESSOR OF AN EXTREMELY RARE POWER:
ASUNA KAGURAZAKA

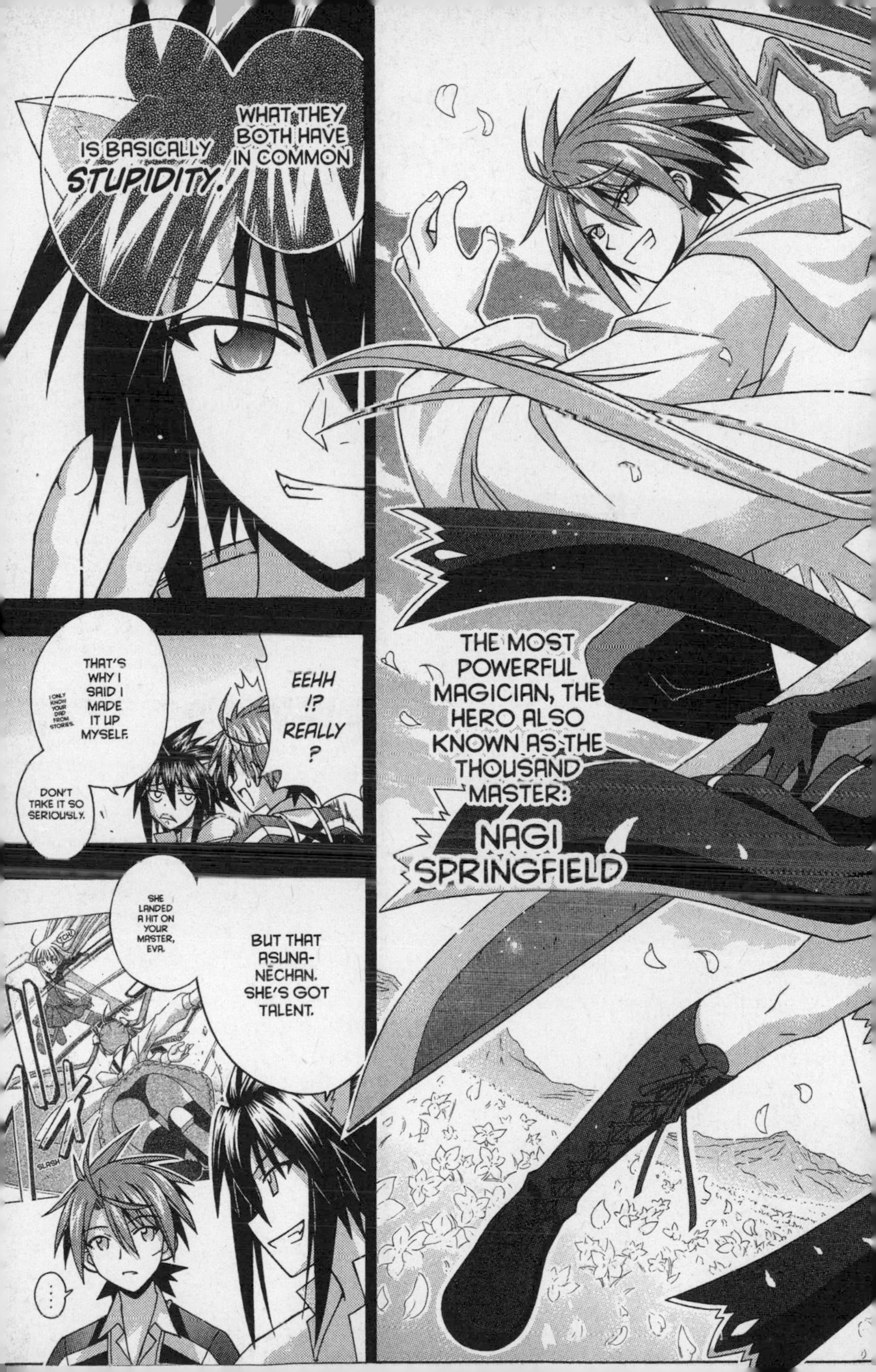
THE MOST POWERFUL MAGICIAN, THE HERO ALSO KNOWN AS THE THOUSAND MASTER:
NAGI SPRINGFIELD
WHAT THEY BOTH HAVE IN COMMON
IS BASICALLY STUPIDITY.
EEHH !? REALLY ?
THAT'S WHY I SAID I MADE IT UP MYSELF.
I ONLY KNOW YOUR DAD FROM STORIES.
DON'T TAKE IT SO SERIOUSLY.
BUT THAT ASUNA-NĒCHAN. SHE'S GOT TALENT.
SHE LANDED A HIT ON YOUR MASTER, EVA.
TCH
SLASH
...

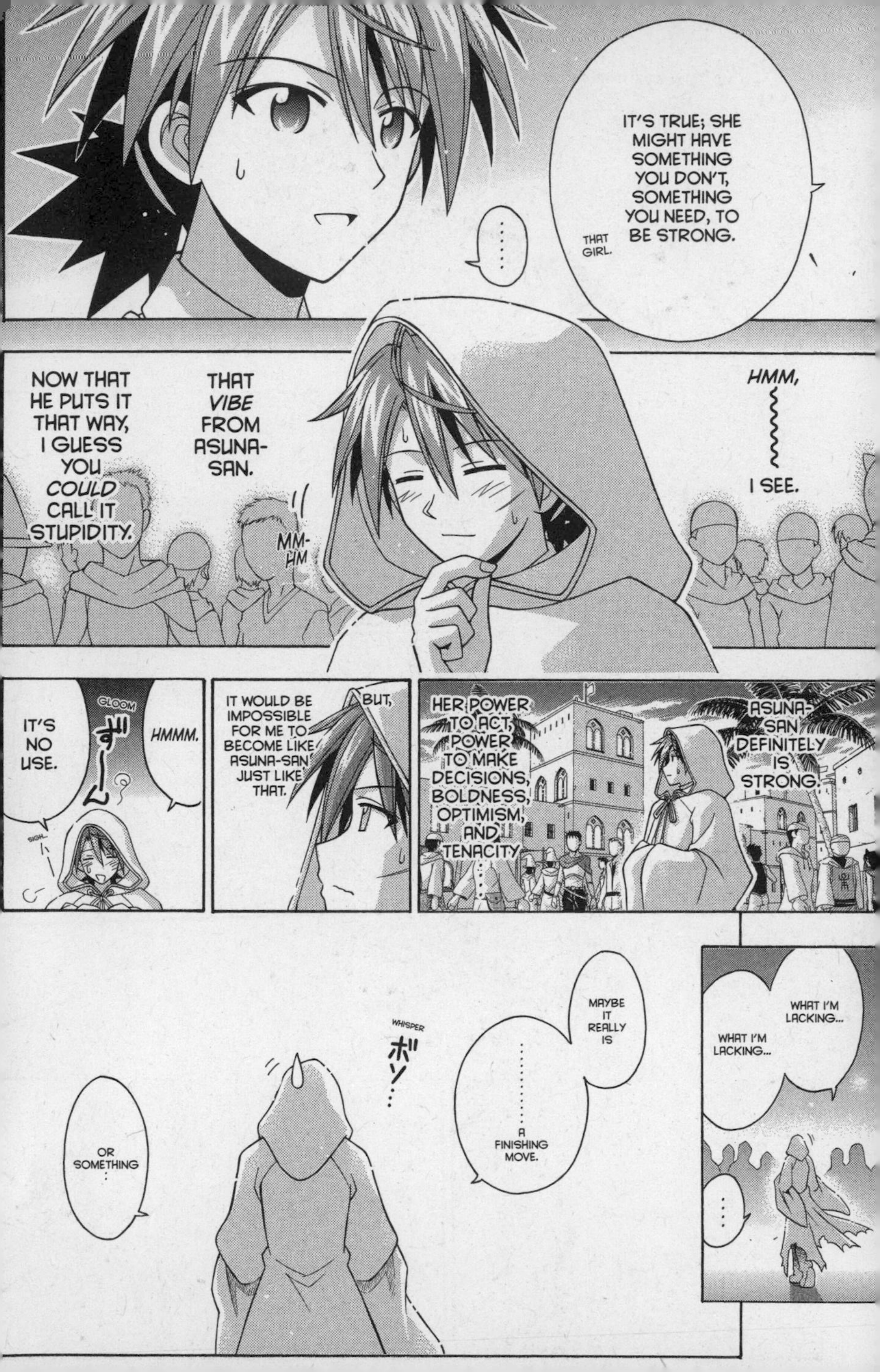
IT'S TRUE; SHE MIGHT HAVE SOMETHING YOU DON'T, SOMETHING YOU NEED, TO BE STRONG.
THAT GIRL.
......
HMM, I SEE.
THAT VIBE FROM ASUNA-SAN.
MM-HM
NOW THAT HE PUTS IT THAT WAY, I GUESS YOU COULD CALL IT STUPIDITY.
ASUNA-SAN DEFINITELY IS STRONG.
HER POWER TO ACT, POWER TO MAKE DECISIONS, BOLDNESS, OPTIMISM, AND TENACITY.
BUT,
IT WOULD BE IMPOSSIBLE FOR ME TO BECOME LIKE ASUNA-SAN JUST LIKE THAT.
HMMM.
GLOOM
ずーん
IT'S NO USE.
SIGH...
WHAT I'M LACKING...
WHAT I'M LACKING...
....
MAYBE IT REALLY IS ...... A FINISHING MOVE.
WHISPER
ボソ…
OR SOMETHING...

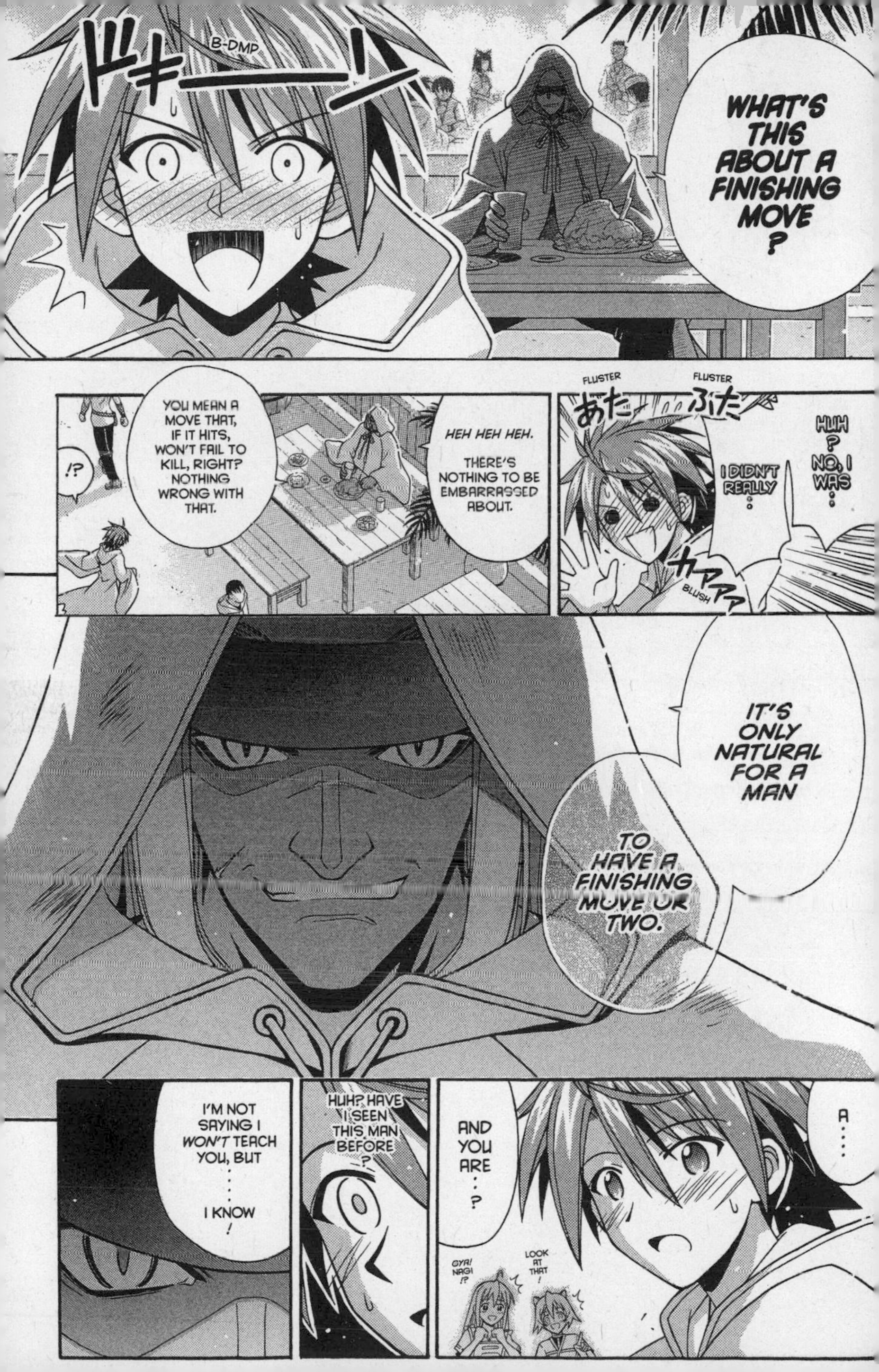
WHAT'S THIS ABOUT A FINISHING MOVE?
ドキーン
B-DMP
FLUSTER
あた
FLUSTER
ぶた
HUH? NO, I WAS...
I DIDN'T REALLY...
カァァ
BLUSH
HEH HEH HEH.
THERE'S NOTHING TO BE EMBARRASSED ABOUT.
YOU MEAN A MOVE THAT, IF IT HITS, WON'T FAIL TO KILL, RIGHT? NOTHING WRONG WITH THAT.
!?
IT'S ONLY NATURAL FOR A MAN
TO HAVE A FINISHING MOVE OR TWO.
A...
AND YOU ARE...?
LOOK AT THAT!
GYA! NAGI!?
HUH? HAVE I SEEN THIS MAN BEFORE?
I'M NOT SAYING I WON'T TEACH YOU, BUT...
I KNOW!

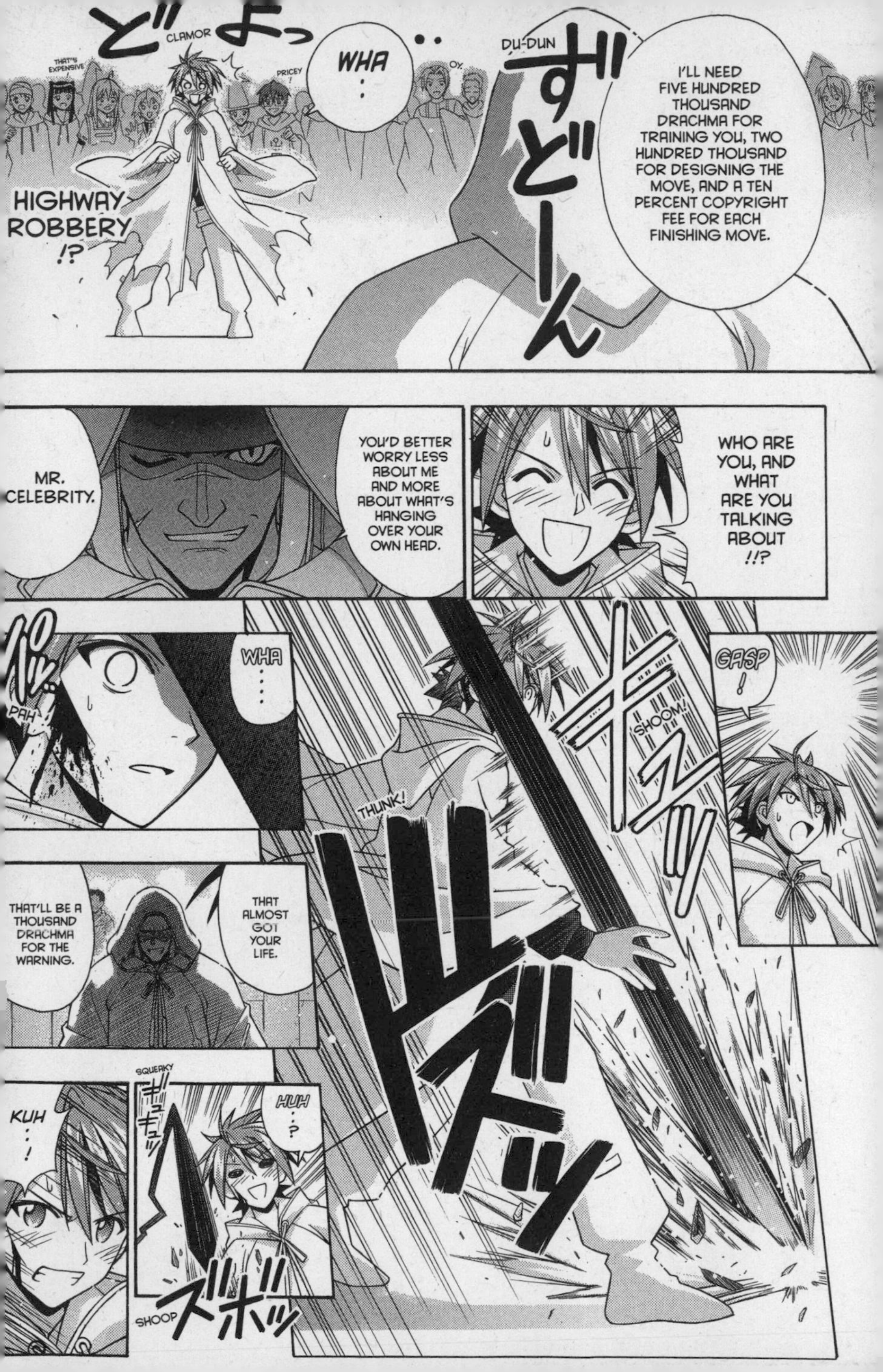
I'LL NEED FIVE HUNDRED THOUSAND DRACHMA FOR TRAINING YOU, TWO HUNDRED THOUSAND FOR DESIGNING THE MOVE, AND A TEN PERCENT COPYRIGHT FEE FOR EACH FINISHING MOVE.
ずどーん
DU-DUN
WHA ..
OY.
PRICEY!
どよっ
CLAMOR
THAT'S EXPENSIVE!
HIGHWAY ROBBERY!?
WHO ARE YOU, AND WHAT ARE YOU TALKING ABOUT!!?
YOU'D BETTER WORRY LESS ABOUT ME AND MORE ABOUT WHAT'S HANGING OVER YOUR OWN HEAD.
MR. CELEBRITY.
GASP!
SHOOM!
THUNK!
WHA....
PAH
THAT ALMOST GOT YOUR LIFE.
THAT'LL BE A THOUSAND DRACHMA FOR THE WARNING.
HUH..?
SQUEAKY
SHOOP
KUH..!

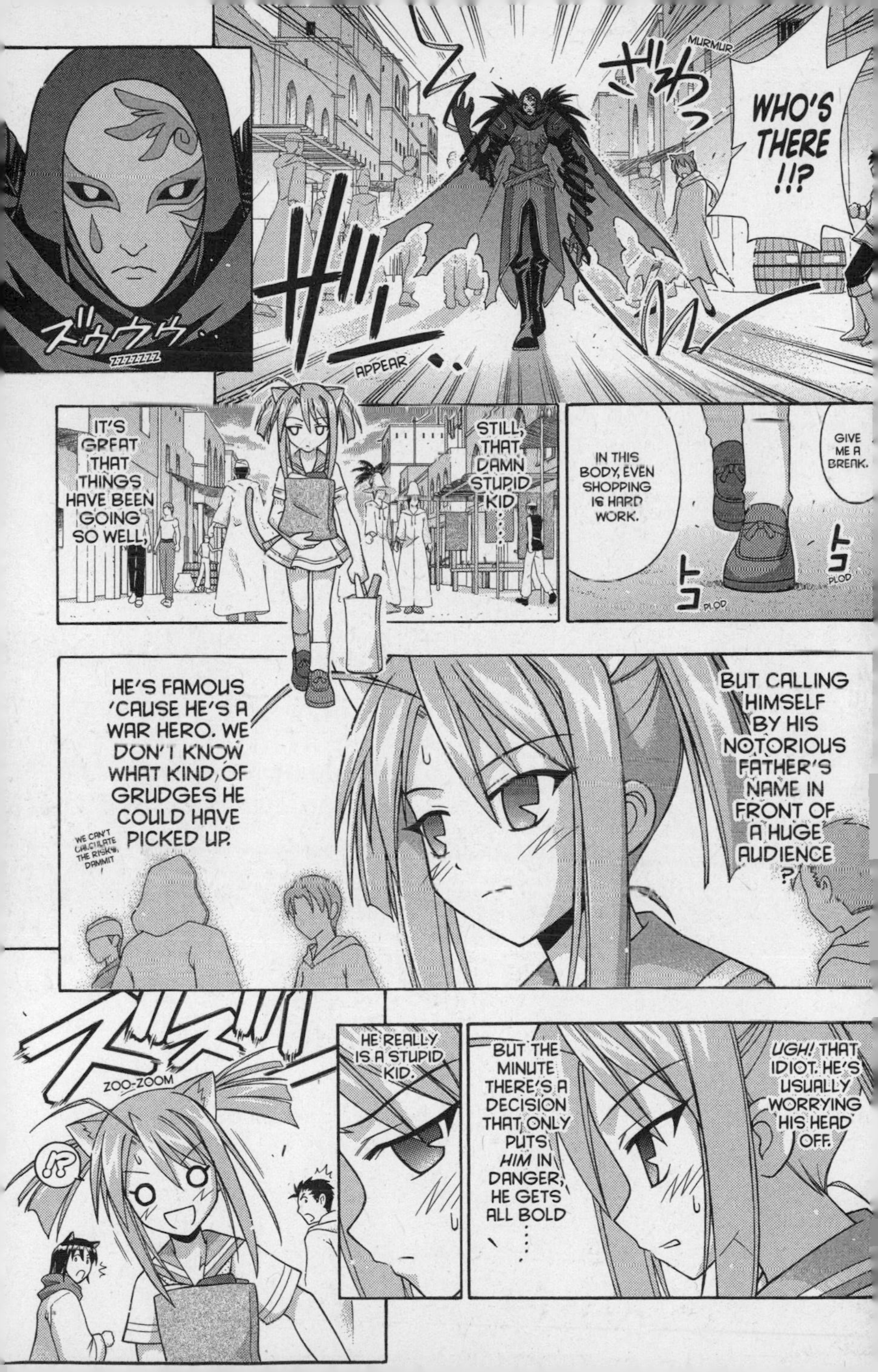
MURMUR
WHO'S THERE !!?
APPEAR
ZZZZZZZ
GIVE ME A BREAK.
IN THIS BODY, EVEN SHOPPING IS HARD WORK.
PLOD
PLOD
STILL, THAT DAMN STUPID KID . . .
IT'S GREAT THAT THINGS HAVE BEEN GOING SO WELL,
BUT CALLING HIMSELF BY HIS NOTORIOUS FATHER'S NAME IN FRONT OF A HUGE AUDIENCE ?
HE'S FAMOUS 'CAUSE HE'S A WAR HERO. WE DON'T KNOW WHAT KIND OF GRUDGES HE COULD HAVE PICKED UP.
WE CAN'T CALCULATE THE RISKS, DAMMIT
UGH! THAT IDIOT. HE'S USUALLY WORRYING HIS HEAD OFF.
BUT THE MINUTE THERE'S A DECISION THAT ONLY PUTS HIM IN DANGER, HE GETS ALL BOLD . . . . . .
HE REALLY IS A STUPID KID.
ZOO-ZOOM
!?

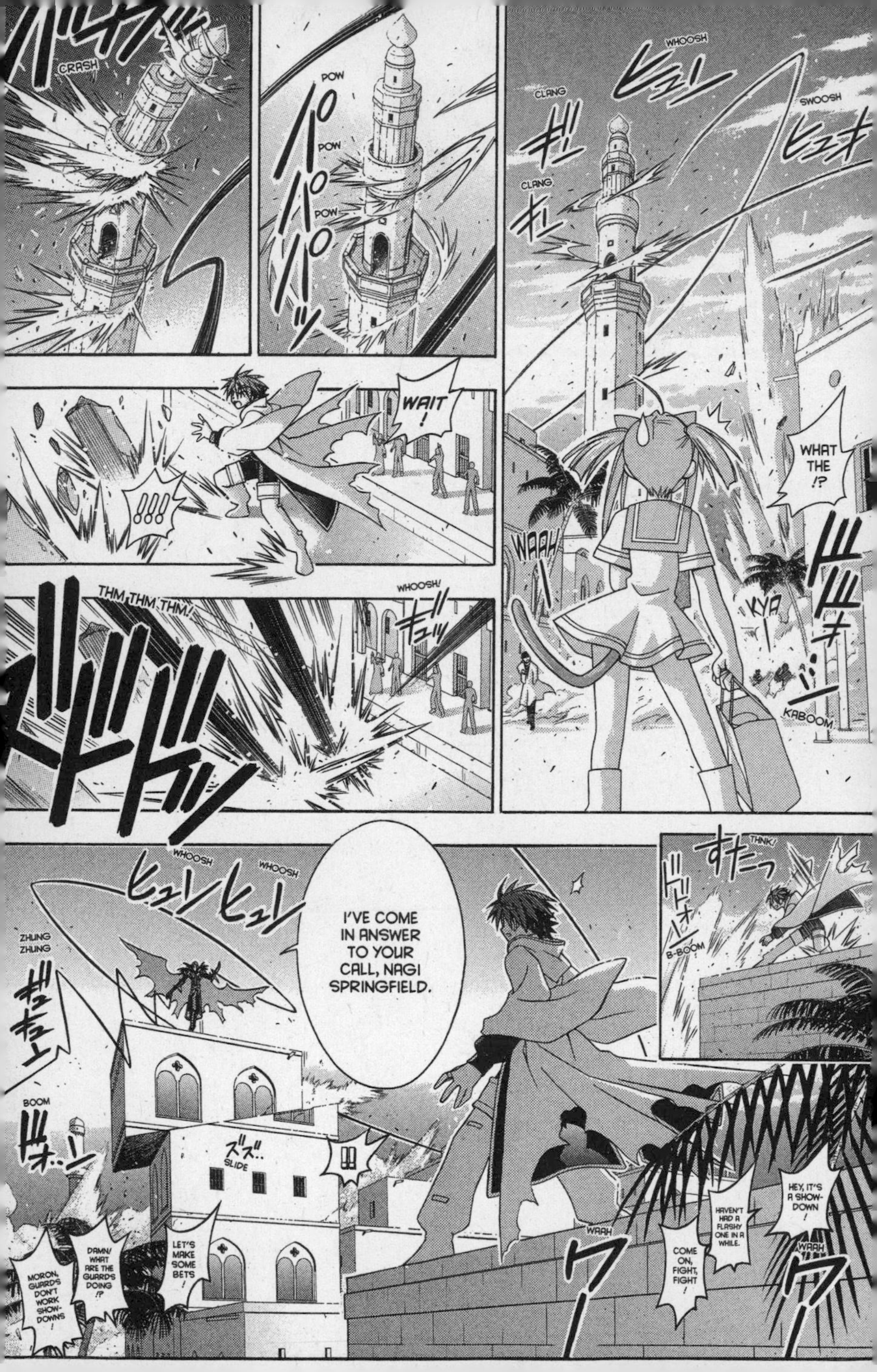
WHOOSH
SWOOSH
CLANG
CLANG
WHAT THE !?
WAAH
KYA
KABOOM
POW
POW
POW
CRASH
WAIT!
!!!!
WHOOSH!
THM THM THM!
THNK!
B-BOOM
WHOOSH
WHOOSH
I'VE COME IN ANSWER TO YOUR CALL, NAGI SPRINGFIELD.
ZHUNG ZHUNG
BOOM
SLIDE
!!
HEY, IT'S A SHOW-DOWN!
WAAH
HAVEN'T HAD A FLASHY ONE IN A WHILE.
COME ON, FIGHT, FIGHT!
WAAH
LET'S MAKE SOME BETS
DAMN! WHAT ARE THE GUARDS DOING!?
MORON, GUARDS DON'T WORK SHOW-DOWNS!

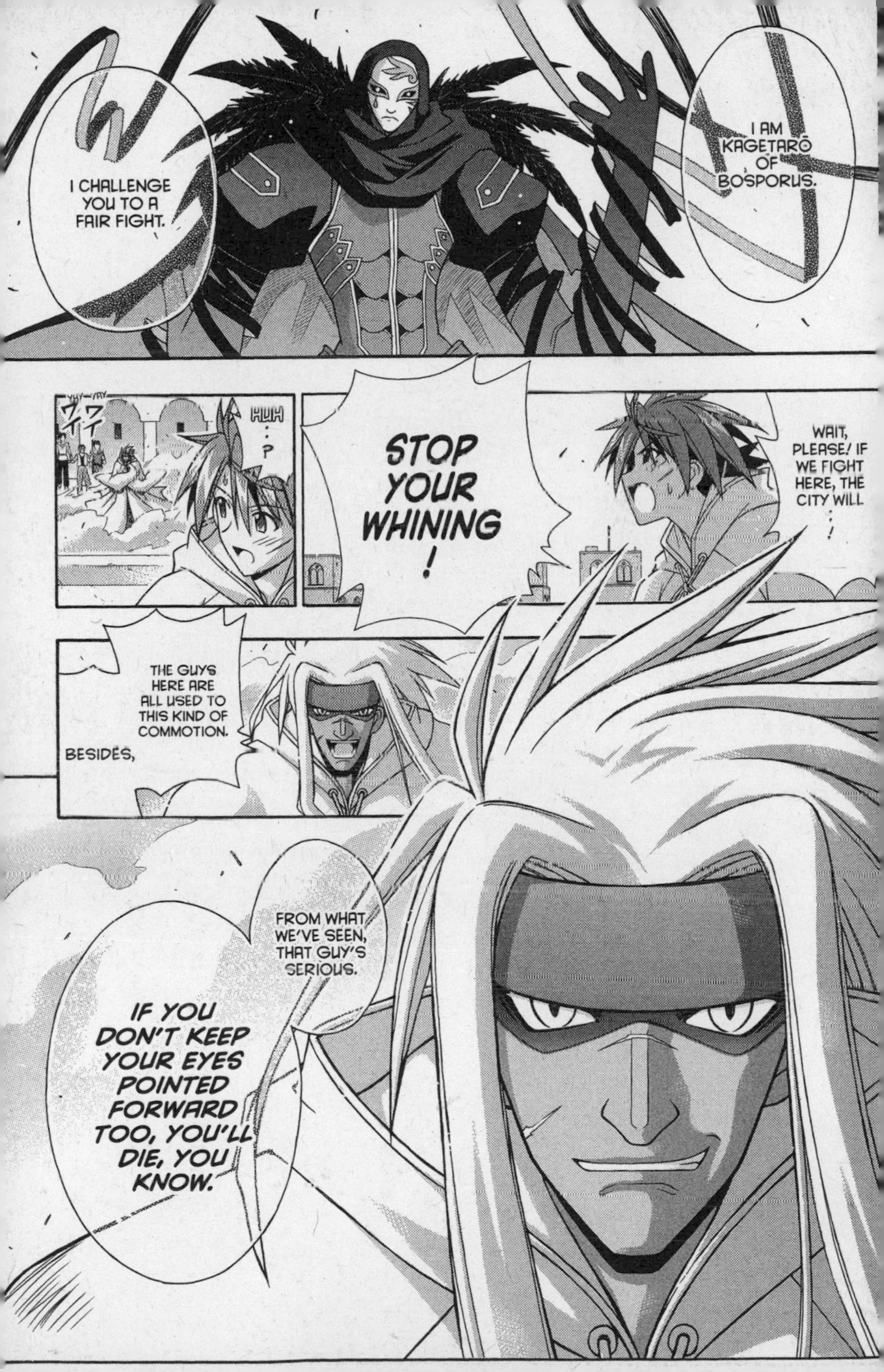
I AM KAGETARŌ OF BOSPORUS.
I CHALLENGE YOU TO A FAIR FIGHT.
WAIT, PLEASE! IF WE FIGHT HERE, THE CITY WILL
STOP YOUR WHINING!
YAY-YAY
ワイワイ
HUH...?
THE GUYS HERE ARE ALL USED TO THIS KIND OF COMMOTION.
BESIDES,
FROM WHAT WE'VE SEEN, THAT GUY'S SERIOUS.
IF YOU DON'T KEEP YOUR EYES POINTED FORWARD TOO, YOU'LL DIE, YOU KNOW.

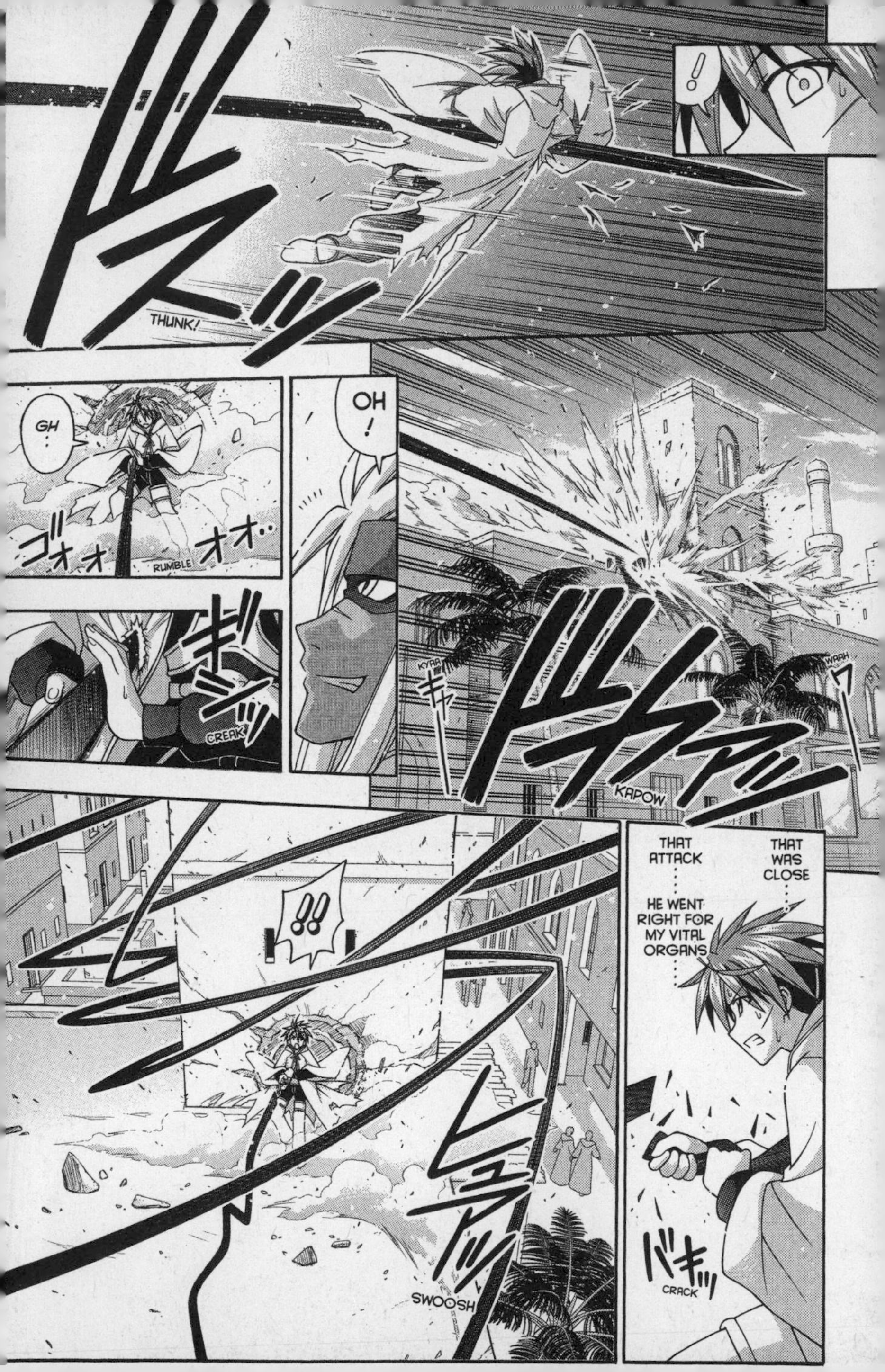
!
THUNK!
KAPOW
KYAA
WAAH
OH!
GH...
RUMBLE
CREAK
THAT WAS CLOSE...
THAT ATTACK... HE WENT RIGHT FOR MY VITAL ORGANS...
CRACK
!!
SWOOSH

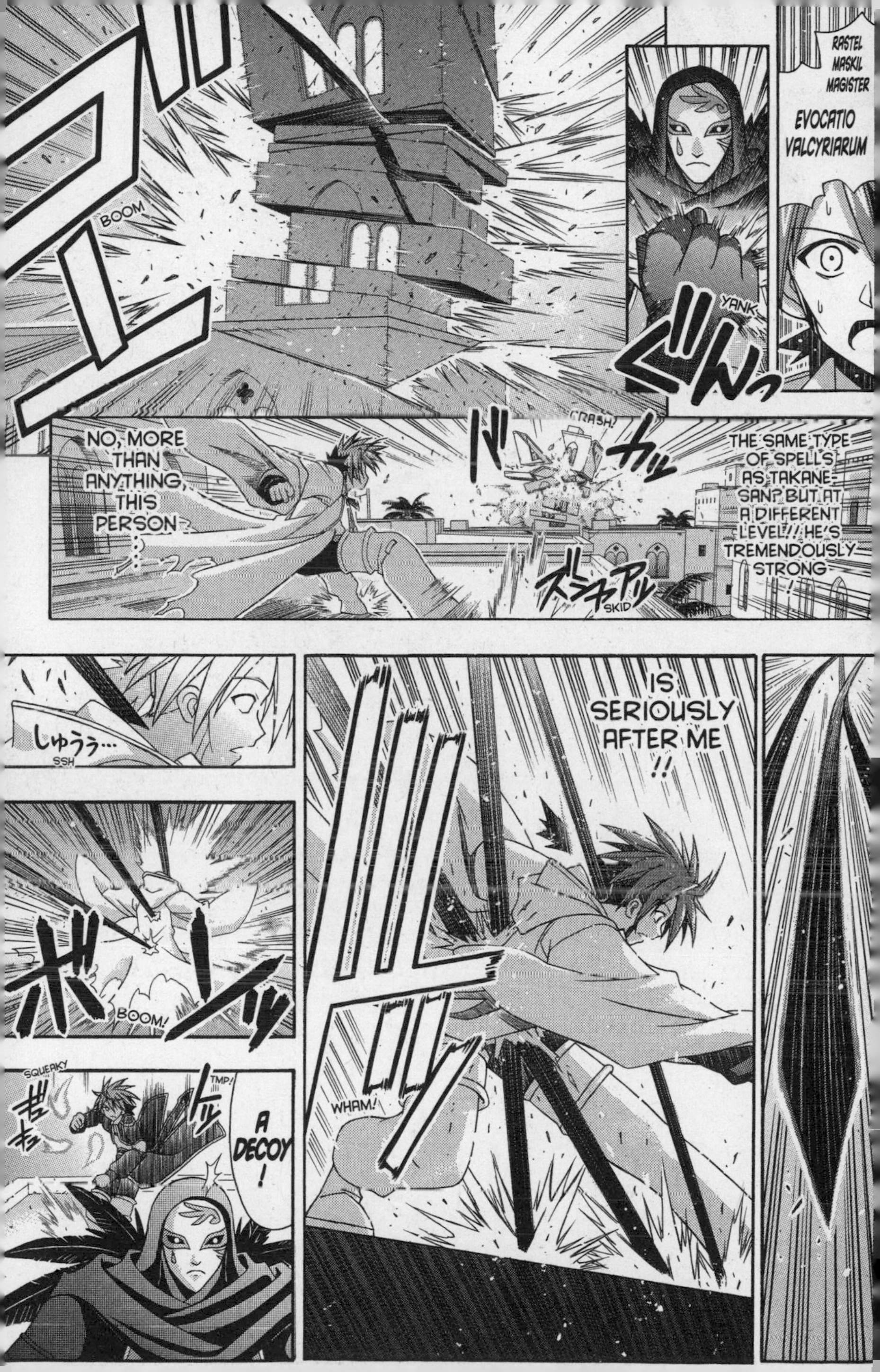
RASTEL MASKIL MAGISTER
EVOCATIO VALCYRIARUM
YANK
BOOM
THE SAME TYPE OF SPELLS AS TAKANE-SAN? BUT AT A DIFFERENT LEVEL!! HE'S TREMENDOUSLY STRONG!
CRASH!
SKID
NO, MORE THAN ANYTHING, THIS PERSON...
IS SERIOUSLY AFTER ME!!
WHAM!
じゅうう…
SSH
BOOM!
SQUEAKY
TMP!
A DECOY!

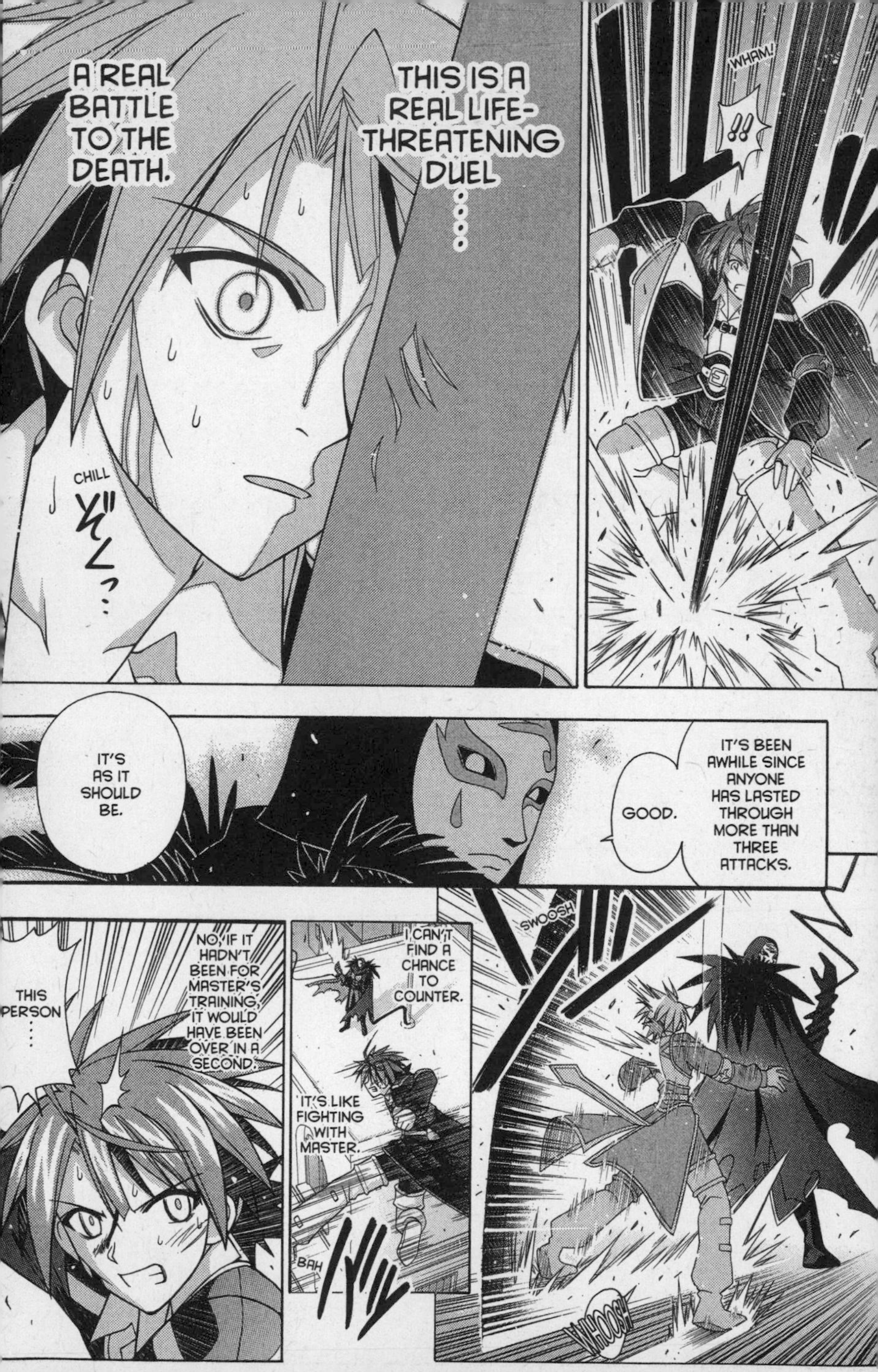
WHAM!
!!
THIS IS A REAL LIFE-THREATENING DUEL....
A REAL BATTLE TO THE DEATH.
CHILL
GOOD.
IT'S BEEN AWHILE SINCE ANYONE HAS LASTED THROUGH MORE THAN THREE ATTACKS.
IT'S AS IT SHOULD BE.
SWOOSH
WHOOSH
I CAN'T FIND A CHANCE TO COUNTER.
IT'S LIKE FIGHTING WITH MASTER.
BAH
NO, IF IT HADN'T BEEN FOR MASTER'S TRAINING, IT WOULD HAVE BEEN OVER IN A SECOND.
THIS PERSON....

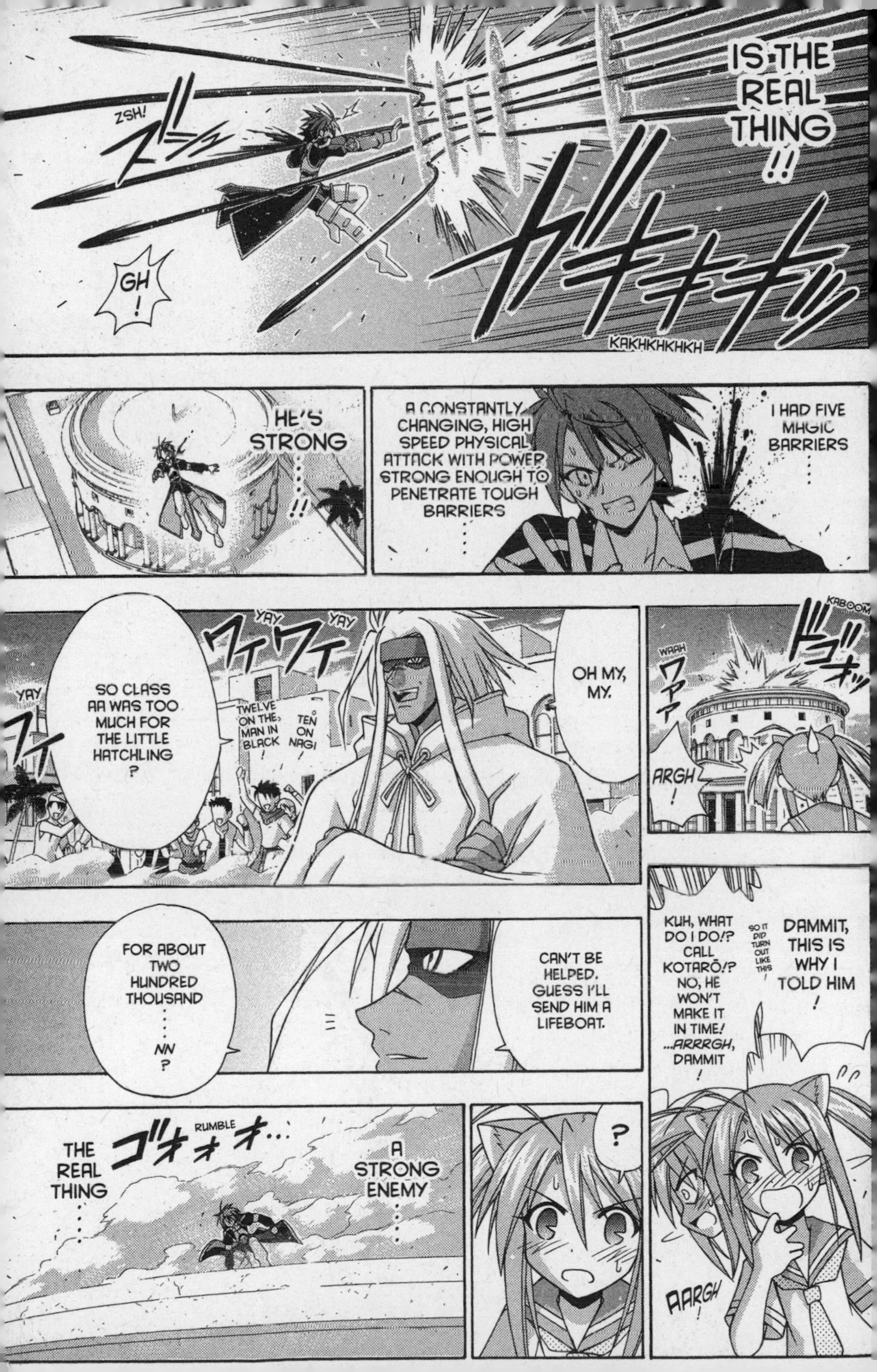
IS THE REAL THING !!
ZSH!
KAKHKHKHKH
GH!
I HAD FIVE MAGIC BARRIERS ......
A CONSTANTLY CHANGING, HIGH SPEED PHYSICAL ATTACK WITH POWER STRONG ENOUGH TO PENETRATE TOUGH BARRIERS ......
HE'S STRONG ......!!
KABOOM
WAAH
ARGH!
OH MY, MY.
YAY
YAY
TEN ON NAGI!
TWELVE ON THE MAN IN BLACK!
SO CLASS AA WAS TOO MUCH FOR THE LITTLE HATCHLING?
YAY
DAMMIT, THIS IS WHY I TOLD HIM!
SO IT DID TURN OUT LIKE THIS!
KUH, WHAT DO I DO!? CALL KOTARŌ!? NO, HE WON'T MAKE IT IN TIME! ...ARRRGH, DAMMIT!
AARGH!
CAN'T BE HELPED. GUESS I'LL SEND HIM A LIFEBOAT.
FOR ABOUT TWO HUNDRED THOUSAND ...... NN?
?
A STRONG ENEMY ......
RUMBLE
THE REAL THING ......

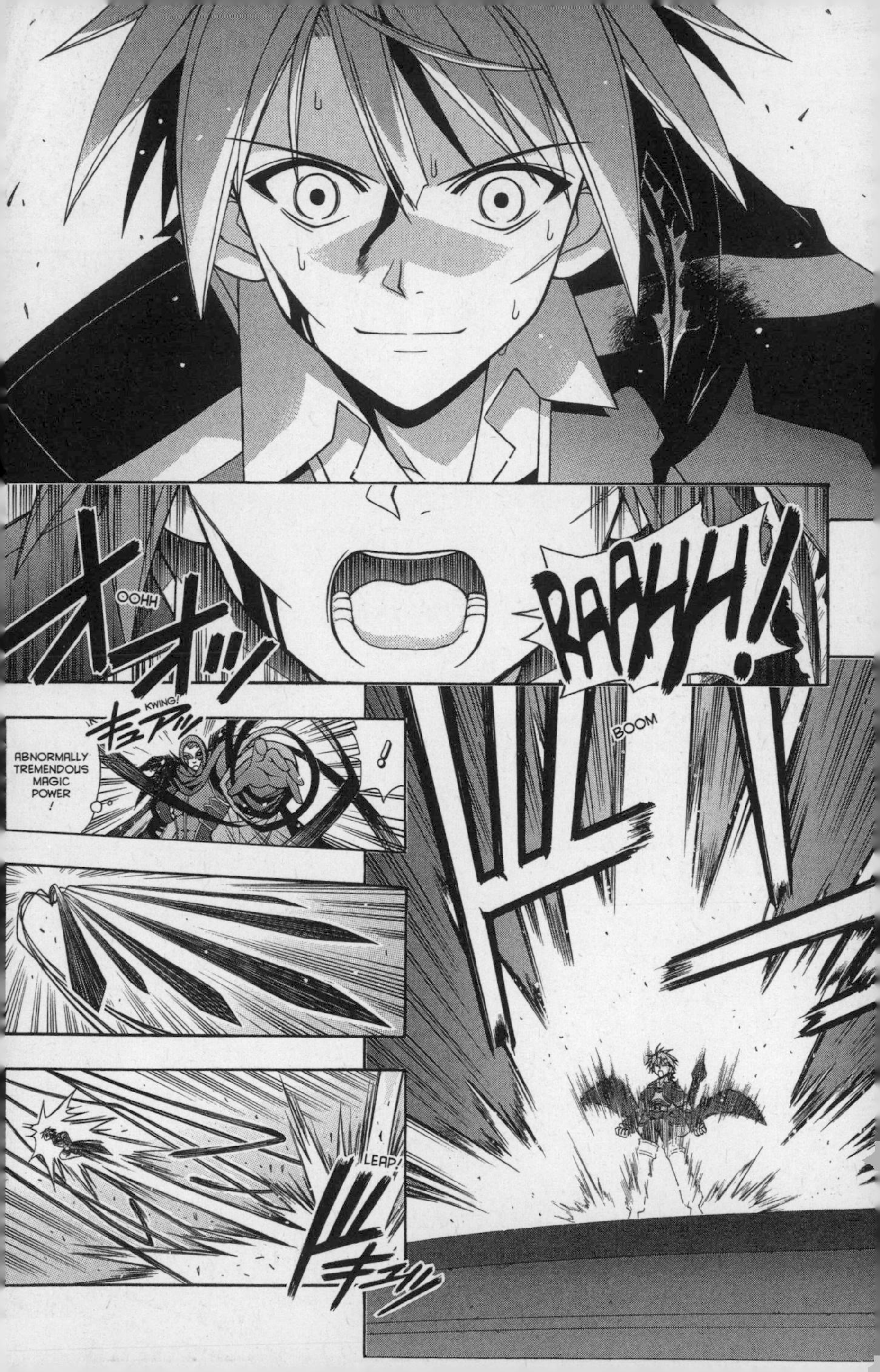
OOHH
RAAHH!!
BOOM
KWING!
ABNORMALLY TREMENDOUS MAGIC POWER!
LEAP!

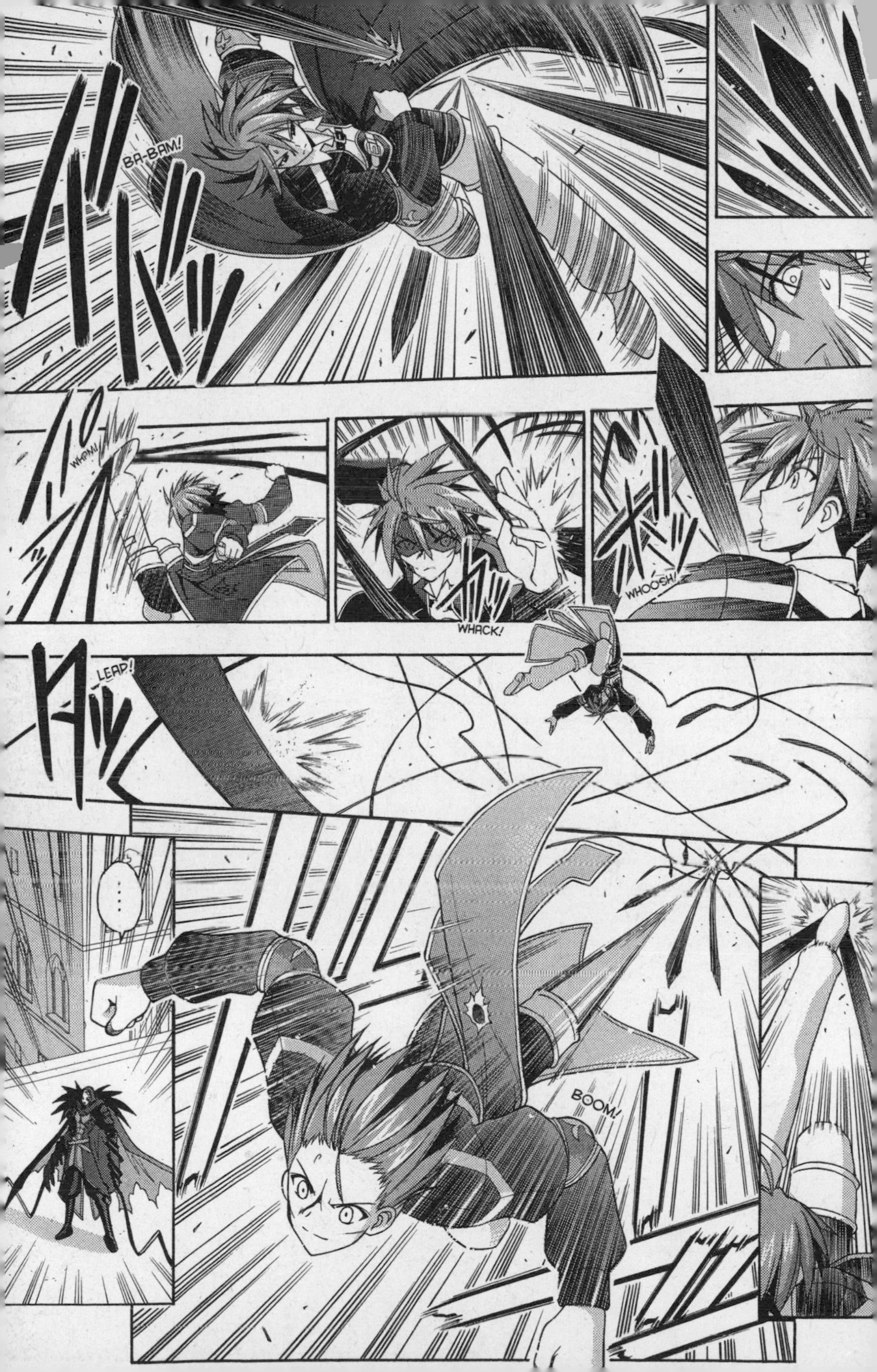
BA-BAM!
WHOOSH!
WHACK!
WHAM!
LEAP!
BOOM!
.....

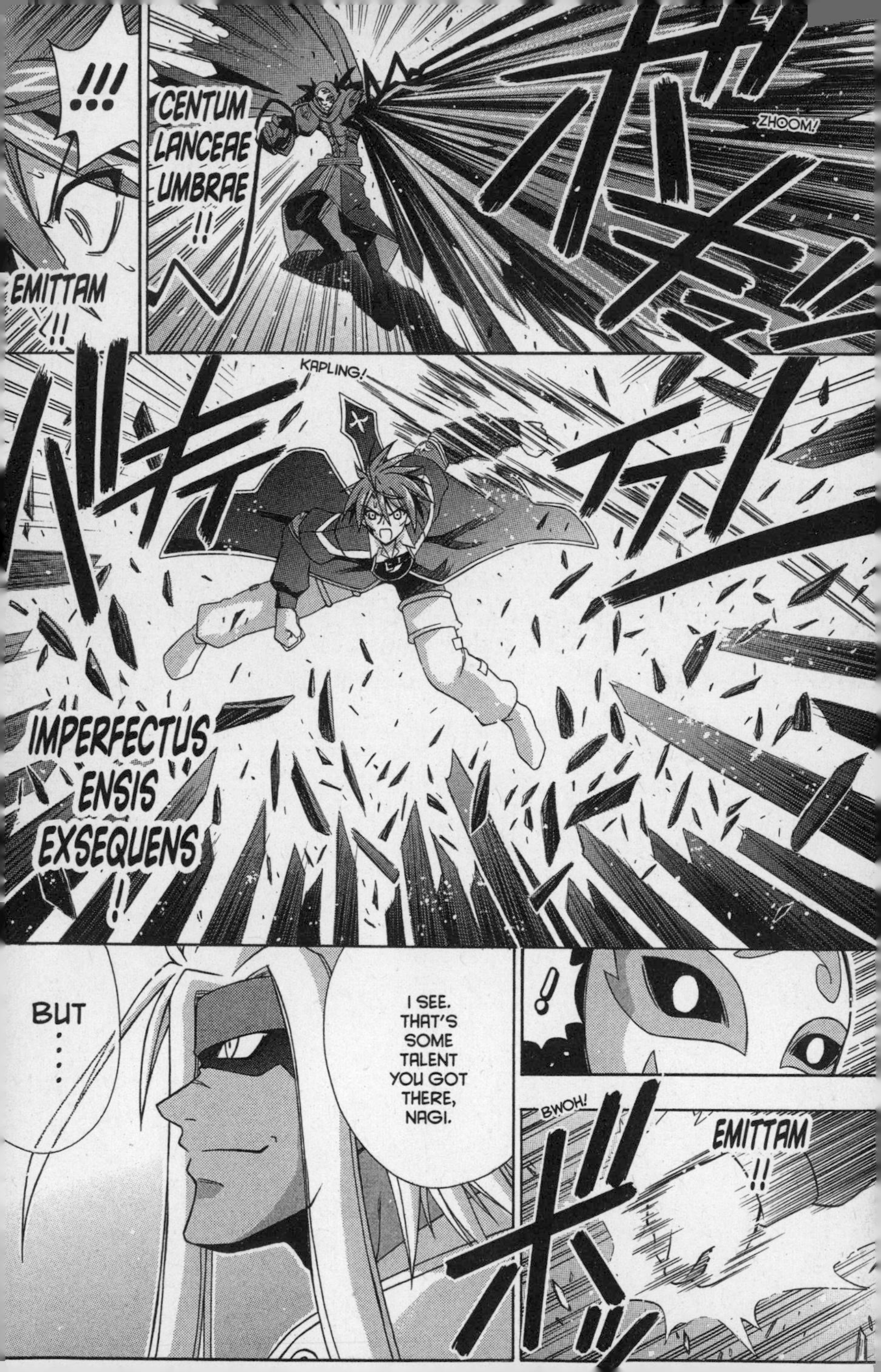
ZHOOM!
CENTUM LANCEAE UMBRAE!!
!!!
EMITTAM!!
KAPLING!
IMPERFECTUS ENSIS EXSEQUENS!!
!
BWOH!
EMITTAM!!
I SEE. THAT'S SOME TALENT YOU GOT THERE, NAGI.
BUT......

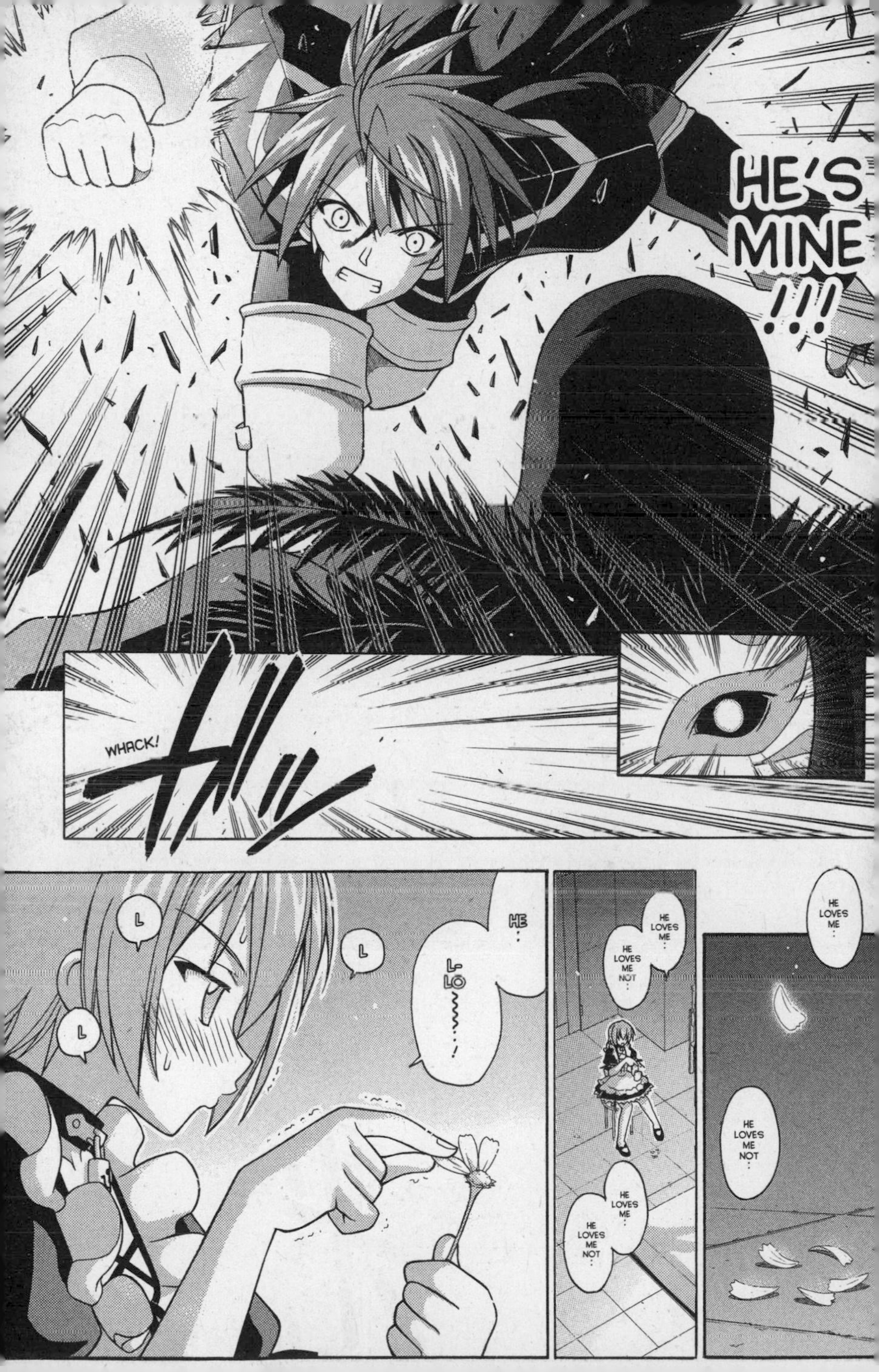
HE'S MINE !!!
WHACK!
HE LOVES ME...
HE LOVES ME NOT...
HE LOVES ME...
HE LOVES ME NOT...
HE LOVES ME...
HE LOVES ME NOT...
HE...
L-LO~~...!
L
L
L

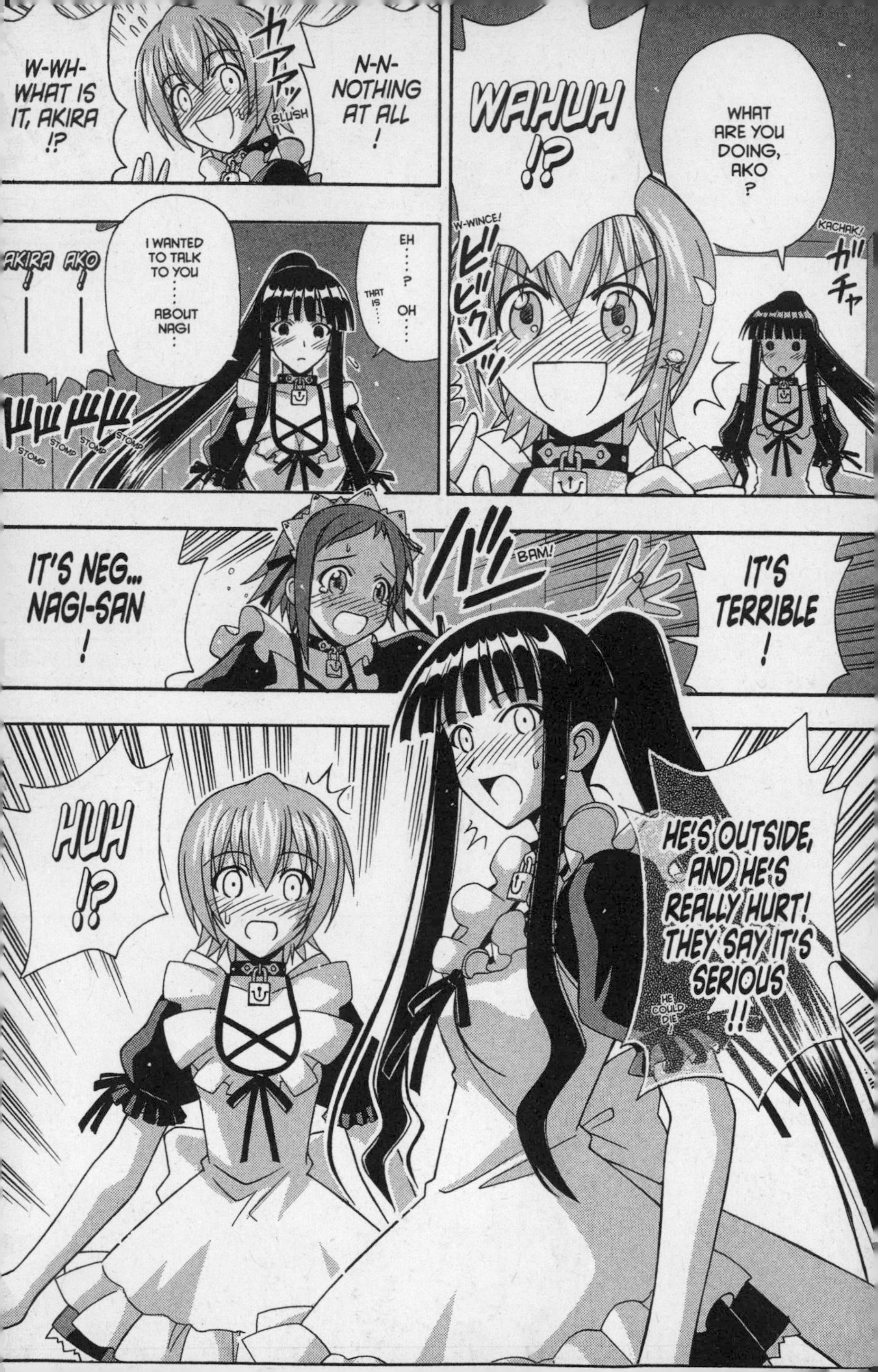
WHAT ARE YOU DOING, AKO?
KACHAK!
WAHUH!?
W-WINCE!
N-N-NOTHING AT ALL!
BLUSH
W-WH-WHAT IS IT, AKIRA!?
EH...? OH...
THAT IS...
I WANTED TO TALK TO YOU... ABOUT NAGI...
AKO!
AKIRA!
STOMP
STOMP
STOMP
STOMP
IT'S TERRIBLE!
BAM!
IT'S NEG... NAGI-SAN!
HE'S OUTSIDE, AND HE'S REALLY HURT! THEY SAY IT'S SERIOUS!!
HE COULD DIE!
HUH!?

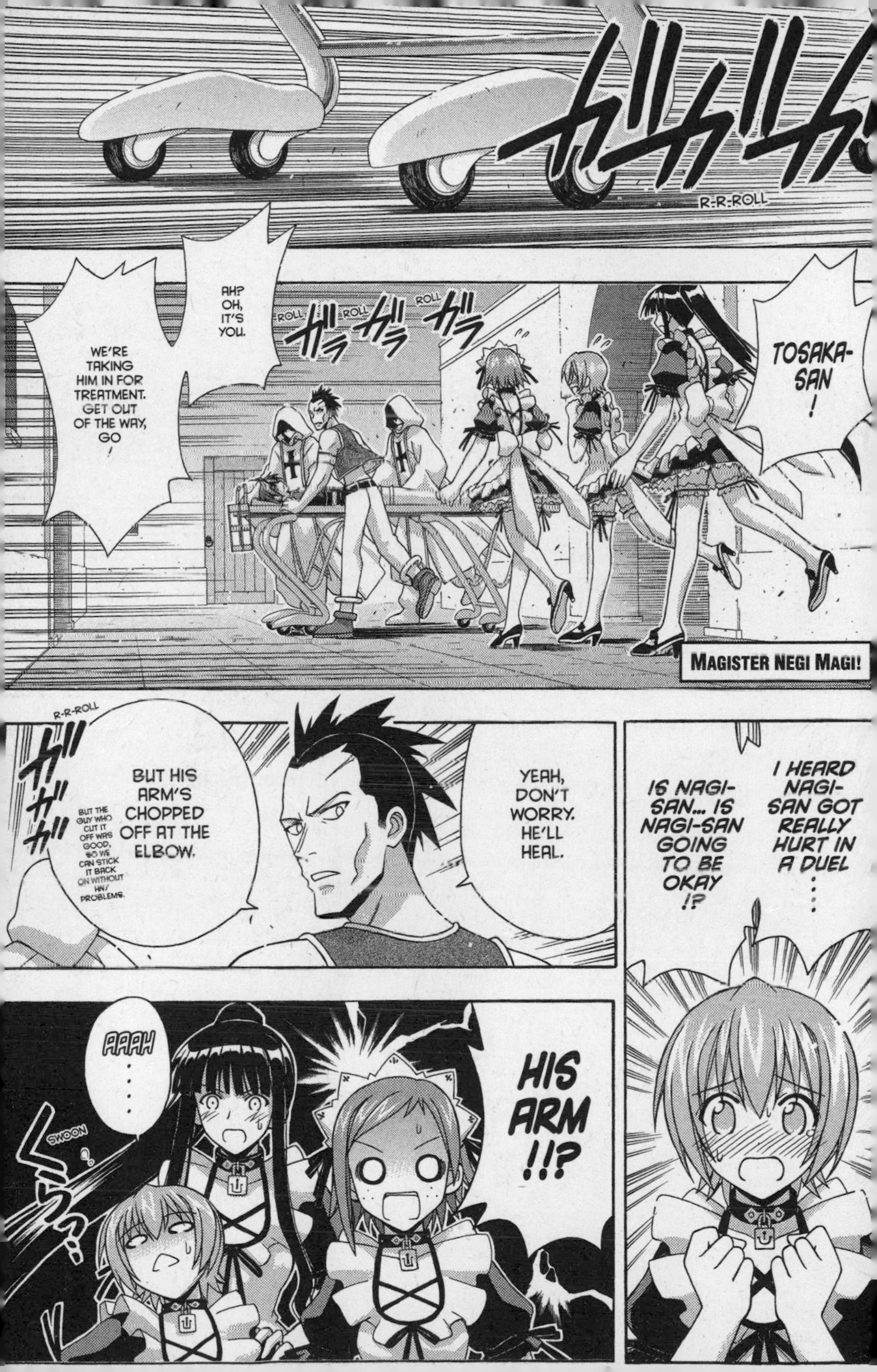
R-R-ROLL
TOSAKA-SAN!
AH? OH, IT'S YOU.
ROLL ROLL ROLL
WE'RE TAKING HIM IN FOR TREATMENT. GET OUT OF THE WAY, GO!
MAGISTER NEGI MAGI!
I HEARD NAGI-SAN GOT REALLY HURT IN A DUEL...
IS NAGI-SAN... IS NAGI-SAN GOING TO BE OKAY!?
YEAH, DON'T WORRY. HE'LL HEAL.
BUT HIS ARM'S CHOPPED OFF AT THE ELBOW.
BUT THE GUY WHO CUT IT OFF WAS GOOD, SO WE CAN STICK IT BACK ON WITHOUT ANY PROBLEMS.
R-R-ROLL
HIS ARM!!?
AAAH...
SWOON

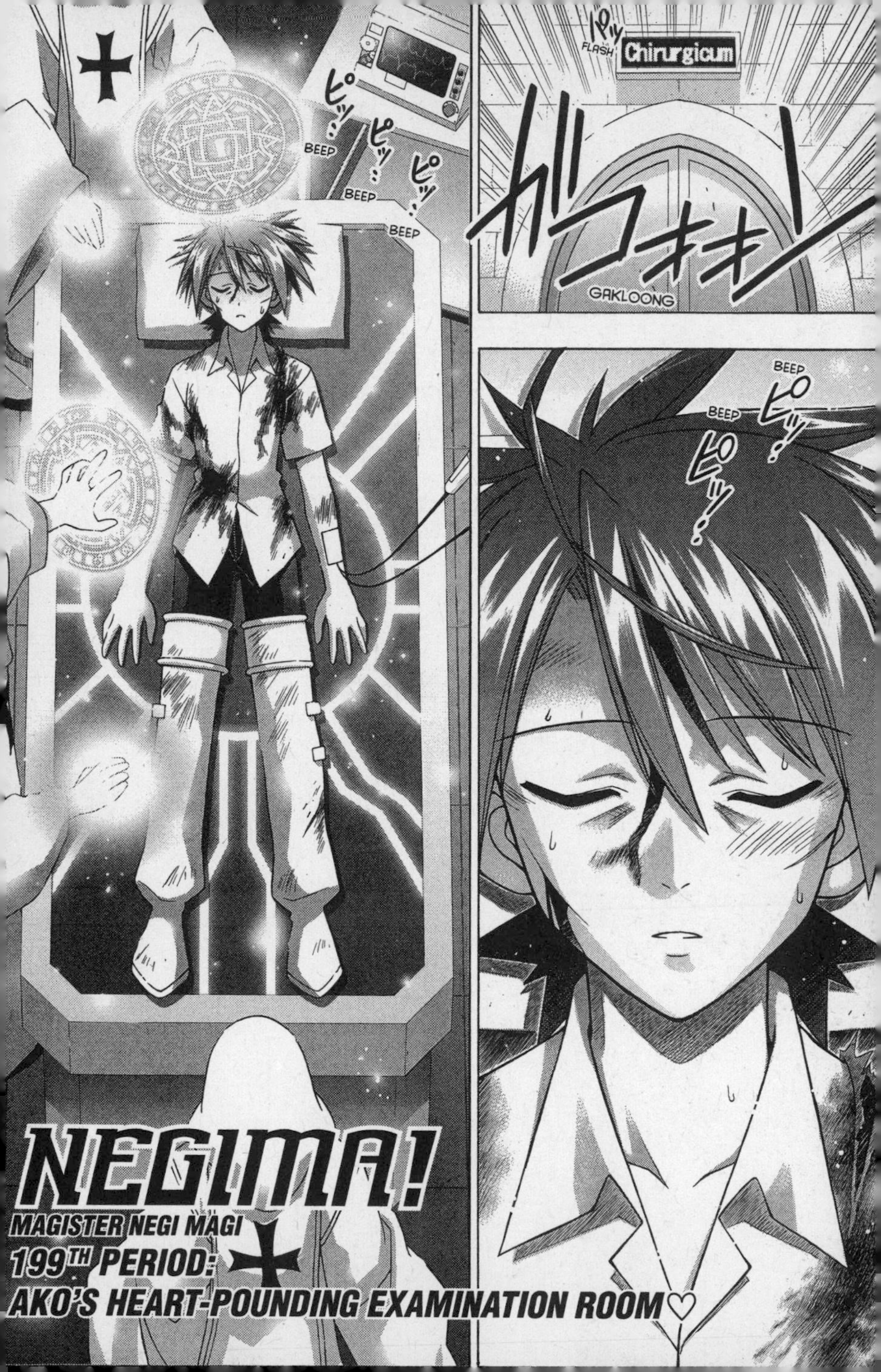
FLASH
Chirurgicum
GAKLOONG
BEEP
BEEP
BEEP
BEEP
BEEP
NEGIMA!
MAGISTER NEGI MAGI
199TH PERIOD:
AKO'S HEART-POUNDING EXAMINATION ROOM♡

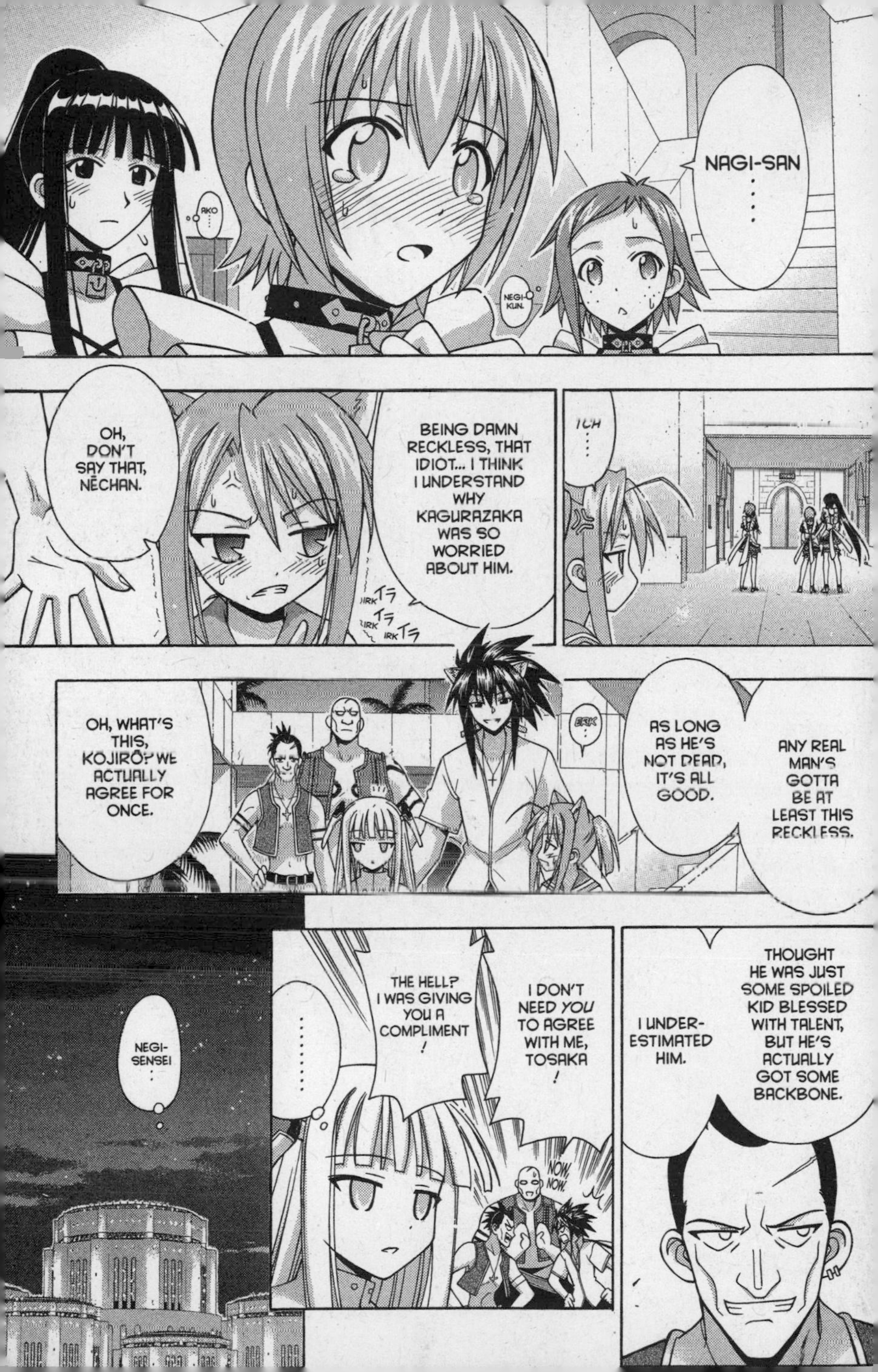
NAGI-SAN ....
NEGI-KUN.
AKO ...
TCH ...
BEING DAMN RECKLESS, THAT IDIOT... I THINK I UNDERSTAND WHY KAGURAZAKA WAS SO WORRIED ABOUT HIM.
IRK IRK IRK
OH, DON'T SAY THAT, NĒCHAN.
ANY REAL MAN'S GOTTA BE AT LEAST THIS RECKLESS.
AS LONG AS HE'S NOT DEAD, IT'S ALL GOOD.
ERK ...
OH, WHAT'S THIS, KOJIRŌ? WE ACTUALLY AGREE FOR ONCE.
THOUGHT HE WAS JUST SOME SPOILED KID BLESSED WITH TALENT, BUT HE'S ACTUALLY GOT SOME BACKBONE.
I UNDER-ESTIMATED HIM.
I DON'T NEED *YOU* TO AGREE WITH ME, TOSAKA!
THE HELL? I WAS GIVING YOU A COMPLIMENT!
NOW, NOW.
......
NEGI-SENSEI ...

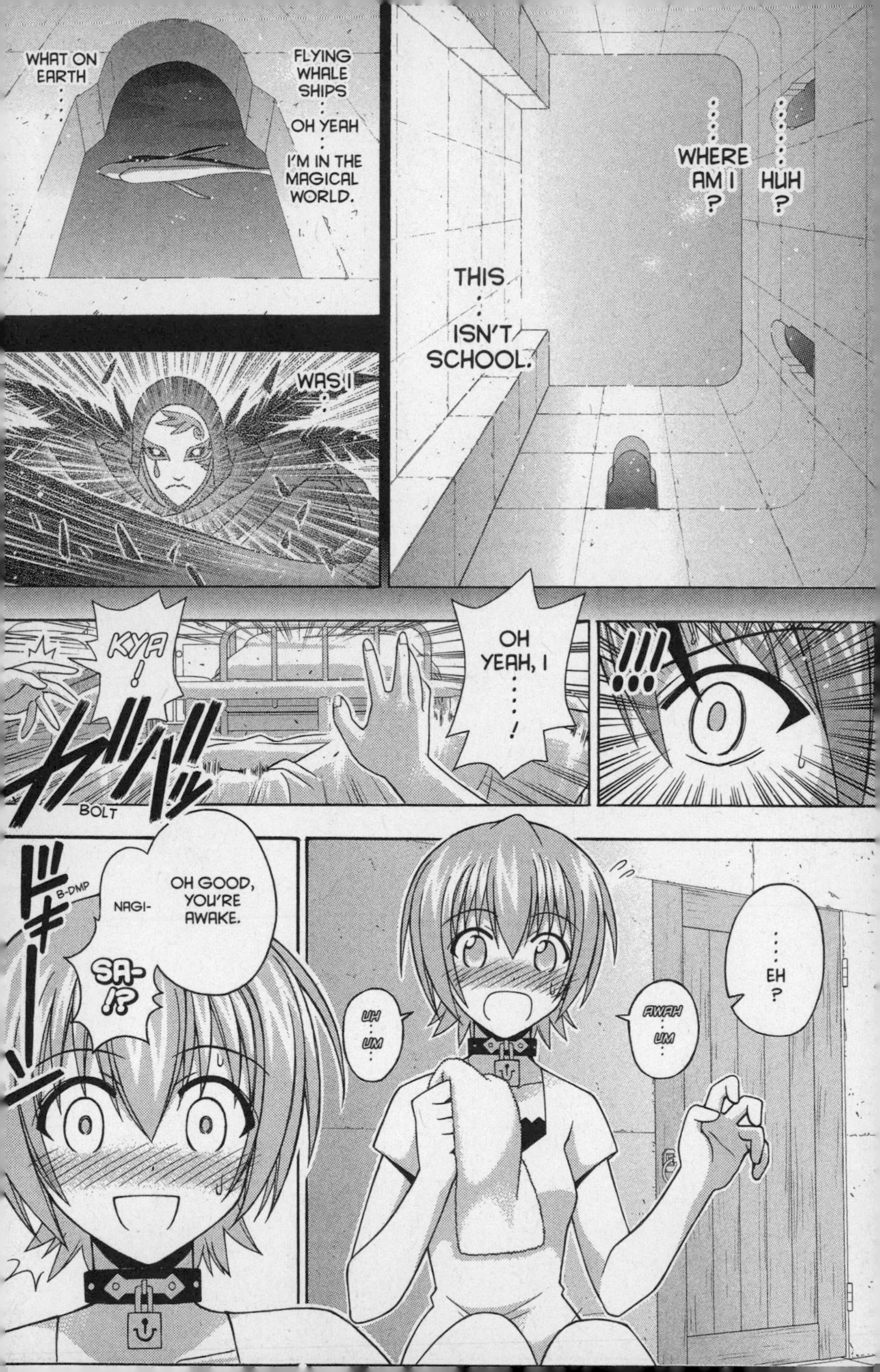

......HUH?
......WHERE AM I?
THIS... ISN'T SCHOOL.
FLYING WHALE SHIPS... OH YEAH... I'M IN THE MAGICAL WORLD.
WHAT ON EARTH...
WAS I...
!!!
OH YEAH, I.....!
KYA!
BOLT
.....EH?
AWAH... UM...
UH... UM...
OH GOOD, YOU'RE AWAKE.
NAGI-
SA-!?
B-DMP

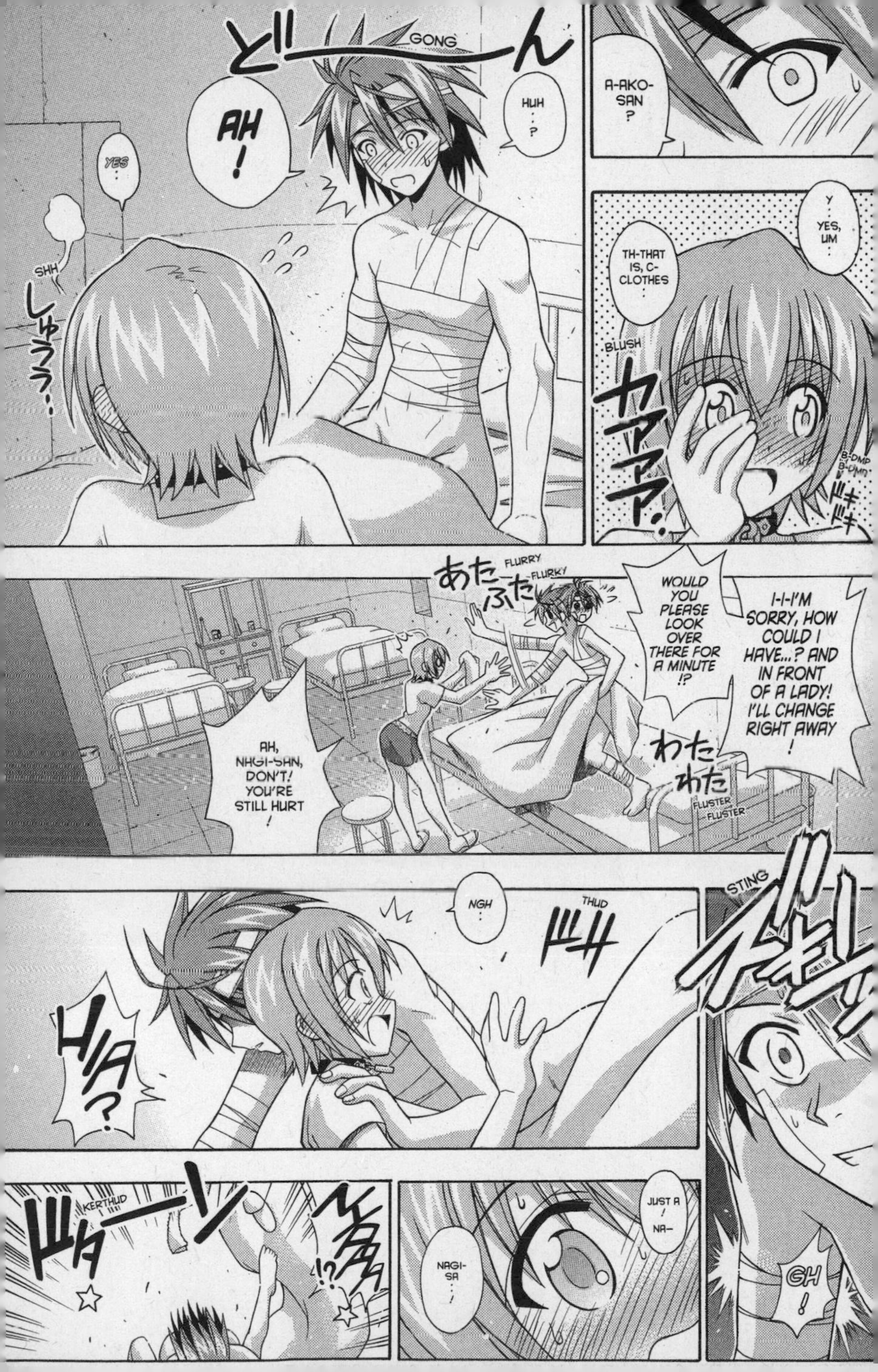
A-AKO-SAN?
Y... YES, UM
TH-THAT IS, C-CLOTHES...
BLUSH
カァァァ
B-DMP B-DMP
ドキドキ
どーーん
GONG
HUH...?
AH!
YES...
SHH
しゅるる...
I-I-I'M SORRY, HOW COULD I HAVE...? AND IN FRONT OF A LADY! I'LL CHANGE RIGHT AWAY!
WOULD YOU PLEASE LOOK OVER THERE FOR A MINUTE!?
あたふた
FLURRY FLURRY
わたわた
FLUSTER FLUSTER
AH, NAGI-SAN, DON'T! YOU'RE STILL HURT!
STING
GH!
NGH...
THUD
HYA?
JUST A! NA—
NAGI-SA...!
KERTHUD
!?

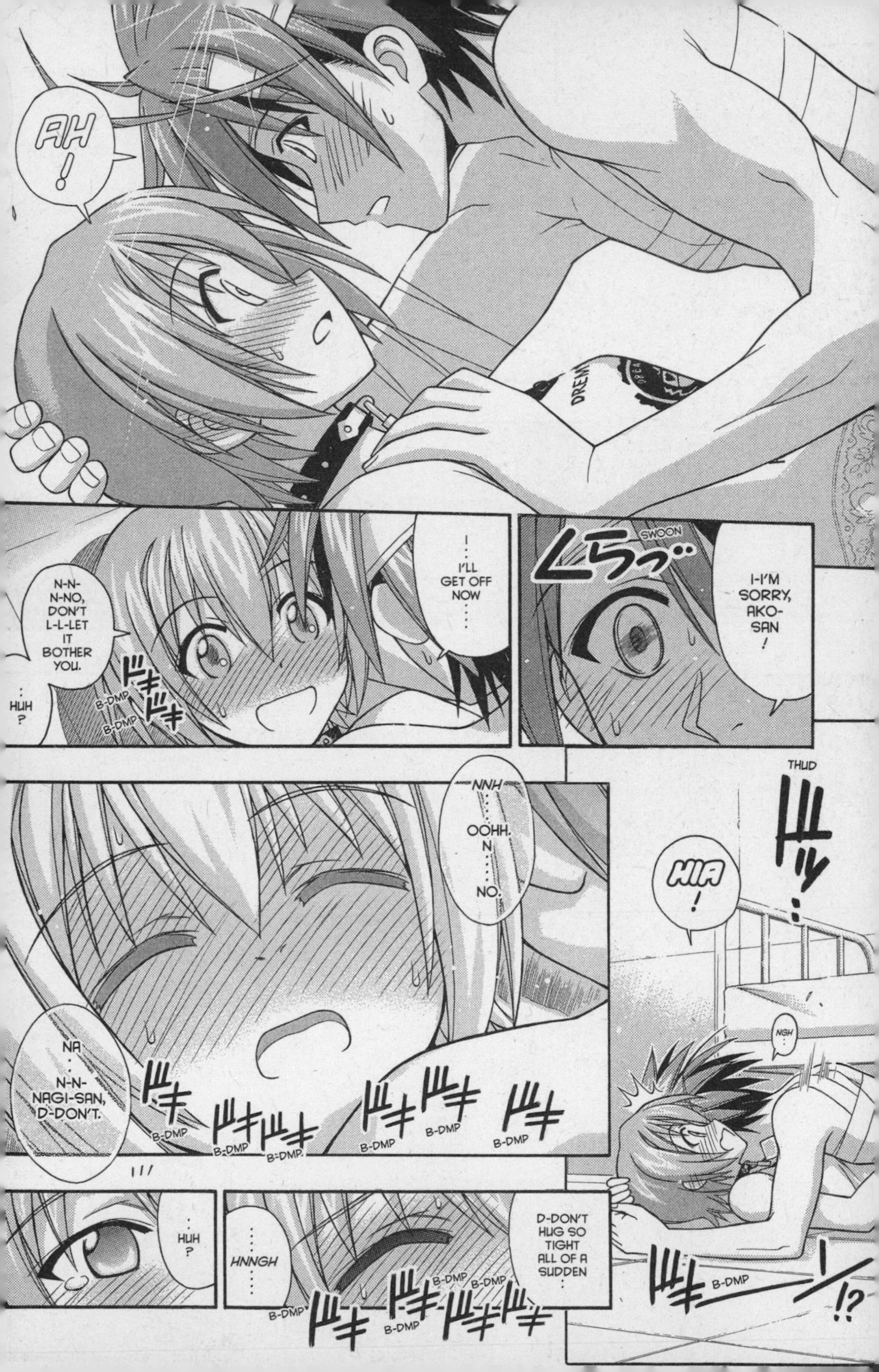
AH!
SWOON
くらっ
I-I'M SORRY, AKO-SAN!
I... I'LL GET OFF NOW......
N-N-N-NO, DON'T L-L-LET IT BOTHER YOU.
ドキドキ
B-DMP B-DMP
...HUH?
THUD
ドッ
HIA!
NGH...
NNH... OOHH. N... NO.
NA... N-N-NAGI-SAN, D-DON'T.
ドキ
B-DMP
ドキドキ
B-DMP B-DMP
ドキ
B-DMP
ドキ
B-DMP
ドキ
B-DMP
!?
D-DON'T HUG SO TIGHT ALL OF A SUDDEN...
...HNNGH......
...HUH?
ドキドキドキドキ
B-DMP B-DMP B-DMP B-DMP

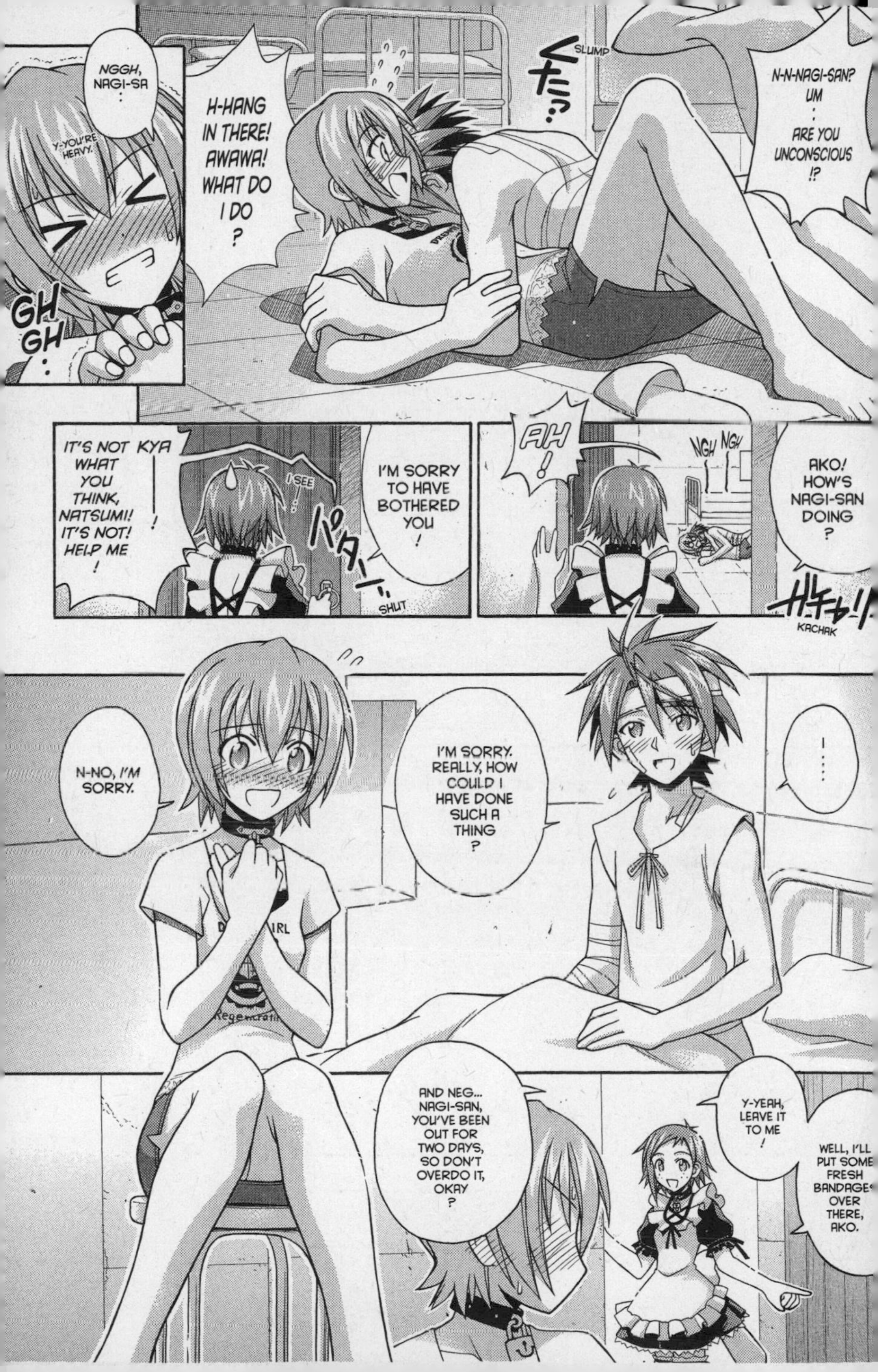
N-N-NAGI-SAN? UM... ARE YOU UNCONSCIOUS!?
SLUMP
H-HANG IN THERE! AWAWA! WHAT DO I DO?
NGGH, NAGI-SA...
Y-YOU'RE HEAVY.
GH GH...
AKO! HOW'S NAGI-SAN DOING?
KACHAK
AH!
NGH NGH
I'M SORRY TO HAVE BOTHERED YOU!
SHUT
I SEE
IT'S NOT WHAT YOU THINK, NATSUMI! IT'S NOT! HELP ME!
KYA!
!....
I'M SORRY. REALLY, HOW COULD I HAVE DONE SUCH A THING?
N-NO, I'M SORRY.
WELL, I'LL PUT SOME FRESH BANDAGES OVER THERE, AKO.
Y-YEAH, LEAVE IT TO ME!
AND NEG... NAGI-SAN, YOU'VE BEEN OUT FOR TWO DAYS, SO DON'T OVERDO IT, OKAY?

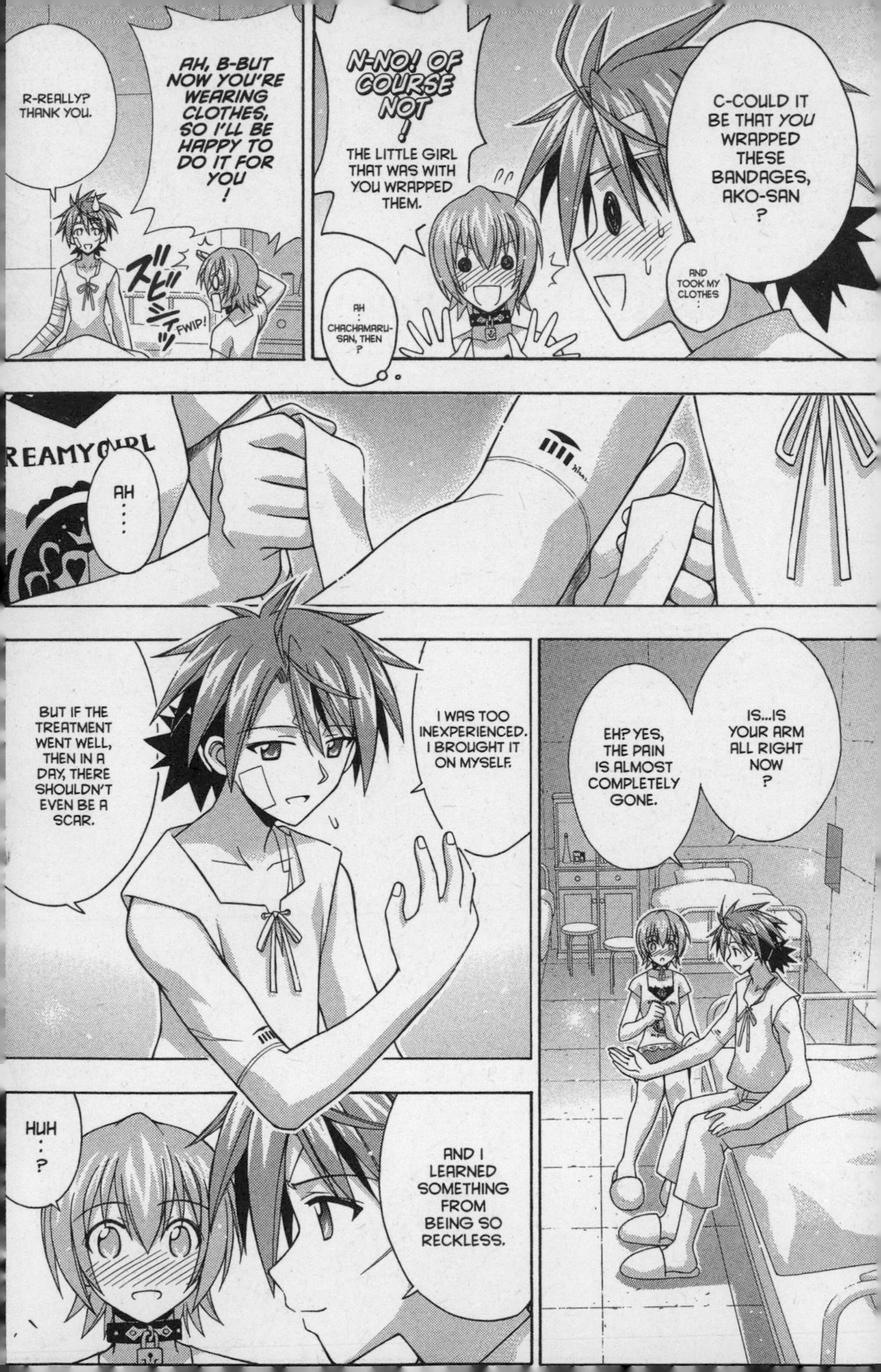
C-COULD IT BE THAT YOU WRAPPED THESE BANDAGES, AKO-SAN?
AND TOOK MY CLOTHES...
N-NO! OF COURSE NOT!
THE LITTLE GIRL THAT WAS WITH YOU WRAPPED THEM.
AH... CHACHAMARU-SAN, THEN?
AH, B-BUT NOW YOU'RE WEARING CLOTHES, SO I'LL BE HAPPY TO DO IT FOR YOU!
FWIP!
R-REALLY? THANK YOU.
REAMYGIRL
AH....
IS...IS YOUR ARM ALL RIGHT NOW?
EH? YES, THE PAIN IS ALMOST COMPLETELY GONE.
I WAS TOO INEXPERIENCED. I BROUGHT IT ON MYSELF.
BUT IF THE TREATMENT WENT WELL, THEN IN A DAY, THERE SHOULDN'T EVEN BE A SCAR.
AND I LEARNED SOMETHING FROM BEING SO RECKLESS.
HUH...?

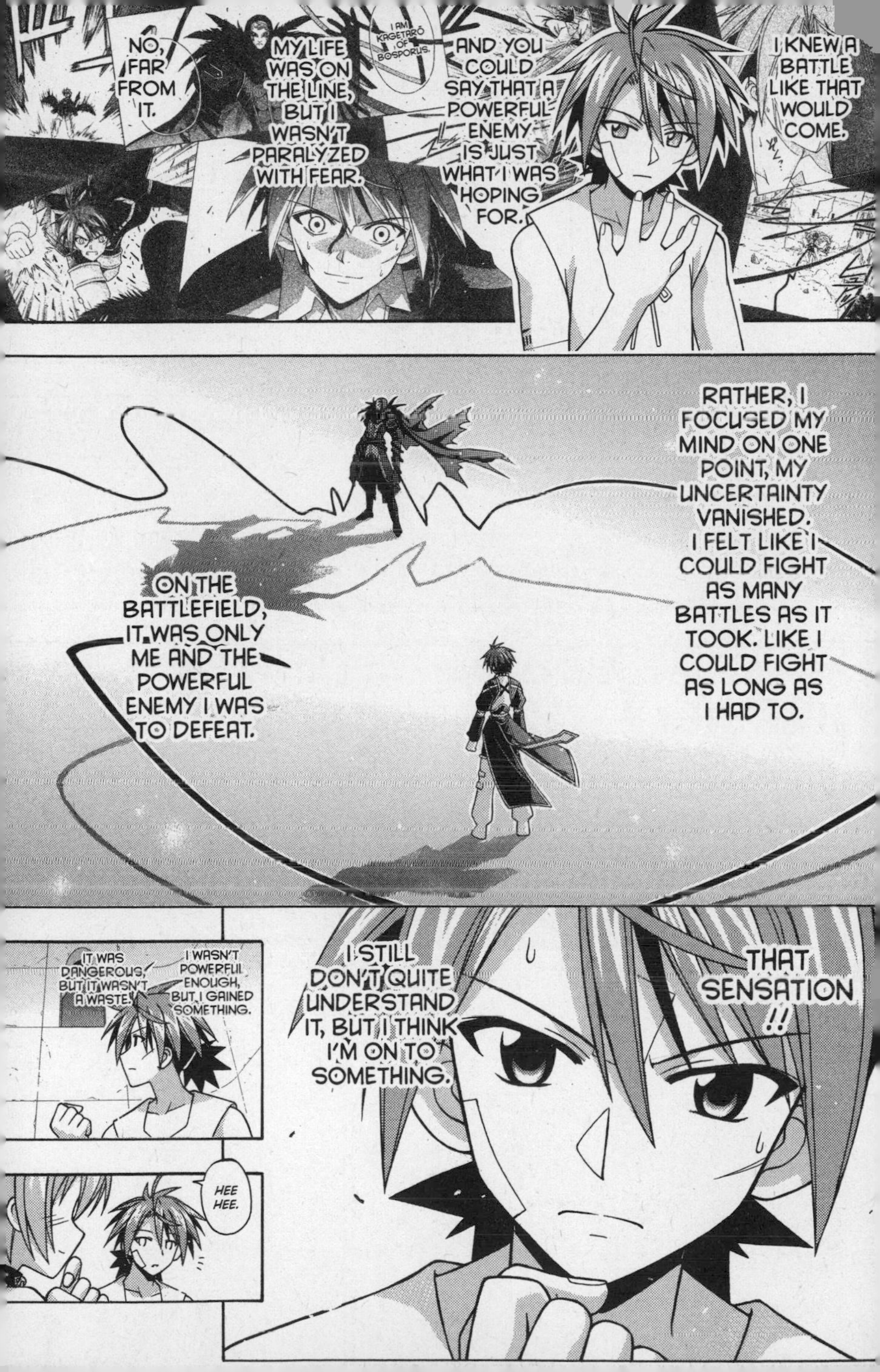
I KNEW A BATTLE LIKE THAT WOULD COME.
AND YOU COULD SAY THAT A POWERFUL ENEMY IS JUST WHAT I WAS HOPING FOR.
I AM KAGETARŌ OF BOSPORUS.
MY LIFE WAS ON THE LINE, BUT I WASN'T PARALYZED WITH FEAR.
NO, FAR FROM IT.
RATHER, I FOCUSED MY MIND ON ONE POINT, MY UNCERTAINTY VANISHED. I FELT LIKE I COULD FIGHT AS MANY BATTLES AS IT TOOK. LIKE I COULD FIGHT AS LONG AS I HAD TO.
ON THE BATTLEFIELD, IT WAS ONLY ME AND THE POWERFUL ENEMY I WAS TO DEFEAT.
THAT SENSATION!!
I STILL DON'T QUITE UNDERSTAND IT, BUT I THINK I'M ON TO SOMETHING.
I WASN'T POWERFUL ENOUGH, BUT I GAINED SOMETHING.
IT WAS DANGEROUS, BUT IT WASN'T A WASTE.
HEE HEE.

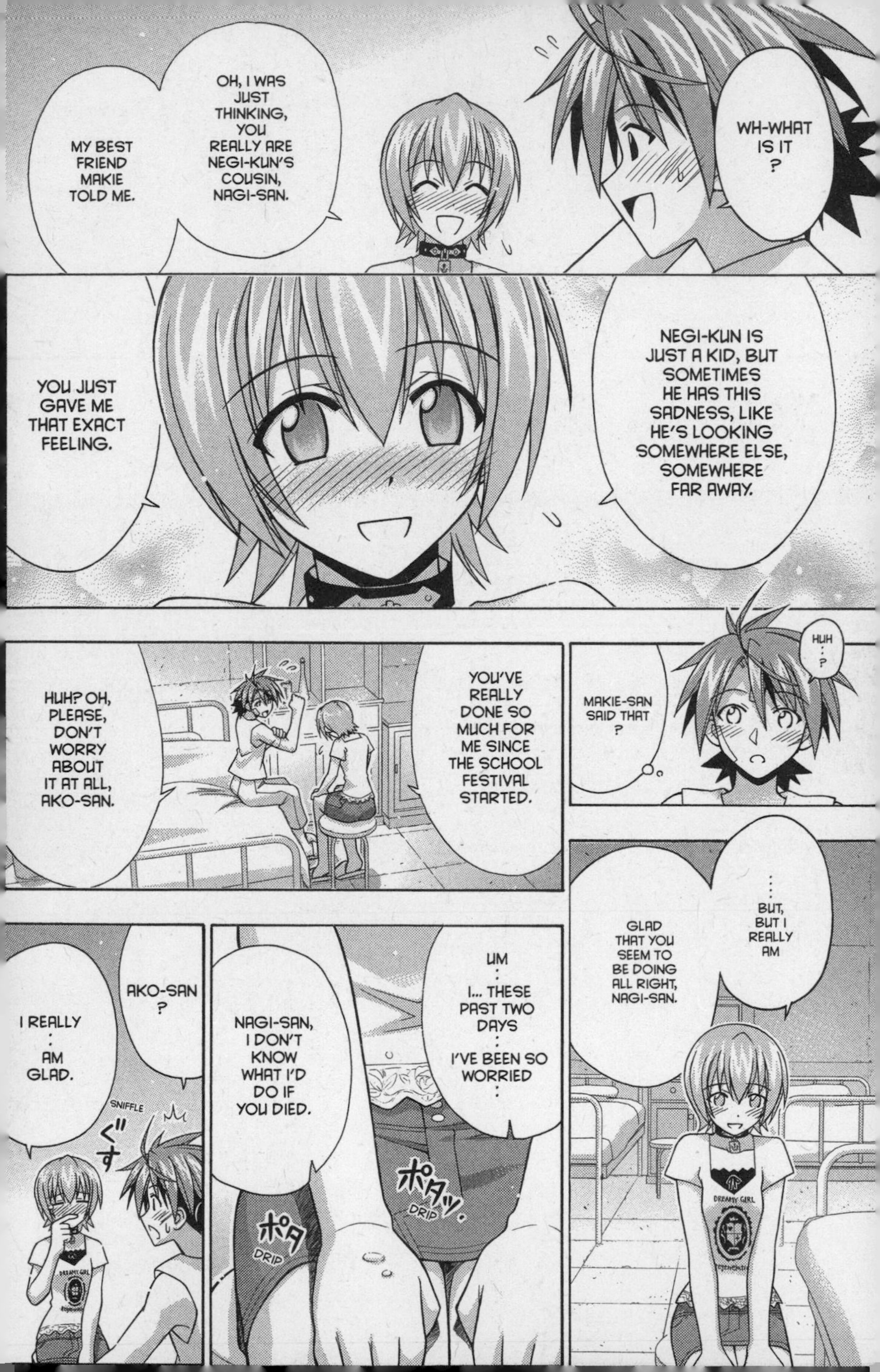
WH-WHAT IS IT?
OH, I WAS JUST THINKING, YOU REALLY ARE NEGI-KUN'S COUSIN, NAGI-SAN.
MY BEST FRIEND MAKIE TOLD ME.
NEGI-KUN IS JUST A KID, BUT SOMETIMES HE HAS THIS SADNESS, LIKE HE'S LOOKING SOMEWHERE ELSE, SOMEWHERE FAR AWAY.
YOU JUST GAVE ME THAT EXACT FEELING.
HUH..?
MAKIE-SAN SAID THAT?
YOU'VE REALLY DONE SO MUCH FOR ME SINCE THE SCHOOL FESTIVAL STARTED.
HUH? OH, PLEASE, DON'T WORRY ABOUT IT AT ALL, AKO-SAN.
...BUT, BUT I REALLY AM
GLAD THAT YOU SEEM TO BE DOING ALL RIGHT, NAGI-SAN.
UM... I... THESE PAST TWO DAYS... I'VE BEEN SO WORRIED...
NAGI-SAN, I DON'T KNOW WHAT I'D DO IF YOU DIED.
ポタッ DRIP
ポタ DRIP
AKO-SAN?
I REALLY... AM GLAD.
ぐす SNIFFLE

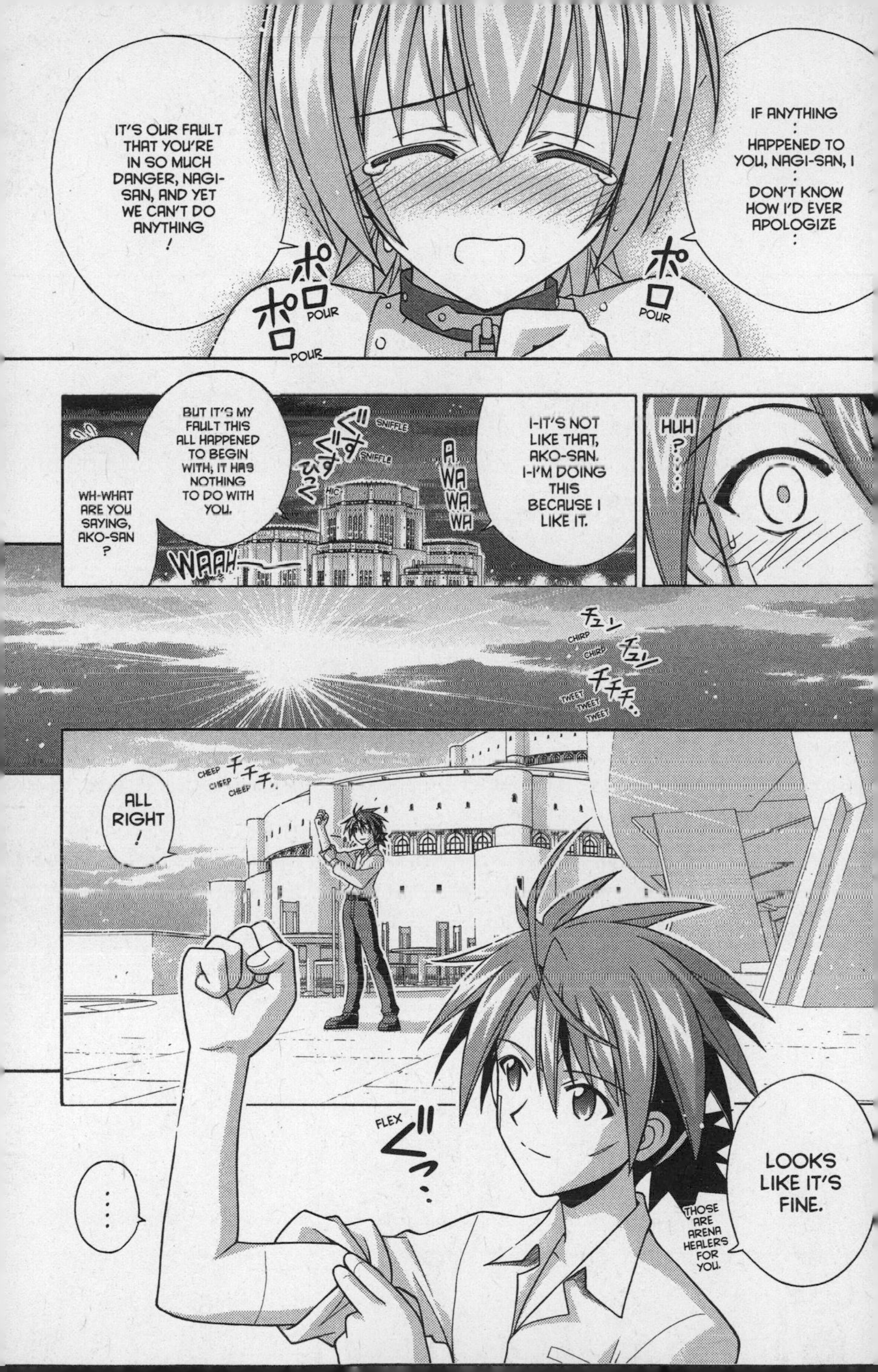
IF ANYTHING... HAPPENED TO YOU, NAGI-SAN, I... DON'T KNOW HOW I'D EVER APOLOGIZE...
ポロ POUR
IT'S OUR FAULT THAT YOU'RE IN SO MUCH DANGER, NAGI-SAN, AND YET WE CAN'T DO ANYTHING!
ポロポロ POUR POUR
HUH?.....
I-IT'S NOT LIKE THAT, AKO-SAN. I-I'M DOING THIS BECAUSE I LIKE IT.
AWAWAWA
ぐすぐす SNIFFLE SNIFFLE
ひっく HIC
BUT IT'S MY FAULT THIS ALL HAPPENED TO BEGIN WITH; IT HAS NOTHING TO DO WITH YOU.
WH-WHAT ARE YOU SAYING, AKO-SAN?
WAAH—
チュン CHIRP
チュン CHIRP
チチチ TWEET TWEET TWEET
チチチ CHEEP CHEEP CHEEP
ALL RIGHT!
ぐっ FLEX
LOOKS LIKE IT'S FINE.
THOSE ARE ARENA HEALERS FOR YOU.
....

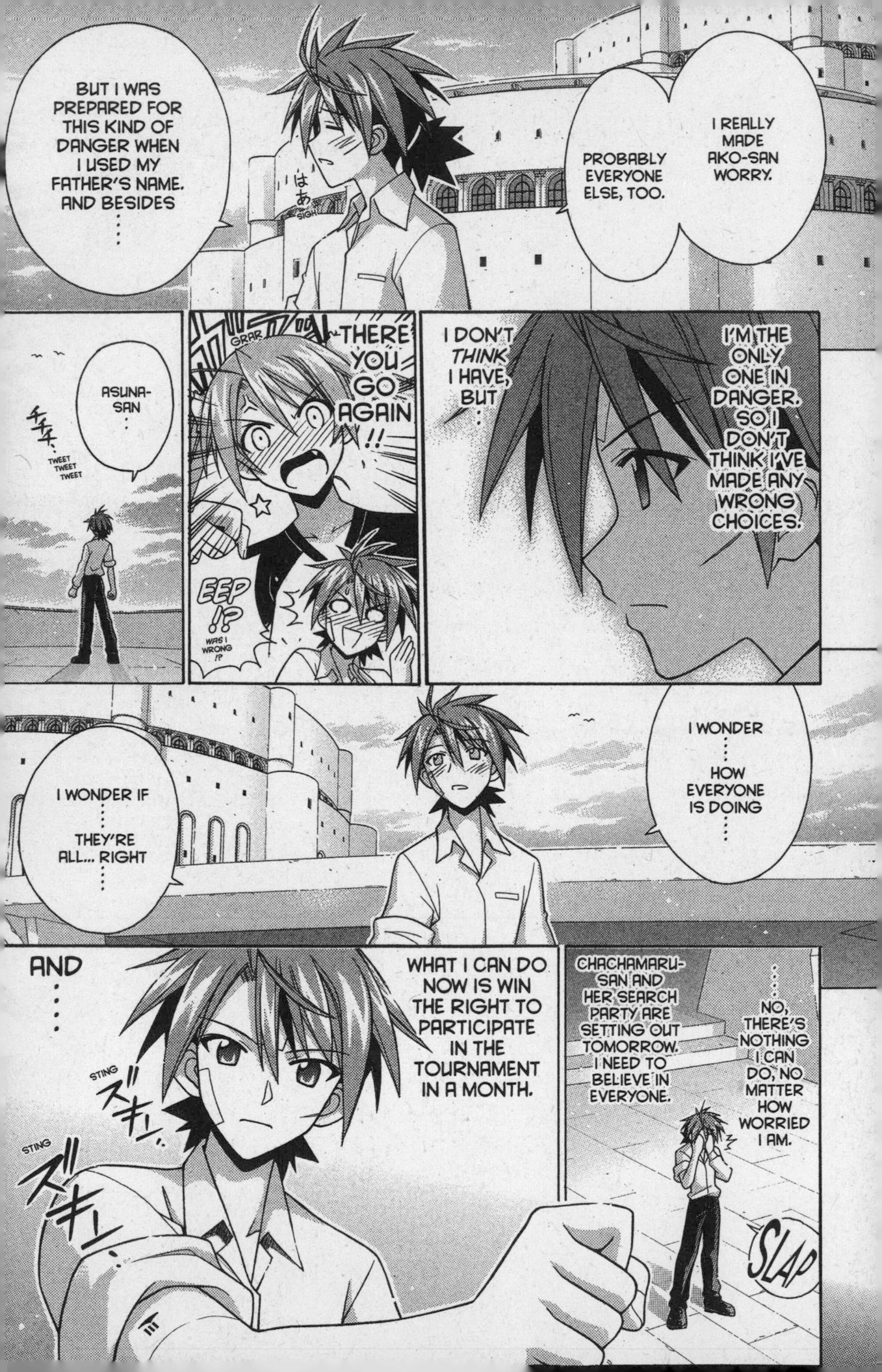
I REALLY MADE AKO-SAN WORRY.
PROBABLY EVERYONE ELSE, TOO.
はあ
SIGH
BUT I WAS PREPARED FOR THIS KIND OF DANGER WHEN I USED MY FATHER'S NAME. AND BESIDES ....
I'M THE ONLY ONE IN DANGER. SO I DON'T THINK I'VE MADE ANY WRONG CHOICES.
I DON'T THINK I HAVE, BUT ...
GRAR
THERE YOU GO AGAIN!!
EEP!?
WAS I WRONG!?
ASUNA-SAN ...
チチチ
TWEET TWEET TWEET
I WONDER ... HOW EVERYONE IS DOING ...
I WONDER IF ... THEY'RE ALL... RIGHT ...
... NO, THERE'S NOTHING I CAN DO, NO MATTER HOW WORRIED I AM.
CHACHAMARU-SAN AND HER SEARCH PARTY ARE SETTING OUT TOMORROW. I NEED TO BELIEVE IN EVERYONE.
SLAP
WHAT I CAN DO NOW IS WIN THE RIGHT TO PARTICIPATE IN THE TOURNAMENT IN A MONTH.
AND ....
ズキン
STING
ズキン
STING

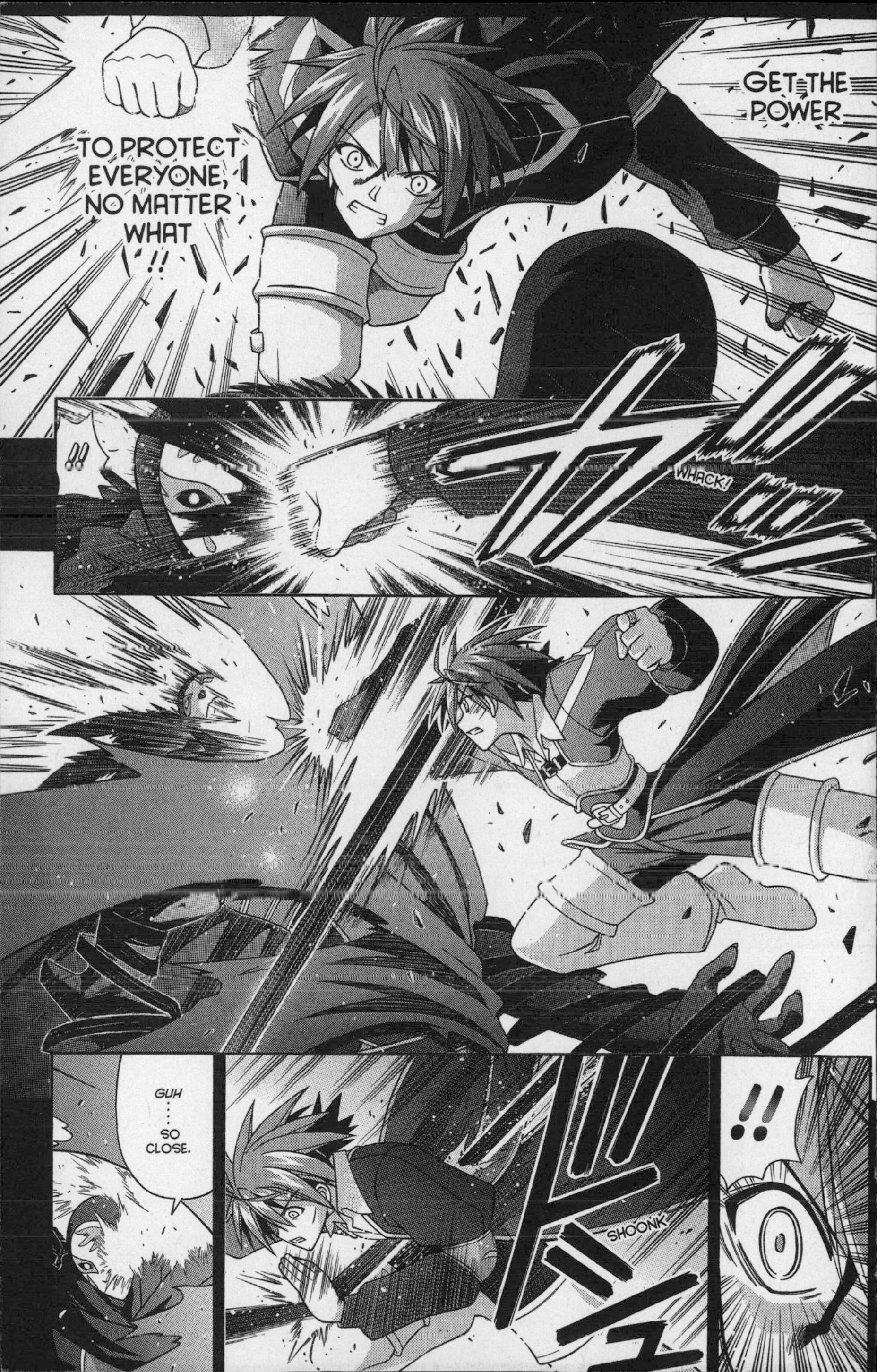
GET THE POWER
TO PROTECT EVERYONE, NO MATTER WHAT !!
WHACK!
!!
!!
SHOONK
GUH ..... SO CLOSE.

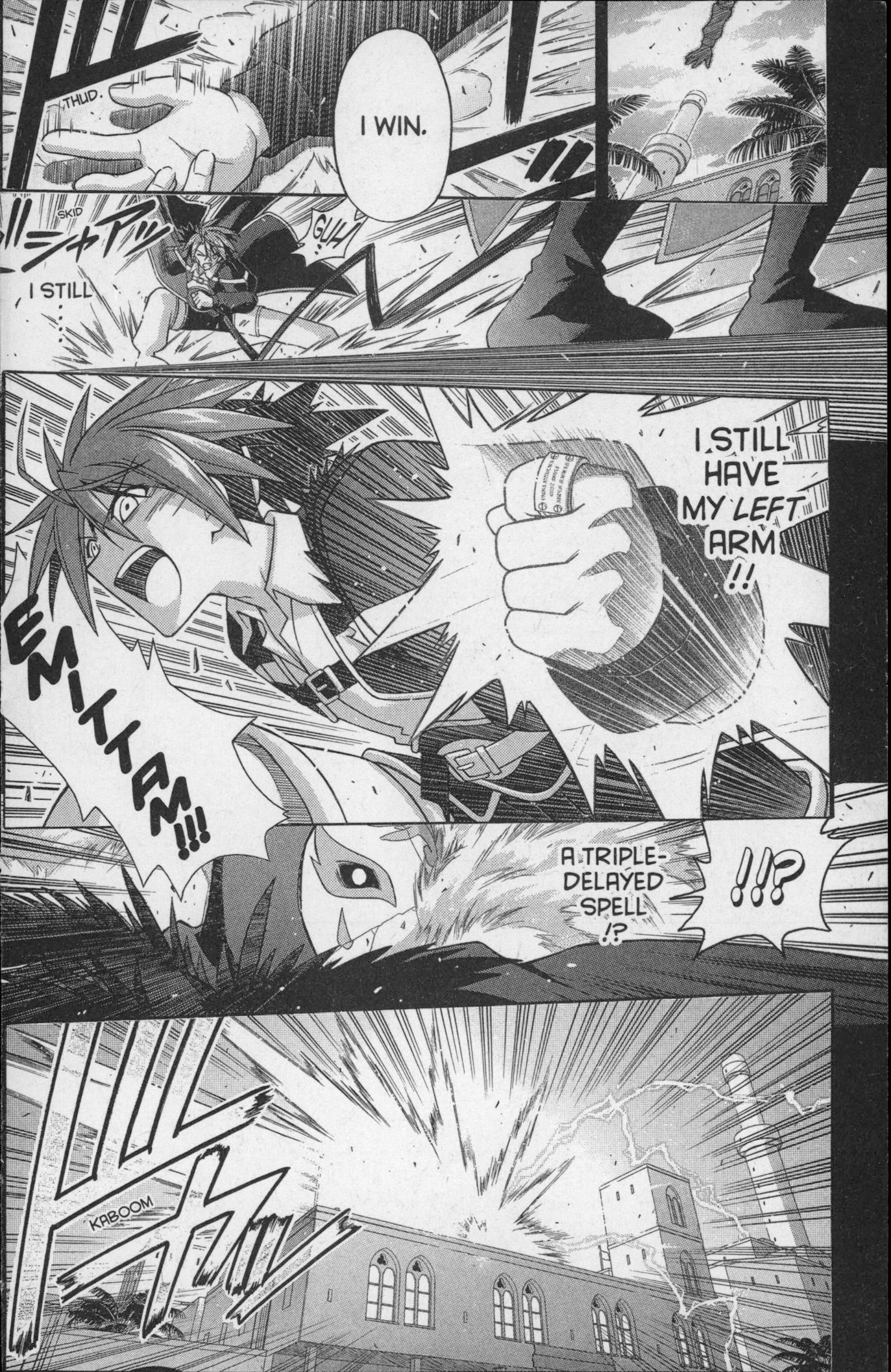
I WIN.
THUD.
GUH
SKID
I STILL ...
I STILL HAVE MY LEFT ARM !!
EMITTAM!!!
!!?
A TRIPLE-DELAYED SPELL !?
KABOOM

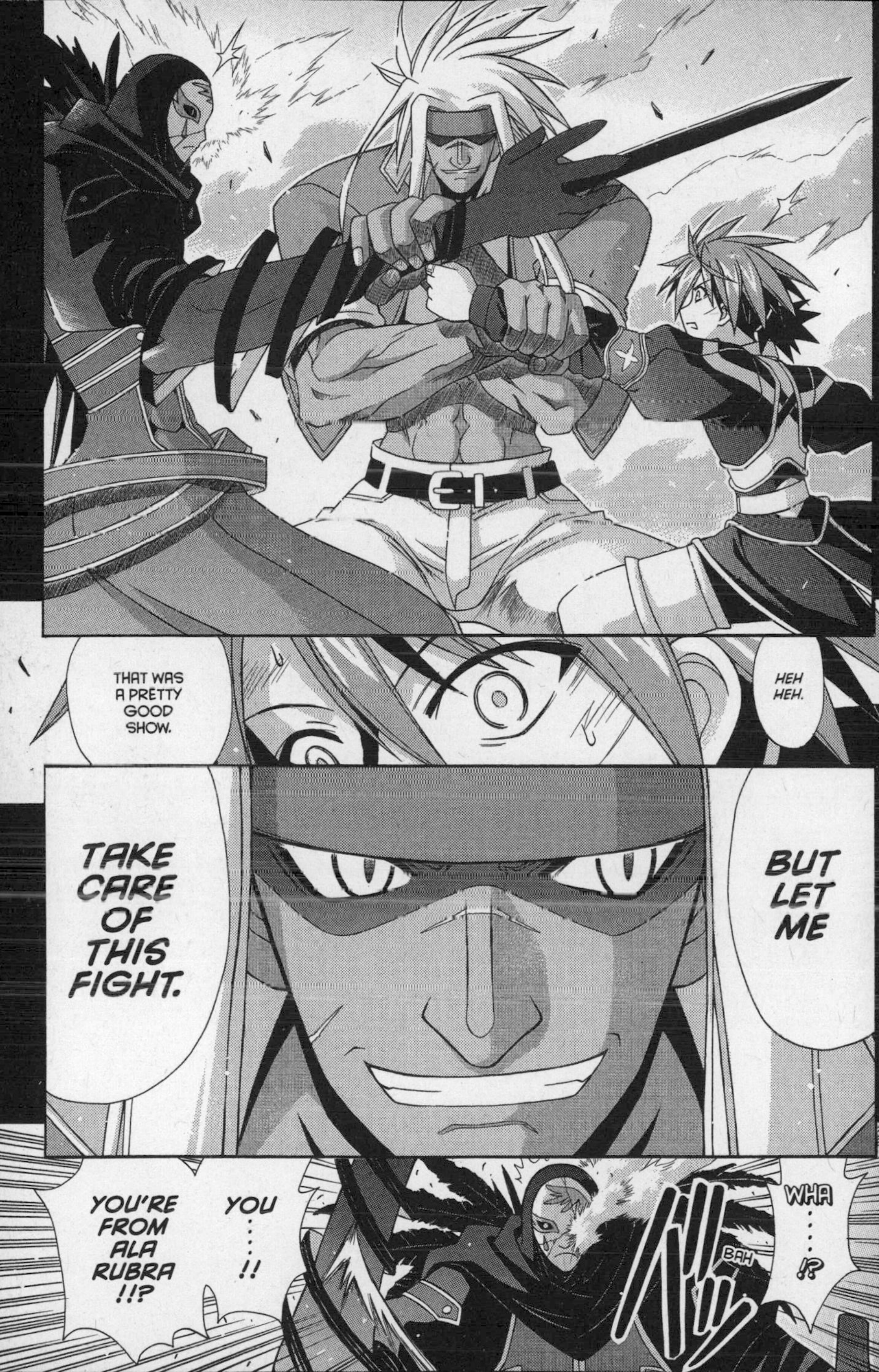
HEH HEH.
THAT WAS A PRETTY GOOD SHOW.
BUT LET ME
TAKE CARE OF THIS FIGHT.
WHA......!?
BAH
YOU.....!!
YOU'RE FROM ALA RUBRA!!?

# ERMINE MATH

## HOW MUCH IS A DRACHMA?

YO! LONG TIME NO SEE, EVERYBODY. THIS IS ALBERT CHAMOMILE, THE ERMINE ELF. YOU ALL KNOW THAT IN THE MAGICAL WORLD, THEY USE A UNIT OF CURRENCY CALLED A DRACHMA (DRACHMA MARK), RIGHT? LET'S THINK ABOUT THIS TODAY. OUR TEACHER WILL BE THE LEADER OF THE BAKA RANGERS, YUECCHI.

 HELLO, I'M SEAT 4, YUE AYASE. NOW, A DRACHMA IS A COIN THAT WAS USED IN ANCIENT GREECE, MADE OF APPROXIMATELY 4.37 GRAMS OF SILVER.

 WOW. AND ABOUT HOW MANY YEN IS THAT?

 PRICES IN GENERAL CHANGED DEPENDING ON TIME AND PLACE, SO I COULDN'T SAY DEFINITIVELY. BUT IN A PLAY BY ARISTOPHANES, THERE'S A TRANSACTION IN WHICH SOMEONE WENT INTO DEBT FOR 1200 DRACHMA TO BUY A FAMOUS RACEHORSE. *1

 WHOA, WHOA!

 ALSO, ACCORDING TO HERODOTUS, DARIUS I, KING OF THE ACHAEMENID PERSIAN EMPIRE, COLLECTED 87,360,000 DRACHMA IN TAXES EVERY YEAR. *2

 THAT AMOUNT IS TOO BIG; THAT DOESN'T TELL ME ANYTHING!

 GOING FORWARD IN TIME TO ROME, IN THE BIBLE'S "PARABLE OF THE WORKERS IN THE VINEYARD," ONE DAY'S WORK WAS WORTH ONE DRACHMA. THE THEORY THAT ONE DRACHMA EQUALS ONE DAY'S WAGES HOLDS UP COMPARATIVELY WELL. *3

 I EARN ABOUT 166 YEN (ABOUT $1.60) A DAY.

 IT IS SAID THAT JESUS WAS SOLD FOR 30 PIECES OF SILVER, BUT IT ONLY SAYS "PIECES OF SILVER," SO WE DON'T KNOW WHICH OF THE FOUR TYPES OF SILVER COINS WERE USED IN THAT ERA—DINARIUS (1 DRACHMA MARK), DRACHMA, DIDRACHMA (2 DRACHMA MARKS), OR STATER (4 DRACHMA MARKS)—THE 30 PIECES WERE. WHICHEVER IT WAS, JESUS WOULD HAVE BEEN SOLD FOR 30 TO 120 DRACHMA. *4

 SO THAT WOULD BE THE AMOUNT OF MONEY YOU WOULD SELL YOUR FRIEND AND TEACHER FOR. OF COURSE JUDAS'S PERSONAL CHARACTER IS ANOTHER PROBLEM.

 FURTHERMORE, ACCORDING TO PLUTARCH, IN 75BC, CAESAR, A ROMAN STATESMAN, WAS KIDNAPPED BY PIRATES AND RANSOMED FOR 300,000 DRACHMA. *5

 WHOA. THE REWARD OUT FOR ANIKI WAS 300,000 DRACHMA. BY THE WAY, YUECCHI, THIS IS MORE ABOUT ANCIENT CIVILIZATIONS THAN MATH, DON'T YOU THINK?

 ....

*1: *THE CLOUDS* 21. *2: *THE HISTORIES* VOLUME 3, CHAPTER 95. *3: "THE GOSPEL ACCORDING TO MATTHEW," 20:1-16. *4: THE SAME, 26:14-16. *5: *PARALLEL LIVES*, CAESAR 2.

* 1 TALENT IS APPROXIMATELY 6,000 DRACHMA. 1 DINARIUS IS EQUAL TO A DRACHMA.

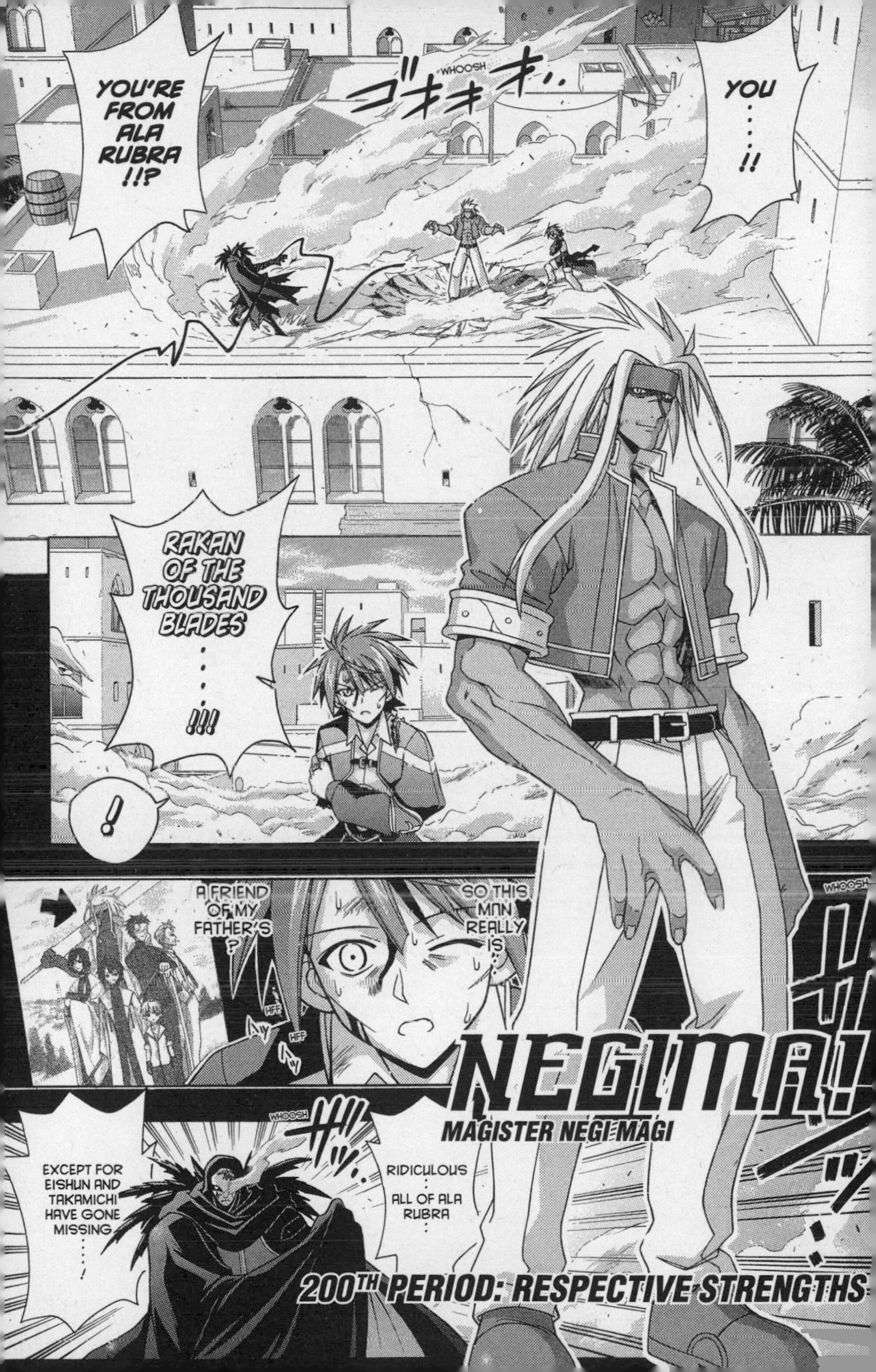
YOU.......!!
WHOOSH
YOU'RE FROM ALA RUBRA!!?
RAKAN OF THE THOUSAND BLADES.......!!!
!
WHOOSH
SO THIS MAN REALLY IS...
A FRIEND OF MY FATHER'S?
HFF
HFF
NEGIMA!
MAGISTER NEGI MAGI
WHOOSH
RIDICULOUS... ALL OF ALA RUBRA...
EXCEPT FOR EISHUN AND TAKAMICHI HAVE GONE MISSING......!
200TH PERIOD: RESPECTIVE STRENGTHS

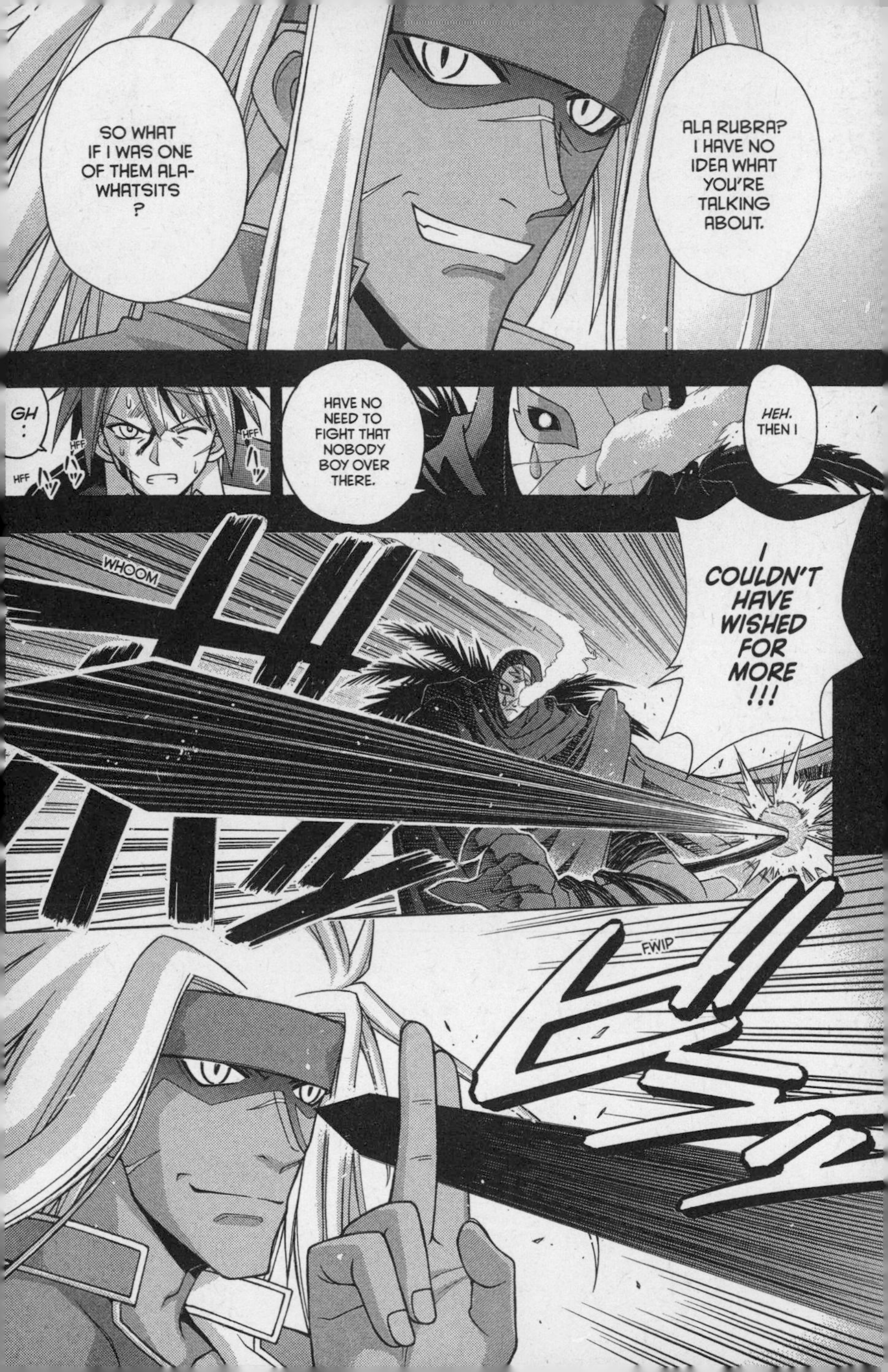
ALA RUBRA? I HAVE NO IDEA WHAT YOU'RE TALKING ABOUT.
SO WHAT IF I WAS ONE OF THEM ALA-WHATSITS ?
HEH. THEN I
HAVE NO NEED TO FIGHT THAT NOBODY BOY OVER THERE.
GH ...
HFF
HFF
HFF
HFF
I COULDN'T HAVE WISHED FOR MORE !!!
WHOOM
FWIP

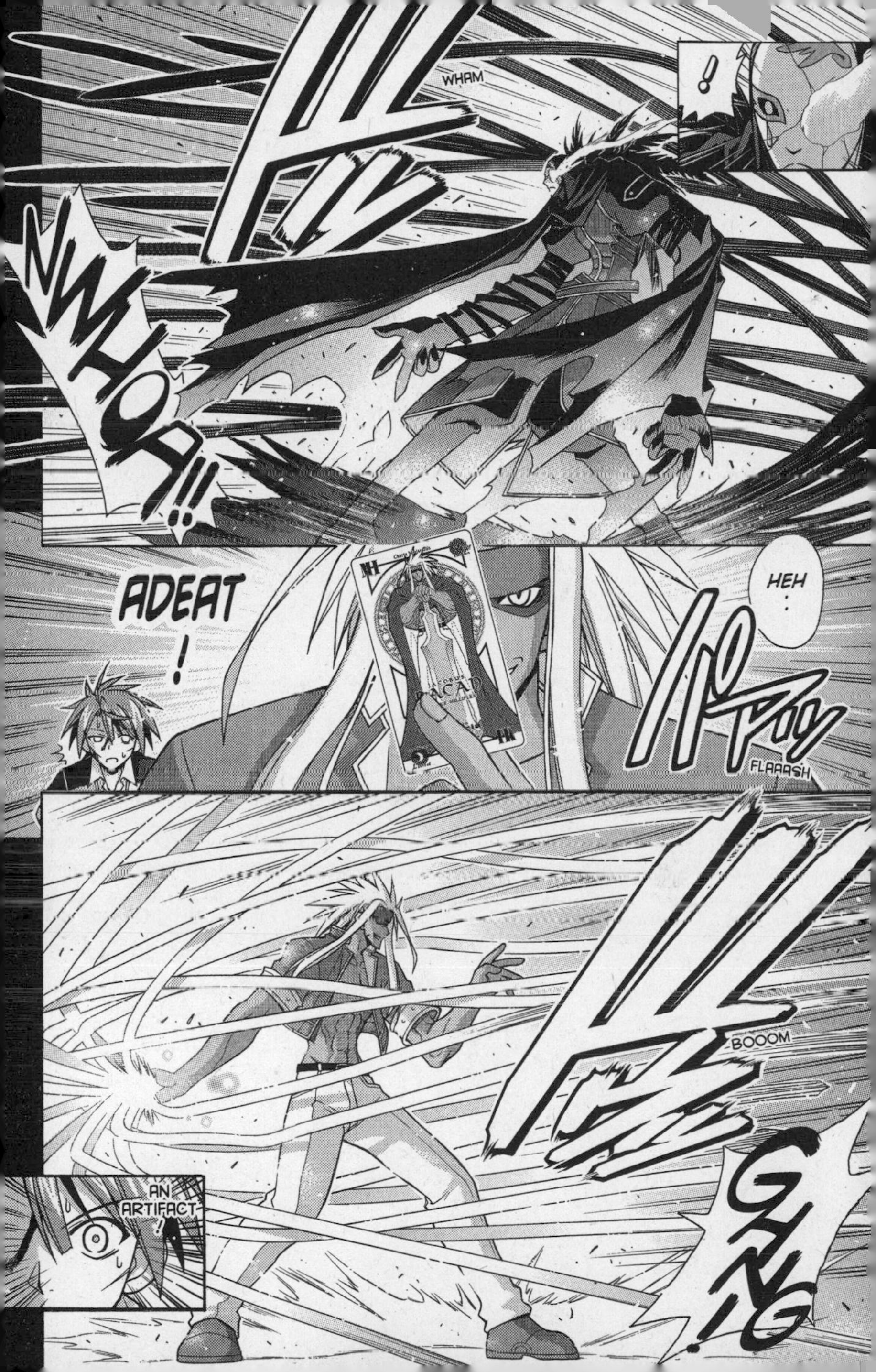
!
WHAM
WHOA!!!
HEH...
FLAAASH
ADEAT!
BOOOM
GANG!
AN ARTIFACT...!

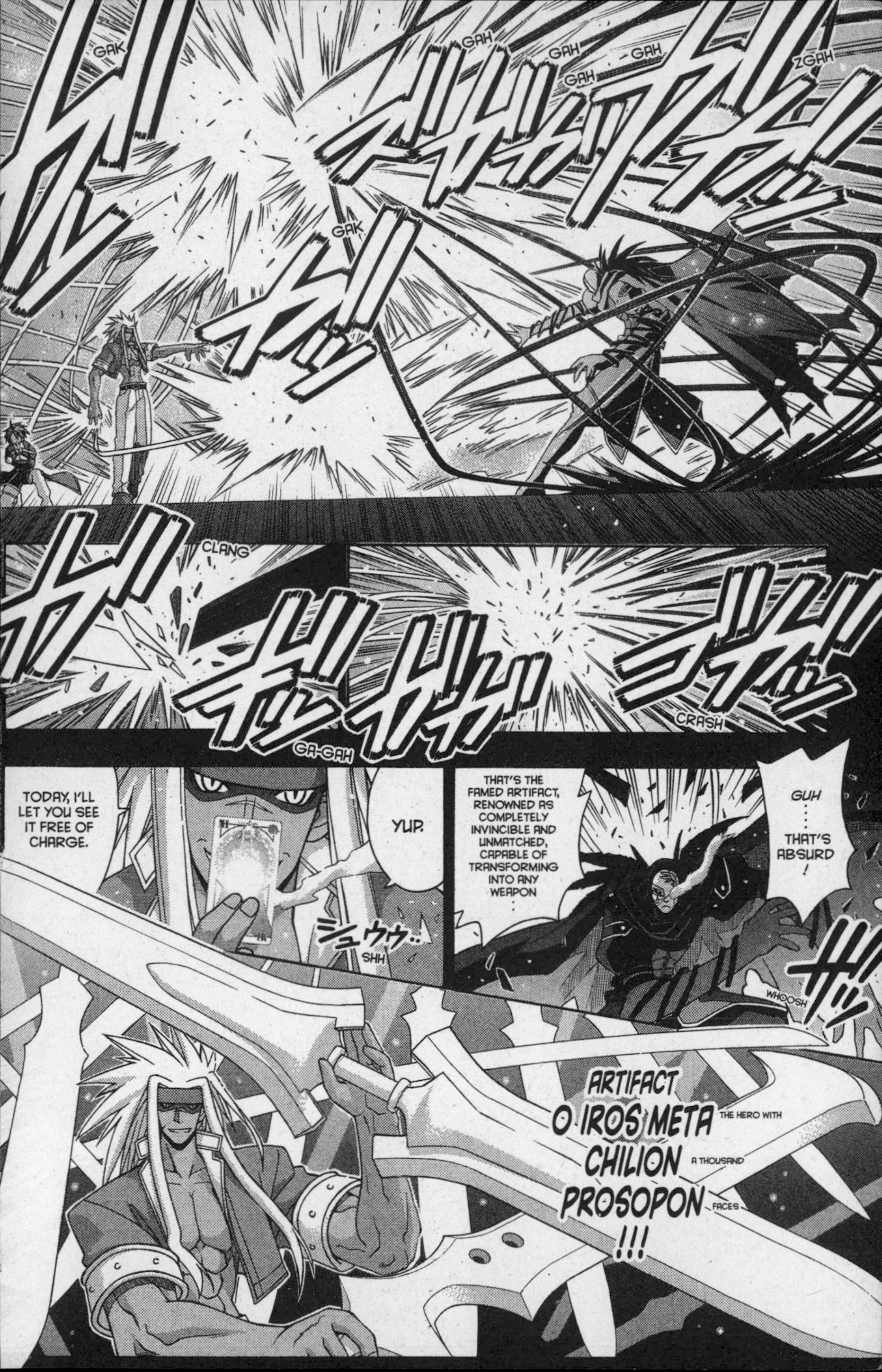
ZGAH
GAH
GAH
GAH
GAH
GAK
GAK
CRASH
CLANG
GA-GAH
GUH... THAT'S ABSURD!
THAT'S THE FAMED ARTIFACT, RENOWNED AS COMPLETELY INVINCIBLE AND UNMATCHED, CAPABLE OF TRANSFORMING INTO ANY WEAPON.
WHOOSH
YUP.
TODAY, I'LL LET YOU SEE IT FREE OF CHARGE.
SHH
ARTIFACT O IROS META CHILION PROSOPON!!!
THE HERO WITH A THOUSAND FACES

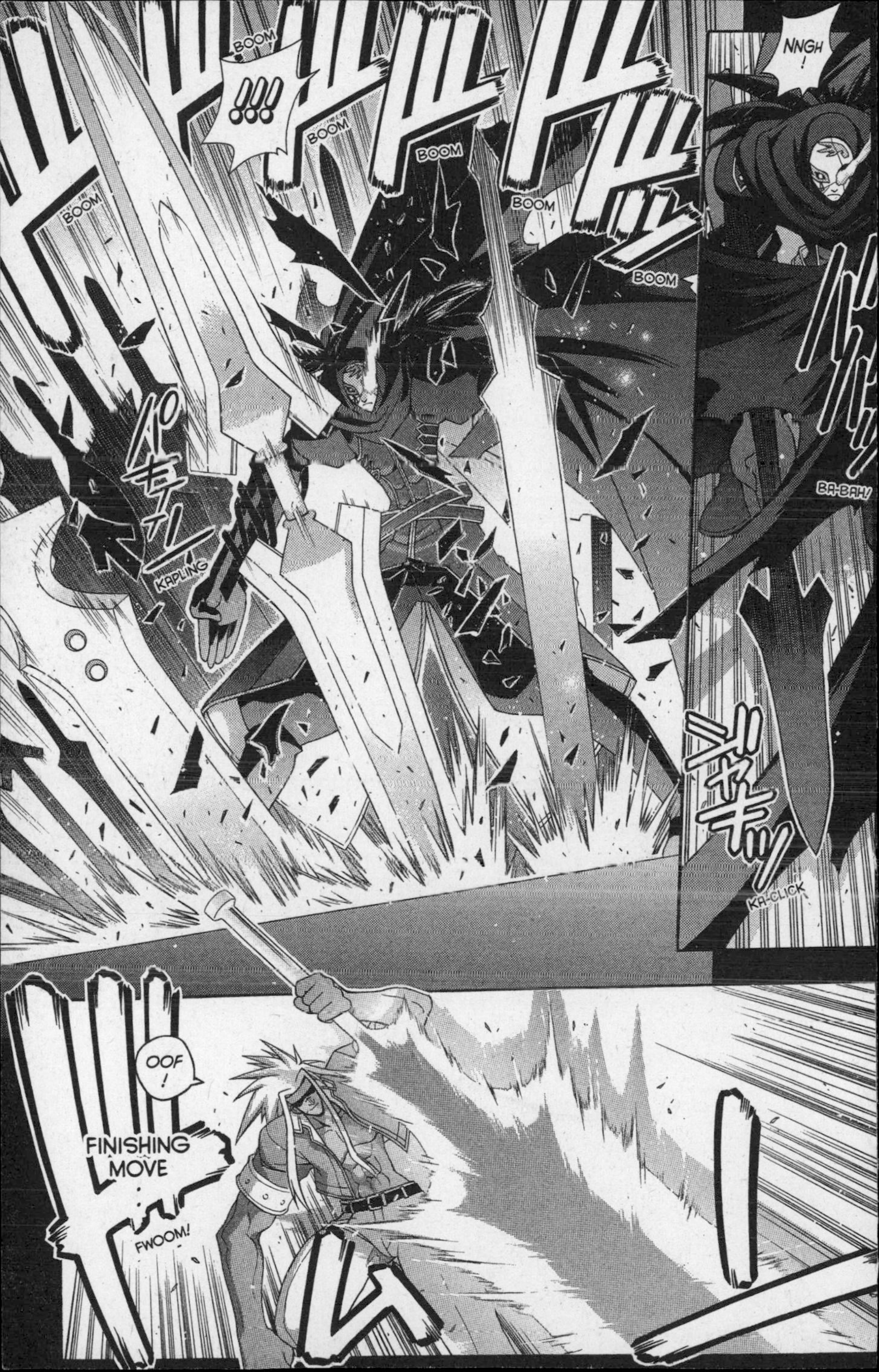
NNGH!
BA-BAH!
KA-CLICK
BOOM
!!!
BOOM
BOOM
BOOM
BOOM
BOOM
KAPLING
OOF!
FINISHING MOVE
FWOOM!

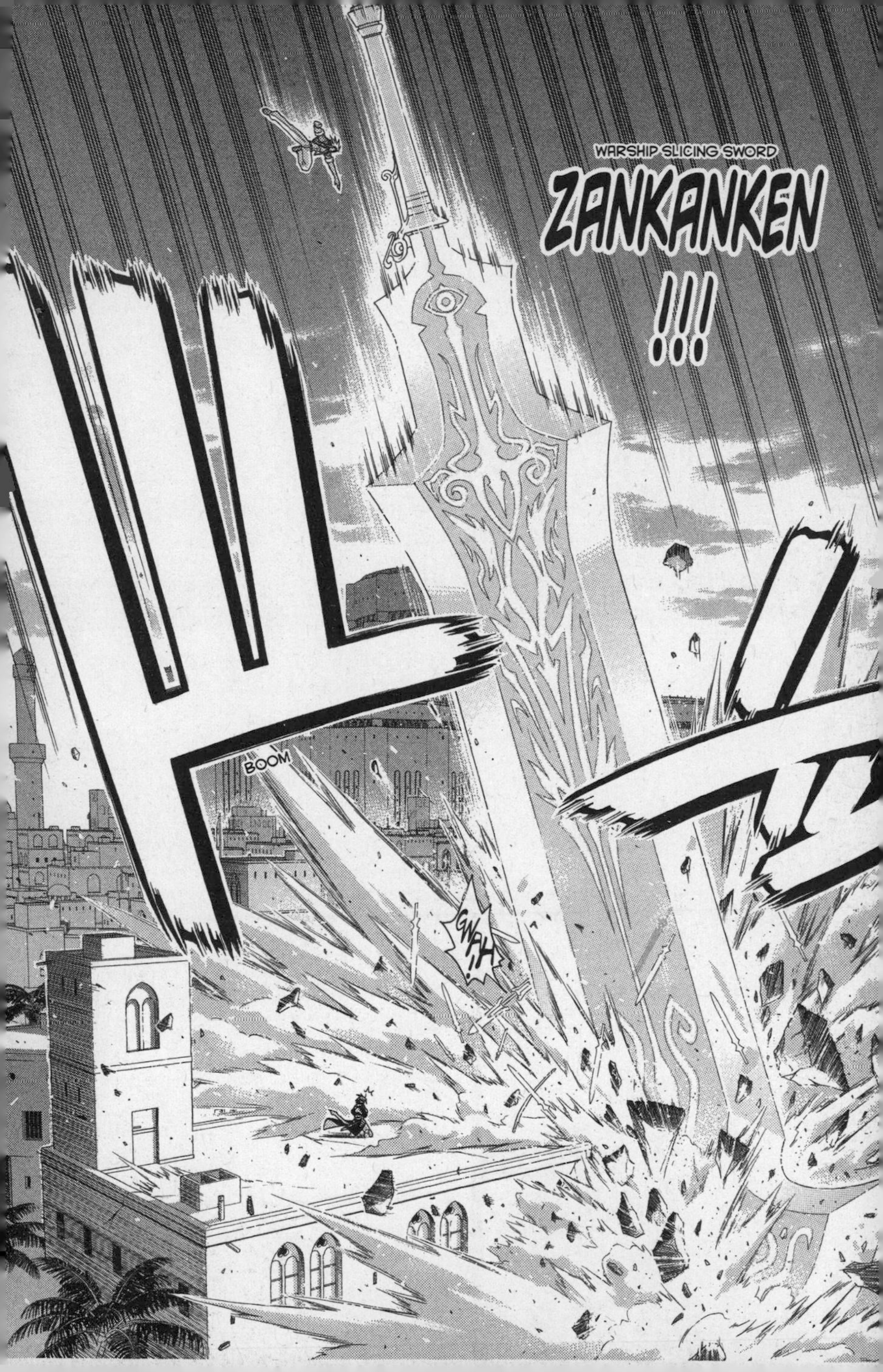
WARSHIP SLICING SWORD
ZANKANKEN !!!
BOOM
GWAH!!

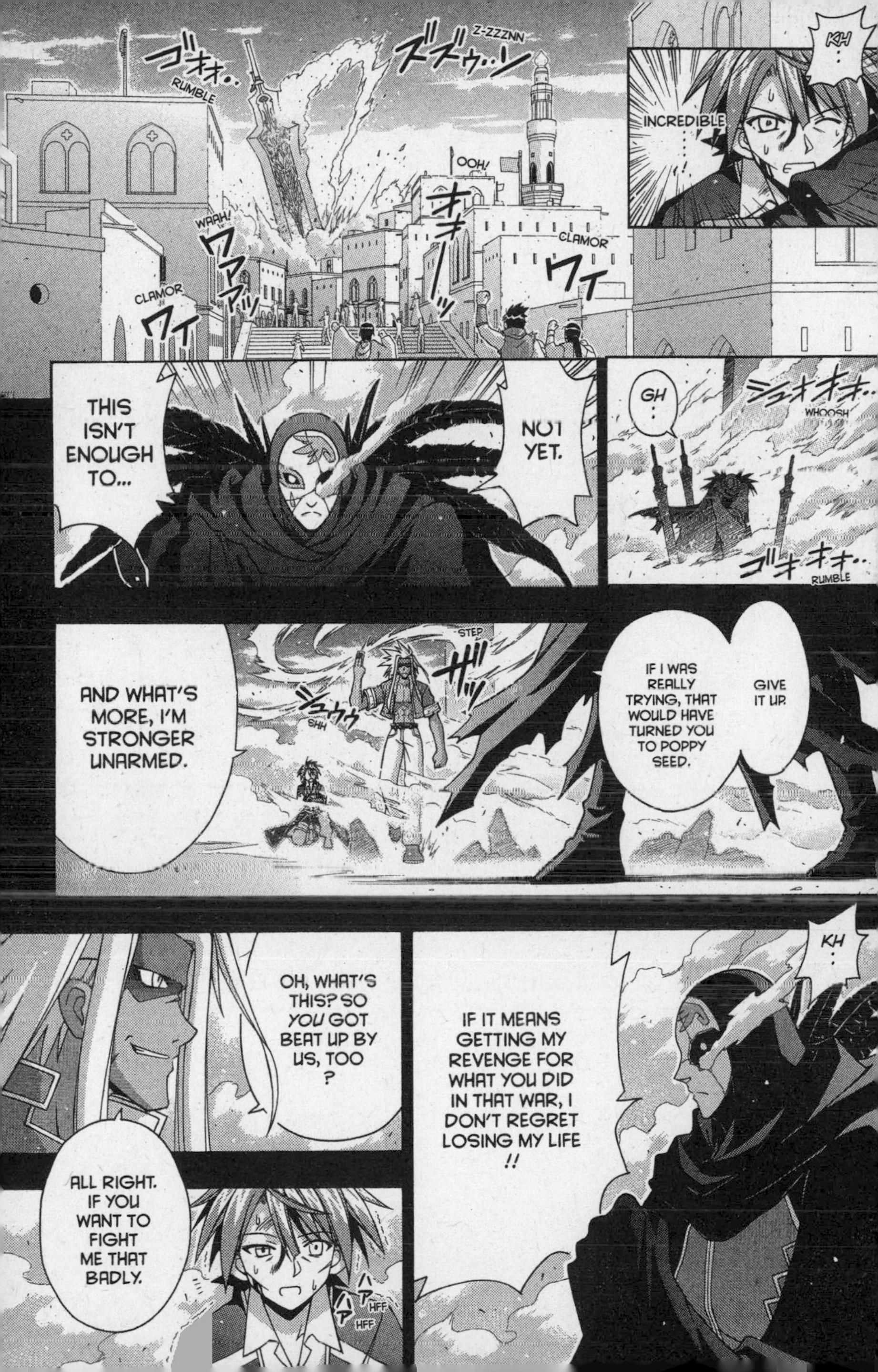
KH...
INCREDIBLE...
Z-ZZZNN
RUMBLE
OOH!
CLAMOR
WAAH!
CLAMOR
GH...
WHOOSH
RUMBLE
NOT YET.
THIS ISN'T ENOUGH TO...
GIVE IT UP.
IF I WAS REALLY TRYING, THAT WOULD HAVE TURNED YOU TO POPPY SEED.
STEP
SHH
AND WHAT'S MORE, I'M STRONGER UNARMED.
KH...
IF IT MEANS GETTING MY REVENGE FOR WHAT YOU DID IN THAT WAR, I DON'T REGRET LOSING MY LIFE!!
OH, WHAT'S THIS? SO *YOU* GOT BEAT UP BY US, TOO?
ALL RIGHT. IF YOU WANT TO FIGHT ME THAT BADLY.
HFF
HFF

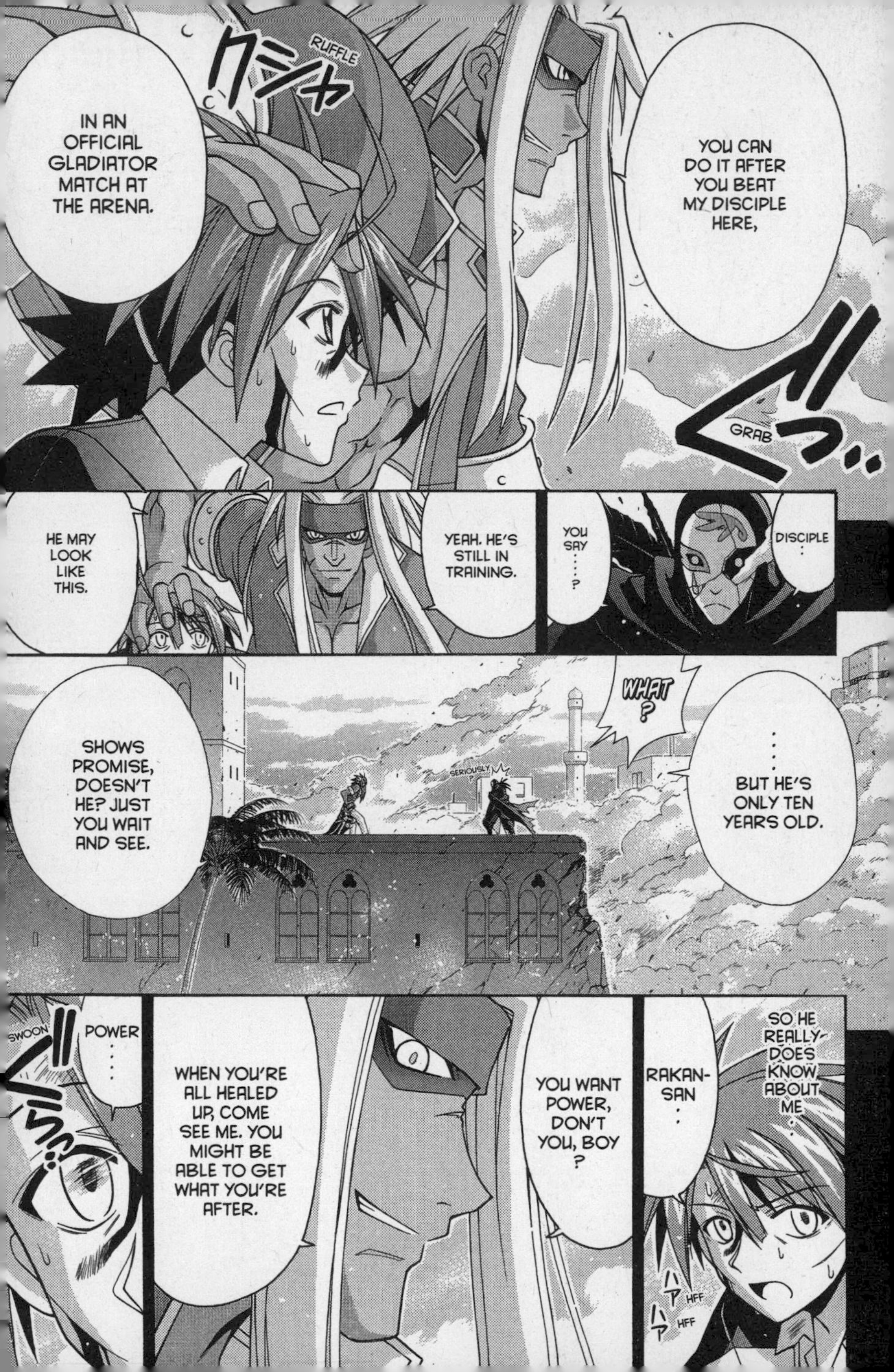
YOU CAN DO IT AFTER YOU BEAT MY DISCIPLE HERE,
GRAB
RUFFLE
IN AN OFFICIAL GLADIATOR MATCH AT THE ARENA.
DISCIPLE...
YOU SAY.....?
YEAH. HE'S STILL IN TRAINING.
HE MAY LOOK LIKE THIS.
....BUT HE'S ONLY TEN YEARS OLD.
WHAT?
SERIOUSLY?
SHOWS PROMISE, DOESN'T HE? JUST YOU WAIT AND SEE.
SO HE REALLY DOES KNOW ABOUT ME...
RAKAN-SAN...
HFF
HFF
YOU WANT POWER, DON'T YOU, BOY?
WHEN YOU'RE ALL HEALED UP, COME SEE ME. YOU MIGHT BE ABLE TO GET WHAT YOU'RE AFTER.
POWER....
SWOON

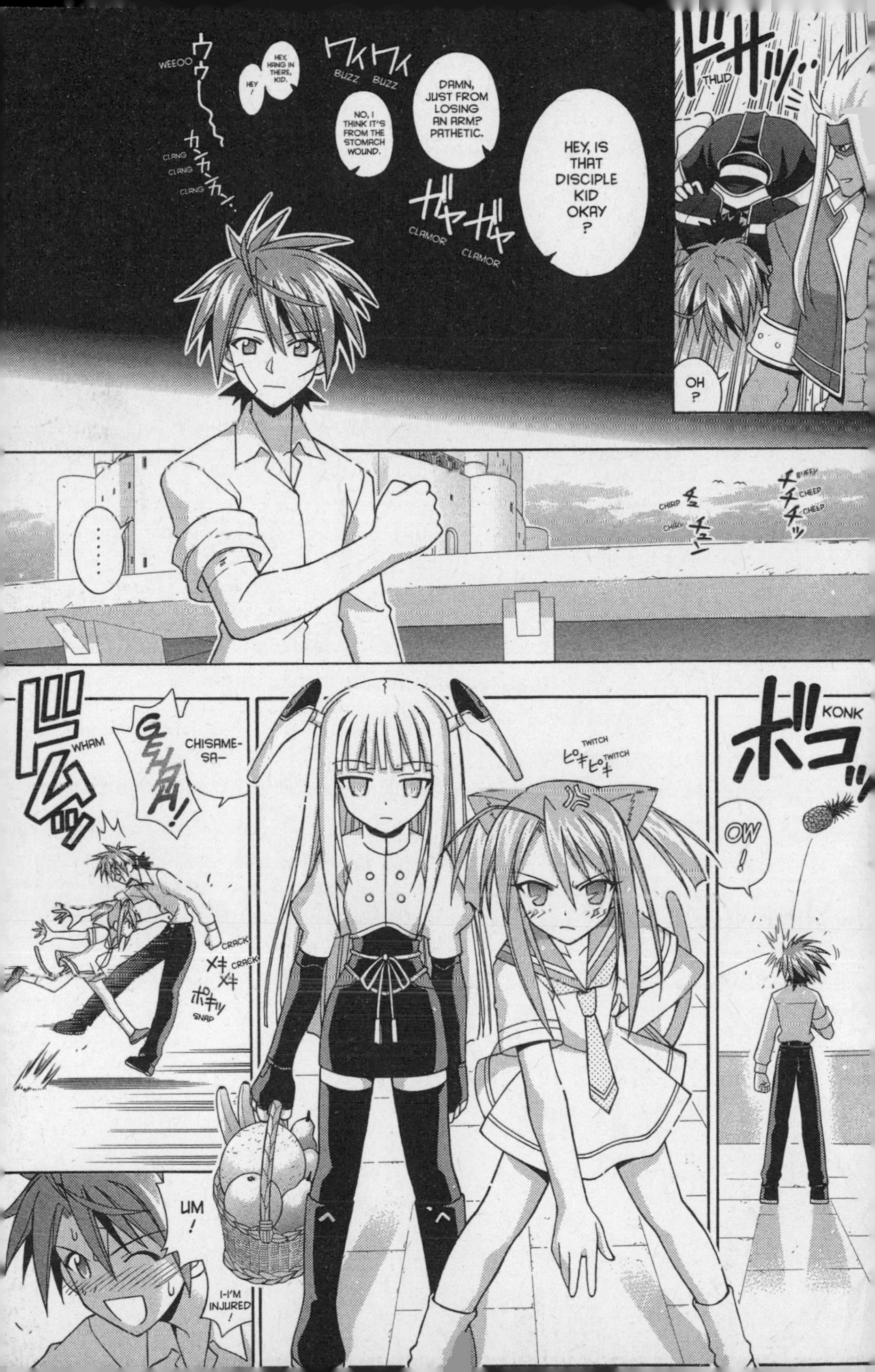
THUD
OH?
HEY, IS THAT DISCIPLE KID OKAY?
CLAMOR CLAMOR
DAMN, JUST FROM LOSING AN ARM? PATHETIC.
NO, I THINK IT'S FROM THE STOMACH WOUND.
BUZZ BUZZ
HEY, HANG IN THERE, KID.
HEY!
WEEOO
CLANG CLANG CLANG
CHEEP CHEEP CHEEP
CHIRP CHIRP
......
KONK
OW!
TWITCH TWITCH
CHISAME-SA–
GEHAA!
WHAM
CRACK CRACK
SNAP
UM!
I-I'M INJURED!

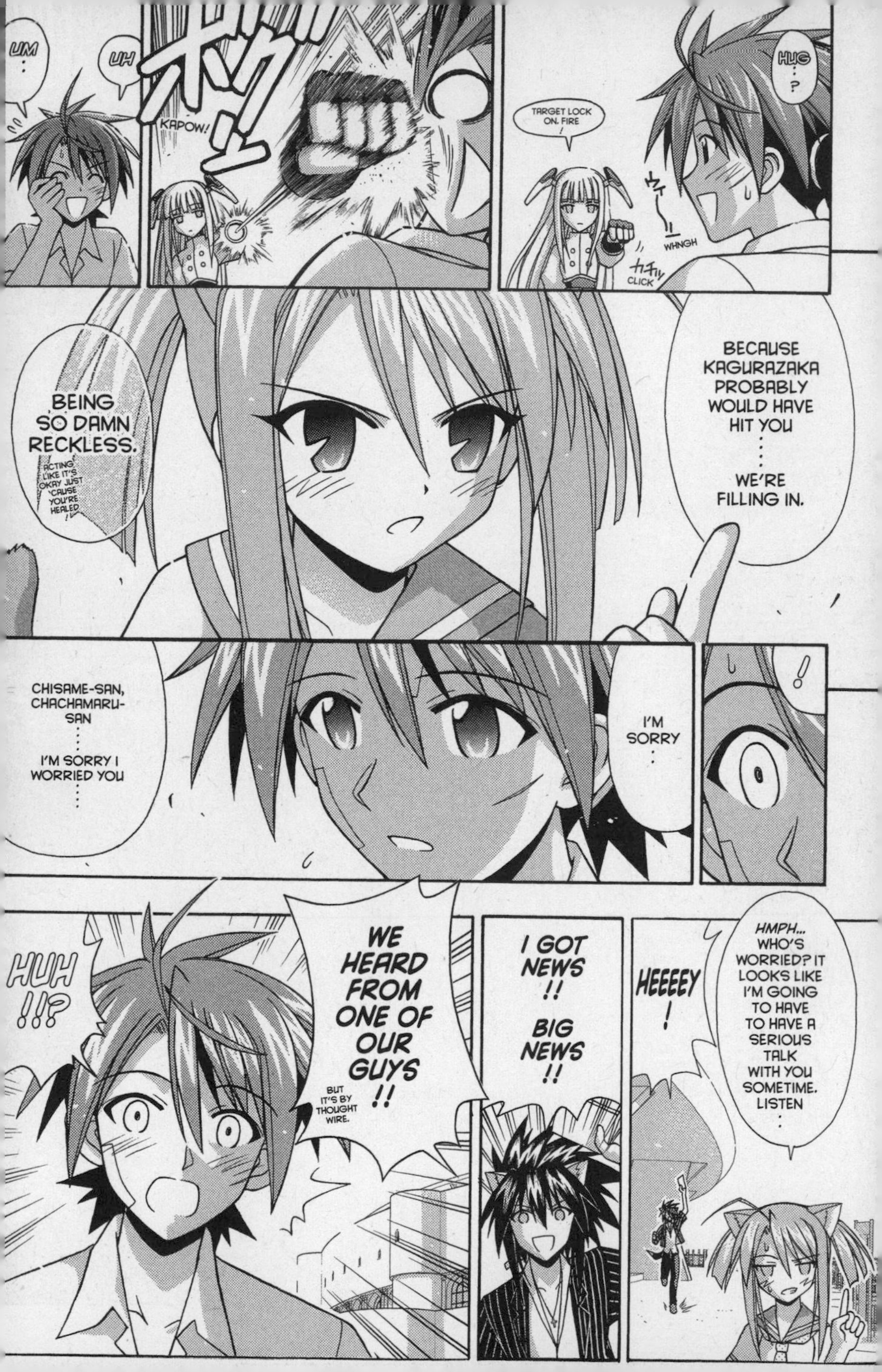
HUG...?
TARGET LOCK ON. FIRE!
WHNGH
CLICK
KAPOW!
UH
UM...
BECAUSE KAGURAZAKA PROBABLY WOULD HAVE HIT YOU... WE'RE FILLING IN.
BEING SO DAMN RECKLESS.
ACTING LIKE IT'S OKAY JUST 'CAUSE YOU'RE HEALED!
!
I'M SORRY...
CHISAME-SAN, CHACHAMARU-SAN... I'M SORRY I WORRIED YOU...
HMPH... WHO'S WORRIED? IT LOOKS LIKE I'M GOING TO HAVE TO HAVE A SERIOUS TALK WITH YOU SOMETIME. LISTEN...
HEEEEY!
I GOT NEWS!! BIG NEWS!!
WE HEARD FROM ONE OF OUR GUYS!!
BUT IT'S BY THOUGHT WIRE.
HUH!!?

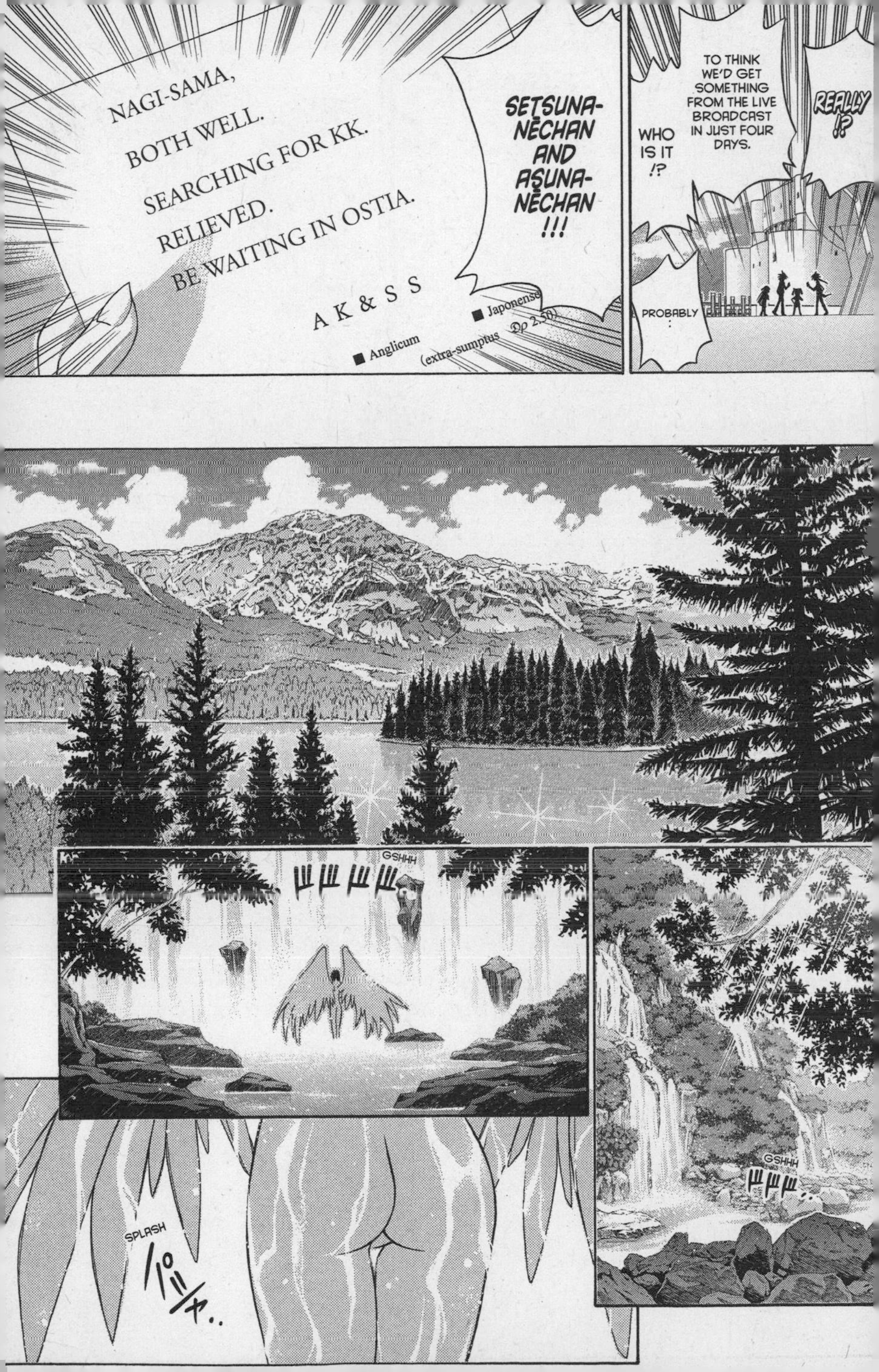
REALLY!?
TO THINK WE'D GET SOMETHING FROM THE LIVE BROADCAST IN JUST FOUR DAYS.
WHO IS IT!?
PROBABLY:
SETSUNA-NĒCHAN AND ASUNA-NĒCHAN!!!
NAGI-SAMA,
BOTH WELL.
SEARCHING FOR KK.
RELIEVED.
BE WAITING IN OSTIA.
A K & S S
■ Japonense
■ Anglicum
(extra-sumptus Ɖp 2.50)
GSHHH
GSHHH
SPLASH

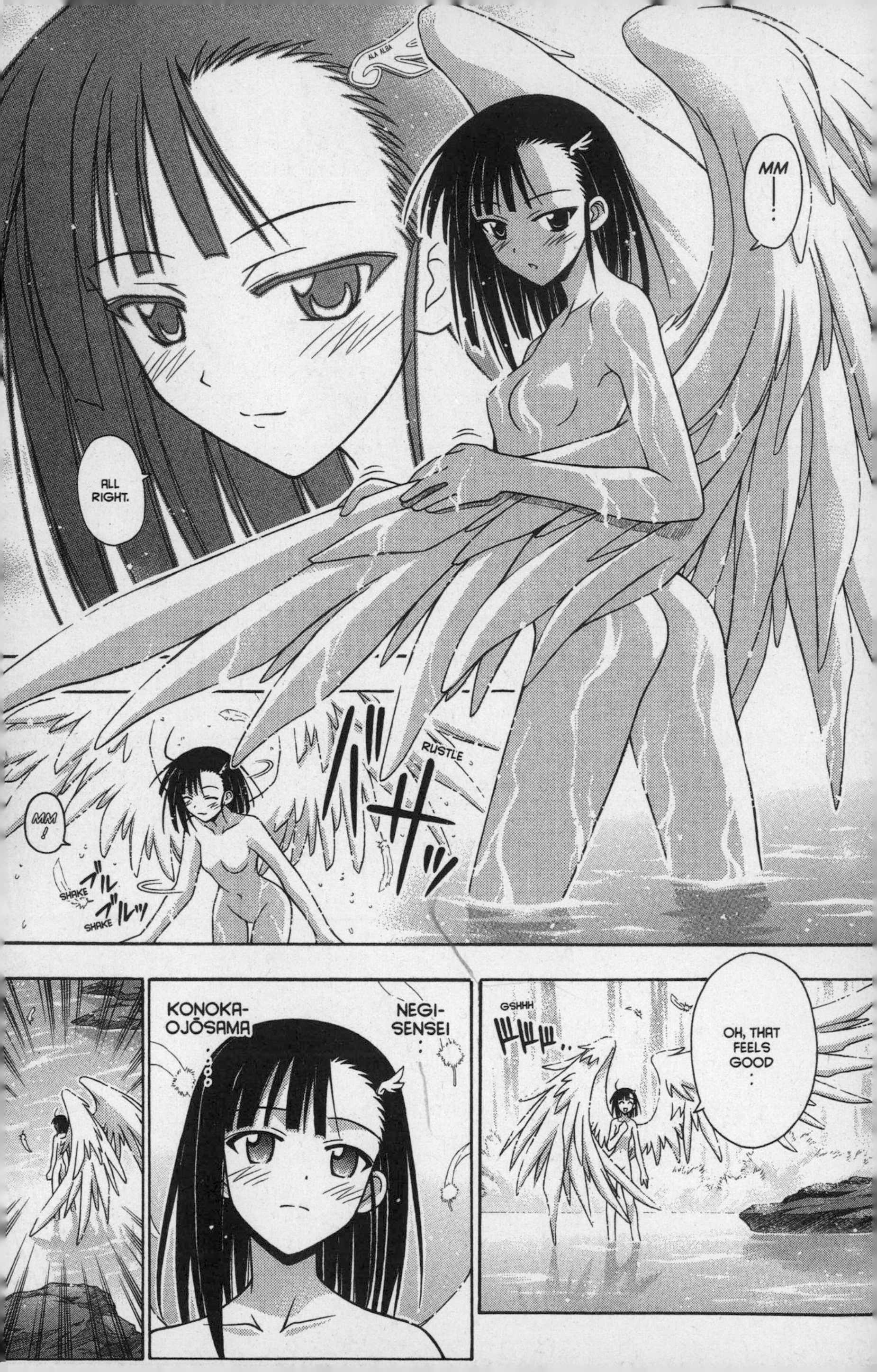
MM...!
ALA ALBA
ALL RIGHT.
RUSTLE
MM!
SHAKE
SHAKE
OH, THAT FEELS GOOD...
GSHHH
NEGI-SENSEI...
KONOKA-OJŌSAMA...

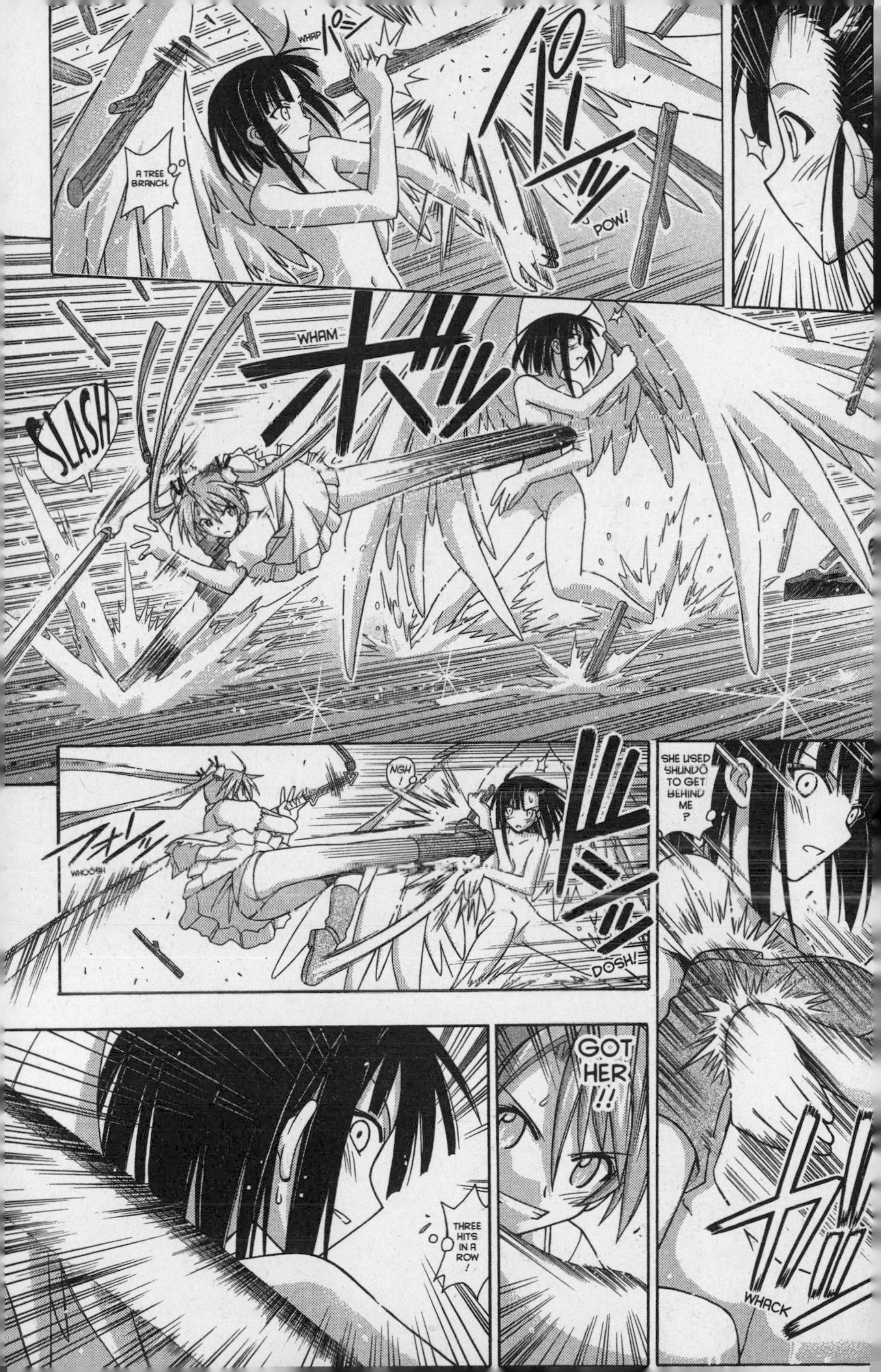
WHAP
A TREE BRANCH.
POW!
WHAM
SLASH
SHE USED SHUNDŌ TO GET BEHIND ME?
NGH!
DOSH!
WHOOSH
WHACK
GOT HER!!
THREE HITS IN A ROW!

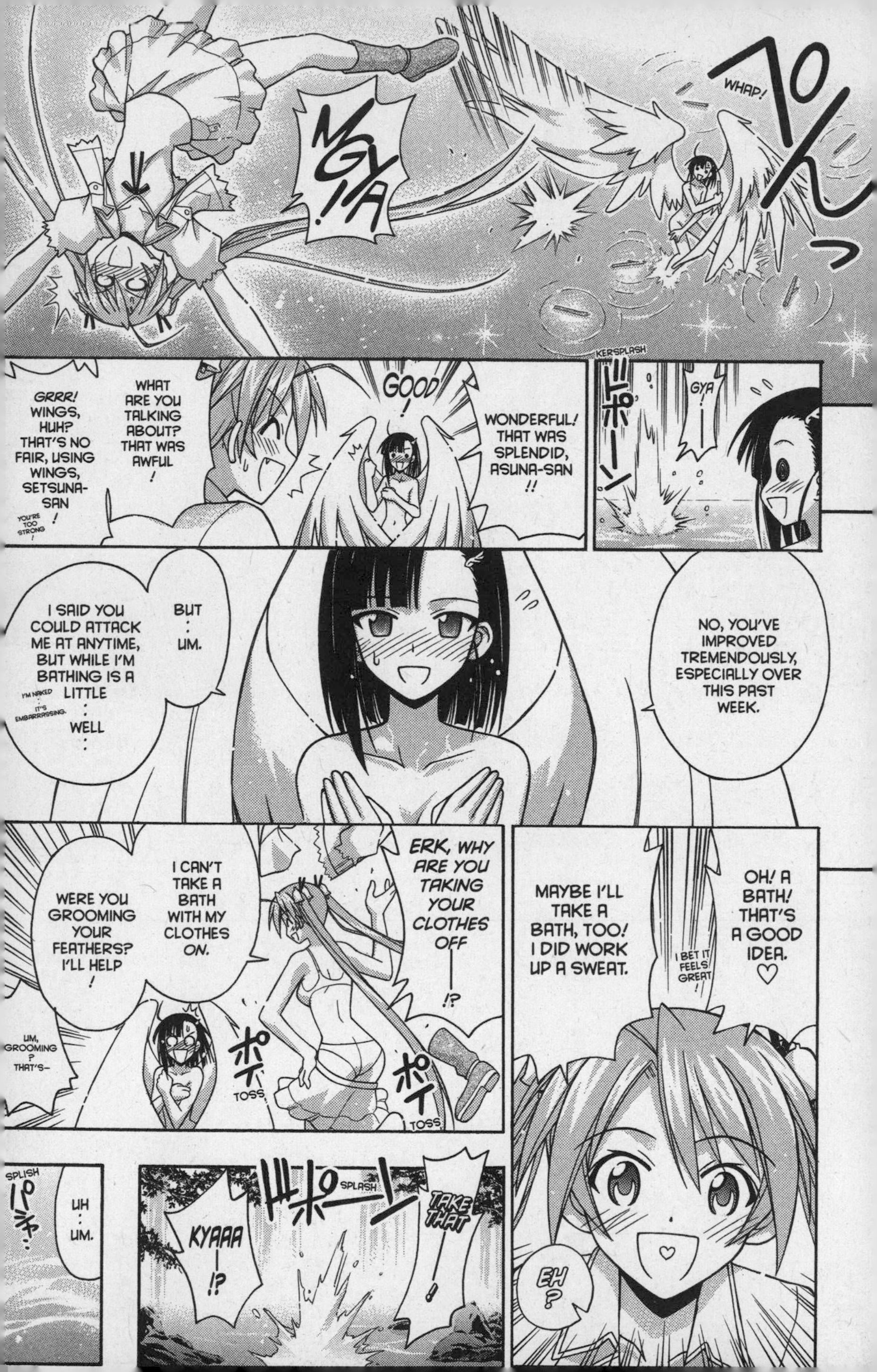
ぺんっ
WHAP!
MGYA!?
ドボーーン
KERSPLASH
GYA!
WONDERFUL! THAT WAS SPLENDID, ASUNA-SAN!!
GOOD!
WHAT ARE YOU TALKING ABOUT? THAT WAS AWFUL!
GRRR! WINGS, HUH? THAT'S NO FAIR, USING WINGS, SETSUNA-SAN!
YOU'RE TOO STRONG!
NO, YOU'VE IMPROVED TREMENDOUSLY, ESPECIALLY OVER THIS PAST WEEK.
BUT... UM.
I SAID YOU COULD ATTACK ME AT ANYTIME, BUT WHILE I'M BATHING IS A LITTLE... WELL...
I'M NAKED... IT'S EMBARRRASSING.
OH! A BATH! THAT'S A GOOD IDEA. ♡
MAYBE I'LL TAKE A BATH, TOO! I DID WORK UP A SWEAT.
I BET IT FEELS GREAT!
EH?
ERK, WHY ARE YOU TAKING YOUR CLOTHES OFF!?
I CAN'T TAKE A BATH WITH MY CLOTHES ON.
WERE YOU GROOMING YOUR FEATHERS? I'LL HELP!
ポイ
TOSS
ポイ
TOSS
UM, GROOMING? THAT'S—
ザボーン
SPLASH
TAKE THAT!
KYAAA!?
パシャ
SPLASH
UH... UM.

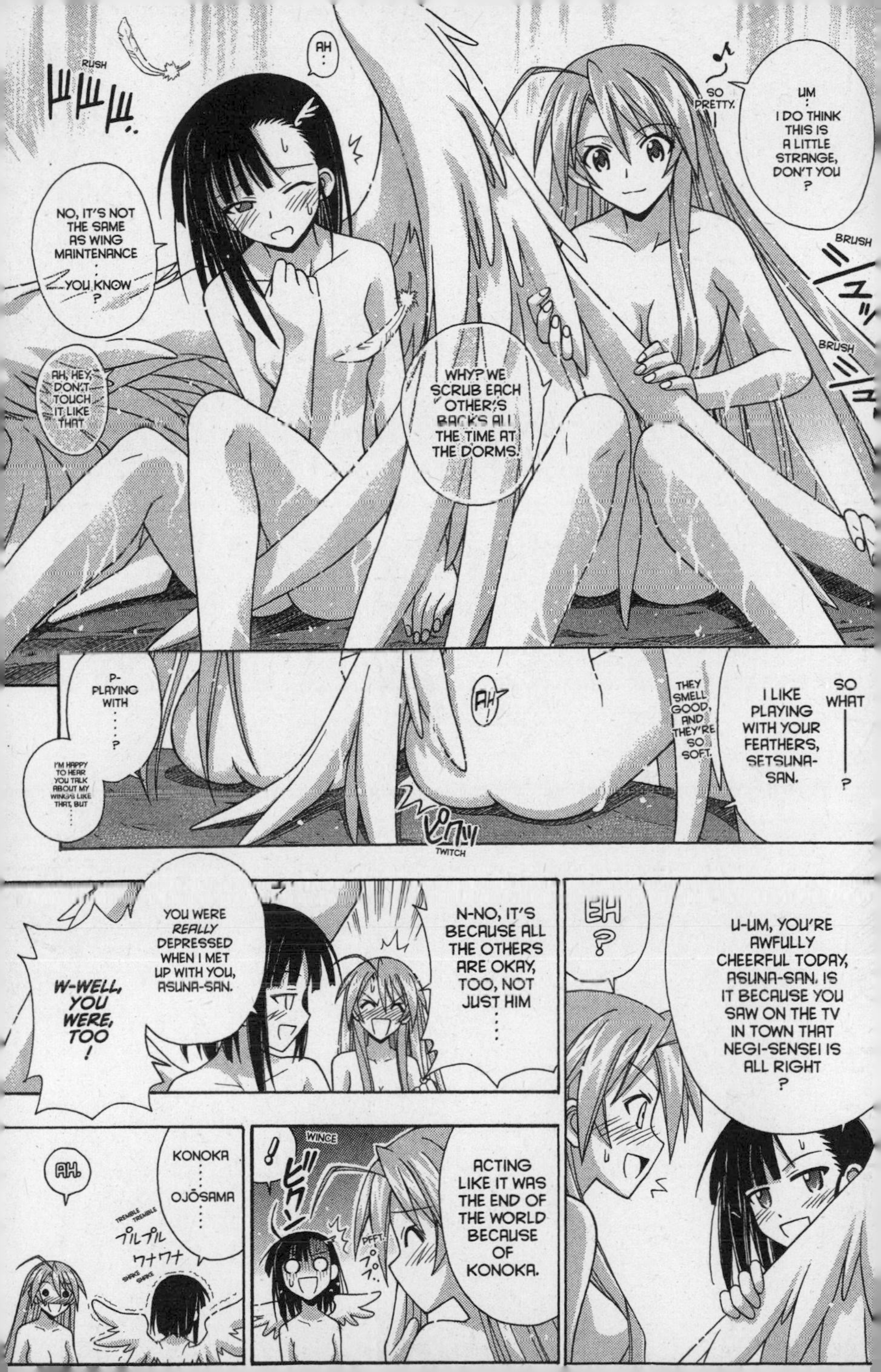
UM : I DO THINK THIS IS A LITTLE STRANGE, DON'T YOU ?
SO PRETTY.
BRUSH
BRUSH
AH :
RUSH
NO, IT'S NOT THE SAME AS WING MAINTENANCE : YOU KNOW ?
WHY? WE SCRUB EACH OTHER'S BACKS ALL THE TIME AT THE DORMS.
AH, HEY, DON'T TOUCH IT LIKE THAT
SO WHAT ?
I LIKE PLAYING WITH YOUR FEATHERS, SETSUNA-SAN.
THEY SMELL GOOD, AND THEY'RE SO SOFT.
AH
TWITCH
P-PLAYING WITH .... ?
I'M HAPPY TO HEAR YOU TALK ABOUT MY WINGS LIKE THAT, BUT ....
U-UM, YOU'RE AWFULLY CHEERFUL TODAY, ASUNA-SAN. IS IT BECAUSE YOU SAW ON THE TV IN TOWN THAT NEGI-SENSEI IS ALL RIGHT ?
EH ?
N-NO, IT'S BECAUSE ALL THE OTHERS ARE OKAY, TOO, NOT JUST HIM ....
YOU WERE *REALLY* DEPRESSED WHEN I MET UP WITH YOU, ASUNA-SAN.
W-WELL, YOU WERE, TOO !
ACTING LIKE IT WAS THE END OF THE WORLD BECAUSE OF KONOKA.
WINCE
!
PFFT.
KONOKA .... OJŌSAMA ....
AH.
TREMBLE TREMBLE
プルプル
ワナワナ
SHAKE SHAKE

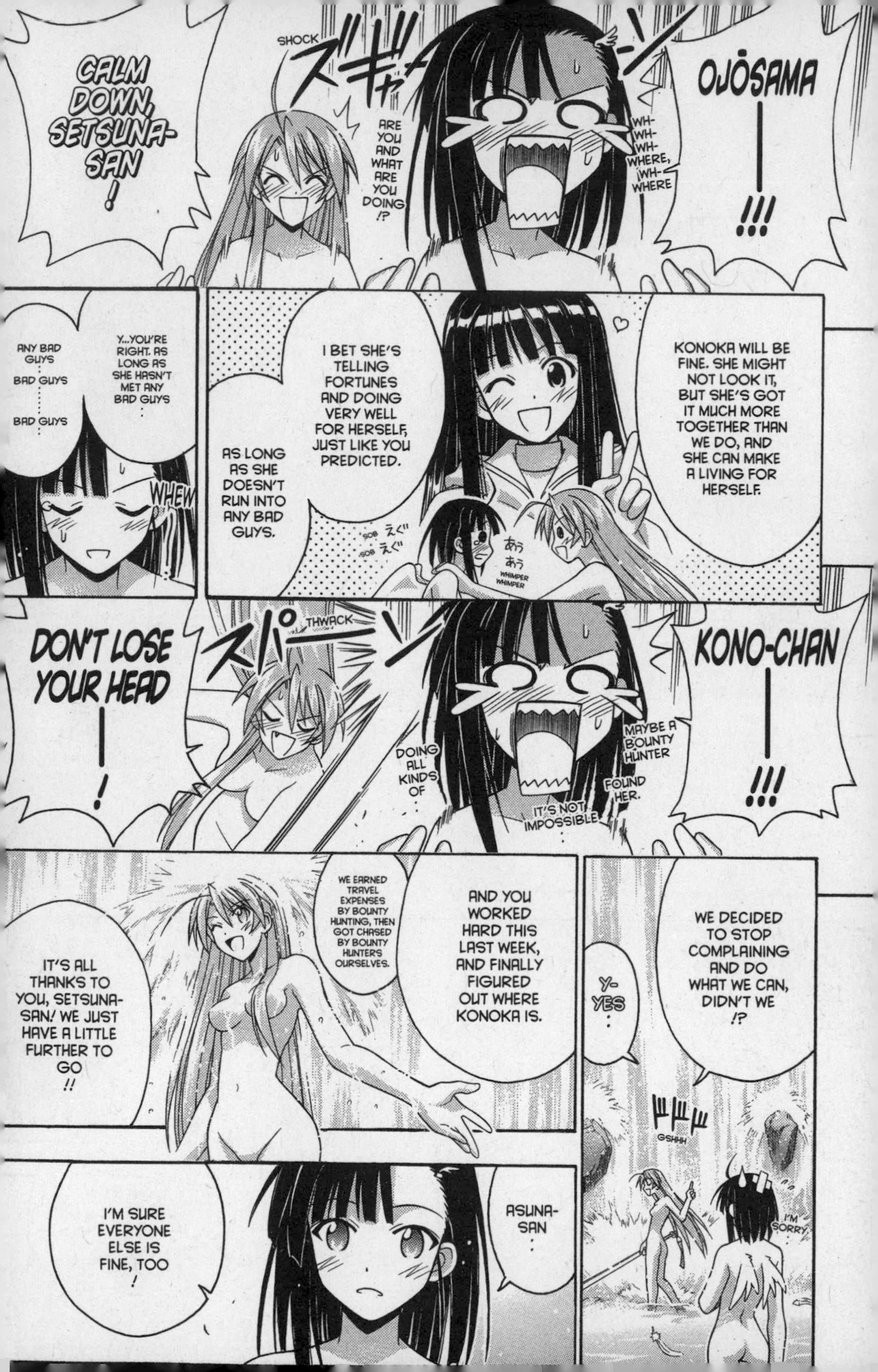
OJŌSAMA — !!!
WH-WH-WH-WHERE, WH-WHERE
SHOCK
ARE YOU AND WHAT ARE YOU DOING!?
CALM DOWN, SETSUNA-SAN!
KONOKA WILL BE FINE. SHE MIGHT NOT LOOK IT, BUT SHE'S GOT IT MUCH MORE TOGETHER THAN WE DO, AND SHE CAN MAKE A LIVING FOR HERSELF.
I BET SHE'S TELLING FORTUNES AND DOING VERY WELL FOR HERSELF, JUST LIKE YOU PREDICTED.
AS LONG AS SHE DOESN'T RUN INTO ANY BAD GUYS.
SOB えぐ SOB えぐ
あう あう WHIMPER WHIMPER
Y...YOU'RE RIGHT. AS LONG AS SHE HASN'T MET ANY BAD GUYS...
ANY BAD GUYS... BAD GUYS... BAD GUYS...
WHEW
KONO-CHAN — !!!
MAYBE A BOUNTY HUNTER FOUND HER.
IT'S NOT IMPOSSIBLE...
DOING ALL KINDS OF...
THWACK
DON'T LOSE YOUR HEAD — !
WE DECIDED TO STOP COMPLAINING AND DO WHAT WE CAN, DIDN'T WE!?
Y-YES...
GSHHH
I'M SORRY
AND YOU WORKED HARD THIS LAST WEEK, AND FINALLY FIGURED OUT WHERE KONOKA IS.
WE EARNED TRAVEL EXPENSES BY BOUNTY HUNTING, THEN GOT CHASED BY BOUNTY HUNTERS OURSELVES.
IT'S ALL THANKS TO YOU, SETSUNA-SAN! WE JUST HAVE A LITTLE FURTHER TO GO!!
ASUNA-SAN...
I'M SURE EVERYONE ELSE IS FINE, TOO!

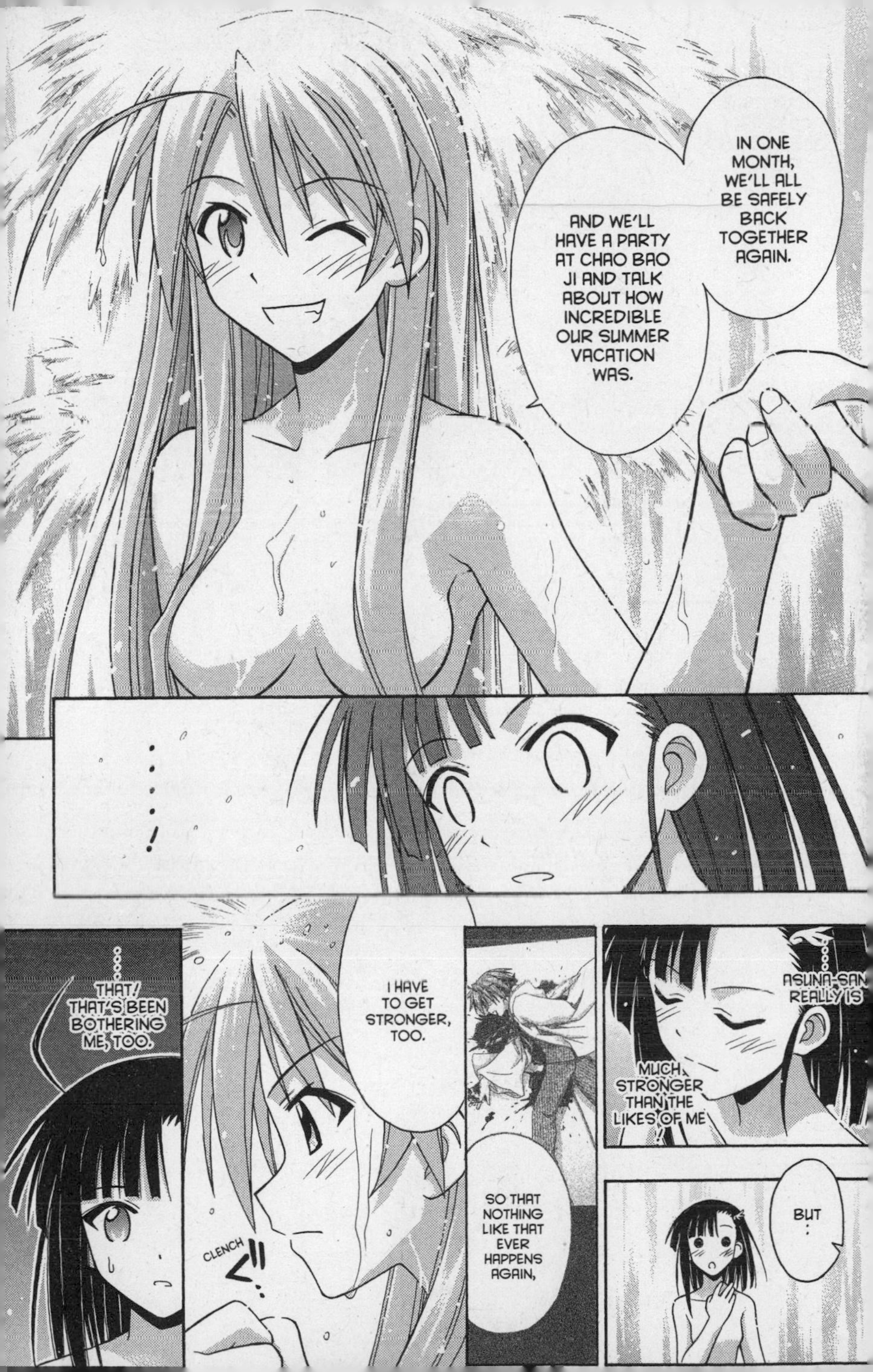
IN ONE MONTH, WE'LL ALL BE SAFELY BACK TOGETHER AGAIN.
AND WE'LL HAVE A PARTY AT CHAO BAO JI AND TALK ABOUT HOW INCREDIBLE OUR SUMMER VACATION WAS.
......!
ASUNA-SAN REALLY IS
MUCH STRONGER THAN THE LIKES OF ME!
BUT...
SO THAT NOTHING LIKE THAT EVER HAPPENS AGAIN,
I HAVE TO GET STRONGER, TOO.
CLENCH
...THAT! THAT'S BEEN BOTHERING ME, TOO.

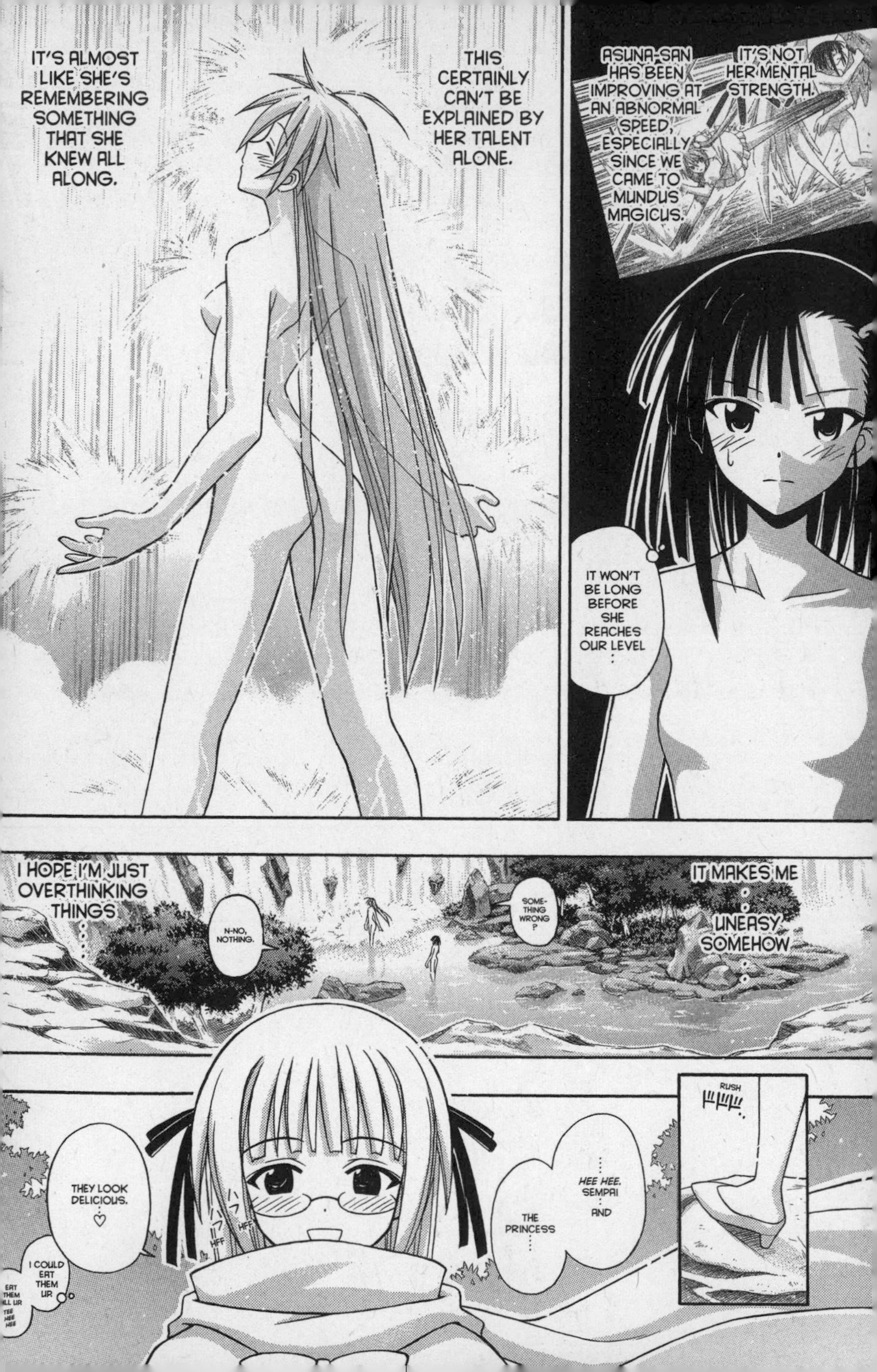
IT'S NOT HER MENTAL STRENGTH.
ASUNA-SAN HAS BEEN IMPROVING AT AN ABNORMAL SPEED, ESPECIALLY SINCE WE CAME TO MUNDUS MAGICUS.
IT WON'T BE LONG BEFORE SHE REACHES OUR LEVEL...
THIS CERTAINLY CAN'T BE EXPLAINED BY HER TALENT ALONE.
IT'S ALMOST LIKE SHE'S REMEMBERING SOMETHING THAT SHE KNEW ALL ALONG.
IT MAKES ME... UNEASY SOMEHOW...
SOMETHING WRONG?
N-NO, NOTHING.
I HOPE I'M JUST OVERTHINKING THINGS...
RUSH
...HEE HEE. SEMPAI... AND
THE PRINCESS......
THEY LOOK DELICIOUS... ♡
HFF HFF
I COULD EAT THEM UP.

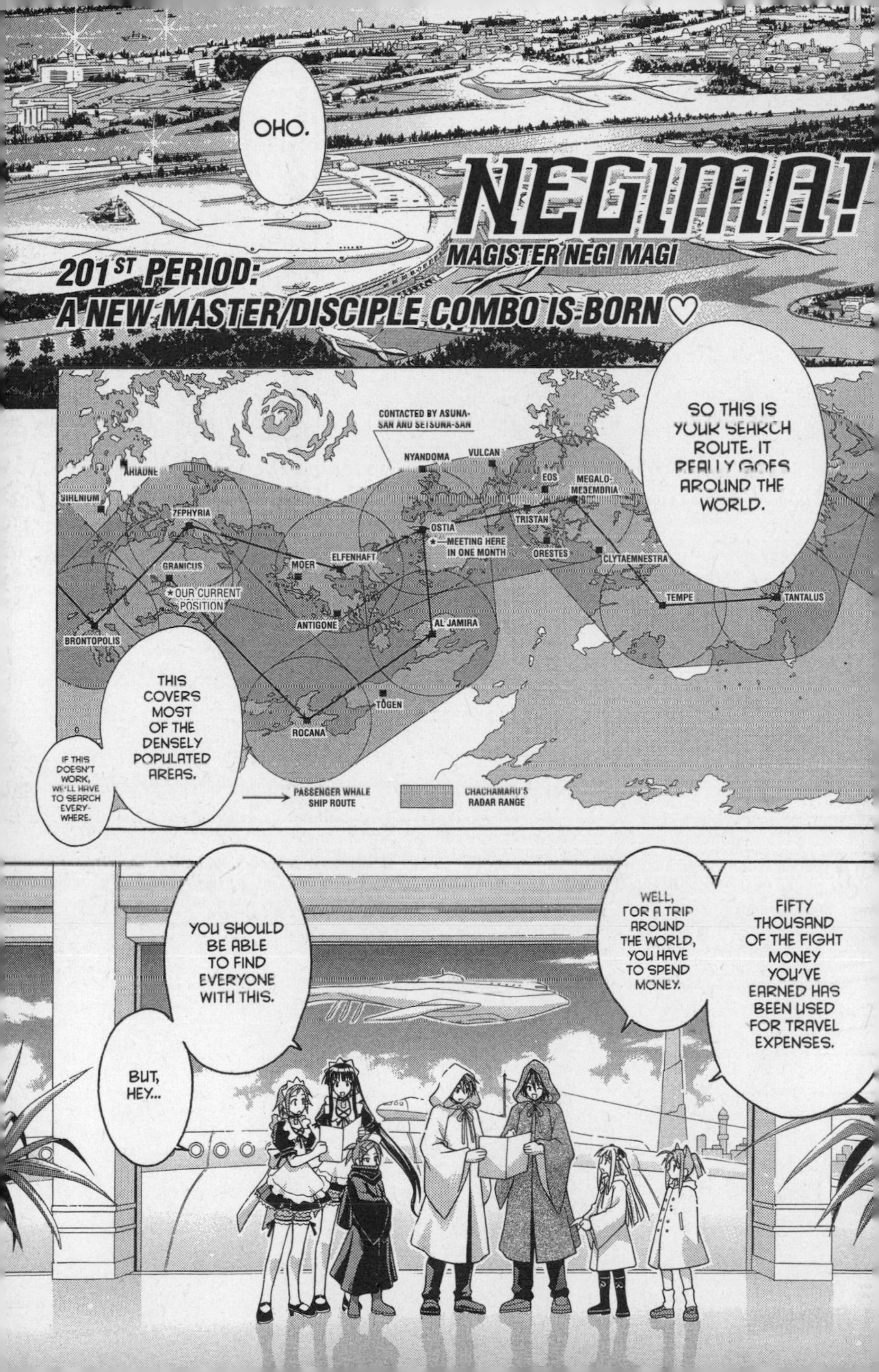
OHO.
NEGIMA!
MAGISTER NEGI MAGI
201ST PERIOD:
A NEW MASTER/DISCIPLE COMBO IS BORN ♡
SO THIS IS YOUR SEARCH ROUTE. IT REALLY GOES AROUND THE WORLD.
CONTACTED BY ASUNA-SAN AND SETSUNA-SAN
NYANDOMA
VULCAN
EOS
MEGALO-MESEMBRIA
ARIADNE
ZEPHYRIA
OSTIA
★—MEETING HERE IN ONE MONTH
TRISTAN
ORESTES
CLYTAEMNESTRA
GRANICUS
MOER
ELFENHAFT
★OUR CURRENT POSITION
TEMPE
TANTALUS
ANTIGONE
AL JAMIRA
BRONTOPOLIS
TŌGEN
ROCANA
PASSENGER WHALE SHIP ROUTE
CHACHAMARU'S RADAR RANGE
THIS COVERS MOST OF THE DENSELY POPULATED AREAS.
IF THIS DOESN'T WORK, WE'LL HAVE TO SEARCH EVERY-WHERE.
FIFTY THOUSAND OF THE FIGHT MONEY YOU'VE EARNED HAS BEEN USED FOR TRAVEL EXPENSES.
WELL, FOR A TRIP AROUND THE WORLD, YOU HAVE TO SPEND MONEY.
YOU SHOULD BE ABLE TO FIND EVERYONE WITH THIS.
BUT, HEY...

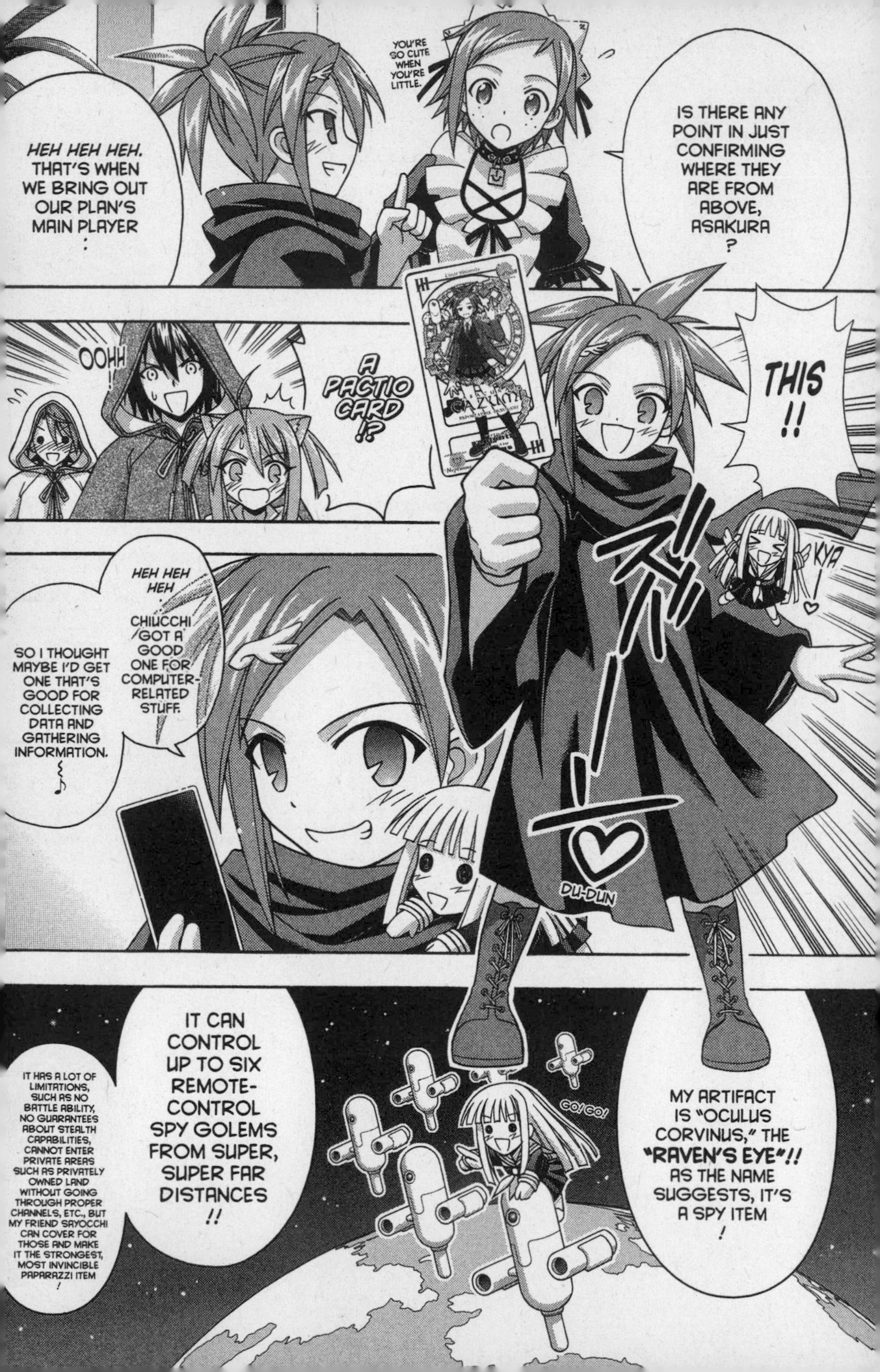
IS THERE ANY POINT IN JUST CONFIRMING WHERE THEY ARE FROM ABOVE, ASAKURA?
YOU'RE SO CUTE WHEN YOU'RE LITTLE.
HEH HEH HEH. THAT'S WHEN WE BRING OUT OUR PLAN'S MAIN PLAYER:
THIS!!
A PACTIO CARD!?
OOHH!
KYA! ♡
DU-DUN
HEH HEH HEH. CHIUCCHI GOT A GOOD ONE FOR COMPUTER-RELATED STUFF.
SO I THOUGHT MAYBE I'D GET ONE THAT'S GOOD FOR COLLECTING DATA AND GATHERING INFORMATION. ♪
MY ARTIFACT IS "OCULUS CORVINUS," THE "RAVEN'S EYE"!! AS THE NAME SUGGESTS, IT'S A SPY ITEM!
GO! GO!
IT CAN CONTROL UP TO SIX REMOTE-CONTROL SPY GOLEMS FROM SUPER, SUPER FAR DISTANCES!!
IT HAS A LOT OF LIMITATIONS, SUCH AS NO BATTLE ABILITY, NO GUARANTEES ABOUT STEALTH CAPABILITIES, CANNOT ENTER PRIVATE AREAS SUCH AS PRIVATELY OWNED LAND WITHOUT GOING THROUGH PROPER CHANNELS, ETC., BUT MY FRIEND SAYOCCHI CAN COVER FOR THOSE AND MAKE IT THE STRONGEST, MOST INVINCIBLE PAPARAZZI ITEM!

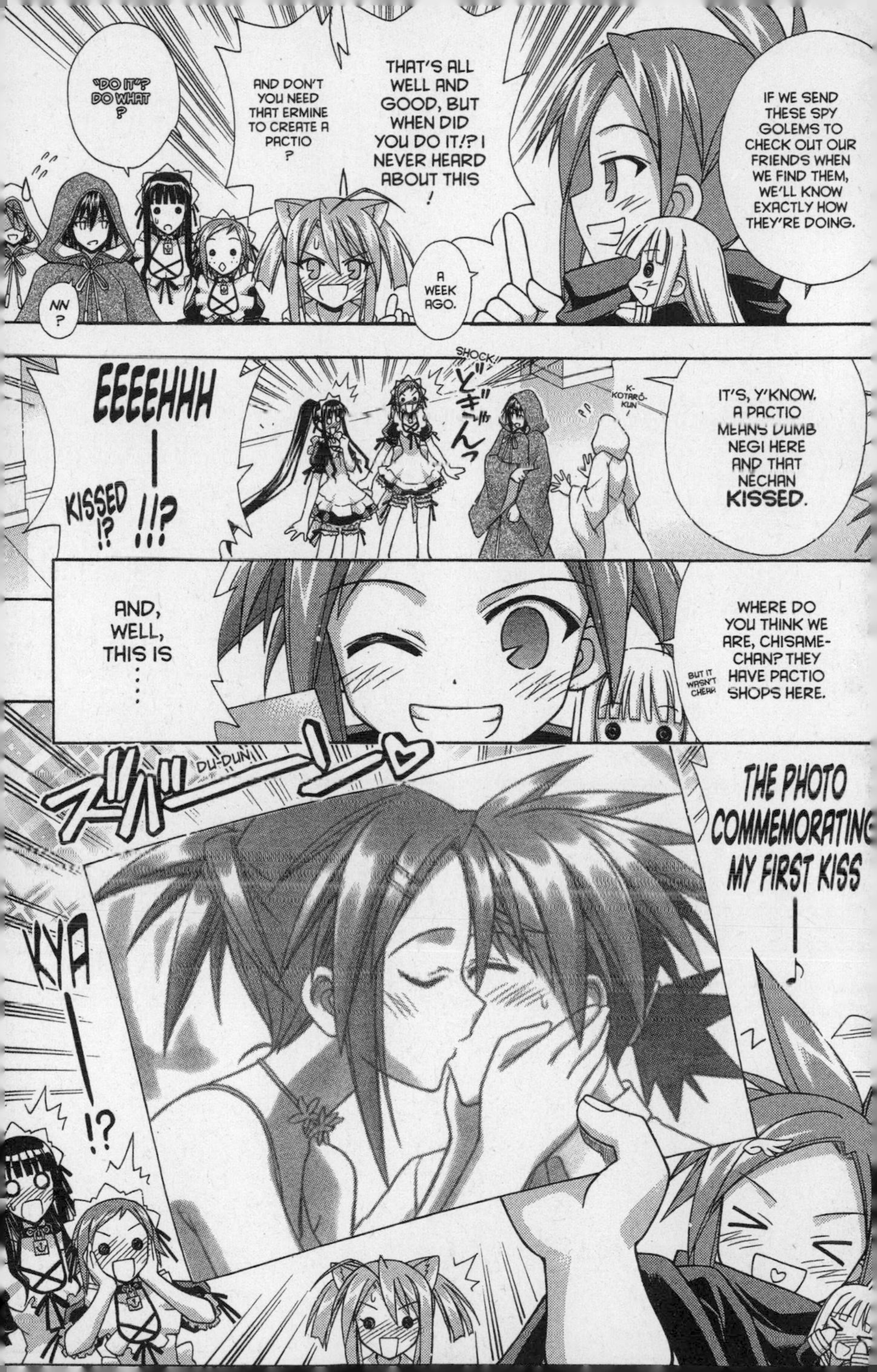
IF WE SEND THESE SPY GOLEMS TO CHECK OUT OUR FRIENDS WHEN WE FIND THEM, WE'LL KNOW EXACTLY HOW THEY'RE DOING.
THAT'S ALL WELL AND GOOD, BUT WHEN DID YOU DO IT!? I NEVER HEARD ABOUT THIS!
AND DON'T YOU NEED THAT ERMINE TO CREATE A PACTIO?
A WEEK AGO.
"DO IT"? DO WHAT?
NN?
IT'S, Y'KNOW. A PACTIO MEANS DUMB NEGI HERE AND THAT NECHAN KISSED.
K-KOTARŌ-KUN!
SHOCK!!
EEEEHHH—!!?
KISSED!?
WHERE DO YOU THINK WE ARE, CHISAME-CHAN? THEY HAVE PACTIO SHOPS HERE.
BUT IT WASN'T CHEAP.
AND, WELL, THIS IS....
THE PHOTO COMMEMORATING MY FIRST KISS—♪
DU-DUN
KYA—!?

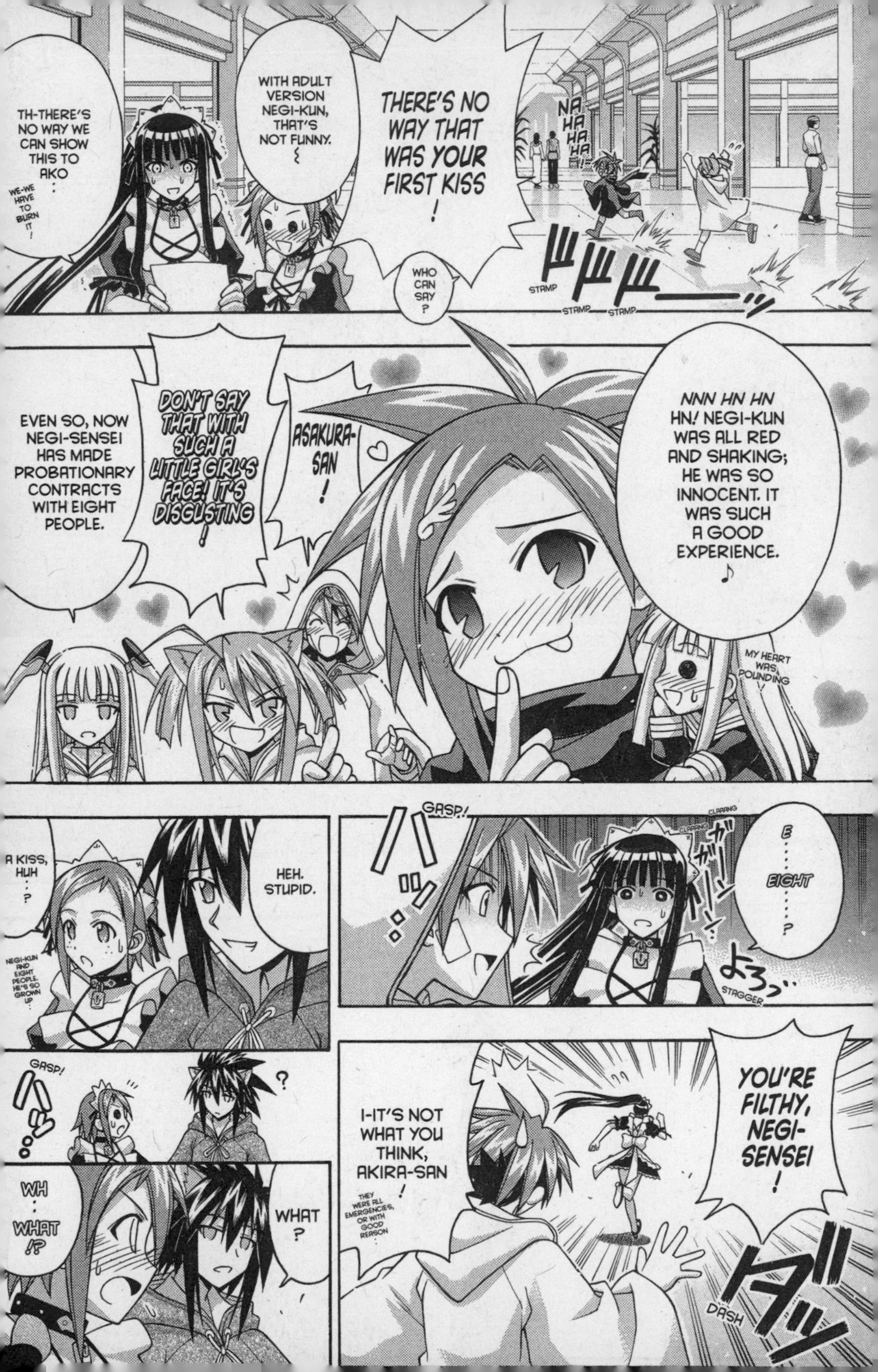
NA HA HA HA!!
STAMP
STAMP
STAMP
THERE'S NO WAY THAT WAS YOUR FIRST KISS!
WHO CAN SAY?
WITH ADULT VERSION NEGI-KUN, THAT'S NOT FUNNY.
TH-THERE'S NO WAY WE CAN SHOW THIS TO AKO...
WE-WE HAVE TO BURN IT!
NNN HN HN HN! NEGI-KUN WAS ALL RED AND SHAKING; HE WAS SO INNOCENT. IT WAS SUCH A GOOD EXPERIENCE. ♪
MY HEART WAS POUNDING!
ASAKURA-SAN ♡!
DON'T SAY THAT WITH SUCH A LITTLE GIRL'S FACE! IT'S DISGUSTING!
EVEN SO, NOW NEGI-SENSEI HAS MADE PROBATIONARY CONTRACTS WITH EIGHT PEOPLE.
E... EIGHT...?
CLAANG
CLAANG
GASP!
よろっ
STAGGER
A KISS, HUH...?
HEH. STUPID.
NEGI-KUN AND EIGHT PEOPLE. HE'S SO GROWN UP...
YOU'RE FILTHY, NEGI-SENSEI!
I-IT'S NOT WHAT YOU THINK, AKIRA-SAN!
THEY WERE ALL EMERGENCIES, OR WITH GOOD REASON
DASH
GASP!
?
WH... WHAT!?
WHAT?

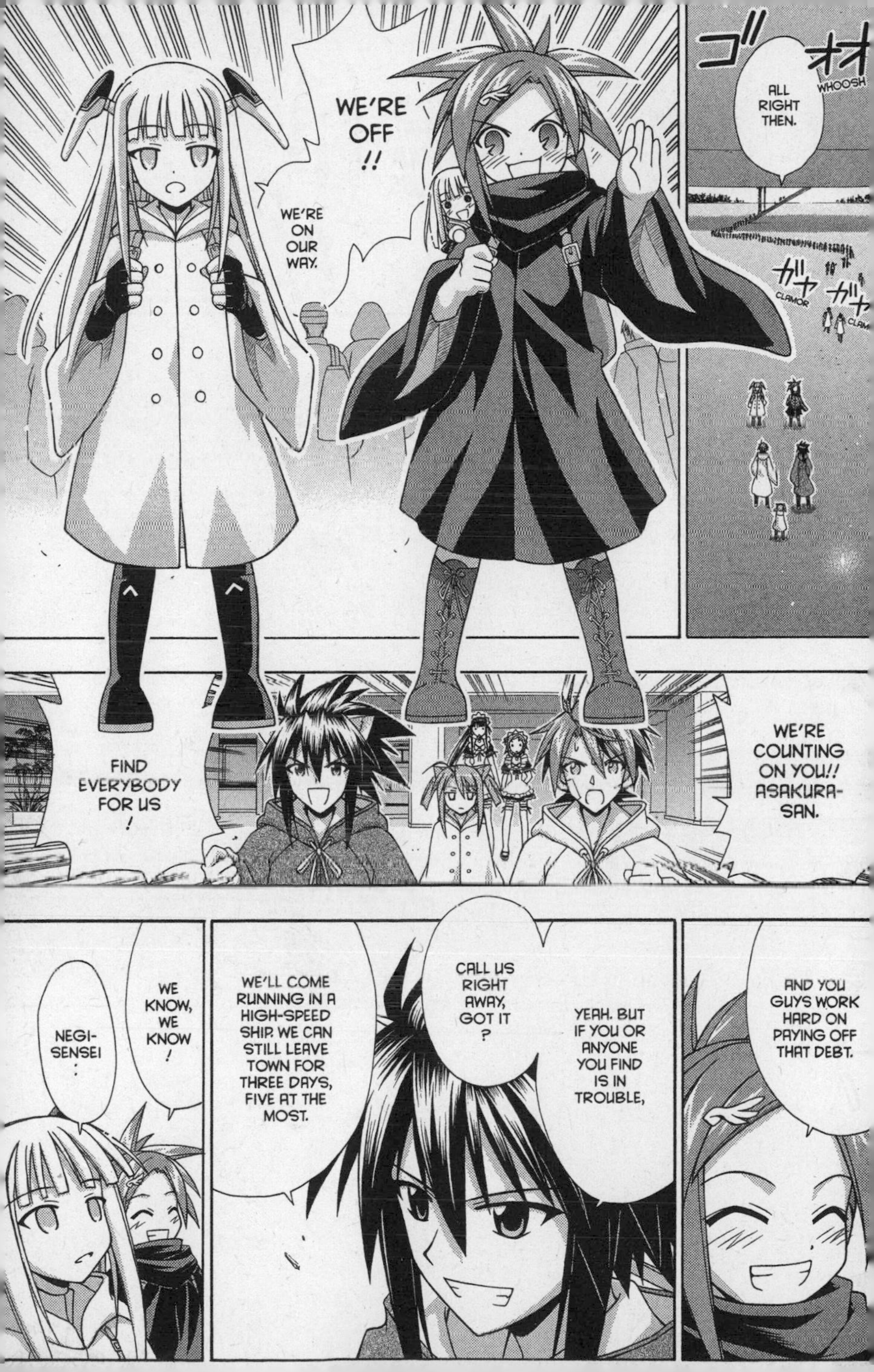
WHOOSH
ALL RIGHT THEN.
CLAMOR CLAMOR
WE'RE OFF!!
WE'RE ON OUR WAY.
WE'RE COUNTING ON YOU!! ASAKURA-SAN.
FIND EVERYBODY FOR US!
AND YOU GUYS WORK HARD ON PAYING OFF THAT DEBT.
YEAH. BUT IF YOU OR ANYONE YOU FIND IS IN TROUBLE,
CALL US RIGHT AWAY, GOT IT?
WE'LL COME RUNNING IN A HIGH-SPEED SHIP. WE CAN STILL LEAVE TOWN FOR THREE DAYS, FIVE AT THE MOST.
WE KNOW, WE KNOW!
NEGI-SENSEI...

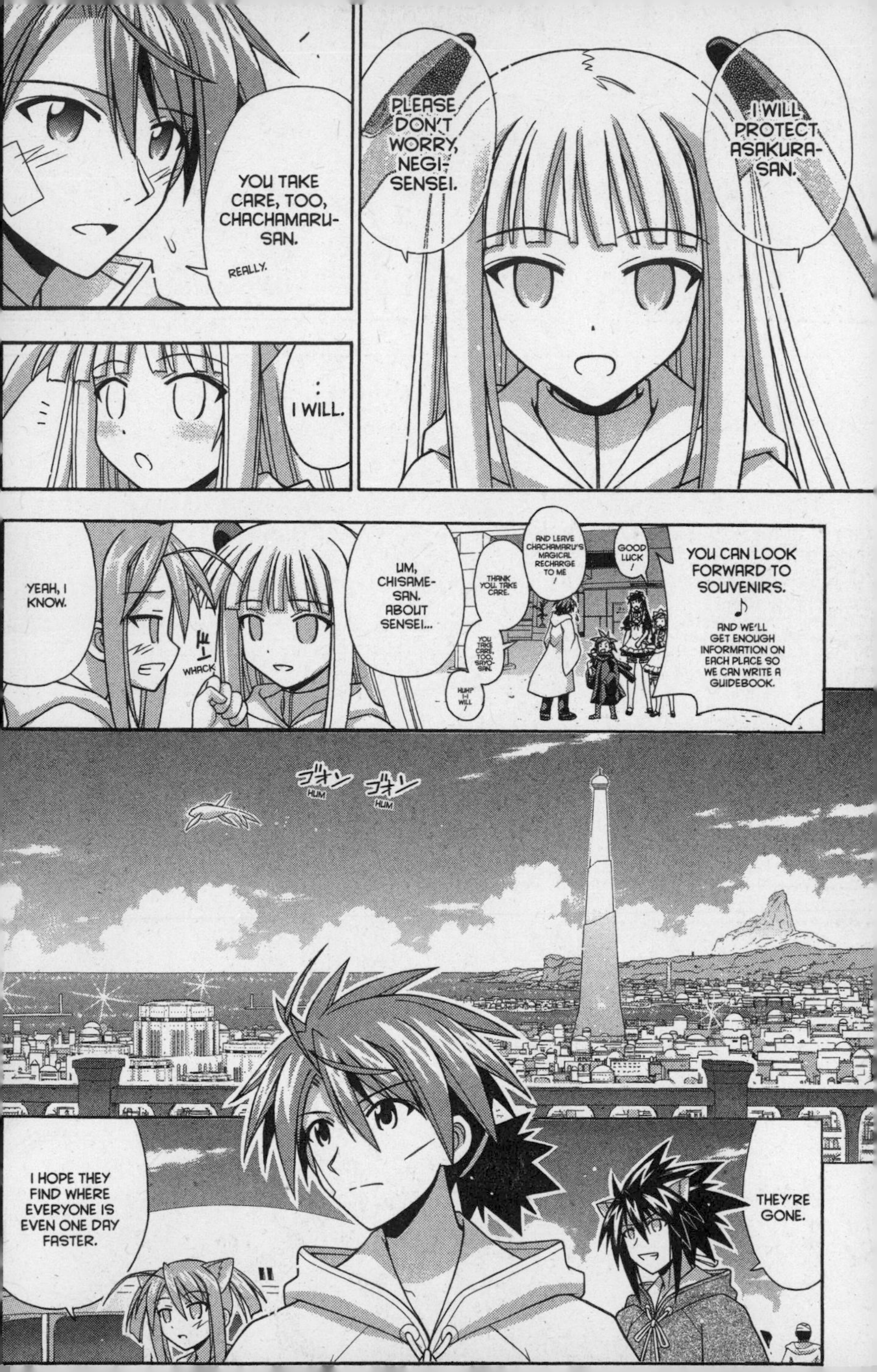
I WILL PROTECT ASAKURA-SAN.
PLEASE DON'T WORRY, NEGI-SENSEI.
YOU TAKE CARE, TOO, CHACHAMARU-SAN.
REALLY.
I WILL.
YOU CAN LOOK FORWARD TO SOUVENIRS. ♪
AND WE'LL GET ENOUGH INFORMATION ON EACH PLACE SO WE CAN WRITE A GUIDEBOOK.
GOOD LUCK!
AND LEAVE CHACHAMARU'S MAGICAL RECHARGE TO ME!
THANK YOU. TAKE CARE.
YOU TAKE CARE, TOO, SAYO-SAN.
HUMP I-I WILL!
UM, CHISAME-SAN. ABOUT SENSEI...
WHACK
YEAH, I KNOW.
ゴォン HUM
ゴォン HUM
THEY'RE GONE.
I HOPE THEY FIND WHERE EVERYONE IS EVEN ONE DAY FASTER.

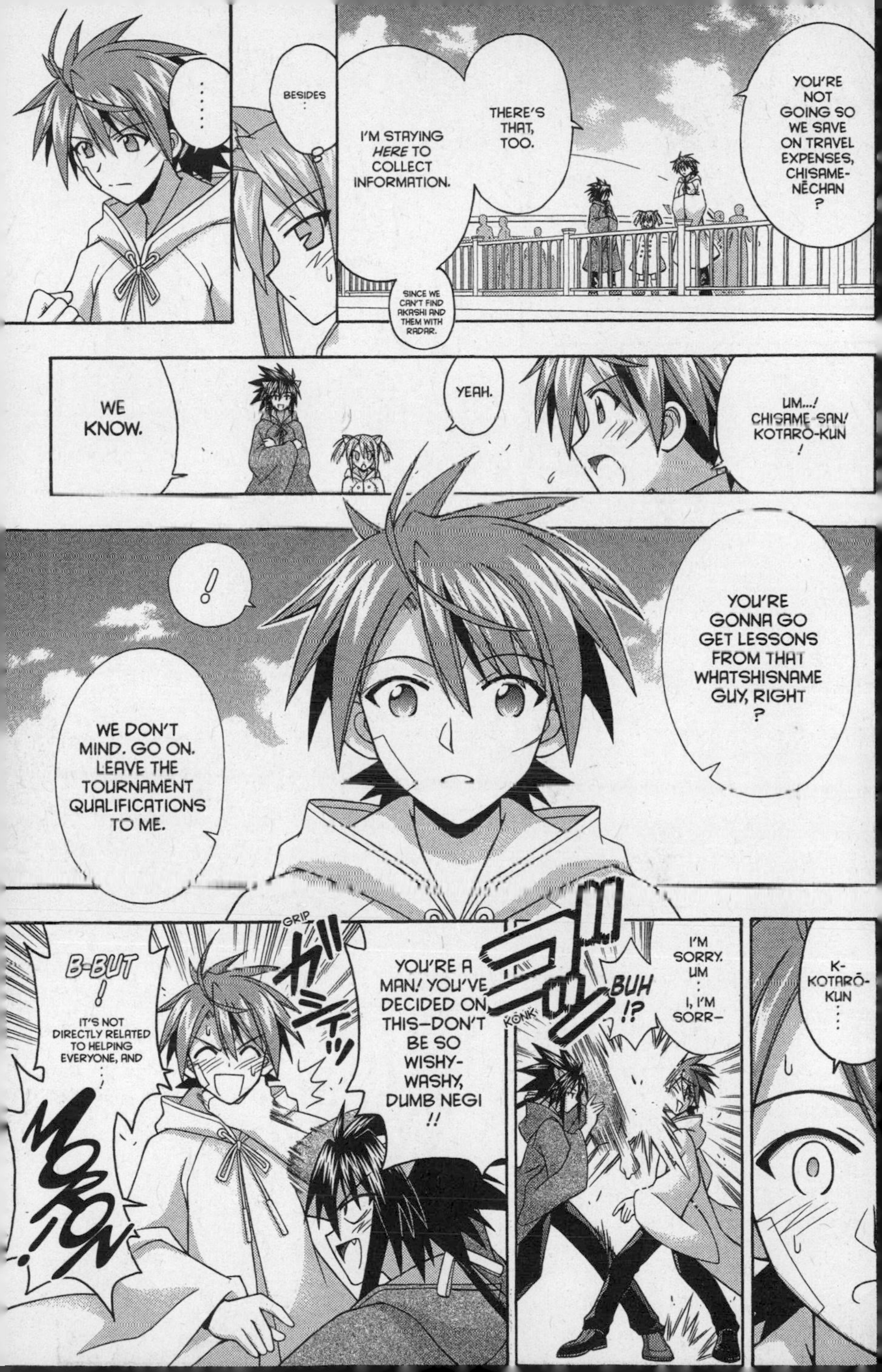
YOU'RE NOT GOING SO WE SAVE ON TRAVEL EXPENSES, CHISAME-NĒCHAN ?
THERE'S THAT, TOO.
I'M STAYING *HERE* TO COLLECT INFORMATION.
SINCE WE CAN'T FIND AKASHI AND THEM WITH RADAR.
BESIDES ...
......
UM...! CHISAME-SAN! KOTARO-KUN !
YEAH.
WE KNOW.
YOU'RE GONNA GO GET LESSONS FROM THAT WHATSHISNAME GUY, RIGHT ?
!
WE DON'T MIND. GO ON. LEAVE THE TOURNAMENT QUALIFICATIONS TO ME.
K-KOTARŌ-KUN ....
I'M SORRY. UM ... I, I'M SORR—
BUH !?
KONK
YOU'RE A MAN! YOU'VE DECIDED ON THIS—DON'T BE SO WISHY-WASHY, DUMB NEGI !!
GRIP
B-BUT !
IT'S NOT DIRECTLY RELATED TO HELPING EVERYONE, AND ...
MORON !

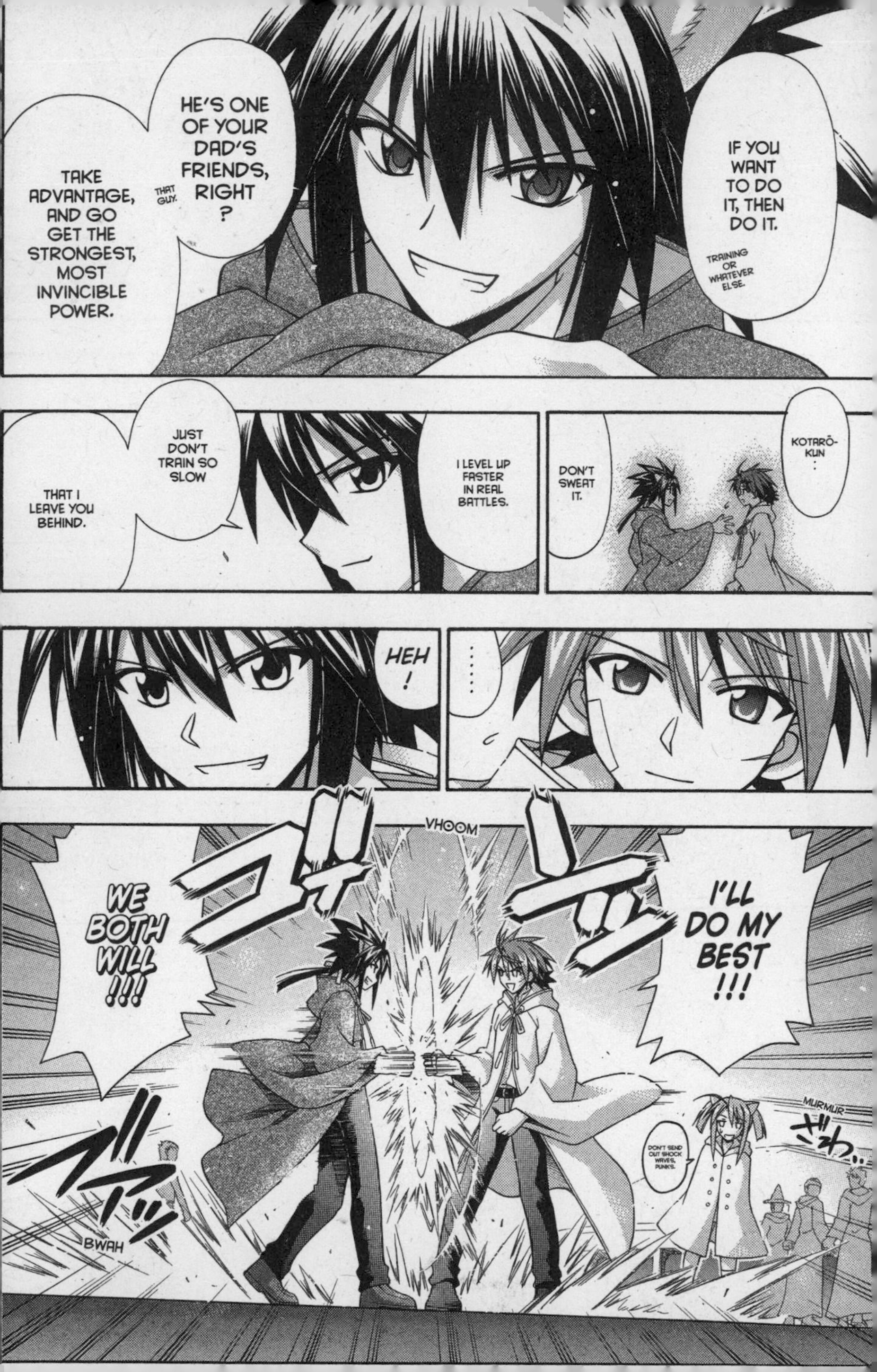

IF YOU WANT TO DO IT, THEN DO IT.
TRAINING OR WHATEVER ELSE.
HE'S ONE OF YOUR DAD'S FRIENDS, RIGHT?
THAT GUY.
TAKE ADVANTAGE, AND GO GET THE STRONGEST, MOST INVINCIBLE POWER.
KOTARŌ-KUN...
DON'T SWEAT IT.
I LEVEL UP FASTER IN REAL BATTLES.
JUST DON'T TRAIN SO SLOW
THAT I LEAVE YOU BEHIND.
......
HEH!
VHOOM
I'LL DO MY BEST!!!
WE BOTH WILL!!!
MURMUR
DON'T SEND OUT SHOCK WAVES, PUNKS.
BWAH

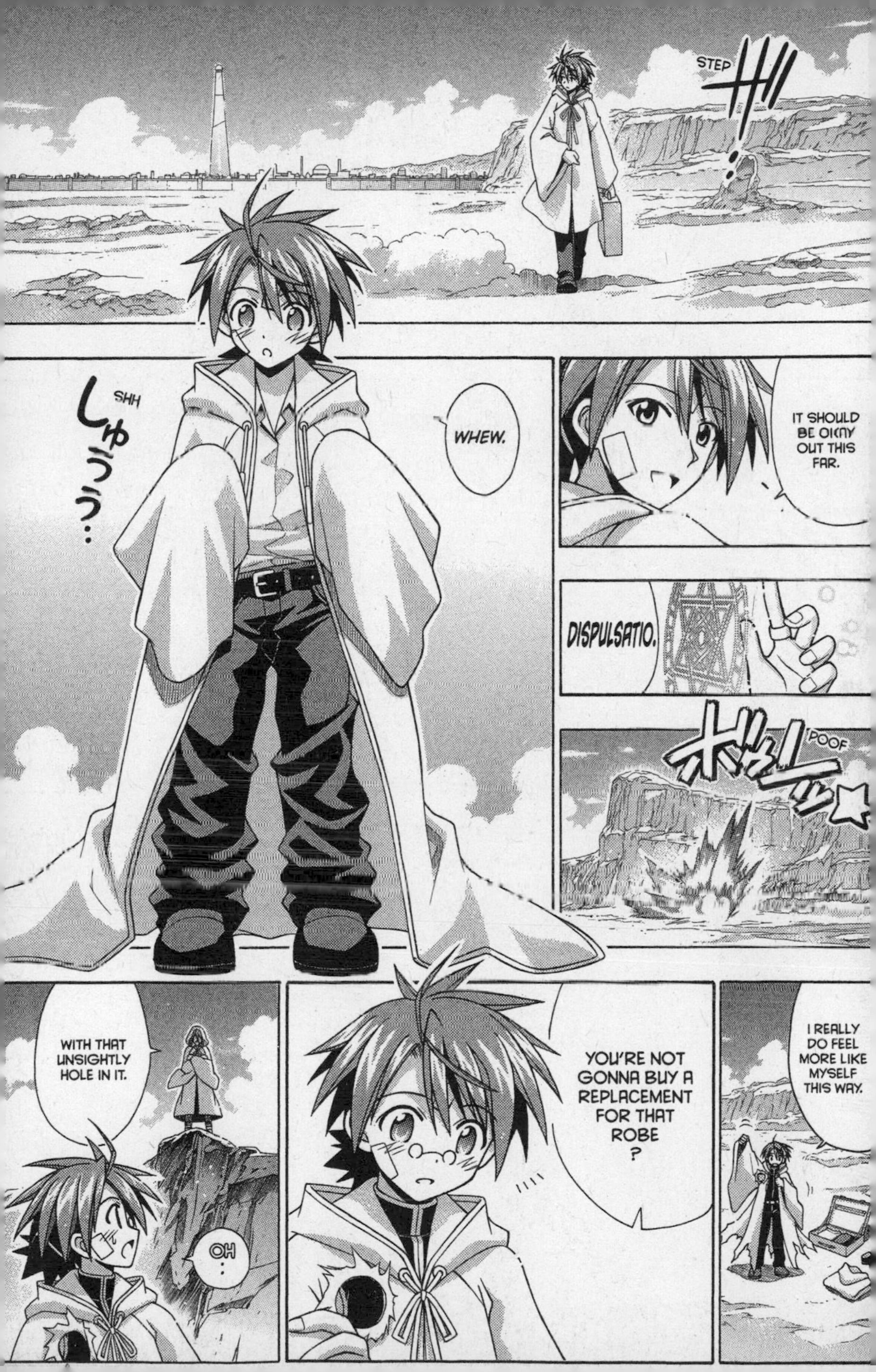
STEP
IT SHOULD BE OKAY OUT THIS FAR.
DISPULSATIO.
POOF
SHH
しゅううう..
WHEW.
I REALLY DO FEEL MORE LIKE MYSELF THIS WAY.
YOU'RE NOT GONNA BUY A REPLACEMENT FOR THAT ROBE
?
WITH THAT UNSIGHTLY HOLE IN IT.
OH...

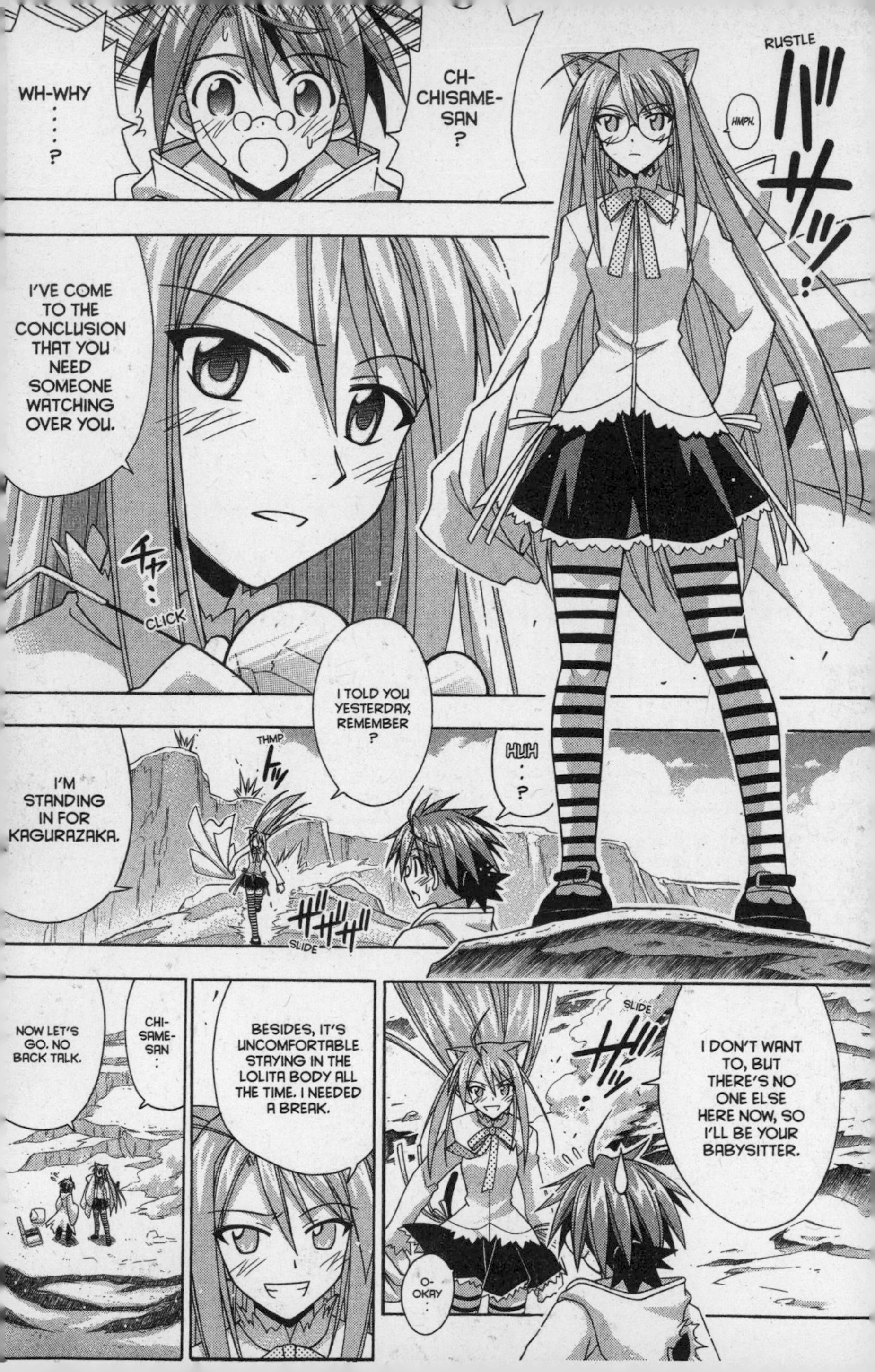
RUSTLE
HMPH.
CH-CHISAME-SAN?
WH-WHY...?
I'VE COME TO THE CONCLUSION THAT YOU NEED SOMEONE WATCHING OVER YOU.
CLICK
HUH...?
I TOLD YOU YESTERDAY, REMEMBER?
THMP
I'M STANDING IN FOR KAGURAZAKA.
SLIDE
SLIDE
I DON'T WANT TO, BUT THERE'S NO ONE ELSE HERE NOW, SO I'LL BE YOUR BABYSITTER.
O-OKAY...
BESIDES, IT'S UNCOMFORTABLE STAYING IN THE LOLITA BODY ALL THE TIME. I NEEDED A BREAK.
CHI-SAME-SAN...
NOW LET'S GO. NO BACK TALK.

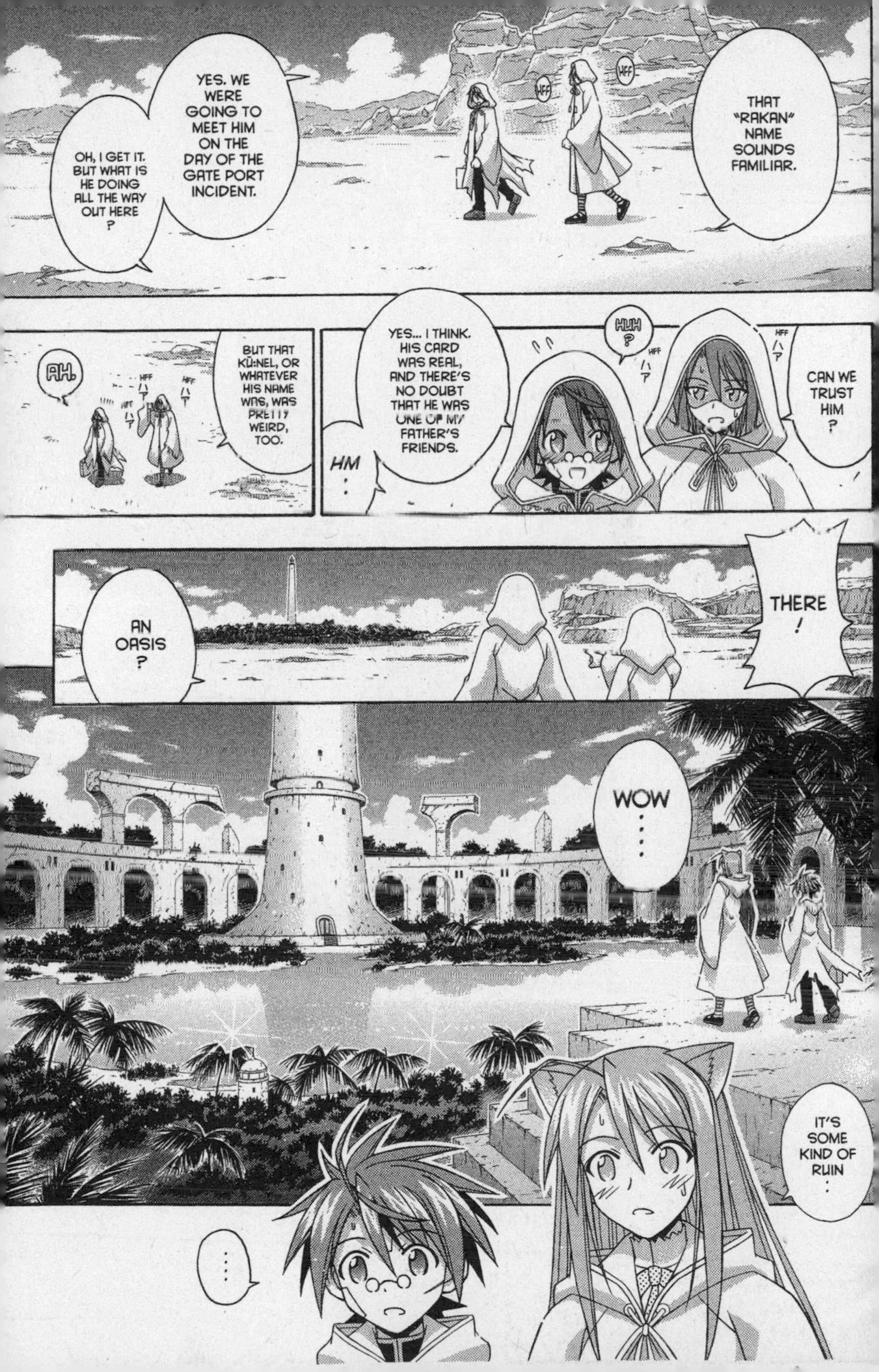
THAT "RAKAN" NAME SOUNDS FAMILIAR.
HFF
HFF
YES. WE WERE GOING TO MEET HIM ON THE DAY OF THE GATE PORT INCIDENT.
OH, I GET IT. BUT WHAT IS HE DOING ALL THE WAY OUT HERE ?
CAN WE TRUST HIM ?
HFF
HUH ?
HFF
YES... I THINK. HIS CARD WAS REAL, AND THERE'S NO DOUBT THAT HE WAS ONE OF MY FATHER'S FRIENDS.
HM :
BUT THAT KÜ:NEL, OR WHATEVER HIS NAME WAS, WAS PRETTY WEIRD, TOO.
HFF
HFF
HFF
AH.
THERE !
AN OASIS ?
WOW ....
IT'S SOME KIND OF RUIN :
....

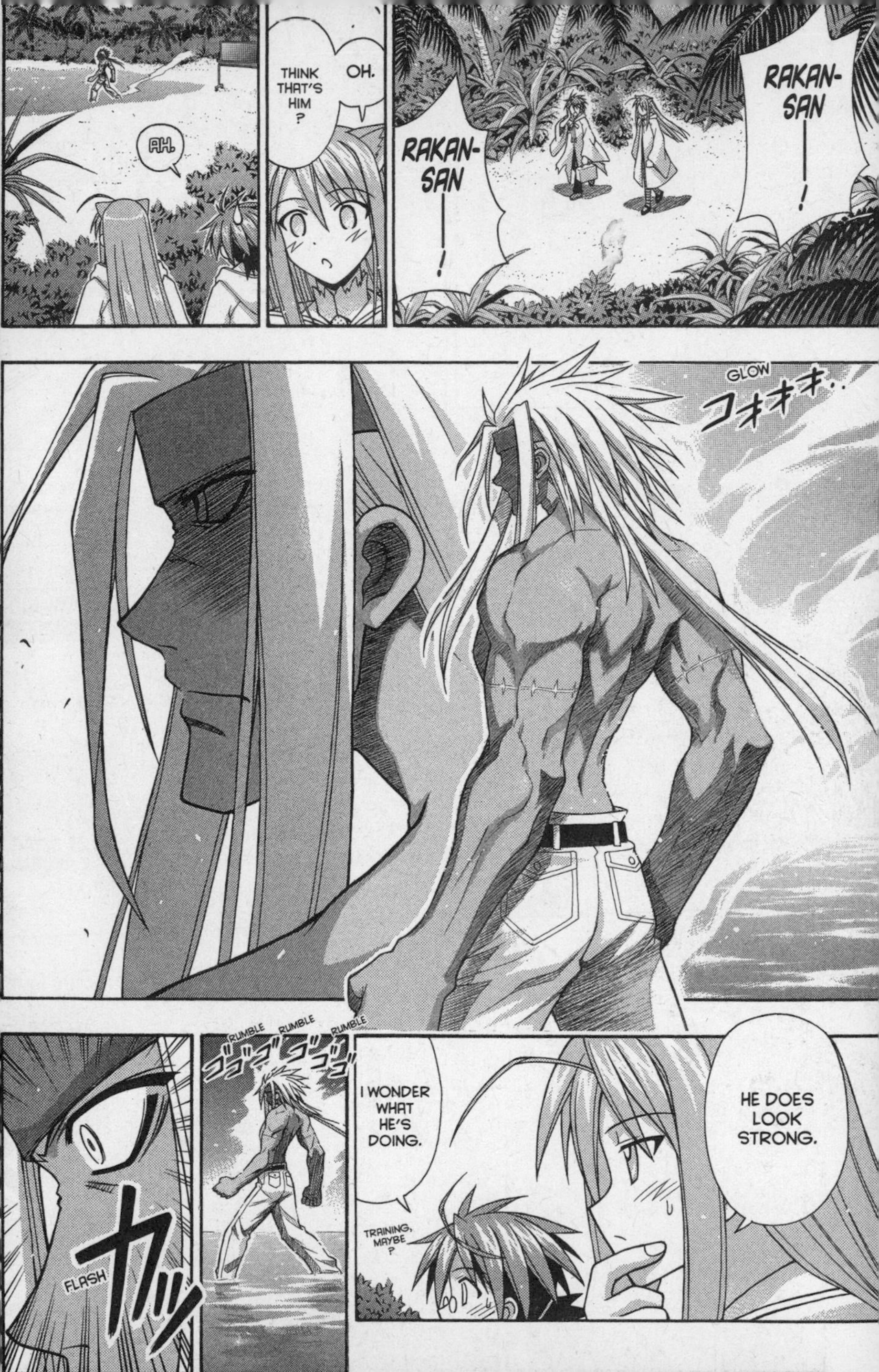
RAKAN-SAN—!
RAKAN-SAN—!
OH.
THINK THAT'S HIM?
AH.
GLOW
コオオオ…
HE DOES LOOK STRONG.
I WONDER WHAT HE'S DOING.
TRAINING, MAYBE?
RUMBLE RUMBLE RUMBLE
ゴゴゴゴゴゴ
FLASH
カッ

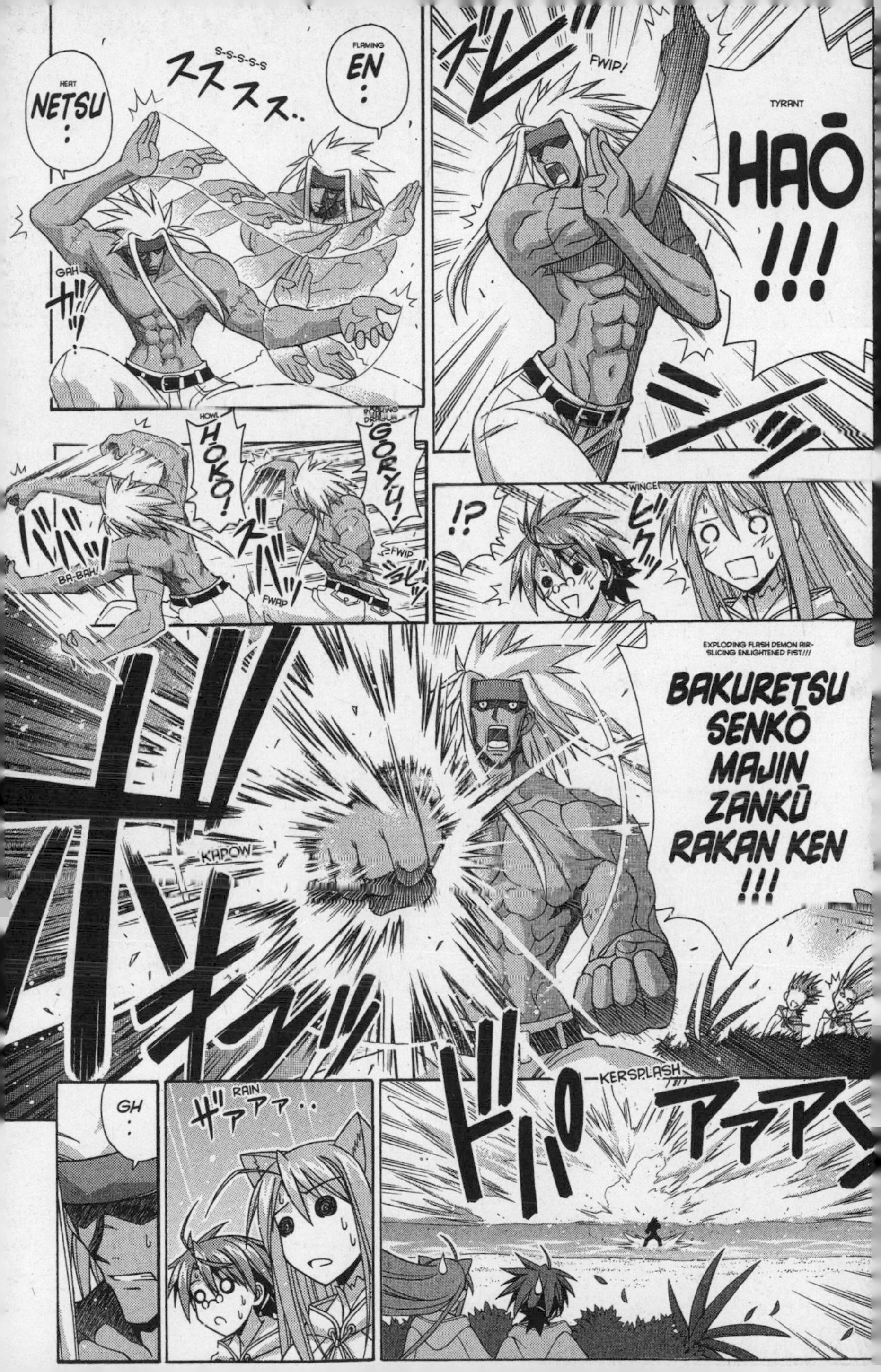
FWIP!
TYRANT
HAŌ!!!
FLAMING
EN...
S-S-S-S-S
HEAT
NETSU...
GAH
WINCE
!?
ROARING DRAGON
GORYU!
FWIP
HOWL
HŌKŌ!
FWAP
BA-BAH!
EXPLODING FLASH DEMON AIR-SLICING ENLIGHTENED FIST!!!
BAKURETSU SENKŌ MAJIN ZANKŪ RAKAN KEN!!!
KAPOW
KERSPLASH
RAIN
GH...

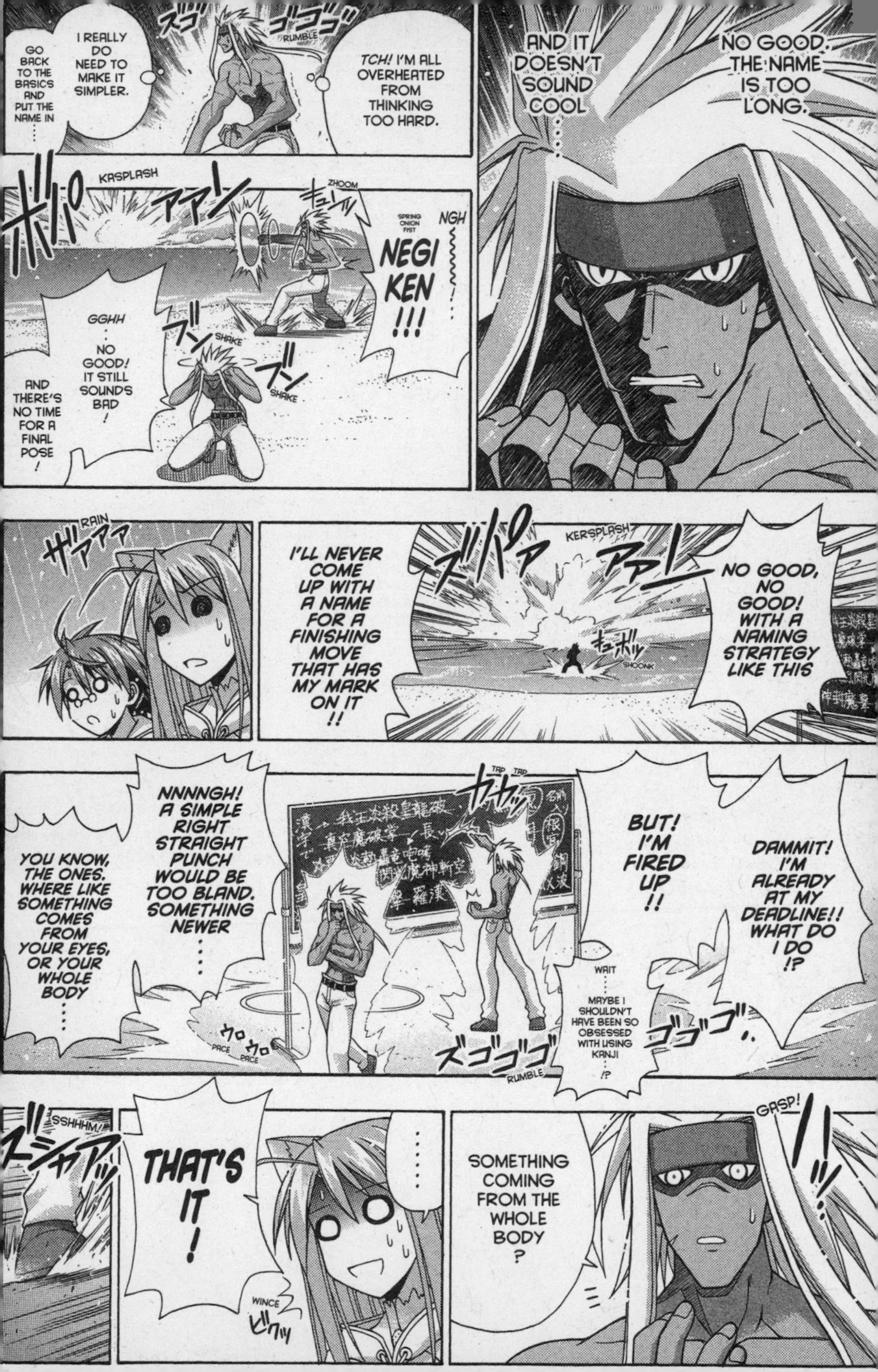

NO GOOD. THE NAME IS TOO LONG.
AND IT DOESN'T SOUND COOL ......
TCH! I'M ALL OVERHEATED FROM THINKING TOO HARD.
RUMBLE
I REALLY DO NEED TO MAKE IT SIMPLER.
GO BACK TO THE BASICS AND PUT THE NAME IN ...
NGH ...!
SPRING ONION FIST
NEGI KEN!!!
ZHOOM
KASPLASH
SHAKE
SHAKE
GGHH ... NO GOOD! IT STILL SOUNDS BAD!
AND THERE'S NO TIME FOR A FINAL POSE!
NO GOOD, NO GOOD! WITH A NAMING STRATEGY LIKE THIS
KERSPLASH
SHOONK
I'LL NEVER COME UP WITH A NAME FOR A FINISHING MOVE THAT HAS MY MARK ON IT!!
RAIN
DAMMIT! I'M ALREADY AT MY DEADLINE!! WHAT DO I DO!?
BUT! I'M FIRED UP!!
WAIT ... MAYBE I SHOULDN'T HAVE BEEN SO OBSESSED WITH USING KANJI ...!?
RUMBLE
TAP TAP
NNNNGH! A SIMPLE RIGHT STRAIGHT PUNCH WOULD BE TOO BLAND. SOMETHING NEWER ....
YOU KNOW, THE ONES. WHERE LIKE SOMETHING COMES FROM YOUR EYES, OR YOUR WHOLE BODY ....
PACE PACE
GASP!
SOMETHING COMING FROM THE WHOLE BODY?
......
THAT'S IT!
WINCE
SSHHHM!

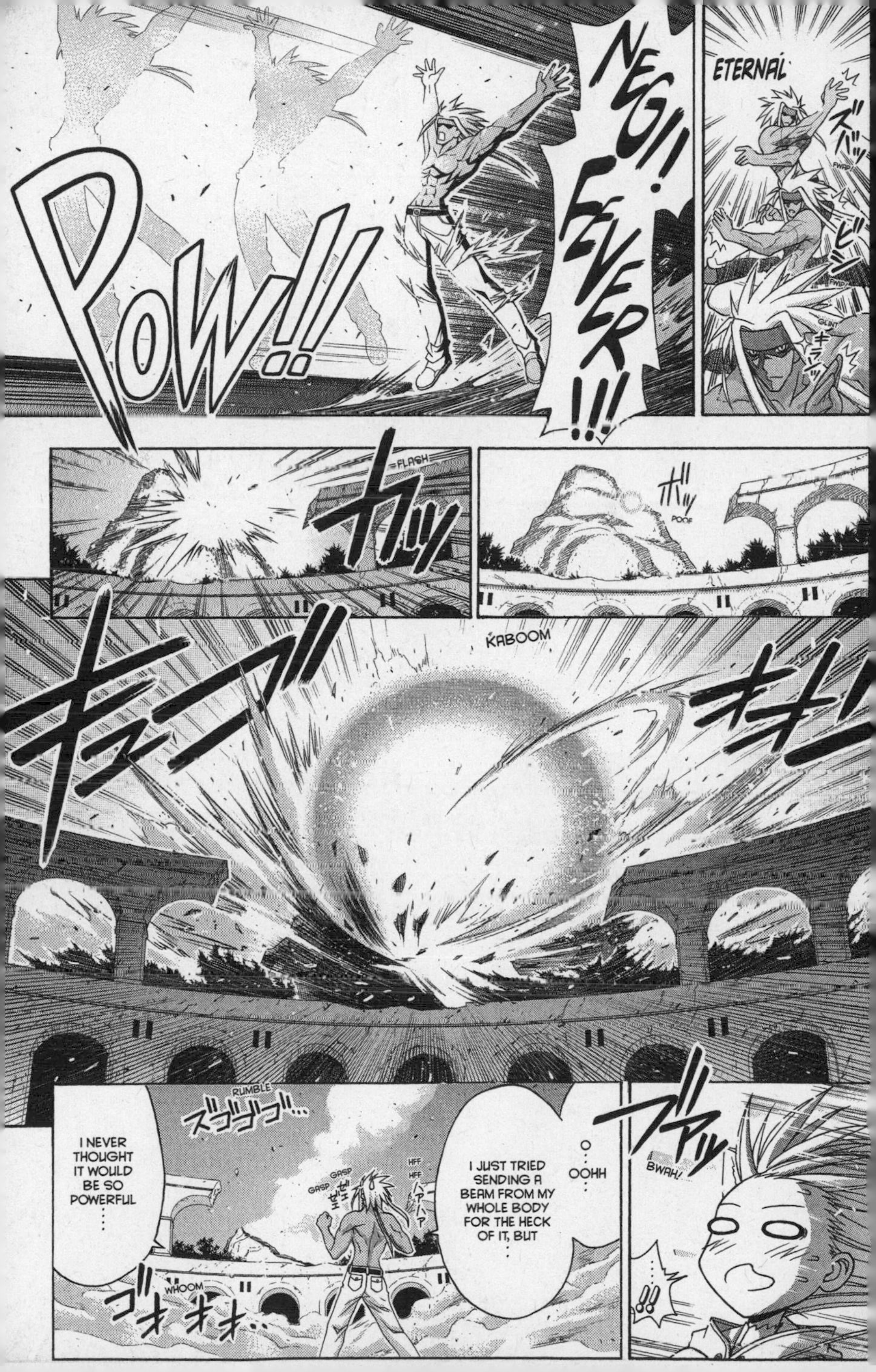

ETERNAL
ズバッ
FWIP
ビシ
FWIP
GLINT
キラッ
NEGI!! FEVER!!!
POW!!
ボッ
POOF
FLASH
カッ
KABOOM
キュゴオォ
ブアッ
BWAH!
......!!
O......OOHH
I JUST TRIED SENDING A BEAM FROM MY WHOLE BODY FOR THE HECK OF IT, BUT......
I NEVER THOUGHT IT WOULD BE SO POWERFUL......
RUMBLE
ズゴゴゴ...
HFF HFF
ハァハァ
GASP GASP
ゼェゼェ
WHOOM
ゴォォォ...

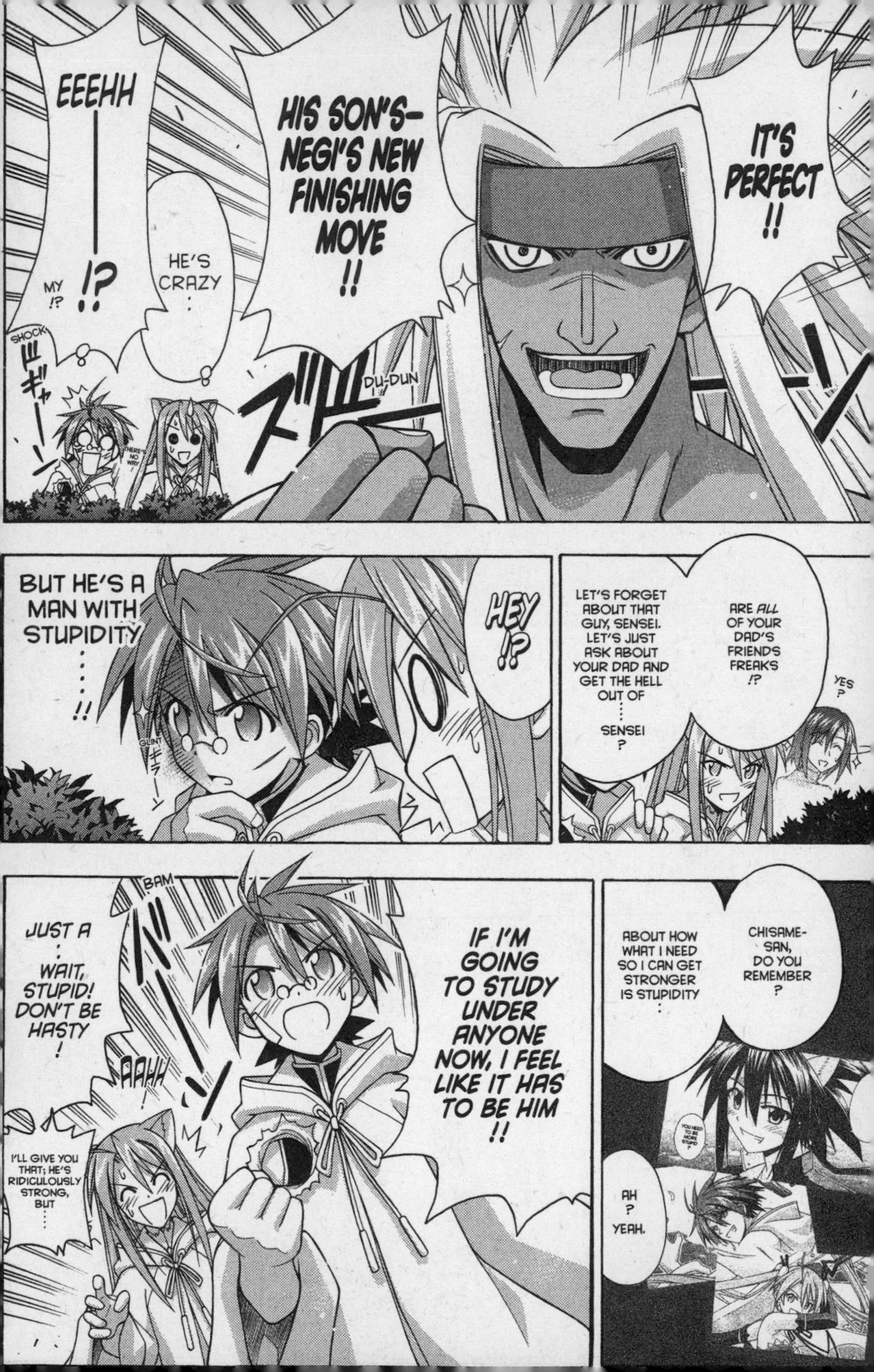

IT'S PERFECT !!
HIS SON'S— NEGI'S NEW FINISHING MOVE !!
DU-DUN
EEEHH——!?
HE'S CRAZY :
MY !?
SHOCK
THERE'S NO WAY
ARE ALL OF YOUR DAD'S FRIENDS FREAKS !?
LET'S FORGET ABOUT THAT GUY, SENSEI. LET'S JUST ASK ABOUT YOUR DAD AND GET THE HELL OUT OF ... SENSEI ?
YES ?
HEY !?
BUT HE'S A MAN WITH STUPIDITY ......!!
GLINT
CHISAME-SAN, DO YOU REMEMBER ?
ABOUT HOW WHAT I NEED SO I CAN GET STRONGER IS STUPIDITY :
YOU NEED TO BE MORE STUPID ?
AH ? YEAH.
IF I'M GOING TO STUDY UNDER ANYONE NOW, I FEEL LIKE IT HAS TO BE HIM !!
BAM
JUST A : WAIT, STUPID! DON'T BE HASTY !
AAHH !
I'LL GIVE YOU THAT; HE'S RIDICULOUSLY STRONG, BUT ...

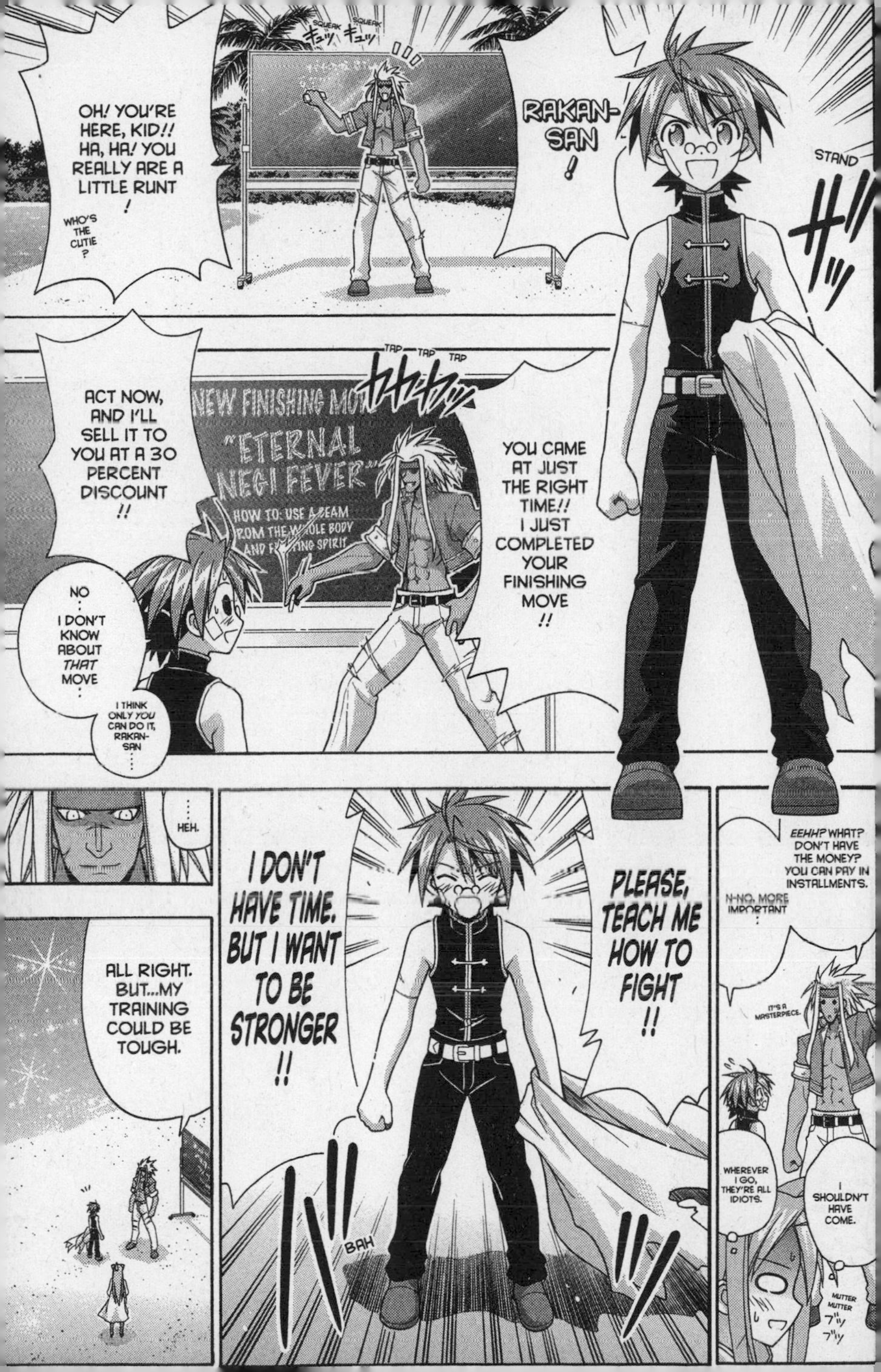
RAKAN-SAN!
STAND
SQUEAK SQUEAK
OH! YOU'RE HERE, KID!! HA, HA! YOU REALLY ARE A LITTLE RUNT!
WHO'S THE CUTIE?
YOU CAME AT JUST THE RIGHT TIME!! I JUST COMPLETED YOUR FINISHING MOVE!!
TAP TAP TAP
NEW FINISHING MO
"ETERNAL NEGI FEVER"
ACT NOW, AND I'LL SELL IT TO YOU AT A 30 PERCENT DISCOUNT!!
NO... I DON'T KNOW ABOUT THAT MOVE...
I THINK ONLY YOU CAN DO IT, RAKAN-SAN...
EEHH? WHAT? DON'T HAVE THE MONEY? YOU CAN PAY IN INSTALLMENTS.
N-NO, MORE IMPORTANT...
IT'S A MASTERPIECE.
I SHOULDN'T HAVE COME.
WHEREVER I GO, THEY'RE ALL IDIOTS.
MUTTER MUTTER
PLEASE, TEACH ME HOW TO FIGHT!!
I DON'T HAVE TIME. BUT I WANT TO BE STRONGER!!
BAH
...HEH.
ALL RIGHT. BUT...MY TRAINING COULD BE TOUGH.

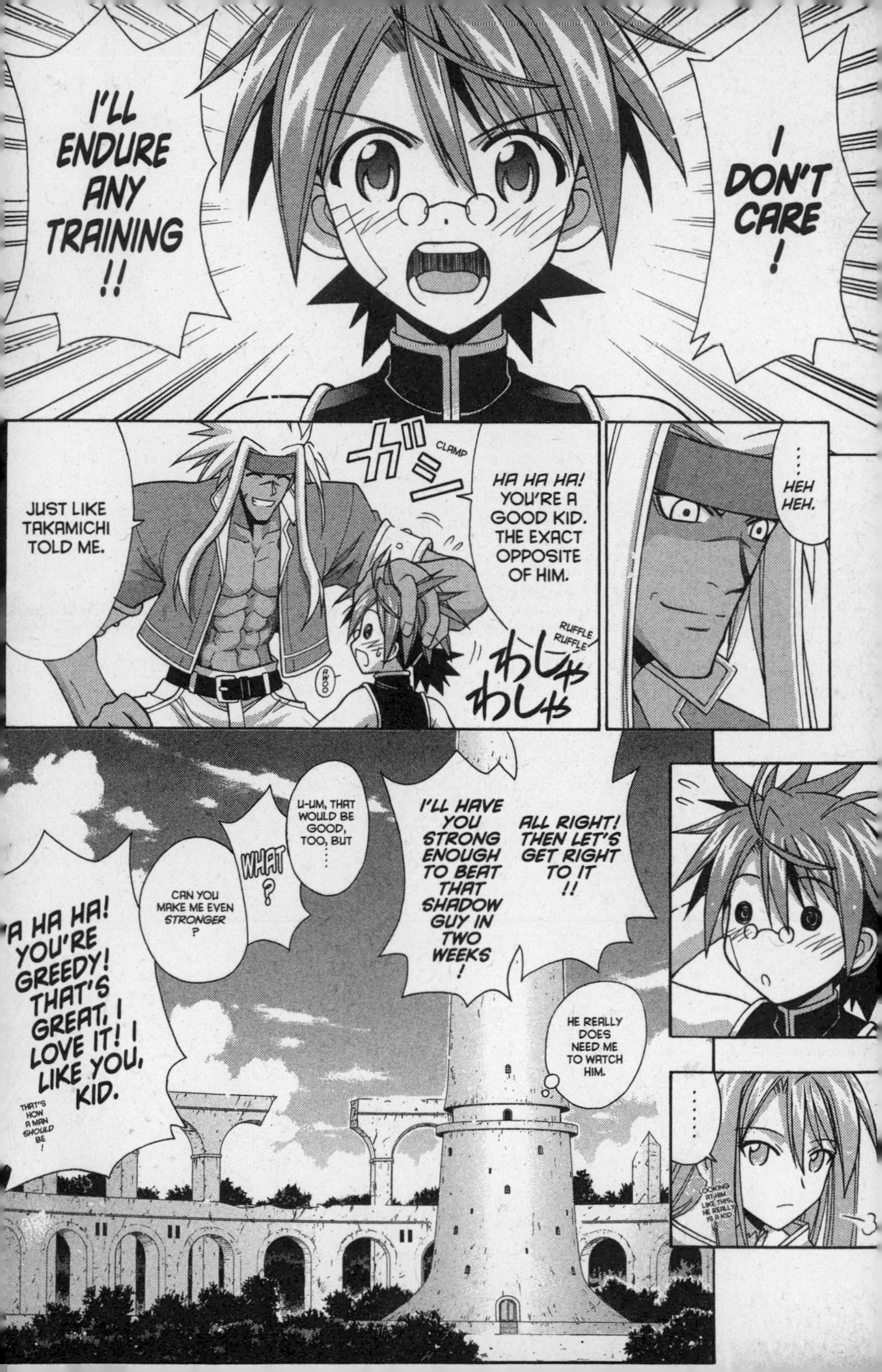
I DON'T CARE!
I'LL ENDURE ANY TRAINING!!
......HEH HEH.
HA HA HA! YOU'RE A GOOD KID. THE EXACT OPPOSITE OF HIM.
CLAMP
RUFFLE RUFFLE
JUST LIKE TAKAMICHI TOLD ME.
AWOO
ALL RIGHT! THEN LET'S GET RIGHT TO IT!!
I'LL HAVE YOU STRONG ENOUGH TO BEAT THAT SHADOW GUY IN TWO WEEKS!
WHAT?
U-UM, THAT WOULD BE GOOD, TOO, BUT......
CAN YOU MAKE ME EVEN STRONGER?
A HA HA! YOU'RE GREEDY! THAT'S GREAT, I LOVE IT! I LIKE YOU, KID.
THAT'S HOW A MAN SHOULD BE!
HE REALLY DOES NEED ME TO WATCH HIM.
......
LOOKING AT HIM LIKE THIS, HE REALLY IS A KID.

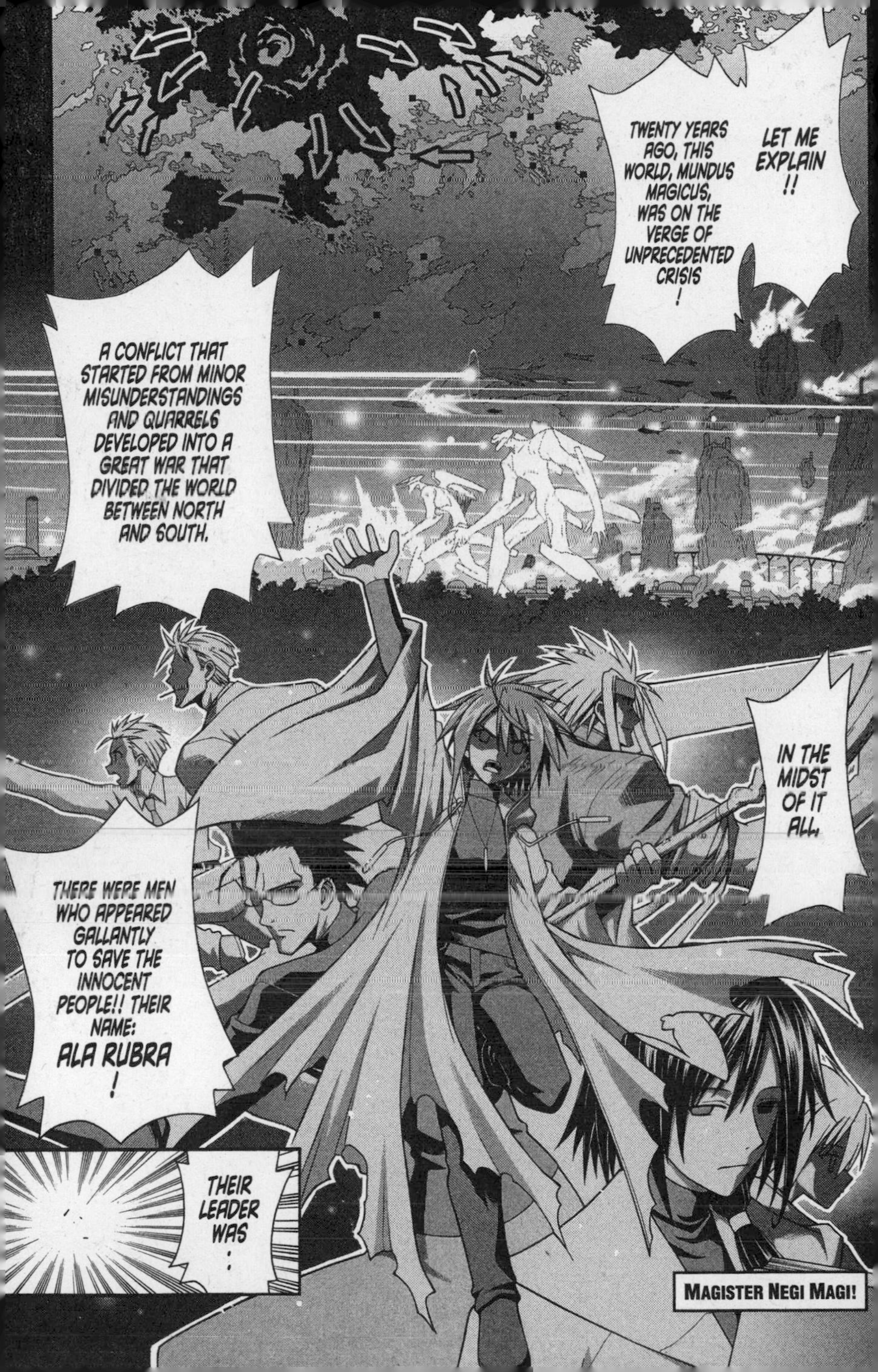
LET ME EXPLAIN!!
TWENTY YEARS AGO, THIS WORLD, MUNDUS MAGICUS, WAS ON THE VERGE OF UNPRECEDENTED CRISIS!
A CONFLICT THAT STARTED FROM MINOR MISUNDERSTANDINGS AND QUARRELS DEVELOPED INTO A GREAT WAR THAT DIVIDED THE WORLD BETWEEN NORTH AND SOUTH.
IN THE MIDST OF IT ALL,
THERE WERE MEN WHO APPEARED GALLANTLY TO SAVE THE INNOCENT PEOPLE!! THEIR NAME: ALA RUBRA!
THEIR LEADER WAS...
MAGISTER NEGI MAGI!

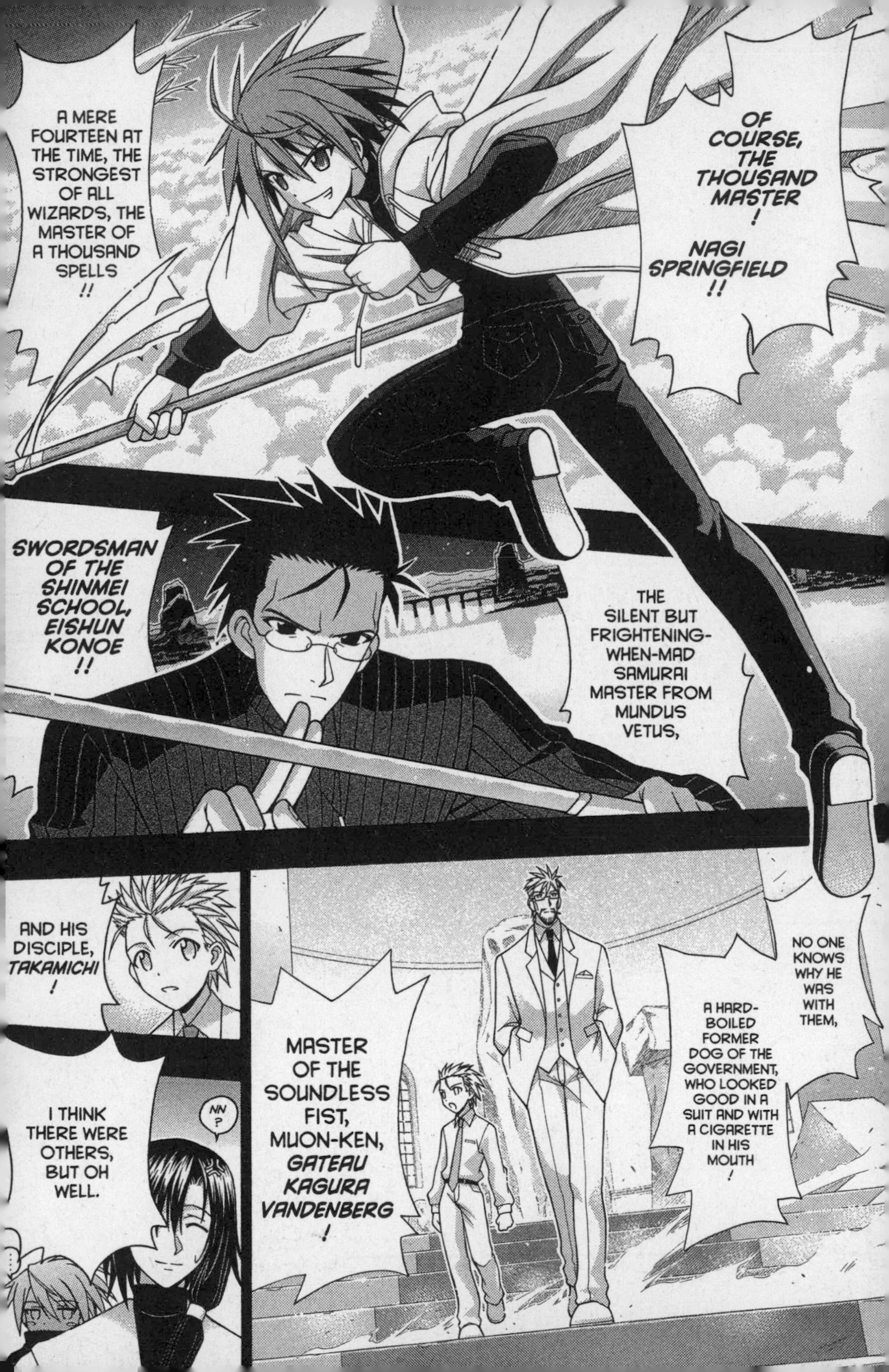
OF COURSE, THE THOUSAND MASTER! NAGI SPRINGFIELD!!
A MERE FOURTEEN AT THE TIME, THE STRONGEST OF ALL WIZARDS, THE MASTER OF A THOUSAND SPELLS!!
THE SILENT BUT FRIGHTENING-WHEN-MAD SAMURAI MASTER FROM MUNDUS VETUS,
SWORDSMAN OF THE SHINMEI SCHOOL, EISHUN KONOE!!
NO ONE KNOWS WHY HE WAS WITH THEM,
A HARD-BOILED FORMER DOG OF THE GOVERNMENT, WHO LOOKED GOOD IN A SUIT AND WITH A CIGARETTE IN HIS MOUTH!
MASTER OF THE SOUNDLESS FIST, MUON-KEN, GATEAU KAGURA VANDENBERG!
AND HIS DISCIPLE, TAKAMICHI!
NN?
I THINK THERE WERE OTHERS, BUT OH WELL.

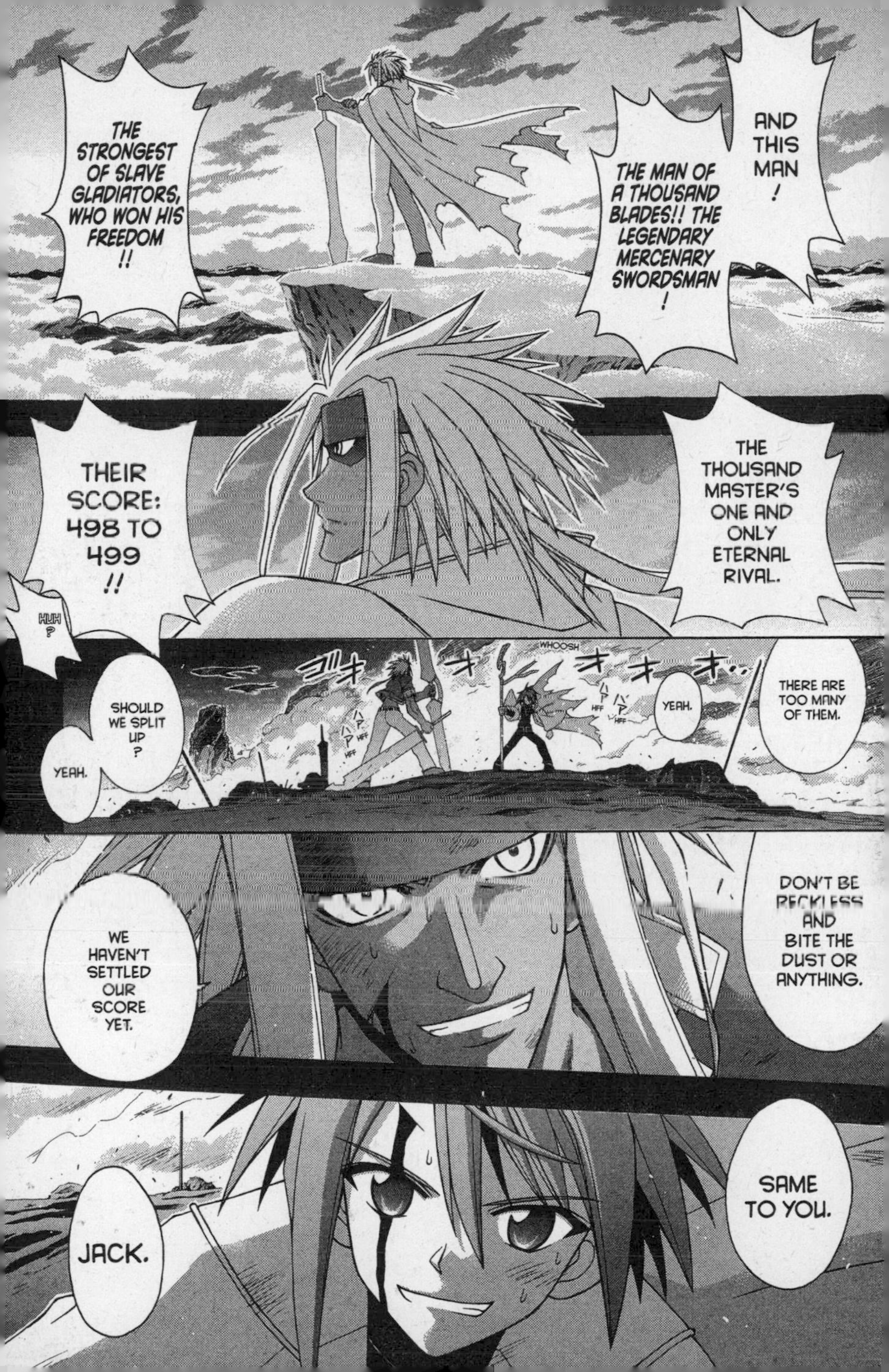
AND THIS MAN!
THE MAN OF A THOUSAND BLADES!! THE LEGENDARY MERCENARY SWORDSMAN!
THE STRONGEST OF SLAVE GLADIATORS, WHO WON HIS FREEDOM!!
THE THOUSAND MASTER'S ONE AND ONLY ETERNAL RIVAL.
THEIR SCORE: 498 TO 499!!
HUH?
THERE ARE TOO MANY OF THEM.
YEAH.
WHOOSH
HFF HFF
HFF HFF
SHOULD WE SPLIT UP?
YEAH.
DON'T BE RECKLESS AND BITE THE DUST OR ANYTHING.
WE HAVEN'T SETTLED OUR SCORE YET.
SAME TO YOU.
JACK.

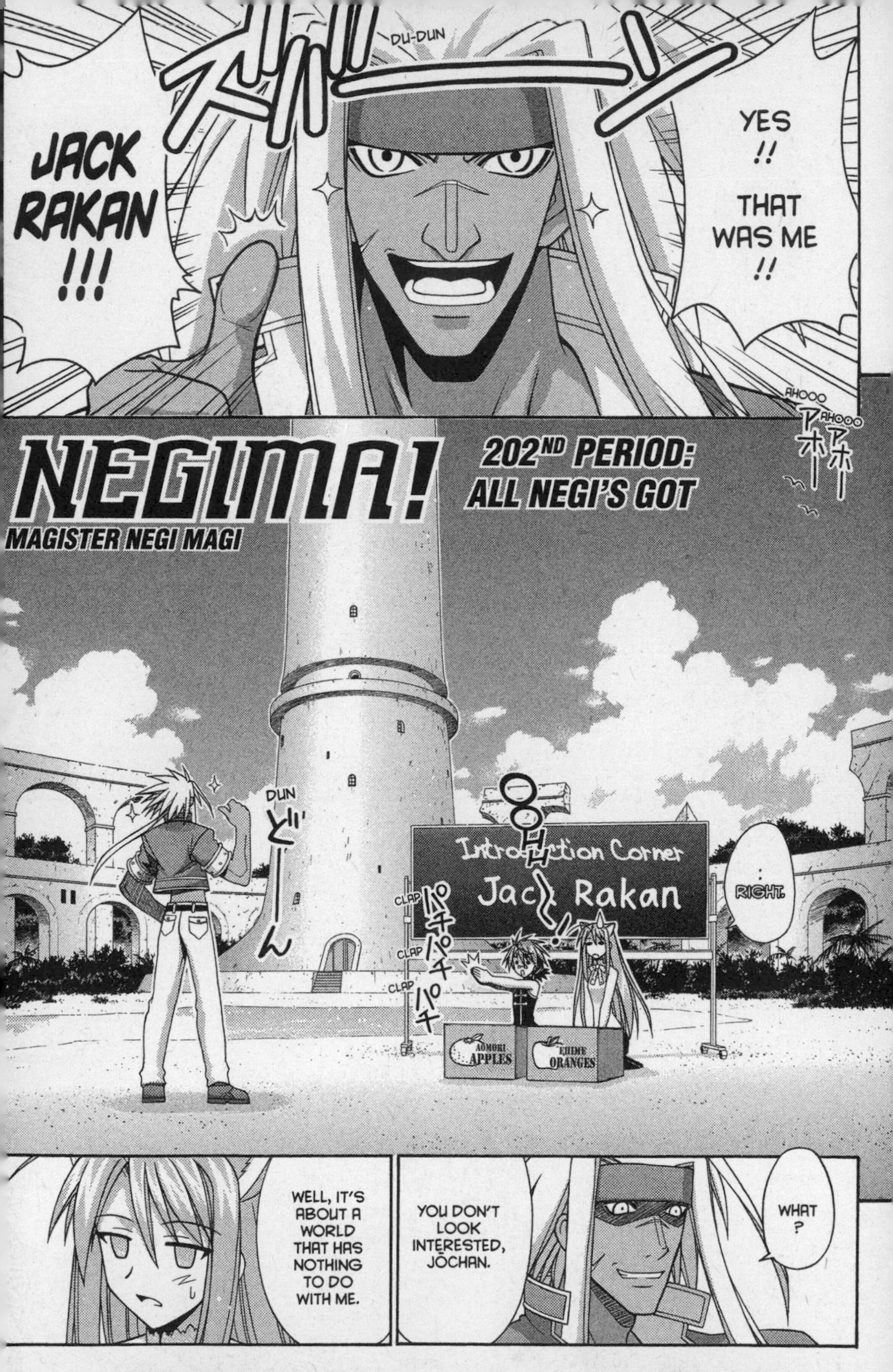

DU-DUN
YES!! THAT WAS ME!!
JACK RAKAN!!!
AHOOO
AHOOO
202ND PERIOD: ALL NEGI'S GOT
NEGIMA!
MAGISTER NEGI MAGI
: RIGHT.
Introduction Corner
Jack Rakan
CLAP
CLAP
CLAP
DUN
APPLES
ORANGES
WHAT?
YOU DON'T LOOK INTERESTED, JŌCHAN.
WELL, IT'S ABOUT A WORLD THAT HAS NOTHING TO DO WITH ME.

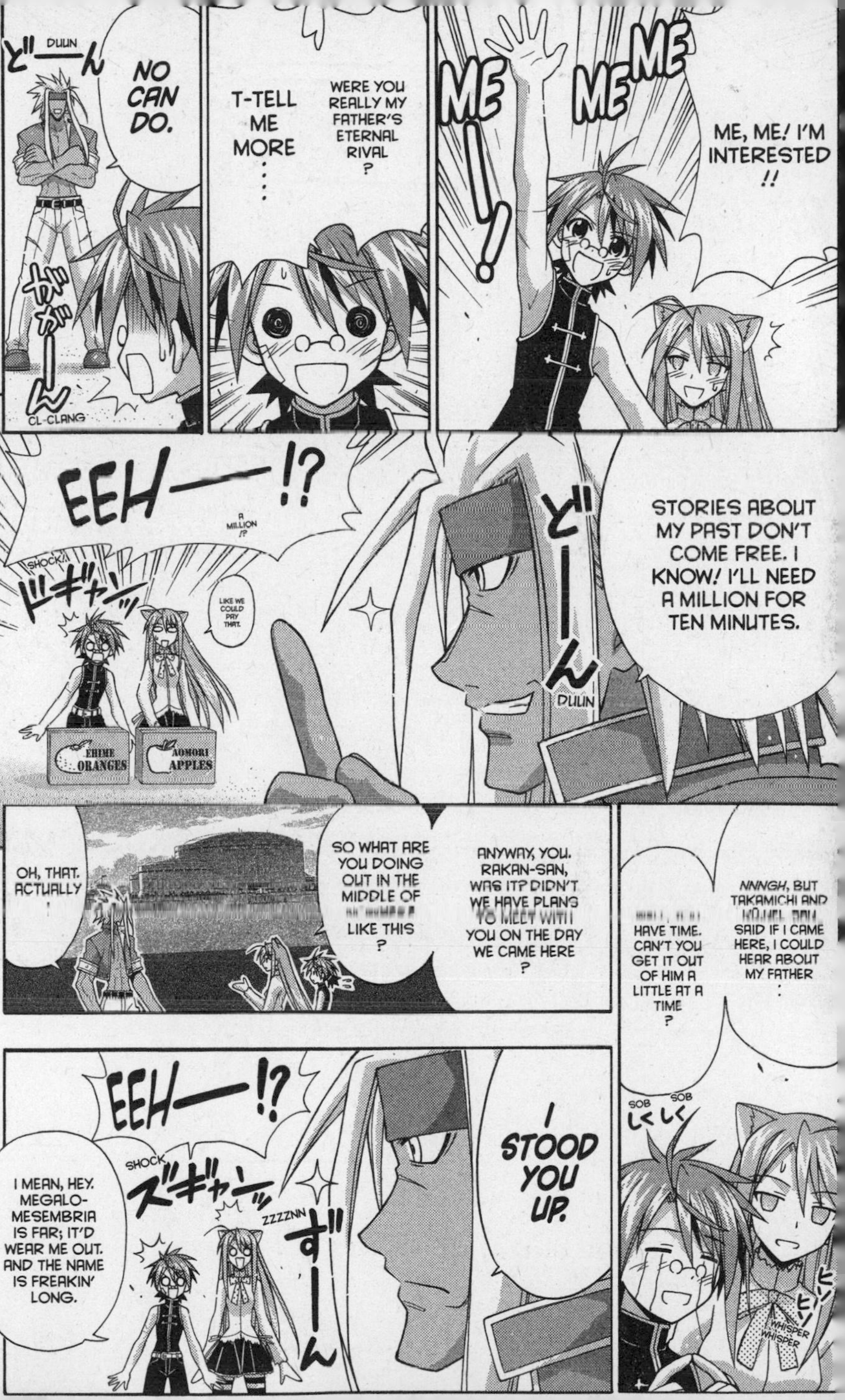
ME ME ME
ME, ME! I'M INTERESTED !!
WERE YOU REALLY MY FATHER'S ETERNAL RIVAL ?
T-TELL ME MORE ...
DUUN
NO CAN DO.
CL-CLANG
STORIES ABOUT MY PAST DON'T COME FREE. I KNOW! I'LL NEED A MILLION FOR TEN MINUTES.
DULIN
EEH——!?
A MILLION !?
LIKE WE COULD PAY THAT.
SHOCK!!
EHIME ORANGES
AOMORI APPLES
NNNGH, BUT TAKAMICHI AND SAID IF I CAME HERE, I COULD HEAR ABOUT MY FATHER ...
HAVE TIME. CAN'T YOU GET IT OUT OF HIM A LITTLE AT A TIME ?
SOB SOB
WHISPER WHISPER
ANYWAY, YOU. RAKAN-SAN, WAS IT? DIDN'T WE HAVE PLANS TO MEET WITH YOU ON THE DAY WE CAME HERE ?
SO WHAT ARE YOU DOING OUT IN THE MIDDLE OF LIKE THIS ?
OH, THAT. ACTUALLY ...
I STOOD YOU UP.
EEH—!?
SHOCK
ZZZZNN
I MEAN, HEY. MEGALO-MESEMBRIA IS FAR; IT'D WEAR ME OUT. AND THE NAME IS FREAKIN' LONG.

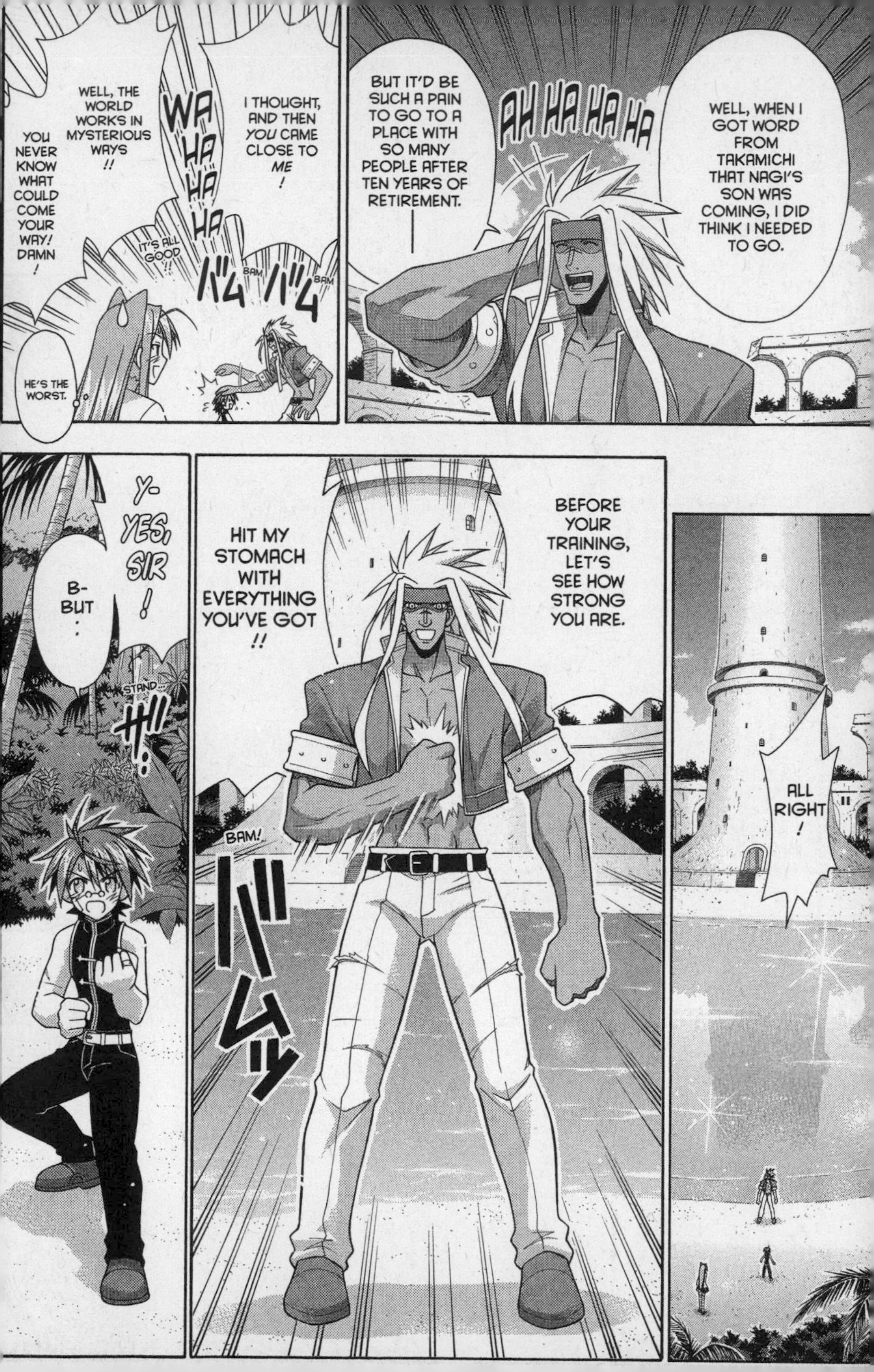

WELL, WHEN I GOT WORD FROM TAKAMICHI THAT NAGI'S SON WAS COMING, I DID THINK I NEEDED TO GO.
AH HA HA HA HA
BUT IT'D BE SUCH A PAIN TO GO TO A PLACE WITH SO MANY PEOPLE AFTER TEN YEARS OF RETIREMENT.
I THOUGHT, AND THEN *YOU* CAME CLOSE TO *ME*!
WA HA HA HA
WELL, THE WORLD WORKS IN MYSTERIOUS WAYS!!
YOU NEVER KNOW WHAT COULD COME YOUR WAY! DAMN!
IT'S ALL GOOD!!
BAM
BAM
HE'S THE WORST.
ALL RIGHT!
BEFORE YOUR TRAINING, LET'S SEE HOW STRONG YOU ARE.
HIT MY STOMACH WITH EVERYTHING YOU'VE GOT!!
BAM!
Y-YES, SIR!
B-BUT...
STAND...

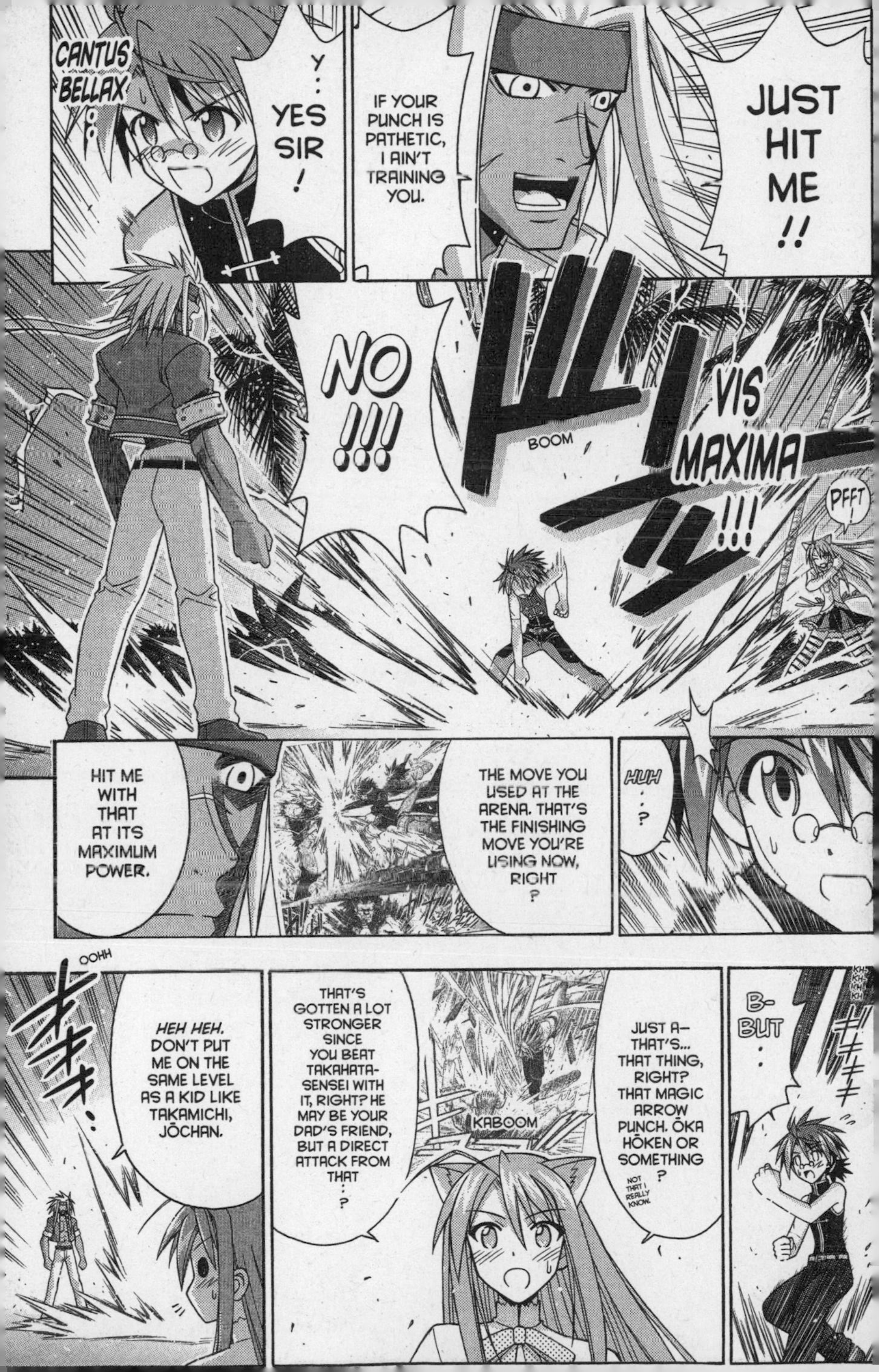
JUST HIT ME!!
IF YOUR PUNCH IS PATHETIC, I AIN'T TRAINING YOU.
Y... YES SIR!
CANTUS BELLAX...
PFFT!
VIS MAXIMA!!!
BOOM
NO!!!
HUH...?
THE MOVE YOU USED AT THE ARENA. THAT'S THE FINISHING MOVE YOU'RE USING NOW, RIGHT?
HIT ME WITH THAT AT ITS MAXIMUM POWER.
B-BUT...
JUST A— THAT'S... THAT THING, RIGHT? THAT MAGIC ARROW PUNCH. ŌKA HŌKEN OR SOMETHING?
NOT THAT I REALLY KNOW.
KABOOM
THAT'S GOTTEN A LOT STRONGER SINCE YOU BEAT TAKAHATA-SENSEI WITH IT, RIGHT? HE MAY BE YOUR DAD'S FRIEND, BUT A DIRECT ATTACK FROM THAT...?
OOHH
HEH HEH. DON'T PUT ME ON THE SAME LEVEL AS A KID LIKE TAKAMICHI, JŌCHAN.

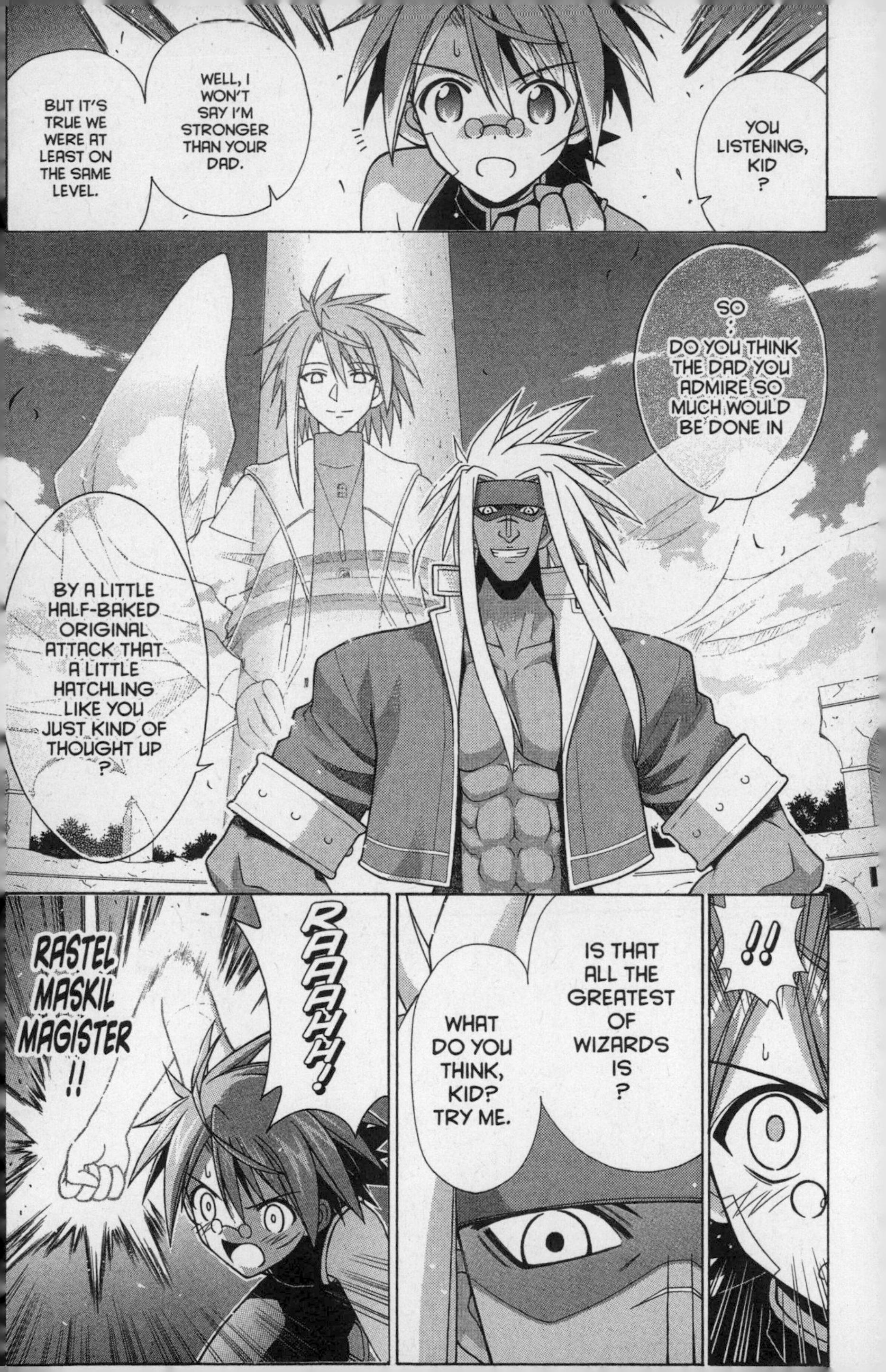
YOU LISTENING, KID?
WELL, I WON'T SAY I'M STRONGER THAN YOUR DAD.
BUT IT'S TRUE WE WERE AT LEAST ON THE SAME LEVEL.
SO... DO YOU THINK THE DAD YOU ADMIRE SO MUCH WOULD BE DONE IN
BY A LITTLE HALF-BAKED ORIGINAL ATTACK THAT A LITTLE HATCHLING LIKE YOU JUST KIND OF THOUGHT UP?
!!
IS THAT ALL THE GREATEST OF WIZARDS IS?
WHAT DO YOU THINK, KID? TRY ME.
RAAAHH!
RASTEL MASKIL MAGISTER!!

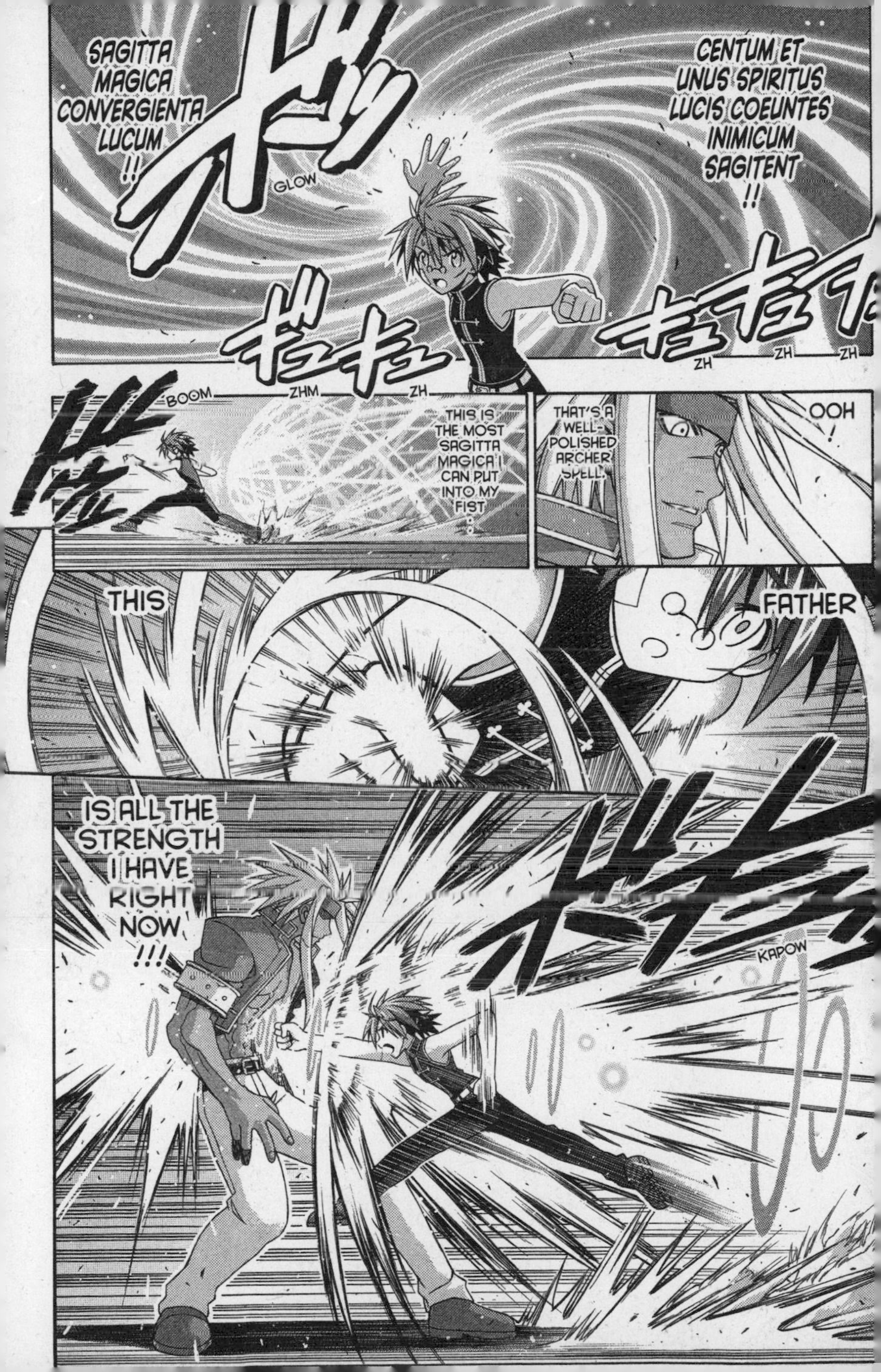
CENTUM ET UNUS SPIRITUS LUCIS COEUNTES INIMICUM SAGITENT !!
SAGITTA MAGICA CONVERGIENTA LUCUM !!
GLOW
ZH
ZH
ZH
ZHM
ZH
OOH !
THAT'S A WELL-POLISHED ARCHER SPELL.
BOOM
THIS IS THE MOST SAGITTA MAGICA I CAN PUT INTO MY FIST...
FATHER
THIS
IS ALL THE STRENGTH I HAVE RIGHT NOW !!!
KAPOW

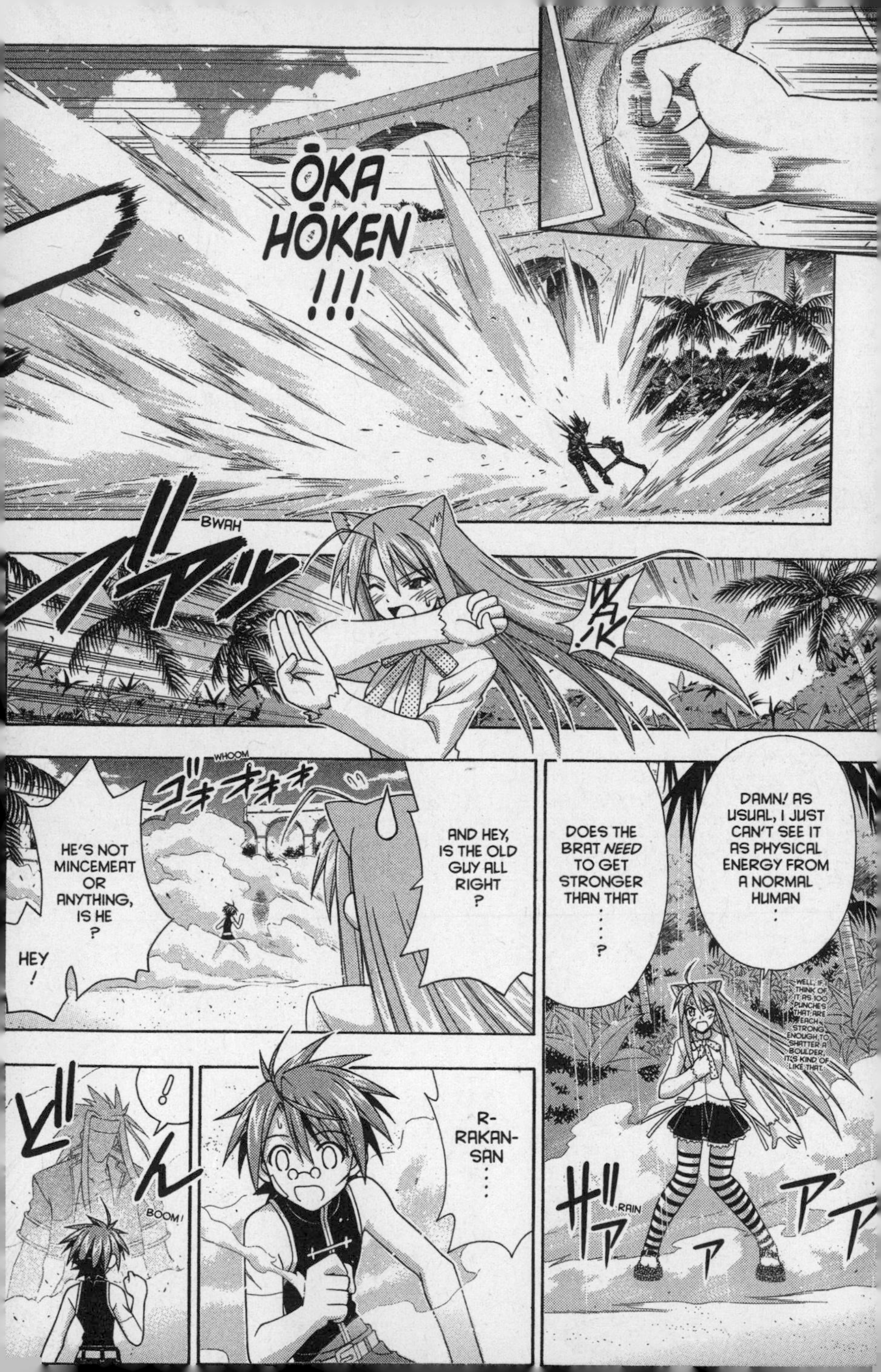
ŌKA HŌKEN !!!
BWAH
WAK!
DAMN! AS USUAL, I JUST CAN'T SEE IT AS PHYSICAL ENERGY FROM A NORMAL HUMAN...
DOES THE BRAT NEED TO GET STRONGER THAN THAT.....?
WELL, IF I THINK OF IT AS 100 PUNCHES THAT ARE EACH STRONG ENOUGH TO SHATTER A BOULDER, IT'S KIND OF LIKE THAT.
RAIN
WHOOM
AND HEY, IS THE OLD GUY ALL RIGHT?
HE'S NOT MINCEMEAT OR ANYTHING, IS HE?
HEY!
R-RAKAN-SAN....
!
BOOM!

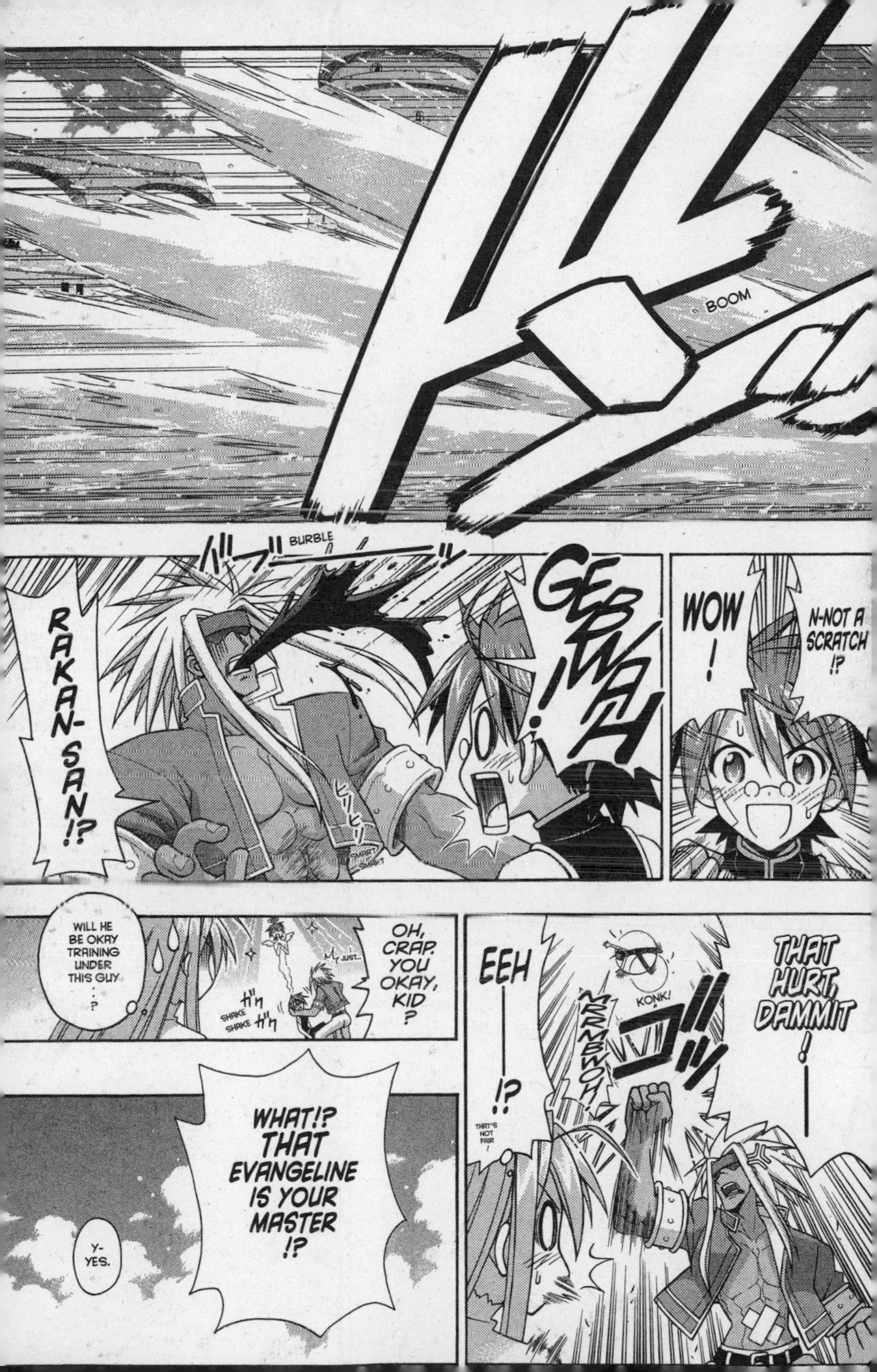
BOOM
WOW!
N-NOT A SCRATCH!?
BURBLE
GEBWAH!
RAKAN-SAN!?
SMART SMART
THAT HURT, DAMMIT!
KONK!
EEH!?
MRRMBWOH!
THAT'S NOT FAIR!
OH, CRAP. YOU OKAY, KID?
JUST...
SHAKE SHAKE
WILL HE BE OKAY TRAINING UNDER THIS GUY...?
WHAT!? THAT EVANGELINE IS YOUR MASTER!?
Y-YES.

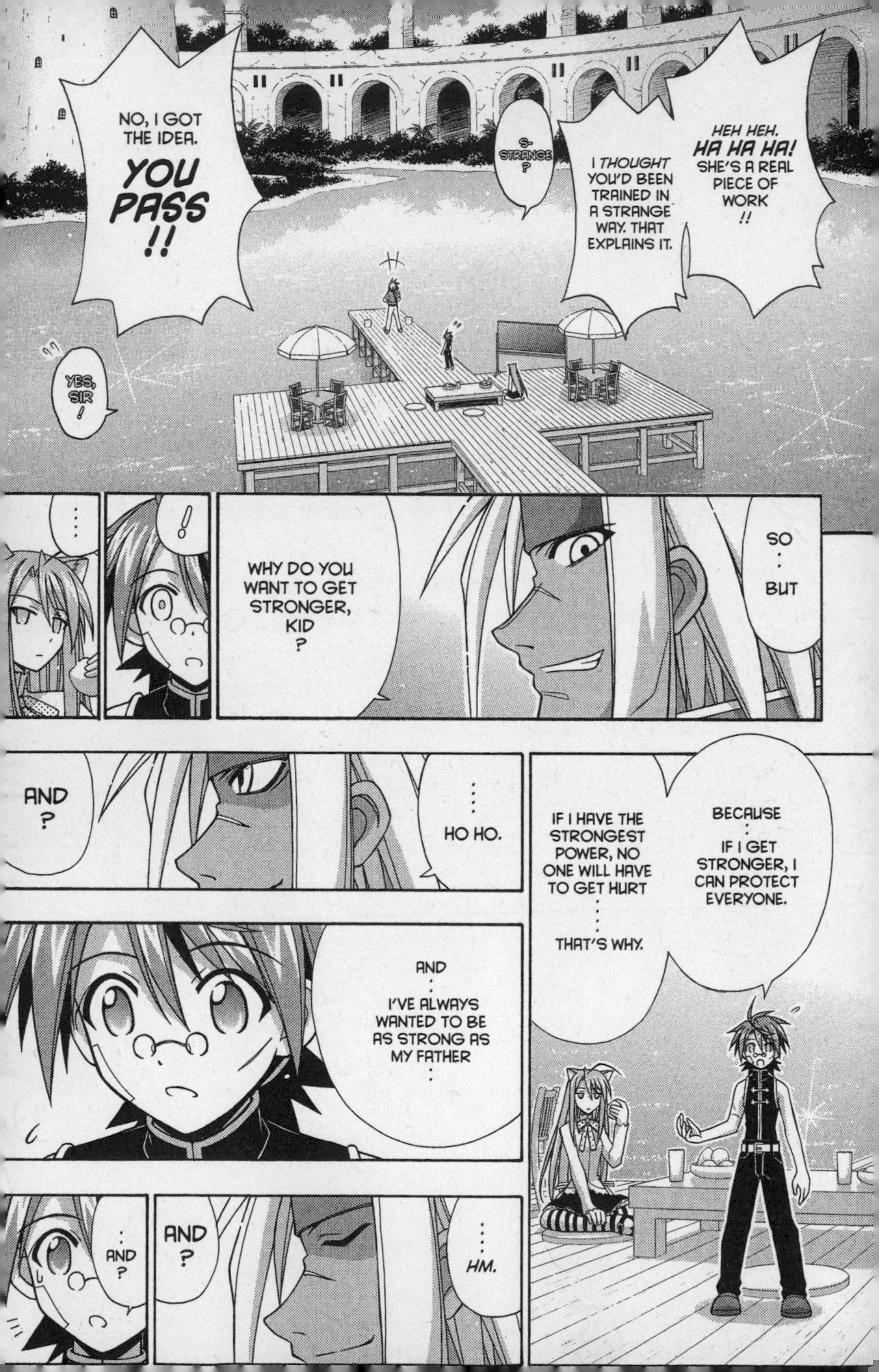
HEH HEH. HA HA HA! SHE'S A REAL PIECE OF WORK!!
I THOUGHT YOU'D BEEN TRAINED IN A STRANGE WAY. THAT EXPLAINS IT.
S-STRANGE?
NO, I GOT THE IDEA. YOU PASS!!
YES, SIR!
SO... BUT
WHY DO YOU WANT TO GET STRONGER, KID?
!
...
BECAUSE... IF I GET STRONGER, I CAN PROTECT EVERYONE.
IF I HAVE THE STRONGEST POWER, NO ONE WILL HAVE TO GET HURT... THAT'S WHY.
... HO HO.
AND?
AND... I'VE ALWAYS WANTED TO BE AS STRONG AS MY FATHER...
... HM.
AND?
...AND?

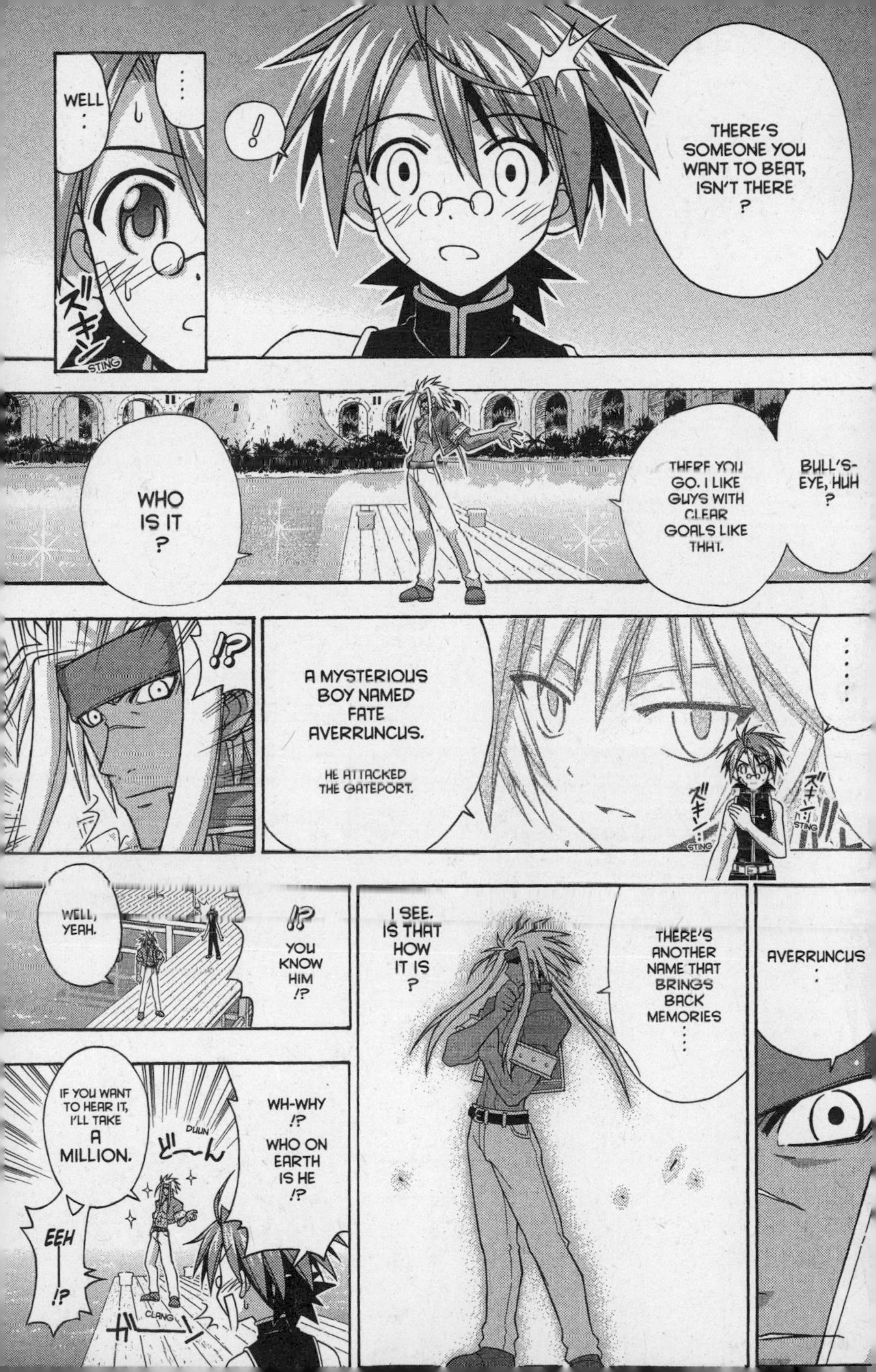
THERE'S SOMEONE YOU WANT TO BEAT, ISN'T THERE?
!
....
WELL...
ズキン
STING
BULL'S-EYE, HUH?
THERE YOU GO. I LIKE GUYS WITH CLEAR GOALS LIKE THAT.
WHO IS IT?
......
A MYSTERIOUS BOY NAMED FATE AVERRUNCUS.
HE ATTACKED THE GATEPORT.
STING
STING
!?
AVERRUNCUS...
THERE'S ANOTHER NAME THAT BRINGS BACK MEMORIES....
I SEE. IS THAT HOW IT IS?
!? YOU KNOW HIM!?
WELL, YEAH.
WH-WHY!? WHO ON EARTH IS HE!?
DUUN
どーん
IF YOU WANT TO HEAR IT, I'LL TAKE A MILLION.
EEH—!?
CLANG

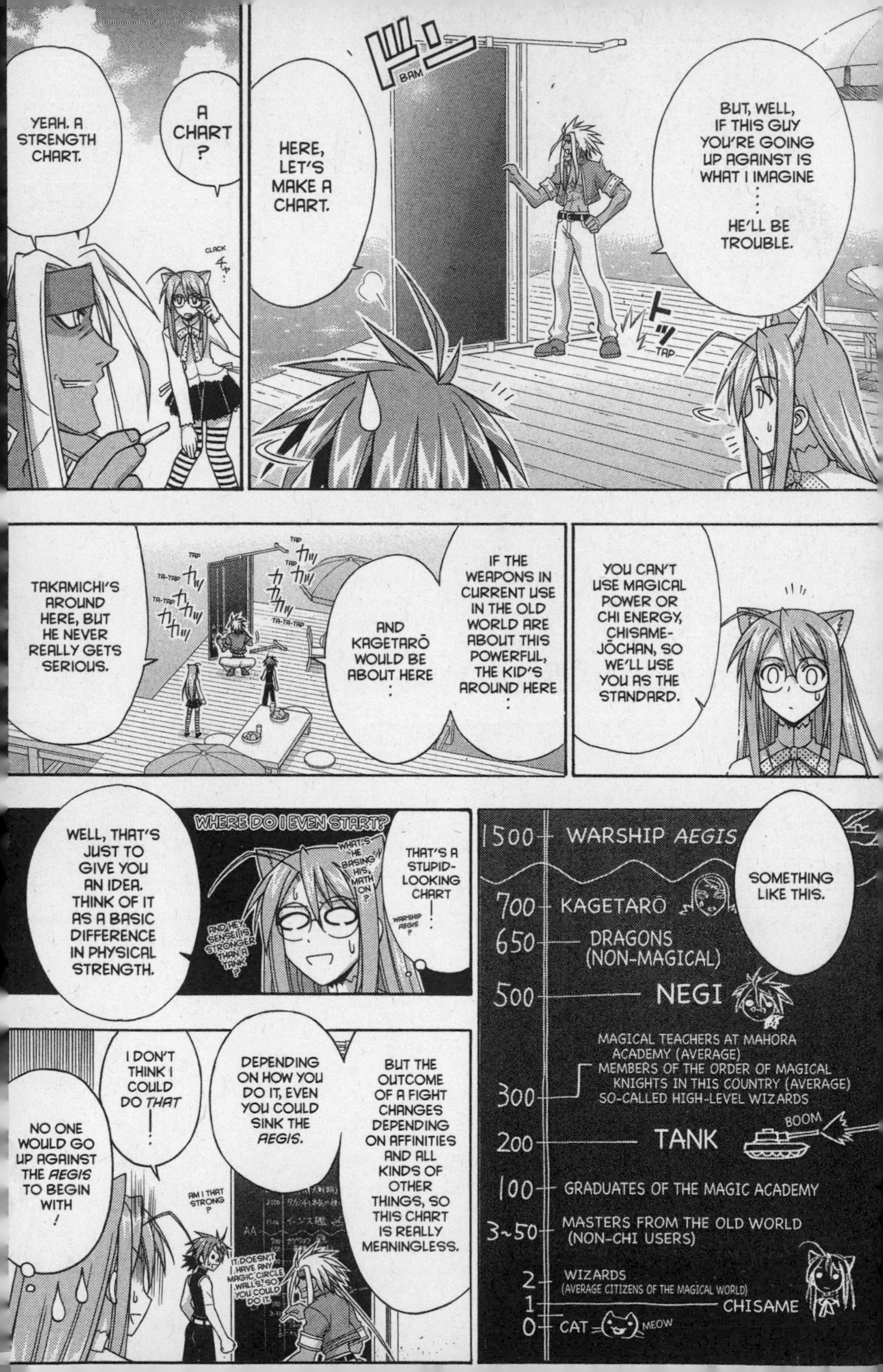
BUT, WELL, IF THIS GUY YOU'RE GOING UP AGAINST IS WHAT I IMAGINE... HE'LL BE TROUBLE.
BAM
HERE, LET'S MAKE A CHART.
TAP
A CHART?
YEAH. A STRENGTH CHART.
CLACK
YOU CAN'T USE MAGICAL POWER OR CHI ENERGY, CHISAME-JŌCHAN, SO WE'LL USE YOU AS THE STANDARD.
IF THE WEAPONS IN CURRENT USE IN THE OLD WORLD ARE ABOUT THIS POWERFUL, THE KID'S AROUND HERE...
AND KAGETARŌ WOULD BE ABOUT HERE...
TAP
TAP
TA-TAP
TA-TAP
TA-TA-TAP
TAKAMICHI'S AROUND HERE, BUT HE NEVER REALLY GETS SERIOUS.
SOMETHING LIKE THIS.
1500 WARSHIP AEGIS
700 KAGETARŌ
650 DRAGONS (NON-MAGICAL)
500 NEGI
MAGICAL TEACHERS AT MAHORA ACADEMY (AVERAGE)
MEMBERS OF THE ORDER OF MAGICAL KNIGHTS IN THIS COUNTRY (AVERAGE)
300 SO-CALLED HIGH-LEVEL WIZARDS
200 TANK
BOOM
100 GRADUATES OF THE MAGIC ACADEMY
3~50 MASTERS FROM THE OLD WORLD (NON-CHI USERS)
2 WIZARDS (AVERAGE CITIZENS OF THE MAGICAL WORLD)
1 CHISAME
0 CAT
MEOW
THAT'S A STUPID-LOOKING CHART!
WARSHIP AEGIS?
WHAT'S HE BASING HIS MATH ON?
WHERE DO I EVEN START?
AND HEY, SENSEI IS STRONGER THAN A TANK?
WELL, THAT'S JUST TO GIVE YOU AN IDEA. THINK OF IT AS A BASIC DIFFERENCE IN PHYSICAL STRENGTH.
BUT THE OUTCOME OF A FIGHT CHANGES DEPENDING ON AFFINITIES AND ALL KINDS OF OTHER THINGS, SO THIS CHART IS REALLY MEANINGLESS.
DEPENDING ON HOW YOU DO IT, EVEN YOU COULD SINK THE AEGIS.
I DON'T THINK I COULD DO THAT!
NO ONE WOULD GO UP AGAINST THE AEGIS TO BEGIN WITH!
AM I THAT STRONG?
IT DOESN'T HAVE ANY MAGIC CIRCLE WALLS, SO YOU COULD DO IT.

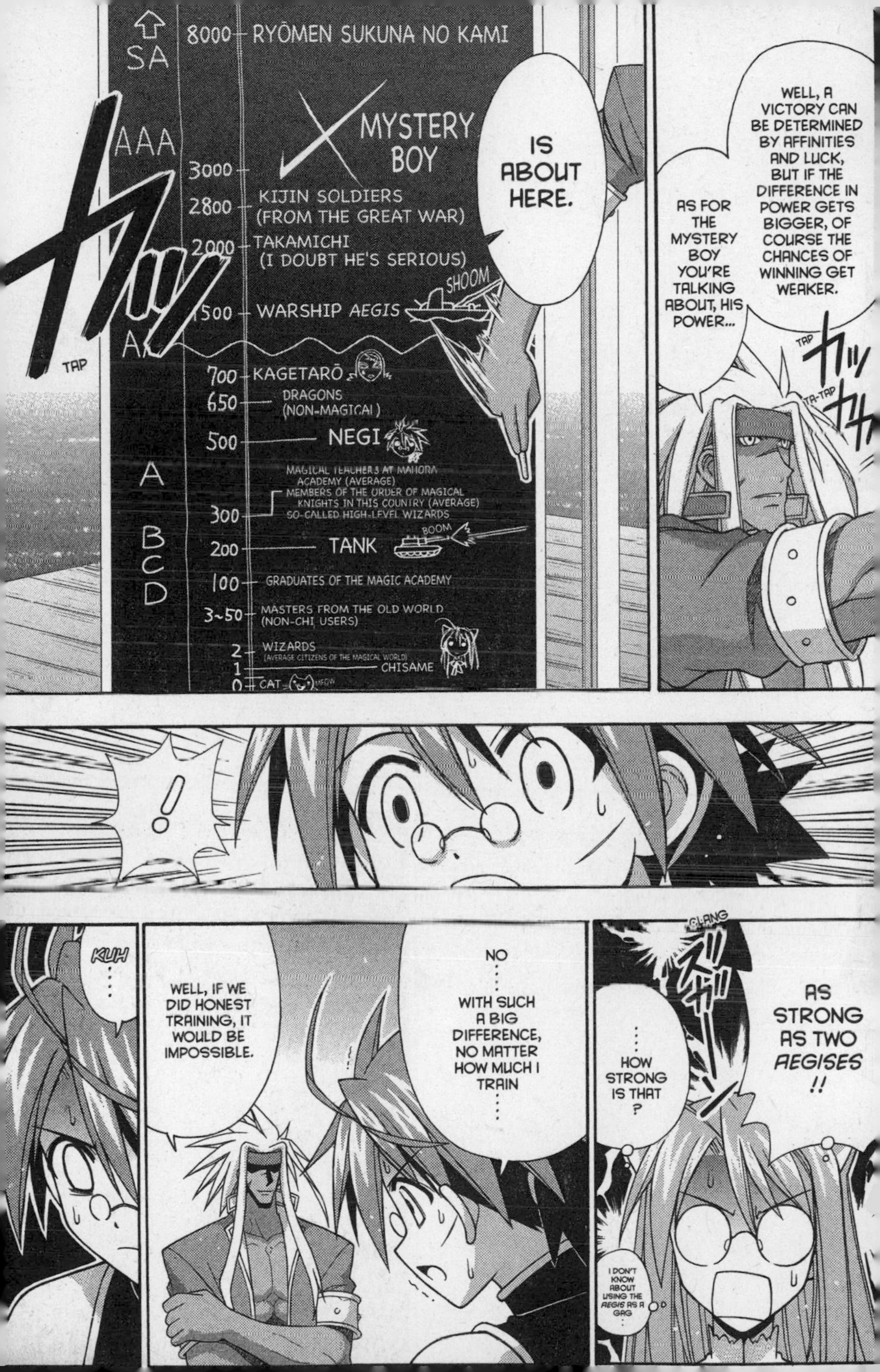
WELL, A VICTORY CAN BE DETERMINED BY AFFINITIES AND LUCK, BUT IF THE DIFFERENCE IN POWER GETS BIGGER, OF COURSE THE CHANCES OF WINNING GET WEAKER.
AS FOR THE MYSTERY BOY YOU'RE TALKING ABOUT, HIS POWER...
TAP
TA-TAP
IS ABOUT HERE.
TAP
SA
8000 RYŌMEN SUKUNA NO KAMI
AAA
MYSTERY BOY
3000
2800 KIJIN SOLDIERS (FROM THE GREAT WAR)
2000 TAKAMICHI (I DOUBT HE'S SERIOUS)
1500 WARSHIP AEGIS
SHOOM
AA
700 KAGETARŌ
650 DRAGONS (NON-MAGICAL)
500 NEGI
A
MAGICAL TEACHERS AT MAHORA ACADEMY (AVERAGE)
MEMBERS OF THE ORDER OF MAGICAL KNIGHTS IN THIS COUNTRY (AVERAGE)
300 SO-CALLED HIGH-LEVEL WIZARDS
B
200 TANK
BOOM
C
D
100 GRADUATES OF THE MAGIC ACADEMY
3~50 MASTERS FROM THE OLD WORLD (NON-CHI USERS)
2 WIZARDS (AVERAGE CITIZENS OF THE MAGICAL WORLD)
1 CHISAME
0 CAT
!
CLANG
AS STRONG AS TWO AEGISES!!
...HOW STRONG IS THAT?
I DON'T KNOW ABOUT USING THE AEGIS AS A GAG...
NO... WITH SUCH A BIG DIFFERENCE, NO MATTER HOW MUCH I TRAIN...
WELL, IF WE DID HONEST TRAINING, IT WOULD BE IMPOSSIBLE.
KUH...

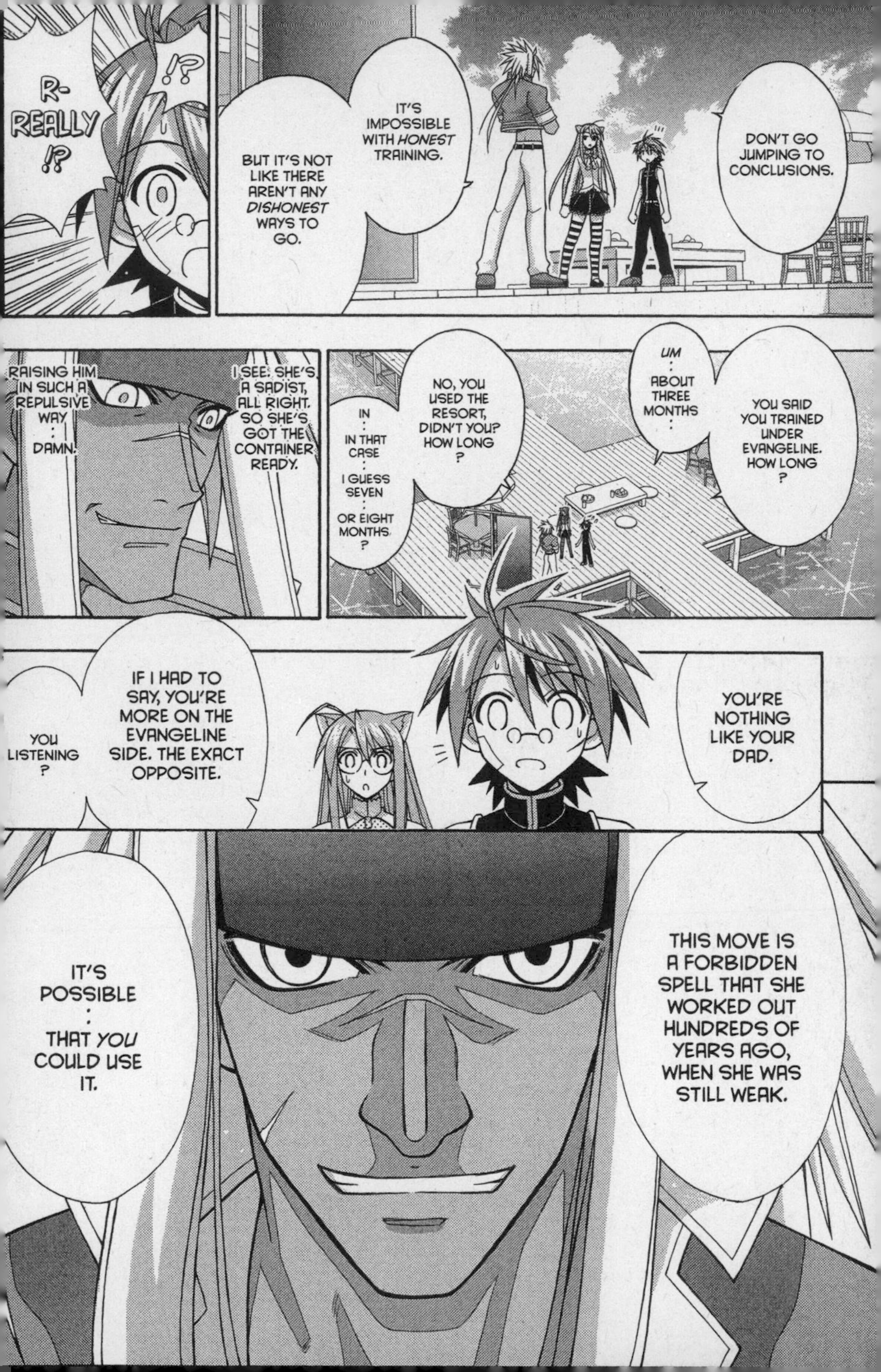
DON'T GO JUMPING TO CONCLUSIONS.
IT'S IMPOSSIBLE WITH *HONEST* TRAINING.
BUT IT'S NOT LIKE THERE AREN'T ANY *DISHONEST* WAYS TO GO.
!?
R-REALLY !?
YOU SAID YOU TRAINED UNDER EVANGELINE. HOW LONG ?
*UM* : ABOUT THREE MONTHS :
NO, YOU USED THE RESORT, DIDN'T YOU? HOW LONG ?
IN : IN THAT CASE : I GUESS SEVEN : OR EIGHT MONTHS ?
I SEE. SHE'S A SADIST, ALL RIGHT. SO SHE'S GOT THE CONTAINER READY.
RAISING HIM IN SUCH A REPULSIVE WAY : DAMN.
YOU'RE NOTHING LIKE YOUR DAD.
IF I HAD TO SAY, YOU'RE MORE ON THE EVANGELINE SIDE. THE EXACT OPPOSITE.
YOU LISTENING ?
THIS MOVE IS A FORBIDDEN SPELL THAT SHE WORKED OUT HUNDREDS OF YEARS AGO, WHEN SHE WAS STILL WEAK.
IT'S POSSIBLE : THAT *YOU* COULD USE IT.

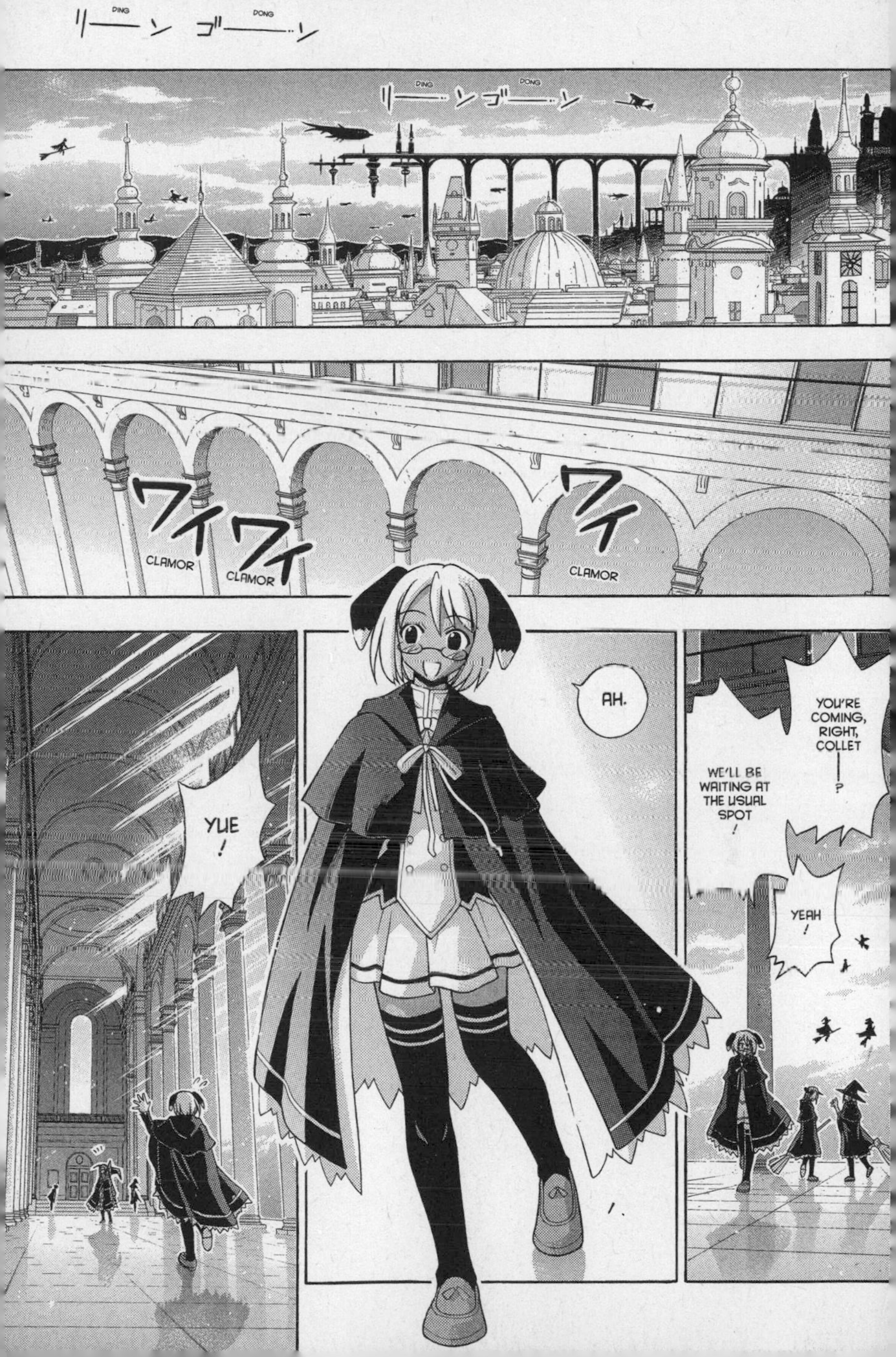
DING DONG
リーン ゴーーン
DING DONG
リーンゴーーン
ワイ CLAMOR
ワイワイ CLAMOR
CLAMOR
YOU'RE COMING, RIGHT, COLLET—?
WE'LL BE WAITING AT THE USUAL SPOT!
YEAH!
AH.
YUE!

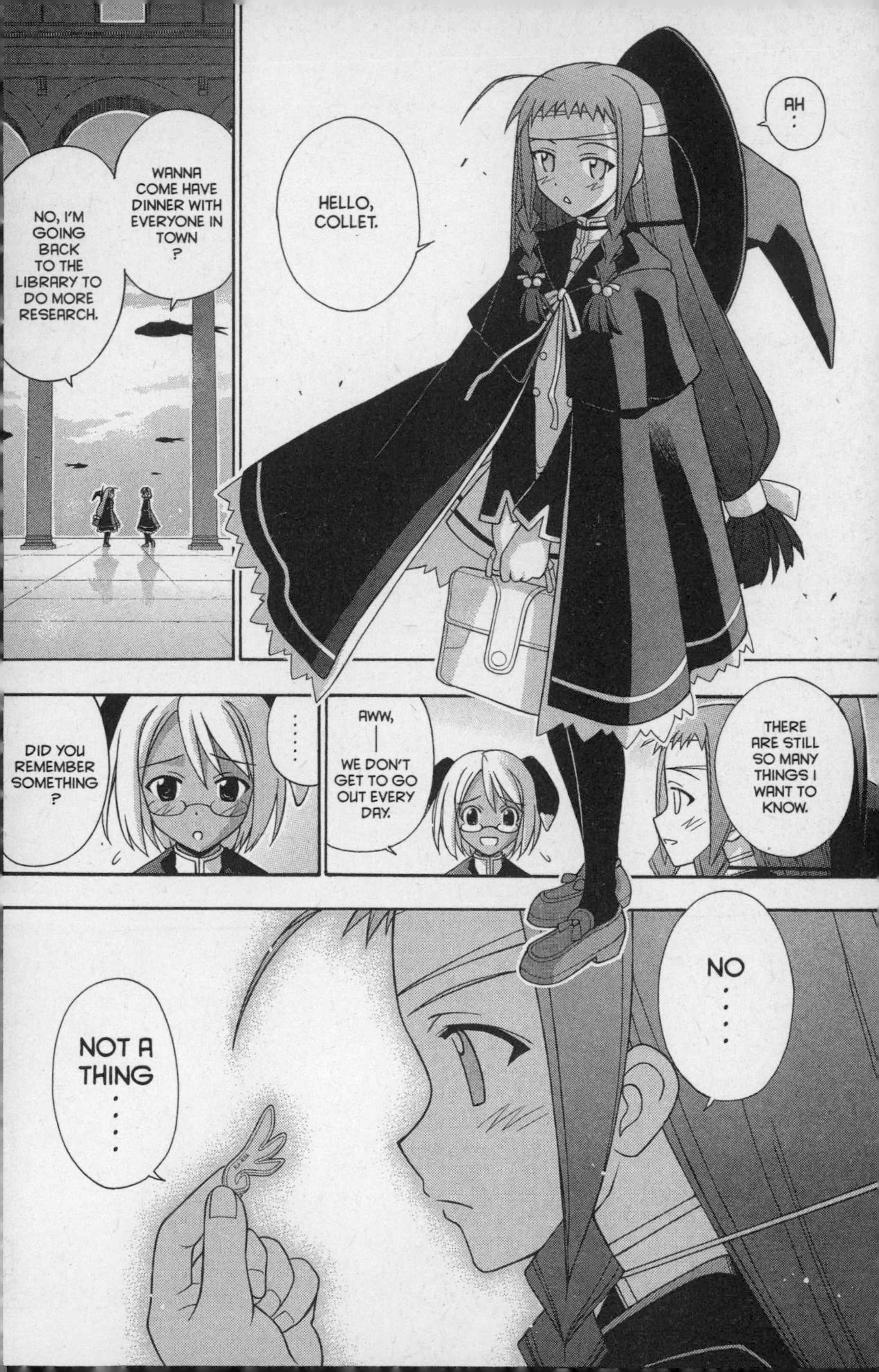
AH...
HELLO, COLLET.
WANNA COME HAVE DINNER WITH EVERYONE IN TOWN?
NO, I'M GOING BACK TO THE LIBRARY TO DO MORE RESEARCH.
THERE ARE STILL SO MANY THINGS I WANT TO KNOW.
AWW, — WE DON'T GET TO GO OUT EVERY DAY.
......
DID YOU REMEMBER SOMETHING?
NO....
NOT A THING....

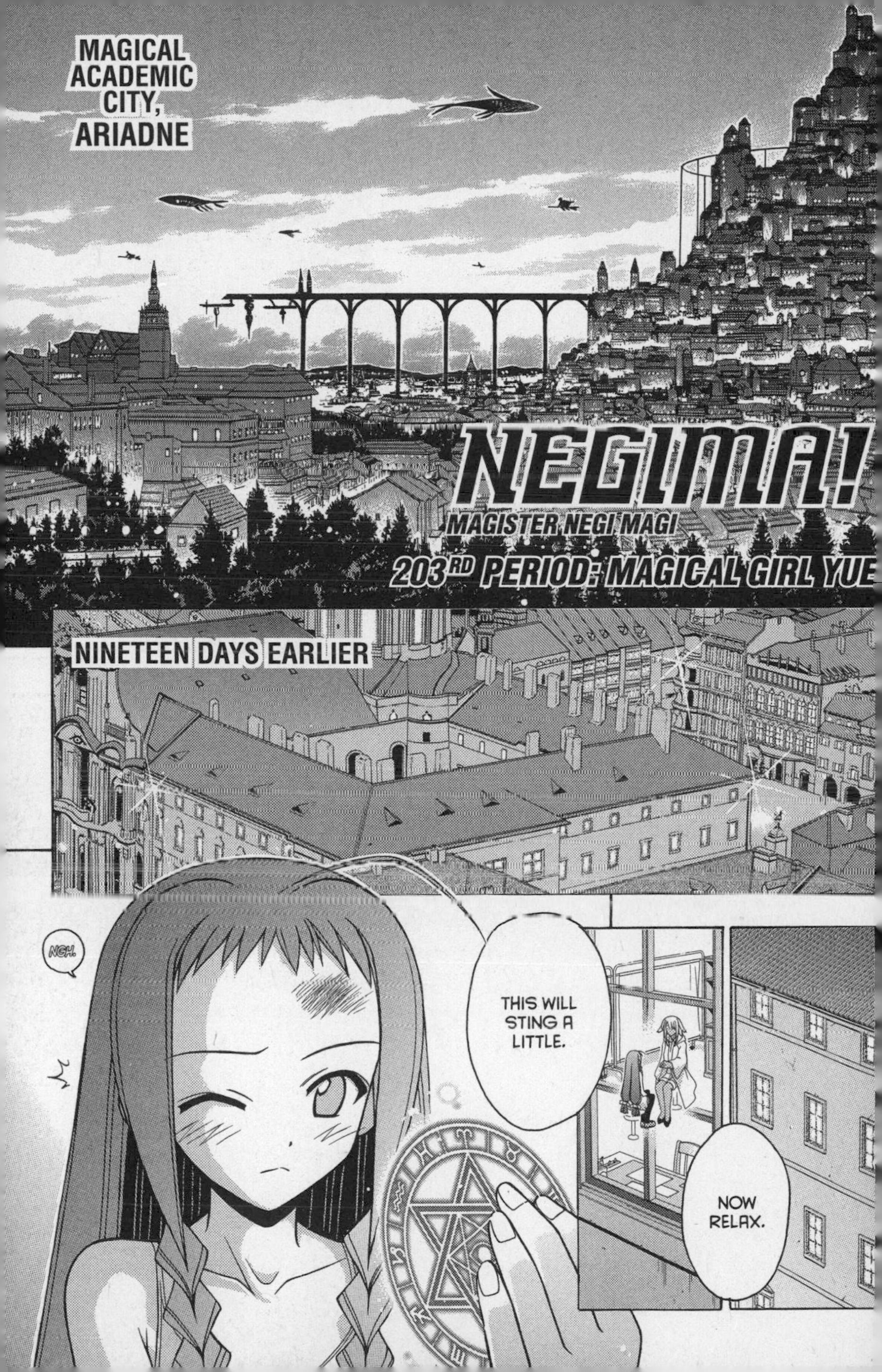
MAGICAL ACADEMIC CITY, ARIADNE
NEGIMA!
MAGISTER NEGI MAGI
203RD PERIOD: MAGICAL GIRL YUE
NINETEEN DAYS EARLIER
THIS WILL STING A LITTLE.
NOW RELAX.
NGH.

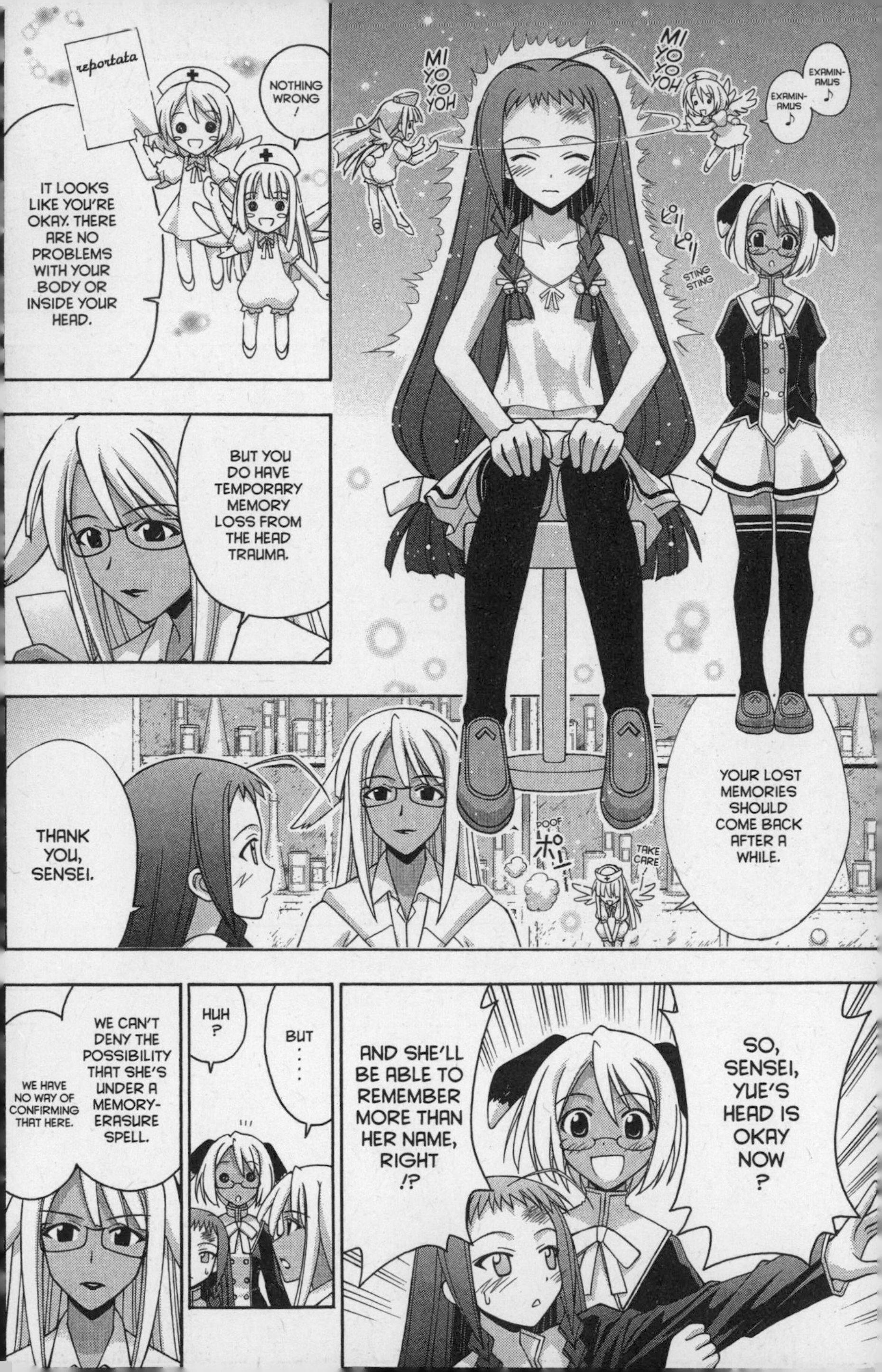
MI YO YO YOH
MI YO YO YOH
EXAMIN-AMUS ♪
EXAMIN-AMUS ♪
ピリ ピリ
STING STING
reportata
NOTHING WRONG!
IT LOOKS LIKE YOU'RE OKAY. THERE ARE NO PROBLEMS WITH YOUR BODY OR INSIDE YOUR HEAD.
BUT YOU DO HAVE TEMPORARY MEMORY LOSS FROM THE HEAD TRAUMA.
YOUR LOST MEMORIES SHOULD COME BACK AFTER A WHILE.
TAKE CARE!
POOF
ポン
THANK YOU, SENSEI.
SO, SENSEI, YUE'S HEAD IS OKAY NOW?
AND SHE'LL BE ABLE TO REMEMBER MORE THAN HER NAME, RIGHT!?
BUT...
HUH?
WE CAN'T DENY THE POSSIBILITY THAT SHE'S UNDER A MEMORY-ERASURE SPELL.
WE HAVE NO WAY OF CONFIRMING THAT HERE.

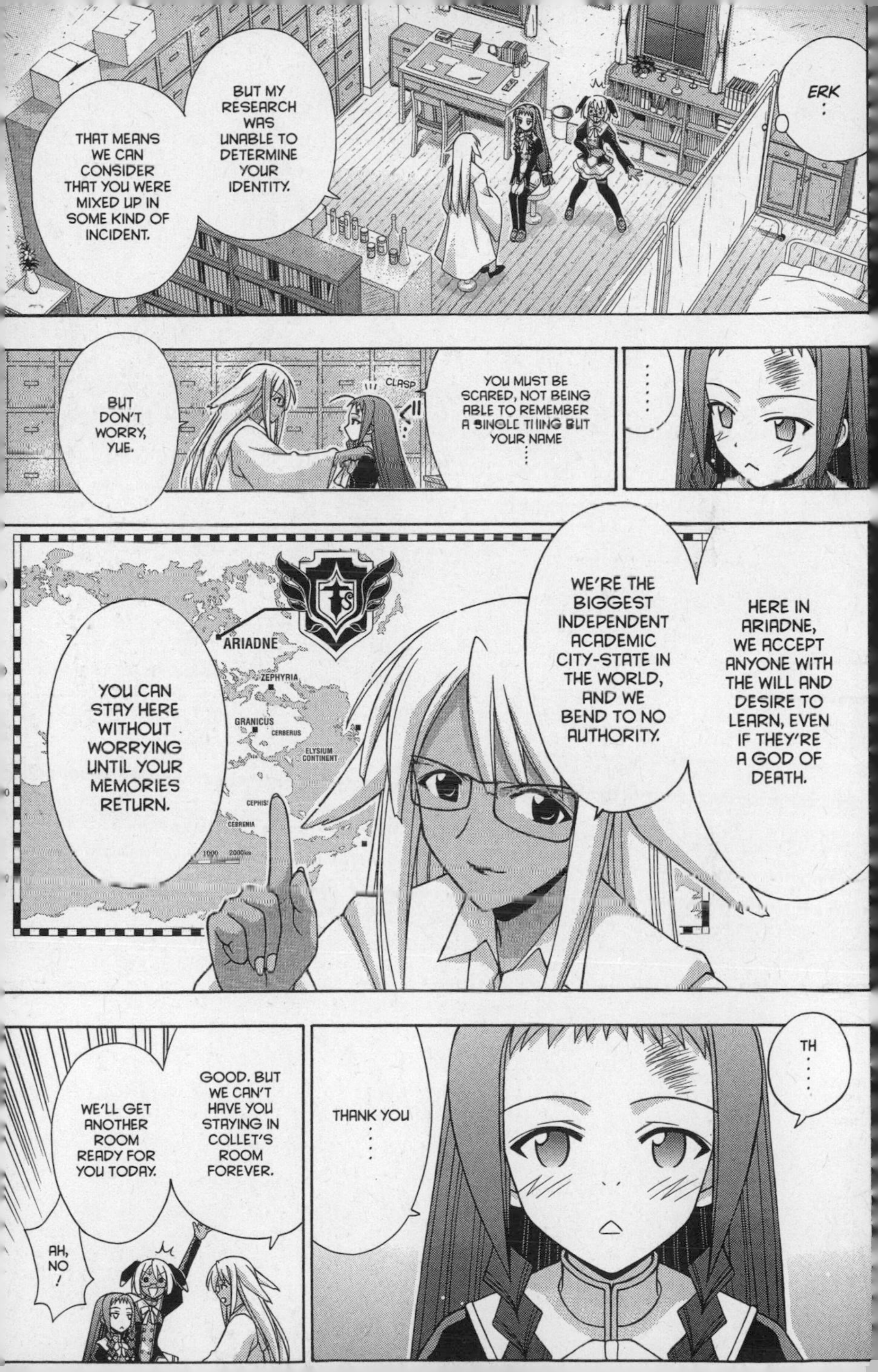
ERK...
BUT MY RESEARCH WAS UNABLE TO DETERMINE YOUR IDENTITY.
THAT MEANS WE CAN CONSIDER THAT YOU WERE MIXED UP IN SOME KIND OF INCIDENT.
......
YOU MUST BE SCARED, NOT BEING ABLE TO REMEMBER A SINGLE THING BUT YOUR NAME...
CLASP
BUT DON'T WORRY, YUE.
HERE IN ARIADNE, WE ACCEPT ANYONE WITH THE WILL AND DESIRE TO LEARN, EVEN IF THEY'RE A GOD OF DEATH.
WE'RE THE BIGGEST INDEPENDENT ACADEMIC CITY-STATE IN THE WORLD, AND WE BEND TO NO AUTHORITY.
ARIADNE
ZEPHYRIA
GRANICUS
CERBERUS
ELYSIUM CONTINENT
CEPHIS
CEBRENIA
1000 2000km
YOU CAN STAY HERE WITHOUT WORRYING UNTIL YOUR MEMORIES RETURN.
TH......
THANK YOU...
GOOD. BUT WE CAN'T HAVE YOU STAYING IN COLLET'S ROOM FOREVER.
WE'LL GET ANOTHER ROOM READY FOR YOU TODAY.
AH, NO!

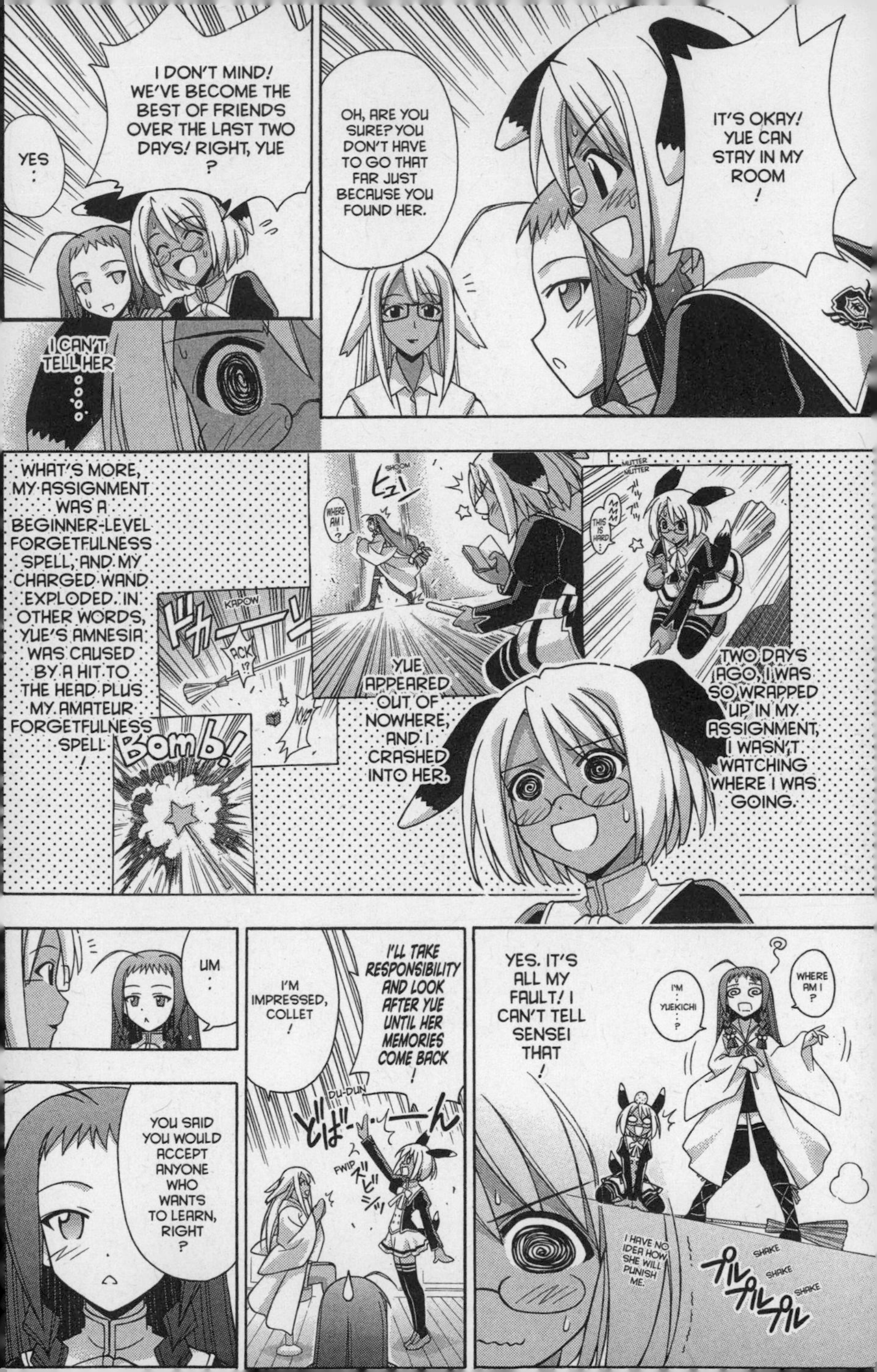

IT'S OKAY! YUE CAN STAY IN MY ROOM!
OH, ARE YOU SURE? YOU DON'T HAVE TO GO THAT FAR JUST BECAUSE YOU FOUND HER.
I DON'T MIND! WE'VE BECOME THE BEST OF FRIENDS OVER THE LAST TWO DAYS! RIGHT, YUE?
YES...
I CAN'T TELL HER......
TWO DAYS AGO, I WAS SO WRAPPED UP IN MY ASSIGNMENT, I WASN'T WATCHING WHERE I WAS GOING.
MUTTER MUTTER
THIS IS HARD...
SHOOM
WHERE AM I...?
YUE APPEARED OUT OF NOWHERE, AND I CRASHED INTO HER.
KAPOW
ACK!?
WHAT'S MORE, MY ASSIGNMENT WAS A BEGINNER-LEVEL FORGETFULNESS SPELL, AND MY CHARGED WAND EXPLODED. IN OTHER WORDS, YUE'S AMNESIA WAS CAUSED BY A HIT TO THE HEAD PLUS MY AMATEUR FORGETFULNESS SPELL!
Bomb!
WHERE AM I?
I'M... YUEKICHI...?
YES. IT'S ALL MY FAULT! I CAN'T TELL SENSEI THAT!
I HAVE NO IDEA HOW SHE WILL PUNISH ME.
SHAKE
SHAKE
SHAKE
I'LL TAKE RESPONSIBILITY AND LOOK AFTER YUE UNTIL HER MEMORIES COME BACK!
I'M IMPRESSED, COLLET!
DU-DUN
FWIP
UM...
YOU SAID YOU WOULD ACCEPT ANYONE WHO WANTS TO LEARN, RIGHT?

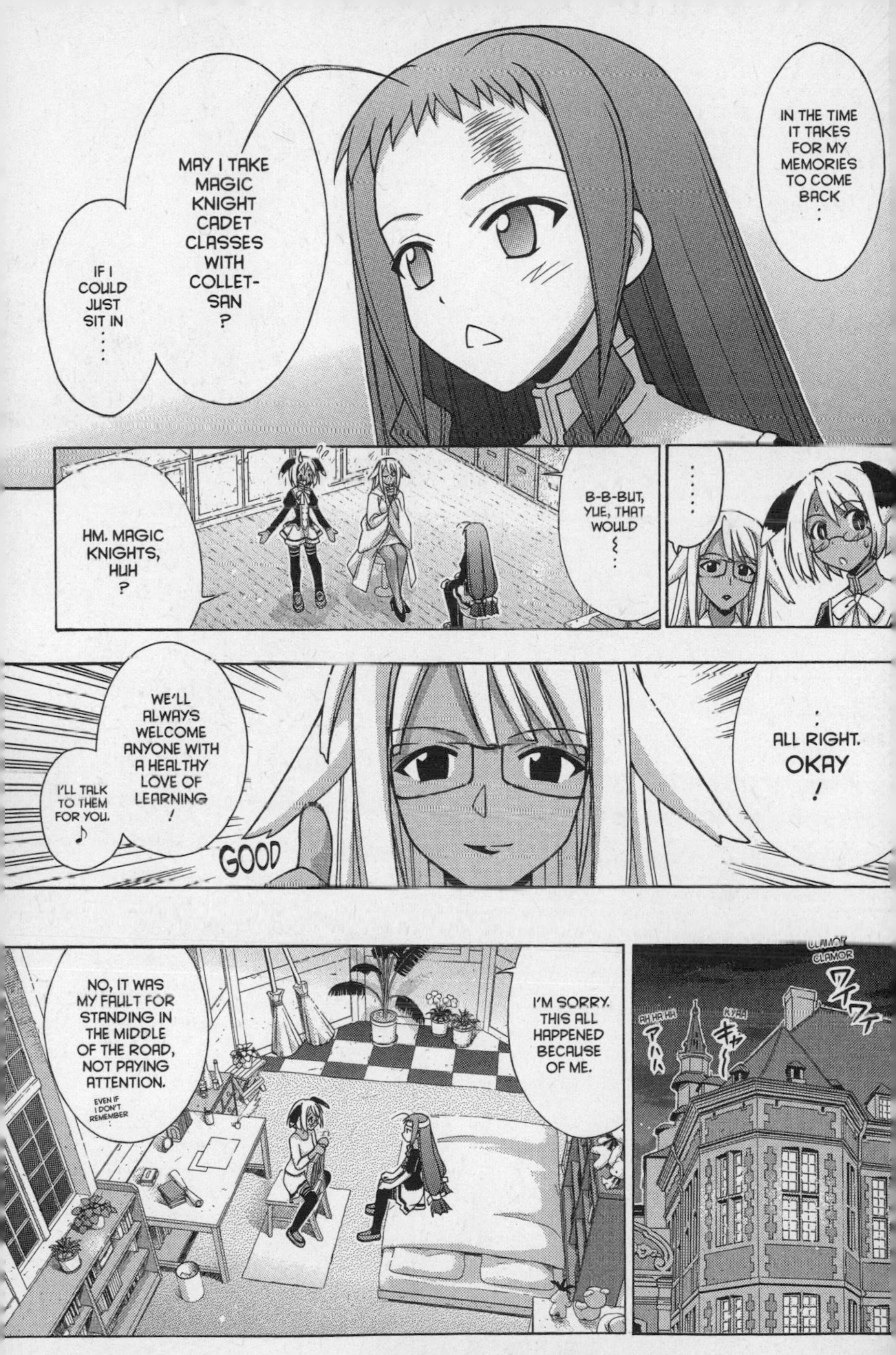
IN THE TIME IT TAKES FOR MY MEMORIES TO COME BACK...
MAY I TAKE MAGIC KNIGHT CADET CLASSES WITH COLLET-SAN?
IF I COULD JUST SIT IN....
......
B-B-BUT, YUE, THAT WOULD~...
HM. MAGIC KNIGHTS, HUH?
:ALL RIGHT. OKAY!
WE'LL ALWAYS WELCOME ANYONE WITH A HEALTHY LOVE OF LEARNING!
GOOD
I'LL TALK TO THEM FOR YOU. ♪
CLAMOR CLAMOR
KYHA
AH HA HA
I'M SORRY. THIS ALL HAPPENED BECAUSE OF ME.
NO, IT WAS MY FAULT FOR STANDING IN THE MIDDLE OF THE ROAD, NOT PAYING ATTENTION.
EVEN IF I DON'T REMEMBER:

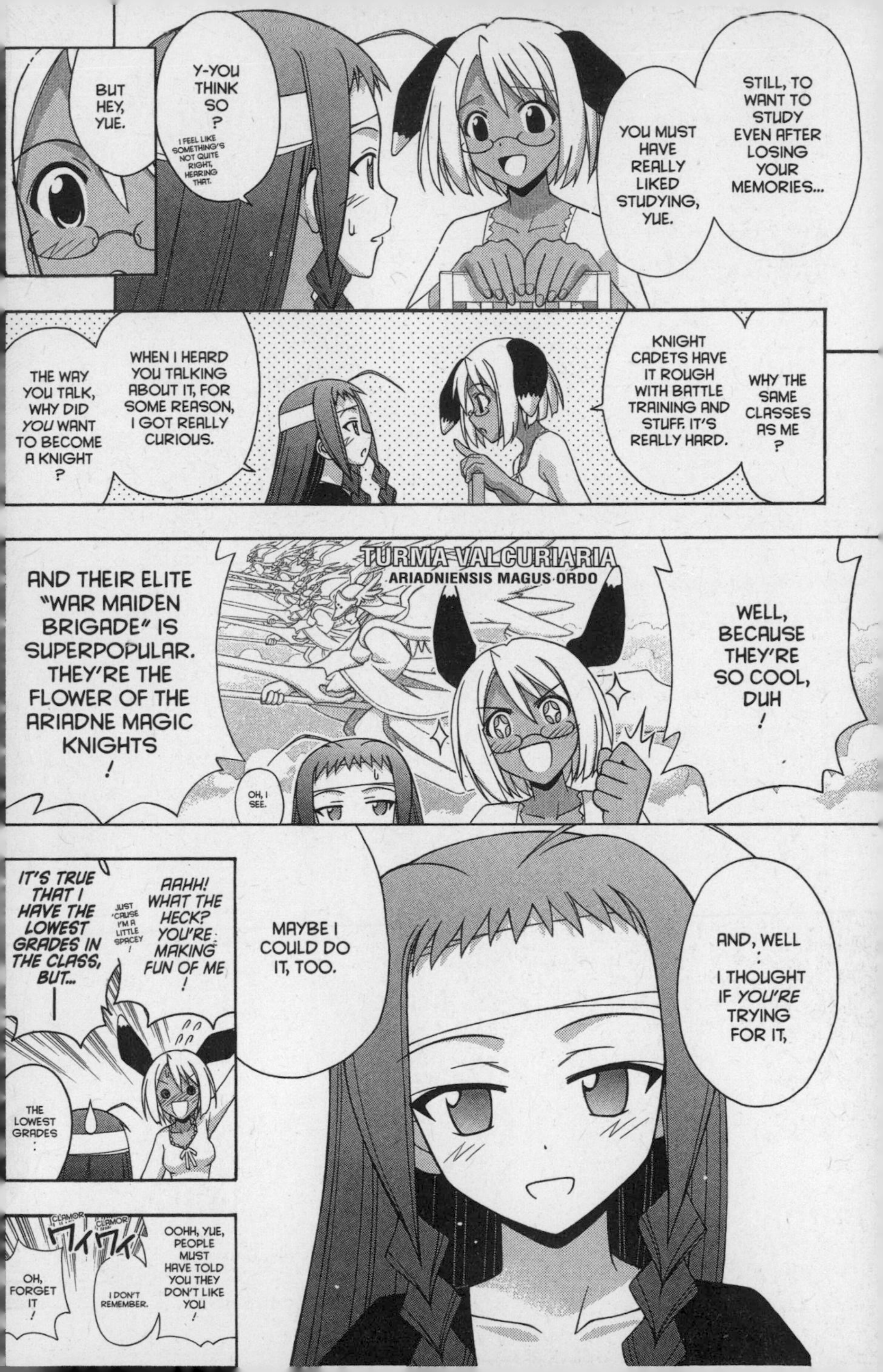
STILL, TO WANT TO STUDY EVEN AFTER LOSING YOUR MEMORIES...
YOU MUST HAVE REALLY LIKED STUDYING, YUE.
Y-YOU THINK SO?
I FEEL LIKE SOMETHING'S NOT QUITE RIGHT, HEARING THAT.
BUT HEY, YUE.
WHY THE SAME CLASSES AS ME?
KNIGHT CADETS HAVE IT ROUGH WITH BATTLE TRAINING AND STUFF. IT'S REALLY HARD.
WHEN I HEARD YOU TALKING ABOUT IT, FOR SOME REASON, I GOT REALLY CURIOUS.
THE WAY YOU TALK, WHY DID *YOU* WANT TO BECOME A KNIGHT?
WELL, BECAUSE THEY'RE SO COOL, DUH!
TURMA VALCURIARIA
ARIADNIENSIS MAGUS ORDO
AND THEIR ELITE "WAR MAIDEN BRIGADE" IS SUPERPOPULAR. THEY'RE THE FLOWER OF THE ARIADNE MAGIC KNIGHTS!
OH, I SEE.
AND, WELL: I THOUGHT IF *YOU'RE* TRYING FOR IT,
MAYBE I COULD DO IT, TOO.
AAHH! WHAT THE HECK? YOU'RE MAKING FUN OF ME!
JUST 'CAUSE I'M A LITTLE SPACEY!
IT'S TRUE THAT I HAVE THE LOWEST GRADES IN THE CLASS, BUT...
THE LOWEST GRADES:
CLAMOR
CLAMOR
ワイワイ
OOHH, YUE, PEOPLE MUST HAVE TOLD YOU THEY DON'T LIKE YOU!
I DON'T REMEMBER.
OH, FORGET IT!

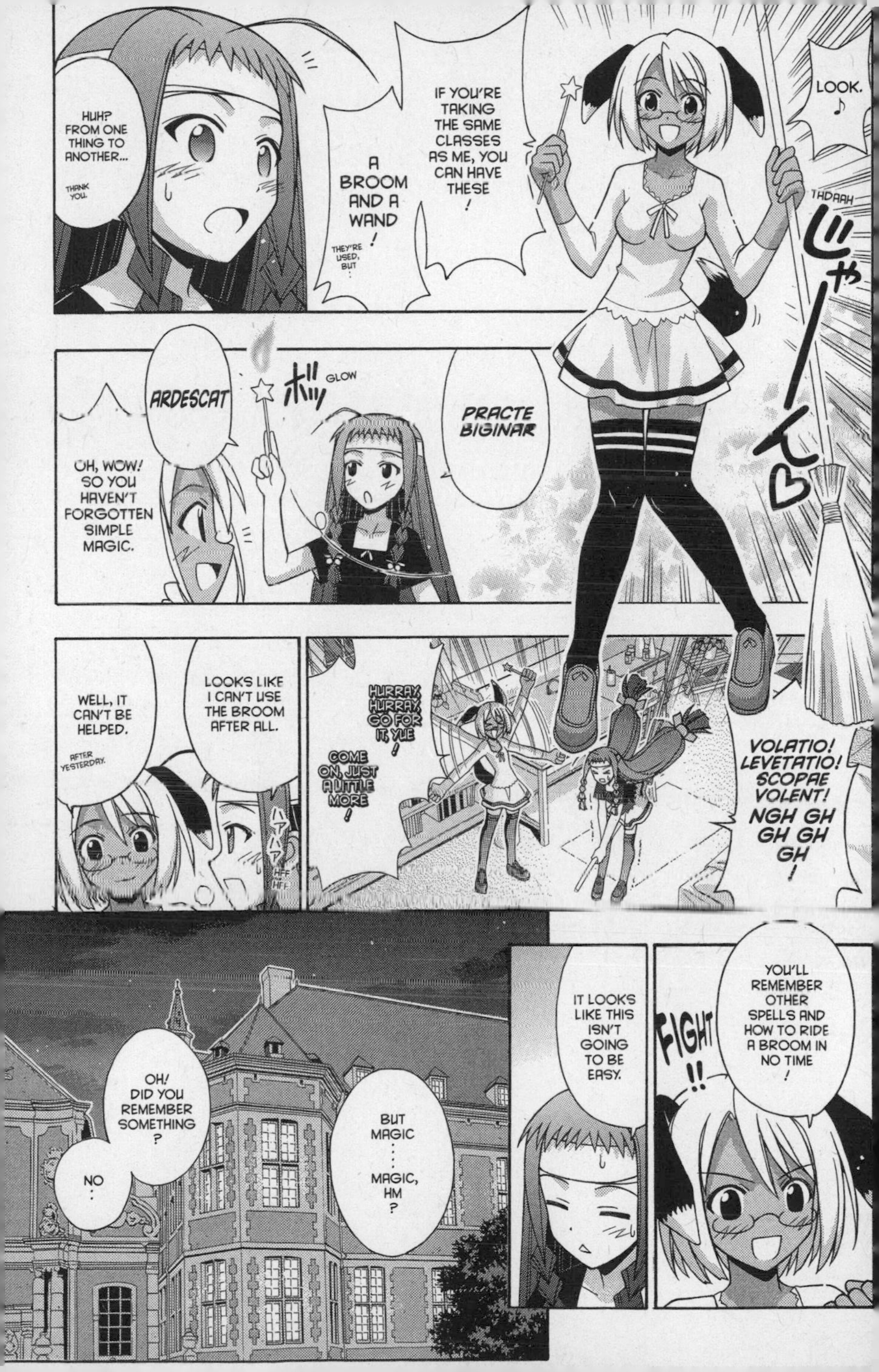
LOOK. ♪
THDAAH
IF YOU'RE TAKING THE SAME CLASSES AS ME, YOU CAN HAVE THESE!
A BROOM AND A WAND!
THEY'RE USED, BUT...
HUH? FROM ONE THING TO ANOTHER...
THANK YOU.
PRACTE BIGINAR
GLOW
ARDESCAT
OH, WOW! SO YOU HAVEN'T FORGOTTEN SIMPLE MAGIC.
VOLATIO! LEVETATIO! SCOPAE VOLENT! NGH GH GH GH GH!
HURRAY, HURRAY, GO FOR IT, YUE!
COME ON, JUST A LITTLE MORE!
LOOKS LIKE I CAN'T USE THE BROOM AFTER ALL.
WELL, IT CAN'T BE HELPED.
AFTER YESTERDAY.
HFF HFF
YOU'LL REMEMBER OTHER SPELLS AND HOW TO RIDE A BROOM IN NO TIME!
FIGHT!!
IT LOOKS LIKE THIS ISN'T GOING TO BE EASY.
BUT MAGIC... MAGIC, HM?
OH! DID YOU REMEMBER SOMETHING?
NO...

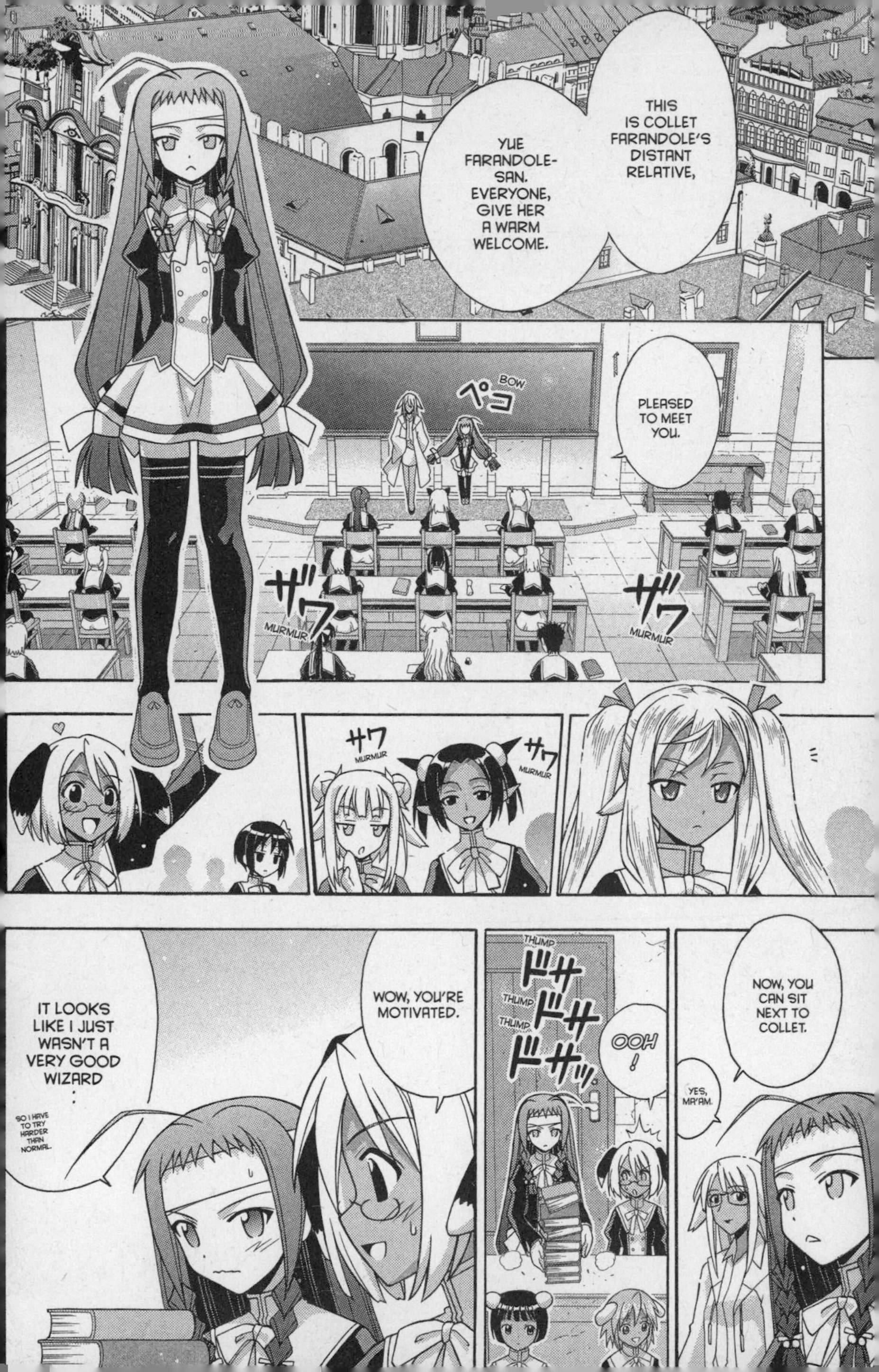
THIS IS COLLET FARANDOLE'S DISTANT RELATIVE,
YUE FARANDOLE-SAN. EVERYONE, GIVE HER A WARM WELCOME.
PLEASED TO MEET YOU.
ペコ
BOW
ザワ
MURMUR
ザワ
MURMUR
サワ
MURMUR
サワ
MURMUR
NOW, YOU CAN SIT NEXT TO COLLET.
YES, MA'AM.
OOH!
ドサ
THUMP
ドサ
THUMP
ドサッ
THUMP
WOW, YOU'RE MOTIVATED.
IT LOOKS LIKE I JUST WASN'T A VERY GOOD WIZARD...
SO I HAVE TO TRY HARDER THAN NORMAL.

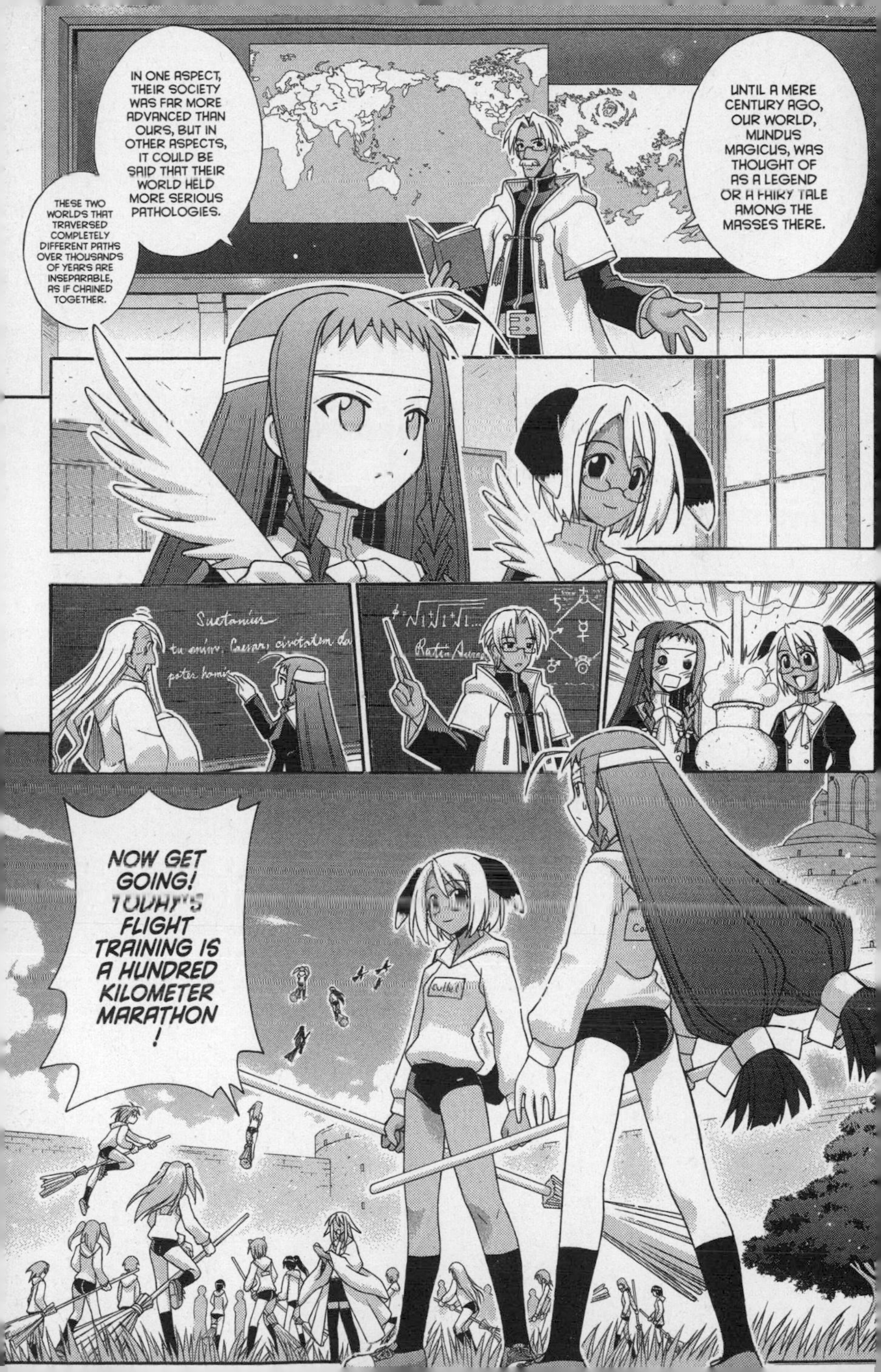
UNTIL A MERE CENTURY AGO, OUR WORLD, MUNDUS MAGICUS, WAS THOUGHT OF AS A LEGEND OR A FAIRY TALE AMONG THE MASSES THERE.
IN ONE ASPECT, THEIR SOCIETY WAS FAR MORE ADVANCED THAN OURS, BUT IN OTHER ASPECTS, IT COULD BE SAID THAT THEIR WORLD HELD MORE SERIOUS PATHOLOGIES.
THESE TWO WORLDS THAT TRAVERSED COMPLETELY DIFFERENT PATHS OVER THOUSANDS OF YEARS ARE INSEPARABLE, AS IF CHAINED TOGETHER.
NOW GET GOING! TODAY'S FLIGHT TRAINING IS A HUNDRED KILOMETER MARATHON!

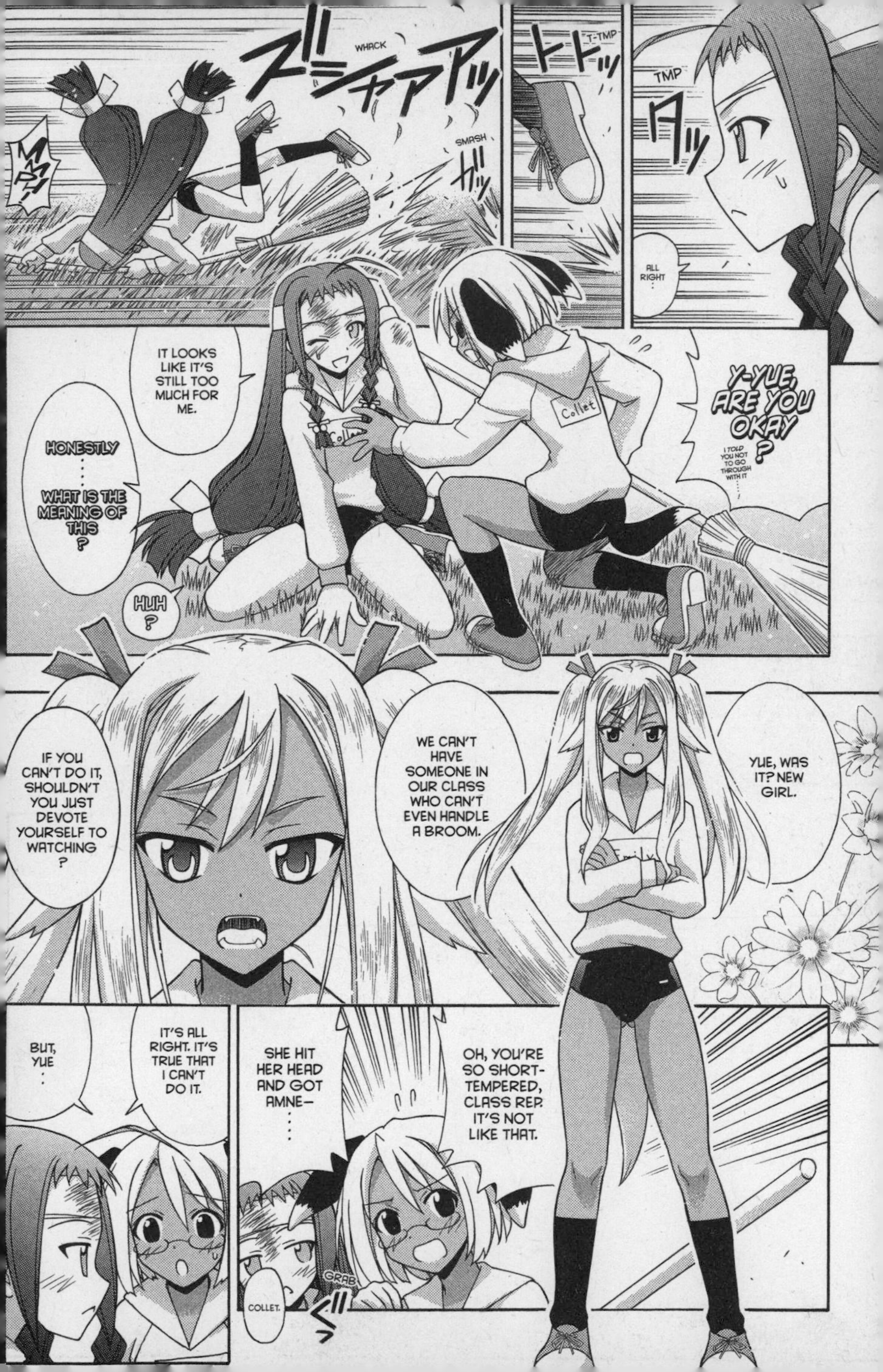
TMP
タッ
ALL RIGHT...
T-TMP
トトッ
WHACK
ズシャアアッ
SMASH
ガッ
MMPH!
Y-YUE, ARE YOU OKAY?
I TOLD YOU NOT TO GO THROUGH WITH IT...
IT LOOKS LIKE IT'S STILL TOO MUCH FOR ME.
HONESTLY... WHAT IS THE MEANING OF THIS?
HUH?
YUE, WAS IT? NEW GIRL.
WE CAN'T HAVE SOMEONE IN OUR CLASS WHO CAN'T EVEN HANDLE A BROOM.
IF YOU CAN'T DO IT, SHOULDN'T YOU JUST DEVOTE YOURSELF TO WATCHING?
OH, YOU'RE SO SHORT-TEMPERED, CLASS REP. IT'S NOT LIKE THAT.
SHE HIT HER HEAD AND GOT AMNE—...
GRAB
COLLET.
IT'S ALL RIGHT. IT'S TRUE THAT I CAN'T DO IT.
BUT, YUE...

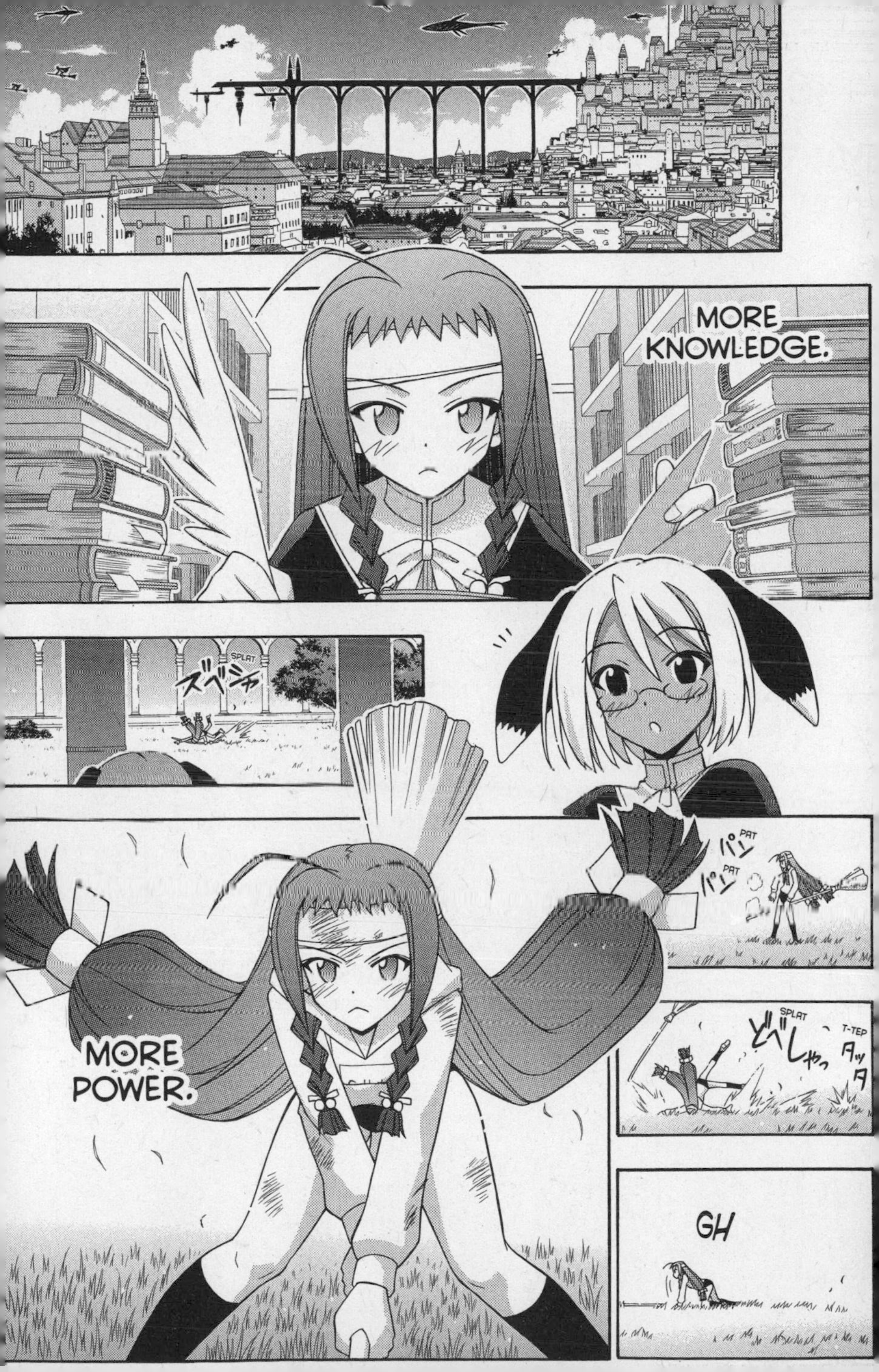
MORE KNOWLEDGE.
SPLAT
ズベシャ
PAT
パン
PAT
パン
SPLAT
どべしゃっ
T-TEP
タッタ
GH
MORE POWER.

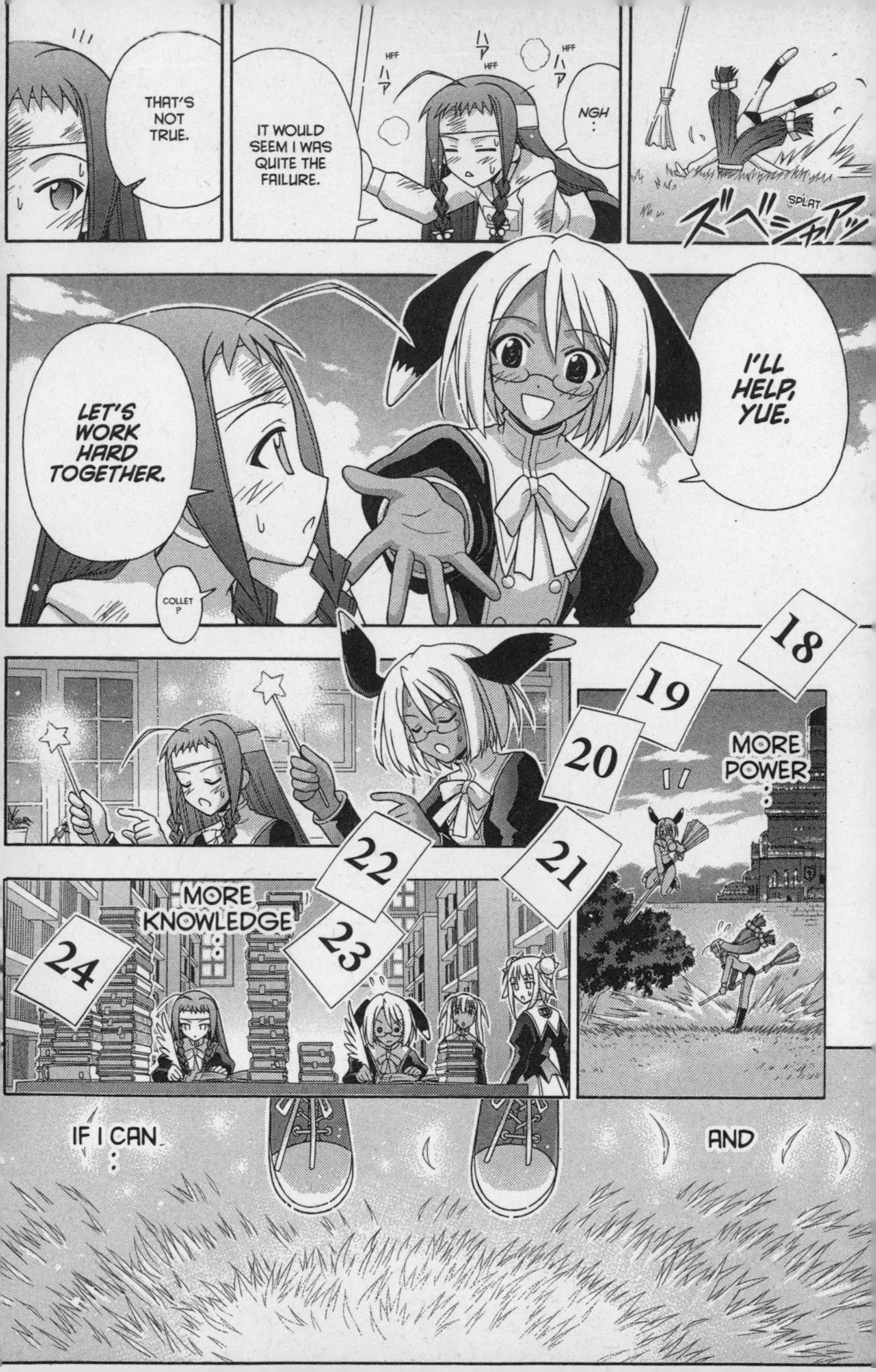
ズベシャアッ
SPLAT
HFF
HFF
NGH...
HFF
IT WOULD SEEM I WAS QUITE THE FAILURE.
THAT'S NOT TRUE.
I'LL HELP, YUE.
LET'S WORK HARD TOGETHER.
COLLET?
18
19
20
MORE POWER...
21
22
23
MORE KNOWLEDGE...
24
AND
IF I CAN...

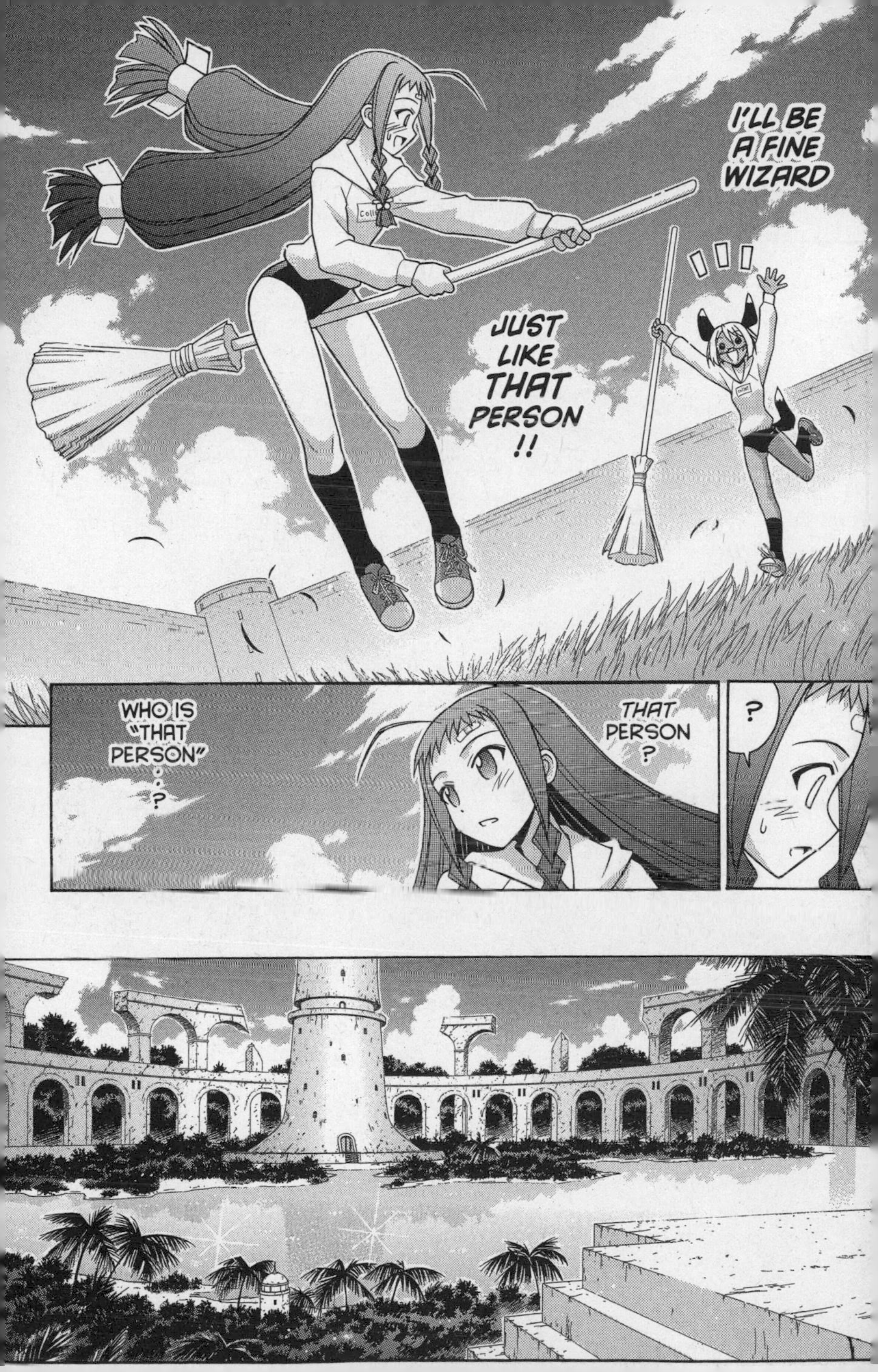
I'LL BE A FINE WIZARD
JUST LIKE THAT PERSON !!
?
THAT PERSON ?
WHO IS "THAT PERSON" . . . ?

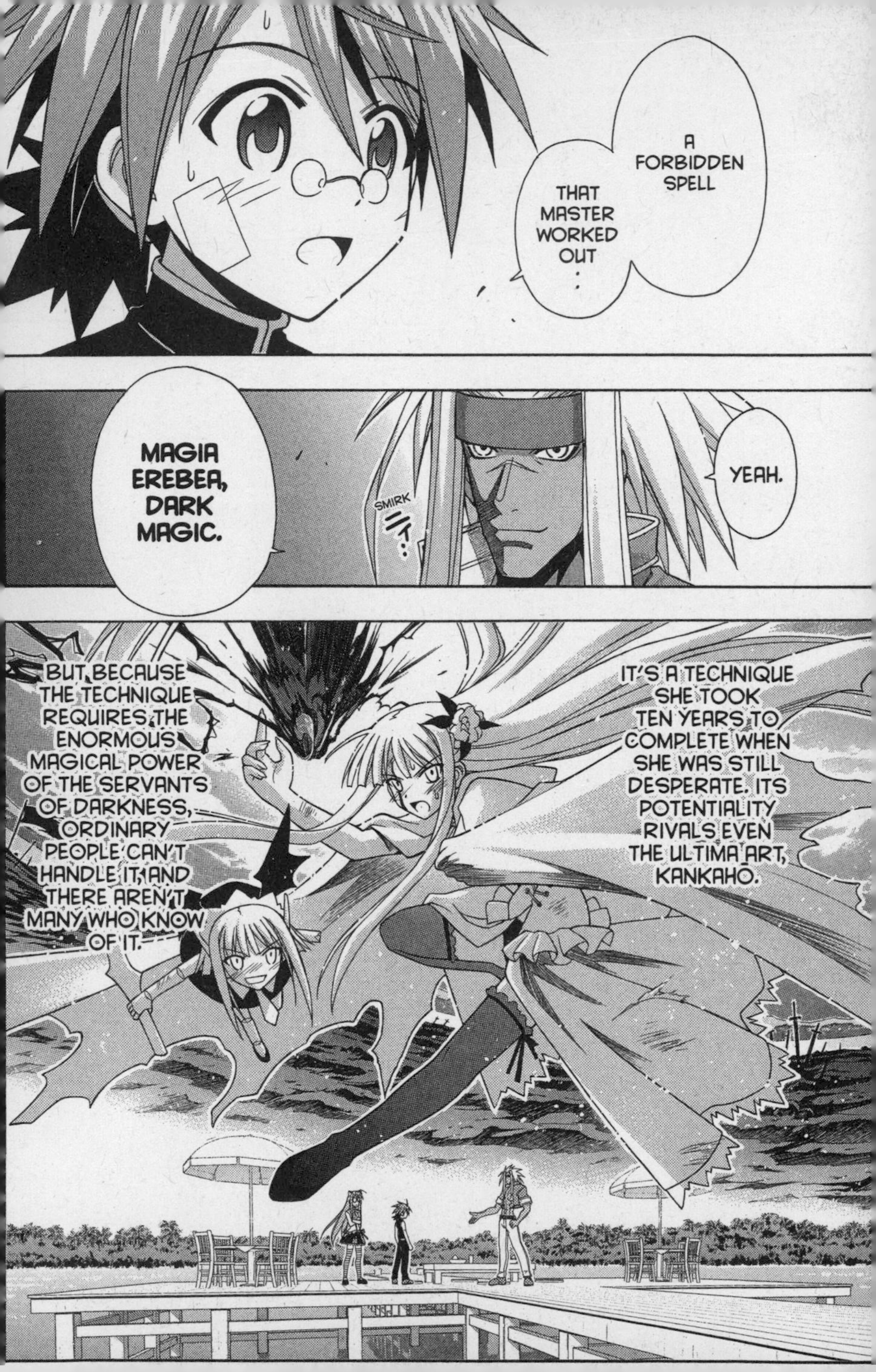
A FORBIDDEN SPELL
THAT MASTER WORKED OUT...
YEAH.
SMIRK
MAGIA EREBEA, DARK MAGIC.
IT'S A TECHNIQUE SHE TOOK TEN YEARS TO COMPLETE WHEN SHE WAS STILL DESPERATE. ITS POTENTIALITY RIVALS EVEN THE ULTIMA ART, KANKAHO.
BUT BECAUSE THE TECHNIQUE REQUIRES THE ENORMOUS MAGICAL POWER OF THE SERVANTS OF DARKNESS, ORDINARY PEOPLE CAN'T HANDLE IT, AND THERE AREN'T MANY WHO KNOW OF IT.

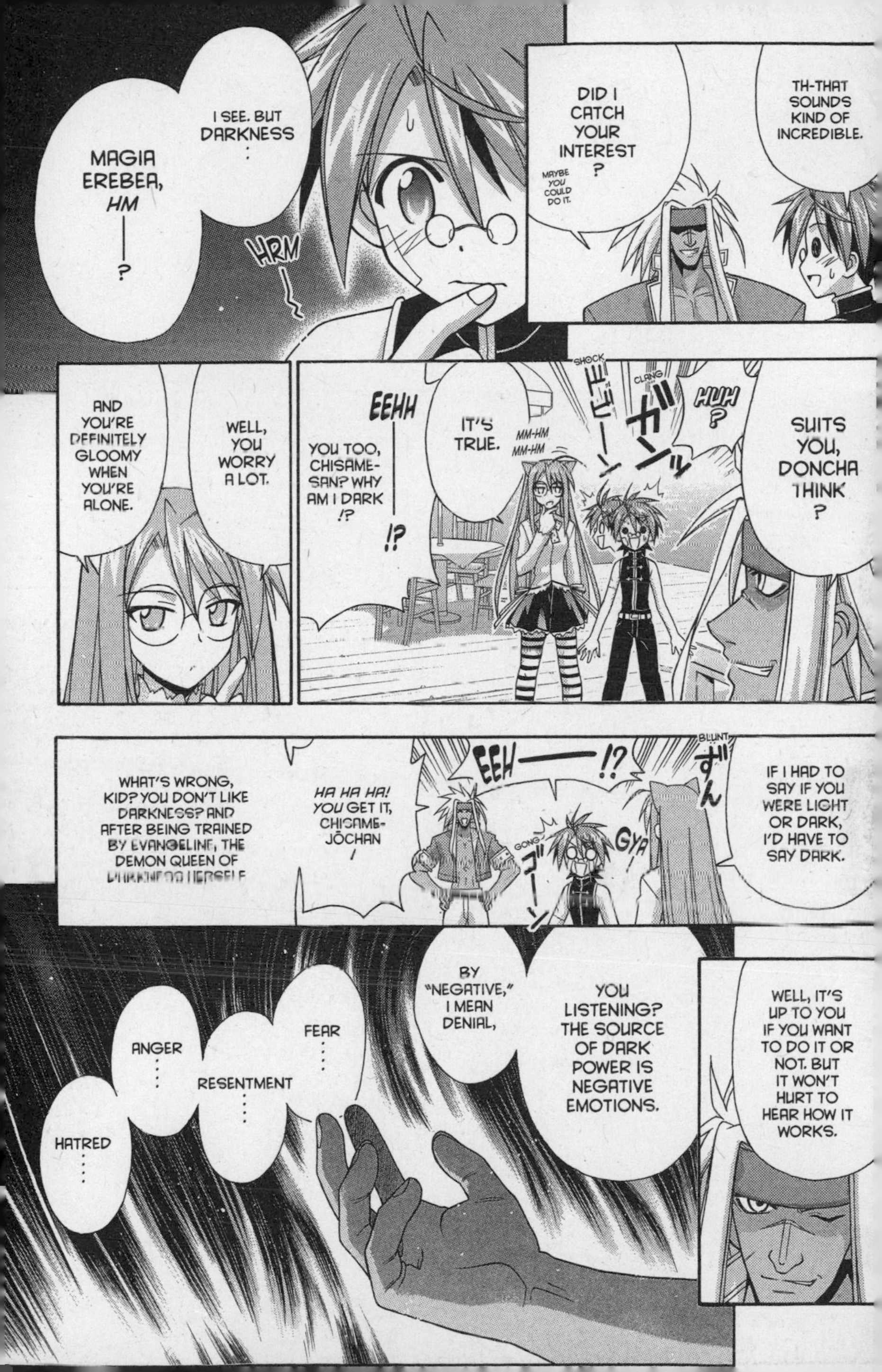
TH-THAT SOUNDS KIND OF INCREDIBLE.
DID I CATCH YOUR INTEREST ?
MAYBE YOU COULD DO IT.
I SEE. BUT DARKNESS ...
MAGIA EREBEA, HM —?
HRM
HUH?
SUITS YOU, DONCHA THINK ?
SHOCK
CLANG
MM-HM MM-HM
IT'S TRUE.
EEHH —!?
YOU TOO, CHISAME-SAN? WHY AM I DARK !?
WELL, YOU WORRY A LOT.
AND YOU'RE DEFINITELY GLOOMY WHEN YOU'RE ALONE.
IF I HAD TO SAY IF YOU WERE LIGHT OR DARK, I'D HAVE TO SAY DARK.
BLUNT
GYA
GONG
EEH—!?
HA HA HA! YOU GET IT, CHISAME-JŌCHAN!
WHAT'S WRONG, KID? YOU DON'T LIKE DARKNESS? AND AFTER BEING TRAINED BY EVANGELINE, THE DEMON QUEEN OF DARKNESS HERSELF
WELL, IT'S UP TO YOU IF YOU WANT TO DO IT OR NOT. BUT IT WON'T HURT TO HEAR HOW IT WORKS.
YOU LISTENING? THE SOURCE OF DARK POWER IS NEGATIVE EMOTIONS.
BY "NEGATIVE," I MEAN DENIAL,
FEAR ...
RESENTMENT ...
ANGER ...
HATRED ...

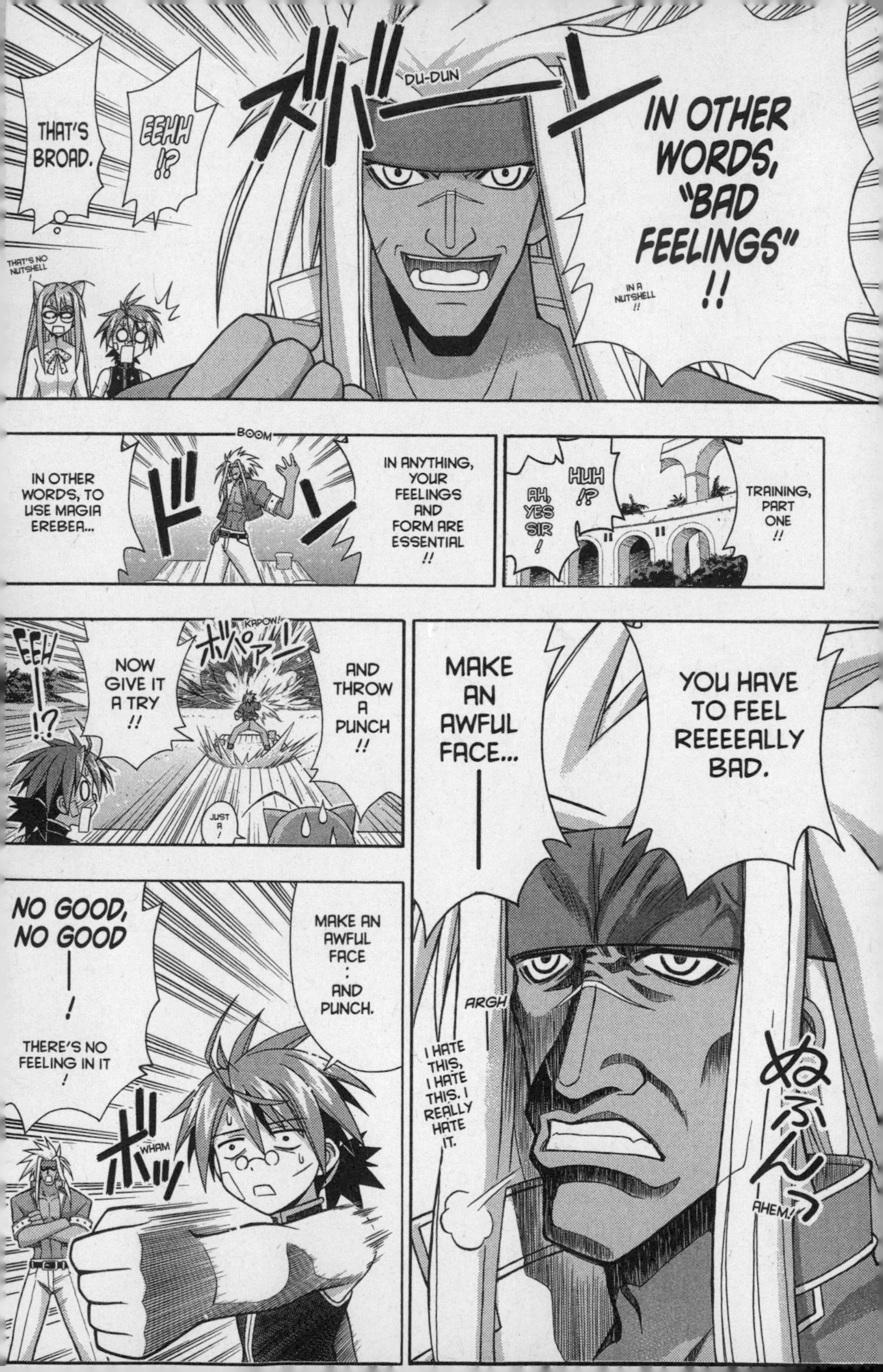
IN OTHER WORDS, "BAD FEELINGS"!!
IN A NUTSHELL!!
DU-DUN
EEHH!?
THAT'S BROAD.
THAT'S NO NUTSHELL!
TRAINING, PART ONE!!
HUH!?
AH, YES SIR!
IN ANYTHING, YOUR FEELINGS AND FORM ARE ESSENTIAL!!
BOOM
IN OTHER WORDS, TO USE MAGIA EREBEA...
YOU HAVE TO FEEL REEEEALLY BAD.
MAKE AN AWFUL FACE...—
AHEM!
I HATE THIS, I HATE THIS. I REALLY HATE IT.
ARGH
AND THROW A PUNCH!!
KAPOW!
NOW GIVE IT A TRY!!
EEH—!?
JUST A!
MAKE AN AWFUL FACE : AND PUNCH.
NO GOOD, NO GOOD—!
THERE'S NO FEELING IN IT!
WHAM

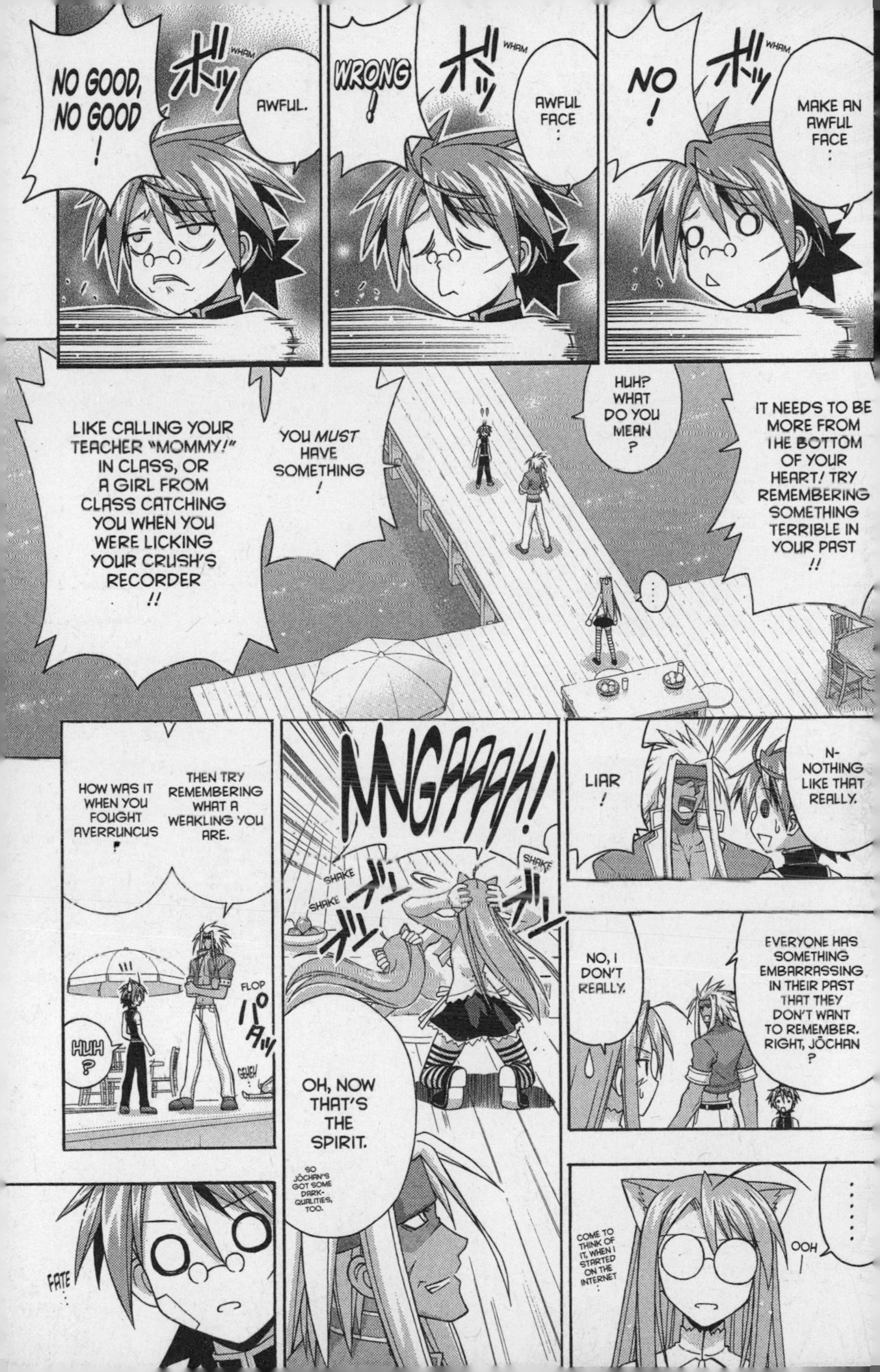
MAKE AN AWFUL FACE . . .
NO!
WHAM
AWFUL FACE . . .
WRONG!
WHAM
AWFUL.
NO GOOD, NO GOOD!
WHAM
IT NEEDS TO BE MORE FROM THE BOTTOM OF YOUR HEART! TRY REMEMBERING SOMETHING TERRIBLE IN YOUR PAST!!
HUH? WHAT DO YOU MEAN?
. . .
YOU *MUST* HAVE SOMETHING!
LIKE CALLING YOUR TEACHER "MOMMY!" IN CLASS, OR A GIRL FROM CLASS CATCHING YOU WHEN YOU WERE LICKING YOUR CRUSH'S RECORDER!!
N-NOTHING LIKE THAT REALLY.
LIAR!
EVERYONE HAS SOMETHING EMBARRASSING IN THEIR PAST THAT THEY DON'T WANT TO REMEMBER. RIGHT, JŌCHAN?
NO, I DON'T REALLY.
MNGAAAH!
SHAKE
SHAKE
SHAKE
OH, NOW THAT'S THE SPIRIT.
THEN TRY REMEMBERING WHAT A WEAKLING YOU ARE.
HOW WAS IT WHEN YOU FOUGHT AVERRUNCUS?
FLOP
HUH?
GEHEH
. . . . . .
OOH!
COME TO THINK OF IT, WHEN I STARTED ON THE INTERNET . . .
SO JŌCHAN'S GOT SOME DARK-QUALITIES, TOO.
FATE . . .

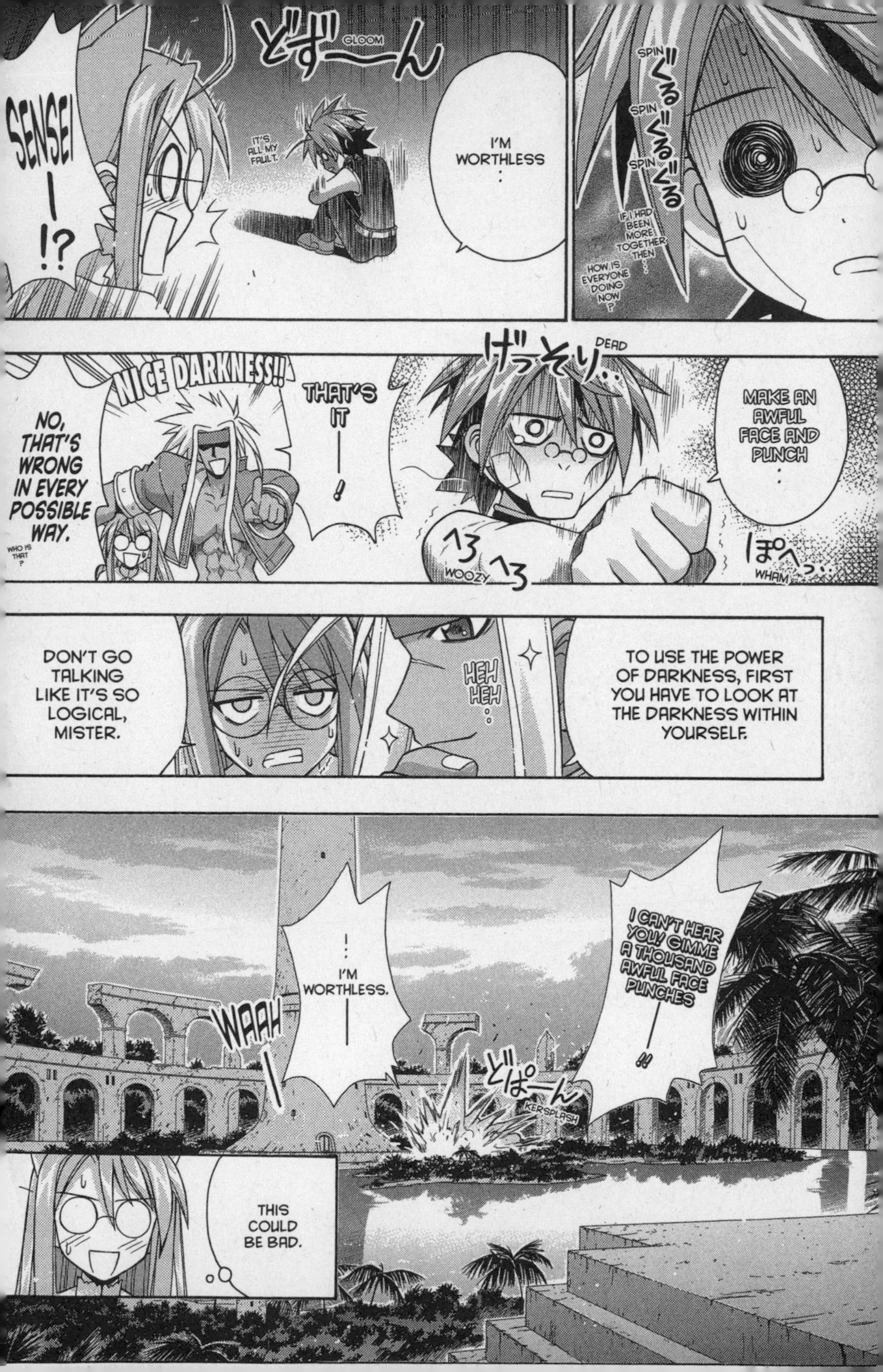

SPIN ぐる
SPIN ぐる
SPIN ぐる
IF I HAD BEEN MORE TOGETHER THEN...
HOW IS EVERYONE DOING NOW?
どずーん GLOOM
I'M WORTHLESS
IT'S ALL MY FAULT.
SENSEI—!?
MAKE AN AWFUL FACE AND PUNCH
ぽへっ WHAM
げっそり DEAD
へろ へろ WOOZY
THAT'S IT—!
NICE DARKNESS!!
NO, THAT'S WRONG IN EVERY POSSIBLE WAY.
WHO IS THAT?
TO USE THE POWER OF DARKNESS, FIRST YOU HAVE TO LOOK AT THE DARKNESS WITHIN YOURSELF.
HEH HEH
DON'T GO TALKING LIKE IT'S SO LOGICAL, MISTER.
I CAN'T HEAR YOU! GIMME A THOUSAND AWFUL FACE PUNCHES—!!
どぱーん KERSPLASH
!! I'M WORTHLESS.—
WAAH—
THIS COULD BE BAD.

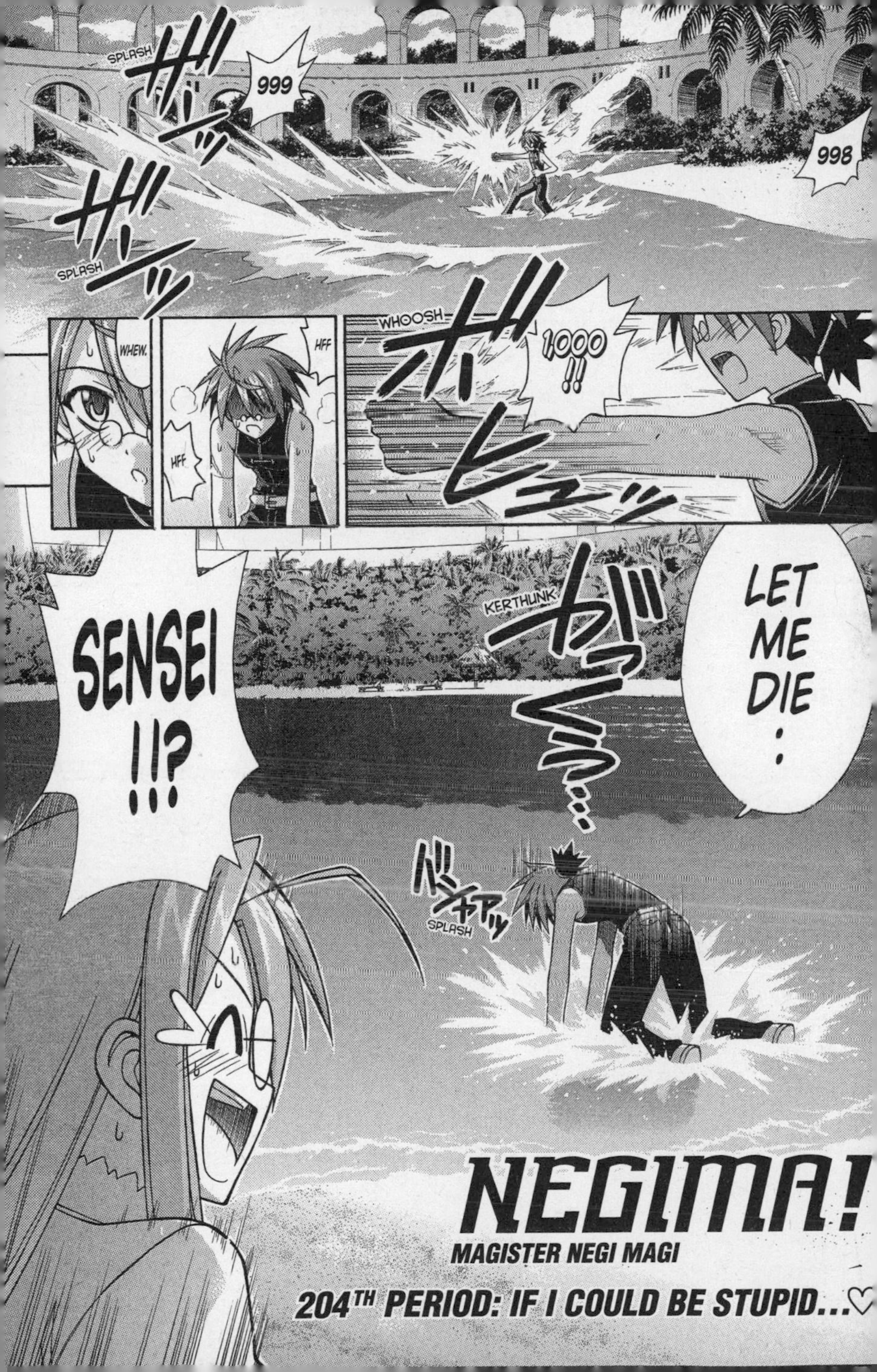
998
999
SPLASH
SPLASH
WHOOSH
1,000!!
HFF
HFF
WHEW.
LET ME DIE
:
KERTHUNK
SENSEI!!?
SPLASH
NEGIMA!
MAGISTER NEGI MAGI
204TH PERIOD: IF I COULD BE STUPID...♡

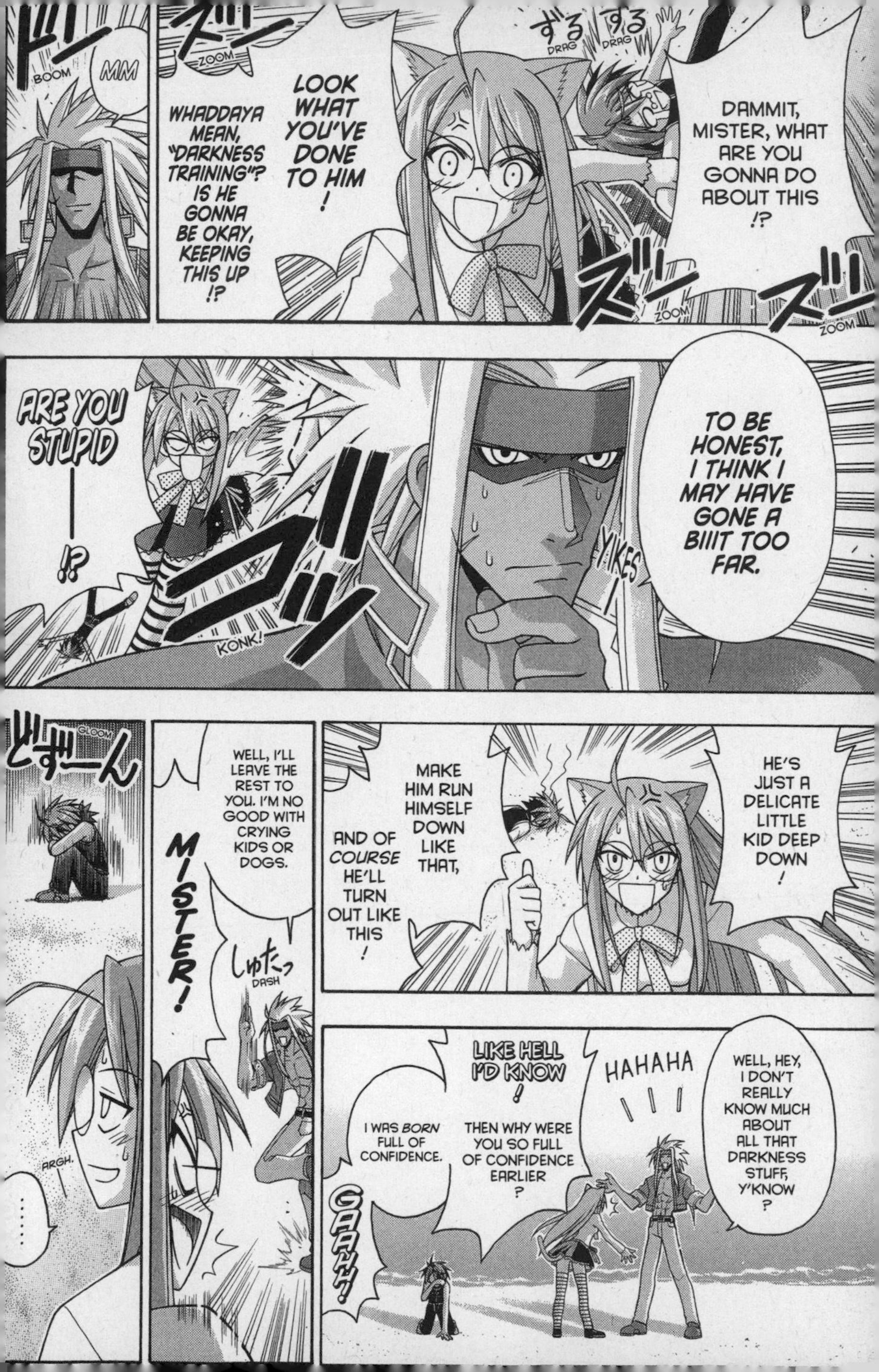
ずる
DRAG
する
DRAG
DAMMIT, MISTER, WHAT ARE YOU GONNA DO ABOUT THIS!?
ズー
ZOOM
ズー
ZOOM
ズー
ZOOM
LOOK WHAT YOU'VE DONE TO HIM!
WHADDAYA MEAN, "DARKNESS TRAINING"? IS HE GONNA BE OKAY, KEEPING THIS UP!?
ドン
BOOM
MM
TO BE HONEST, I THINK I MAY HAVE GONE A BIIIT TOO FAR.
YIKES!
ARE YOU STUPID—!?
ゴッ
KONK!
HE'S JUST A DELICATE LITTLE KID DEEP DOWN!
MAKE HIM RUN HIMSELF DOWN LIKE THAT,
AND OF COURSE HE'LL TURN OUT LIKE THIS!
WELL, HEY, I DON'T REALLY KNOW MUCH ABOUT ALL THAT DARKNESS STUFF, Y'KNOW?
HAHAHA
LIKE HELL I'D KNOW!
THEN WHY WERE YOU SO FULL OF CONFIDENCE EARLIER?
I WAS BORN FULL OF CONFIDENCE.
GAAAH!
WELL, I'LL LEAVE THE REST TO YOU. I'M NO GOOD WITH CRYING KIDS OR DOGS.
MISTER!
しゅたっ
DASH
どずーん
GLOOM
ARGH.
……

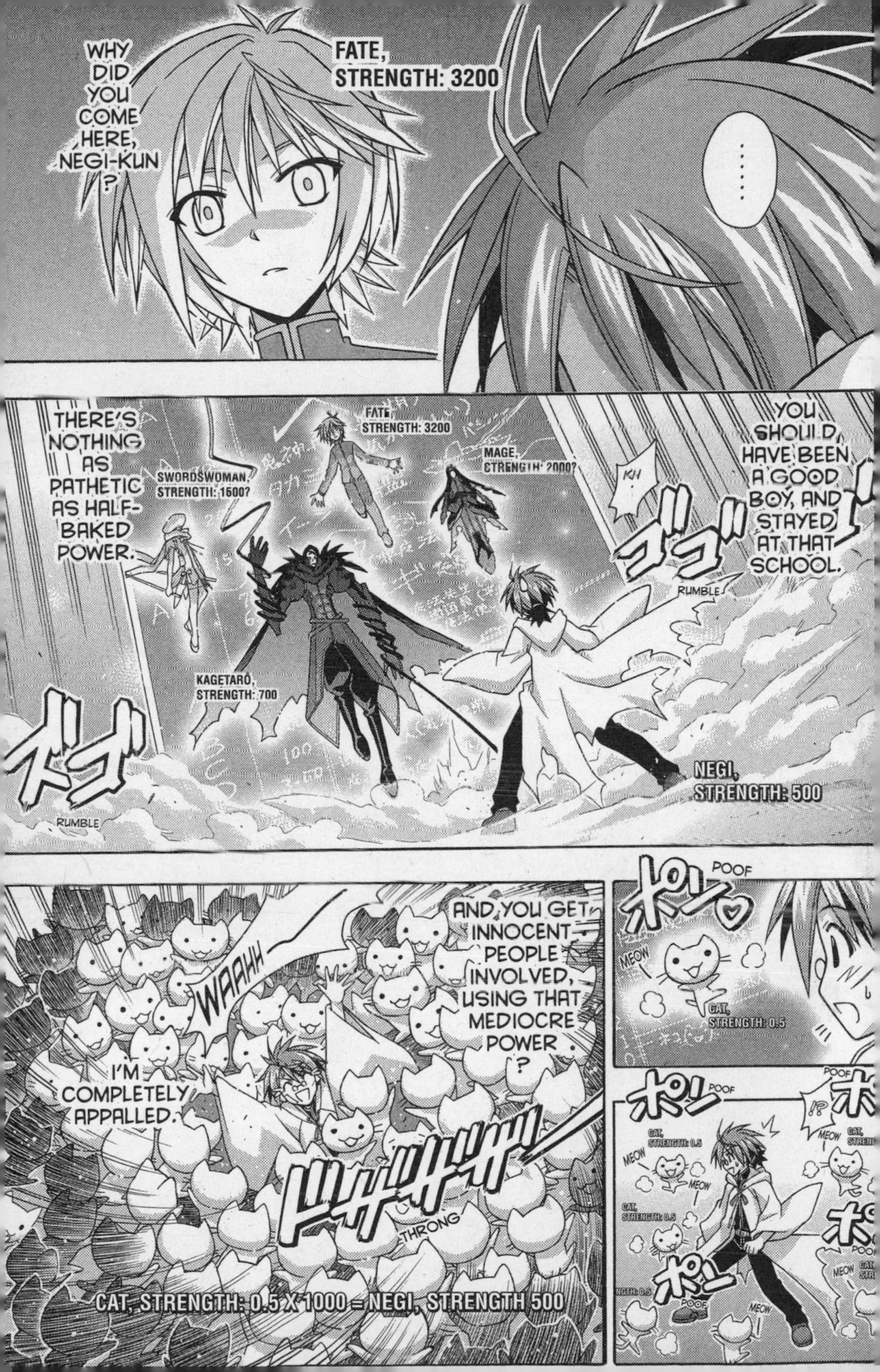
……
FATE, STRENGTH: 3200
WHY DID YOU COME HERE, NEGI-KUN?
YOU SHOULD HAVE BEEN A GOOD BOY, AND STAYED AT THAT SCHOOL.
KU
ゴゴ
RUMBLE
FATE STRENGTH: 3200
MAGE, STRENGTH: 2000?
SWORDSWOMAN, STRENGTH: 1500?
THERE'S NOTHING AS PATHETIC AS HALF-BAKED POWER.
KAGETARO, STRENGTH: 700
NEGI, STRENGTH: 500
ズゴ
RUMBLE
ポン
POOF
MEOW
CAT, STRENGTH: 0.5
ポン
POOF
!?
MEOW
CAT, STRENGTH: 0.5
MEOW
MEOW
CAT, STRENGTH: 0.5
ポン
POOF
MEOW
AND YOU GET INNOCENT PEOPLE INVOLVED, USING THAT MEDIOCRE POWER?
WAAHH
I'M COMPLETELY APPALLED.
ドザザザ
THRONG
CAT, STRENGTH: 0.5 X 1000 = NEGI, STRENGTH 500

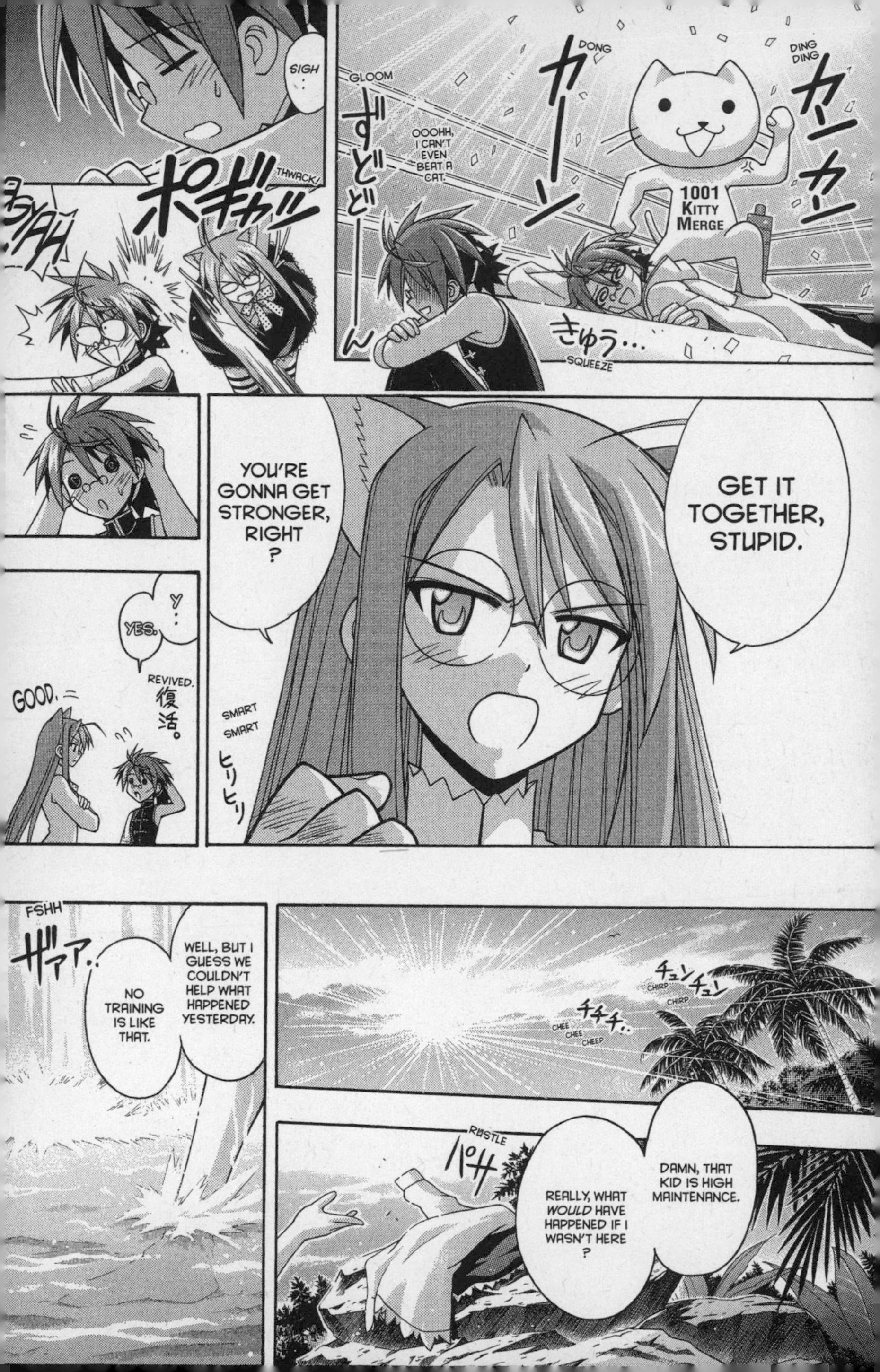
DING DING
カーンカーン
DONG
カーン
1001 KITTY MERGE
GLOOM
ずどーん
OOOHH, I CAN'T EVEN BEAT A CAT.
きゅう…
SQUEEZE
SIGH . .
THWACK!
ポギャッ
YAH
GET IT TOGETHER, STUPID.
YOU'RE GONNA GET STRONGER, RIGHT?
Y . . YES.
REVIVED.
復活。
SMART SMART
ヒリヒリ
GOOD.
チュンチュン
CHIRP CHIRP
チチチ..
CHEE CHEE CHEEP
RUSTLE
パサ
DAMN, THAT KID IS HIGH MAINTENANCE.
REALLY, WHAT *WOULD* HAVE HAPPENED IF I WASN'T HERE?
FSHH
ザァア..
WELL, BUT I GUESS WE COULDN'T HELP WHAT HAPPENED YESTERDAY.
NO TRAINING IS LIKE THAT.

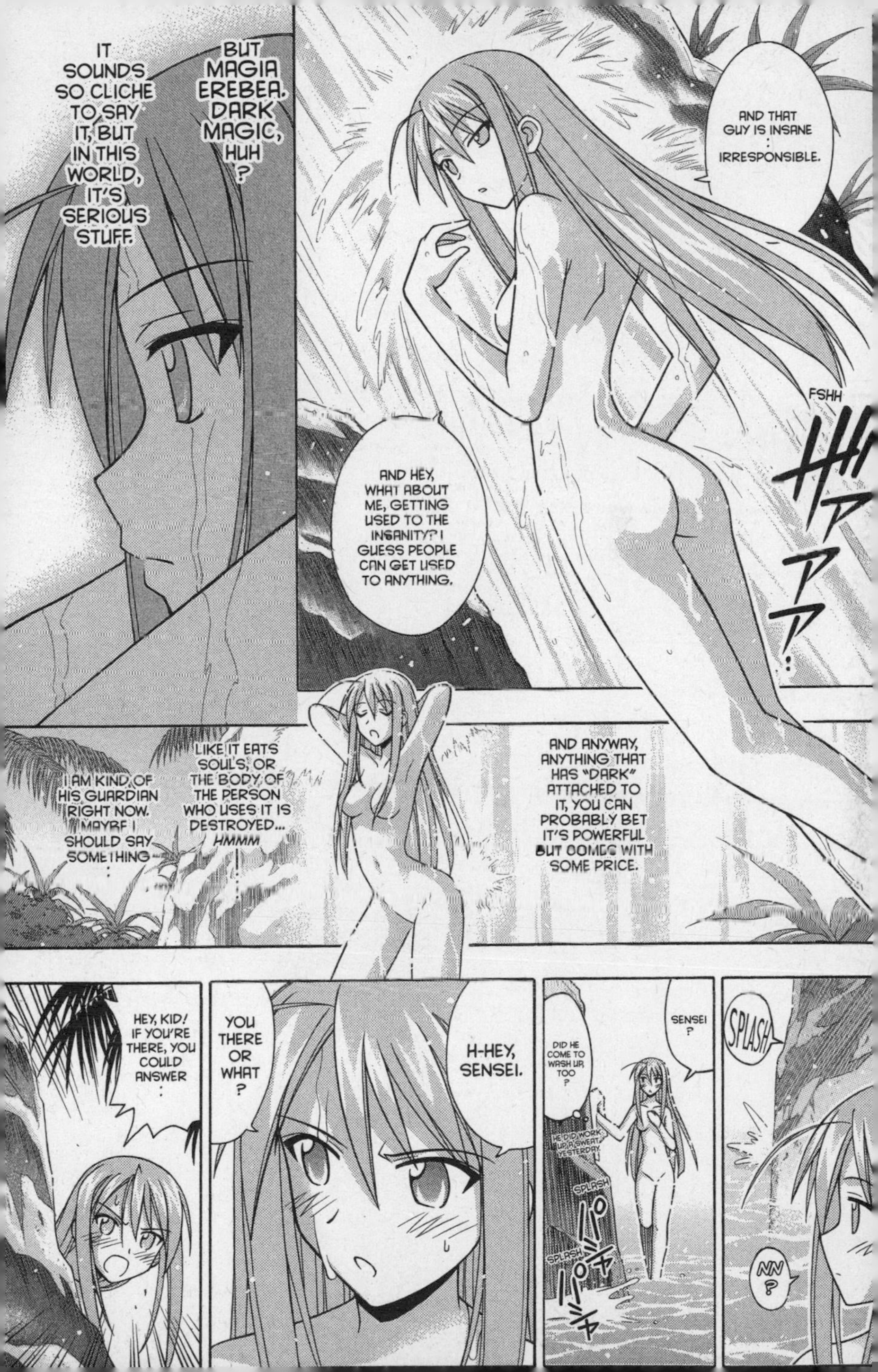
AND THAT GUY IS INSANE : IRRESPONSIBLE.
FSHH
AND HEY, WHAT ABOUT ME, GETTING USED TO THE INSANITY? I GUESS PEOPLE CAN GET USED TO ANYTHING.
BUT MAGIA EREBEA. DARK MAGIC, HUH ?
IT SOUNDS SO CLICHE TO SAY IT, BUT IN THIS WORLD, IT'S SERIOUS STUFF.
AND ANYWAY, ANYTHING THAT HAS "DARK" ATTACHED TO IT, YOU CAN PROBABLY BET IT'S POWERFUL BUT COMES WITH SOME PRICE.
LIKE IT EATS SOULS, OR THE BODY OF THE PERSON WHO USES IT IS DESTROYED... HMMM ......
I AM KIND OF HIS GUARDIAN RIGHT NOW. MAYBE I SHOULD SAY SOMETHING :
SPLASH
NN ?
SENSEI ?
DID HE COME TO WASH UP, TOO ?
HE DID WORK UP A SWEAT YESTERDAY.
SPLASH
SPLASH
H-HEY, SENSEI.
YOU THERE OR WHAT ?
HEY, KID! IF YOU'RE THERE, YOU COULD ANSWER :

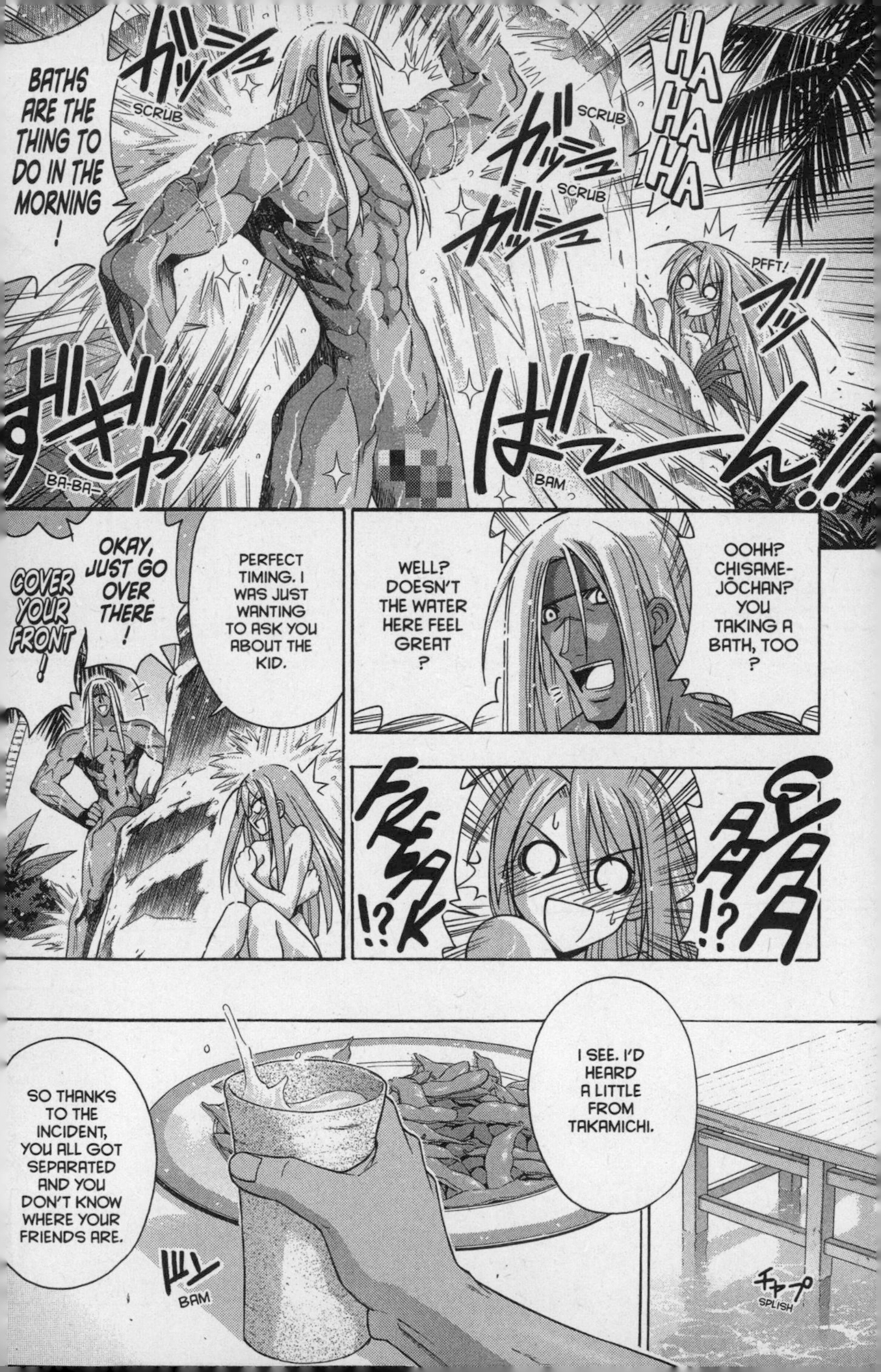
HA HA HA HA
SCRUB
SCRUB
SCRUB
BATHS ARE THE THING TO DO IN THE MORNING!
PFFT!
BAM
BA-BA-
OOHH? CHISAME-JŌCHAN? YOU TAKING A BATH, TOO?
WELL? DOESN'T THE WATER HERE FEEL GREAT?
GAAAA!?
FREAK!?
PERFECT TIMING. I WAS JUST WANTING TO ASK YOU ABOUT THE KID.
OKAY, JUST GO OVER THERE!
COVER YOUR FRONT!
I SEE. I'D HEARD A LITTLE FROM TAKAMICHI.
SPLISH
SO THANKS TO THE INCIDENT, YOU ALL GOT SEPARATED AND YOU DON'T KNOW WHERE YOUR FRIENDS ARE.
BAM

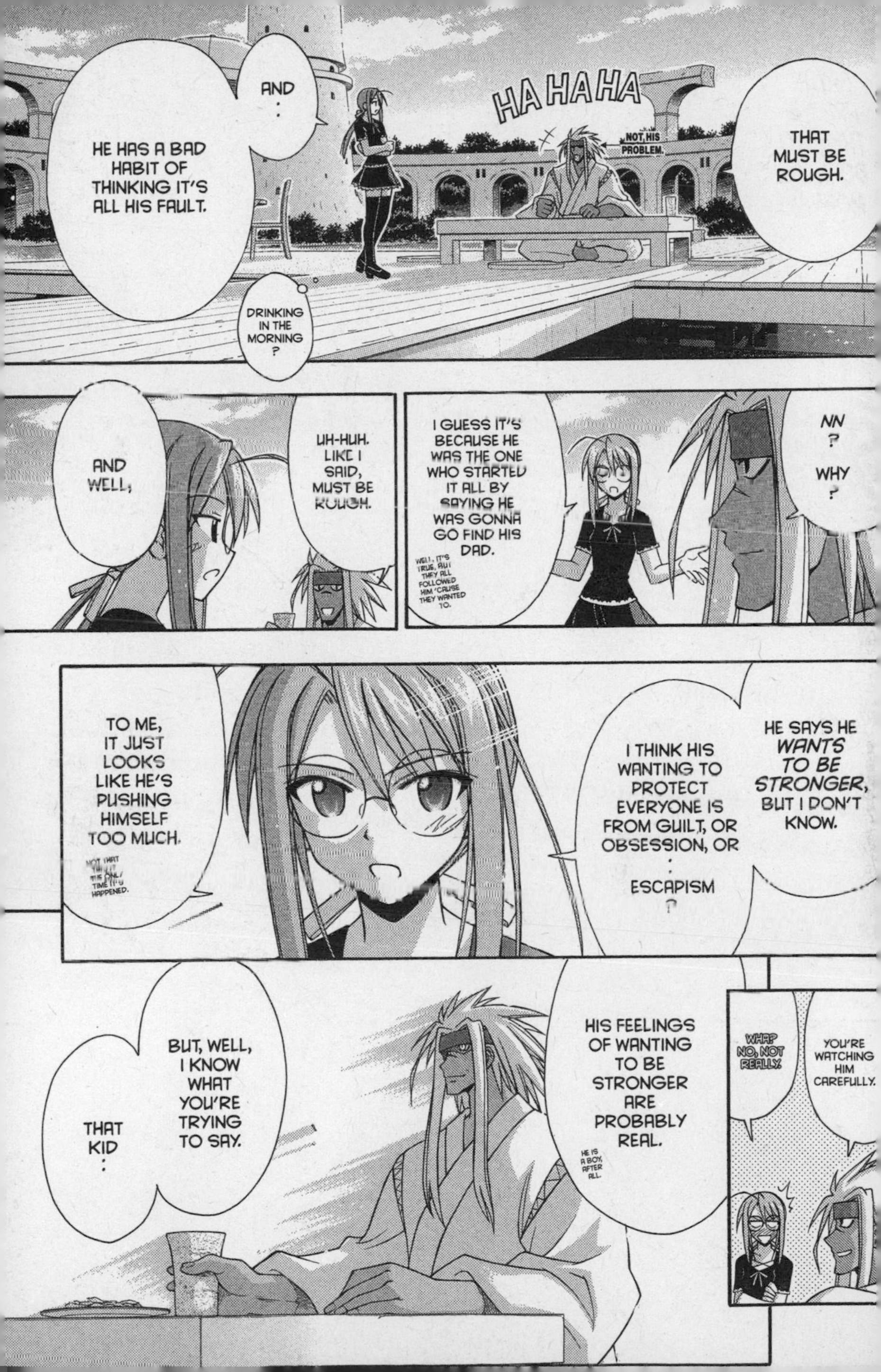
THAT MUST BE ROUGH.
NOT, HIS PROBLEM.
HA HA HA
AND :
HE HAS A BAD HABIT OF THINKING IT'S ALL HIS FAULT.
DRINKING IN THE MORNING ?
NN ? WHY ?
I GUESS IT'S BECAUSE HE WAS THE ONE WHO STARTED IT ALL BY SAYING HE WAS GONNA GO FIND HIS DAD.
WELL, IT'S TRUE, BUT THEY ALL FOLLOWED HIM 'CAUSE THEY WANTED TO.
UH-HUH. LIKE I SAID, MUST BE ROUGH.
AND WELL,
HE SAYS HE WANTS TO BE STRONGER, BUT I DON'T KNOW.
I THINK HIS WANTING TO PROTECT EVERYONE IS FROM GUILT, OR OBSESSION, OR : ESCAPISM ?
TO ME, IT JUST LOOKS LIKE HE'S PUSHING HIMSELF TOO MUCH.
YOU'RE WATCHING HIM CAREFULLY.
WHA? NO, NOT REALLY.
HIS FEELINGS OF WANTING TO BE STRONGER ARE PROBABLY REAL.
HE IS A BOY, AFTER ALL.
BUT, WELL, I KNOW WHAT YOU'RE TRYING TO SAY.
THAT KID :

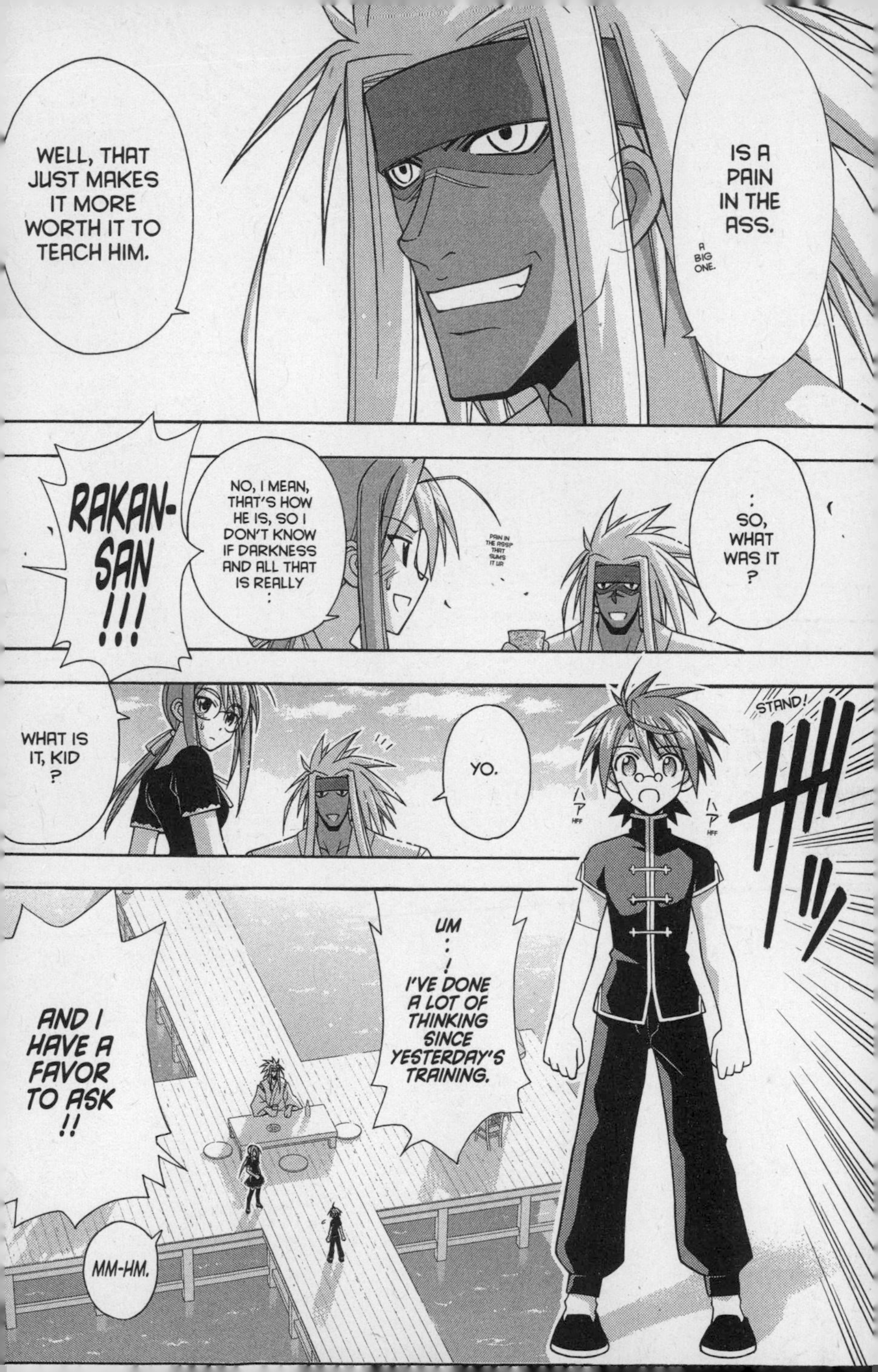

IS A PAIN IN THE ASS.
A BIG ONE.
WELL, THAT JUST MAKES IT MORE WORTH IT TO TEACH HIM.
...SO, WHAT WAS IT?
PAIN IN THE ASS? THAT SUMS IT UP.
NO, I MEAN, THAT'S HOW HE IS, SO I DON'T KNOW IF DARKNESS AND ALL THAT IS REALLY...
RAKAN-SAN!!!
STAND!
ハァ HFF
ハァ HFF
YO.
WHAT IS IT, KID?
UM...! I'VE DONE A LOT OF THINKING SINCE YESTERDAY'S TRAINING.
AND I HAVE A FAVOR TO ASK!!
MM-HM.

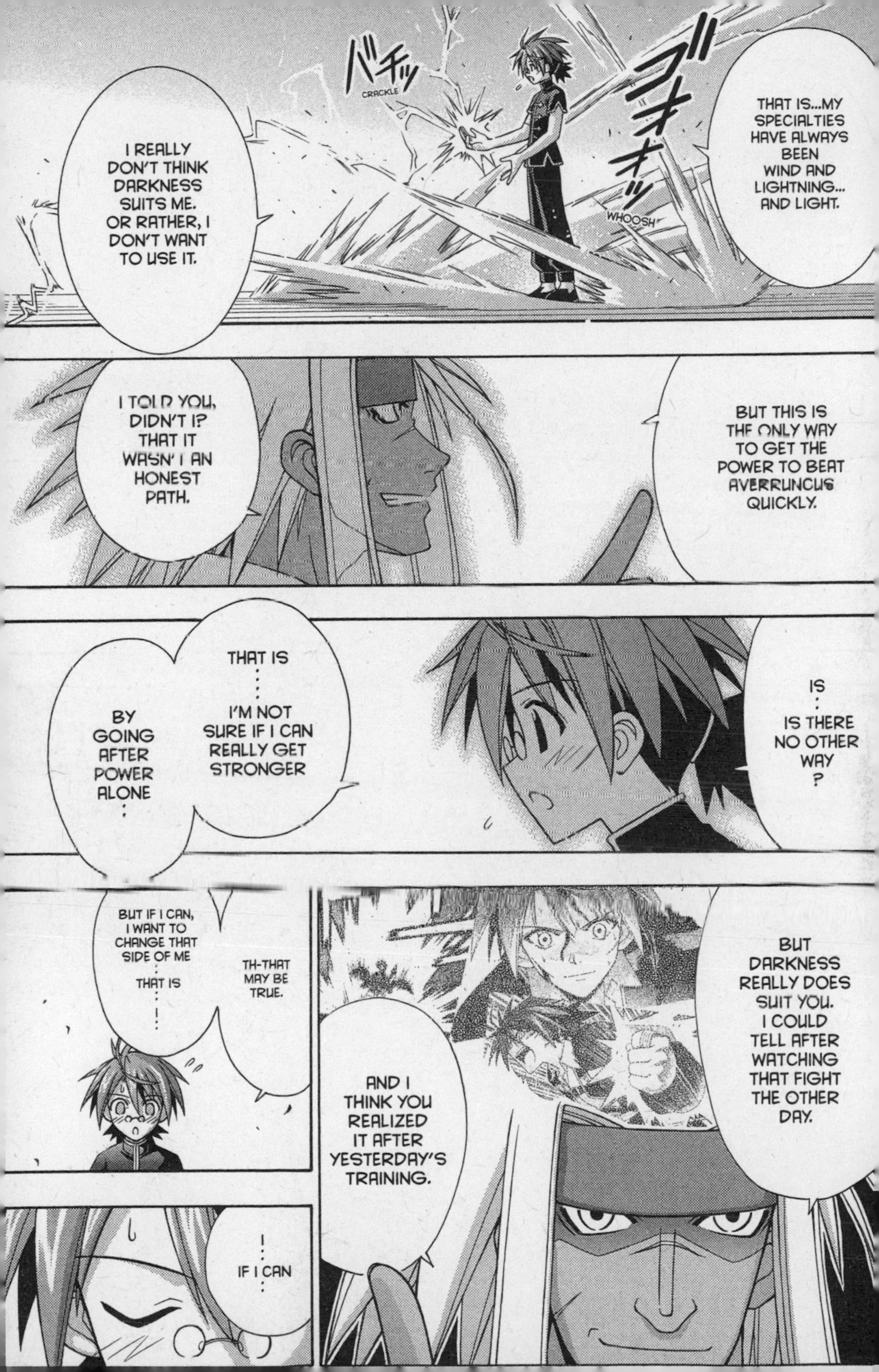
THAT IS...MY SPECIALTIES HAVE ALWAYS BEEN WIND AND LIGHTNING... AND LIGHT.
WHOOSH
CRACKLE
I REALLY DON'T THINK DARKNESS SUITS ME. OR RATHER, I DON'T WANT TO USE IT.
BUT THIS IS THE ONLY WAY TO GET THE POWER TO BEAT AVERRUNCUS QUICKLY.
I TOLD YOU, DIDN'T I? THAT IT WASN'T AN HONEST PATH.
IS... IS THERE NO OTHER WAY?
THAT IS... I'M NOT SURE IF I CAN REALLY GET STRONGER BY GOING AFTER POWER ALONE...
BUT DARKNESS REALLY DOES SUIT YOU. I COULD TELL AFTER WATCHING THAT FIGHT THE OTHER DAY.
AND I THINK YOU REALIZED IT AFTER YESTERDAY'S TRAINING.
TH-THAT MAY BE TRUE.
BUT IF I CAN, I WANT TO CHANGE THAT SIDE OF ME... THAT IS...!
!... IF I CAN...

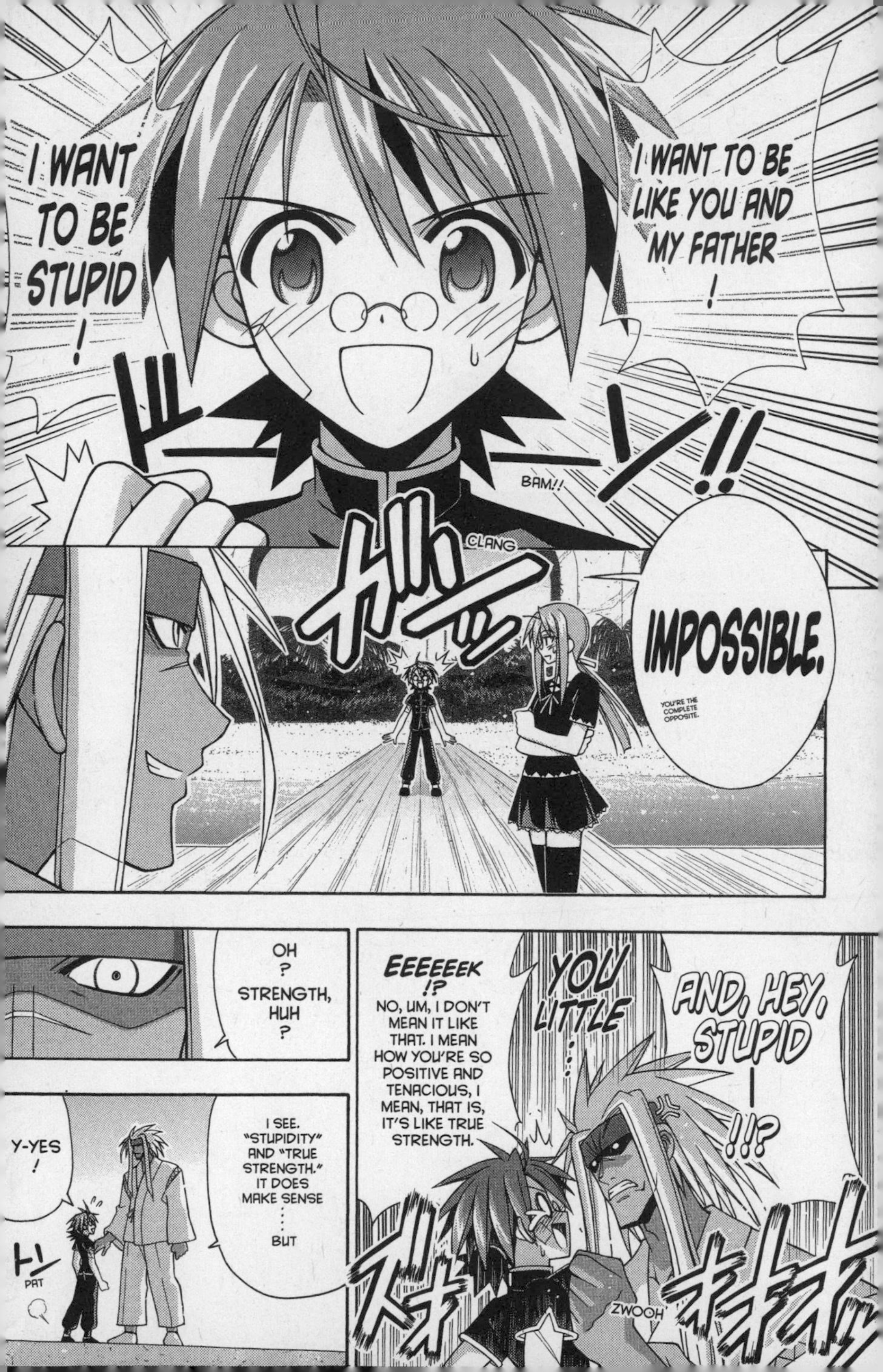
I WANT TO BE LIKE YOU AND MY FATHER!
I WANT TO BE STUPID!
BAM!!
IMPOSSIBLE.
YOU'RE THE COMPLETE OPPOSITE.
CLANG
AND, HEY, STUPID—!!?
YOU LITTLE...
EEEEEEK!? NO, UM, I DON'T MEAN IT LIKE THAT. I MEAN HOW YOU'RE SO POSITIVE AND TENACIOUS, I MEAN, THAT IS, IT'S LIKE TRUE STRENGTH.
ZWOOH
OH? STRENGTH, HUH?
I SEE. "STUPIDITY" AND "TRUE STRENGTH." IT DOES MAKE SENSE.... BUT
Y-YES!
PAT

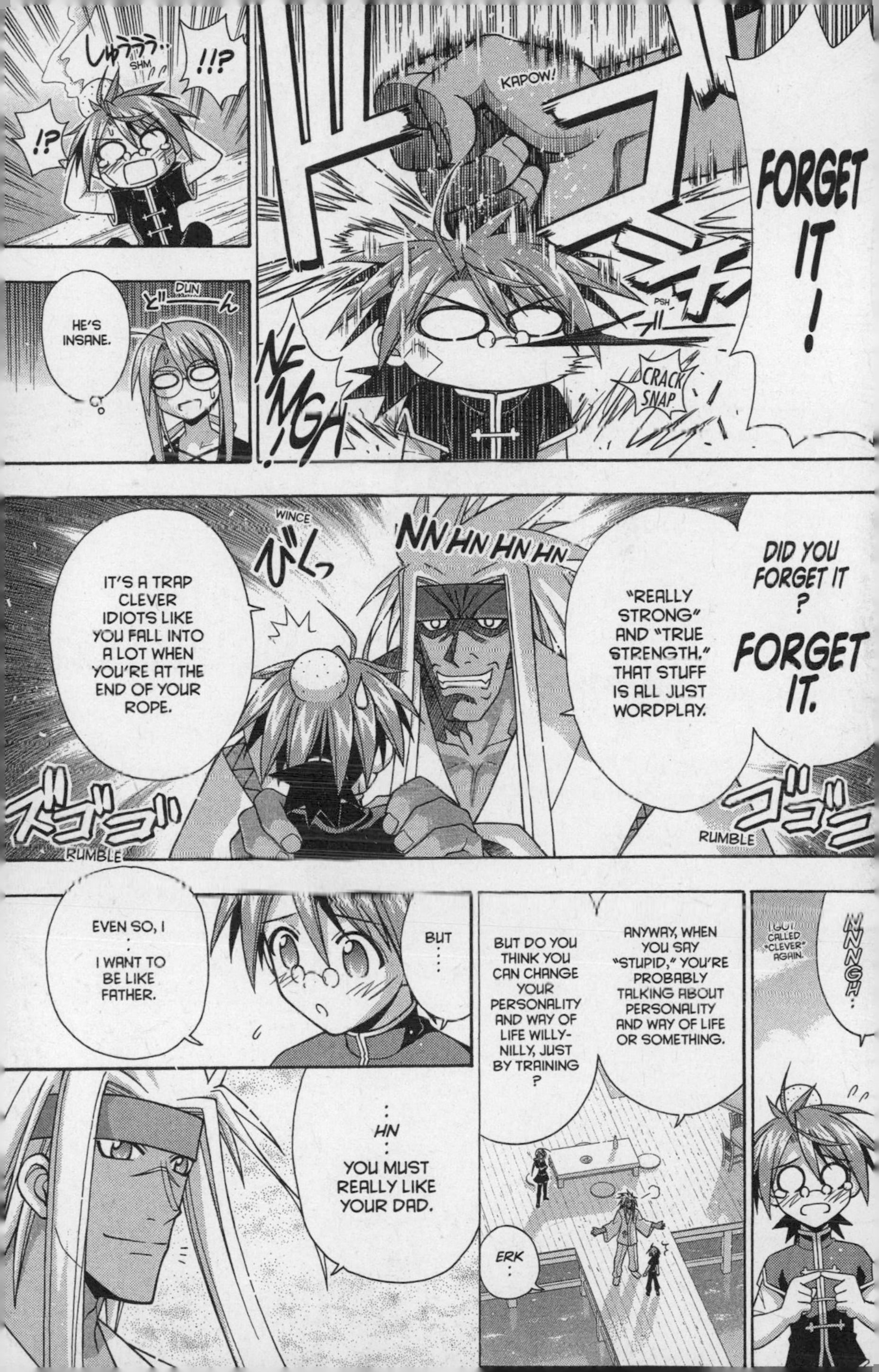
FORGET IT!
KAPOW!
PSH
CRACK SNAP
NNMGH!
SHM
!!?
!?
DUN
HE'S INSANE.
DID YOU FORGET IT? FORGET IT.
"REALLY STRONG" AND "TRUE STRENGTH." THAT STUFF IS ALL JUST WORDPLAY.
NN HN HN HN
WINCE
IT'S A TRAP CLEVER IDIOTS LIKE YOU FALL INTO A LOT WHEN YOU'RE AT THE END OF YOUR ROPE.
RUMBLE
RUMBLE
MNNNGH...
I GOT CALLED "CLEVER" AGAIN.
ANYWAY, WHEN YOU SAY "STUPID," YOU'RE PROBABLY TALKING ABOUT PERSONALITY AND WAY OF LIFE OR SOMETHING.
BUT DO YOU THINK YOU CAN CHANGE YOUR PERSONALITY AND WAY OF LIFE WILLY-NILLY, JUST BY TRAINING?
ERK...
BUT...
EVEN SO, I... I WANT TO BE LIKE FATHER.
...HN...
YOU MUST REALLY LIKE YOUR DAD.

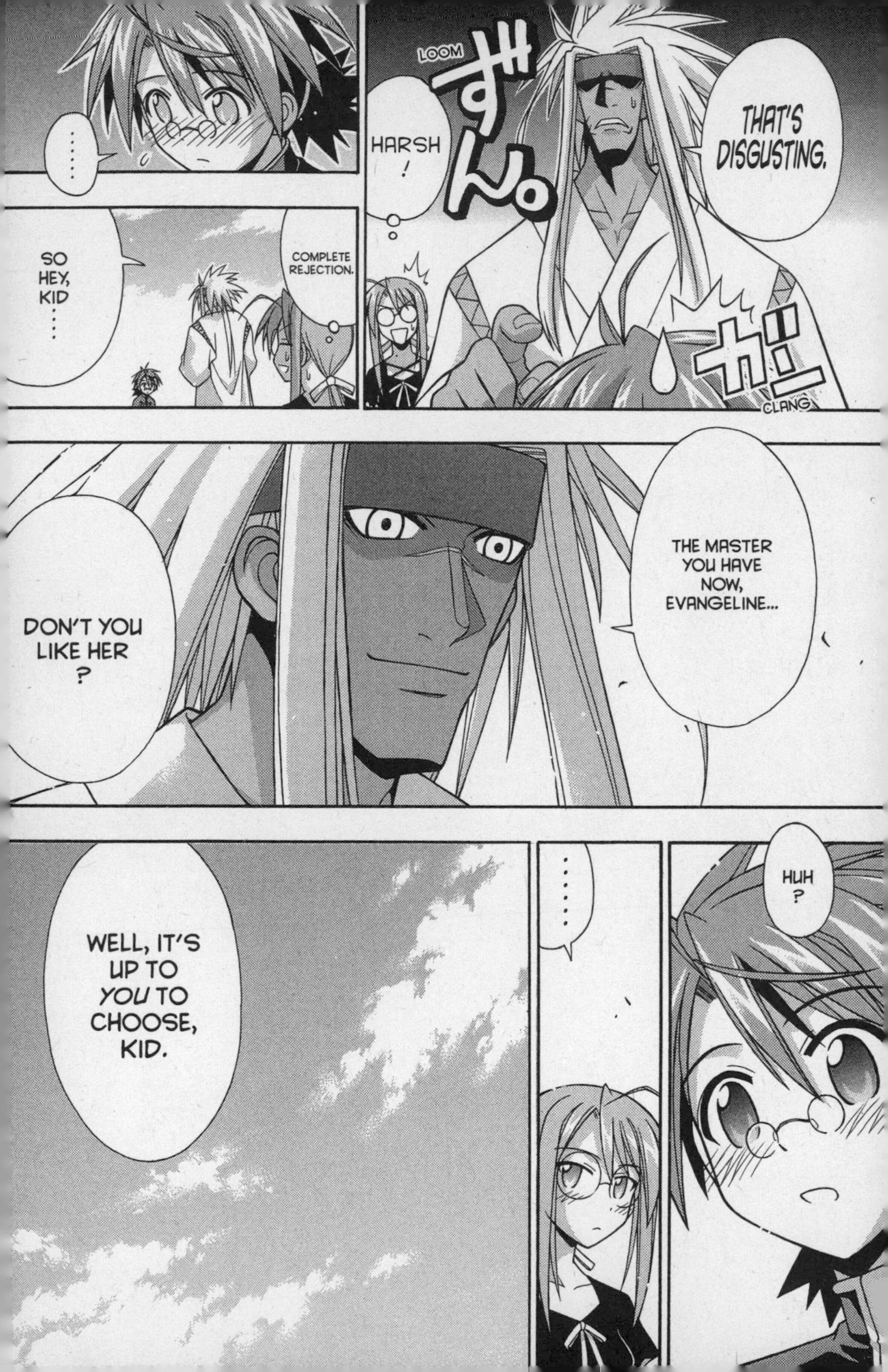

THAT'S DISGUSTING.
ずん。
LOOM
HARSH!
カン
CLANG
......
COMPLETE REJECTION.
SO HEY, KID....
THE MASTER YOU HAVE NOW, EVANGELINE...
DON'T YOU LIKE HER?
HUH?
......
WELL, IT'S UP TO *YOU* TO CHOOSE, KID.

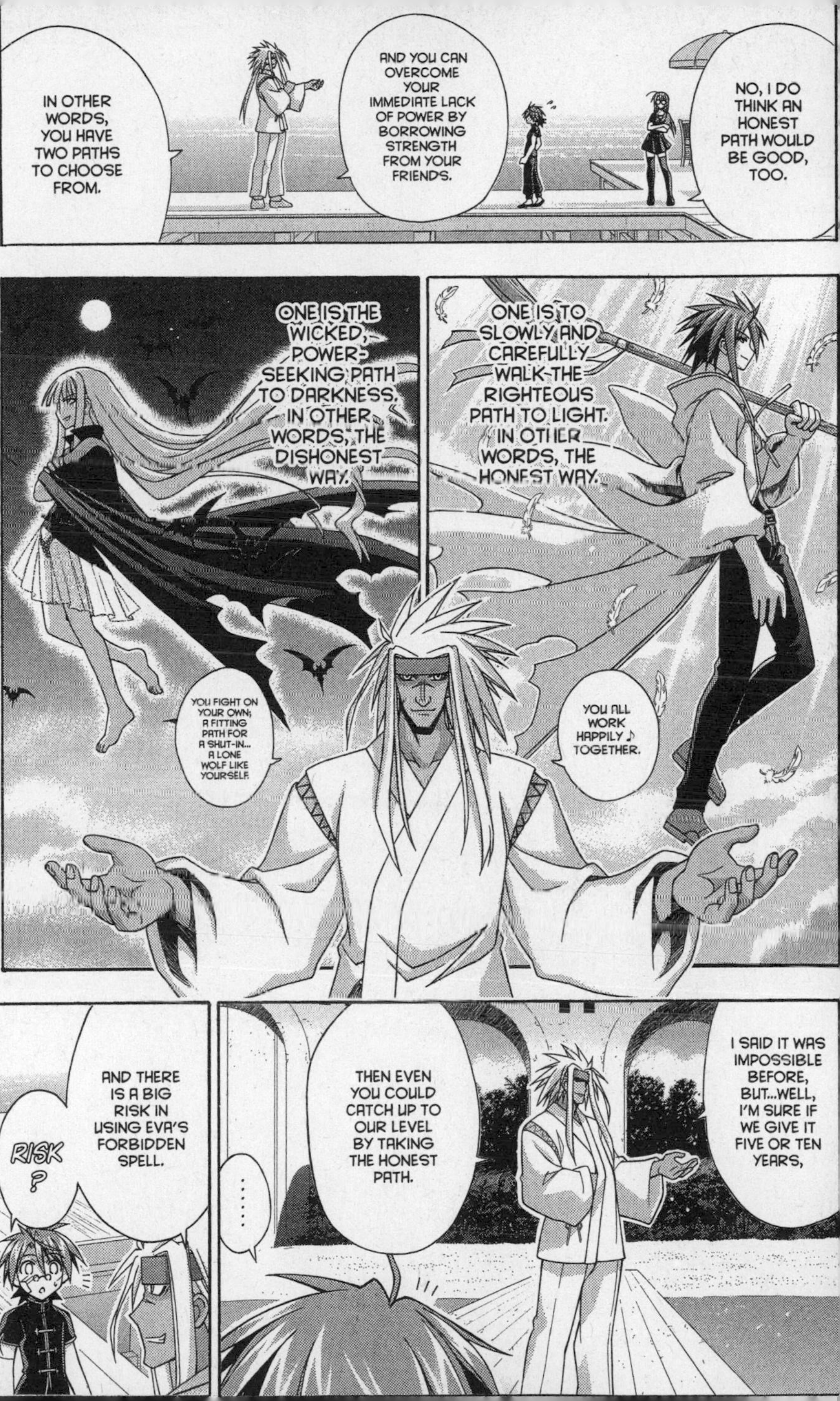
NO, I DO THINK AN HONEST PATH WOULD BE GOOD, TOO.
AND YOU CAN OVERCOME YOUR IMMEDIATE LACK OF POWER BY BORROWING STRENGTH FROM YOUR FRIENDS.
IN OTHER WORDS, YOU HAVE TWO PATHS TO CHOOSE FROM.
ONE IS TO SLOWLY AND CAREFULLY WALK THE RIGHTEOUS PATH TO LIGHT. IN OTHER WORDS, THE HONEST WAY.
ONE IS THE WICKED, POWER-SEEKING PATH TO DARKNESS. IN OTHER WORDS, THE DISHONEST WAY.
YOU ALL WORK HAPPILY ♪ TOGETHER.
YOU FIGHT ON YOUR OWN; A FITTING PATH FOR A SHUT-IN... A LONE WOLF LIKE YOURSELF.
I SAID IT WAS IMPOSSIBLE BEFORE, BUT...WELL, I'M SURE IF WE GIVE IT FIVE OR TEN YEARS,
THEN EVEN YOU COULD CATCH UP TO OUR LEVEL BY TAKING THE HONEST PATH.
......
AND THERE IS A BIG RISK IN USING EVA'S FORBIDDEN SPELL.
RISK?

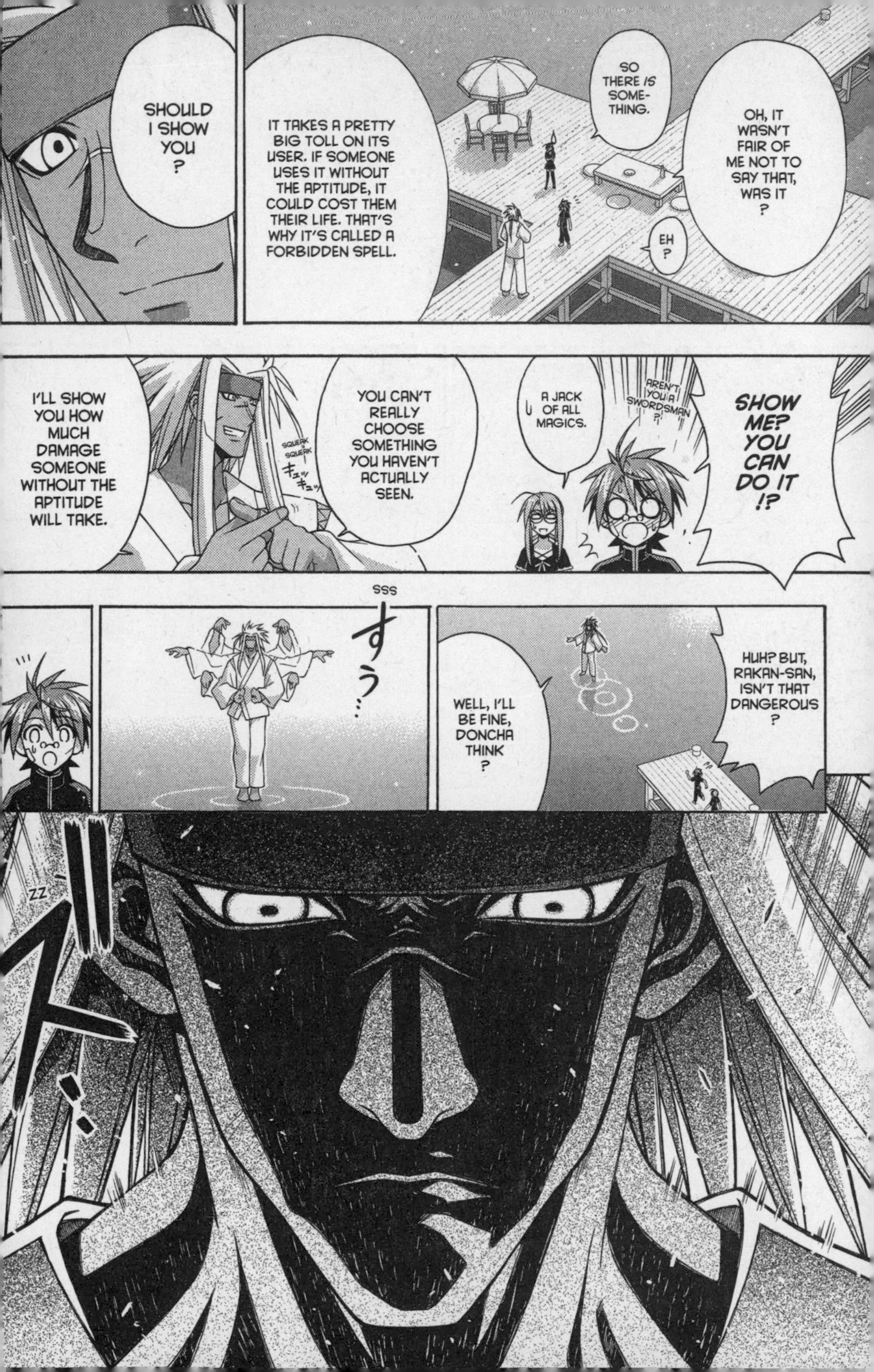
OH, IT WASN'T FAIR OF ME NOT TO SAY THAT, WAS IT?
SO THERE IS SOME-THING.
EH?
IT TAKES A PRETTY BIG TOLL ON ITS USER. IF SOMEONE USES IT WITHOUT THE APTITUDE, IT COULD COST THEM THEIR LIFE. THAT'S WHY IT'S CALLED A FORBIDDEN SPELL.
SHOULD I SHOW YOU?
SHOW ME? YOU CAN DO IT!?
AREN'T YOU A SWORDSMAN?
A JACK OF ALL MAGICS.
YOU CAN'T REALLY CHOOSE SOMETHING YOU HAVEN'T ACTUALLY SEEN.
SQUEAK SQUEAK
キュッキュッ
I'LL SHOW YOU HOW MUCH DAMAGE SOMEONE WITHOUT THE APTITUDE WILL TAKE.
HUH? BUT, RAKAN-SAN, ISN'T THAT DANGEROUS?
WELL, I'LL BE FINE, DONCHA THINK?
SSS
すぅ…
ZZ

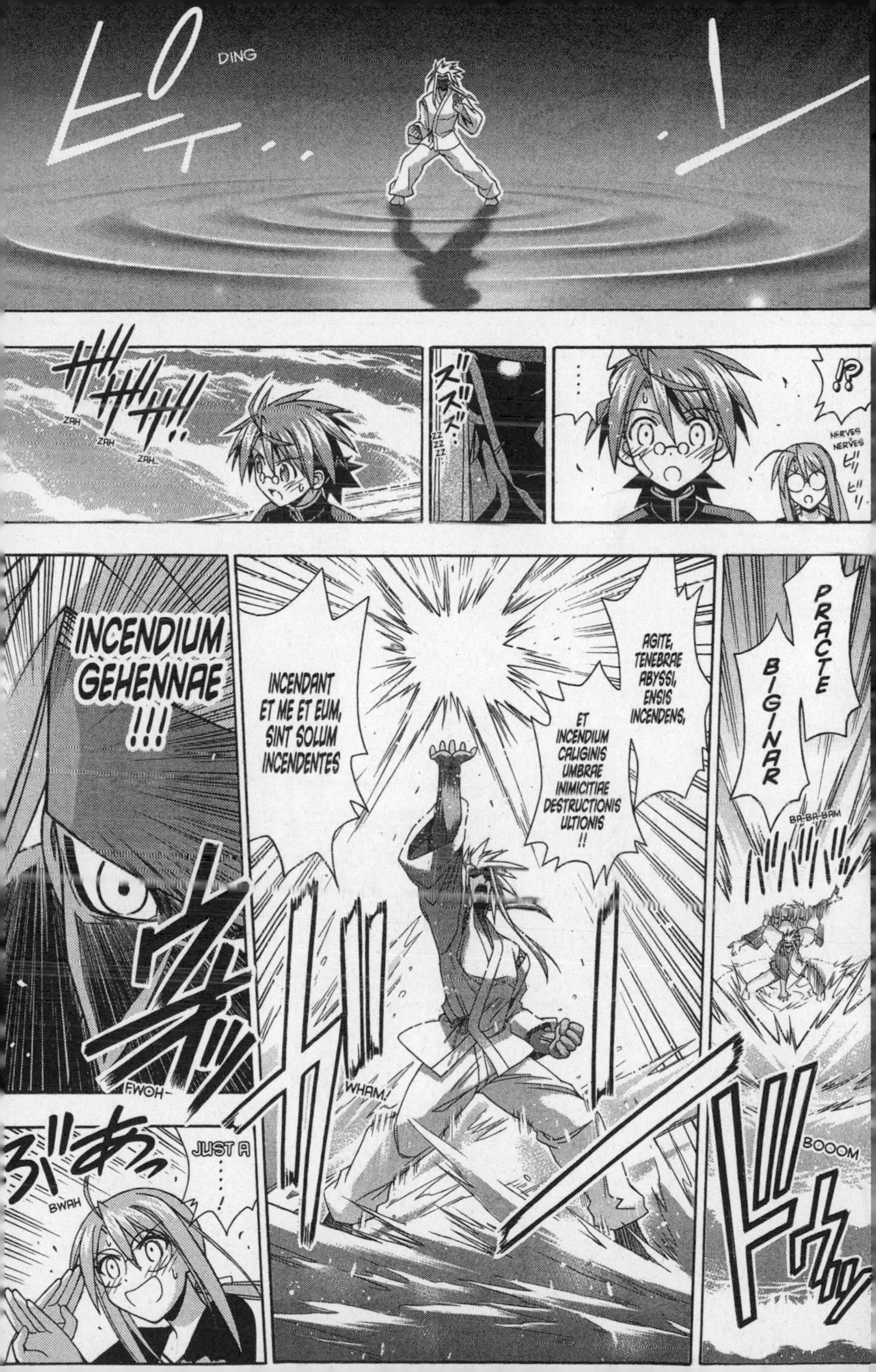

DING
!?
NERVES NERVES
ZZ ZZ ZZ
ZAH ZAH ZAH..
PRACTE BIGINAR
BA-BA-BAM
AGITE, TENEBRAE ABYSSI, ENSIS INCENDENS,
ET INCENDIUM CALIGINIS UMBRAE INIMICITIAE DESTRUCTIONIS ULTIONIS !!
INCENDANT ET ME ET EUM, SINT SOLUM INCENDENTES
WHAM!
BOOOM
INCENDIUM GEHENNAE !!!
FWOH
JUST A ......!
BWAH

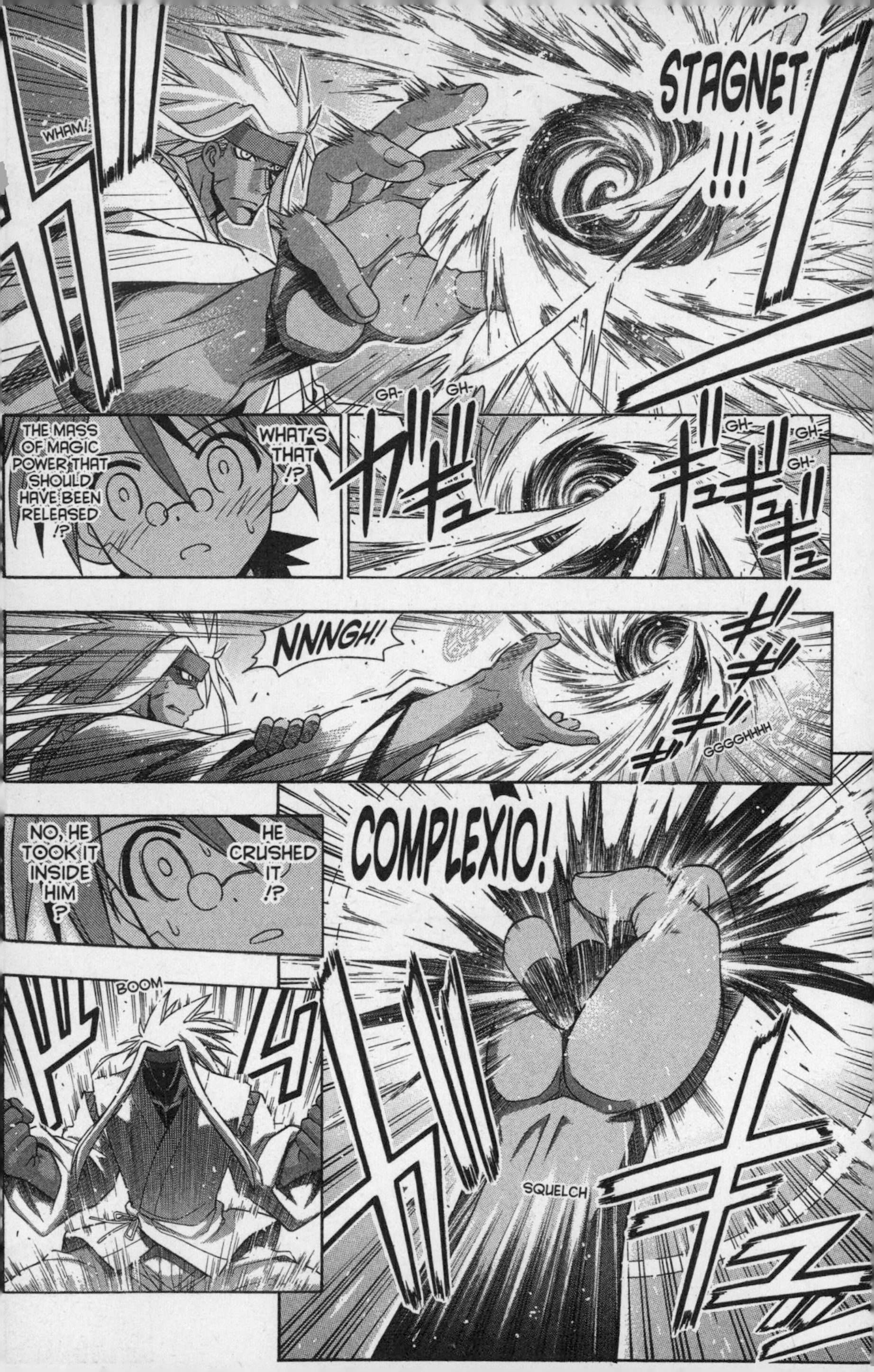
STAGNET !!!
WHAM!
GA-
GH-
GH-
GH-
GH-
WHAT'S THAT !?
THE MASS OF MAGIC POWER THAT SHOULD HAVE BEEN RELEASED !?
GGGGHHHH
NNNGH!
COMPLEXIO!
HE CRUSHED IT !?
NO, HE TOOK IT INSIDE HIM ?
SQUELCH
BOOM

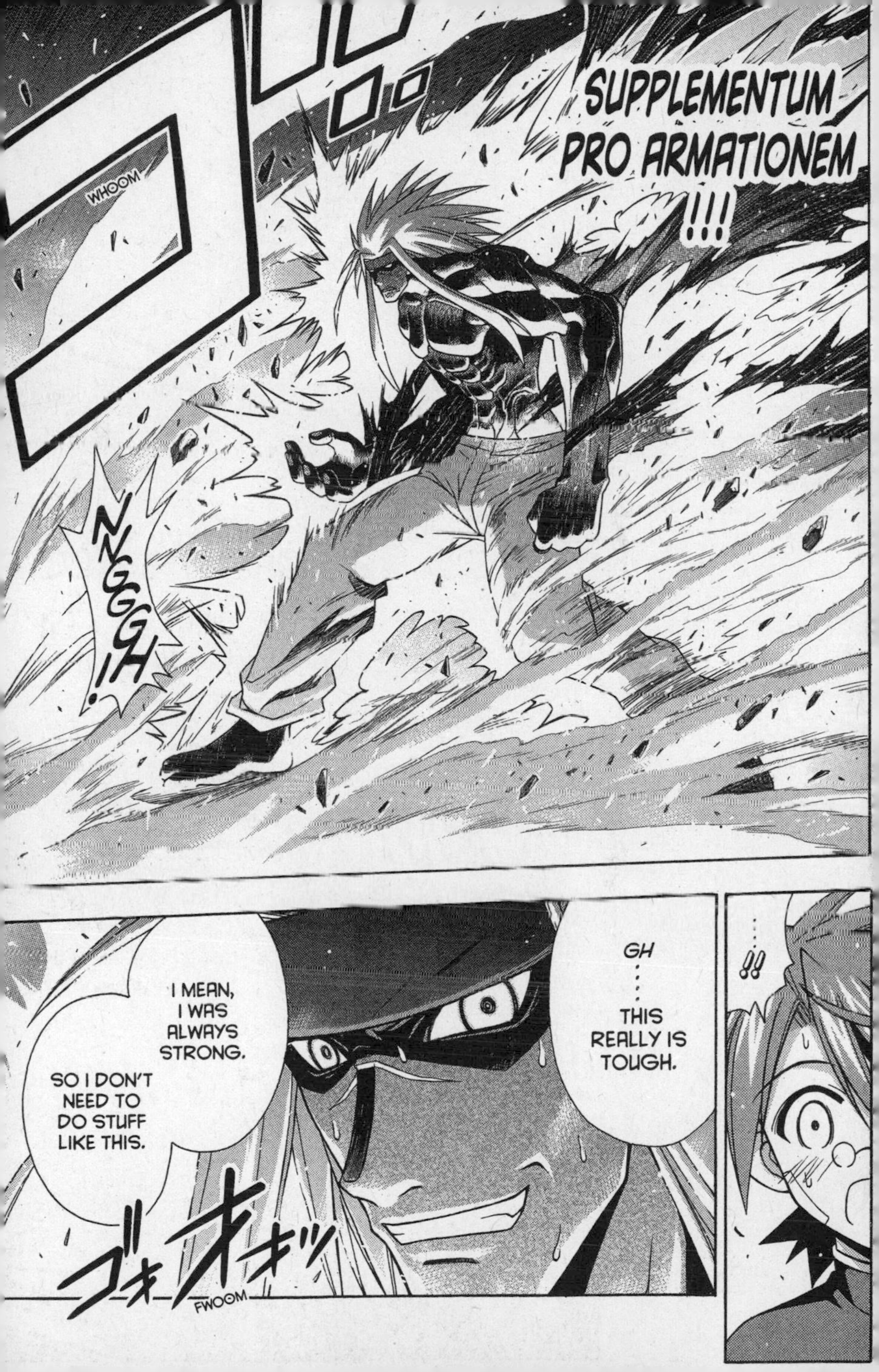
SUPPLEMENTUM PRO ARMATIONEM !!!
WHOOM
NNGGGH!
...!!
GH... THIS REALLY IS TOUGH.
I MEAN, I WAS ALWAYS STRONG.
SO I DON'T NEED TO DO STUFF LIKE THIS.
ゴォオオッ
FWOOM

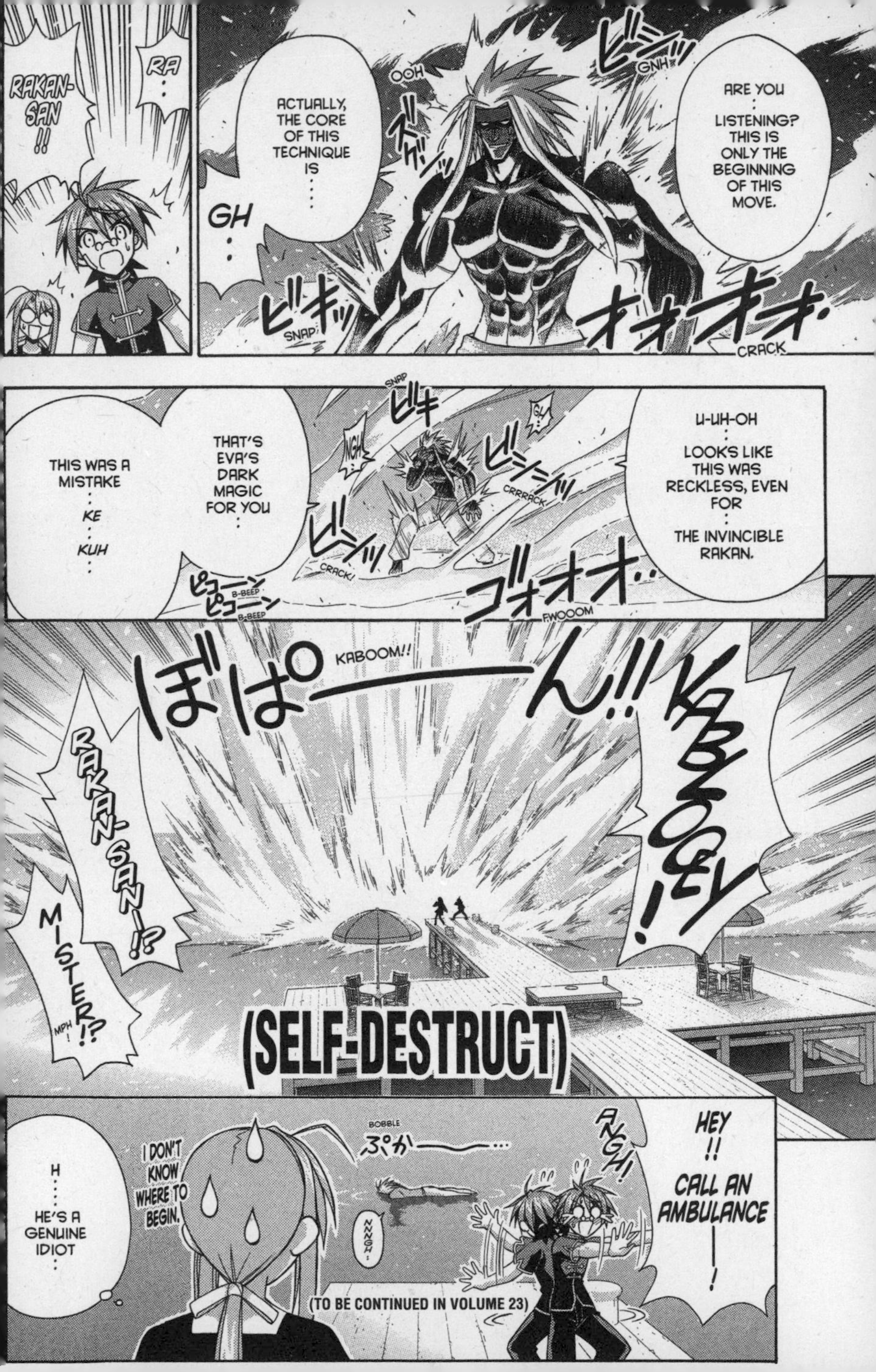
ARE YOU... LISTENING? THIS IS ONLY THE BEGINNING OF THIS MOVE.
GNH
OOH
ACTUALLY, THE CORE OF THIS TECHNIQUE IS......
GH..
SNAP
CRACK
RA...
RAKAN-SAN!!
U-UH-OH... LOOKS LIKE THIS WAS RECKLESS, EVEN FOR... THE INVINCIBLE RAKAN.
SNAP
GU...
NGH
CRRRACK
CRACK!
THAT'S EVA'S DARK MAGIC FOR YOU...
THIS WAS A MISTAKE... KE... KUH...
ピコーン B-BEEP
ピコーン B-BEEP
ゴォオオ FWOOOM
ぼぱーーん!! KABOOM!!
KABLOOEY!
RAKAN-SAN!!?
MISTER!!?
MPH!
(SELF-DESTRUCT)
HEY!! CALL AN AMBULANCE—!
ANGH!
ぷかーー... BOBBLE
NNNGH...
I DON'T KNOW WHERE TO BEGIN.
H.... HE'S A GENUINE IDIOT
(TO BE CONTINUED IN VOLUME 23)

# A Word from the Author

Presenting *Negima!* volume 23! While split up in the Magical World, each of the members of the Negi Party powers up. Meanwhile, our main character Negi...!?

There are still a lot of battles, but we're keeping track of the class-mates that stayed behind, too. (laugh) Because this is *Negima*, with its thirty-one classmates, after all. (^^)

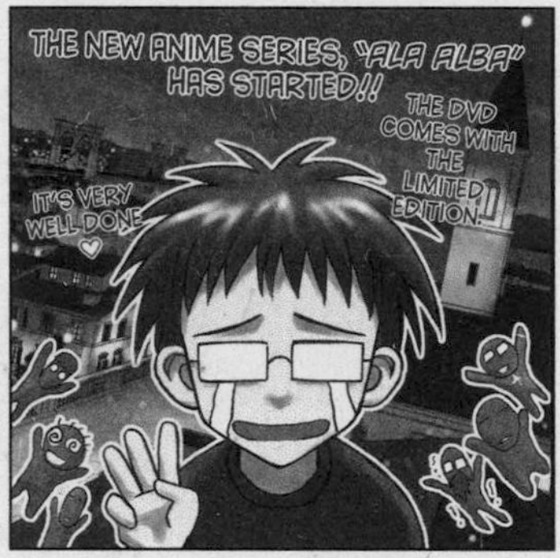
THE NEW ANIME SERIES, "ALA ALBA" HAS STARTED!!
THE DVD COMES WITH THE LIMITED EDITION.
IT'S VERY WELL DONE ♥

The new anime series, completely based on the manga, *Magister Negi Magi ~ Ala Alba ~* has started! DVDs come with the limited editions of volumes 23–25! For details, check my homepage.

Ken Akamatsu
www.ailove.net

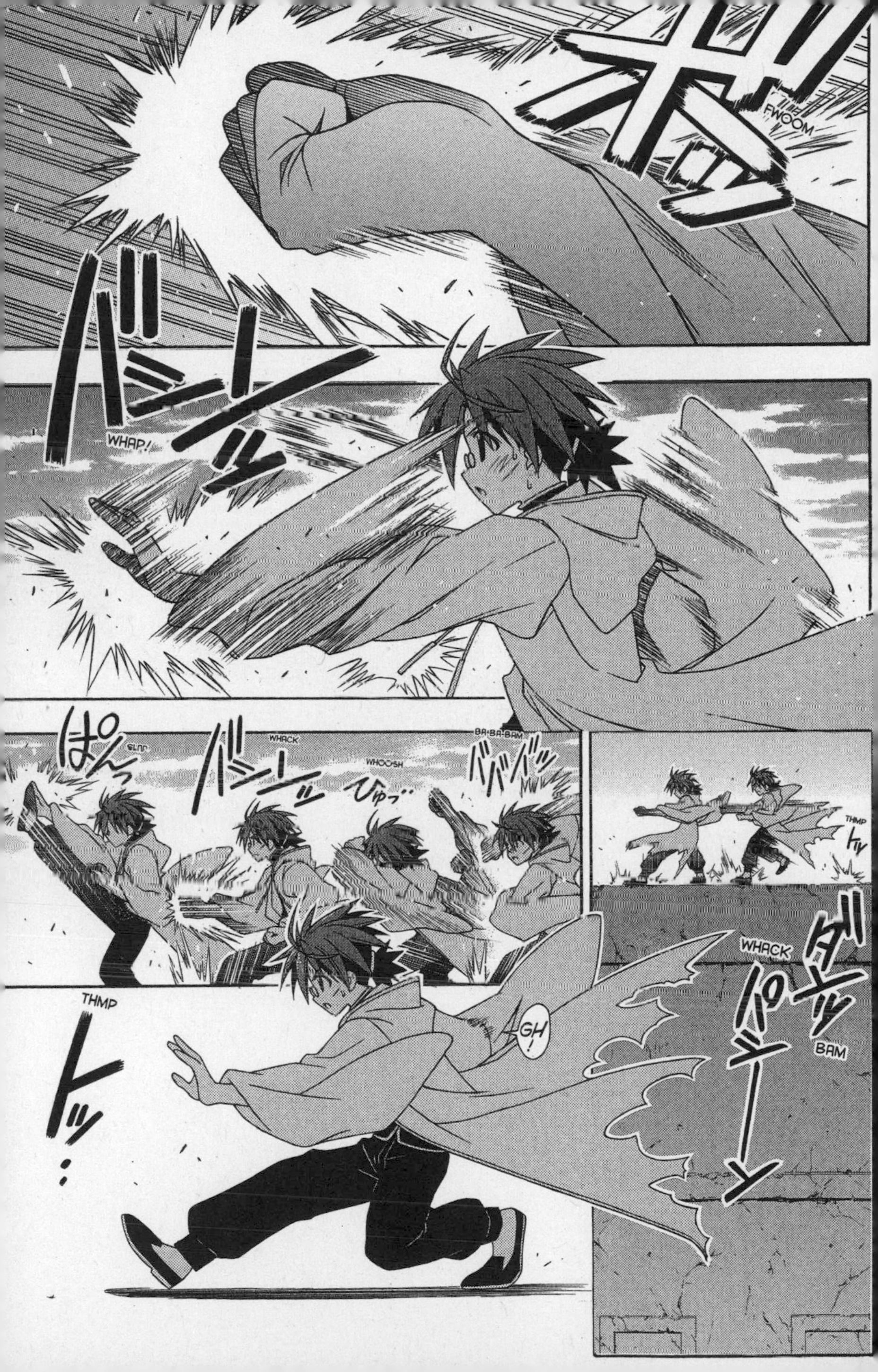
FWOOM
WHAP!
THMP
BA-BA-BAM
WHOOSH
WHACK
BAM
WHACK
GH!
THMP

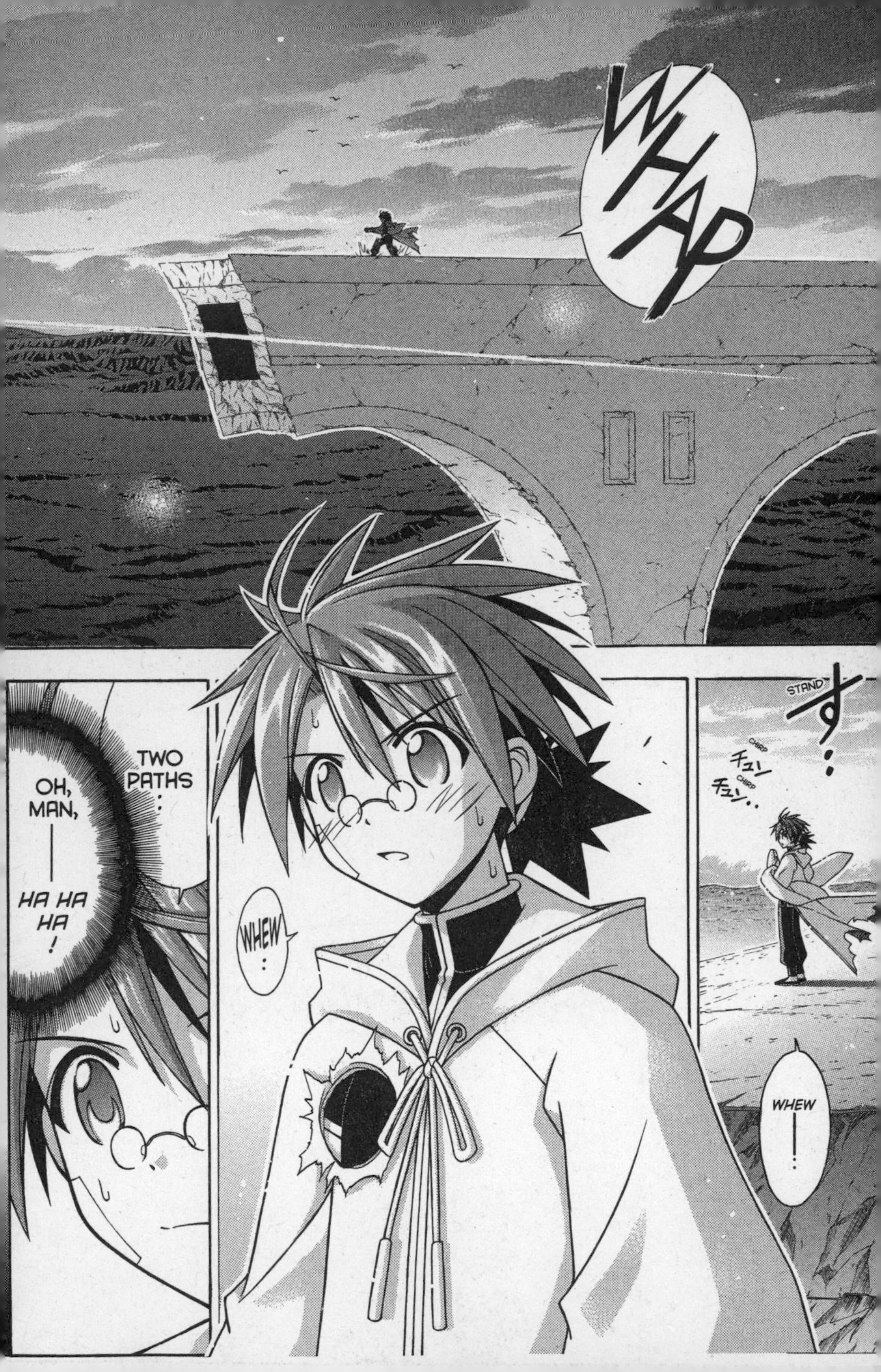
WHAP
STAND す..
CHIRP チュン
CHIRP チュン..
WHEW—!..
WHEW...
TWO PATHS...
OH, MAN, — HA HA HA!

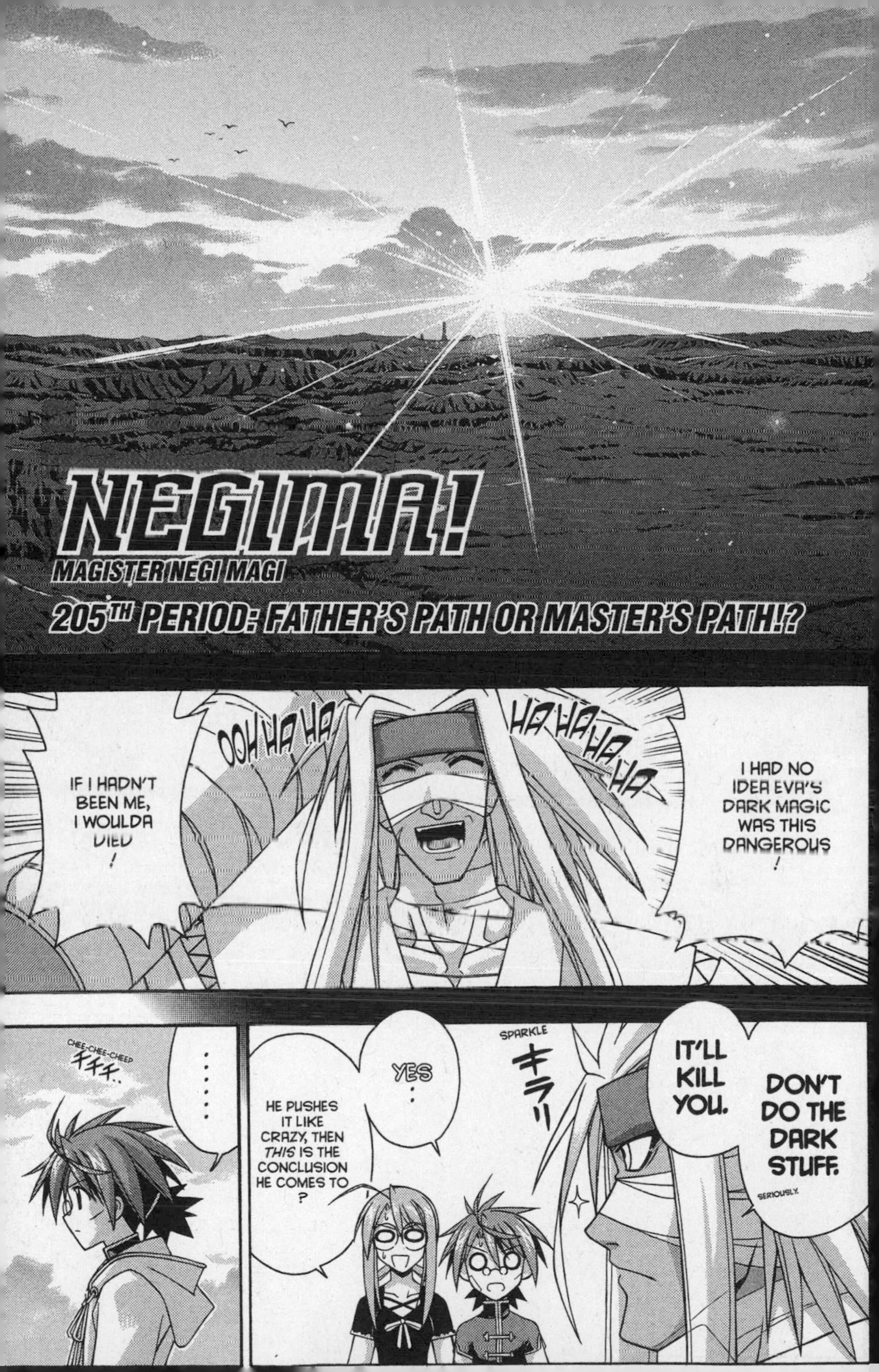
NEGIMA!
MAGISTER NEGI MAGI
205TH PERIOD: FATHER'S PATH OR MASTER'S PATH!?
I HAD NO IDEA EVA'S DARK MAGIC WAS THIS DANGEROUS!
HA HA HA HA HA
OOH HA HA
IF I HADN'T BEEN ME, I WOULDA DIED!
DON'T DO THE DARK STUFF.
IT'LL KILL YOU.
SERIOUSLY.
SPARKLE
YES...
HE PUSHES IT LIKE CRAZY, THEN *THIS* IS THE CONCLUSION HE COMES TO?
......
CHEE-CHEE-CHEEP

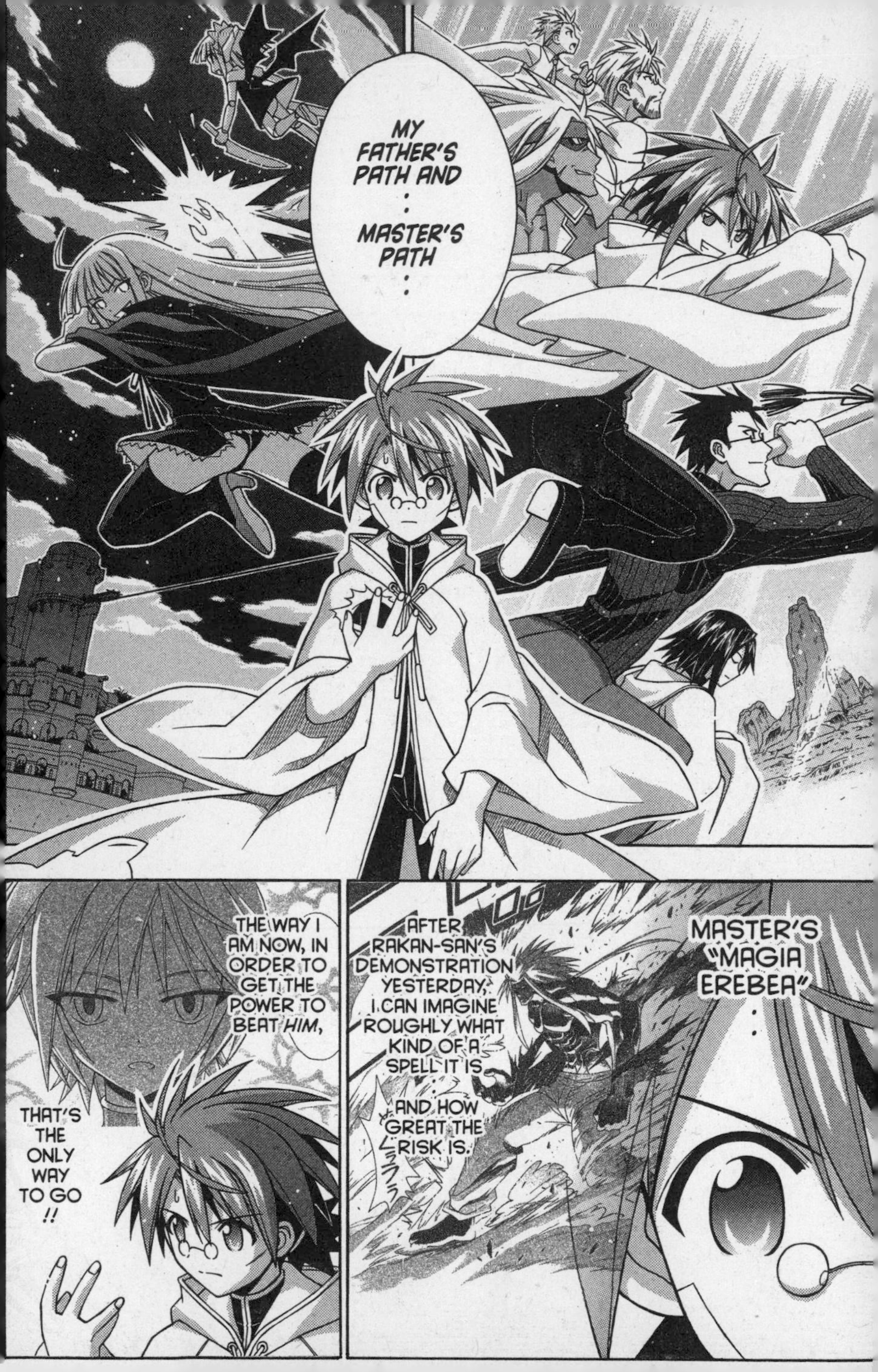
MY FATHER'S PATH AND
: MASTER'S PATH :
MASTER'S "MAGIA EREBEA" :
AFTER RAKAN-SAN'S DEMONSTRATION YESTERDAY, I CAN IMAGINE ROUGHLY WHAT KIND OF A SPELL IT IS
: AND HOW GREAT THE RISK IS.
THE WAY I AM NOW, IN ORDER TO GET THE POWER TO BEAT HIM,
THAT'S THE ONLY WAY TO GO !!

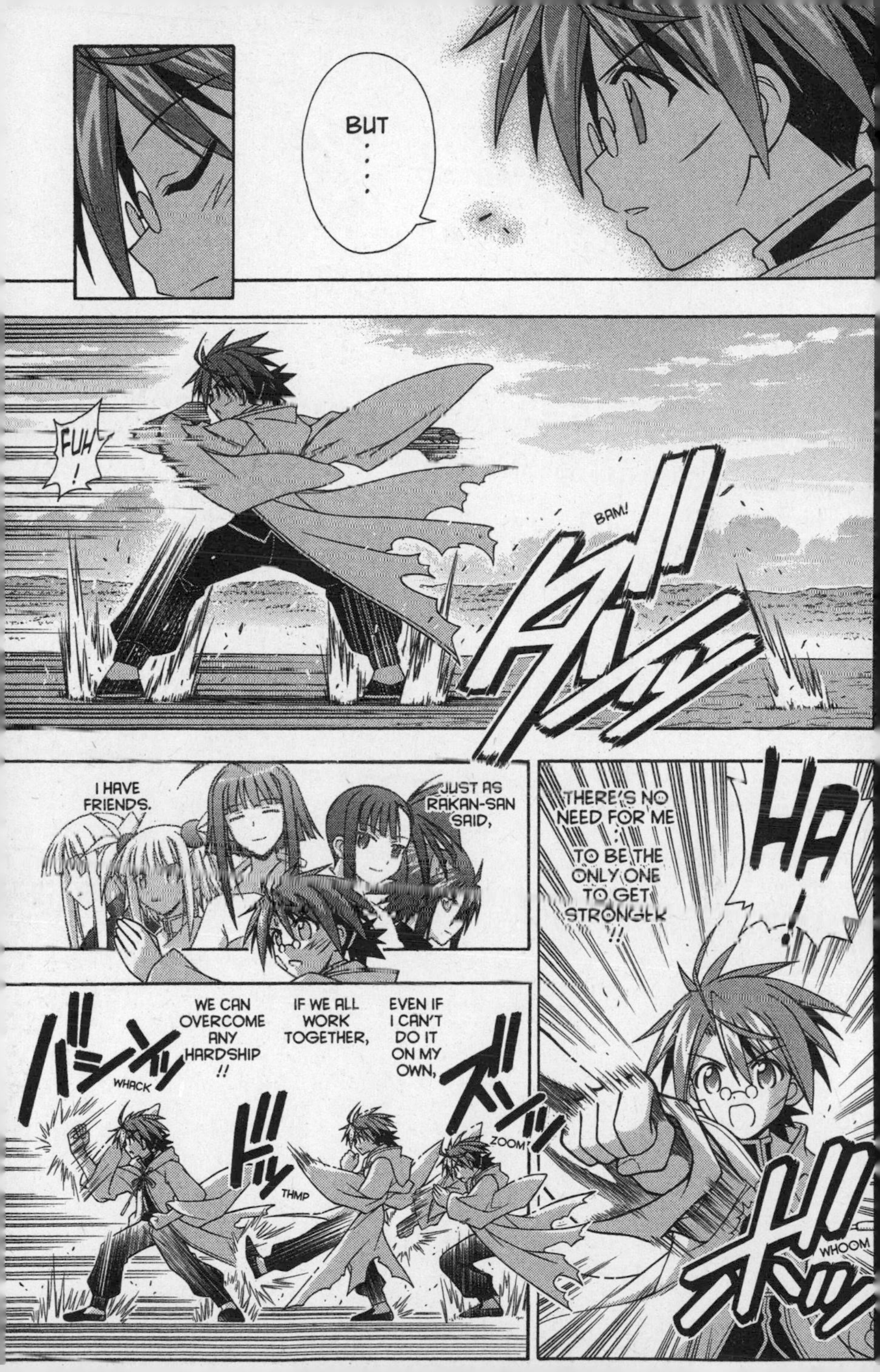
BUT
....
FUH!
BAM!
HA!
THERE'S NO NEED FOR ME TO BE THE ONLY ONE TO GET STRONGER!!
WHOOM
JUST AS RAKAN-SAN SAID,
I HAVE FRIENDS.
EVEN IF I CAN'T DO IT ON MY OWN,
IF WE ALL WORK TOGETHER,
WE CAN OVERCOME ANY HARDSHIP!!
ZOOM
THMP
WHACK

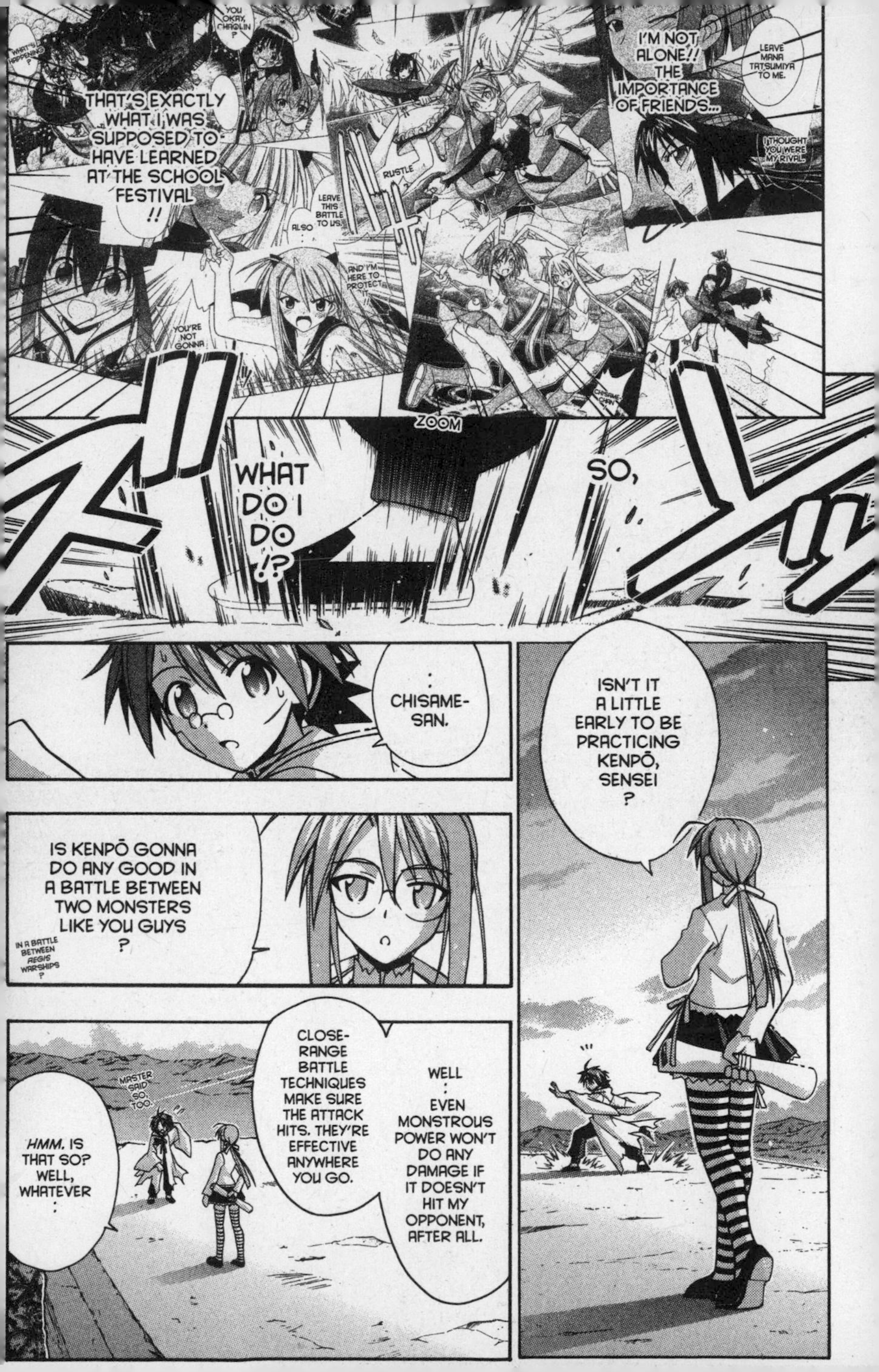
I'M NOT ALONE!! THE IMPORTANCE OF FRIENDS...
LEAVE MANA TATSUMIYA TO ME.
I THOUGHT YOU WERE MY RIVAL.
RUSTLE
CHISAME-CHAN!
LEAVE THIS BATTLE TO US.
ALSO :
AND I'M HERE TO PROTECT IT!!
YOU'RE NOT GONNA
YOU OKAY, CHAOLIN?
WHAT'S HAPPENING?
THAT'S EXACTLY WHAT I WAS SUPPOSED TO HAVE LEARNED AT THE SCHOOL FESTIVAL!!
ZOOM
SO,
WHAT DO I DO!?
ISN'T IT A LITTLE EARLY TO BE PRACTICING KENPŌ, SENSEI?
: CHISAME-SAN.
IS KENPŌ GONNA DO ANY GOOD IN A BATTLE BETWEEN TWO MONSTERS LIKE YOU GUYS?
IN A BATTLE BETWEEN AEGIS WARSHIPS?
WELL : EVEN MONSTROUS POWER WON'T DO ANY DAMAGE IF IT DOESN'T HIT MY OPPONENT, AFTER ALL.
CLOSE-RANGE BATTLE TECHNIQUES MAKE SURE THE ATTACK HITS. THEY'RE EFFECTIVE ANYWHERE YOU GO.
MASTER SAID SO, TOO.
HMM. IS THAT SO? WELL, WHATEVER :

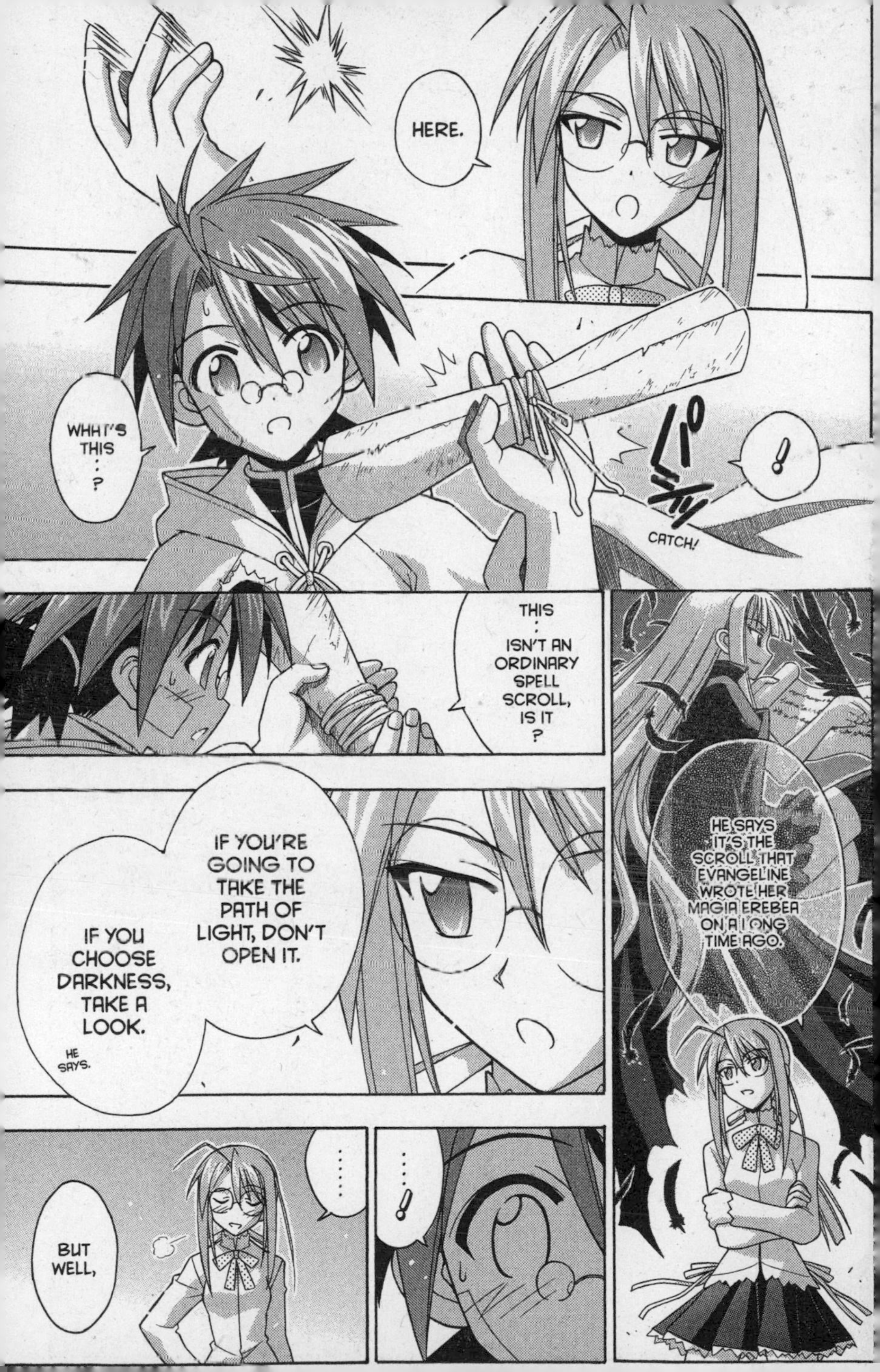
HERE.
!
CATCH!
WHAT'S THIS . . ?
HE SAYS IT'S THE SCROLL THAT EVANGELINE WROTE HER MAGIA EREBEA ON A LONG TIME AGO.
THIS . . ISN'T AN ORDINARY SPELL SCROLL, IS IT ?
IF YOU'RE GOING TO TAKE THE PATH OF LIGHT, DON'T OPEN IT.
IF YOU CHOOSE DARKNESS, TAKE A LOOK.
HE SAYS.
. . . . . . !
. . . . . .
BUT WELL,

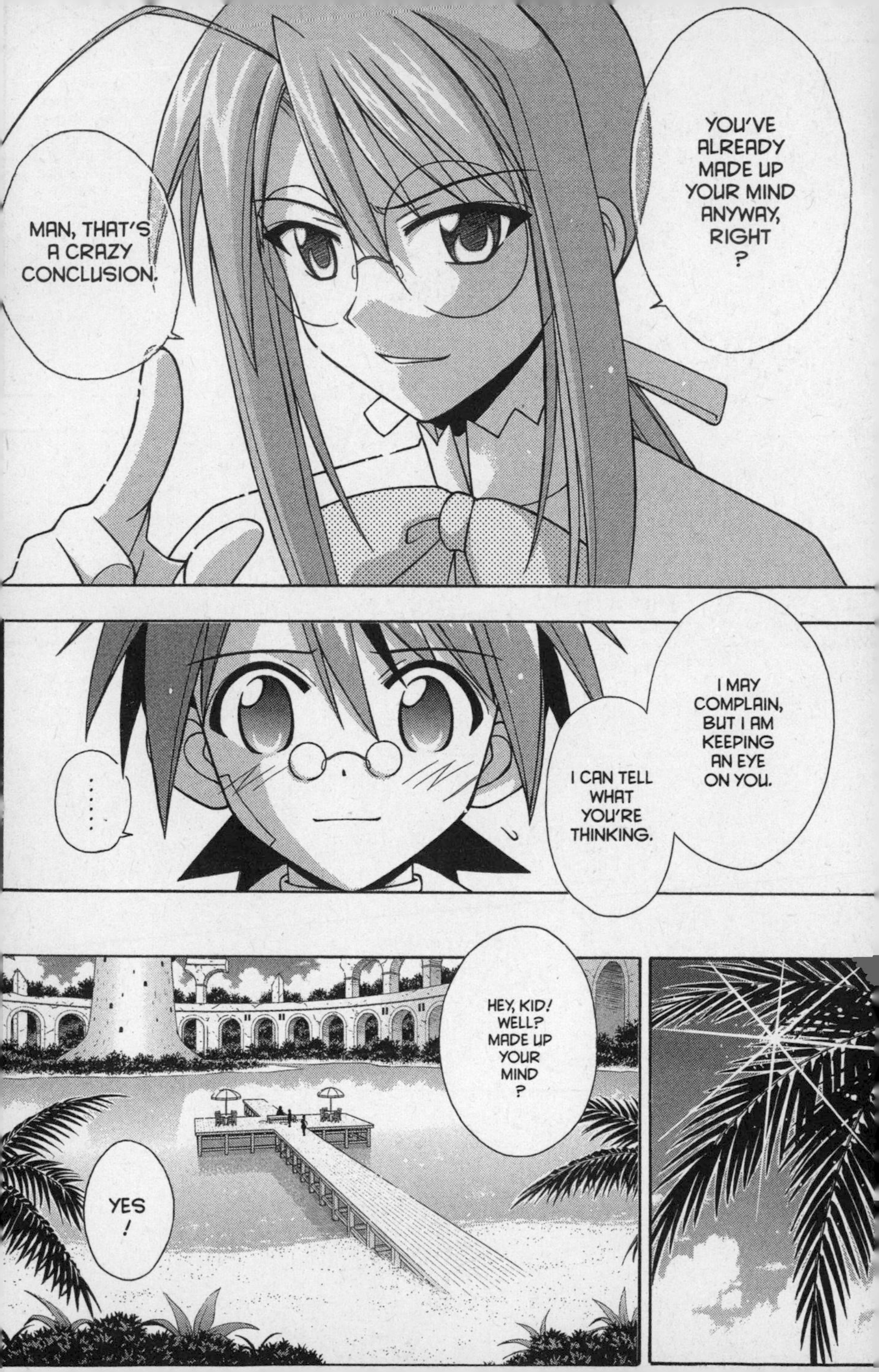
YOU'VE ALREADY MADE UP YOUR MIND ANYWAY, RIGHT?
MAN, THAT'S A CRAZY CONCLUSION.
I MAY COMPLAIN, BUT I AM KEEPING AN EYE ON YOU.
I CAN TELL WHAT YOU'RE THINKING.
......
HEY, KID! WELL? MADE UP YOUR MIND?
YES!

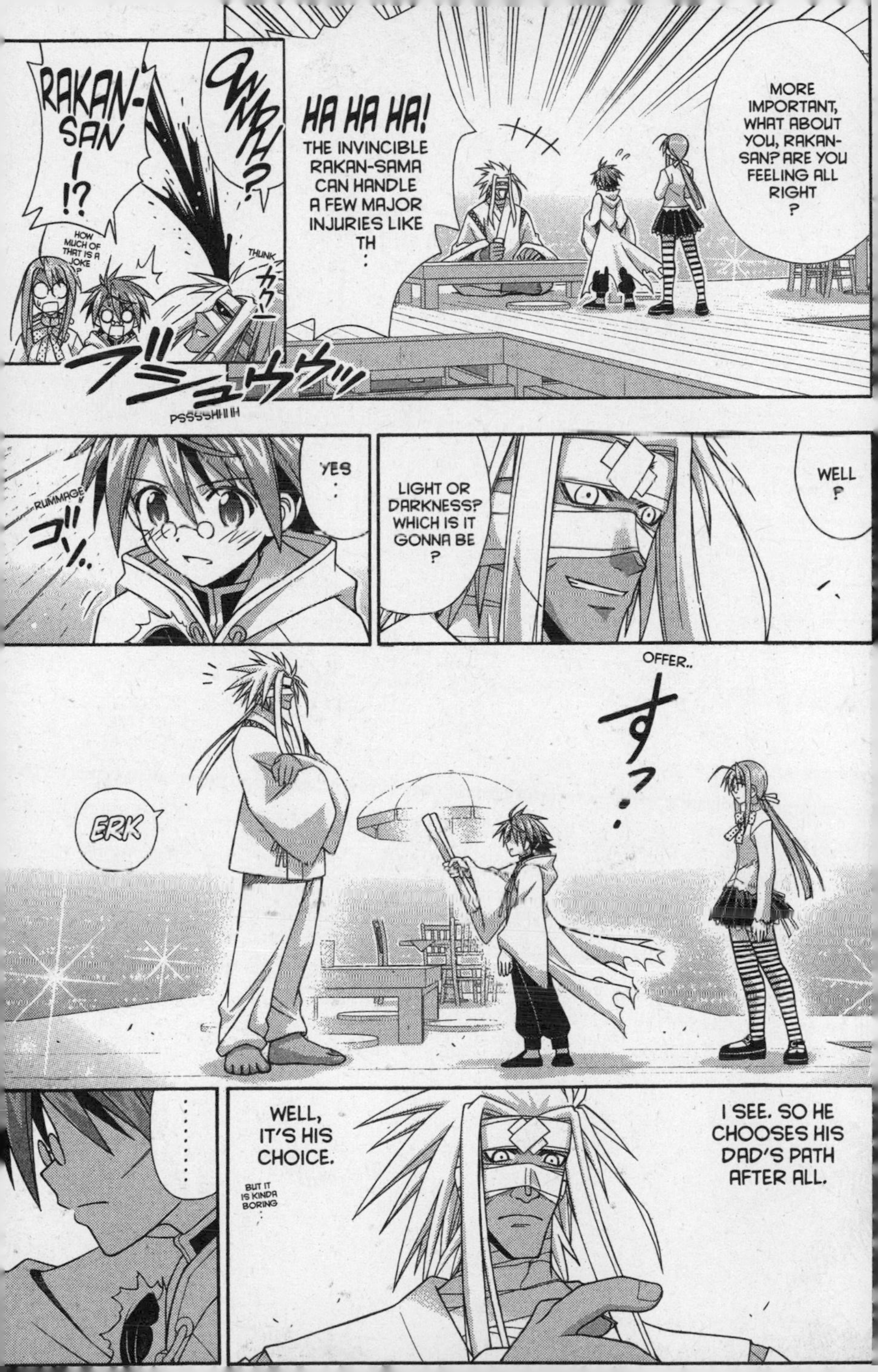

MORE IMPORTANT, WHAT ABOUT YOU, RAKAN-SAN? ARE YOU FEELING ALL RIGHT ?
HA HA HA! THE INVINCIBLE RAKAN-SAMA CAN HANDLE A FEW MAJOR INJURIES LIKE TH . . .
GWARH?!
THUNK
RAKAN-SAN!!?
HOW MUCH OF THAT IS A JOKE ?
PSSSSHHHH
WELL ?
LIGHT OR DARKNESS? WHICH IS IT GONNA BE ?
YES . . .
RUMMAGE
OFFER..
ERK
I SEE. SO HE CHOOSES HIS DAD'S PATH AFTER ALL.
WELL, IT'S HIS CHOICE.
BUT IT IS KINDA BORING . . .
......

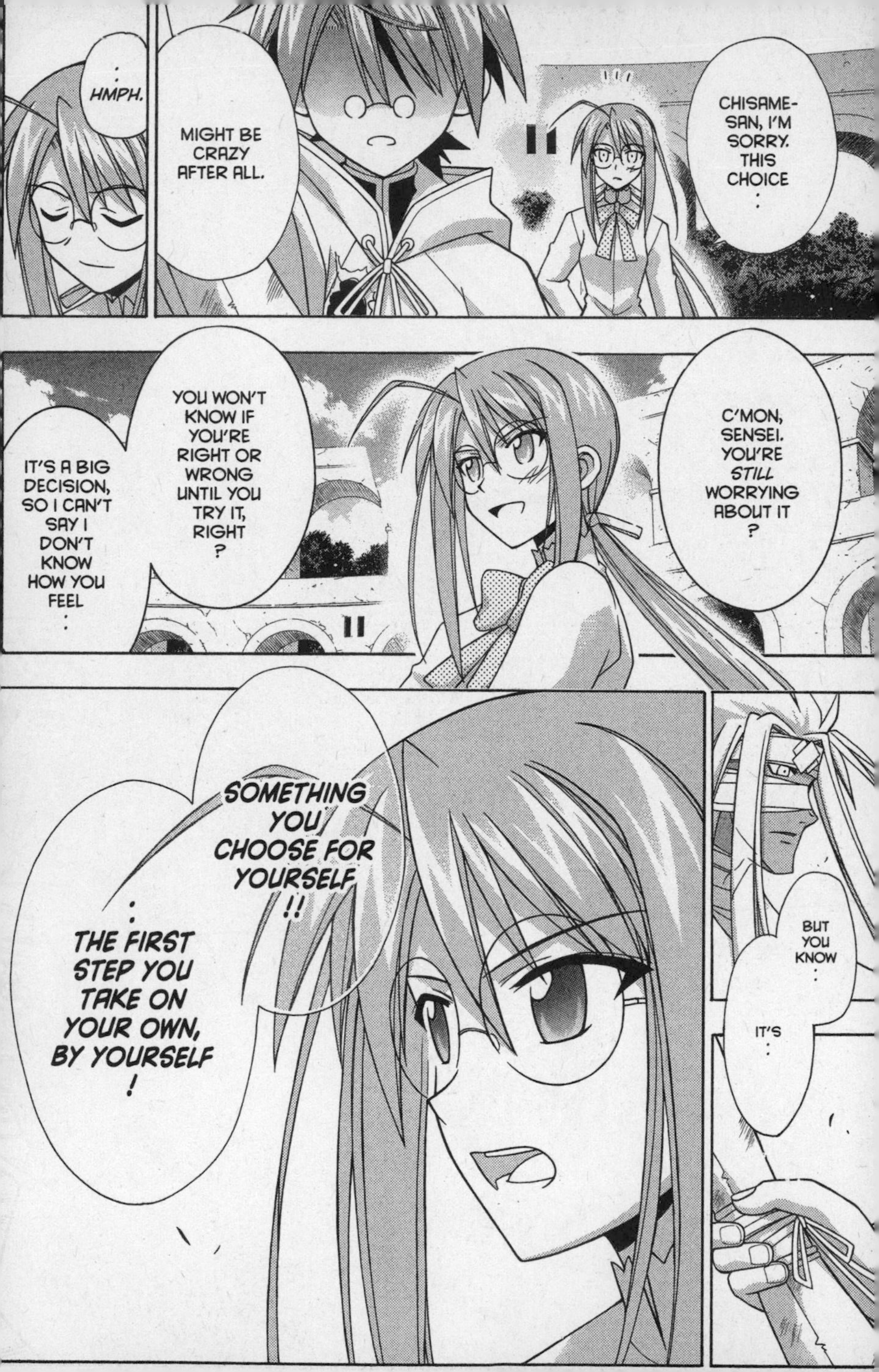
CHISAME-SAN, I'M SORRY. THIS CHOICE :
MIGHT BE CRAZY AFTER ALL.
: HMPH.
C'MON, SENSEI. YOU'RE STILL WORRYING ABOUT IT ?
YOU WON'T KNOW IF YOU'RE RIGHT OR WRONG UNTIL YOU TRY IT, RIGHT ?
IT'S A BIG DECISION, SO I CAN'T SAY I DON'T KNOW HOW YOU FEEL :
BUT YOU KNOW :
IT'S :
SOMETHING YOU CHOOSE FOR YOURSELF !!
: THE FIRST STEP YOU TAKE ON YOUR OWN, BY YOURSELF !

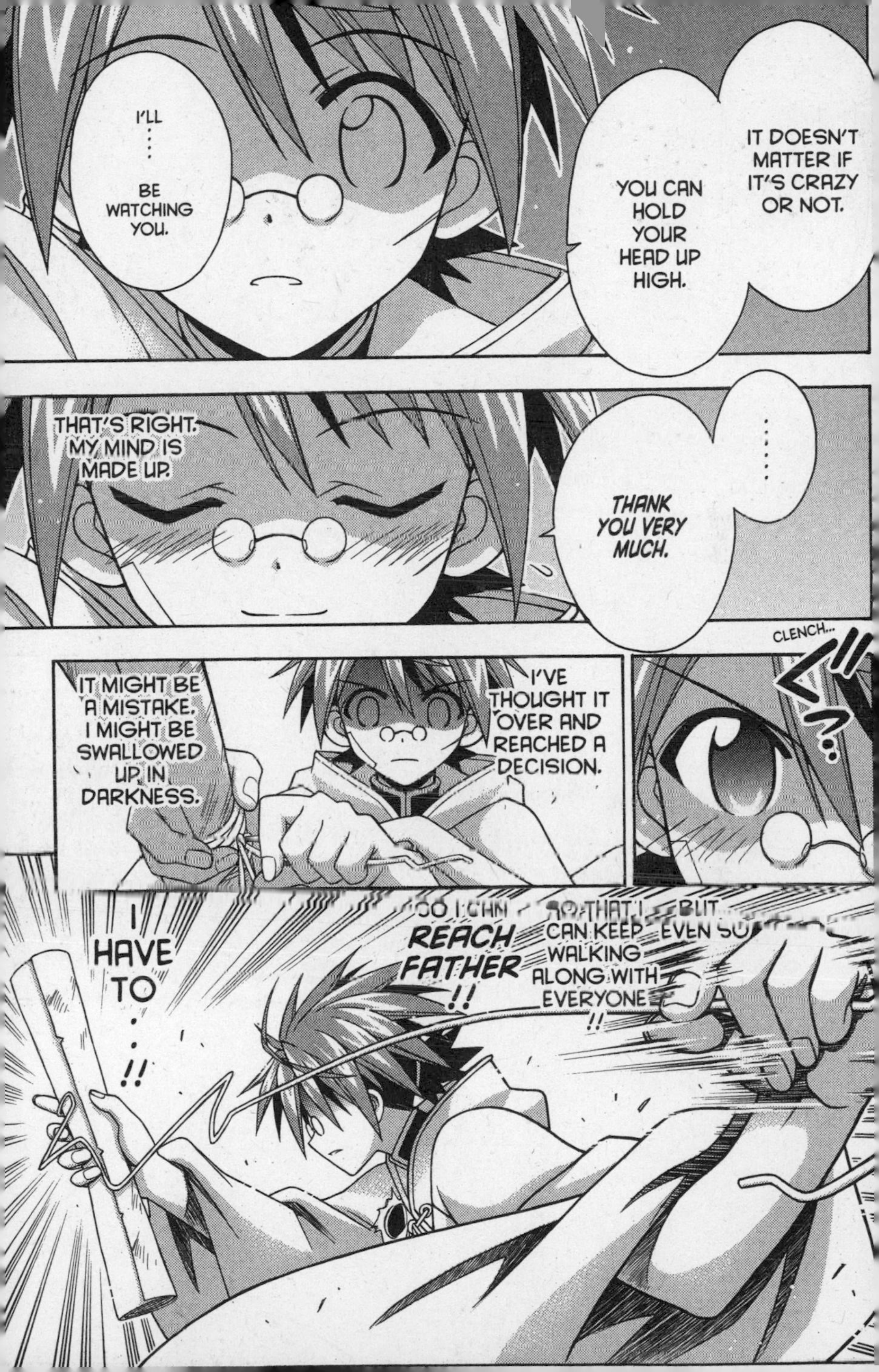
IT DOESN'T MATTER IF IT'S CRAZY OR NOT.
YOU CAN HOLD YOUR HEAD UP HIGH.
I'LL ... BE WATCHING YOU.
......
THANK YOU VERY MUCH.
THAT'S RIGHT. MY MIND IS MADE UP.
CLENCH...
I'VE THOUGHT IT OVER AND REACHED A DECISION.
IT MIGHT BE A MISTAKE. I MIGHT BE SWALLOWED UP IN DARKNESS.
BUT EVEN SO...
SO THAT I CAN KEEP WALKING ALONG WITH EVERYONE!!
SO I CAN REACH FATHER!!
I HAVE TO...!!

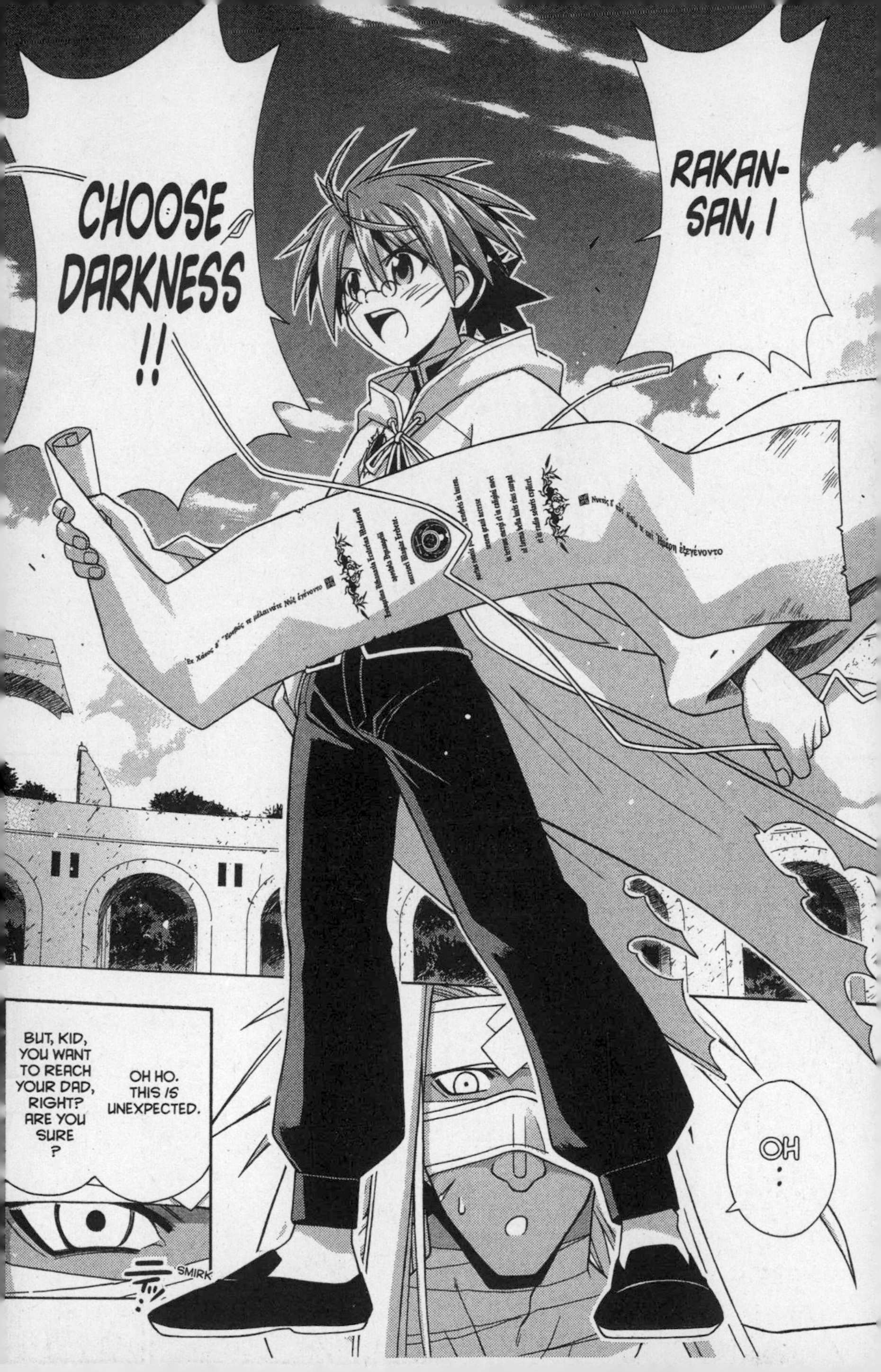
RAKAN-SAN, I
CHOOSE DARKNESS!!
OH...
OH HO. THIS *IS* UNEXPECTED.
BUT, KID, YOU WANT TO REACH YOUR DAD, RIGHT? ARE YOU SURE?
SMIRK

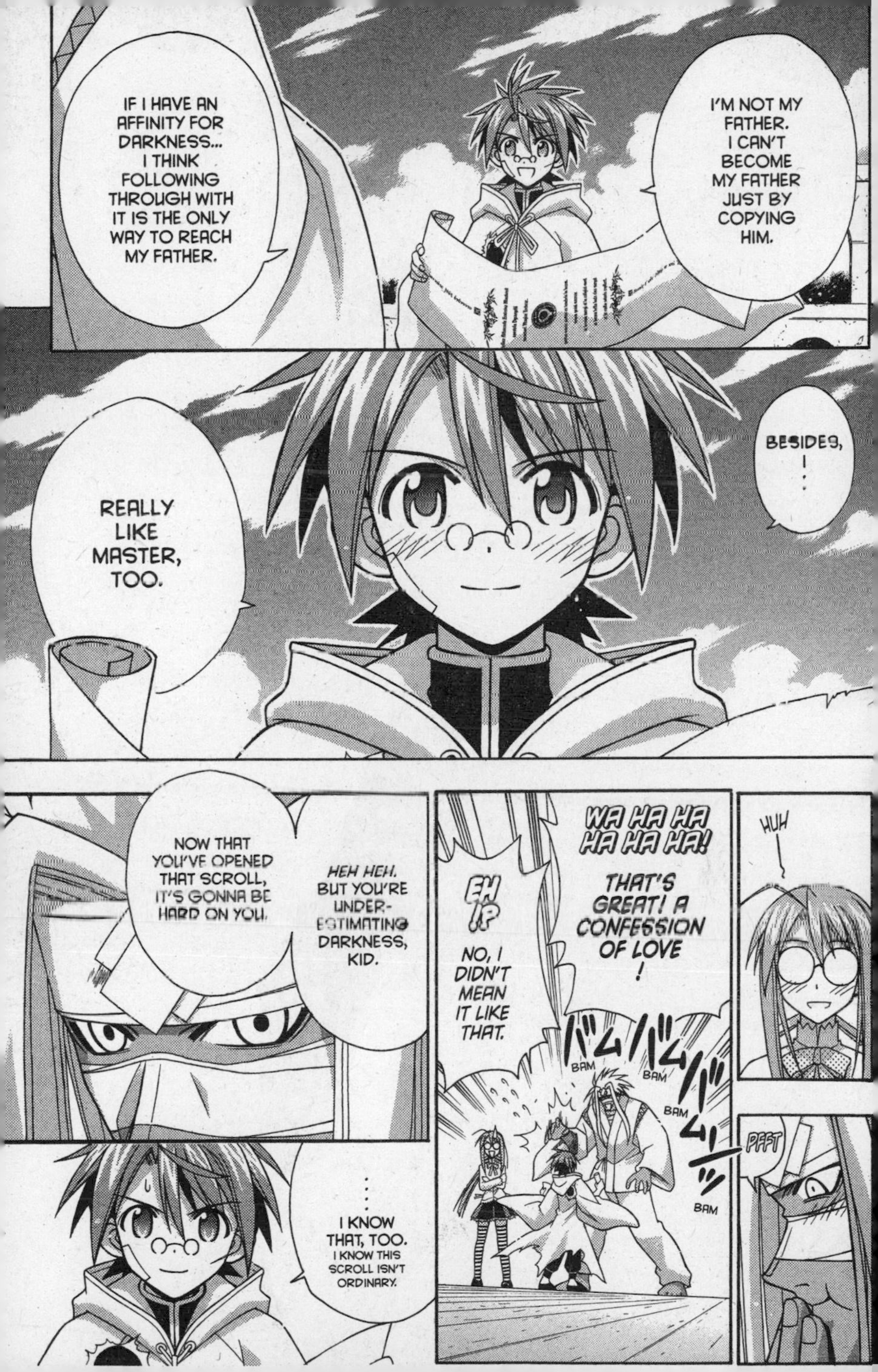
I'M NOT MY FATHER. I CAN'T BECOME MY FATHER JUST BY COPYING HIM.
IF I HAVE AN AFFINITY FOR DARKNESS... I THINK FOLLOWING THROUGH WITH IT IS THE ONLY WAY TO REACH MY FATHER.
BESIDES, I...
REALLY LIKE MASTER, TOO.
HUH!
PFFT
WA HA HA HA HA HA!
THAT'S GREAT! A CONFESSION OF LOVE!
EH!?
NO, I DIDN'T MEAN IT LIKE THAT.
BAM
BAM
BAM
BAM
HEH HEH. BUT YOU'RE UNDER-ESTIMATING DARKNESS, KID.
NOW THAT YOU'VE OPENED THAT SCROLL, IT'S GONNA BE HARD ON YOU.
... I KNOW THAT, TOO.
I KNOW THIS SCROLL ISN'T ORDINARY.

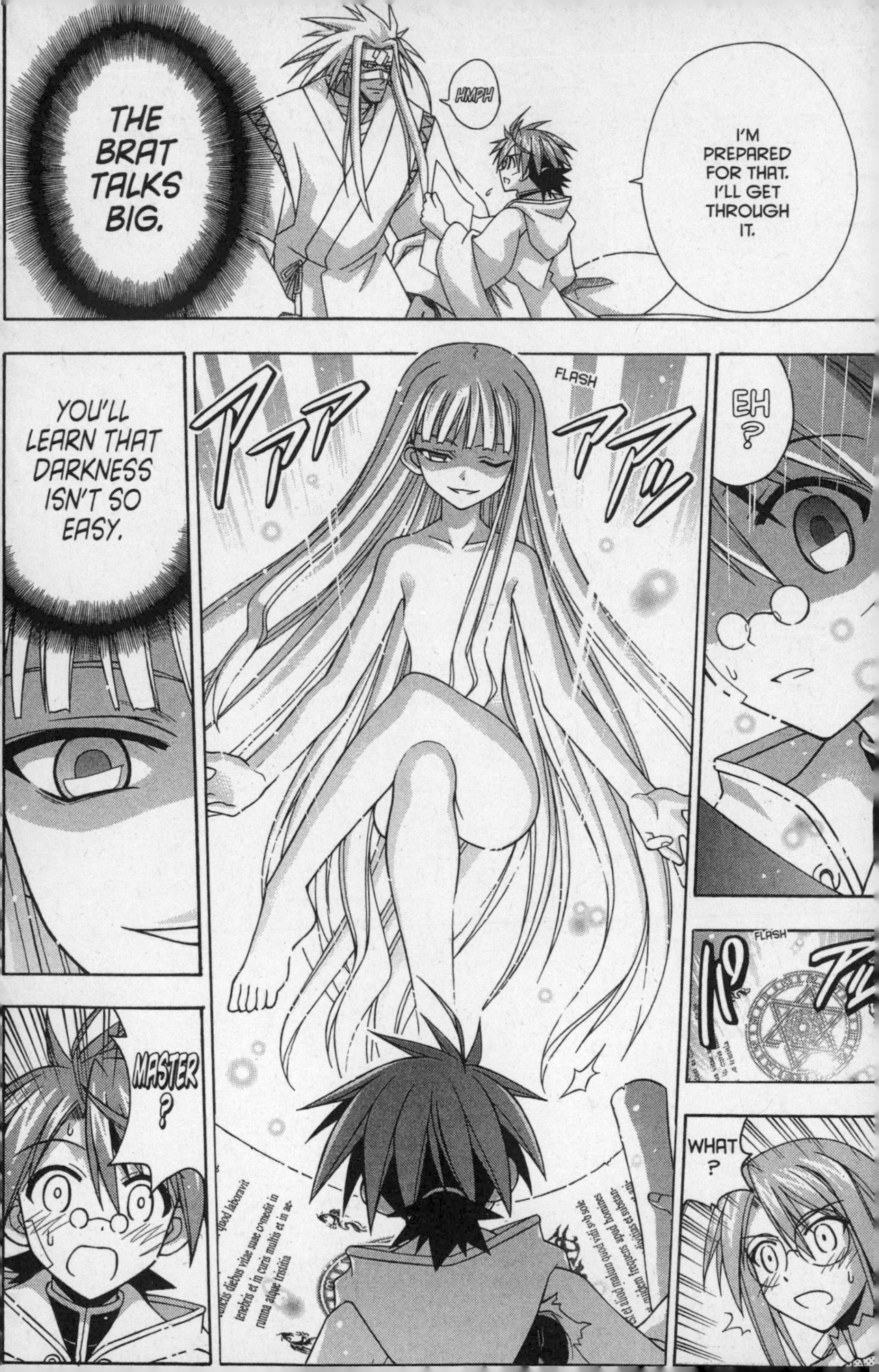
I'M PREPARED FOR THAT. I'LL GET THROUGH IT.
HMPH
THE BRAT TALKS BIG.
EH?
FLASH
YOU'LL LEARN THAT DARKNESS ISN'T SO EASY.
FLASH
WHAT?
MASTER?

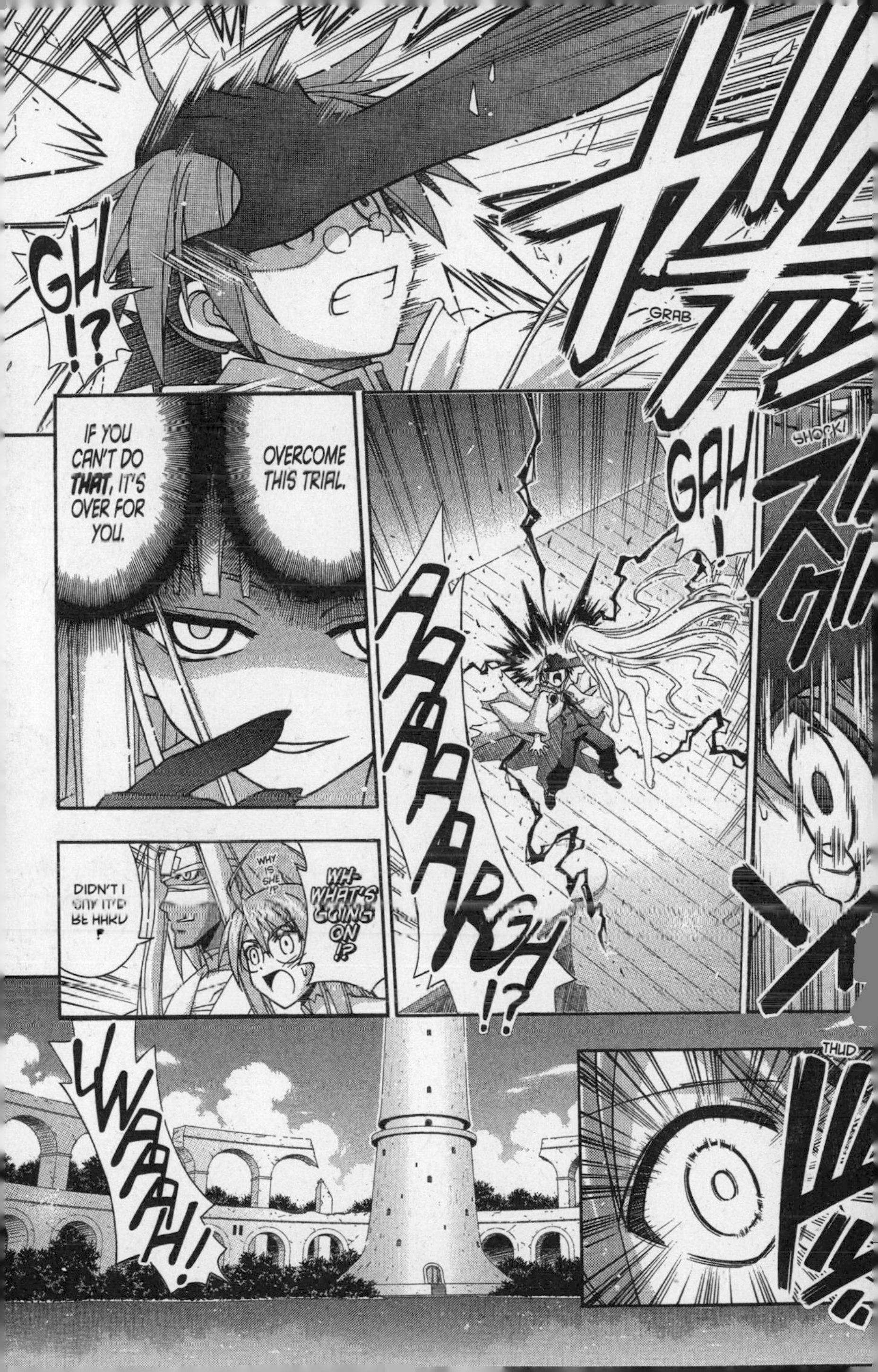
GRAB
GH!?
SHOCK!
GAH!
AAAAAARGH!?
OVERCOME THIS TRIAL.
IF YOU CAN'T DO THAT, IT'S OVER FOR YOU.
WH-WHAT'S GOING ON!?
WHY IS SHE!?
DIDN'T I SAY IT'D BE HARD?
THUD
UWAAAH!

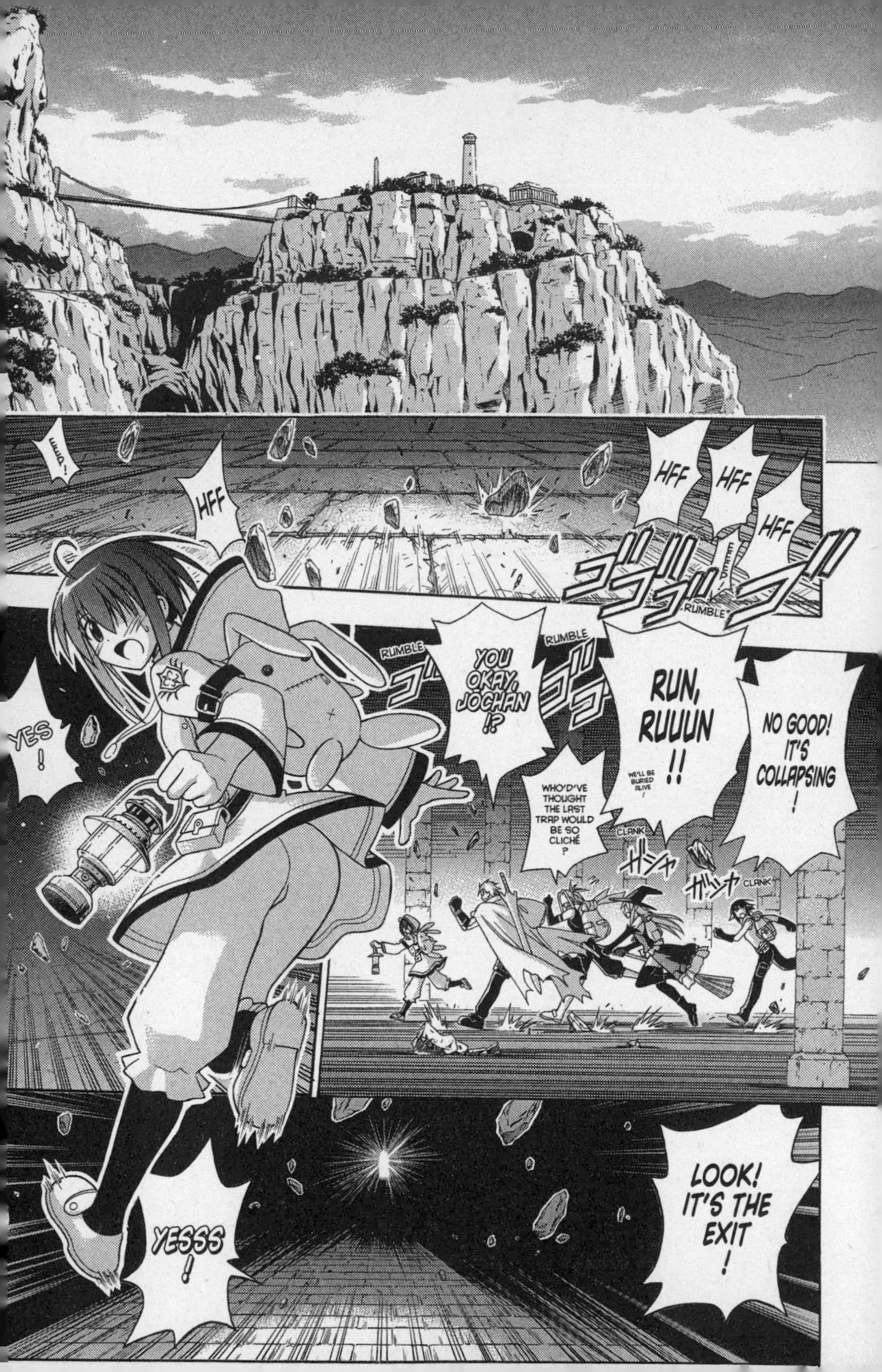
HFF
HFF
HFF
EEEP!
RUMBLE
HFF
EEEP!
NO GOOD! IT'S COLLAPSING!
RUN, RUUUN!!
WE'LL BE BURIED ALIVE!
RUMBLE
YOU OKAY, JOCHAN!?
RUMBLE
WHO'D'VE THOUGHT THE LAST TRAP WOULD BE SO CLICHÉ?
ガシャ CLANK
ガシャ CLANK
YES!
LOOK! IT'S THE EXIT!
YESSS!

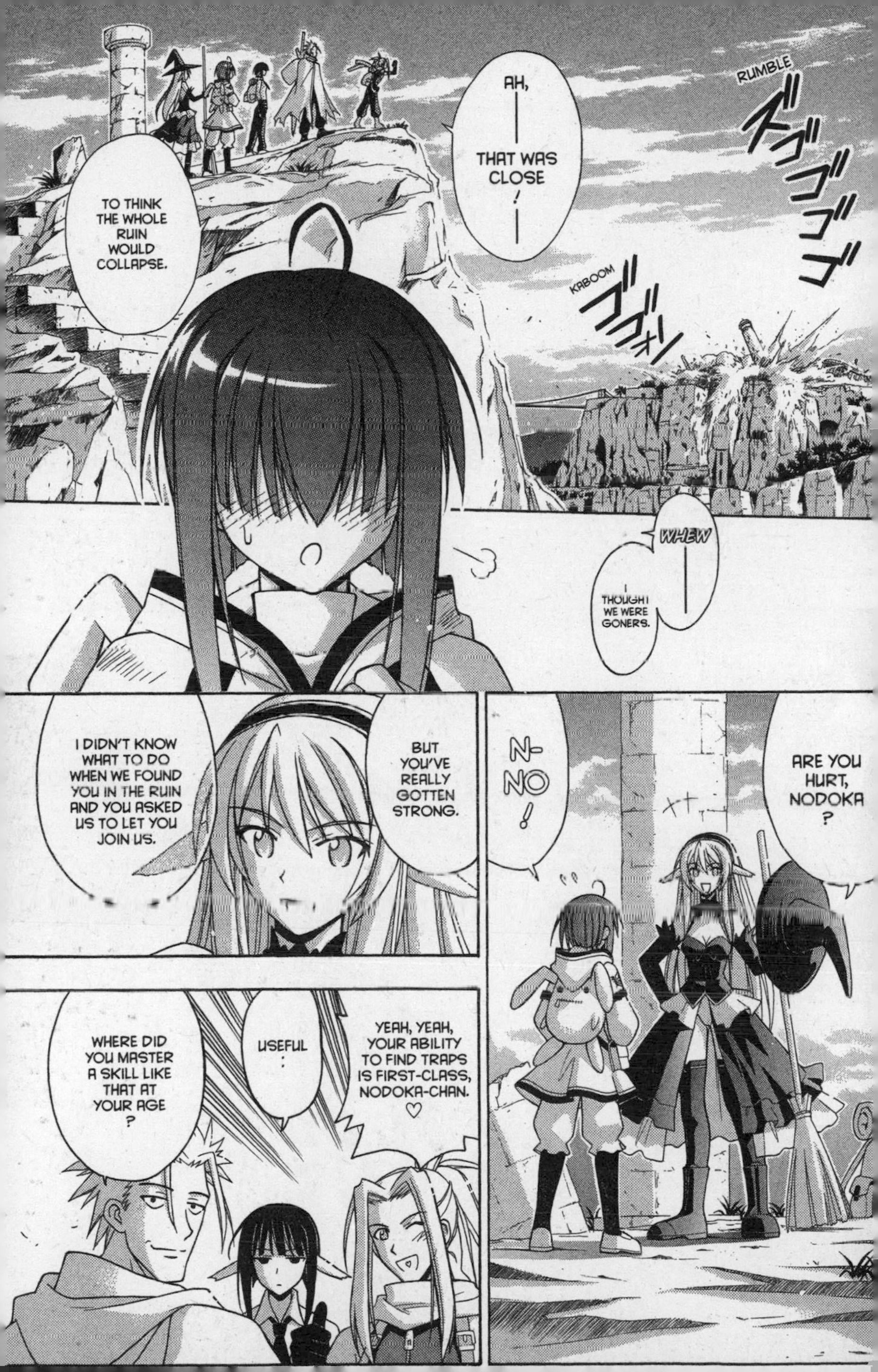
RUMBLE
ズゴゴゴ
AH, —— THAT WAS CLOSE! ——
KABOOM
ゴゴォン
TO THINK THE WHOLE RUIN WOULD COLLAPSE.
WHEW —— I THOUGHT WE WERE GONERS.
ARE YOU HURT, NODOKA?
N-NO!
BUT YOU'VE REALLY GOTTEN STRONG.
I DIDN'T KNOW WHAT TO DO WHEN WE FOUND YOU IN THE RUIN AND YOU ASKED US TO LET YOU JOIN US.
YEAH, YEAH, YOUR ABILITY TO FIND TRAPS IS FIRST-CLASS, NODOKA-CHAN. ♡
USEFUL:
WHERE DID YOU MASTER A SKILL LIKE THAT AT YOUR AGE?

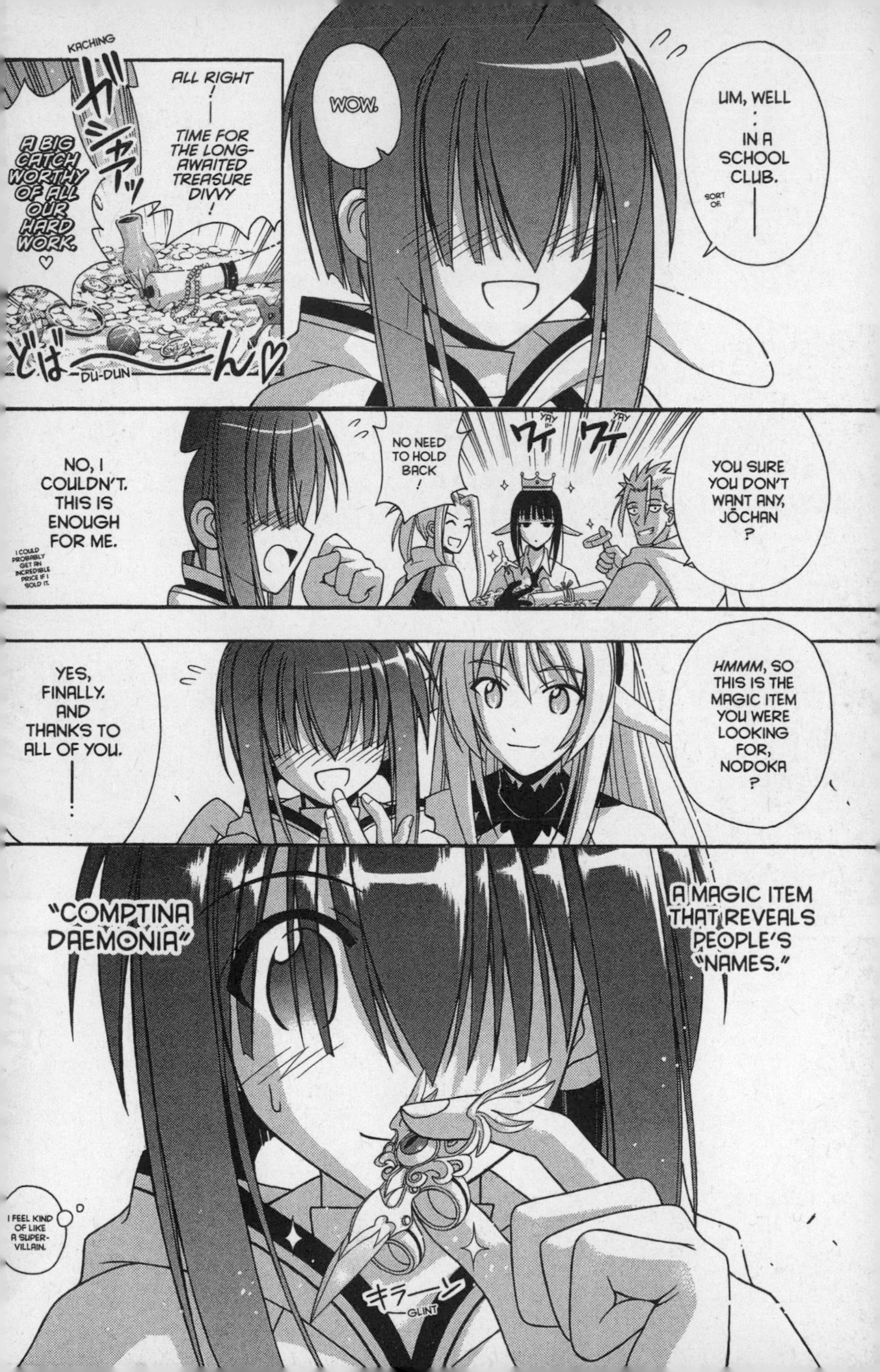
WOW.
UM, WELL: IN A SCHOOL CLUB.
SORT OF.
KACHING
ALL RIGHT! TIME FOR THE LONG-AWAITED TREASURE DIVVY!
A BIG CATCH WORTHY OF ALL OUR HARD WORK. ♡
DU-DUN
YOU SURE YOU DON'T WANT ANY, JŌCHAN?
YAY
YAY
NO NEED TO HOLD BACK!
NO, I COULDN'T. THIS IS ENOUGH FOR ME.
I COULD PROBABLY GET AN INCREDIBLE PRICE IF I SOLD IT.
HMMM, SO THIS IS THE MAGIC ITEM YOU WERE LOOKING FOR, NODOKA?
YES, FINALLY. AND THANKS TO ALL OF YOU.
A MAGIC ITEM THAT REVEALS PEOPLE'S "NAMES."
"COMPTINA DAEMONIA"
GLINT
I FEEL KIND OF LIKE A SUPER-VILLAIN.

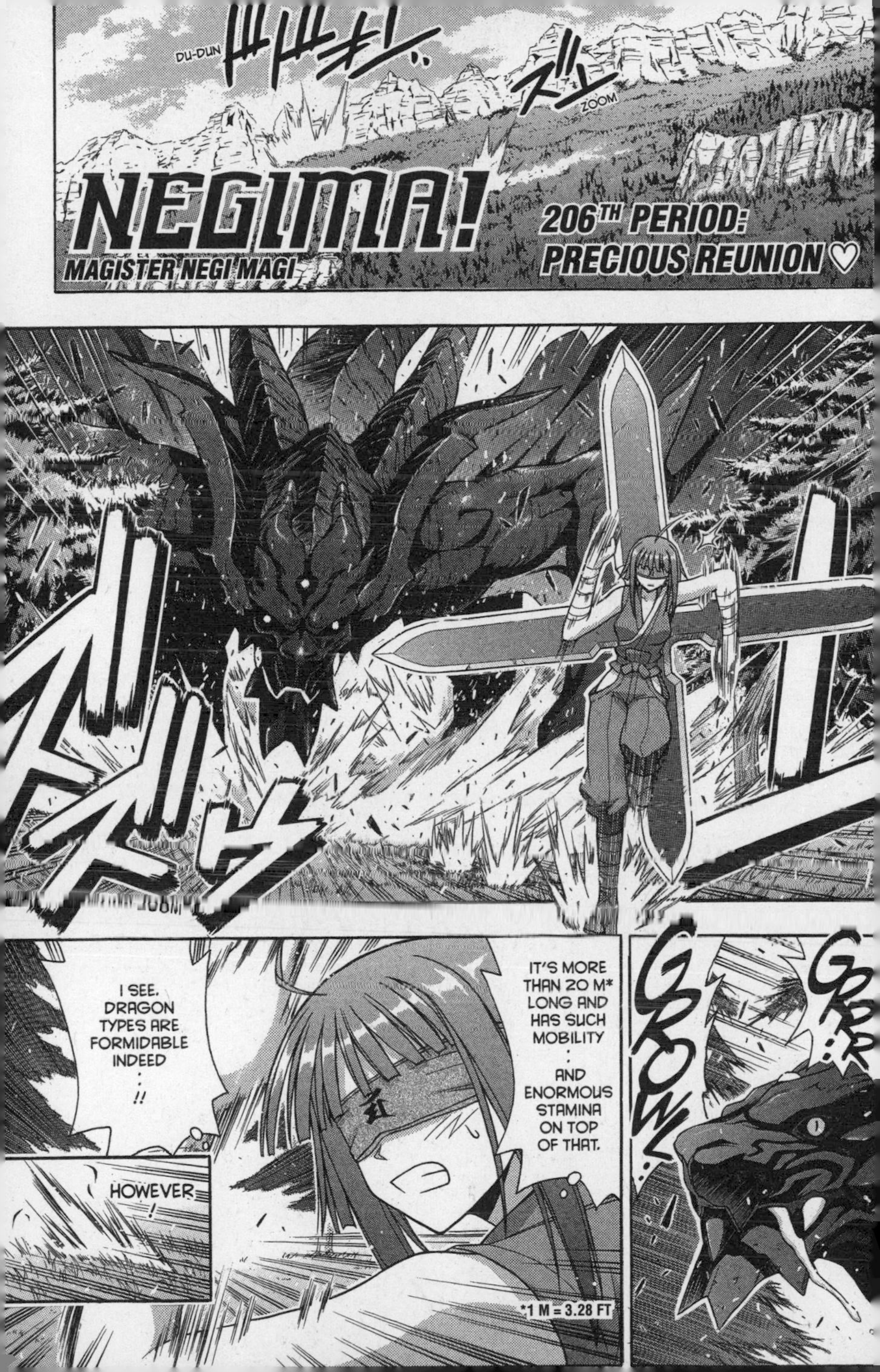
ZOOM
DU-DUN
NEGIMA!
MAGISTER NEGI MAGI
206TH PERIOD: PRECIOUS REUNION ♡
GRRR
GROWL
IT'S MORE THAN 20 M* LONG AND HAS SUCH MOBILITY . . . AND ENORMOUS STAMINA ON TOP OF THAT.
I SEE. DRAGON TYPES ARE FORMIDABLE INDEED . . . !!
HOWEVER !
*1 M = 3.28 FT

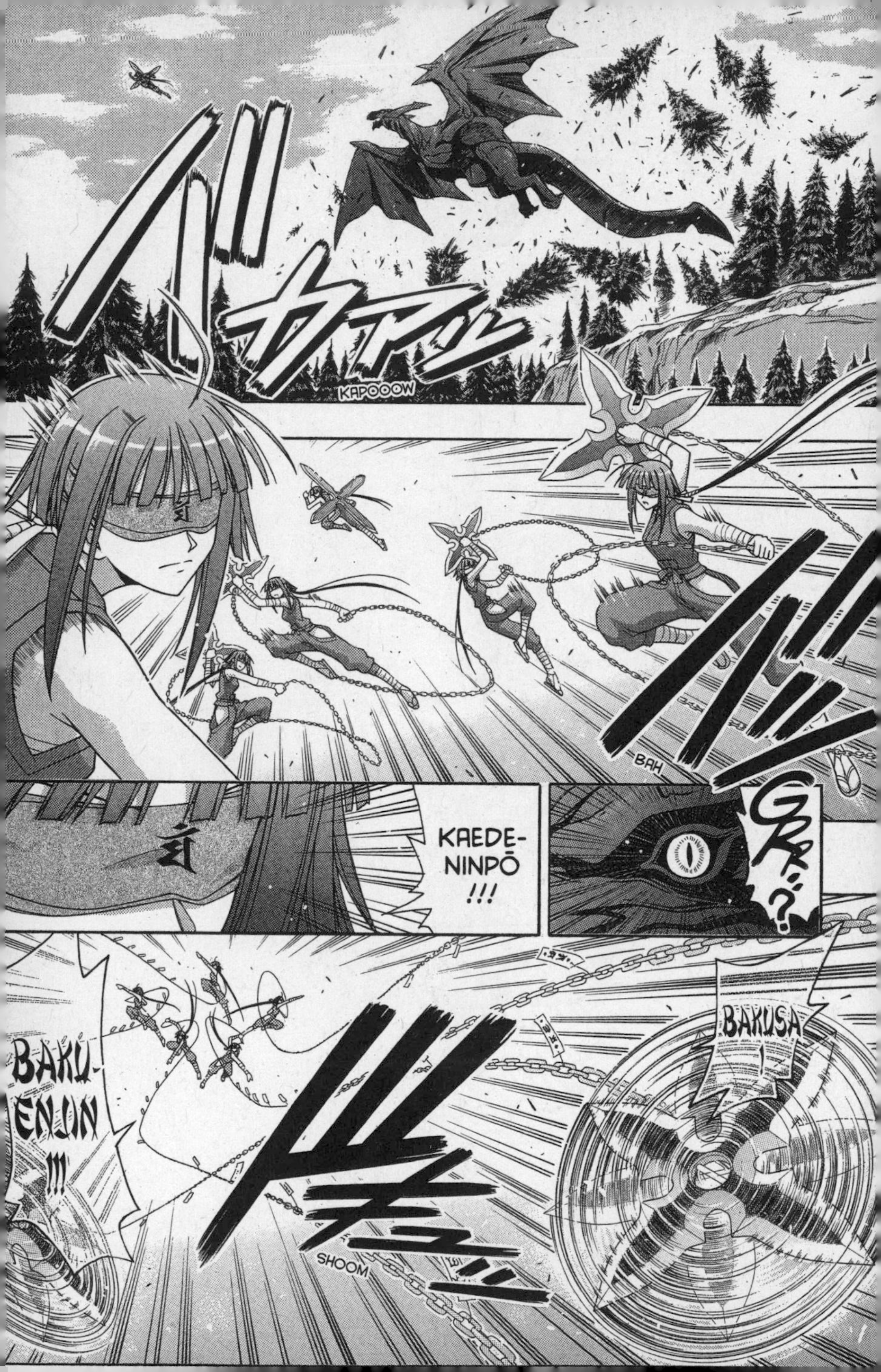
KAPOOOW
BAH
GRR...?
KAEDE-NINPŌ!!!
BAKUSA
SHOOM
BAKU-ENJIN!!!

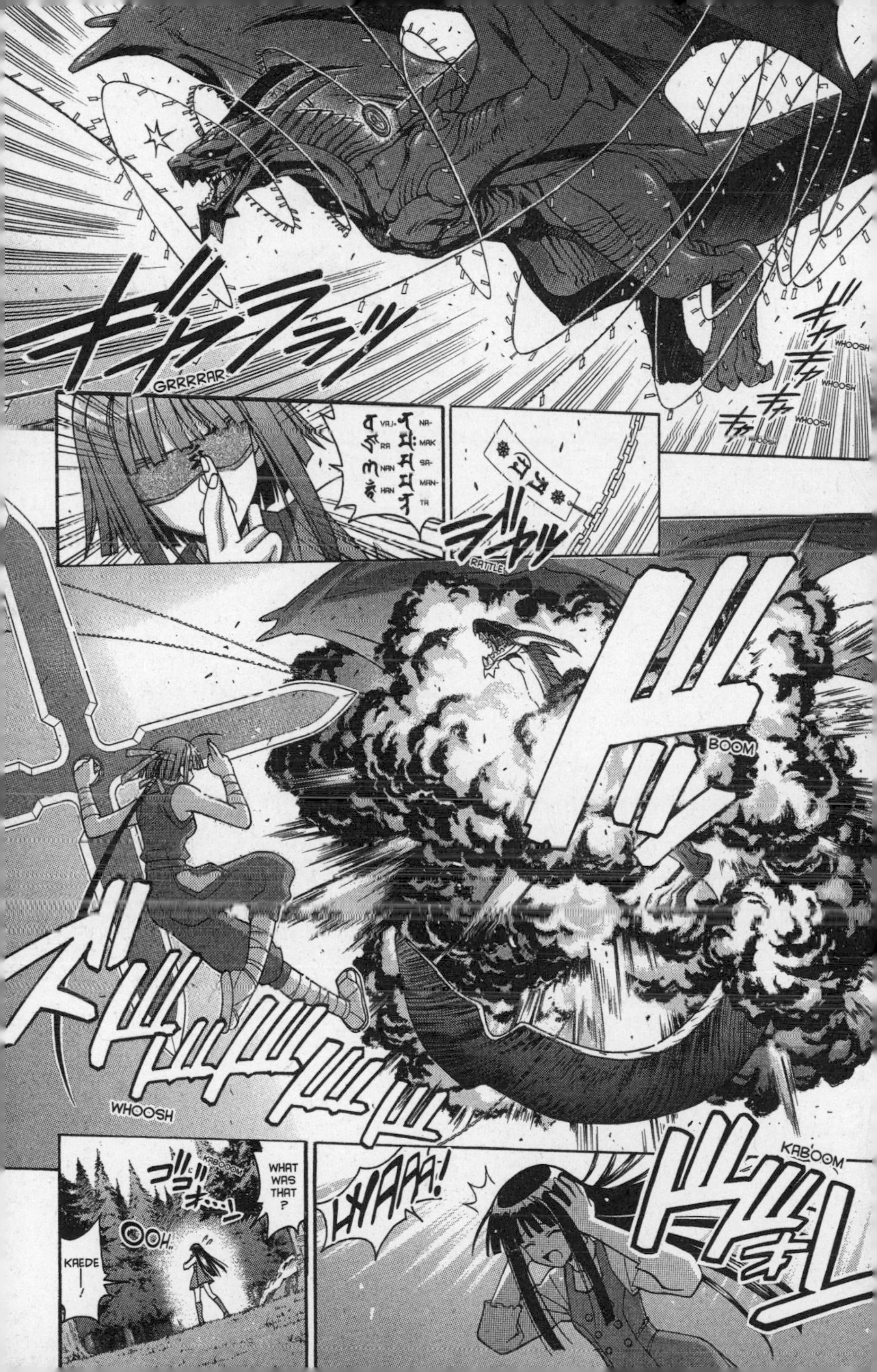
WHOOSH
WHOOSH
WHOOSH
WHOOSH
GRRRRAR
RATTLE
NA-MAK SA-MAN-TA VAJ-RA NAN HAN
BOOM
WHOOSH
KABOOM
HYAAA!
WHAT WAS THAT?
KABOOOM
OOH...
KAEDE!

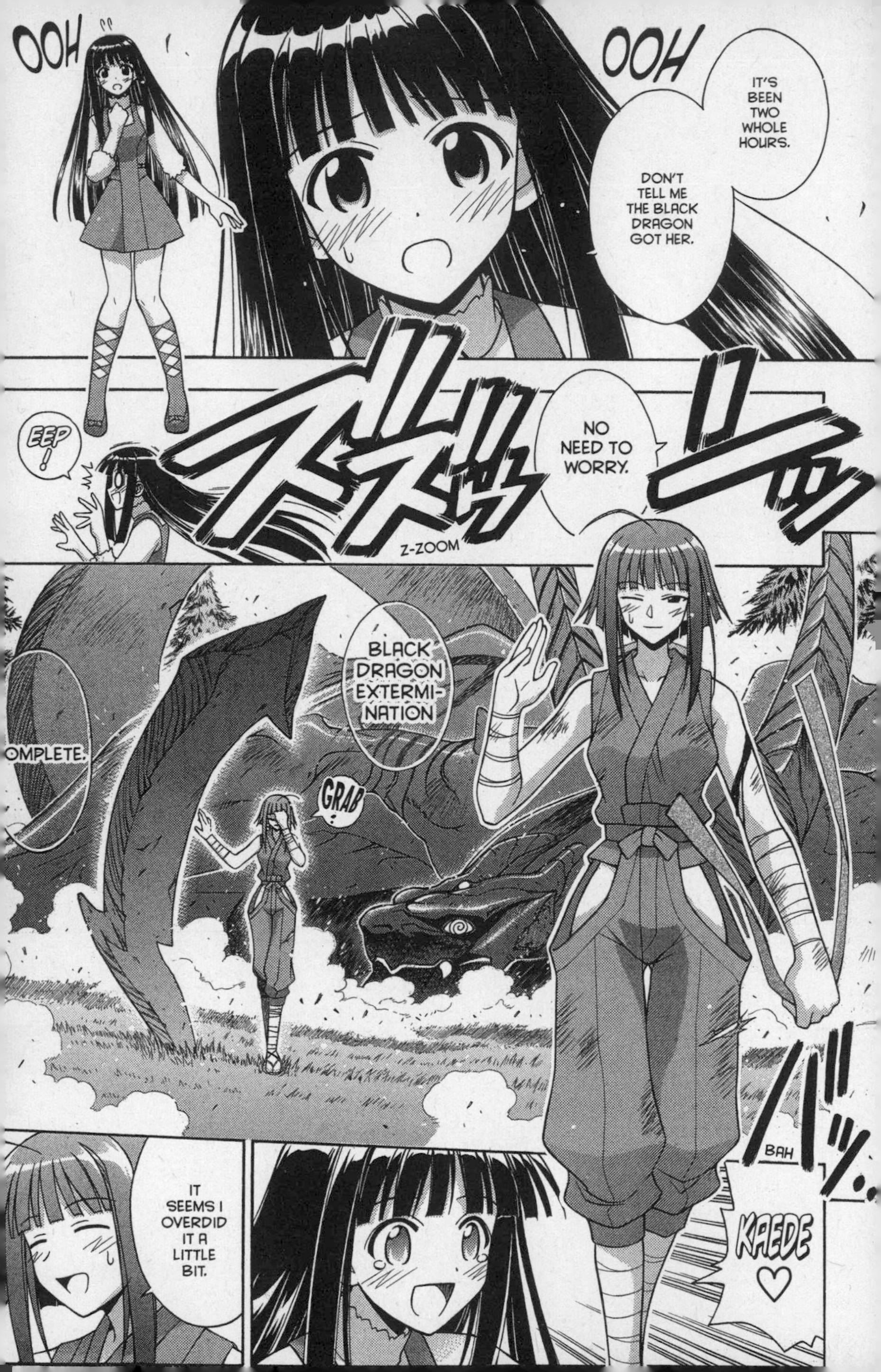
OOH
IT'S BEEN TWO WHOLE HOURS.
DON'T TELL ME THE BLACK DRAGON GOT HER.
OOH
NO NEED TO WORRY.
Z-ZOOM
EEP!
BLACK DRAGON EXTERMI-NATION
OMPLETE.
GRAB
BAH
KAEDE ♥
IT SEEMS I OVERDID IT A LITTLE BIT.

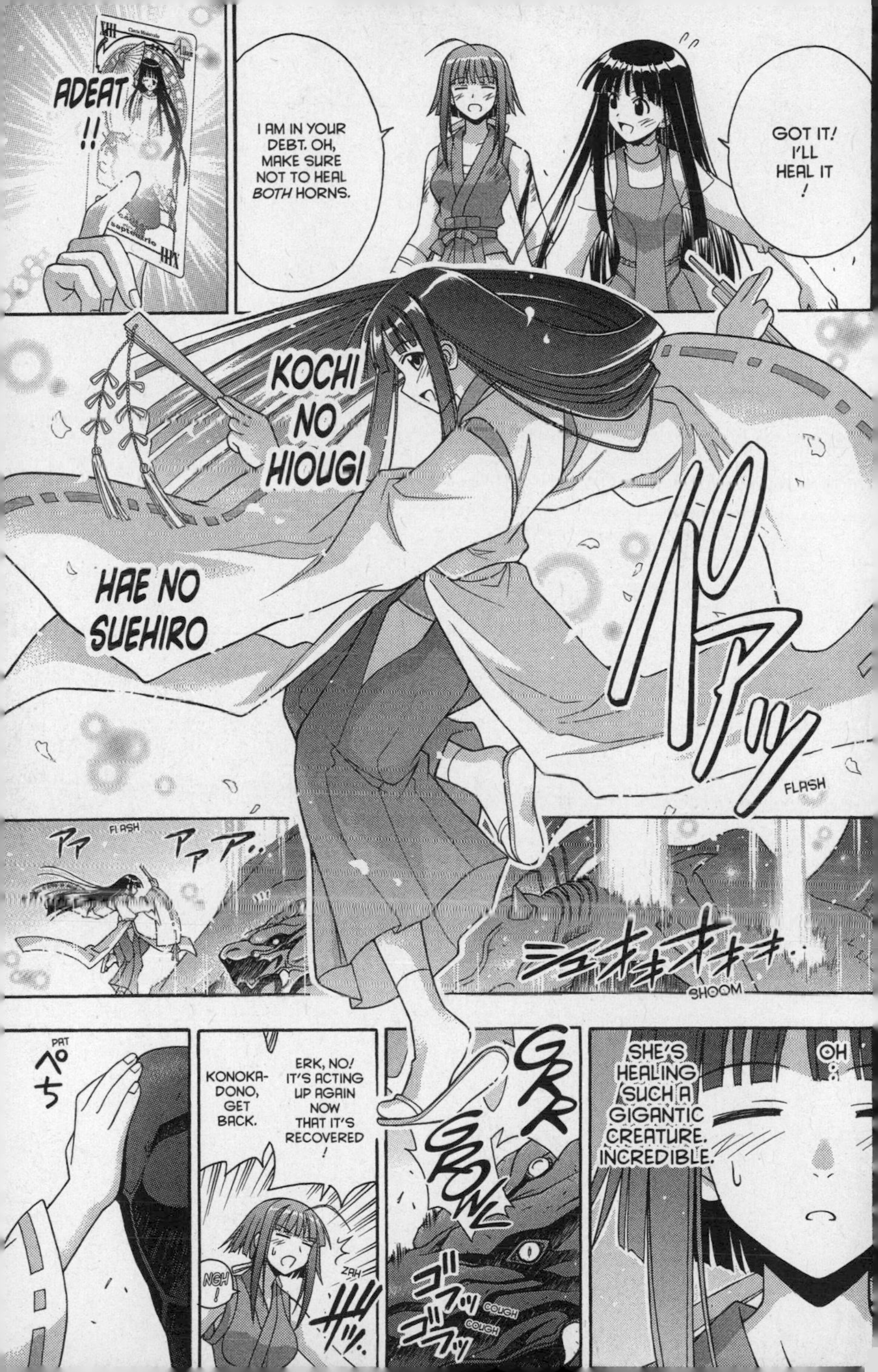
I AM IN YOUR DEBT. OH, MAKE SURE NOT TO HEAL *BOTH* HORNS.
GOT IT! I'LL HEAL IT!
ADEAT!!
KOCHI NO HIOUGI
HAE NO SUEHIRO
パアッ
FLASH
シュオォォォォォ..
SHOOM
アァ
FLASH
アァア..
OH
SHE'S HEALING SUCH A GIGANTIC CREATURE. INCREDIBLE.
GRR
GROWL
ゴフッ
COUGH
ゴフッ
COUGH
ERK, NO! IT'S ACTING UP AGAIN NOW THAT IT'S RECOVERED!
KONOKA-DONO, GET BACK.
ZAH
ザッ
NGH!
PAT
ぺち

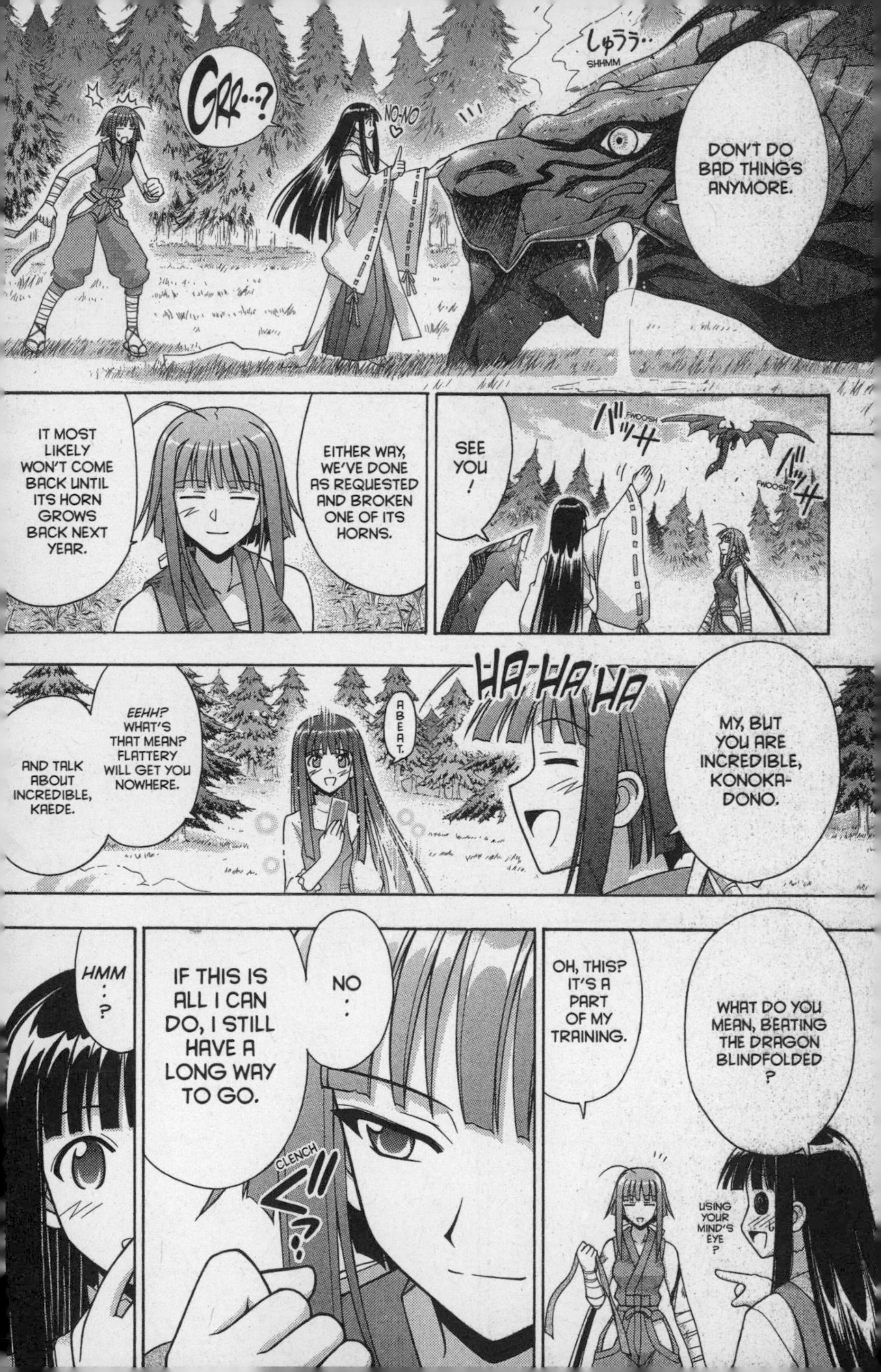
しゅララ・・
SHHMM
DON'T DO BAD THINGS ANYMORE.
NO-NO
GRR...?
SEE YOU!
FWOOSH
FWOOSH
EITHER WAY, WE'VE DONE AS REQUESTED AND BROKEN ONE OF ITS HORNS.
IT MOST LIKELY WON'T COME BACK UNTIL ITS HORN GROWS BACK NEXT YEAR.
MY, BUT YOU ARE INCREDIBLE, KONOKA-DONO.
HA HA HA HA
A BEAT.
EEHH? WHAT'S THAT MEAN? FLATTERY WILL GET YOU NOWHERE.
AND TALK ABOUT INCREDIBLE, KAEDE.
WHAT DO YOU MEAN, BEATING THE DRAGON BLINDFOLDED?
USING YOUR MIND'S EYE?
OH, THIS? IT'S A PART OF MY TRAINING.
NO...
IF THIS IS ALL I CAN DO, I STILL HAVE A LONG WAY TO GO.
CLENCH
HMM...?

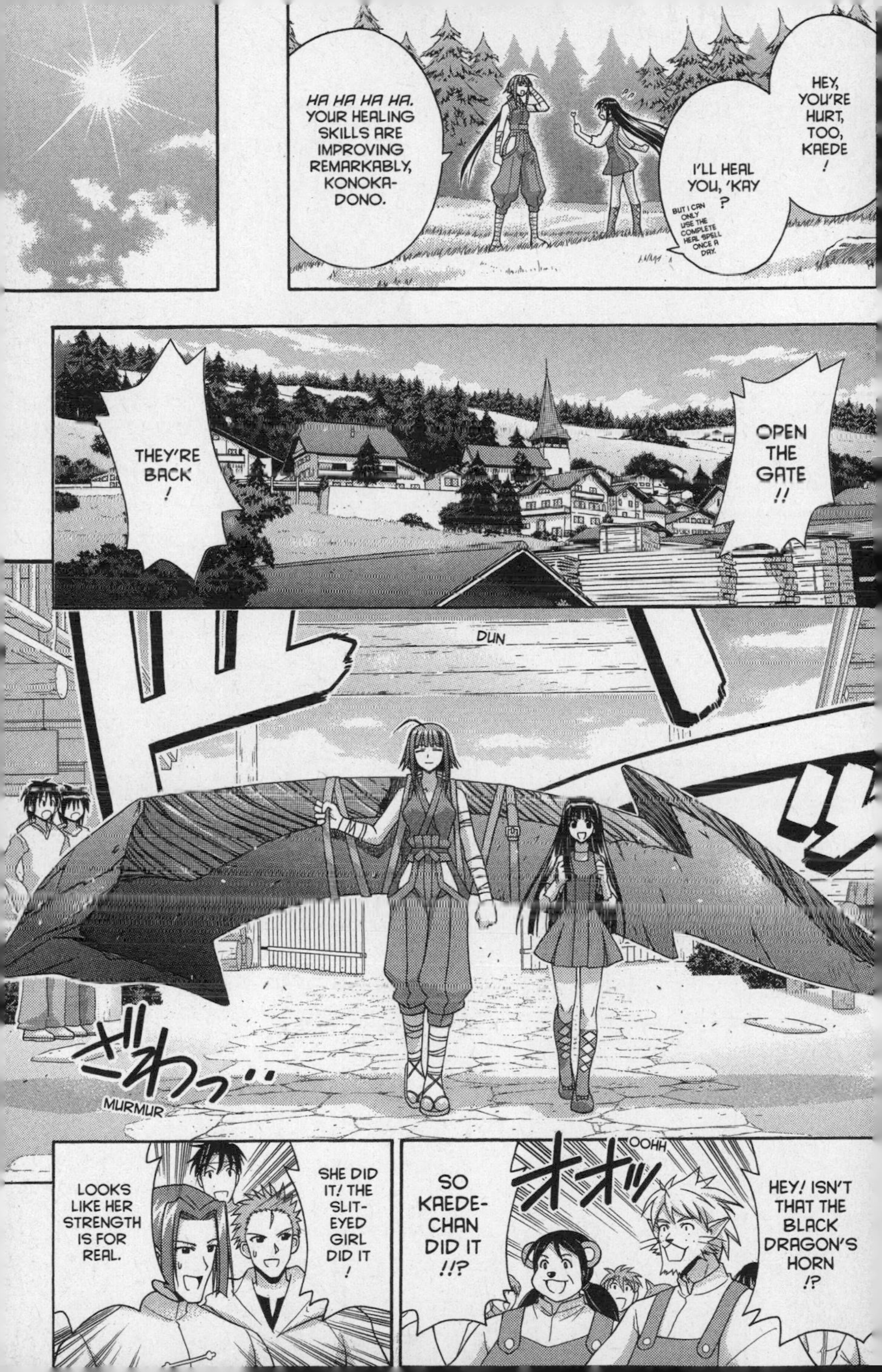
HEY, YOU'RE HURT, TOO, KAEDE!
I'LL HEAL YOU, 'KAY?
BUT I CAN ONLY USE THE COMPLETE HEAL SPELL ONCE A DAY.
HA HA HA HA. YOUR HEALING SKILLS ARE IMPROVING REMARKABLY, KONOKA-DONO.
OPEN THE GATE!!
THEY'RE BACK!
DUN
ざわっ..
MURMUR
オオッ
OOHH
HEY! ISN'T THAT THE BLACK DRAGON'S HORN!?
SO KAEDE-CHAN DID IT!!?
SHE DID IT! THE SLIT-EYED GIRL DID IT!
LOOKS LIKE HER STRENGTH IS FOR REAL.

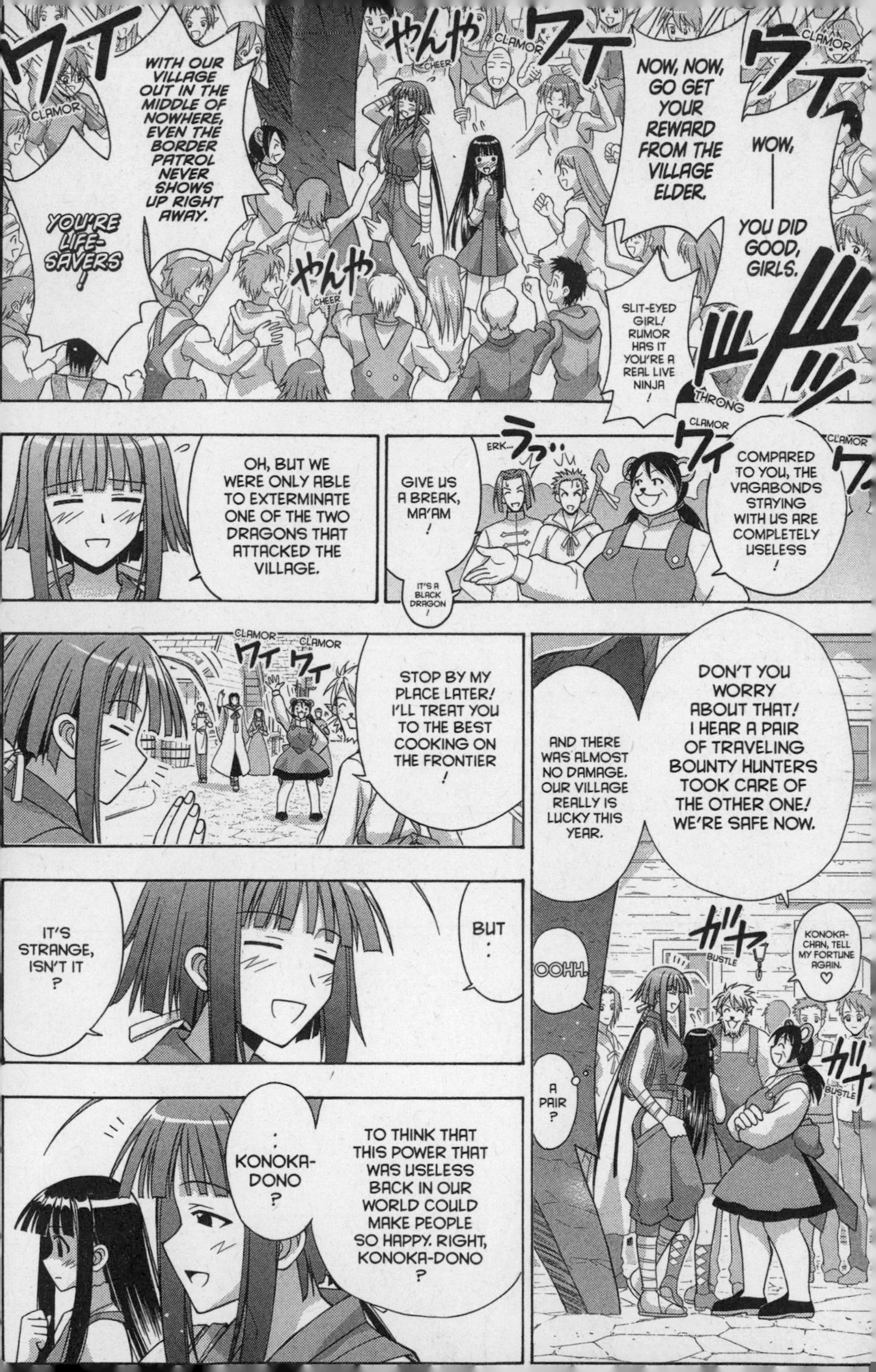
ワイ
CLAMOR
WOW, — YOU DID GOOD, GIRLS.
NOW, NOW, GO GET YOUR REWARD FROM THE VILLAGE ELDER.
ワイ
CLAMOR
やんや
CHEER
WITH OUR VILLAGE OUT IN THE MIDDLE OF NOWHERE, EVEN THE BORDER PATROL NEVER SHOWS UP RIGHT AWAY.
ワイ
CLAMOR
YOU'RE LIFE-SAVERS!
ドドッ
THRONG
SLIT-EYED GIRL! RUMOR HAS IT YOU'RE A REAL LIVE NINJA!
やんや
CHEER
ワ
CLAMOR
COMPARED TO YOU, THE VAGABONDS STAYING WITH US ARE COMPLETELY USELESS!
ワイ
CLAMOR
うっ
ERK...
GIVE US A BREAK, MA'AM!
IT'S A BLACK DRAGON!
OH, BUT WE WERE ONLY ABLE TO EXTERMINATE ONE OF THE TWO DRAGONS THAT ATTACKED THE VILLAGE.
DON'T YOU WORRY ABOUT THAT! I HEAR A PAIR OF TRAVELING BOUNTY HUNTERS TOOK CARE OF THE OTHER ONE! WE'RE SAFE NOW.
AND THERE WAS ALMOST NO DAMAGE. OUR VILLAGE REALLY IS LUCKY THIS YEAR.
OOHH.
KONOKA-CHAN, TELL MY FORTUNE AGAIN. ♡
ガヤ
BUSTLE
ガヤ
BUSTLE
A PAIR?
ワイ
CLAMOR
ワイ
CLAMOR
STOP BY MY PLACE LATER! I'LL TREAT YOU TO THE BEST COOKING ON THE FRONTIER!
BUT...
IT'S STRANGE, ISN'T IT?
TO THINK THAT THIS POWER THAT WAS USELESS BACK IN OUR WORLD COULD MAKE PEOPLE SO HAPPY. RIGHT, KONOKA-DONO?
...KONOKA-DONO?

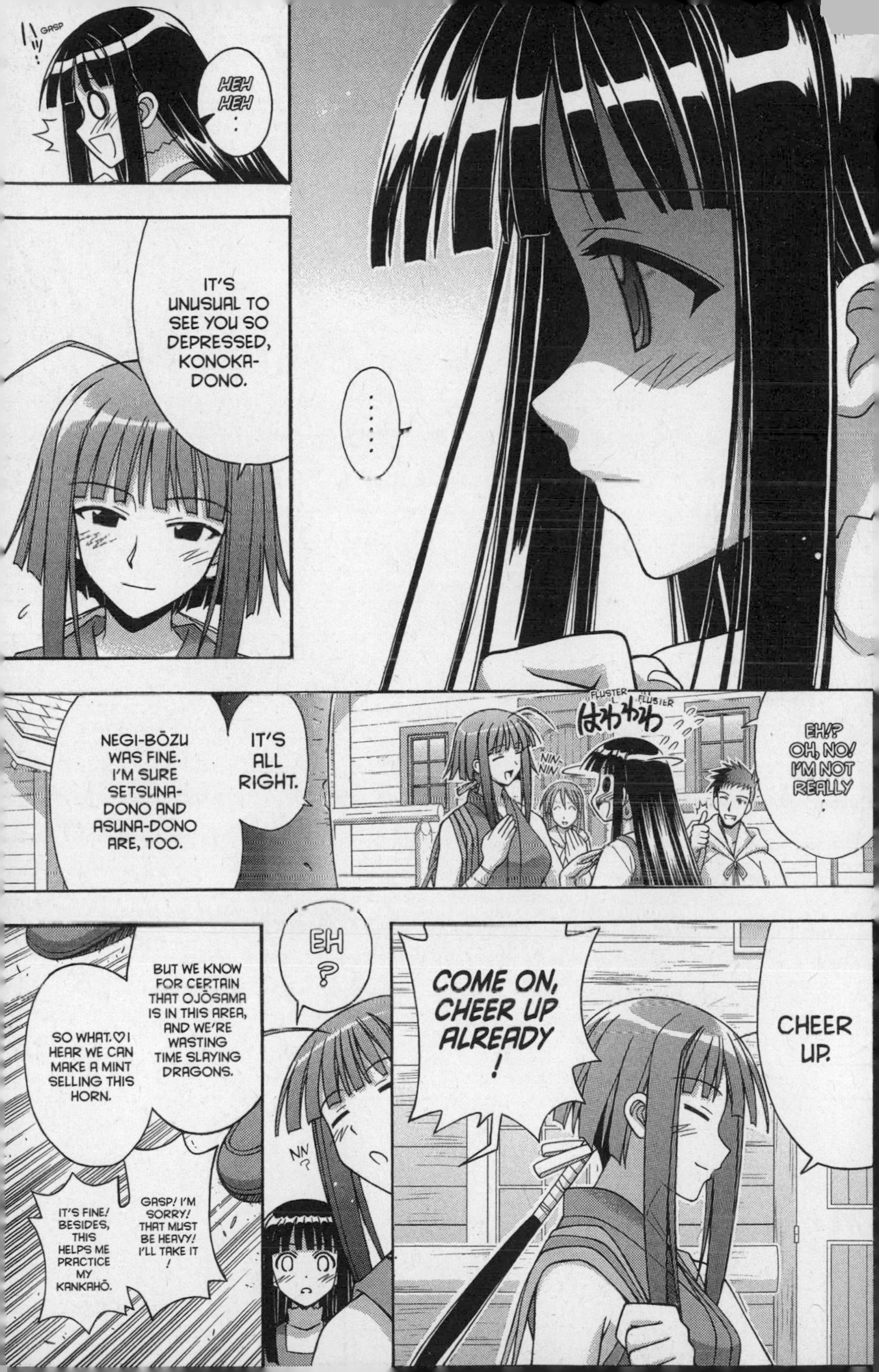
......
GASP
HEH HEH...
IT'S UNUSUAL TO SEE YOU SO DEPRESSED, KONOKA-DONO.
EH!? OH, NO! I'M NOT REALLY:
FLUSTER FLUSTER
はわわわ
NIN NIN
IT'S ALL RIGHT.
NEGI-BŌZU WAS FINE. I'M SURE SETSUNA-DONO AND ASUNA-DONO ARE, TOO.
CHEER UP.
COME ON, CHEER UP ALREADY!
EH?
BUT WE KNOW FOR CERTAIN THAT OJŌSAMA IS IN THIS AREA, AND WE'RE WASTING TIME SLAYING DRAGONS.
SO WHAT.♡ I HEAR WE CAN MAKE A MINT SELLING THIS HORN.
NN?
GASP! I'M SORRY! THAT MUST BE HEAVY! I'LL TAKE IT!
IT'S FINE! BESIDES, THIS HELPS ME PRACTICE MY KANKAHŌ.

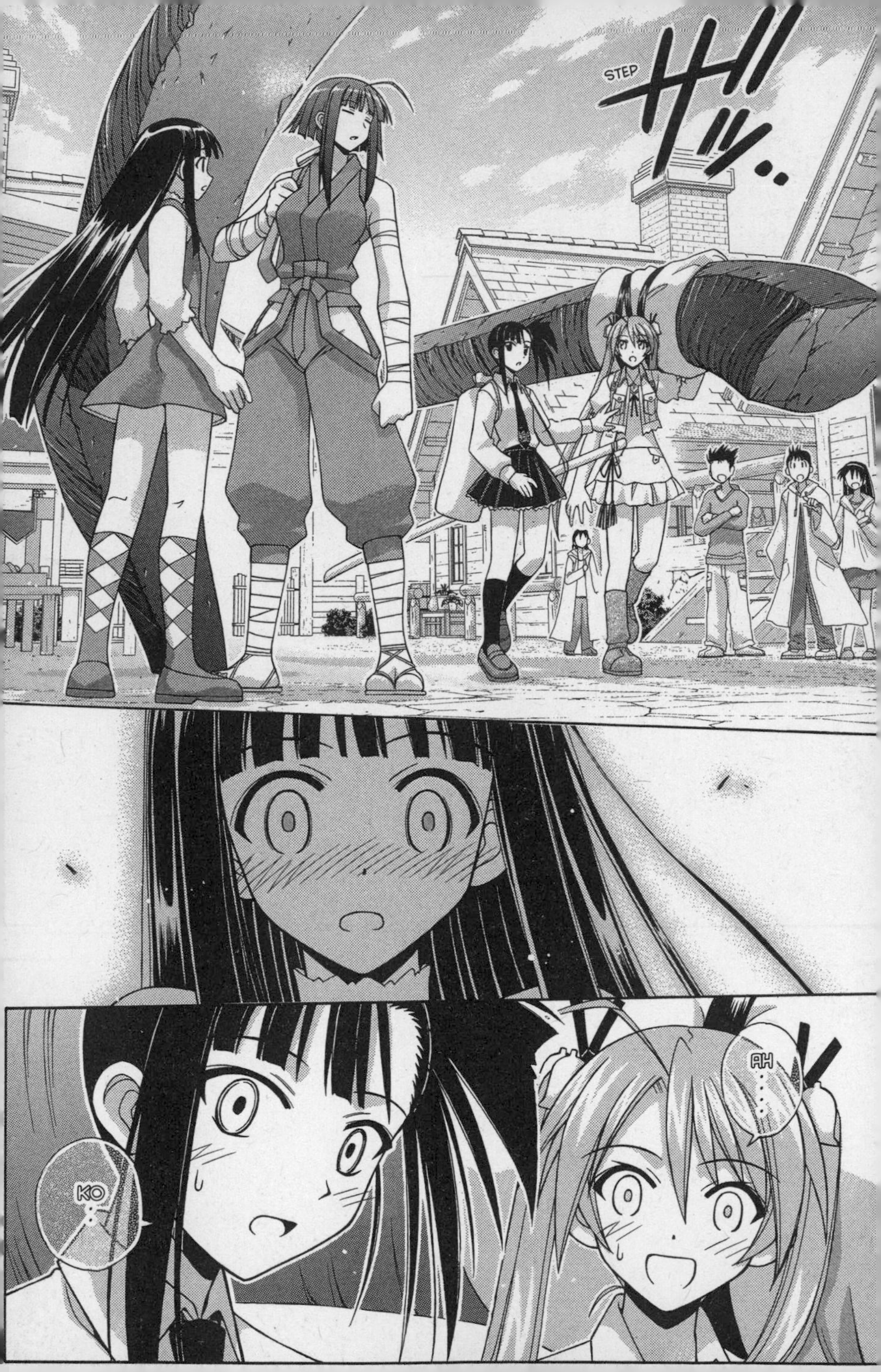
STEP
AH.....
KO..

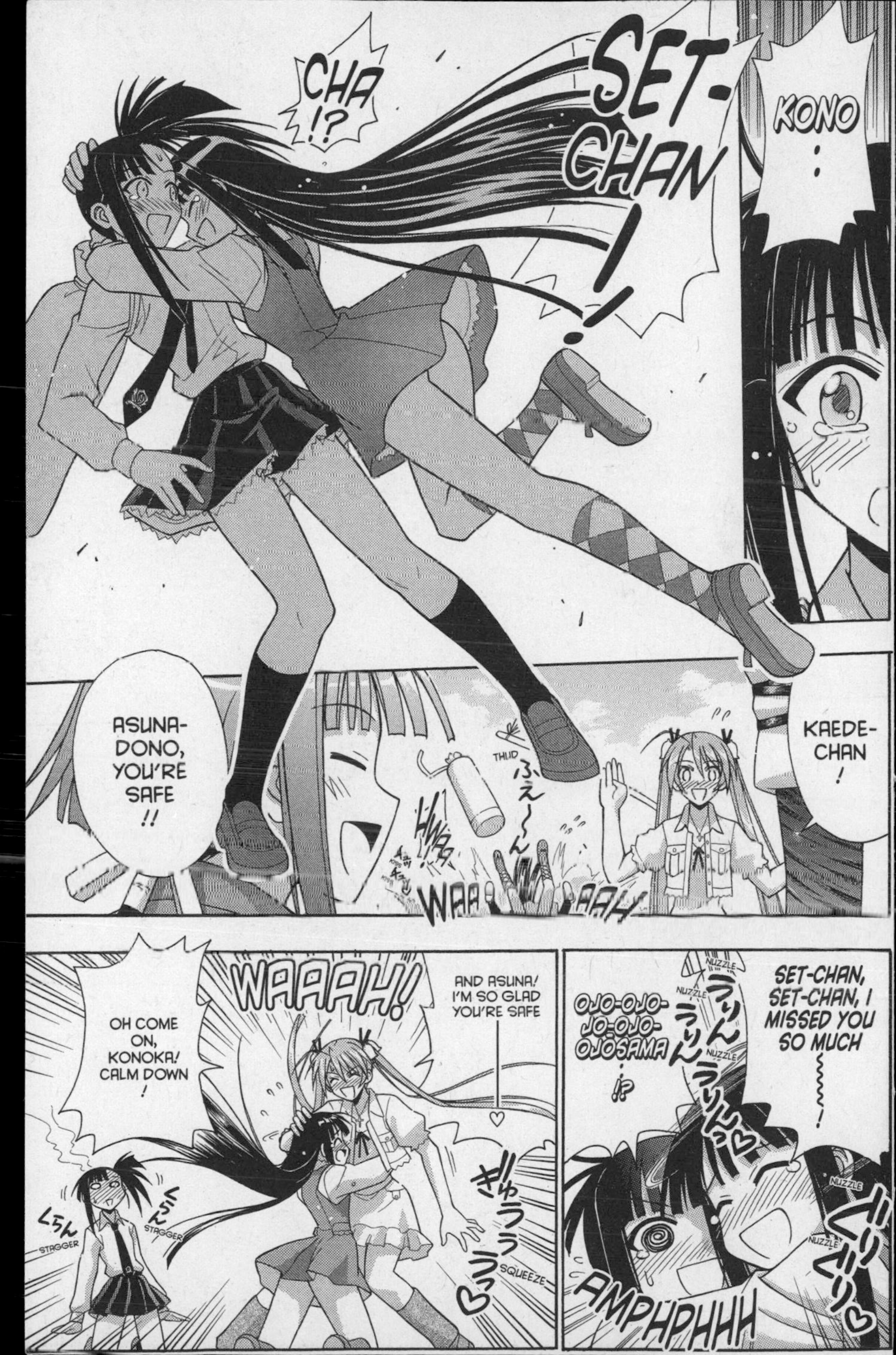
KONO : :
SET-CHAN !!
CHA !?
KAEDE-CHAN !
ASUNA-DONO, YOU'RE SAFE !!
THUD
ふえ〜ん
HWAA
WAA AAH
SET-CHAN, SET-CHAN, I MISSED YOU SO MUCH ~~~!
OJO-OJO-JO-OJO-OJOSAMA !?
NUZZLE
うりんうりん
AMPHPHHH
ぐりぐり
WAAAH!
AND ASUNA! I'M SO GLAD YOU'RE SAFE ♡
OH COME ON, KONOKA! CALM DOWN !
SQUEEZE
くらん
STAGGER

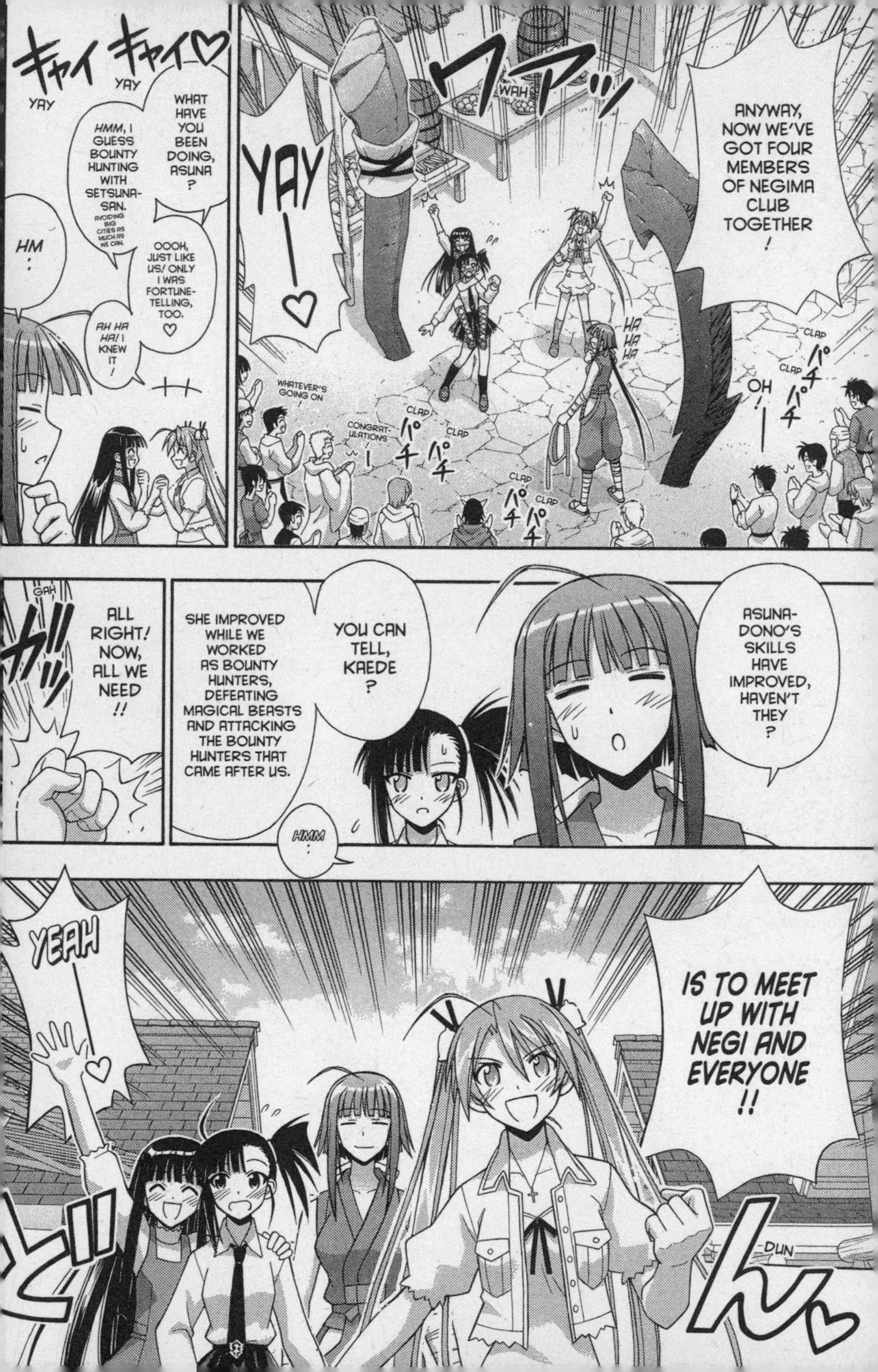
ANYWAY, NOW WE'VE GOT FOUR MEMBERS OF NEGIMA CLUB TOGETHER!
ワァッ WAH
YAY!♡
HA HA HA
パチ CLAP パチ CLAP
OH!
WHATEVER'S GOING ON!
CONGRATULATIONS!
パチ CLAP パチ CLAP
パチ CLAP パチ CLAP
キャイ キャイ♡ YAY YAY
WHAT HAVE YOU BEEN DOING, ASUNA?
HMM, I GUESS BOUNTY HUNTING WITH SETSUNA-SAN. AVOIDING BIG CITIES AS MUCH AS WE CAN.
OOOH, JUST LIKE US! ONLY I WAS FORTUNE-TELLING, TOO. ♡
AH HA HA! I KNEW IT!
HM...
ASUNA-DONO'S SKILLS HAVE IMPROVED, HAVEN'T THEY?
YOU CAN TELL, KAEDE?
SHE IMPROVED WHILE WE WORKED AS BOUNTY HUNTERS, DEFEATING MAGICAL BEASTS AND ATTACKING THE BOUNTY HUNTERS THAT CAME AFTER US.
HMM...
GAH
ALL RIGHT! NOW, ALL WE NEED!!
IS TO MEET UP WITH NEGI AND EVERYONE!!
YEAH!♡
-DUN

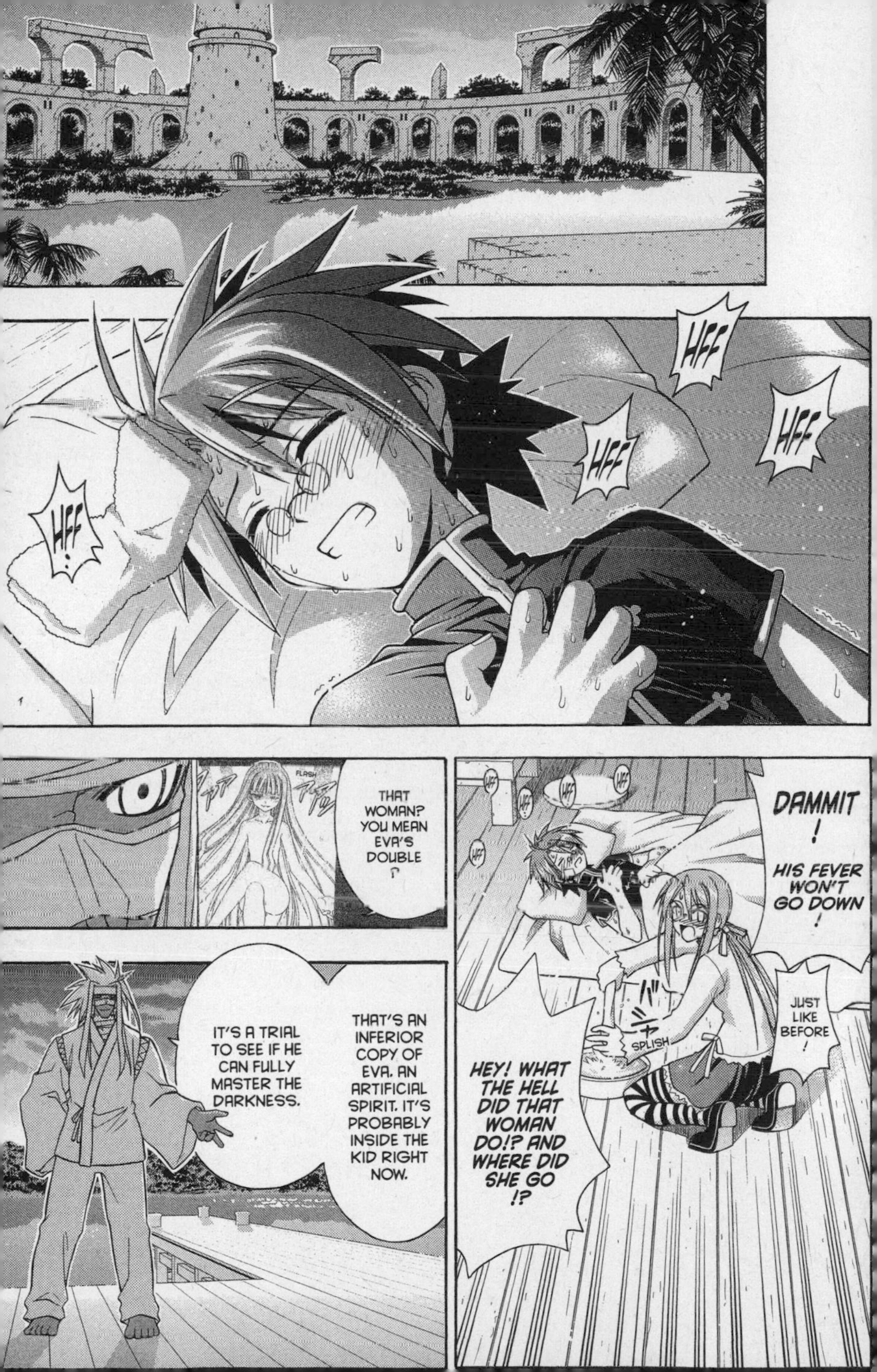
HFF
HFF
HFF
HFF!
HFF
HFF
HFF
HFF
DAMMIT!
HIS FEVER WON'T GO DOWN!
JUST LIKE BEFORE!
SPLISH
HEY! WHAT THE HELL DID THAT WOMAN DO!? AND WHERE DID SHE GO!?
FLASH
THAT WOMAN? YOU MEAN EVA'S DOUBLE?
THAT'S AN INFERIOR COPY OF EVA. AN ARTIFICIAL SPIRIT. IT'S PROBABLY INSIDE THE KID RIGHT NOW.
IT'S A TRIAL TO SEE IF HE CAN FULLY MASTER THE DARKNESS.

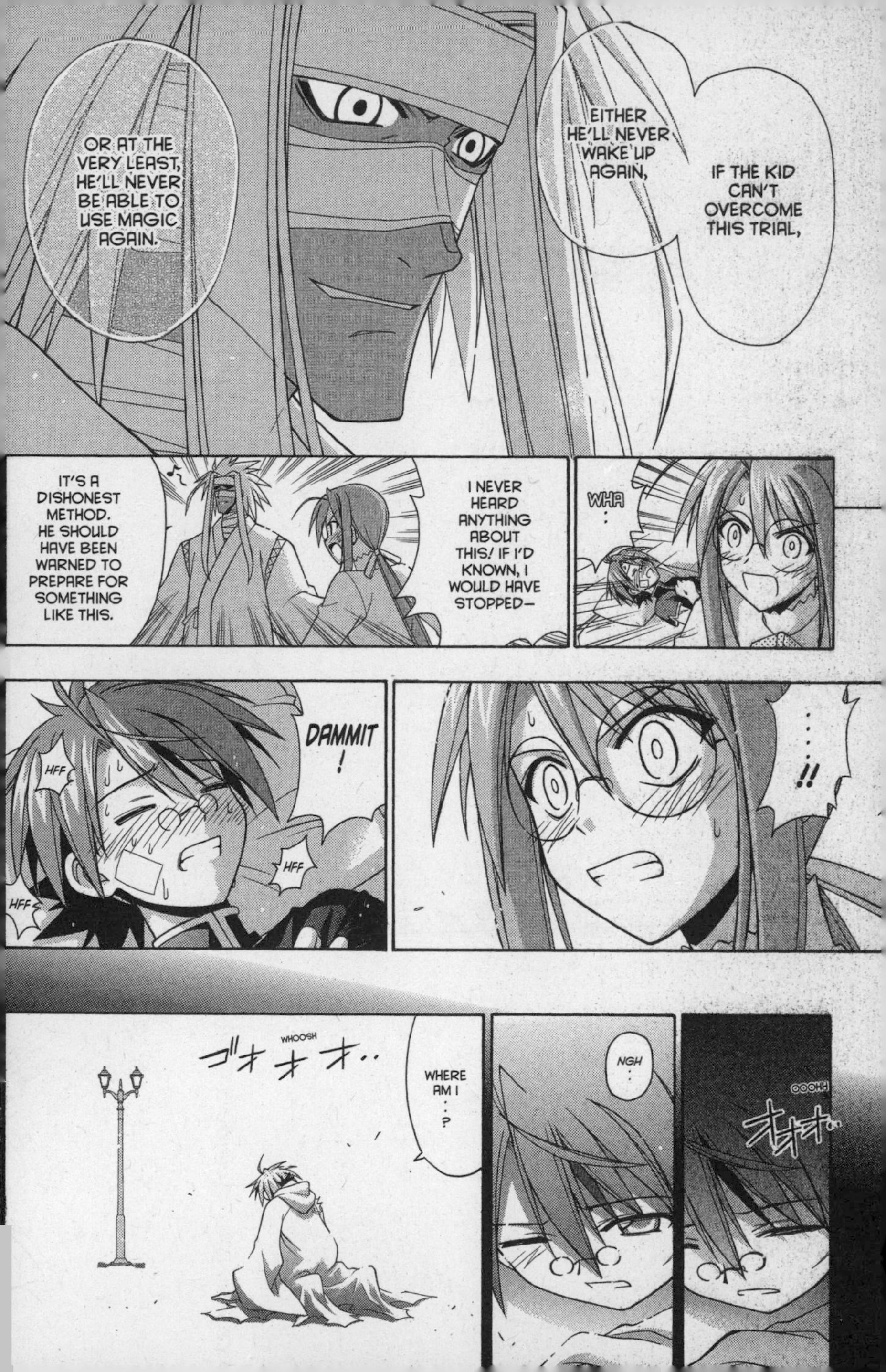
IF THE KID CAN'T OVERCOME THIS TRIAL,
EITHER HE'LL NEVER WAKE UP AGAIN,
OR AT THE VERY LEAST, HE'LL NEVER BE ABLE TO USE MAGIC AGAIN.
WHA...
I NEVER HEARD ANYTHING ABOUT THIS! IF I'D KNOWN, I WOULD HAVE STOPPED—
IT'S A DISHONEST METHOD. HE SHOULD HAVE BEEN WARNED TO PREPARE FOR SOMETHING LIKE THIS.
...!!
DAMMIT!
HFF
HFF
HFF
OOOHH
NGH...
WHERE AM I...?
WHOOSH

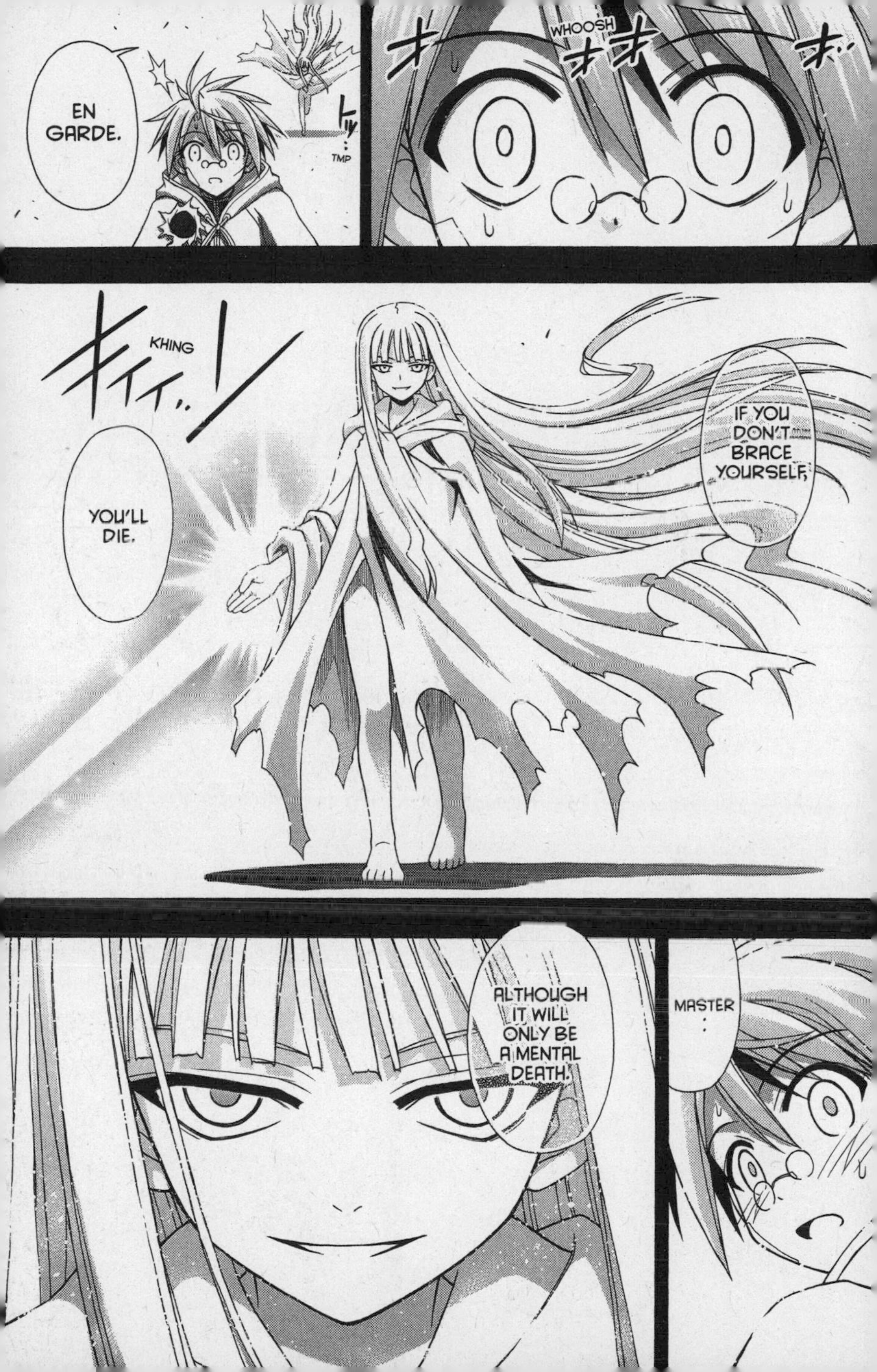
WHOOSH
EN GARDE.
TMP
IF YOU DON'T BRACE YOURSELF,
KHING
YOU'LL DIE.
MASTER
...
ALTHOUGH IT WILL ONLY BE A MENTAL DEATH.

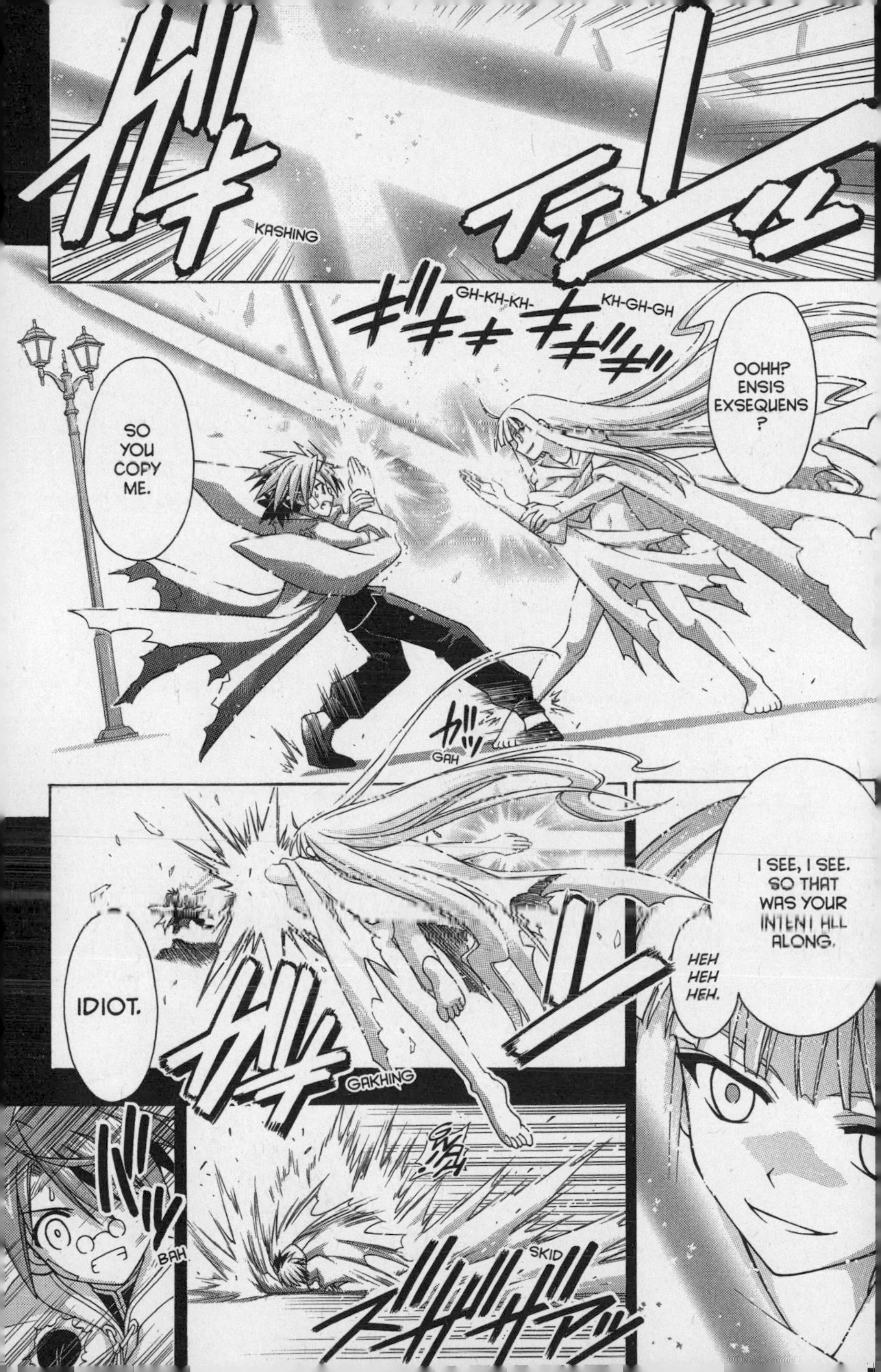
KASHING
GH-KH-KH-
KH-GH-GH
OOHH? ENSIS EXSEQUENS ?
SO YOU COPY ME.
GAH
I SEE, I SEE. SO THAT WAS YOUR INTENT ALL ALONG.
HEH HEH HEH.
IDIOT.
GAKHING
GWAH!
SKID
BAH

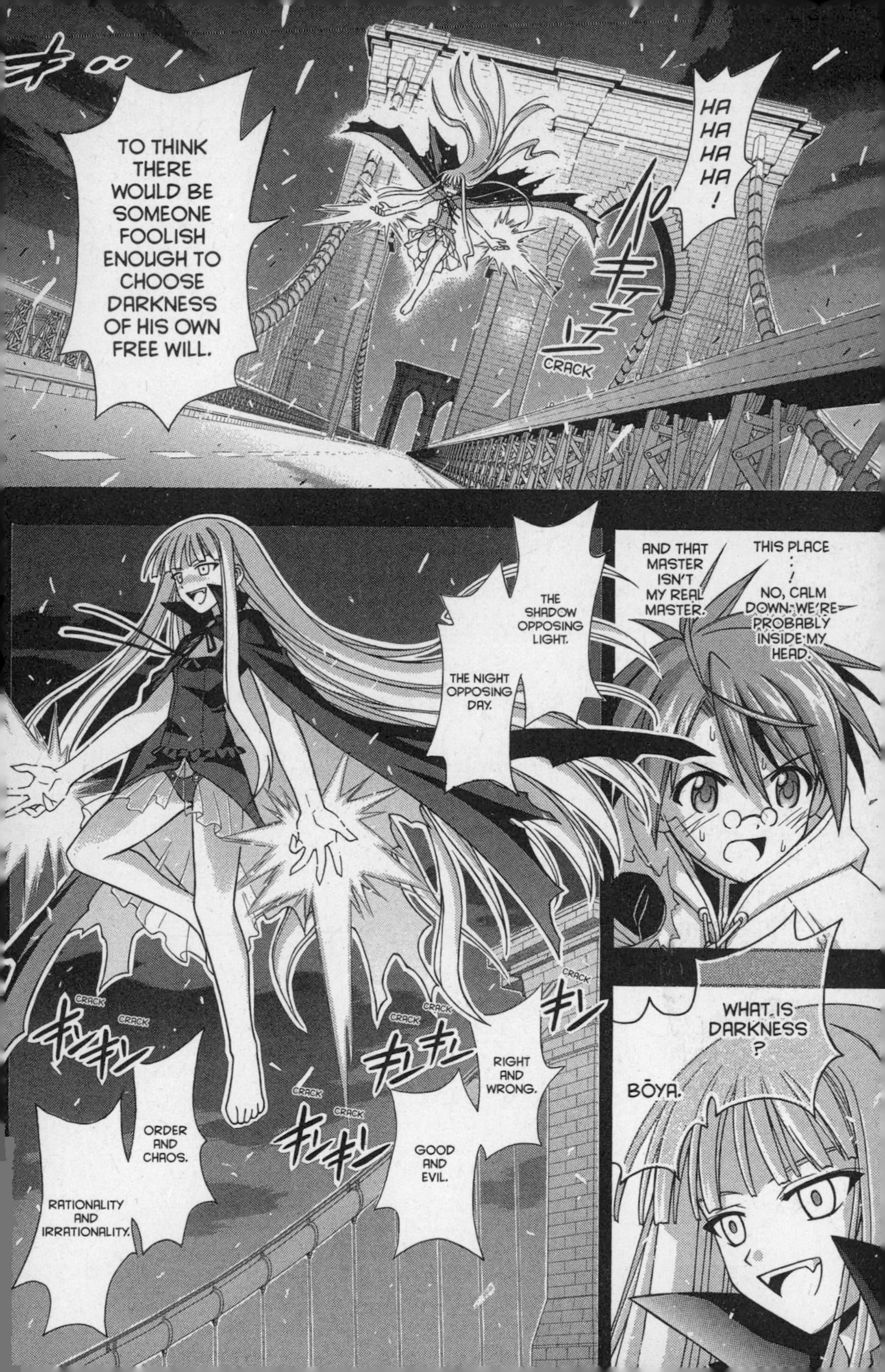
HA HA HA HA!
CRACK
TO THINK THERE WOULD BE SOMEONE FOOLISH ENOUGH TO CHOOSE DARKNESS OF HIS OWN FREE WILL.
THIS PLACE...!
NO, CALM DOWN. WE'RE PROBABLY INSIDE MY HEAD.
AND THAT MASTER ISN'T MY REAL MASTER.
WHAT IS DARKNESS?
BŌYA.
THE SHADOW OPPOSING LIGHT.
THE NIGHT OPPOSING DAY.
CRACK
RIGHT AND WRONG.
CRACK
CRACK
CRACK
CRACK
CRACK
CRACK
GOOD AND EVIL.
ORDER AND CHAOS.
RATIONALITY AND IRRATIONALITY.

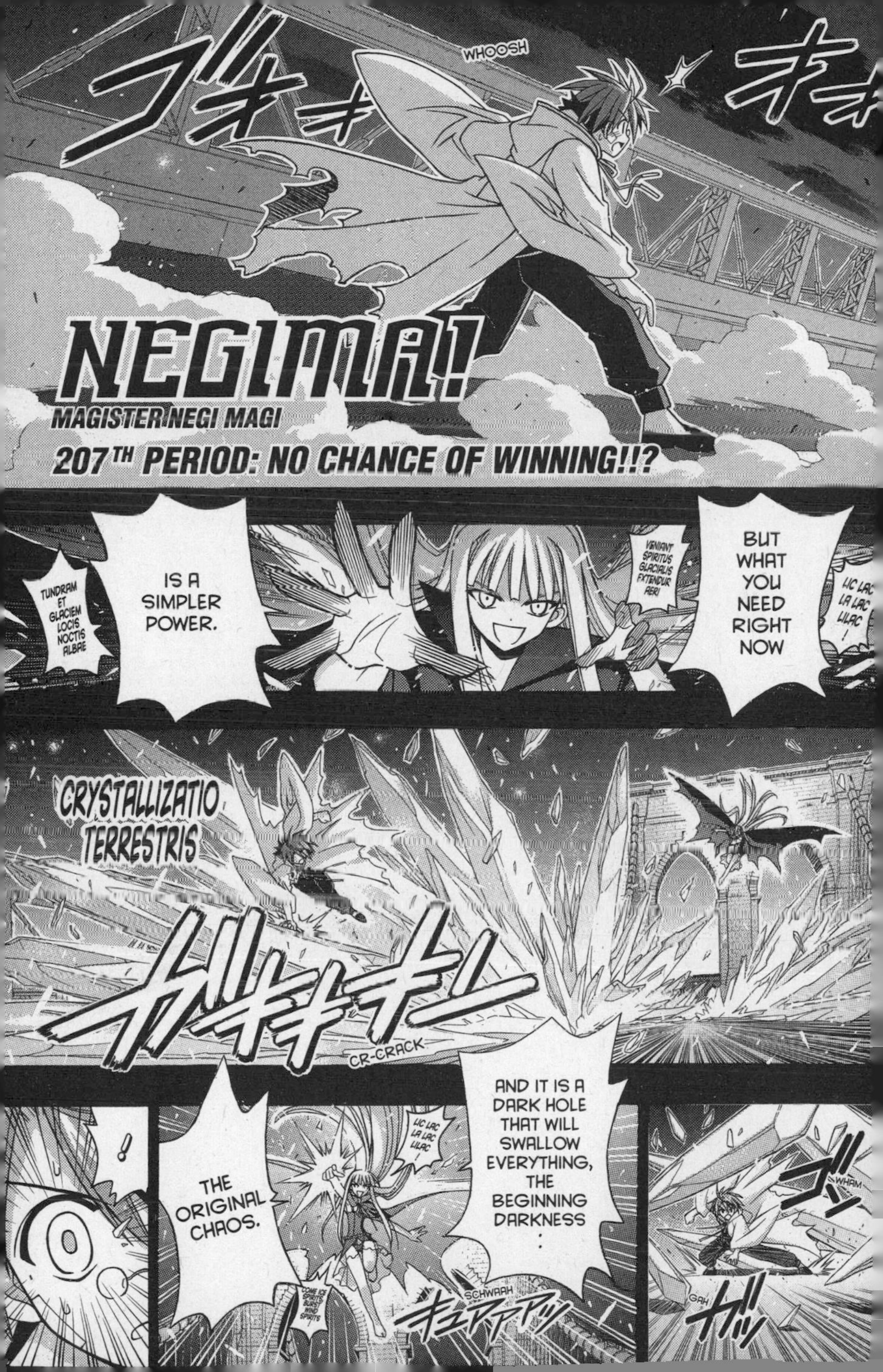
WHOOSH
NEGIMA!
MAGISTER NEGI MAGI
207TH PERIOD: NO CHANCE OF WINNING!!?
LIC LAC LA LAC LILAC!
BUT WHAT YOU NEED RIGHT NOW
VENIANT SPIRITUS GLACIALIS EXTENDUR AER!
IS A SIMPLER POWER.
TUNDRAM ET GLACIEM LOCIS NOCTIS ALBAE
CRYSTALLIZATIO TERRESTRIS
CR-CRACK
WHAM
GAH
AND IT IS A DARK HOLE THAT WILL SWALLOW EVERYTHING, THE BEGINNING DARKNESS:
LIC LAC LA LAC LILAC!
THE ORIGINAL CHAOS.
COME ICE SPIRITS BURST WIND SPIRITS!
SCHWAAH
!

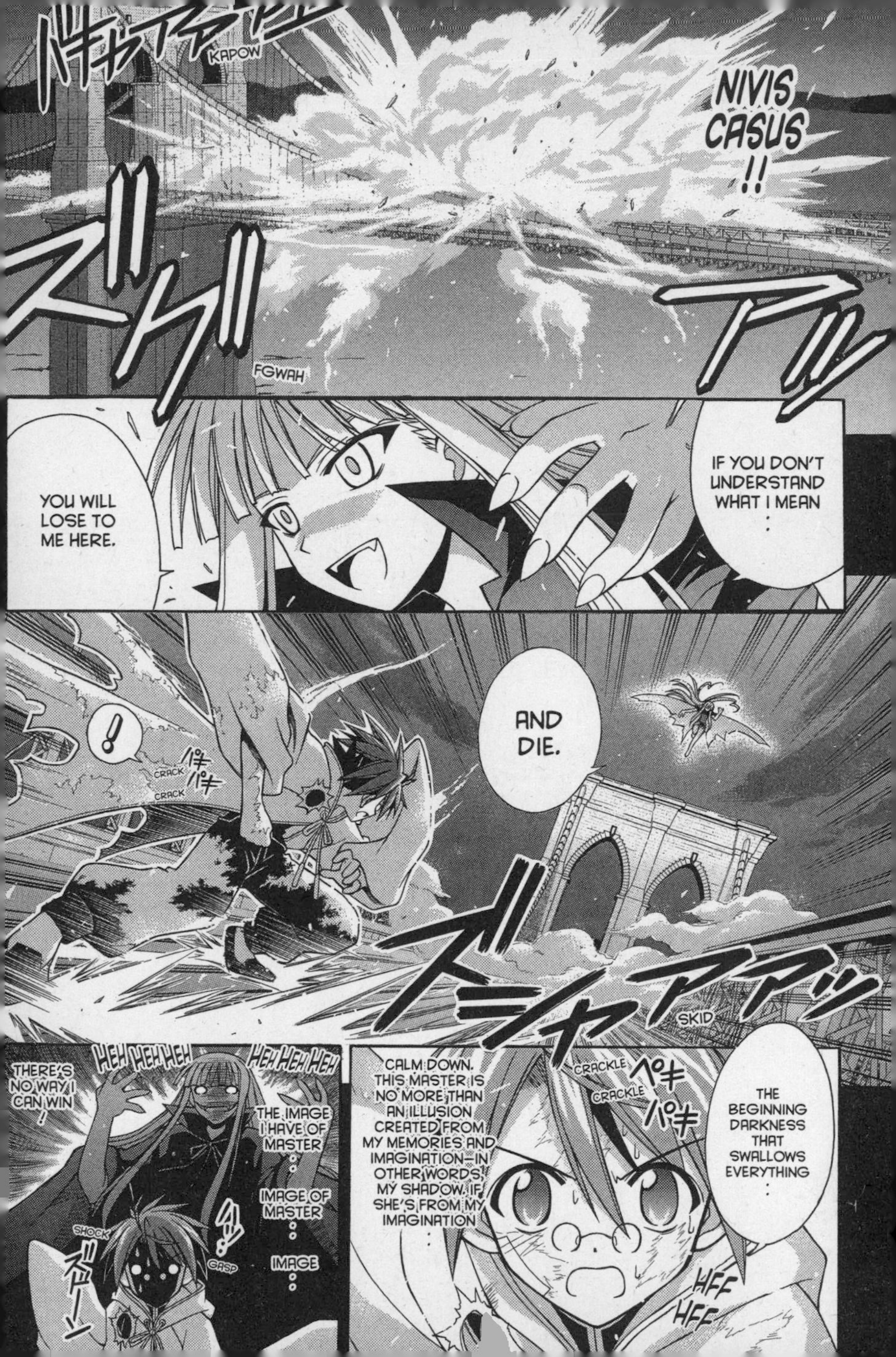
NIVIS CASUS !!
KAPOW
FGWAH
IF YOU DON'T UNDERSTAND WHAT I MEAN . . .
YOU WILL LOSE TO ME HERE.
AND DIE.
!
CRACK
CRACK
SKID
CRACKLE
CRACKLE
THE BEGINNING DARKNESS THAT SWALLOWS EVERYTHING . . .
CALM DOWN. THIS MASTER IS NO MORE THAN AN ILLUSION CREATED FROM MY MEMORIES AND IMAGINATION—IN OTHER WORDS, MY SHADOW. IF SHE'S FROM MY IMAGINATION . . .
HFF
HFF
HEH HEH HEH
HEH HEH HEH
THE IMAGE I HAVE OF MASTER . . .
IMAGE OF MASTER . . .
IMAGE . . .
THERE'S NO WAY I CAN WIN!
SHOCK
GASP

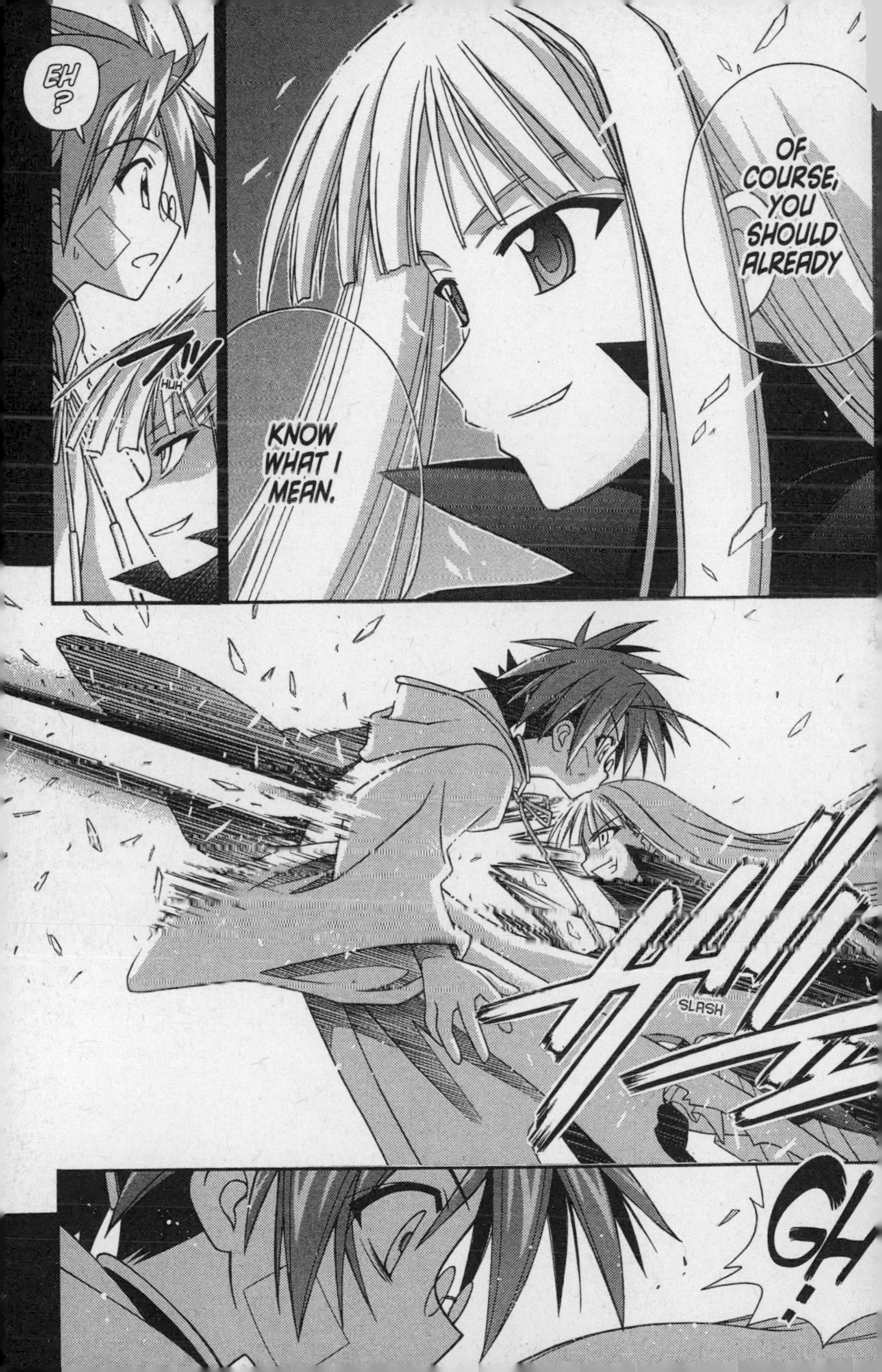
OF COURSE, YOU SHOULD ALREADY
KNOW WHAT I MEAN.
EH?
HUH
SLASH
GH..!

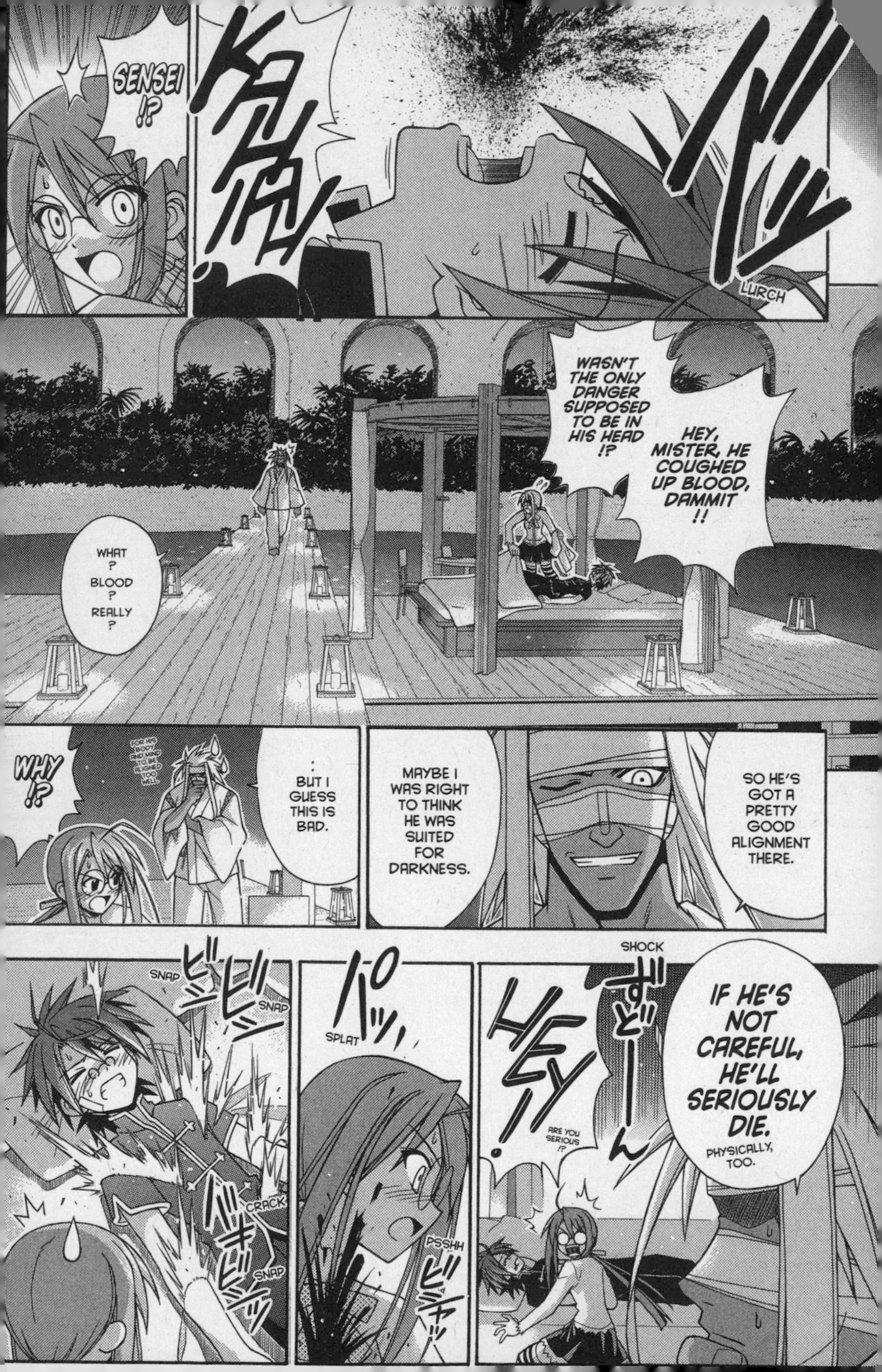
LURCH
KAHAK!
SENSEI !?
HEY, MISTER, HE COUGHED UP BLOOD, DAMMIT !!
WASN'T THE ONLY DANGER SUPPOSED TO BE IN HIS HEAD !?
WHAT ? BLOOD ? REALLY ?
SO HE'S GOT A PRETTY GOOD ALIGNMENT THERE.
MAYBE I WAS RIGHT TO THINK HE WAS SUITED FOR DARKNESS.
: BUT I GUESS THIS IS BAD.
FOR HIS BODY AND MIND TO BE ALIGNED TOO WELL.
WHY !?
IF HE'S NOT CAREFUL, HE'LL SERIOUSLY DIE.
PHYSICALLY, TOO.
SHOCK
HEY !!
ARE YOU SERIOUS !?
SPLAT
PSSHH
SNAP
SNAP
CRACK
SNAP

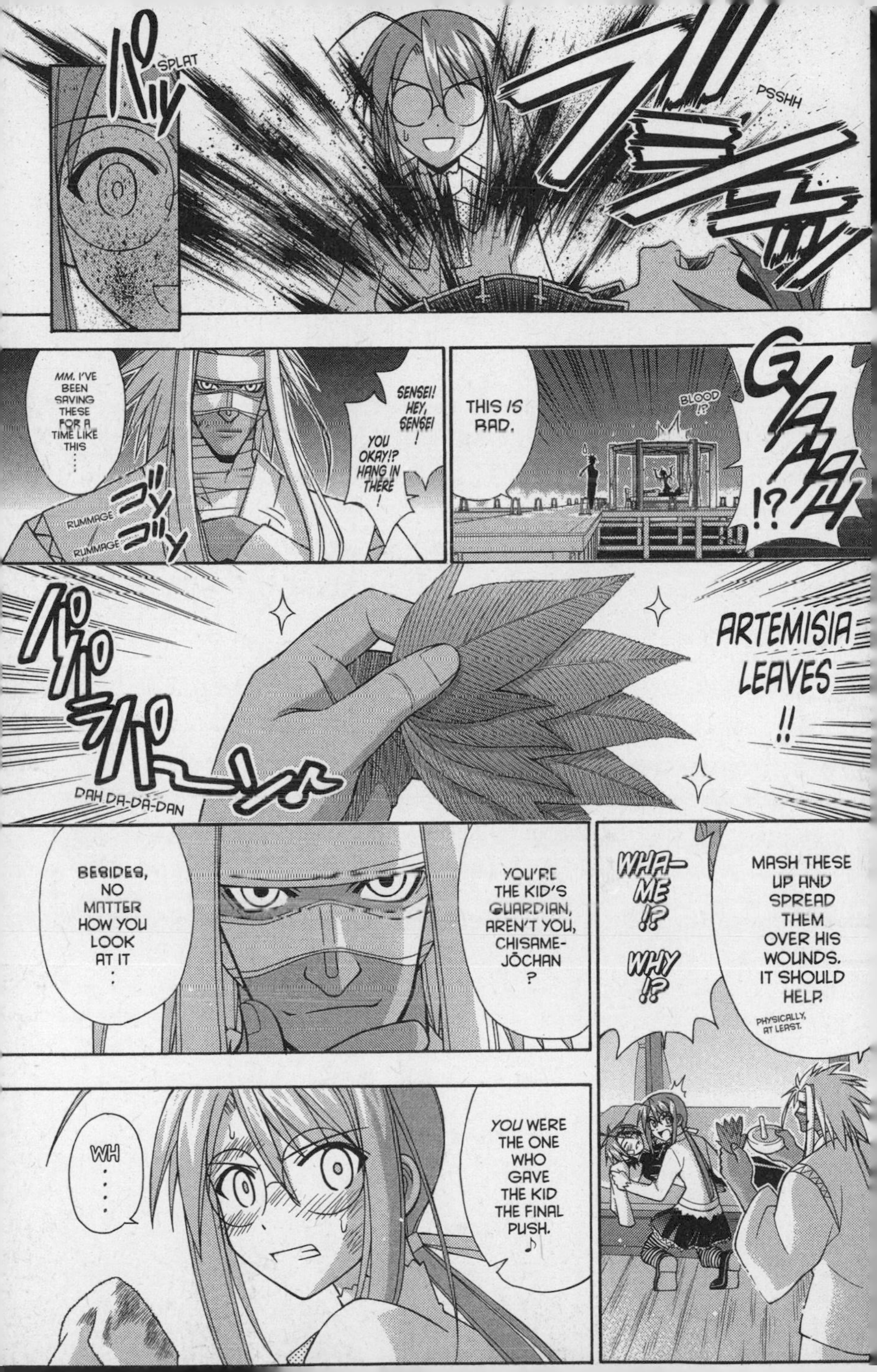
PSSHH
SPLAT
GYAAAH!?
BLOOD!?
THIS IS BAD.
SENSEI! HEY, SENSEI!
YOU OKAY!? HANG IN THERE!
MM. I'VE BEEN SAVING THESE FOR A TIME LIKE THIS...
RUMMAGE
RUMMAGE
ARTEMISIA LEAVES!!
DAH DA-DA-DAN
MASH THESE UP AND SPREAD THEM OVER HIS WOUNDS. IT SHOULD HELP.
PHYSICALLY, AT LEAST.
WHA- ME!?
WHY!?
YOU'RE THE KID'S GUARDIAN, AREN'T YOU, CHISAME-JŌCHAN?
BESIDES, NO MATTER HOW YOU LOOK AT IT...
YOU WERE THE ONE WHO GAVE THE KID THE FINAL PUSH. ♪
WH...

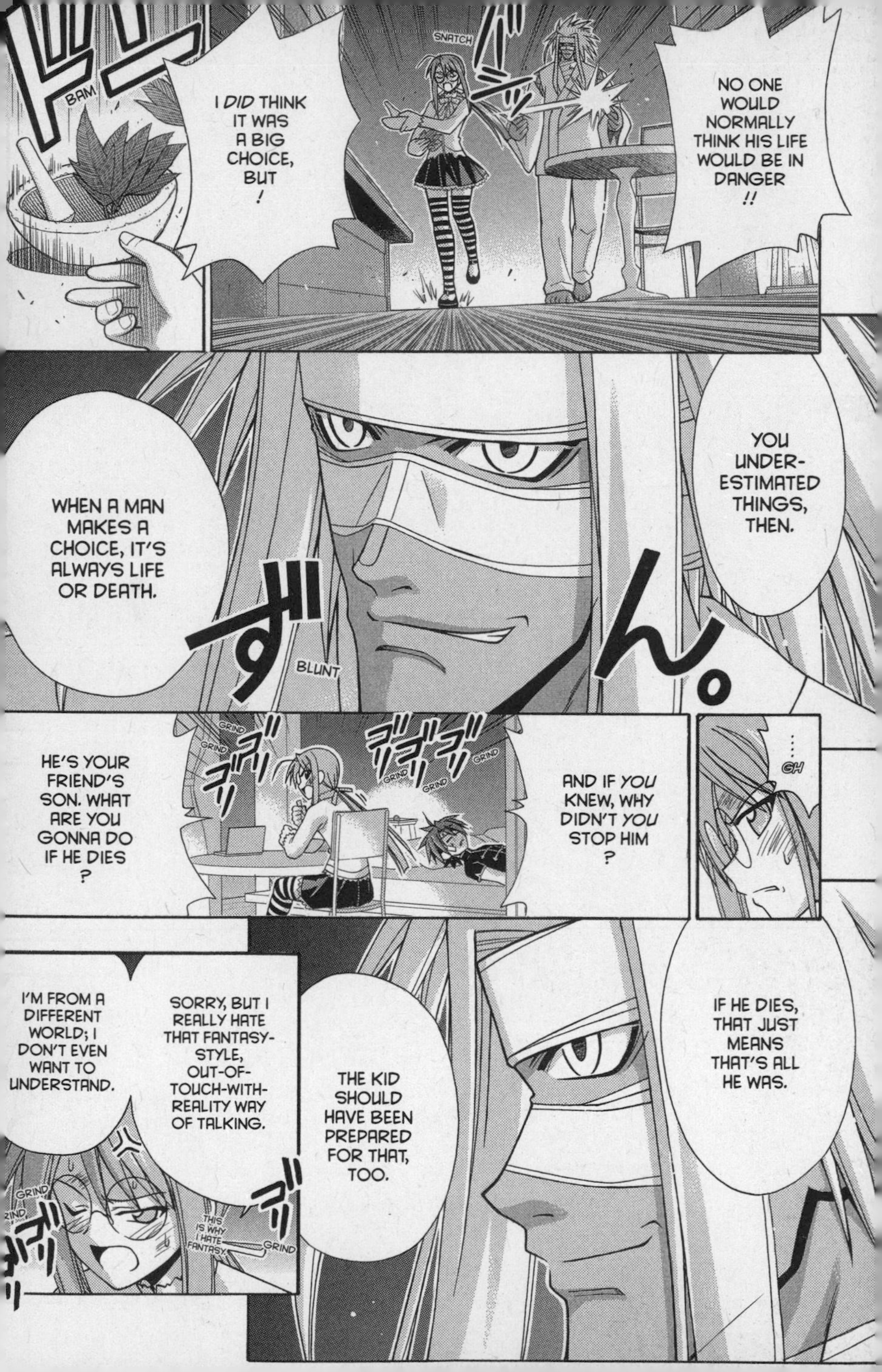
SNATCH
NO ONE WOULD NORMALLY THINK HIS LIFE WOULD BE IN DANGER!!
I *DID* THINK IT WAS A BIG CHOICE, BUT!
BAM
YOU UNDER-ESTIMATED THINGS, THEN.
WHEN A MAN MAKES A CHOICE, IT'S ALWAYS LIFE OR DEATH.
BLUNT
...GH
AND IF *YOU* KNEW, WHY DIDN'T *YOU* STOP HIM?
GRIND
GRIND
HE'S YOUR FRIEND'S SON. WHAT ARE YOU GONNA DO IF HE DIES?
GRIND
GRIND
IF HE DIES, THAT JUST MEANS THAT'S ALL HE WAS.
THE KID SHOULD HAVE BEEN PREPARED FOR THAT, TOO.
SORRY, BUT I REALLY HATE THAT FANTASY-STYLE, OUT-OF-TOUCH-WITH-REALITY WAY OF TALKING.
I'M FROM A DIFFERENT WORLD; I DON'T EVEN WANT TO UNDERSTAND.
GRIND
THIS IS WHY I HATE FANTASY.
GRIND

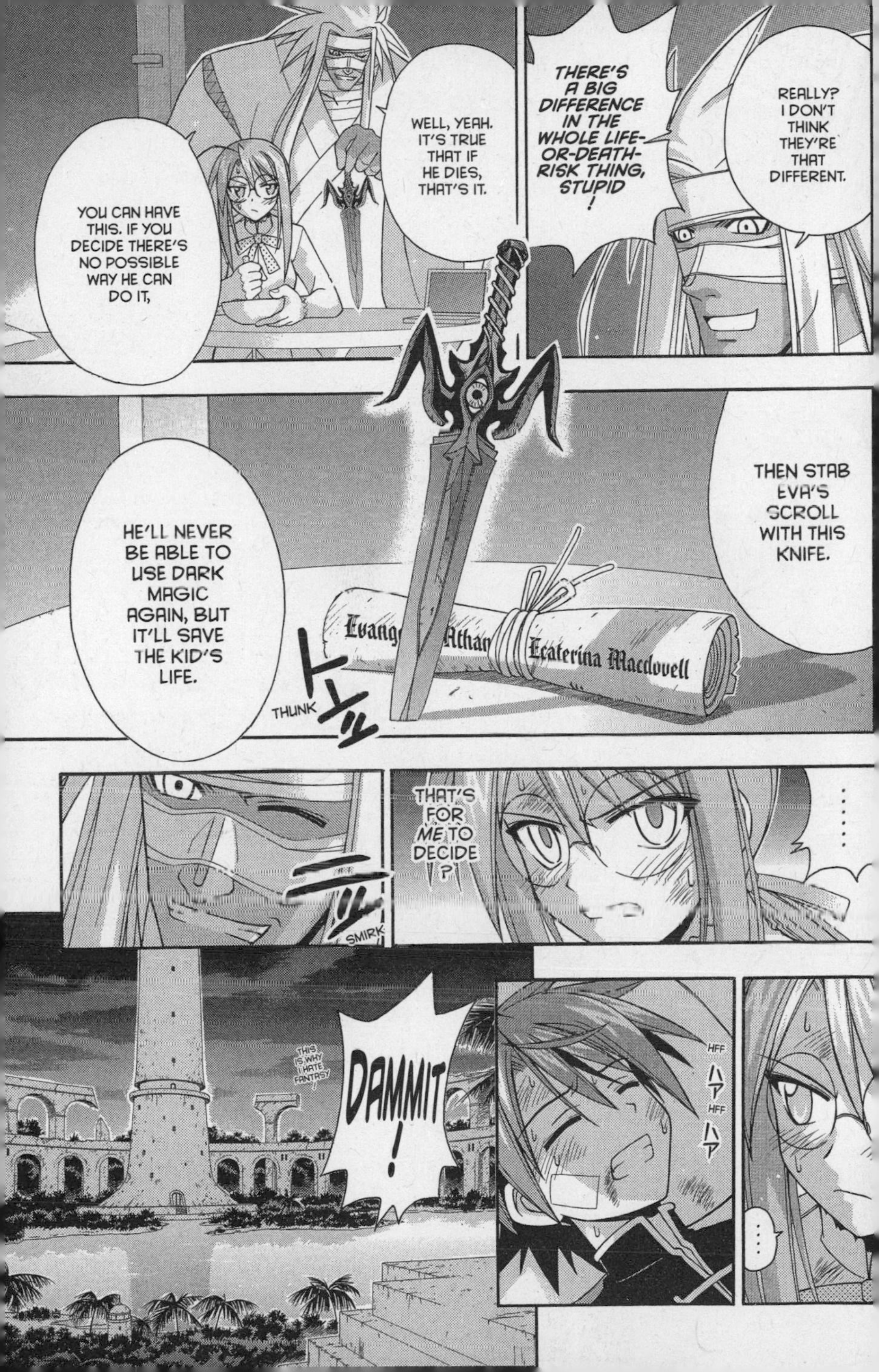
REALLY? I DON'T THINK THEY'RE THAT DIFFERENT.
THERE'S A BIG DIFFERENCE IN THE WHOLE LIFE-OR-DEATH-RISK THING, STUPID!
WELL, YEAH. IT'S TRUE THAT IF HE DIES, THAT'S IT.
YOU CAN HAVE THIS. IF YOU DECIDE THERE'S NO POSSIBLE WAY HE CAN DO IT,
THEN STAB EVA'S SCROLL WITH THIS KNIFE.
HE'LL NEVER BE ABLE TO USE DARK MAGIC AGAIN, BUT IT'LL SAVE THE KID'S LIFE.
Ecaterina Macdovell
THUNK
.....
THAT'S FOR ME TO DECIDE?
SMIRK
.....
HFF
HFF
DAMMIT!
THIS IS WHY I HATE FANTASY

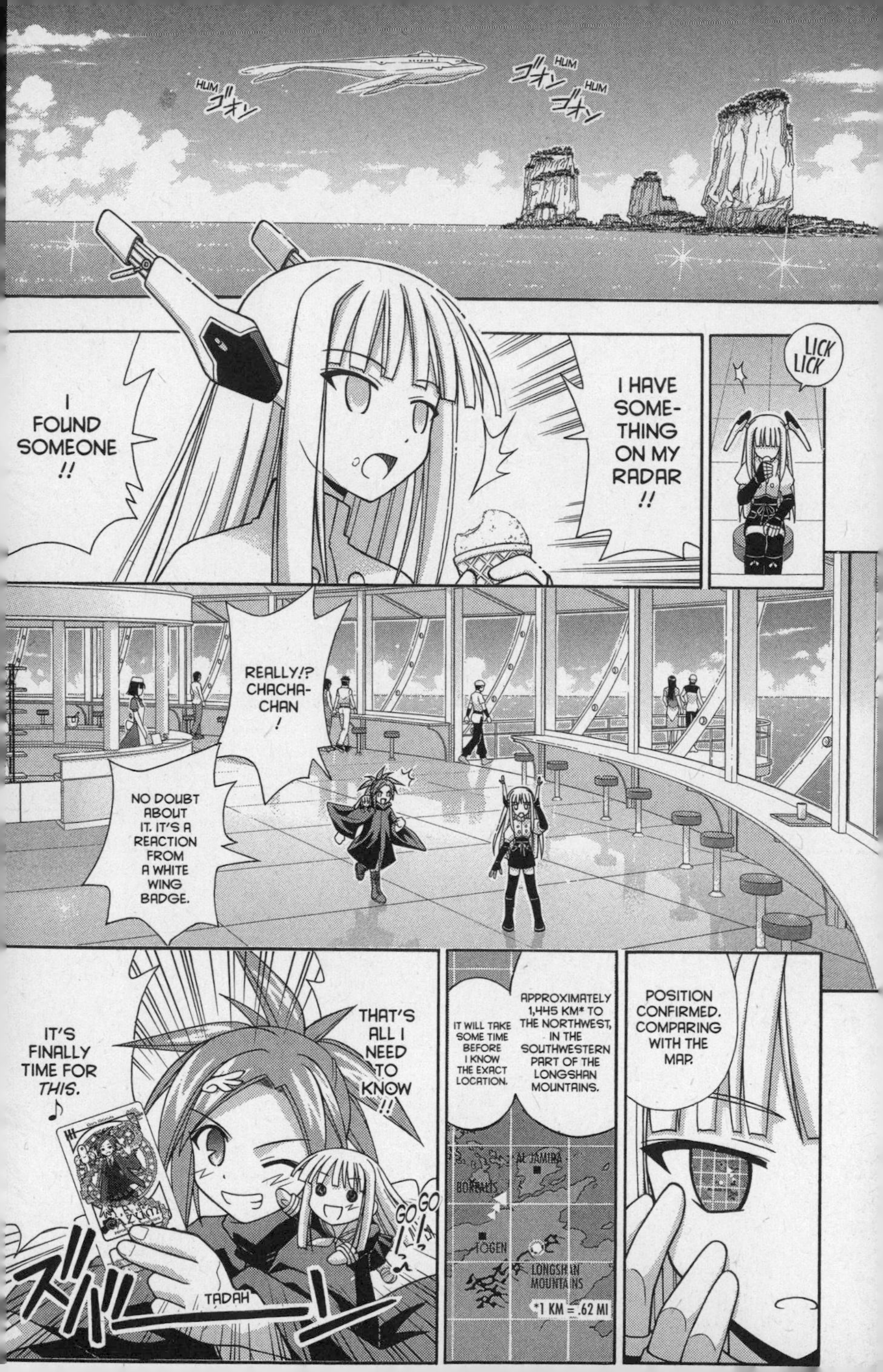
HUM
ゴオン
HUM
ゴオン
HUM
ゴオン
LICK LICK
I HAVE SOME-THING ON MY RADAR !!
I FOUND SOMEONE !!
REALLY!? CHACHA-CHAN !
NO DOUBT ABOUT IT. IT'S A REACTION FROM A WHITE WING BADGE.
POSITION CONFIRMED. COMPARING WITH THE MAP.
APPROXIMATELY 1,445 KM* TO THE NORTHWEST, IN THE SOUTHWESTERN PART OF THE LONGSHAN MOUNTAINS.
IT WILL TAKE SOME TIME BEFORE I KNOW THE EXACT LOCATION.
AL JAMIRA
BOREALIS
TŌGEN
LONGSHAN MOUNTAINS
*1 KM = .62 MI
THAT'S ALL I NEED TO KNOW !!
IT'S FINALLY TIME FOR THIS. ♪
GO GO
TADAH

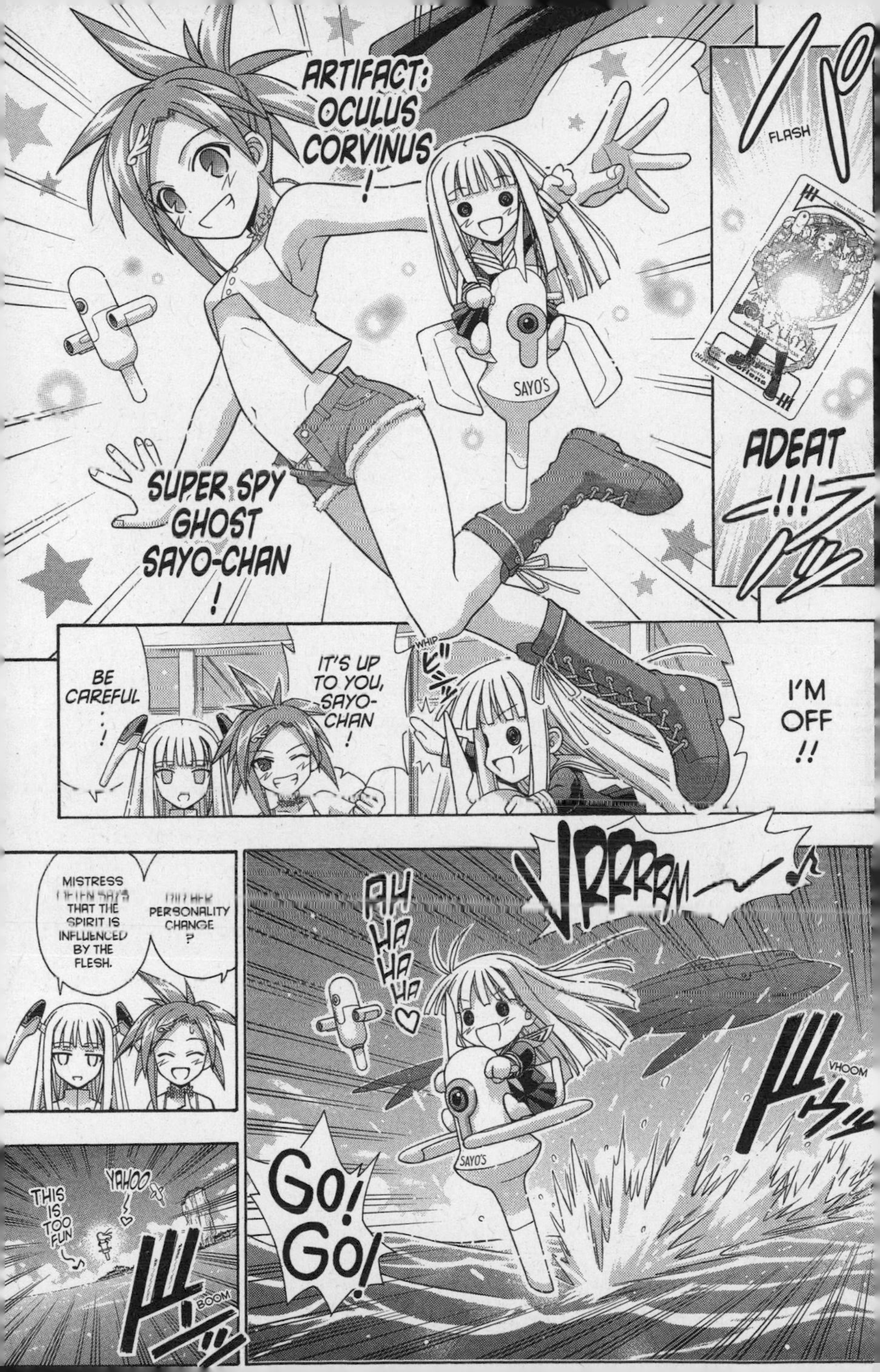
FLASH
ADEAT!!!
ARTIFACT: OCULUS CORVINUS!
SUPER SPY GHOST SAYO-CHAN!
SAYO'S
I'M OFF!!
WHIP
IT'S UP TO YOU, SAYO-CHAN!
BE CAREFUL...!
VRRRRM
AH HA HA HA ♡
VHOOM
SAYO'S
GO! GO!
RATHER PERSONALITY CHANGE?
MISTRESS OFTEN SAYS THAT THE SPIRIT IS INFLUENCED BY THE FLESH.
YAHOO ♡
THIS IS TOO FUN
BOOM

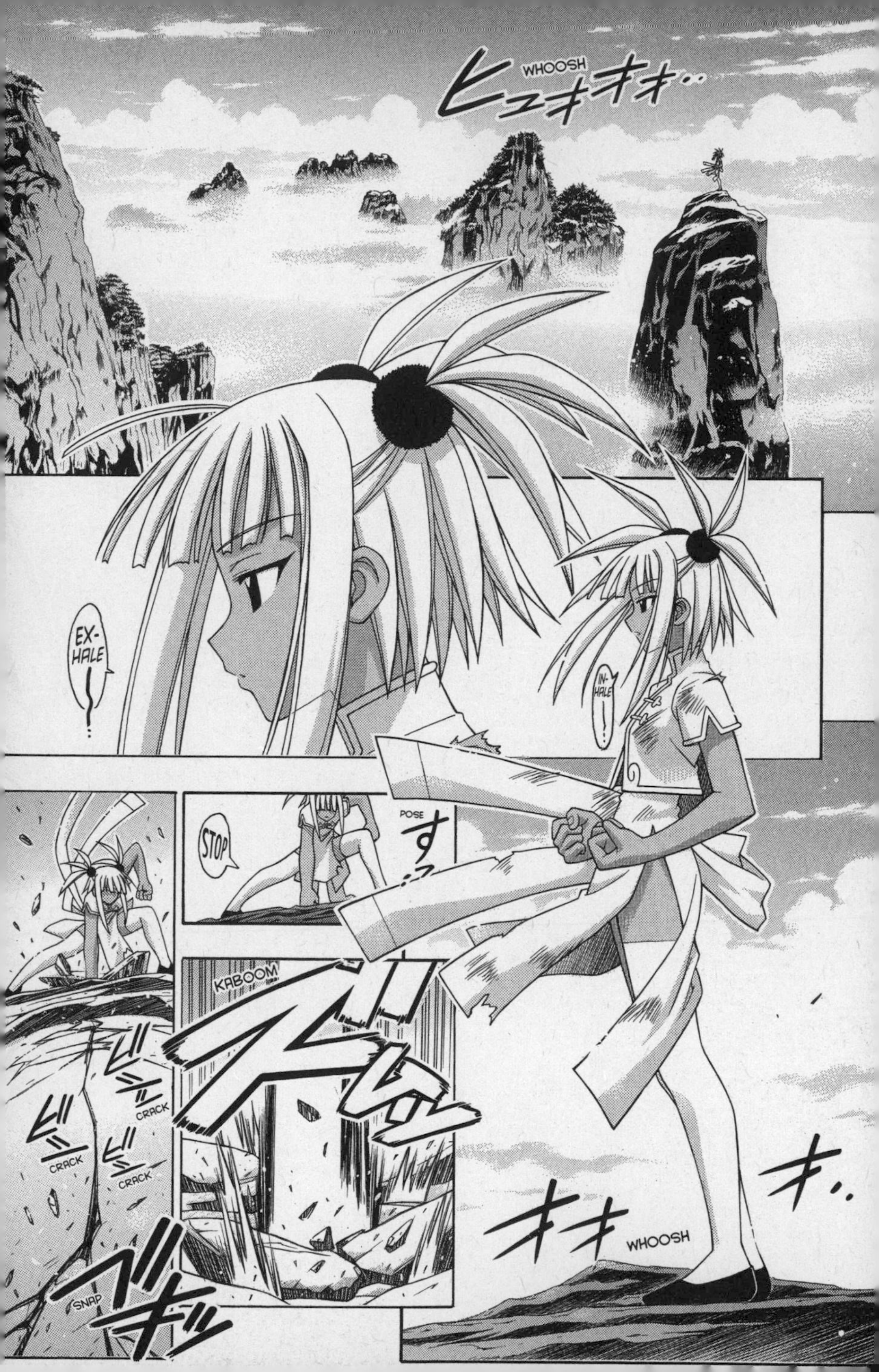
WHOOSH
ヒュォォォ..
IN-HALE!
EX-HALE!
POSE
す..
STOP
WHOOSH
ォォォ..
KABOOM
CRACK
CRACK
CRACK
SNAP

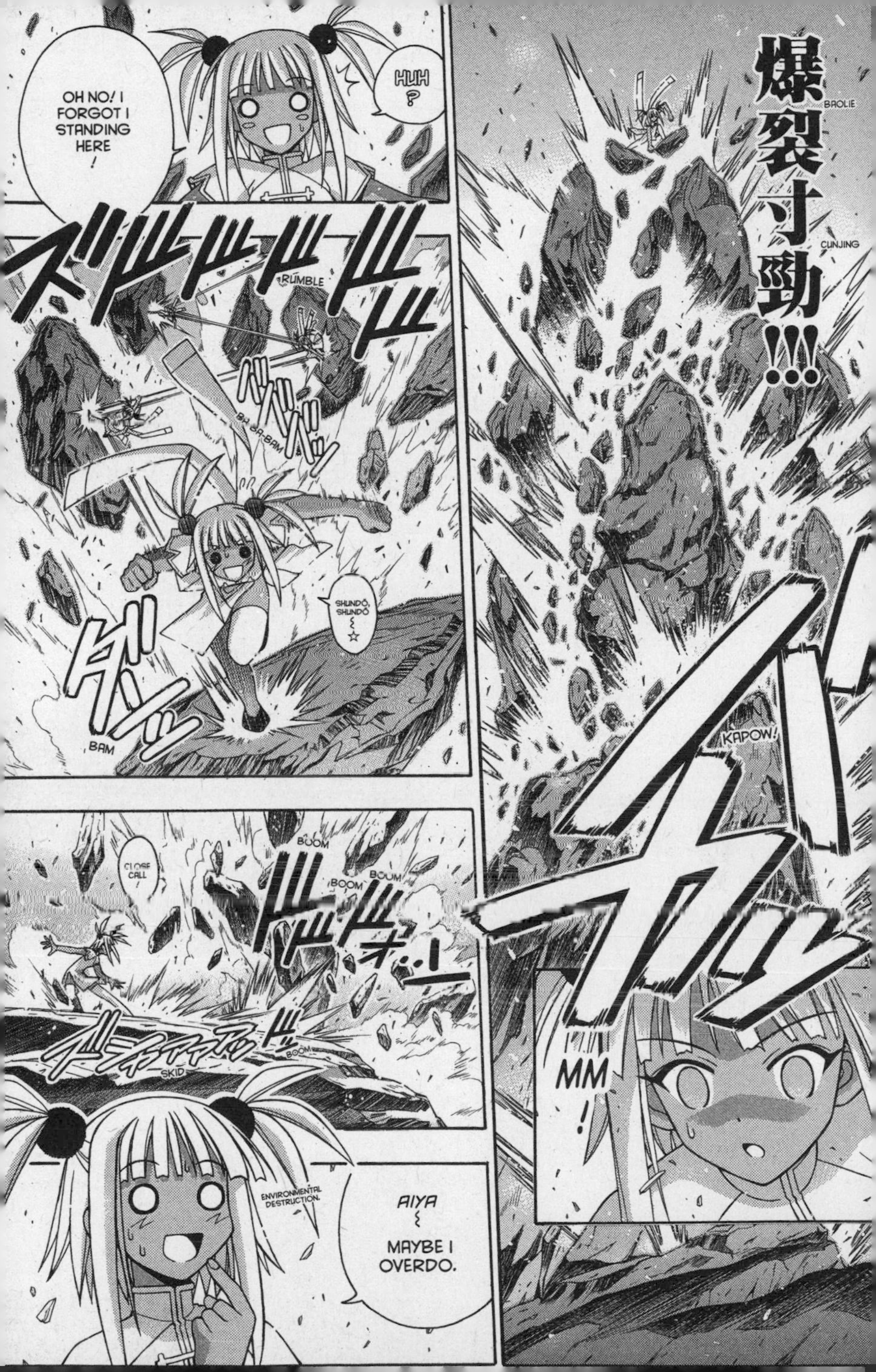

爆裂寸勁!!!
BROLIE
CUNJING
KAPOW!
MM!
HUH?
OH NO! I FORGOT I STANDING HERE!
RUMBLE
BA BA-BAM
SHUNDO, SHUNDO~☆
BAM
BOOM
BOOM
BOOM
CLOSE CALL!
BOOM
SKID
AIYA~ MAYBE I OVERDO.
ENVIRONMENTAL DESTRUCTION.

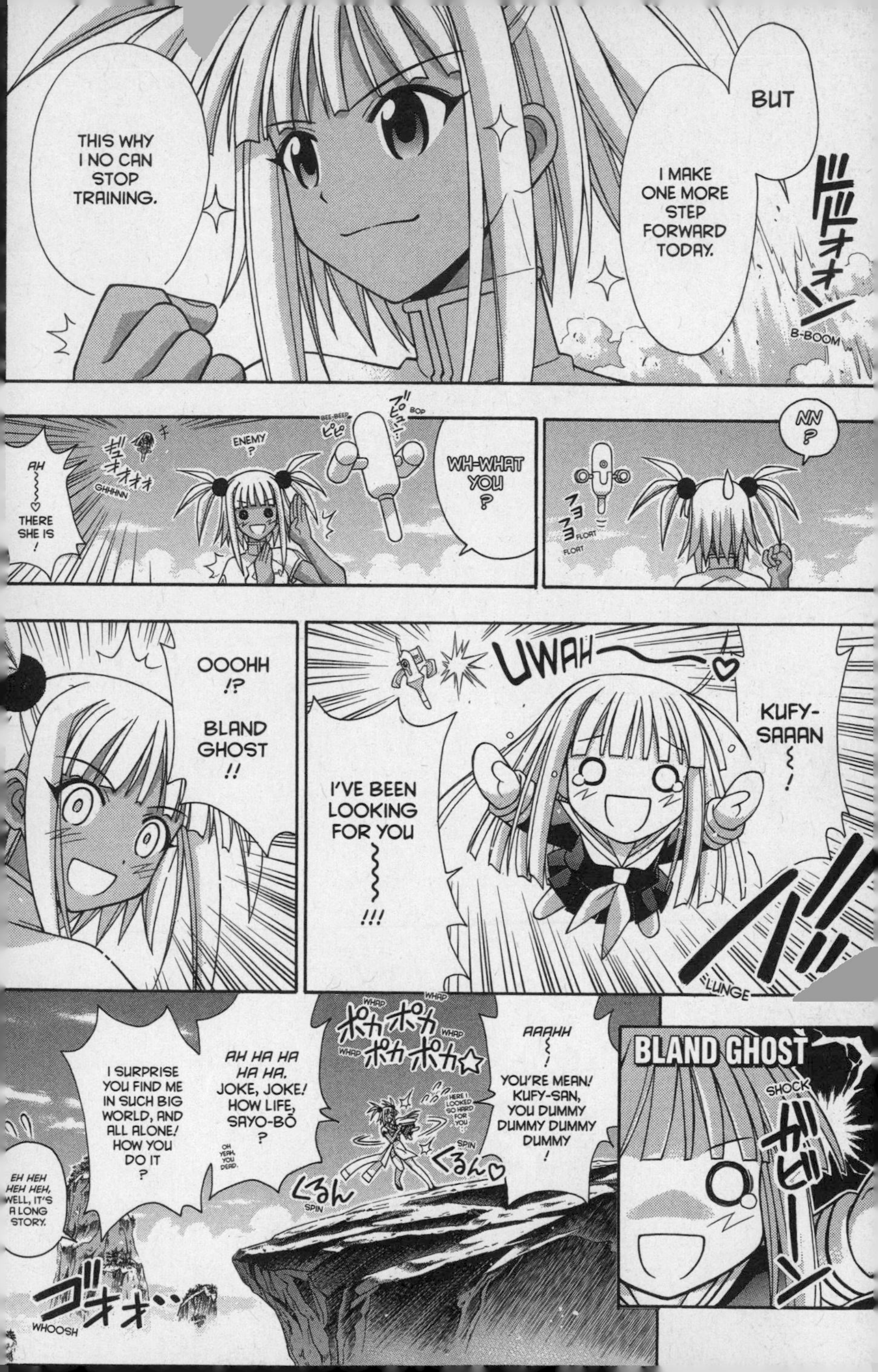
BUT
I MAKE ONE MORE STEP FORWARD TODAY.
B-BOOM
THIS WHY I NO CAN STOP TRAINING.
NN?
FLOAT
FLOAT
WH-WHAT YOU?
BOP
BEE-BEEP
ENEMY?
GHHHNN
AH~~♡ THERE SHE IS!
UWAH~♡
KUFY-SAAAN~!
I'VE BEEN LOOKING FOR YOU~!!!
LUNGE
OOOHH!?
BLAND GHOST!!
BLAND GHOST
SHOCK
AAAHH~!
YOU'RE MEAN! KUFY-SAN, YOU DUMMY DUMMY DUMMY DUMMY!
WHAP WHAP WHAP WHAP
HERE I LOOKED SO HARD FOR YOU
SPIN
SPIN
AH HA HA HA HA. JOKE, JOKE! HOW LIFE, SAYO-BŌ?
OH YEAH, YOU DEAD.
I SURPRISE YOU FIND ME IN SUCH BIG WORLD, AND ALL ALONE! HOW YOU DO IT?
EH HEH HEH HEH, WELL, IT'S A LONG STORY.
WHOOSH

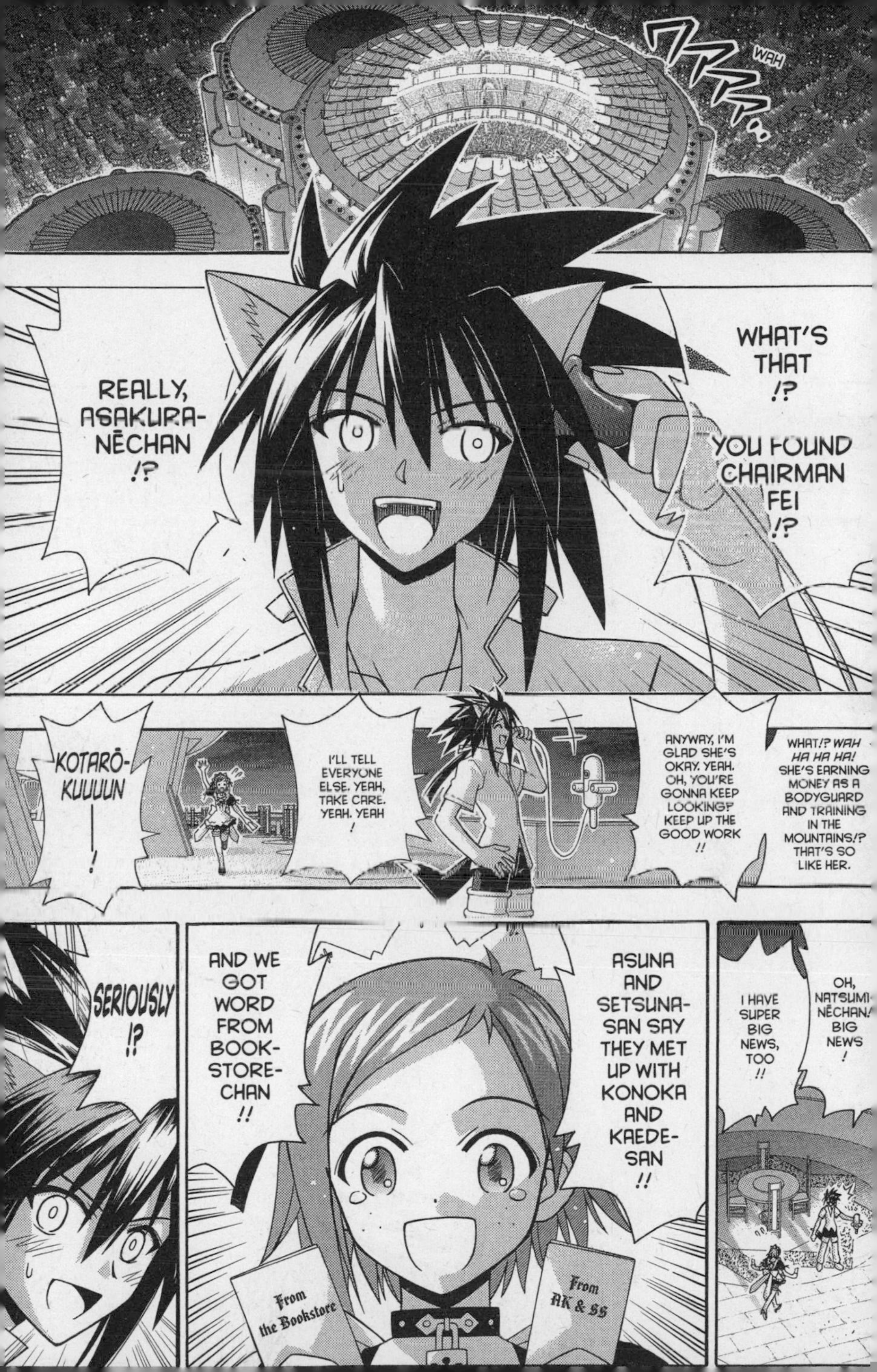
WAH
WHAT'S THAT !? YOU FOUND CHAIRMAN FEI !?
REALLY, ASAKURA-NĒCHAN !?
WHAT!? WAH HA HA HA! SHE'S EARNING MONEY AS A BODYGUARD AND TRAINING IN THE MOUNTAINS!? THAT'S SO LIKE HER.
ANYWAY, I'M GLAD SHE'S OKAY. YEAH. OH, YOU'RE GONNA KEEP LOOKING!? KEEP UP THE GOOD WORK !!
I'LL TELL EVERYONE ELSE. YEAH, TAKE CARE. YEAH. YEAH !
KOTARŌ-KUUUUN —— !
OH, NATSUMI-NĒCHAN! BIG NEWS !
I HAVE SUPER BIG NEWS, TOO !!
ASUNA AND SETSUNA-SAN SAY THEY MET UP WITH KONOKA AND KAEDE-SAN !!
From AK & SS
AND WE GOT WORD FROM BOOKSTORE-CHAN !!
From the Bookstore
SERIOUSLY !?

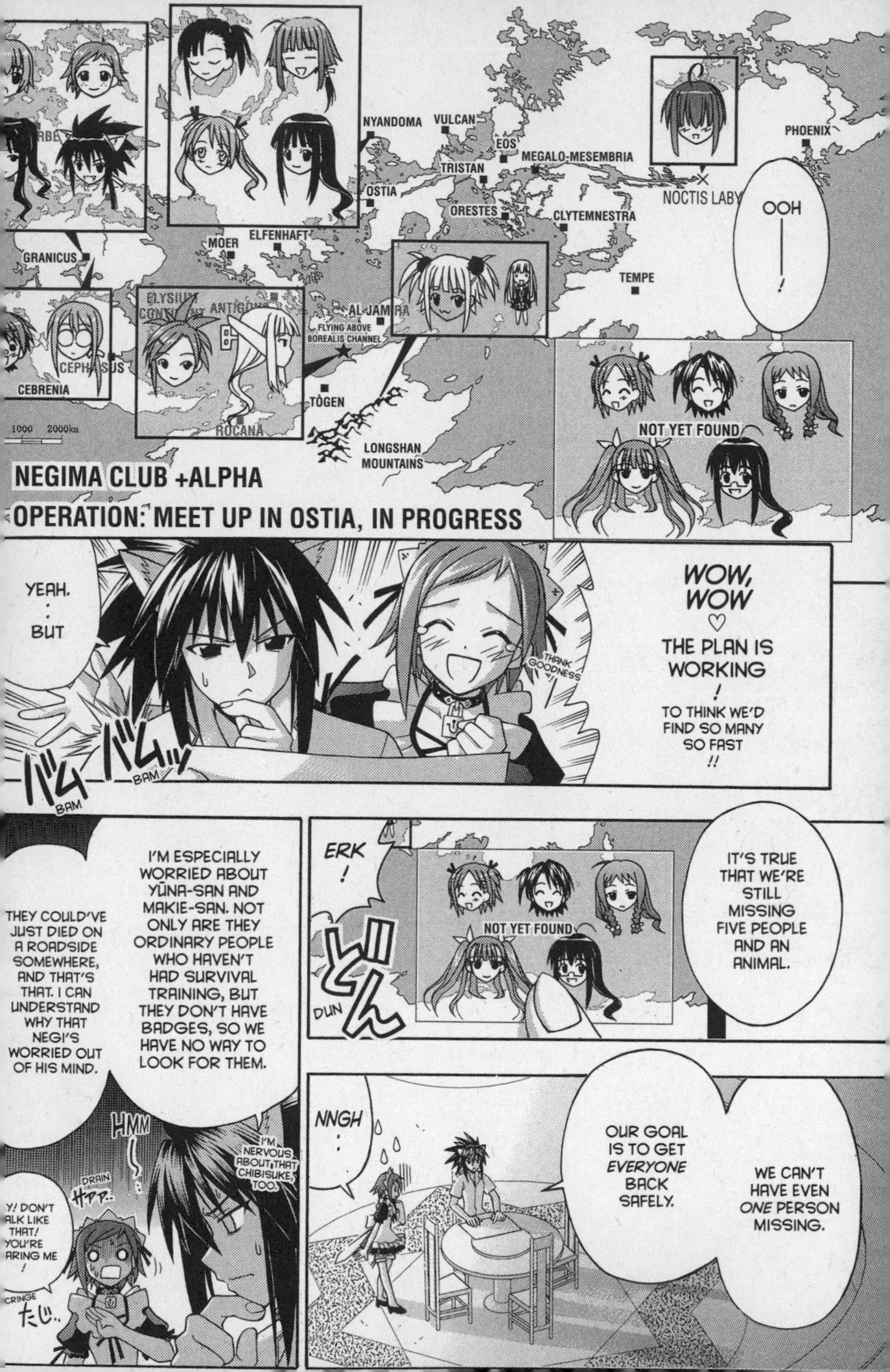

OOH—!
PHOENIX
NOCTIS LABY
MEGALO-MESEMBRIA
EOS
VULCAN
TRISTAN
NYANDOMA
OSTIA
ORESTES
CLYTEMNESTRA
ELFENHAFT
MOER
GRANICUS
TEMPE
AL JAMRA
FLYING ABOVE BOREALIS CHANNEL
ANTIGONE
CEPHISSUS
CEBRENIA
TŌGEN
ROCANA
LONGSHAN MOUNTAINS
1000 2000km
NOT YET FOUND
NEGIMA CLUB +ALPHA
OPERATION: MEET UP IN OSTIA, IN PROGRESS
WOW, WOW ♡ THE PLAN IS WORKING!
TO THINK WE'D FIND SO MANY SO FAST!!
THANK GOODNESS!!
YEAH. : BUT
BAM
BAM
IT'S TRUE THAT WE'RE STILL MISSING FIVE PEOPLE AND AN ANIMAL.
NOT YET FOUND
ERK!
DUN
I'M ESPECIALLY WORRIED ABOUT YŪNA-SAN AND MAKIE-SAN. NOT ONLY ARE THEY ORDINARY PEOPLE WHO HAVEN'T HAD SURVIVAL TRAINING, BUT THEY DON'T HAVE BADGES, SO WE HAVE NO WAY TO LOOK FOR THEM.
THEY COULD'VE JUST DIED ON A ROADSIDE SOMEWHERE, AND THAT'S THAT. I CAN UNDERSTAND WHY THAT NEGI'S WORRIED OUT OF HIS MIND.
WE CAN'T HAVE EVEN ONE PERSON MISSING.
OUR GOAL IS TO GET EVERYONE BACK SAFELY.
NNGH :
HMM~
I'M NERVOUS ABOUT THAT CHIBISUKE, TOO.
DRAIN
Y! DON'T ALK LIKE THAT! YOU'RE ARING ME!
CRINGE

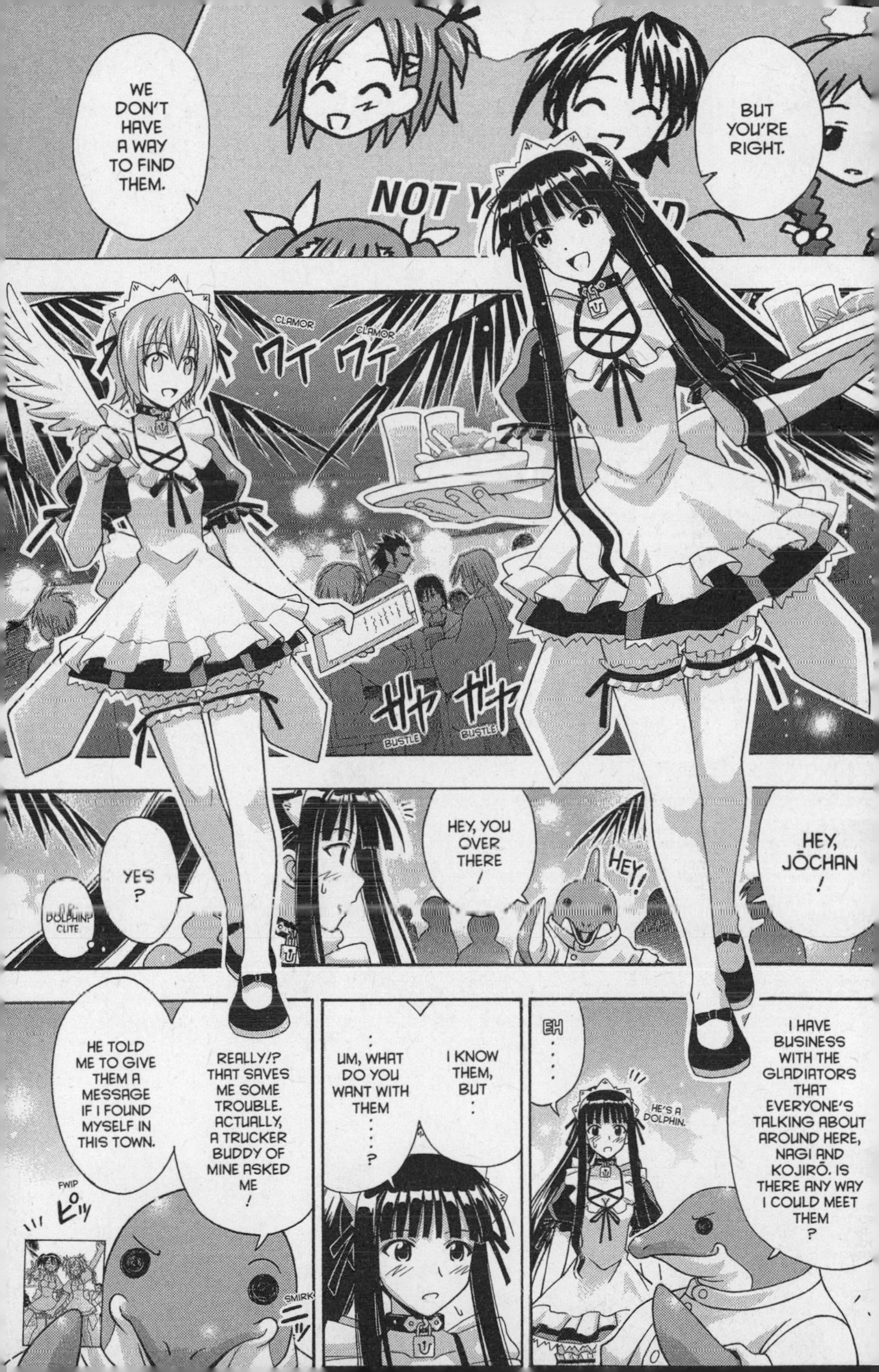
BUT YOU'RE RIGHT.
WE DON'T HAVE A WAY TO FIND THEM.
CLAMOR
CLAMOR
BUSTLE
BUSTLE
HEY, JŌCHAN!
HEY!
HEY, YOU OVER THERE!
YES?
DOLPHIN? CUTE
I HAVE BUSINESS WITH THE GLADIATORS THAT EVERYONE'S TALKING ABOUT AROUND HERE, NAGI AND KOJIRŌ. IS THERE ANY WAY I COULD MEET THEM?
EH....
HE'S A DOLPHIN.
I KNOW THEM, BUT...
UM, WHAT DO YOU WANT WITH THEM.....?
REALLY!? THAT SAVES ME SOME TROUBLE. ACTUALLY, A TRUCKER BUDDY OF MINE ASKED ME!
HE TOLD ME TO GIVE THEM A MESSAGE IF I FOUND MYSELF IN THIS TOWN.
FWIP
SMIRK

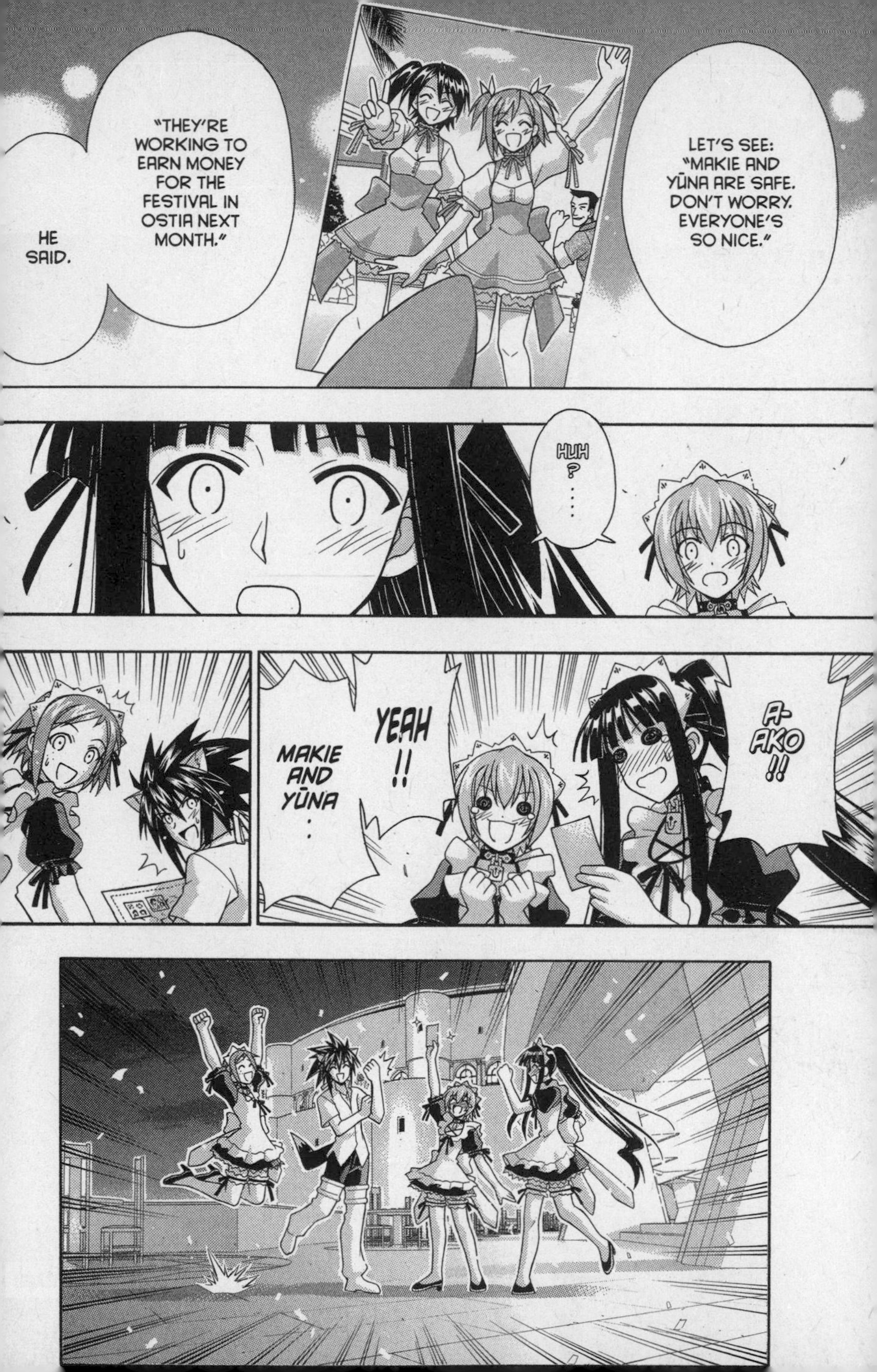
LET'S SEE: "MAKIE AND YŪNA ARE SAFE. DON'T WORRY. EVERYONE'S SO NICE."
"THEY'RE WORKING TO EARN MONEY FOR THE FESTIVAL IN OSTIA NEXT MONTH."
HE SAID.
HUH?.....
A-AKO!!
YEAH!!
MAKIE AND YŪNA...

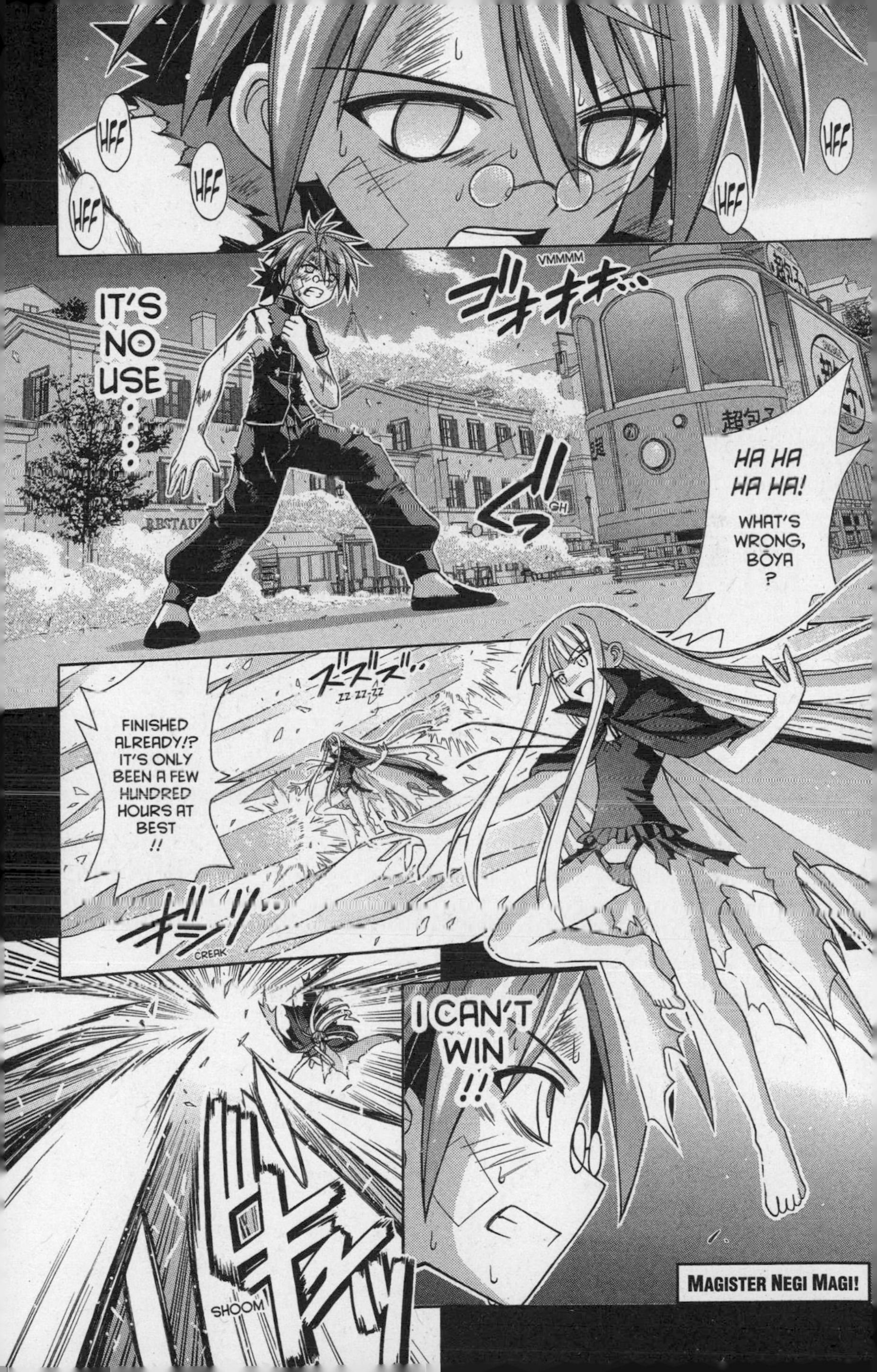

HFF
HFF
HFF
HFF
HFF
VMMMM
HA HA HA HA! WHAT'S WRONG, BŌYA?
IT'S NO USE......
GH
ZZ ZZ ZZ
FINISHED ALREADY!? IT'S ONLY BEEN A FEW HUNDRED HOURS AT BEST!!
CREAK
I CAN'T WIN!!
MAGISTER NEGI MAGI!
SHOOM

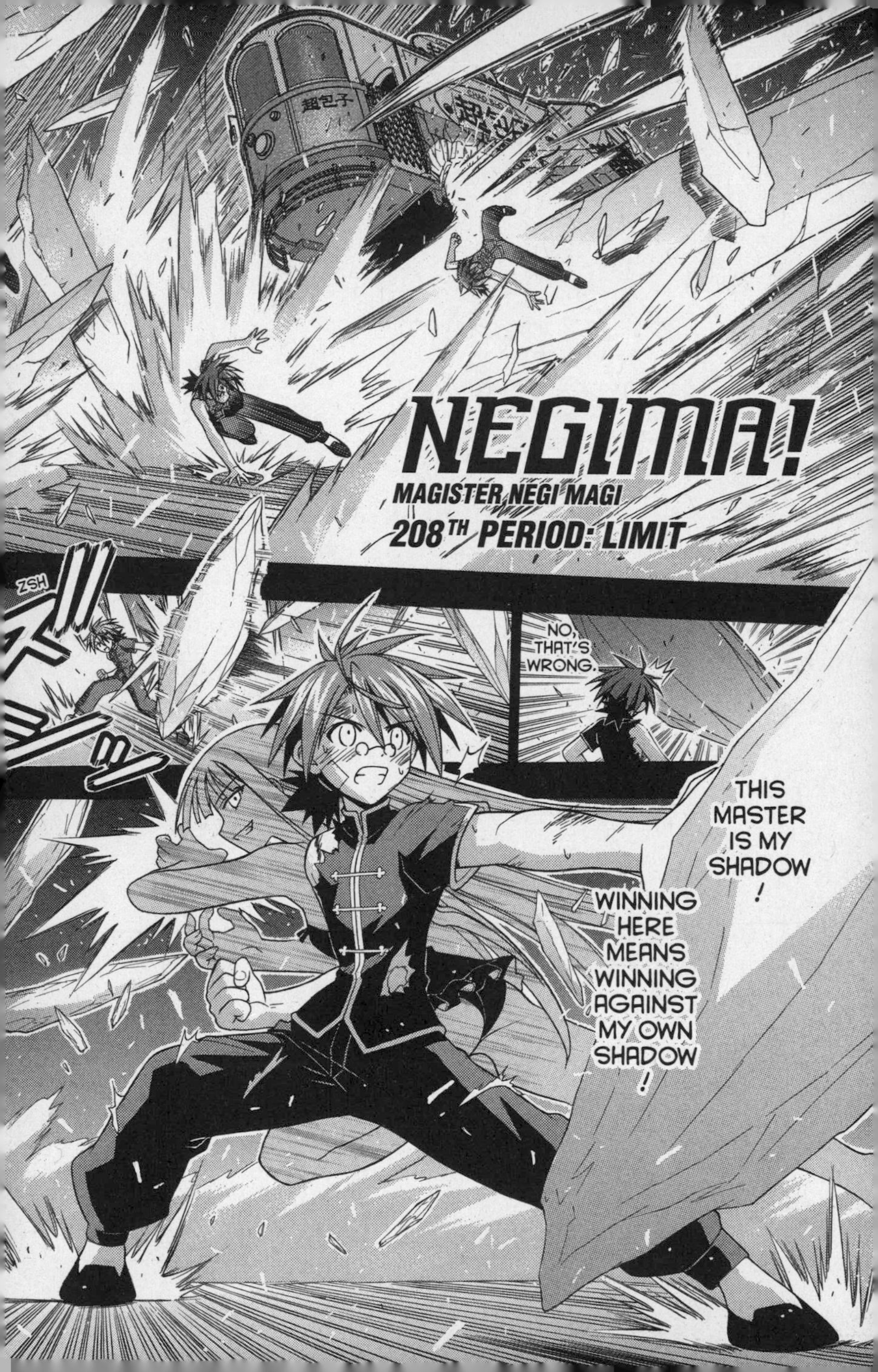

超包子
NEGIMA!
MAGISTER NEGI MAGI
208TH PERIOD: LIMIT
ZSH
NO, THAT'S WRONG.
THIS MASTER IS MY SHADOW!
WINNING HERE MEANS WINNING AGAINST MY OWN SHADOW!

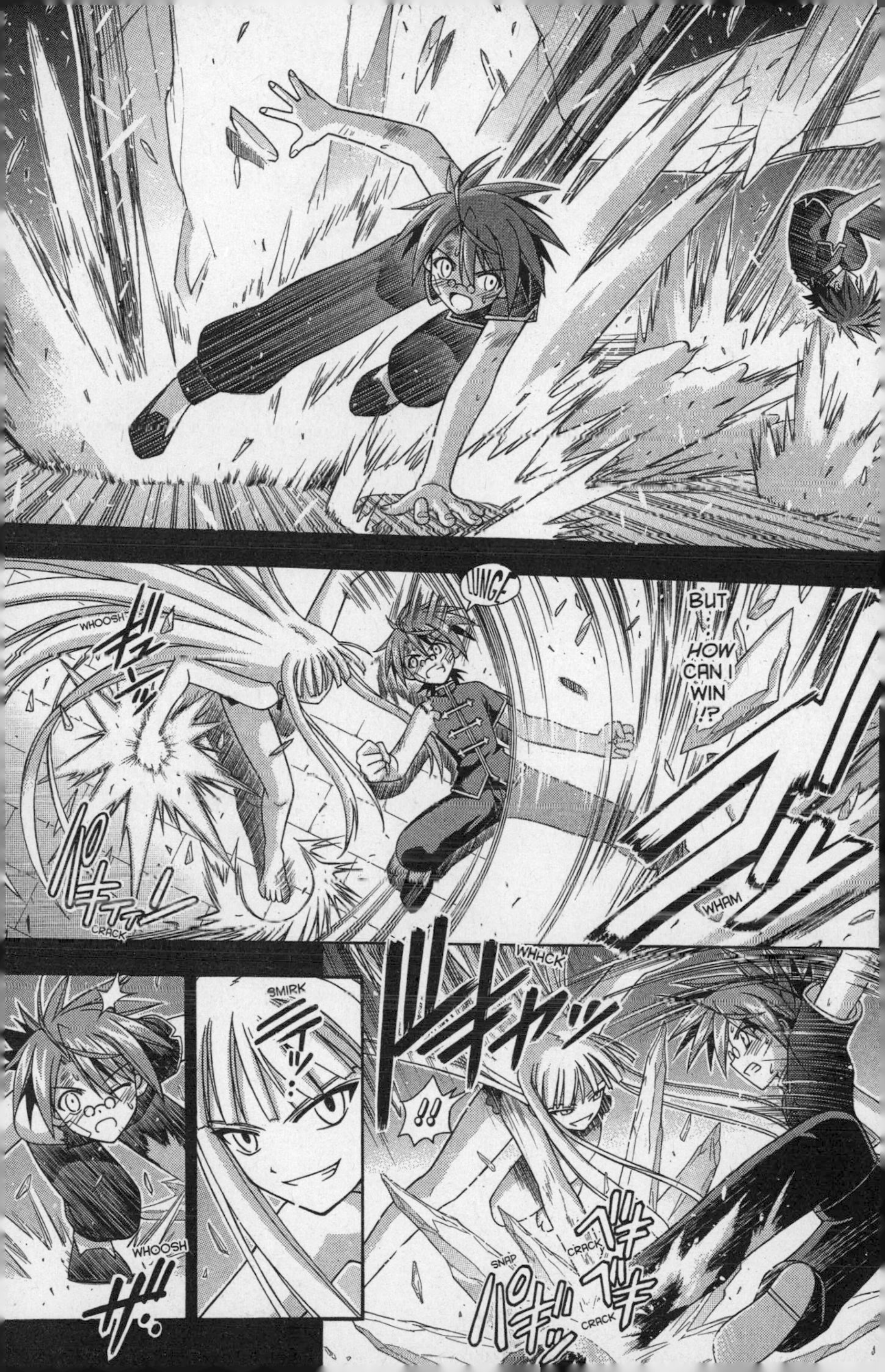
BUT... HOW CAN I WIN!?
LUNGE
WHAM
WHOOSH
CRACK
WHHCK
!!
CRACK
SNAP
CRACK
SMIRK
WHOOSH

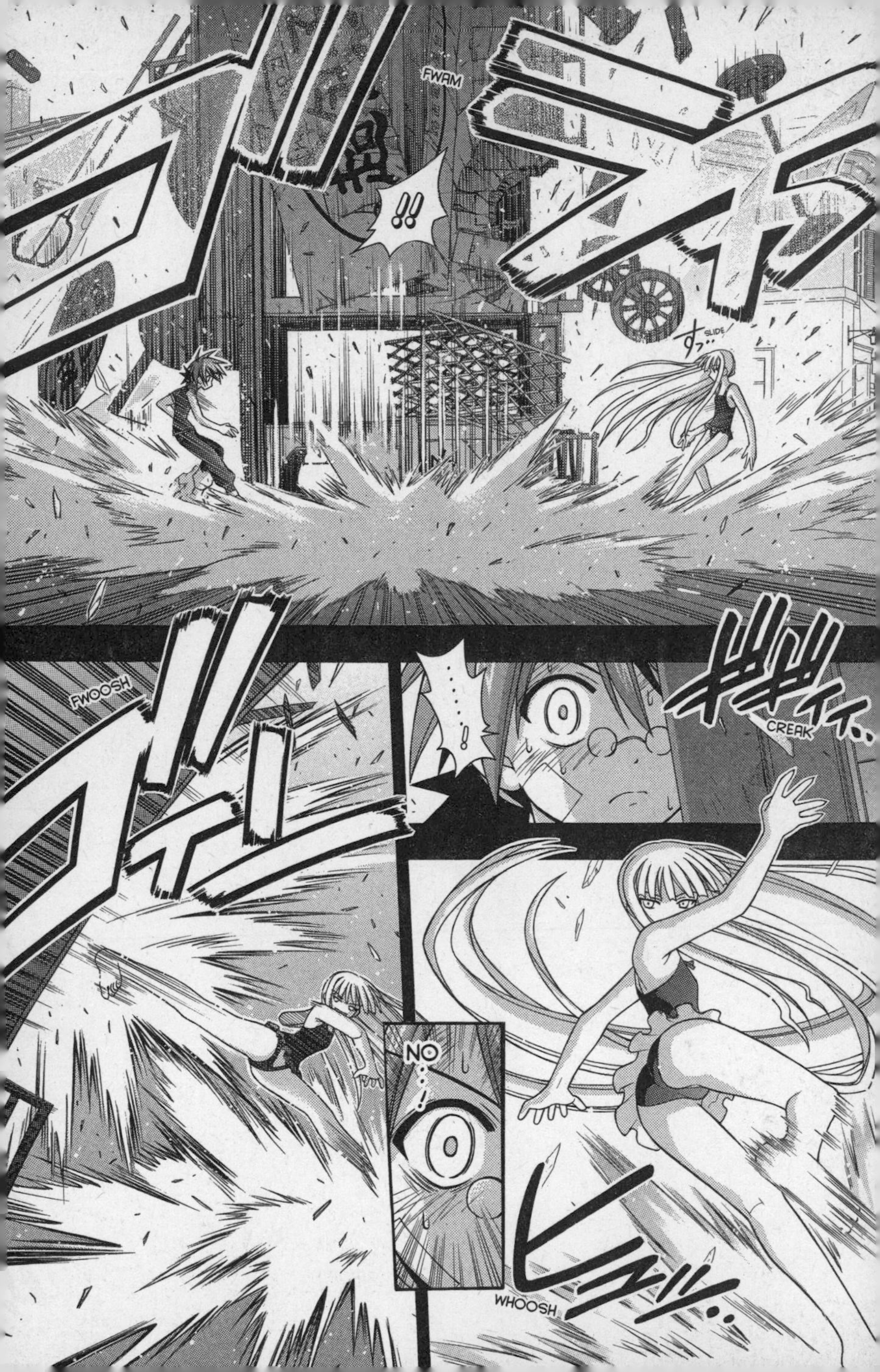
FWAM
!!
すっ SLIDE
.....!
CREAK
WHOOSH
NO...!
FWOOSH

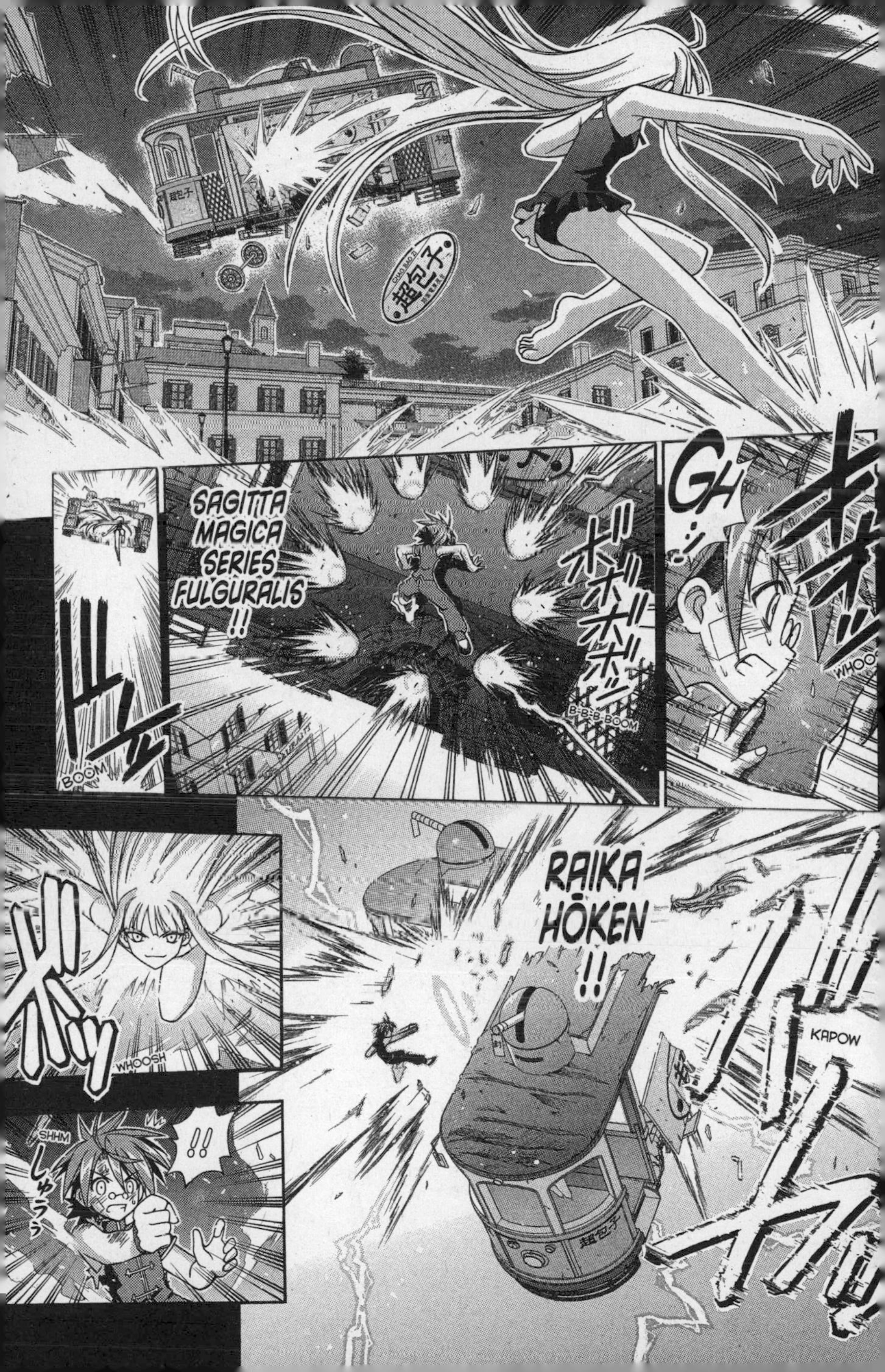

超包子
GH
WHOOSH
SAGITTA MAGICA SERIES FULGURALIS !!
B-B-B-BOOM
BOOM
RAIKA HÖKEN !!
KAPOW
WHOOSH
SHHM
!!

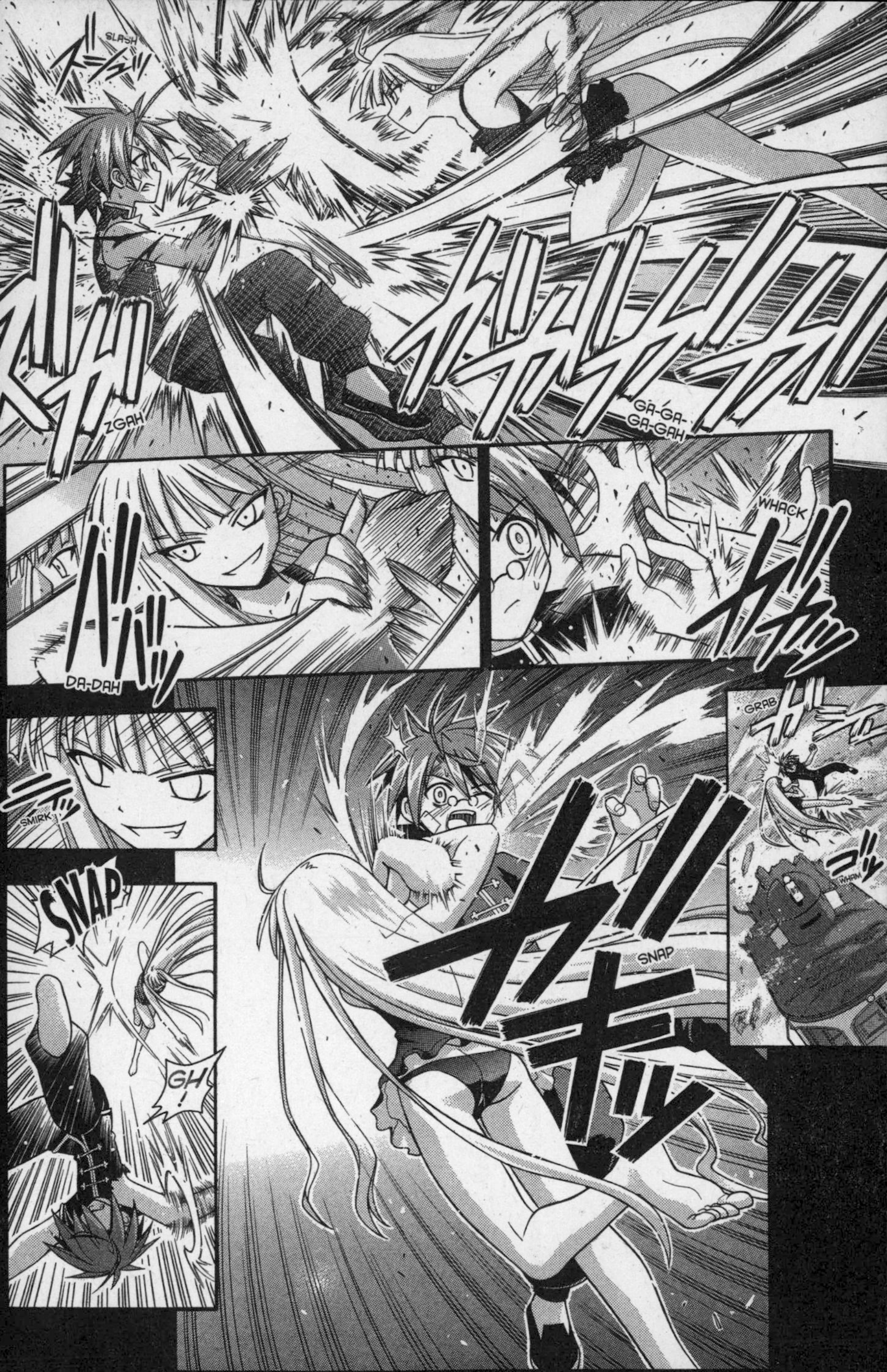
SLASH
GA-GA-GA-GAH
ZGAH
WHACK
DA-DAH
GRAB
WHAM
SNAP
SMIRK
SNAP
GH!

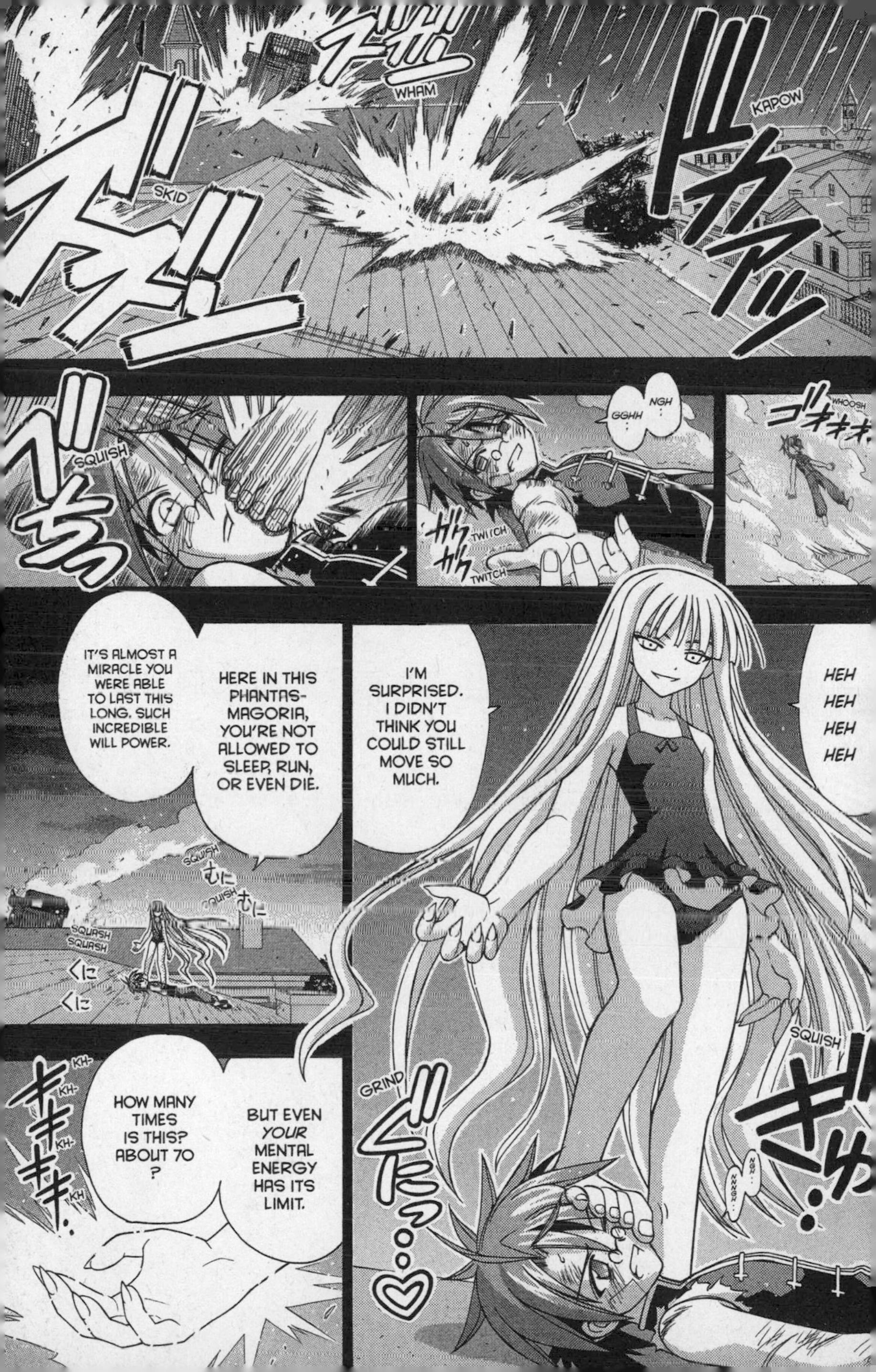
KAPOW
WHAM
SKID
WHOOSH
NGH...
GGHH...
TWITCH
TWITCH
SQUISH
HEH HEH HEH HEH
I'M SURPRISED. I DIDN'T THINK YOU COULD STILL MOVE SO MUCH.
SQUISH
NGH...
NNNGH...
GRIND
HERE IN THIS PHANTAS-MAGORIA, YOU'RE NOT ALLOWED TO SLEEP, RUN, OR EVEN DIE.
IT'S ALMOST A MIRACLE YOU WERE ABLE TO LAST THIS LONG. SUCH INCREDIBLE WILL POWER.
SQUISH
SQUISH
SQUASH
SQUASH
BUT EVEN *YOUR* MENTAL ENERGY HAS ITS LIMIT.
HOW MANY TIMES IS THIS? ABOUT 70?
KH-
KH-
KH-
KH

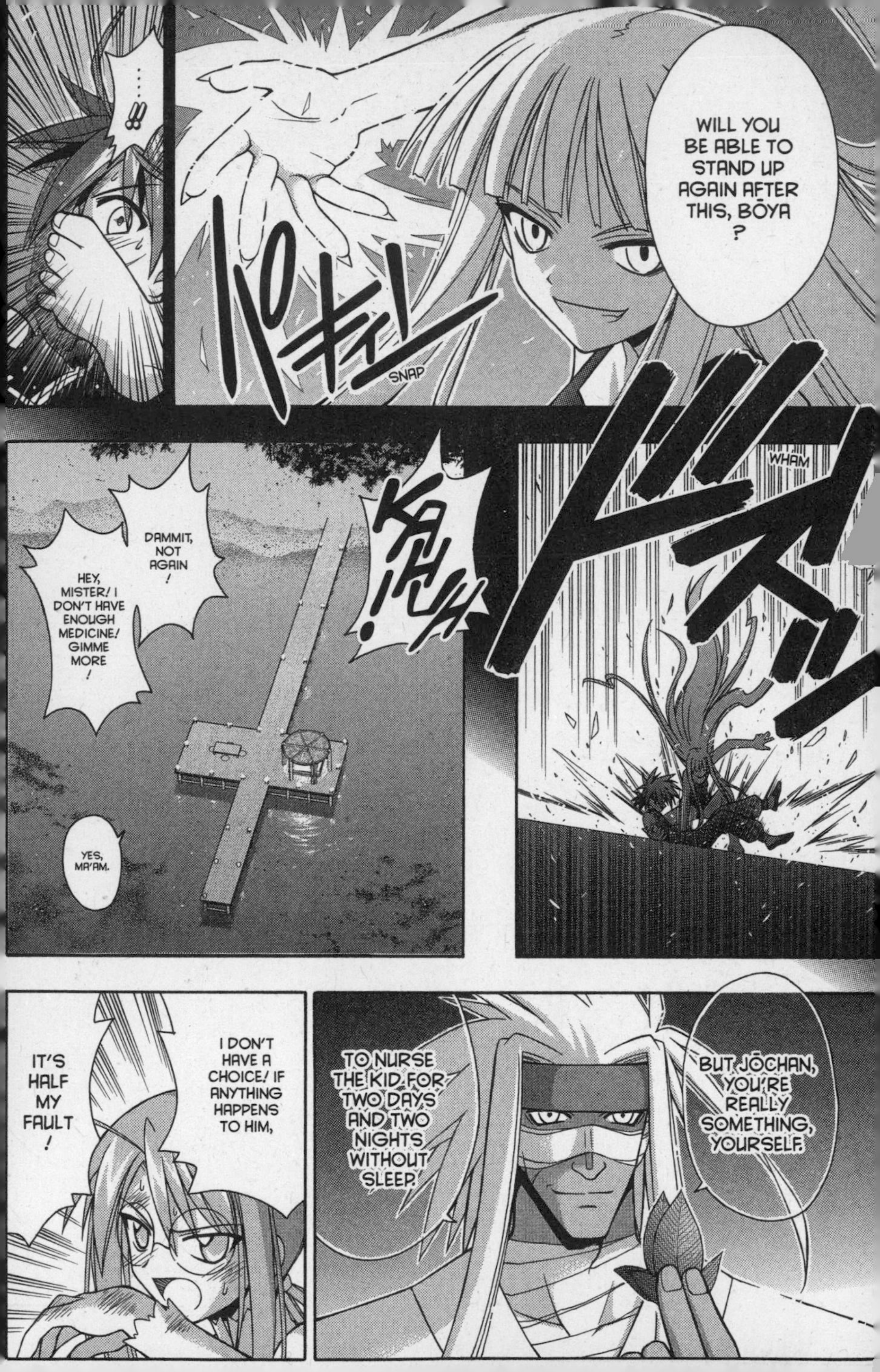
WILL YOU BE ABLE TO STAND UP AGAIN AFTER THIS, BŌYA?
SNAP
……!!
WHAM
DAMMIT, NOT AGAIN!
HEY, MISTER! I DON'T HAVE ENOUGH MEDICINE! GIMME MORE!
YES, MA'AM.
BUT JŌCHAN, YOU'RE REALLY SOMETHING, YOURSELF.
TO NURSE THE KID FOR TWO DAYS AND TWO NIGHTS WITHOUT SLEEP.
I DON'T HAVE A CHOICE! IF ANYTHING HAPPENS TO HIM,
IT'S HALF MY FAULT!

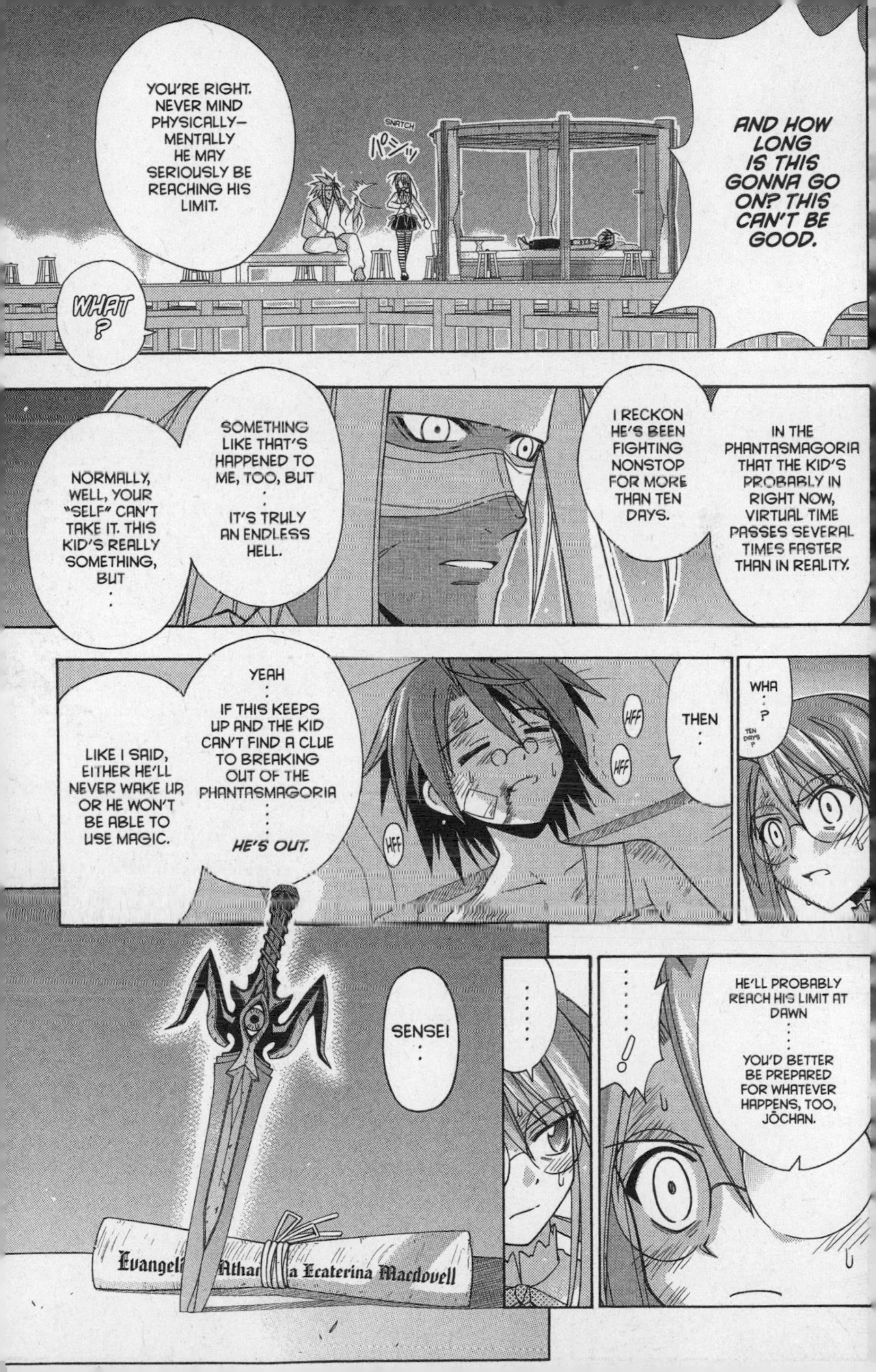
AND HOW LONG IS THIS GONNA GO ON? THIS CAN'T BE GOOD.
SNATCH
YOU'RE RIGHT. NEVER MIND PHYSICALLY— MENTALLY HE MAY SERIOUSLY BE REACHING HIS LIMIT.
WHAT?
IN THE PHANTASMAGORIA THAT THE KID'S PROBABLY IN RIGHT NOW, VIRTUAL TIME PASSES SEVERAL TIMES FASTER THAN IN REALITY.
I RECKON HE'S BEEN FIGHTING NONSTOP FOR MORE THAN TEN DAYS.
SOMETHING LIKE THAT'S HAPPENED TO ME, TOO, BUT... IT'S TRULY AN ENDLESS HELL.
NORMALLY, WELL, YOUR "SELF" CAN'T TAKE IT. THIS KID'S REALLY SOMETHING, BUT...
WHA...?
TEN DAYS?
THEN...
HFF
HFF
HFF
YEAH... IF THIS KEEPS UP AND THE KID CAN'T FIND A CLUE TO BREAKING OUT OF THE PHANTASMAGORIA... HE'S OUT.
LIKE I SAID, EITHER HE'LL NEVER WAKE UP, OR HE WON'T BE ABLE TO USE MAGIC.
HE'LL PROBABLY REACH HIS LIMIT AT DAWN... YOU'D BETTER BE PREPARED FOR WHATEVER HAPPENS, TOO, JŌCHAN.
......!
......
SENSEI...
Ecaterina Macdovell

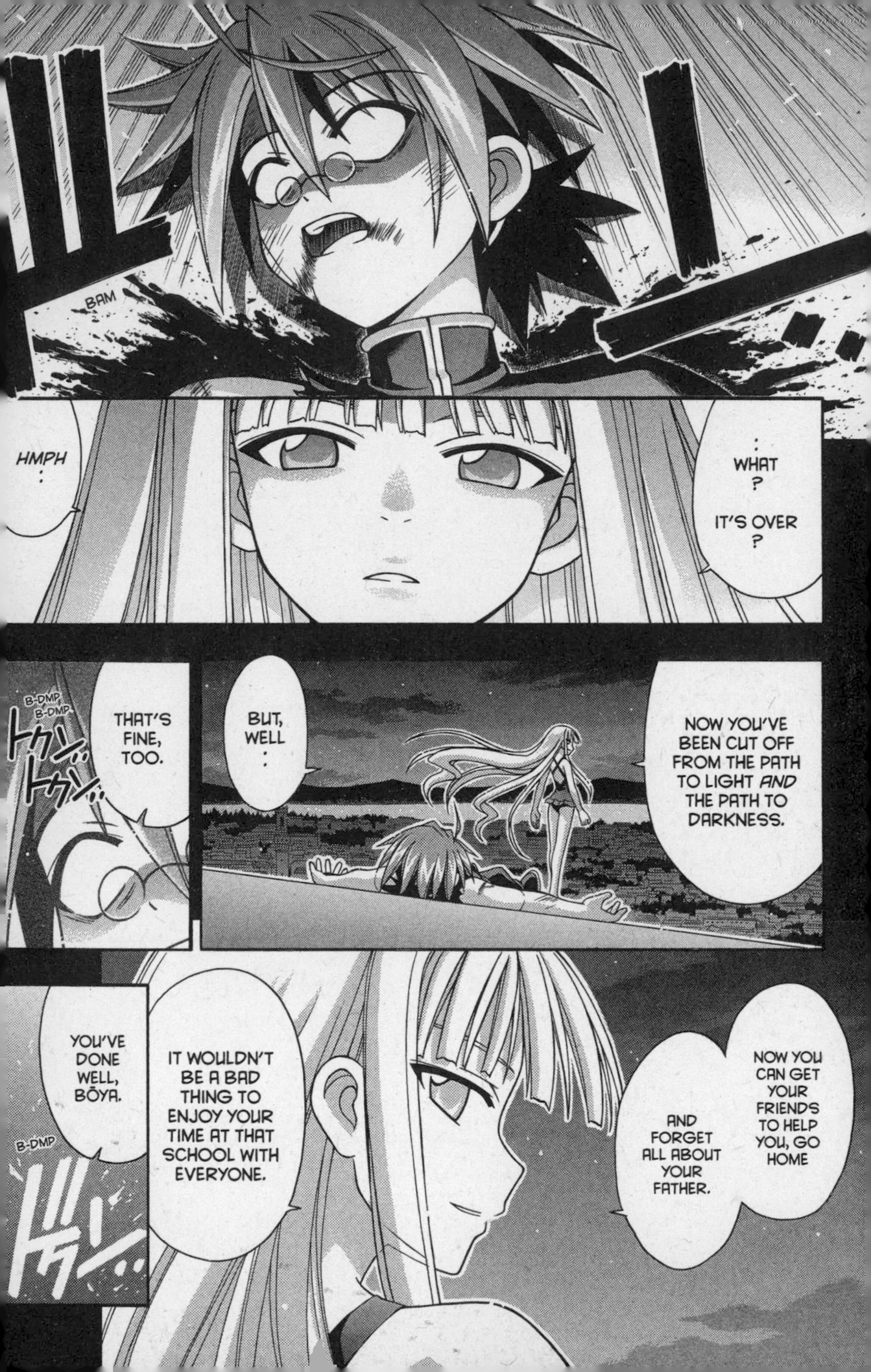
BAM
... WHAT? IT'S OVER?
HMPH ...
NOW YOU'VE BEEN CUT OFF FROM THE PATH TO LIGHT *AND* THE PATH TO DARKNESS.
BUT, WELL ...
THAT'S FINE, TOO.
B-DMP B-DMP
トクン トクン
NOW YOU CAN GET YOUR FRIENDS TO HELP YOU, GO HOME
AND FORGET ALL ABOUT YOUR FATHER.
IT WOULDN'T BE A BAD THING TO ENJOY YOUR TIME AT THAT SCHOOL WITH EVERYONE.
YOU'VE DONE WELL, BŌYA.
B-DMP
ドクン...

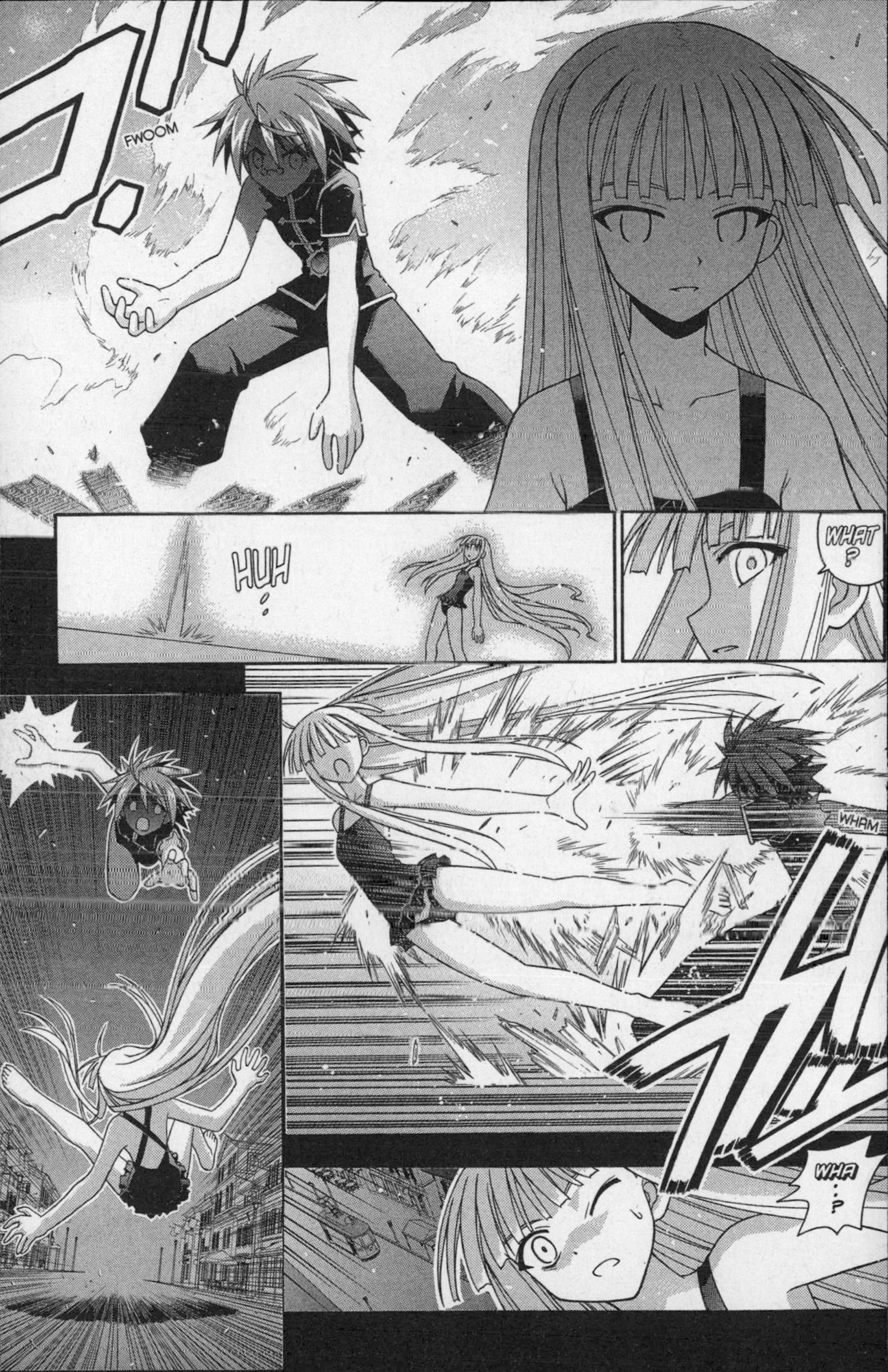
FWOOM
WHAT ?
HUH
WHAM
WHA...?

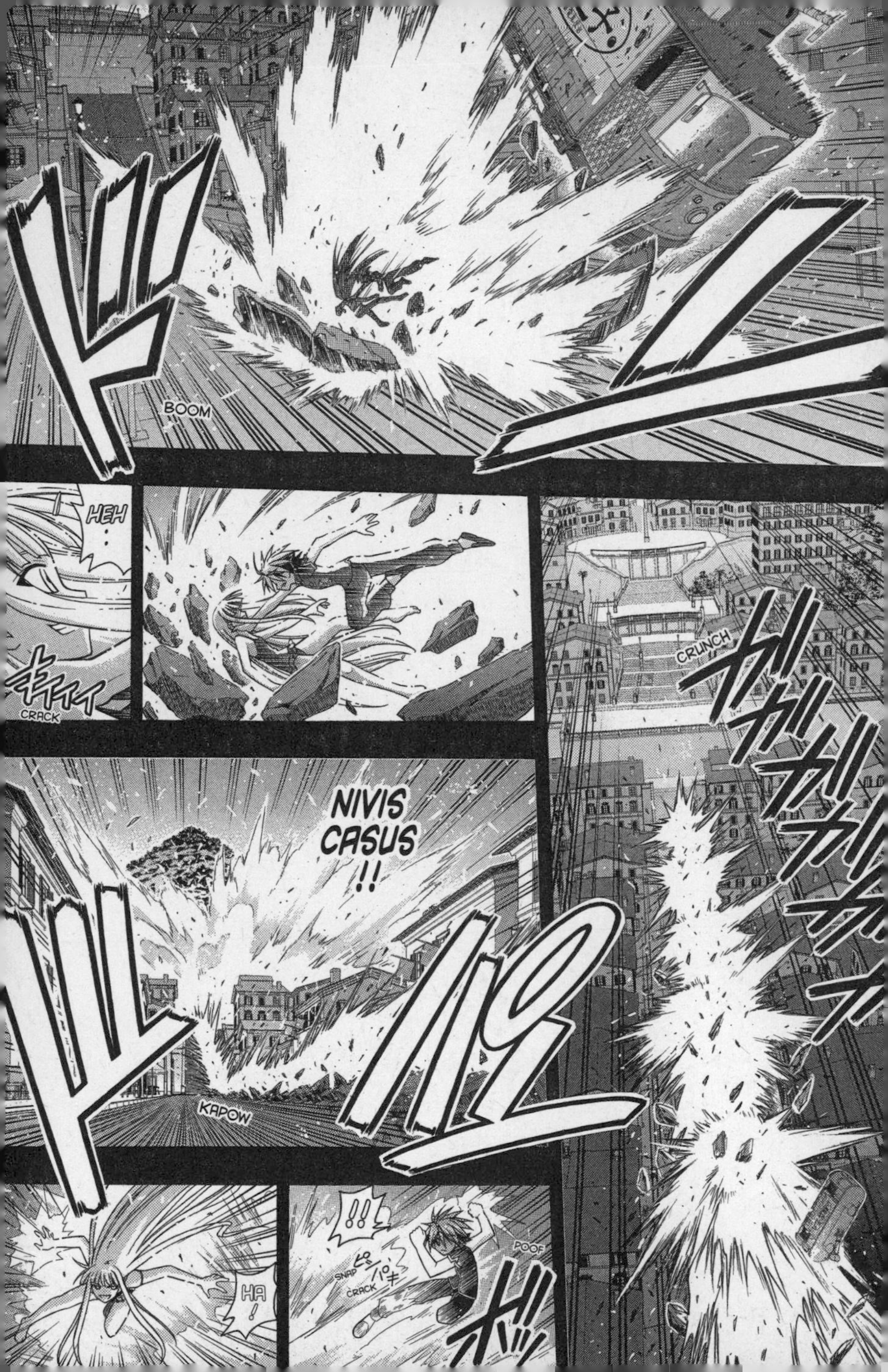
BOOM
CRUNCH
HEH
CRACK
NIVIS CASUS !!
KAPOW
!!
SNAP
CRACK
POOF
HA !

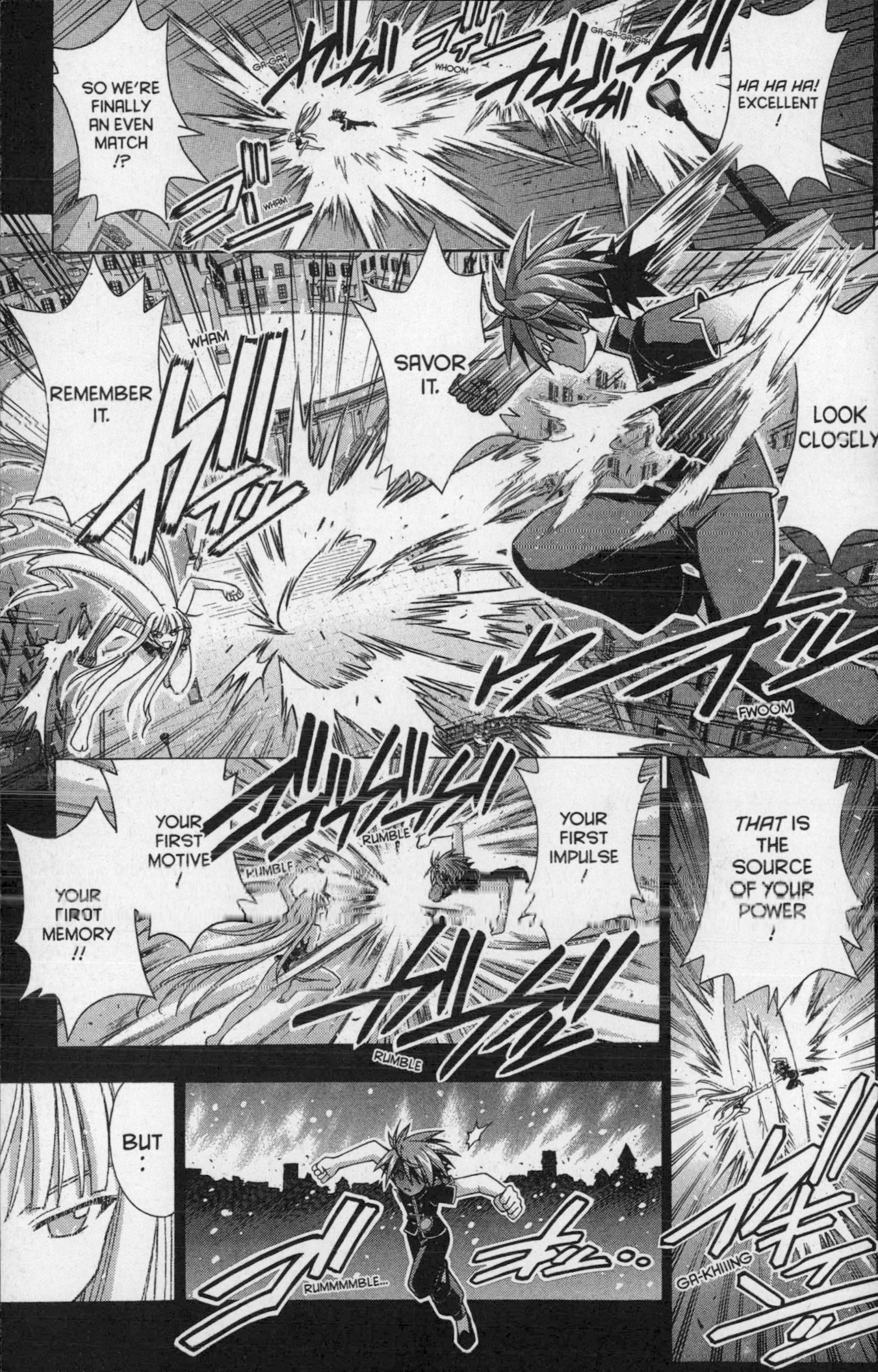

HA HA HA! EXCELLENT!
GA-GA-GA-GAH
WHOOM
GA-GAH
SO WE'RE FINALLY AN EVEN MATCH!?
WHAM
LOOK CLOSELY
SAVOR IT.
REMEMBER IT.
WHAM
FWOOM
THAT IS THE SOURCE OF YOUR POWER!
GA-KHIING
YOUR FIRST IMPULSE!
RUMBLE
YOUR FIRST MOTIVE!
RUMBLE
YOUR FIRST MEMORY!!
RUMBLE
BUT...
RUMMMMBLE...

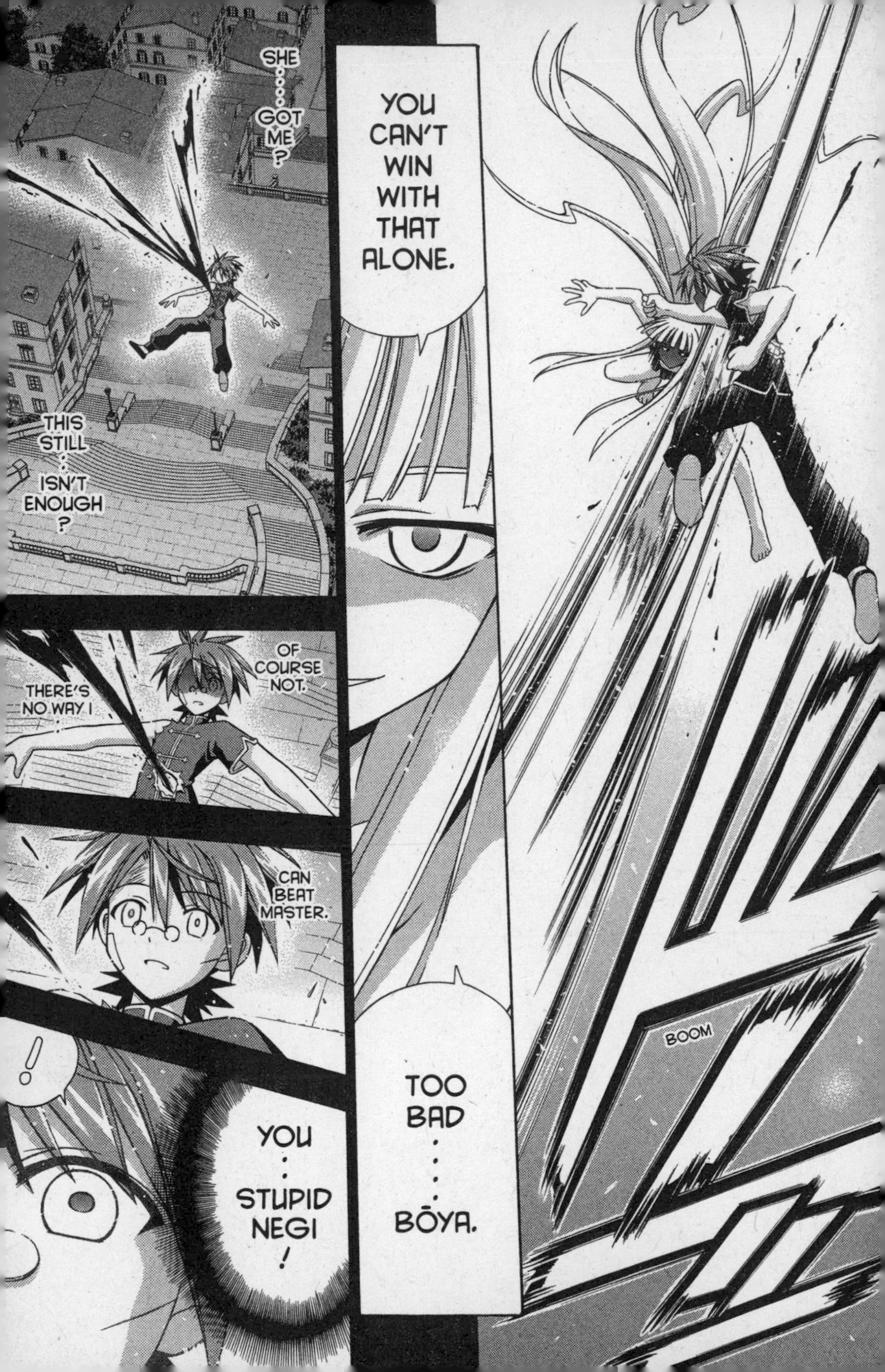
BOOM
YOU CAN'T WIN WITH THAT ALONE.
TOO BAD . . . . BŌYA.
SHE . . . . GOT ME ?
THIS STILL . . ISN'T ENOUGH ?
OF COURSE NOT.
THERE'S NO WAY I
CAN BEAT MASTER.
!
YOU . . STUPID NEGI !

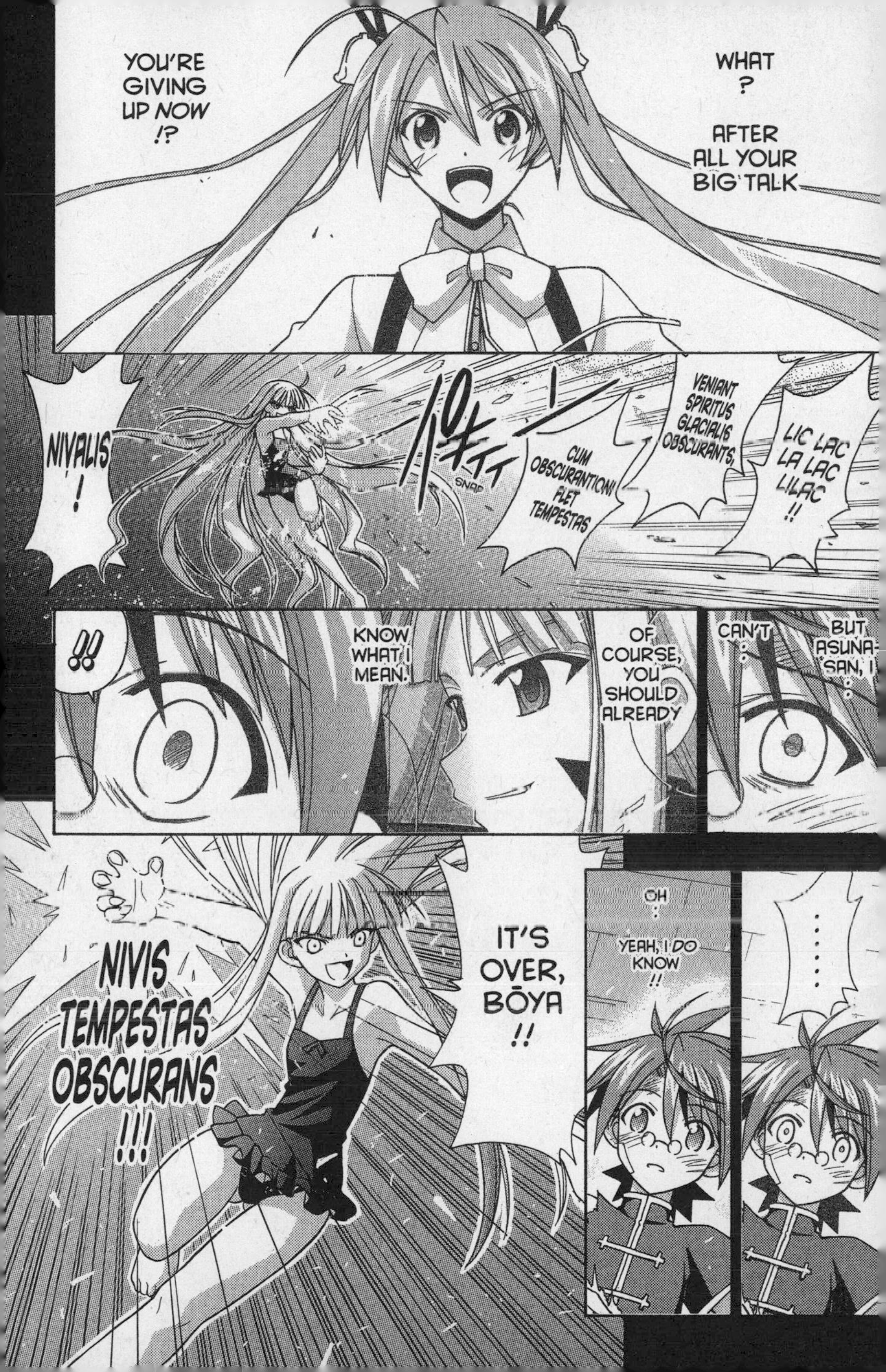
WHAT?
AFTER ALL YOUR BIG TALK
YOU'RE GIVING UP NOW !?
LIC LAC LA LAC LILAC !!
VENIANT SPIRITUS GLACIALIS OBSCURANTS,
CUM OBSCURANTIONI FLET TEMPESTAS
NIVALIS !
BUT ASUNA-SAN, I ...
CAN'T ...
OF COURSE, YOU SHOULD ALREADY
KNOW WHAT I MEAN.
!!
......
OH ...
YEAH, I DO KNOW !!
IT'S OVER, BŌYA !!
NIVIS TEMPESTAS OBSCURANS !!!

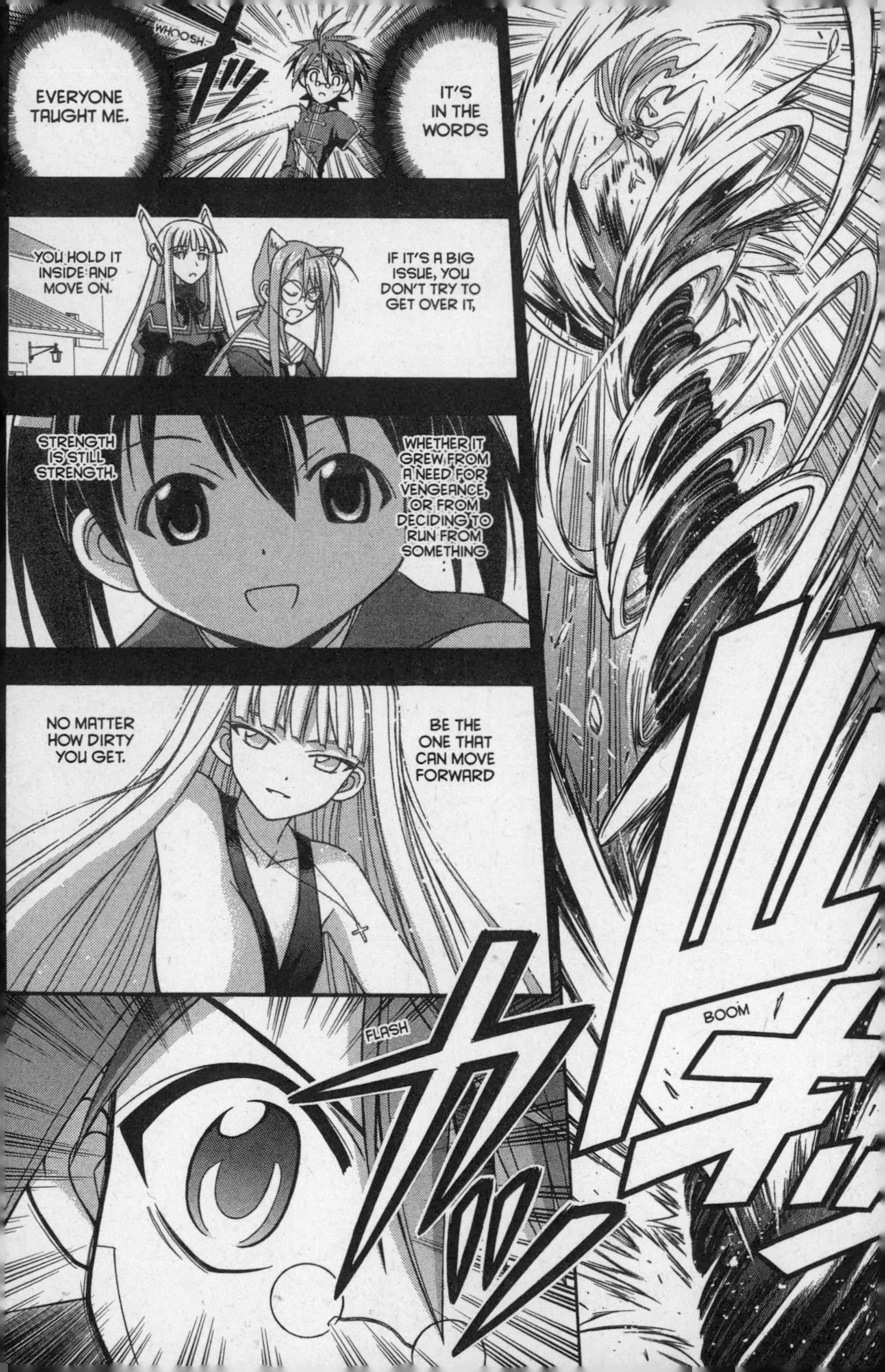
BOOM
WHOOSH
IT'S IN THE WORDS
EVERYONE TAUGHT ME.
IF IT'S A BIG ISSUE, YOU DON'T TRY TO GET OVER IT,
YOU HOLD IT INSIDE AND MOVE ON.
WHETHER IT GREW FROM A NEED FOR VENGEANCE, OR FROM DECIDING TO RUN FROM SOMETHING
STRENGTH IS STILL STRENGTH.
BE THE ONE THAT CAN MOVE FORWARD
NO MATTER HOW DIRTY YOU GET.
FLASH

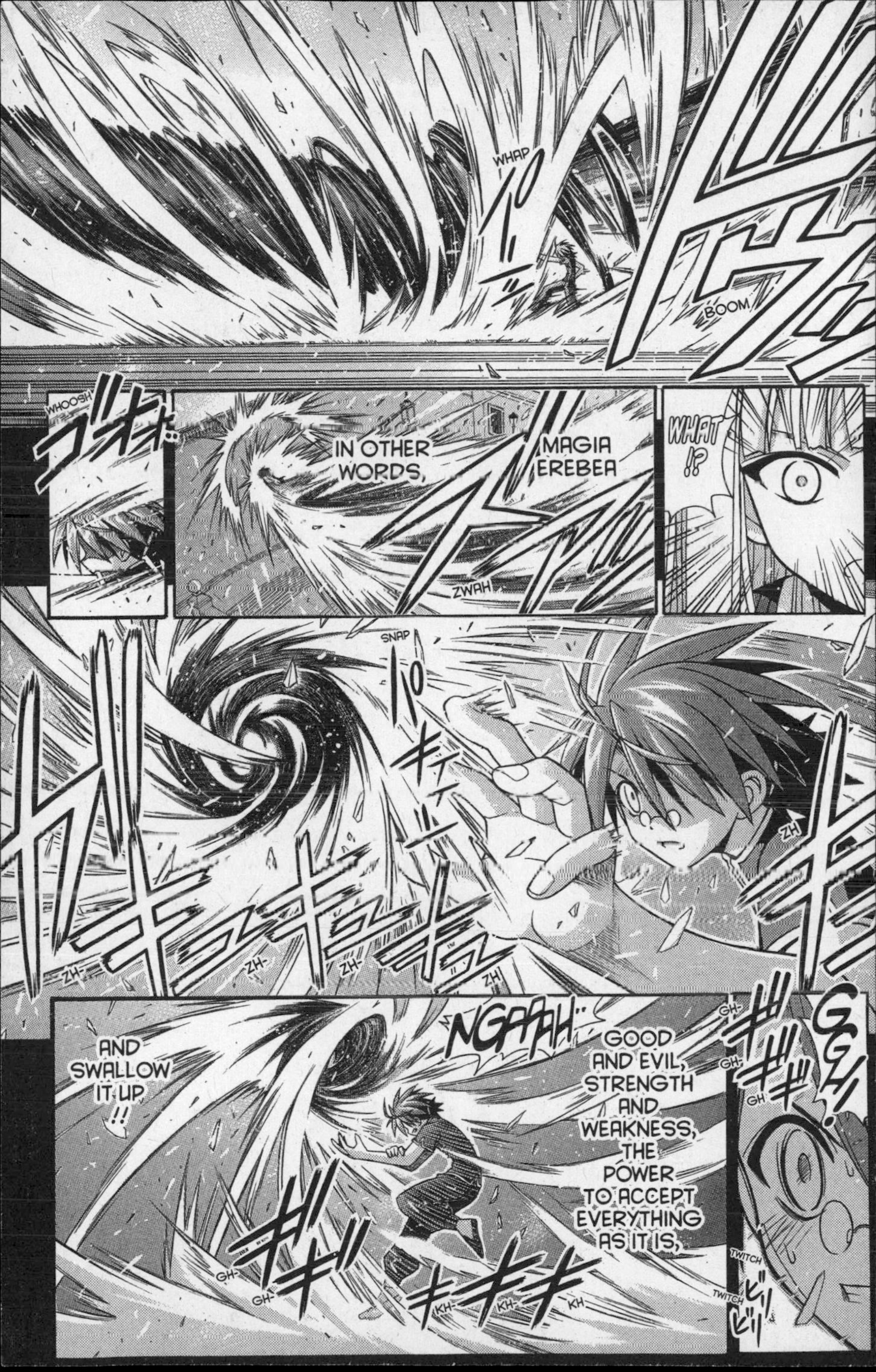

WHAP
BOOM
WHAT !?
IN OTHER WORDS,
MAGIA EREBEA
ZWAH
WHOOSH
SNAP
ZH
ZH-
ZH-
ZH-
ZH
GGH!
GH-
GH-
GH
TWITCH
TWITCH
NGAAAH
GOOD AND EVIL, STRENGTH AND WEAKNESS, THE POWER TO ACCEPT EVERYTHING AS IT IS,
AND SWALLOW IT UP !!
GH-
GH-
KH-
KH-
KH

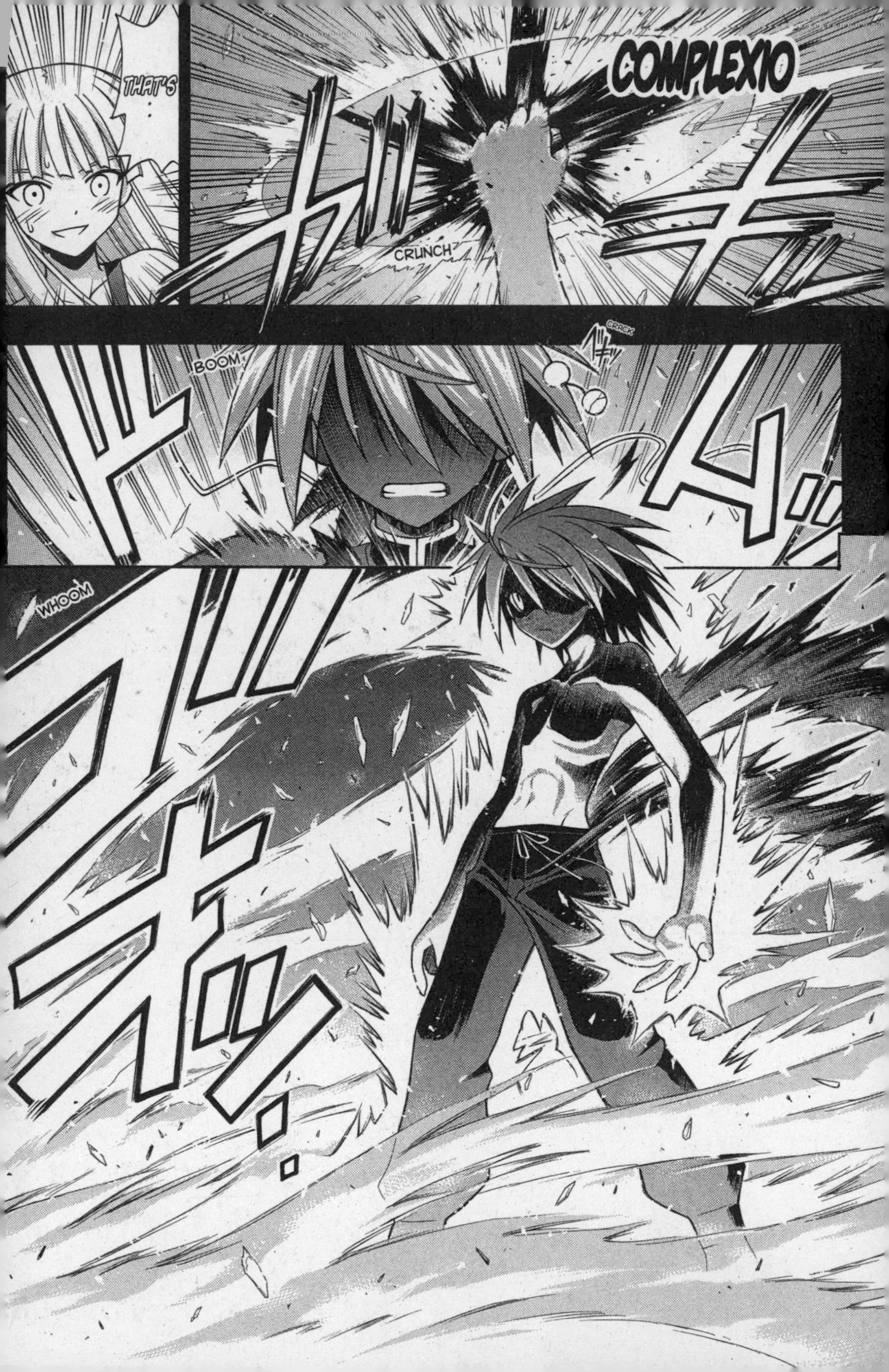
COMPLEXIO
CRUNCH
THAT'S
...
CRACK
BOOM
WHOOM

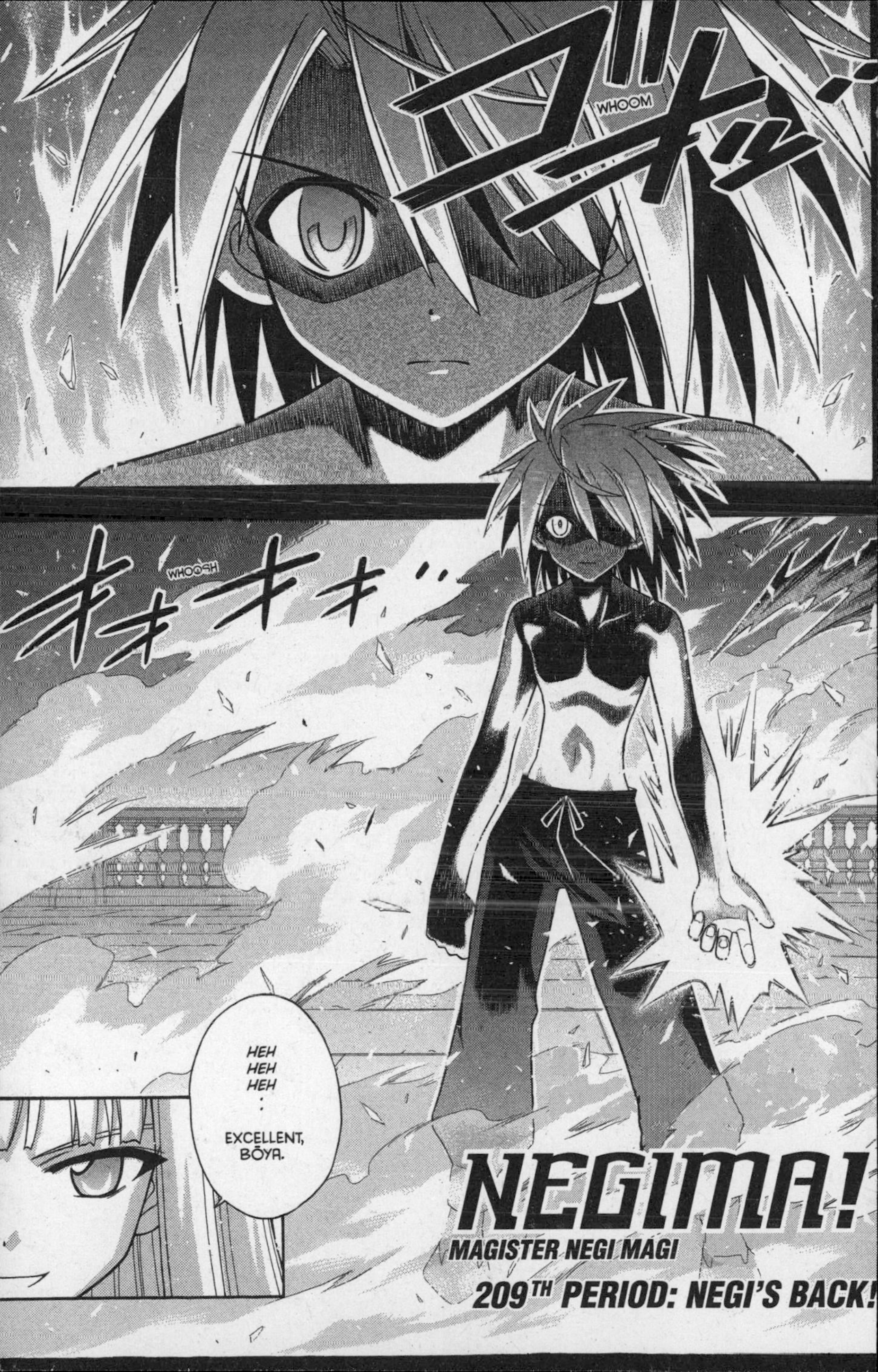
WHOOM
WHOOSH
HEH HEH HEH
:
EXCELLENT, BŌYA.
NEGIMA!
MAGISTER NEGI MAGI
209TH PERIOD: NEGI'S BACK!

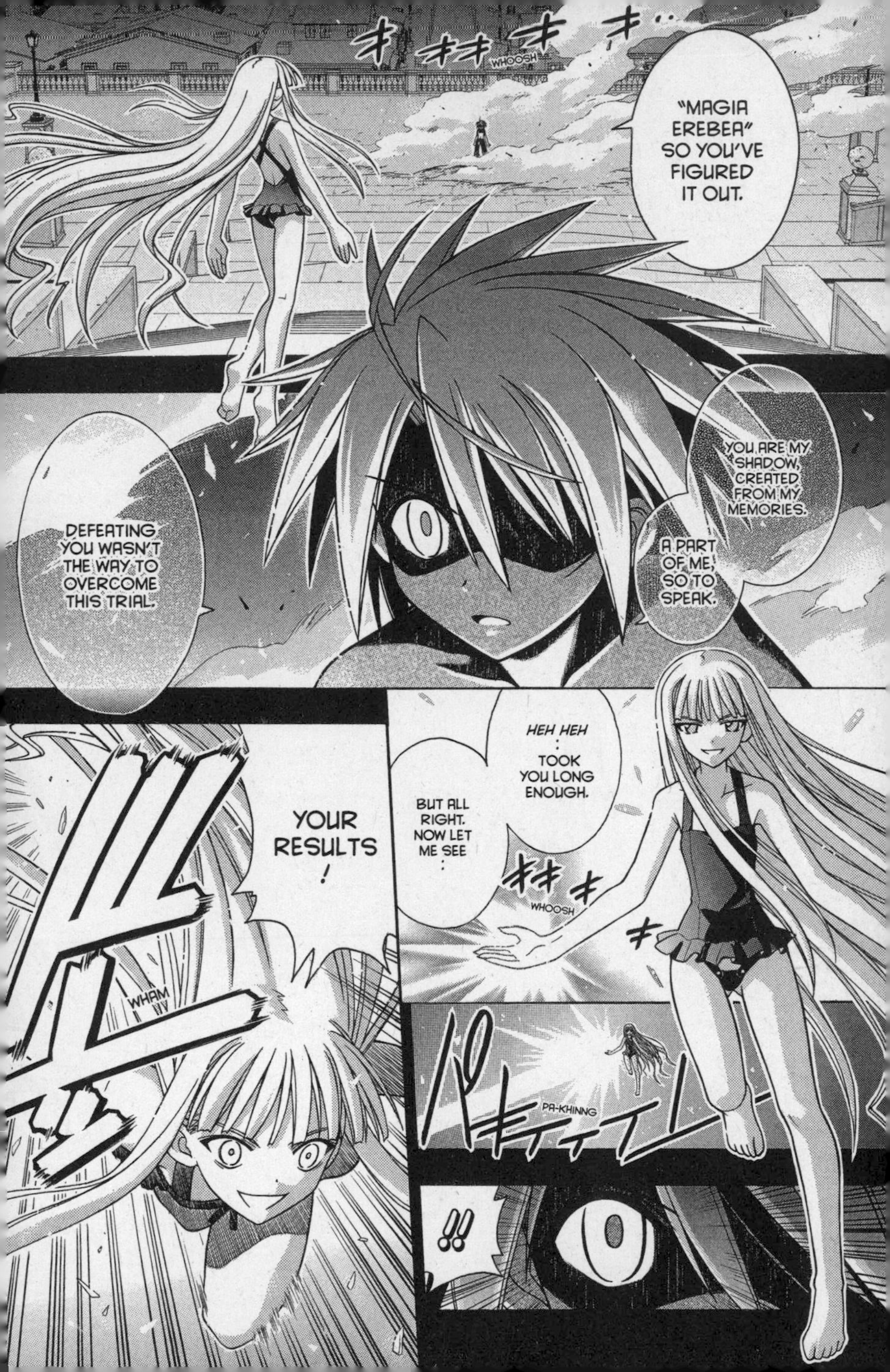
WHOOSH
"MAGIA EREBEA" SO YOU'VE FIGURED IT OUT.
YOU ARE MY SHADOW, CREATED FROM MY MEMORIES.
A PART OF ME, SO TO SPEAK.
DEFEATING YOU WASN'T THE WAY TO OVERCOME THIS TRIAL.
HEH HEH... TOOK YOU LONG ENOUGH.
BUT ALL RIGHT. NOW LET ME SEE...
WHOOSH
PA-KHINNG
!!
YOUR RESULTS!
WHAM

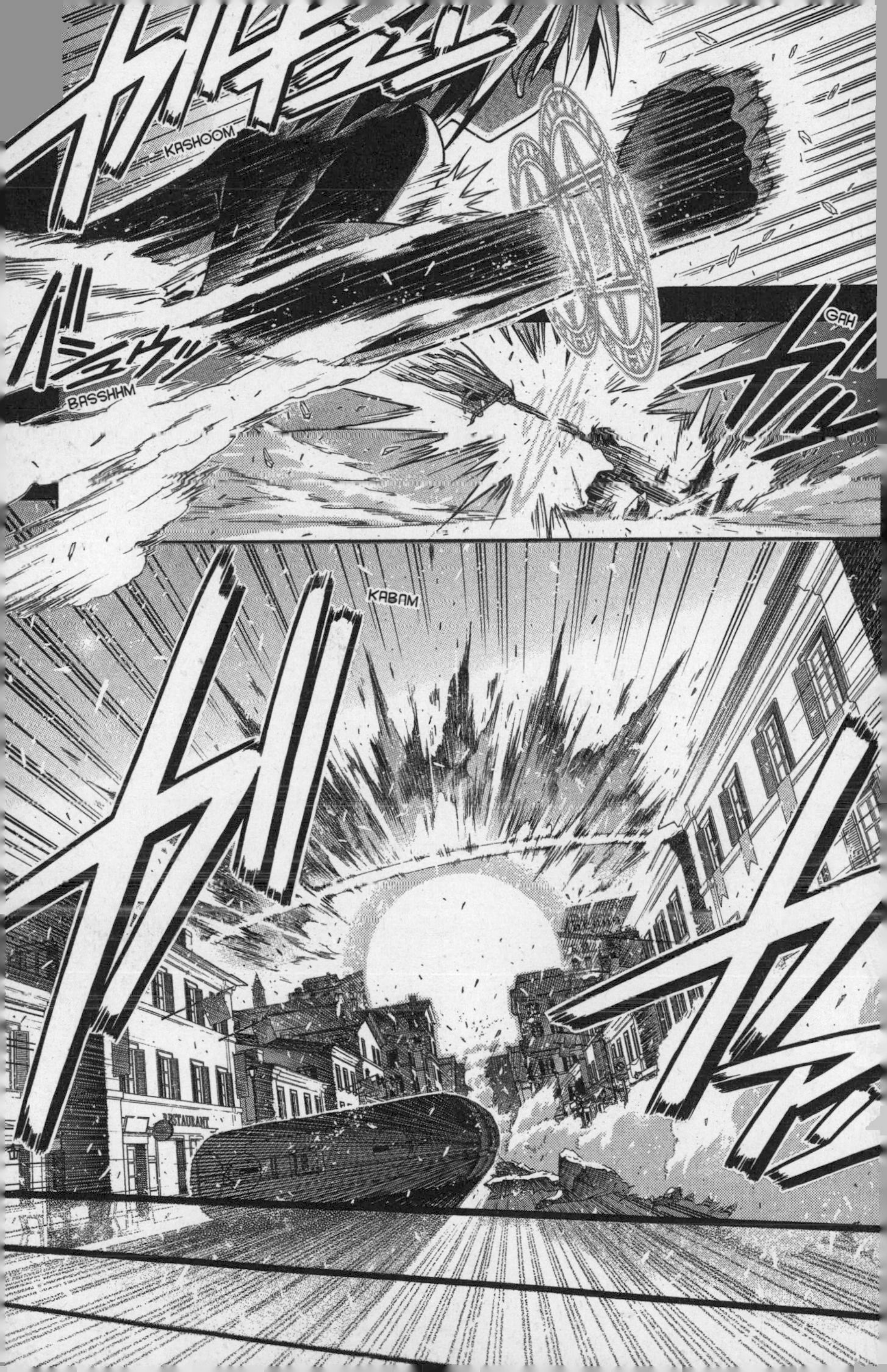
KASHOOM
BASSHHM
GAH
KABAM
RESTAURANT

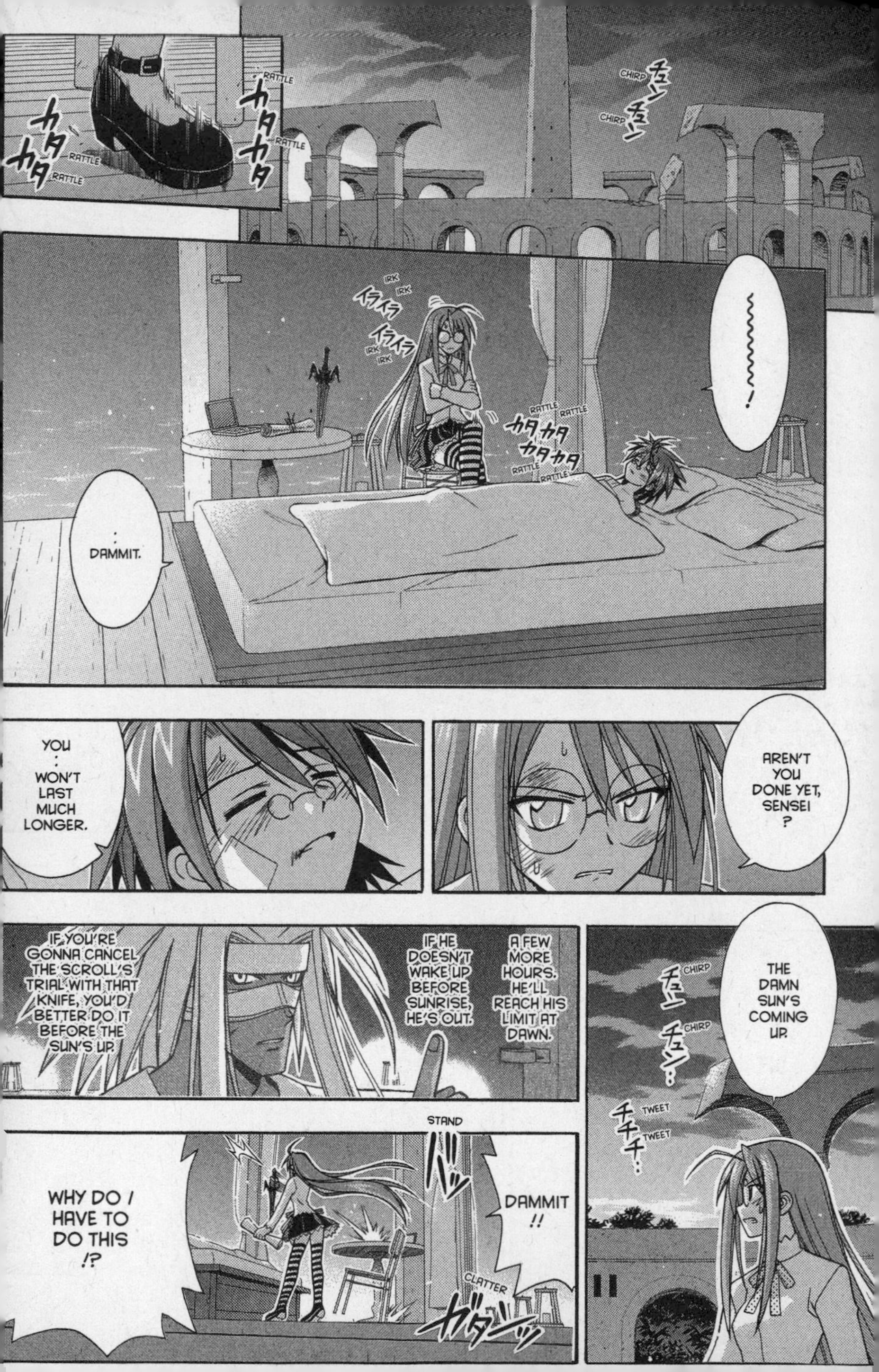

チュンチュン
CHIRP
CHIRP
カタカタ
RATTLE
RATTLE
カタカタ
RATTLE
RATTLE
~~~~!
イライラ
IRK
IRK
イライラ
IRK
IRK
カタカタ
RATTLE
RATTLE
カタカタ
RATTLE
RATTLE
: DAMMIT.
AREN'T YOU DONE YET, SENSEI ?
YOU : WON'T LAST MUCH LONGER.
THE DAMN SUN'S COMING UP.
CHIRP
CHIRP
TWEET
TWEET
A FEW MORE HOURS. HE'LL REACH HIS LIMIT AT DAWN.
IF HE DOESN'T WAKE UP BEFORE SUNRISE, HE'S OUT.
IF YOU'RE GONNA CANCEL THE SCROLL'S TRIAL WITH THAT KNIFE, YOU'D BETTER DO IT BEFORE THE SUN'S UP.
STAND
DAMMIT !!
WHY DO I HAVE TO DO THIS !?
CLATTER
~~~~

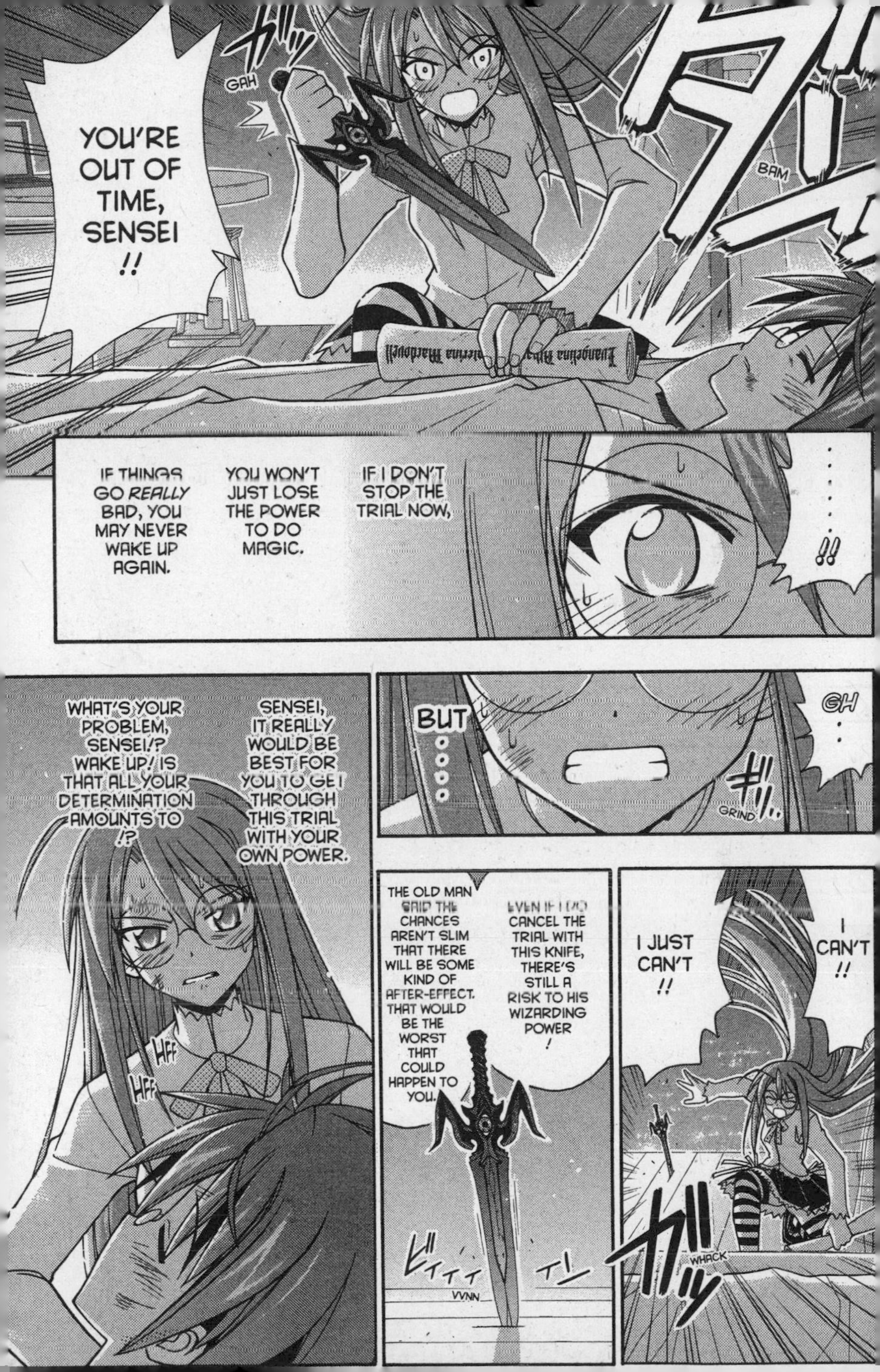
BAM
GAH
YOU'RE OUT OF TIME, SENSEI!!
......!!
IF I DON'T STOP THE TRIAL NOW,
YOU WON'T JUST LOSE THE POWER TO DO MAGIC.
IF THINGS GO *REALLY* BAD, YOU MAY NEVER WAKE UP AGAIN.
GH...
GRIND
BUT....
I CAN'T!!
I JUST CAN'T!!
WHACK
EVEN IF I DO CANCEL THE TRIAL WITH THIS KNIFE, THERE'S STILL A RISK TO HIS WIZARDING POWER!
THE OLD MAN SAID THE CHANCES AREN'T SLIM THAT THERE WILL BE SOME KIND OF AFTER-EFFECT. THAT WOULD BE THE WORST THAT COULD HAPPEN TO YOU.
VVNN
SENSEI, IT REALLY WOULD BE BEST FOR YOU TO GET THROUGH THIS TRIAL WITH YOUR OWN POWER.
WHAT'S YOUR PROBLEM, SENSEI!? WAKE UP! IS THAT ALL YOUR DETERMINATION AMOUNTS TO!?
HFF
HFF

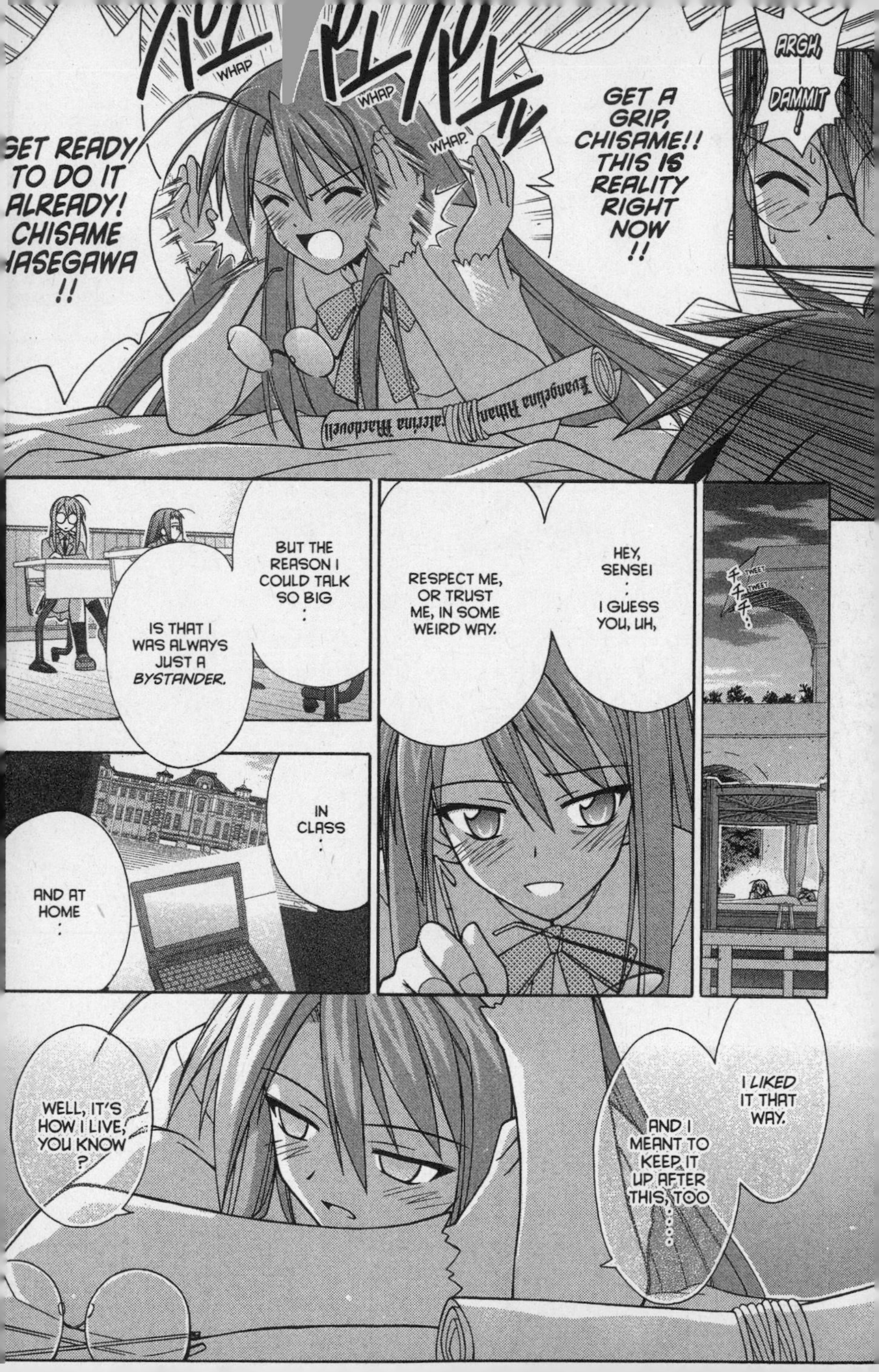
ARGH, DAMMIT!
GET A GRIP, CHISAME!! THIS IS REALITY RIGHT NOW!!
WHAP
WHAP
WHAP
GET READY TO DO IT ALREADY! CHISAME HASEGAWA!!
チチチ…
TWEET TWEET
HEY, SENSEI... I GUESS YOU, UH,
RESPECT ME, OR TRUST ME, IN SOME WEIRD WAY.
BUT THE REASON I COULD TALK SO BIG...
IS THAT I WAS ALWAYS JUST A BYSTANDER.
IN CLASS...
AND AT HOME...
I LIKED IT THAT WAY.
AND I MEANT TO KEEP IT UP AFTER THIS, TOO......
WELL, IT'S HOW I LIVE, YOU KNOW?

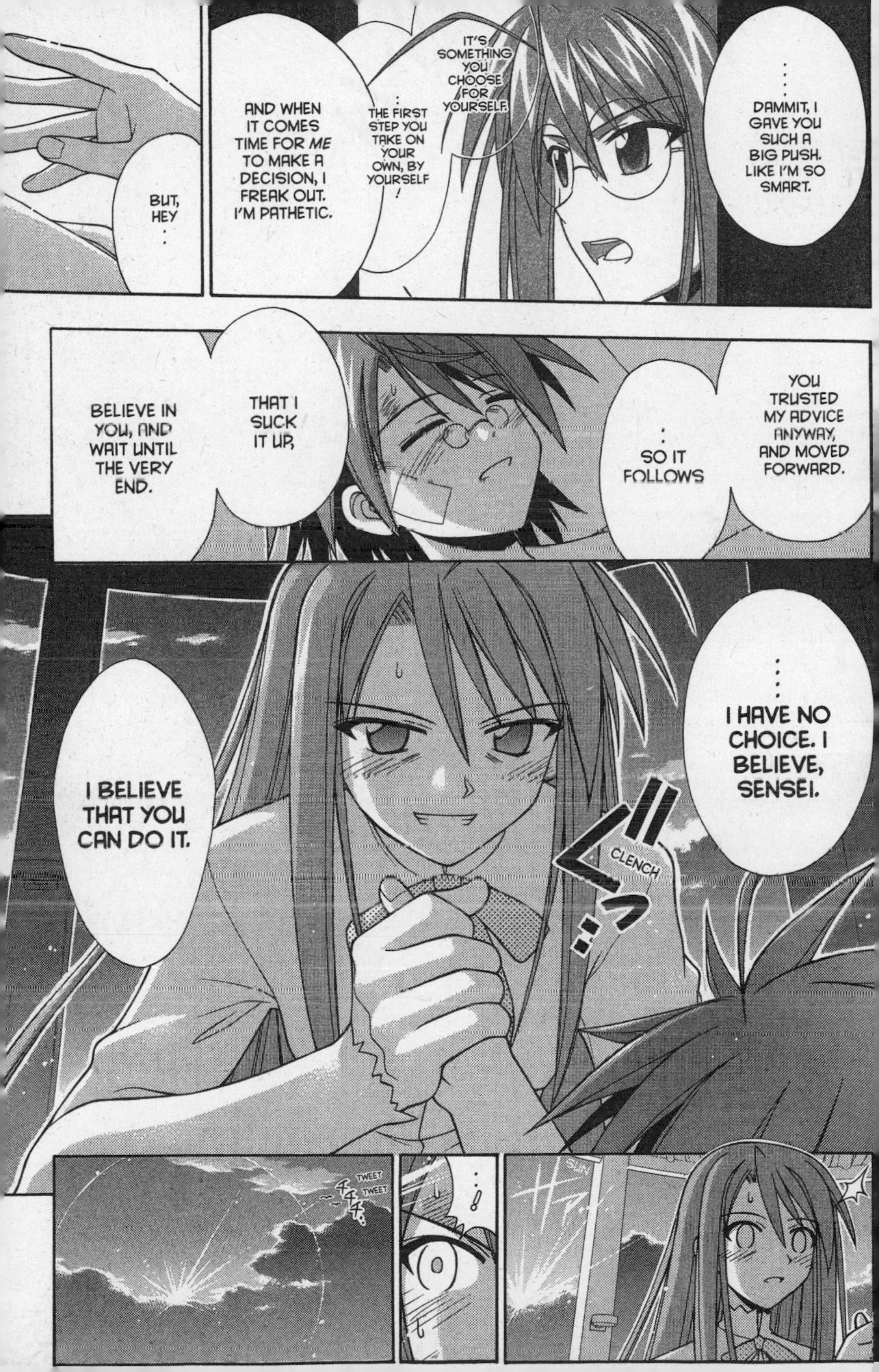
...DAMMIT, I GAVE YOU SUCH A BIG PUSH. LIKE I'M SO SMART.
IT'S SOMETHING YOU CHOOSE FOR YOURSELF.
: THE FIRST STEP YOU TAKE ON YOUR OWN, BY YOURSELF !
AND WHEN IT COMES TIME FOR *ME* TO MAKE A DECISION, I FREAK OUT. I'M PATHETIC.
BUT, HEY ...
YOU TRUSTED MY ADVICE ANYWAY, AND MOVED FORWARD.
: SO IT FOLLOWS
THAT I SUCK IT UP,
BELIEVE IN YOU, AND WAIT UNTIL THE VERY END.
...I HAVE NO CHOICE. I BELIEVE, SENSEI.
CLENCH
I BELIEVE THAT YOU CAN DO IT.
: !
TWEET TWEET

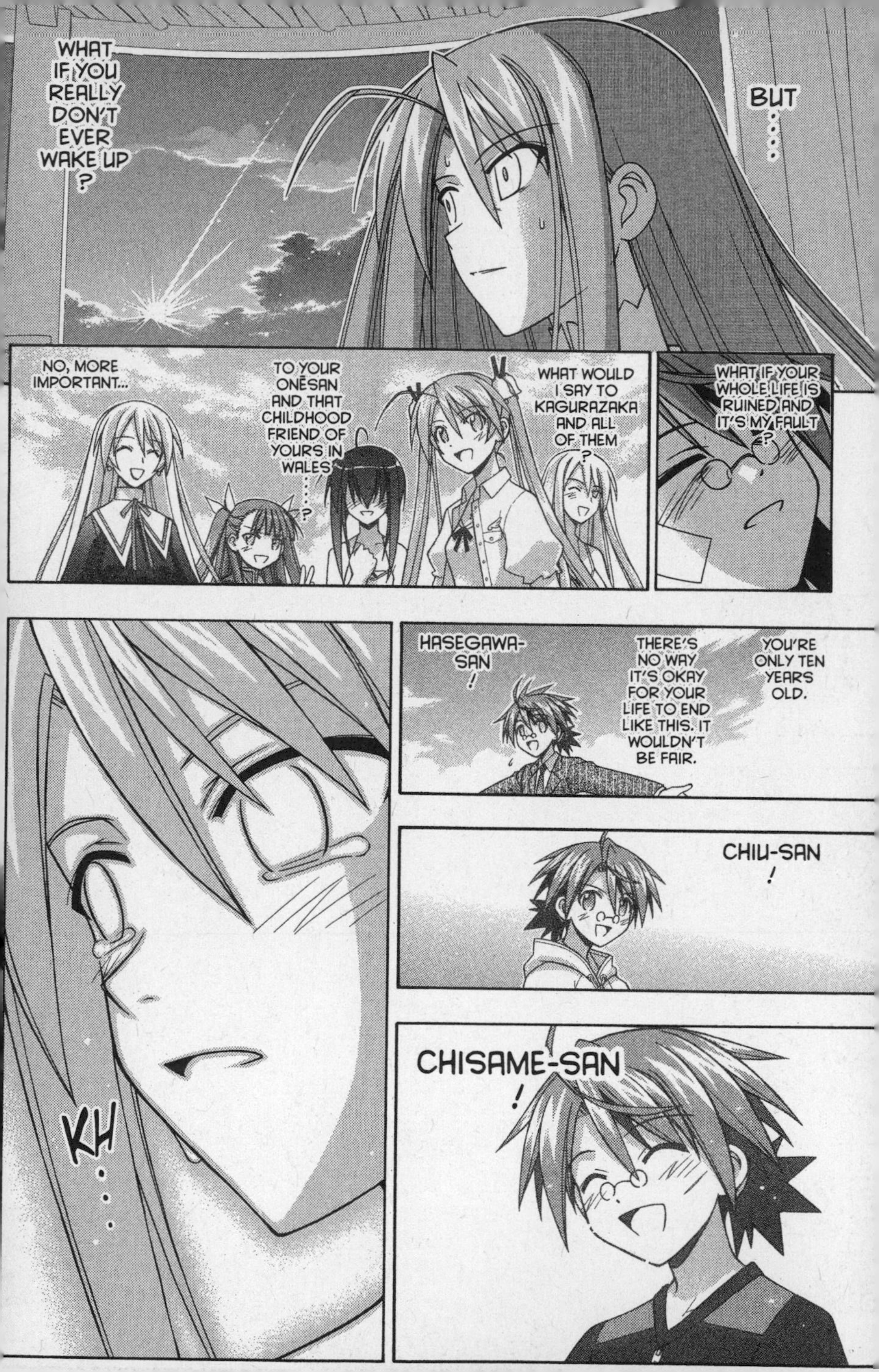
BUT....
WHAT IF YOU REALLY DON'T EVER WAKE UP?
WHAT IF YOUR WHOLE LIFE IS RUINED AND IT'S MY FAULT?
WHAT WOULD I SAY TO KAGURAZAKA AND ALL OF THEM?
TO YOUR ONĒSAN AND THAT CHILDHOOD FRIEND OF YOURS IN WALES...?
NO, MORE IMPORTANT...
YOU'RE ONLY TEN YEARS OLD.
THERE'S NO WAY IT'S OKAY FOR YOUR LIFE TO END LIKE THIS. IT WOULDN'T BE FAIR.
HASEGAWA-SAN!
CHIU-SAN!
CHISAME-SAN!
KH...

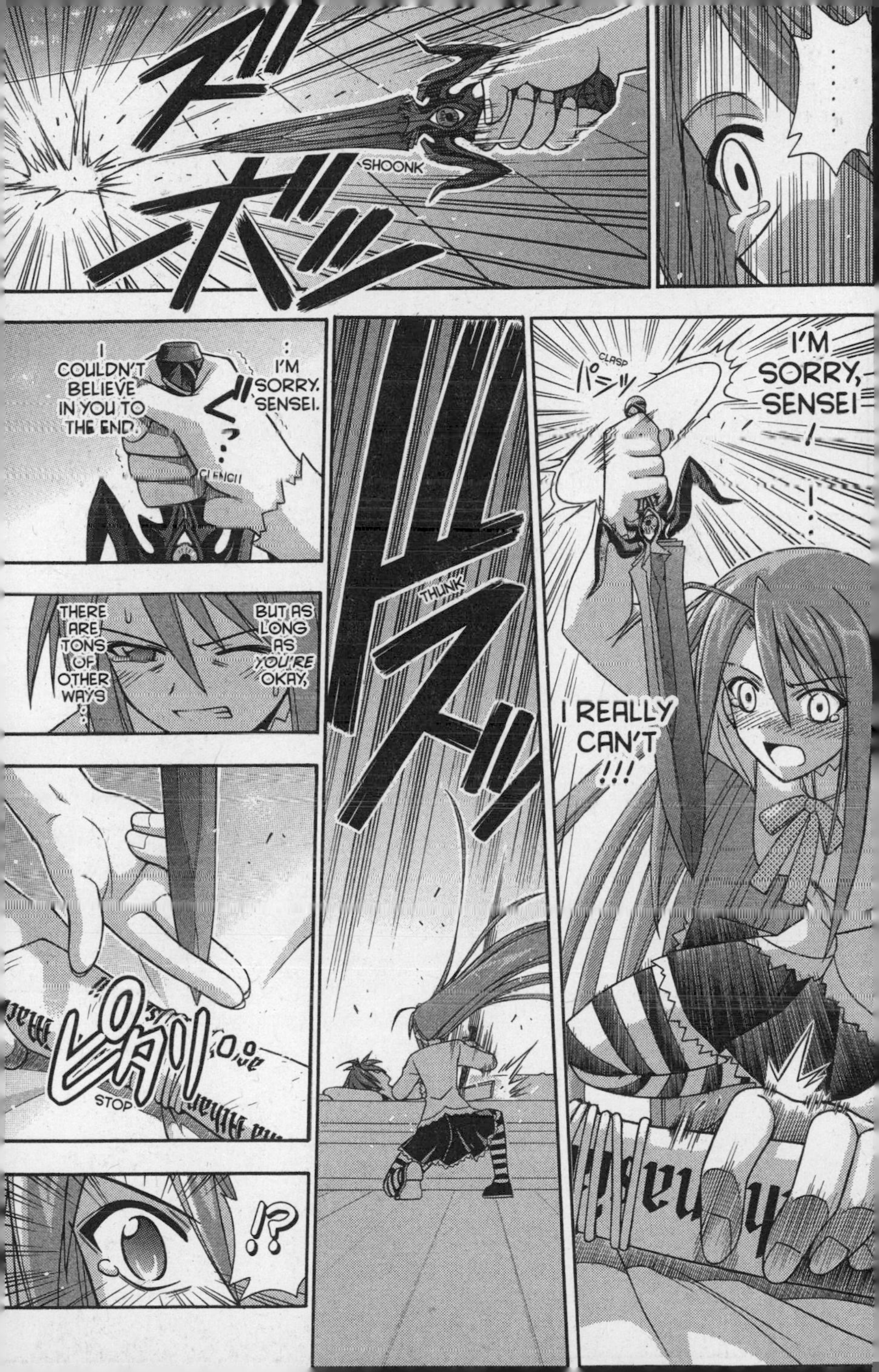
SHOONK
CLASP
I'M SORRY, SENSEI!
I REALLY CAN'T!!!
THUNK
I'M SORRY. SENSEI.
I COULDN'T BELIEVE IN YOU TO THE END.
CLENCH
BUT AS LONG AS YOU'RE OKAY,
THERE ARE TONS OF OTHER WAYS...
STOP
!?

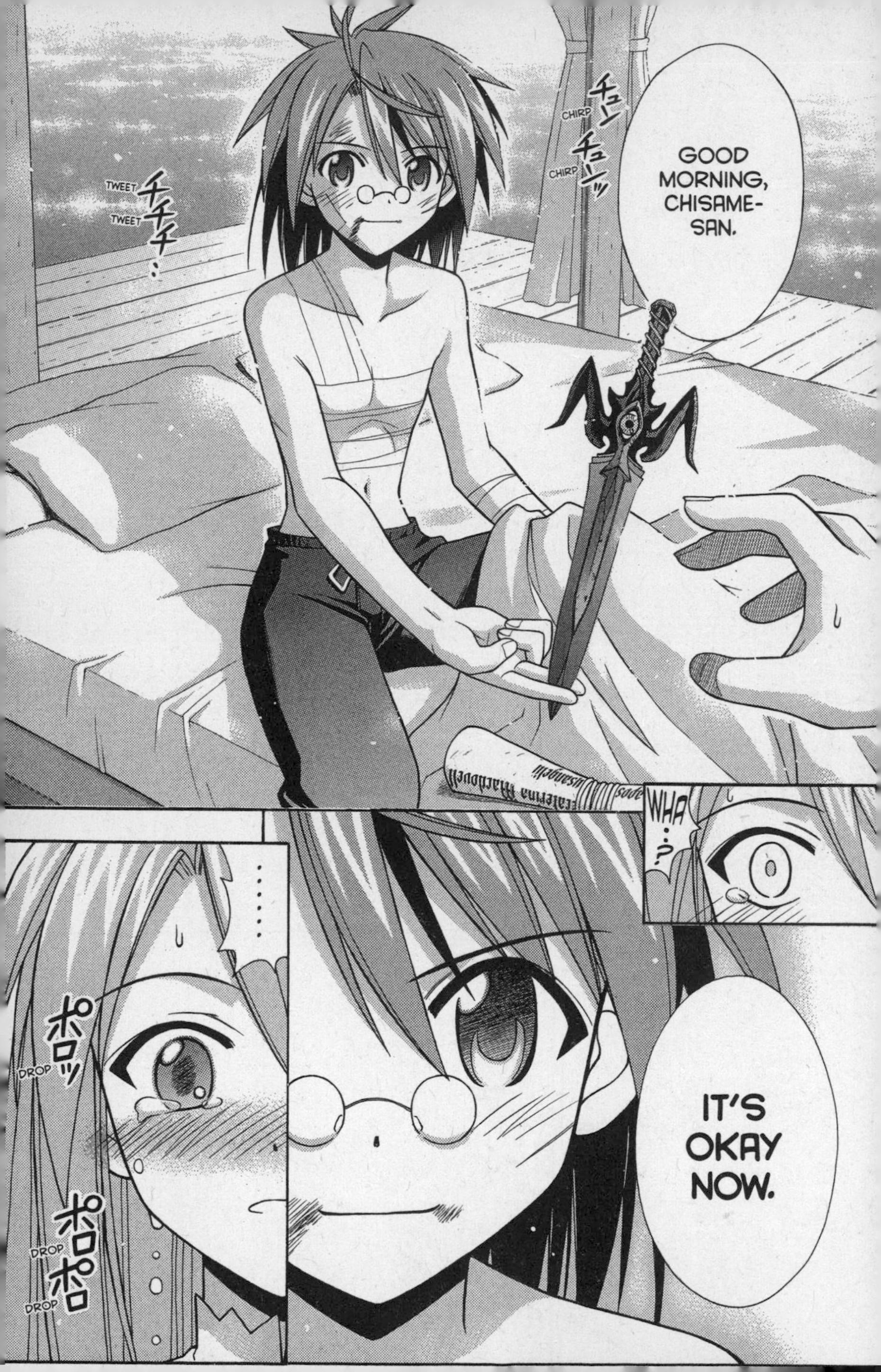
GOOD MORNING, CHISAME-SAN.
チュン チュンッ
CHIRP CHIRP
チチチ…
TWEET TWEET
WHA...?
IT'S OKAY NOW.
......
ポロッ
DROP
ポロポロ
DROP DROP

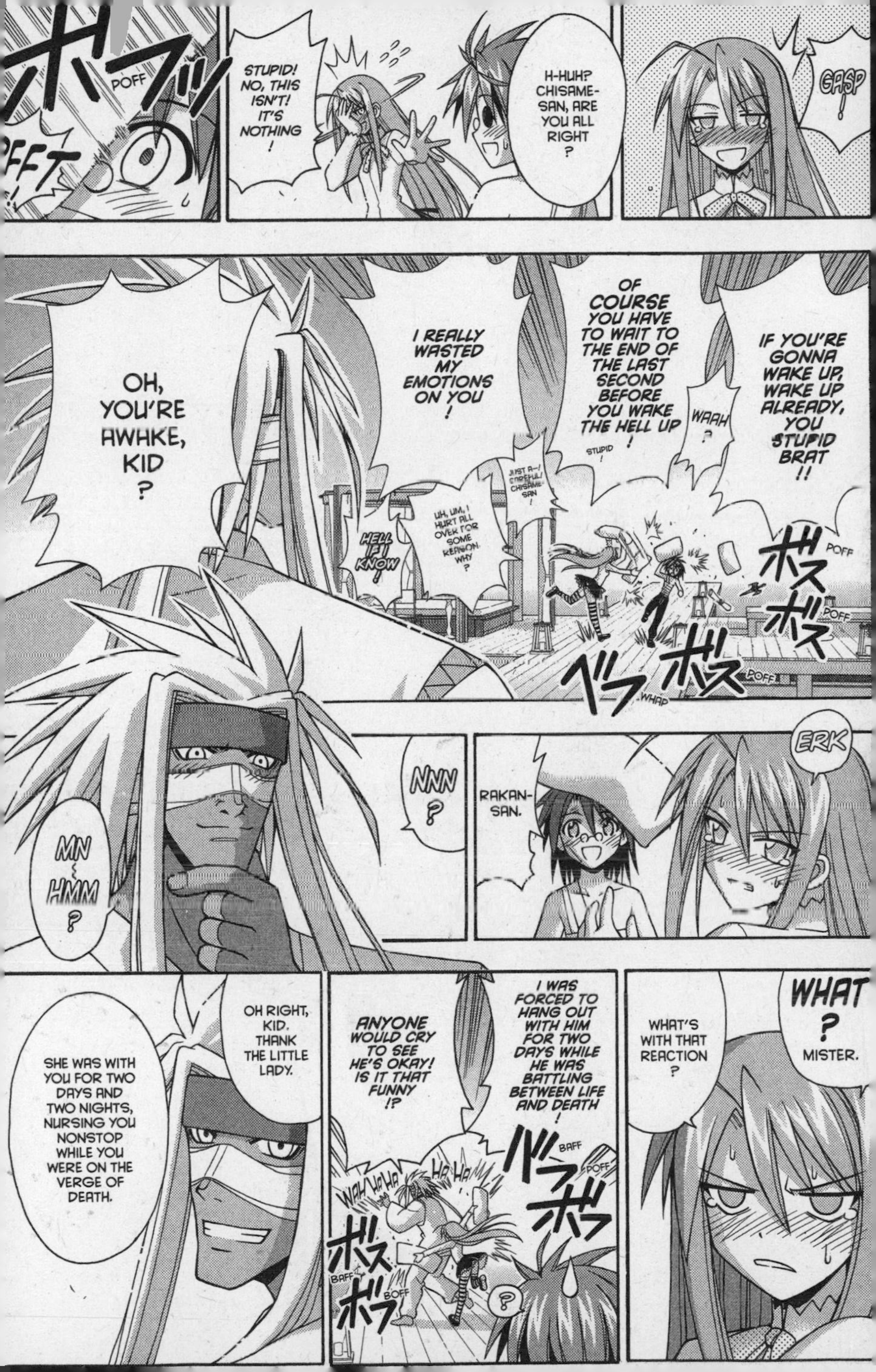
GASP!
H-HUH? CHISAME-SAN, ARE YOU ALL RIGHT?
STUPID! NO, THIS ISN'T! IT'S NOTHING!
POFF
PFFT!
IF YOU'RE GONNA WAKE UP, WAKE UP ALREADY, YOU STUPID BRAT!!
WAAH?
OF COURSE YOU HAVE TO WAIT TO THE END OF THE LAST SECOND BEFORE YOU WAKE THE HELL UP!
STUPID!
I REALLY WASTED MY EMOTIONS ON YOU!
JUST A-! CAREFUL! CHISAME-SAN!
UH, UM, I HURT ALL OVER FOR SOME REASON. WHY?
HELL IF I KNOW!
POFF
POFF
POFF
WHAP
OH, YOU'RE AWHKE, KID?
ERK
RAKAN-SAN.
NNN?
MN~HMM?
WHAT? MISTER.
WHAT'S WITH THAT REACTION?
I WAS FORCED TO HANG OUT WITH HIM FOR TWO DAYS WHILE HE WAS BATTLING BETWEEN LIFE AND DEATH!
BAFF
POFF
ANYONE WOULD CRY TO SEE HE'S OKAY! IS IT THAT FUNNY!?
HA HA
WAH HAHA
BAFF
BOFF
?
OH RIGHT, KID. THANK THE LITTLE LADY.
SHE WAS WITH YOU FOR TWO DAYS AND TWO NIGHTS, NURSING YOU NONSTOP WHILE YOU WERE ON THE VERGE OF DEATH.

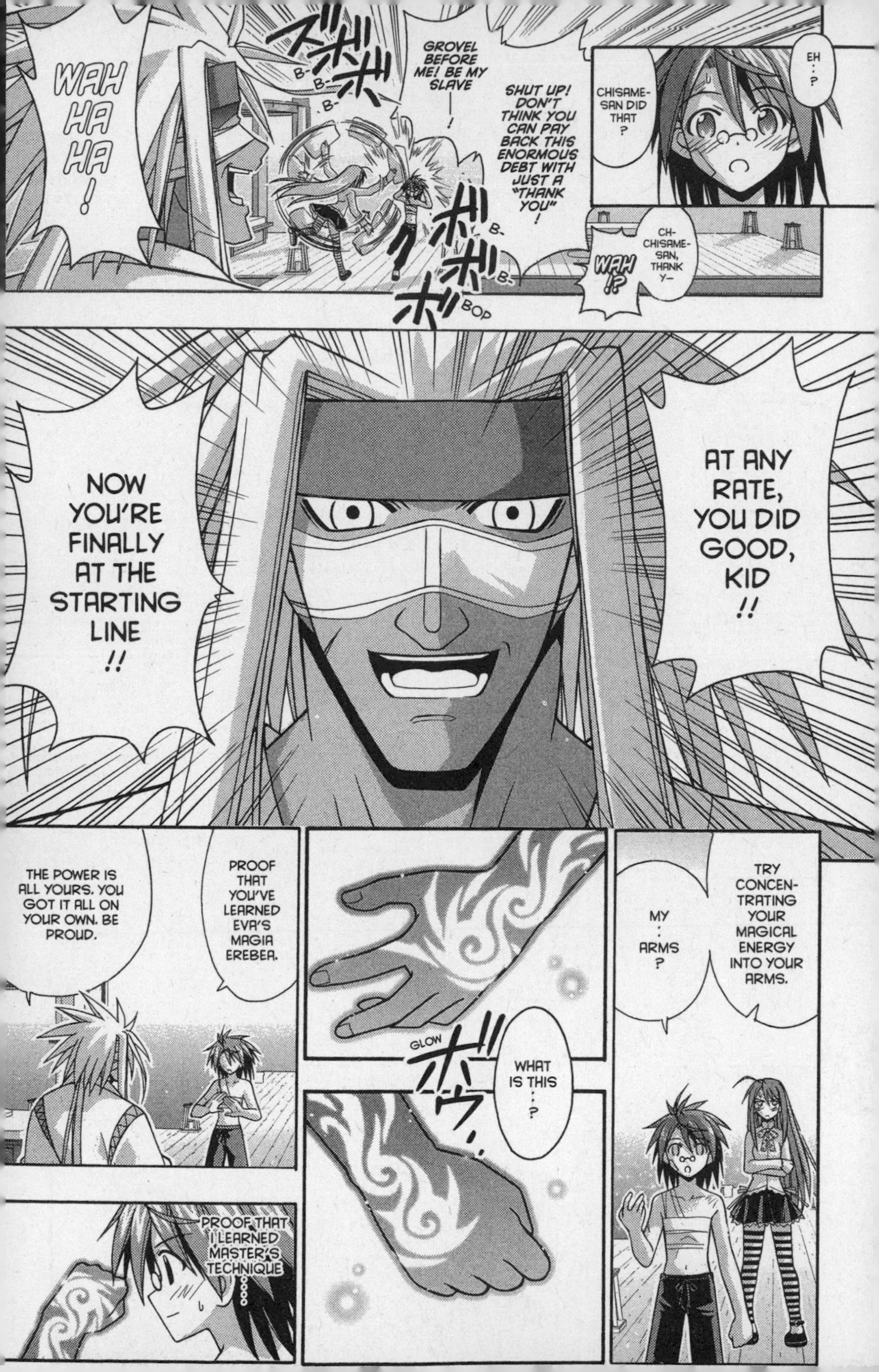
EH...?
CHISAME-SAN DID THAT?
CH-CHISAME-SAN, THANK Y—
WAH!?
SHUT UP! DON'T THINK YOU CAN PAY BACK THIS ENORMOUS DEBT WITH JUST A "THANK YOU"!
GROVEL BEFORE ME! BE MY SLAVE—!
B-B-B-
B-B-BOP
WAH HA HA!
AT ANY RATE, YOU DID GOOD, KID!!
NOW YOU'RE FINALLY AT THE STARTING LINE!!
TRY CONCENTRATING YOUR MAGICAL ENERGY INTO YOUR ARMS.
MY... ARMS?
GLOW
WHAT IS THIS...?
PROOF THAT YOU'VE LEARNED EVA'S MAGIA EREBEA.
THE POWER IS ALL YOURS. YOU GOT IT ALL ON YOUR OWN. BE PROUD.
PROOF THAT I LEARNED MASTER'S TECHNIQUE....

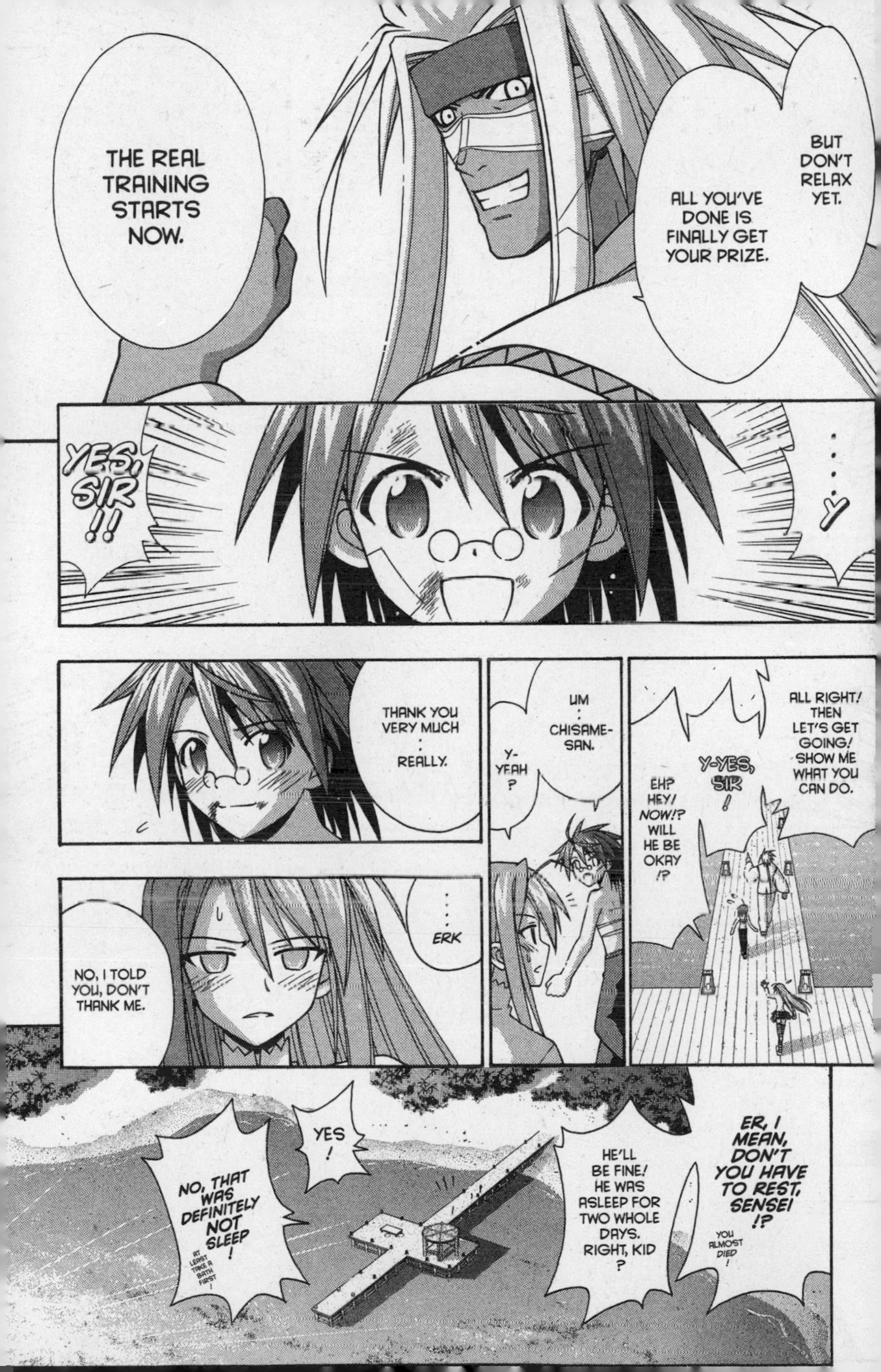
BUT DON'T RELAX YET.
ALL YOU'VE DONE IS FINALLY GET YOUR PRIZE.
THE REAL TRAINING STARTS NOW.
...Y
YES, SIR!!
ALL RIGHT! THEN LET'S GET GOING! SHOW ME WHAT YOU CAN DO.
Y-YES, SIR!
EH? HEY! NOW!? WILL HE BE OKAY!?
UM... CHISAME-SAN.
Y-YEAH?
THANK YOU VERY MUCH... REALLY.
...ERK
NO, I TOLD YOU, DON'T THANK ME.
ER, I MEAN, DON'T YOU HAVE TO REST, SENSEI!?
YOU ALMOST DIED!
HE'LL BE FINE! HE WAS ASLEEP FOR TWO WHOLE DAYS. RIGHT, KID?
YES!
NO, THAT WAS DEFINITELY NOT SLEEP!
AT LEAST TAKE A BATH FIRST!

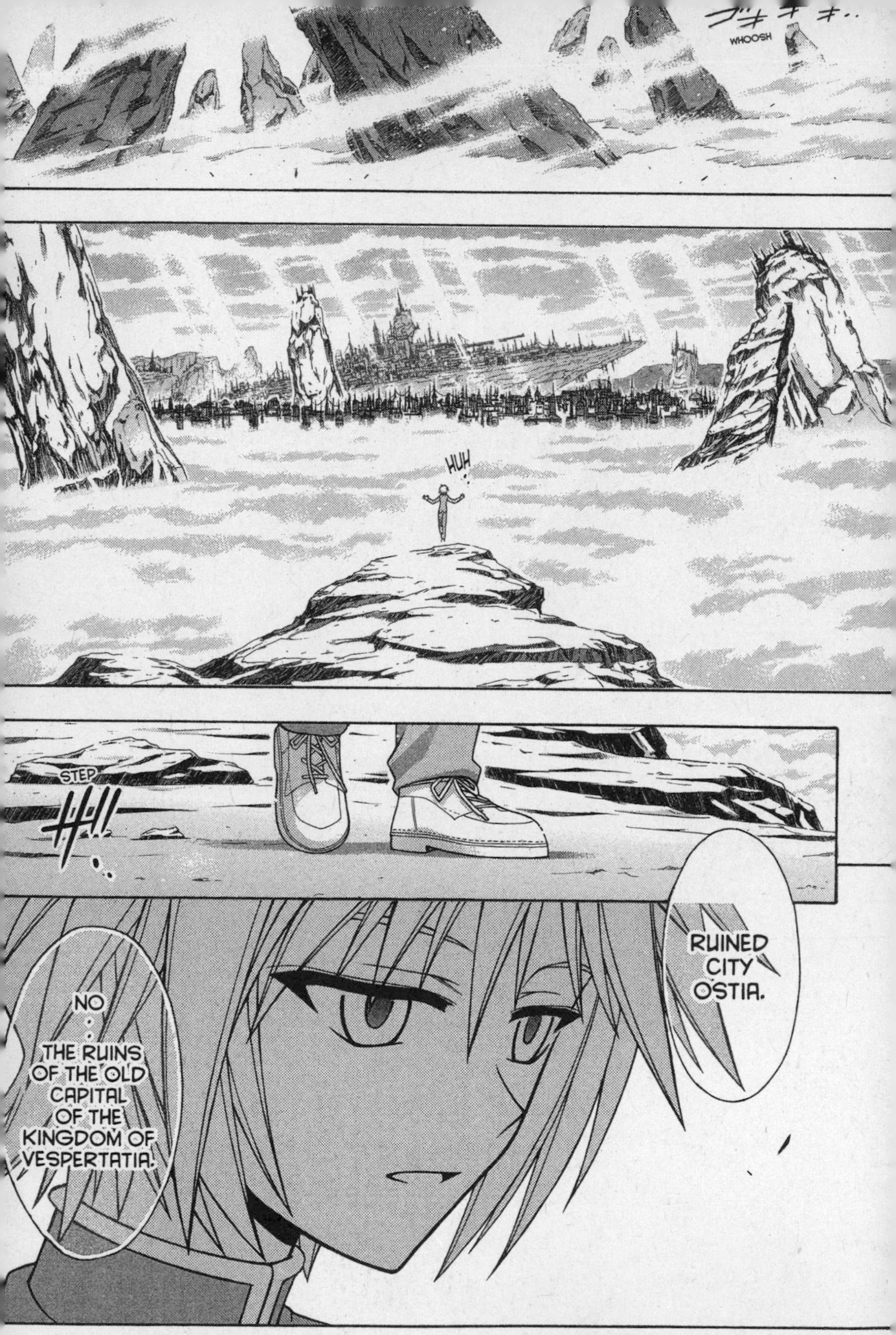
WHOOSH
HUH
STEP
RUINED CITY OSTIA.
NO... THE RUINS OF THE OLD CAPITAL OF THE KINGDOM OF VESPERTATIA.

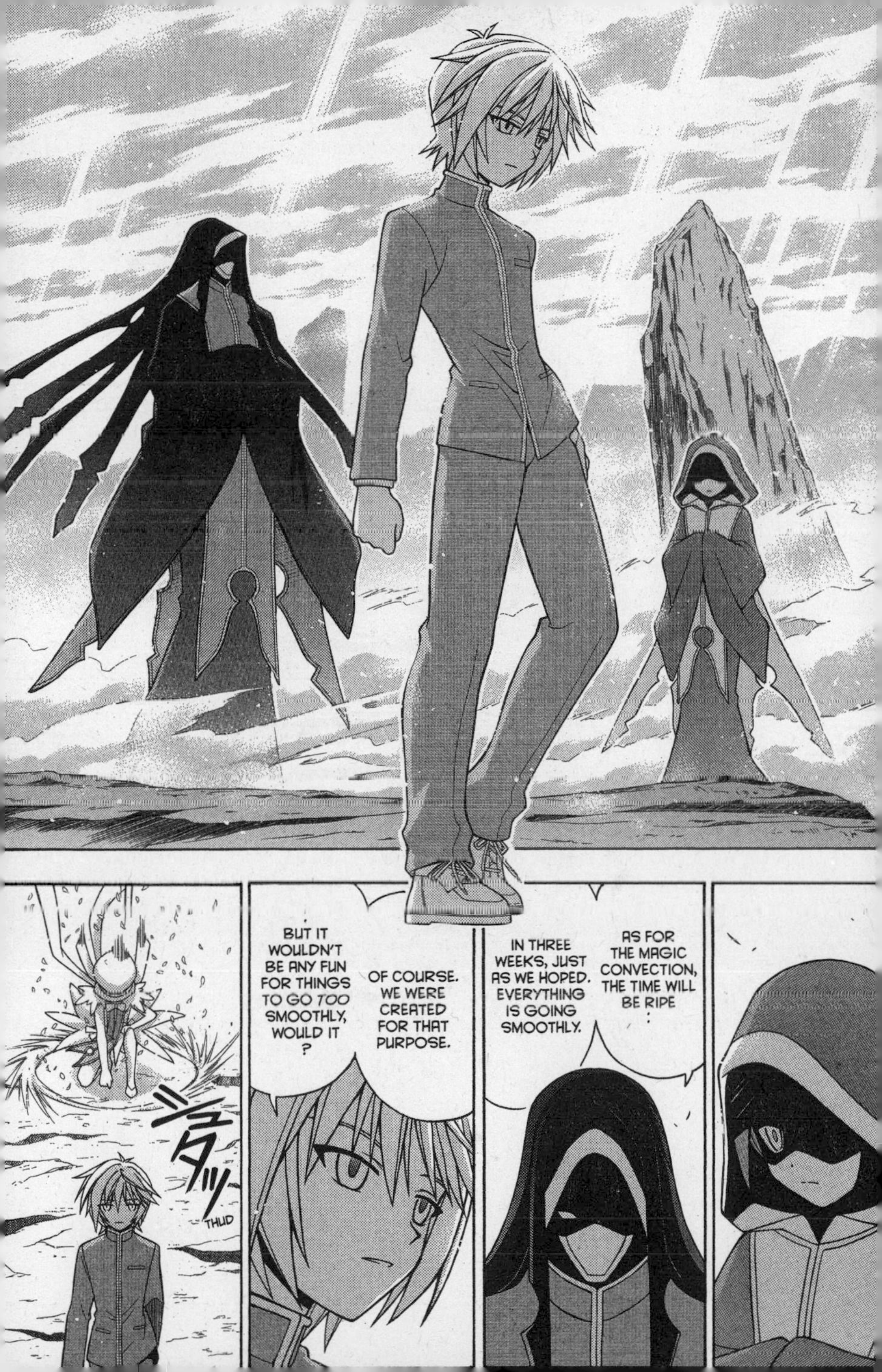
AS FOR THE MAGIC CONVECTION, THE TIME WILL BE RIPE...
IN THREE WEEKS, JUST AS WE HOPED. EVERYTHING IS GOING SMOOTHLY.
OF COURSE. WE WERE CREATED FOR THAT PURPOSE.
BUT IT WOULDN'T BE ANY FUN FOR THINGS TO GO *TOO* SMOOTHLY, WOULD IT?
シュタッ
THUD

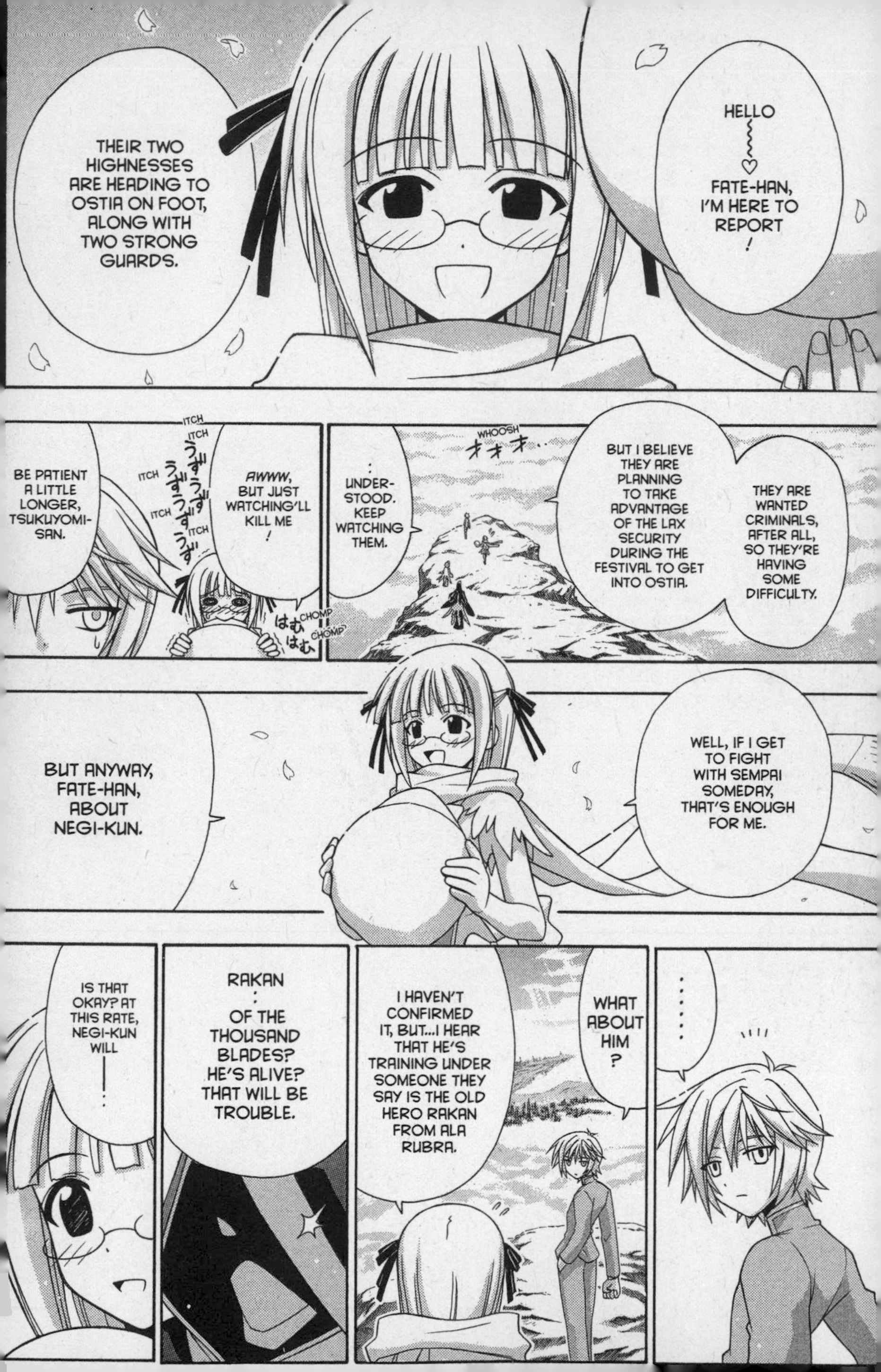
HELLO~♡ FATE-HAN, I'M HERE TO REPORT!
THEIR TWO HIGHNESSES ARE HEADING TO OSTIA ON FOOT, ALONG WITH TWO STRONG GUARDS.
THEY ARE WANTED CRIMINALS, AFTER ALL, SO THEY'RE HAVING SOME DIFFICULTY.
BUT I BELIEVE THEY ARE PLANNING TO TAKE ADVANTAGE OF THE LAX SECURITY DURING THE FESTIVAL TO GET INTO OSTIA.
WHOOSH オオオ…
: UNDERSTOOD. KEEP WATCHING THEM.
AWWW, BUT JUST WATCHING'LL KILL ME!
ITCH うず ITCH うず ITCH うず ITCH うず
はむ CHOMP はむ CHOMP
BE PATIENT A LITTLE LONGER, TSUKUYOMI-SAN.
WELL, IF I GET TO FIGHT WITH SEMPAI SOMEDAY, THAT'S ENOUGH FOR ME.
BUT ANYWAY, FATE-HAN, ABOUT NEGI-KUN.
......
WHAT ABOUT HIM?
I HAVEN'T CONFIRMED IT, BUT...I HEAR THAT HE'S TRAINING UNDER SOMEONE THEY SAY IS THE OLD HERO RAKAN FROM ALA RUBRA.
RAKAN : OF THE THOUSAND BLADES? HE'S ALIVE? THAT WILL BE TROUBLE.
IS THAT OKAY? AT THIS RATE, NEGI-KUN WILL —...

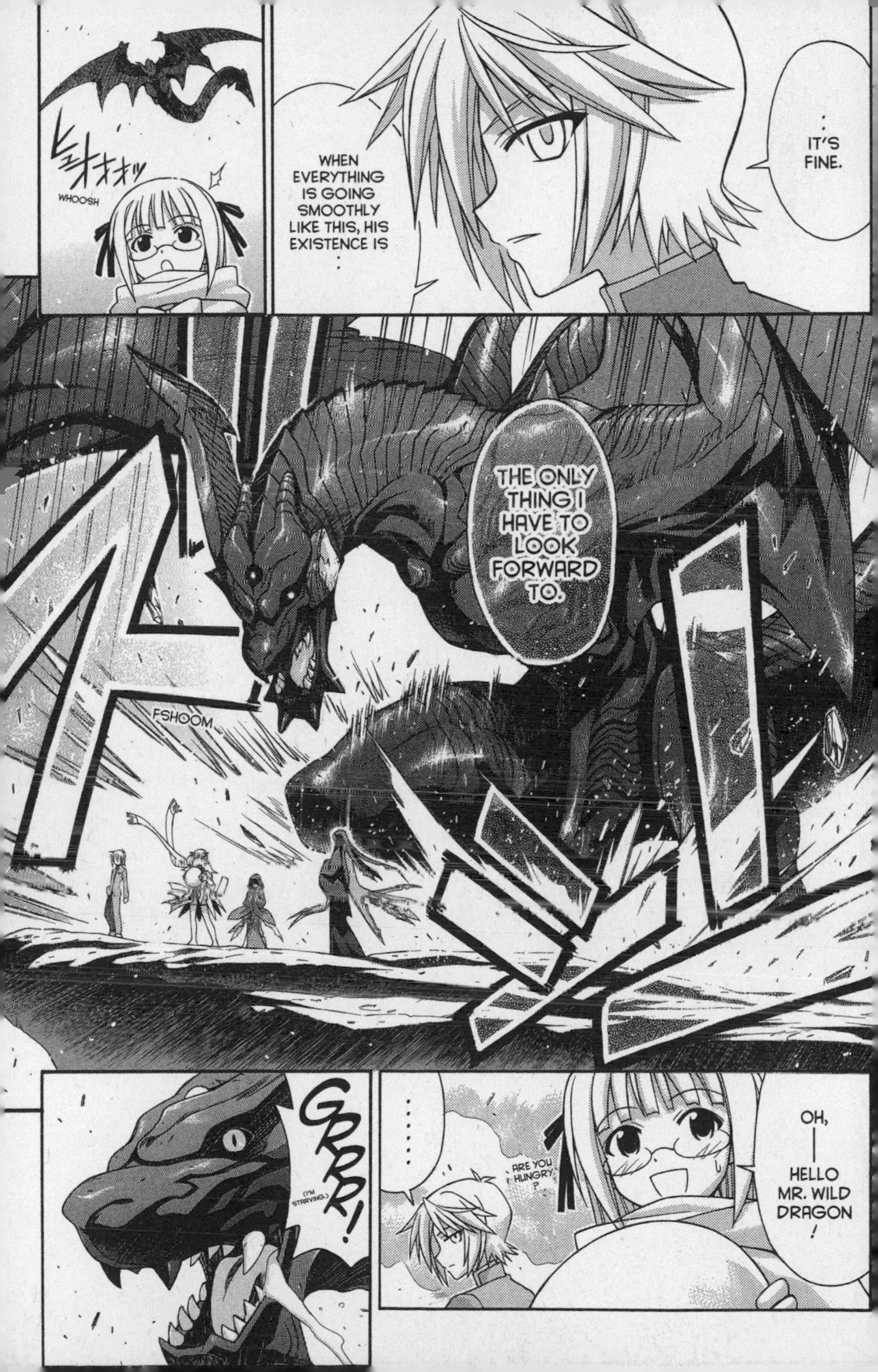

: IT'S FINE.
WHEN EVERYTHING IS GOING SMOOTHLY LIKE THIS, HIS EXISTENCE IS :
ヒュオオオッ
WHOOSH
THE ONLY THING I HAVE TO LOOK FORWARD TO.
FSHOOM
OH, — HELLO MR. WILD DRAGON!
ARE YOU HUNGRY?
......
GRRR!
(I'M STARVING.)

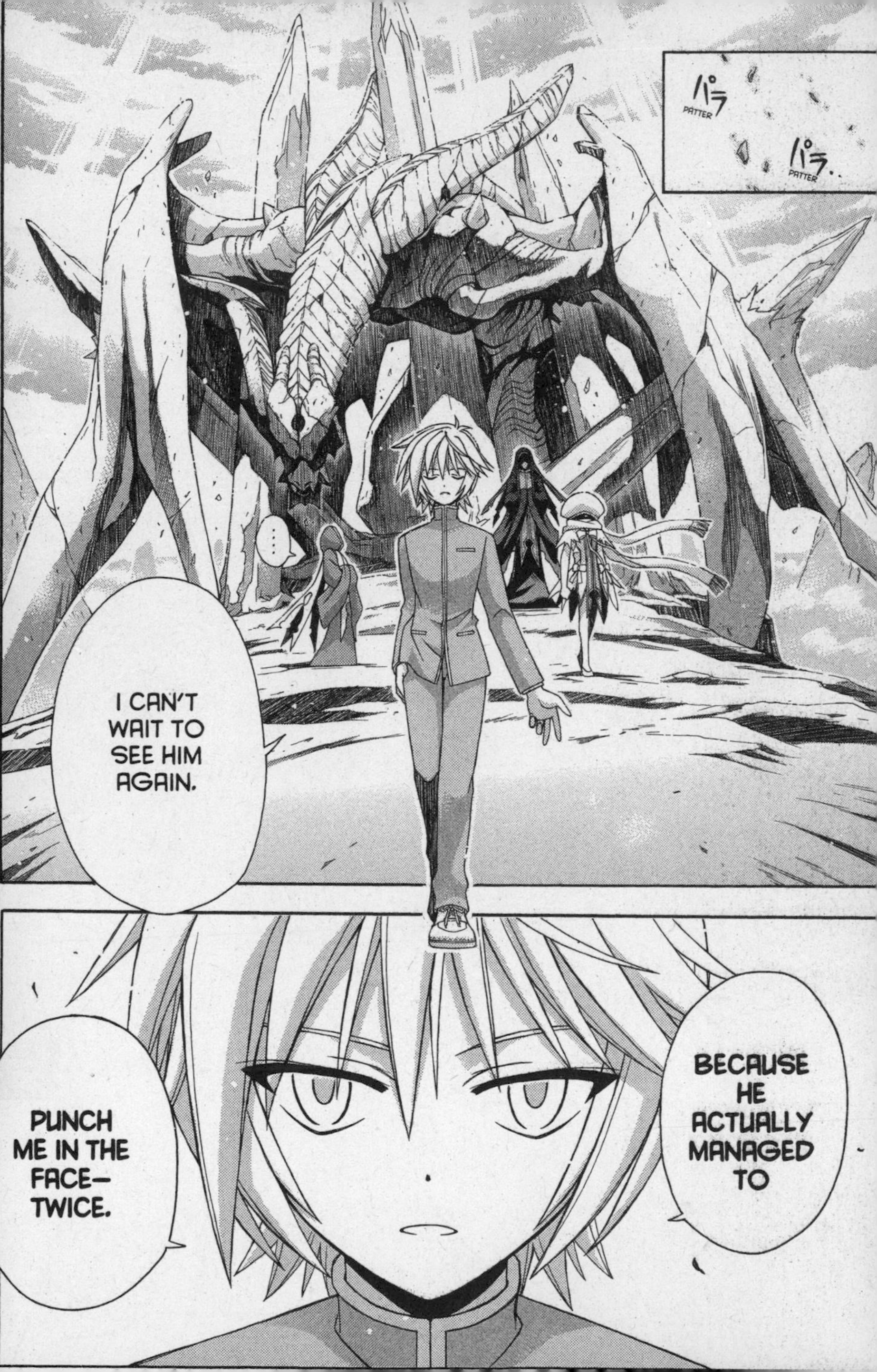
パラ PATTER
パラ PATTER..
...
I CAN'T WAIT TO SEE HIM AGAIN.
BECAUSE HE ACTUALLY MANAGED TO
PUNCH ME IN THE FACE—TWICE.

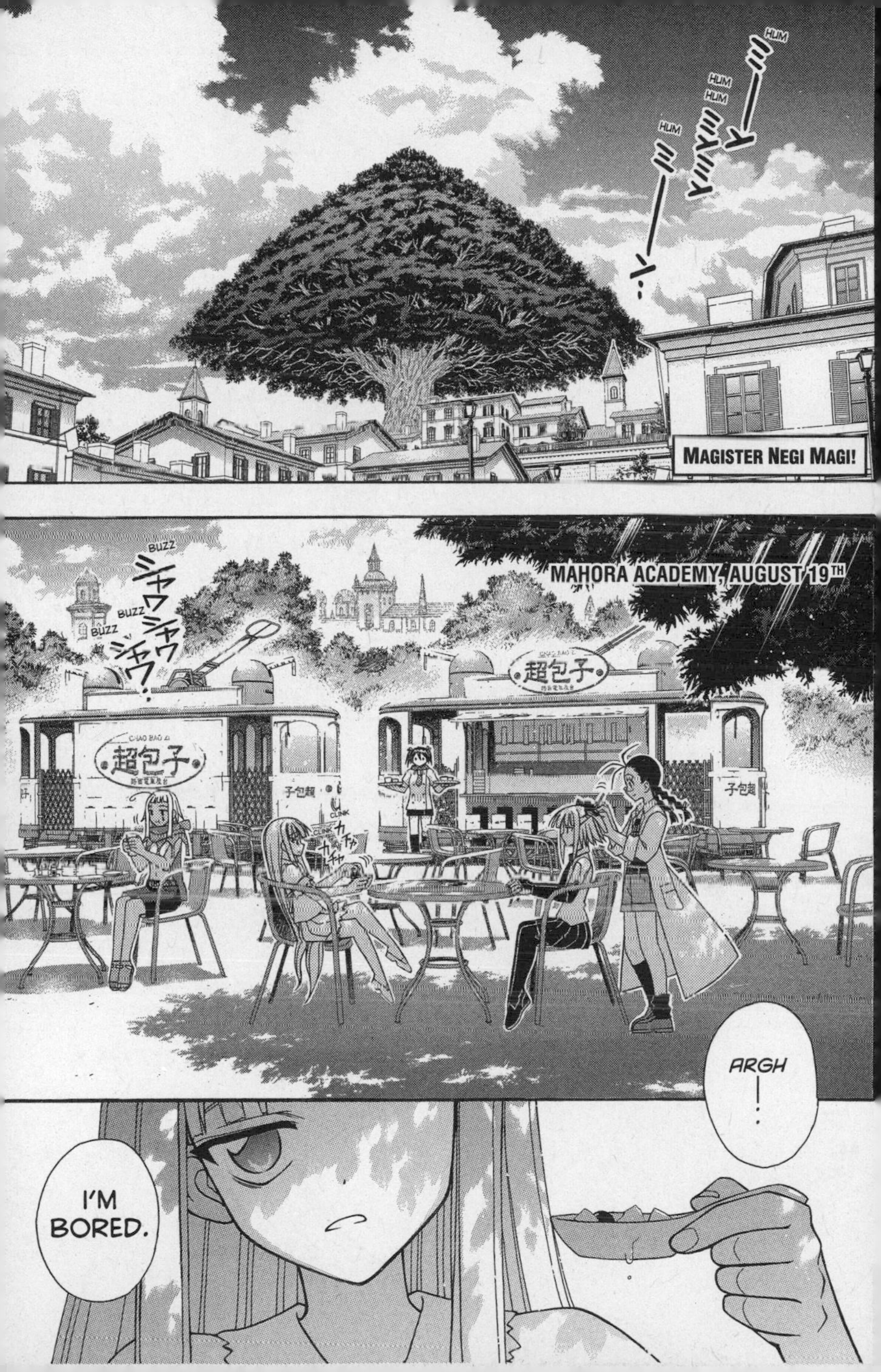
HUM
HUM
HUM
HUM
Magister Negi Magi!
MAHORA ACADEMY, AUGUST 19TH
超包子
CLINK
CLINK
BUZZ
BUZZ
BUZZ
ARGH
I'M BORED.

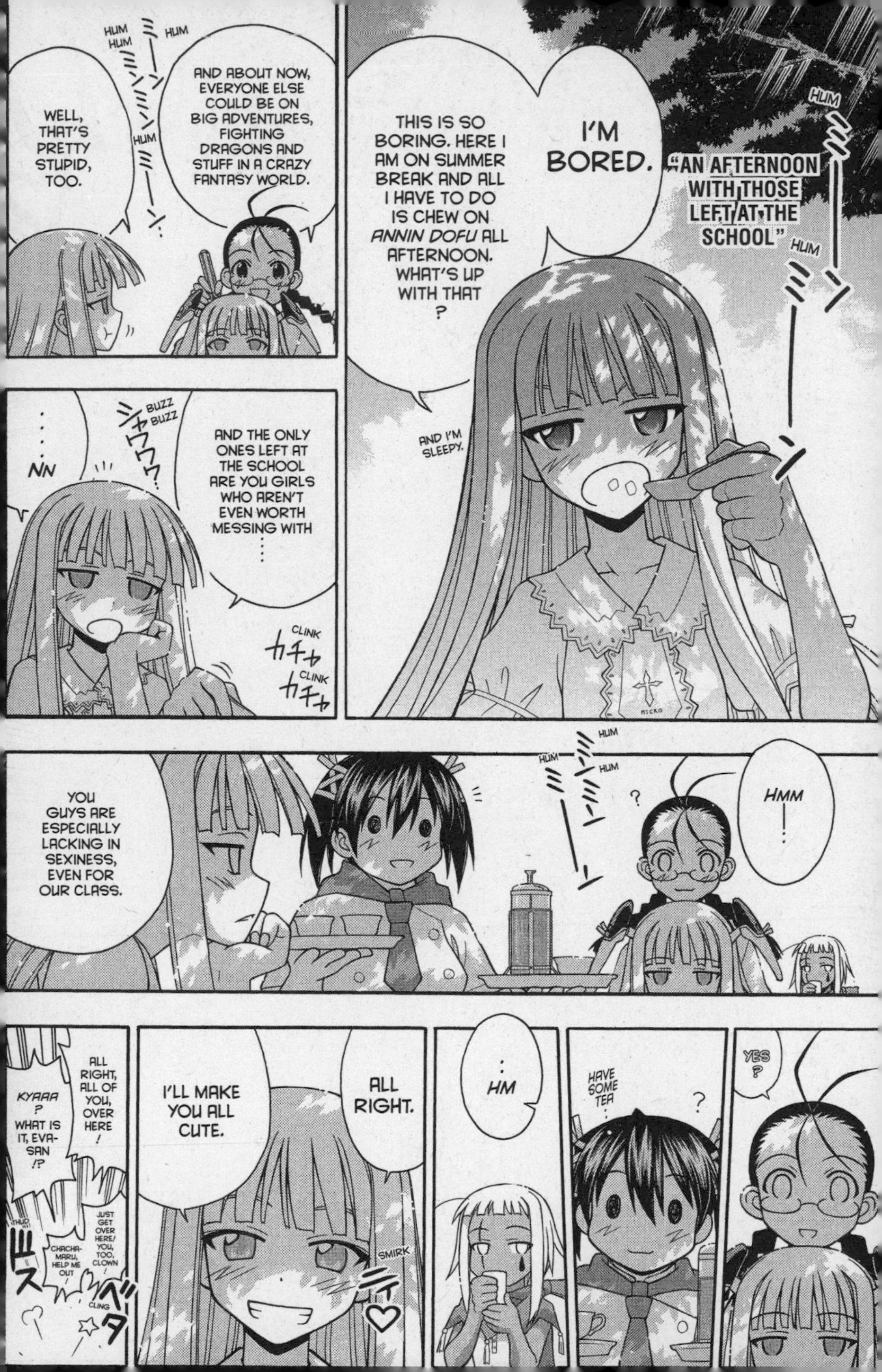

HUM
HUM
"AN AFTERNOON WITH THOSE LEFT AT THE SCHOOL"
I'M BORED.
THIS IS SO BORING. HERE I AM ON SUMMER BREAK AND ALL I HAVE TO DO IS CHEW ON ANNIN DOFU ALL AFTERNOON. WHAT'S UP WITH THAT?
AND I'M SLEEPY.
HUM HUM HUM
AND ABOUT NOW, EVERYONE ELSE COULD BE ON BIG ADVENTURES, FIGHTING DRAGONS AND STUFF IN A CRAZY FANTASY WORLD.
HUM
WELL, THAT'S PRETTY STUPID, TOO.
BUZZ BUZZ
AND THE ONLY ONES LEFT AT THE SCHOOL ARE YOU GIRLS WHO AREN'T EVEN WORTH MESSING WITH...
...NN
CLINK
CLINK
HUM
HUM
HUM
HMM!
?
YOU GUYS ARE ESPECIALLY LACKING IN SEXINESS, EVEN FOR OUR CLASS.
YES?
HAVE SOME TEA?
:HM
ALL RIGHT.
I'LL MAKE YOU ALL CUTE.
SMIRK
ALL RIGHT, ALL OF YOU, OVER HERE!
JUST GET OVER HERE! YOU, TOO, CLOWN!
KYAAA? WHAT IS IT, EVA-SAN!?
CHACHA-MARU, HELP ME OUT!
THUD
CLING

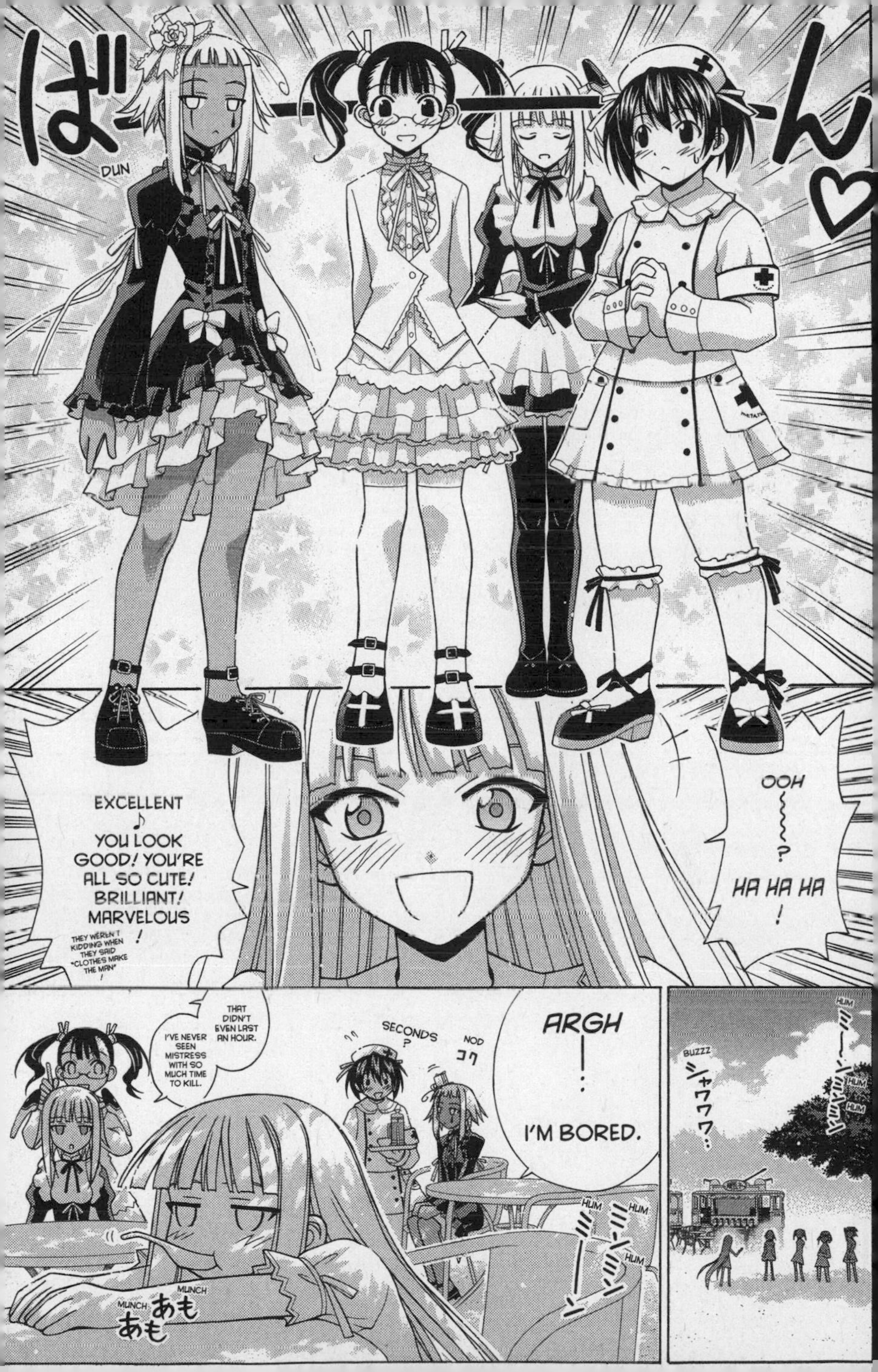
ばーーーん♡
DUN
OOH~~~? HA HA HA!
EXCELLENT ♪ YOU LOOK GOOD! YOU'RE ALL SO CUTE! BRILLIANT! MARVELOUS!
THEY WEREN'T KIDDING WHEN THEY SAID "CLOTHES MAKE THE MAN"!
HUM ミ〜ンミンミン HUM HUM
BUZZZ シャワワ…
ARGH—…
I'M BORED.
HUM ミ〜ンミンミ〜ン HUM HUM
NOD コク
SECONDS?
THAT DIDN'T EVEN LAST AN HOUR.
I'VE NEVER SEEN MISTRESS WITH SO MUCH TIME TO KILL.
MUNCH あも MUNCH あも

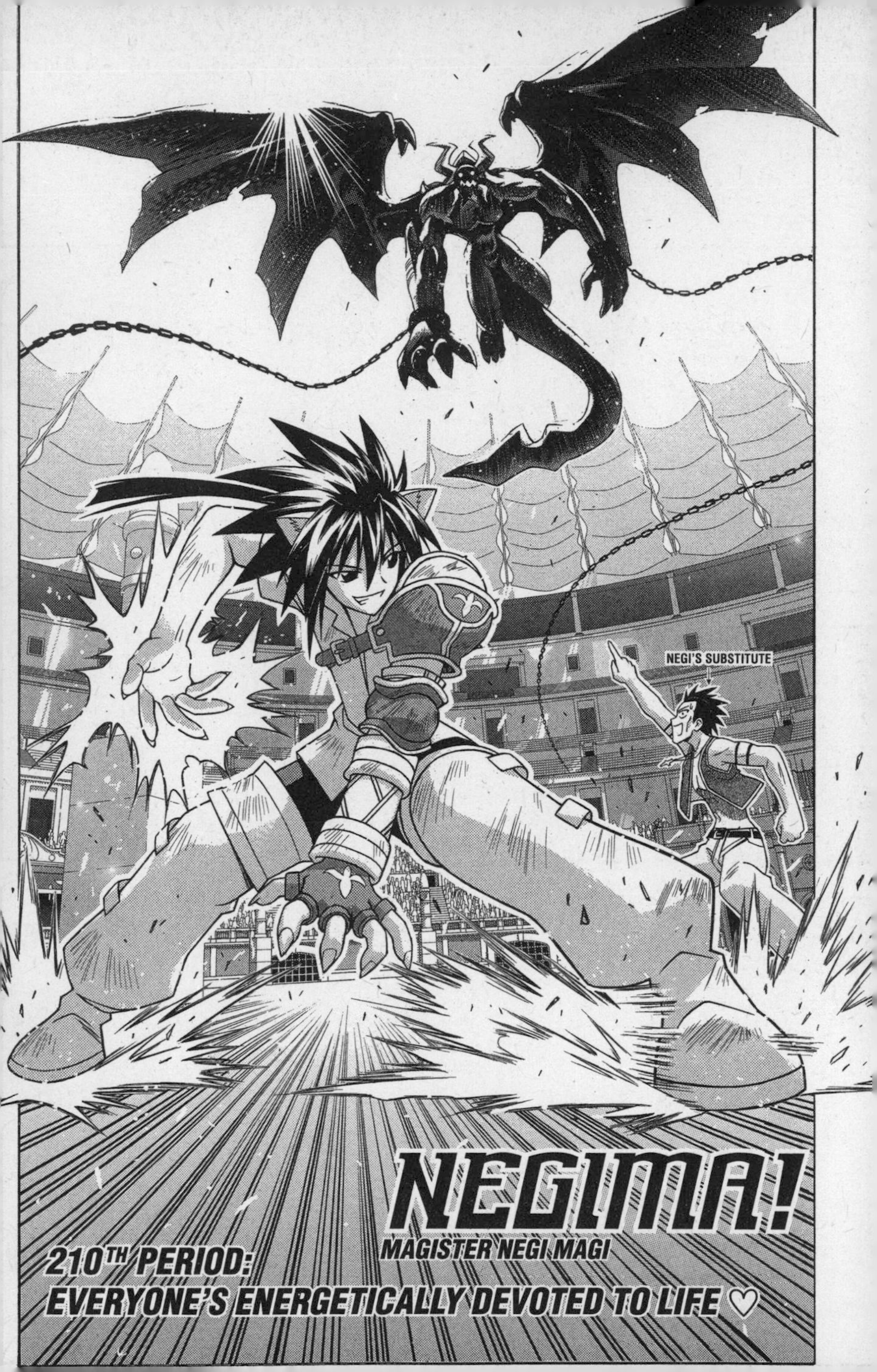
NEGI'S SUBSTITUTE
NEGIMA!
MAGISTER NEGI MAGI
210TH PERIOD:
EVERYONE'S ENERGETICALLY DEVOTED TO LIFE ♡

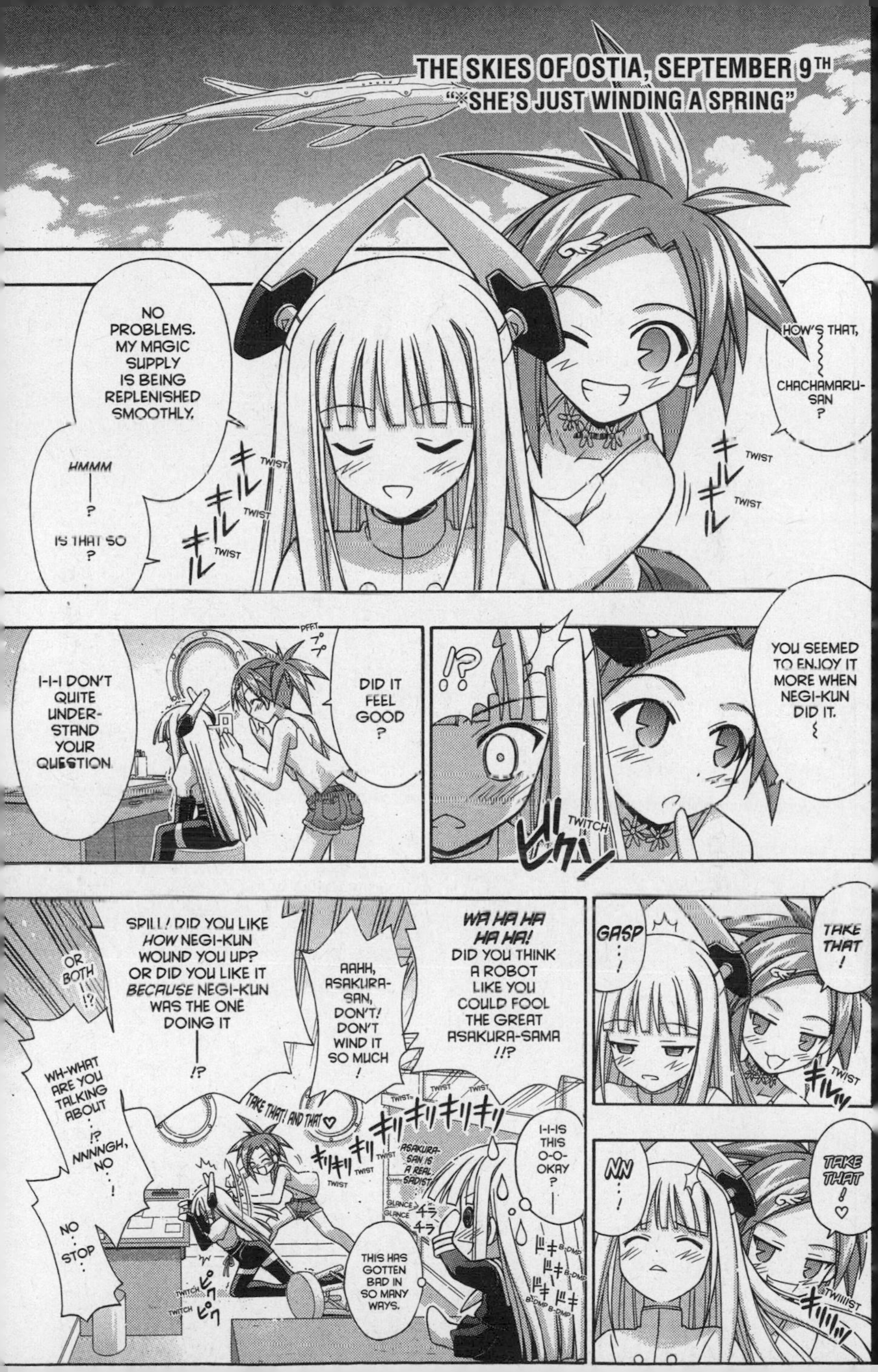
THE SKIES OF OSTIA, SEPTEMBER 9TH
"※SHE'S JUST WINDING A SPRING"
HOW'S THAT, CHACHAMARU-SAN?
TWIST
TWIST
NO PROBLEMS. MY MAGIC SUPPLY IS BEING REPLENISHED SMOOTHLY.
TWIST
TWIST
TWIST
HMMM—? IS THAT SO?
YOU SEEMED TO ENJOY IT MORE WHEN NEGI-KUN DID IT.
!?
TWITCH
PFFT
DID IT FEEL GOOD?
I-I-I DON'T QUITE UNDERSTAND YOUR QUESTION
TAKE THAT!
GASP...!
TWIST
TAKE THAT! ♥
NN...!
TWIIIIST
WA HA HA HA HA! DID YOU THINK A ROBOT LIKE YOU COULD FOOL THE GREAT ASAKURA-SAMA!!?
AAHH, ASAKURA-SAN, DON'T! DON'T WIND IT SO MUCH!
SPILL! DID YOU LIKE HOW NEGI-KUN WOUND YOU UP? OR DID YOU LIKE IT BECAUSE NEGI-KUN WAS THE ONE DOING IT—!?
OR BOTH—!?
I-I-IS THIS O-O-OKAY?—
ASAKURA-SAN IS A REAL SADIST
GLANCE
GLANCE
B-DMP
B-DMP
B-DMP B-DMP
THIS HAS GOTTEN BAD IN SO MANY WAYS.
TAKE THAT! AND THAT ♥
TWIST
TWIST
TWIST
TWIST
TWIST
WH-WHAT ARE YOU TALKING ABOUT...!? NNNNGH, NO...!
NO... STOP...
TWITCH
TWITCH

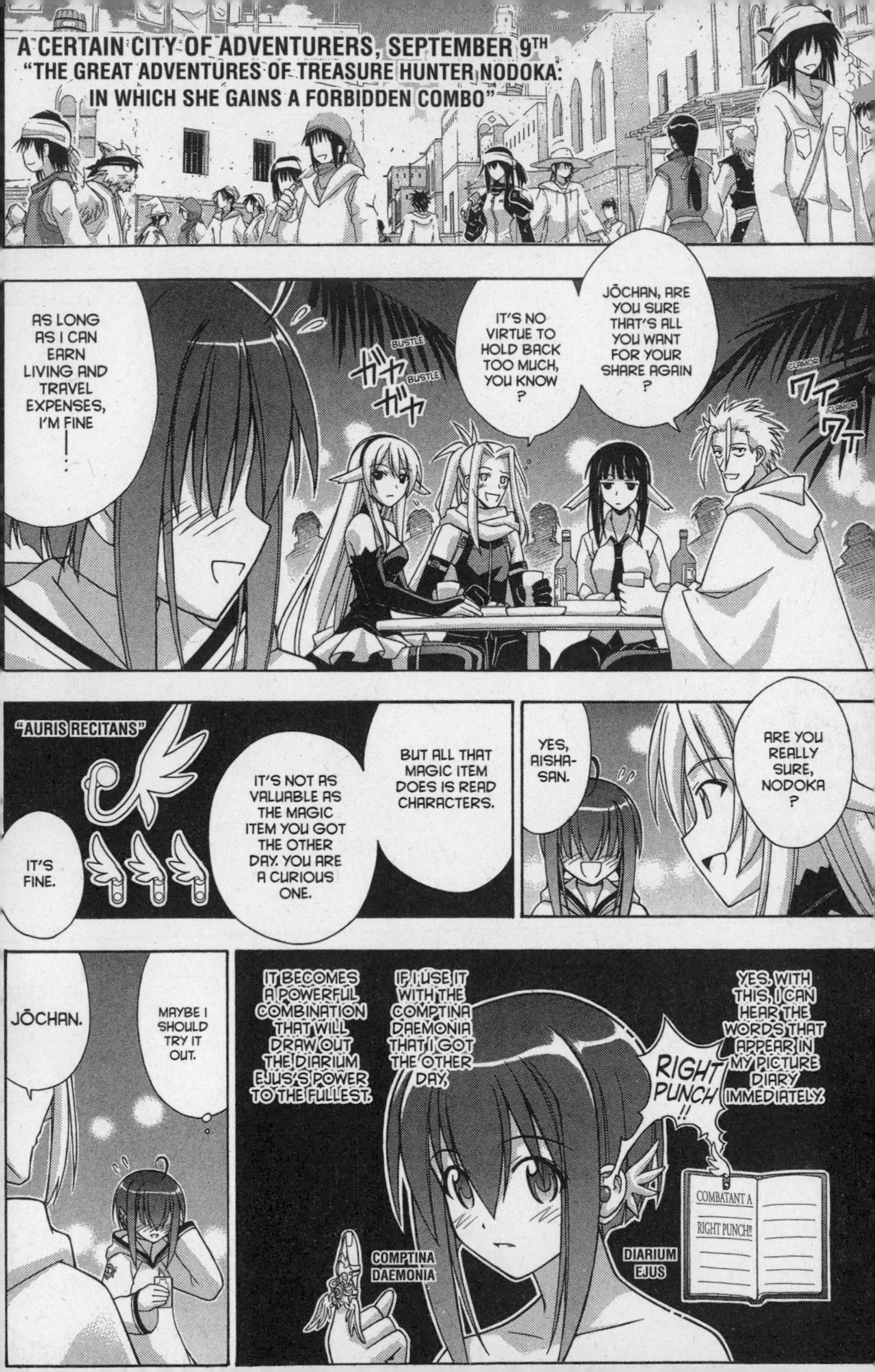
A CERTAIN CITY OF ADVENTURERS, SEPTEMBER 9TH
"THE GREAT ADVENTURES OF TREASURE HUNTER NODOKA: IN WHICH SHE GAINS A FORBIDDEN COMBO"
JŌCHAN, ARE YOU SURE THAT'S ALL YOU WANT FOR YOUR SHARE AGAIN?
CLAMOR CLAMOR
IT'S NO VIRTUE TO HOLD BACK TOO MUCH, YOU KNOW?
BUSTLE BUSTLE
AS LONG AS I CAN EARN LIVING AND TRAVEL EXPENSES, I'M FINE…!
ARE YOU REALLY SURE, NODOKA?
YES, AISHA-SAN.
BUT ALL THAT MAGIC ITEM DOES IS READ CHARACTERS.
IT'S NOT AS VALUABLE AS THE MAGIC ITEM YOU GOT THE OTHER DAY. YOU ARE A CURIOUS ONE.
"AURIS RECITANS"
IT'S FINE.
YES. WITH THIS, I CAN HEAR THE WORDS THAT APPEAR IN MY PICTURE DIARY IMMEDIATELY.
IF I USE IT WITH THE COMPTINA DAEMONIA THAT I GOT THE OTHER DAY,
IT BECOMES A POWERFUL COMBINATION THAT WILL DRAW OUT THE DIARIUM EJUS'S POWER TO THE FULLEST.
RIGHT PUNCH!!
COMBATANT A
RIGHT PUNCH!!
DIARIUM EJUS
COMPTINA DAEMONIA
MAYBE I SHOULD TRY IT OUT.
JŌCHAN.

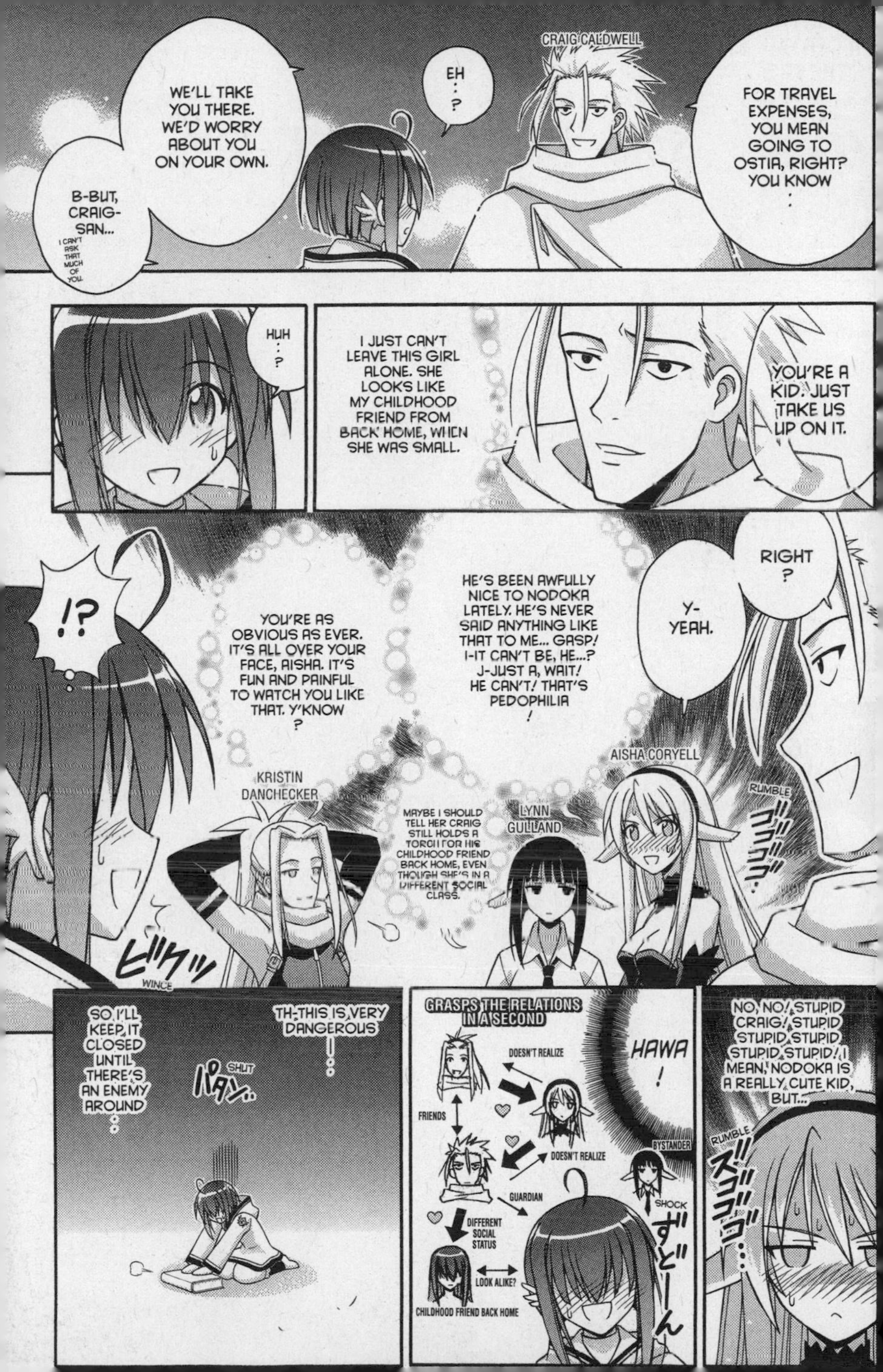
CRAIG CALDWELL
FOR TRAVEL EXPENSES, YOU MEAN GOING TO OSTIA, RIGHT? YOU KNOW :
EH..?
WE'LL TAKE YOU THERE. WE'D WORRY ABOUT YOU ON YOUR OWN.
B-BUT, CRAIG-SAN...
I CAN'T ASK THAT MUCH OF YOU.
YOU'RE A KID. JUST TAKE US UP ON IT.
I JUST CAN'T LEAVE THIS GIRL ALONE. SHE LOOKS LIKE MY CHILDHOOD FRIEND FROM BACK HOME, WHEN SHE WAS SMALL.
HUH..?
RIGHT?
Y-YEAH.
HE'S BEEN AWFULLY NICE TO NODOKA LATELY. HE'S NEVER SAID ANYTHING LIKE THAT TO ME... GASP! I-IT CAN'T BE, HE...? J-JUST A, WAIT! HE CAN'T! THAT'S PEDOPHILIA!
YOU'RE AS OBVIOUS AS EVER. IT'S ALL OVER YOUR FACE, AISHA. IT'S FUN AND PAINFUL TO WATCH YOU LIKE THAT. Y'KNOW?
!?
AISHA CORYELL
RUMBLE
LYNN GULLAND
MAYBE I SHOULD TELL HER CRAIG STILL HOLDS A TORCH FOR HIS CHILDHOOD FRIEND BACK HOME, EVEN THOUGH SHE'S IN A DIFFERENT SOCIAL CLASS.
KRISTIN DANCHECKER
WINCE
NO, NO! STUPID CRAIG! STUPID STUPID STUPID STUPID STUPID! I MEAN, NODOKA IS A REALLY CUTE KID, BUT...
RUMBLE
HAWA!
GRASPS THE RELATIONS IN A SECOND
DOESN'T REALIZE
FRIENDS
DOESN'T REALIZE
BYSTANDER
GUARDIAN
DIFFERENT SOCIAL STATUS
LOOK ALIKE?
CHILDHOOD FRIEND BACK HOME
SHOCK
TH-THIS IS VERY DANGEROUS...
SO, I'LL KEEP IT CLOSED UNTIL THERE'S AN ENEMY AROUND..
SHUT

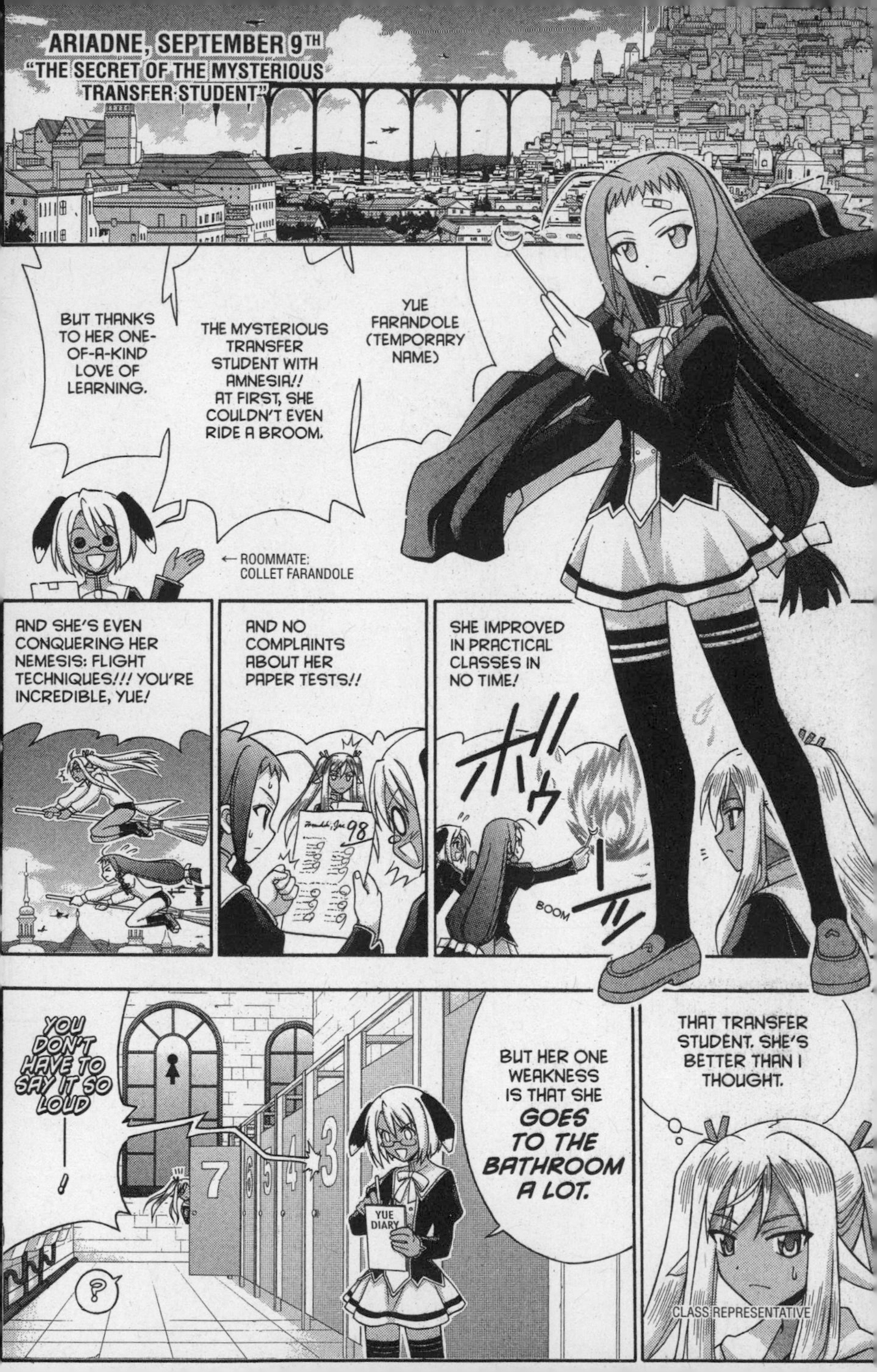
ARIADNE, SEPTEMBER 9TH
"THE SECRET OF THE MYSTERIOUS TRANSFER STUDENT"
YUE FARANDOLE (TEMPORARY NAME)
THE MYSTERIOUS TRANSFER STUDENT WITH AMNESIA!! AT FIRST, SHE COULDN'T EVEN RIDE A BROOM.
BUT THANKS TO HER ONE-OF-A-KIND LOVE OF LEARNING.
← ROOMMATE: COLLET FARANDOLE
SHE IMPROVED IN PRACTICAL CLASSES IN NO TIME!
BOOM
AND NO COMPLAINTS ABOUT HER PAPER TESTS!!
98
AND SHE'S EVEN CONQUERING HER NEMESIS: FLIGHT TECHNIQUES!!! YOU'RE INCREDIBLE, YUE!
THAT TRANSFER STUDENT. SHE'S BETTER THAN I THOUGHT.
CLASS REPRESENTATIVE
BUT HER ONE WEAKNESS IS THAT SHE GOES TO THE BATHROOM A LOT.
YUE DIARY
YOU DON'T HAVE TO SAY IT SO LOUD—!
7
3
?

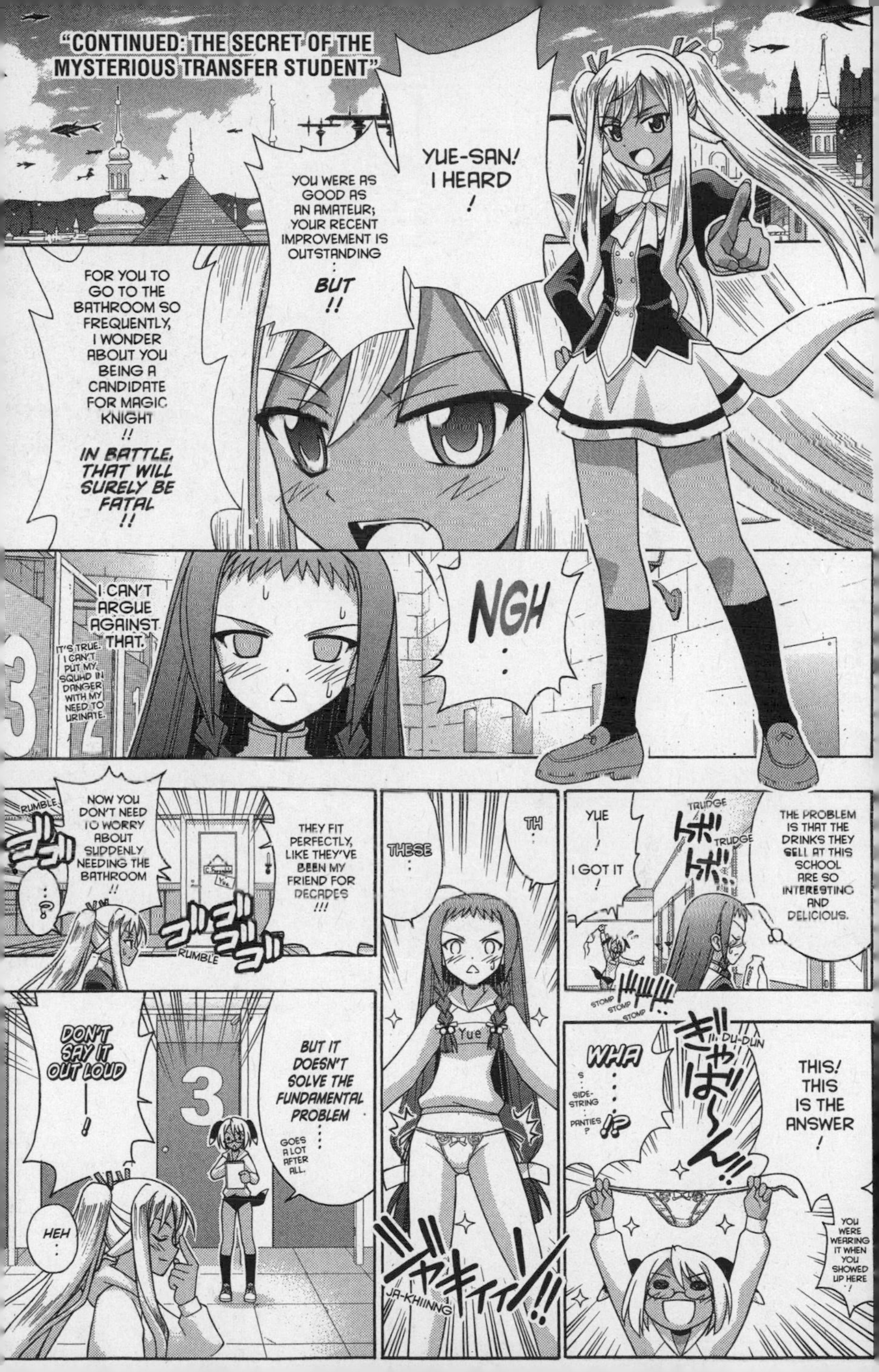
"CONTINUED: THE SECRET OF THE MYSTERIOUS TRANSFER STUDENT"
YUE-SAN! I HEARD!
YOU WERE AS GOOD AS AN AMATEUR; YOUR RECENT IMPROVEMENT IS OUTSTANDING... BUT!!
FOR YOU TO GO TO THE BATHROOM SO FREQUENTLY, I WONDER ABOUT YOU BEING A CANDIDATE FOR MAGIC KNIGHT!!
IN BATTLE, THAT WILL SURELY BE FATAL!!
NGH...
I CAN'T ARGUE AGAINST THAT.
IT'S TRUE. I CAN'T PUT MY SQUAD IN DANGER WITH MY NEED TO URINATE.
THE PROBLEM IS THAT THE DRINKS THEY SELL AT THIS SCHOOL ARE SO INTERESTING AND DELICIOUS.
TRUDGE
TRUDGE
YUE! I GOT IT!
STOMP STOMP STOMP
THIS! THIS IS THE ANSWER!
DU-DUN
WHA...
S... SIDE-STRING PANTIES?!
YOU WERE WEARING IT WHEN YOU SHOWED UP HERE!
TH...
THESE...
THEY FIT PERFECTLY, LIKE THEY'VE BEEN MY FRIEND FOR DECADES!!!
JA-KHIINNG
NOW YOU DON'T NEED TO WORRY ABOUT SUDDENLY NEEDING THE BATHROOM!!
RUMBLE
RUMBLE
...?
BUT IT DOESN'T SOLVE THE FUNDAMENTAL PROBLEM...
GOES A LOT AFTER ALL.
DON'T SAY IT OUT LOUD—!
HEH...

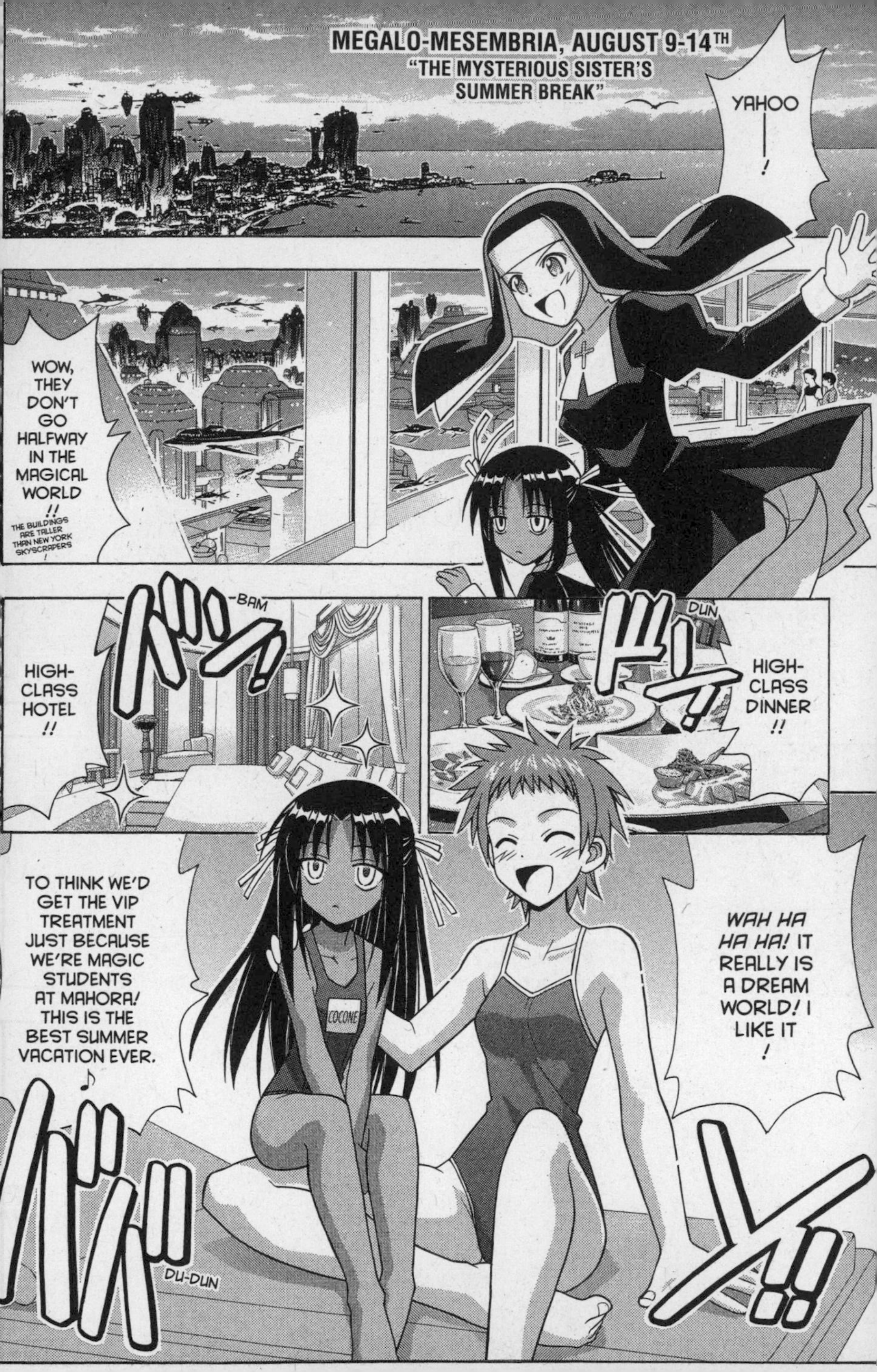
MEGALO-MESEMBRIA, AUGUST 9-14TH
"THE MYSTERIOUS SISTER'S SUMMER BREAK"
YAHOO——!
WOW, THEY DON'T GO HALFWAY IN THE MAGICAL WORLD!!
THE BUILDINGS ARE TALLER THAN NEW YORK SKYSCRAPERS!
DUN
HIGH-CLASS DINNER!!
-BAM
HIGH-CLASS HOTEL!!
WAH HA HA HA! IT REALLY IS A DREAM WORLD! I LIKE IT!
TO THINK WE'D GET THE VIP TREATMENT JUST BECAUSE WE'RE MAGIC STUDENTS AT MAHORA! THIS IS THE BEST SUMMER VACATION EVER. ♪
COCONE
DU-DUN

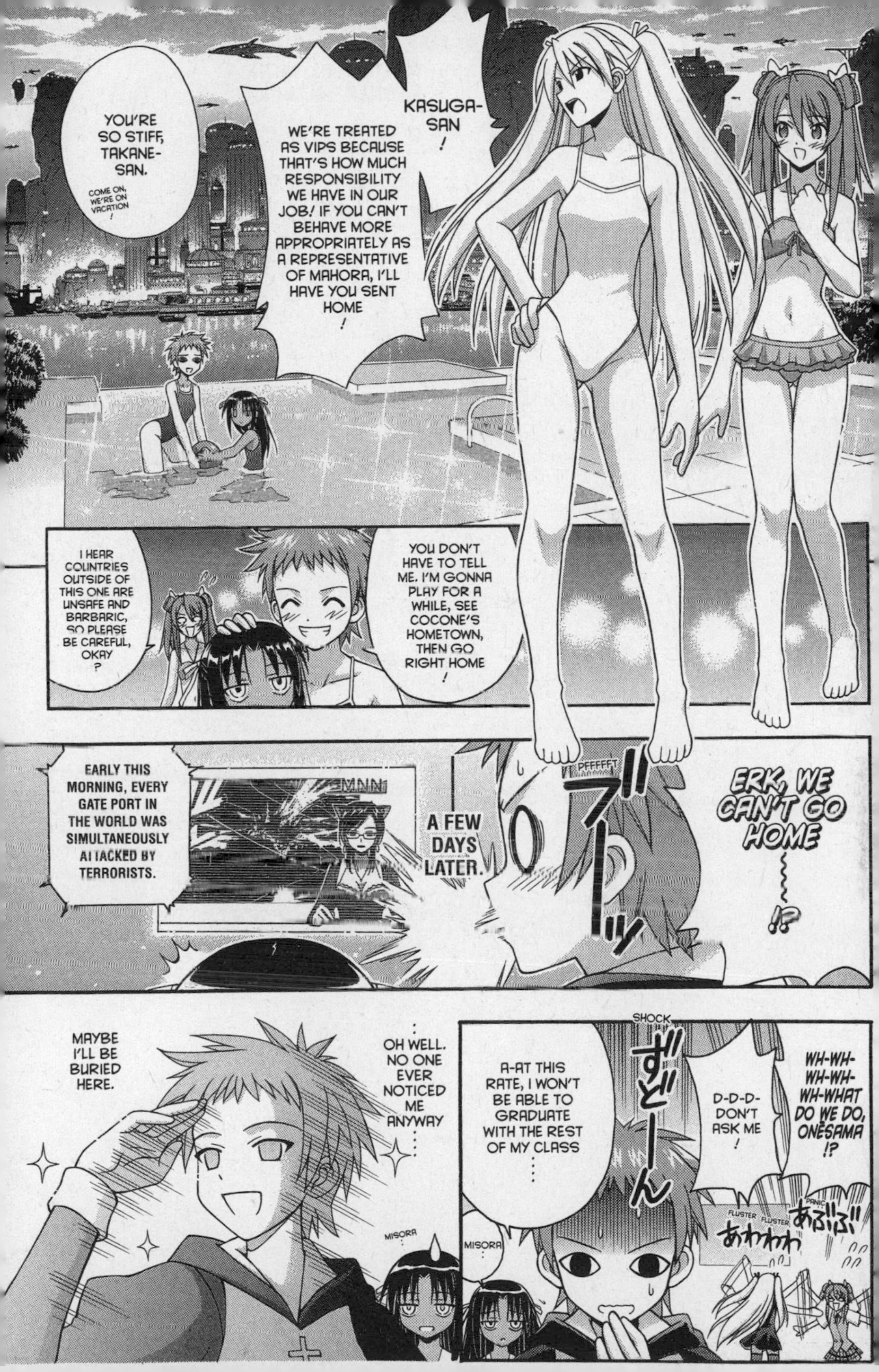
KASUGA-SAN!
WE'RE TREATED AS VIPS BECAUSE THAT'S HOW MUCH RESPONSIBILITY WE HAVE IN OUR JOB! IF YOU CAN'T BEHAVE MORE APPROPRIATELY AS A REPRESENTATIVE OF MAHORA, I'LL HAVE YOU SENT HOME!
YOU'RE SO STIFF, TAKANE-SAN.
COME ON, WE'RE ON VACATION!
YOU DON'T HAVE TO TELL ME. I'M GONNA PLAY FOR A WHILE, SEE COCONE'S HOMETOWN, THEN GO RIGHT HOME!
I HEAR COUNTRIES OUTSIDE OF THIS ONE ARE UNSAFE AND BARBARIC, SO PLEASE BE CAREFUL, OKAY?
ERK, WE CAN'T GO HOME~~~!?
PFFFFFT
ブーッ
A FEW DAYS LATER.
EARLY THIS MORNING, EVERY GATE PORT IN THE WORLD WAS SIMULTANEOUSLY ATTACKED BY TERRORISTS.
WH-WH-WH-WH-WH-WHAT DO WE DO, ONESAMA!?
D-D-D-DON'T ASK ME!
PANIC
あぷぷ!!
FLUSTER FLUSTER
あわわわ
SHOCK
ずどーん
A-AT THIS RATE, I WON'T BE ABLE TO GRADUATE WITH THE REST OF MY CLASS....
MISORA...
OH WELL. NO ONE EVER NOTICED ME ANYWAY......
MISORA...
MAYBE I'LL BE BURIED HERE.

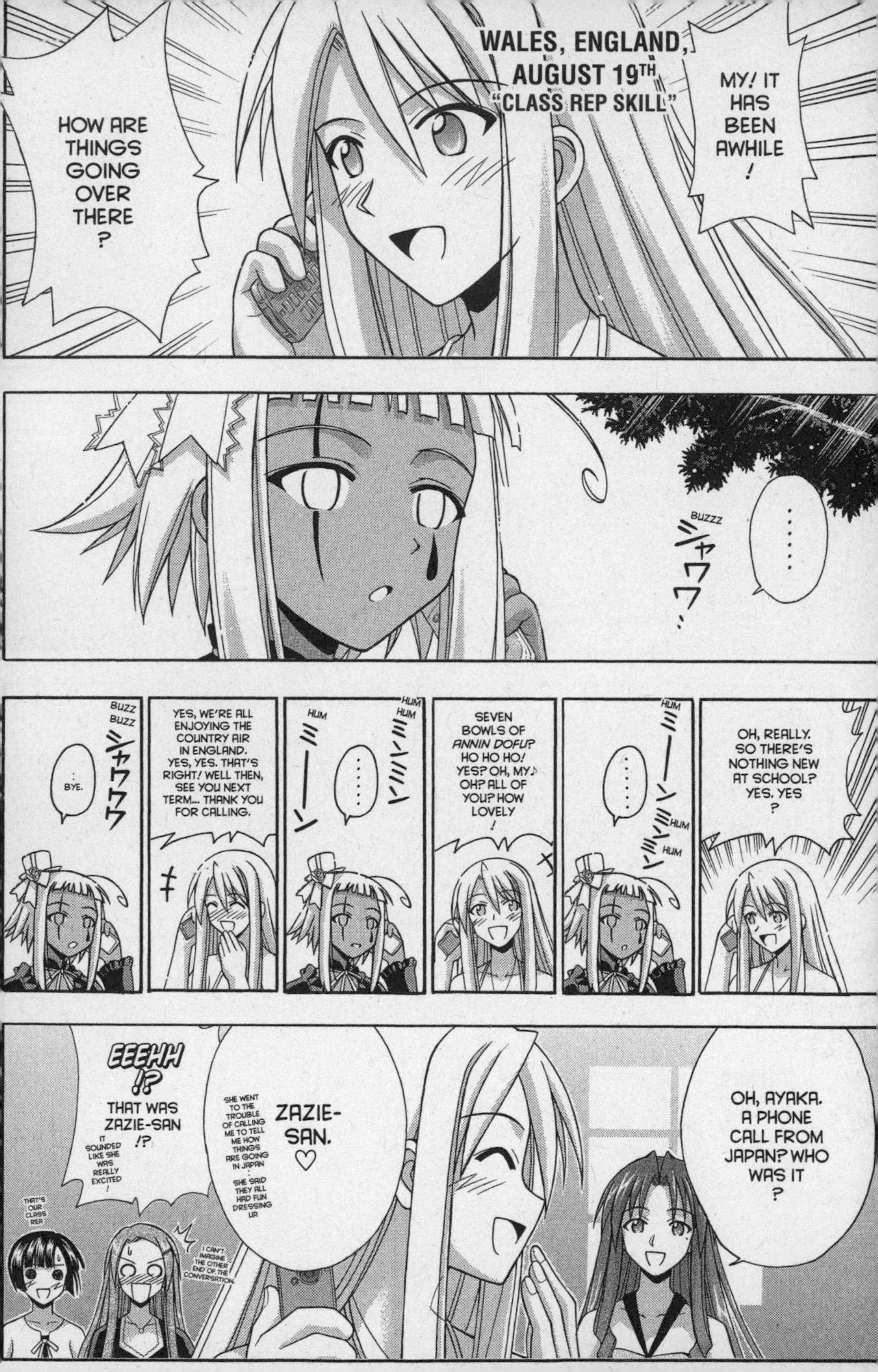
WALES, ENGLAND, AUGUST 19TH "CLASS REP SKILL"
MY! IT HAS BEEN AWHILE!
HOW ARE THINGS GOING OVER THERE?
BUZZZ
......
OH, REALLY. SO THERE'S NOTHING NEW AT SCHOOL? YES. YES?
HUM HUM
HUM
......
SEVEN BOWLS OF ANNIN DOFU? HO HO HO! YES? OH, MY♪ OH? ALL OF YOU? HOW LOVELY!
HUM HUM
HUM
......
YES, WE'RE ALL ENJOYING THE COUNTRY AIR IN ENGLAND. YES, YES. THAT'S RIGHT! WELL THEN, SEE YOU NEXT TERM... THANK YOU FOR CALLING.
BUZZ BUZZ
: BYE.
OH, AYAKA. A PHONE CALL FROM JAPAN? WHO WAS IT?
ZAZIE-SAN. ♡
SHE WENT TO THE TROUBLE OF CALLING ME TO TELL ME HOW THINGS ARE GOING IN JAPAN: SHE SAID THEY ALL HAD FUN DRESSING UP
EEEHH!?
THAT WAS ZAZIE-SAN!?
IT SOUNDED LIKE SHE WAS REALLY EXCITED!
I CAN'T IMAGINE THE OTHER END OF THE CONVERSATION.
THAT'S OUR CLASS REP.

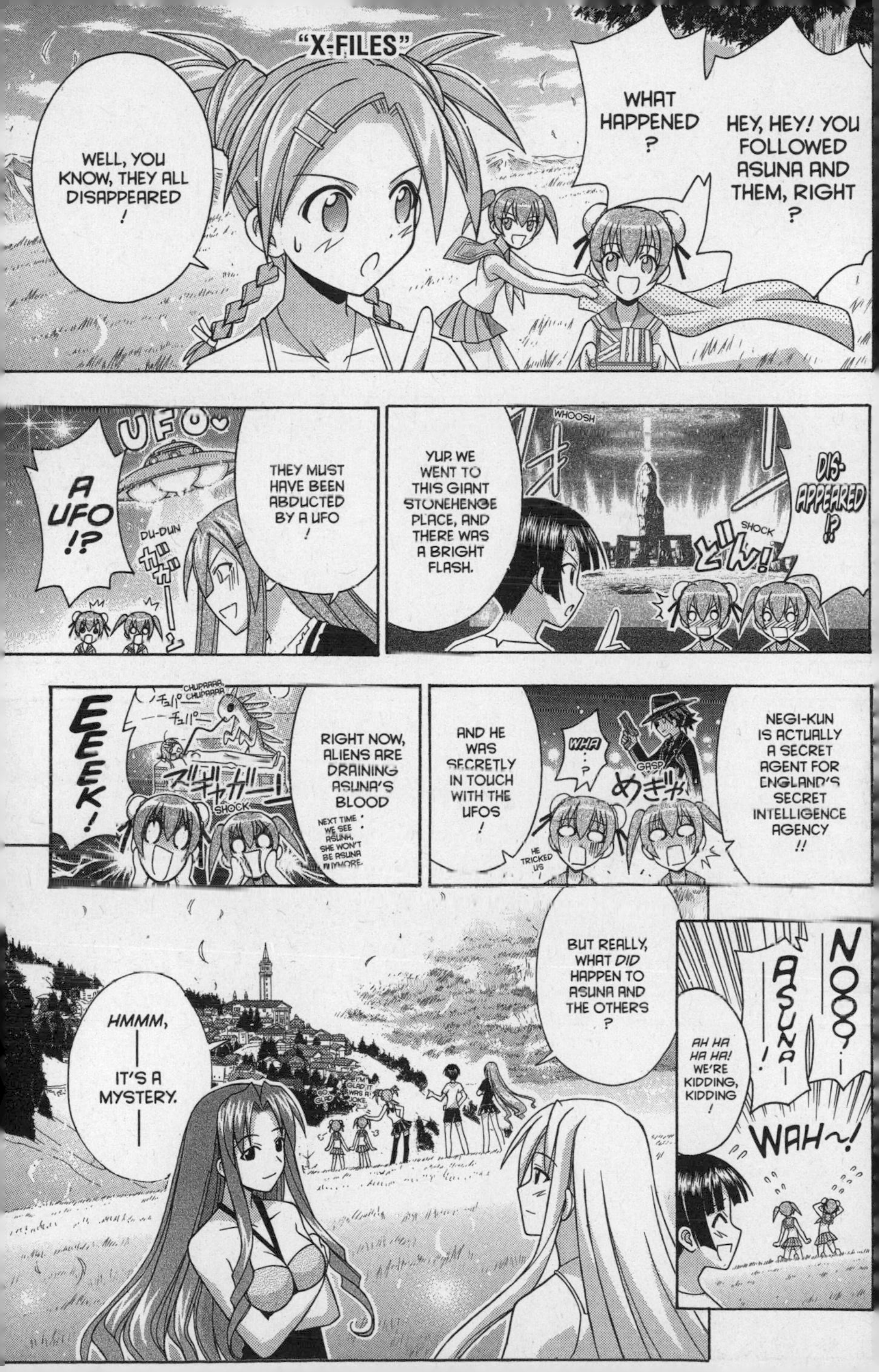
"X-FILES"
HEY, HEY! YOU FOLLOWED ASUNA AND THEM, RIGHT?
WHAT HAPPENED?
WELL, YOU KNOW, THEY ALL DISAPPEARED!
WHOOSH
DIS-APPEARED!?
SHOCK
どん!
YUP. WE WENT TO THIS GIANT STONEHENGE PLACE, AND THERE WAS A BRIGHT FLASH.
THEY MUST HAVE BEEN ABDUCTED BY A UFO!
UFO
A UFO!?
DU-DUN
NEGI-KUN IS ACTUALLY A SECRET AGENT FOR ENGLAND'S SECRET INTELLIGENCE AGENCY!!
AND HE WAS SECRETLY IN TOUCH WITH THE UFOS!
WHA...?
GASP
めぎゃ
HE TRICKED US!
RIGHT NOW, ALIENS ARE DRAINING ASUNA'S BLOOD
NEXT TIME WE SEE ASUNA, SHE WON'T BE ASUNA ANYMORE.
CHUPAAAA, CHUPAAAA
EEEEK!
SHOCK
NOOO—!
ASUNA—!
AH HA HA HA! WE'RE KIDDING, KIDDING!
WAH~!
BUT REALLY, WHAT DID HAPPEN TO ASUNA AND THE OTHERS?
HMMM, — IT'S A MYSTERY. —

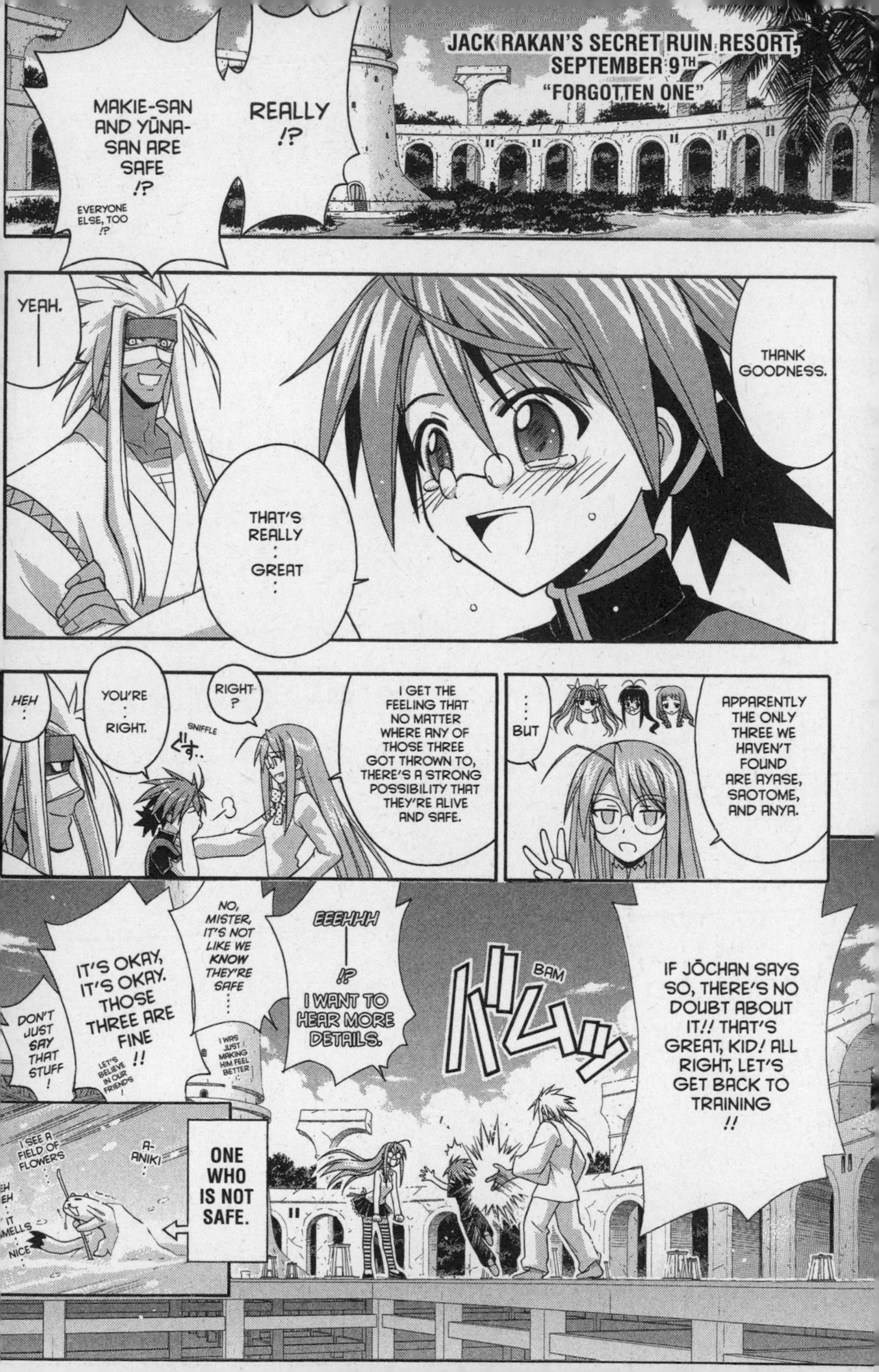

JACK RAKAN'S SECRET RUIN RESORT, SEPTEMBER 9TH
"FORGOTTEN ONE"
REALLY !?
MAKIE-SAN AND YŪNA-SAN ARE SAFE !?
EVERYONE ELSE, TOO !?
THANK GOODNESS.
THAT'S REALLY... GREAT...
YEAH. —
APPARENTLY THE ONLY THREE WE HAVEN'T FOUND ARE AYASE, SAOTOME, AND ANYA.
... BUT
I GET THE FEELING THAT NO MATTER WHERE ANY OF THOSE THREE GOT THROWN TO, THERE'S A STRONG POSSIBILITY THAT THEY'RE ALIVE AND SAFE.
RIGHT ?
SNIFFLE
ぐす..
YOU'RE ... RIGHT.
HEH ...
IF JŌCHAN SAYS SO, THERE'S NO DOUBT ABOUT IT!! THAT'S GREAT, KID! ALL RIGHT, LET'S GET BACK TO TRAINING !!
BAM
EEEHHH — !? I WANT TO HEAR MORE DETAILS.
NO, MISTER, IT'S NOT LIKE WE KNOW THEY'RE SAFE ...
I WAS JUST MAKING HIM FEEL BETTER
IT'S OKAY, IT'S OKAY. THOSE THREE ARE FINE !!
LET'S BELIEVE IN OUR FRIENDS !
DON'T JUST SAY THAT STUFF !
ONE WHO IS NOT SAFE.
A- ANIKI
I SEE A FIELD OF FLOWERS
NICE

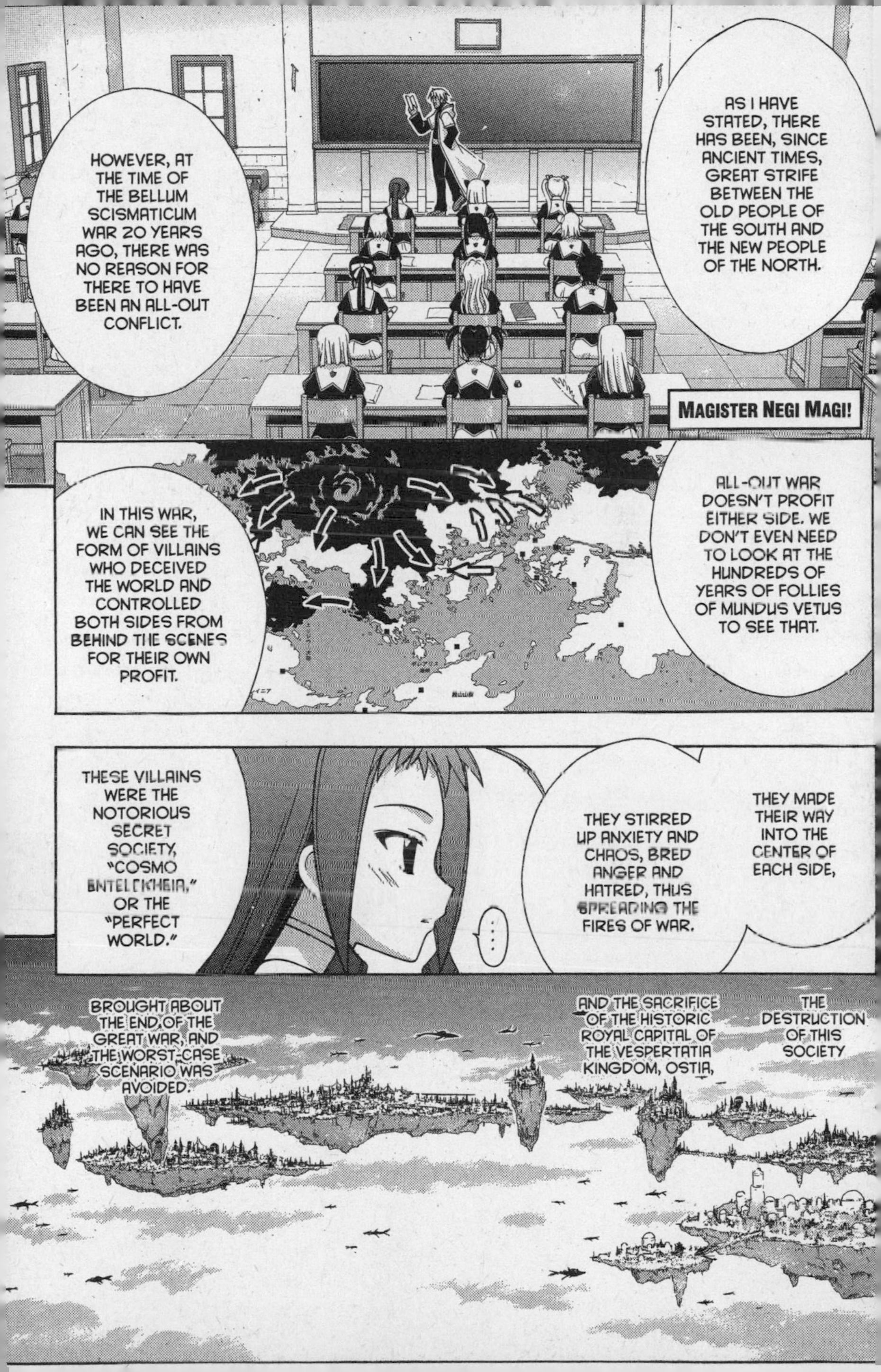
AS I HAVE STATED, THERE HAS BEEN, SINCE ANCIENT TIMES, GREAT STRIFE BETWEEN THE OLD PEOPLE OF THE SOUTH AND THE NEW PEOPLE OF THE NORTH.
HOWEVER, AT THE TIME OF THE BELLUM SCISMATICUM WAR 20 YEARS AGO, THERE WAS NO REASON FOR THERE TO HAVE BEEN AN ALL-OUT CONFLICT.
MAGISTER NEGI MAGI!
ALL-OUT WAR DOESN'T PROFIT EITHER SIDE. WE DON'T EVEN NEED TO LOOK AT THE HUNDREDS OF YEARS OF FOLLIES OF MUNDUS VETUS TO SEE THAT.
IN THIS WAR, WE CAN SEE THE FORM OF VILLAINS WHO DECEIVED THE WORLD AND CONTROLLED BOTH SIDES FROM BEHIND THE SCENES FOR THEIR OWN PROFIT.
THEY MADE THEIR WAY INTO THE CENTER OF EACH SIDE,
THEY STIRRED UP ANXIETY AND CHAOS, BRED ANGER AND HATRED, THUS SPREADING THE FIRES OF WAR.
...
THESE VILLAINS WERE THE NOTORIOUS SECRET SOCIETY, "COSMO ENTELEKHEIA," OR THE "PERFECT WORLD."
THE DESTRUCTION OF THIS SOCIETY
AND THE SACRIFICE OF THE HISTORIC ROYAL CAPITAL OF THE VESPERTATIA KINGDOM, OSTIA,
BROUGHT ABOUT THE END OF THE GREAT WAR, AND THE WORST-CASE SCENARIO WAS AVOIDED.

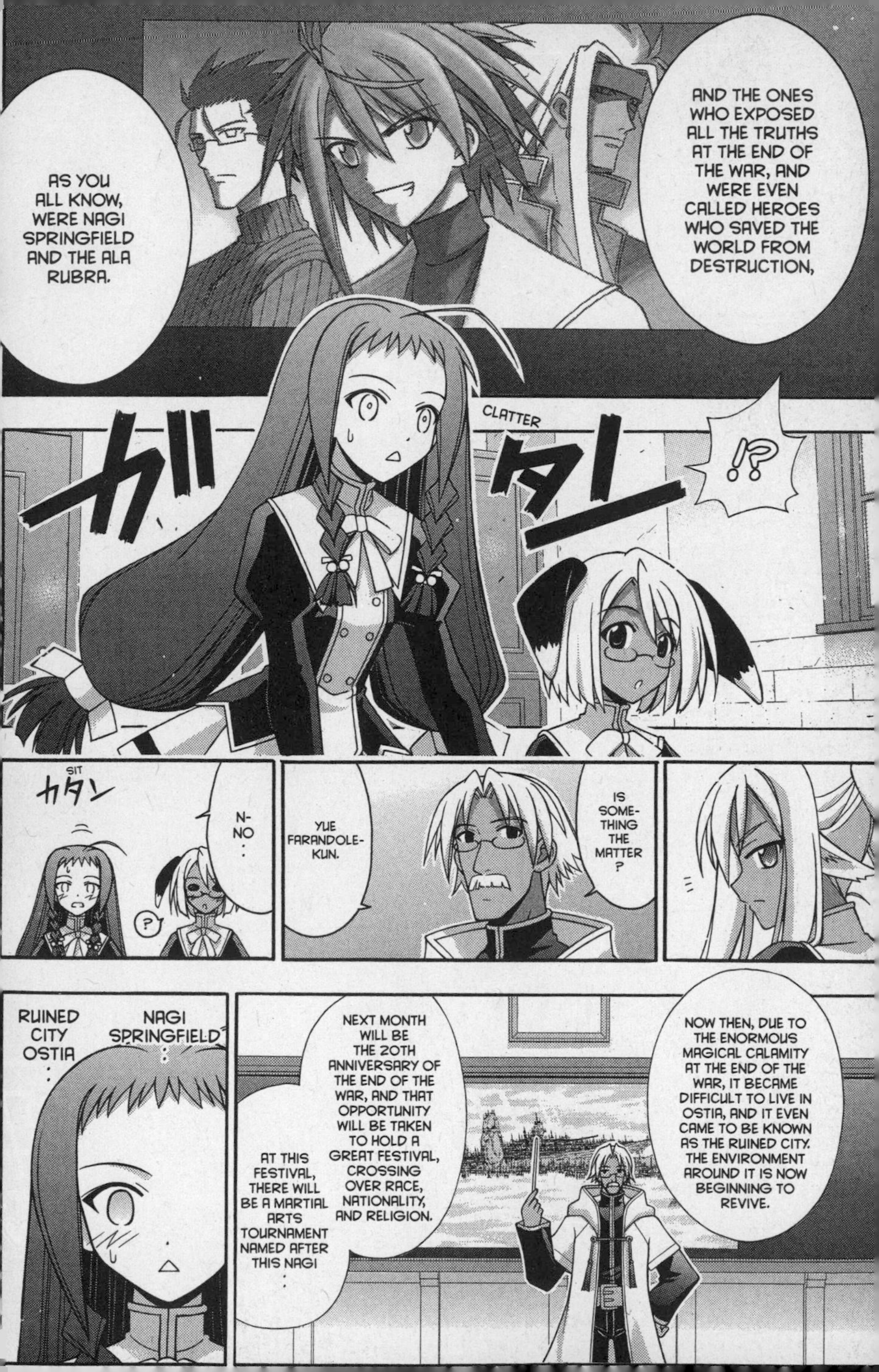

AND THE ONES WHO EXPOSED ALL THE TRUTHS AT THE END OF THE WAR, AND WERE EVEN CALLED HEROES WHO SAVED THE WORLD FROM DESTRUCTION,
AS YOU ALL KNOW, WERE NAGI SPRINGFIELD AND THE ALA RUBRA.
!?
ガタン
CLATTER
IS SOMETHING THE MATTER?
YUE FARANDOLE-KUN.
N-NO...
カタン
SIT
?
NOW THEN, DUE TO THE ENORMOUS MAGICAL CALAMITY AT THE END OF THE WAR, IT BECAME DIFFICULT TO LIVE IN OSTIA, AND IT EVEN CAME TO BE KNOWN AS THE RUINED CITY. THE ENVIRONMENT AROUND IT IS NOW BEGINNING TO REVIVE.
NEXT MONTH WILL BE THE 20TH ANNIVERSARY OF THE END OF THE WAR, AND THAT OPPORTUNITY WILL BE TAKEN TO HOLD A GREAT FESTIVAL, CROSSING OVER RACE, NATIONALITY, AND RELIGION.
AT THIS FESTIVAL, THERE WILL BE A MARTIAL ARTS TOURNAMENT NAMED AFTER THIS NAGI...
NAGI SPRINGFIELD...
RUINED CITY OSTIA...

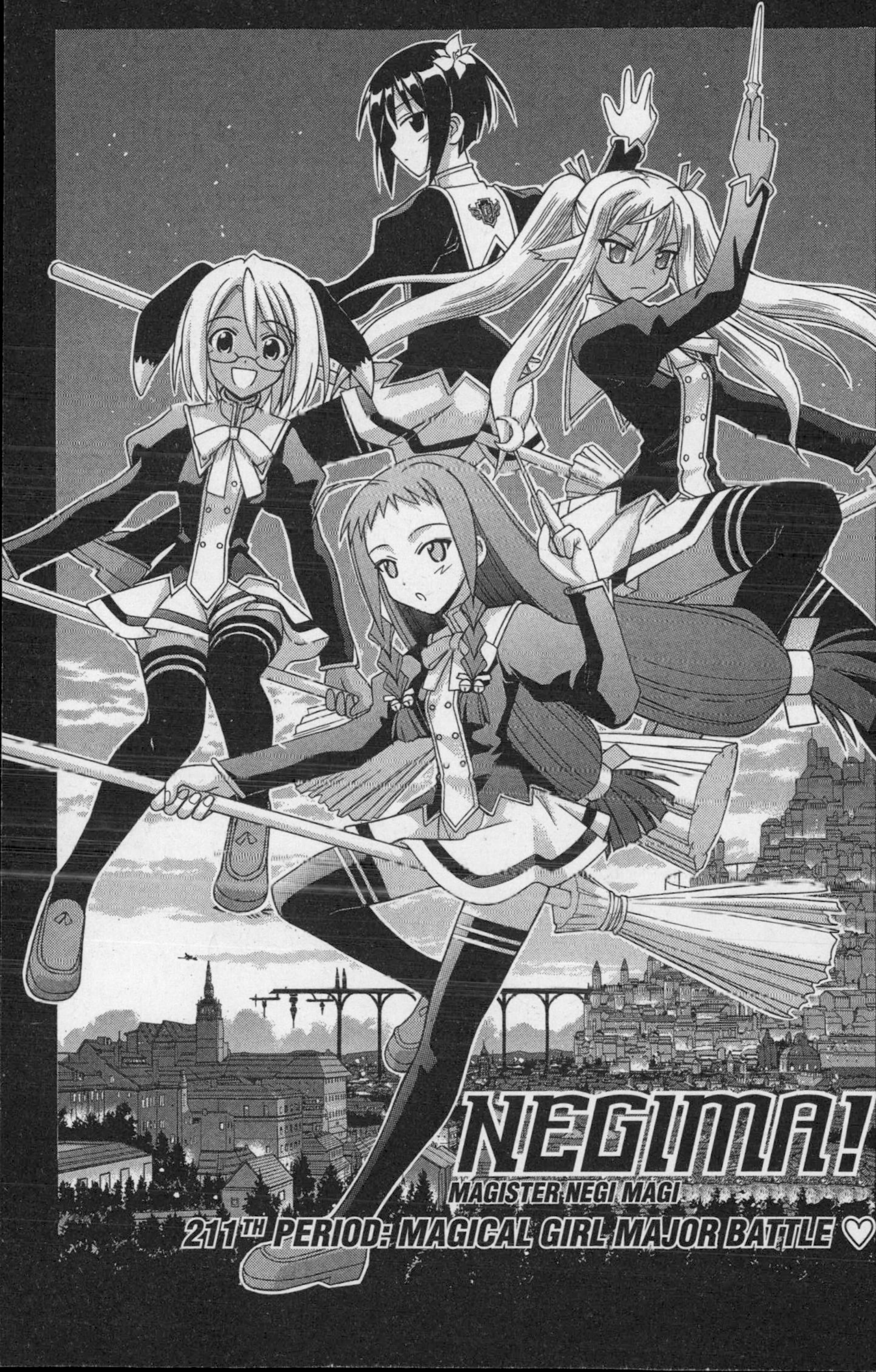
NEGIMA!
MAGISTER NEGI MAGI
211TH PERIOD: MAGICAL GIRL MAJOR BATTLE ♡

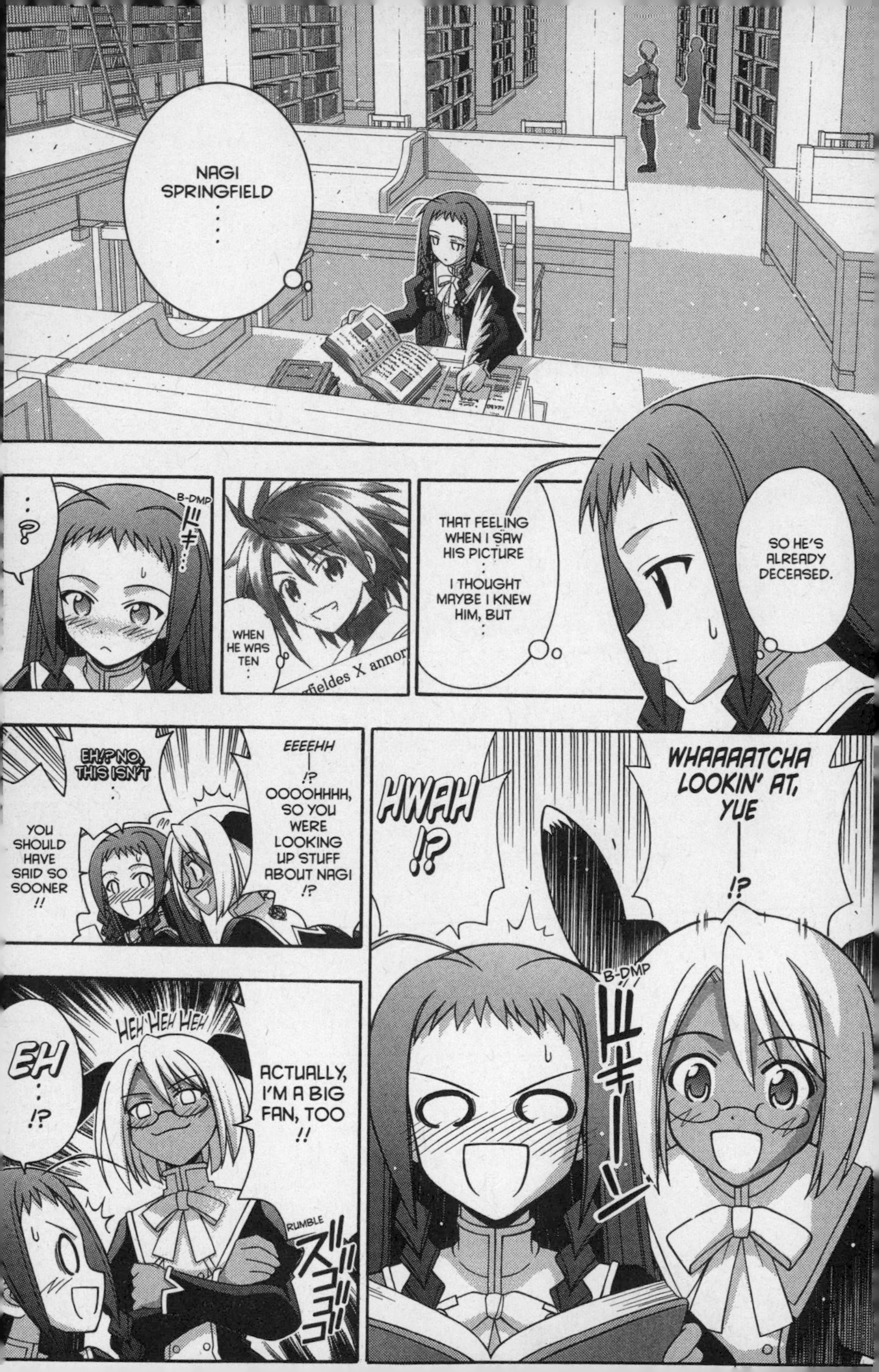
NAGI SPRINGFIELD
...
SO HE'S ALREADY DECEASED.
THAT FEELING WHEN I SAW HIS PICTURE...
I THOUGHT MAYBE I KNEW HIM, BUT...
WHEN HE WAS TEN...
fieldes X annor
B-DMP
...?
WHAAAATCHA LOOKIN' AT, YUE—!?
HWAH!?
B-DMP
EEEEHH—!? OOOOHHHH, SO YOU WERE LOOKING UP STUFF ABOUT NAGI!?
EH!? NO, THIS ISN'T...
YOU SHOULD HAVE SAID SO SOONER!!
HEH HEH HEH
ACTUALLY, I'M A BIG FAN, TOO!!
RUMBLE
EH...!?

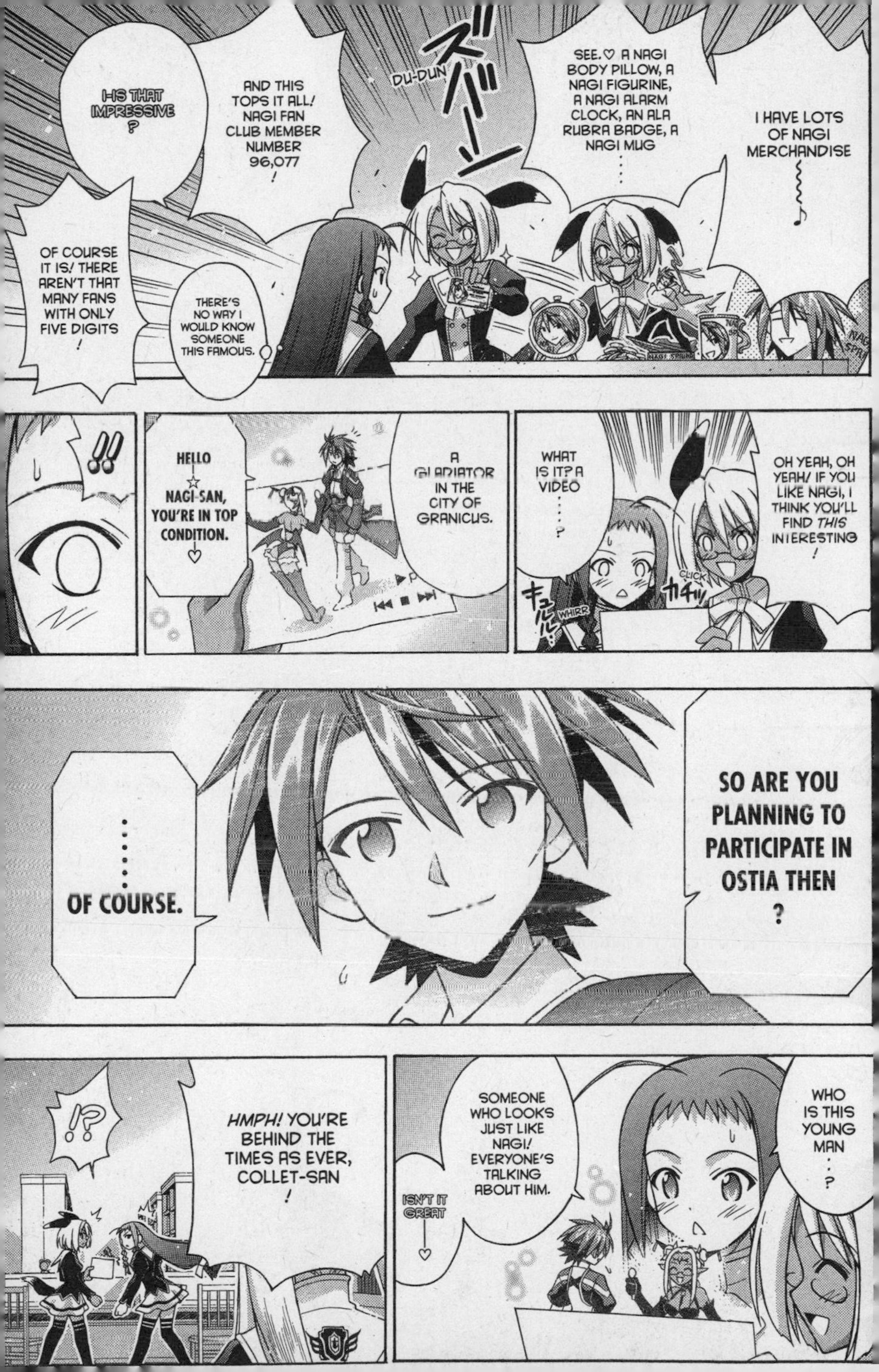
I HAVE LOTS OF NAGI MERCHANDISE ~♪
SEE.♡ A NAGI BODY PILLOW, A NAGI FIGURINE, A NAGI ALARM CLOCK, AN ALA RUBRA BADGE, A NAGI MUG...
DU-DUN
AND THIS TOPS IT ALL! NAGI FAN CLUB MEMBER NUMBER 96,077!
I-IS THAT IMPRESSIVE?
THERE'S NO WAY I WOULD KNOW SOMEONE THIS FAMOUS.
OF COURSE IT IS! THERE AREN'T THAT MANY FANS WITH ONLY FIVE DIGITS!
OH YEAH, OH YEAH! IF YOU LIKE NAGI, I THINK YOU'LL FIND *THIS* INTERESTING!
WHAT IS IT? A VIDEO...?
CLICK
WHIRR
A GLADIATOR IN THE CITY OF GRANICUS.
HELLO☆ NAGI-SAN, YOU'RE IN TOP CONDITION.♡
!!
SO ARE YOU PLANNING TO PARTICIPATE IN OSTIA THEN?
......OF COURSE.
WHO IS THIS YOUNG MAN...?
SOMEONE WHO LOOKS JUST LIKE NAGI! EVERYONE'S TALKING ABOUT HIM.
ISN'T IT GREAT♡
*HMPH!* YOU'RE BEHIND THE TIMES AS EVER, COLLET-SAN!
!?

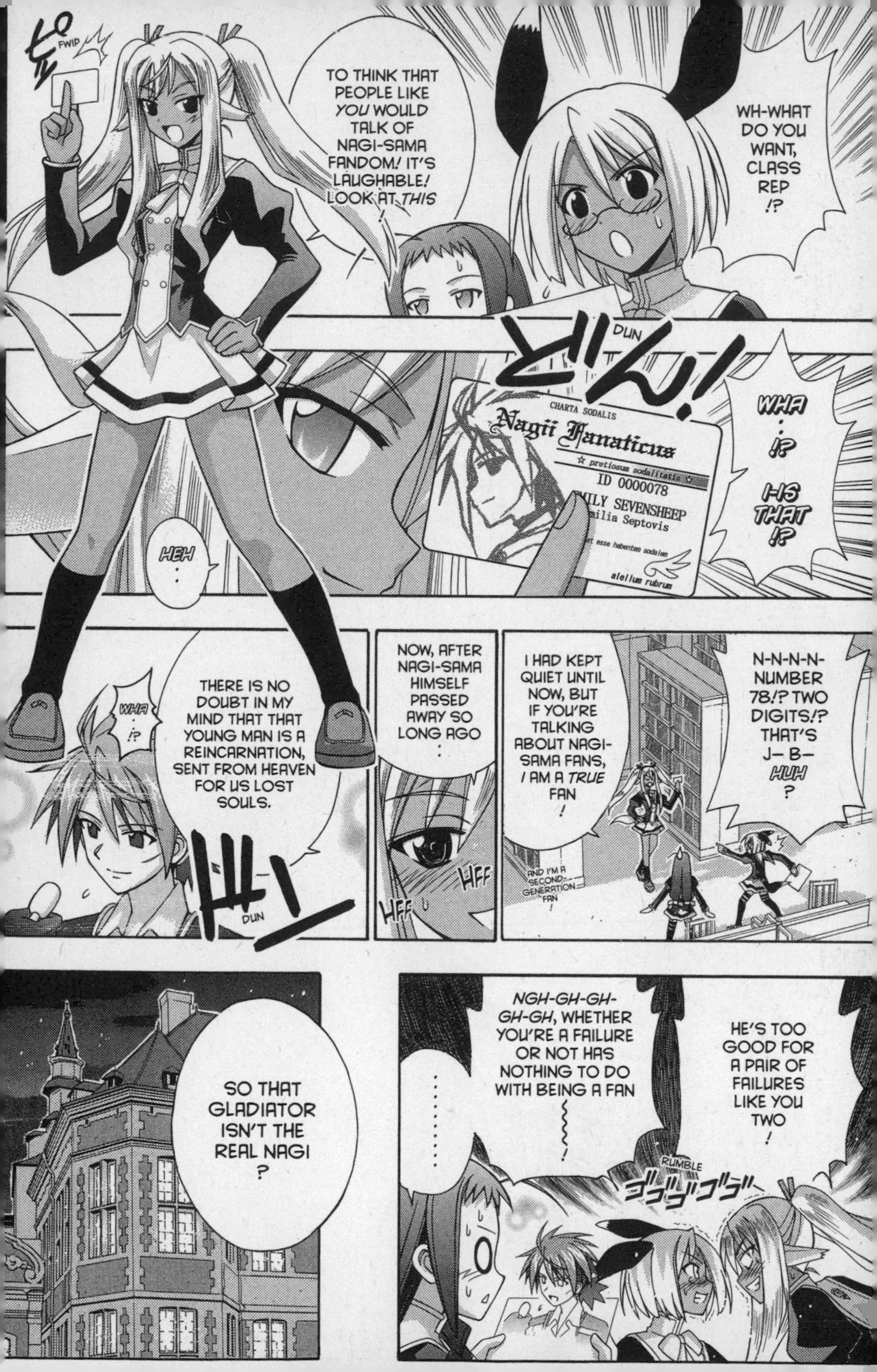WH-WHAT DO YOU WANT, CLASS REP !?
FWIP
TO THINK THAT PEOPLE LIKE *YOU* WOULD TALK OF NAGI-SAMA FANDOM! IT'S LAUGHABLE! LOOK AT *THIS* !
DUN
WHA . . !? I-IS THAT !?
CHARTA SODALIS
Nagii Fanaticus
pretiosum sodalitatis
ID 0000078
MILY SEVENSHEEP
ailia Septovis
et esse habentem sodalem
alellum rubrum
HEH . . .
N-N-N-N-NUMBER 78!? TWO DIGITS!? THAT'S J— B— *HUH* ?
I HAD KEPT QUIET UNTIL NOW, BUT IF YOU'RE TALKING ABOUT NAGI-SAMA FANS, *I* AM A *TRUE* FAN !
AND I'M A SECOND-GENERATION FAN !
NOW, AFTER NAGI-SAMA HIMSELF PASSED AWAY SO LONG AGO . . .
HFF
HFF
THERE IS NO DOUBT IN MY MIND THAT THAT YOUNG MAN IS A REINCARNATION, SENT FROM HEAVEN FOR US LOST SOULS.
WHA . . !?
DUN
HE'S TOO GOOD FOR A PAIR OF FAILURES LIKE YOU TWO !
*NGH-GH-GH-GH-GH*, WHETHER YOU'RE A FAILURE OR NOT HAS NOTHING TO DO WITH BEING A FAN ~~~ !
. . . . . . . . .
RUMBLE
SO THAT GLADIATOR ISN'T THE REAL NAGI ?

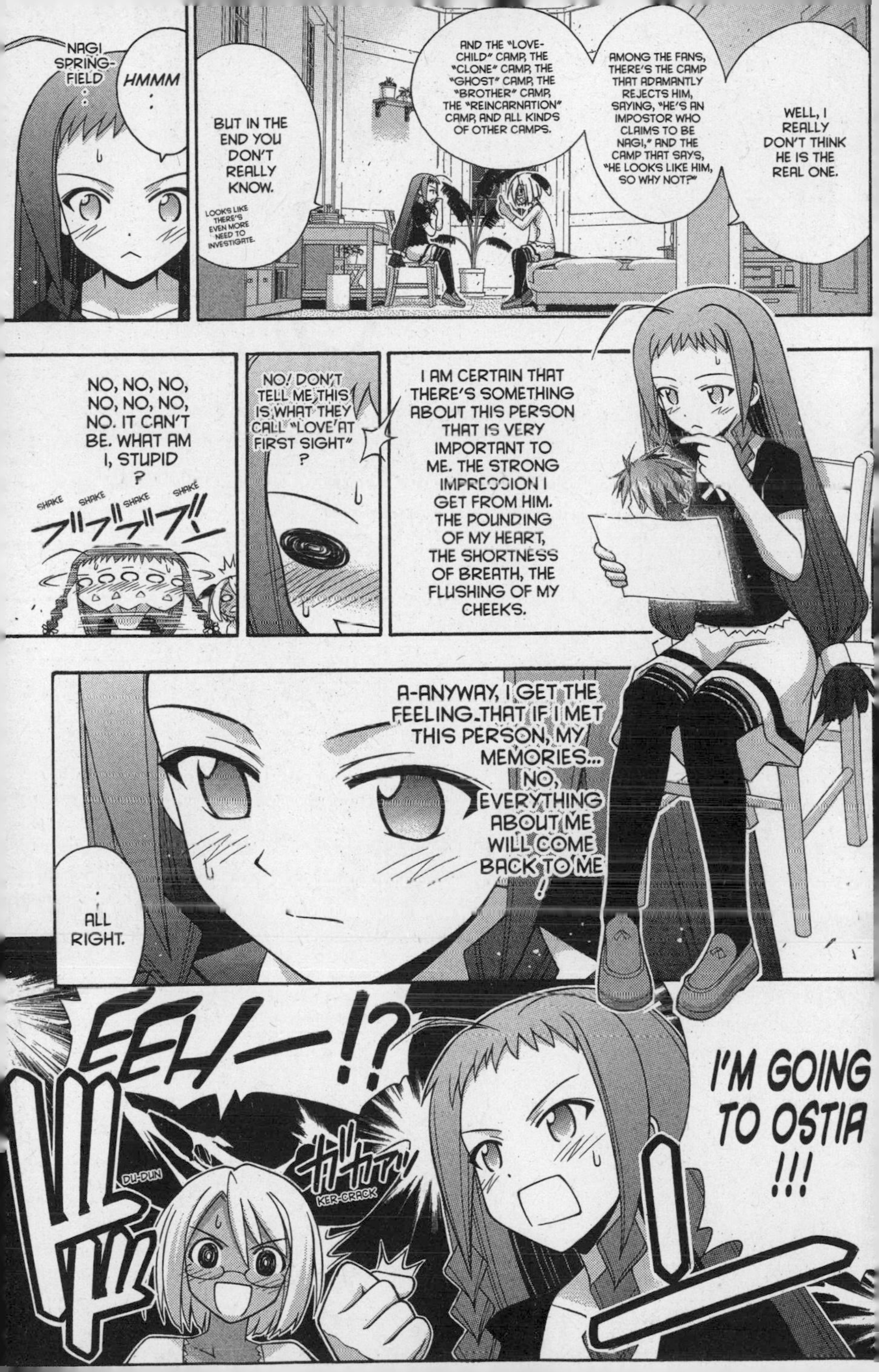
WELL, I REALLY DON'T THINK HE IS THE REAL ONE.
AMONG THE FANS, THERE'S THE CAMP THAT ADAMANTLY REJECTS HIM, SAYING, "HE'S AN IMPOSTOR WHO CLAIMS TO BE NAGI," AND THE CAMP THAT SAYS, "HE LOOKS LIKE HIM, SO WHY NOT?"
AND THE "LOVE-CHILD" CAMP, THE "CLONE" CAMP, THE "GHOST" CAMP, THE "BROTHER" CAMP, THE "REINCARNATION" CAMP, AND ALL KINDS OF OTHER CAMPS.
BUT IN THE END YOU DON'T REALLY KNOW.
LOOKS LIKE THERE'S EVEN MORE NEED TO INVESTIGATE.
HMMM :
NAGI SPRING-FIELD ...
I AM CERTAIN THAT THERE'S SOMETHING ABOUT THIS PERSON THAT IS VERY IMPORTANT TO ME. THE STRONG IMPRESSION I GET FROM HIM. THE POUNDING OF MY HEART, THE SHORTNESS OF BREATH, THE FLUSHING OF MY CHEEKS.
NO! DON'T TELL ME THIS IS WHAT THEY CALL "LOVE AT FIRST SIGHT" ?
NO, NO, NO, NO, NO, NO, NO. IT CAN'T BE. WHAT AM I, STUPID ?
SHAKE SHAKE SHAKE SHAKE
A-ANYWAY, I GET THE FEELING THAT IF I MET THIS PERSON, MY MEMORIES... NO, EVERYTHING ABOUT ME WILL COME BACK TO ME !
... ALL RIGHT.
I'M GOING TO OSTIA !!!
KER-CRACK
EEH—!?
DU-DUN

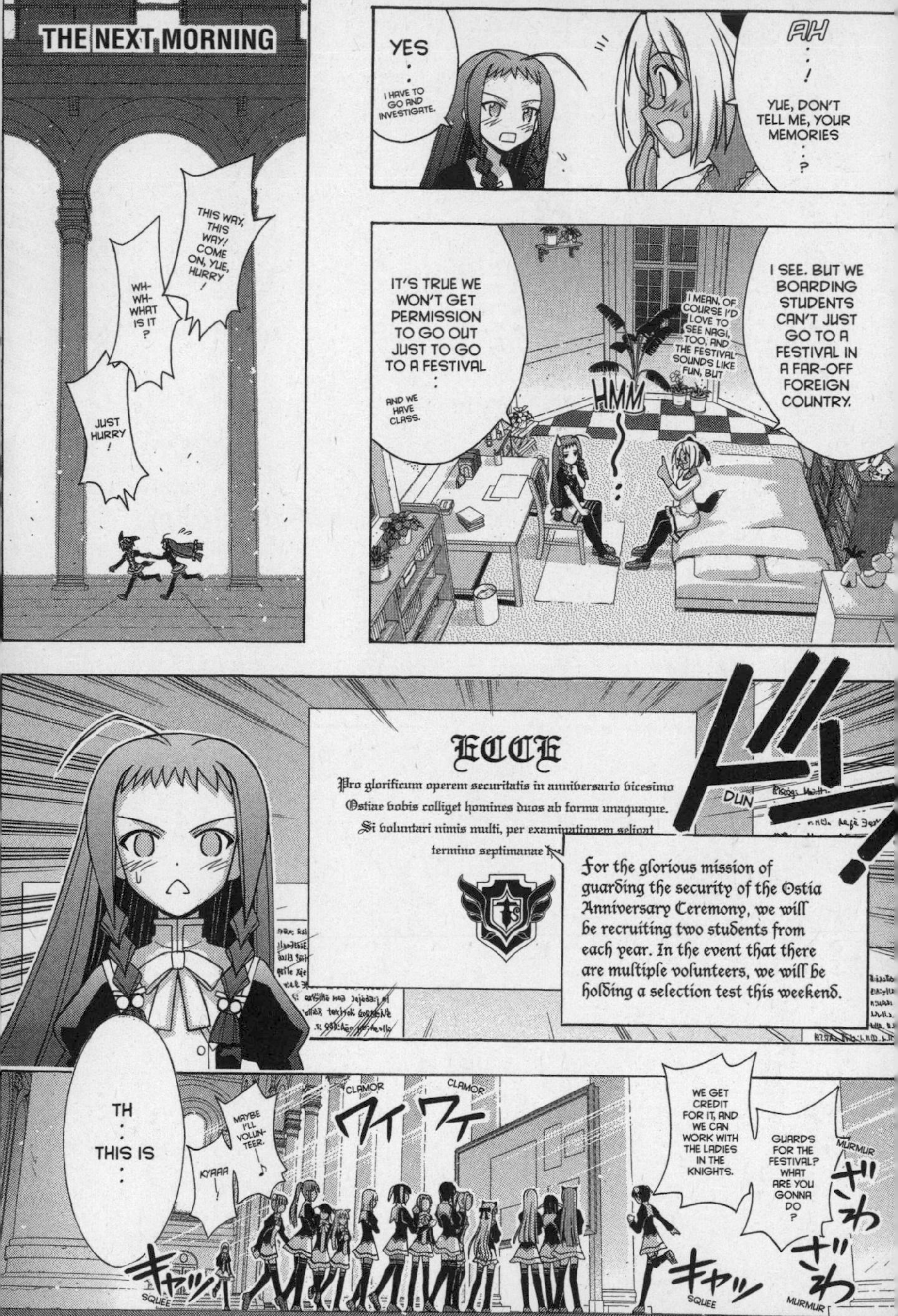
AH . . . !
YUE, DON'T TELL ME, YOUR MEMORIES . . . ?
YES . I HAVE TO GO AND INVESTIGATE.
I SEE. BUT WE BOARDING STUDENTS CAN'T JUST GO TO A FESTIVAL IN A FAR-OFF FOREIGN COUNTRY.
I MEAN, OF COURSE I'D LOVE TO SEE NAGI, TOO, AND THE FESTIVAL SOUNDS LIKE FUN, BUT
HMM
IT'S TRUE WE WON'T GET PERMISSION TO GO OUT JUST TO GO TO A FESTIVAL : AND WE HAVE CLASS.
THE NEXT MORNING
THIS WAY, THIS WAY! COME ON, YUE, HURRY!
WH-WH-WHAT IS IT?
JUST HURRY!
DUN
ECCE
Pro glorificum operem securitatis in anniversario vicesimo
Ostiae vobis colliget homines duos ab forma unaquaque.
Si voluntari nimis multi, per examinationem seligat
termino septimanae
For the glorious mission of guarding the security of the Ostia Anniversary Ceremony, we will be recruiting two students from each year. In the event that there are multiple volunteers, we will be holding a selection test this weekend.
MURMUR
GUARDS FOR THE FESTIVAL? WHAT ARE YOU GONNA DO?
WE GET CREDIT FOR IT, AND WE CAN WORK WITH THE LADIES IN THE KNIGHTS.
SQUEE
CLAMOR
CLAMOR
MAYBE I'LL VOLUNTEER.
KYAAA!
SQUEE
TH . . THIS IS . . .

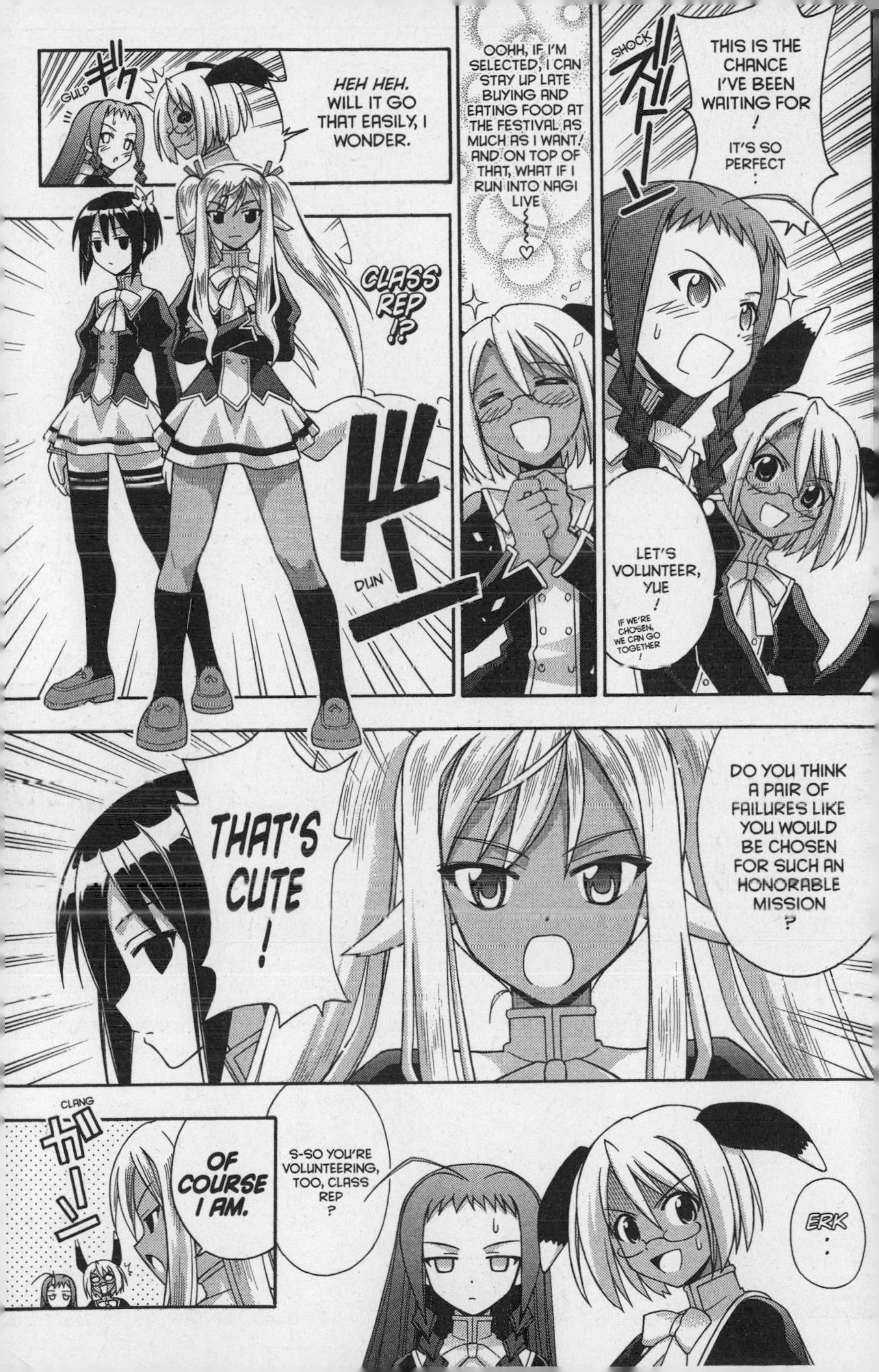
SHOCK
THIS IS THE CHANCE I'VE BEEN WAITING FOR! IT'S SO PERFECT:
LET'S VOLUNTEER, YUE!
IF WE'RE CHOSEN, WE CAN GO TOGETHER!
OOHH, IF I'M SELECTED, I CAN STAY UP LATE BUYING AND EATING FOOD AT THE FESTIVAL AS MUCH AS I WANT! AND ON TOP OF THAT, WHAT IF I RUN INTO NAGI LIVE
GULP
HEH HEH. WILL IT GO THAT EASILY, I WONDER.
CLASS REP!?
DUN
DO YOU THINK A PAIR OF FAILURES LIKE YOU WOULD BE CHOSEN FOR SUCH AN HONORABLE MISSION?
THAT'S CUTE!
ERK..
S-SO YOU'RE VOLUNTEERING, TOO, CLASS REP?
OF COURSE I AM.
CLANG

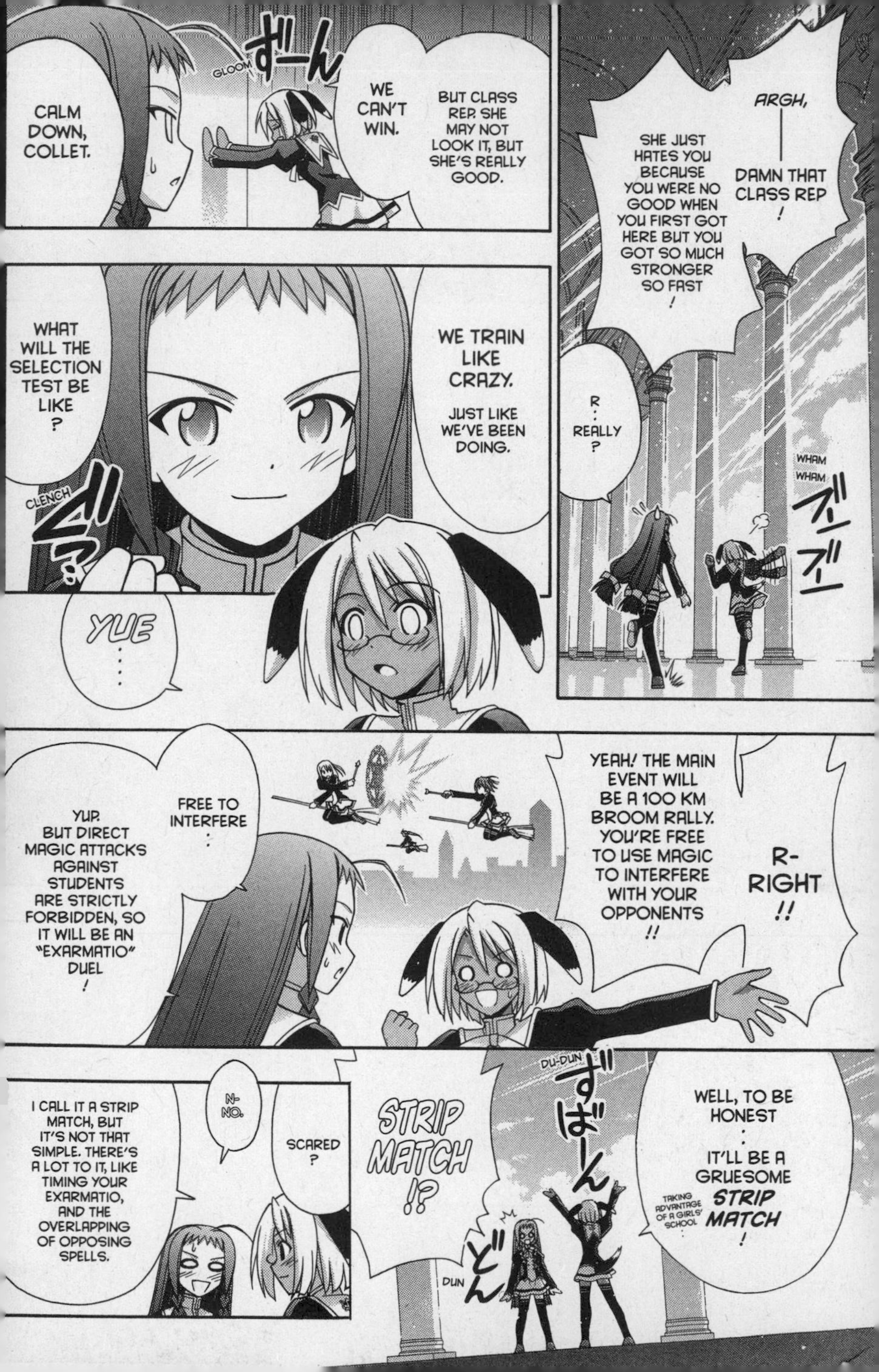
ARGH, DAMN THAT CLASS REP!
SHE JUST HATES YOU BECAUSE YOU WERE NO GOOD WHEN YOU FIRST GOT HERE BUT YOU GOT SO MUCH STRONGER SO FAST!
R... REALLY?
WHAM WHAM
ずーん
GLOOM
BUT CLASS REP. SHE MAY NOT LOOK IT, BUT SHE'S REALLY GOOD.
WE CAN'T WIN.
CALM DOWN, COLLET.
WE TRAIN LIKE CRAZY.
JUST LIKE WE'VE BEEN DOING.
WHAT WILL THE SELECTION TEST BE LIKE?
CLENCH
YUE....
R-RIGHT!!
YEAH! THE MAIN EVENT WILL BE A 100 KM BROOM RALLY. YOU'RE FREE TO USE MAGIC TO INTERFERE WITH YOUR OPPONENTS!!
FREE TO INTERFERE...
YUP. BUT DIRECT MAGIC ATTACKS AGAINST STUDENTS ARE STRICTLY FORBIDDEN, SO IT WILL BE AN "EXARMATIO" DUEL!
WELL, TO BE HONEST... IT'LL BE A GRUESOME STRIP MATCH!
TAKING ADVANTAGE OF A GIRLS' SCHOOL...
ずばーん
DU-DUN
どん
DUN
STRIP MATCH!?
SCARED?
N-NO.
I CALL IT A STRIP MATCH, BUT IT'S NOT THAT SIMPLE. THERE'S A LOT TO IT, LIKE TIMING YOUR EXARMATIO, AND THE OVERLAPPING OF OPPOSING SPELLS.

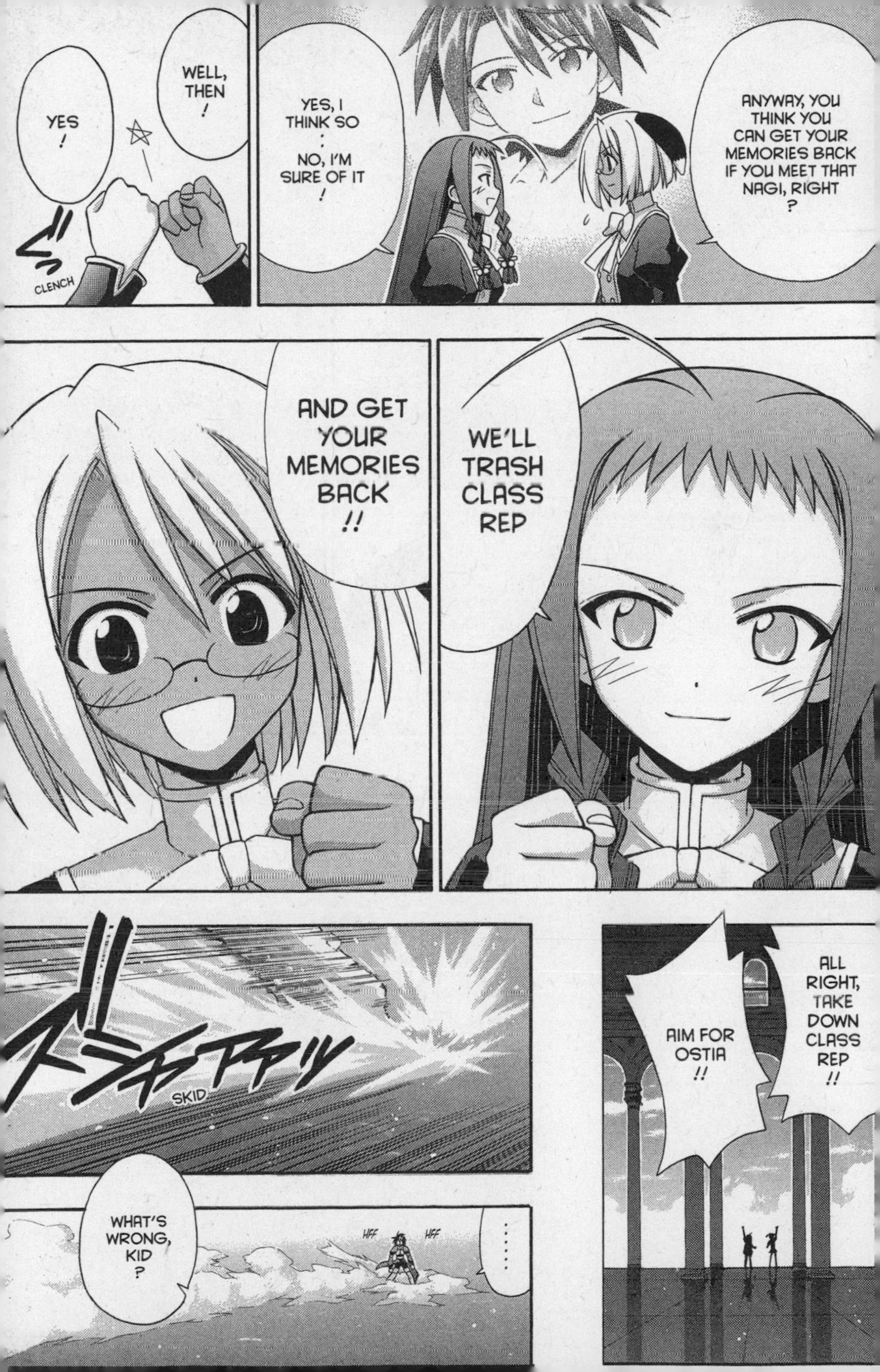
ANYWAY, YOU THINK YOU CAN GET YOUR MEMORIES BACK IF YOU MEET THAT NAGI, RIGHT ?
YES, I THINK SO : NO, I'M SURE OF IT !
WELL, THEN !
YES !
CLENCH
WE'LL TRASH CLASS REP
AND GET YOUR MEMORIES BACK !!
ALL RIGHT, TAKE DOWN CLASS REP !!
AIM FOR OSTIA !!
SKID
......
HFF
HFF
WHAT'S WRONG, KID ?

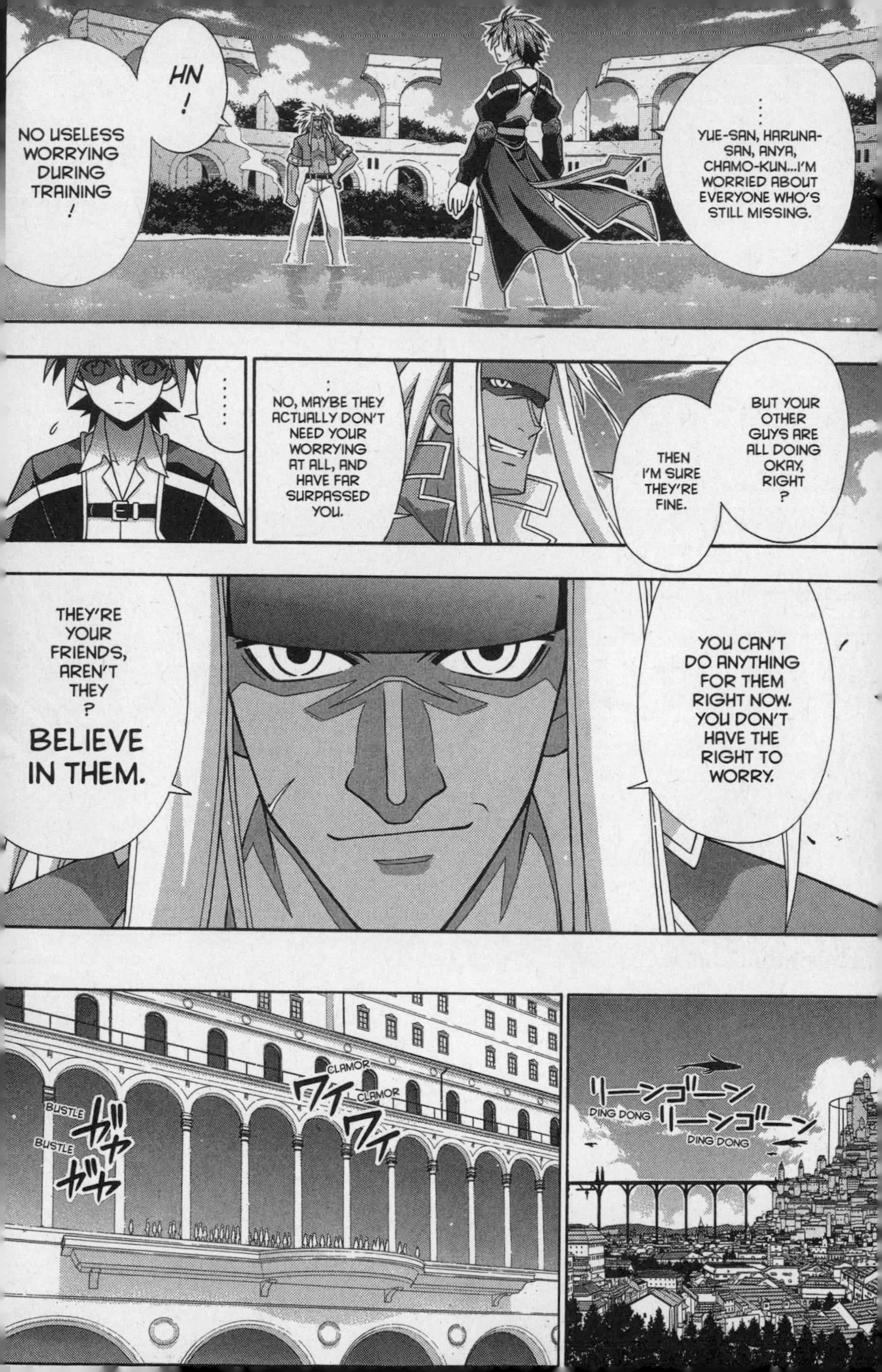
......YUE-SAN, HARUNA-SAN, ANYA, CHAMO-KUN...I'M WORRIED ABOUT EVERYONE WHO'S STILL MISSING.
HN!
NO USELESS WORRYING DURING TRAINING!
BUT YOUR OTHER GUYS ARE ALL DOING OKAY, RIGHT?
THEN I'M SURE THEY'RE FINE.
...NO, MAYBE THEY ACTUALLY DON'T NEED YOUR WORRYING AT ALL, AND HAVE FAR SURPASSED YOU.
......
YOU CAN'T DO ANYTHING FOR THEM RIGHT NOW. YOU DON'T HAVE THE RIGHT TO WORRY.
THEY'RE YOUR FRIENDS, AREN'T THEY? BELIEVE IN THEM.
リーンゴーン
DING DONG
リーンゴーン
DING DONG
ワイ
CLAMOR
ワイ
CLAMOR
ガヤ
BUSTLE
ガヤ
BUSTLE

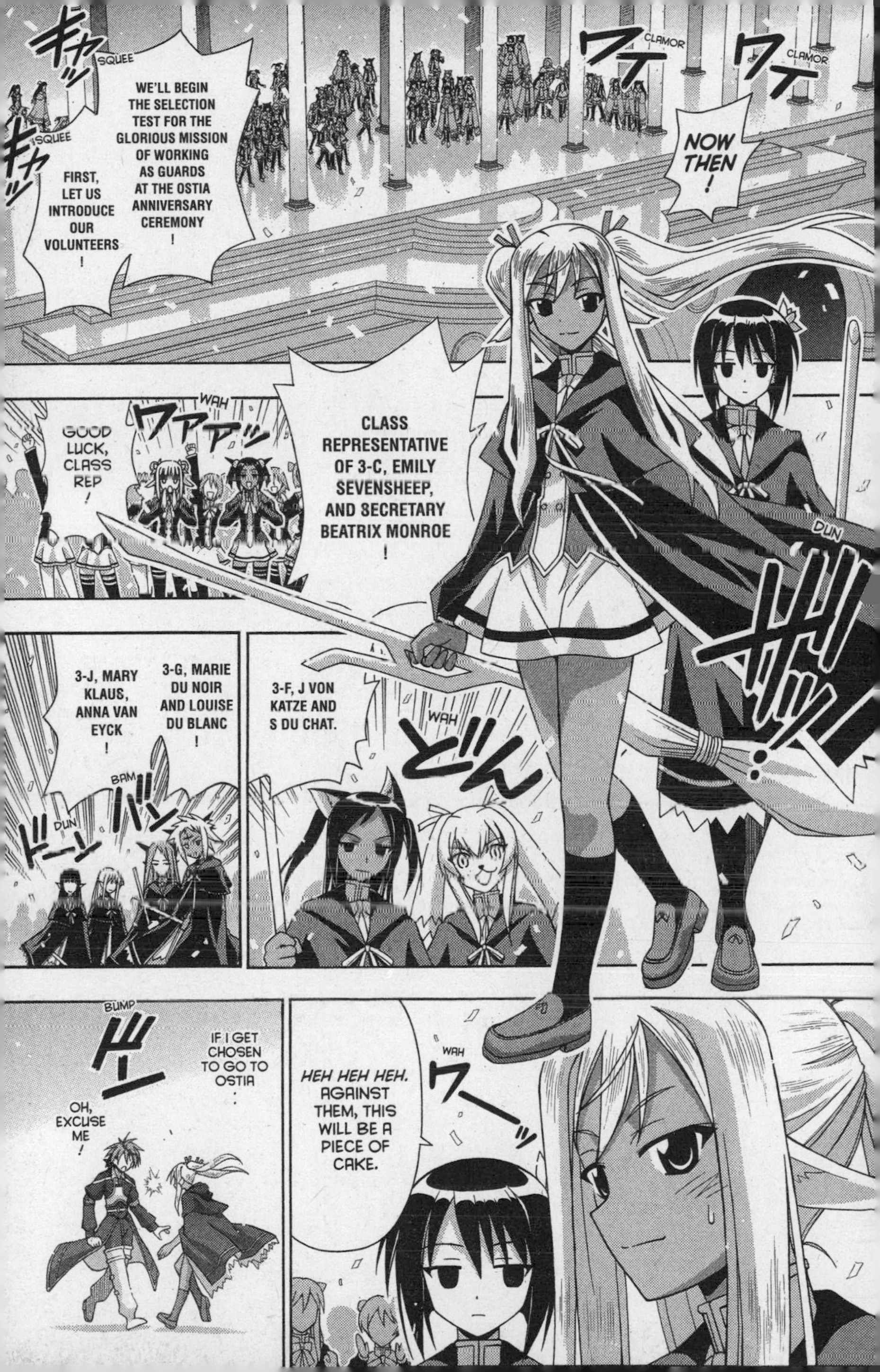
CLAMOR
CLAMOR
NOW THEN!
WE'LL BEGIN THE SELECTION TEST FOR THE GLORIOUS MISSION OF WORKING AS GUARDS AT THE OSTIA ANNIVERSARY CEREMONY!
FIRST, LET US INTRODUCE OUR VOLUNTEERS!
SQUEE
SQUEE
CLASS REPRESENTATIVE OF 3-C, EMILY SEVENSHEEP, AND SECRETARY BEATRIX MONROE!
DUN
WAH
GOOD LUCK, CLASS REP!
3-F, J VON KATZE AND S DU CHAT.
WAH
3-G, MARIE DU NOIR AND LOUISE DU BLANC!
3-J, MARY KLAUS, ANNA VAN EYCK!
BAM
DUN
HEH HEH HEH. AGAINST THEM, THIS WILL BE A PIECE OF CAKE.
WAH
IF I GET CHOSEN TO GO TO OSTIA...
BUMP
OH, EXCUSE ME!

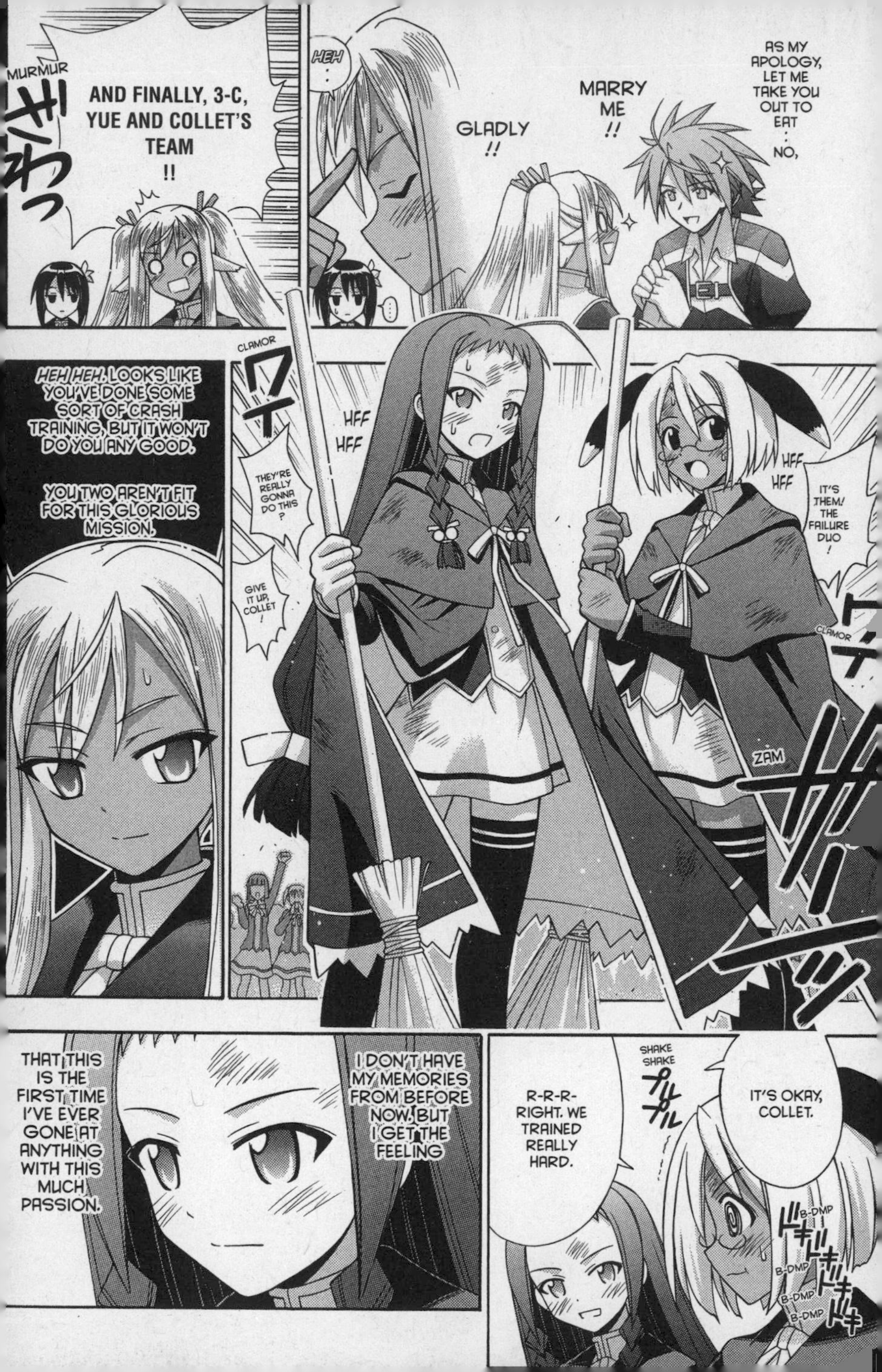
AS MY APOLOGY, LET ME TAKE YOU OUT TO EAT . . NO,
MARRY ME!!
GLADLY!!
HEH . .
MURMUR
AND FINALLY, 3-C, YUE AND COLLET'S TEAM!!
IT'S THEM! THE FAILURE DUO!
CLAMOR
HFF HFF
ZAM
HFF HFF
THEY'RE REALLY GONNA DO THIS?
GIVE IT UP, COLLET!
CLAMOR
HEH HEH. LOOKS LIKE YOU'VE DONE SOME SORT OF CRASH TRAINING, BUT IT WON'T DO YOU ANY GOOD.
YOU TWO AREN'T FIT FOR THIS GLORIOUS MISSION.
IT'S OKAY, COLLET.
SHAKE SHAKE
R-R-R-RIGHT. WE TRAINED REALLY HARD.
B-DMP
B-DMP
B-DMP
B-DMP
I DON'T HAVE MY MEMORIES FROM BEFORE NOW. BUT I GET THE FEELING
THAT THIS IS THE FIRST TIME I'VE EVER GONE AT ANYTHING WITH THIS MUCH PASSION.

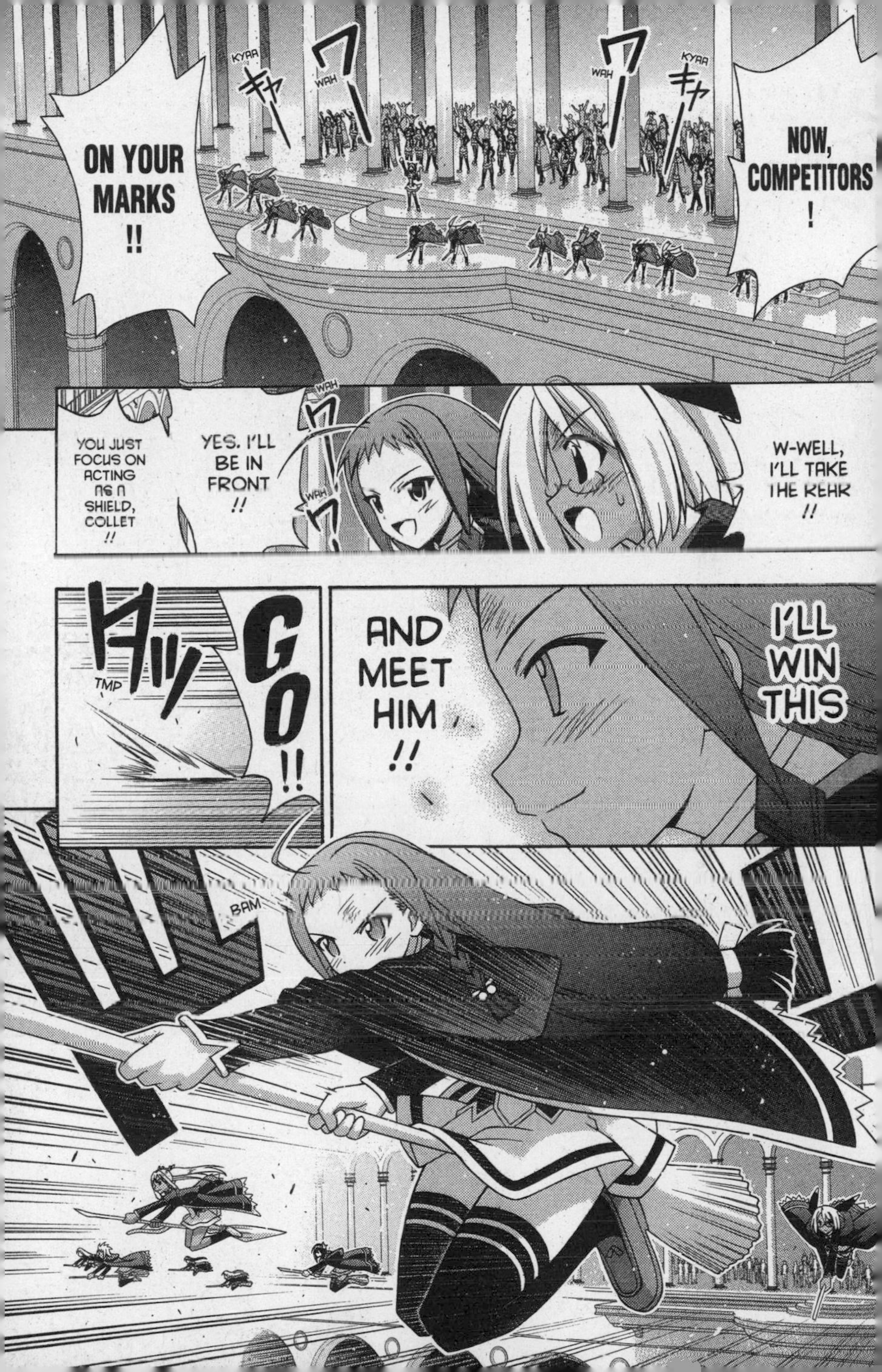
KYAA
WAH
NOW, COMPETITORS !
KYAA
WAH
ON YOUR MARKS !!
W-WELL, I'LL TAKE THE REAR !!
WAH
WAH
YES. I'LL BE IN FRONT !!
YOU JUST FOCUS ON ACTING AS A SHIELD, COLLET !!
I'LL WIN THIS
AND MEET HIM !!
GO !!
TMP
BAM

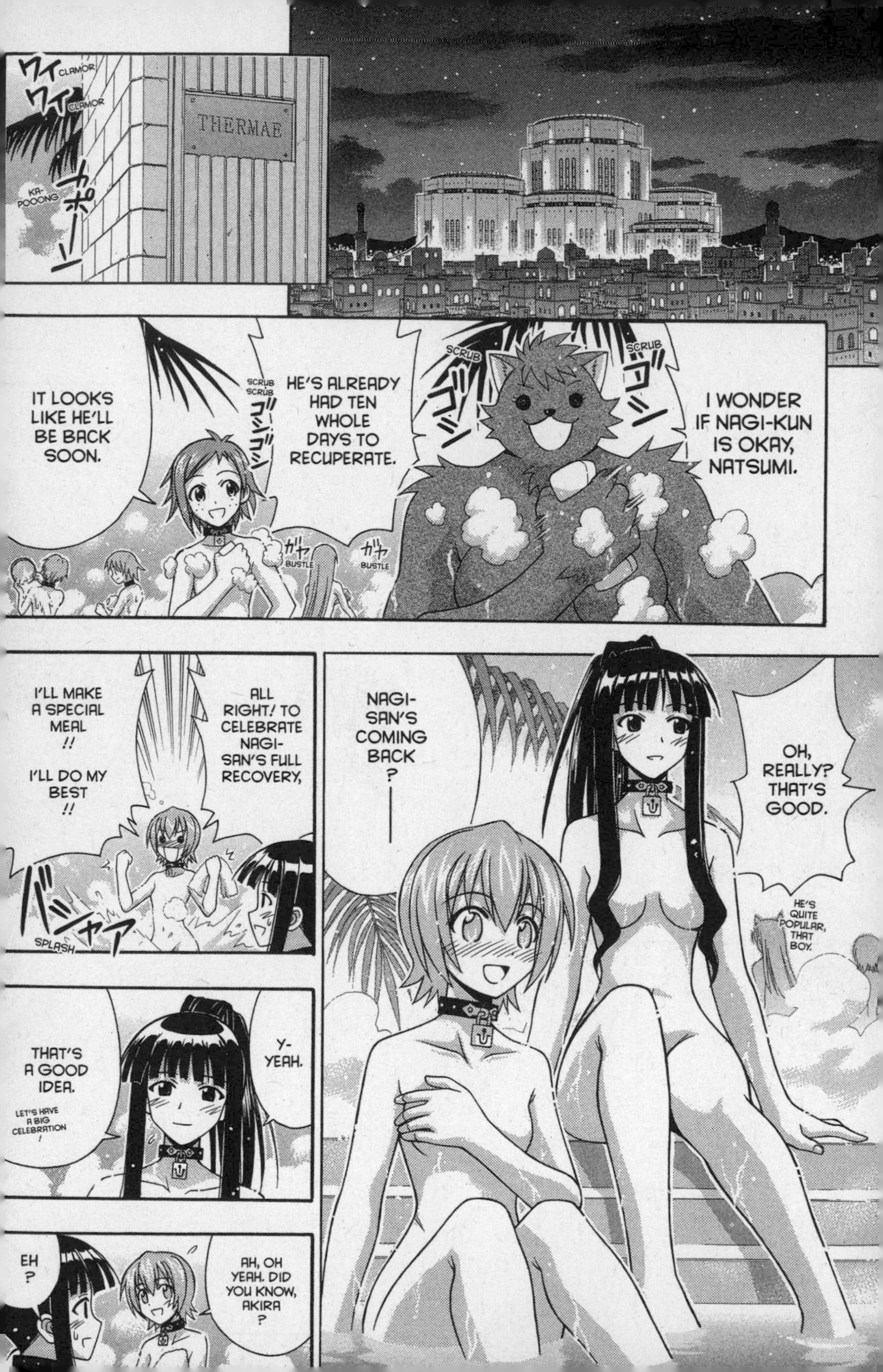
ワイワイ
CLAMOR
CLAMOR
THERMAE
カポーン
KA-POOONG
I WONDER IF NAGI-KUN IS OKAY, NATSUMI.
SCRUB
ゴシ
SCRUB
ゴシ
HE'S ALREADY HAD TEN WHOLE DAYS TO RECUPERATE.
SCRUB SCRUB
ゴシゴシ
IT LOOKS LIKE HE'LL BE BACK SOON.
ガヤ
BUSTLE
ガヤ
BUSTLE
OH, REALLY? THAT'S GOOD.
NAGI-SAN'S COMING BACK?
HE'S QUITE POPULAR, THAT BOY.
ALL RIGHT! TO CELEBRATE NAGI-SAN'S FULL RECOVERY,
I'LL MAKE A SPECIAL MEAL!!
I'LL DO MY BEST!!
バシャア
SPLASH
Y-YEAH.
THAT'S A GOOD IDEA.
LET'S HAVE A BIG CELEBRATION!
AH, OH YEAH. DID YOU KNOW, AKIRA?
EH?

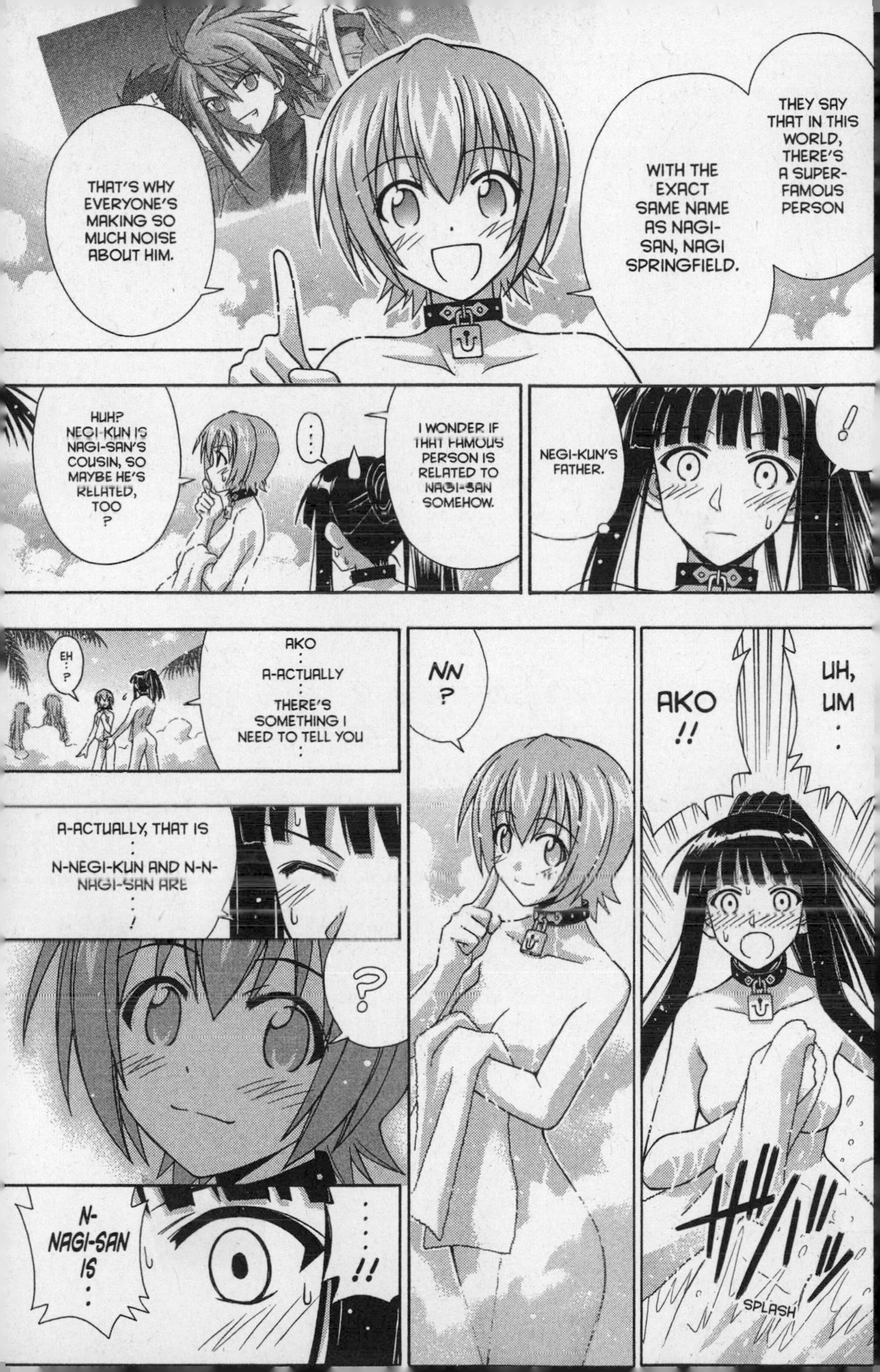
THEY SAY THAT IN THIS WORLD, THERE'S A SUPER-FAMOUS PERSON
WITH THE EXACT SAME NAME AS NAGI-SAN, NAGI SPRINGFIELD.
THAT'S WHY EVERYONE'S MAKING SO MUCH NOISE ABOUT HIM.
!
NEGI-KUN'S FATHER.
I WONDER IF THAT FAMOUS PERSON IS RELATED TO NAGI-SAN SOMEHOW.
. . . .
HUH? NEGI-KUN IS NAGI-SAN'S COUSIN, SO MAYBE HE'S RELATED, TOO?
UH, UM . .
AKO !!
SPLASH
NN ?
AKO . . . A-ACTUALLY . . . THERE'S SOMETHING I NEED TO TELL YOU . .
EH . . ?
A-ACTUALLY, THAT IS . . N-NEGI-KUN AND N-N-NAGI-SAN ARE . . . !
?
N-NAGI-SAN IS . . .
. . . . !!

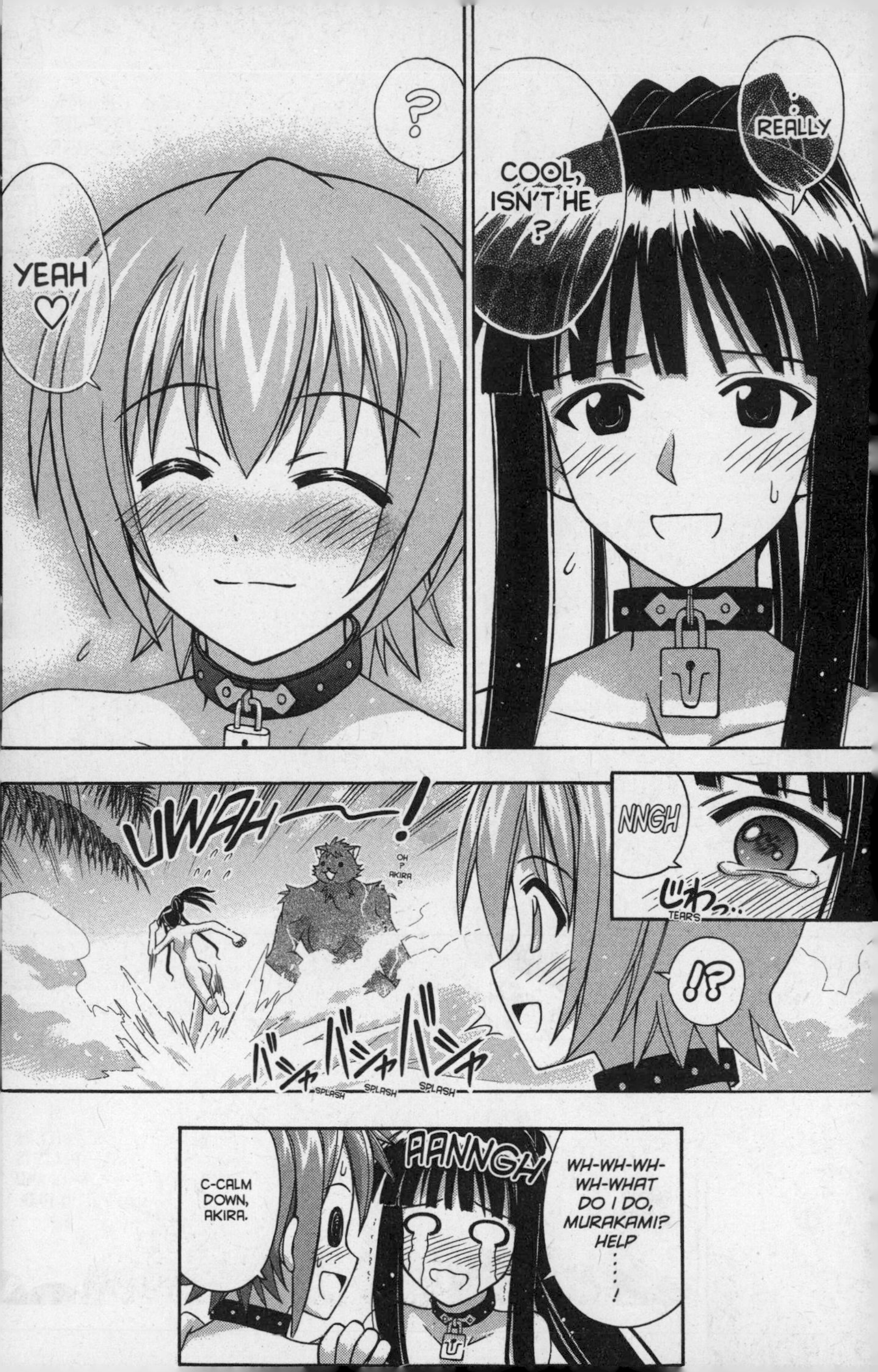
COOL, ISN'T HE ?
...REALLY
?
YEAH ♡
NNGH
じわっ…
TEARS
!?
UWAH—!
OH? AKIRA?
バシャバシャバシャ
SPLASH SPLASH SPLASH
AANNGH
WH-WH-WH-WH-WHAT DO I DO, MURAKAMI? HELP......!
C-CALM DOWN, AKIRA.

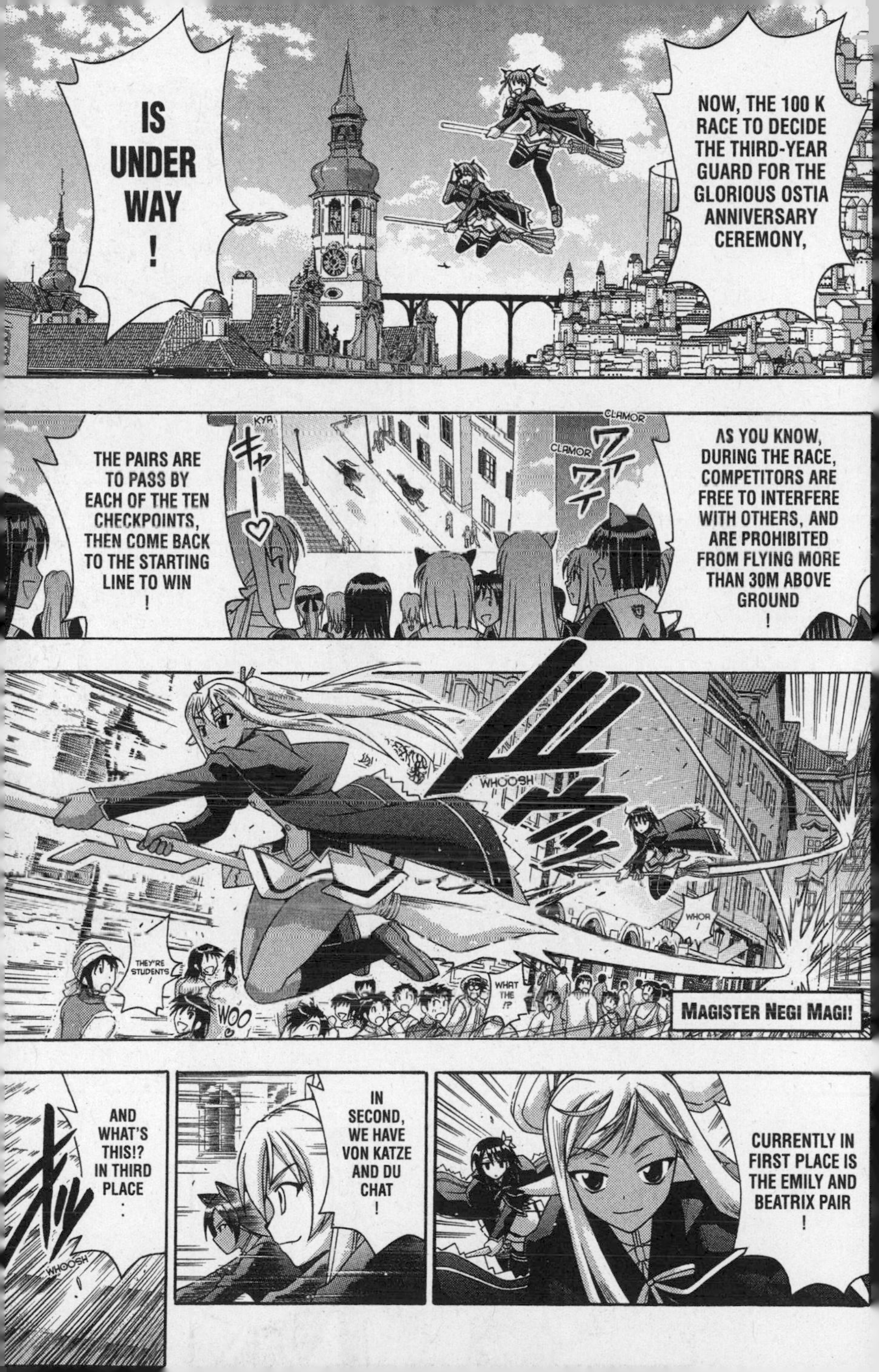
NOW, THE 100 K RACE TO DECIDE THE THIRD-YEAR GUARD FOR THE GLORIOUS OSTIA ANNIVERSARY CEREMONY,
IS UNDER WAY!
AS YOU KNOW, DURING THE RACE, COMPETITORS ARE FREE TO INTERFERE WITH OTHERS, AND ARE PROHIBITED FROM FLYING MORE THAN 30M ABOVE GROUND!
CLAMOR
CLAMOR
KYA
THE PAIRS ARE TO PASS BY EACH OF THE TEN CHECKPOINTS, THEN COME BACK TO THE STARTING LINE TO WIN!
WHOOSH
WHOA!
WHAT THE!?
THEY'RE STUDENTS!
WOO
MAGISTER NEGI MAGI!
CURRENTLY IN FIRST PLACE IS THE EMILY AND BEATRIX PAIR!
IN SECOND, WE HAVE VON KATZE AND DU CHAT!
AND WHAT'S THIS!? IN THIRD PLACE...
WHOOSH

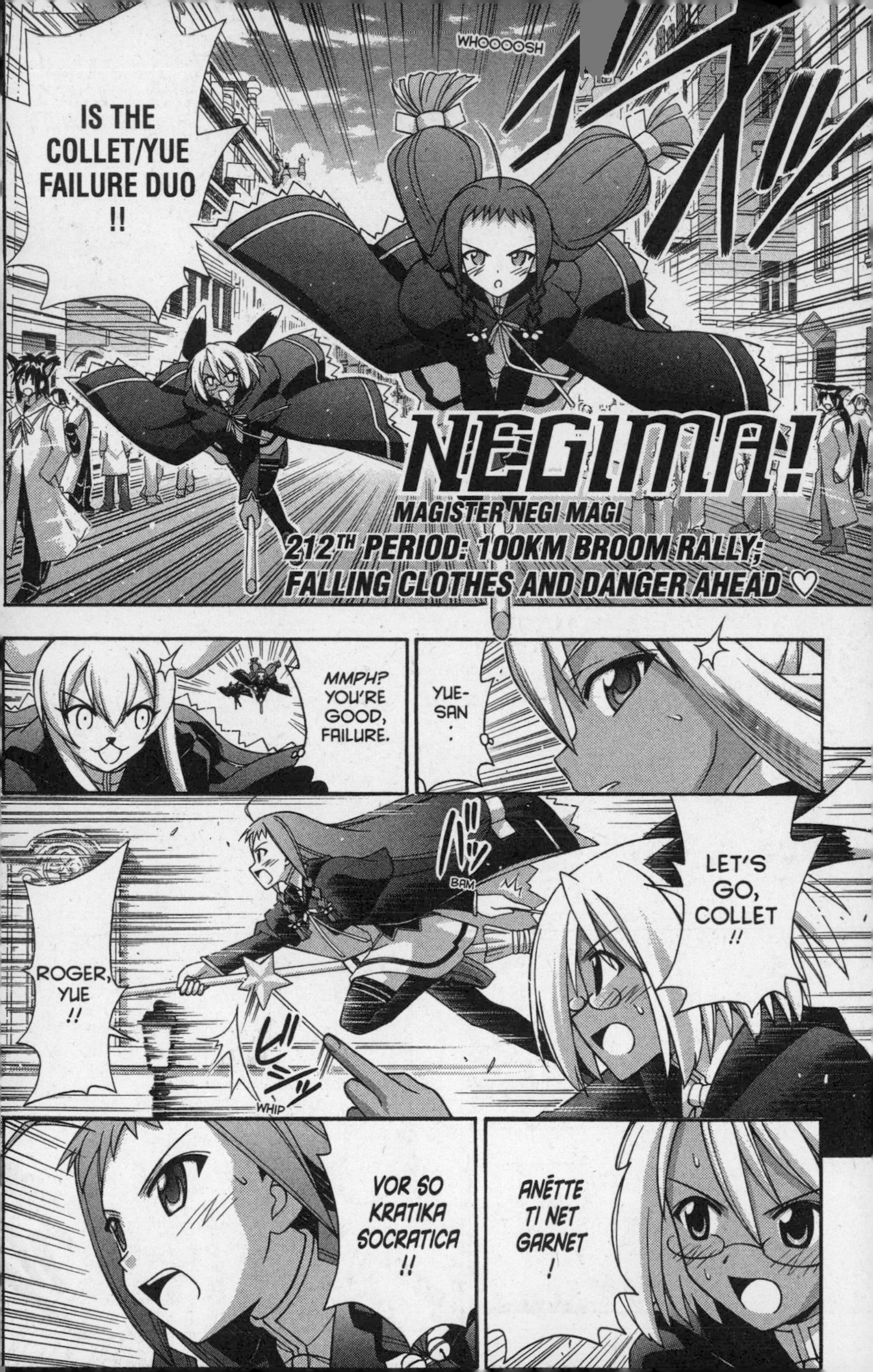
WHOOOOSH
IS THE COLLET/YUE FAILURE DUO !!
NEGIMA!
MAGISTER NEGI MAGI
212TH PERIOD: 100KM BROOM RALLY; FALLING CLOTHES AND DANGER AHEAD ♡
YUE-SAN :
MMPH? YOU'RE GOOD, FAILURE.
LET'S GO, COLLET !!
BAM
ROGER, YUE !!
WHIP
ANÉTTE TI NET GARNET !
VOR SO KRATIKA SOCRATICA !!

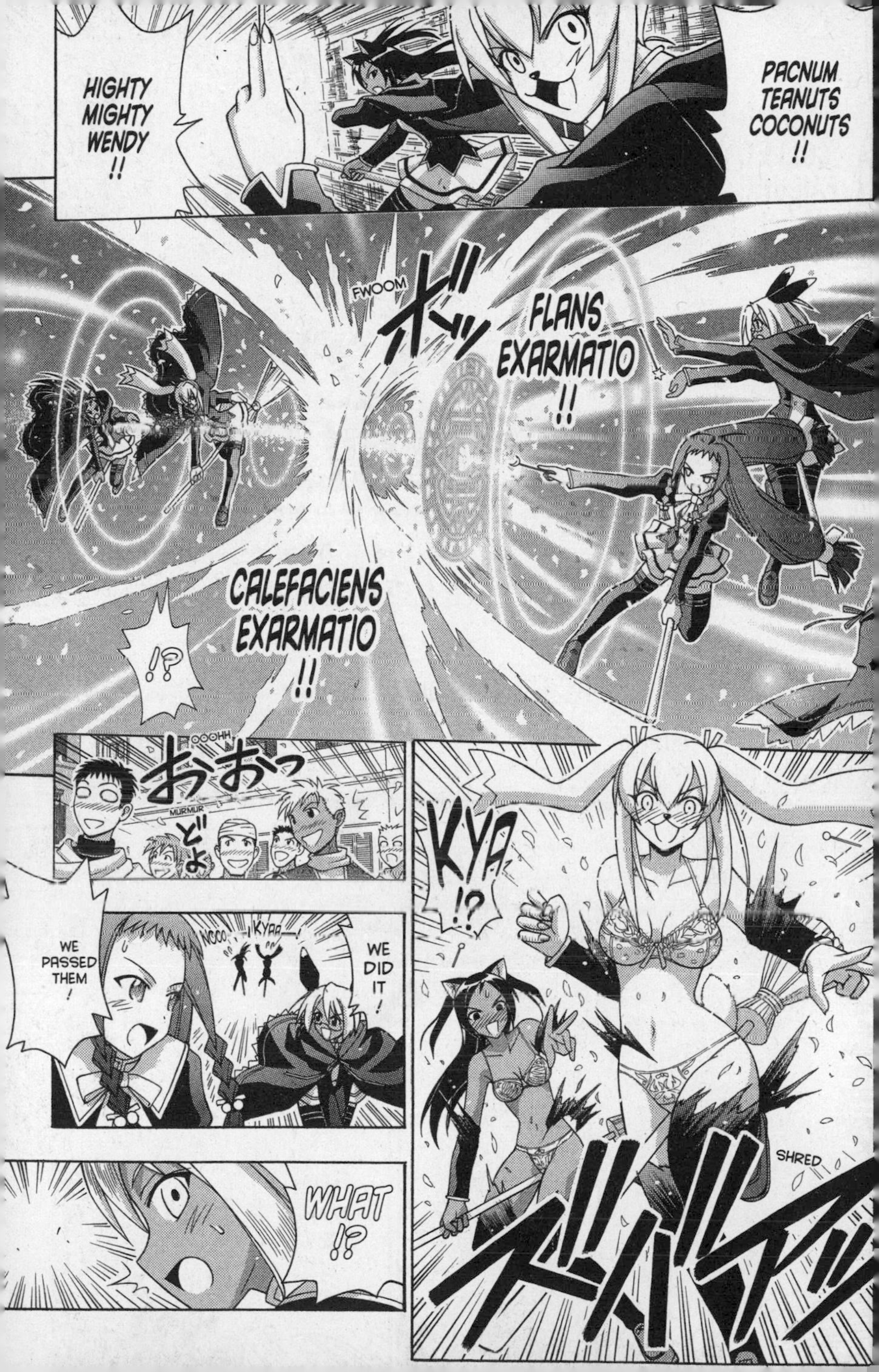
PACNUM TEANUTS COCONUTS !!
HIGHTY MIGHTY WENDY !!
FLANS EXARMATIO !!
FWOOM
CALEFACIENS EXARMATIO !!
!?
KYA !?
SHRED
OOOHH
おおっ
MURMUR
どよ
WE DID IT !
NOOO
KYAA
WE PASSED THEM !
WHAT !?

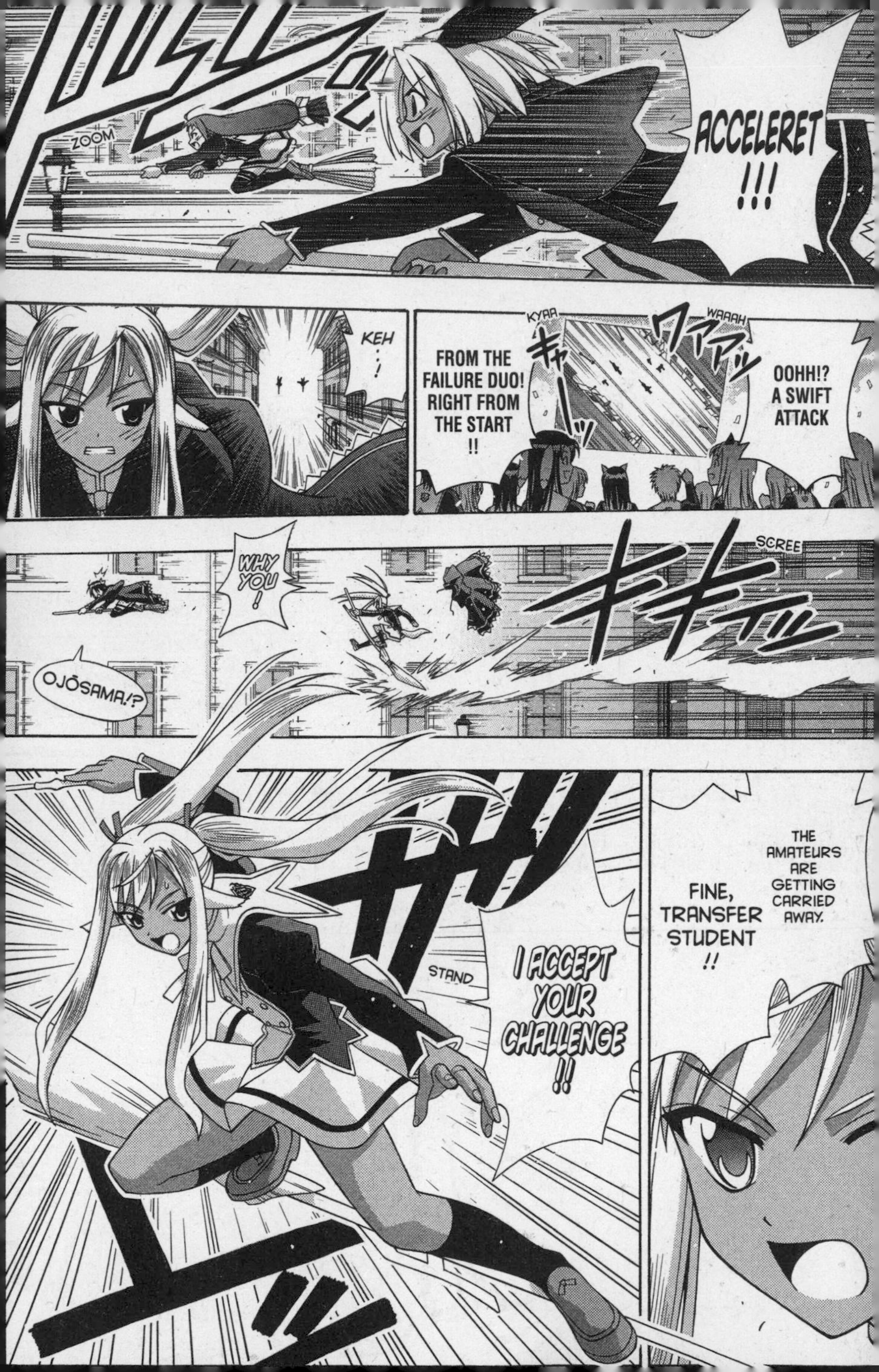
ZOOM
ACCELERET !!!
WAAAH
KYAA
OOHH!? A SWIFT ATTACK
FROM THE FAILURE DUO! RIGHT FROM THE START !!
KEH...!
SCREE
WHY YOU !
OJŌSAMA!?
THE AMATEURS ARE GETTING CARRIED AWAY.
FINE, TRANSFER STUDENT !!
I ACCEPT YOUR CHALLENGE !!
STAND

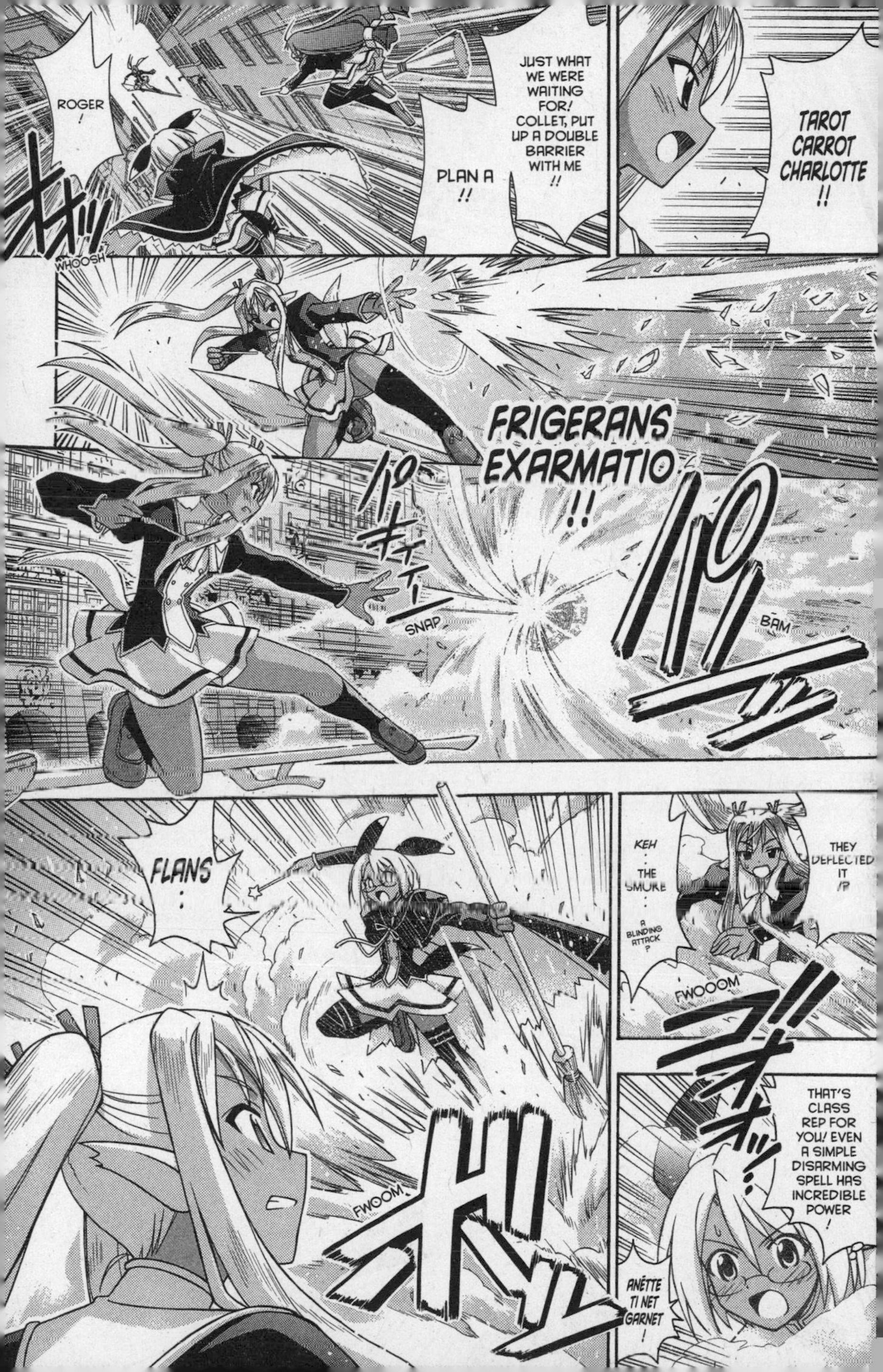
TAROT CARROT CHARLOTTE !!
JUST WHAT WE WERE WAITING FOR! COLLET, PUT UP A DOUBLE BARRIER WITH ME !!
PLAN A !!
ROGER !
WHOOSH
FRIGERANS EXARMATIO !!
BAM
SNAP
THEY DEFLECTED IT !?
KEH ... THE SMOKE ...
A BLINDING ATTACK ?
FWOOOM
THAT'S CLASS REP FOR YOU! EVEN A SIMPLE DISARMING SPELL HAS INCREDIBLE POWER !
ANÉTTE TI NET GARNET !
FLANS ...
FWOOM

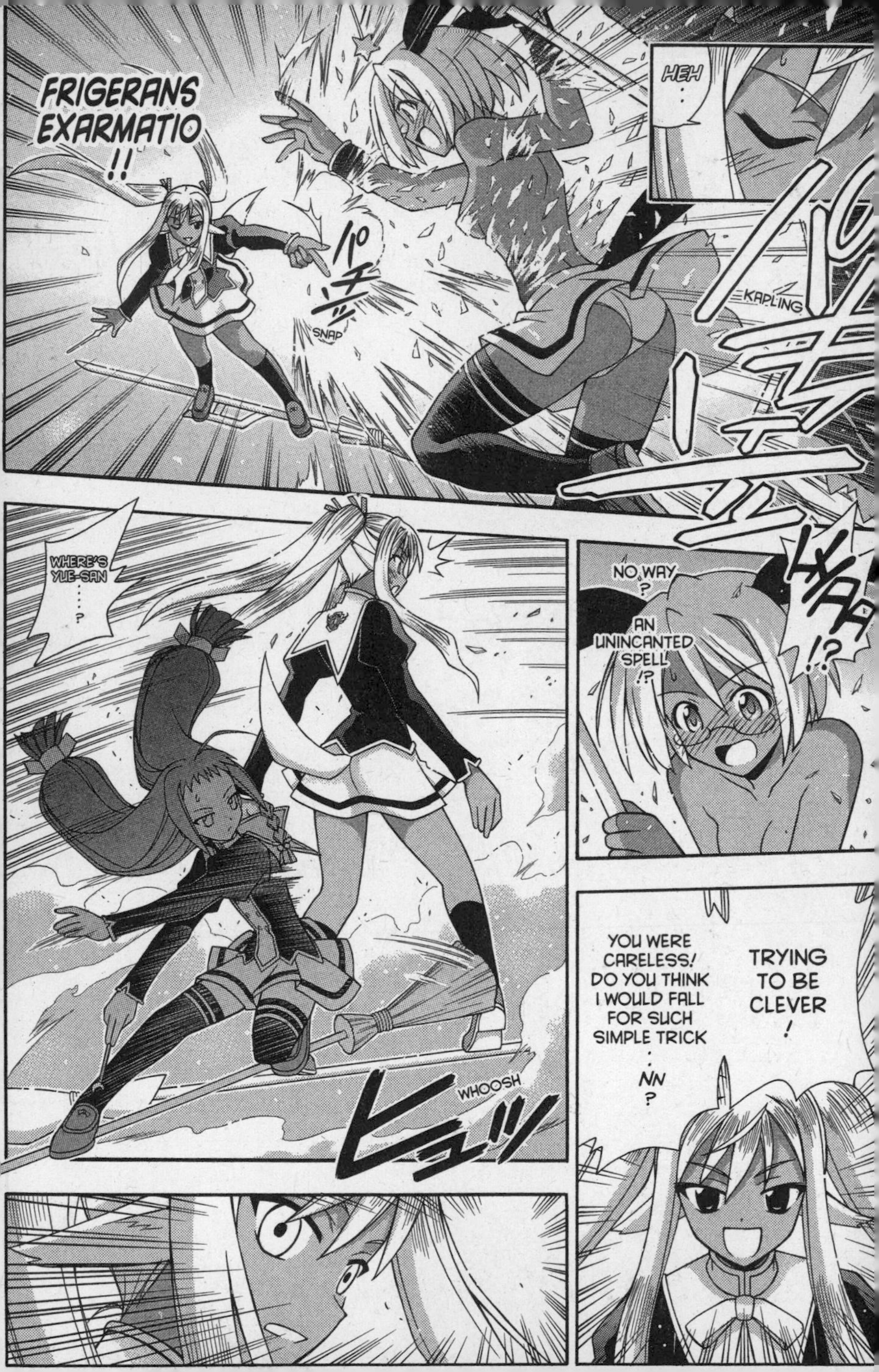
HEH
...
FRIGERANS EXARMATIO!!
SNAP
KAPLING
HYAA!?
NO WAY?
AN UNINCANTED SPELL!?
WHERE'S YUE-SAN.....?
WHOOSH
TRYING TO BE CLEVER!
YOU WERE CARELESS! DO YOU THINK I WOULD FALL FOR SUCH SIMPLE TRICK..
NN?

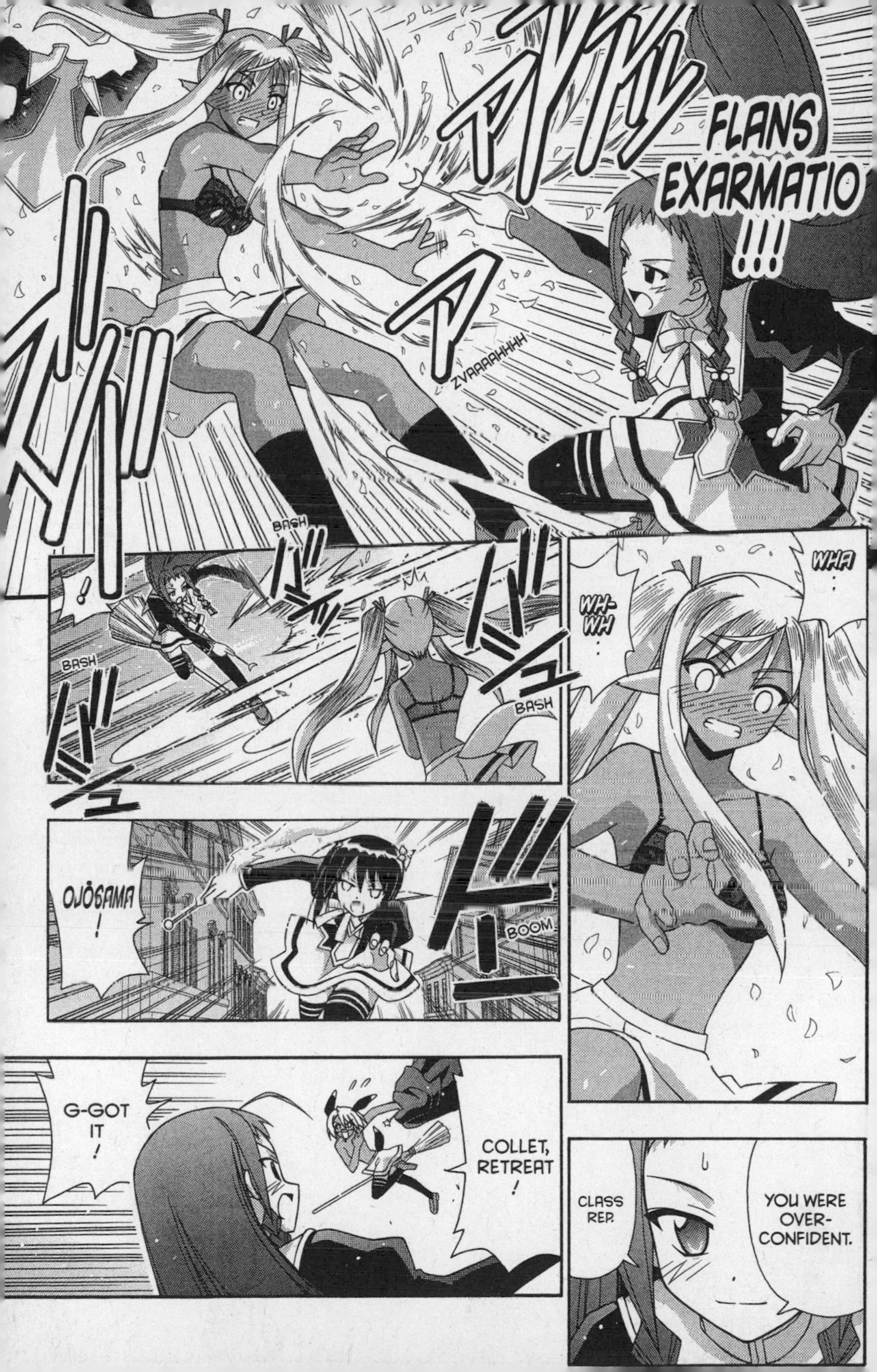
FLANS EXARMATIO !!!
ZVAAAAHHHH
WHA :
WH- WH :
BASH
!
BASH
BASH
OJŌSAMA !
BOOM
YOU WERE OVER-CONFIDENT.
CLASS REP.
COLLET, RETREAT !
G-GOT IT !

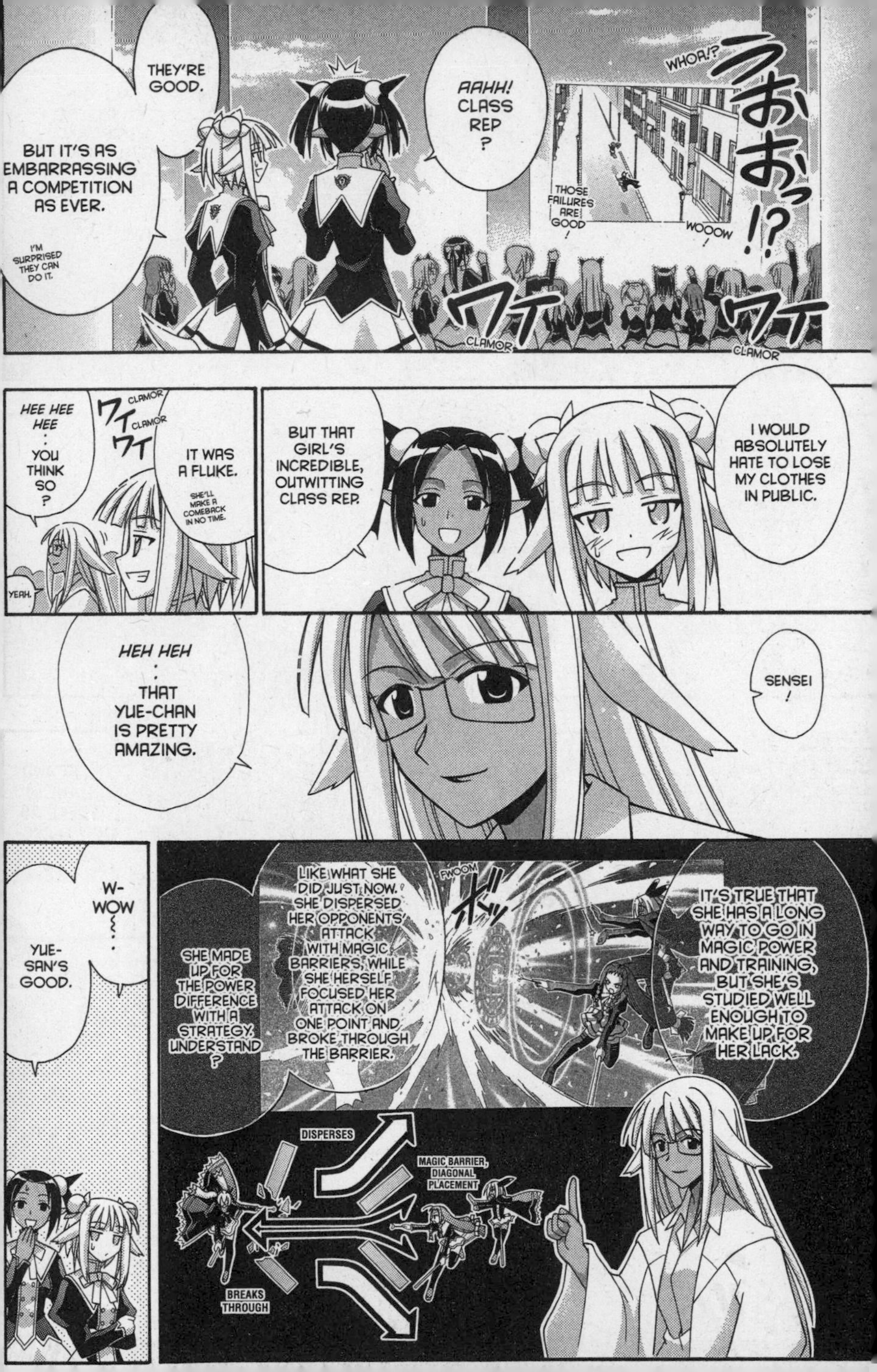
WHOA!?
うおおっ!?
WOOOW!
THOSE FAILURES ARE GOOD!
AAHH! CLASS REP?
THEY'RE GOOD.
BUT IT'S AS EMBARRASSING A COMPETITION AS EVER.
I'M SURPRISED THEY CAN DO IT.
ワイ CLAMOR
ワイ CLAMOR
I WOULD ABSOLUTELY HATE TO LOSE MY CLOTHES IN PUBLIC.
BUT THAT GIRL'S INCREDIBLE, OUTWITTING CLASS REP.
IT WAS A FLUKE.
SHE'LL MAKE A COMEBACK IN NO TIME.
ワイ CLAMOR
ワイ CLAMOR
HEE HEE HEE... YOU THINK SO?
YEAH.
SENSEI!
HEH HEH... THAT YUE-CHAN IS PRETTY AMAZING.
IT'S TRUE THAT SHE HAS A LONG WAY TO GO IN MAGIC POWER AND TRAINING, BUT SHE'S STUDIED WELL ENOUGH TO MAKE UP FOR HER LACK.
ズッ FWOOM
LIKE WHAT SHE DID JUST NOW. SHE DISPERSED HER OPPONENTS' ATTACK WITH MAGIC BARRIERS, WHILE SHE HERSELF FOCUSED HER ATTACK ON ONE POINT AND BROKE THROUGH THE BARRIER.
SHE MADE UP FOR THE POWER DIFFERENCE WITH A STRATEGY. UNDERSTAND?
DISPERSES
MAGIC BARRIER, DIAGONAL PLACEMENT
BREAKS THROUGH
W-WOW~...
YUE-SAN'S GOOD.

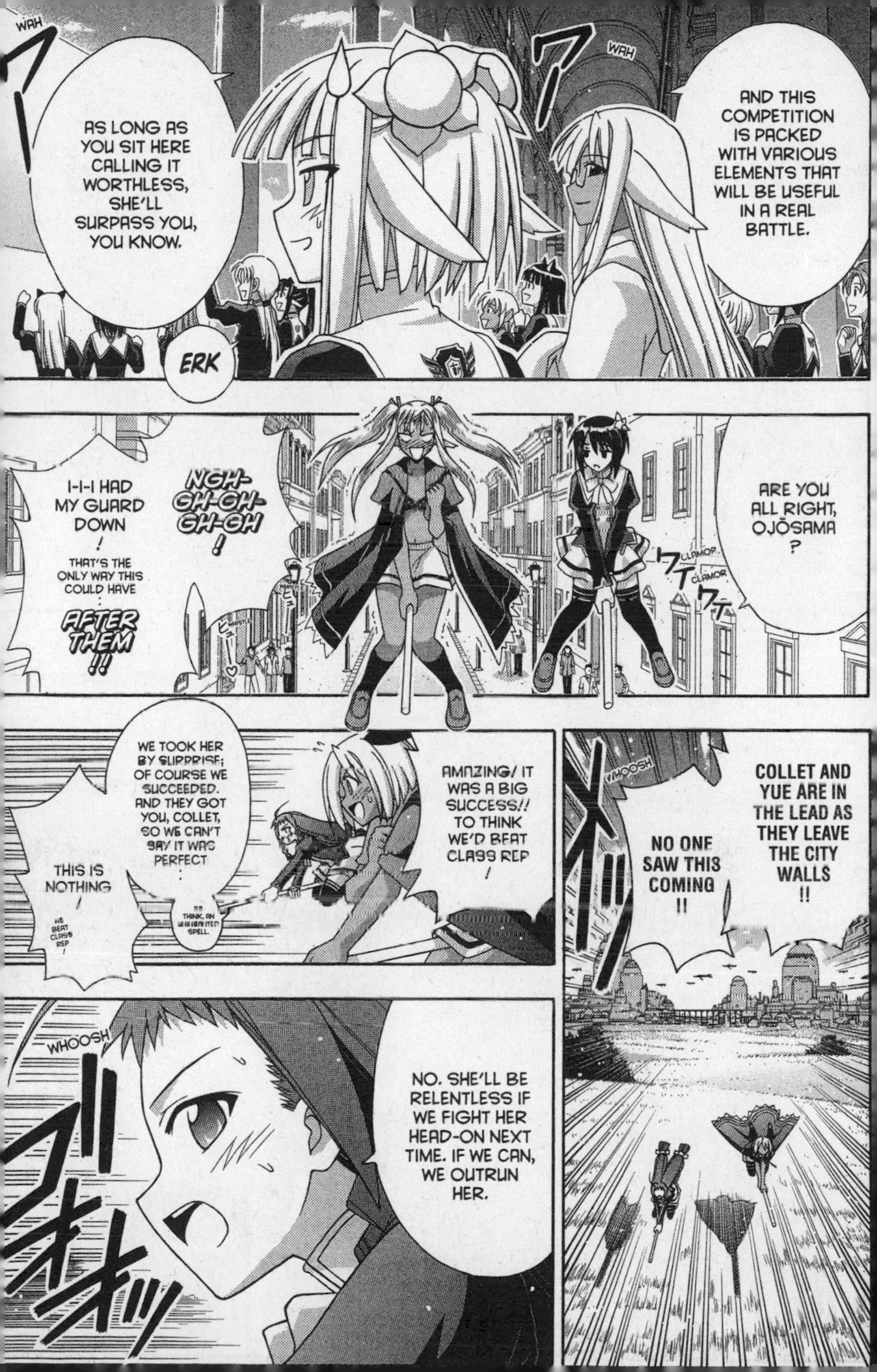
WAH
AND THIS COMPETITION IS PACKED WITH VARIOUS ELEMENTS THAT WILL BE USEFUL IN A REAL BATTLE.
WAH
AS LONG AS YOU SIT HERE CALLING IT WORTHLESS, SHE'LL SURPASS YOU, YOU KNOW.
ERK
ARE YOU ALL RIGHT, OJŌSAMA?
CLAMOR CLAMOR
NGH-GH-GH-GH-GH!
I-I-I HAD MY GUARD DOWN! THAT'S THE ONLY WAY THIS COULD HAVE...
AFTER THEM!!
WHOOSH
COLLET AND YUE ARE IN THE LEAD AS THEY LEAVE THE CITY WALLS!!
NO ONE SAW THIS COMING!!
AMAZING! IT WAS A BIG SUCCESS!! TO THINK WE'D BEAT CLASS REP!
WE TOOK HER BY SURPRISE; OF COURSE WE SUCCEEDED. AND THEY GOT YOU, COLLET, SO WE CAN'T SAY IT WAS PERFECT...
THIS IS NOTHING!
WE BEAT CLASS REP!
WHOOSH
NO. SHE'LL BE RELENTLESS IF WE FIGHT HER HEAD-ON NEXT TIME. IF WE CAN, WE OUTRUN HER.

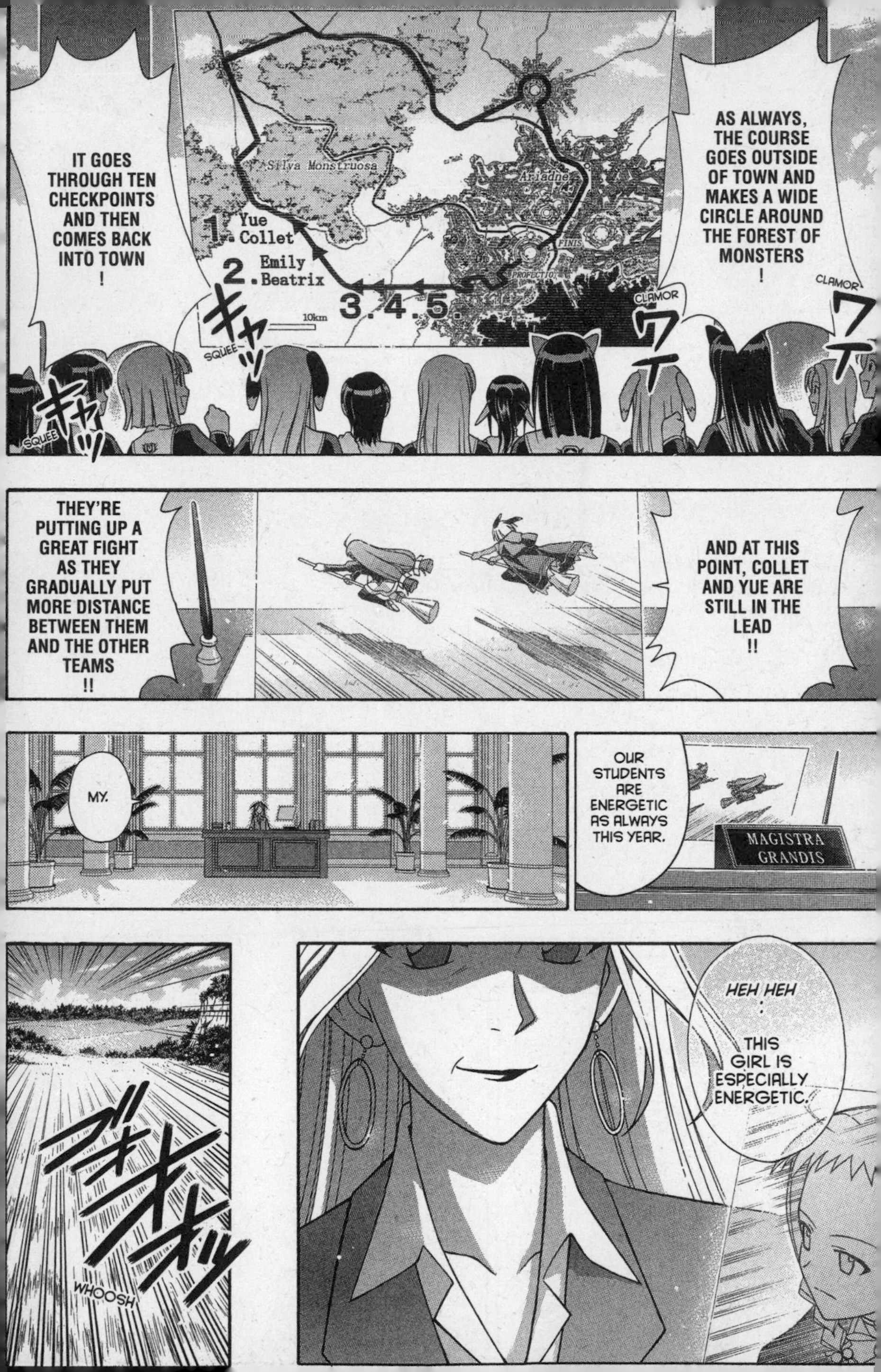

AS ALWAYS, THE COURSE GOES OUTSIDE OF TOWN AND MAKES A WIDE CIRCLE AROUND THE FOREST OF MONSTERS !
CLAMOR
CLAMOR
Ariadne
FINIS
Silva Monstruosa
1. Yue Collet
2. Emily Beatrix
3. 4. 5.
10km
IT GOES THROUGH TEN CHECKPOINTS AND THEN COMES BACK INTO TOWN !
SQUEE
SQUEE
AND AT THIS POINT, COLLET AND YUE ARE STILL IN THE LEAD !!
THEY'RE PUTTING UP A GREAT FIGHT AS THEY GRADUALLY PUT MORE DISTANCE BETWEEN THEM AND THE OTHER TEAMS !!
OUR STUDENTS ARE ENERGETIC AS ALWAYS THIS YEAR.
MAGISTRA GRANDIS
MY.
HEH HEH :
THIS GIRL IS ESPECIALLY ENERGETIC.
WHOOSH

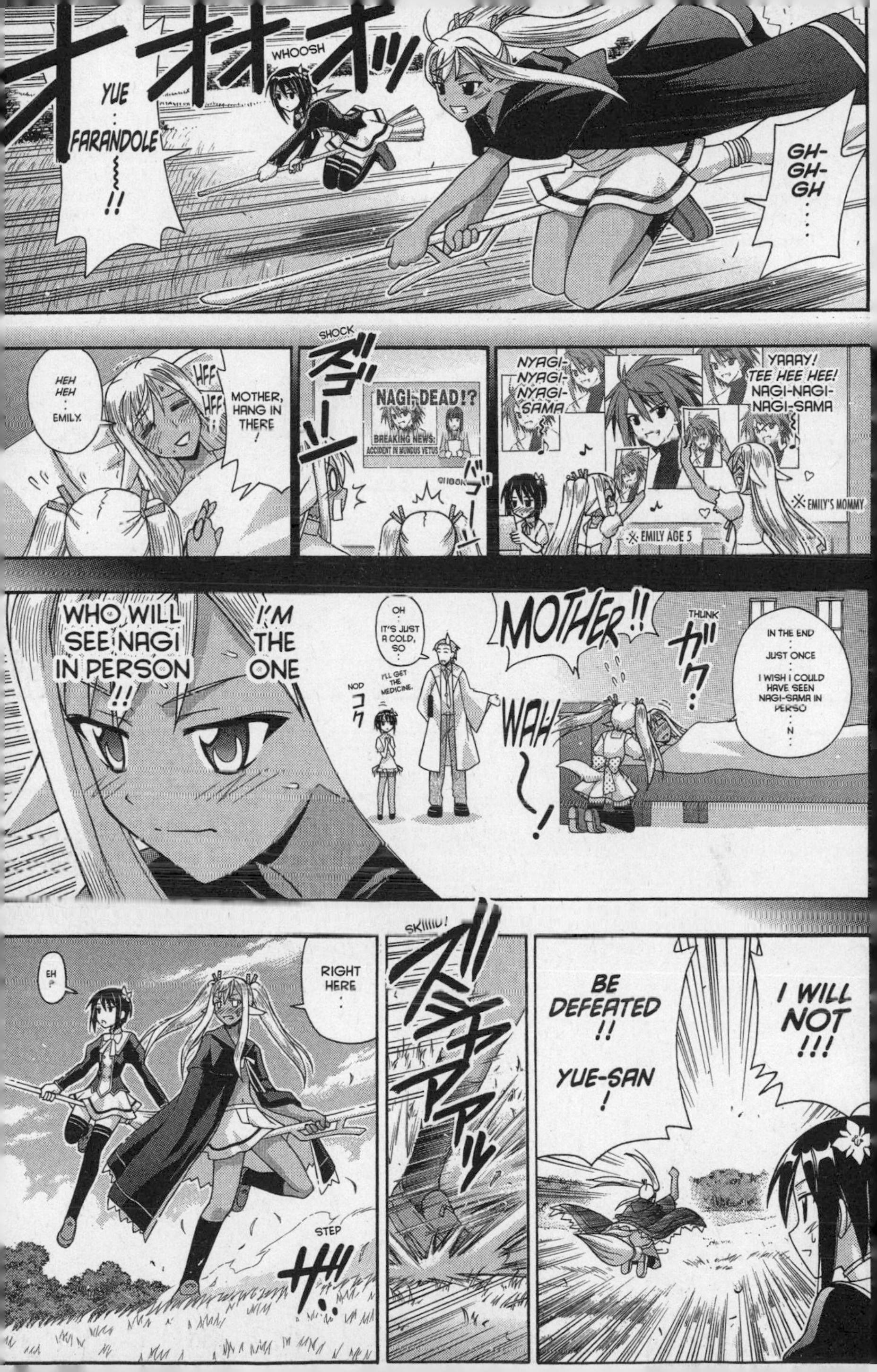
GH-
GH-
GH
. . . .
WHOOSH
YUE
. .
FARANDOLE
~~~
!!
YAAAY!
TEE HEE HEE!
NAGI-NAGI-
NAGI-SAMA
NYAGI-
NYAGI-
NYAGI-
SAMA
※EMILY'S MOMMY
※EMILY AGE 5
SHOCK
NAGI DEAD!?
BREAKING NEWS:
ACCIDENT IN MUNDUS VETUS
MOTHER,
HANG IN
THERE
!
HFF
HFF
HEH
HEH
. .
EMILY.
IN THE END
. .
JUST ONCE
. . .
I WISH I COULD
HAVE SEEN
NAGI-SAMA IN
PERSO
. . . N
. . .
THUNK
MOTHER!!
WAH
~
!
OH
. .
IT'S JUST
A COLD,
SO
. . .
I'LL GET
THE
MEDICINE.
NOD
I'M
THE
ONE
WHO WILL
SEE NAGI
IN PERSON
!!
I WILL
NOT
!!!
BE
DEFEATED
!!
YUE-SAN
!
SKIIID!
RIGHT
HERE
. . .
EH
?
STEP
~~~

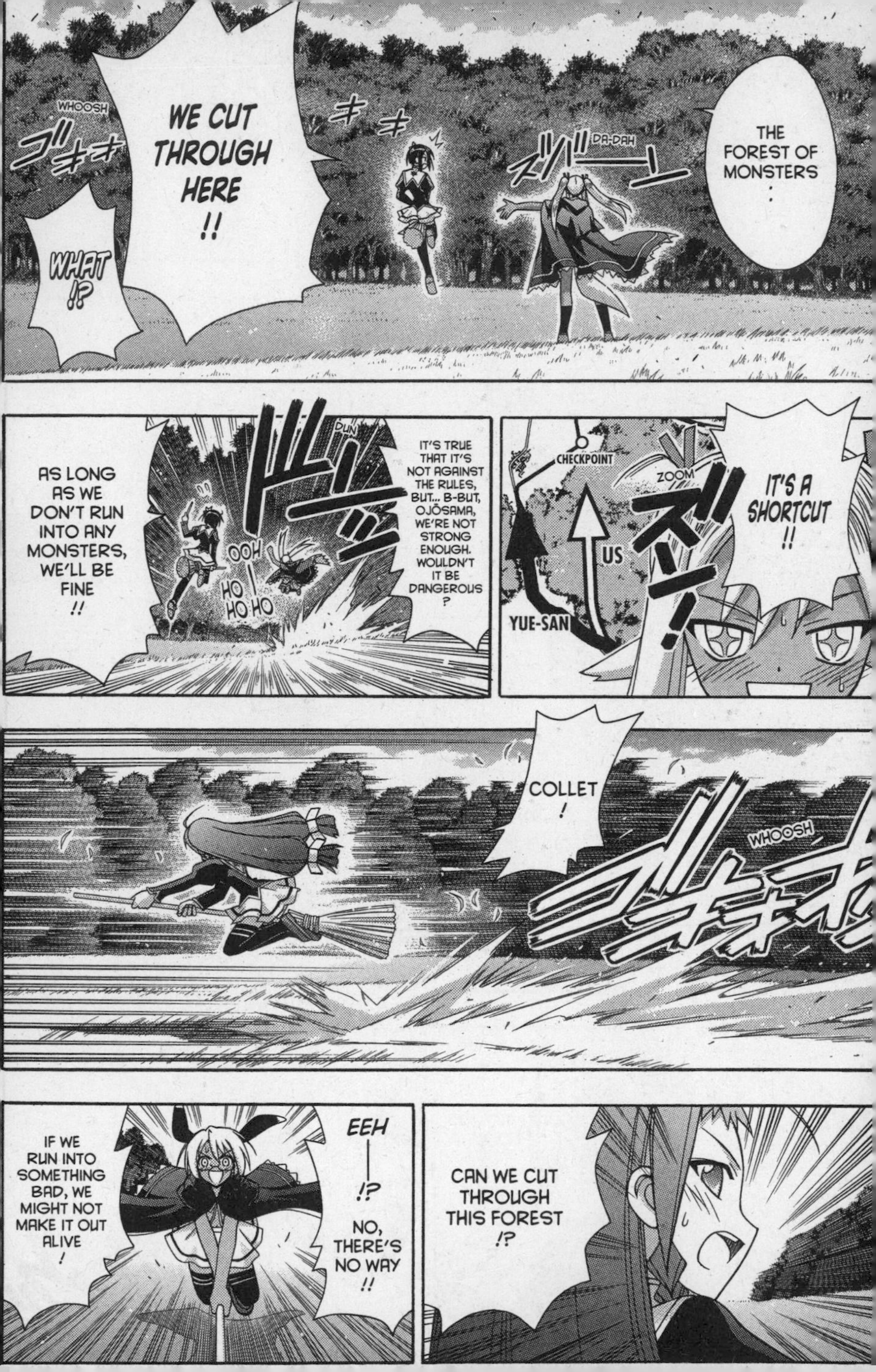
THE FOREST OF MONSTERS :
DA-DAH
WE CUT THROUGH HERE !!
WHOOSH
WHAT !?
IT'S A SHORTCUT !!
ZOOM
CHECKPOINT
US
YUE-SAN
IT'S TRUE THAT IT'S NOT AGAINST THE RULES, BUT... B-BUT, OJŌSAMA, WE'RE NOT STRONG ENOUGH. WOULDN'T IT BE DANGEROUS ?
DUN
OOH HO HO HO
AS LONG AS WE DON'T RUN INTO ANY MONSTERS, WE'LL BE FINE !!
COLLET !
WHOOSH
CAN WE CUT THROUGH THIS FOREST !?
EEH —— !?
NO, THERE'S NO WAY !!
IF WE RUN INTO SOMETHING BAD, WE MIGHT NOT MAKE IT OUT ALIVE !

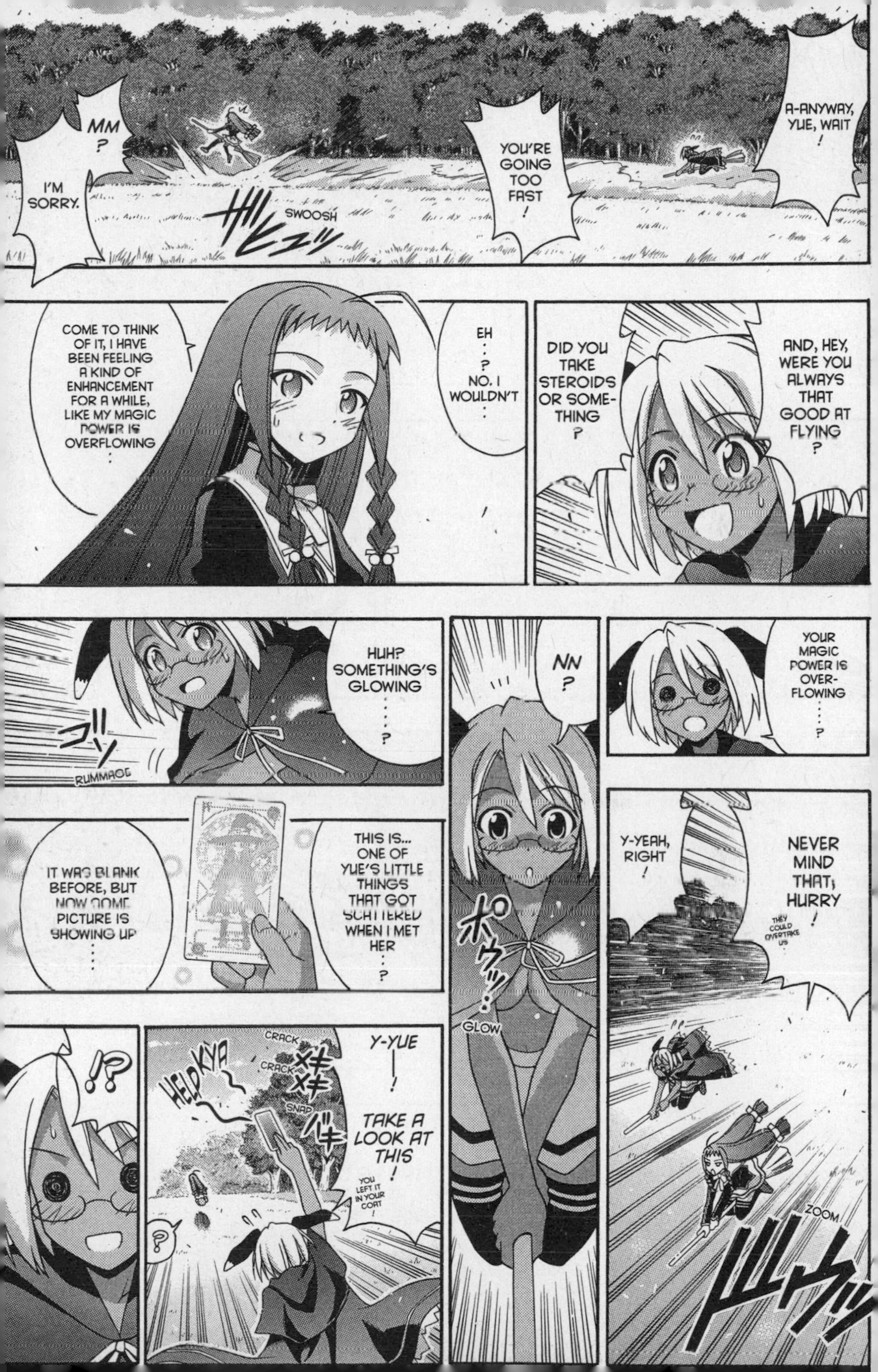
A-ANYWAY, YUE, WAIT!
YOU'RE GOING TOO FAST!
MM?
I'M SORRY.
SWOOSH
AND, HEY, WERE YOU ALWAYS THAT GOOD AT FLYING?
DID YOU TAKE STEROIDS OR SOME-THING?
EH...? NO. I WOULDN'T...
COME TO THINK OF IT, I HAVE BEEN FEELING A KIND OF ENHANCEMENT FOR A WHILE, LIKE MY MAGIC POWER IS OVERFLOWING...
YOUR MAGIC POWER IS OVER-FLOWING....?
NEVER MIND THAT, HURRY!
THEY COULD OVERTAKE US
Y-YEAH, RIGHT!
ZOOM
NN?
GLOW
HUH? SOMETHING'S GLOWING....?
RUMMAGE
THIS IS... ONE OF YUE'S LITTLE THINGS THAT GOT SCATTERED WHEN I MET HER...?
IT WAS BLANK BEFORE, BUT NOW SOME PICTURE IS SHOWING UP....
Y-YUE! TAKE A LOOK AT THIS!
YOU LEFT IT IN YOUR COAT!
CRACK
CRACK
SNAP
HELP
KYA~
!?

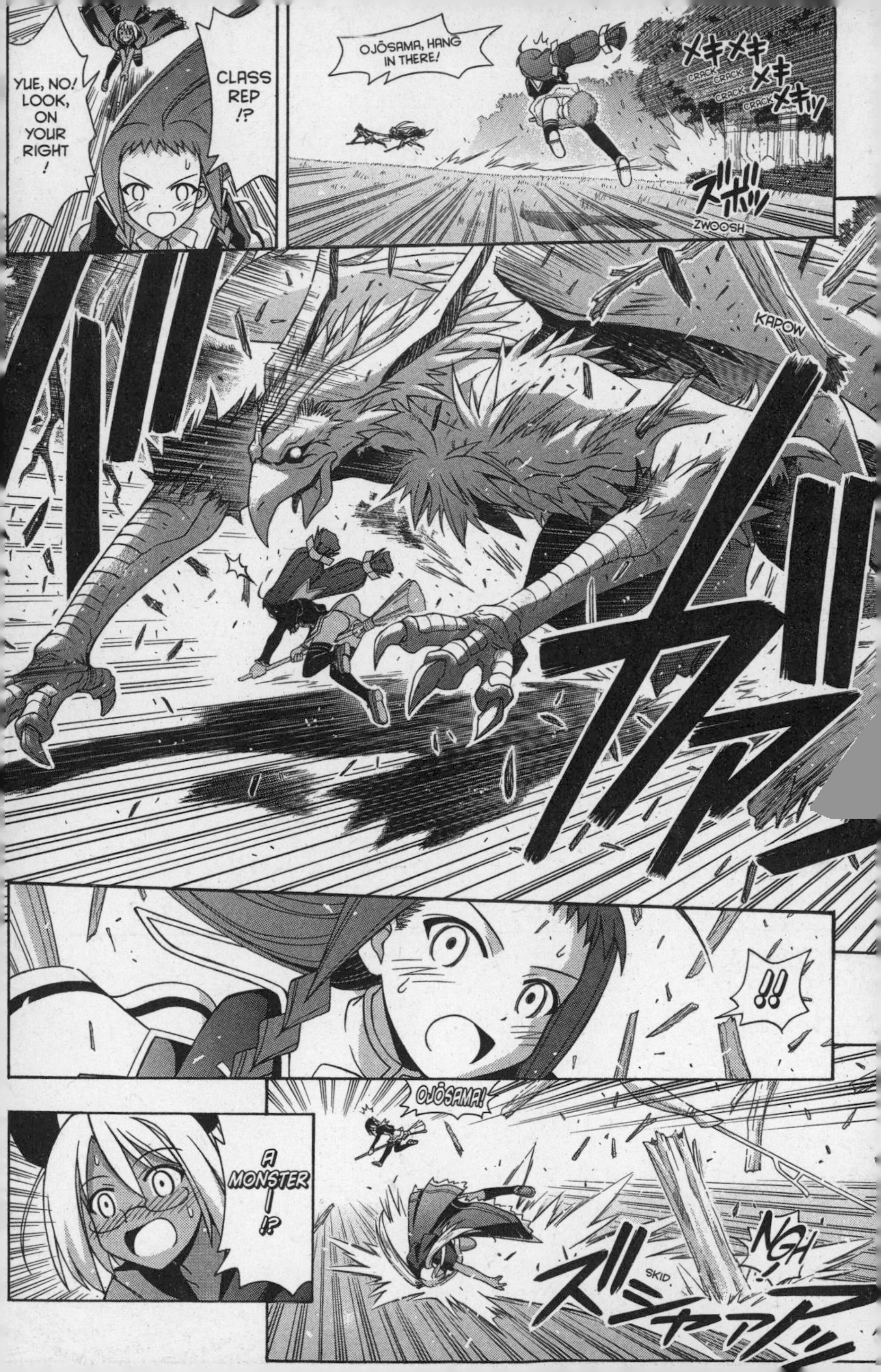
OJŌSAMA, HANG IN THERE!
メキメキメキメキッ
CRACK CRACK CRACK CRACK
ズボッ
ZWOOSH
CLASS REP !?
YUE, NO! LOOK, ON YOUR RIGHT!
KAPOW
!!
OJŌSAMA!
NGH
SKID
A MONSTER—!?

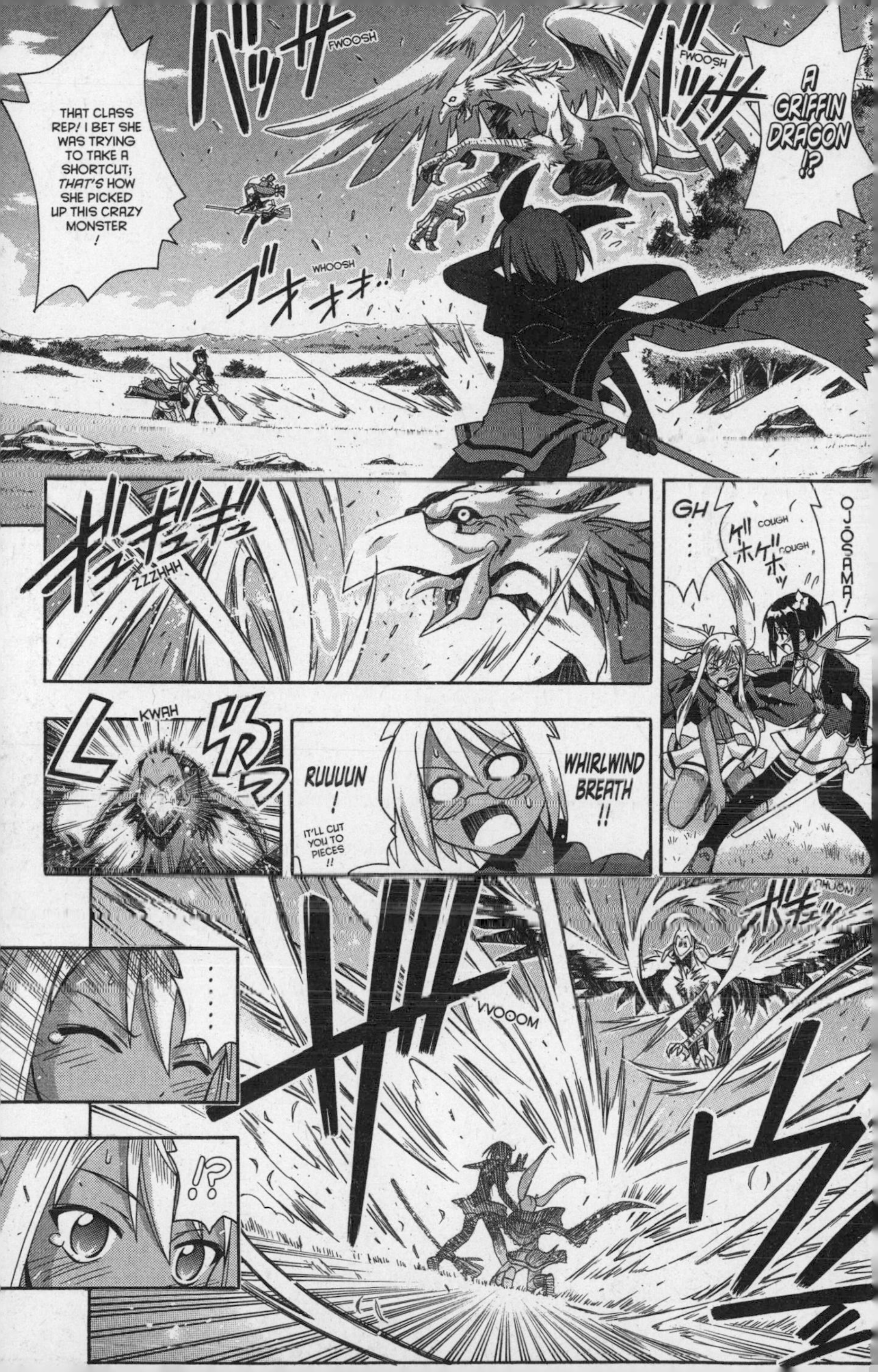
A GRIFFIN DRAGON !?
バッサ
FWOOSH
バッサ
FWOOSH
THAT CLASS REP! I BET SHE WAS TRYING TO TAKE A SHORTCUT; THAT'S HOW SHE PICKED UP THIS CRAZY MONSTER !
ゴオオオ…
WHOOSH
O-JŌSAMA!
GH ...
ゲホゲホッ
COUGH
COUGH
ZZZHHH
WHIRLWIND BREATH !!
RUUUUN !
IT'LL CUT YOU TO PIECES !!
KWAH
VVOOOM
......
!?

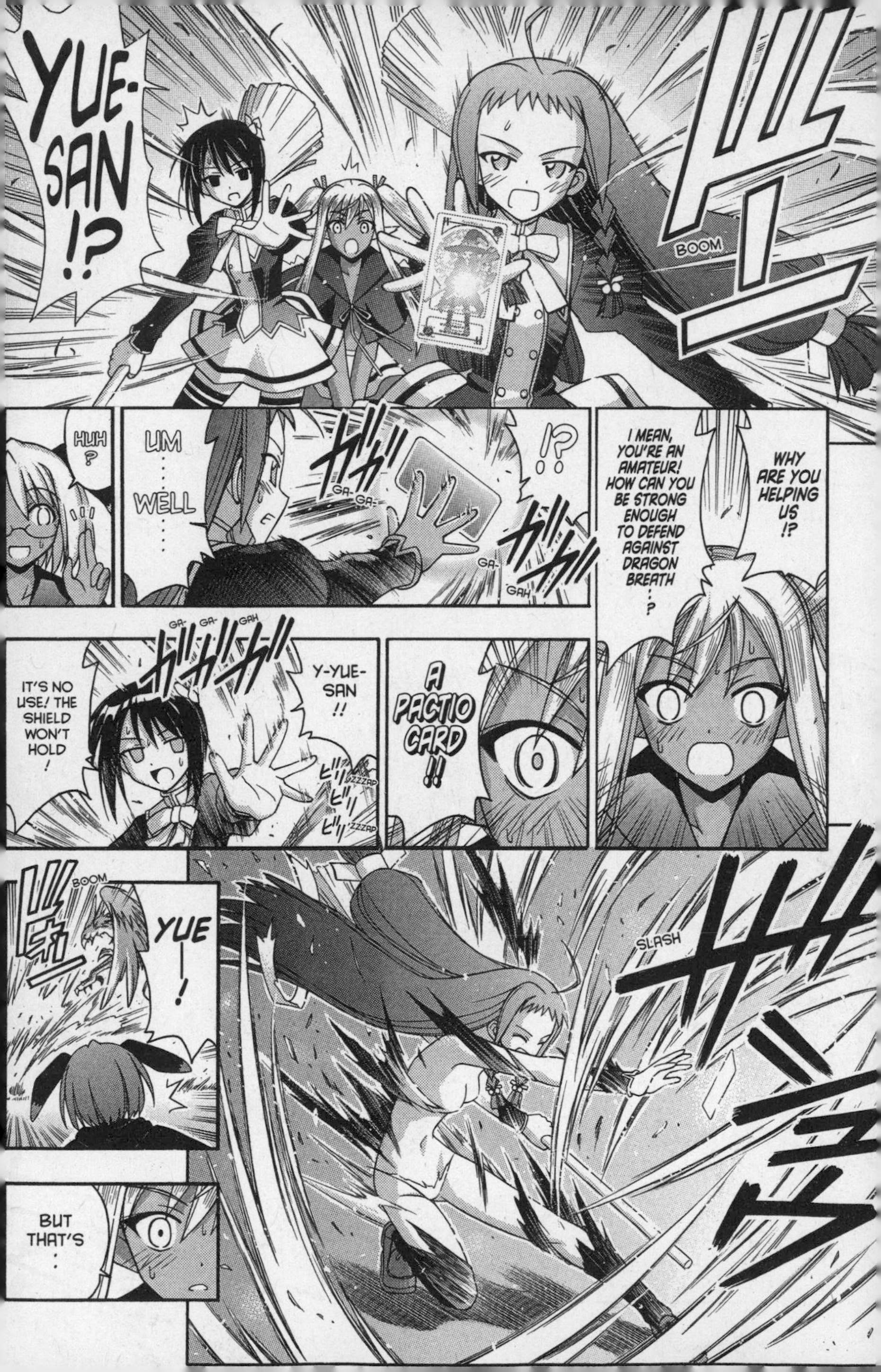
BOOM
YUE-SAN !?
WHY ARE YOU HELPING US !?
I MEAN, YOU'RE AN AMATEUR! HOW CAN YOU BE STRONG ENOUGH TO DEFEND AGAINST DRAGON BREATH...?
!?
GA-GA-
GA-GAH
UM... WELL...
HUH ?
A PACTIO CARD !!
Y-YUE-SAN !!
ZZZAP
ZZZAP
GA-GA-GAH
IT'S NO USE! THE SHIELD WON'T HOLD!
SLASH
BOOM
YUE—!
BUT THAT'S...

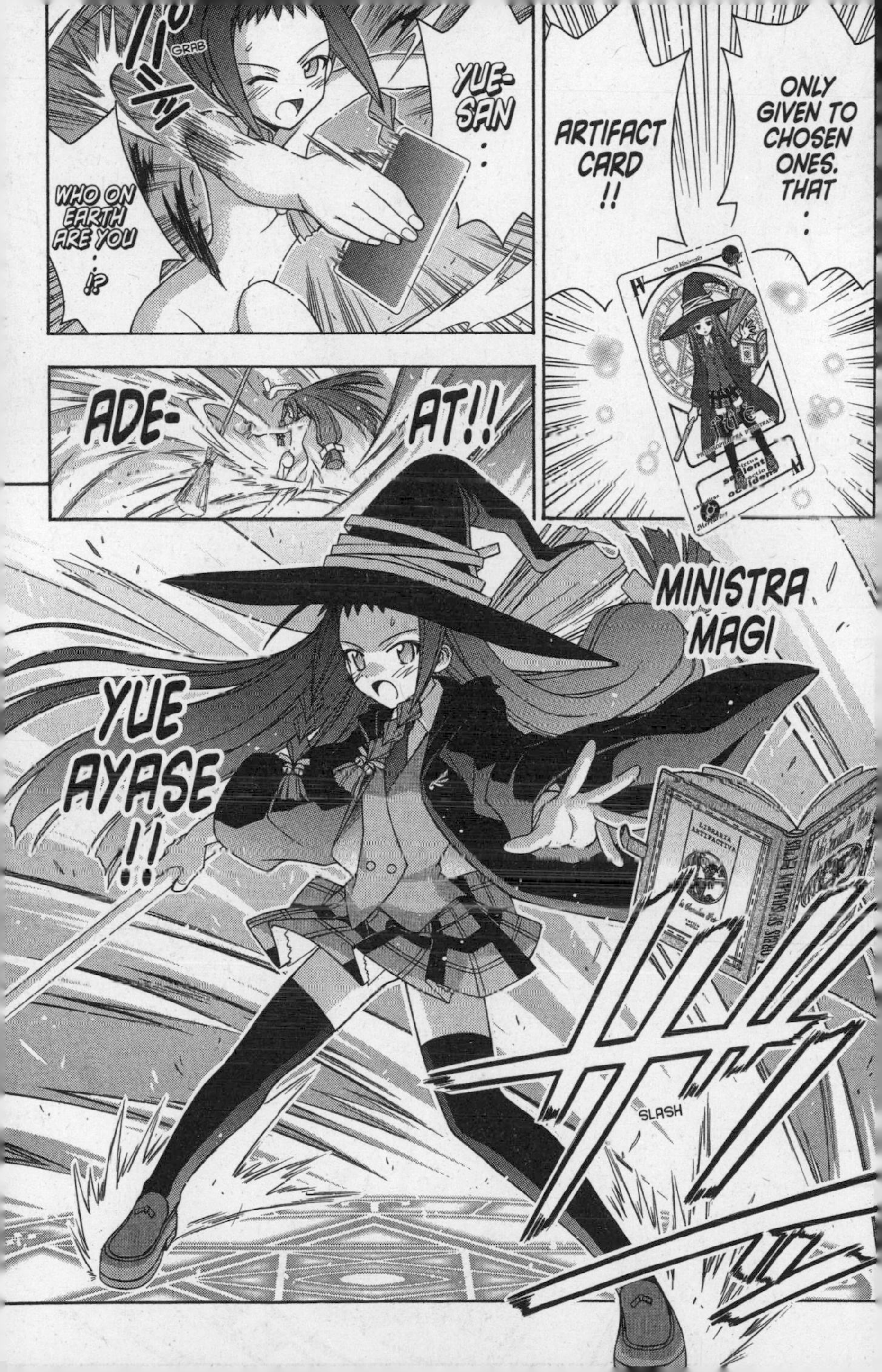
ONLY GIVEN TO CHOSEN ONES. THAT :
ARTIFACT CARD !!
GRAB
YUE-SAN :
WHO ON EARTH ARE YOU :!?
ADE-
AT!!
MINISTRA MAGI
YUE AYASE!!
SLASH

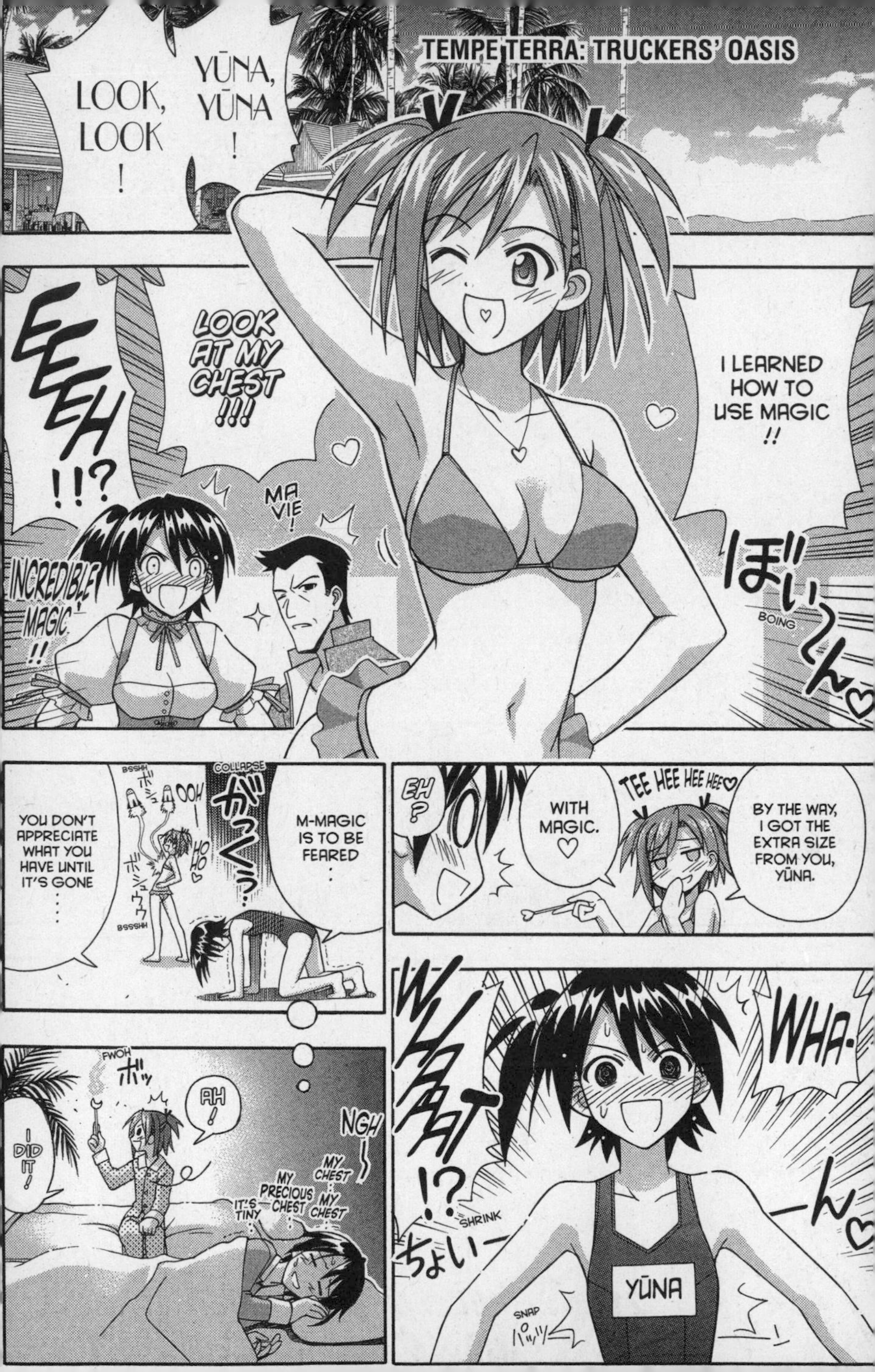
TEMPE TERRA: TRUCKERS' OASIS
YŪNA, YŪNA!
LOOK, LOOK!
I LEARNED HOW TO USE MAGIC!!
ぼいーん♡
BOING
LOOK AT MY CHEST!!!
MA VIE!
EEEEH!!?
INCREDIBLE MAGIC!!
BY THE WAY, I GOT THE EXTRA SIZE FROM YOU, YŪNA.
TEE HEE HEE HEE♡
WITH MAGIC. ♡
EH?
M-MAGIC IS TO BE FEARED...
がっくう
COLLAPSE
OOH HO HO
ボシュ
BSSHH
ボシュウウ
BSSSHH
YOU DON'T APPRECIATE WHAT YOU HAVE UNTIL IT'S GONE...
WHA-
ーん♡
WHAAAT!!?
ちょいー
SHRINK
YŪNA
パッ
SNAP
NGH~
MY CHEST... MY CHEST
MY PRECIOUS CHEST
IT'S TINY
AH!
ボッ
FWOH
I DID IT!

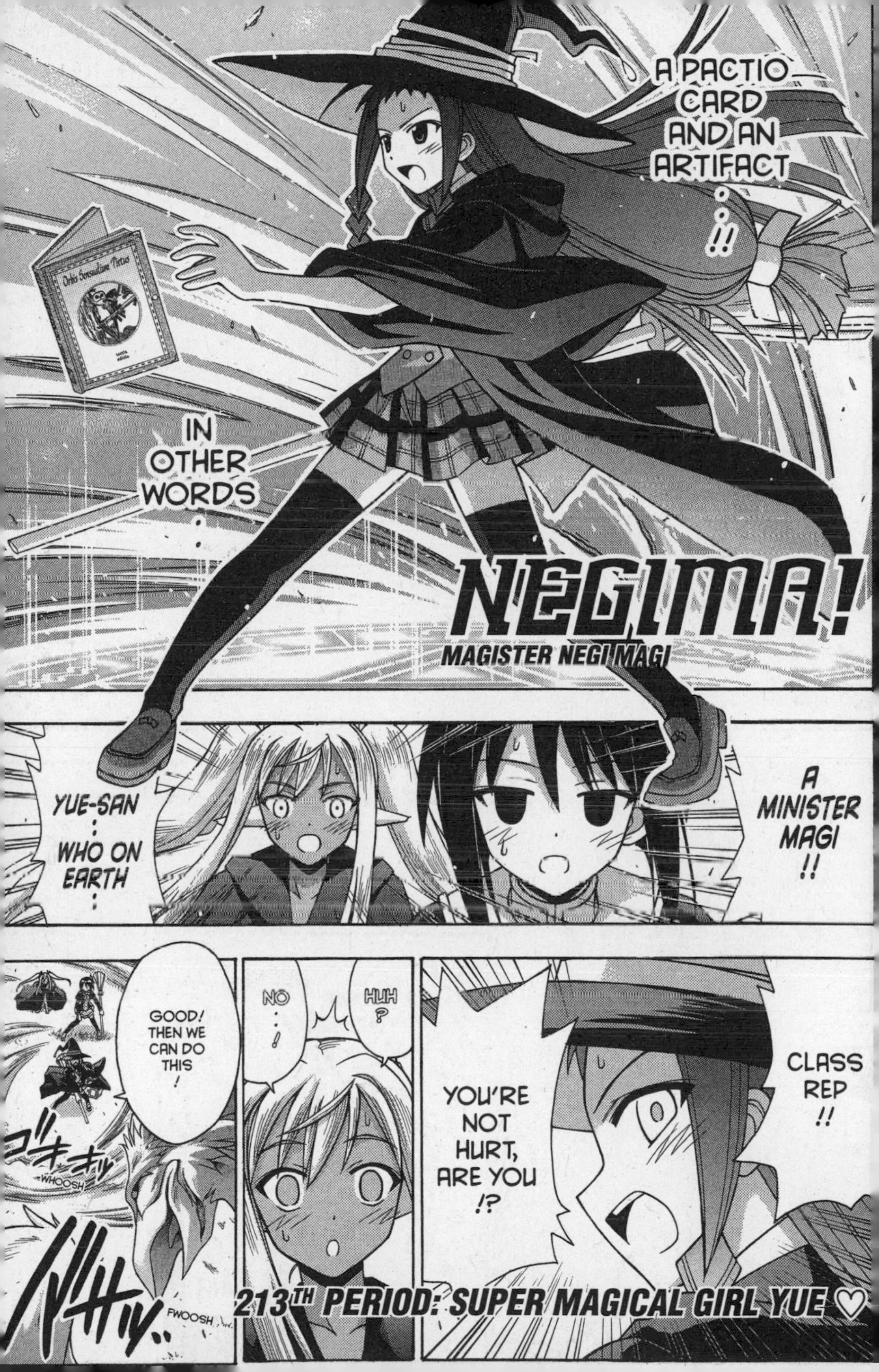
A PACTIO CARD AND AN ARTIFACT . . . !!
IN OTHER WORDS . . .
NEGIMA!
MAGISTER NEGI MAGI
A MINISTER MAGI !!
YUE-SAN . . . WHO ON EARTH . . .
CLASS REP !!
YOU'RE NOT HURT, ARE YOU !?
HUH ?
NO . . . !
GOOD! THEN WE CAN DO THIS !
WHOOSH
FWOOSH
213TH PERIOD: SUPER MAGICAL GIRL YUE ♡

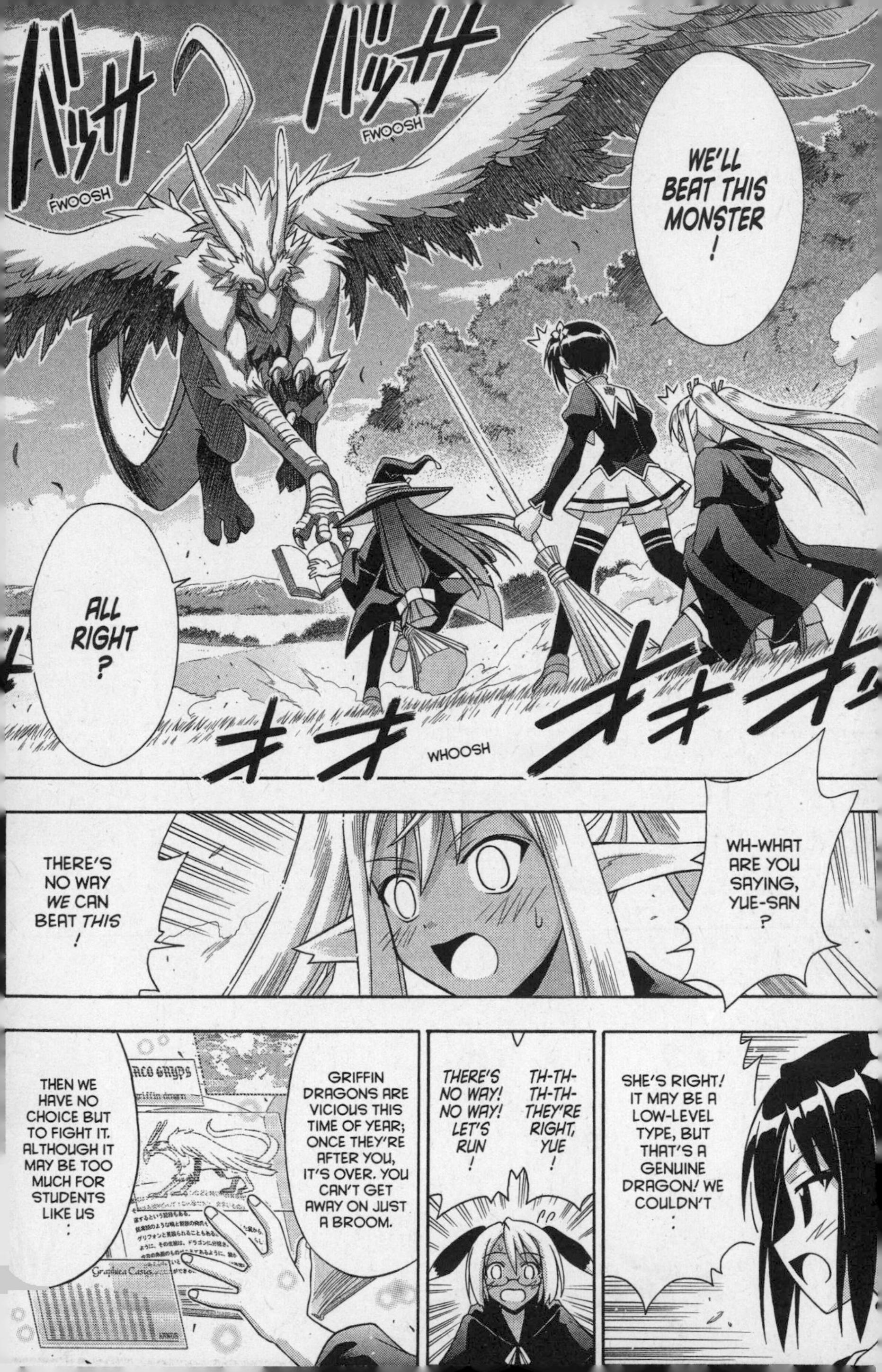
WE'LL BEAT THIS MONSTER!
バッサ
FWOOSH
バッサ
FWOOSH
ALL RIGHT?
WHOOSH
WH-WHAT ARE YOU SAYING, YUE-SAN?
THERE'S NO WAY *WE* CAN BEAT *THIS*!
SHE'S RIGHT! IT MAY BE A LOW-LEVEL TYPE, BUT THAT'S A GENUINE DRAGON! WE COULDN'T...
TH-TH-TH-TH-THEY'RE RIGHT, YUE!
THERE'S NO WAY! NO WAY! LET'S RUN!
GRIFFIN DRAGONS ARE VICIOUS THIS TIME OF YEAR; ONCE THEY'RE AFTER YOU, IT'S OVER. YOU CAN'T GET AWAY ON JUST A BROOM.
THEN WE HAVE NO CHOICE BUT TO FIGHT IT. ALTHOUGH IT MAY BE TOO MUCH FOR STUDENTS LIKE US...

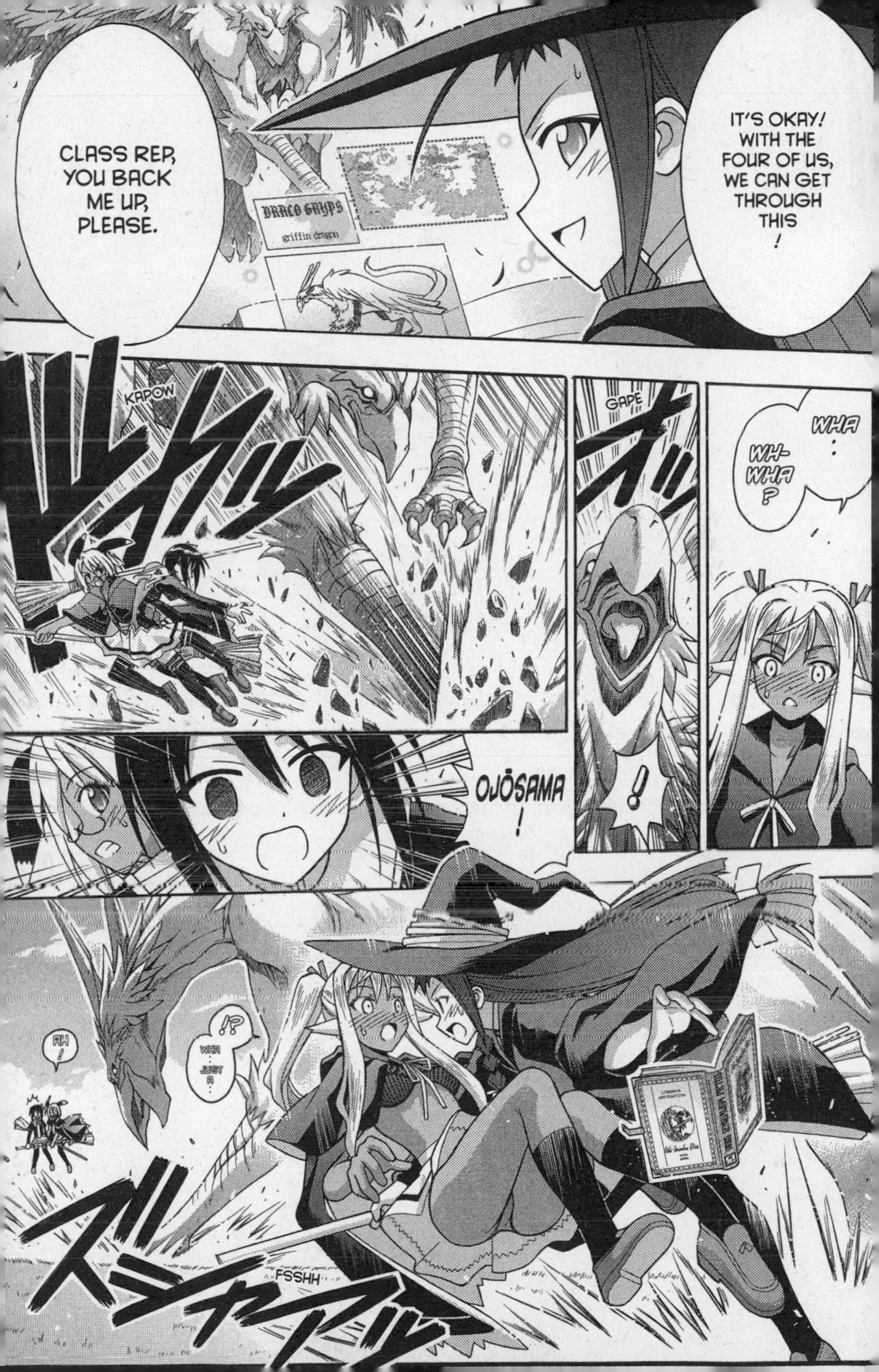
IT'S OKAY! WITH THE FOUR OF US, WE CAN GET THROUGH THIS!
DRACO GRYPS
griffin dragon
CLASS REP, YOU BACK ME UP, PLEASE.
WHA :
WH-WHA ?
GAPE
!
KAPOW
OJŌSAMA !
!?
WHA... JUST A...
AH !
FSSHH

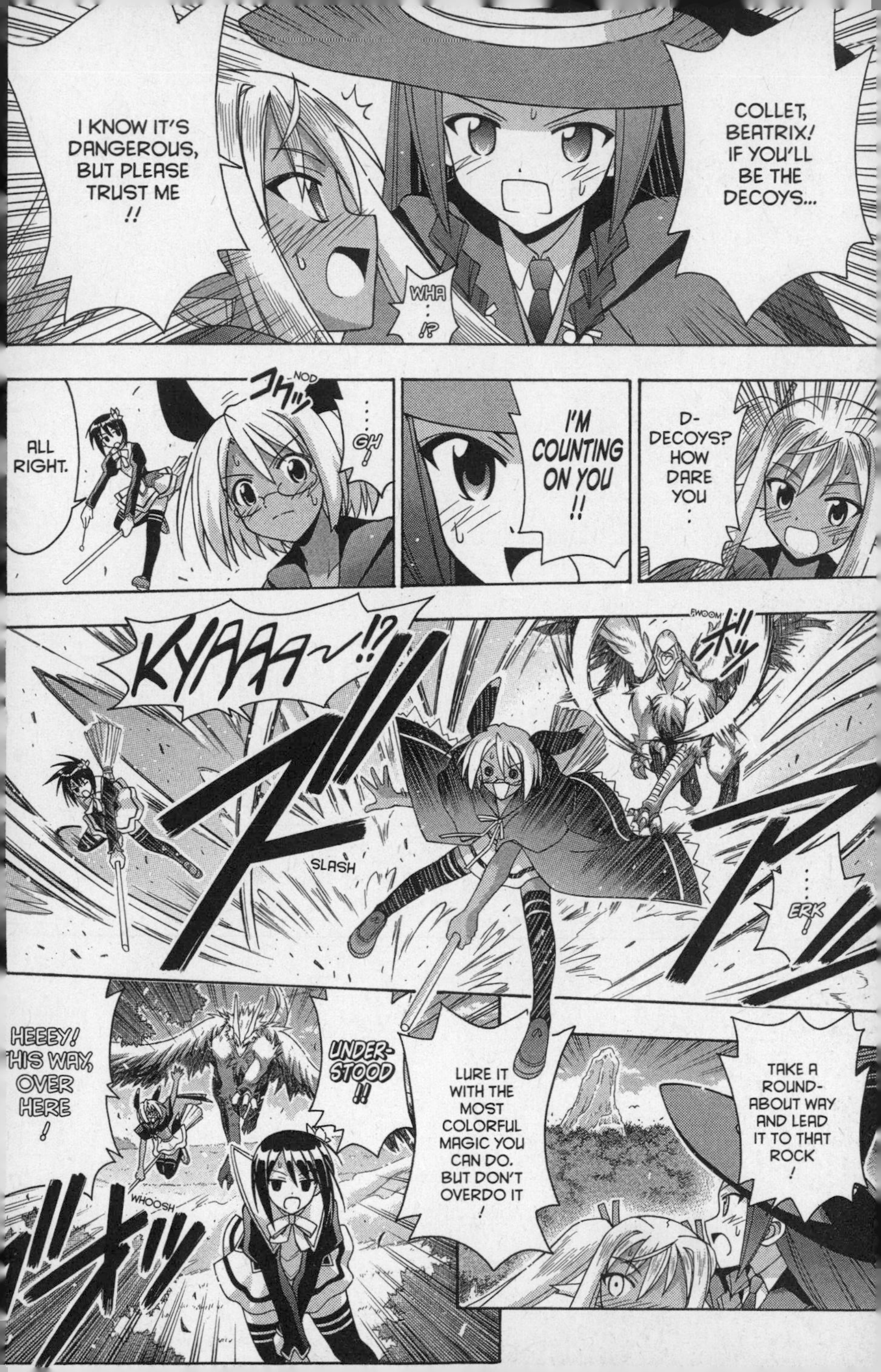
COLLET, BEATRIX! IF YOU'LL BE THE DECOYS...
WHA...!?
I KNOW IT'S DANGEROUS, BUT PLEASE TRUST ME!!
D-DECOYS? HOW DARE YOU...
I'M COUNTING ON YOU!!
NOD
...GH!
ALL RIGHT.
FWOOM
...ERK!
KYAAA~!!?
SLASH
TAKE A ROUND-ABOUT WAY AND LEAD IT TO THAT ROCK!
LURE IT WITH THE MOST COLORFUL MAGIC YOU CAN DO. BUT DON'T OVERDO IT!
UNDER-STOOD!!
HEEEY! THIS WAY, OVER HERE!
WHOOSH

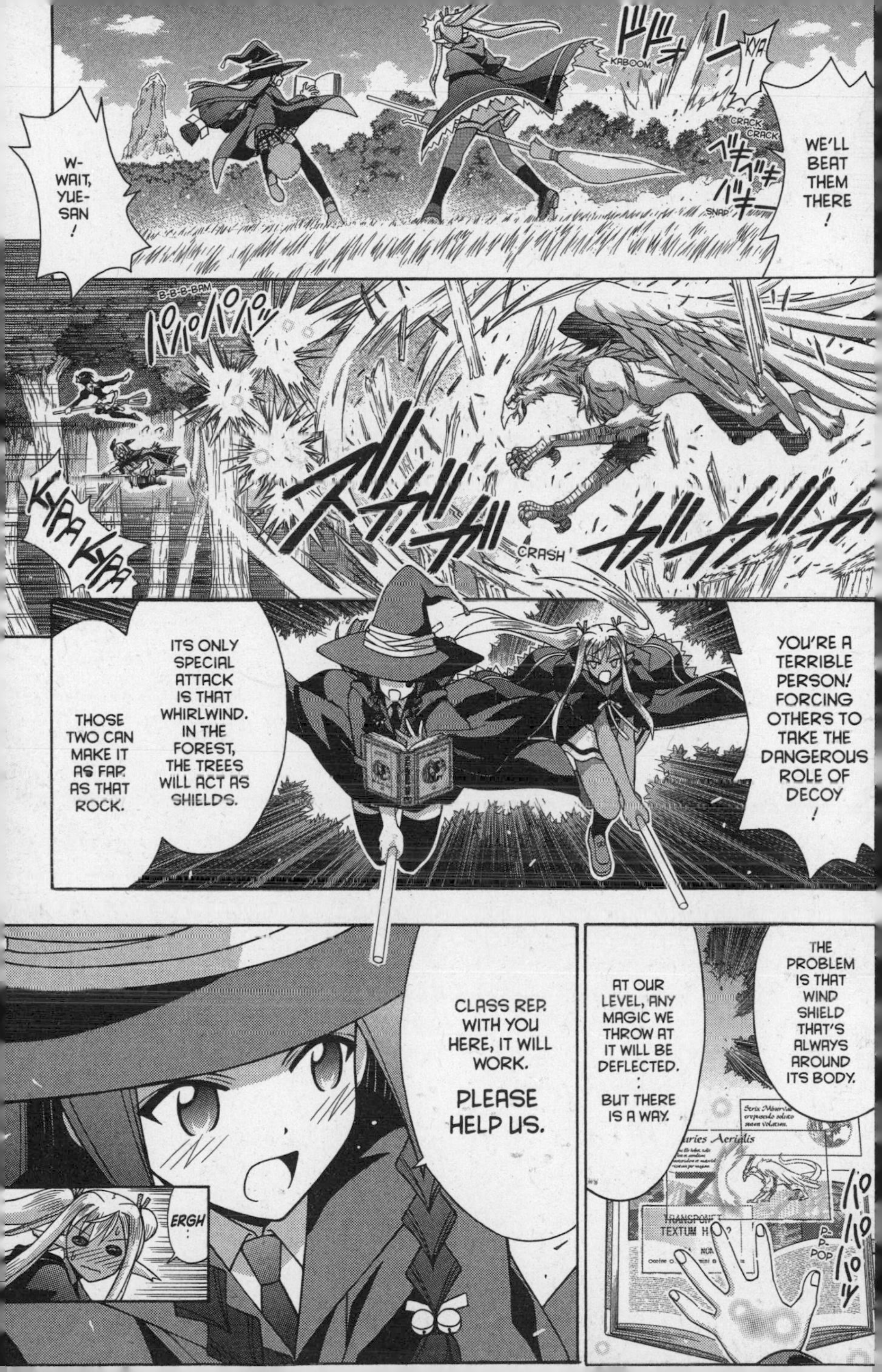
WE'LL BEAT THEM THERE!
KYA!
KABOOM
CRACK CRACK
SNAP
W-WAIT, YUE-SAN!
B-B-B-BAM
CRASH
KYAA KYAA
YOU'RE A TERRIBLE PERSON! FORCING OTHERS TO TAKE THE DANGEROUS ROLE OF DECOY!
ITS ONLY SPECIAL ATTACK IS THAT WHIRLWIND. IN THE FOREST, THE TREES WILL ACT AS SHIELDS.
THOSE TWO CAN MAKE IT AS FAR AS THAT ROCK.
THE PROBLEM IS THAT WIND SHIELD THAT'S ALWAYS AROUND ITS BODY.
P-P-POP
AT OUR LEVEL, ANY MAGIC WE THROW AT IT WILL BE DEFLECTED.
: BUT THERE IS A WAY.
CLASS REP. WITH YOU HERE, IT WILL WORK.
PLEASE HELP US.
ERGH...

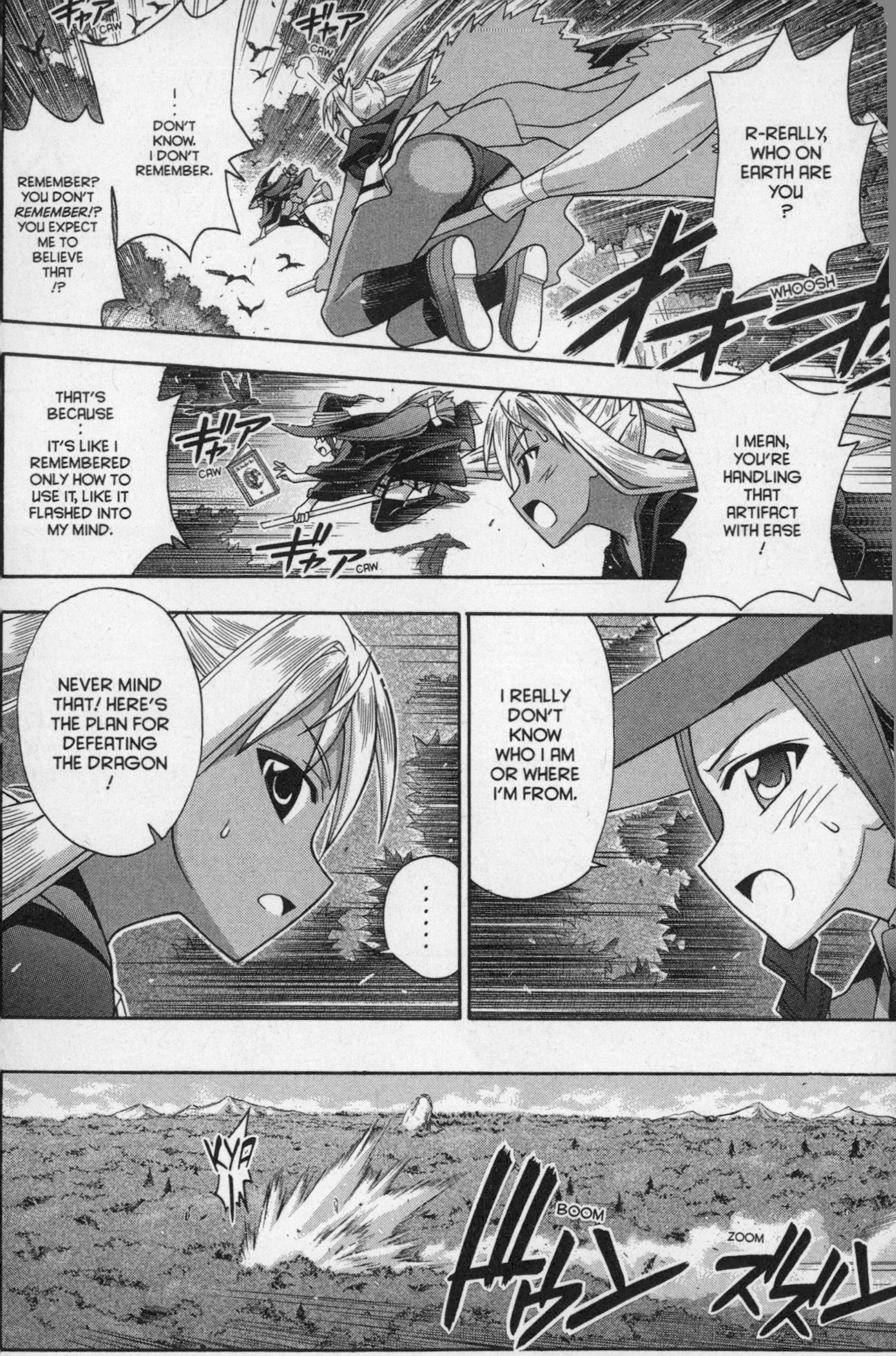
R-REALLY, WHO ON EARTH ARE YOU?
WHOOSH
...DON'T KNOW. I DON'T REMEMBER.
REMEMBER? YOU DON'T *REMEMBER!?* YOU EXPECT ME TO BELIEVE THAT!?
CAW
CAW
I MEAN, YOU'RE HANDLING THAT ARTIFACT WITH EASE!
THAT'S BECAUSE... IT'S LIKE I REMEMBERED ONLY HOW TO USE IT, LIKE IT FLASHED INTO MY MIND.
CAW
CAW
I REALLY DON'T KNOW WHO I AM OR WHERE I'M FROM.
......
NEVER MIND THAT! HERE'S THE PLAN FOR DEFEATING THE DRAGON!
ZOOM
BOOM
KYA!

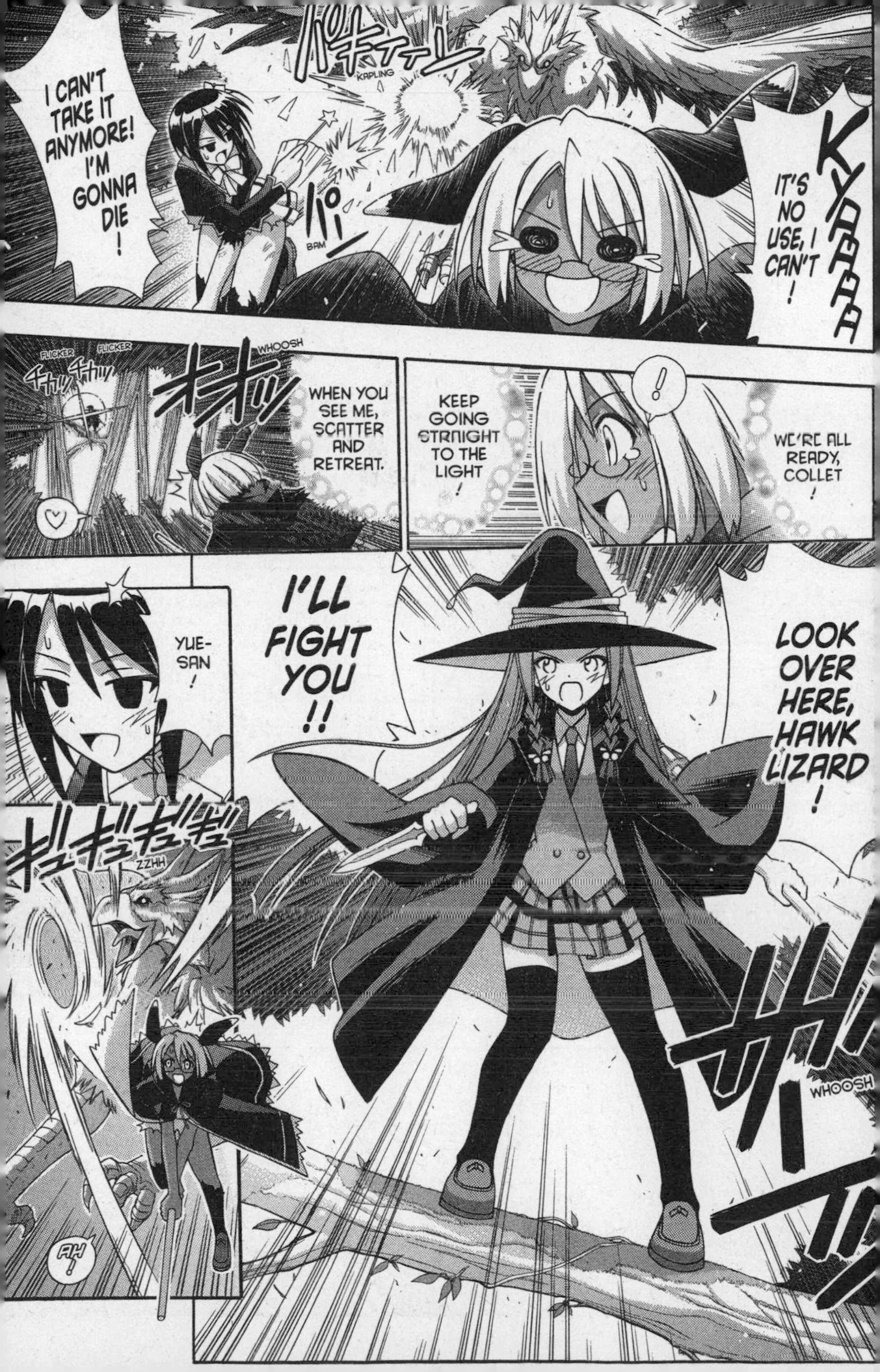

KYAAAAA
IT'S NO USE, I CAN'T!
KAPLING
BAM
I CAN'T TAKE IT ANYMORE! I'M GONNA DIE!
!
WE'RE ALL READY, COLLET!
KEEP GOING STRAIGHT TO THE LIGHT!
WHOOSH
WHEN YOU SEE ME, SCATTER AND RETREAT.
FLICKER
FLICKER
LOOK OVER HERE, HAWK LIZARD!
I'LL FIGHT YOU!!
WHOOSH
YUE-SAN!
ZZHH
AH!

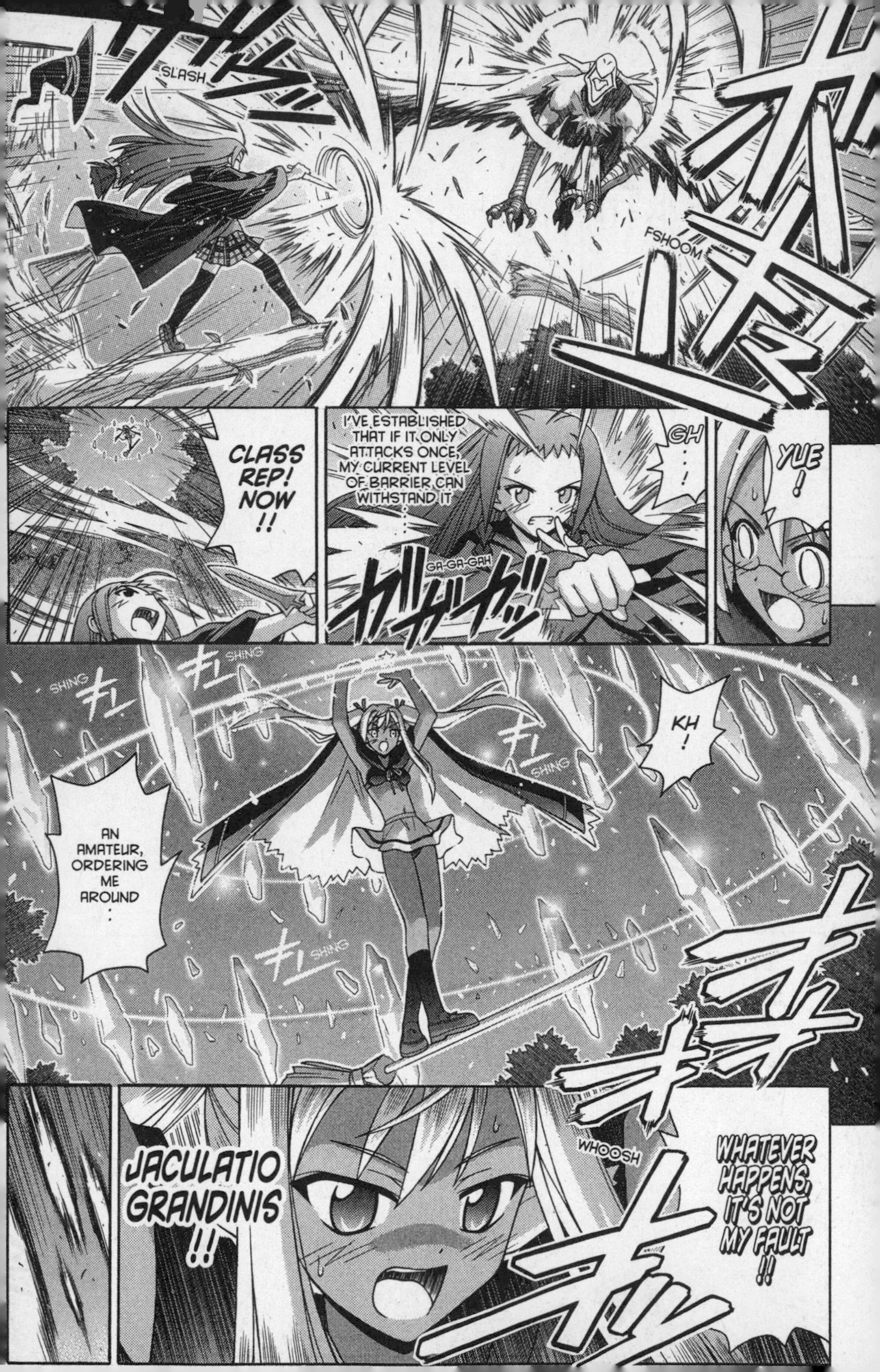
SLASH
FSHOOM
YUE
!
GH
. . !
I'VE ESTABLISHED THAT IF IT ONLY ATTACKS ONCE, MY CURRENT LEVEL OF BARRIER CAN WITHSTAND IT
. . .
GA-GA-GAH
CLASS REP! NOW !!
KH
!
SHING
SHING
SHING
SHING
AN AMATEUR, ORDERING ME AROUND
. . .
WHATEVER HAPPENS, IT'S NOT MY FAULT
!!
WHOOSH
JACULATIO GRANDINIS
!!

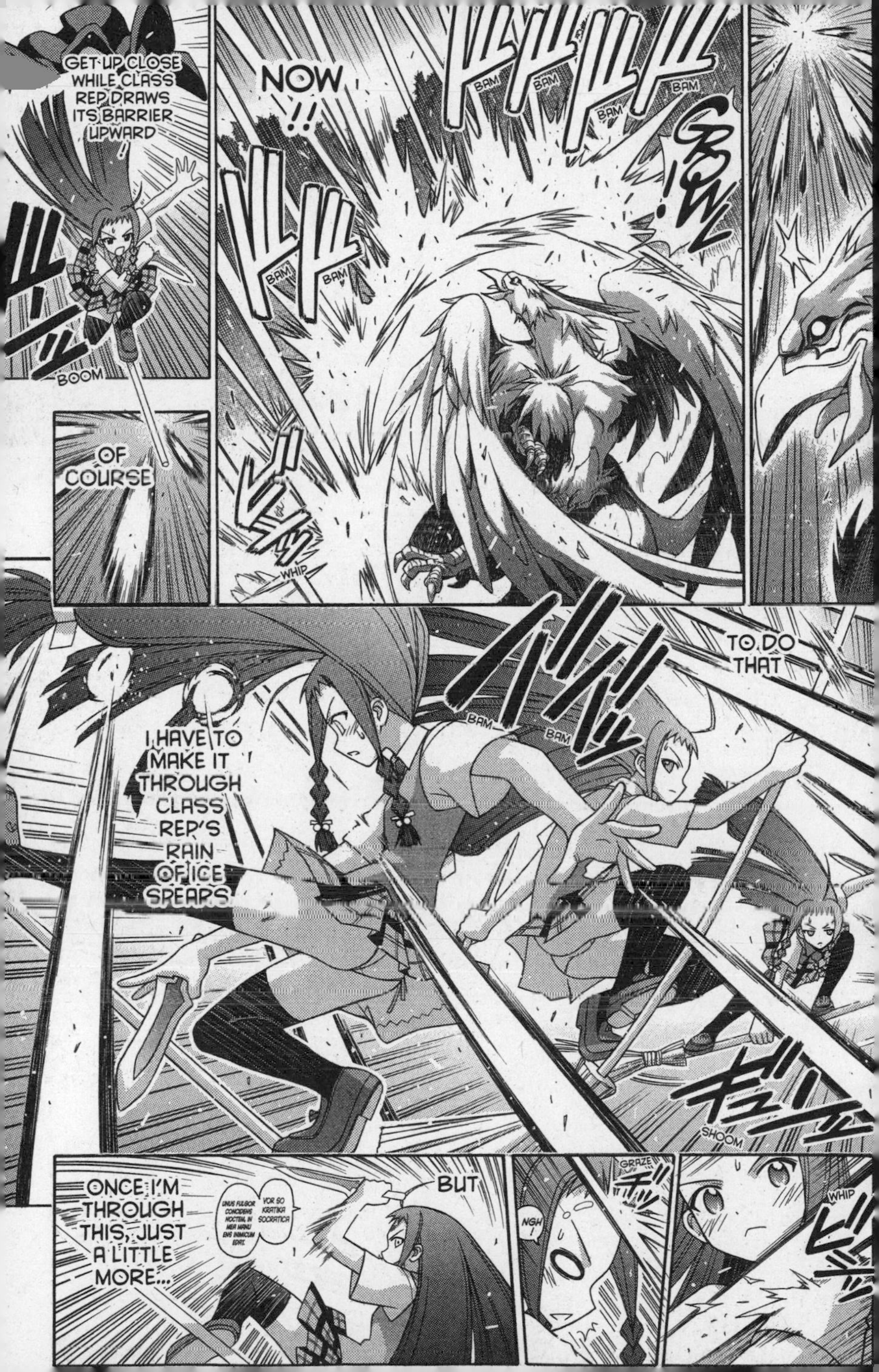
GROWL!
BAM
BAM
BAM
BAM
NOW!!
BAM
BAM
WHIP
GET UP CLOSE WHILE CLASS REP DRAWS ITS BARRIER UPWARD!
BOOM
OF COURSE
TO DO THAT
BAM
BAM
I HAVE TO MAKE IT THROUGH CLASS REP'S RAIN OF ICE SPEARS
SHOOM
WHIP
GRAZE
NGH!
BUT
VOR SO KRATIKA SOCRATICA
UNUS FULGOR CONCIDENS NOCTEM, IN MEA MANU ENS INIMICUM EDAT.
ONCE I'M THROUGH THIS, JUST A LITTLE MORE...

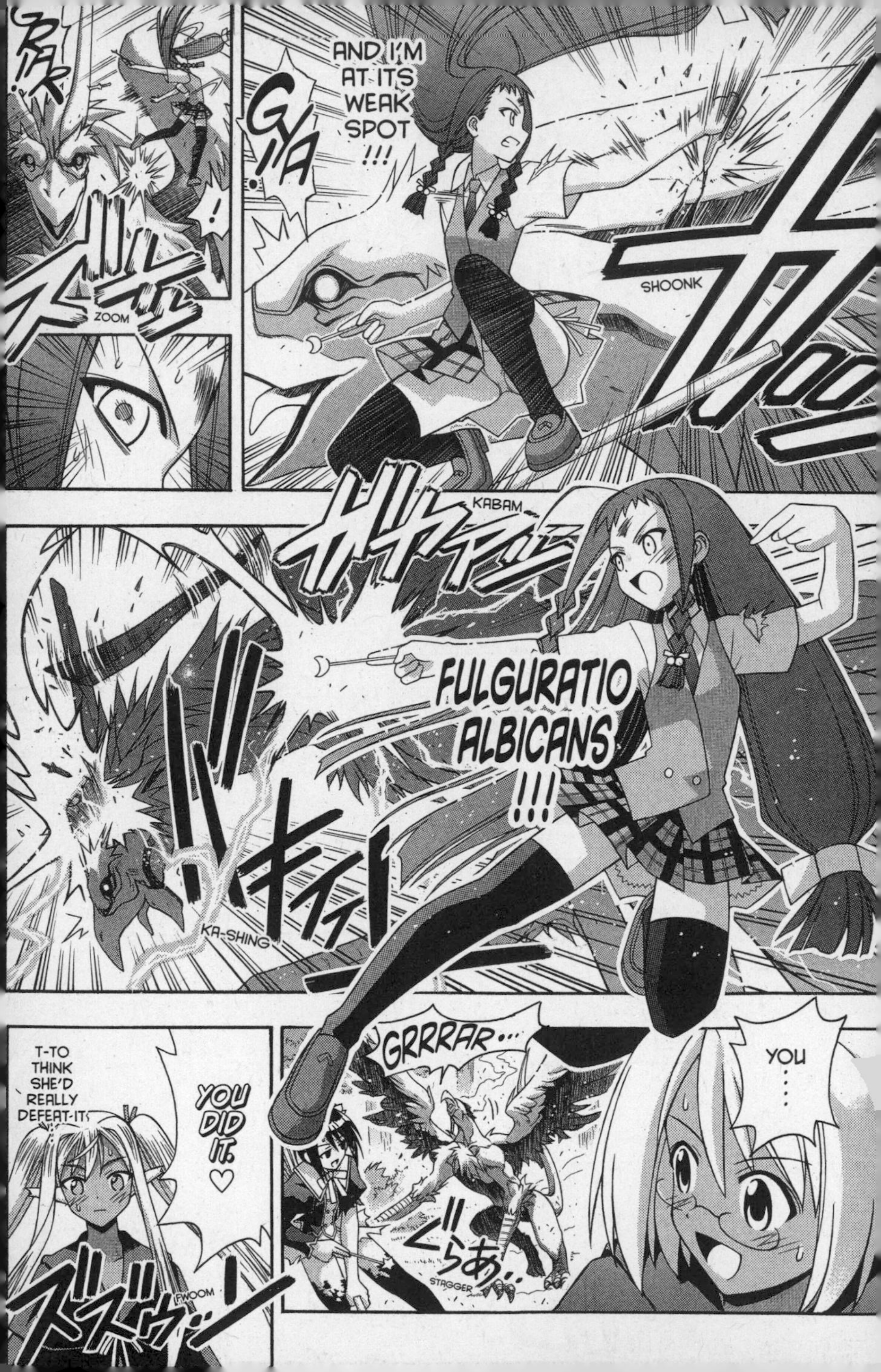
AND I'M AT ITS WEAK SPOT !!!
GYA
SHOONK
ZOOM
KABAM
FULGURATIO ALBICANS !!!
KA-SHING
YOU ....
GRRRAR...
STAGGER
T-TO THINK SHE'D REALLY DEFEAT IT
YOU DID IT. ♥
FWOOM

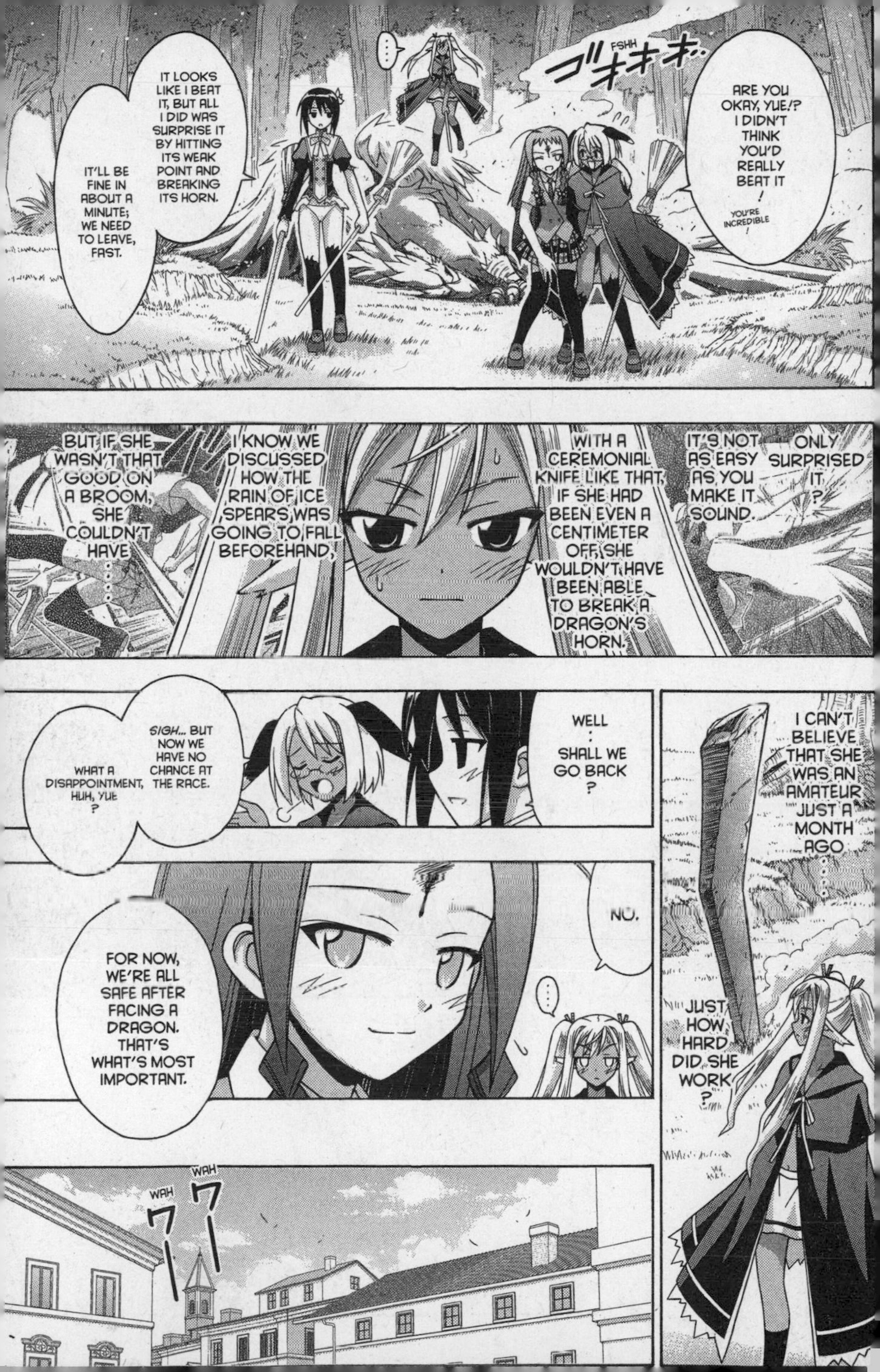
FSHH
ARE YOU OKAY, YUE!? I DIDN'T THINK YOU'D REALLY BEAT IT!
YOU'RE INCREDIBLE!
...
IT LOOKS LIKE I BEAT IT, BUT ALL I DID WAS SURPRISE IT BY HITTING ITS WEAK POINT AND BREAKING ITS HORN.
IT'LL BE FINE IN ABOUT A MINUTE; WE NEED TO LEAVE, FAST.
ONLY SURPRISED IT?
IT'S NOT AS EASY AS YOU MAKE IT SOUND.
WITH A CEREMONIAL KNIFE LIKE THAT, IF SHE HAD BEEN EVEN A CENTIMETER OFF, SHE WOULDN'T HAVE BEEN ABLE TO BREAK A DRAGON'S HORN.
I KNOW WE DISCUSSED HOW THE RAIN OF ICE SPEARS WAS GOING TO FALL BEFOREHAND,
BUT IF SHE WASN'T THAT GOOD ON A BROOM, SHE COULDN'T HAVE......
I CAN'T BELIEVE THAT SHE WAS AN AMATEUR JUST A MONTH AGO...
JUST HOW HARD DID SHE WORK?
WELL: SHALL WE GO BACK?
SIGH... BUT NOW WE HAVE NO CHANCE AT THE RACE.
WHAT A DISAPPOINTMENT, HUH, YUE?
NO.
...
FOR NOW, WE'RE ALL SAFE AFTER FACING A DRAGON. THAT'S WHAT'S MOST IMPORTANT.
WAH
WAH

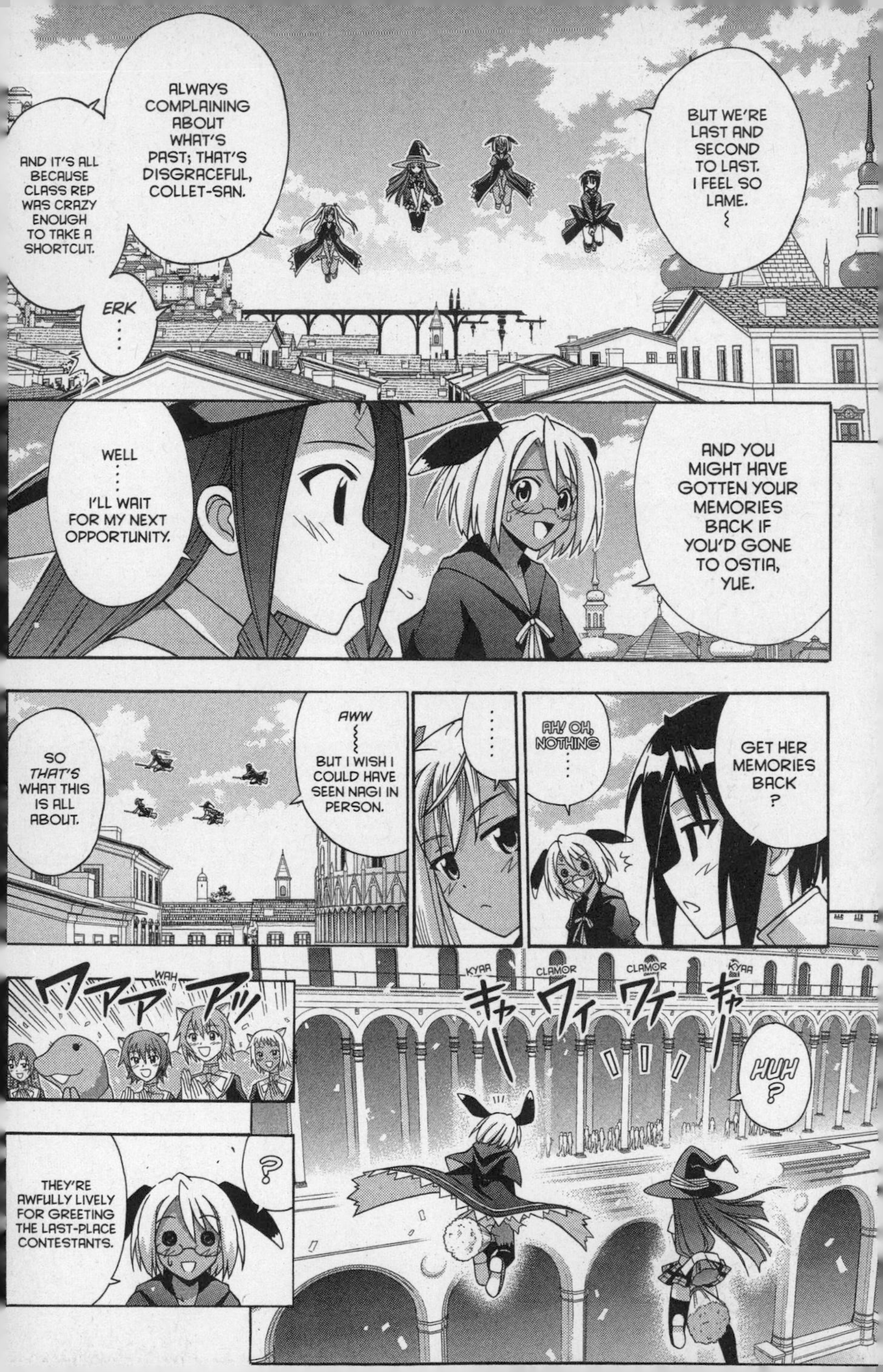
BUT WE'RE LAST AND SECOND TO LAST. I FEEL SO LAME.
ALWAYS COMPLAINING ABOUT WHAT'S PAST; THAT'S DISGRACEFUL, COLLET-SAN.
AND IT'S ALL BECAUSE CLASS REP WAS CRAZY ENOUGH TO TAKE A SHORTCUT.
ERK .....
AND YOU MIGHT HAVE GOTTEN YOUR MEMORIES BACK IF YOU'D GONE TO OSTIA, YUE.
WELL ... I'LL WAIT FOR MY NEXT OPPORTUNITY.
GET HER MEMORIES BACK ?
AH! OH, NOTHING .....
......
AWW ~ BUT I WISH I COULD HAVE SEEN NAGI IN PERSON.
SO THAT'S WHAT THIS IS ALL ABOUT.
キャー ワイ ワイ キャー
KYAA CLAMOR CLAMOR KYAA
HUH ?
ワァァァッ
WAH
?
THEY'RE AWFULLY LIVELY FOR GREETING THE LAST-PLACE CONTESTANTS.

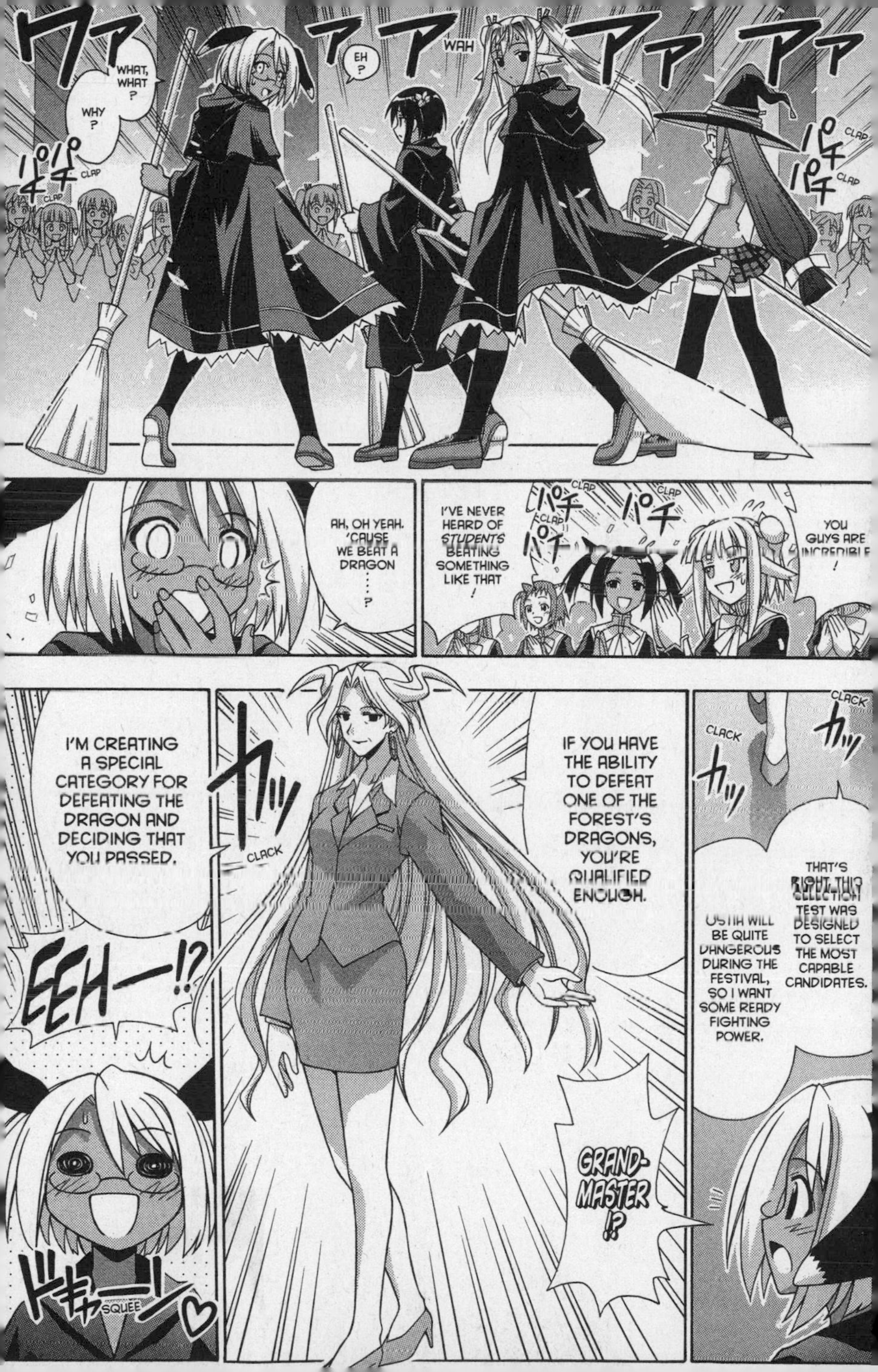
ワァァァァァ
WAH
パチパチ
CLAP
CLAP
EH?
WHAT, WHAT?
WHY?
パチパチ
CLAP
CLAP
YOU GUYS ARE INCREDIBLE!
パチパチパチ
CLAP
CLAP
CLAP
I'VE NEVER HEARD OF STUDENTS BEATING SOMETHING LIKE THAT!
AH, OH YEAH. 'CAUSE WE BEAT A DRAGON.....?
カッ
CLACK
カッ
CLACK
THAT'S RIGHT. THIS SELECTION TEST WAS DESIGNED TO SELECT THE MOST CAPABLE CANDIDATES.
USTIA WILL BE QUITE DANGEROUS DURING THE FESTIVAL, SO I WANT SOME READY FIGHTING POWER.
GRAND-MASTER!?
IF YOU HAVE THE ABILITY TO DEFEAT ONE OF THE FOREST'S DRAGONS, YOU'RE QUALIFIED ENOUGH.
カッ
CLACK
I'M CREATING A SPECIAL CATEGORY FOR DEFEATING THE DRAGON AND DECIDING THAT YOU PASSED.
EEH—!?
ドキャー
SQUEE

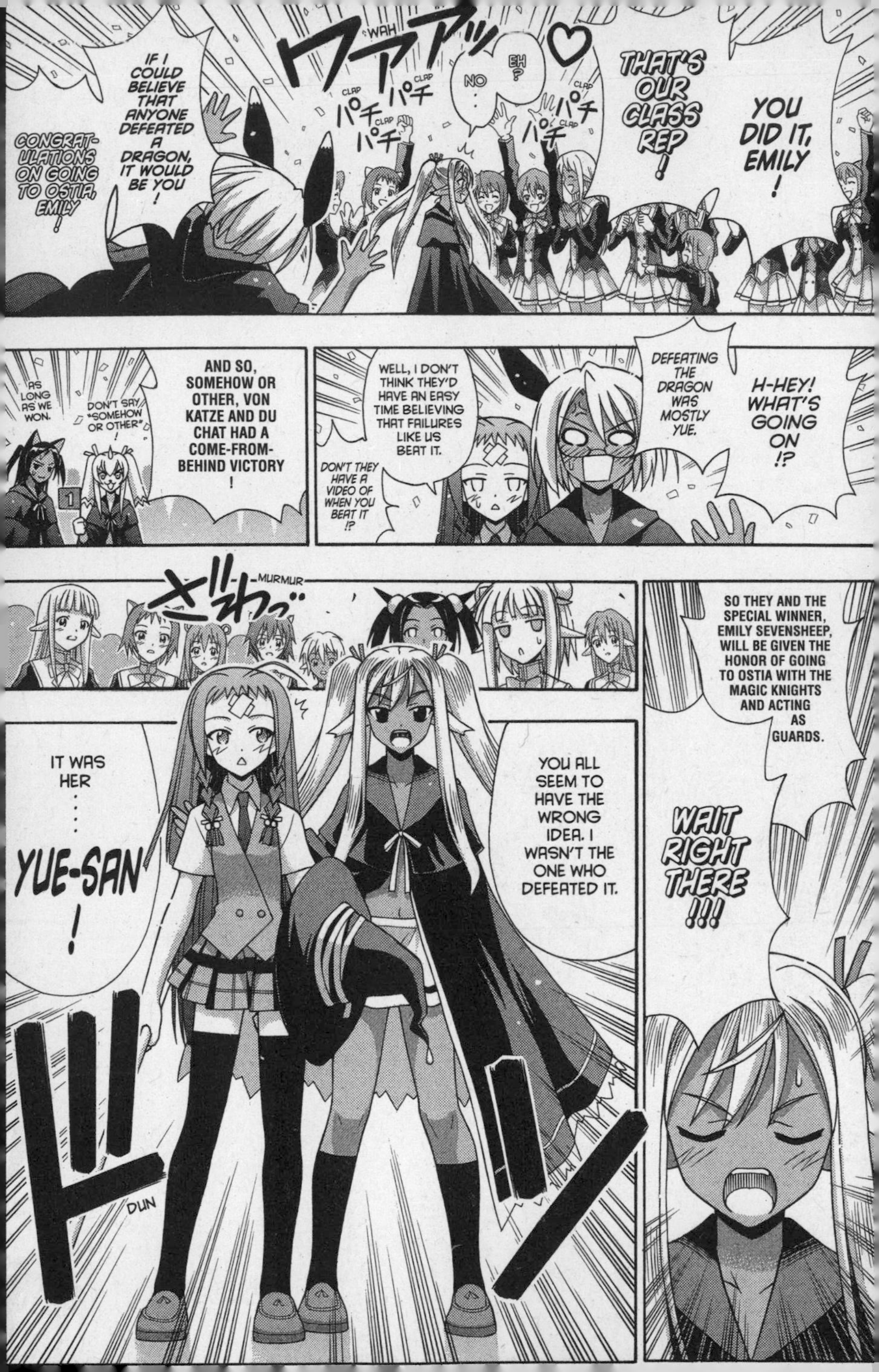
YOU DID IT, EMILY!
THAT'S OUR CLASS REP!
ワアアッ WAH
パチ CLAP パチ CLAP パチ CLAP
パチ CLAP パチ CLAP
EH?
NO...
IF I COULD BELIEVE THAT ANYONE DEFEATED A DRAGON, IT WOULD BE YOU!
CONGRATULATIONS ON GOING TO OSTIA, EMILY!
H-HEY! WHAT'S GOING ON!?
DEFEATING THE DRAGON WAS MOSTLY YUE.
WELL, I DON'T THINK THEY'D HAVE AN EASY TIME BELIEVING THAT FAILURES LIKE US BEAT IT.
DON'T THEY HAVE A VIDEO OF WHEN YOU BEAT IT!?
AND SO, SOMEHOW OR OTHER, VON KATZE AND DU CHAT HAD A COME-FROM-BEHIND VICTORY!
DON'T SAY "SOMEHOW OR OTHER"!
AS LONG AS WE WON.
SO THEY AND THE SPECIAL WINNER, EMILY SEVENSHEEP, WILL BE GIVEN THE HONOR OF GOING TO OSTIA WITH THE MAGIC KNIGHTS AND ACTING AS GUARDS.
WAIT RIGHT THERE!!!
ざわっ MURMUR
YOU ALL SEEM TO HAVE THE WRONG IDEA. I WASN'T THE ONE WHO DEFEATED IT.
IT WAS HER... YUE-SAN!
DUN

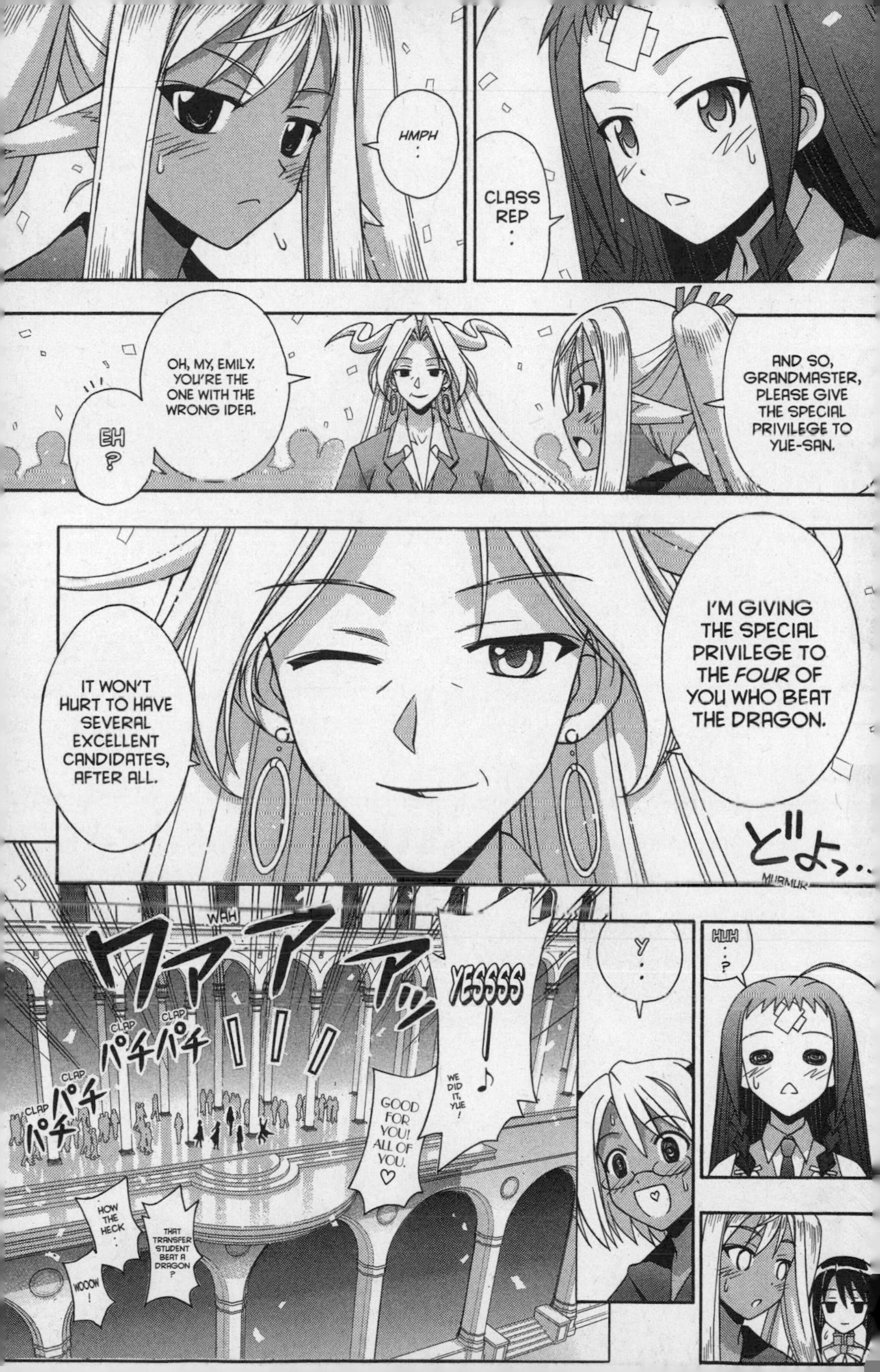
CLASS REP . . .
HMPH . . .
AND SO, GRANDMASTER, PLEASE GIVE THE SPECIAL PRIVILEGE TO YUE-SAN.
OH, MY, EMILY. YOU'RE THE ONE WITH THE WRONG IDEA.
EH ?
I'M GIVING THE SPECIAL PRIVILEGE TO THE *FOUR* OF YOU WHO BEAT THE DRAGON.
IT WON'T HURT TO HAVE SEVERAL EXCELLENT CANDIDATES, AFTER ALL.
どよっ..
MURMUR
HUH . . ?
Y . .
YESSSS ! ♪
ワァァァッ
WAH
WE DID IT, YUE !
GOOD FOR YOU! ALL OF YOU. ♡
パチパチ
CLAP CLAP
パチ
CLAP
パチ
CLAP
HOW THE HECK . .
THAT TRANSFER STUDENT BEAT A DRAGON ?
WOOOW !

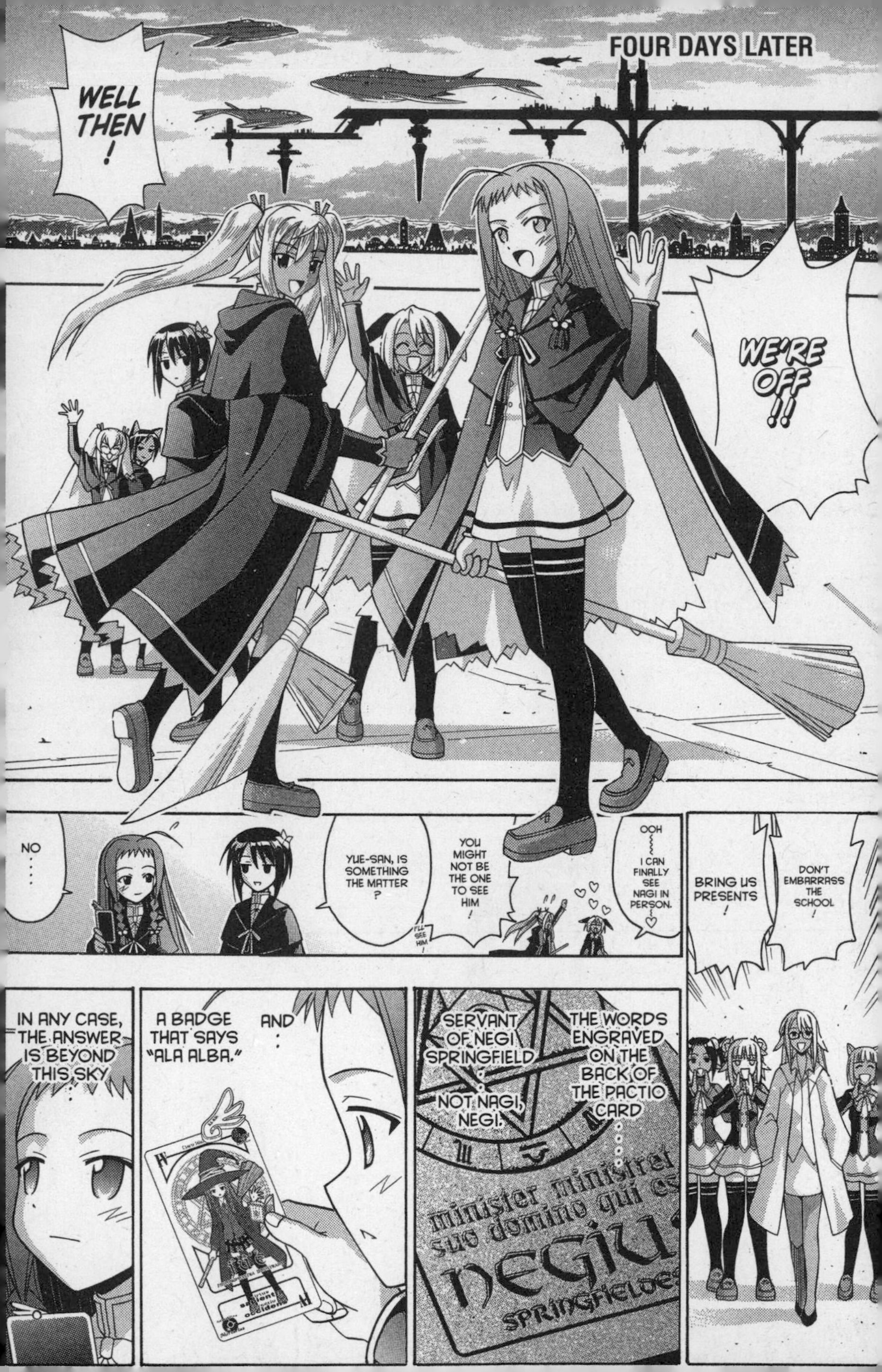
FOUR DAYS LATER
WELL THEN!
WE'RE OFF!!
DON'T EMBARRASS THE SCHOOL!
BRING US PRESENTS!
OOH~ I CAN FINALLY SEE NAGI IN PERSON.♡
YOU MIGHT NOT BE THE ONE TO SEE HIM!
I'LL SEE HIM!
YUE-SAN, IS SOMETHING THE MATTER?
NO...
THE WORDS ENGRAVED ON THE BACK OF THE PACTIO CARD......
SERVANT OF NEGI SPRINGFIELD.
NOT NAGI, NEGI.
minister ministrat
sue domino qui es
NEGIU
SPRINGFIELDE
AND:
A BADGE THAT SAYS "ALA ALBA."
IN ANY CASE, THE ANSWER IS BEYOND THIS SKY

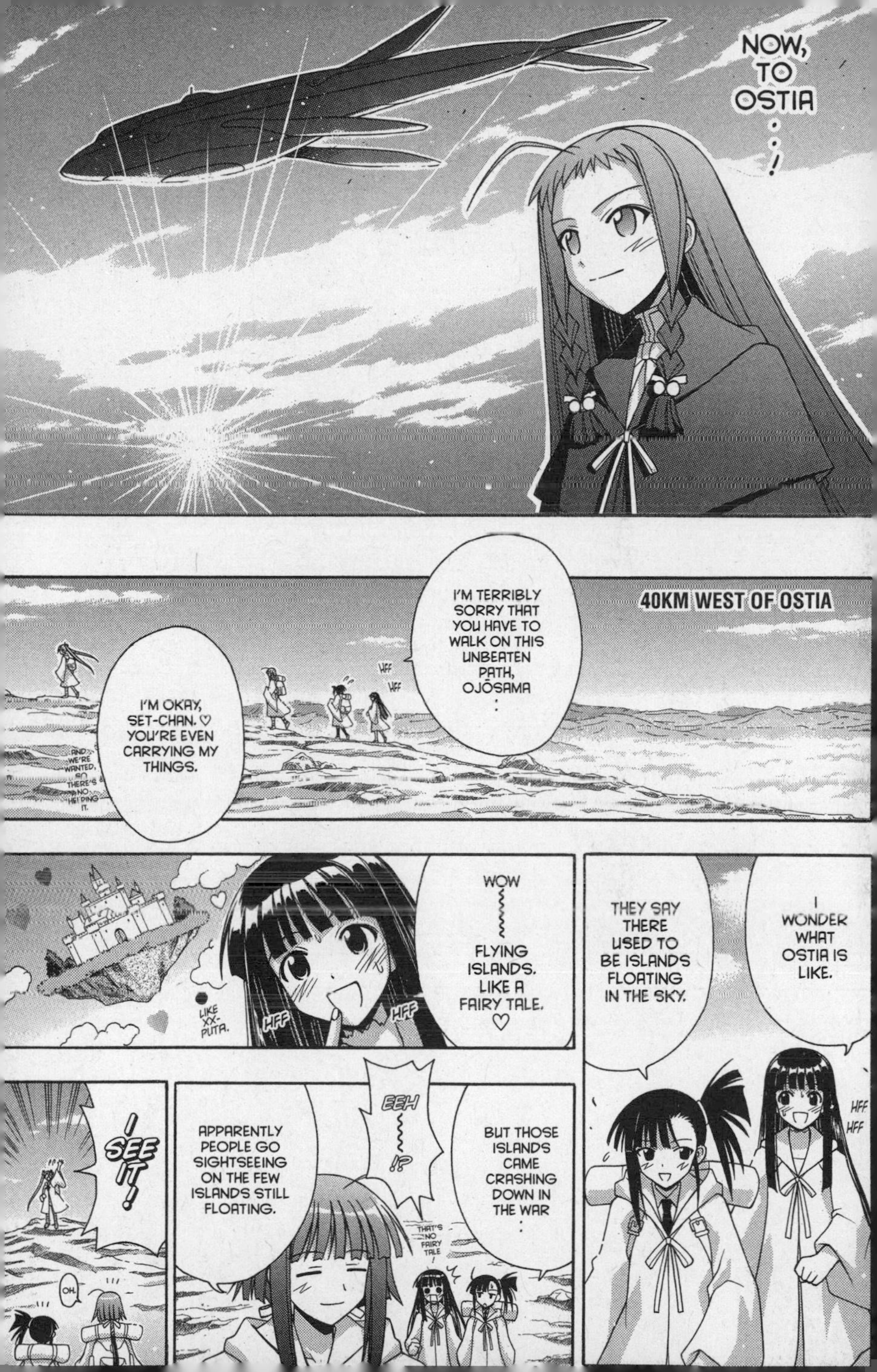
NOW, TO OSTIA . . . !
40KM WEST OF OSTIA
I'M TERRIBLY SORRY THAT YOU HAVE TO WALK ON THIS UNBEATEN PATH, OJŌSAMA :
HFF HFF
I'M OKAY, SET-CHAN. ♡ YOU'RE EVEN CARRYING MY THINGS.
AND WE'RE WANTED, SO THERE'S NO HELPING IT.
I WONDER WHAT OSTIA IS LIKE.
THEY SAY THERE USED TO BE ISLANDS FLOATING IN THE SKY.
HFF HFF
WOW~~~ FLYING ISLANDS. LIKE A FAIRY TALE. ♡
HFF HFF
LIKE XX-PUTA.
BUT THOSE ISLANDS CAME CRASHING DOWN IN THE WAR :
EEH~~~!?
APPARENTLY PEOPLE GO SIGHTSEEING ON THE FEW ISLANDS STILL FLOATING.
THAT'S NO FAIRY TALE!
I SEE IT!
OH.

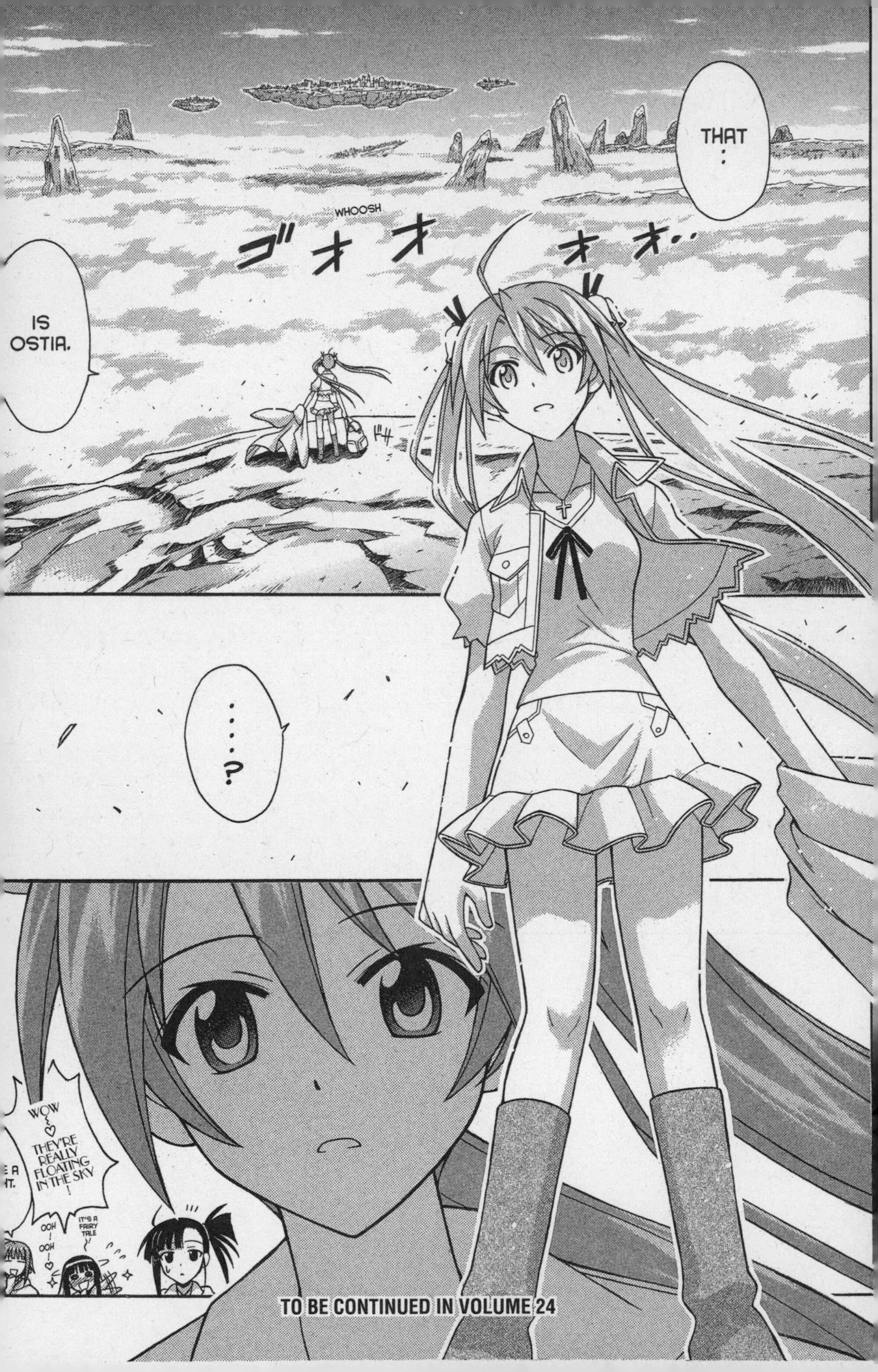
THAT…
WHOOSH
ゴオオ オオ..
IS OSTIA.
….?
IT'S A FAIRY TALE
OOH! OOH! ♡
WOW ♡ THEY'RE REALLY FLOATING IN THE SKY!
TO BE CONTINUED IN VOLUME 24

# A Word from the Author

Presenting *Negima!* volume 24!

Every member of the Negi party has super-powered up. The time has finally come for the real fighting.

Will Negi really use his dark magic?!

And where are the members who haven't been found yet?!

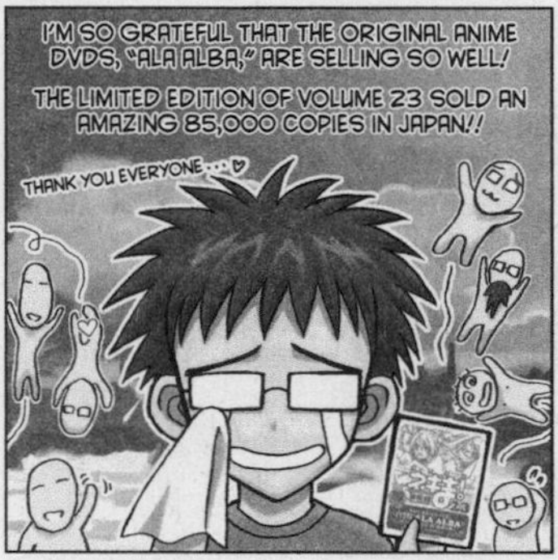
I'M SO GRATEFUL THAT THE ORIGINAL ANIME DVDS, "ALA ALBA," ARE SELLING SO WELL!
THE LIMITED EDITION OF VOLUME 23 SOLD AN AMAZING 85,000 COPIES IN JAPAN!!
THANK YOU EVERYONE...♡

And Fate's adorable backup squad arrives, and the Magical World arc is thrown into big confusion. Is the climax still a long way off?!

The new, all-manga-based anime series, *Magister Negi Magi ~ Ala Alba ~*, has started on Japanese TV. For details, check my home page.

Ken Akamatsu
www.ailove.net

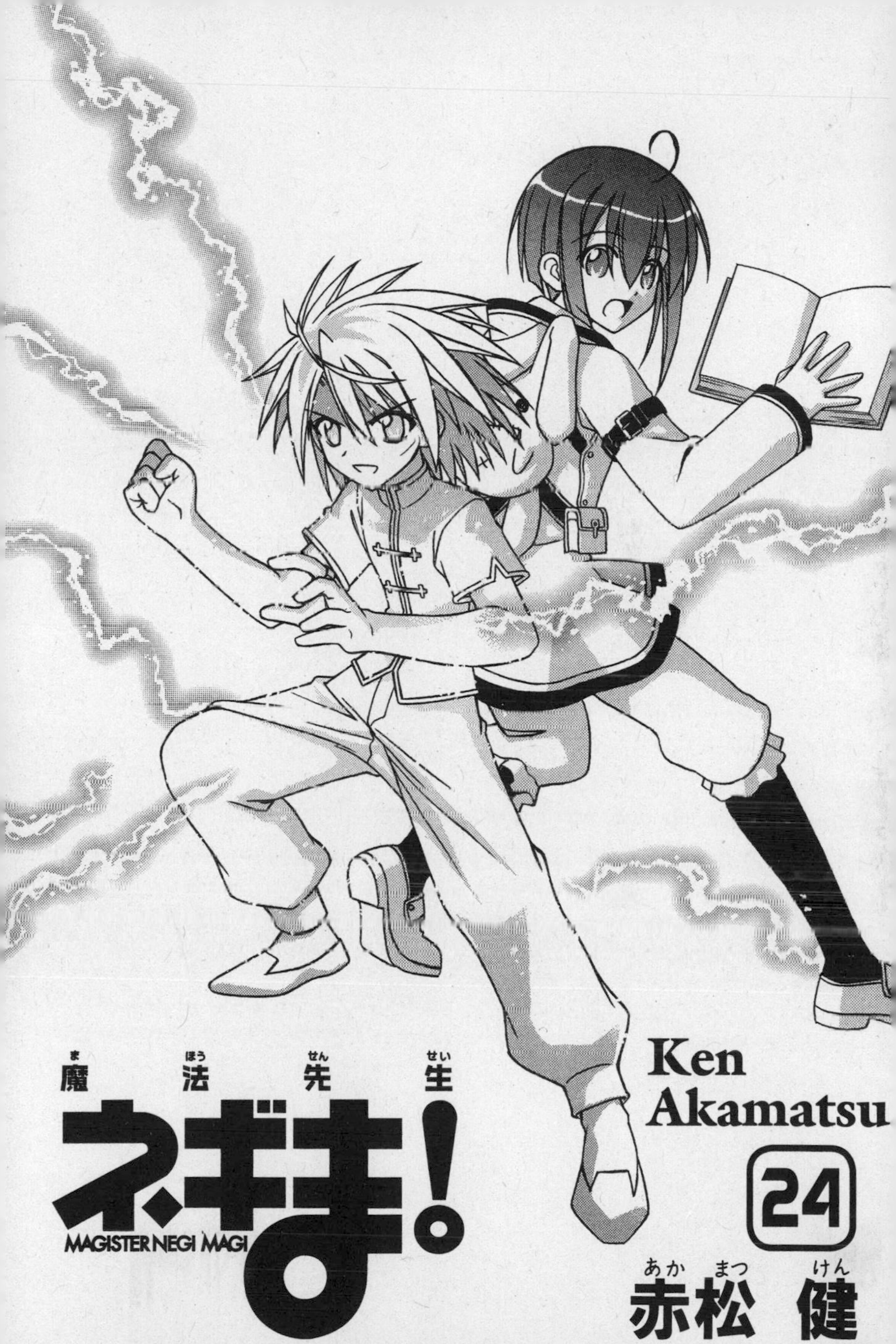

# 魔法先生ネギま!

MAGISTER NEGI MAGI

Ken Akamatsu

24

赤松 健

**CONTENTS**

VII
Charta Ministralis

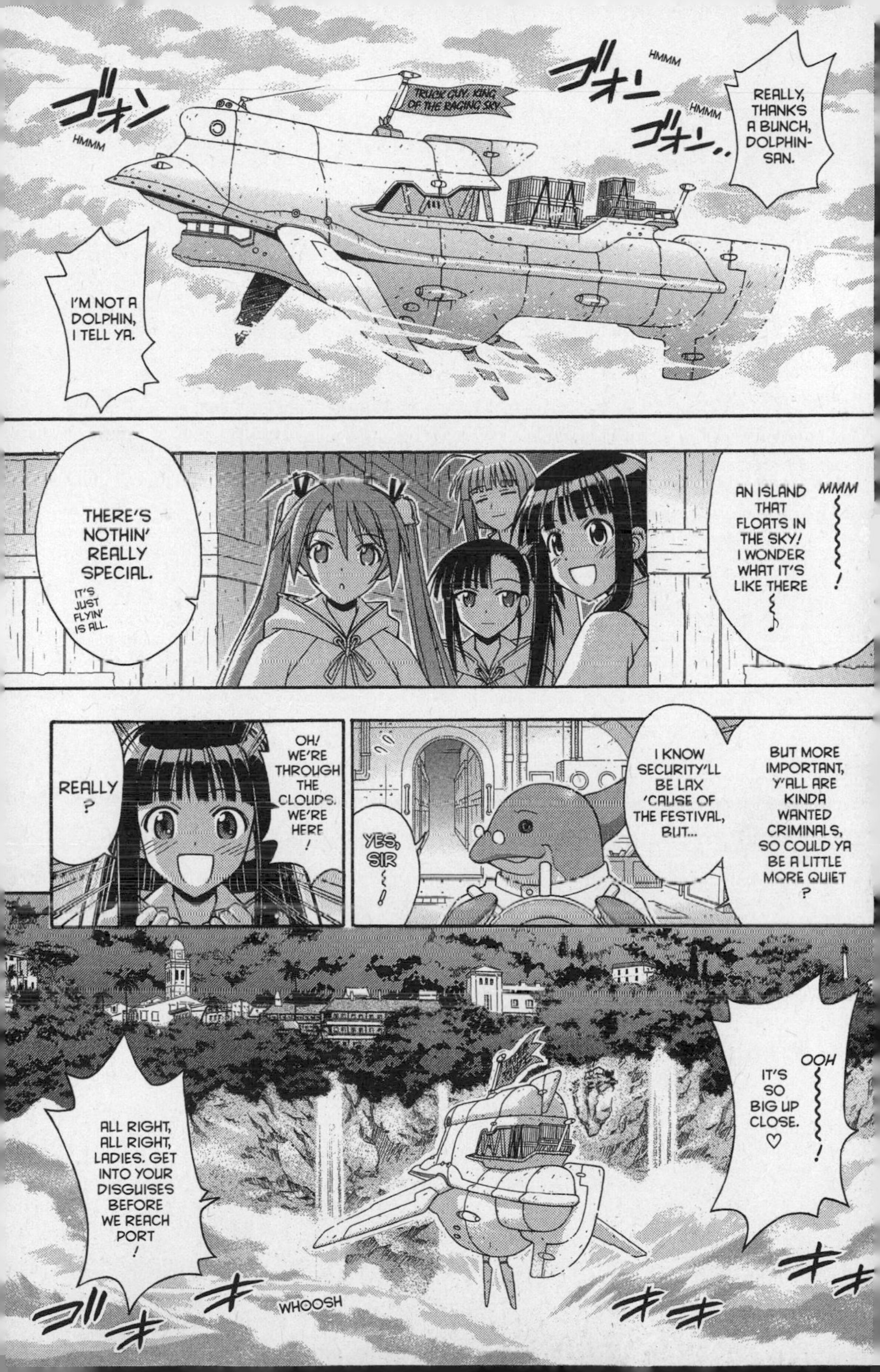
HMMM
HMMM
REALLY, THANKS A BUNCH, DOLPHIN-SAN.
TRUCK GUY, KING OF THE RAGING SKY
HMMM
I'M NOT A DOLPHIN, I TELL YA.
MMM~!
AN ISLAND THAT FLOATS IN THE SKY! I WONDER WHAT IT'S LIKE THERE~♪
THERE'S NOTHIN' REALLY SPECIAL.
IT'S JUST FLYIN' IS ALL.
BUT MORE IMPORTANT, Y'ALL ARE KINDA WANTED CRIMINALS, SO COULD YA BE A LITTLE MORE QUIET?
I KNOW SECURITY'LL BE LAX 'CAUSE OF THE FESTIVAL, BUT...
YES, SIR~!
OH! WE'RE THROUGH THE CLOUDS. WE'RE HERE!
REALLY?
OOH~!
IT'S SO BIG UP CLOSE. ♡
ALL RIGHT, ALL RIGHT, LADIES. GET INTO YOUR DISGUISES BEFORE WE REACH PORT!
WHOOSH

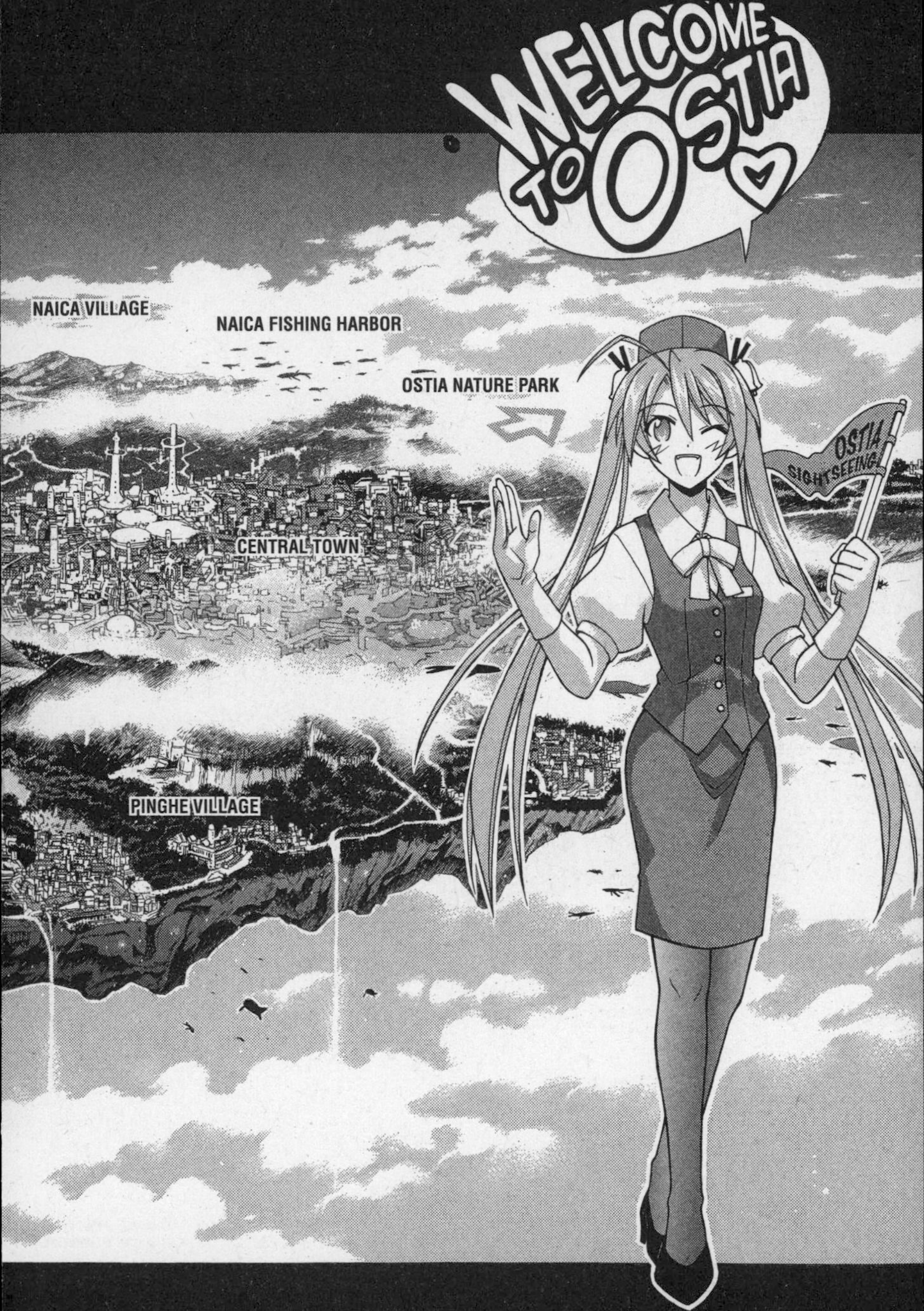
WELCOME TO OSTIA
NAICA VILLAGE
NAICA FISHING HARBOR
OSTIA NATURE PARK
CENTRAL TOWN
PINGHE VILLAGE
OSTIA SIGHTSEEING!

# NEGIMA!
MAGISTER NEGI MAGI

## 214TH PERIOD: I'M SO GLAD TO SEE YOU♡

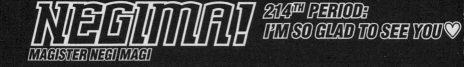

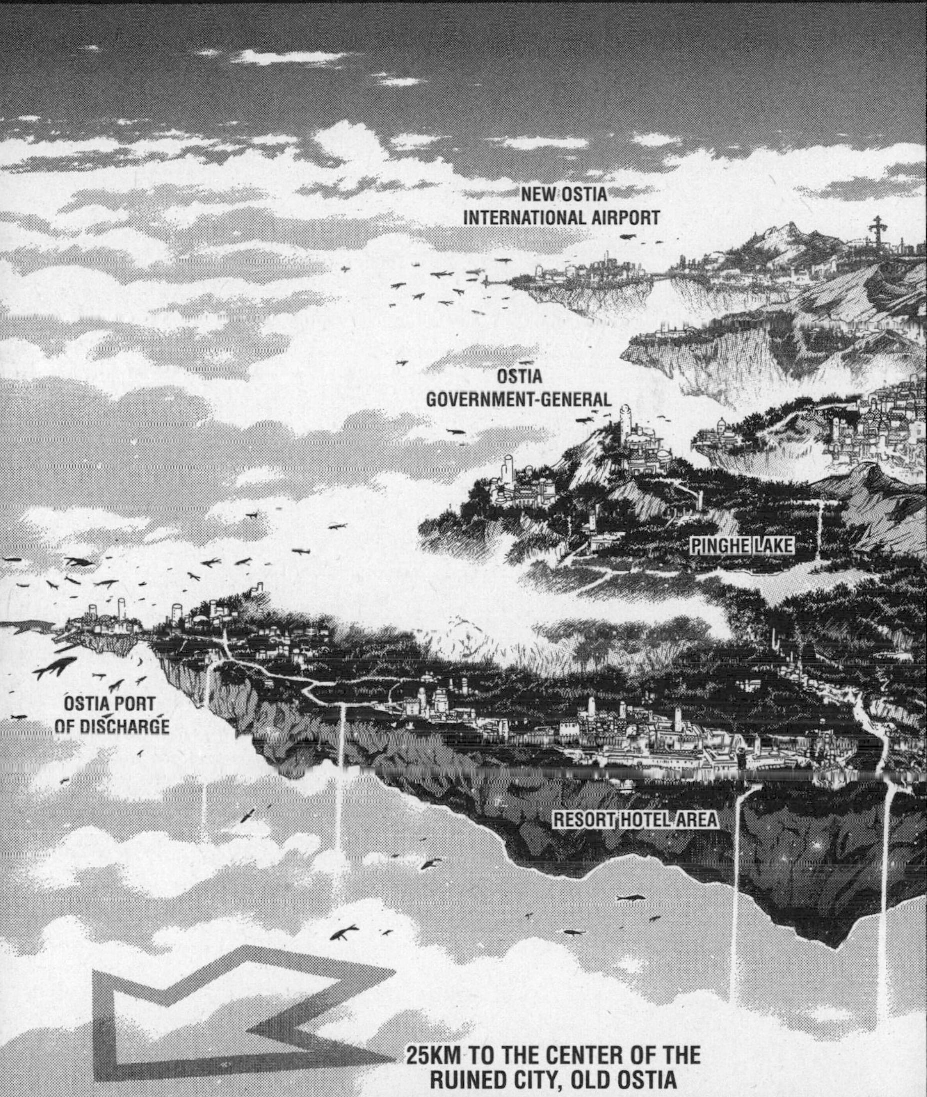
NEW OSTIA INTERNATIONAL AIRPORT
OSTIA GOVERNMENT-GENERAL
PINGHE LAKE
OSTIA PORT OF DISCHARGE
RESORT HOTEL AREA
25KM TO THE CENTER OF THE RUINED CITY, OLD OSTIA
BECAUSE OF LINGERING EFFECTS FROM THE ENORMOUS MAGICAL CALAMITY DURING THE WAR, CIVILIANS ARE NOT PERMITTED INSIDE. (THE CITY MAY BE VIEWED FROM ABOVE FROM SIGHTSEEING SHIPS MANAGED BY THE GOVERNMENT-GENERAL.)

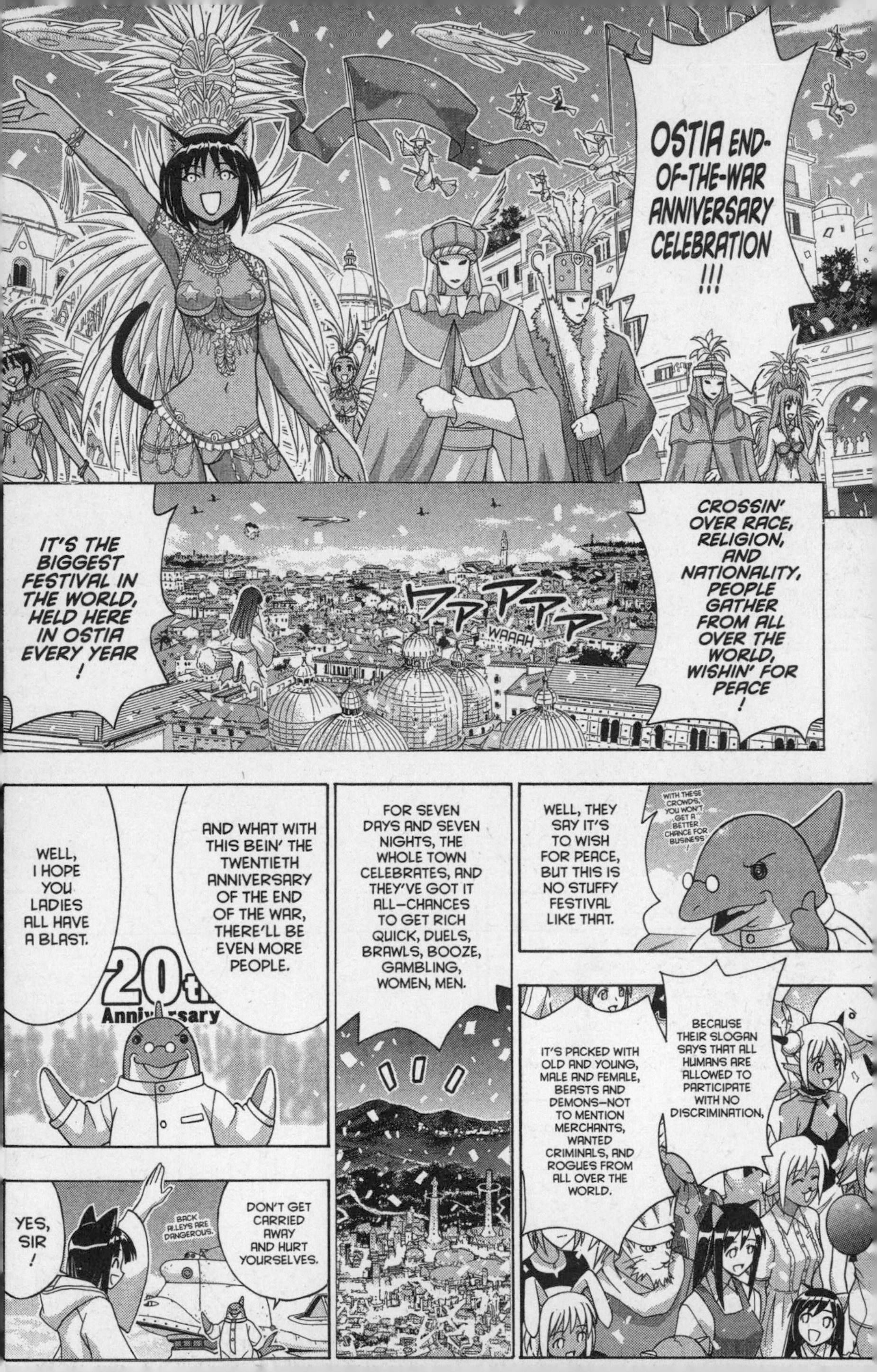
OSTIA END-OF-THE-WAR ANNIVERSARY CELEBRATION!!!
CROSSIN' OVER RACE, RELIGION, AND NATIONALITY, PEOPLE GATHER FROM ALL OVER THE WORLD, WISHIN' FOR PEACE!
ワァァァ
WAAAH
IT'S THE BIGGEST FESTIVAL IN THE WORLD, HELD HERE IN OSTIA EVERY YEAR!
WELL, THEY SAY IT'S TO WISH FOR PEACE, BUT THIS IS NO STUFFY FESTIVAL LIKE THAT.
WITH THESE CROWDS, YOU WON'T GET A BETTER CHANCE FOR BUSINESS!
BECAUSE THEIR SLOGAN SAYS THAT ALL HUMANS ARE ALLOWED TO PARTICIPATE WITH NO DISCRIMINATION,
IT'S PACKED WITH OLD AND YOUNG, MALE AND FEMALE, BEASTS AND DEMONS—NOT TO MENTION MERCHANTS, WANTED CRIMINALS, AND ROGUES FROM ALL OVER THE WORLD.
FOR SEVEN DAYS AND SEVEN NIGHTS, THE WHOLE TOWN CELEBRATES, AND THEY'VE GOT IT ALL—CHANCES TO GET RICH QUICK, DUELS, BRAWLS, BOOZE, GAMBLING, WOMEN, MEN.
!!!
AND WHAT WITH THIS BEIN' THE TWENTIETH ANNIVERSARY OF THE END OF THE WAR, THERE'LL BE EVEN MORE PEOPLE.
WELL, I HOPE YOU LADIES ALL HAVE A BLAST.
20th Anniversary
DON'T GET CARRIED AWAY AND HURT YOURSELVES.
BACK ALLEYS ARE DANGEROUS.
YES, SIR!

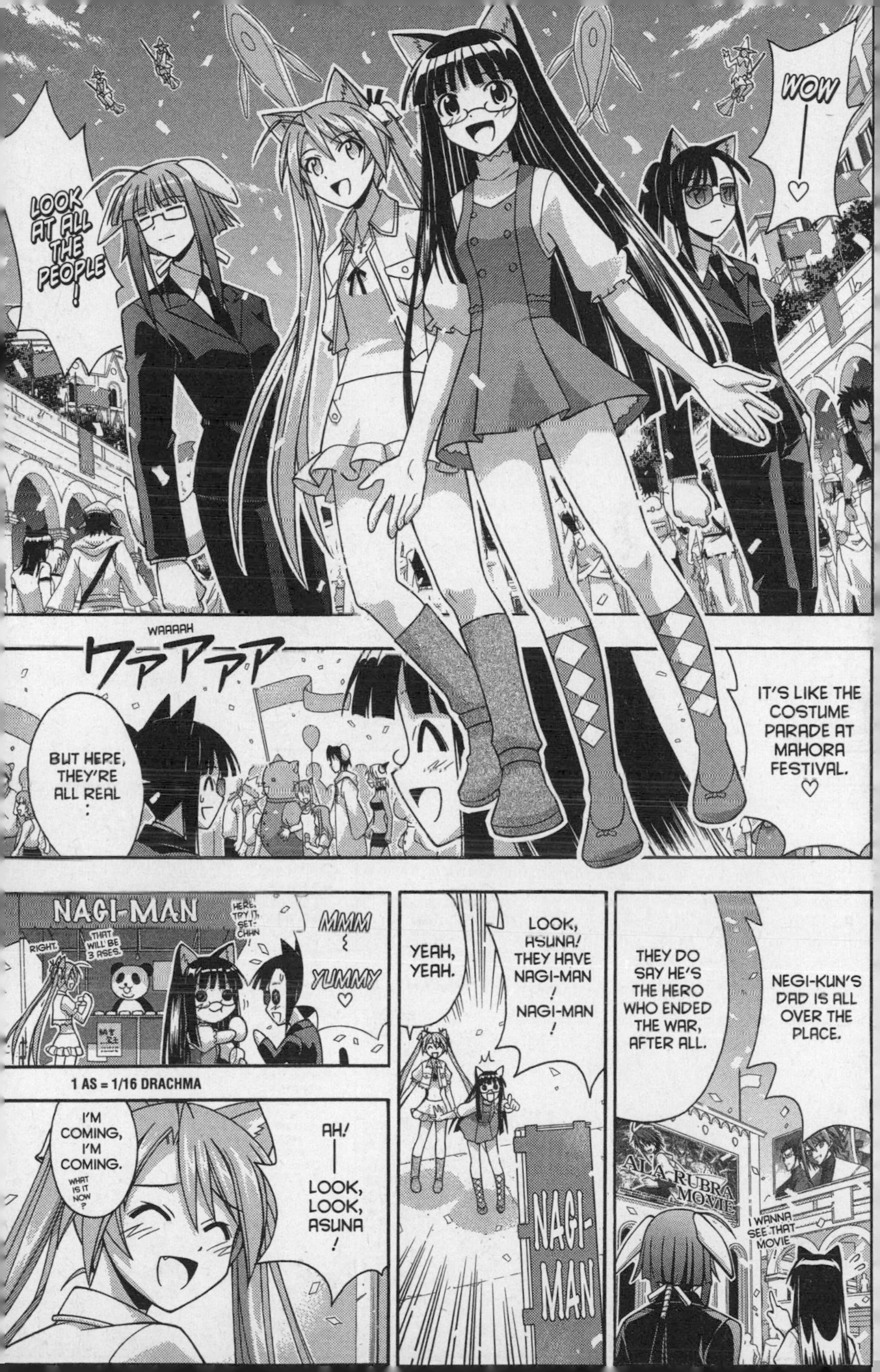
WOW — ♡
LOOK AT ALL THE PEOPLE!
WAAAAH
ワァアアア
IT'S LIKE THE COSTUME PARADE AT MAHORA FESTIVAL. ♡
BUT HERE, THEY'RE ALL REAL...
NEGI-KUN'S DAD IS ALL OVER THE PLACE.
THEY DO SAY HE'S THE HERO WHO ENDED THE WAR, AFTER ALL.
ALA RUBRA MOVIE
I WANNA SEE THAT MOVIE
LOOK, ASUNA! THEY HAVE NAGI-MAN! NAGI-MAN!
YEAH, YEAH.
NAGI-MAN
MMM~ YUMMY ♡
HERE, TRY IT, SET-CHAN!
THAT WILL BE 3 ASES.
RIGHT.
NAGI-MAN
1 AS = 1/16 DRACHMA
AH! — LOOK, LOOK, ASUNA!
I'M COMING, I'M COMING.
WHAT IS IT NOW?

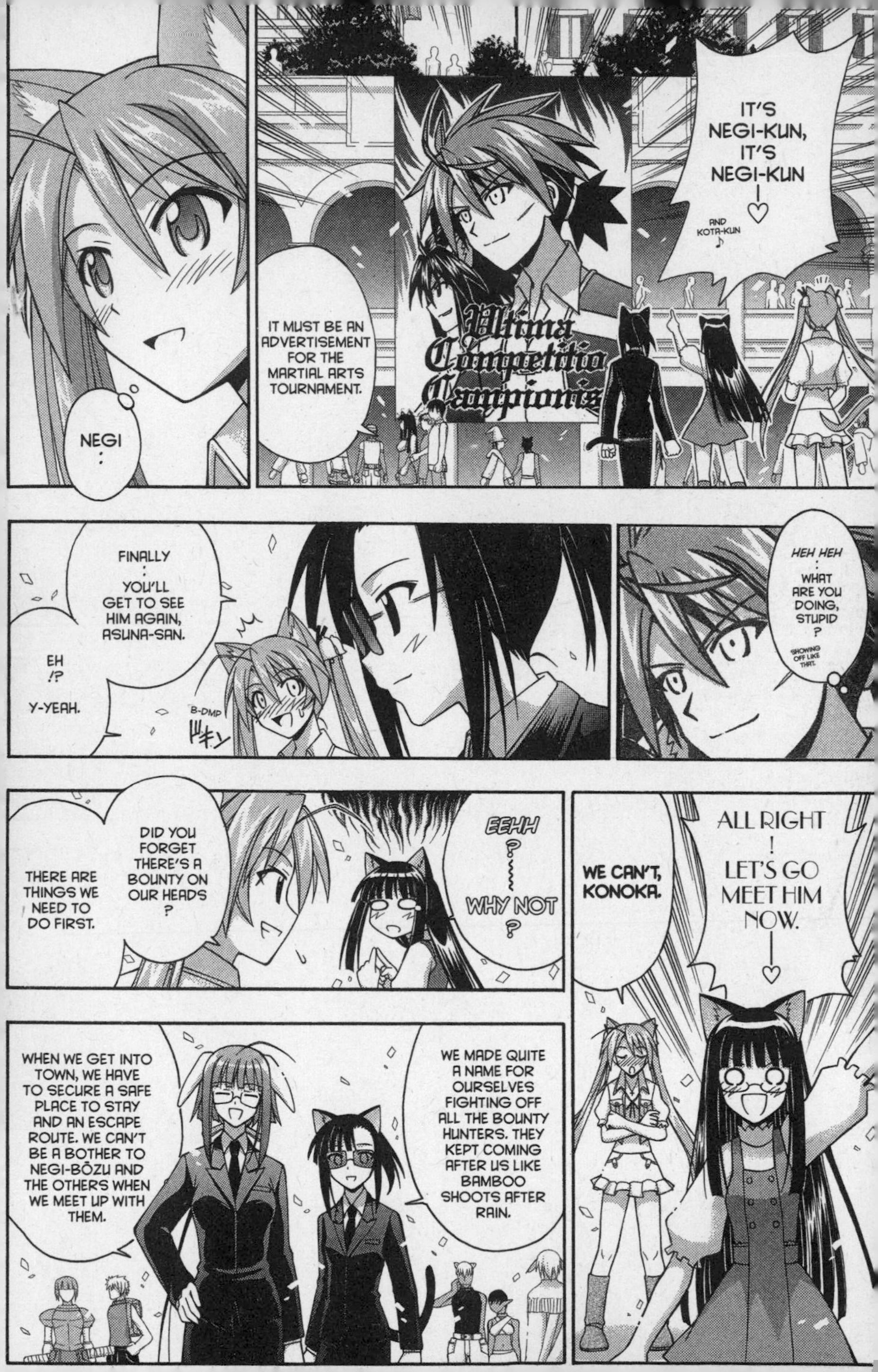
IT'S NEGI-KUN, IT'S NEGI-KUN ♡
AND KOTA-KUN ♪
Ultima Competitio Campionis
IT MUST BE AN ADVERTISEMENT FOR THE MARTIAL ARTS TOURNAMENT.
NEGI :
HEH HEH : WHAT ARE YOU DOING, STUPID ?
SHOWING OFF LIKE THAT.
FINALLY : YOU'LL GET TO SEE HIM AGAIN, ASUNA-SAN.
EH !? Y-YEAH.
B-DMP
ドキン
ALL RIGHT ! LET'S GO MEET HIM NOW. ♡
WE CAN'T, KONOKA.
EEHH ?... WHY NOT ?
DID YOU FORGET THERE'S A BOUNTY ON OUR HEADS ?
THERE ARE THINGS WE NEED TO DO FIRST.
WE MADE QUITE A NAME FOR OURSELVES FIGHTING OFF ALL THE BOUNTY HUNTERS. THEY KEPT COMING AFTER US LIKE BAMBOO SHOOTS AFTER RAIN.
WHEN WE GET INTO TOWN, WE HAVE TO SECURE A SAFE PLACE TO STAY AND AN ESCAPE ROUTE. WE CAN'T BE A BOTHER TO NEGI-BŌZU AND THE OTHERS WHEN WE MEET UP WITH THEM.

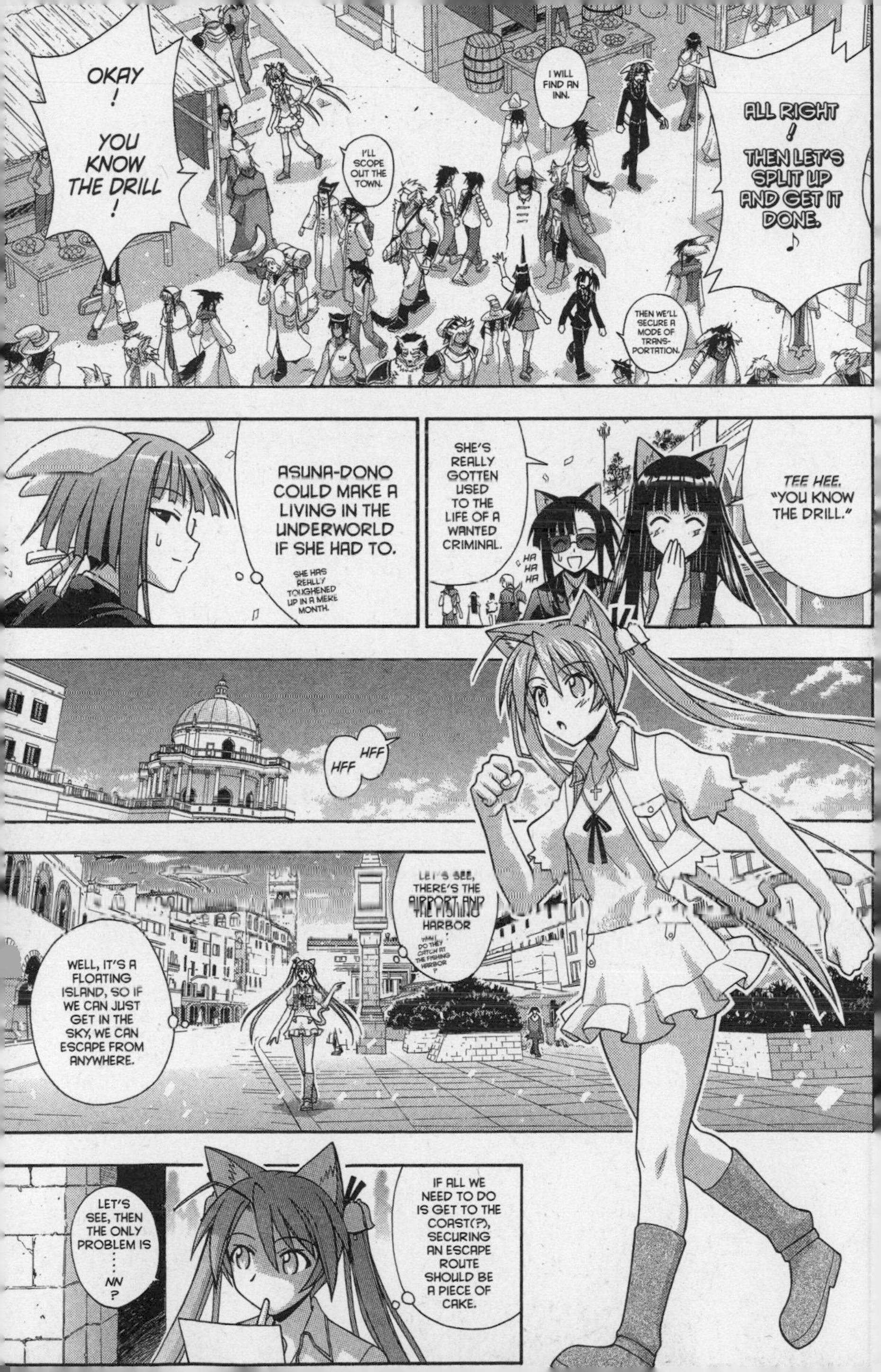
ALL RIGHT! THEN LET'S SPLIT UP AND GET IT DONE. ♪
I WILL FIND AN INN.
THEN WE'LL SECURE A MODE OF TRANS-PORTATION.
I'LL SCOPE OUT THE TOWN.
OKAY! YOU KNOW THE DRILL!
TEE HEE. "YOU KNOW THE DRILL."
SHE'S REALLY GOTTEN USED TO THE LIFE OF A WANTED CRIMINAL.
HA HA HA
ASUNA-DONO COULD MAKE A LIVING IN THE UNDERWORLD IF SHE HAD TO.
SHE HAS REALLY TOUGHENED UP IN A MERE MONTH.
HFF HFF
LET'S SEE, THERE'S THE AIRPORT AND THE FISHING HARBOR
WHAT DO THEY CATCH AT THE FISHING HARBOR?
WELL, IT'S A FLOATING ISLAND, SO IF WE CAN JUST GET IN THE SKY, WE CAN ESCAPE FROM ANYWHERE.
IF ALL WE NEED TO DO IS GET TO THE COAST(?), SECURING AN ESCAPE ROUTE SHOULD BE A PIECE OF CAKE.
LET'S SEE, THEN THE ONLY PROBLEM IS.... NN?

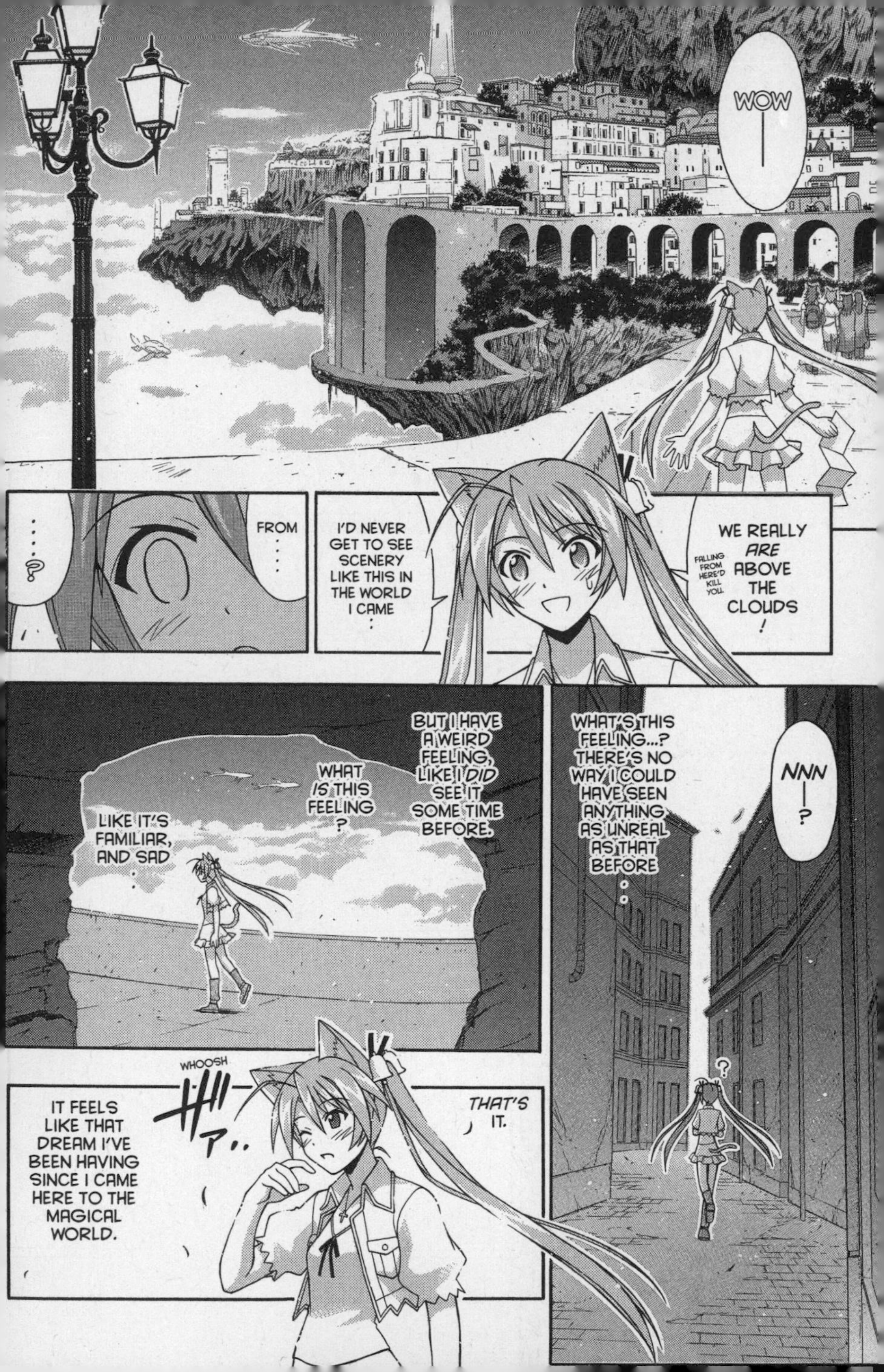
WOW—
WE REALLY *ARE* ABOVE THE CLOUDS!
FALLING FROM HERE'D KILL YOU.
I'D NEVER GET TO SEE SCENERY LIKE THIS IN THE WORLD I CAME FROM....
....?
NNN—?
WHAT'S THIS FEELING...? THERE'S NO WAY I COULD HAVE SEEN ANYTHING AS UNREAL AS THAT BEFORE...
BUT I HAVE A WEIRD FEELING, LIKE I *DID* SEE IT SOME TIME BEFORE.
WHAT *IS* THIS FEELING?
LIKE IT'S FAMILIAR, AND SAD.
THAT'S IT.
WHOOSH
IT FEELS LIKE THAT DREAM I'VE BEEN HAVING SINCE I CAME HERE TO THE MAGICAL WORLD.

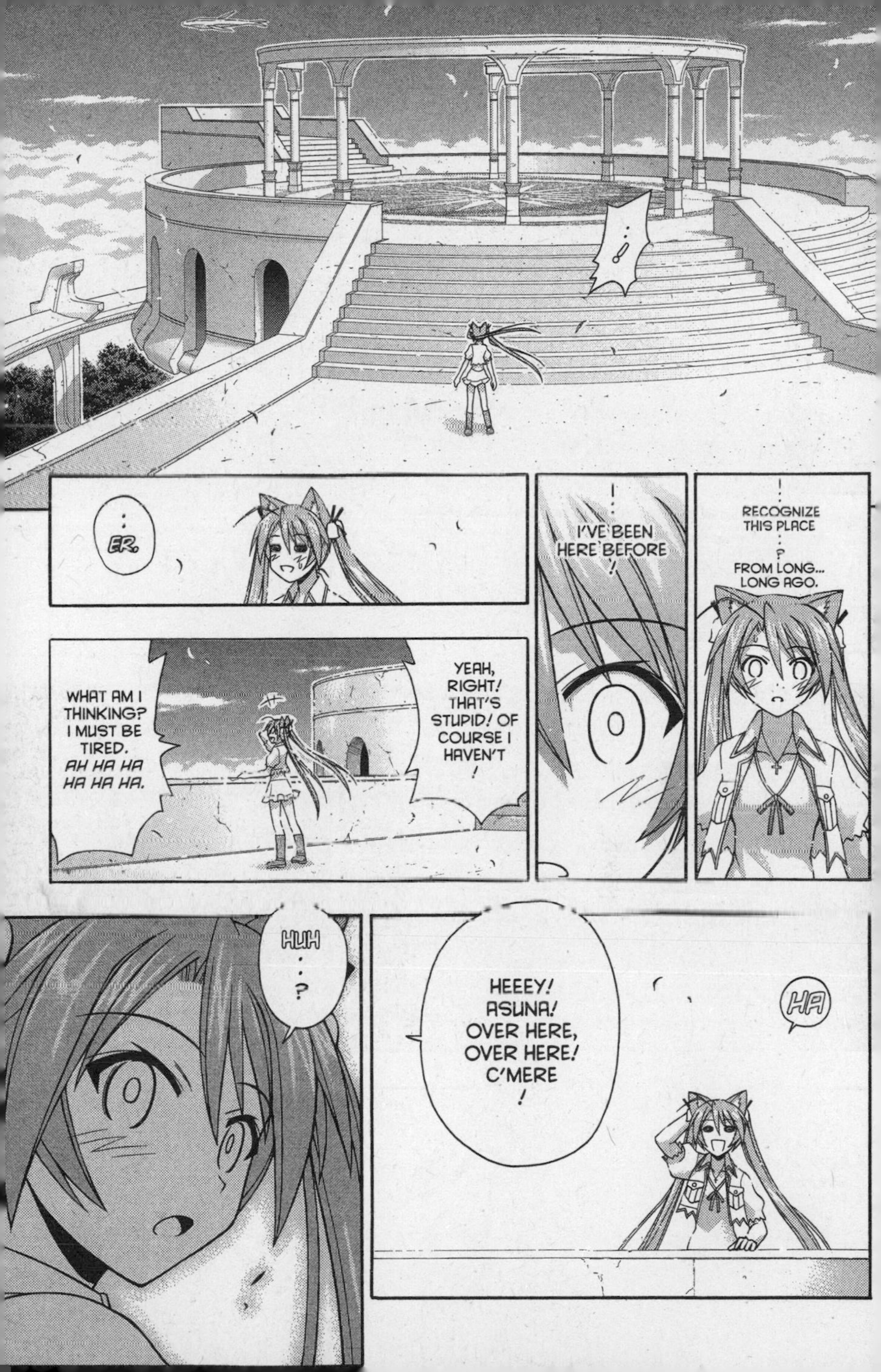
...!
...! RECOGNIZE THIS PLACE...?
FROM LONG... LONG AGO.
...! I'VE BEEN HERE BEFORE!
...ER.
YEAH, RIGHT! THAT'S STUPID! OF COURSE I HAVEN'T!
WHAT AM I THINKING? I MUST BE TIRED. AH HA HA HA HA HA.
HA
HEEEY! ASUNA! OVER HERE, OVER HERE! C'MERE!
HUH...?

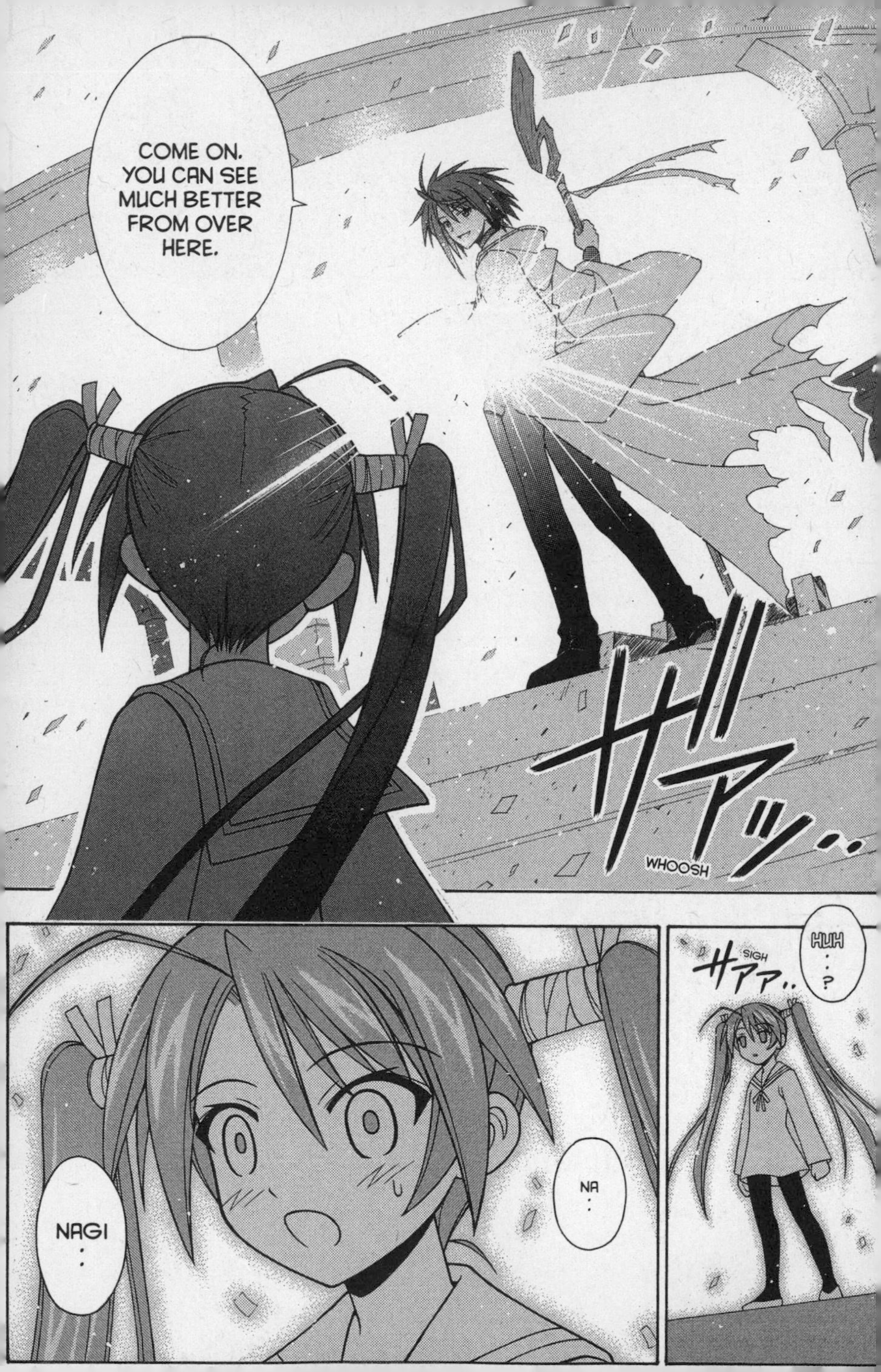
COME ON. YOU CAN SEE MUCH BETTER FROM OVER HERE.
ザアッ..
WHOOSH
サアア..
SIGH
HUH ..?
NA ..
NAGI ..

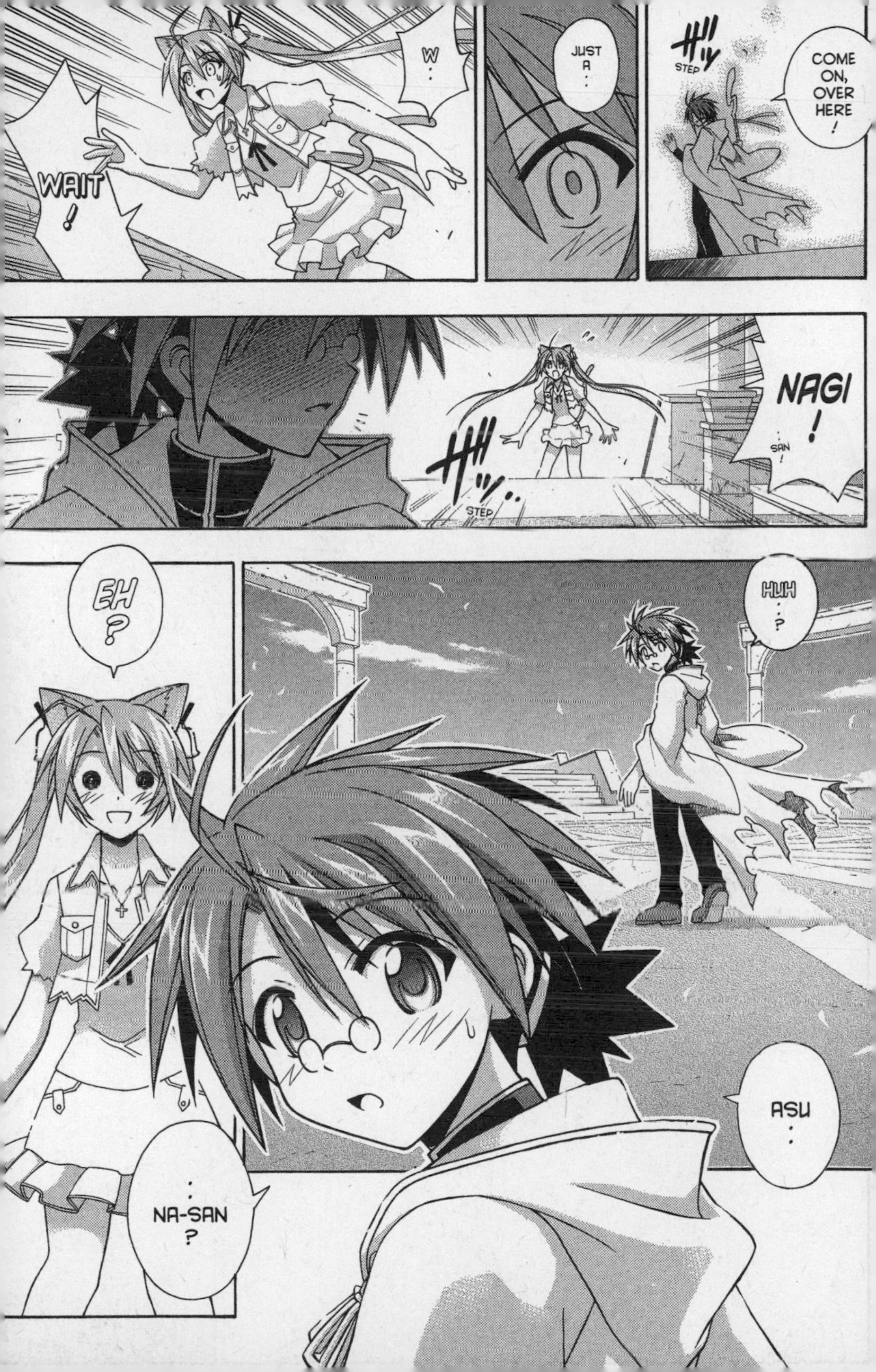
STEP
COME ON, OVER HERE!
JUST A . . .
W . .
WAIT!
NAGI!
. . SAN!
STEP
HUH . . ?
ASU . . .
. . NA-SAN?
EH?

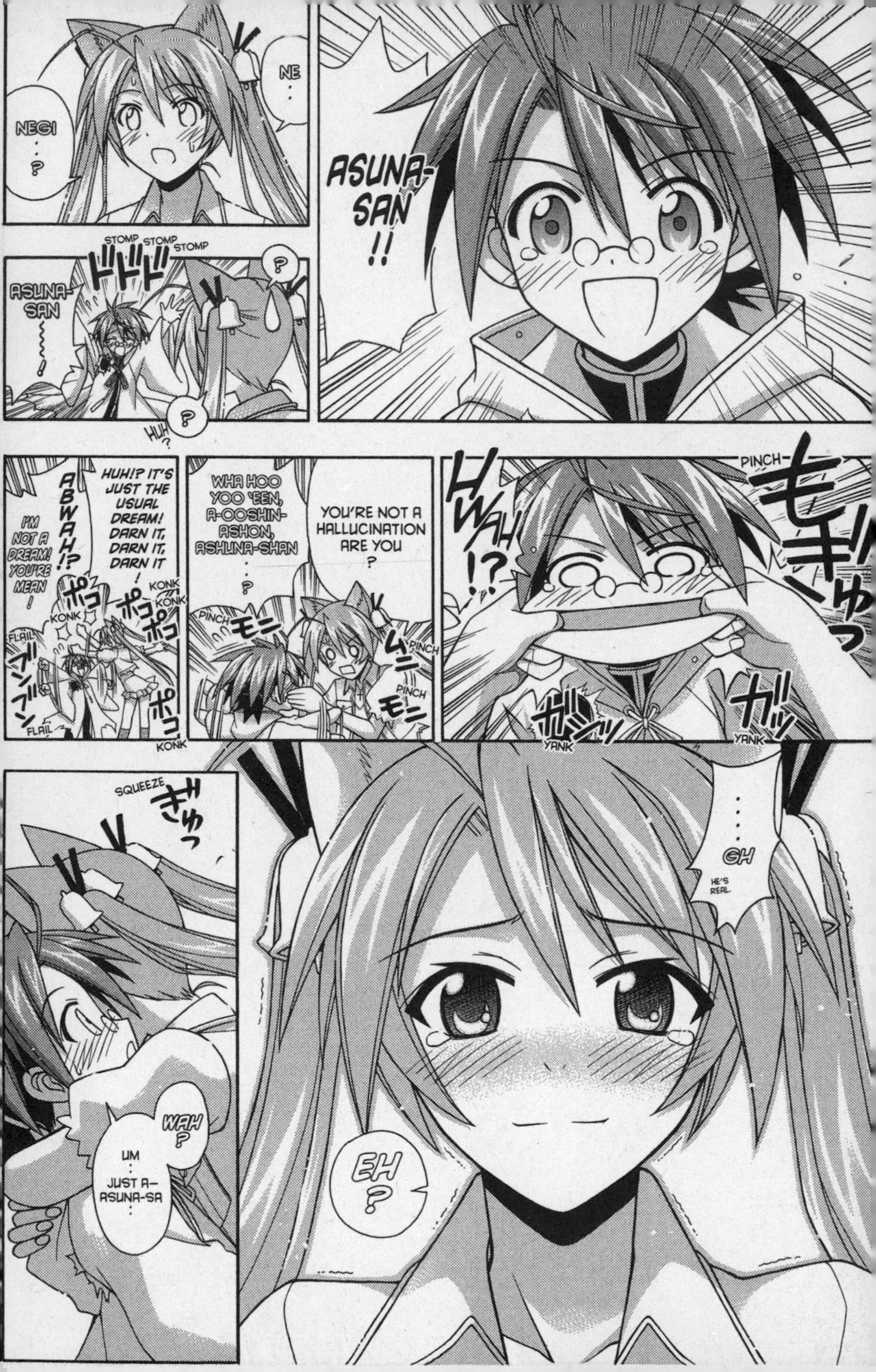
ASUNA-SAN!!
NE...
NEGI...?
STOMP STOMP STOMP
ドドド
?
ASUNA-SAN~!
?
HUH?
PINCH
モギュッ
HWAH!?
ガッ YANK
ガシッ YANK
YOU'RE NOT A HALLUCINATION ARE YOU?
WHA HOO YOO 'EEN, A-OOSHIN-ASHON, ASHUNA-SHAN...?
ムニ PINCH
モニ PINCH
モニ PINCH
HUH!? IT'S JUST THE USUAL DREAM! DARN IT, DARN IT, DARN IT!
ABWAH!?
I'M NOT A DREAM! YOU'RE MEAN!
ポコ KONK
ポコ KONK
ポコ KONK
ポコ KONK
ブンブン FLAIL FLAIL
.....GH
HE'S REAL.
EH?
SQUEEZE
ぎゅっ
WAH?
UM... JUST A-ASUNA-SA...

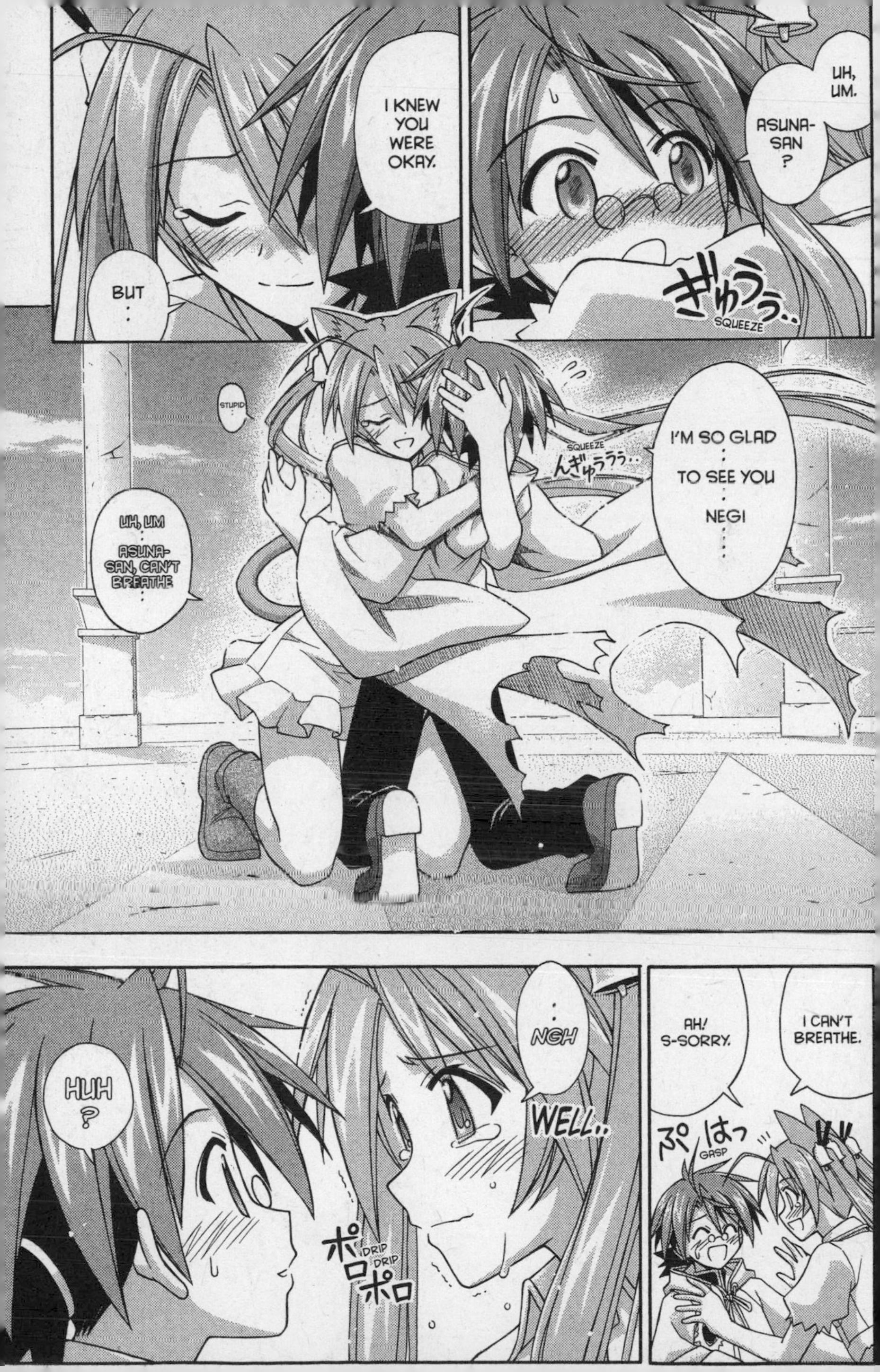
UH, UM.
ASUNA-SAN?
ぎゅうう..
SQUEEZE
I KNEW YOU WERE OKAY.
BUT...
I'M SO GLAD... TO SEE YOU... NEGI...
んぎゅううう..
SQUEEZE
STUPID...
UH, UM... ASUNA-SAN, CAN'T BREATHE...
I CAN'T BREATHE.
AH! S-SORRY.
ぷはっ
GASP
...NGH
WELL..
HUH?
ポロポロ
DRIP DRIP

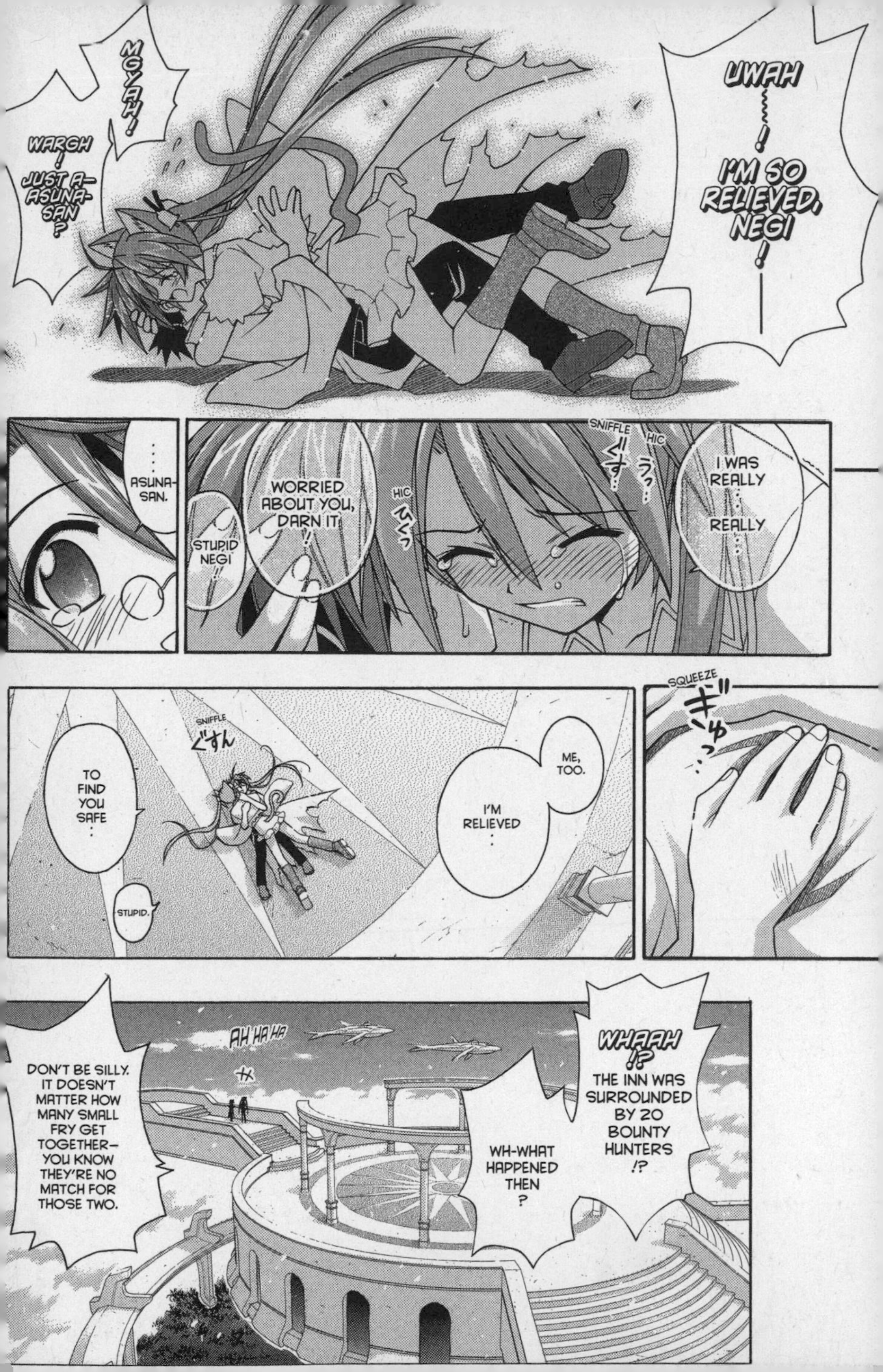
UWAH~~! I'M SO RELIEVED, NEGI!—
MGYAH!
WARGH! JUST A- ASUNA-SAN?
SNIFFLE ぐすっ…
HIC うっ…
I WAS REALLY… REALLY…
WORRIED ABOUT YOU, DARN IT!
HIC ひくっ
STUPID NEGI!
…ASUNA-SAN.
SQUEEZE ぎゅっ
ME, TOO.
I'M RELIEVED…
SNIFFLE ぐすん
TO FIND YOU SAFE…
STUPID.
WHAAH!? THE INN WAS SURROUNDED BY 20 BOUNTY HUNTERS!?
WH-WHAT HAPPENED THEN?
AH HA HA
DON'T BE SILLY. IT DOESN'T MATTER HOW MANY SMALL FRY GET TOGETHER— YOU KNOW THEY'RE NO MATCH FOR THOSE TWO.

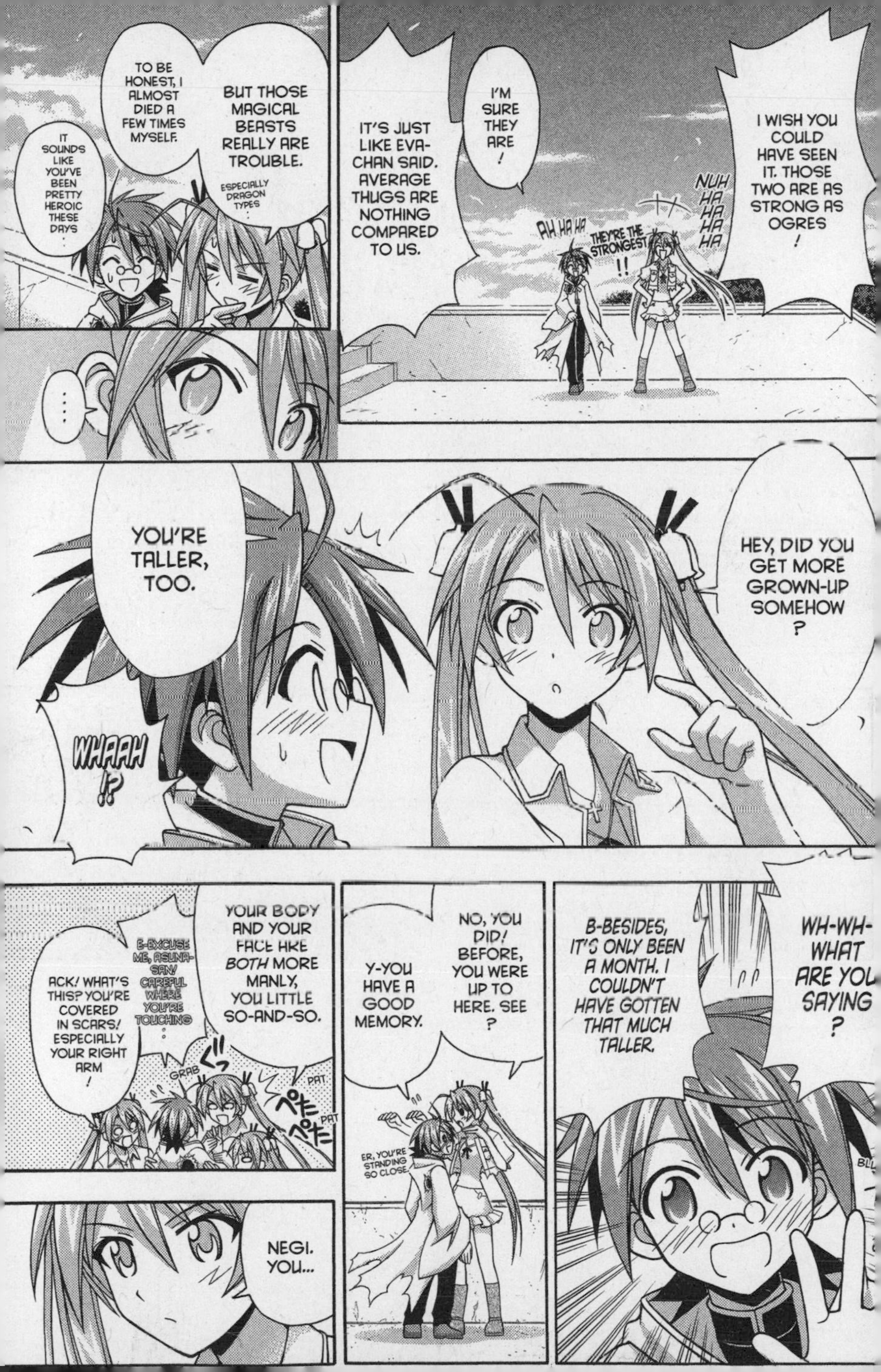
I WISH YOU COULD HAVE SEEN IT. THOSE TWO ARE AS STRONG AS OGRES!
NUH HA HA HA HA
THEY'RE THE STRONGEST!!
AH HA HA
I'M SURE THEY ARE!
IT'S JUST LIKE EVA-CHAN SAID. AVERAGE THUGS ARE NOTHING COMPARED TO US.
BUT THOSE MAGICAL BEASTS REALLY ARE TROUBLE.
ESPECIALLY DRAGON TYPES...
TO BE HONEST, I ALMOST DIED A FEW TIMES MYSELF.
IT SOUNDS LIKE YOU'VE BEEN PRETTY HEROIC THESE DAYS...
.....
HEY, DID YOU GET MORE GROWN-UP SOMEHOW?
YOU'RE TALLER, TOO.
WHAAH!?
WH-WH-WHAT ARE YOU SAYING?
B-BESIDES, IT'S ONLY BEEN A MONTH. I COULDN'T HAVE GOTTEN THAT MUCH TALLER.
NO, YOU DID! BEFORE, YOU WERE UP TO HERE. SEE?
Y-YOU HAVE A GOOD MEMORY.
ER, YOU'RE STANDING SO CLOSE.
YOUR BODY AND YOUR FACE ARE BOTH MORE MANLY, YOU LITTLE SO-AND-SO.
PAT
PAT
E-EXCUSE ME, ASUNA-SAN! CAREFUL WHERE YOU'RE TOUCHING...
ACK! WHAT'S THIS? YOU'RE COVERED IN SCARS! ESPECIALLY YOUR RIGHT ARM!
GRAB
NEGI. YOU...

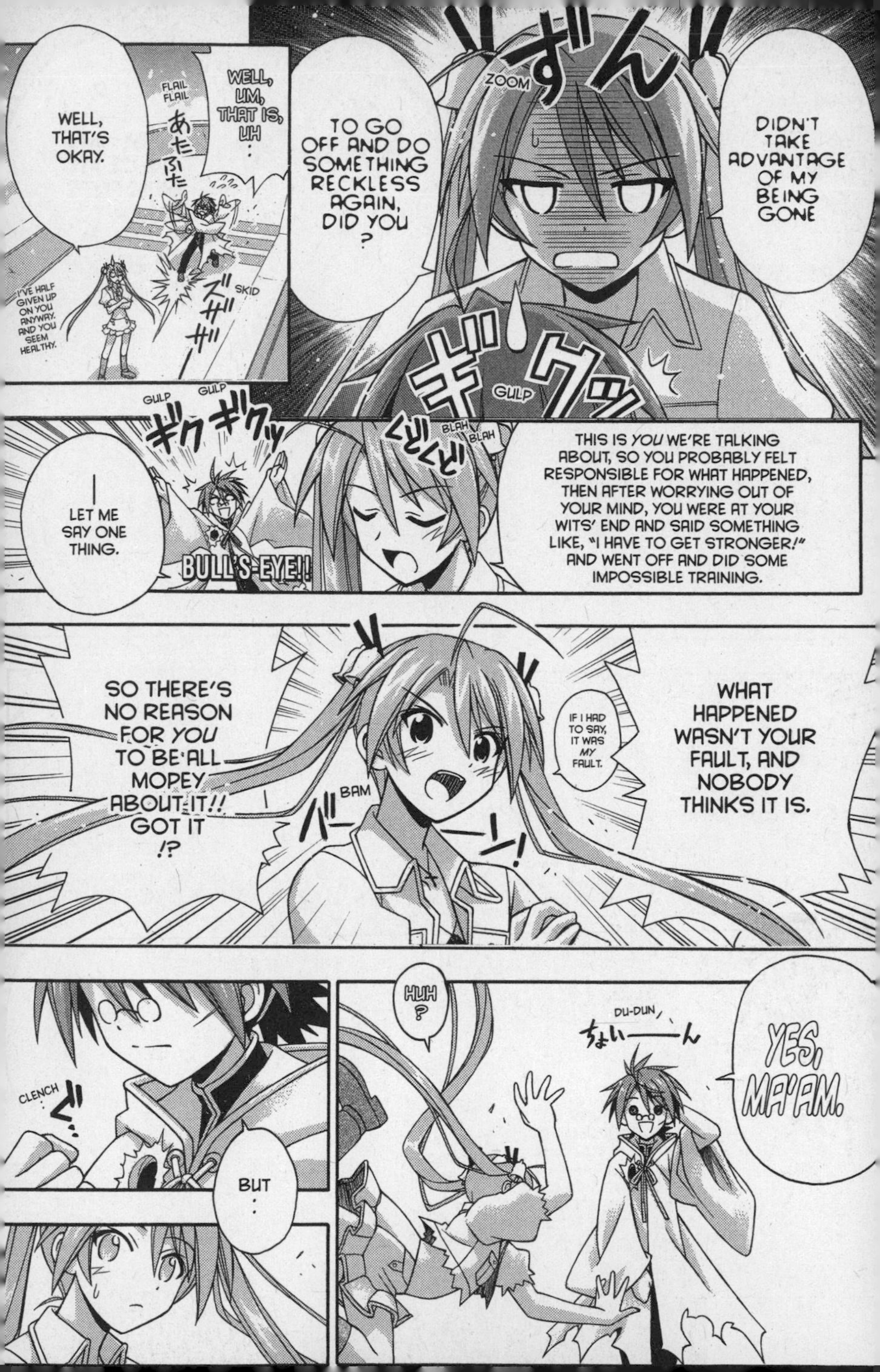
ずん!!
ZOOM
DIDN'T TAKE ADVANTAGE OF MY BEING GONE
TO GO OFF AND DO SOMETHING RECKLESS AGAIN, DID YOU?
ギクッ
GULP
WELL, UM, THAT IS, UH...
FLAIL FLAIL
あたふた
WELL, THAT'S OKAY.
SKID
ズザザザ
I'VE HALF GIVEN UP ON YOU ANYWAY. AND YOU SEEM HEALTHY.
THIS IS *YOU* WE'RE TALKING ABOUT, SO YOU PROBABLY FELT RESPONSIBLE FOR WHAT HAPPENED, THEN AFTER WORRYING OUT OF YOUR MIND, YOU WERE AT YOUR WITS' END AND SAID SOMETHING LIKE, "I HAVE TO GET STRONGER!" AND WENT OFF AND DID SOME IMPOSSIBLE TRAINING.
くどくど
BLAH BLAH
ギクギクッ
GULP GULP
BULL'S-EYE!!
I LET ME SAY ONE THING.
WHAT HAPPENED WASN'T YOUR FAULT, AND NOBODY THINKS IT IS.
IF I HAD TO SAY, IT WAS *MY* FAULT.
バーン!
BAM
SO THERE'S NO REASON FOR *YOU* TO BE ALL MOPEY ABOUT IT!! GOT IT!?
YES, MA'AM.
ちょいーーん
DU-DUN
HUH?
BUT...
CLENCH
ぐ

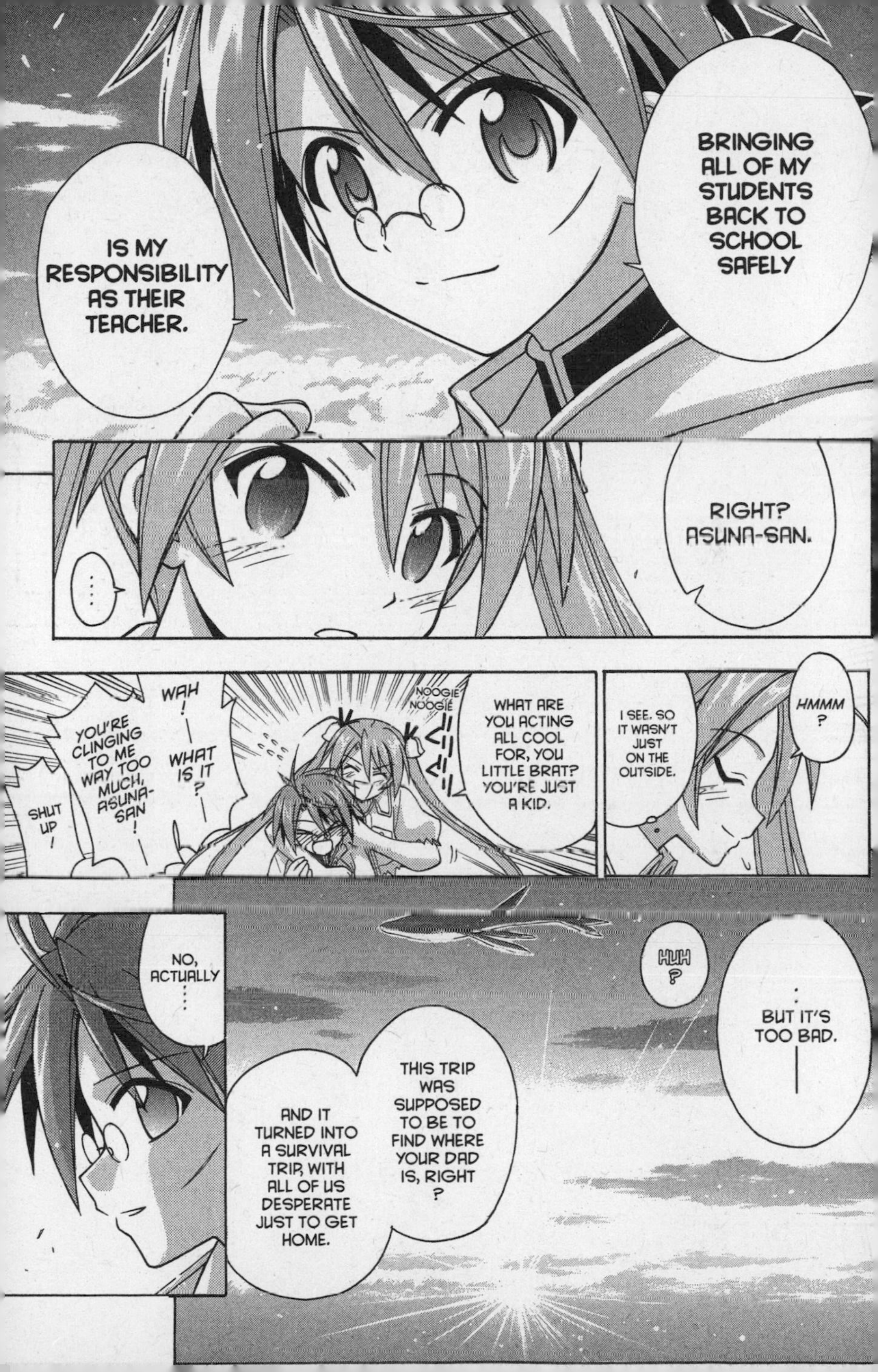
BRINGING ALL OF MY STUDENTS BACK TO SCHOOL SAFELY
IS MY RESPONSIBILITY AS THEIR TEACHER.
RIGHT? ASUNA-SAN.
.....
HMMM?
I SEE. SO IT WASN'T JUST ON THE OUTSIDE.
WHAT ARE YOU ACTING ALL COOL FOR, YOU LITTLE BRAT? YOU'RE JUST A KID.
NOOGIE NOOGIE
WAH! WHAT IS IT?
YOU'RE CLINGING TO ME WAY TOO MUCH, ASUNA-SAN!
SHUT UP!
...BUT IT'S TOO BAD.
HUH?
THIS TRIP WAS SUPPOSED TO BE TO FIND WHERE YOUR DAD IS, RIGHT?
AND IT TURNED INTO A SURVIVAL TRIP, WITH ALL OF US DESPERATE JUST TO GET HOME.
NO, ACTUALLY......

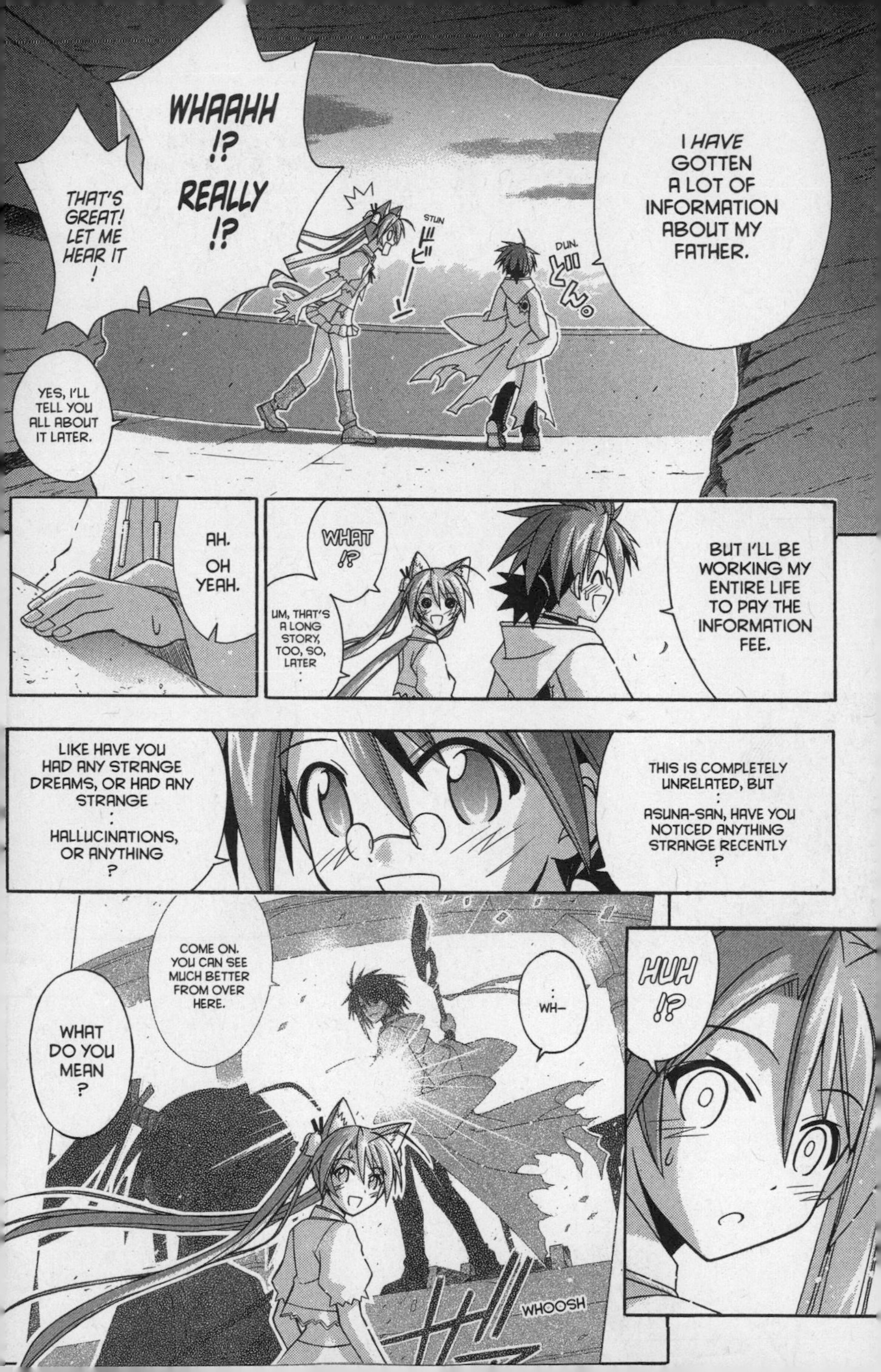
I HAVE GOTTEN A LOT OF INFORMATION ABOUT MY FATHER.
DUN.
STUN
WHAAHH !? REALLY !?
THAT'S GREAT! LET ME HEAR IT !
YES, I'LL TELL YOU ALL ABOUT IT LATER.
BUT I'LL BE WORKING MY ENTIRE LIFE TO PAY THE INFORMATION FEE.
WHAT !?
UM, THAT'S A LONG STORY, TOO, SO, LATER :
AH. OH YEAH.
THIS IS COMPLETELY UNRELATED, BUT : ASUNA-SAN, HAVE YOU NOTICED ANYTHING STRANGE RECENTLY ?
LIKE HAVE YOU HAD ANY STRANGE DREAMS, OR HAD ANY STRANGE : HALLUCINATIONS, OR ANYTHING ?
HUH !?
: WH–
COME ON. YOU CAN SEE MUCH BETTER FROM OVER HERE.
WHAT DO YOU MEAN ?
WHOOSH

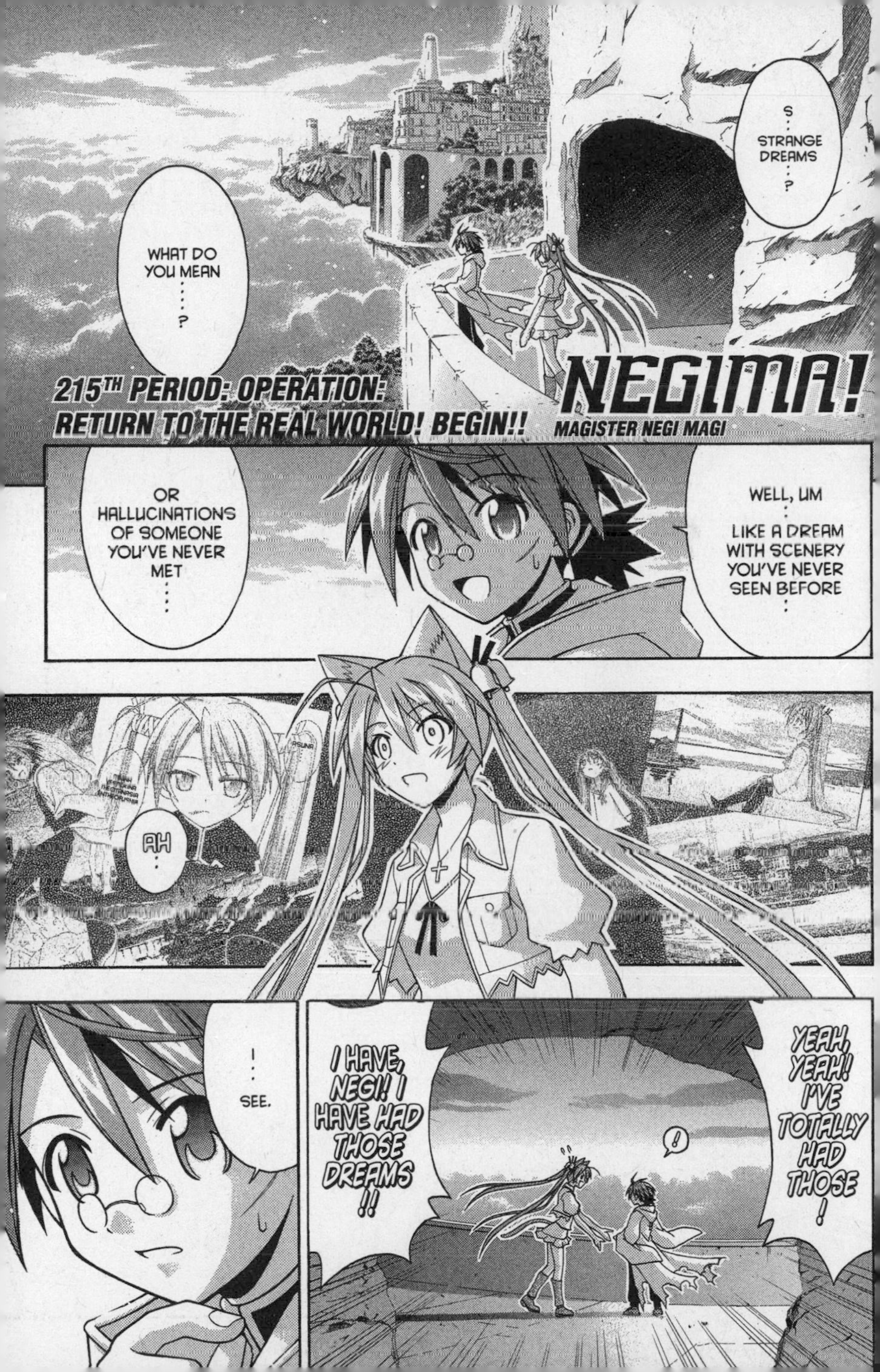
S... STRANGE DREAMS...?
WHAT DO YOU MEAN....?
NEGIMA! MAGISTER NEGI MAGI
215TH PERIOD: OPERATION: RETURN TO THE REAL WORLD! BEGIN!!
WELL, UM: LIKE A DREAM WITH SCENERY YOU'VE NEVER SEEN BEFORE:
OR HALLUCINATIONS OF SOMEONE YOU'VE NEVER MET....
AH...
YEAH, YEAH! I'VE TOTALLY HAD THOSE!
!
I HAVE, NEGI! I HAVE HAD THOSE DREAMS!!
!: SEE.

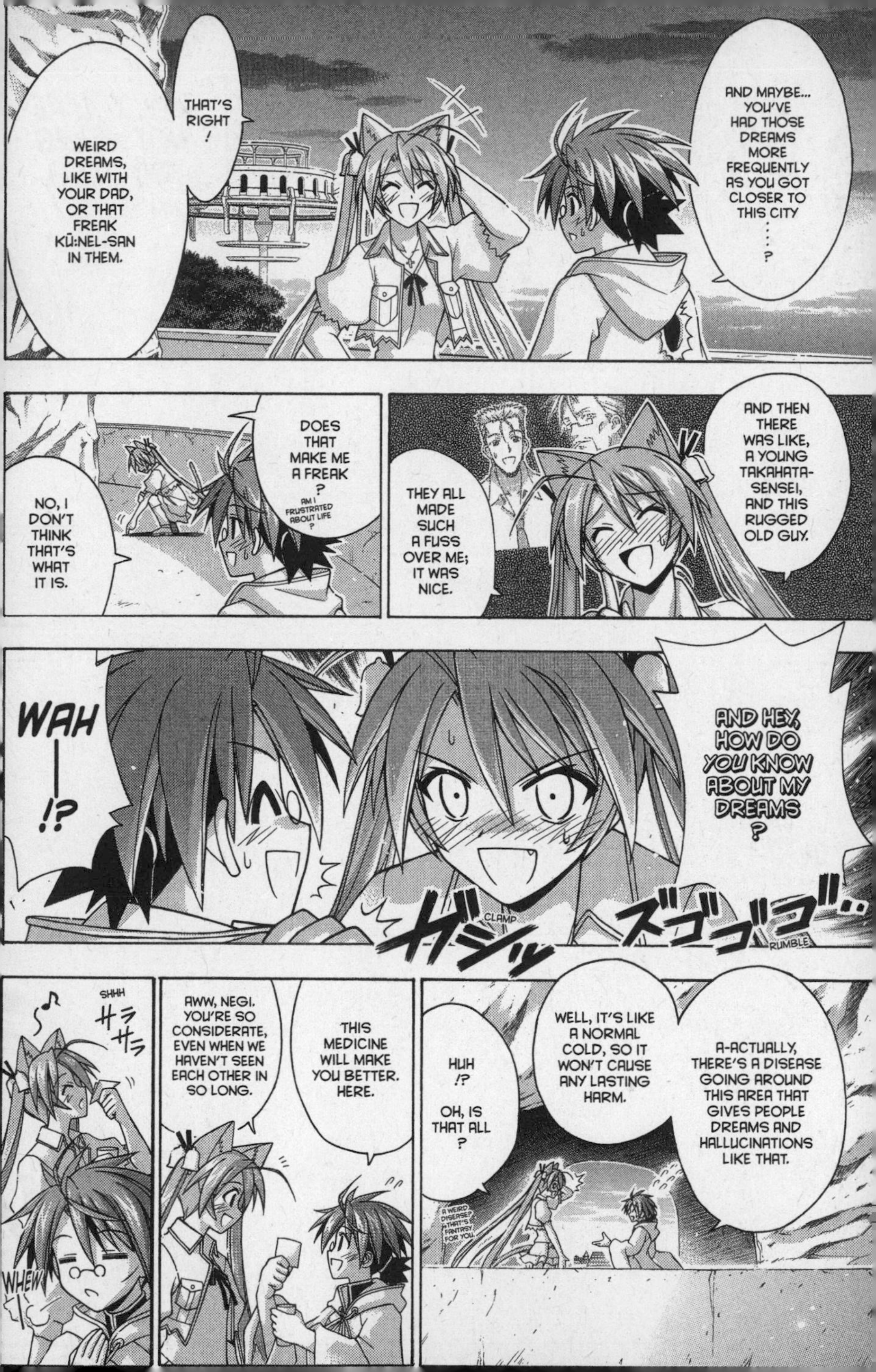
AND MAYBE... YOU'VE HAD THOSE DREAMS MORE FREQUENTLY AS YOU GOT CLOSER TO THIS CITY ....?
THAT'S RIGHT!
WEIRD DREAMS, LIKE WITH YOUR DAD, OR THAT FREAK KŪ:NEL-SAN IN THEM.
AND THEN THERE WAS LIKE, A YOUNG TAKAHATA-SENSEI, AND THIS RUGGED OLD GUY.
THEY ALL MADE SUCH A FUSS OVER ME; IT WAS NICE.
DOES THAT MAKE ME A FREAK?
AM I FRUSTRATED ABOUT LIFE?
NO, I DON'T THINK THAT'S WHAT IT IS.
AND HEY, HOW DO YOU KNOW ABOUT MY DREAMS?
WAH—!?
ガシッ
CLAMP
ズゴゴゴ
RUMBLE
A-ACTUALLY, THERE'S A DISEASE GOING AROUND THIS AREA THAT GIVES PEOPLE DREAMS AND HALLUCINATIONS LIKE THAT.
WELL, IT'S LIKE A NORMAL COLD, SO IT WON'T CAUSE ANY LASTING HARM.
HUH!? OH, IS THAT ALL?
A WEIRD DISEASE? THAT'S FANTASY FOR YOU.
THIS MEDICINE WILL MAKE YOU BETTER. HERE.
AWW, NEGI. YOU'RE SO CONSIDERATE, EVEN WHEN WE HAVEN'T SEEN EACH OTHER IN SO LONG.
SHHH
サラサラ
WHEW

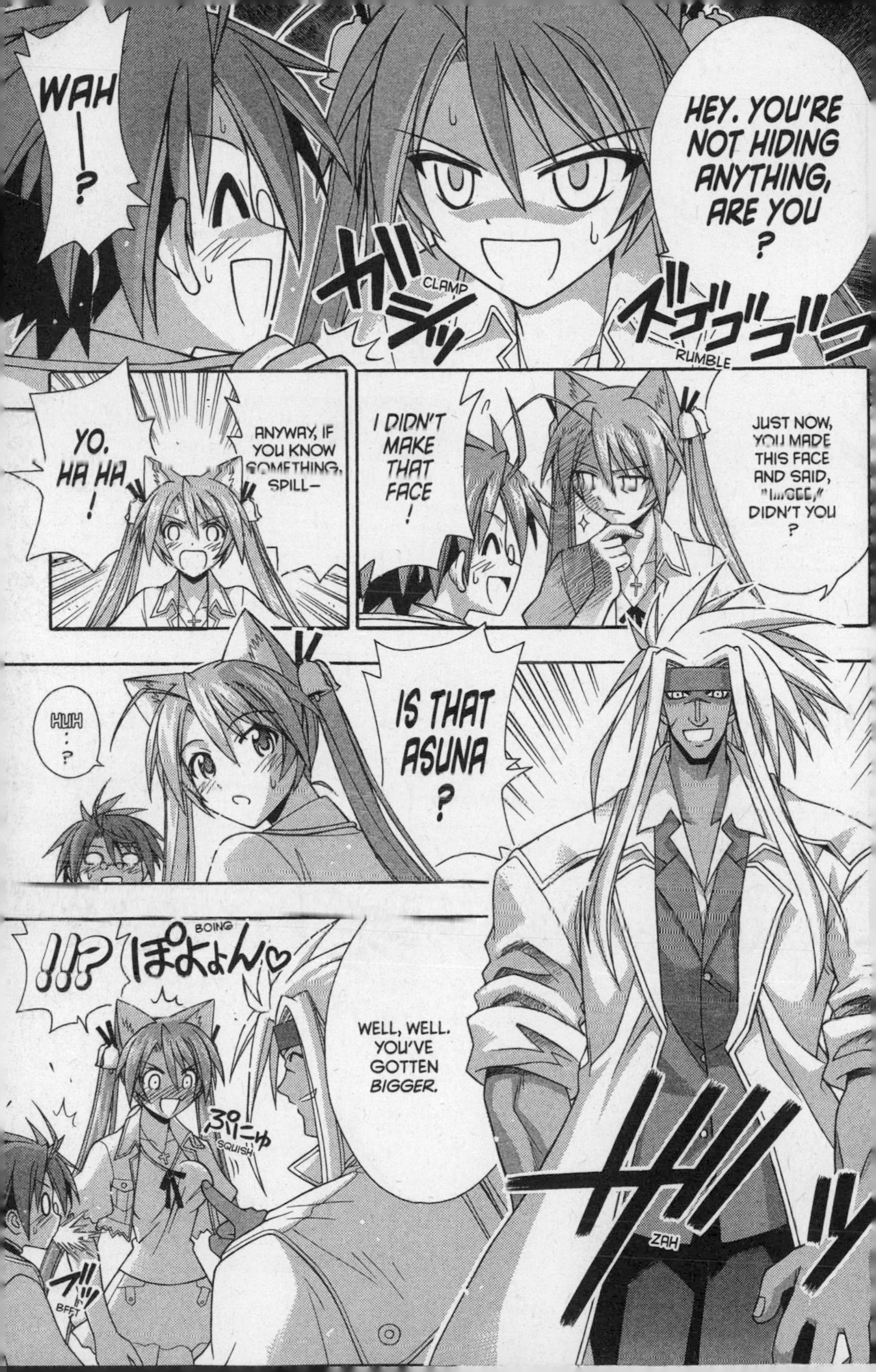
HEY. YOU'RE NOT HIDING ANYTHING, ARE YOU?
RUMBLE
CLAMP
WAH—?
JUST NOW, YOU MADE THIS FACE AND SAID, "I...SEE," DIDN'T YOU?
I DIDN'T MAKE THAT FACE!
ANYWAY, IF YOU KNOW SOMETHING, SPILL—
YO. HA HA!
ZAH
IS THAT ASUNA?
HUH...?
WELL, WELL. YOU'VE GOTTEN BIGGER.
ぽよょん♡
BOING
!!?
ぷにゅ
SQUISH
BFFT

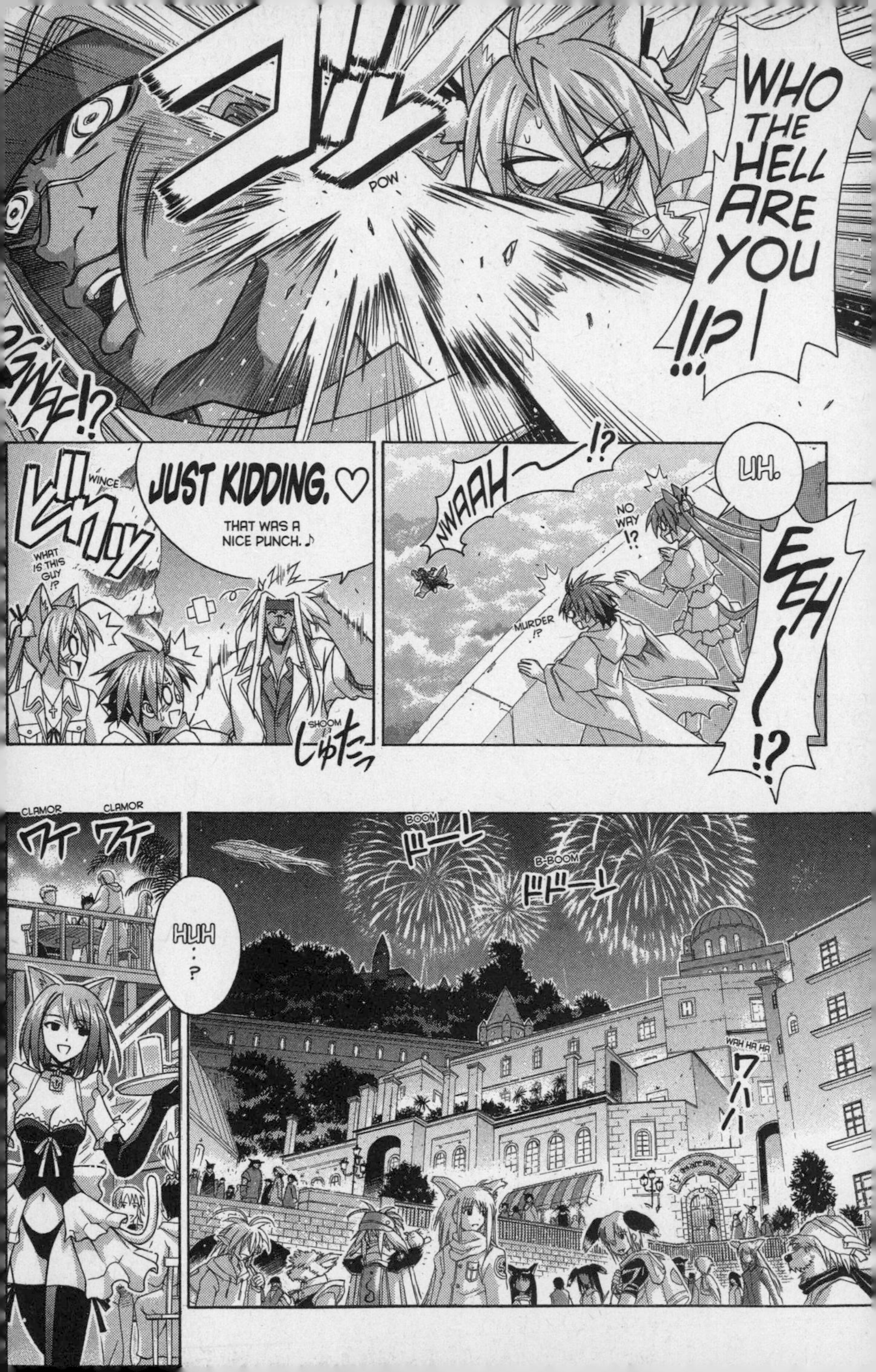
WHO THE HELL ARE YOU!!?
POW
GWAF!?
UH.
EEH~~!?
NO WAY!?
NWAAH~~!?
MURDER!?
JUST KIDDING. ♡
THAT WAS A NICE PUNCH. ♪
WINCE
WHAT IS THIS GUY!?
SHOOM
BOOM
B-BOOM
WAH HA HA
CLAMOR CLAMOR
HUH...?

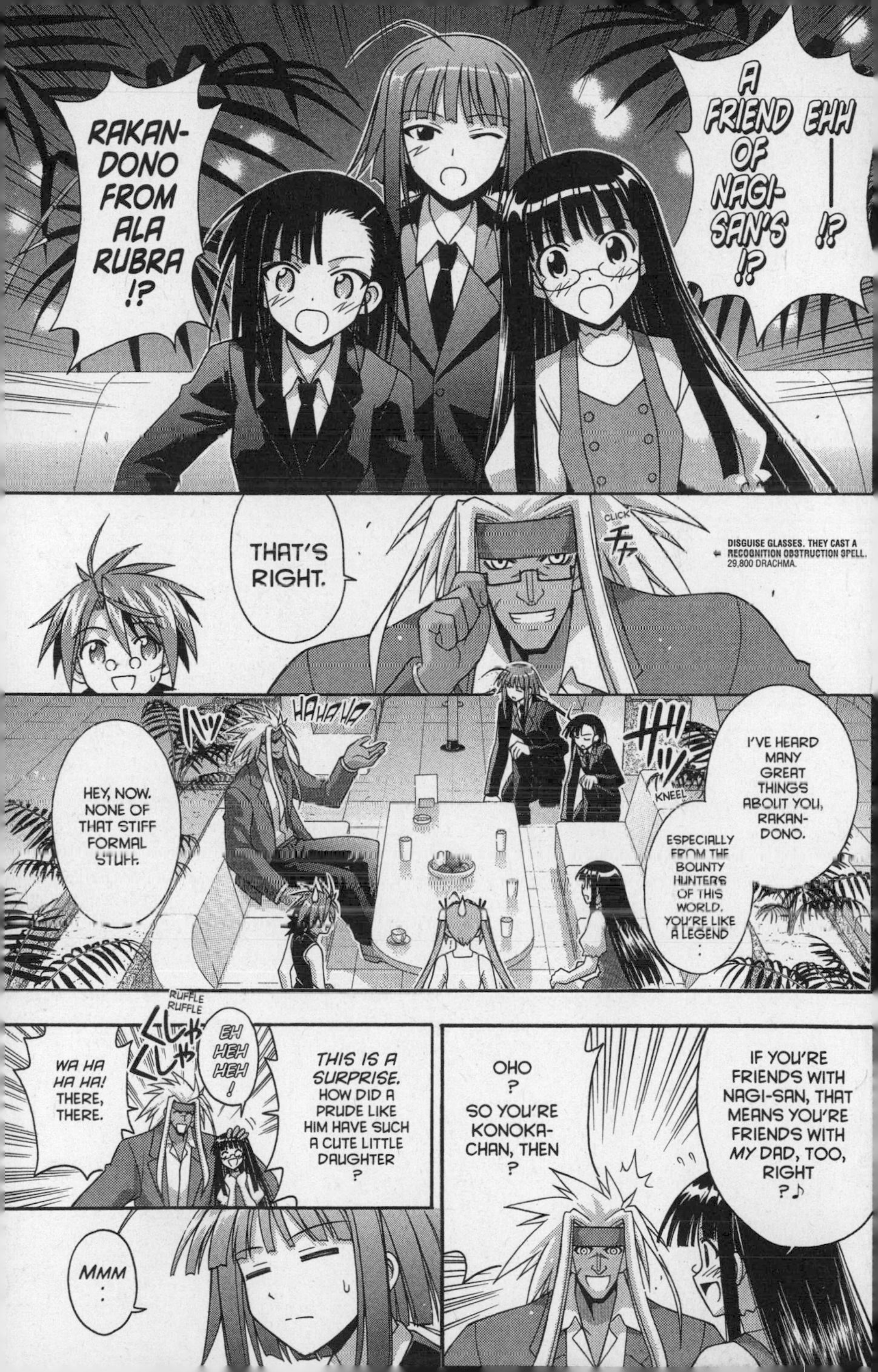

A FRIEND OF NAGI-SAN'S !?
EHH —— !?
RAKAN-DONO FROM ALA RUBRA !?
← DISGUISE GLASSES. THEY CAST A RECOGNITION OBSTRUCTION SPELL. 29,800 DRACHMA.
CLICK
チャ
THAT'S RIGHT.
I'VE HEARD MANY GREAT THINGS ABOUT YOU, RAKAN-DONO.
ESPECIALLY FROM THE BOUNTY HUNTERS OF THIS WORLD. YOU'RE LIKE A LEGEND :
ザッ
KNEEL
HAHAHA
ハッ
HEY, NOW. NONE OF THAT STIFF FORMAL STUFF.
IF YOU'RE FRIENDS WITH NAGI-SAN, THAT MEANS YOU'RE FRIENDS WITH MY DAD, TOO, RIGHT ?♪
OHO ?
SO YOU'RE KONOKA-CHAN, THEN ?
THIS IS A SURPRISE. HOW DID A PRUDE LIKE HIM HAVE SUCH A CUTE LITTLE DAUGHTER ?
EH HEH HEH !
RUFFLE RUFFLE
くしゃくしゃ
WA HA HA HA! THERE, THERE.
MMM :

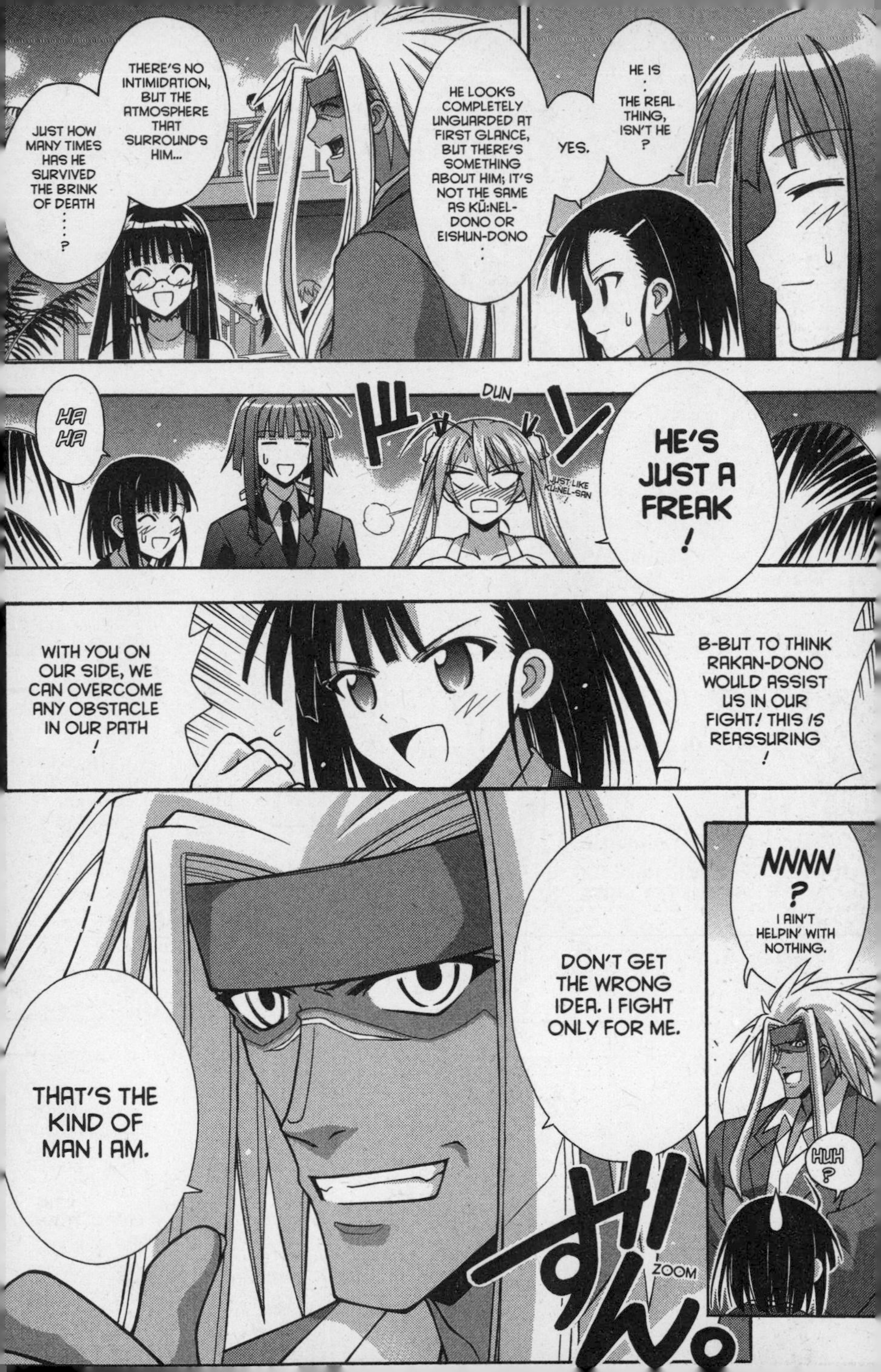
HE IS . THE REAL THING, ISN'T HE ?
YES.
HE LOOKS COMPLETELY UNGUARDED AT FIRST GLANCE, BUT THERE'S SOMETHING ABOUT HIM; IT'S NOT THE SAME AS KŪ:NEL-DONO OR EISHUN-DONO . .
THERE'S NO INTIMIDATION, BUT THE ATMOSPHERE THAT SURROUNDS HIM...
JUST HOW MANY TIMES HAS HE SURVIVED THE BRINK OF DEATH . . . . ?
HE'S JUST A FREAK !
DUN
JUST LIKE KŪ:NEL-SAN !
HA HA
B-BUT TO THINK RAKAN-DONO WOULD ASSIST US IN OUR FIGHT! THIS IS REASSURING !
WITH YOU ON OUR SIDE, WE CAN OVERCOME ANY OBSTACLE IN OUR PATH !
NNNN ?
I AIN'T HELPIN' WITH NOTHING.
HUH ?
DON'T GET THE WRONG IDEA. I FIGHT ONLY FOR ME.
THAT'S THE KIND OF MAN I AM.
すん。
ZOOM

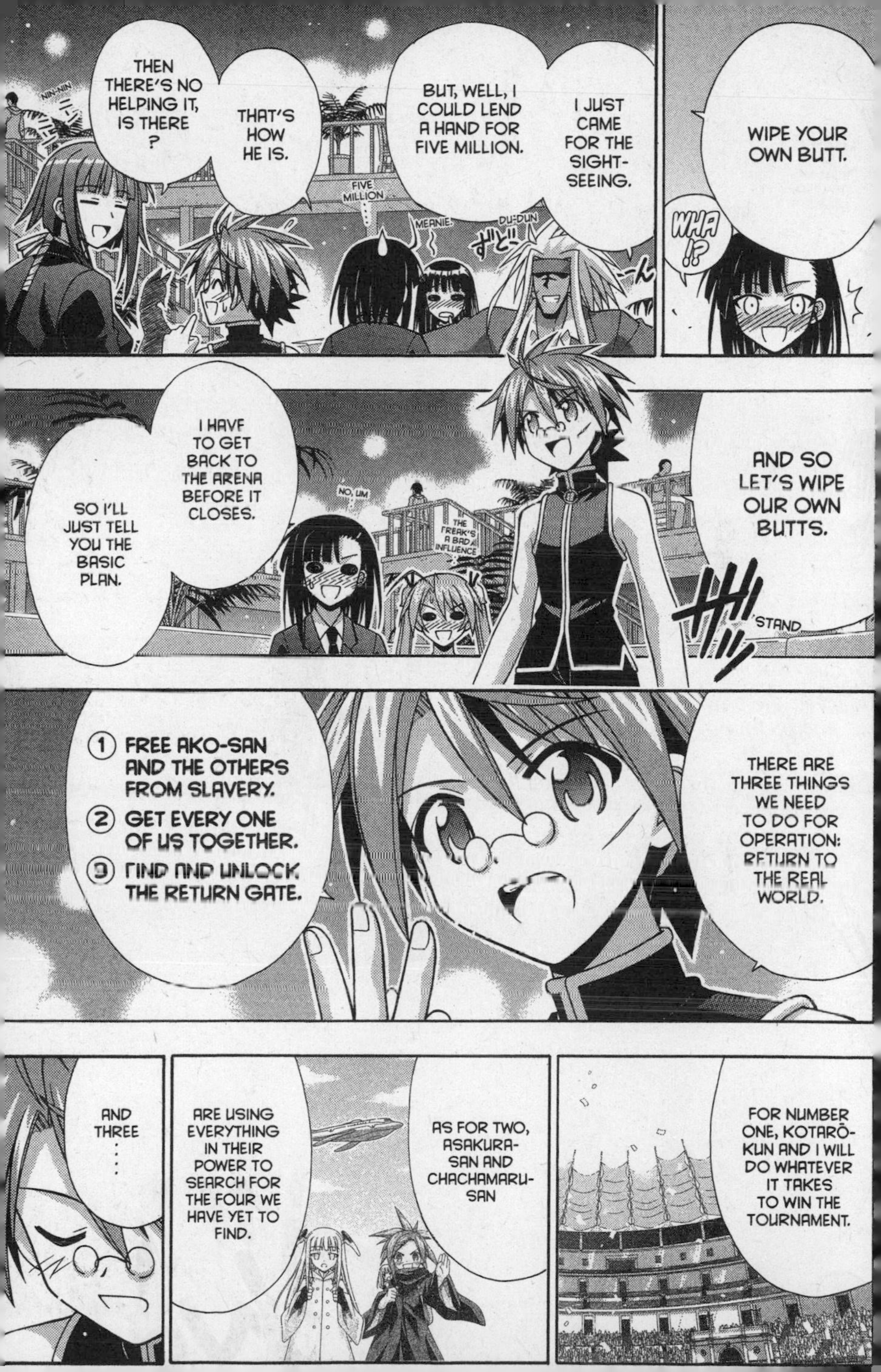
WIPE YOUR OWN BUTT.
WHA !?
I JUST CAME FOR THE SIGHT-SEEING.
BUT, WELL, I COULD LEND A HAND FOR FIVE MILLION.
DU-DUN
MEANIE.
FIVE MILLION...
THAT'S HOW HE IS.
THEN THERE'S NO HELPING IT, IS THERE?
NIN-NIN
AND SO LET'S WIPE OUR OWN BUTTS.
STAND
THE FREAK'S A BAD INFLUENCE
NO, UM
I HAVE TO GET BACK TO THE ARENA BEFORE IT CLOSES.
SO I'LL JUST TELL YOU THE BASIC PLAN.
THERE ARE THREE THINGS WE NEED TO DO FOR OPERATION: RETURN TO THE REAL WORLD.
① FREE AKO-SAN AND THE OTHERS FROM SLAVERY.
② GET EVERY ONE OF US TOGETHER.
③ FIND AND UNLOCK THE RETURN GATE.
FOR NUMBER ONE, KOTARŌ-KUN AND I WILL DO WHATEVER IT TAKES TO WIN THE TOURNAMENT.
AS FOR TWO, ASAKURA-SAN AND CHACHAMARU-SAN
ARE USING EVERYTHING IN THEIR POWER TO SEARCH FOR THE FOUR WE HAVE YET TO FIND.
AND THREE...

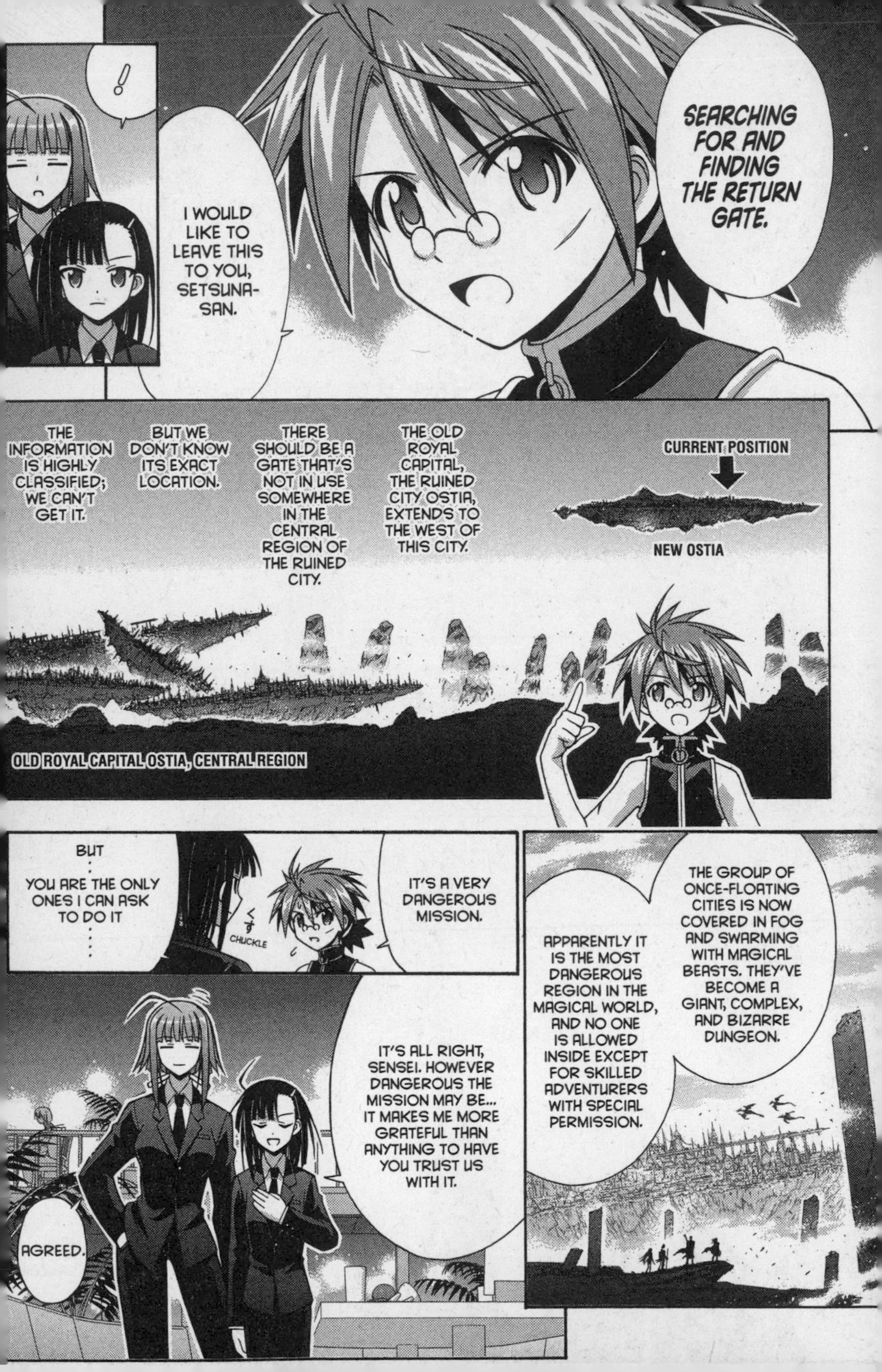
SEARCHING FOR AND FINDING THE RETURN GATE.
I WOULD LIKE TO LEAVE THIS TO YOU, SETSUNA-SAN.
!
CURRENT POSITION
NEW OSTIA
THE OLD ROYAL CAPITAL, THE RUINED CITY OSTIA, EXTENDS TO THE WEST OF THIS CITY.
THERE SHOULD BE A GATE THAT'S NOT IN USE SOMEWHERE IN THE CENTRAL REGION OF THE RUINED CITY.
BUT WE DON'T KNOW ITS EXACT LOCATION.
THE INFORMATION IS HIGHLY CLASSIFIED; WE CAN'T GET IT.
OLD ROYAL CAPITAL OSTIA, CENTRAL REGION
THE GROUP OF ONCE-FLOATING CITIES IS NOW COVERED IN FOG AND SWARMING WITH MAGICAL BEASTS. THEY'VE BECOME A GIANT, COMPLEX, AND BIZARRE DUNGEON.
APPARENTLY IT IS THE MOST DANGEROUS REGION IN THE MAGICAL WORLD, AND NO ONE IS ALLOWED INSIDE EXCEPT FOR SKILLED ADVENTURERS WITH SPECIAL PERMISSION.
IT'S A VERY DANGEROUS MISSION.
くす
CHUCKLE
BUT... YOU ARE THE ONLY ONES I CAN ASK TO DO IT...
IT'S ALL RIGHT, SENSEI. HOWEVER DANGEROUS THE MISSION MAY BE... IT MAKES ME MORE GRATEFUL THAN ANYTHING TO HAVE YOU TRUST US WITH IT.
AGREED.

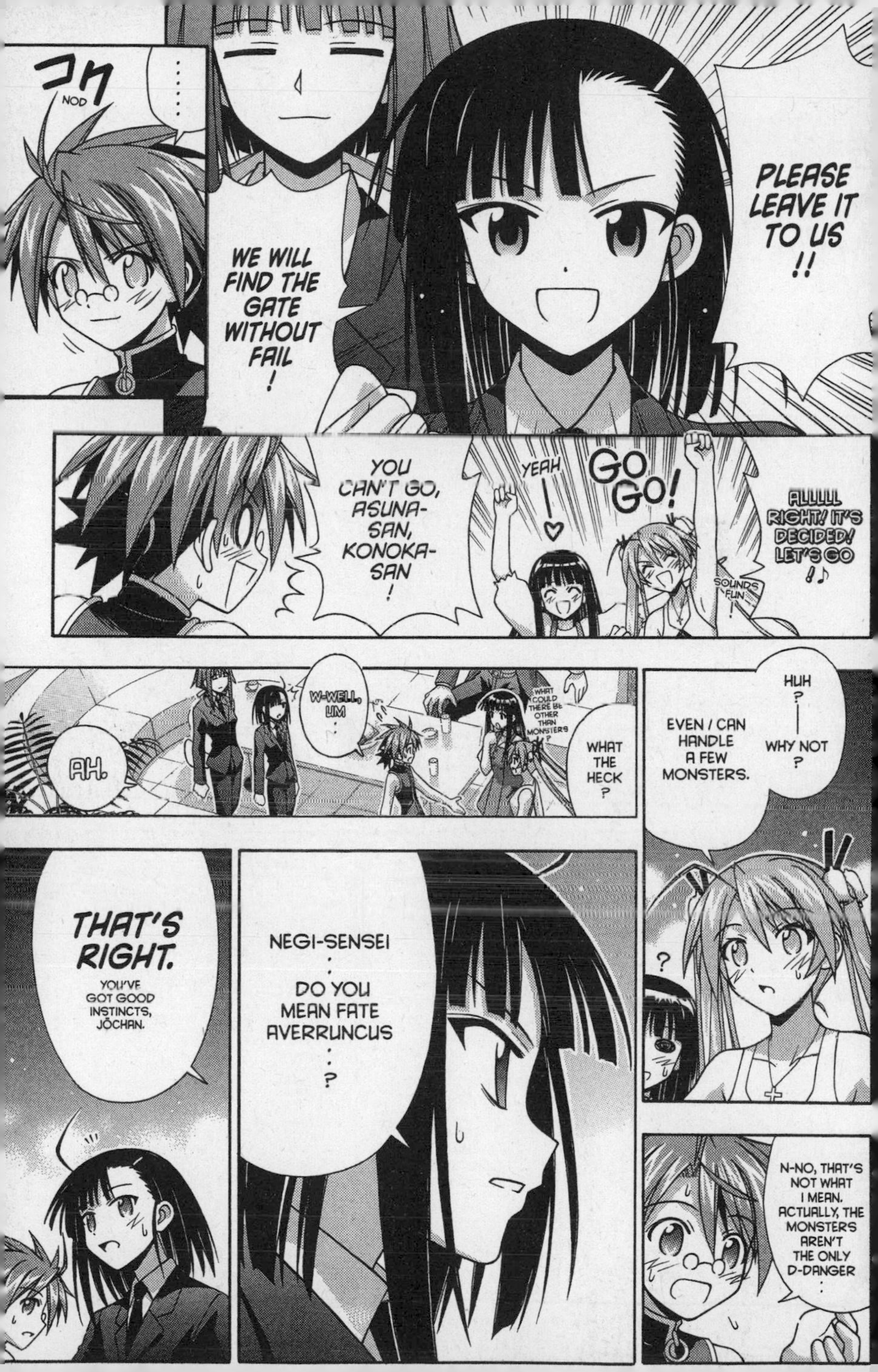
PLEASE LEAVE IT TO US !!
WE WILL FIND THE GATE WITHOUT FAIL !
. . . . .
コク
NOD
ALLLLL RIGHT! IT'S DECIDED! LET'S GO !♪
SOUNDS FUN !
GO GO!
YEAH ♥
YOU CAN'T GO, ASUNA-SAN, KONOKA-SAN !
HUH ? WHY NOT ?
EVEN I CAN HANDLE A FEW MONSTERS.
WHAT THE HECK ?
WHAT COULD THERE BE OTHER THAN MONSTERS ?
W-WELL, UM . .
AH.
?
N-NO, THAT'S NOT WHAT I MEAN. ACTUALLY, THE MONSTERS AREN'T THE ONLY D-DANGER . .
NEGI-SENSEI . . DO YOU MEAN FATE AVERRUNCUS . . . ?
THAT'S RIGHT.
YOU'VE GOT GOOD INSTINCTS, JŌCHAN.

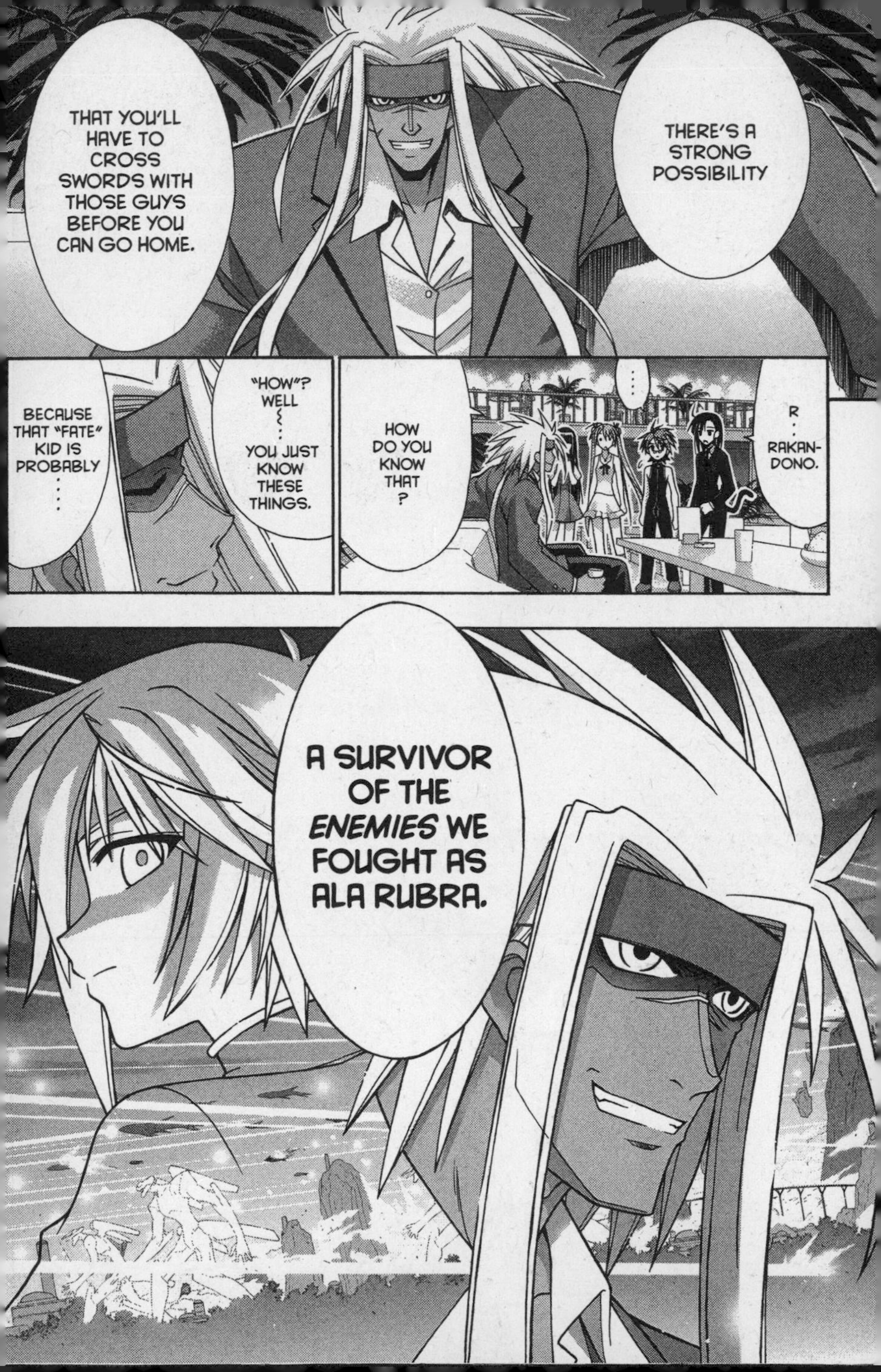
THERE'S A STRONG POSSIBILITY
THAT YOU'LL HAVE TO CROSS SWORDS WITH THOSE GUYS BEFORE YOU CAN GO HOME.
R... RAKAN-DONO.
...
HOW DO YOU KNOW THAT?
"HOW"? WELL... YOU JUST KNOW THESE THINGS.
BECAUSE THAT "FATE" KID IS PROBABLY...
A SURVIVOR OF THE *ENEMIES* WE FOUGHT AS ALA RUBRA.

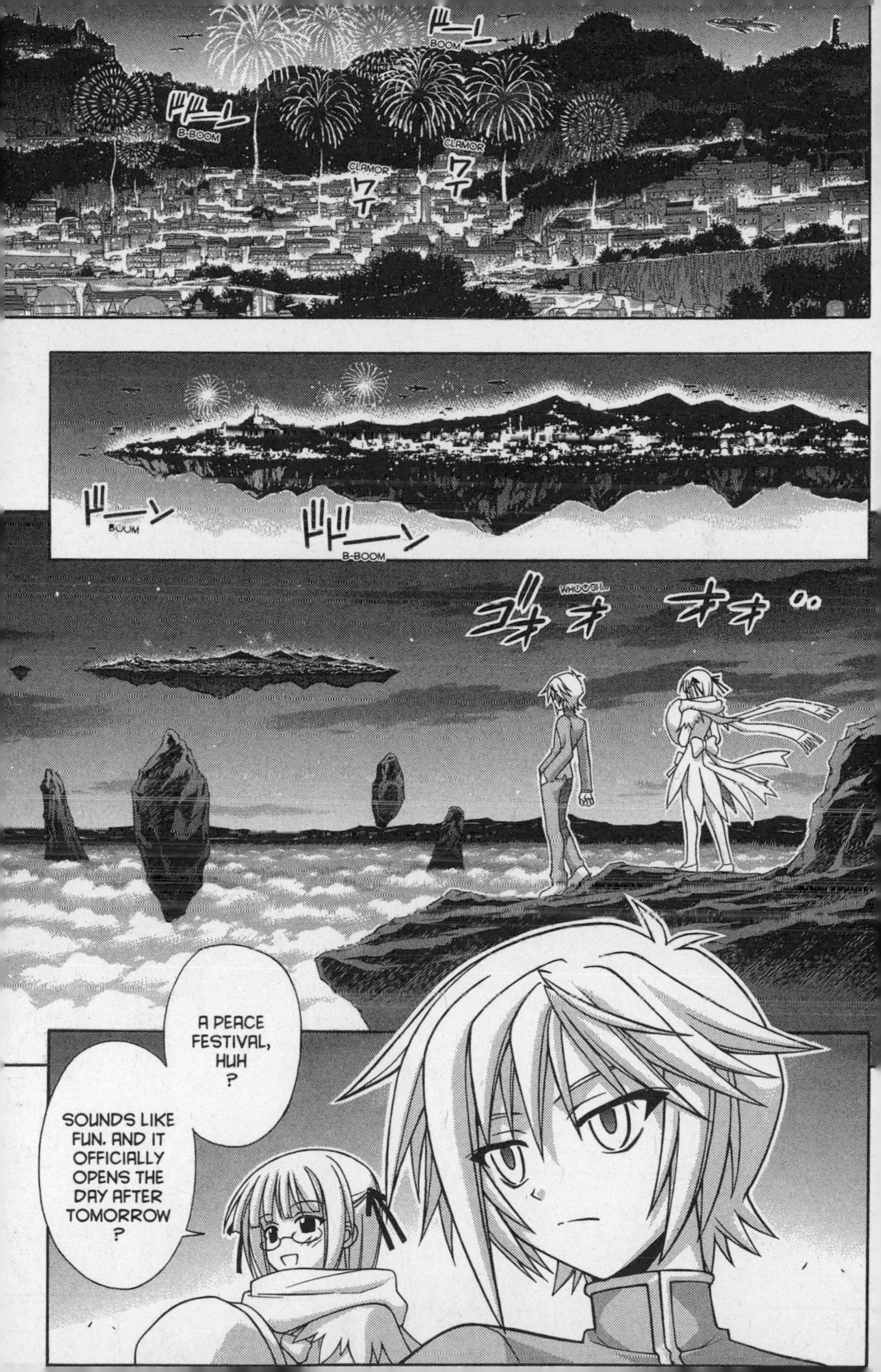
BOOM
CLAMOR
CLAMOR
B-BOOM
B-BOOM
BOOM
WHOOSH...
A PEACE FESTIVAL, HUH?
SOUNDS LIKE FUN. AND IT OFFICIALLY OPENS THE DAY AFTER TOMORROW?

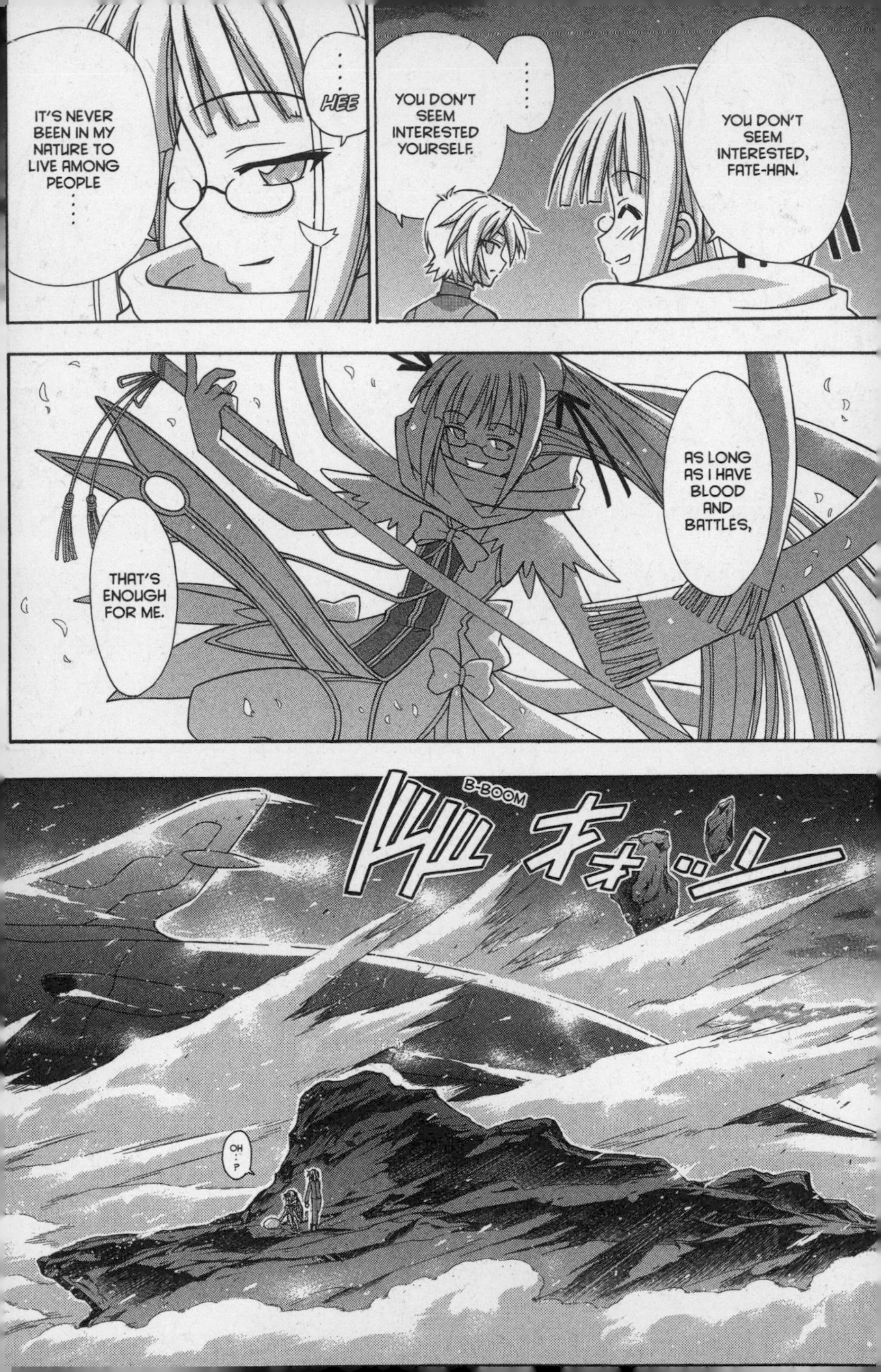
YOU DON'T SEEM INTERESTED, FATE-HAN.
.....
YOU DON'T SEEM INTERESTED YOURSELF.
..... HEE
IT'S NEVER BEEN IN MY NATURE TO LIVE AMONG PEOPLE .....
AS LONG AS I HAVE BLOOD AND BATTLES,
THAT'S ENOUGH FOR ME.
B-BOOM
OH...?

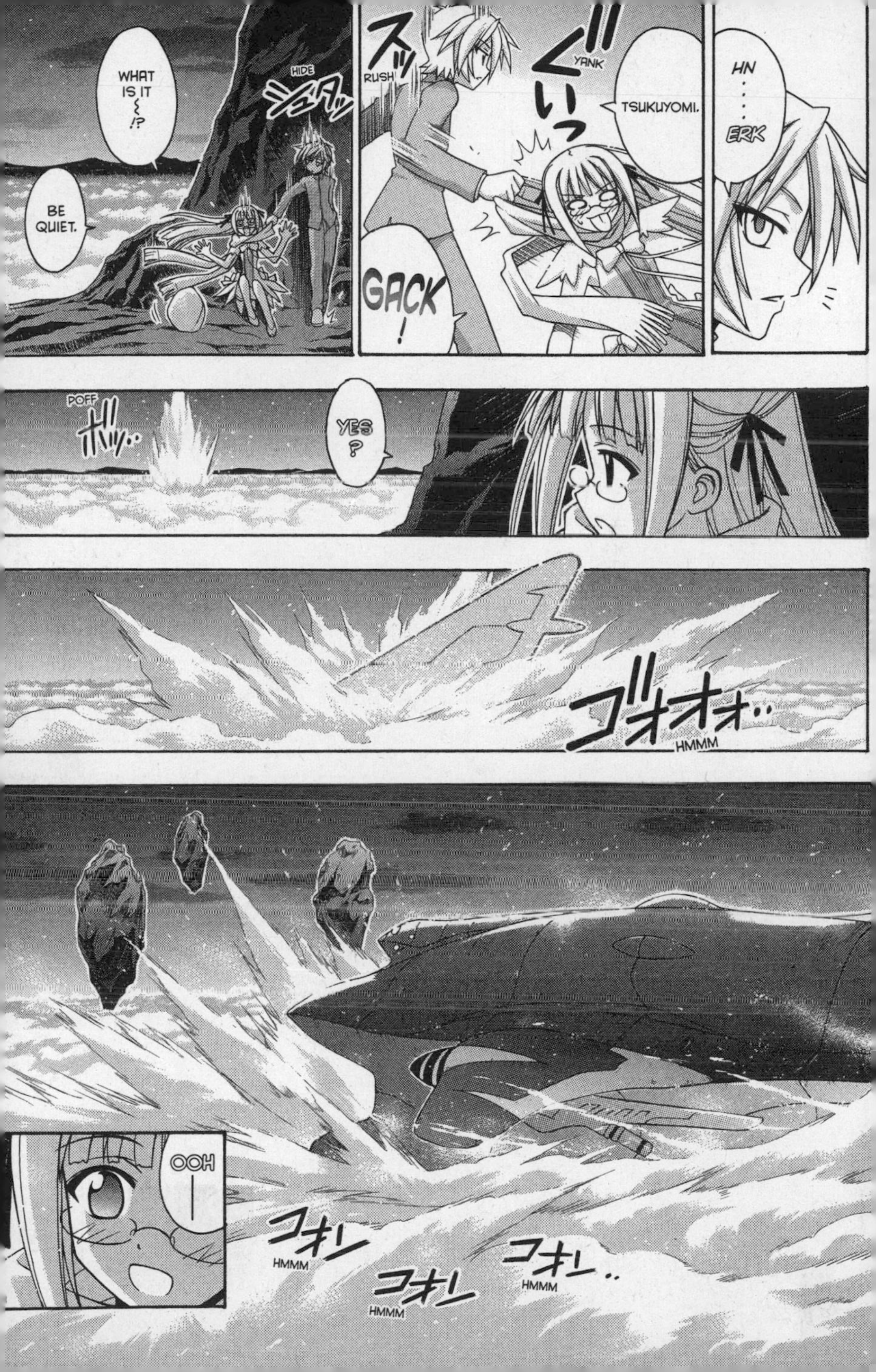
HN . . . . ERK
YANK
TSUKUYOMI.
RUSH
GACK!
HIDE
WHAT IS IT ~!?
BE QUIET.
YES?
POFF
HMMM
OOH —
HMMM
HMMM
HMMM

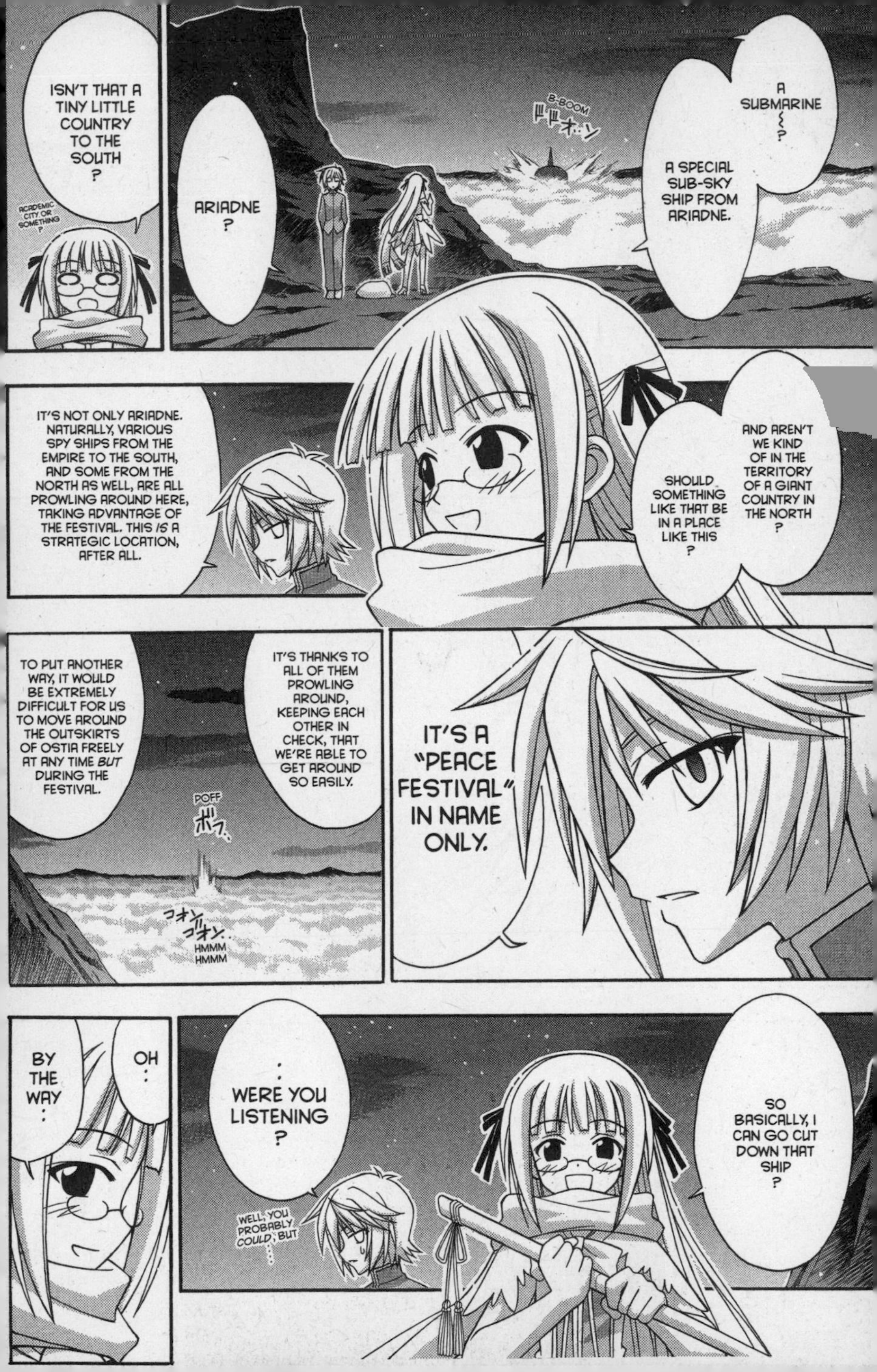
A SUBMARINE ~~?
B-BOOM
A SPECIAL SUB-SKY SHIP FROM ARIADNE.
ARIADNE?
ISN'T THAT A TINY LITTLE COUNTRY TO THE SOUTH?
ACADEMIC CITY OR SOMETHING?
AND AREN'T WE KIND OF IN THE TERRITORY OF A GIANT COUNTRY IN THE NORTH?
SHOULD SOMETHING LIKE THAT BE IN A PLACE LIKE THIS?
IT'S NOT ONLY ARIADNE. NATURALLY, VARIOUS SPY SHIPS FROM THE EMPIRE TO THE SOUTH, AND SOME FROM THE NORTH AS WELL, ARE ALL PROWLING AROUND HERE, TAKING ADVANTAGE OF THE FESTIVAL. THIS *IS* A STRATEGIC LOCATION, AFTER ALL.
IT'S A "PEACE FESTIVAL" IN NAME ONLY.
IT'S THANKS TO ALL OF THEM PROWLING AROUND, KEEPING EACH OTHER IN CHECK, THAT WE'RE ABLE TO GET AROUND SO EASILY.
TO PUT ANOTHER WAY, IT WOULD BE EXTREMELY DIFFICULT FOR US TO MOVE AROUND THE OUTSKIRTS OF OSTIA FREELY AT ANY TIME *BUT* DURING THE FESTIVAL.
POFF
HMMM HMMM
SO BASICALLY, I CAN GO CUT DOWN THAT SHIP?
WELL, YOU PROBABLY *COULD*, BUT...
...WERE YOU LISTENING?
OH:
BY THE WAY:

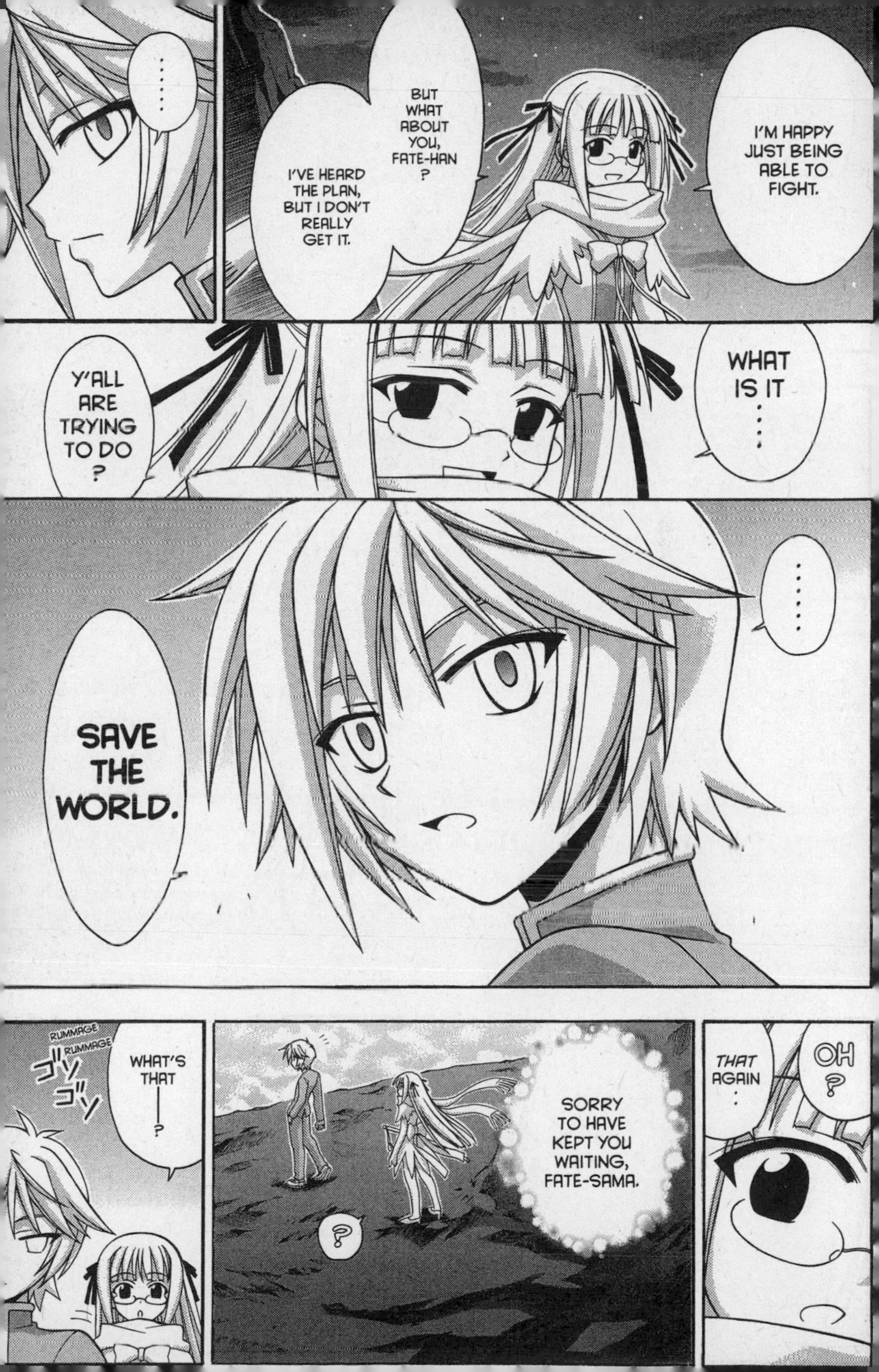
I'M HAPPY JUST BEING ABLE TO FIGHT.
BUT WHAT ABOUT YOU, FATE-HAN?
I'VE HEARD THE PLAN, BUT I DON'T REALLY GET IT.
......
WHAT IS IT ......
Y'ALL ARE TRYING TO DO?
......
SAVE THE WORLD.
OH?
*THAT* AGAIN...
SORRY TO HAVE KEPT YOU WAITING, FATE-SAMA.
?
RUMMAGE RUMMAGE
ゴソゴソ
WHAT'S THAT—?

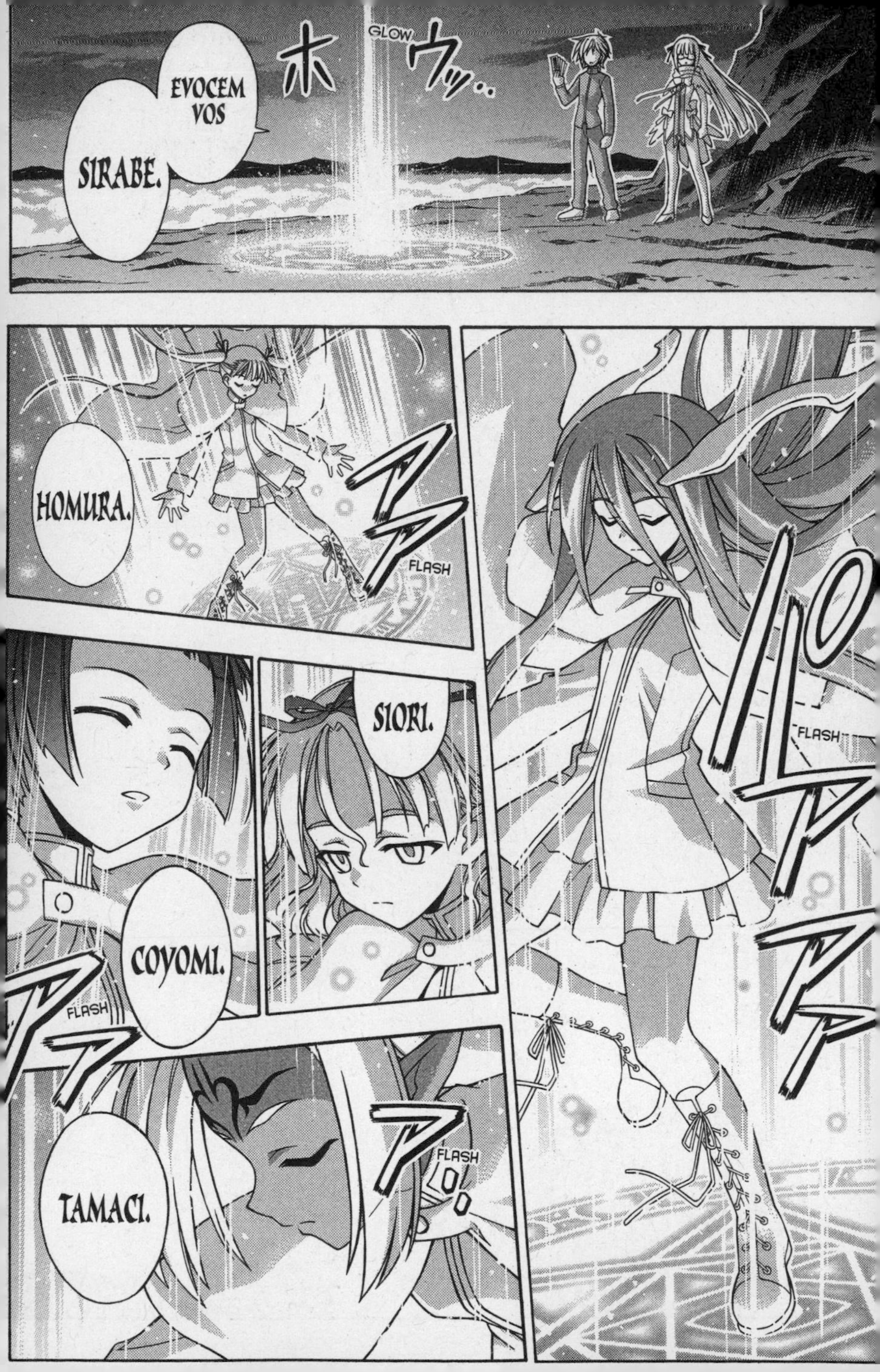
ホウッ..
GLOW
EVOCEM VOS
SIRABE.
FLASH
HOMURA.
FLASH
SIORI.
COYOMI.
FLASH
TAMACI.
FLASH

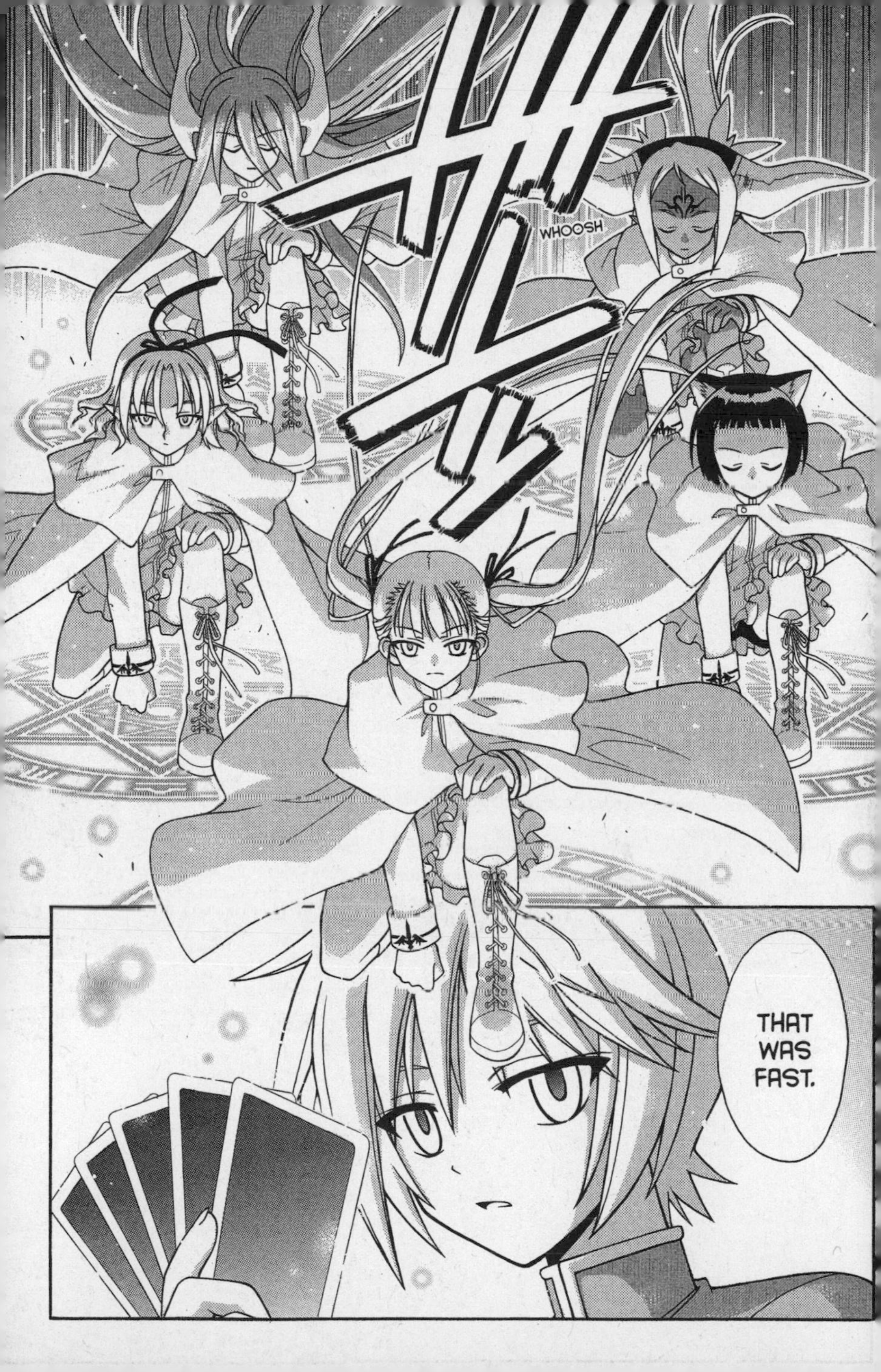
WHOOSH
THAT WAS FAST.

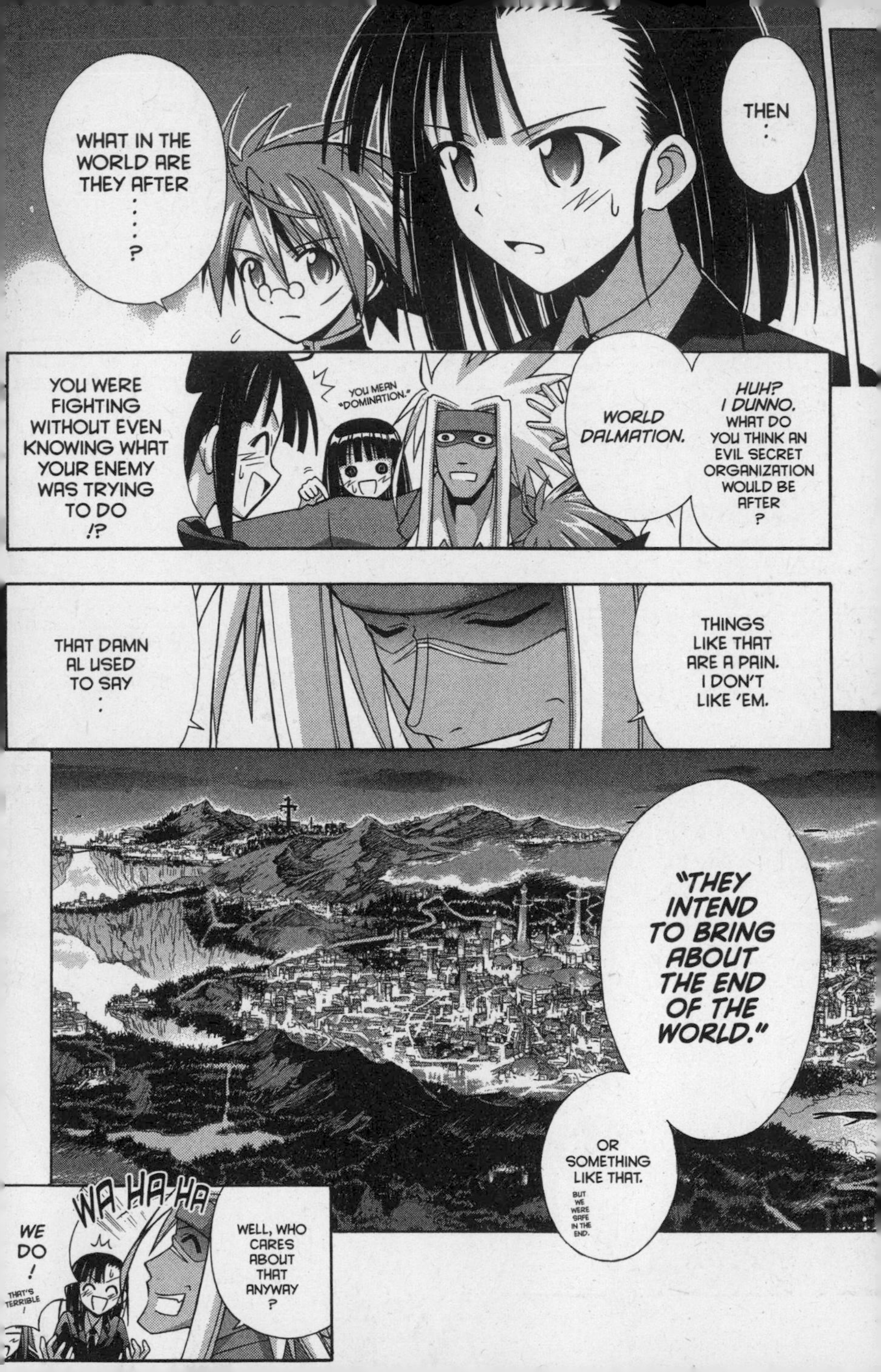
THEN...
WHAT IN THE WORLD ARE THEY AFTER.....?
HUH? I DUNNO. WHAT DO YOU THINK AN EVIL SECRET ORGANIZATION WOULD BE AFTER?
WORLD DALMATION.
YOU MEAN "DOMINATION."
YOU WERE FIGHTING WITHOUT EVEN KNOWING WHAT YOUR ENEMY WAS TRYING TO DO!?
THINGS LIKE THAT ARE A PAIN. I DON'T LIKE 'EM.
THAT DAMN AL USED TO SAY:
"THEY INTEND TO BRING ABOUT THE END OF THE WORLD."
OR SOMETHING LIKE THAT.
BUT WE WERE SAFE IN THE END.
WA HA HA
WELL, WHO CARES ABOUT THAT ANYWAY?
WE DO!
THAT'S TERRIBLE!

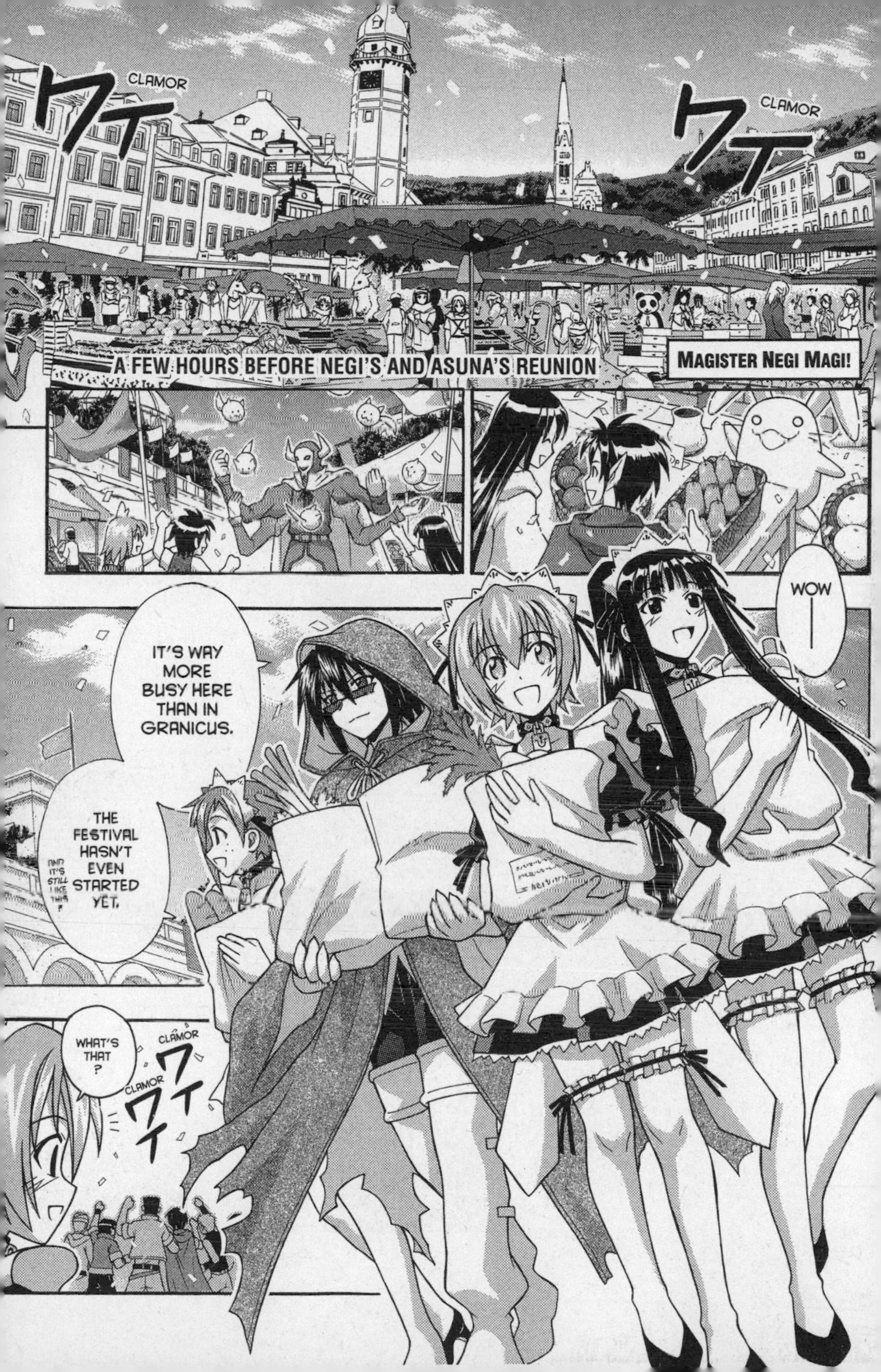
ワイ
CLAMOR
Magister Negi Magi!
ワイ
CLAMOR
A FEW HOURS BEFORE NEGI'S AND ASUNA'S REUNION
WOW
IT'S WAY MORE BUSY HERE THAN IN GRANICUS.
THE FESTIVAL HASN'T EVEN STARTED YET.
AND IT'S STILL LIKE THIS?
WHAT'S THAT?
ワイ
CLAMOR
ワイ
CLAMOR

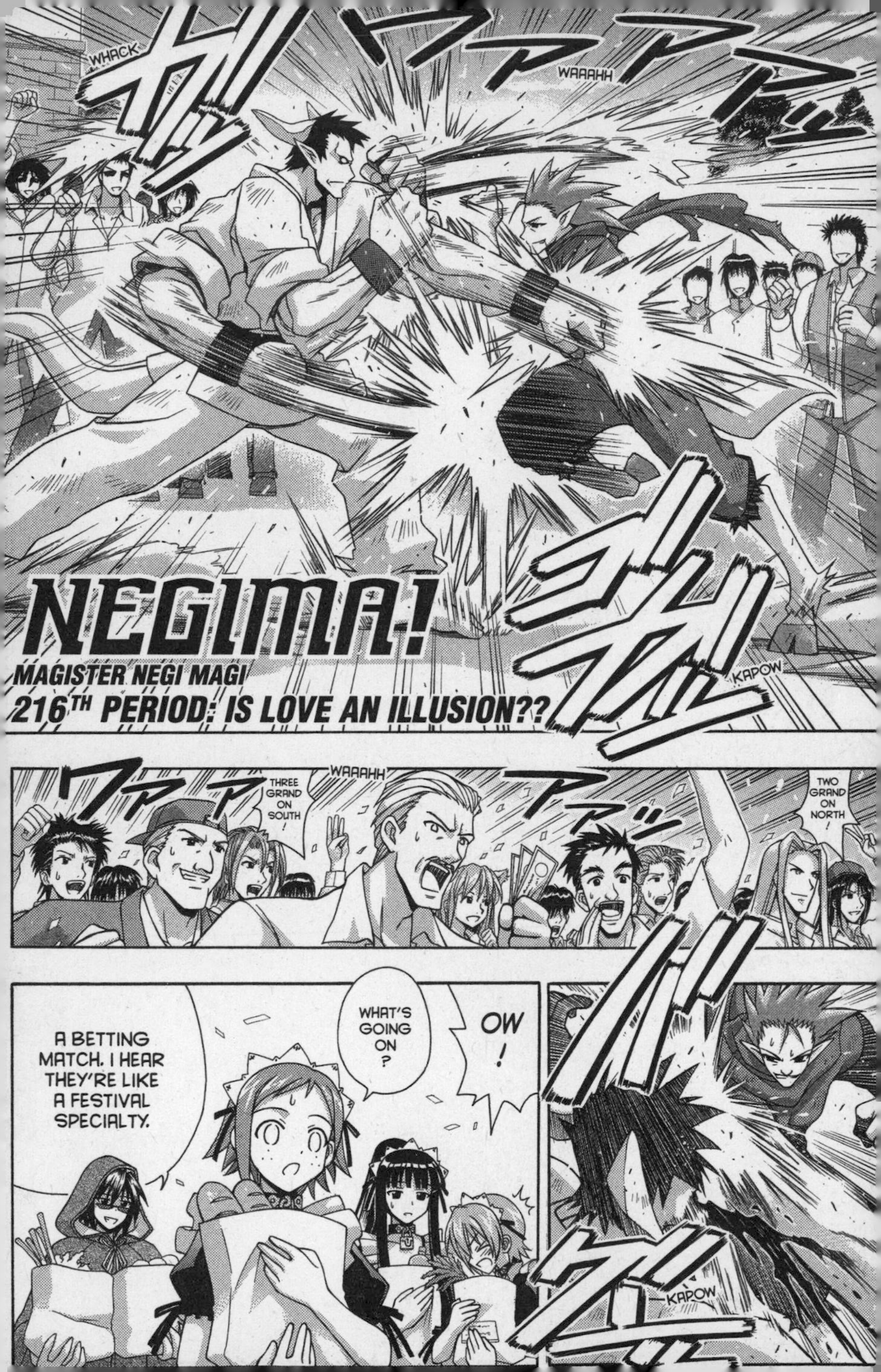
WHACK
WAAAHH
NEGIMA!
MAGISTER NEGI MAGI
216TH PERIOD: IS LOVE AN ILLUSION??
KAPOW
TWO GRAND ON NORTH!
WAAAHH
THREE GRAND ON SOUTH!
KAPOW
OW!
WHAT'S GOING ON?
A BETTING MATCH. I HEAR THEY'RE LIKE A FESTIVAL SPECIALTY.

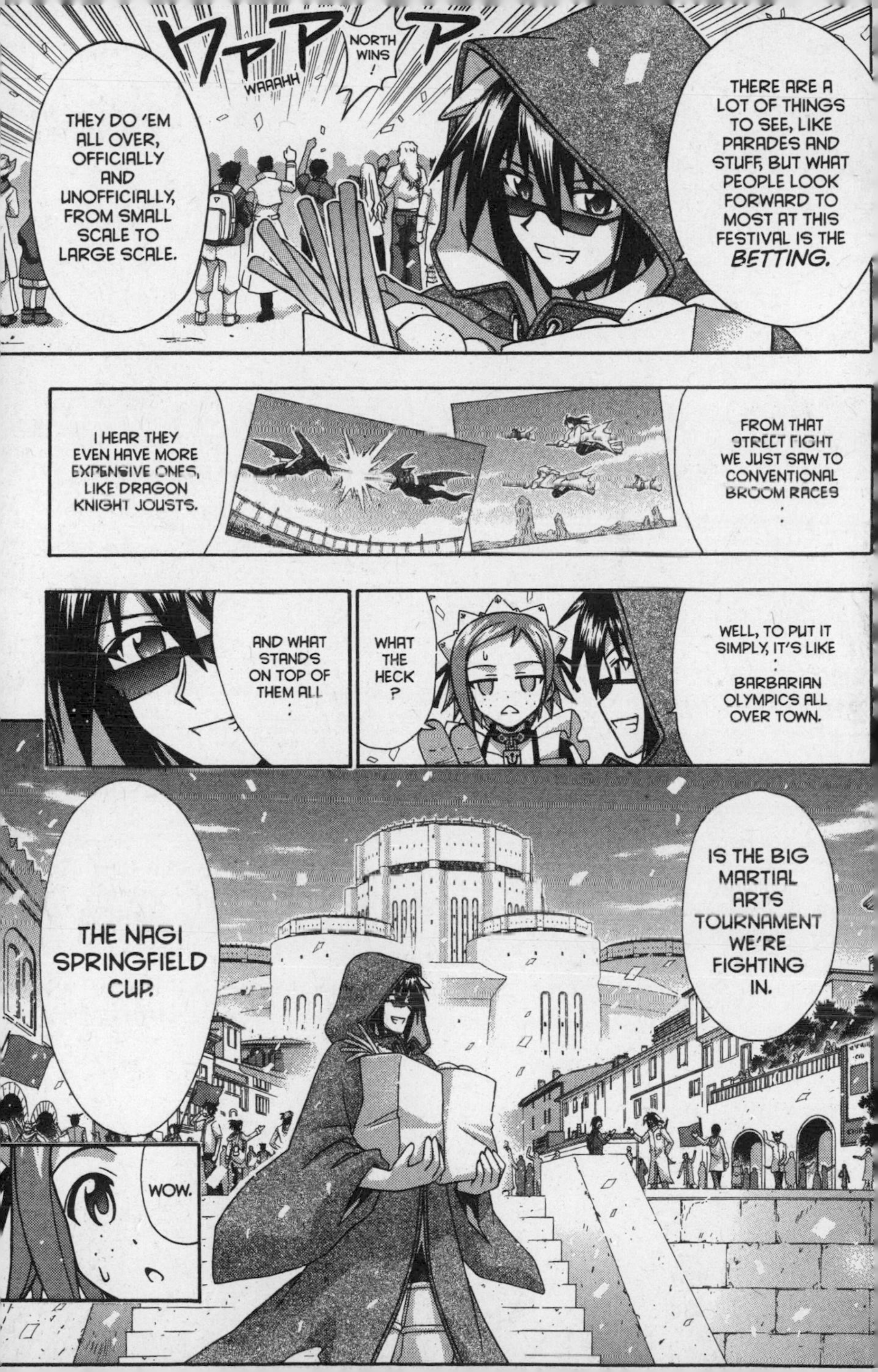
THERE ARE A LOT OF THINGS TO SEE, LIKE PARADES AND STUFF, BUT WHAT PEOPLE LOOK FORWARD TO MOST AT THIS FESTIVAL IS THE *BETTING.*
NORTH WINS!
WAAAAHH
THEY DO 'EM ALL OVER, OFFICIALLY AND UNOFFICIALLY, FROM SMALL SCALE TO LARGE SCALE.
FROM THAT STREET FIGHT WE JUST SAW TO CONVENTIONAL BROOM RACES...
I HEAR THEY EVEN HAVE MORE EXPENSIVE ONES, LIKE DRAGON KNIGHT JOUSTS.
WELL, TO PUT IT SIMPLY, IT'S LIKE... BARBARIAN OLYMPICS ALL OVER TOWN.
WHAT THE HECK?
AND WHAT STANDS ON TOP OF THEM ALL...
IS THE BIG MARTIAL ARTS TOURNAMENT WE'RE FIGHTING IN.
THE NAGI SPRINGFIELD CUP.
WOW.

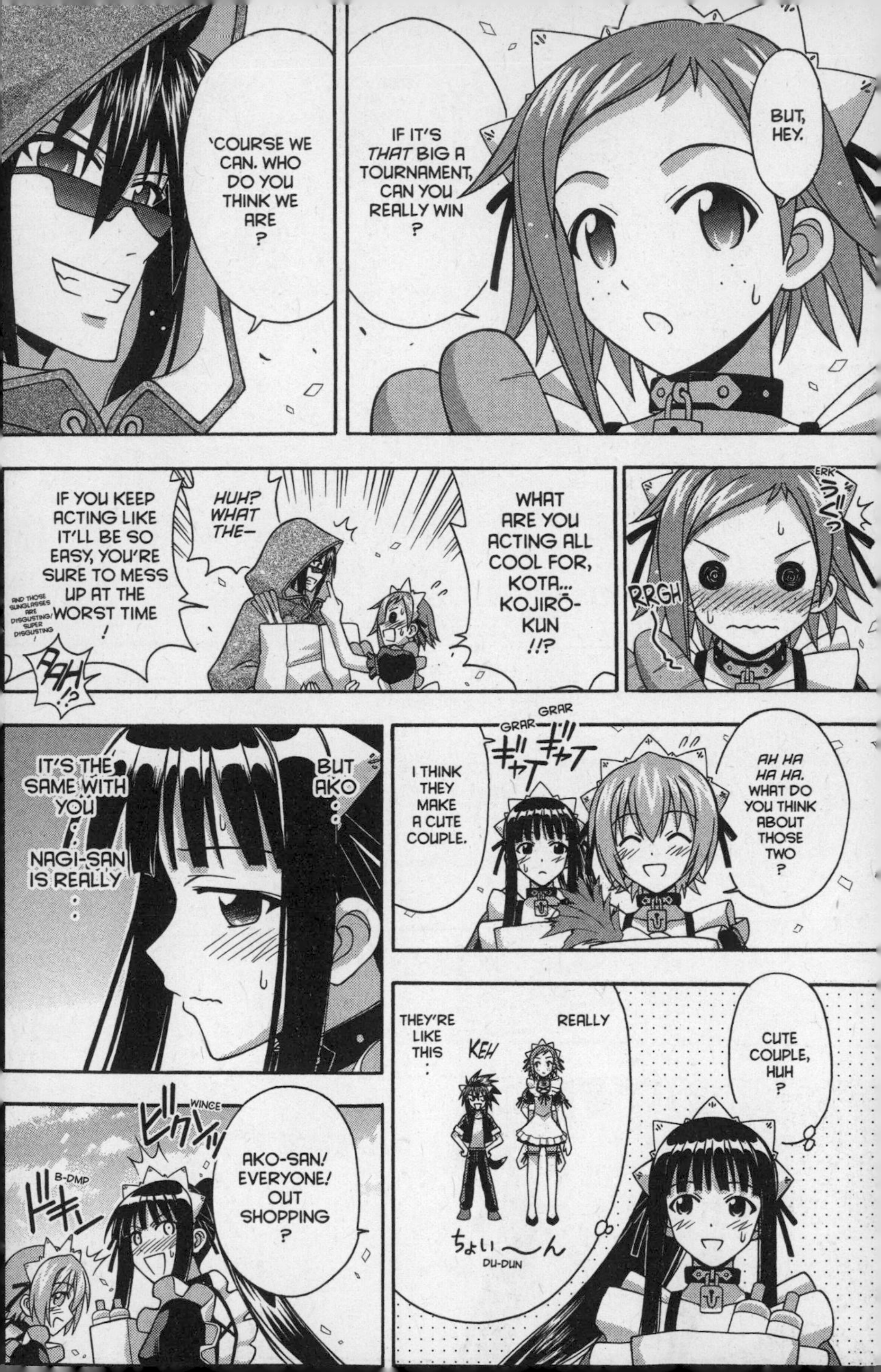
BUT, HEY.
IF IT'S *THAT* BIG A TOURNAMENT, CAN YOU REALLY WIN?
'COURSE WE CAN. WHO DO YOU THINK WE ARE?
ERK
RRGH
WHAT ARE YOU ACTING ALL COOL FOR, KOTA... KOJIRŌ-KUN!!?
*HUH? WHAT THE–*
IF YOU KEEP ACTING LIKE IT'LL BE SO EASY, YOU'RE SURE TO MESS UP AT THE WORST TIME!
AND THOSE SUNGLASSES ARE DISGUSTING/ SUPER DISGUSTING!
AAH!!?
*AH HA HA HA.* WHAT DO YOU THINK ABOUT THOSE TWO?
GRAR GRAR
I THINK THEY MAKE A CUTE COUPLE.
CUTE COUPLE, HUH?
REALLY
THEY'RE LIKE THIS:
*KEH*
ちょい〜ん
DU-DUN
BUT AKO...
NAGI-SAN IS REALLY...
IT'S THE SAME WITH YOU...
WINCE
AKO-SAN! EVERYONE! OUT SHOPPING?
B-DMP

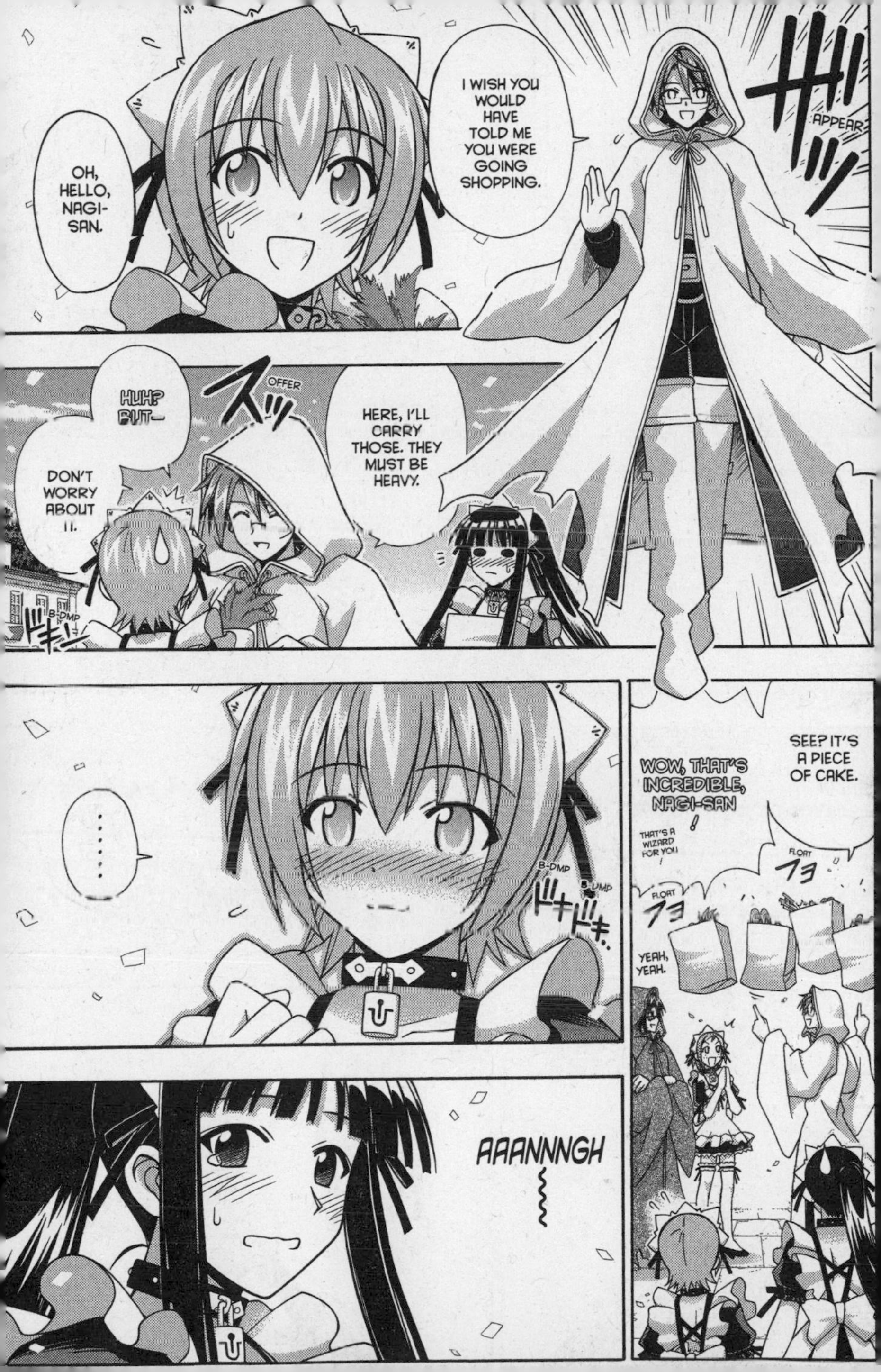
APPEAR
I WISH YOU WOULD HAVE TOLD ME YOU WERE GOING SHOPPING.
OH, HELLO, NAGI-SAN.
OFFER
HERE, I'LL CARRY THOSE. THEY MUST BE HEAVY.
HUH? BUT—
DON'T WORRY ABOUT IT.
B-DMP
SEE? IT'S A PIECE OF CAKE.
FLOAT
WOW, THAT'S INCREDIBLE, NAGI-SAN!
THAT'S A WIZARD FOR YOU!
FLOAT
YEAH, YEAH.
......
B-DMP
B-DMP
AAANNNGH

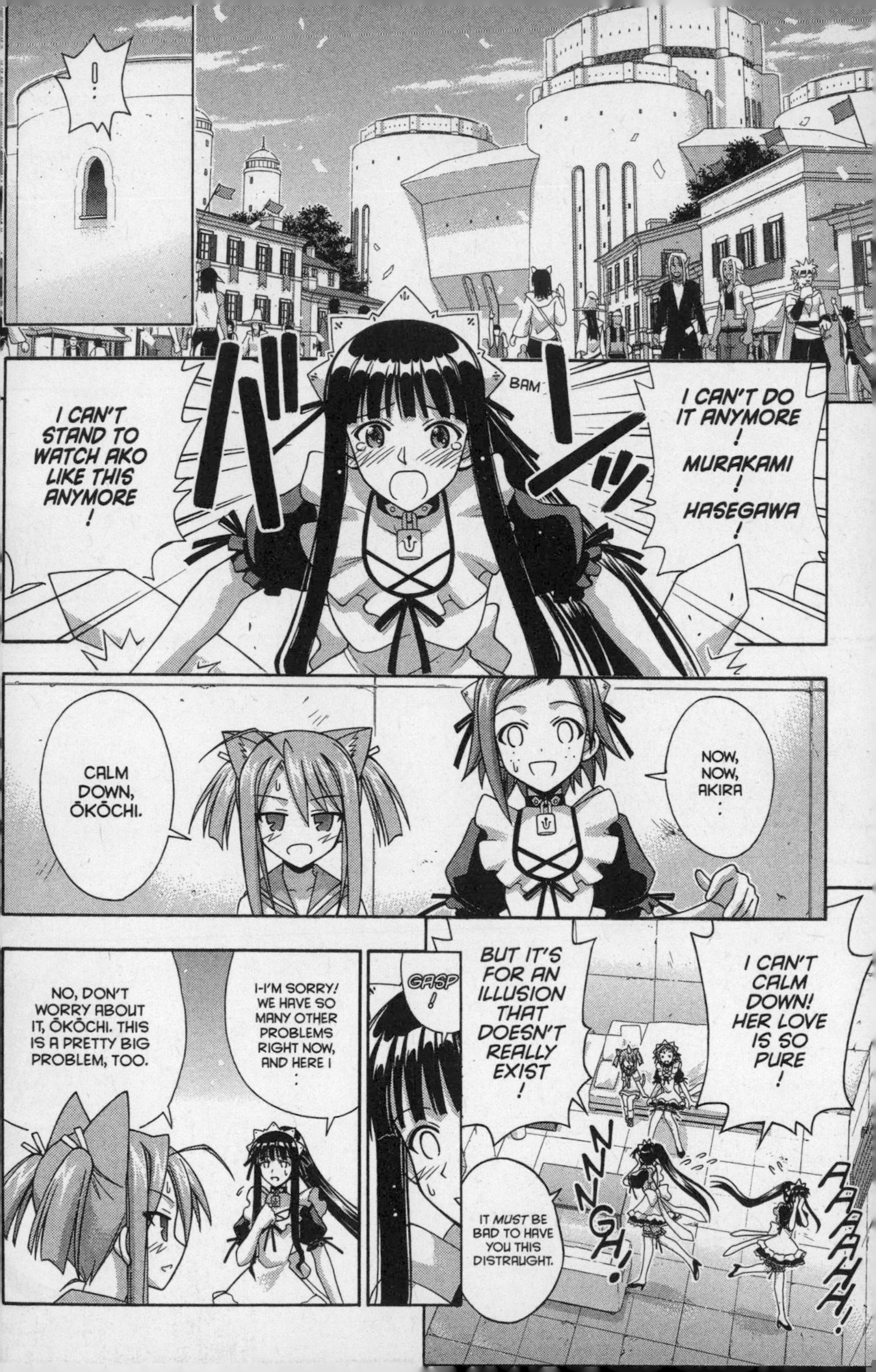
!:
BAM
I CAN'T DO IT ANYMORE! MURAKAMI! HASEGAWA!
I CAN'T STAND TO WATCH AKO LIKE THIS ANYMORE!
NOW, NOW, AKIRA:
CALM DOWN, ŌKŌCHI.
I CAN'T CALM DOWN! HER LOVE IS SO PURE!
BUT IT'S FOR AN ILLUSION THAT DOESN'T REALLY EXIST!
AAAAHH!
NNNGH!
IT MUST BE BAD TO HAVE YOU THIS DISTRAUGHT.
GASP!
I-I'M SORRY! WE HAVE SO MANY OTHER PROBLEMS RIGHT NOW, AND HERE I:
NO, DON'T WORRY ABOUT IT, ŌKŌCHI. THIS IS A PRETTY BIG PROBLEM, TOO.

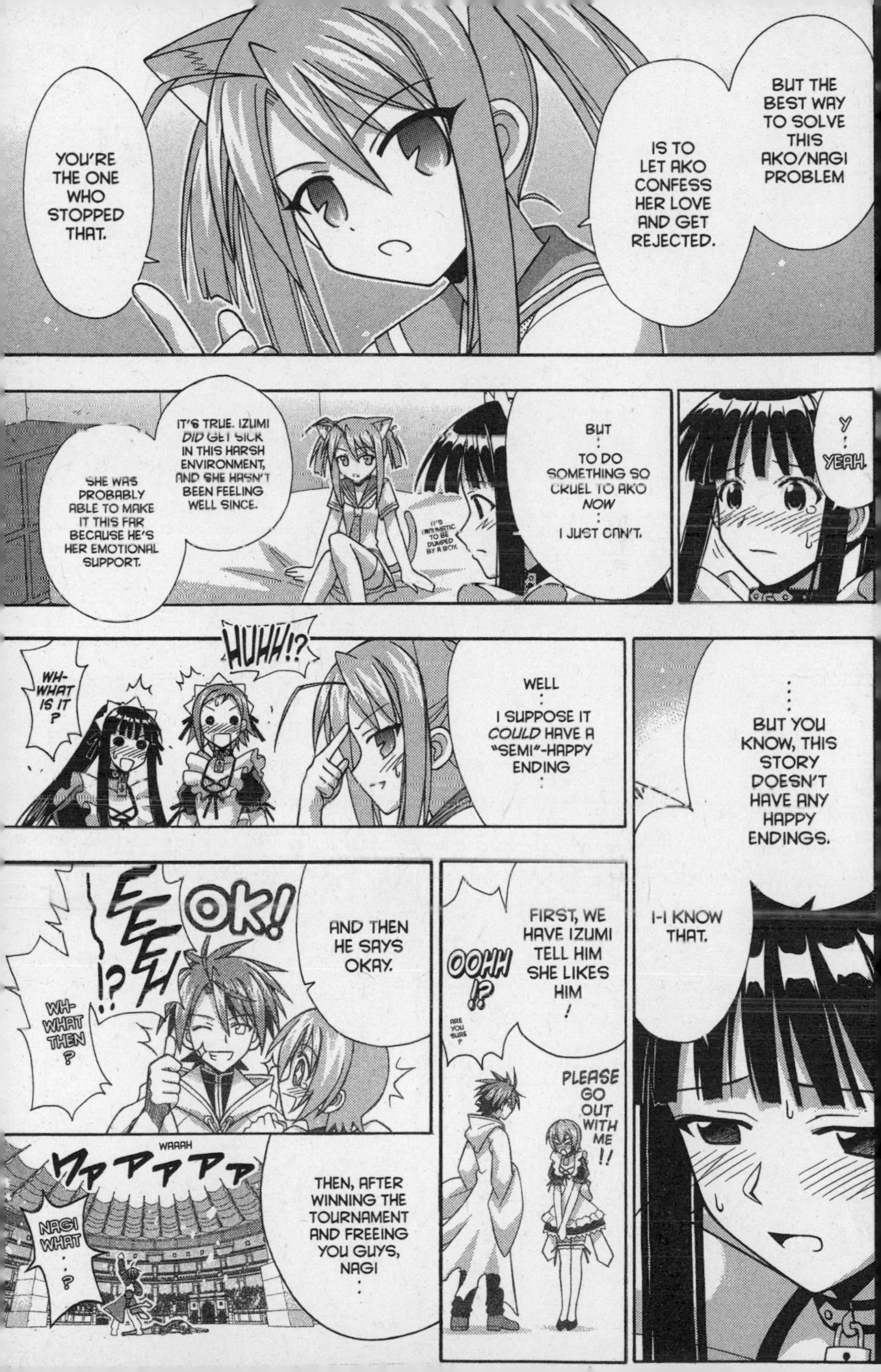
BUT THE BEST WAY TO SOLVE THIS AKO/NAGI PROBLEM
IS TO LET AKO CONFESS HER LOVE AND GET REJECTED.
YOU'RE THE ONE WHO STOPPED THAT.
Y... YEAH.
BUT... TO DO SOMETHING SO CRUEL TO AKO *NOW*... I JUST CAN'T.
IT'S TRAUMATIC TO BE DUMPED BY A BOY.
IT'S TRUE. IZUMI *DID* GET SICK IN THIS HARSH ENVIRONMENT, AND SHE HASN'T BEEN FEELING WELL SINCE.
SHE WAS PROBABLY ABLE TO MAKE IT THIS FAR BECAUSE HE'S HER EMOTIONAL SUPPORT.
... BUT YOU KNOW, THIS STORY DOESN'T HAVE ANY HAPPY ENDINGS.
I-I KNOW THAT.
WELL... I SUPPOSE IT *COULD* HAVE A "SEMI"-HAPPY ENDING...
HUHH!?
WH-WHAT IS IT?
FIRST, WE HAVE IZUMI TELL HIM SHE LIKES HIM!
PLEASE GO OUT WITH ME!!
OOHH!?
ARE YOU SURE?
AND THEN HE SAYS OKAY.
OK!
EEEEH!?
WH-WHAT THEN?
THEN, AFTER WINNING THE TOURNAMENT AND FREEING YOU GUYS, NAGI...
WAAAH
NAGI WHAT...?

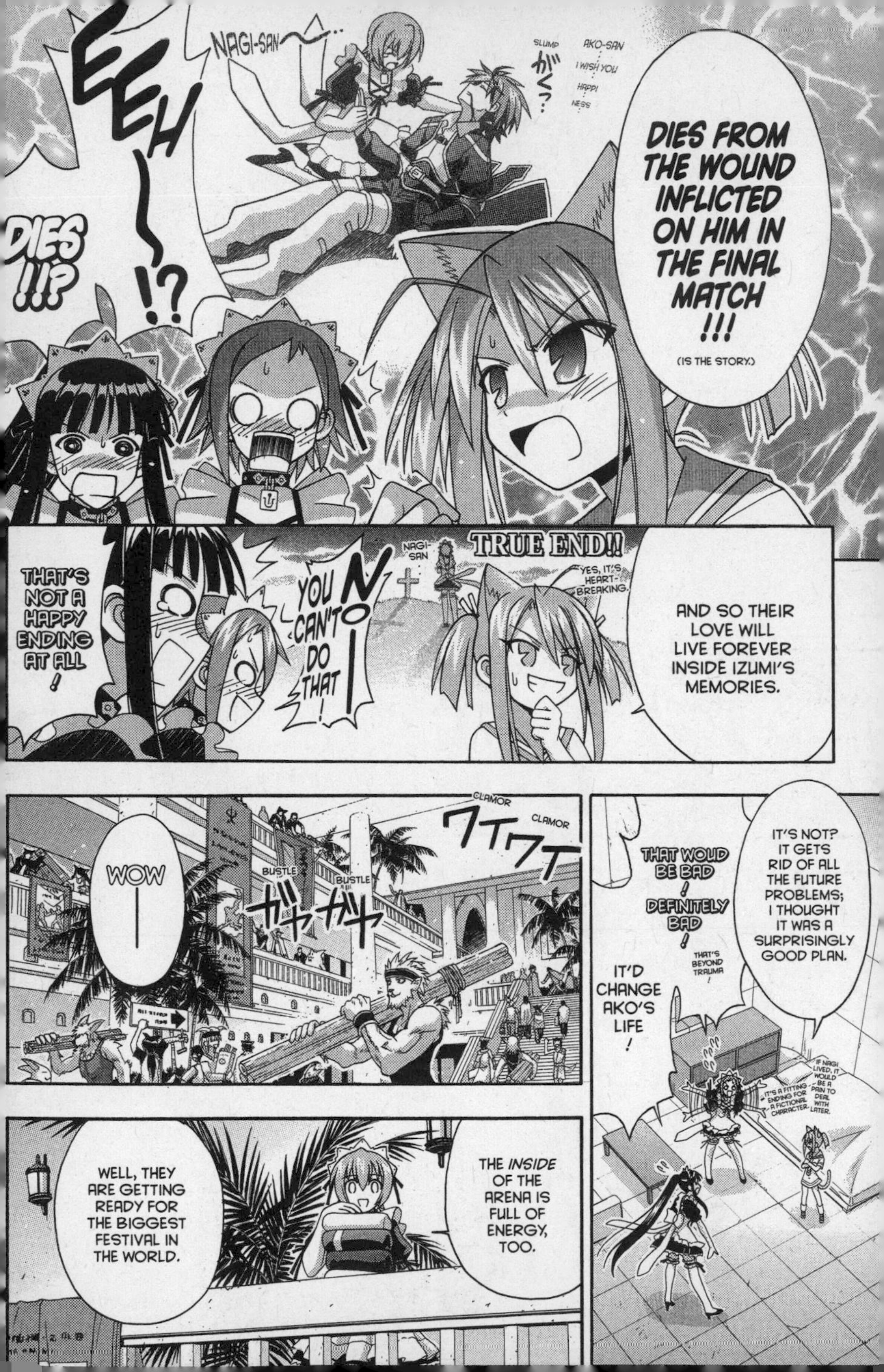
DIES FROM THE WOUND INFLICTED ON HIM IN THE FINAL MATCH!!!
(IS THE STORY.)
AKO-SAN... I WISH YOU HAPPI NESS...
SLUMP
がくっ
NAGI-SAN~
EEEH~~!?
DIES!!?
AND SO THEIR LOVE WILL LIVE FOREVER INSIDE IZUMI'S MEMORIES.
YES, IT'S HEART-BREAKING.
TRUE END!!
NAGI-SAN...
NO! YOU CAN'T DO THAT!
THAT'S NOT A HAPPY ENDING AT ALL!
IT'S NOT? IT GETS RID OF ALL THE FUTURE PROBLEMS; I THOUGHT IT WAS A SURPRISINGLY GOOD PLAN.
THAT WOUD BE BAD! DEFINITELY BAD!
THAT'S BEYOND TRAUMA!
IT'D CHANGE AKO'S LIFE!
IF NAGI LIVED, IT WOULD BE A PAIN TO DEAL WITH LATER.
IT'S A FITTING ENDING FOR A FICTIONAL CHARACTER.
CLAMOR
CLAMOR
ワイワイ
BUSTLE
BUSTLE
ガヤガヤ
WOW—
THE INSIDE OF THE ARENA IS FULL OF ENERGY, TOO.
WELL, THEY ARE GETTING READY FOR THE BIGGEST FESTIVAL IN THE WORLD.

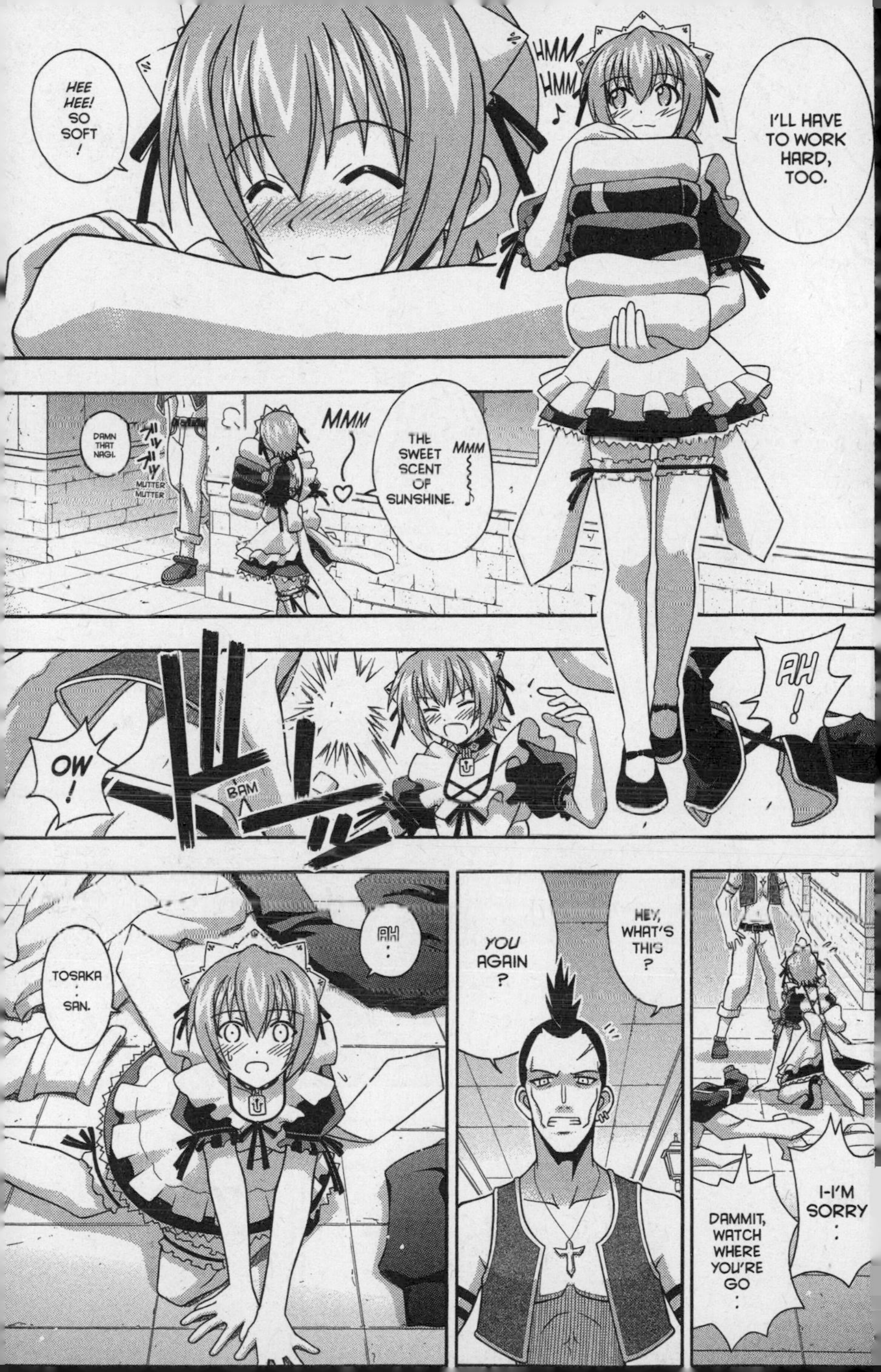
HMMM HMMM ♪
I'LL HAVE TO WORK HARD, TOO.
HEE HEE! SO SOFT!
MMM ♡
THE SWEET SCENT OF SUNSHINE.
MMM ♪
DAMN THAT NAGI.
MUTTER MUTTER
AH!
BAM
OW!
I-I'M SORRY...
DAMMIT, WATCH WHERE YOU'RE GO...
HEY, WHAT'S THIS?
YOU AGAIN?
AH...
TOSAKA... SAN.

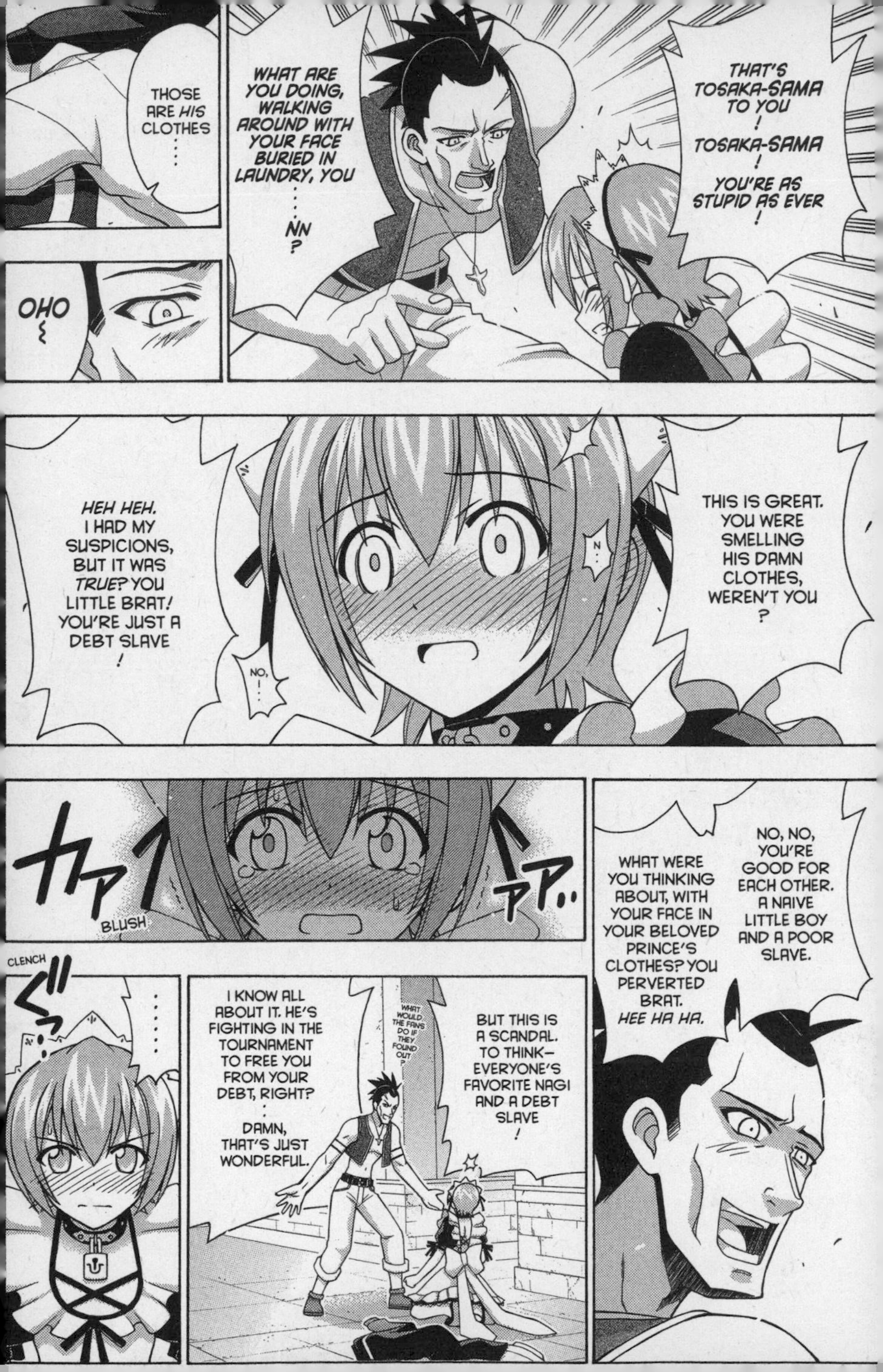
THAT'S TOSAKA-SAMA TO YOU! TOSAKA-SAMA! YOU'RE AS STUPID AS EVER!
WHAT ARE YOU DOING, WALKING AROUND WITH YOUR FACE BURIED IN LAUNDRY, YOU...
NN?
THOSE ARE HIS CLOTHES...
OHO~
THIS IS GREAT. YOU WERE SMELLING HIS DAMN CLOTHES, WEREN'T YOU?
N...
HEH HEH. I HAD MY SUSPICIONS, BUT IT WAS TRUE? YOU LITTLE BRAT! YOU'RE JUST A DEBT SLAVE!
NO, !...
NO, NO, YOU'RE GOOD FOR EACH OTHER. A NAIVE LITTLE BOY AND A POOR SLAVE.
WHAT WERE YOU THINKING ABOUT, WITH YOUR FACE IN YOUR BELOVED PRINCE'S CLOTHES? YOU PERVERTED BRAT. HEE HA HA.
BLUSH
BUT THIS IS A SCANDAL. TO THINK— EVERYONE'S FAVORITE NAGI AND A DEBT SLAVE!
WHAT WOULD THE FANS DO IF THEY FOUND OUT?
I KNOW ALL ABOUT IT. HE'S FIGHTING IN THE TOURNAMENT TO FREE YOU FROM YOUR DEBT, RIGHT?
DAMN, THAT'S JUST WONDERFUL.
CLENCH
......

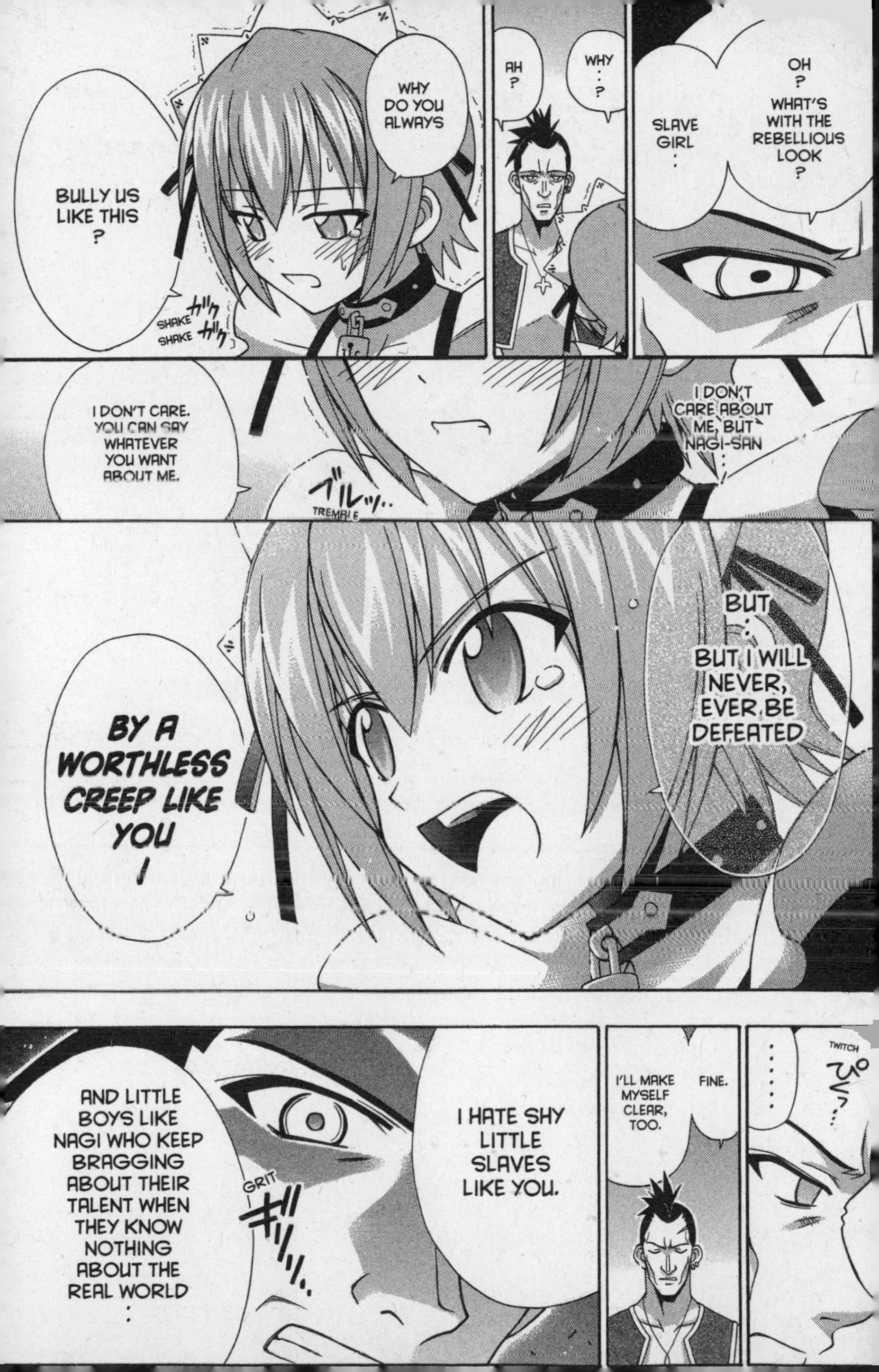
OH? WHAT'S WITH THE REBELLIOUS LOOK?
SLAVE GIRL...
WHY...?
AH?
WHY DO YOU ALWAYS
BULLY US LIKE THIS?
SHAKE SHAKE
I DON'T CARE ABOUT ME, BUT NAGI-SAN...
TREMBLE
I DON'T CARE. YOU CAN SAY WHATEVER YOU WANT ABOUT ME.
BUT... BUT I WILL NEVER, EVER BE DEFEATED
BY A WORTHLESS CREEP LIKE YOU!
......
TWITCH
FINE.
I'LL MAKE MYSELF CLEAR, TOO.
I HATE SHY LITTLE SLAVES LIKE YOU.
AND LITTLE BOYS LIKE NAGI WHO KEEP BRAGGING ABOUT THEIR TALENT WHEN THEY KNOW NOTHING ABOUT THE REAL WORLD...
GRIT

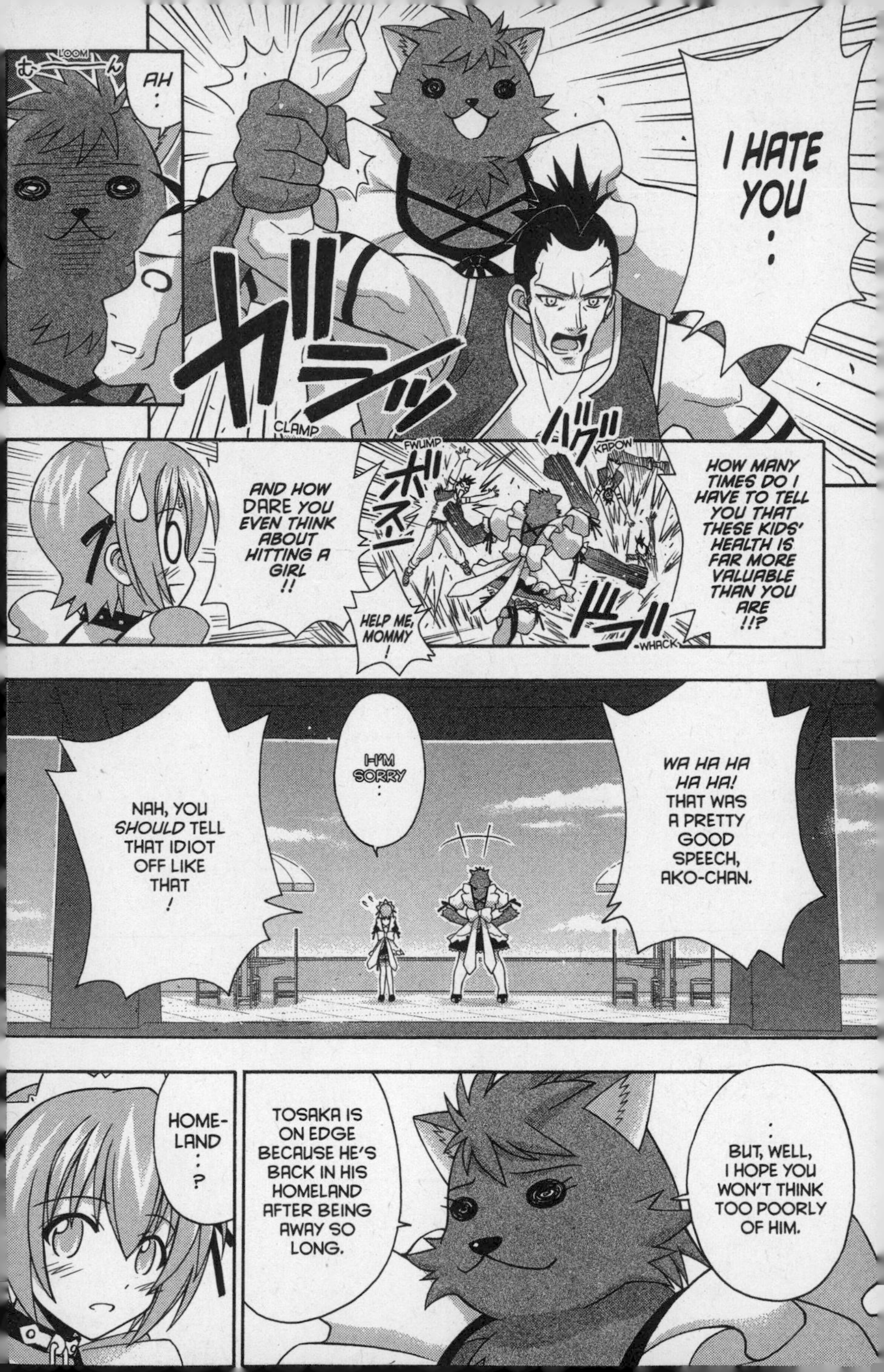
I HATE YOU :
CLAMP
LOOM
AH :
HOW MANY TIMES DO I HAVE TO TELL YOU THAT THESE KIDS' HEALTH IS FAR MORE VALUABLE THAN YOU ARE !!?
KAPOW
FWUMP
WHACK
HELP ME, MOMMY !
AND HOW DARE YOU EVEN THINK ABOUT HITTING A GIRL !!
WA HA HA HA HA! THAT WAS A PRETTY GOOD SPEECH, AKO-CHAN.
I-I'M SORRY :
NAH, YOU SHOULD TELL THAT IDIOT OFF LIKE THAT !
: BUT, WELL, I HOPE YOU WON'T THINK TOO POORLY OF HIM.
TOSAKA IS ON EDGE BECAUSE HE'S BACK IN HIS HOMELAND AFTER BEING AWAY SO LONG.
HOME-LAND . . . ?

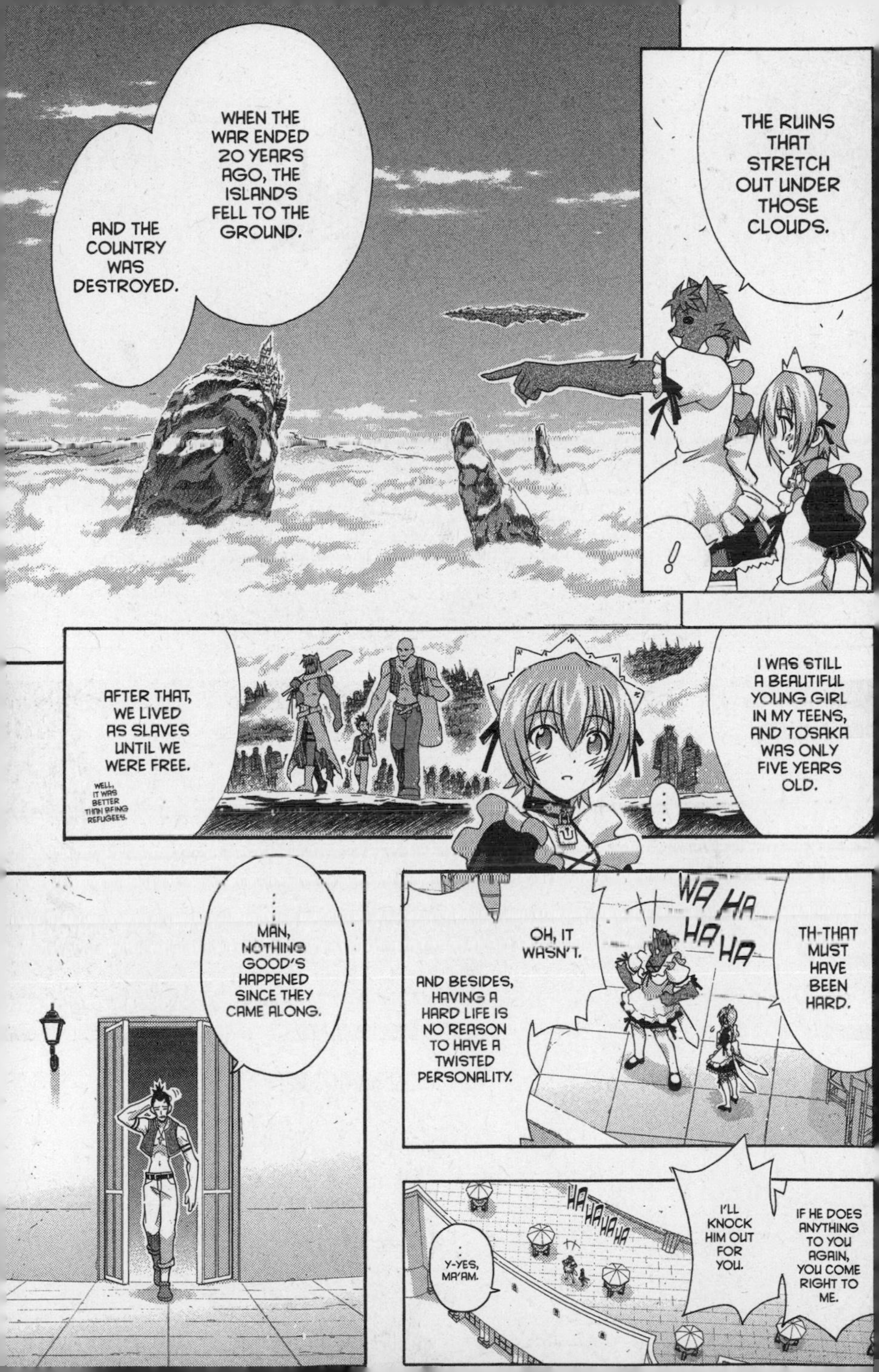
THE RUINS THAT STRETCH OUT UNDER THOSE CLOUDS.
!
WHEN THE WAR ENDED 20 YEARS AGO, THE ISLANDS FELL TO THE GROUND.
AND THE COUNTRY WAS DESTROYED.
I WAS STILL A BEAUTIFUL YOUNG GIRL IN MY TEENS, AND TOSAKA WAS ONLY FIVE YEARS OLD.
.....
AFTER THAT, WE LIVED AS SLAVES UNTIL WE WERE FREE.
WELL, IT WAS BETTER THAN BEING REFUGEES.
TH-THAT MUST HAVE BEEN HARD.
WA HA HA HA HA
OH, IT WASN'T.
AND BESIDES, HAVING A HARD LIFE IS NO REASON TO HAVE A TWISTED PERSONALITY.
IF HE DOES ANYTHING TO YOU AGAIN, YOU COME RIGHT TO ME.
I'LL KNOCK HIM OUT FOR YOU.
HA HA HA HA HA
: Y-YES, MA'AM.
...... MAN, NOTHING GOOD'S HAPPENED SINCE THEY CAME ALONG.

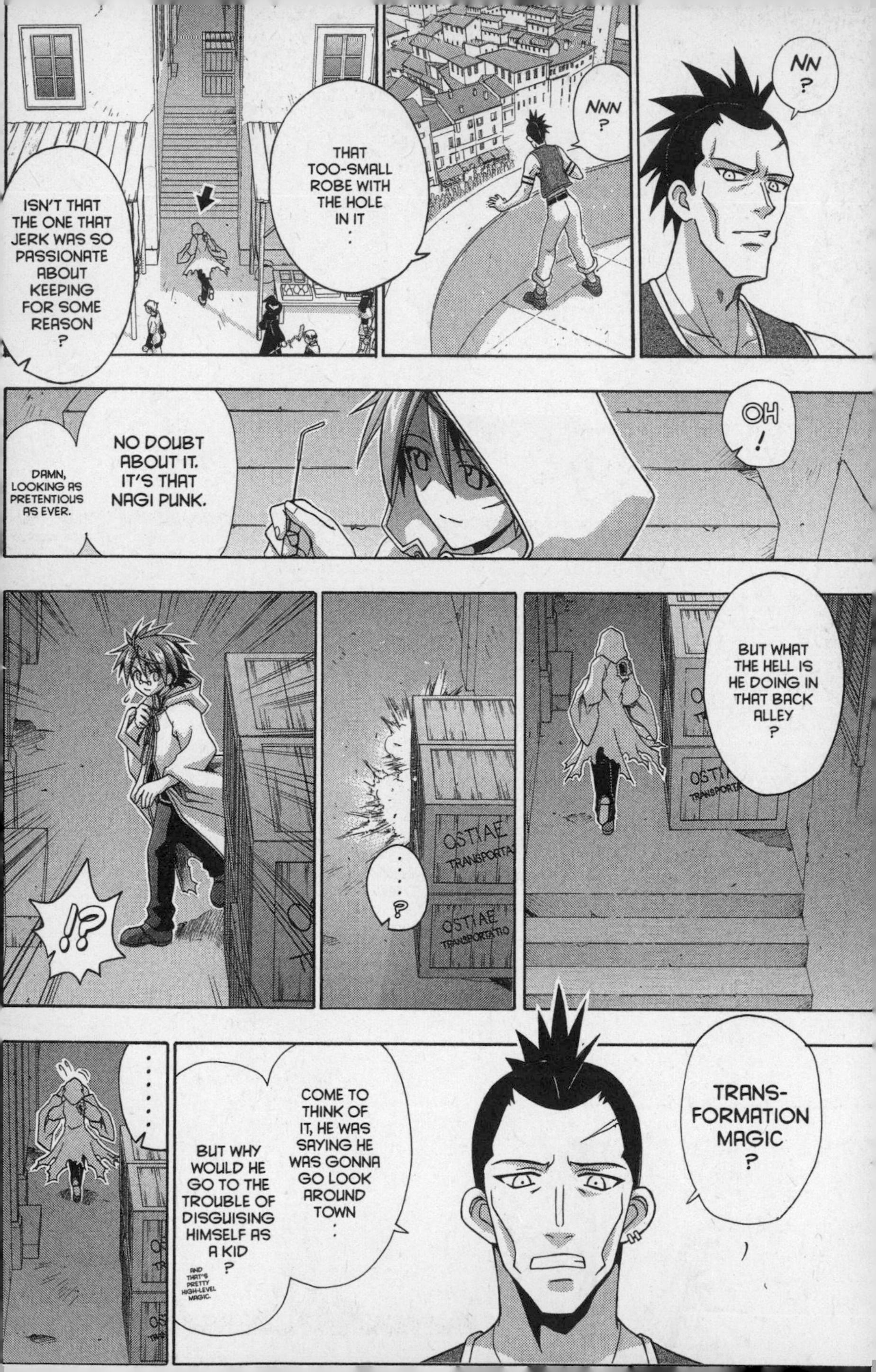
NN ?
NNN ?
THAT TOO-SMALL ROBE WITH THE HOLE IN IT ...
ISN'T THAT THE ONE THAT JERK WAS SO PASSIONATE ABOUT KEEPING FOR SOME REASON ?
OH !
NO DOUBT ABOUT IT. IT'S THAT NAGI PUNK.
DAMN, LOOKING AS PRETENTIOUS AS EVER.
BUT WHAT THE HELL IS HE DOING IN THAT BACK ALLEY ?
....?
OSTIAE
!?
TRANS-FORMATION MAGIC ?
COME TO THINK OF IT, HE WAS SAYING HE WAS GONNA GO LOOK AROUND TOWN ...
BUT WHY WOULD HE GO TO THE TROUBLE OF DISGUISING HIMSELF AS A KID ?
AND THAT'S PRETTY HIGH-LEVEL MAGIC.
......

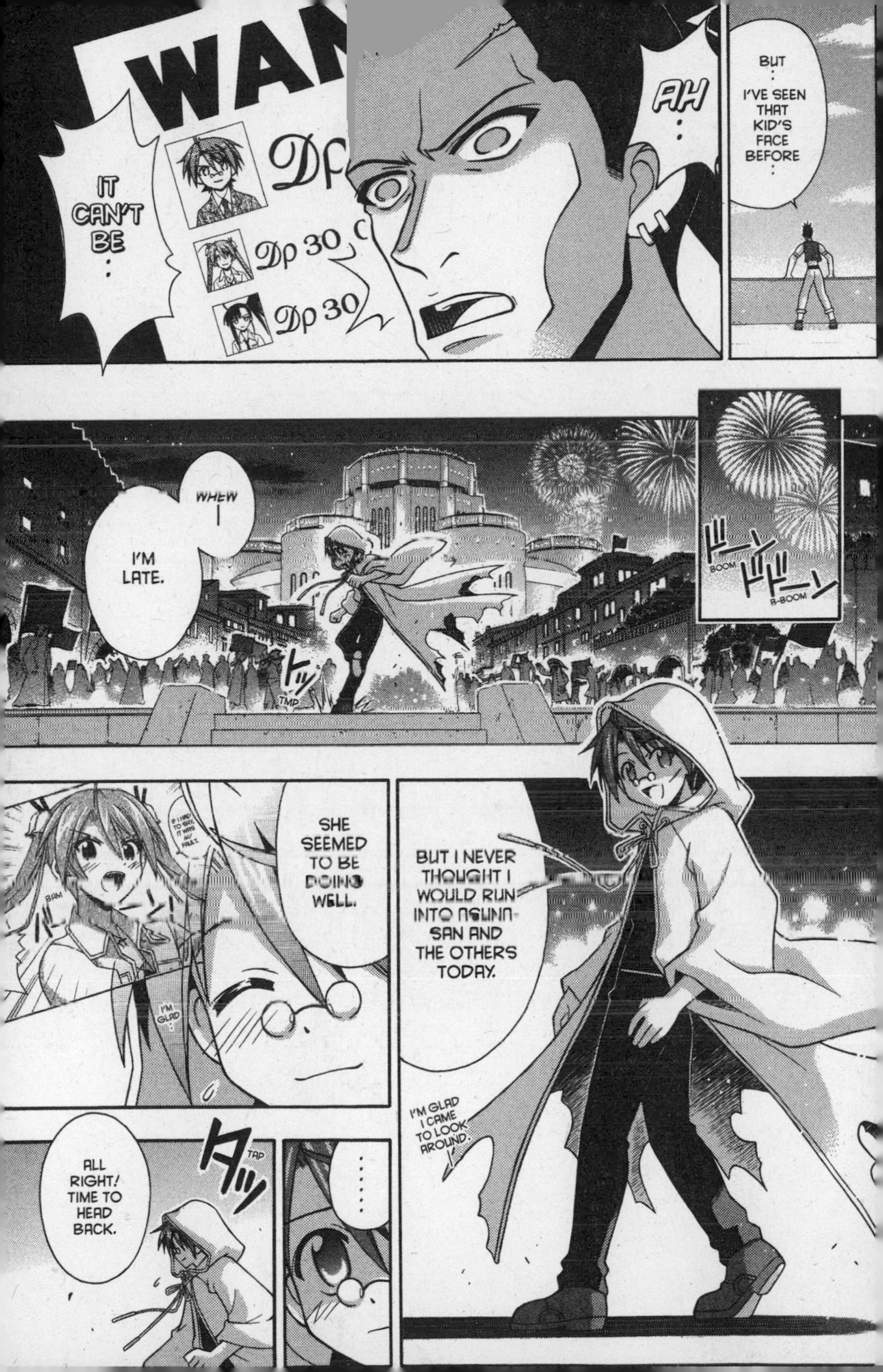
BUT : I'VE SEEN THAT KID'S FACE BEFORE :
AH :
WAN
Dp
Dp 30
Dp 30
IT CAN'T BE :
ドーン
BOOM
ドドーン
B-BOOM
WHEW I'M LATE.
トッ
TMP
BUT I NEVER THOUGHT I WOULD RUN INTO ASUNA-SAN AND THE OTHERS TODAY.
I'M GLAD I CAME TO LOOK AROUND.
SHE SEEMED TO BE DOING WELL.
IF I HAD TO SAY, IT WAS MY FAULT.
BAM
I'M GLAD :
......
タッ
TAP
ALL RIGHT! TIME TO HEAD BACK.

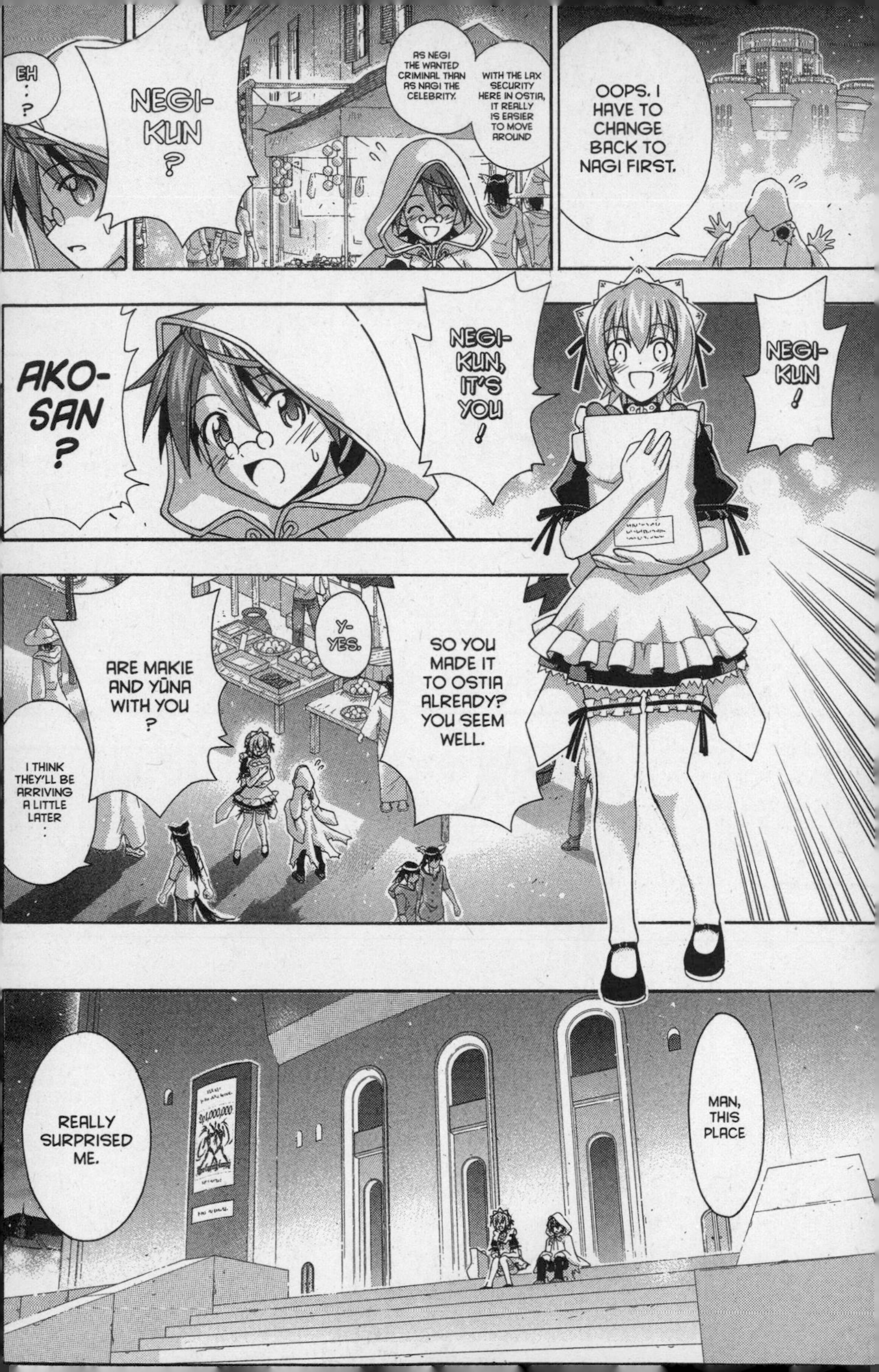
OOPS. I HAVE TO CHANGE BACK TO NAGI FIRST.
WITH THE LAX SECURITY HERE IN OSTIA, IT REALLY IS EASIER TO MOVE AROUND
AS NEGI THE WANTED CRIMINAL THAN AS NAGI THE CELEBRITY.
NEGI-KUN?
EH...?
NEGI-KUN!
NEGI-KUN, IT'S YOU!
AKO-SAN?
SO YOU MADE IT TO OSTIA ALREADY? YOU SEEM WELL.
Y-YES.
ARE MAKIE AND YŪNA WITH YOU?
I THINK THEY'LL BE ARRIVING A LITTLE LATER...
MAN, THIS PLACE
REALLY SURPRISED ME.

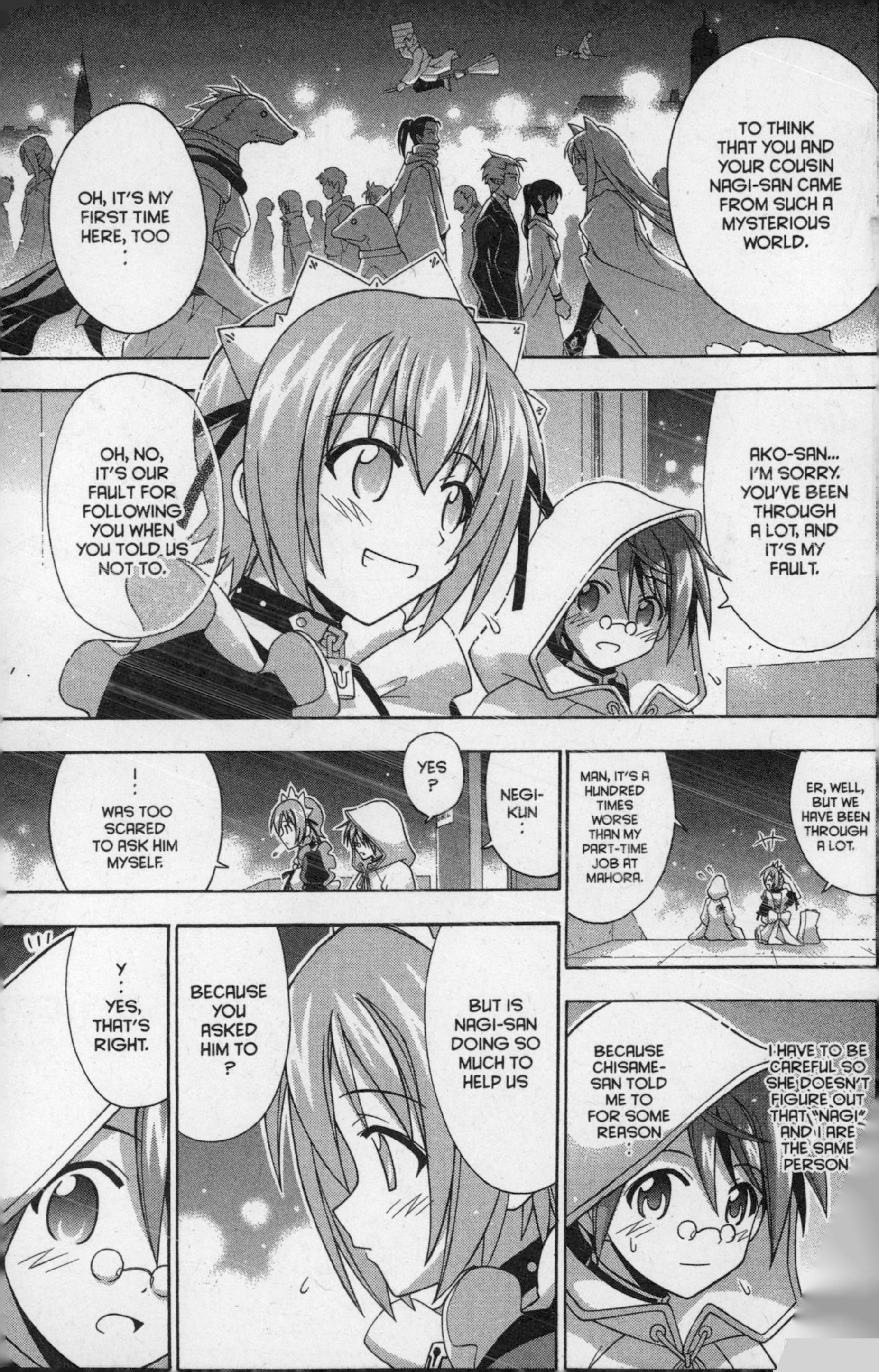
TO THINK THAT YOU AND YOUR COUSIN NAGI-SAN CAME FROM SUCH A MYSTERIOUS WORLD.
OH, IT'S MY FIRST TIME HERE, TOO...
AKO-SAN... I'M SORRY. YOU'VE BEEN THROUGH A LOT, AND IT'S MY FAULT.
OH, NO, IT'S OUR FAULT FOR FOLLOWING YOU WHEN YOU TOLD US NOT TO.
ER, WELL, BUT WE HAVE BEEN THROUGH A LOT.
MAN, IT'S A HUNDRED TIMES WORSE THAN MY PART-TIME JOB AT MAHORA.
NEGI-KUN...
YES?
I... WAS TOO SCARED TO ASK HIM MYSELF.
BUT IS NAGI-SAN DOING SO MUCH TO HELP US
BECAUSE YOU ASKED HIM TO?
Y... YES, THAT'S RIGHT.
BECAUSE CHISAME-SAN TOLD ME TO FOR SOME REASON...
I HAVE TO BE CAREFUL SO SHE DOESN'T FIGURE OUT THAT "NAGI" AND I ARE THE SAME PERSON

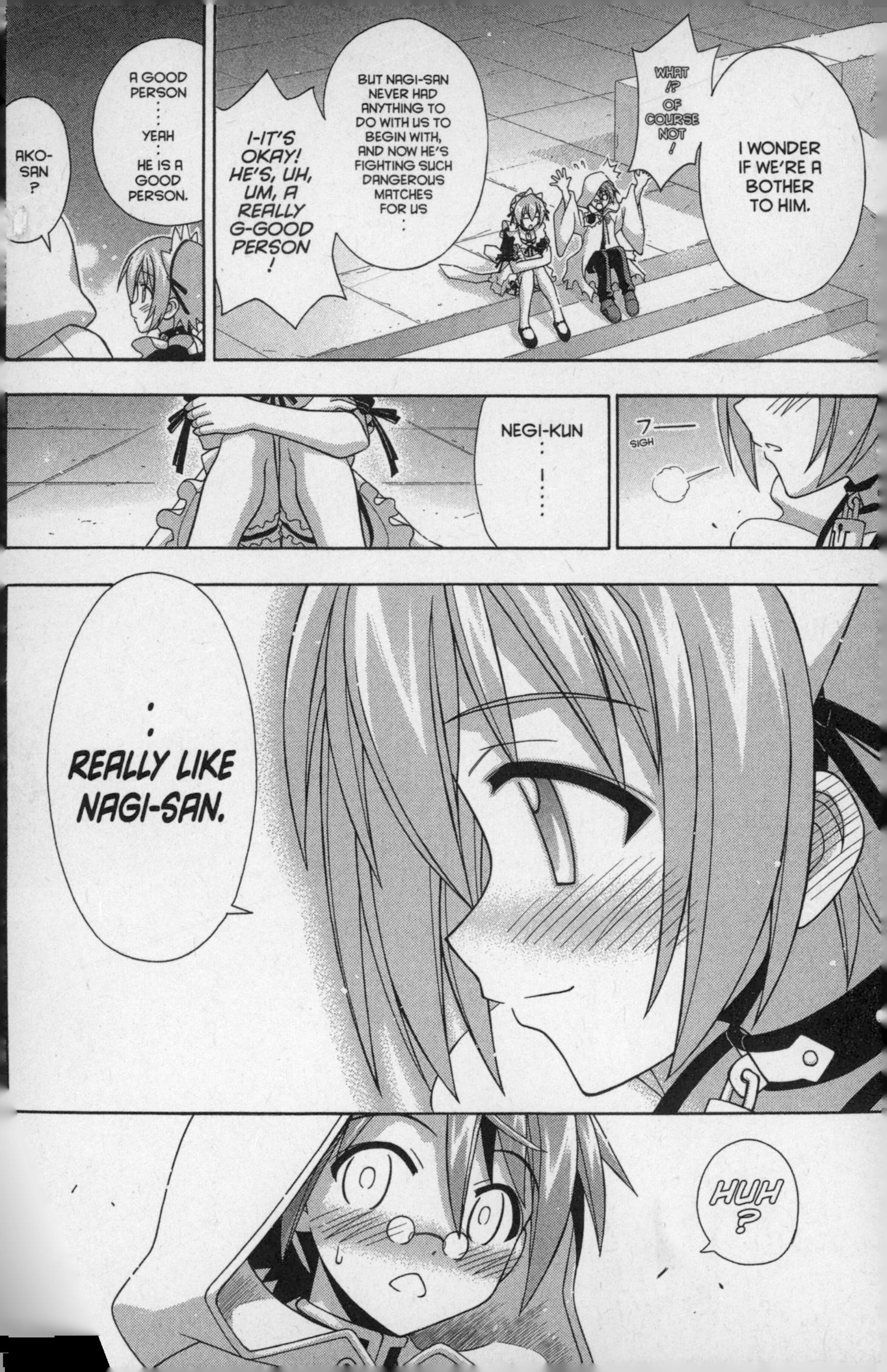
I WONDER IF WE'RE A BOTHER TO HIM.
WHAT!? OF COURSE NOT!
BUT NAGI-SAN NEVER HAD ANYTHING TO DO WITH US TO BEGIN WITH, AND NOW HE'S FIGHTING SUCH DANGEROUS MATCHES FOR US...
I-IT'S OKAY! HE'S, UH, UM, A REALLY G-GOOD PERSON!
A GOOD PERSON... YEAH HE IS A GOOD PERSON.
AKO-SAN?
SIGH
NEGI-KUN... I...
: REALLY LIKE NAGI-SAN.
HUH?

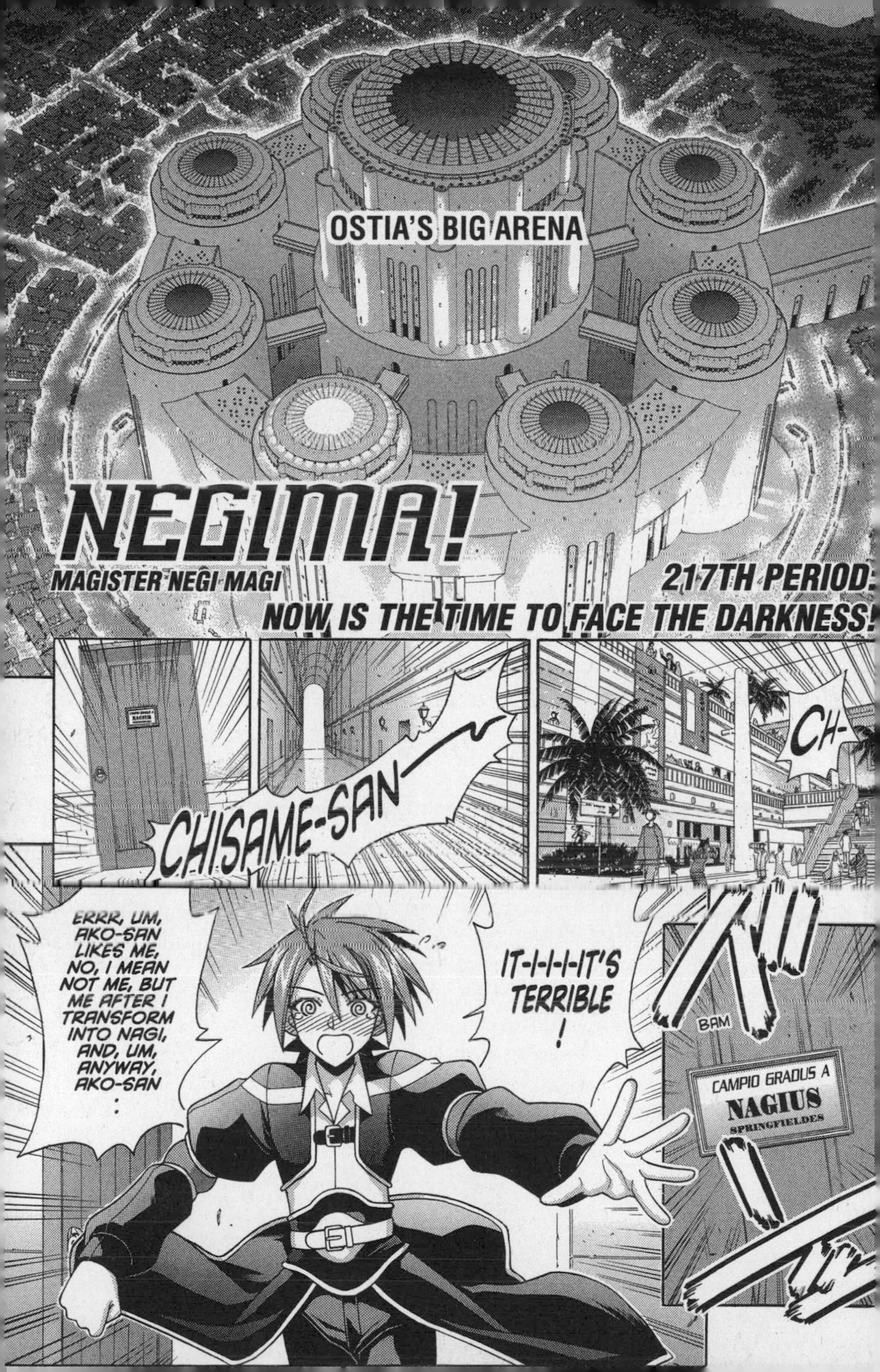
OSTIA'S BIG ARENA
NEGIMA!
MAGISTER NEGI MAGI
217TH PERIOD:
NOW IS THE TIME TO FACE THE DARKNESS!
CH-
CHISAME-SAN
BAM
CAMPIO GRADUS A
NAGIUS
SPRINGFIELDES
IT-I-I-I-IT'S TERRIBLE!
ERRR, UM, AKO-SAN LIKES ME, NO, I MEAN NOT ME, BUT ME AFTER I TRANSFORM INTO NAGI, AND, UM, ANYWAY, AKO-SAN:

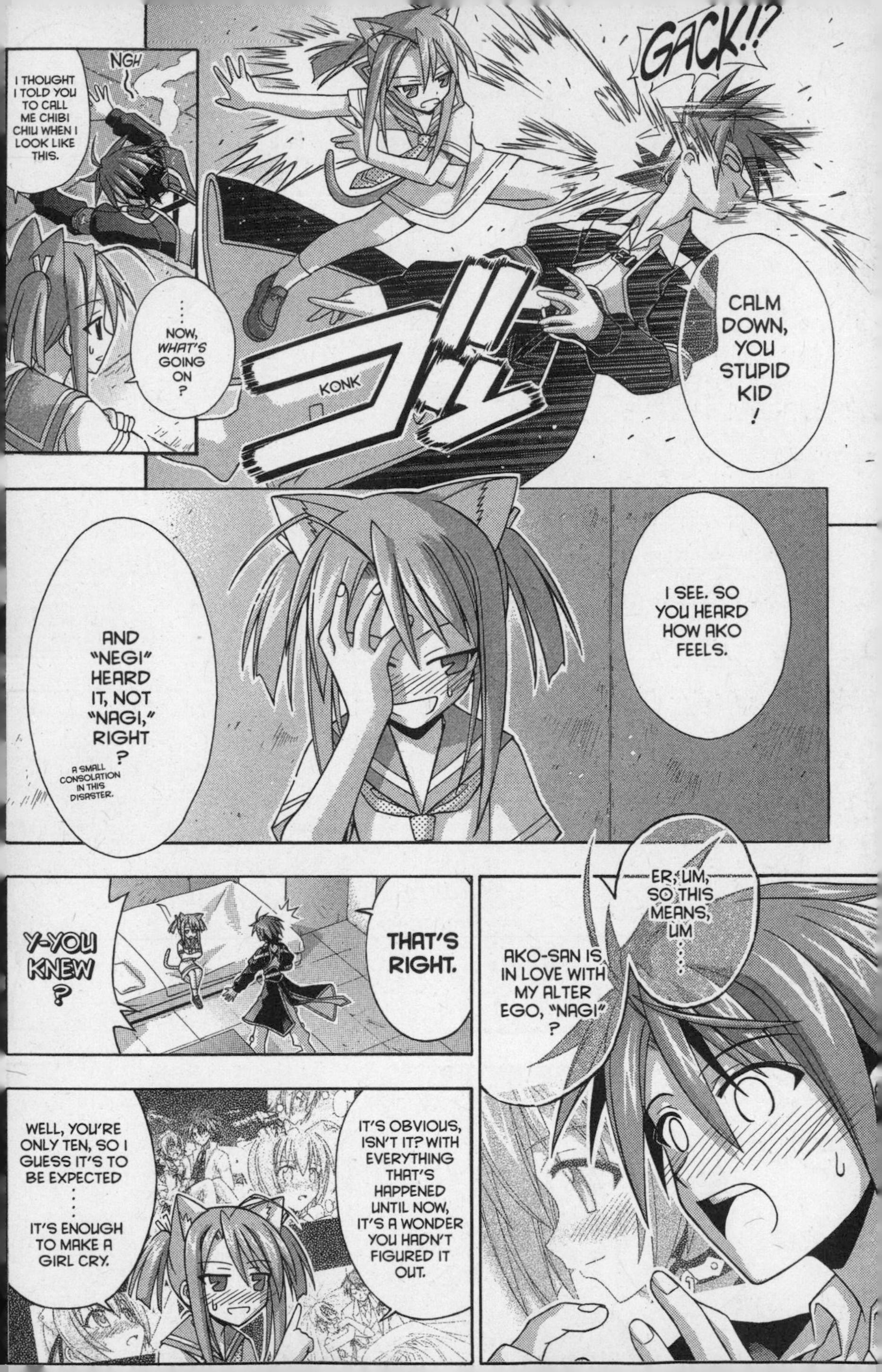
GACK!!?
CALM DOWN, YOU STUPID KID!
KONK
NGH
I THOUGHT I TOLD YOU TO CALL ME CHIBI CHIU WHEN I LOOK LIKE THIS.
... NOW, WHAT'S GOING ON?
I SEE. SO YOU HEARD HOW AKO FEELS.
AND "NEGI" HEARD IT, NOT "NAGI," RIGHT?
A SMALL CONSOLATION IN THIS DISASTER.
ER, UM, SO THIS MEANS, UM.....
AKO-SAN IS IN LOVE WITH MY ALTER EGO, "NAGI"?
THAT'S RIGHT.
Y-YOU KNEW?
IT'S OBVIOUS, ISN'T IT? WITH EVERYTHING THAT'S HAPPENED UNTIL NOW, IT'S A WONDER YOU HADN'T FIGURED IT OUT.
WELL, YOU'RE ONLY TEN, SO I GUESS IT'S TO BE EXPECTED ... IT'S ENOUGH TO MAKE A GIRL CRY.

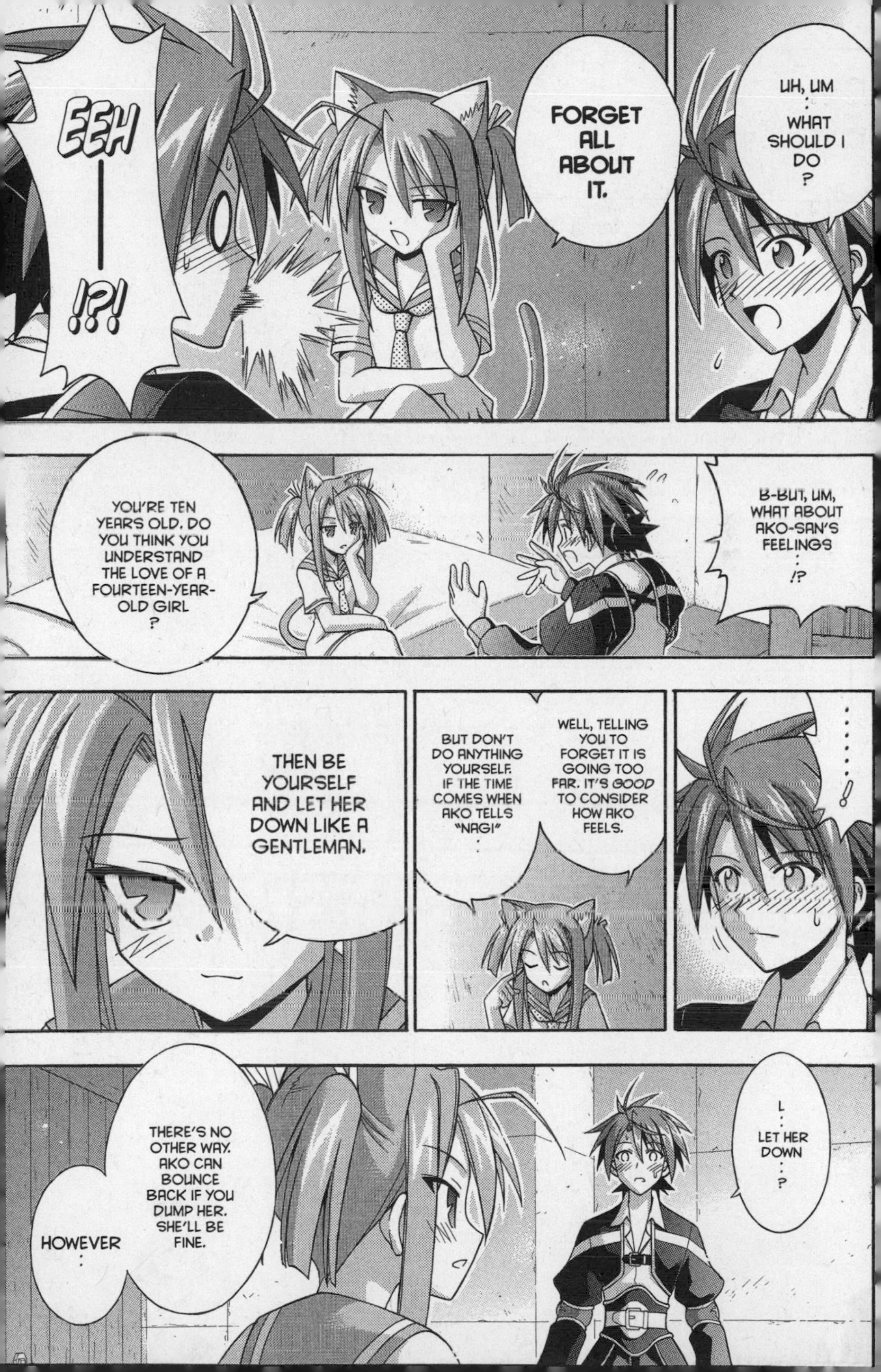
UH, UM : WHAT SHOULD I DO ?
FORGET ALL ABOUT IT.
EEH —— !?!
B-BUT, UM, WHAT ABOUT AKO-SAN'S FEELINGS : !?
YOU'RE TEN YEARS OLD. DO YOU THINK YOU UNDERSTAND THE LOVE OF A FOURTEEN-YEAR-OLD GIRL ?
......!
WELL, TELLING YOU TO FORGET IT IS GOING TOO FAR. IT'S *GOOD* TO CONSIDER HOW AKO FEELS.
BUT DON'T DO ANYTHING YOURSELF. IF THE TIME COMES WHEN AKO TELLS "NAGI" :
THEN BE YOURSELF AND LET HER DOWN LIKE A GENTLEMAN.
L.. LET HER DOWN .. ?
THERE'S NO OTHER WAY. AKO CAN BOUNCE BACK IF YOU DUMP HER. SHE'LL BE FINE.
HOWEVER :

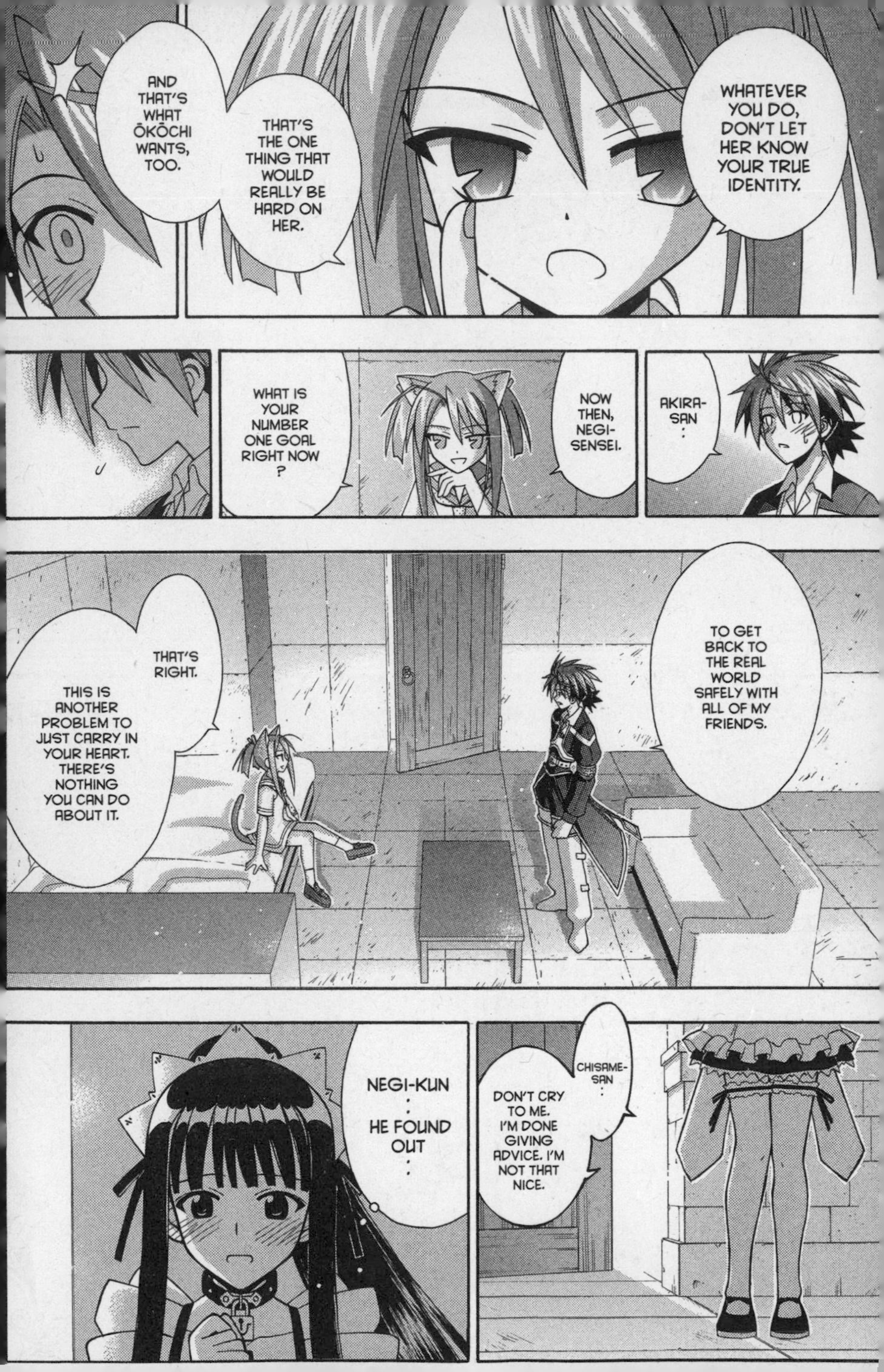

WHATEVER YOU DO, DON'T LET HER KNOW YOUR TRUE IDENTITY.
THAT'S THE ONE THING THAT WOULD REALLY BE HARD ON HER.
AND THAT'S WHAT ŌKŌCHI WANTS, TOO.
AKIRA-SAN :
NOW THEN, NEGI-SENSEI.
WHAT IS YOUR NUMBER ONE GOAL RIGHT NOW ?
TO GET BACK TO THE REAL WORLD SAFELY WITH ALL OF MY FRIENDS.
THAT'S RIGHT.
THIS IS ANOTHER PROBLEM TO JUST CARRY IN YOUR HEART. THERE'S NOTHING YOU CAN DO ABOUT IT.
CHISAME-SAN :
DON'T CRY TO ME. I'M DONE GIVING ADVICE. I'M NOT THAT NICE.
NEGI-KUN :
HE FOUND OUT :

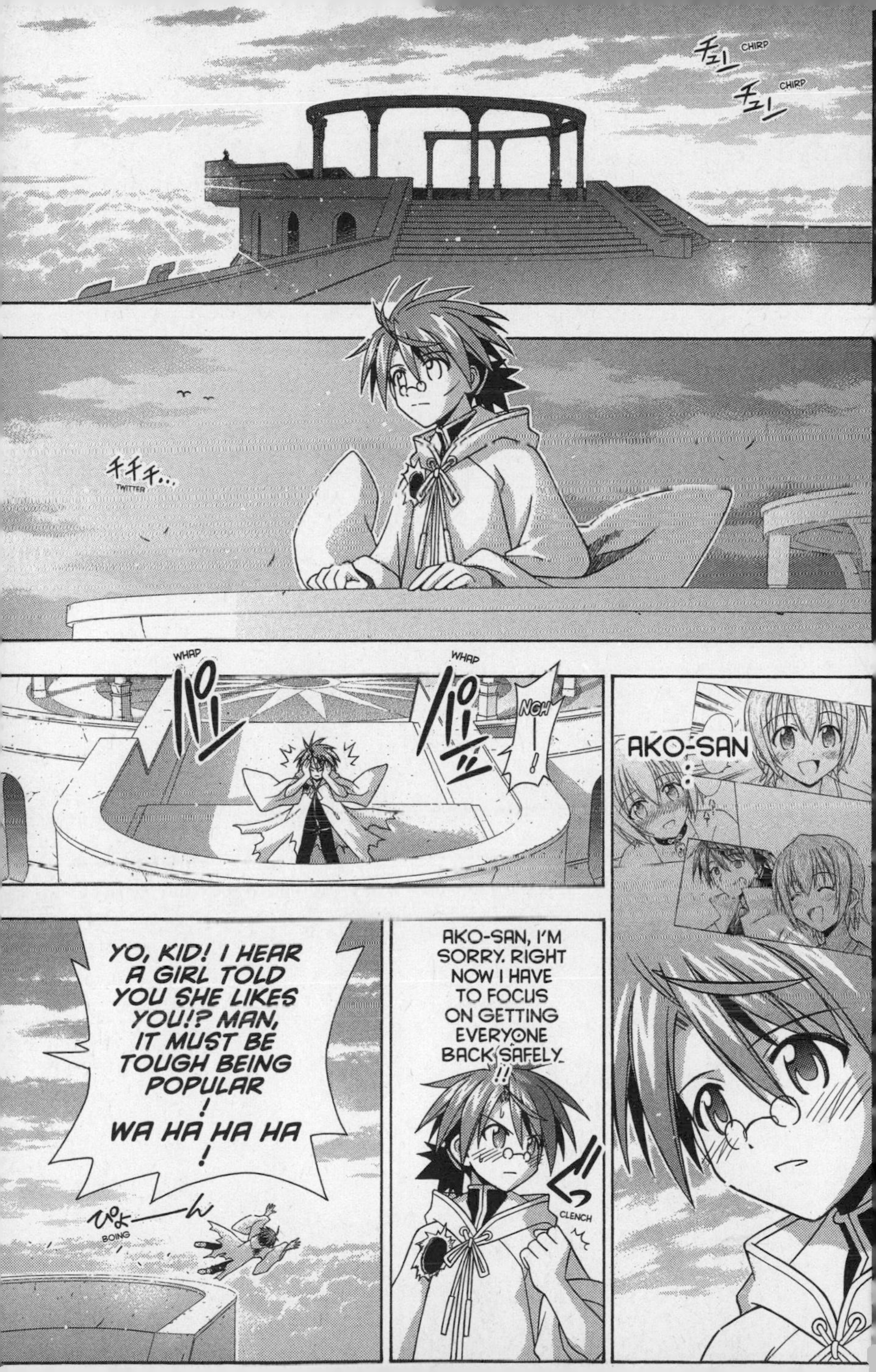

チュー CHIRP
チュー CHIRP
チチチ… TWITTER
AKO-SAN
…
WHAP
パン
WHAP
パンッ
NGH!
AKO-SAN, I'M SORRY. RIGHT NOW I HAVE TO FOCUS ON GETTING EVERYONE BACK SAFELY.
!!
くっ CLENCH
YO, KID! I HEAR A GIRL TOLD YOU SHE LIKES YOU!? MAN, IT MUST BE TOUGH BEING POPULAR! WA HA HA HA!
ぴょーーん BOING

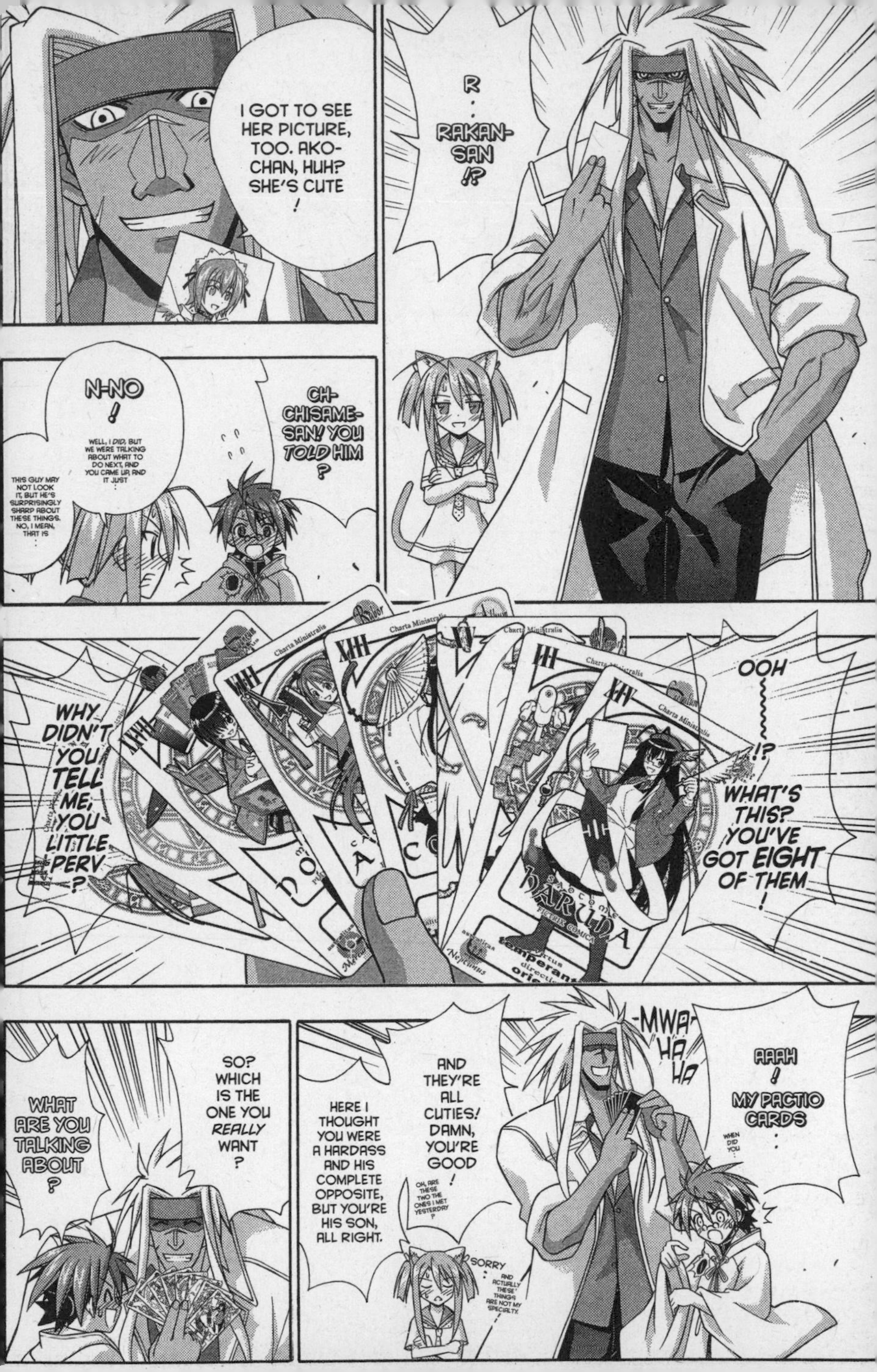
R... RAKAN-SAN!?
I GOT TO SEE HER PICTURE, TOO. AKO-CHAN, HUH? SHE'S CUTE!
CH-CHISAME-SAN! YOU TOLD HIM?
N-NO!
WELL, I DID, BUT WE WERE TALKING ABOUT WHAT TO DO NEXT, AND YOU CAME UP, AND IT JUST...
THIS GUY MAY NOT LOOK IT, BUT HE'S SURPRISINGLY SHARP ABOUT THESE THINGS. NO, I MEAN, THAT IS...
OOH~!? WHAT'S THIS? YOU'VE GOT EIGHT OF THEM!
WHY DIDN'T YOU TELL ME, YOU LITTLE PERV?
-MWAHAHA
AAAH! MY PACTIO CARDS...
WHEN DID YOU...
AND THEY'RE ALL CUTIES! DAMN, YOU'RE GOOD!
HERE I THOUGHT YOU WERE A HARDASS AND HIS COMPLETE OPPOSITE, BUT YOU'RE HIS SON, ALL RIGHT.
OH, ARE THESE THE ONES I MET YESTERDAY?
SORRY...
AND ACTUALLY THESE THINGS ARE NOT MY SPECIALTY.
SO? WHICH IS THE ONE YOU REALLY WANT?
WHAT ARE YOU TALKING ABOUT?

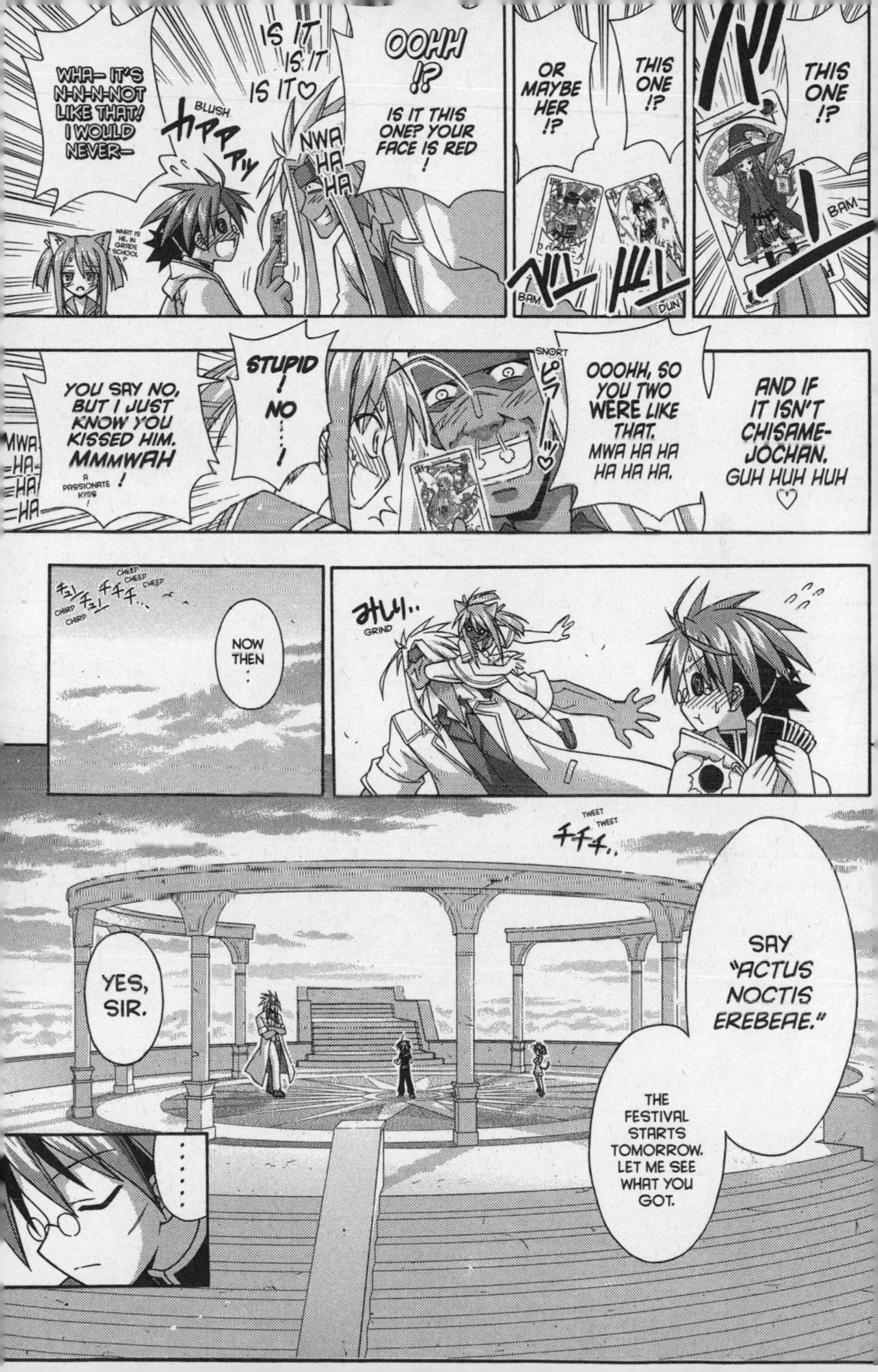
THIS ONE !?
BAM
THIS ONE !?
OR MAYBE HER !?
BAM
DUN
OOHH !?
IS IT THIS ONE? YOUR FACE IS RED !
IS IT IS IT IS IT♡
NWA HA HA
BLUSH
WHA– IT'S N-N-N-NOT LIKE THAT! I WOULD NEVER–
WHAT IS HE, IN GRADE SCHOOL ?
AND IF IT ISN'T CHISAME-JOCHAN. GUH HUH HUH ♡
OOOHH, SO YOU TWO WERE LIKE THAT. MWA HA HA HA HA HA.
SNORT
STUPID ! NO ...!
YOU SAY NO, BUT I JUST KNOW YOU KISSED HIM. MMMWAH !
A PASSIONATE KISS !
MWA-HA-HA-HA
GRIND
CHEEP CHEEP CHEEP
CHIRP CHIRP
NOW THEN ...
TWEET TWEET
SAY "ACTUS NOCTIS EREBEAE."
THE FESTIVAL STARTS TOMORROW. LET ME SEE WHAT YOU GOT.
YES, SIR.
......

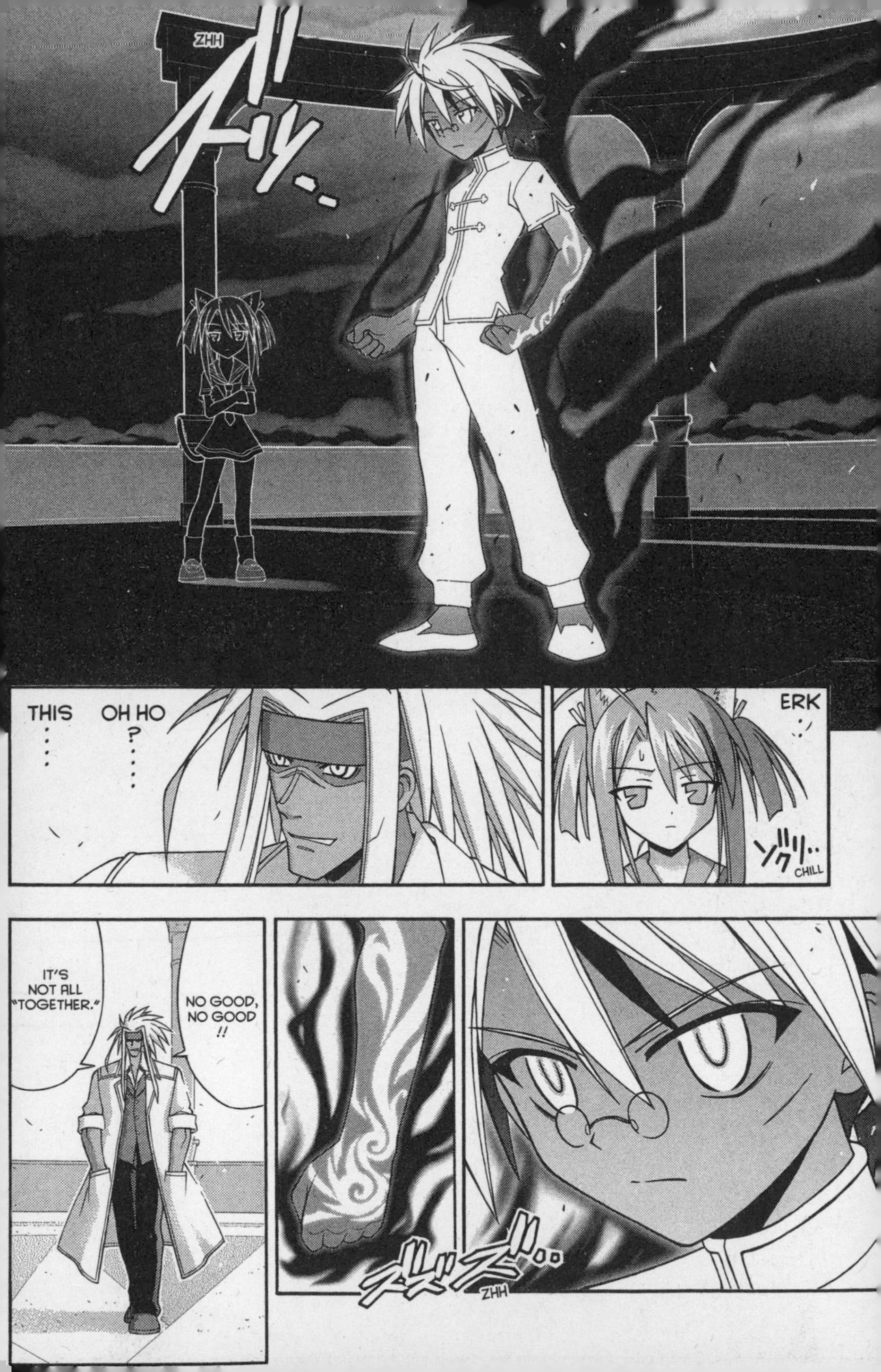
ZHH
ERK
CHILL
OH HO?
THIS...
ZHH
NO GOOD, NO GOOD!!
IT'S NOT ALL "TOGETHER."

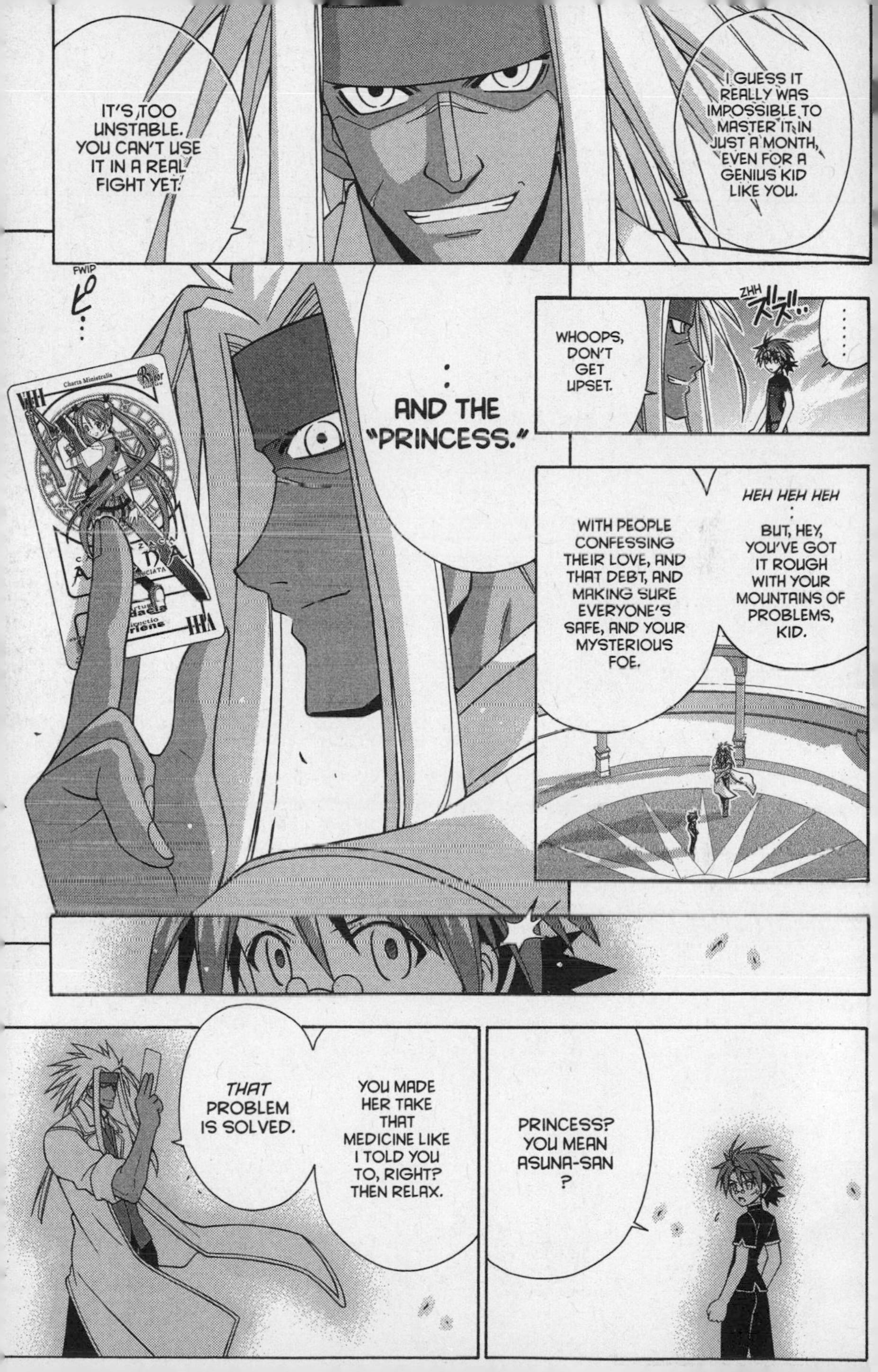
I GUESS IT REALLY WAS IMPOSSIBLE TO MASTER IT IN JUST A MONTH, EVEN FOR A GENIUS KID LIKE YOU.
IT'S TOO UNSTABLE. YOU CAN'T USE IT IN A REAL FIGHT YET.
......
ZHH
ズズ...
WHOOPS, DON'T GET UPSET.
HEH HEH HEH
:
BUT, HEY, YOU'VE GOT IT ROUGH WITH YOUR MOUNTAINS OF PROBLEMS, KID.
WITH PEOPLE CONFESSING THEIR LOVE, AND THAT DEBT, AND MAKING SURE EVERYONE'S SAFE, AND YOUR MYSTERIOUS FOE.
:
:
AND THE "PRINCESS."
FWIP
ピ...
Charta Ministralis
PRINCESS? YOU MEAN ASUNA-SAN ?
YOU MADE HER TAKE THAT MEDICINE LIKE I TOLD YOU TO, RIGHT? THEN RELAX.
THAT PROBLEM IS SOLVED.

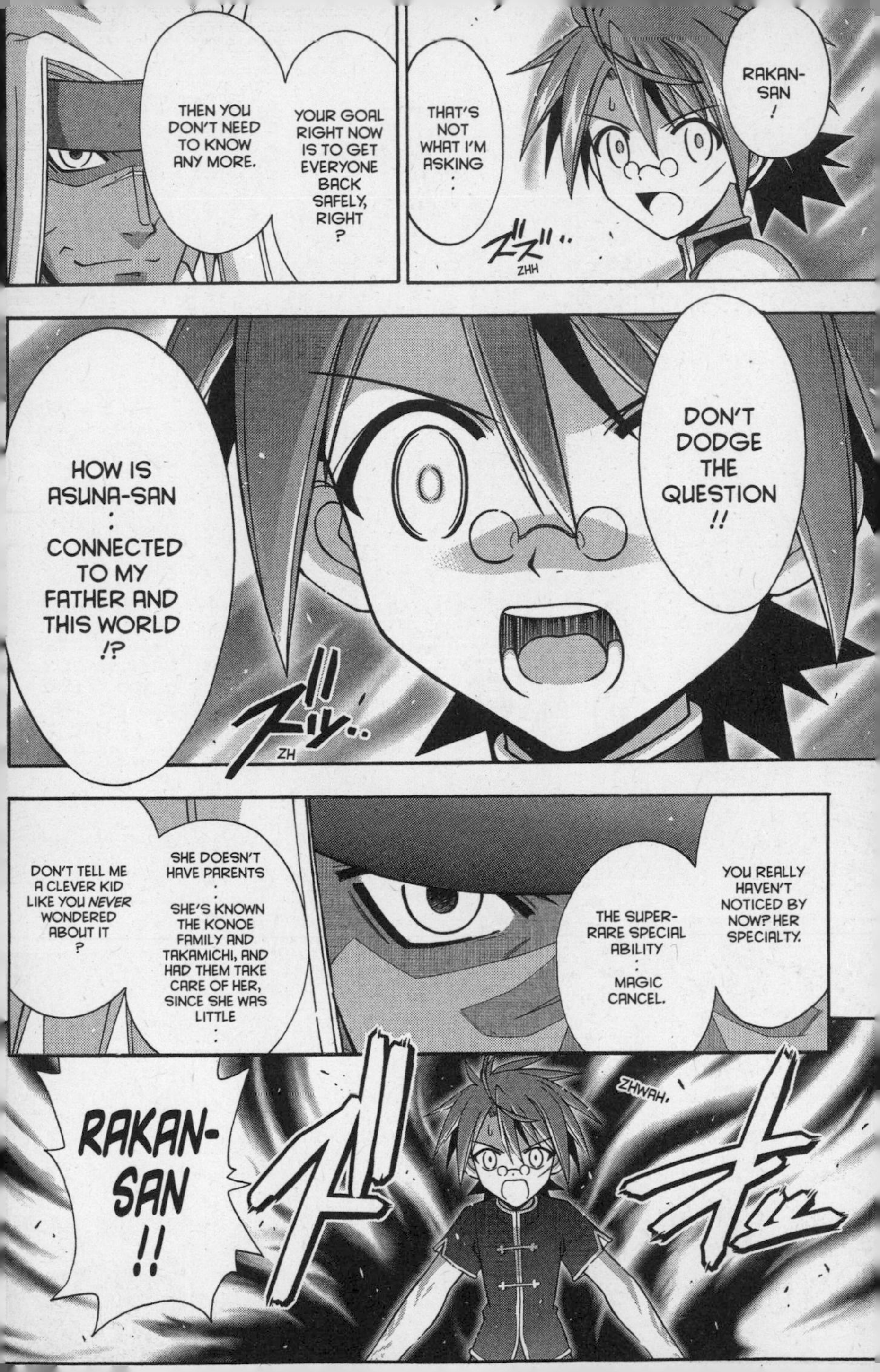
RAKAN-SAN!
THAT'S NOT WHAT I'M ASKING...
ZHH
YOUR GOAL RIGHT NOW IS TO GET EVERYONE BACK SAFELY, RIGHT?
THEN YOU DON'T NEED TO KNOW ANY MORE.
DON'T DODGE THE QUESTION!!
HOW IS ASUNA-SAN... CONNECTED TO MY FATHER AND THIS WORLD!?
ZH
YOU REALLY HAVEN'T NOTICED BY NOW? HER SPECIALTY.
THE SUPER-RARE SPECIAL ABILITY... MAGIC CANCEL.
SHE DOESN'T HAVE PARENTS... SHE'S KNOWN THE KONOE FAMILY AND TAKAMICHI, AND HAD THEM TAKE CARE OF HER, SINCE SHE WAS LITTLE...
DON'T TELL ME A CLEVER KID LIKE YOU *NEVER* WONDERED ABOUT IT?
ZHWAH
RAKAN-SAN!!

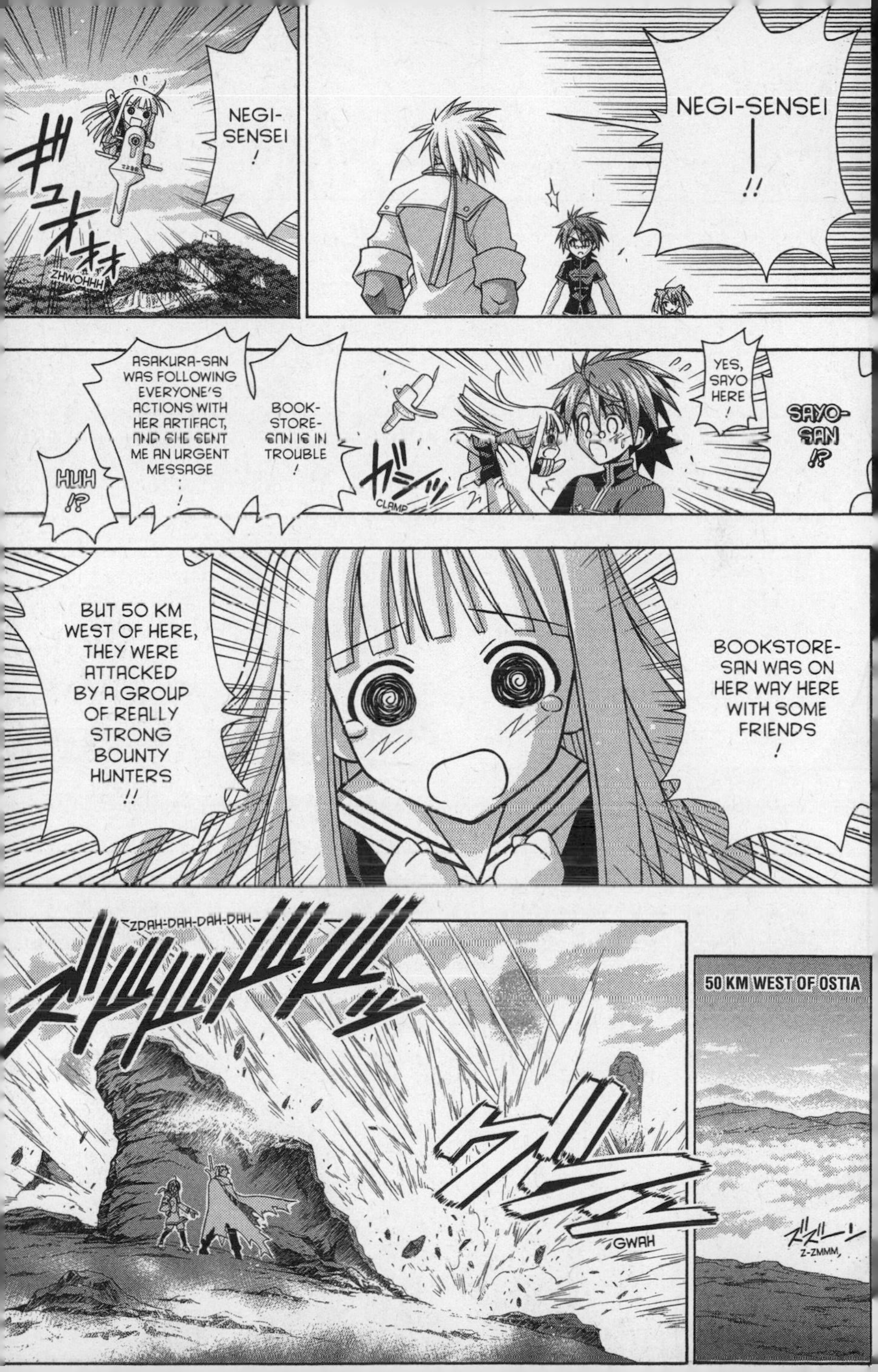
NEGI-SENSEI —!!
NEGI-SENSEI!
ZHWOHHH
SAYO-SAN!?
YES, SAYO HERE!
CLAMP
BOOK-STORE-SAN IS IN TROUBLE!
ASAKURA-SAN WAS FOLLOWING EVERYONE'S ACTIONS WITH HER ARTIFACT, AND SHE SENT ME AN URGENT MESSAGE...!
HUH!?
BOOKSTORE-SAN WAS ON HER WAY HERE WITH SOME FRIENDS!
BUT 50 KM WEST OF HERE, THEY WERE ATTACKED BY A GROUP OF REALLY STRONG BOUNTY HUNTERS!!
50 KM WEST OF OSTIA
Z-ZMMM,
ZDAH-DAH-DAH-DAH
GWAH

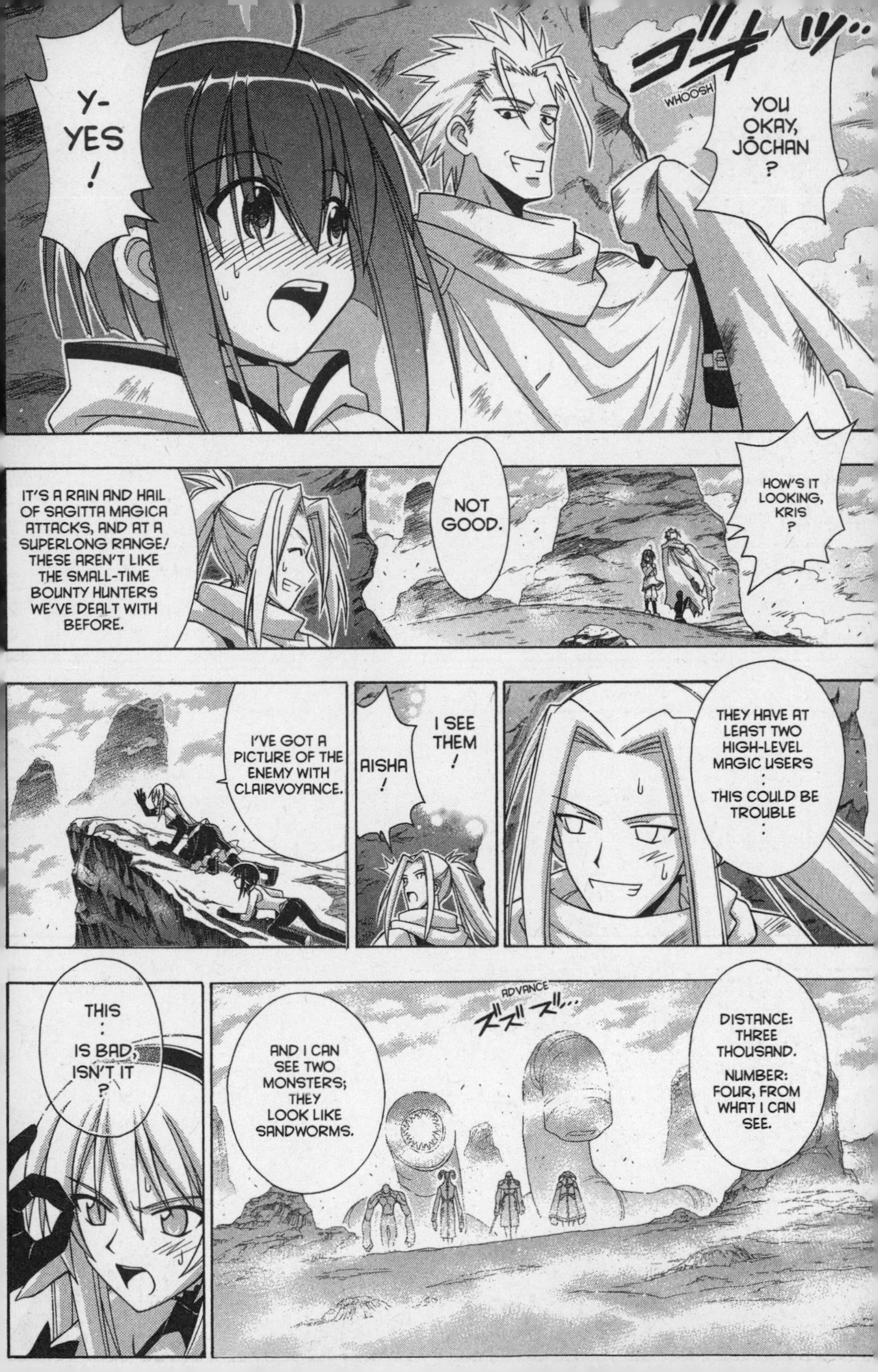
WHOOSH
YOU OKAY, JŌCHAN?
Y-YES!
HOW'S IT LOOKING, KRIS?
NOT GOOD.
IT'S A RAIN AND HAIL OF SAGITTA MAGICA ATTACKS, AND AT A SUPERLONG RANGE! THESE AREN'T LIKE THE SMALL-TIME BOUNTY HUNTERS WE'VE DEALT WITH BEFORE.
THEY HAVE AT LEAST TWO HIGH-LEVEL MAGIC USERS... THIS COULD BE TROUBLE...
I SEE THEM!
AISHA!
I'VE GOT A PICTURE OF THE ENEMY WITH CLAIRVOYANCE.
ADVANCE
DISTANCE: THREE THOUSAND. NUMBER: FOUR, FROM WHAT I CAN SEE.
AND I CAN SEE TWO MONSTERS; THEY LOOK LIKE SANDWORMS.
THIS... IS BAD, ISN'T IT?

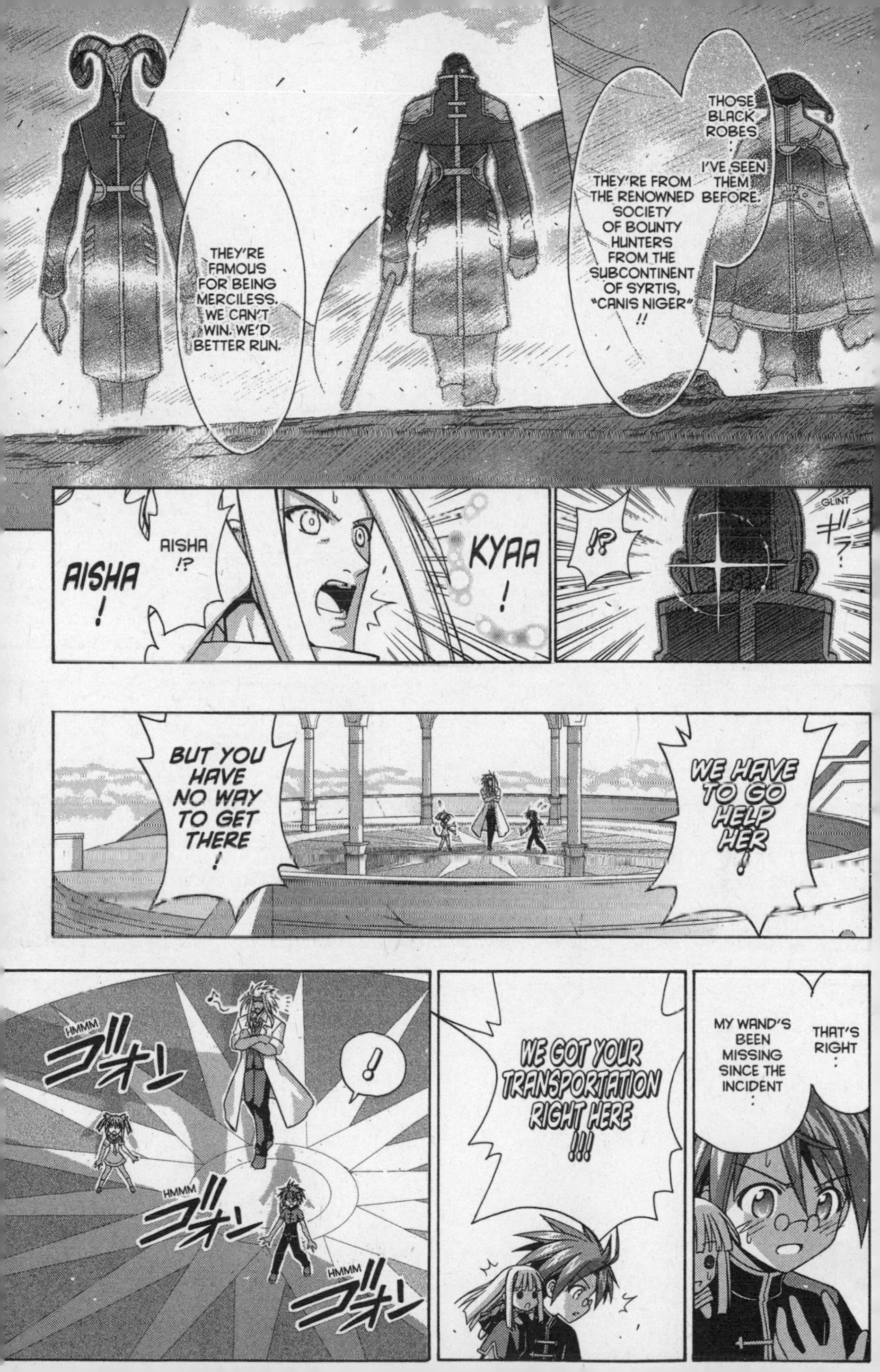
THOSE BLACK ROBES... I'VE SEEN THEM BEFORE.
THEY'RE FROM THE RENOWNED SOCIETY OF BOUNTY HUNTERS FROM THE SUBCONTINENT OF SYRTIS, "CANIS NIGER"!!
THEY'RE FAMOUS FOR BEING MERCILESS. WE CAN'T WIN. WE'D BETTER RUN.
GLINT
!?
KYAA!
AISHA!?
AISHA!
WE HAVE TO GO HELP HER!
BUT YOU HAVE NO WAY TO GET THERE!
THAT'S RIGHT...
MY WAND'S BEEN MISSING SINCE THE INCIDENT...
WE GOT YOUR TRANSPORTATION RIGHT HERE!!!
!
HMMM
HMMM
HMMM

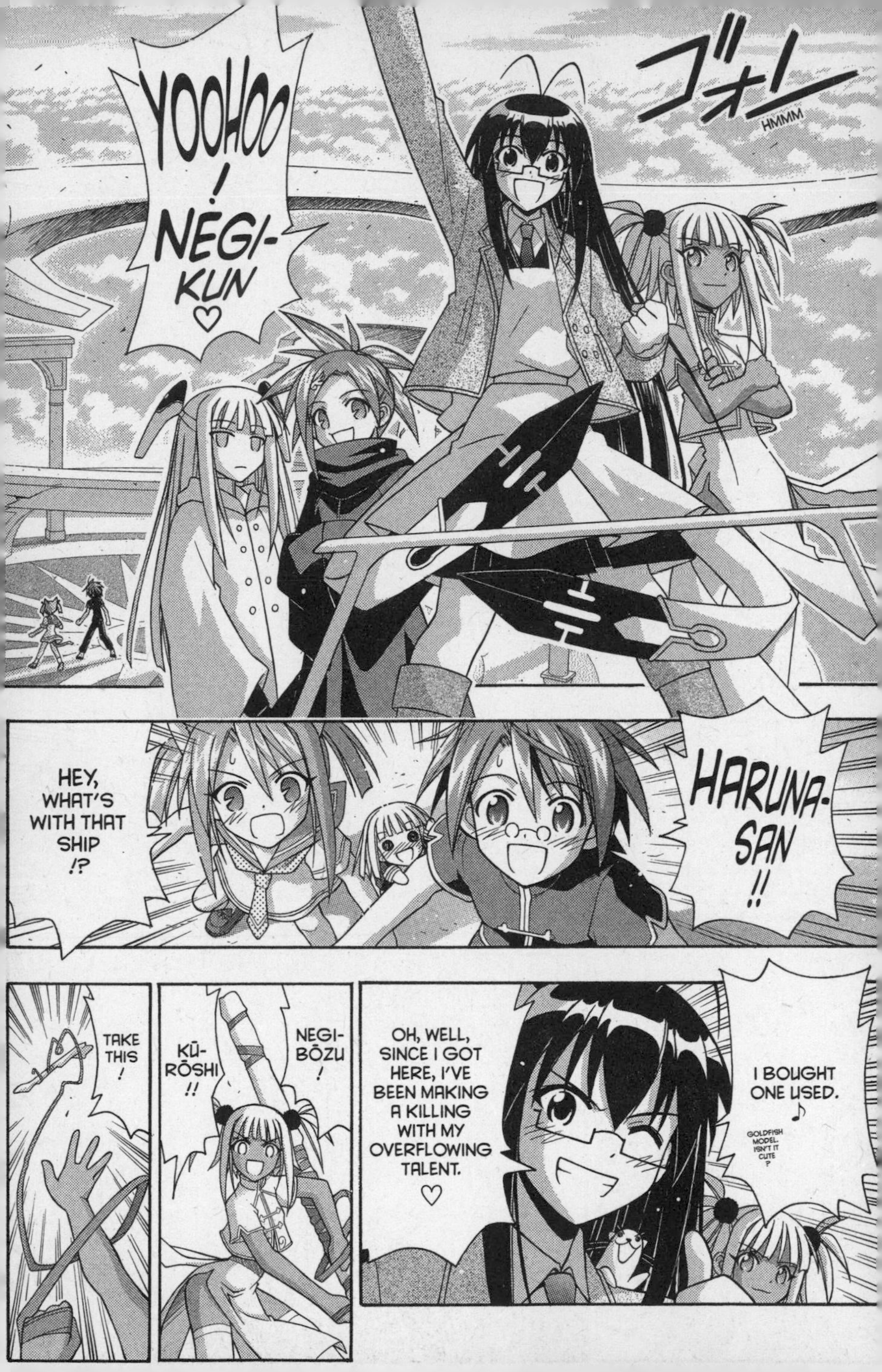
ゴォン
HMMM
YOOHOO! NEGI-KUN ♡
HARUNA-SAN!!
HEY, WHAT'S WITH THAT SHIP!?
I BOUGHT ONE USED. ♪
GOLDFISH MODEL. ISN'T IT CUTE?
OH, WELL, SINCE I GOT HERE, I'VE BEEN MAKING A KILLING WITH MY OVERFLOWING TALENT. ♡
NEGI-BŌZU!
KŪ-RŌSHI!!
TAKE THIS!

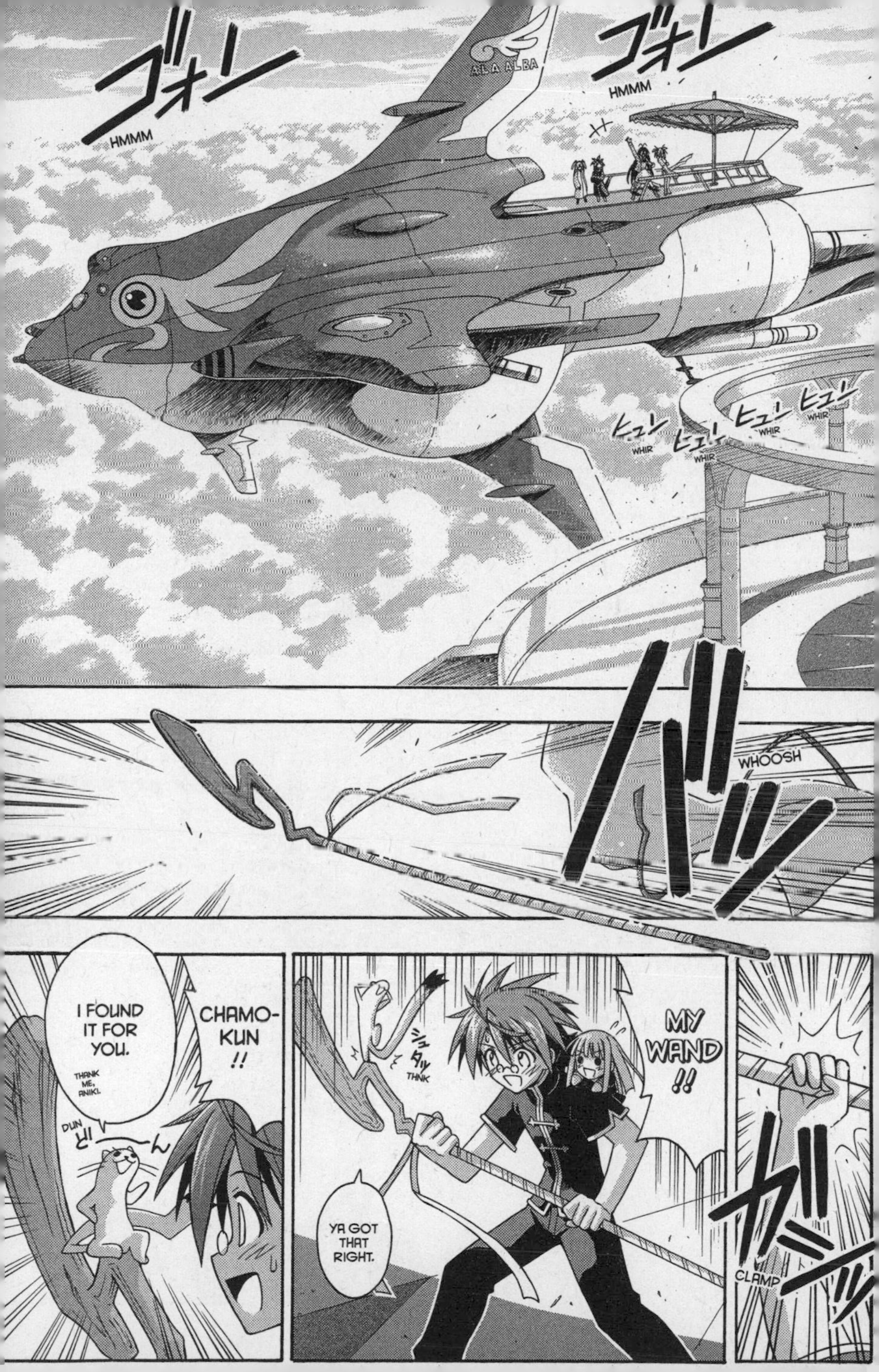

HMMM
ALA ALBA
HMMM
WHIR
WHIR
WHIR
WHIR
WHOOSH
CLAMP
MY WAND!!
THNK
YA GOT THAT RIGHT.
CHAMO-KUN!!
I FOUND IT FOR YOU.
THANK ME, ANIKI.
DUN

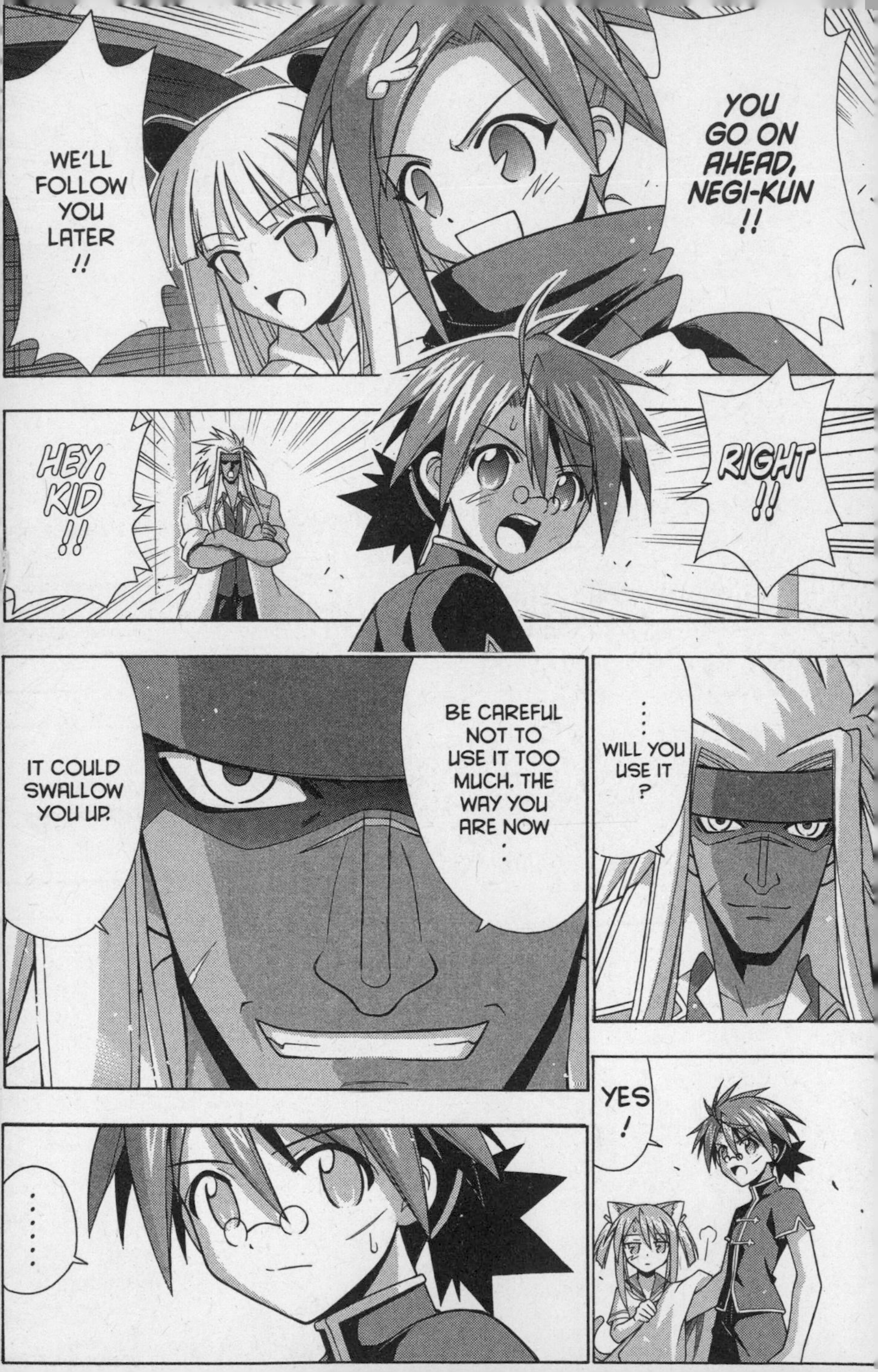
YOU GO ON AHEAD, NEGI-KUN !!
WE'LL FOLLOW YOU LATER !!
RIGHT !!
HEY, KID !!
.... WILL YOU USE IT ?
BE CAREFUL NOT TO USE IT TOO MUCH. THE WAY YOU ARE NOW :
IT COULD SWALLOW YOU UP.
YES !
......

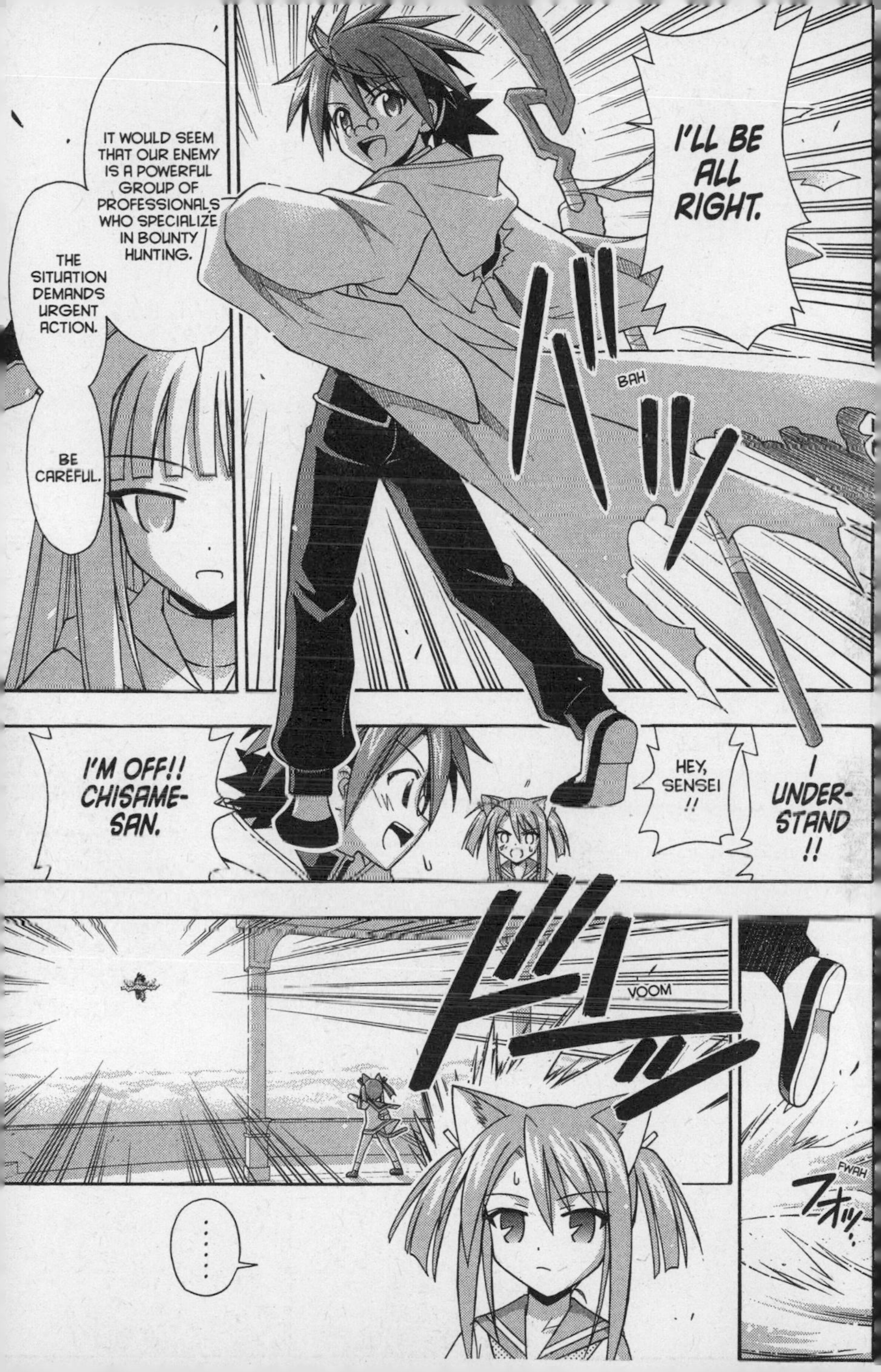

I'LL BE ALL RIGHT.
BAH
IT WOULD SEEM THAT OUR ENEMY IS A POWERFUL GROUP OF PROFESSIONALS WHO SPECIALIZE IN BOUNTY HUNTING.
THE SITUATION DEMANDS URGENT ACTION.
BE CAREFUL.
I UNDER-STAND!!
HEY, SENSEI!!
I'M OFF!! CHISAME-SAN.
VOOM
FWAH
......

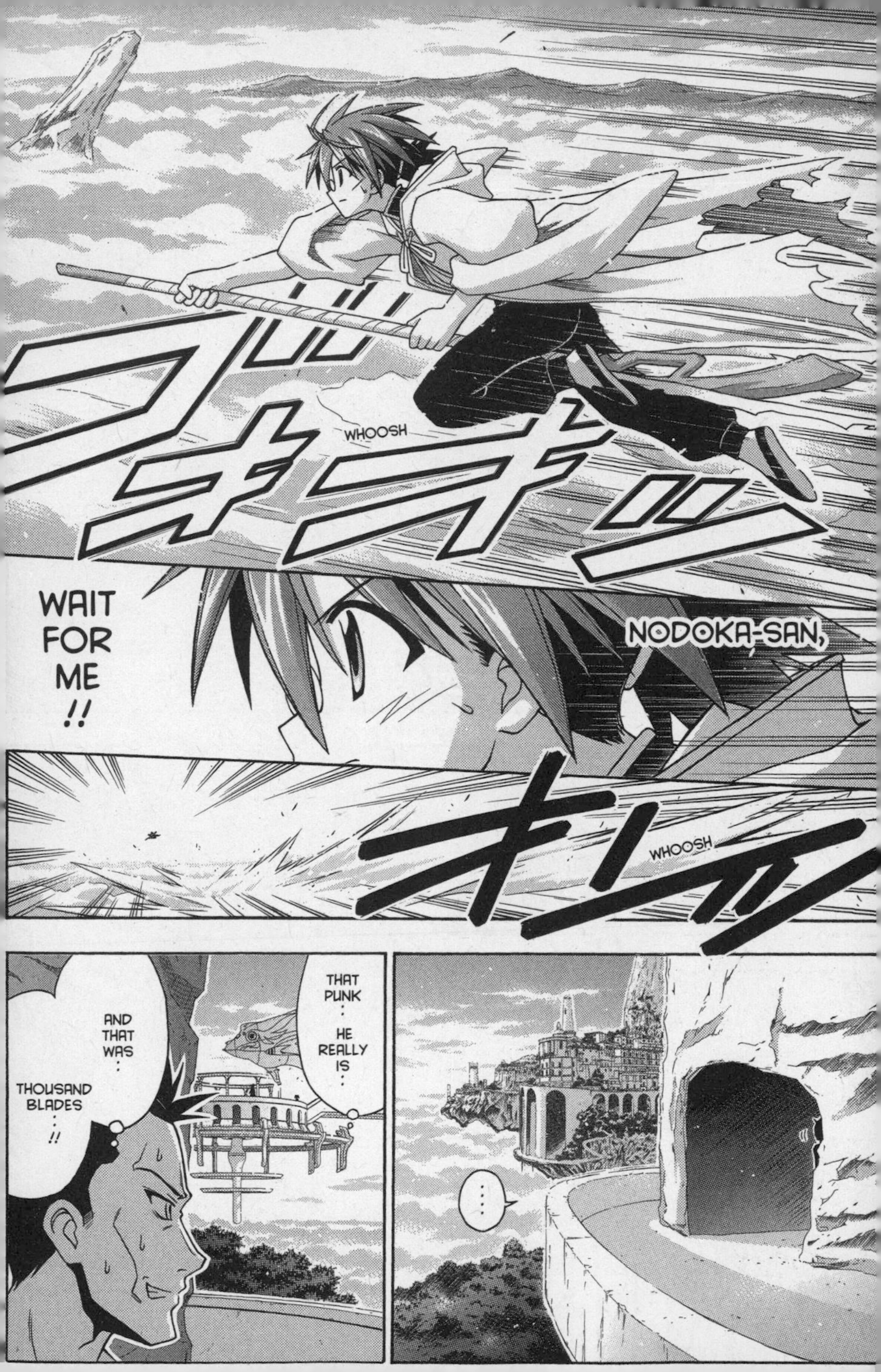
WHOOSH
NODOKA-SAN,
WAIT FOR ME !!
WHOOSH
....
THAT PUNK : HE REALLY IS . .
AND THAT WAS : THOUSAND BLADES . . !!

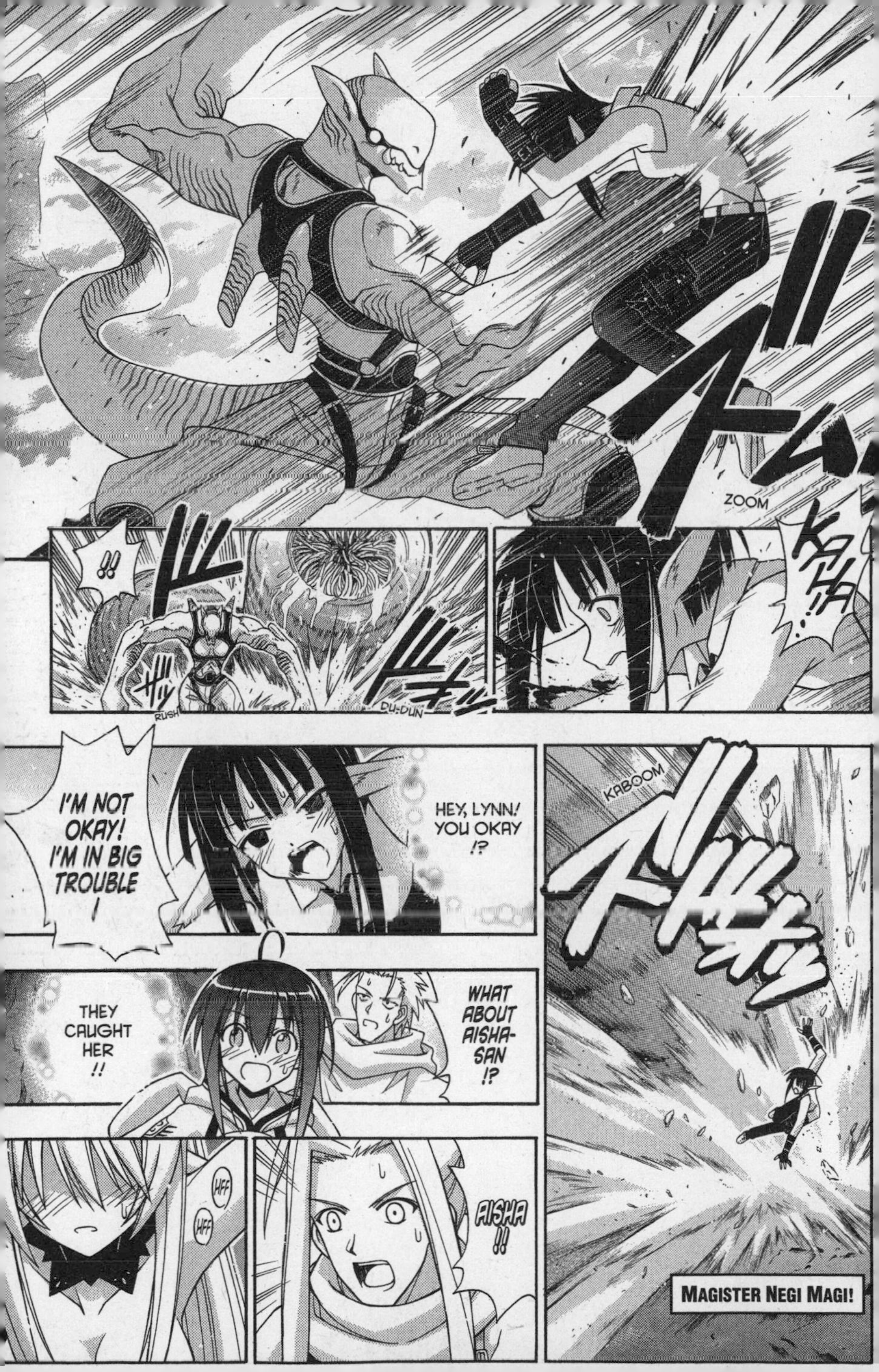
ZOOM
KAHA !!
!!
RUSH
DU-DUN
KABOOM
HEY, LYNN! YOU OKAY !?
I'M NOT OKAY! I'M IN BIG TROUBLE !
WHAT ABOUT AISHA-SAN !?
THEY CAUGHT HER !!
AISHA !!
HFF
HFF
MAGISTER NEGI MAGI!

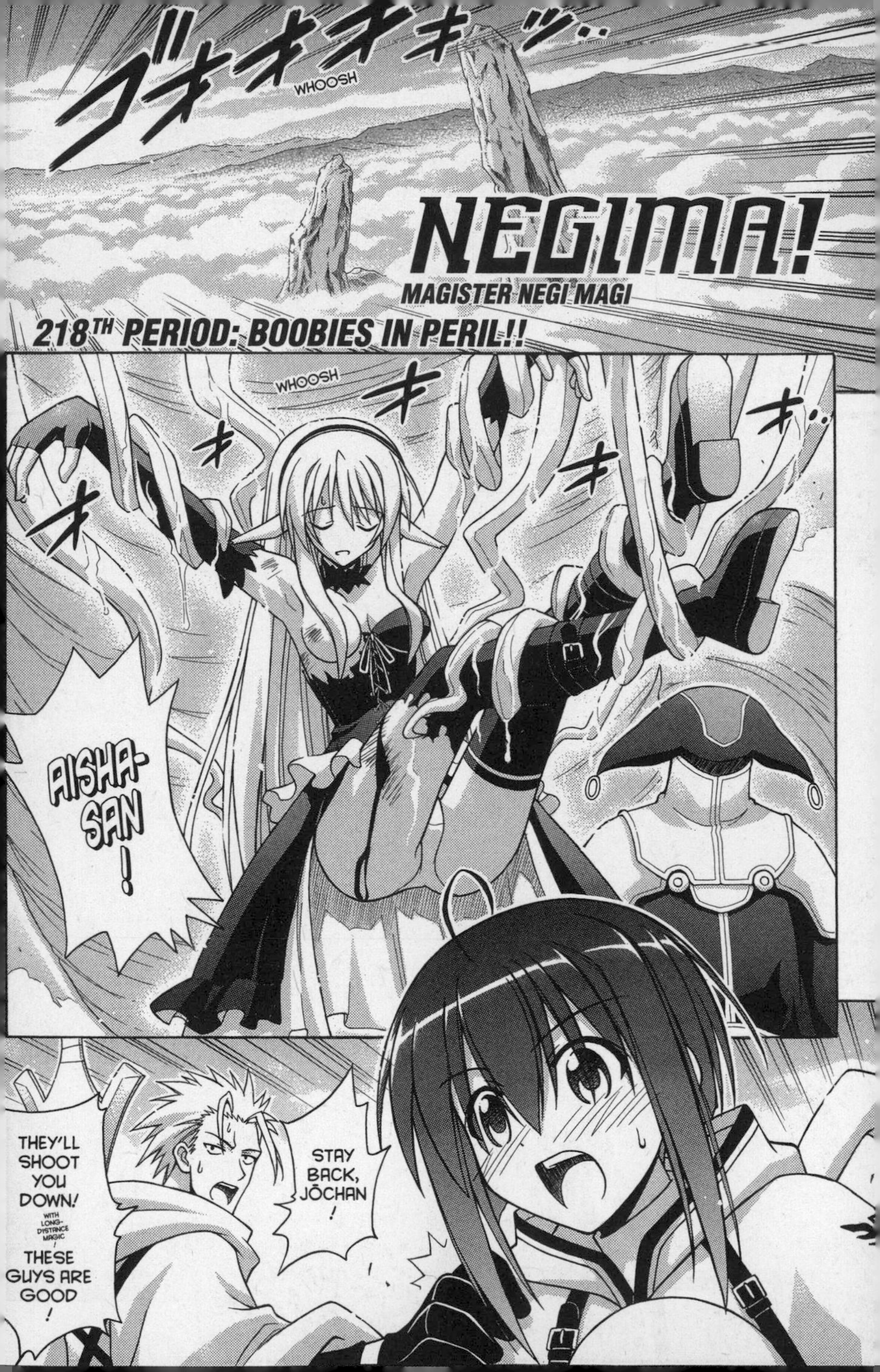
WHOOSH
NEGIMA!
MAGISTER NEGI MAGI
218TH PERIOD: BOOBIES IN PERIL!!
WHOOSH
AISHA-SAN!
STAY BACK, JŌCHAN!
THEY'LL SHOOT YOU DOWN!
WITH LONG-DISTANCE MAGIC!
THESE GUYS ARE GOOD!

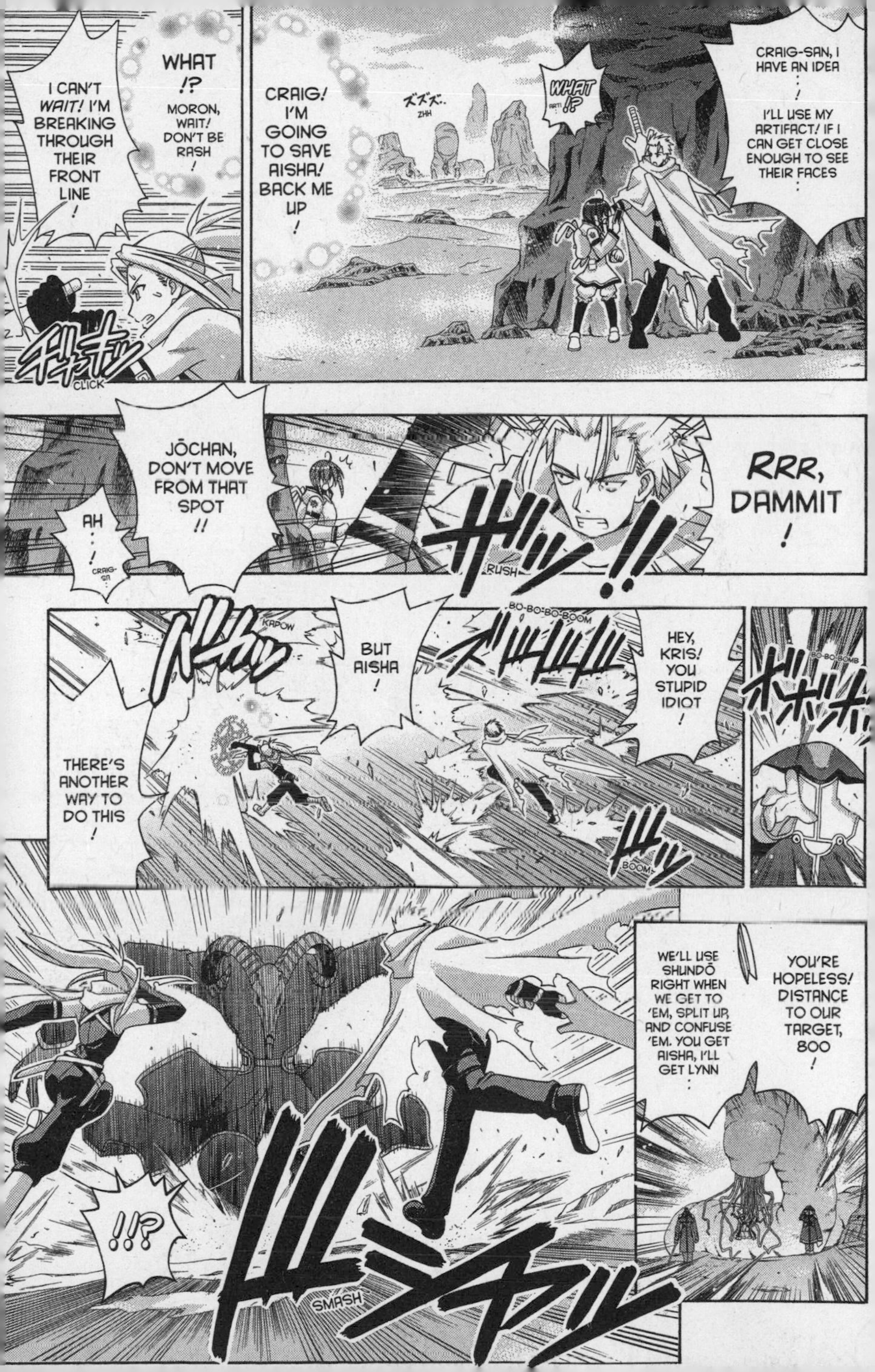
CRAIG-SAN, I HAVE AN IDEA...
I'LL USE MY ARTIFACT! IF I CAN GET CLOSE ENOUGH TO SEE THEIR FACES...
WHAT!? ART!
ZHH
CRAIG! I'M GOING TO SAVE AISHA! BACK ME UP!
WHAT!? MORON, WAIT! DON'T BE RASH!
I CAN'T WAIT! I'M BREAKING THROUGH THEIR FRONT LINE!
CLICK
RRR, DAMMIT!
RUSH
JŌCHAN, DON'T MOVE FROM THAT SPOT!!
AH...! CRAIG-SAN
BO-BO-BOMB
HEY, KRIS! YOU STUPID IDIOT!
BO-BO-BO-BOOM
BOOM
BUT AISHA!
KAPOW
THERE'S ANOTHER WAY TO DO THIS!
YOU'RE HOPELESS! DISTANCE TO OUR TARGET, 800!
WE'LL USE SHUNDŌ RIGHT WHEN WE GET TO 'EM, SPLIT UP, AND CONFUSE 'EM. YOU GET AISHA, I'LL GET LYNN...
SMASH
!!?

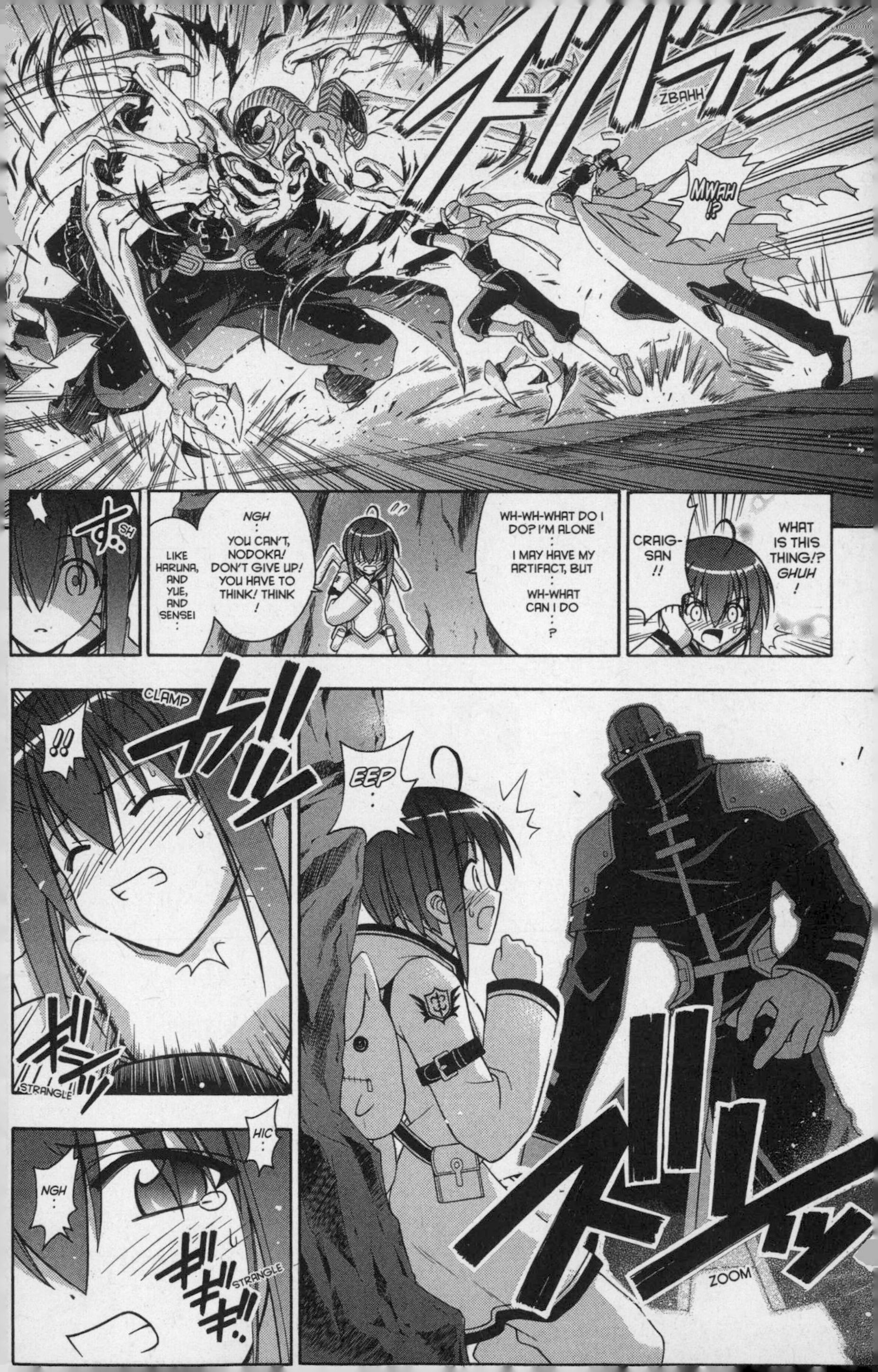
ZBAHH
MWAH !?
CRAIG-SAN !!
WHAT IS THIS THING!? GHUH !
WH-WH-WHAT DO I DO? I'M ALONE ... I MAY HAVE MY ARTIFACT, BUT ... WH-WHAT CAN I DO ...?
NGH ... YOU CAN'T, NODOKA! DON'T GIVE UP! YOU HAVE TO THINK! THINK!
LIKE HARUNA, AND YUE, AND SENSEI ...
SH
EEP ...
ZOOM
CLAMP
!!
STRANGLE
HIC ...
NGH ...
STRANGLE

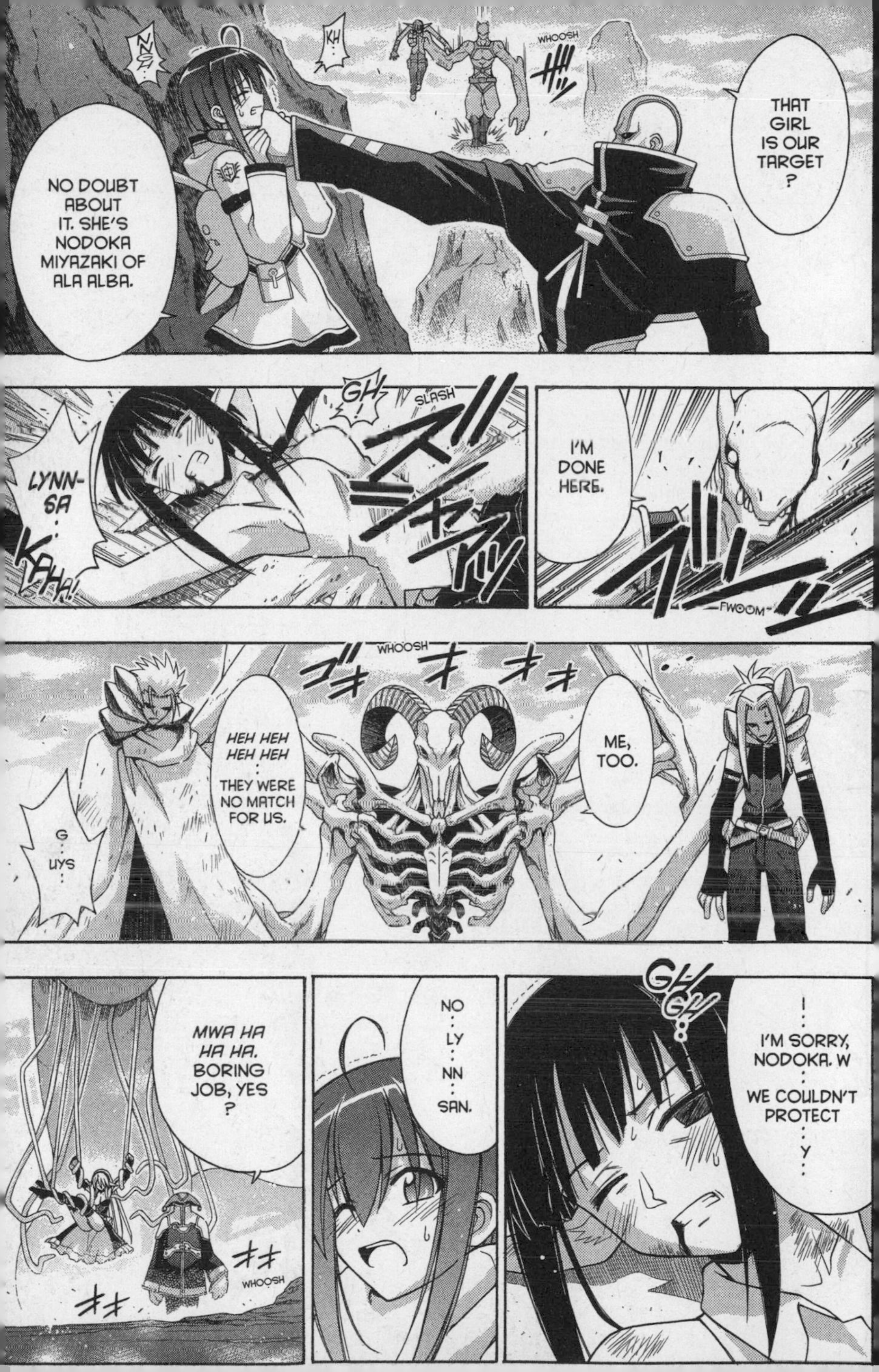
WHOOSH
THAT GIRL IS OUR TARGET?
KH...
NNGH...
NO DOUBT ABOUT IT. SHE'S NODOKA MIYAZAKI OF ALA ALBA.
I'M DONE HERE.
FWOOM
SLASH
GH!
LYNN-SA...
KAHA!
ME, TOO.
WHOOSH
HEH HEH HEH HEH... THEY WERE NO MATCH FOR US.
G... UYS...
GH-GH!
I'M SORRY, NODOKA. W... WE COULDN'T PROTECT... Y...
NO... LY... NN... SAN.
MWA HA HA HA. BORING JOB, YES?
WHOOSH

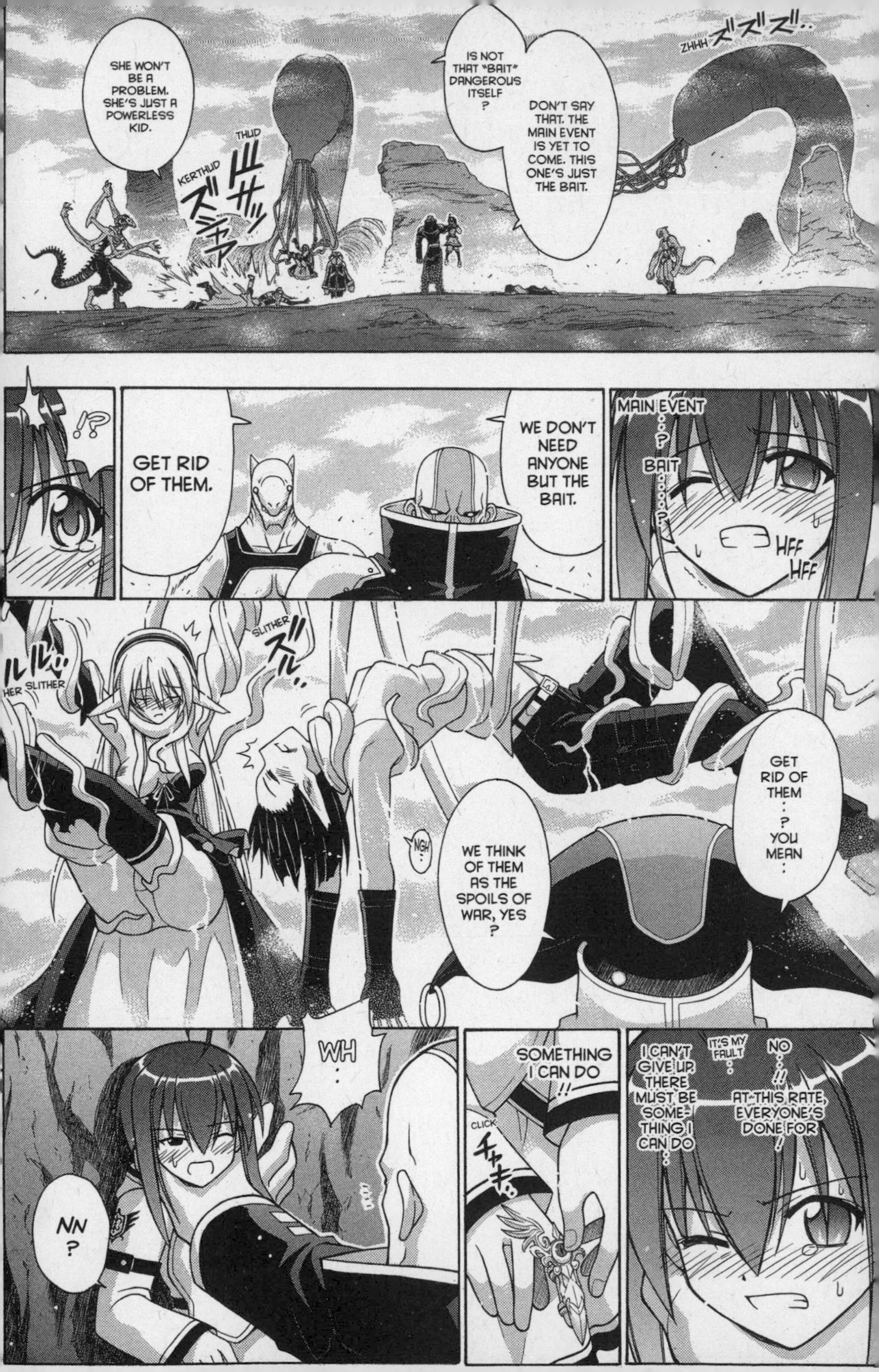
ZHHH ズズズ..
DON'T SAY THAT. THE MAIN EVENT IS YET TO COME. THIS ONE'S JUST THE BAIT.
IS NOT THAT "BAIT" DANGEROUS ITSELF?
THUD ザッ
KERTHUD ズシャア
SHE WON'T BE A PROBLEM. SHE'S JUST A POWERLESS KID.
MAIN EVENT...? BAIT...?
HFF HFF
WE DON'T NEED ANYONE BUT THE BAIT.
GET RID OF THEM.
!?
GET RID OF THEM...? YOU MEAN...
WE THINK OF THEM AS THE SPOILS OF WAR, YES?
NGH...
SLITHER ズル..
HER SLITHER ルル..
NO...!!
AT THIS RATE, EVERYONE'S DONE FOR!
IT'S MY FAULT...
I CAN'T GIVE UP. THERE MUST BE SOMETHING I CAN DO...
SOMETHING I CAN DO!!
CLICK チャキ..
WH...
NN?

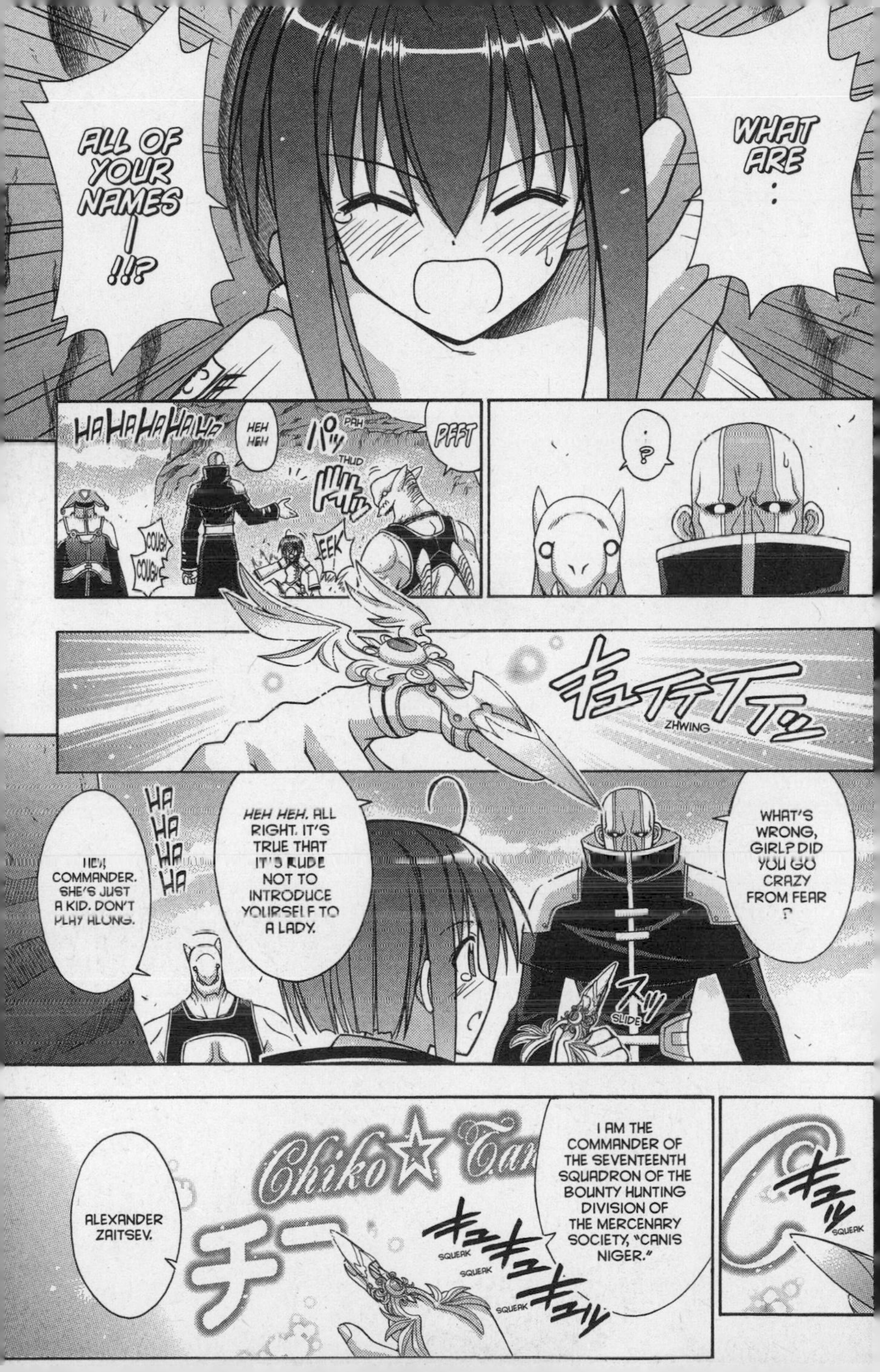
WHAT ARE :
ALL OF YOUR NAMES !!?
?
PFFT
パッ PAH
HEH HEH
ドサッ THUD
HAHAHAHAHAHA
EEK
COUGH COUGH
キュイイイッ ZHWING
WHAT'S WRONG, GIRL? DID YOU GO CRAZY FROM FEAR?
スッ SLIDE
HEH HEH. ALL RIGHT. IT'S TRUE THAT IT'S RUDE NOT TO INTRODUCE YOURSELF TO A LADY.
HA HA HA HA
HEY, COMMANDER. SHE'S JUST A KID. DON'T PLAY ALONG.
キュッ SQUEAK
I AM THE COMMANDER OF THE SEVENTEENTH SQUADRON OF THE BOUNTY HUNTING DIVISION OF THE MERCENARY SOCIETY, "CANIS NIGER."
キュキュキュッ SQUEAK SQUEAK SQUEAK
Chiko☆Tan
チー
ALEXANDER ZAITSEV.

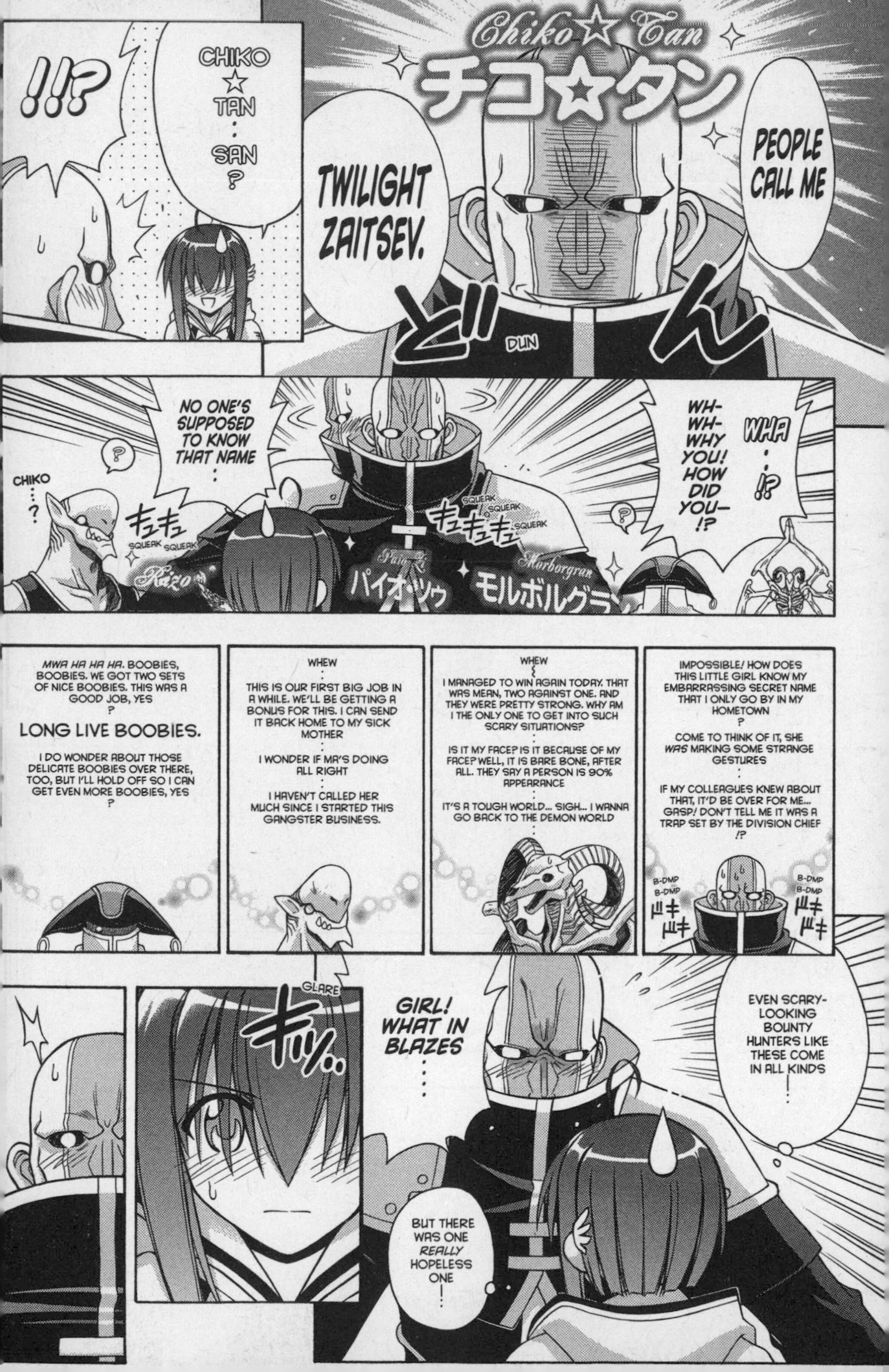

PEOPLE CALL ME
TWILIGHT ZAITSEV.
Chiko☆Tan
チコ☆タン
どん
DUN
CHIKO ☆ TAN ... SAN ?
!!?
WHA ... !?
WH- WH- WHY YOU! HOW DID YOU- !?
?
きゅきゅきゅ
SQUEAK SQUEAK SQUEAK
Morborgran
モルボルグラン
Pai-Tsu
パイオ・ツウ
NO ONE'S SUPPOSED TO KNOW THAT NAME ...
?
キュキュ
SQUEAK SQUEAK
Razo
CHIKO ... ?
IMPOSSIBLE! HOW DOES THIS LITTLE GIRL KNOW MY EMBARRASSING SECRET NAME THAT I ONLY GO BY IN MY HOMETOWN ?
COME TO THINK OF IT, SHE *WAS* MAKING SOME STRANGE GESTURES
IF MY COLLEAGUES KNEW ABOUT THAT, IT'D BE OVER FOR ME... GASP! DON'T TELL ME IT WAS A TRAP SET BY THE DIVISION CHIEF !?
B-DMP B-DMP ドキドキ
B-DMP B-DMP ドキドキ
WHEW ...
I MANAGED TO WIN AGAIN TODAY. THAT WAS MEAN, TWO AGAINST ONE. AND THEY WERE PRETTY STRONG. WHY AM I THE ONLY ONE TO GET INTO SUCH SCARY SITUATIONS? ...
IS IT MY FACE? IS IT BECAUSE OF MY FACE? WELL, IT IS BARE BONE, AFTER ALL. THEY SAY A PERSON IS 90% APPEARANCE
IT'S A TOUGH WORLD... SIGH... I WANNA GO BACK TO THE DEMON WORLD ...
WHEW ...
THIS IS OUR FIRST BIG JOB IN A WHILE. WE'LL BE GETTING A BONUS FOR THIS. I CAN SEND IT BACK HOME TO MY SICK MOTHER
I WONDER IF MA'S DOING ALL RIGHT ...
I HAVEN'T CALLED HER MUCH SINCE I STARTED THIS GANGSTER BUSINESS.
*MWA HA HA HA.* BOOBIES, BOOBIES. WE GOT TWO SETS OF NICE BOOBIES. THIS WAS A GOOD JOB, YES
LONG LIVE BOOBIES.
I DO WONDER ABOUT THOSE DELICATE BOOBIES OVER THERE, TOO, BUT I'LL HOLD OFF SO I CAN GET EVEN MORE BOOBIES, YES ?
EVEN SCARY-LOOKING BOUNTY HUNTERS LIKE THESE COME IN ALL KINDS !
BUT THERE WAS ONE *REALLY* HOPELESS ONE ...!
GIRL! WHAT IN BLAZES ...
GLARE
キッ..

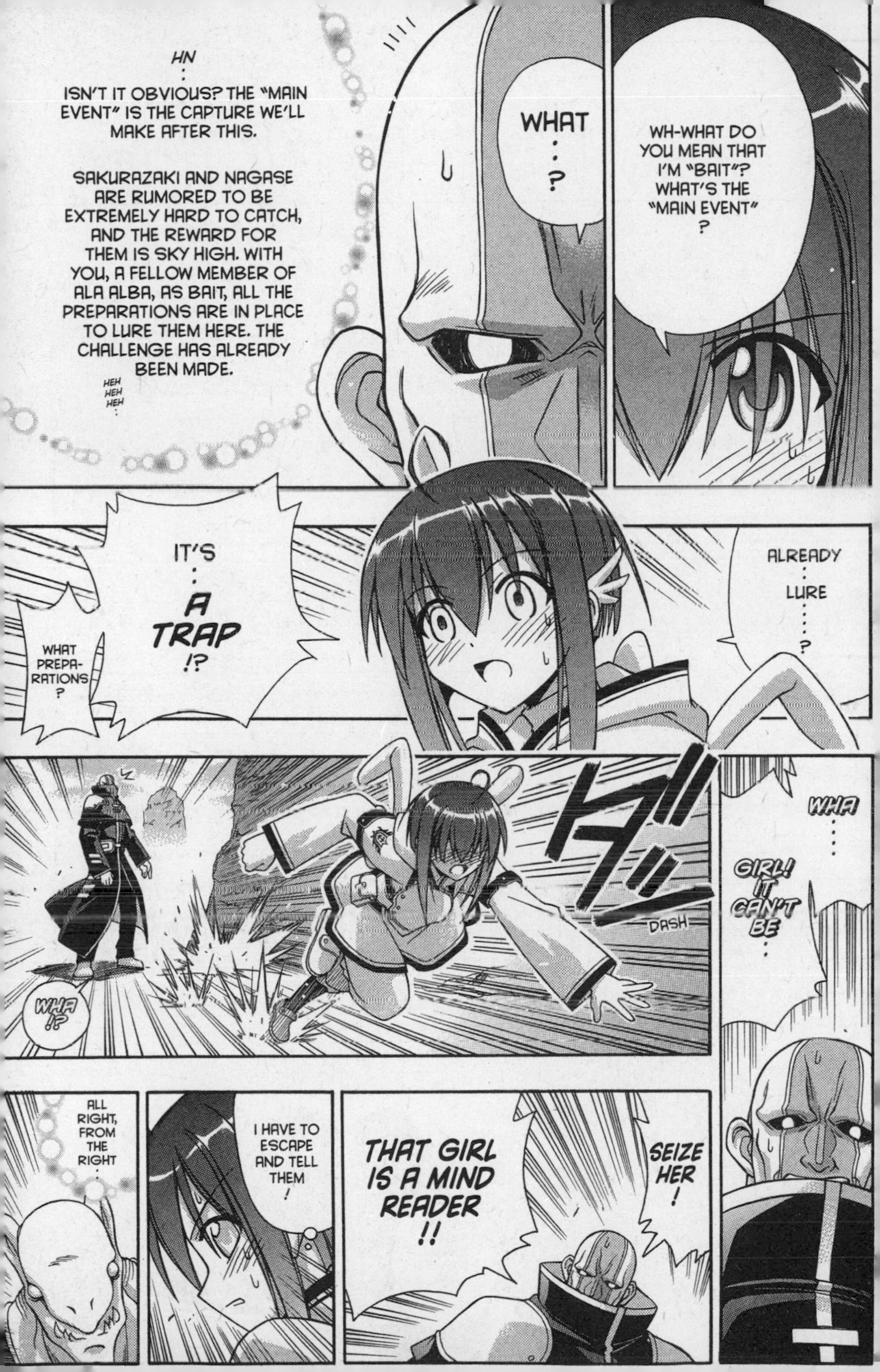
WH-WHAT DO YOU MEAN THAT I'M "BAIT"? WHAT'S THE "MAIN EVENT"?
WHAT...?
HN:
ISN'T IT OBVIOUS? THE "MAIN EVENT" IS THE CAPTURE WE'LL MAKE AFTER THIS.
SAKURAZAKI AND NAGASE ARE RUMORED TO BE EXTREMELY HARD TO CATCH, AND THE REWARD FOR THEM IS SKY HIGH. WITH YOU, A FELLOW MEMBER OF ALA ALBA, AS BAIT, ALL THE PREPARATIONS ARE IN PLACE TO LURE THEM HERE. THE CHALLENGE HAS ALREADY BEEN MADE.
HEH HEH HEH:
ALREADY... LURE......?
IT'S... A TRAP!?
WHAT PREPARATIONS?
WHA...
GIRL! IT CAN'T BE...
DASH
WHA!?
SEIZE HER!
THAT GIRL IS A MIND READER!!
I HAVE TO ESCAPE AND TELL THEM!
ALL RIGHT, FROM THE RIGHT...

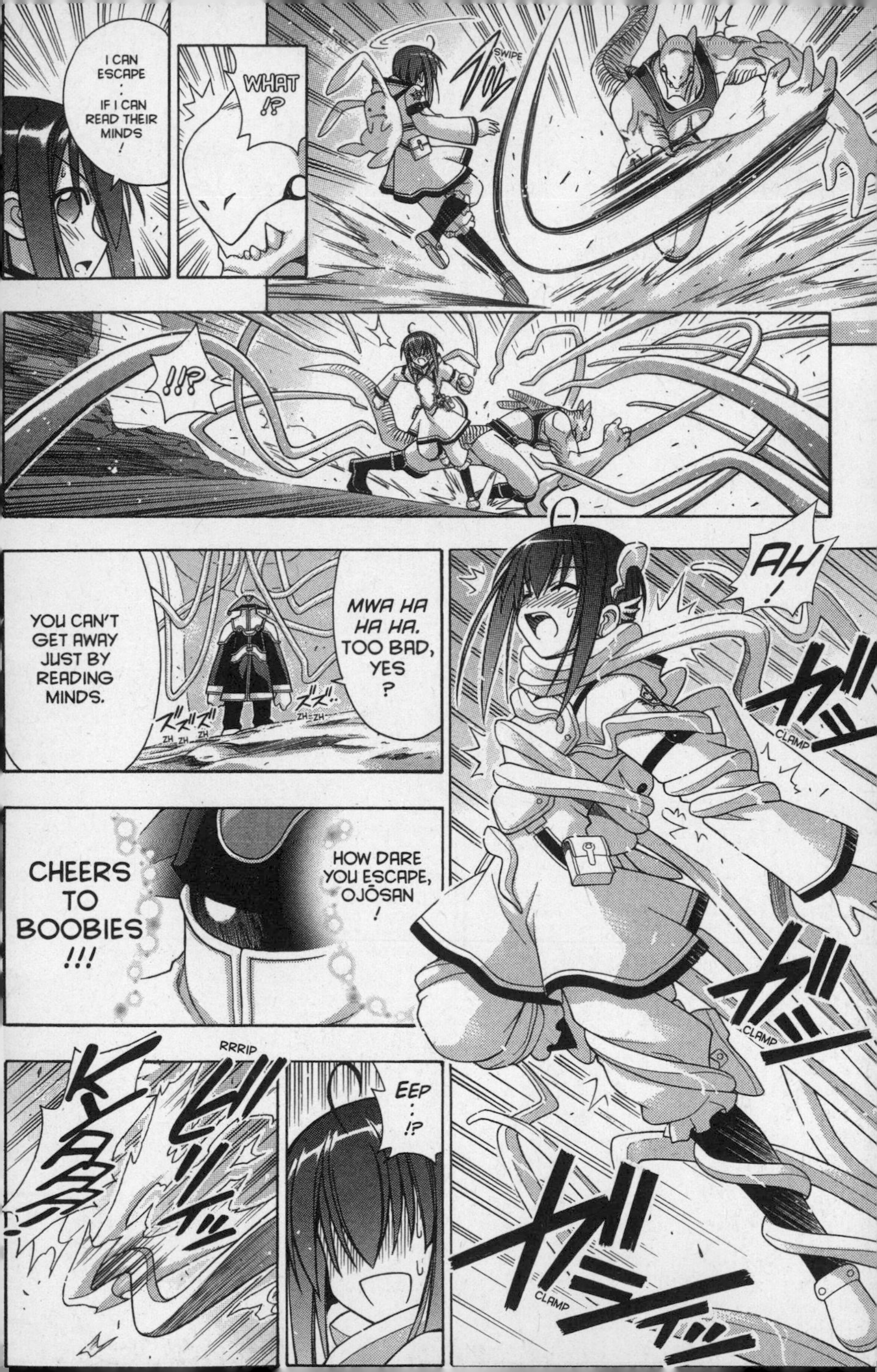
SWIPE
WHAT !?
I CAN ESCAPE ... IF I CAN READ THEIR MINDS !
!!?
AH !
CLAMP
CLAMP
CLAMP
MWA HA HA HA. TOO BAD, YES ?
YOU CAN'T GET AWAY JUST BY READING MINDS.
ZH ZH ZH
ZH ZH
HOW DARE YOU ESCAPE, OJŌSAN !
CHEERS TO BOOBIES !!!
EEP ..!?
RRRIP
KYAAA!

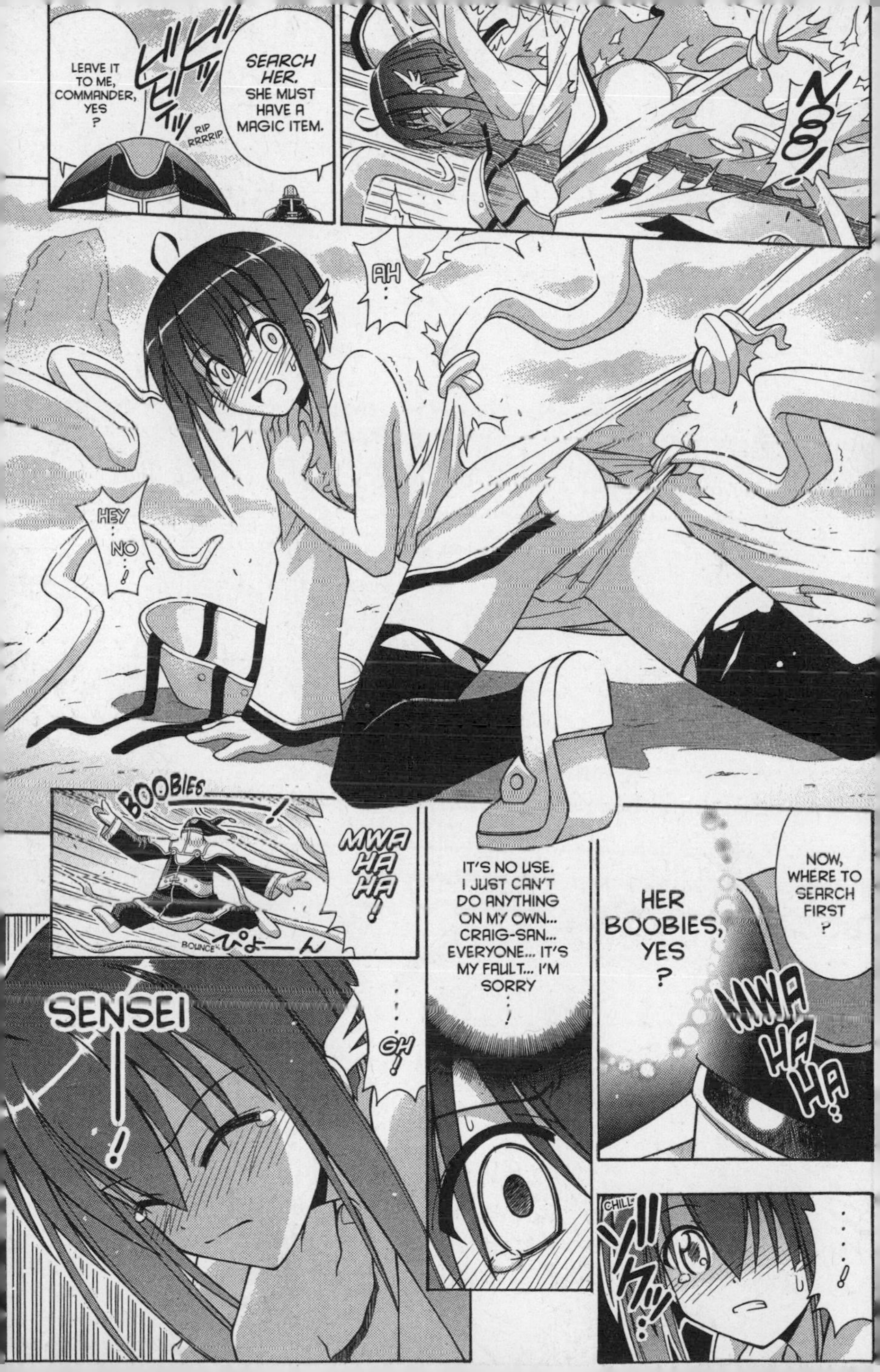
NOOO!
SEARCH HER. SHE MUST HAVE A MAGIC ITEM.
LEAVE IT TO ME, COMMANDER, YES?
RIP RRRRIP
AH...
HEY... NO...!
NOW, WHERE TO SEARCH FIRST?
HER BOOBIES, YES?
MWA HA HA!
CHILL
...!
...GH!
IT'S NO USE. I JUST CAN'T DO ANYTHING ON MY OWN... CRAIG-SAN... EVERYONE... IT'S MY FAULT... I'M SORRY...!
BOOBIES!
MWA HA HA!
BOUNCE ぴよーん
SENSEI!

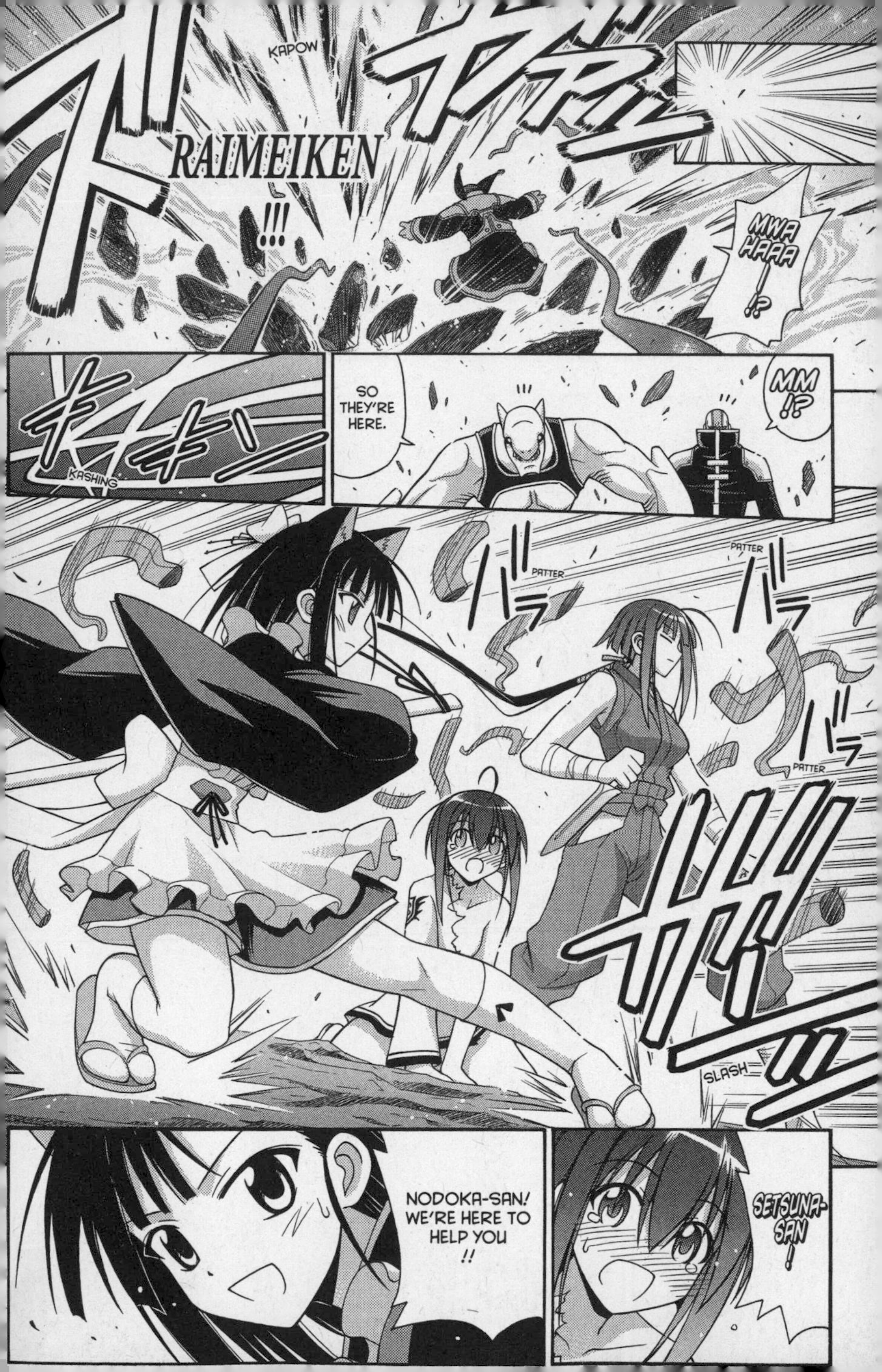
KAPOW
MWA HAAA!!?
RAIMEIKEN
!!!
MM!?
SO THEY'RE HERE.
KASHING
PATTER
PATTER
PATTER
SLASH
SETSUNA-SAN!
NODOKA-SAN! WE'RE HERE TO HELP YOU!!

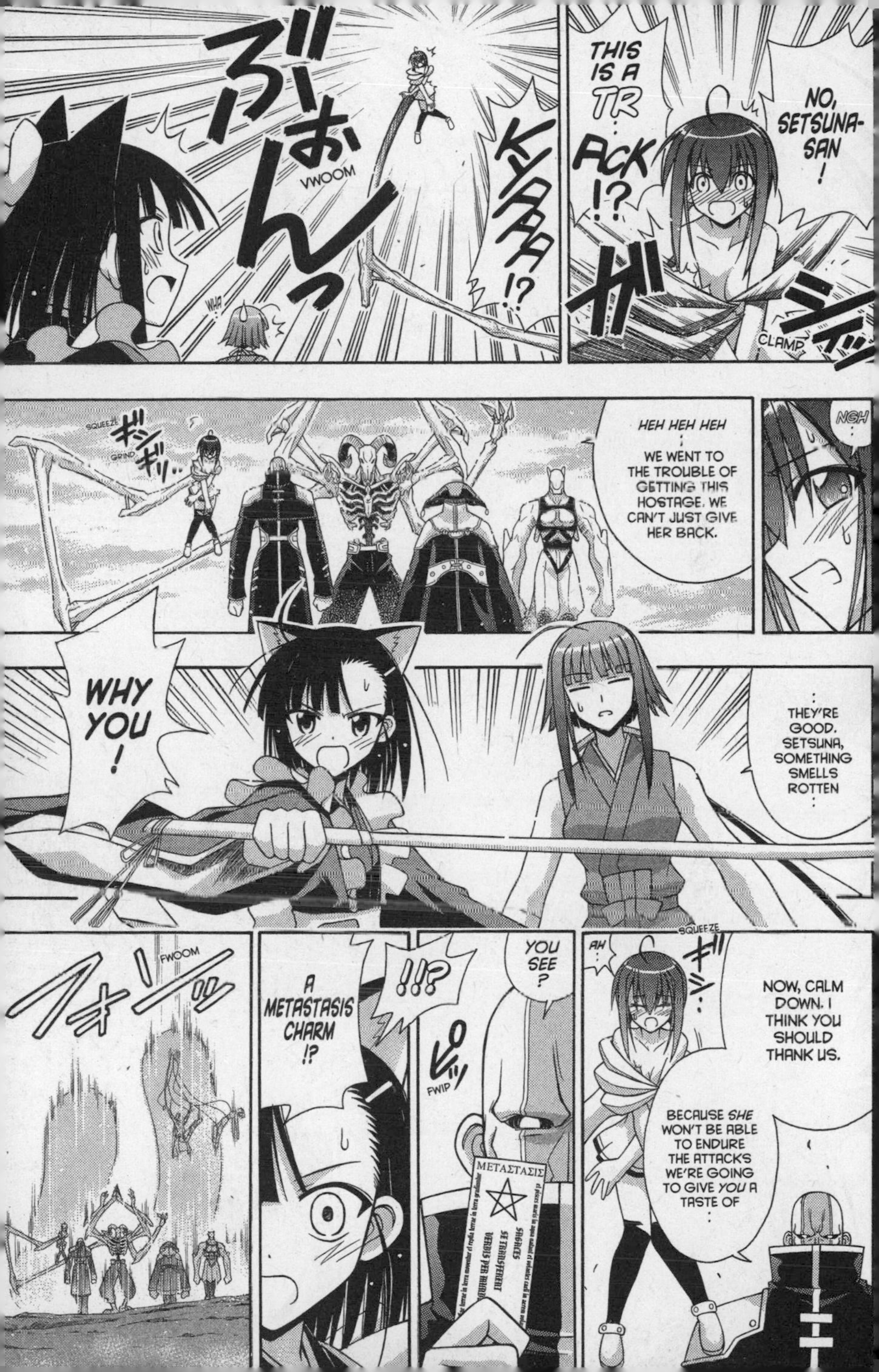
NO, SETSUNA-SAN!
THIS IS A TR... ACK!?
CLAMP
KYAAA!?
VWOOM
WHA
NGH...
HEH HEH HEH... WE WENT TO THE TROUBLE OF GETTING THIS HOSTAGE. WE CAN'T JUST GIVE HER BACK.
SQUEEZE
GRIND
...THEY'RE GOOD. SETSUNA, SOMETHING SMELLS ROTTEN...
WHY YOU!
SQUEEZE
AH...
NOW, CALM DOWN. I THINK YOU SHOULD THANK US.
BECAUSE SHE WON'T BE ABLE TO ENDURE THE ATTACKS WE'RE GOING TO GIVE YOU A TASTE OF...
YOU SEE?
FWIP
ΜΕΤΑΣΤΑΣΙΣ
!!?
A METASTASIS CHARM!?
FWOOM

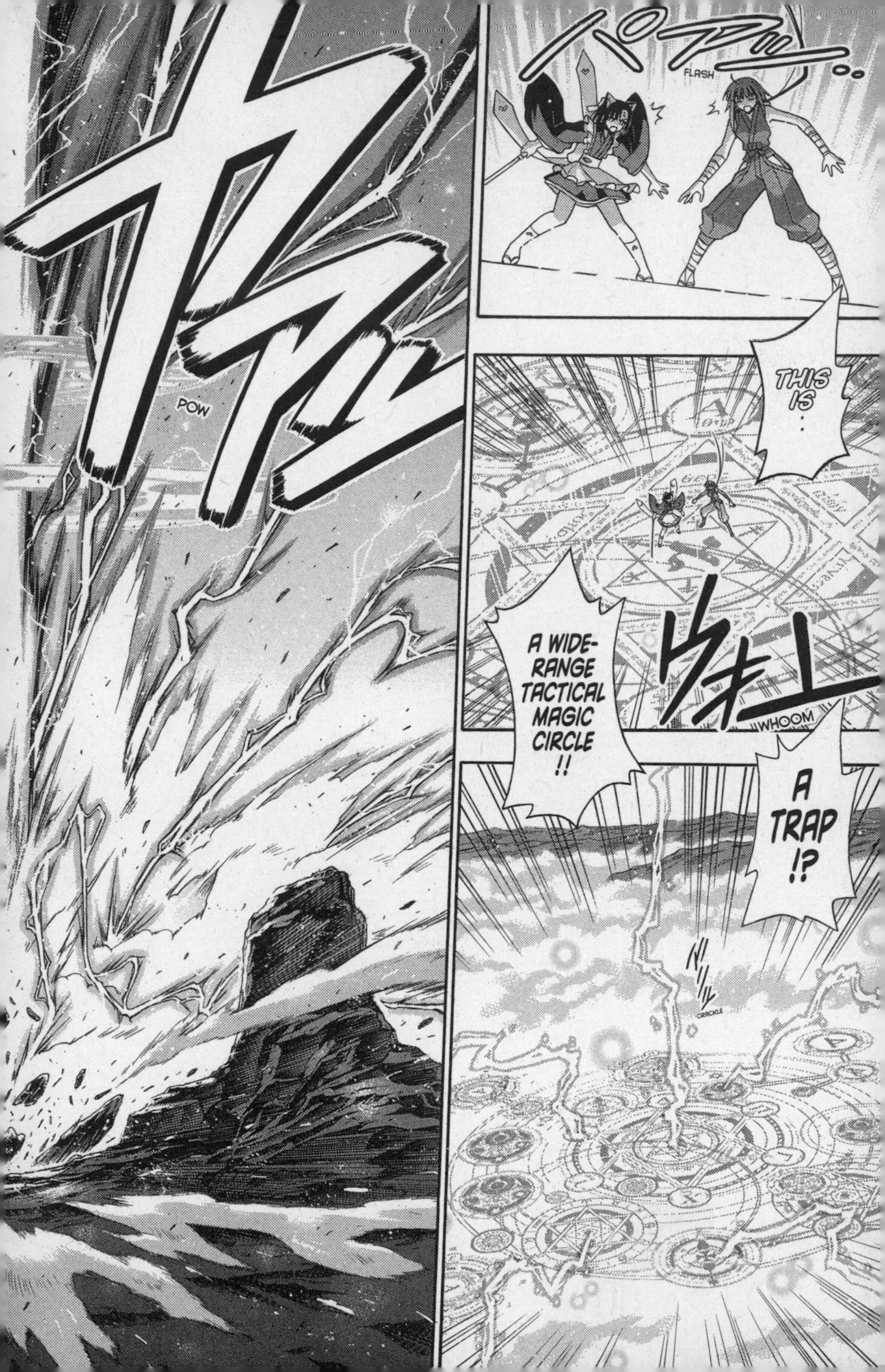
FLASH
THIS IS . .
A WIDE-RANGE TACTICAL MAGIC CIRCLE !!
WHOOM
A TRAP !?
CRACKLE
POW

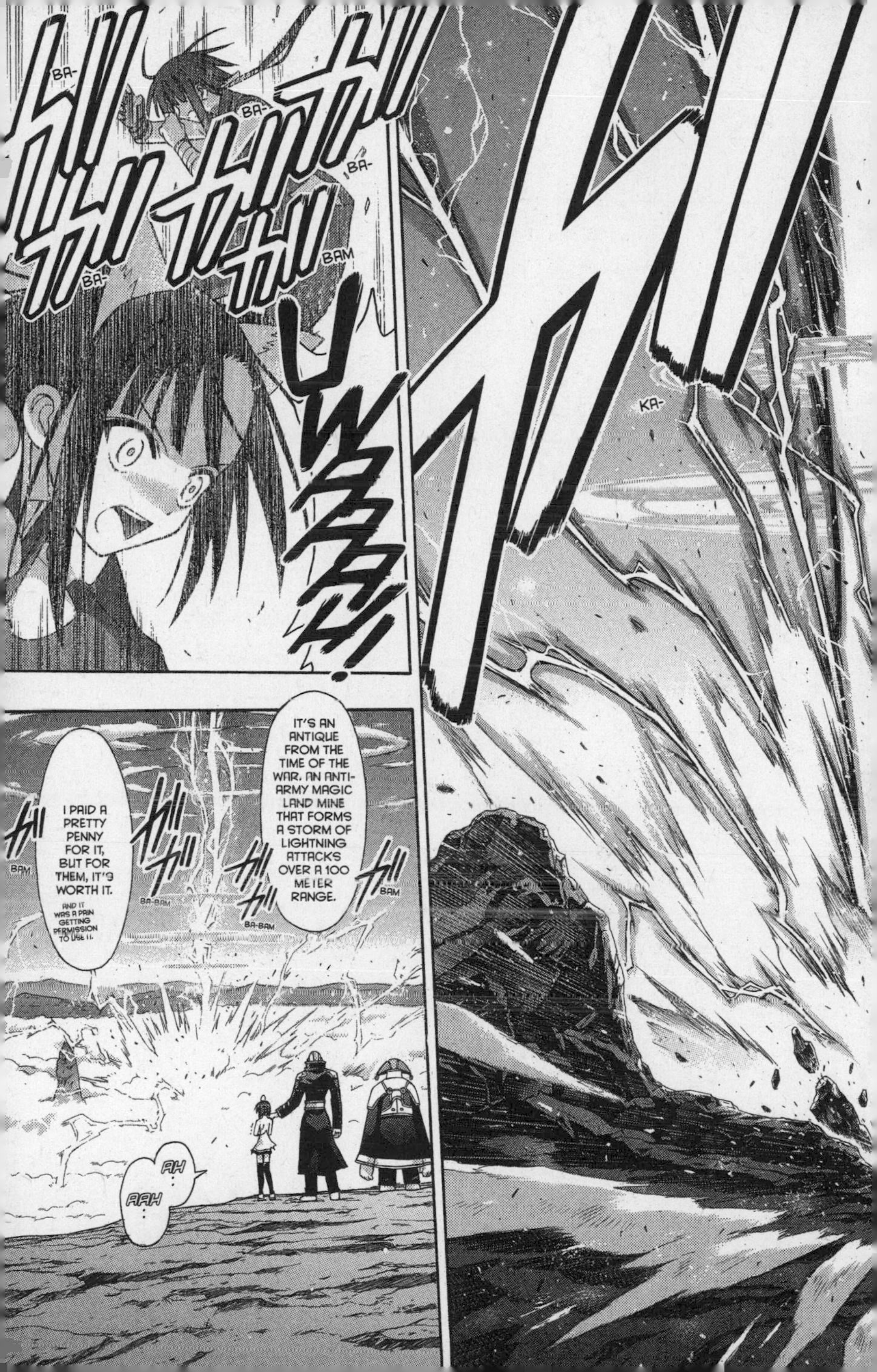
KA-
BA-
BA-
BA-
BAM
BA-
IT'S AN ANTIQUE FROM THE TIME OF THE WAR. AN ANTI-ARMY MAGIC LAND MINE THAT FORMS A STORM OF LIGHTNING ATTACKS OVER A 100 METER RANGE.
BAM
BA-BAM
I PAID A PRETTY PENNY FOR IT, BUT FOR THEM, IT'S WORTH IT.
AND IT WAS A PAIN GETTING PERMISSION TO USE IT.
BA-BAM
BAM
AH...
AAH...

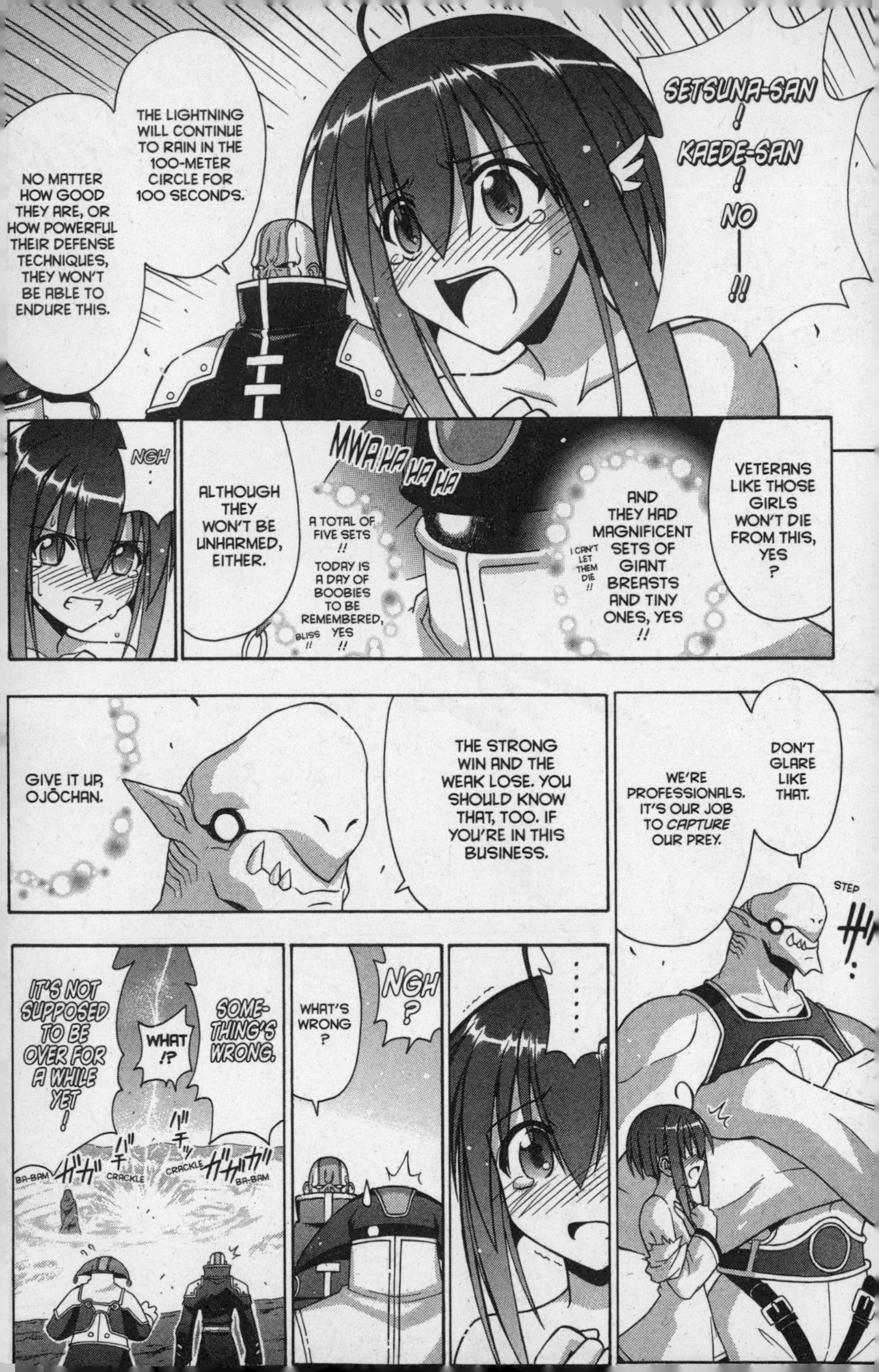
SETSUNA-SAN! KAEDE-SAN! NO—!!
THE LIGHTNING WILL CONTINUE TO RAIN IN THE 100-METER CIRCLE FOR 100 SECONDS.
NO MATTER HOW GOOD THEY ARE, OR HOW POWERFUL THEIR DEFENSE TECHNIQUES, THEY WON'T BE ABLE TO ENDURE THIS.
VETERANS LIKE THOSE GIRLS WON'T DIE FROM THIS, YES?
AND THEY HAD MAGNIFICENT SETS OF GIANT BREASTS AND TINY ONES, YES!!
I CAN'T LET THEM DIE!!
MWAHAHAHA
A TOTAL OF FIVE SETS!!
TODAY IS A DAY OF BOOBIES TO BE REMEMBERED, YES!!
BLISS!!
ALTHOUGH THEY WON'T BE UNHARMED, EITHER.
NGH...
DON'T GLARE LIKE THAT.
WE'RE PROFESSIONALS. IT'S OUR JOB TO *CAPTURE* OUR PREY.
STEP
THE STRONG WIN AND THE WEAK LOSE. YOU SHOULD KNOW THAT, TOO. IF YOU'RE IN THIS BUSINESS.
GIVE IT UP, OJŌCHAN.
......
NGH?
WHAT'S WRONG?
SOME-THING'S WRONG.
WHAT!?
IT'S NOT SUPPOSED TO BE OVER FOR A WHILE YET!
CRACKLE
CRACKLE
BA-BAM
BA-BAM

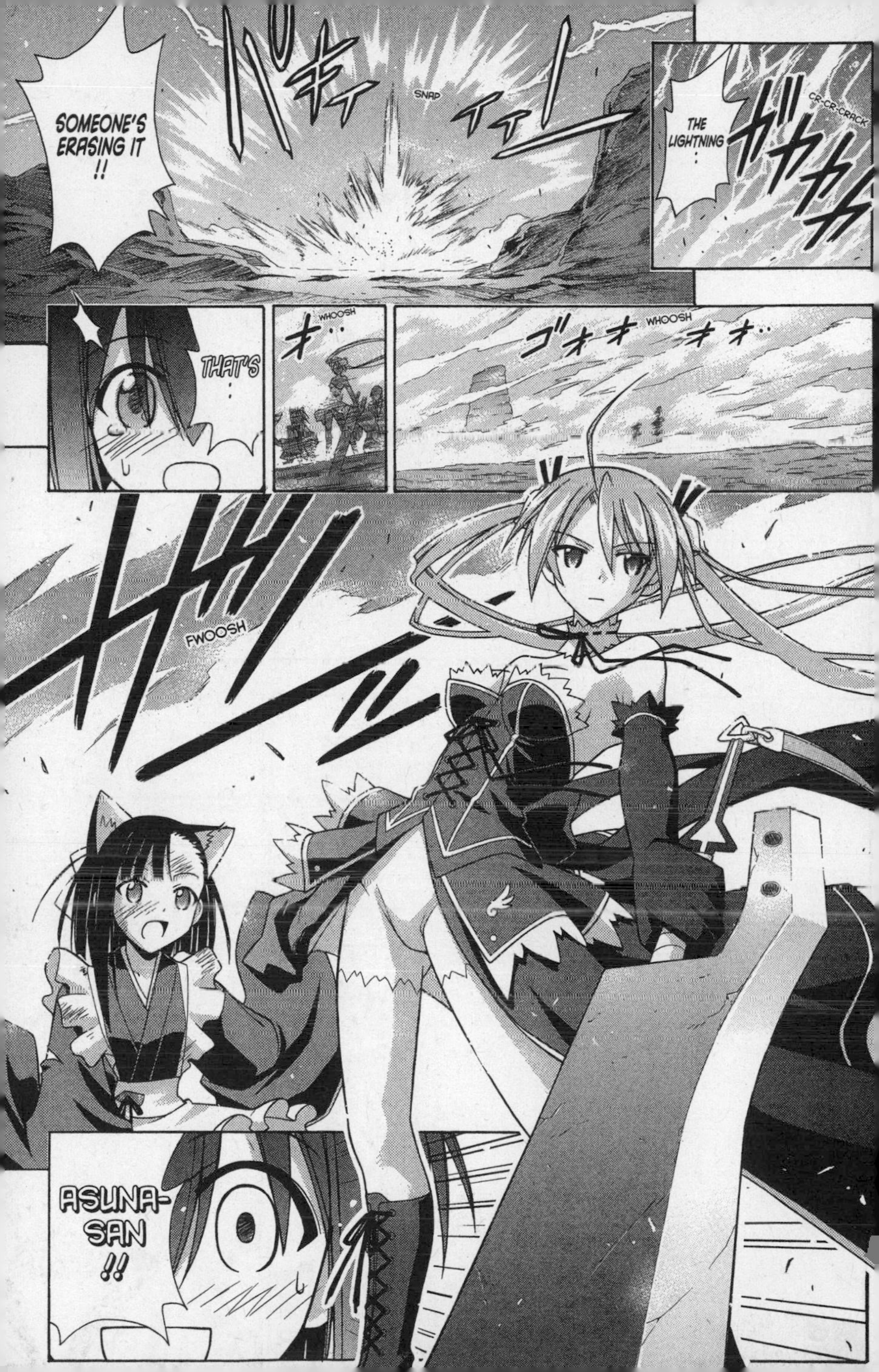
CR-CR-CRACK
THE LIGHTNING :
SNAP
SOMEONE'S ERASING IT !!
WHOOSH
WHOOSH
THAT'S :
FWOOSH
ASUNA-SAN !!

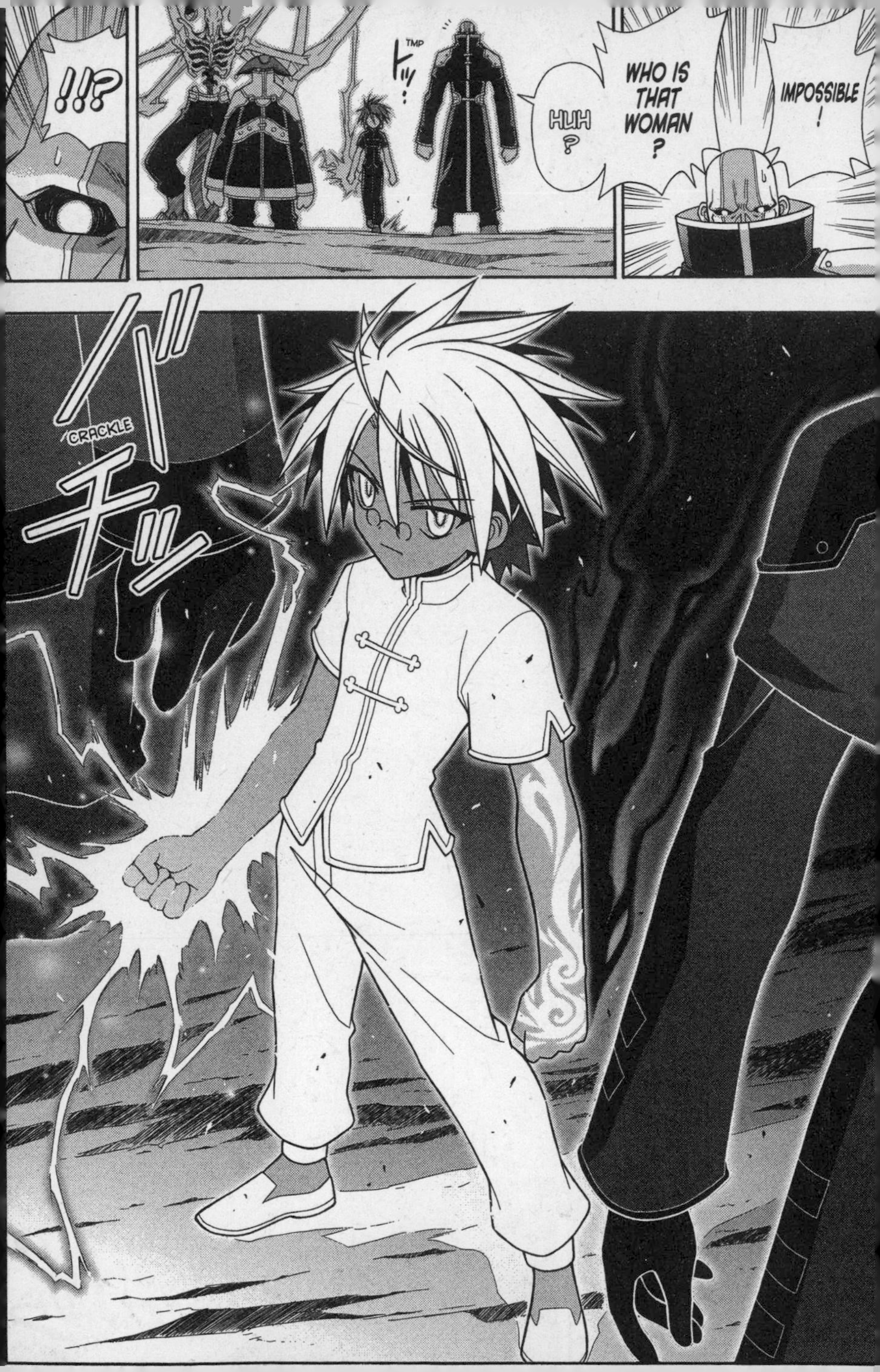

IMPOSSIBLE!
WHO IS THAT WOMAN?
HUH?
TMP
!!?
CRACKLE

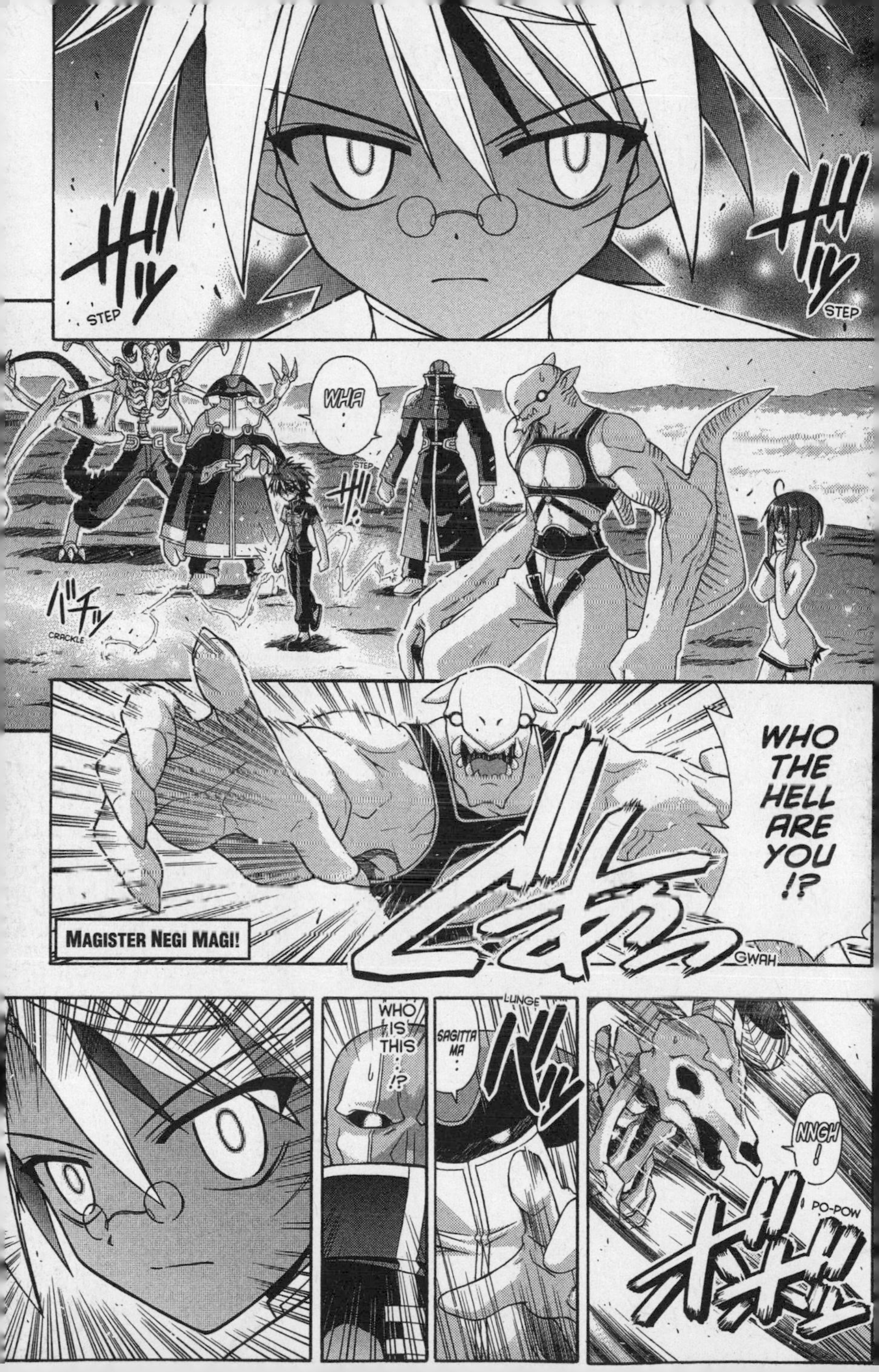
STEP
STEP
WHA...
STEP
バチッ
CRACKLE
WHO THE HELL ARE YOU!?
GWAH
MAGISTER NEGI MAGI!
NNGH!
PO-POW
LUNGE
SAGITTA MA...
WHO IS THIS...!?

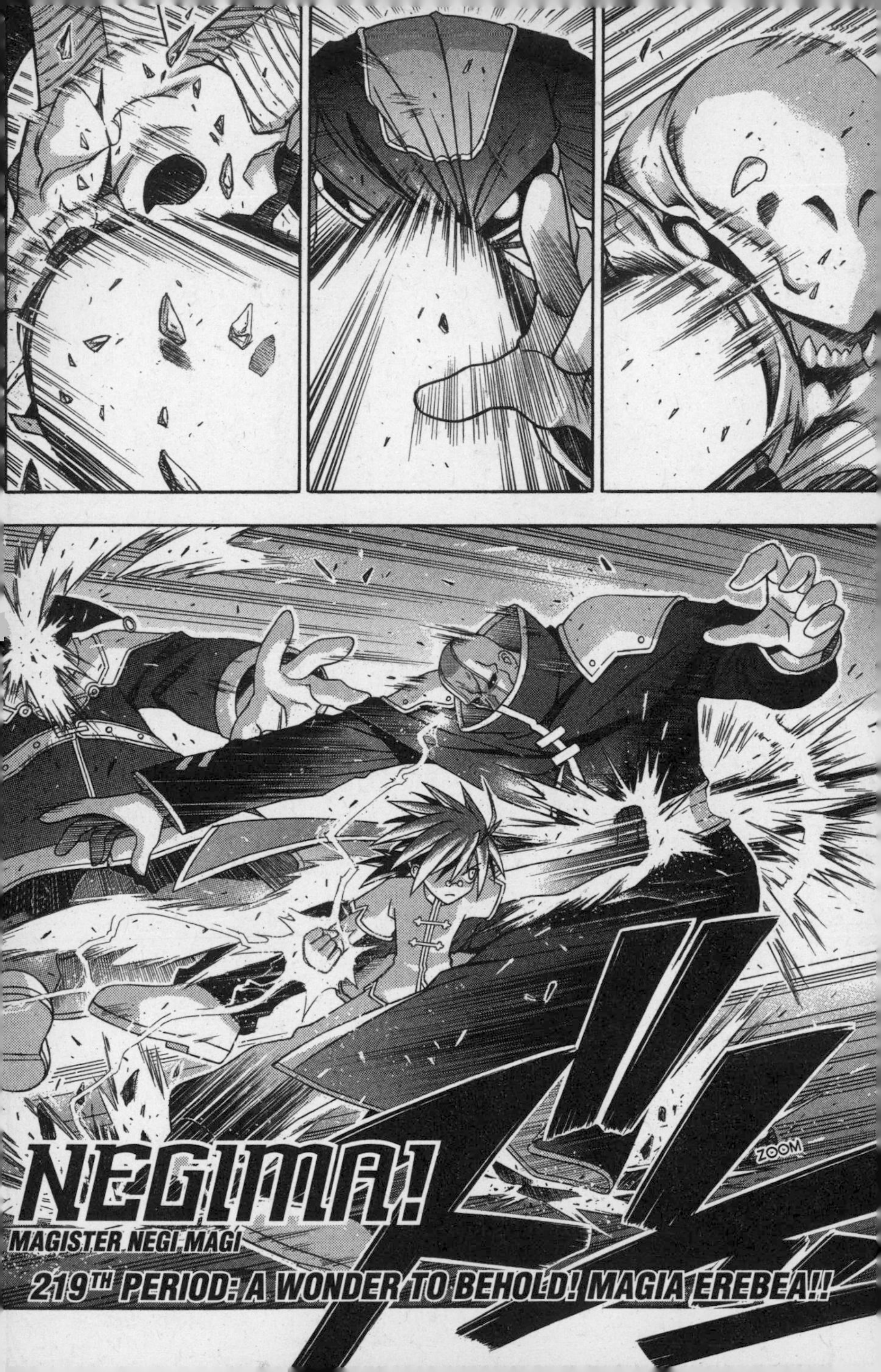
ZOOM
NEGIMA!
MAGISTER NEGI MAGI
219TH PERIOD: A WONDER TO BEHOLD! MAGIA EREBEA!!

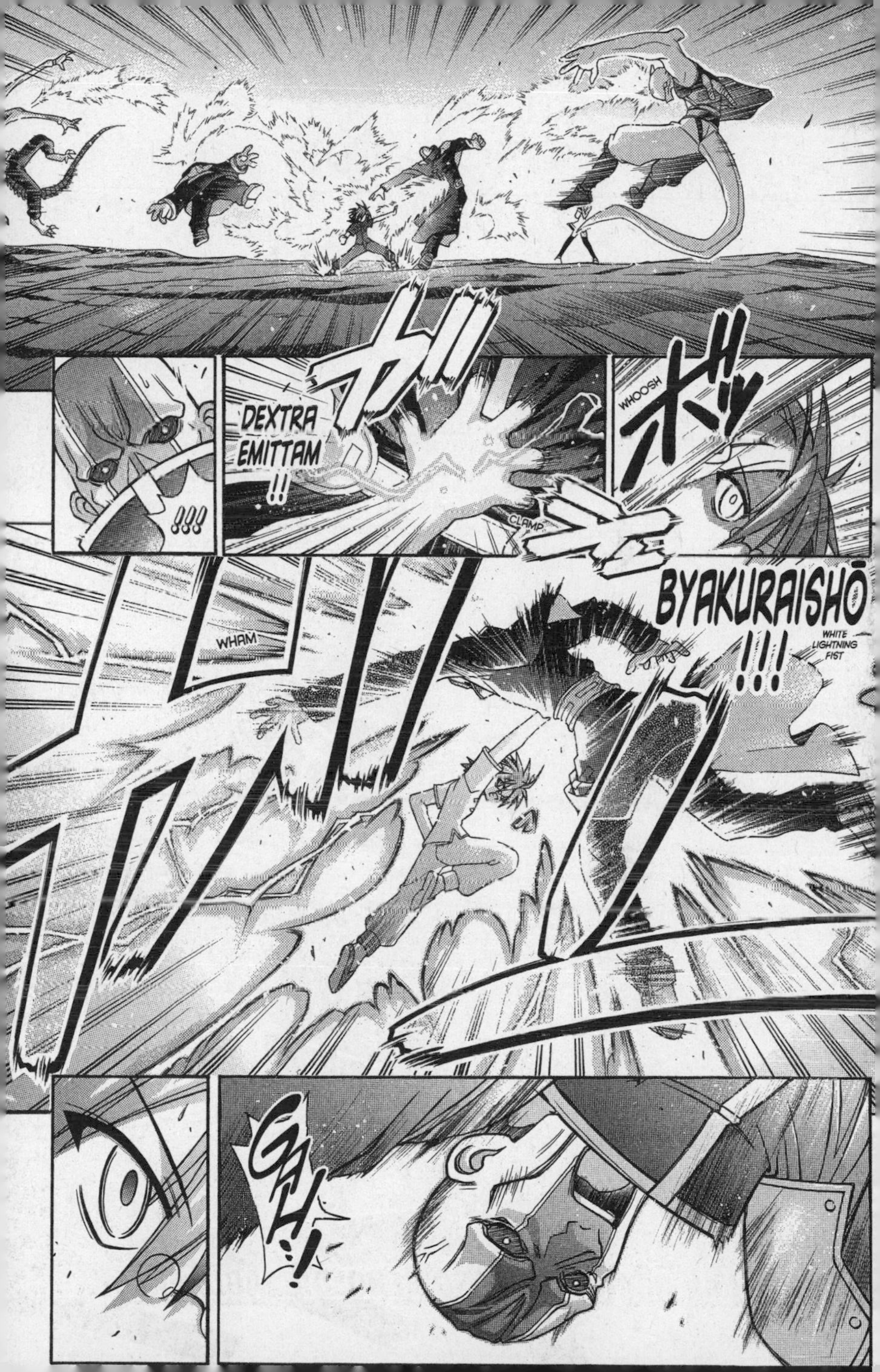

WHOOSH
DEXTRA EMITTAM !!
CLAMP
!!!
BYAKURAISHŌ !!!
WHITE LIGHTNING FIST
WHAM
GAH..!

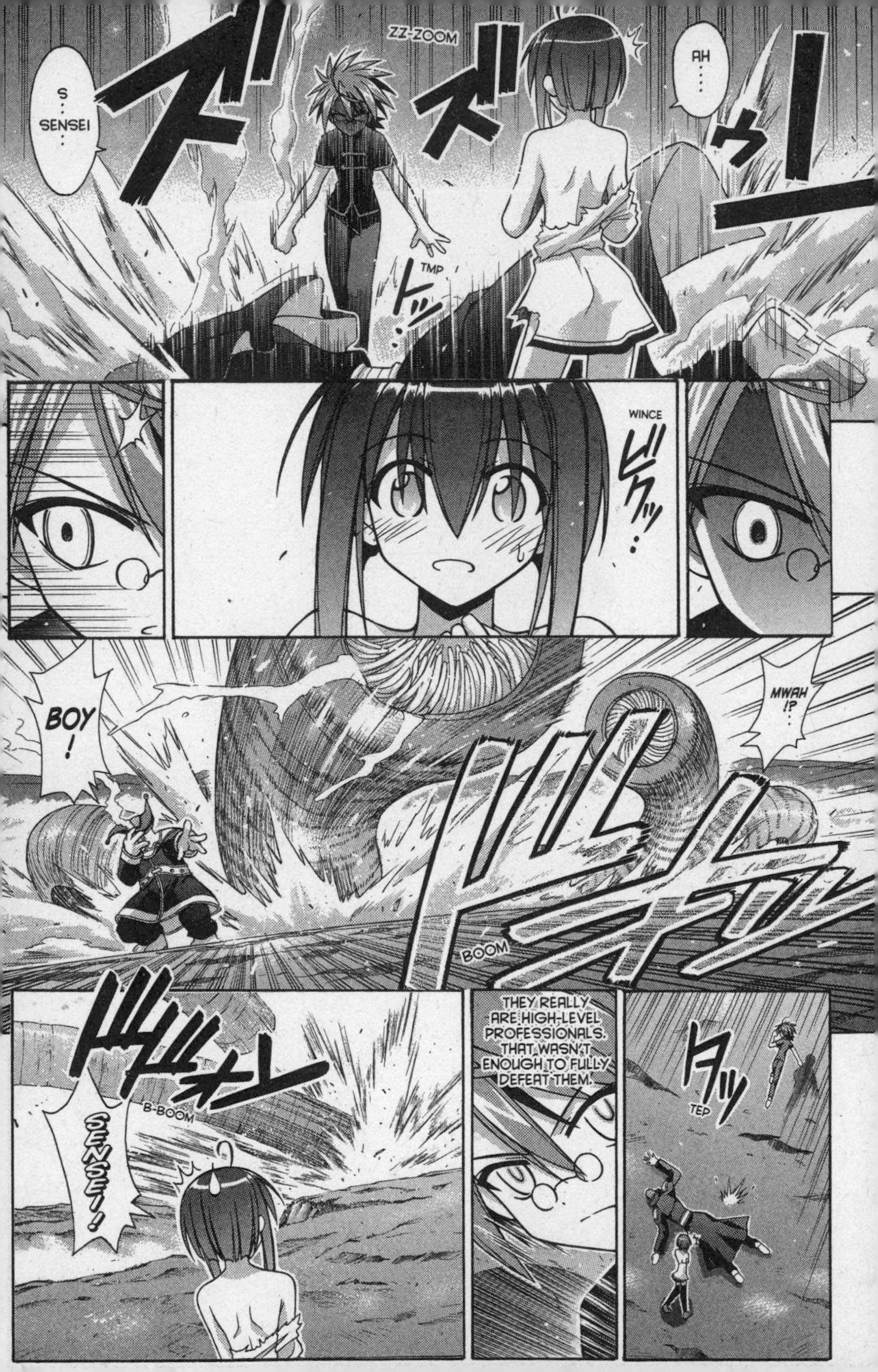
AH ......
ZZ-ZOOM
S... SENSEI...
TMP
WINCE
MWAH !?
BOY !
BOOM
TEP
THEY REALLY ARE HIGH-LEVEL PROFESSIONALS. THAT WASN'T ENOUGH TO FULLY DEFEAT THEM.
B-BOOM
SENSEI!!

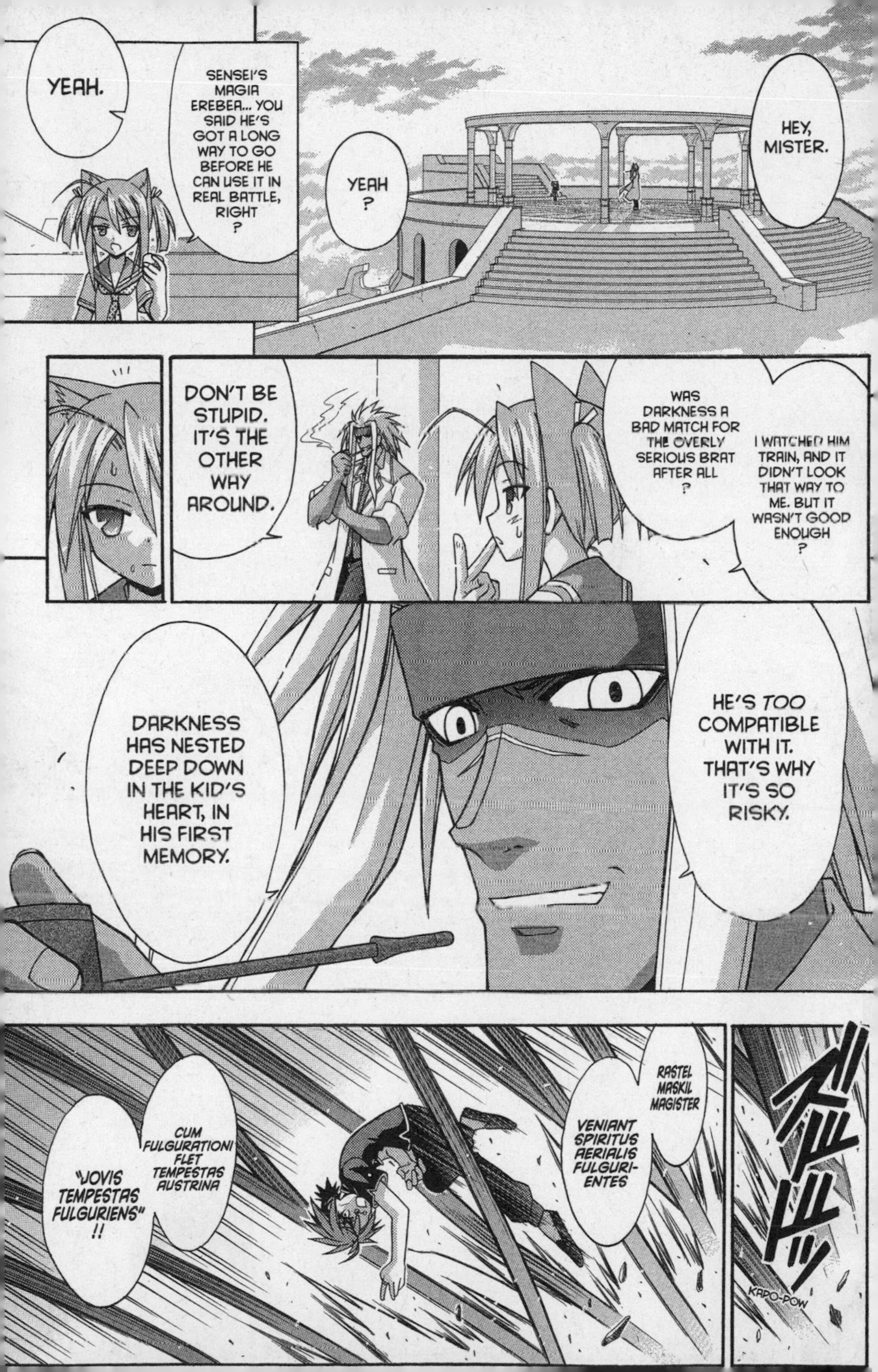
HEY, MISTER.
YEAH ?
SENSEI'S MAGIA EREBEA... YOU SAID HE'S GOT A LONG WAY TO GO BEFORE HE CAN USE IT IN REAL BATTLE, RIGHT ?
YEAH.
I WATCHED HIM TRAIN, AND IT DIDN'T LOOK THAT WAY TO ME. BUT IT WASN'T GOOD ENOUGH ?
WAS DARKNESS A BAD MATCH FOR THE OVERLY SERIOUS BRAT AFTER ALL ?
DON'T BE STUPID. IT'S THE OTHER WAY AROUND.
HE'S *TOO* COMPATIBLE WITH IT. THAT'S WHY IT'S SO RISKY.
DARKNESS HAS NESTED DEEP DOWN IN THE KID'S HEART, IN HIS FIRST MEMORY.
KADO-POW
RASTEL MASKIL MAGISTER
VENIANT SPIRITUS AERIALIS FULGURIENTES
CUM FULGURATIONI FLET TEMPESTAS AUSTRINA
"JOVIS TEMPESTAS FULGURIENS" !!

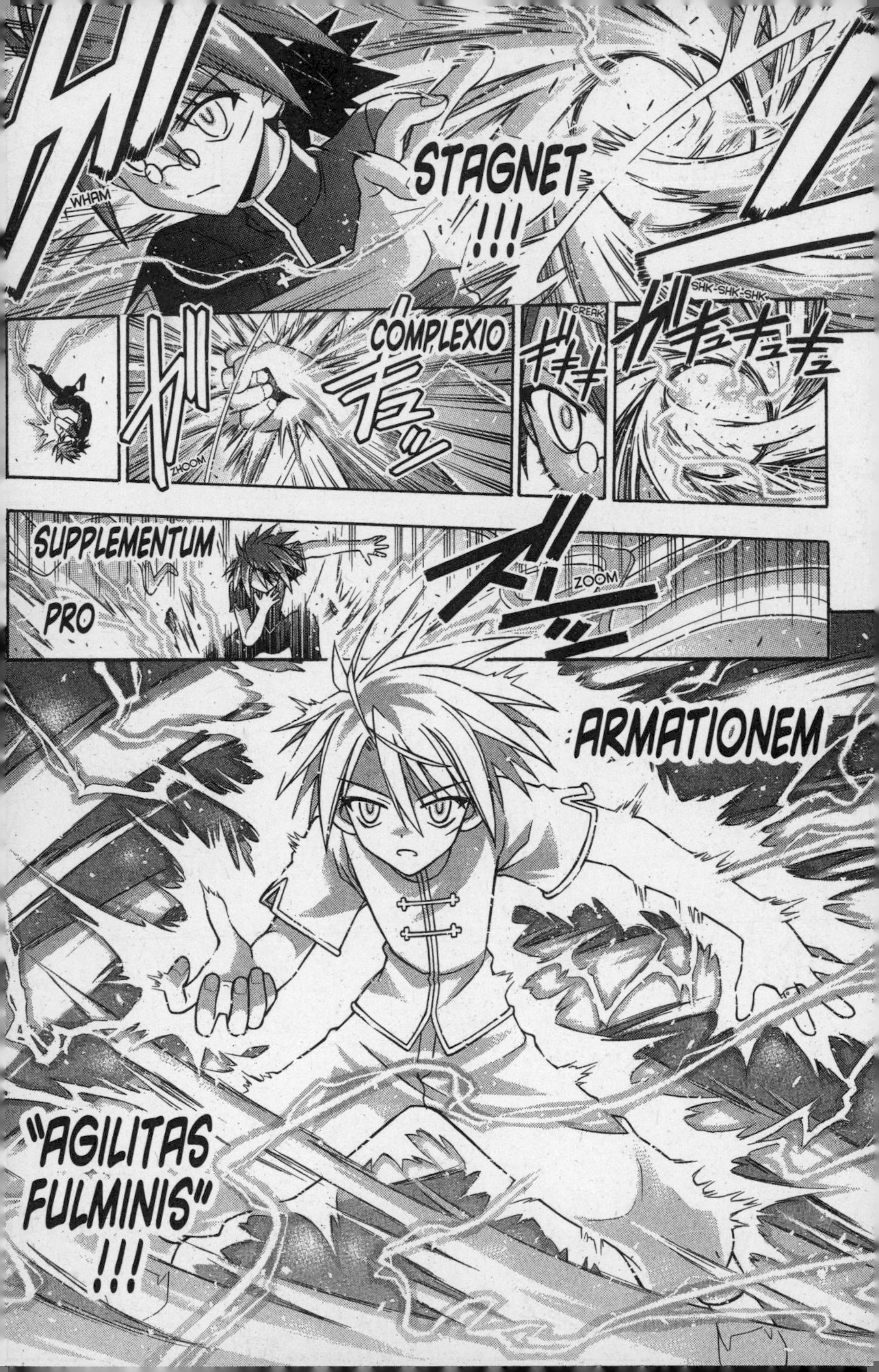
WHAM
STAGNET !!!
SHK-SHK-SHK
CREAK
COMPLEXIO
ZHOOM
ZOOM
SUPPLEMENTUM
PRO
ARMATIONEM
"AGILITAS FULMINIS" !!!

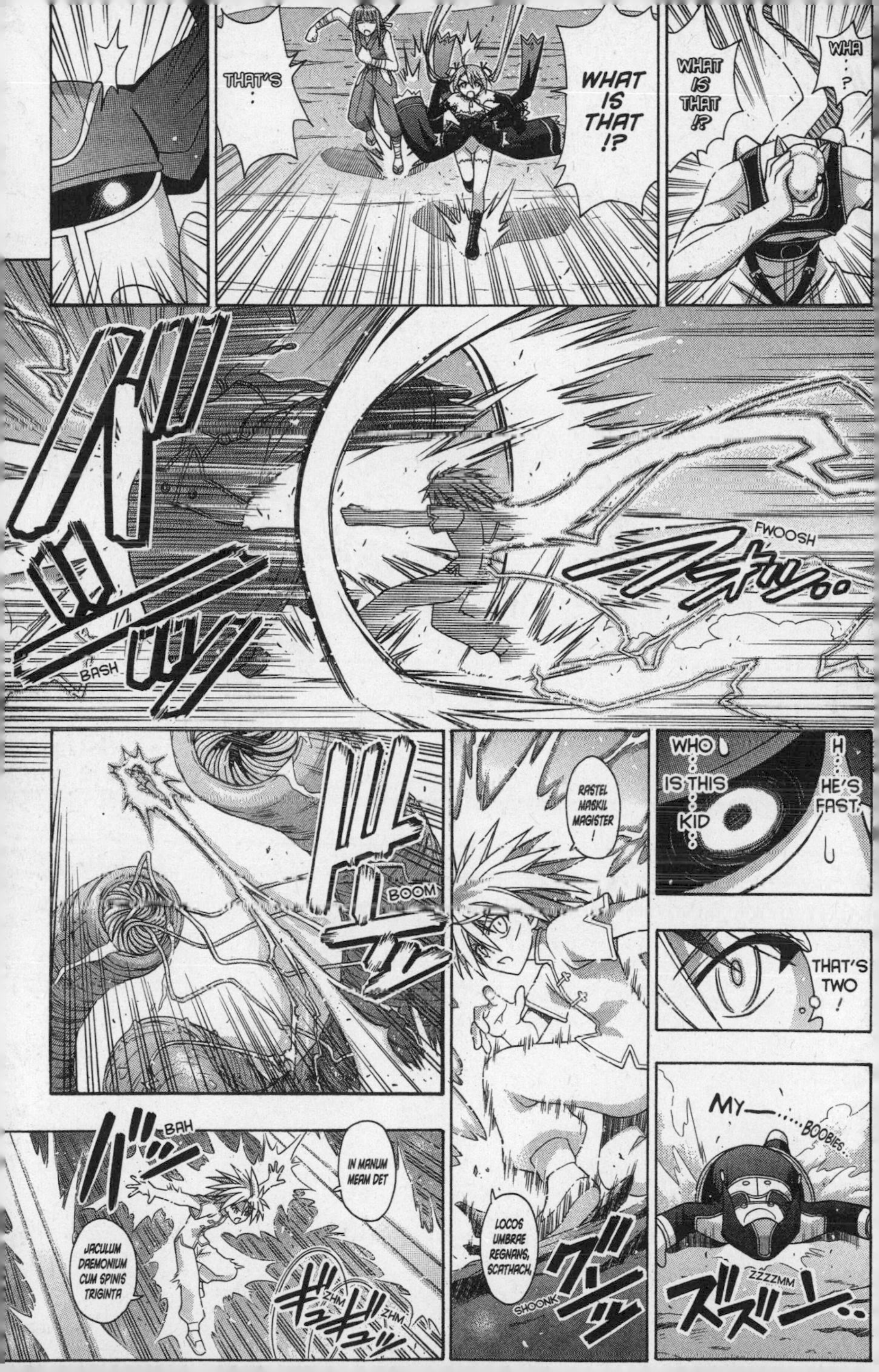
WHA...?
WHAT IS THAT!?
WHAT IS THAT!?
THAT'S...
FWOOSH
BASH
H... HE'S FAST.
WHO... IS THIS... KID...
THAT'S TWO!
MY—......BOOBIES...
ZZZZMM
RASTEL MASKIL MAGISTER!
LOCOS UMBRAE REGNANS, SCATHACH,
SHOONK
BOOM
IN MANUM MEAM DET
JACULUM DAEMONIUM CUM SPINIS TRIGINTA
BAH
ZHM
ZHM

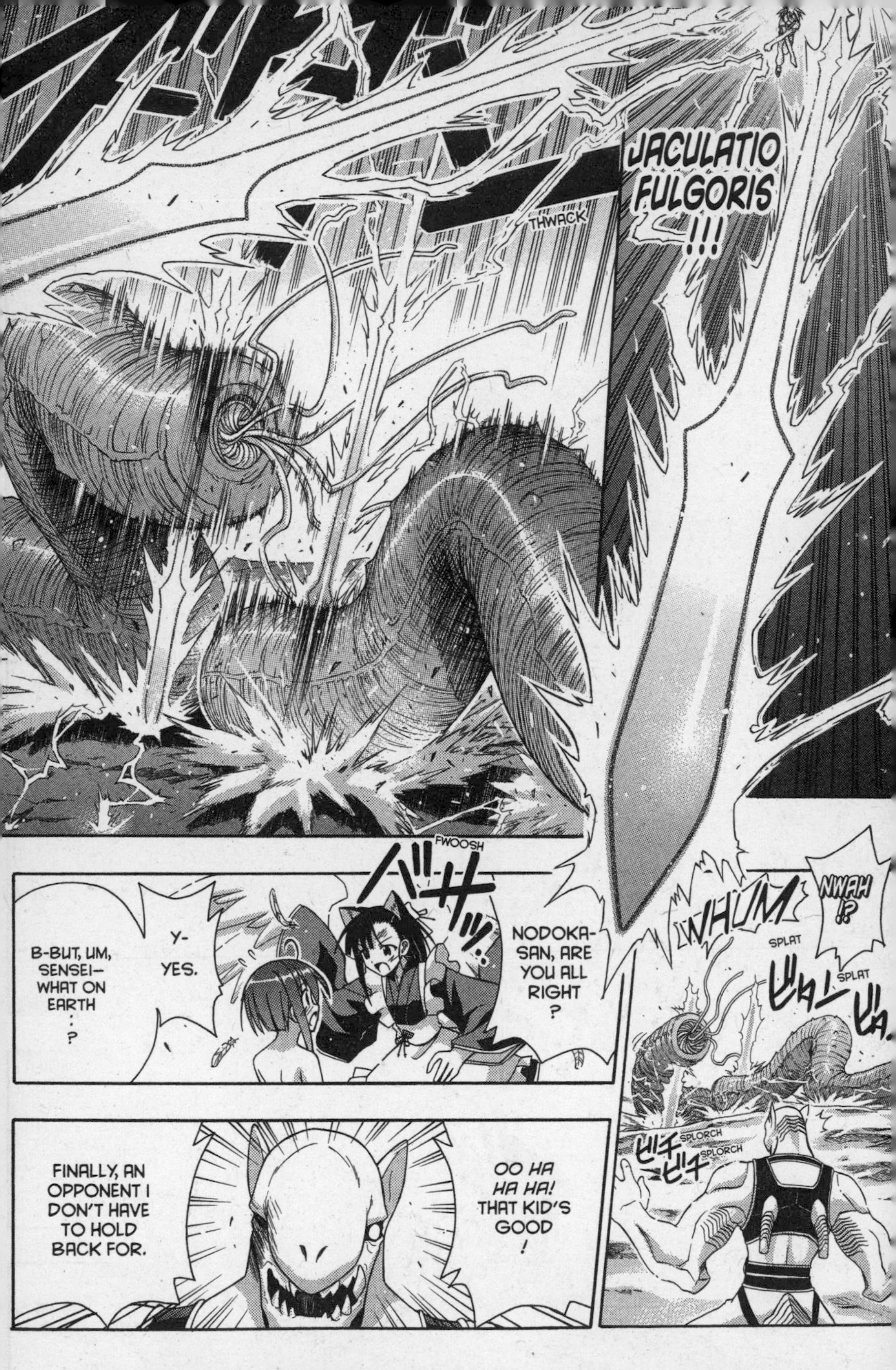
JACULATIO FULGORIS !!!
THWACK
NWAH !?
WHUM
SPLAT
SPLAT
SPLORCH
SPLORCH
FWOOSH
NODOKA-SAN, ARE YOU ALL RIGHT ?
Y-YES.
B-BUT, UM, SENSEI—WHAT ON EARTH . . ?
OO HA HA HA! THAT KID'S GOOD !
FINALLY, AN OPPONENT I DON'T HAVE TO HOLD BACK FOR.

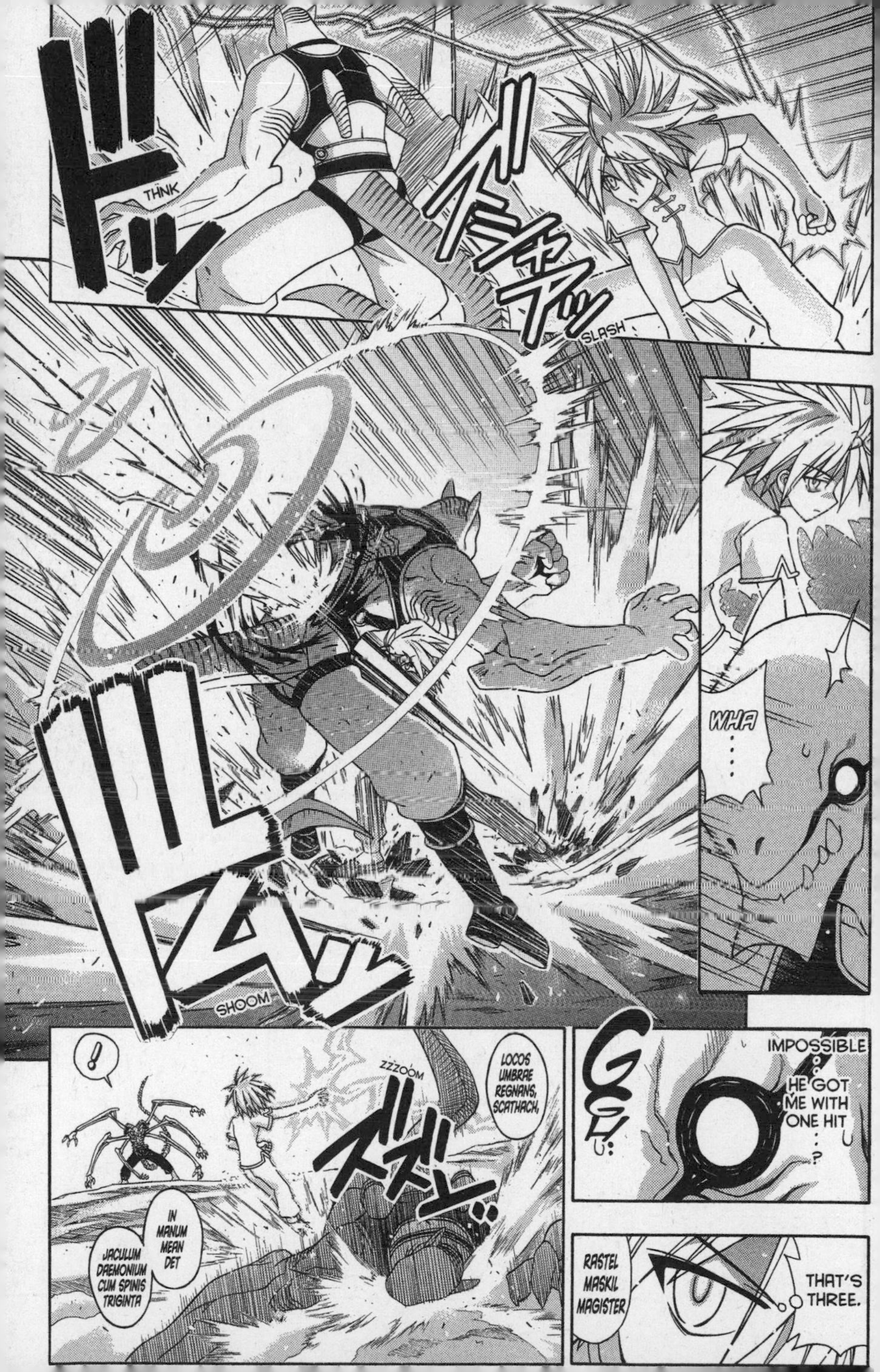
SLASH
THINK
WHA...
SHOOM
IMPOSSIBLE...
HE GOT ME WITH ONE HIT...?
THAT'S THREE.
RASTEL MASKIL MAGISTER
LOCOS UMBRAE REGNANS, SCATHACH,
ZZZOOM
!
IN MANUM MEAN DET
JACULUM DAEMONIUM CUM SPINIS TRIGINTA

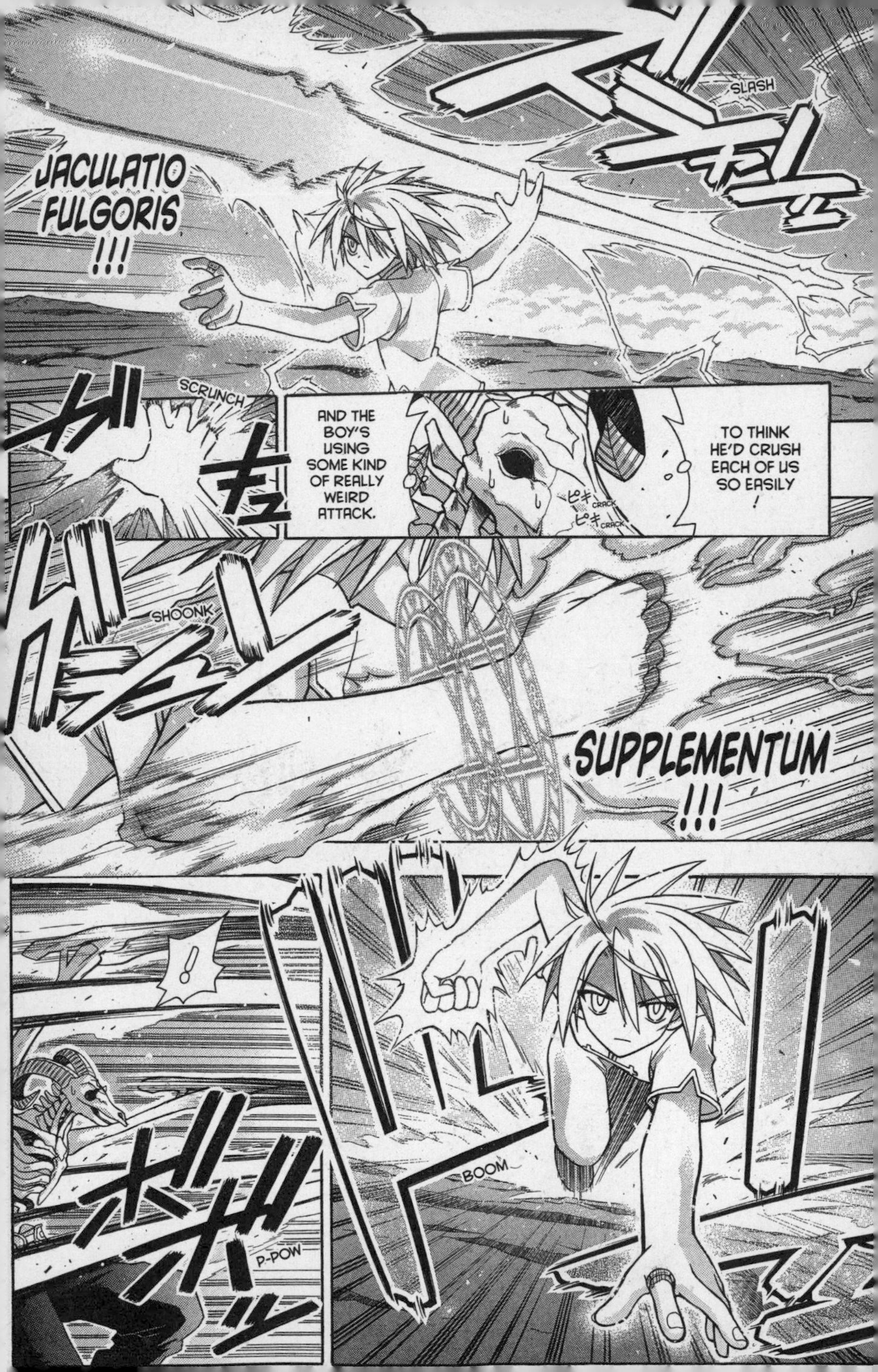
SLASH
JACULATIO FULGORIS !!!
TO THINK HE'D CRUSH EACH OF US SO EASILY!
ピキ CRACK
ピキ CRACK
AND THE BOY'S USING SOME KIND OF REALLY WEIRD ATTACK.
SCRUNCH
SUPPLEMENTUM !!!
SHOONK
BOOM
!
P-POW

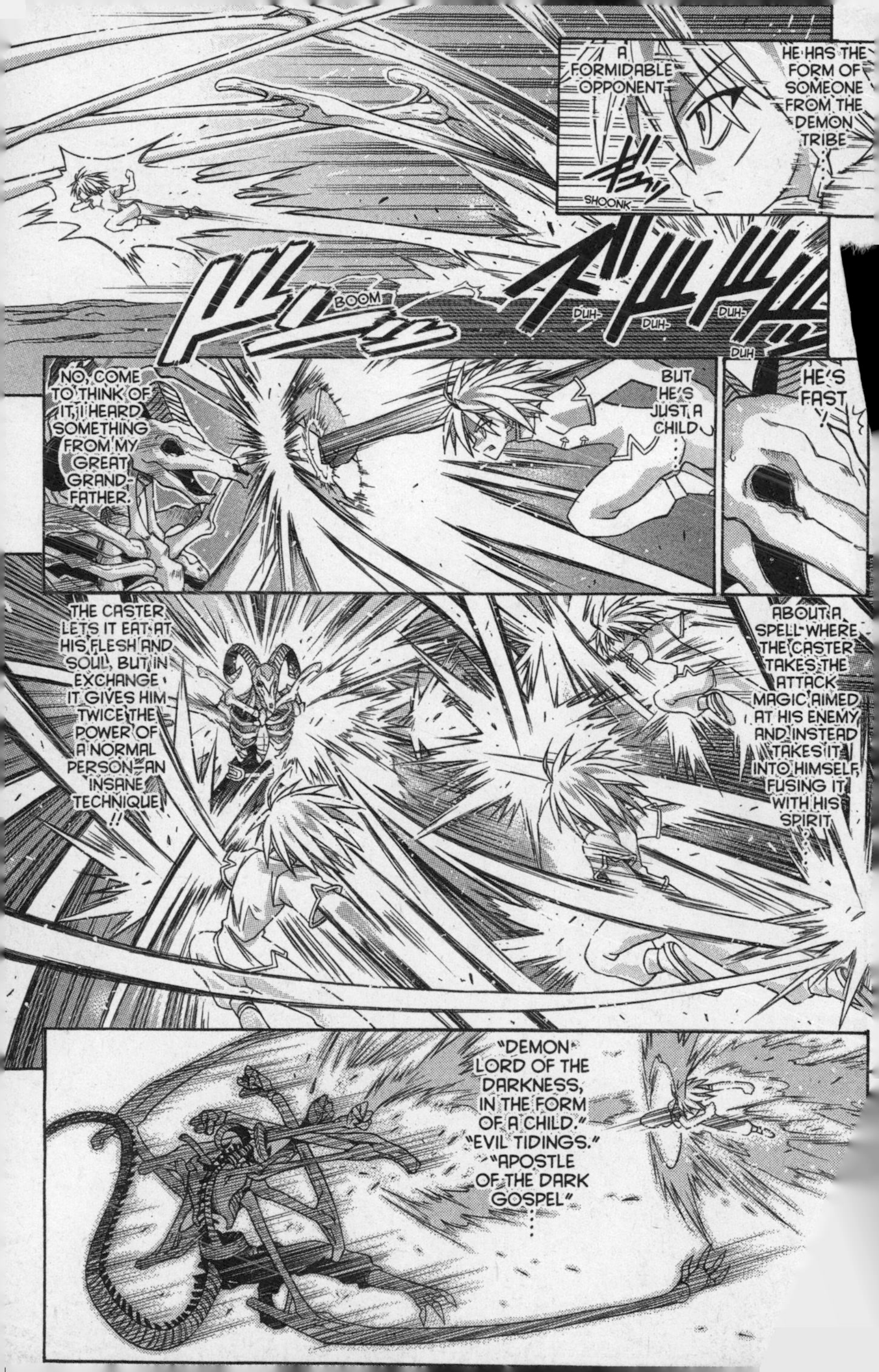
HE HAS THE FORM OF SOMEONE FROM THE DEMON TRIBE
A FORMIDABLE OPPONENT
SHOONK
DUH-DUH-DUH-DUH
BOOM
HE'S FAST!
BUT HE'S JUST A CHILD
NO, COME TO THINK OF IT, I HEARD SOMETHING FROM MY GREAT GRAND-FATHER.
ABOUT A SPELL WHERE THE CASTER TAKES THE ATTACK MAGIC AIMED AT HIS ENEMY AND INSTEAD TAKES IT INTO HIMSELF, FUSING IT WITH HIS SPIRIT...
THE CASTER LETS IT EAT AT HIS FLESH AND SOUL, BUT IN EXCHANGE IT GIVES HIM TWICE THE POWER OF A NORMAL PERSON--AN INSANE TECHNIQUE!!
"DEMON LORD OF THE DARKNESS, IN THE FORM OF A CHILD." "EVIL TIDINGS." "APOSTLE OF THE DARK GOSPEL"...

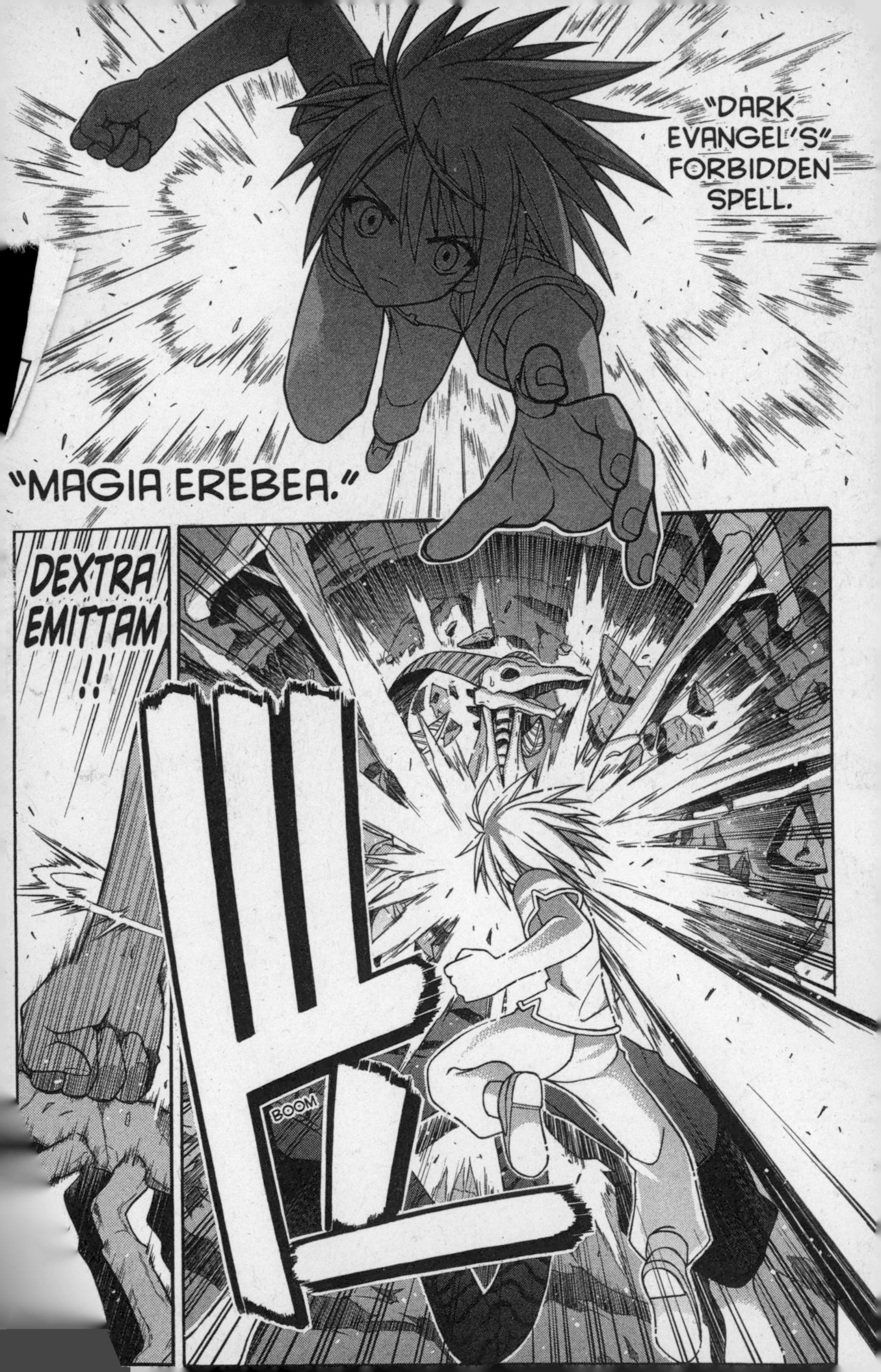
"DARK EVANGEL'S" FORBIDDEN SPELL.
"MAGIA EREBEA."
DEXTRA EMITTAM!!
BOOM

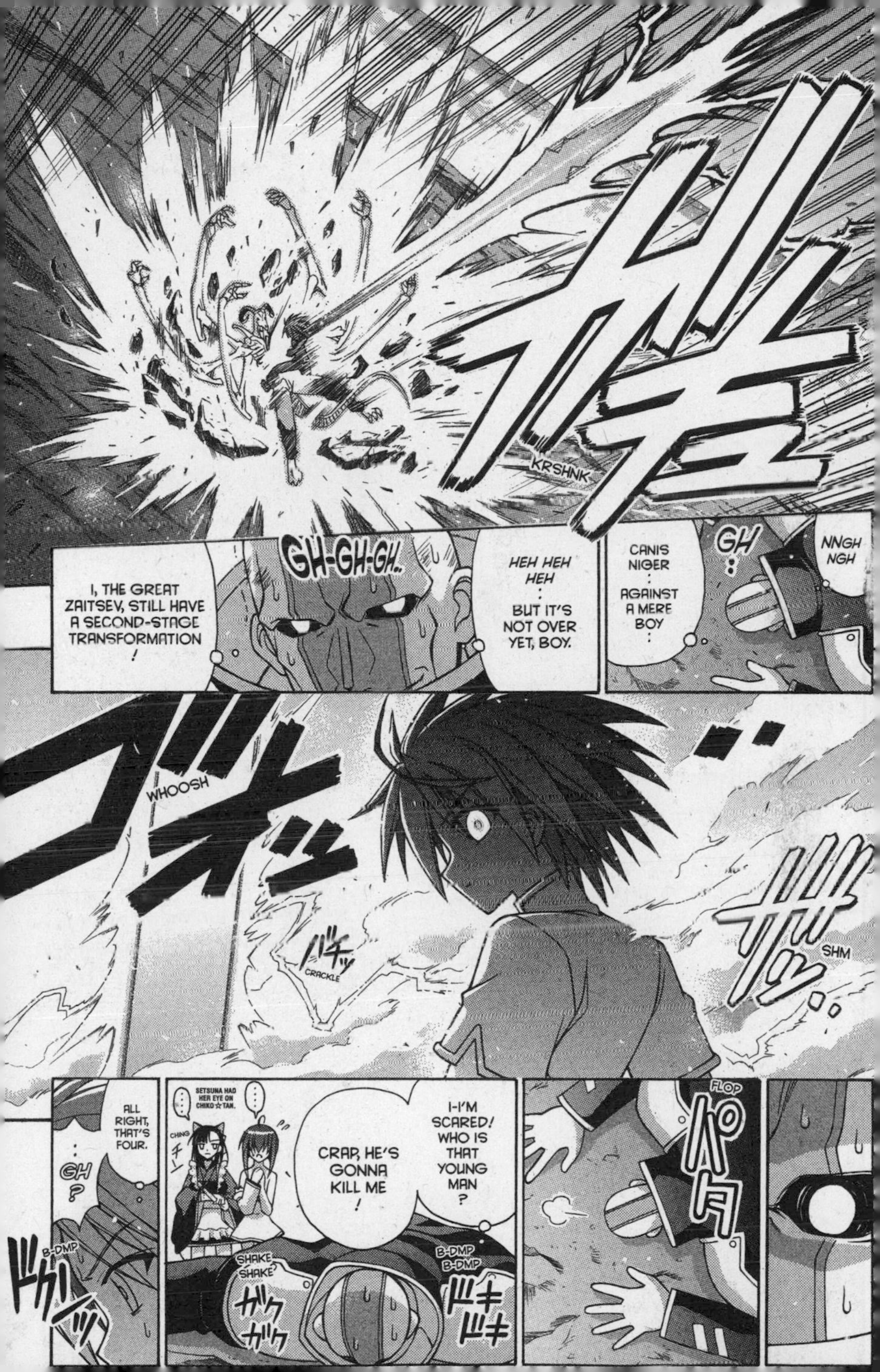
KRSHNK
NNGH NGH
GH...
CANIS NIGER... AGAINST A MERE BOY...
HEH HEH HEH... BUT IT'S NOT OVER YET, BOY.
GH-GH-GH..
I, THE GREAT ZAITSEV, STILL HAVE A SECOND-STAGE TRANSFORMATION!
SHM
CRACKLE
WHOOSH
FLOP
I-I'M SCARED! WHO IS THAT YOUNG MAN?
B-DMP B-DMP
CRAP, HE'S GONNA KILL ME!
SHAKE SHAKE
SETSUNA HAD HER EYE ON CHIKO☆TAN.
CHING
ALL RIGHT, THAT'S FOUR.
GH?
B-DMP

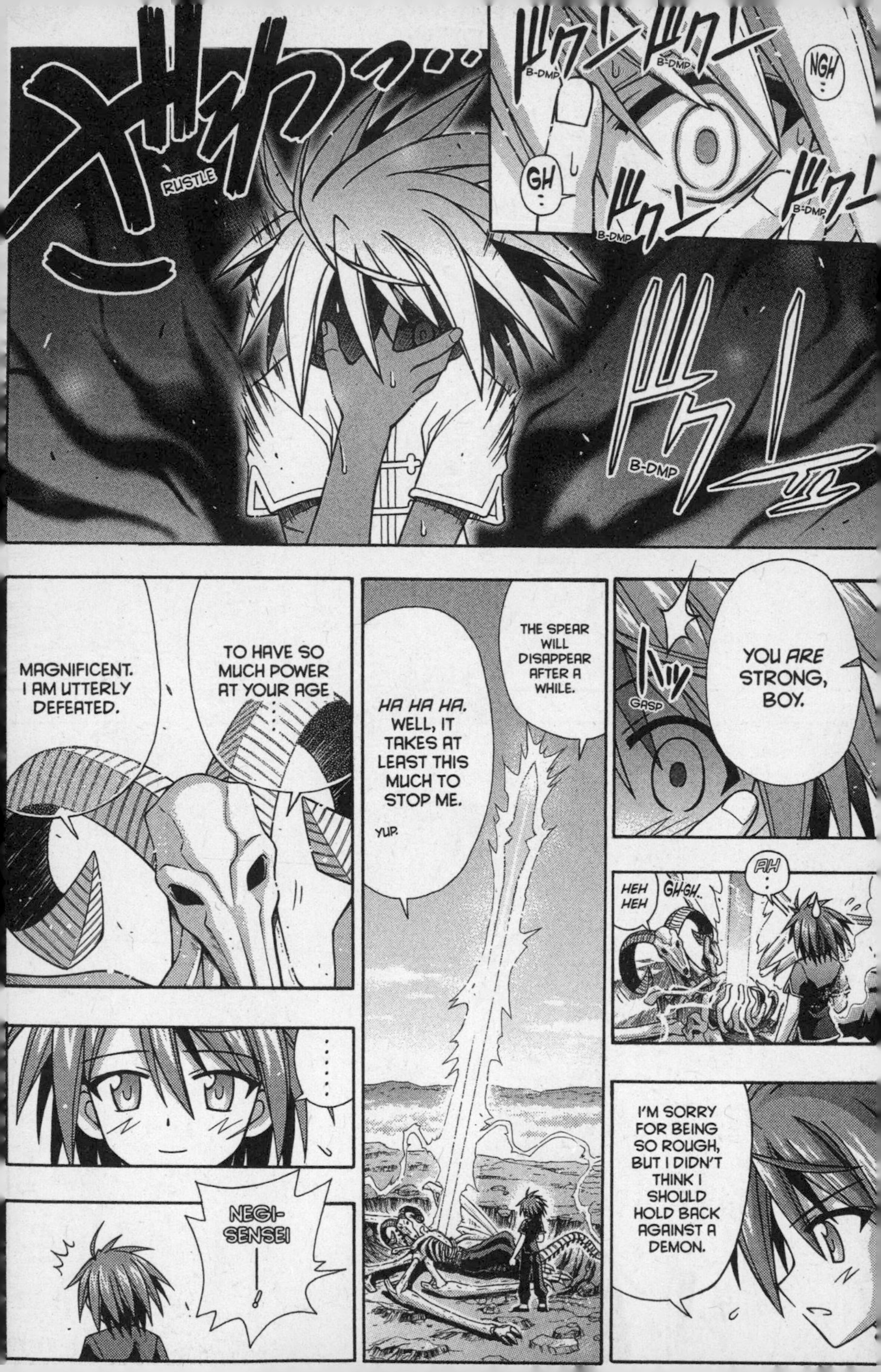
B-DMP
B-DMP
NGH...
GH...
B-DMP
B-DMP
RUSTLE
B-DMP
YOU ARE STRONG, BOY.
GASP
AH...
GH-GH..
HEH HEH
I'M SORRY FOR BEING SO ROUGH, BUT I DIDN'T THINK I SHOULD HOLD BACK AGAINST A DEMON.
THE SPEAR WILL DISAPPEAR AFTER A WHILE.
HA HA HA. WELL, IT TAKES AT LEAST THIS MUCH TO STOP ME.
YUP.
TO HAVE SO MUCH POWER AT YOUR AGE...
MAGNIFICENT. I AM UTTERLY DEFEATED.
......
NEGI-SENSEI...!

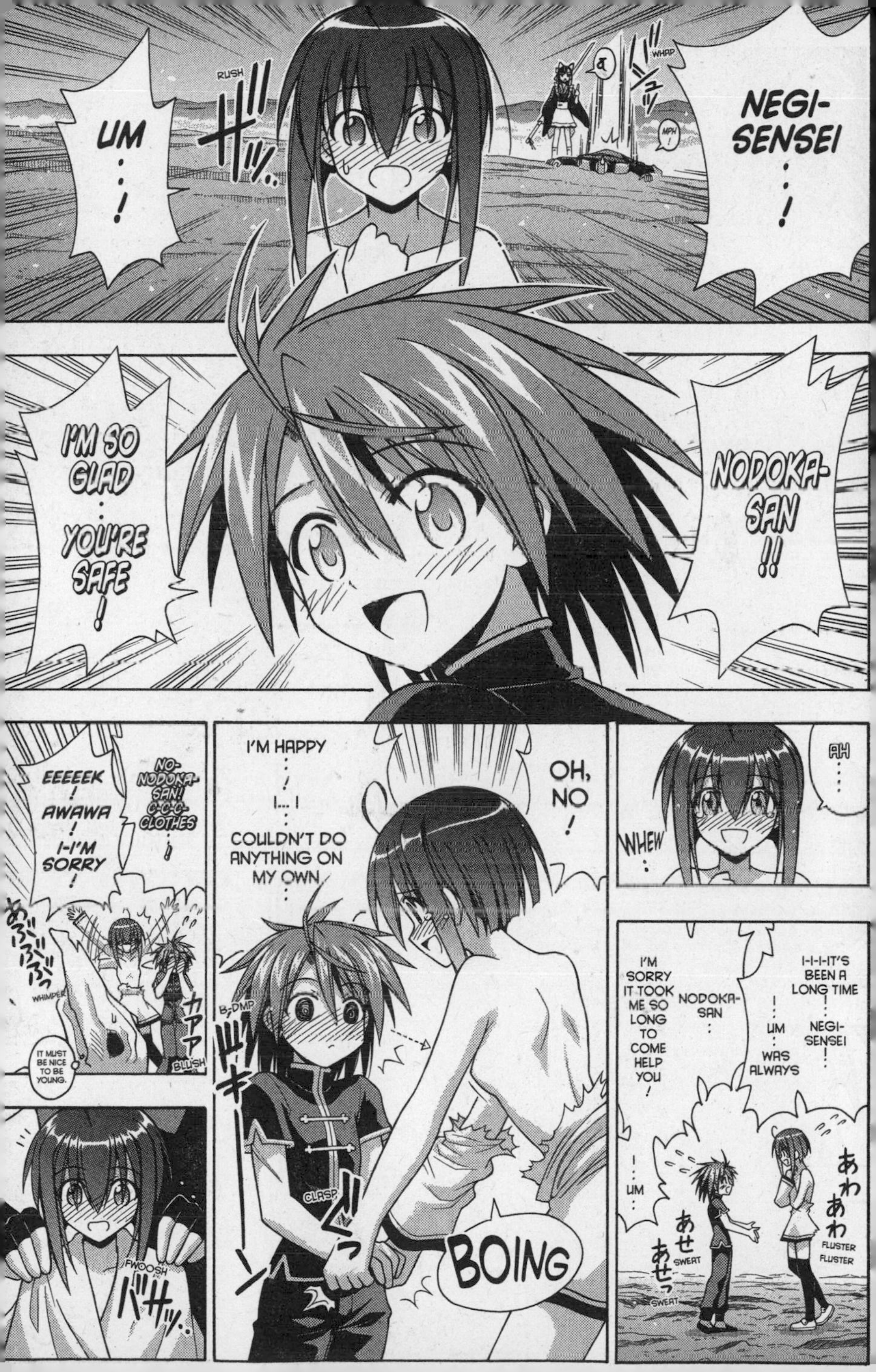
NEGI-SENSEI . . . !
WHAP
MPH !
RUSH
UM . . . !
NODOKA-SAN !!
I'M SO GLAD . . . YOU'RE SAFE !
AH . . . .
WHEW . . .
I-I-I-IT'S BEEN A LONG TIME . . . ! NEGI-SENSEI . . . !
UM . . . WAS ALWAYS
NODOKA-SAN . . .
I'M SORRY IT TOOK ME SO LONG TO COME HELP YOU !
UM . . .
あわあわ
FLUSTER FLUSTER
あせあせっ
SWEAT
SWEAT
OH, NO !
I'M HAPPY . . . I... I . . . COULDN'T DO ANYTHING ON MY OWN . . .
B-DMP
CLASP
BOING
NO-NODOKA-SAN! C-C-C-CLOTHES . . !
EEEEEK ! AWAWA ! I-I'M SORRY !
WHIMPER
BLUSH
IT MUST BE NICE TO BE YOUNG.
FWOOSH

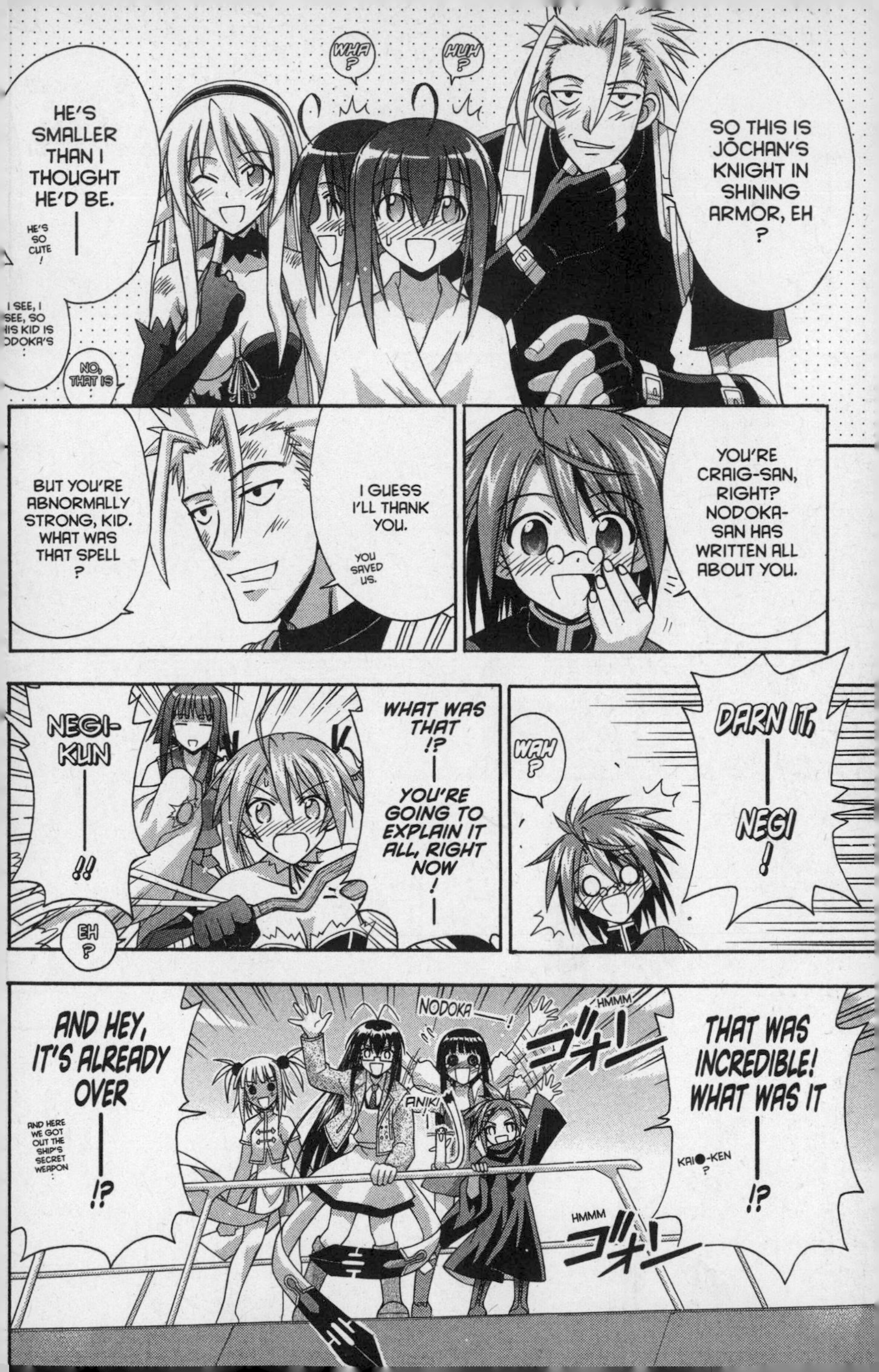
SO THIS IS JŌCHAN'S KNIGHT IN SHINING ARMOR, EH?
HUH?
WHA?
HE'S SMALLER THAN I THOUGHT HE'D BE.
HE'S SO CUTE!
I SEE, I SEE, SO HIS KID IS ODOKA'S
NO, THAT IS
YOU'RE CRAIG-SAN, RIGHT? NODOKA-SAN HAS WRITTEN ALL ABOUT YOU.
I GUESS I'LL THANK YOU.
YOU SAVED US.
BUT YOU'RE ABNORMALLY STRONG, KID. WHAT WAS THAT SPELL?
DARN IT, — NEGI!
WAH?
WHAT WAS THAT!? — YOU'RE GOING TO EXPLAIN IT ALL, RIGHT NOW!
NEGI-KUN — !!
EH?
THAT WAS INCREDIBLE! WHAT WAS IT — !?
KAI●-KEN?
HMMM
ゴォー
NODOKA—!
ANIKI!
AND HEY, IT'S ALREADY OVER — !?
AND HERE WE GOT OUT THE SHIP'S SECRET WEAPON:
HMMM
ゴォー

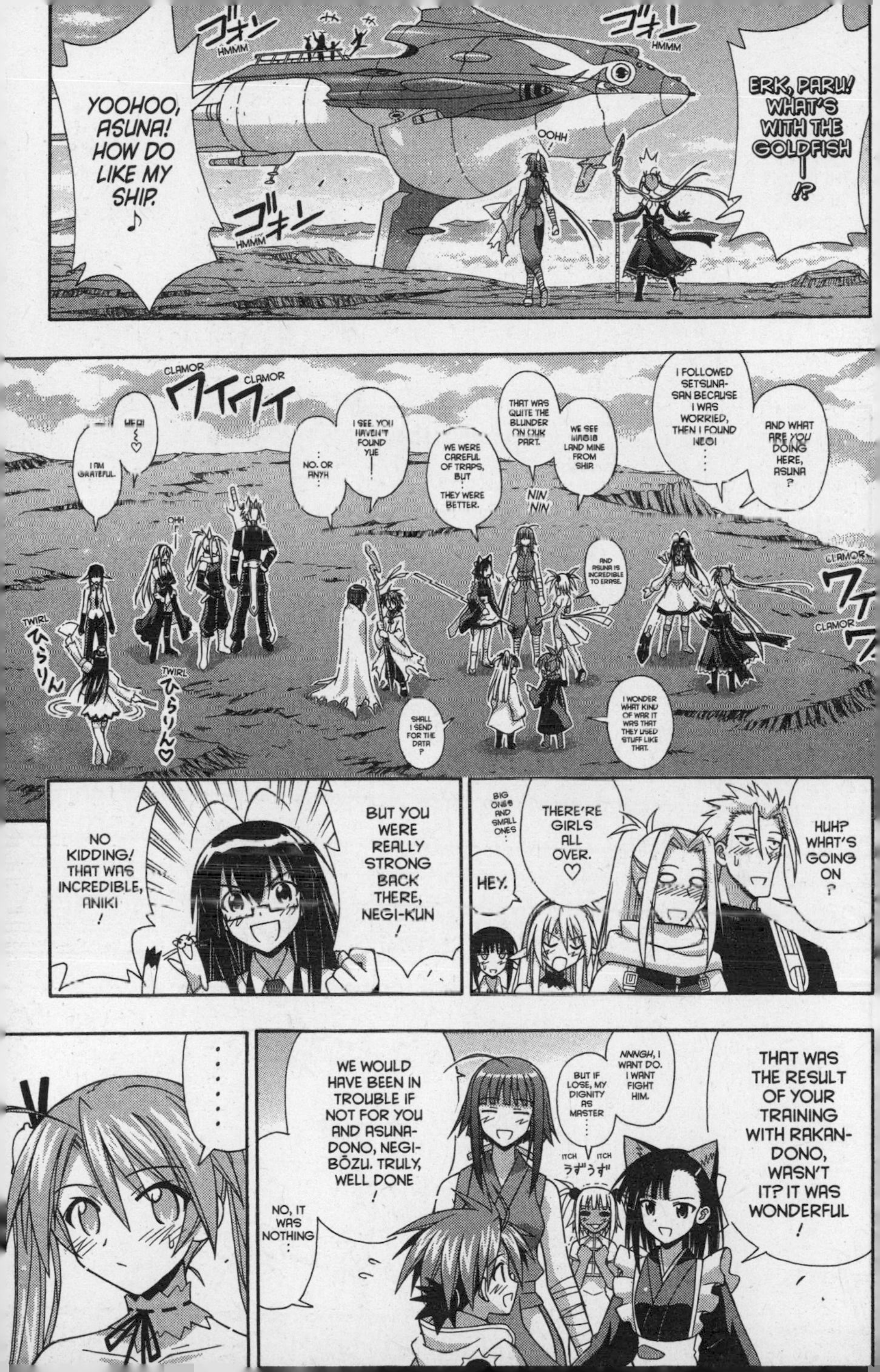

HMMM
HMMM
ERK, PARU! WHAT'S WITH THE GOLDFISH!?
OOHH
HMMM
YOOHOO, ASUNA! HOW DO LIKE MY SHIP. ♪
AND WHAT ARE YOU DOING HERE, ASUNA?
I FOLLOWED SETSUNA-SAN BECAUSE I WAS WORRIED, THEN I FOUND NEGI......
CLAMOR CLAMOR
WE SEE LAND MINE FROM SHIP.
THAT WAS QUITE THE BLUNDER ON OUR PART.
NIN NIN
WE WERE CAREFUL OF TRAPS, BUT... THEY WERE BETTER.
I SEE. YOU HAVEN'T FOUND YUE!
...NO. OR ANY...
AND ASUNA IS INCREDIBLE TO ERASE.
I WONDER WHAT KIND OF WAR IT WAS THAT THEY USED STUFF LIKE THAT.
SHALL I SEND FOR THE DATA?
OHH!
CLAMOR CLAMOR
♡
I AM GRATEFUL.
TWIRL
TWIRL ♡
HUH? WHAT'S GOING ON?
THERE'RE GIRLS ALL OVER. ♡
BIG ONES AND SMALL ONES...
HEY.
BUT YOU WERE REALLY STRONG BACK THERE, NEGI-KUN!
NO KIDDING! THAT WAS INCREDIBLE, ANIKI!
THAT WAS THE RESULT OF YOUR TRAINING WITH RAKAN-DONO, WASN'T IT? IT WAS WONDERFUL!
NNNGH, I WANT DO. I WANT FIGHT HIM.
BUT IF LOSE, MY DIGNITY AS MASTER...
ITCH ITCH
WE WOULD HAVE BEEN IN TROUBLE IF NOT FOR YOU AND ASUNA-DONO, NEGI-BŌZU. TRULY, WELL DONE!
NO, IT WAS NOTHING...
......

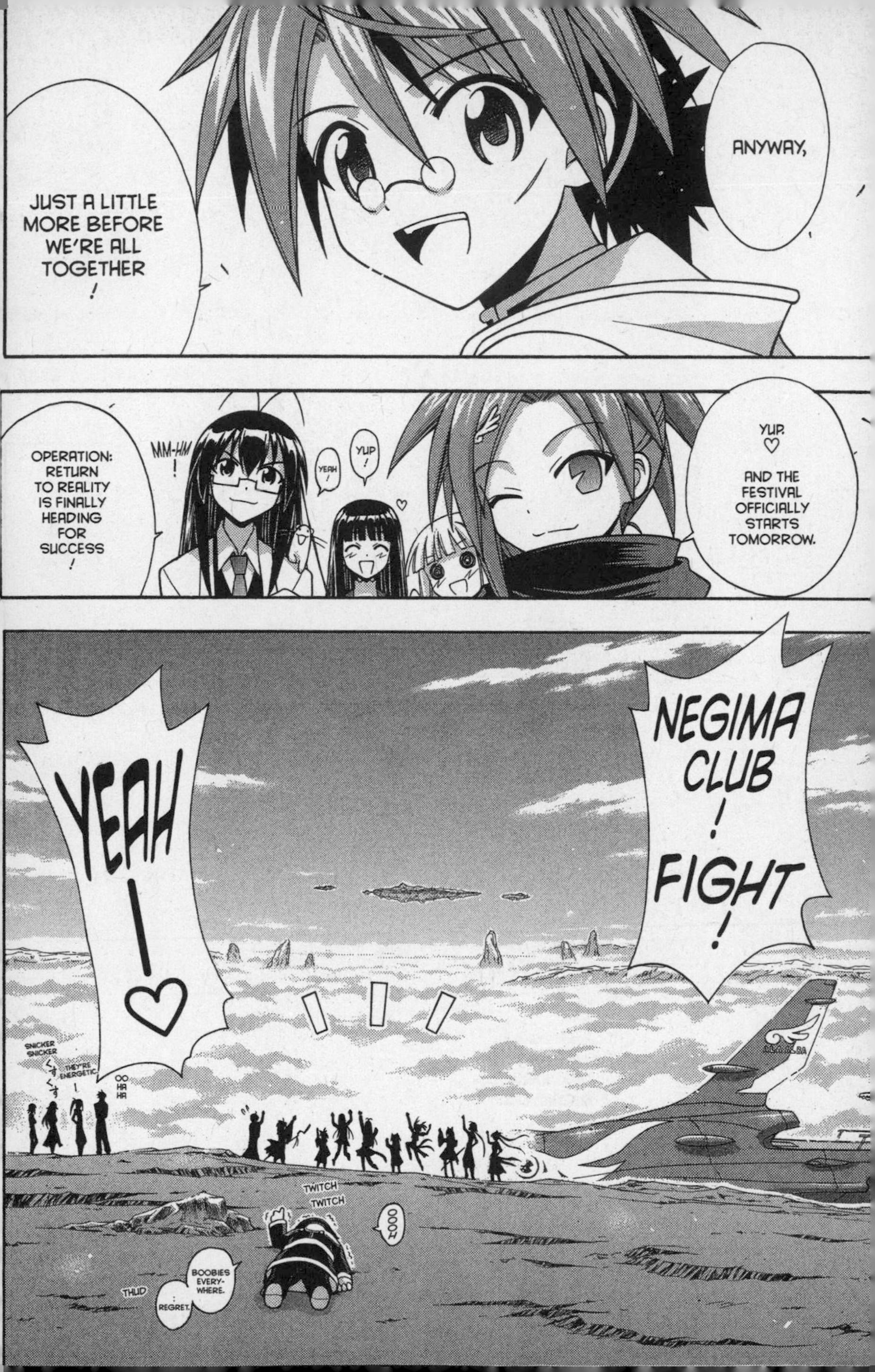
ANYWAY,
JUST A LITTLE MORE BEFORE WE'RE ALL TOGETHER!
YUP. ♡ AND THE FESTIVAL OFFICIALLY STARTS TOMORROW.
YUP!
YEAH!
MM-HM!
OPERATION: RETURN TO REALITY IS FINALLY HEADING FOR SUCCESS!
NEGIMA CLUB! FIGHT!
YEAH! ♡
OO HA HA
THEY'RE ENERGETIC.
SNICKER SNICKER
くすくす
TWITCH TWITCH
OOOH
BOOBIES EVERYWHERE.
: REGRET.
THUD

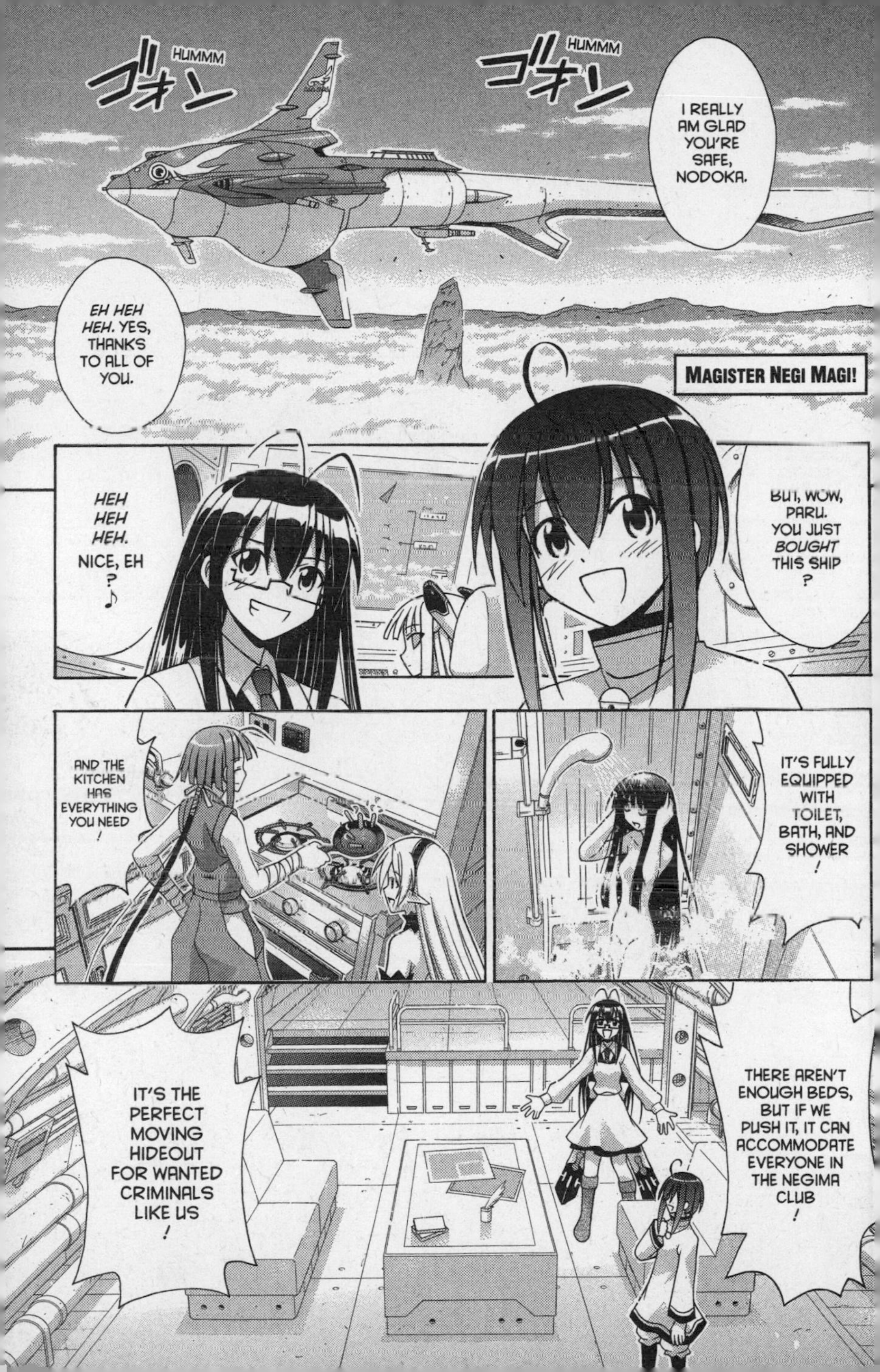

ゴオン HUMMM
ゴオン HUMMM
I REALLY AM GLAD YOU'RE SAFE, NODOKA.
EH HEH HEH. YES, THANKS TO ALL OF YOU.
MAGISTER NEGI MAGI!
BUT, WOW, PARU. YOU JUST *BOUGHT* THIS SHIP?
HEH HEH HEH. NICE, EH?♪
IT'S FULLY EQUIPPED WITH TOILET, BATH, AND SHOWER!
AND THE KITCHEN HAS EVERYTHING YOU NEED!
THERE AREN'T ENOUGH BEDS, BUT IF WE PUSH IT, IT CAN ACCOMMODATE EVERYONE IN THE NEGIMA CLUB!
IT'S THE PERFECT MOVING HIDEOUT FOR WANTED CRIMINALS LIKE US!

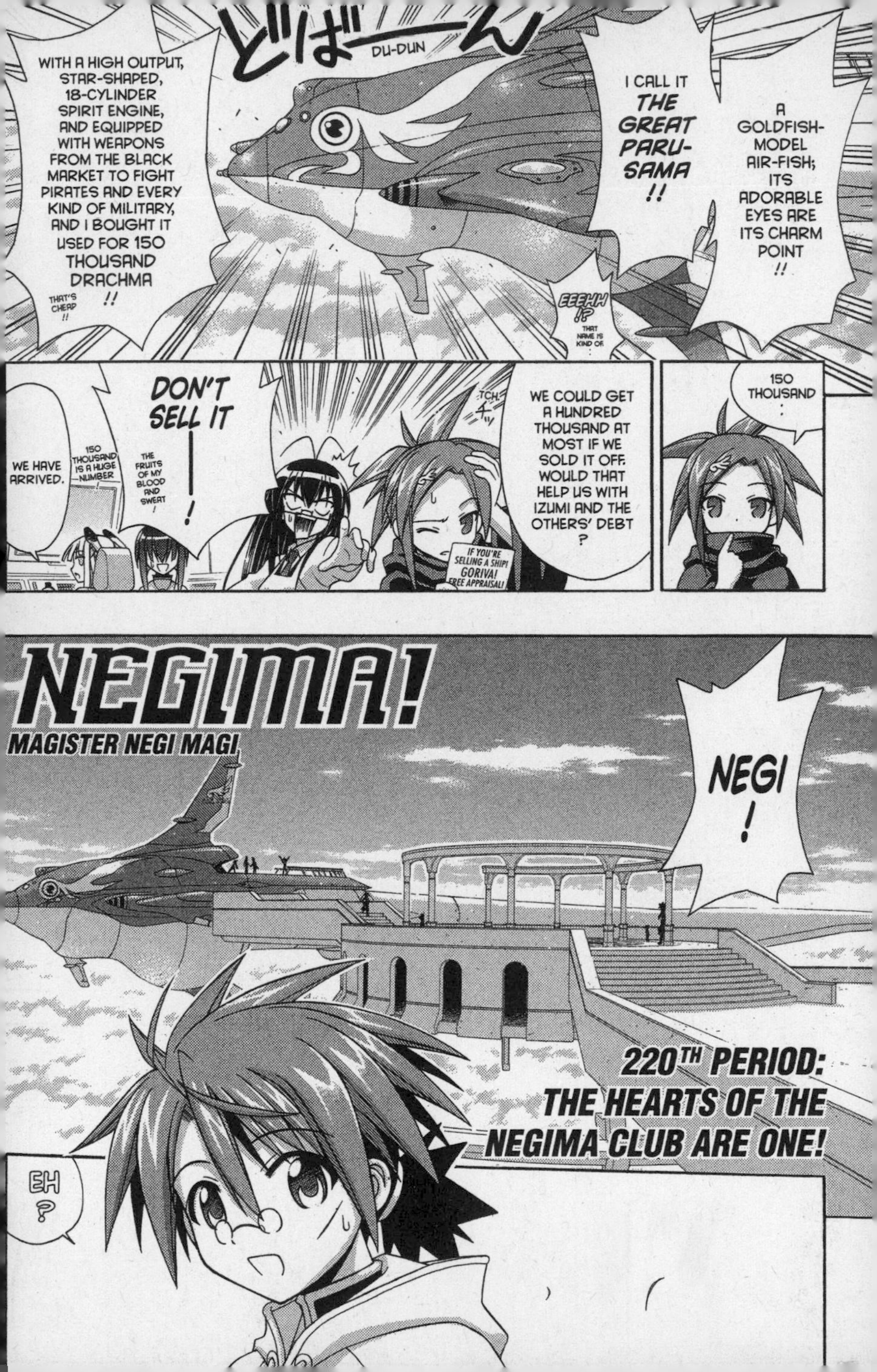
A GOLDFISH-MODEL AIR-FISH; ITS ADORABLE EYES ARE ITS CHARM POINT!!
I CALL IT THE GREAT PARU-SAMA!!
EEEHH!?
THAT NAME IS KIND OF...
どばーーん
DU-DUN
WITH A HIGH OUTPUT, STAR-SHAPED, 18-CYLINDER SPIRIT ENGINE, AND EQUIPPED WITH WEAPONS FROM THE BLACK MARKET TO FIGHT PIRATES AND EVERY KIND OF MILITARY, AND I BOUGHT IT USED FOR 150 THOUSAND DRACHMA!!
THAT'S CHEAP!!
150 THOUSAND...
WE COULD GET A HUNDRED THOUSAND AT MOST IF WE SOLD IT OFF. WOULD THAT HELP US WITH IZUMI AND THE OTHERS' DEBT?
TCH
IF YOU'RE SELLING A SHIP! GORIVA! FREE APPRAISAL!
DON'T SELL IT—!
THE FRUITS OF MY BLOOD AND SWEAT!
150 THOUSAND IS A HUGE NUMBER!
WE HAVE ARRIVED.
NEGIMA!
MAGISTER NEGI MAGI
NEGI!
220TH PERIOD: THE HEARTS OF THE NEGIMA CLUB ARE ONE!
EH?

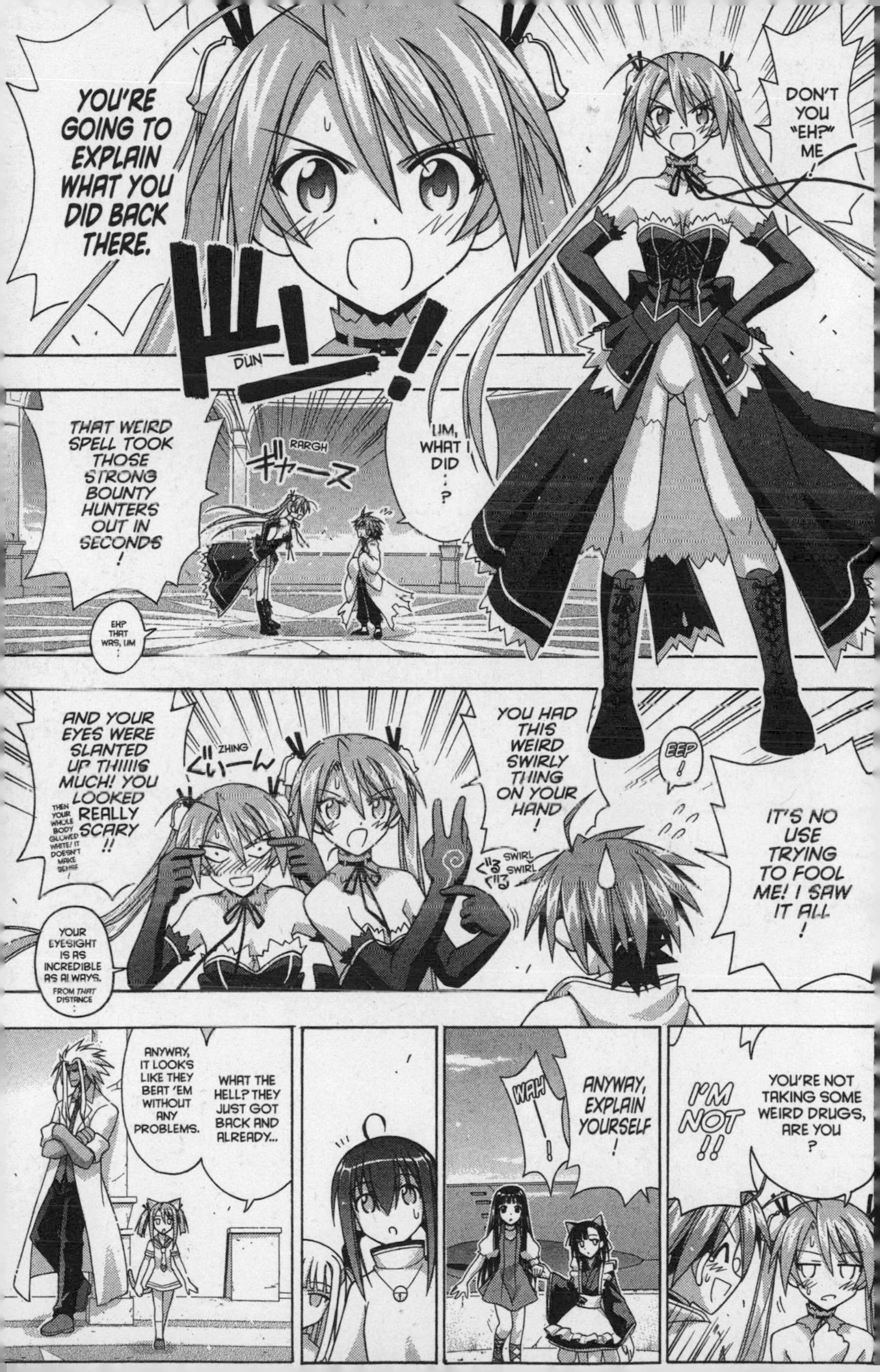
DON'T YOU "EH?" ME!
YOU'RE GOING TO EXPLAIN WHAT YOU DID BACK THERE.
DUN
UM, WHAT I DID...?
THAT WEIRD SPELL TOOK THOSE STRONG BOUNTY HUNTERS OUT IN SECONDS!
ギャース
RARGH
EH? THAT WAS, UM...
EEP!
IT'S NO USE TRYING TO FOOL ME! I SAW IT ALL!
YOU HAD THIS WEIRD SWIRLY THING ON YOUR HAND!
ぐるぐる
SWIRL SWIRL
ぐいーん
ZHING
AND YOUR EYES WERE SLANTED UP THIIIIS MUCH! YOU LOOKED REALLY SCARY!!
THEN YOUR WHOLE BODY GLOWED WHITE! IT DOESN'T MAKE SENSE!
YOUR EYESIGHT IS AS INCREDIBLE AS ALWAYS. FROM THAT DISTANCE...
YOU'RE NOT TAKING SOME WEIRD DRUGS, ARE YOU?
I'M NOT!!
ANYWAY, EXPLAIN YOURSELF!
WAH!
WHAT THE HELL? THEY JUST GOT BACK AND ALREADY...
ANYWAY, IT LOOKS LIKE THEY BEAT 'EM WITHOUT ANY PROBLEMS.

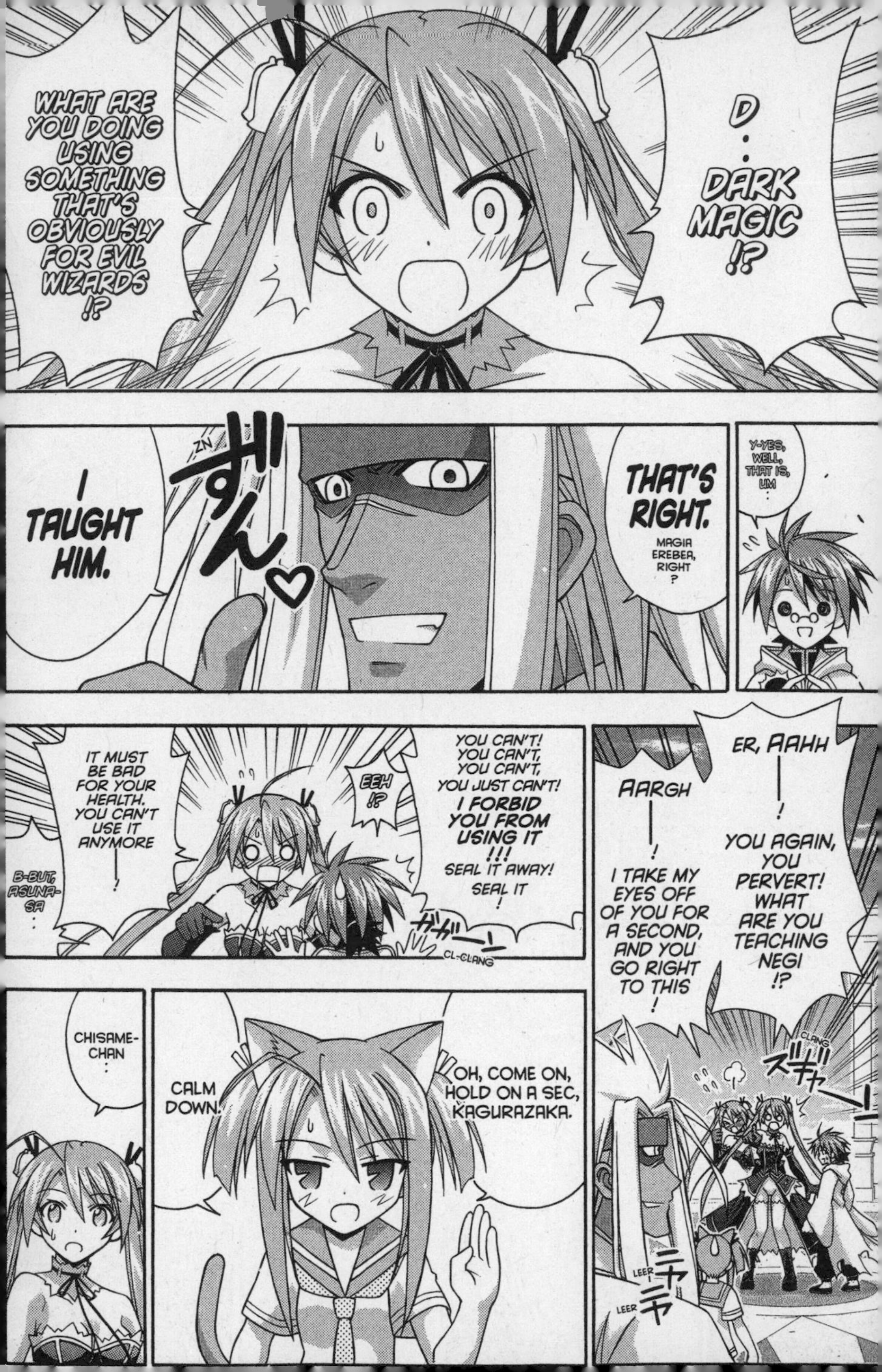
D... DARK MAGIC !?
WHAT ARE YOU DOING USING SOMETHING THAT'S OBVIOUSLY FOR EVIL WIZARDS !?
Y-YES, WELL, THAT IS, UM...
THAT'S RIGHT.
MAGIA EREBEA, RIGHT?
ZN
I TAUGHT HIM.
ER, AAHH—!
YOU AGAIN, YOU PERVERT! WHAT ARE YOU TEACHING NEGI !?
AARGH—! I TAKE MY EYES OFF OF YOU FOR A SECOND, AND YOU GO RIGHT TO THIS!
CLANG
LEER
LEER
YOU CAN'T! YOU CAN'T, YOU CAN'T, YOU JUST CAN'T! I FORBID YOU FROM USING IT!!! SEAL IT AWAY! SEAL IT!
EEH !?
IT MUST BE BAD FOR YOUR HEALTH. YOU CAN'T USE IT ANYMORE—!
B-BUT, ASUNA-SA...
CL-CLANG
OH, COME ON, HOLD ON A SEC, KAGURAZAKA.
CALM DOWN.
CHISAME-CHAN...

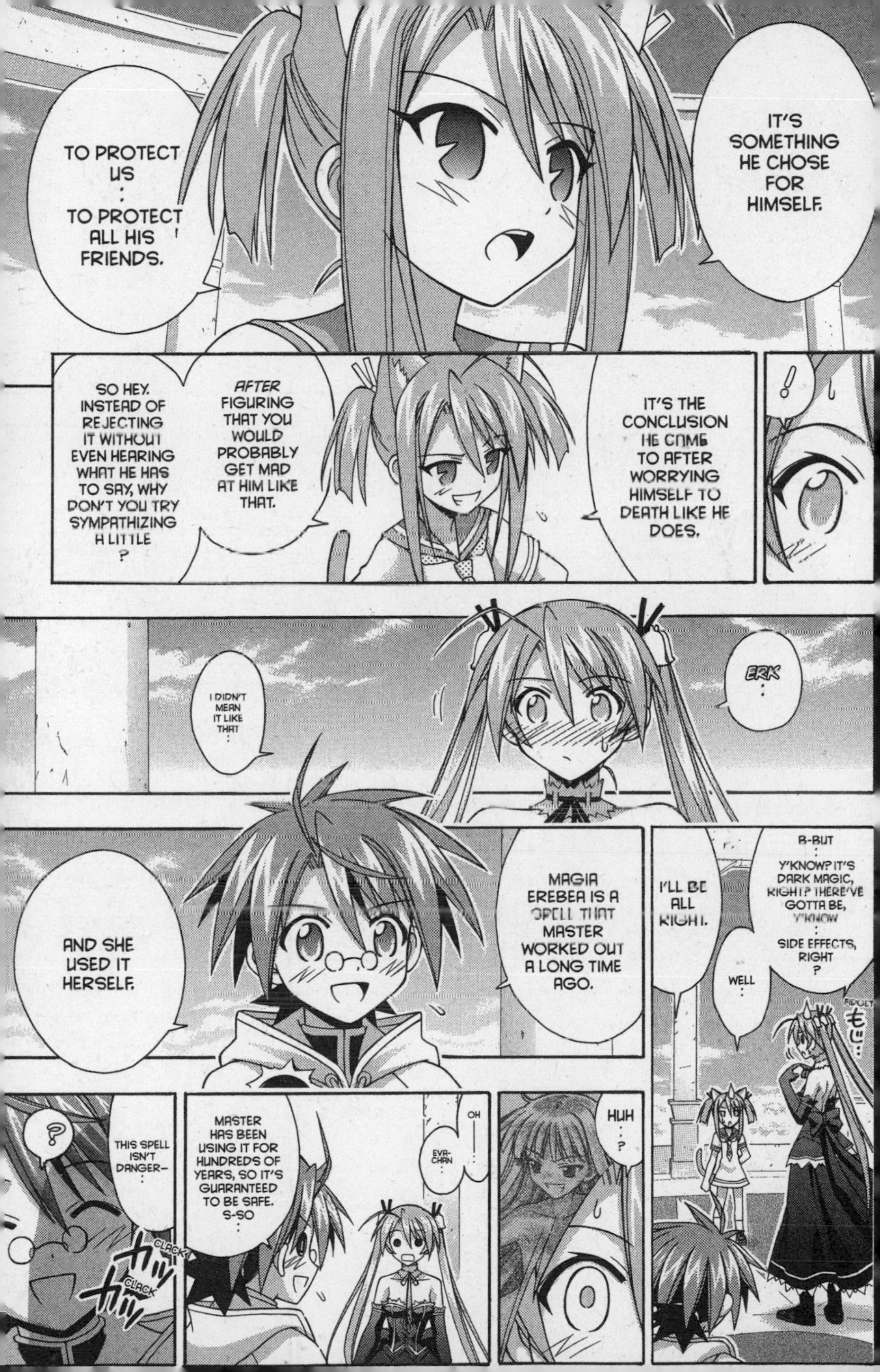
IT'S SOMETHING HE CHOSE FOR HIMSELF.
TO PROTECT US : TO PROTECT ALL HIS FRIENDS.
!
IT'S THE CONCLUSION HE CAME TO AFTER WORRYING HIMSELF TO DEATH LIKE HE DOES.
AFTER FIGURING THAT YOU WOULD PROBABLY GET MAD AT HIM LIKE THAT.
SO HEY. INSTEAD OF REJECTING IT WITHOUT EVEN HEARING WHAT HE HAS TO SAY, WHY DON'T YOU TRY SYMPATHIZING A LITTLE ?
ERK :
I DIDN'T MEAN IT LIKE THAT :
B-BUT : Y'KNOW? IT'S DARK MAGIC, RIGHT? THERE'VE GOTTA BE, Y'KNOW : SIDE EFFECTS, RIGHT ?
WELL :
FIDGET
I'LL BE ALL RIGHT.
MAGIA EREBEA IS A SPELL THAT MASTER WORKED OUT A LONG TIME AGO.
AND SHE USED IT HERSELF.
HUH : ?
OH — :
EVA-CHAN :
MASTER HAS BEEN USING IT FOR HUNDREDS OF YEARS, SO IT'S GUARANTEED TO BE SAFE. S-SO :
?
THIS SPELL ISN'T DANGER— :
CLACK
CLACK

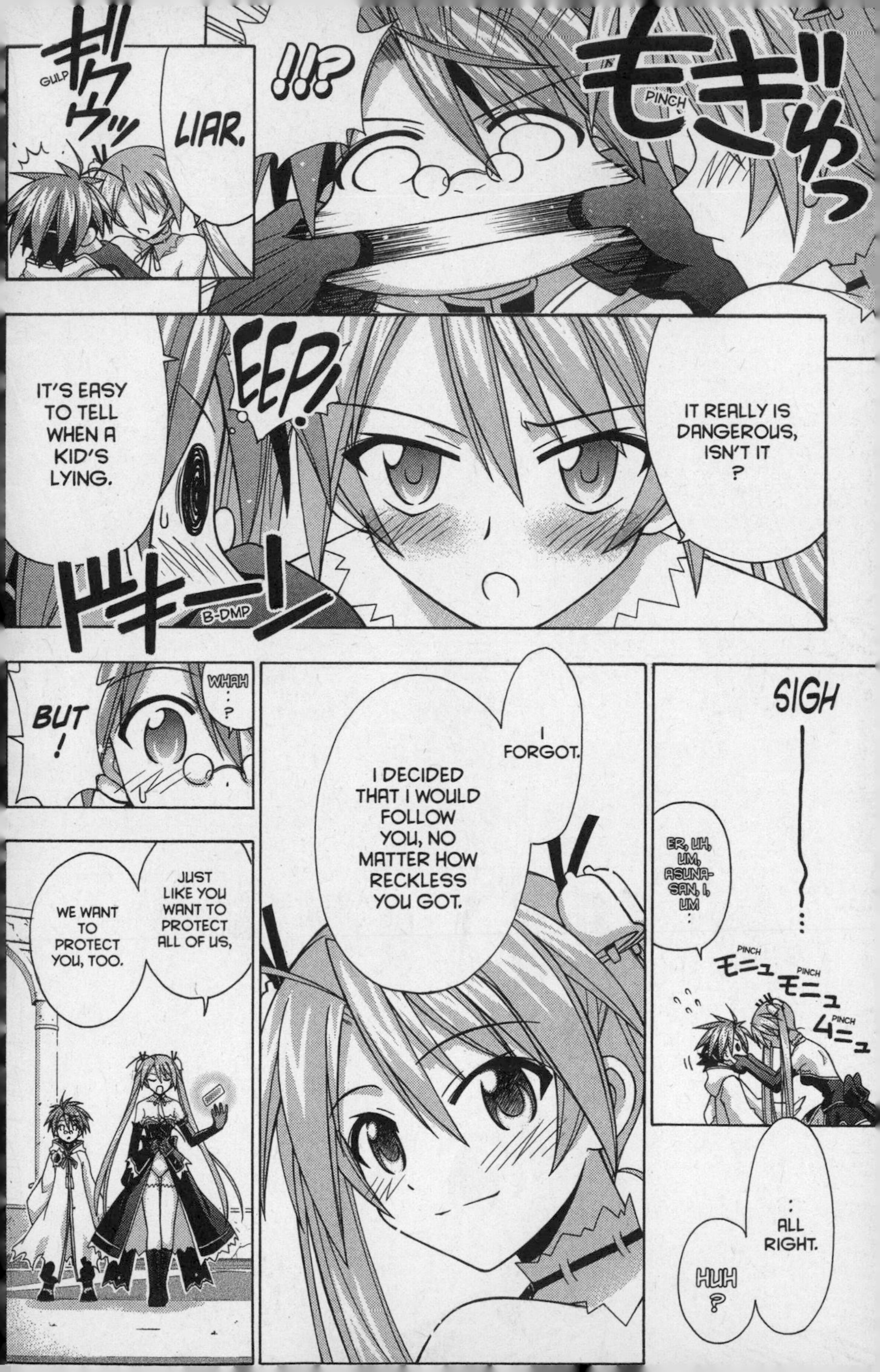
もぎゅっ
PINCH
!!!?
LIAR.
GULP
IT REALLY IS DANGEROUS, ISN'T IT?
EEP!
IT'S EASY TO TELL WHEN A KID'S LYING.
ドキーー
B-DMP
SIGH
......
ER, UH, UM, ASUNA-SAN, I, UM...
モニュ
PINCH
モニュ
PINCH
ムニュ
PINCH
...ALL RIGHT.
HUH?
I FORGOT.
I DECIDED THAT I WOULD FOLLOW YOU, NO MATTER HOW RECKLESS YOU GOT.
WHAH...?
BUT!
JUST LIKE YOU WANT TO PROTECT ALL OF US,
WE WANT TO PROTECT YOU, TOO.

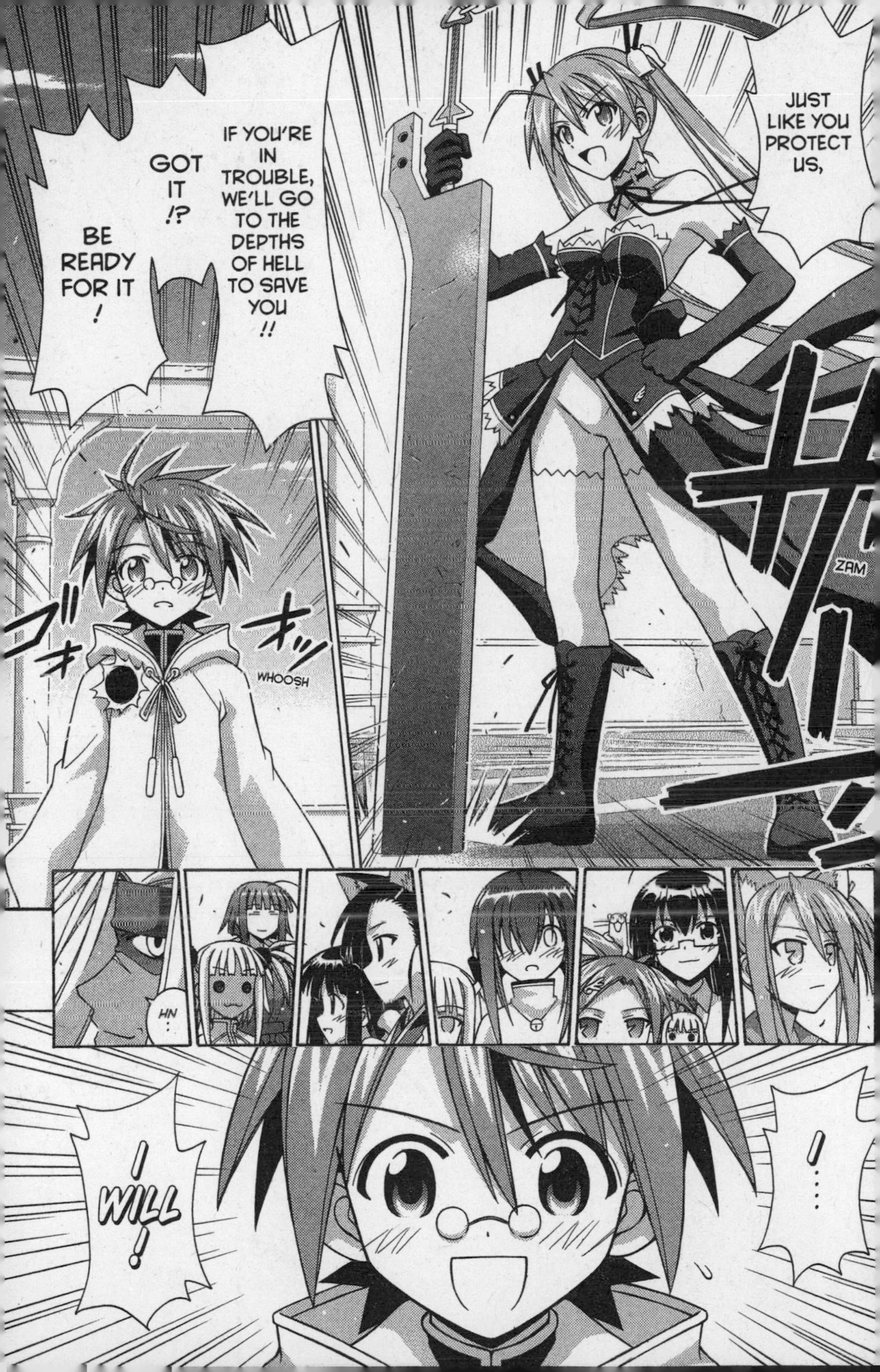
JUST LIKE YOU PROTECT US,
IF YOU'RE IN TROUBLE, WE'LL GO TO THE DEPTHS OF HELL TO SAVE YOU!!
GOT IT!?
BE READY FOR IT!
ZAM
WHOOSH
HN...
!....
I WILL!

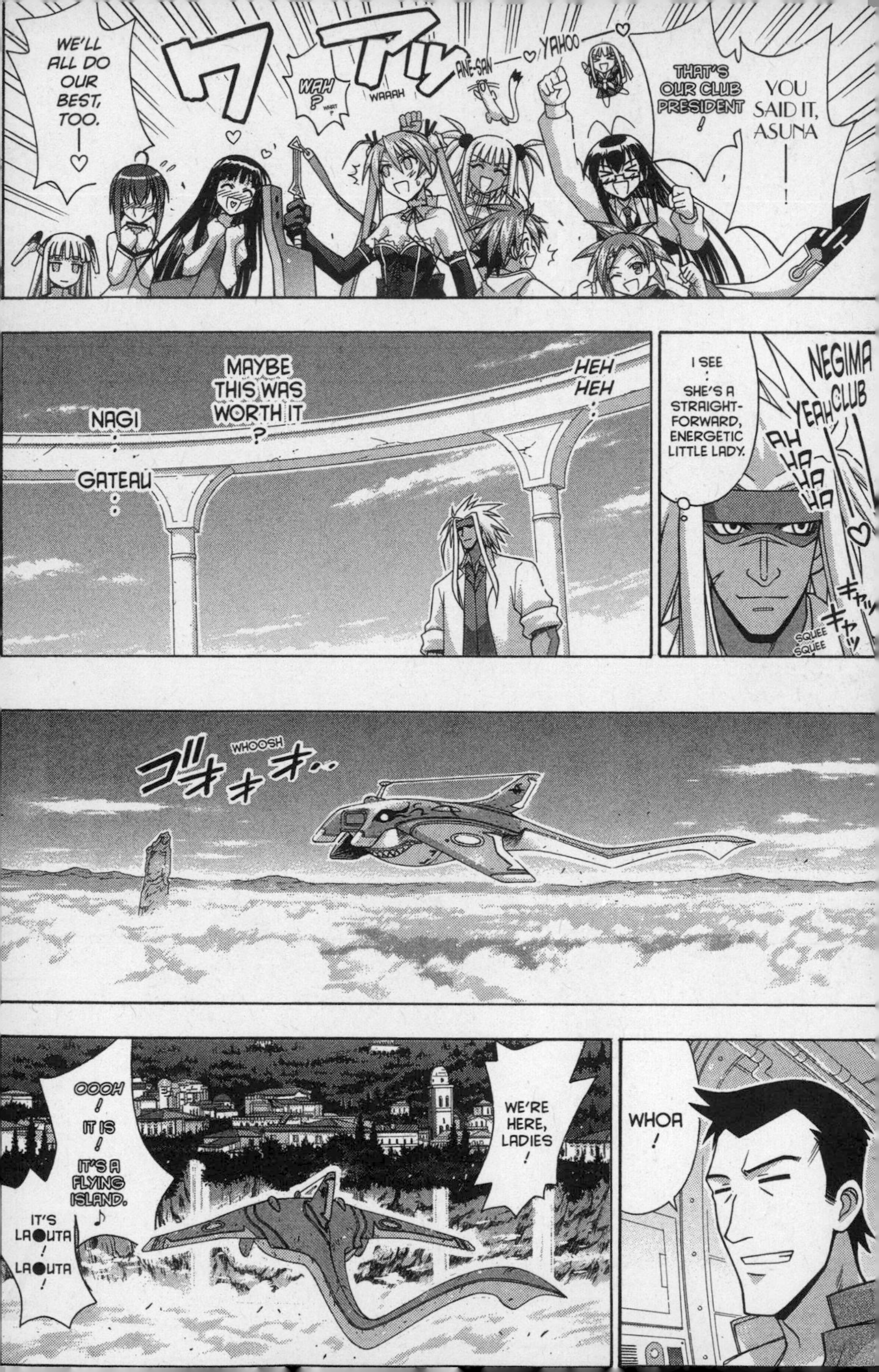
YOU SAID IT, ASUNA!
THAT'S OUR CLUB PRESIDENT!
YAHOO ♡
ANE-SAN ♡
ワアッ
WAAAH
WAH? WAIT?
WE'LL ALL DO OUR BEST, TOO. ♡
NEGIMA CLUB
YEAH
AH HA HA HA ♡
I SEE: SHE'S A STRAIGHT-FORWARD, ENERGETIC LITTLE LADY.
ギャッ ギャッ
SQUEE SQUEE
HEH HEH
MAYBE THIS WAS WORTH IT?
NAGI: GATEAU:
ゴオォオ..
WHOOSH
WHOA!
WE'RE HERE, LADIES!
OOOH! IT IS! IT'S A FLYING ISLAND. ♪
IT'S LA●UTA! LA●UTA!

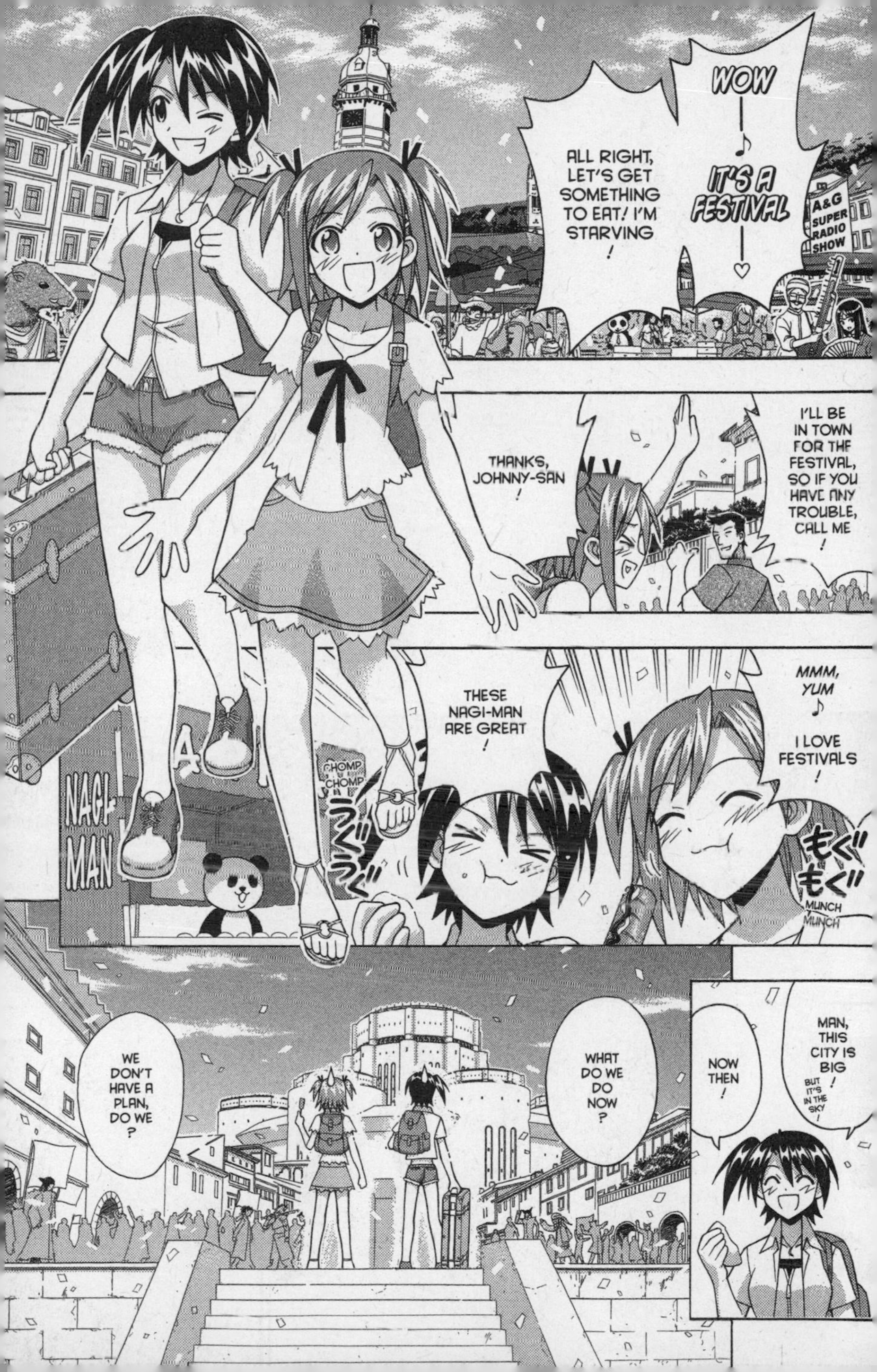
WOW ♪ IT'S A FESTIVAL ♥
A&G SUPER RADIO SHOW
ALL RIGHT, LET'S GET SOMETHING TO EAT! I'M STARVING!
I'LL BE IN TOWN FOR THE FESTIVAL, SO IF YOU HAVE ANY TROUBLE, CALL ME!
THANKS, JOHNNY-SAN!
MMM, YUM ♪ I LOVE FESTIVALS!
もぐもぐ
MUNCH MUNCH
THESE NAGI-MAN ARE GREAT!
うぐうぐ
CHOMP CHOMP
NAGI-MAN
MAN, THIS CITY IS BIG!
BUT IT'S IN THE SKY!
NOW THEN!
WHAT DO WE DO NOW?
WE DON'T HAVE A PLAN, DO WE?

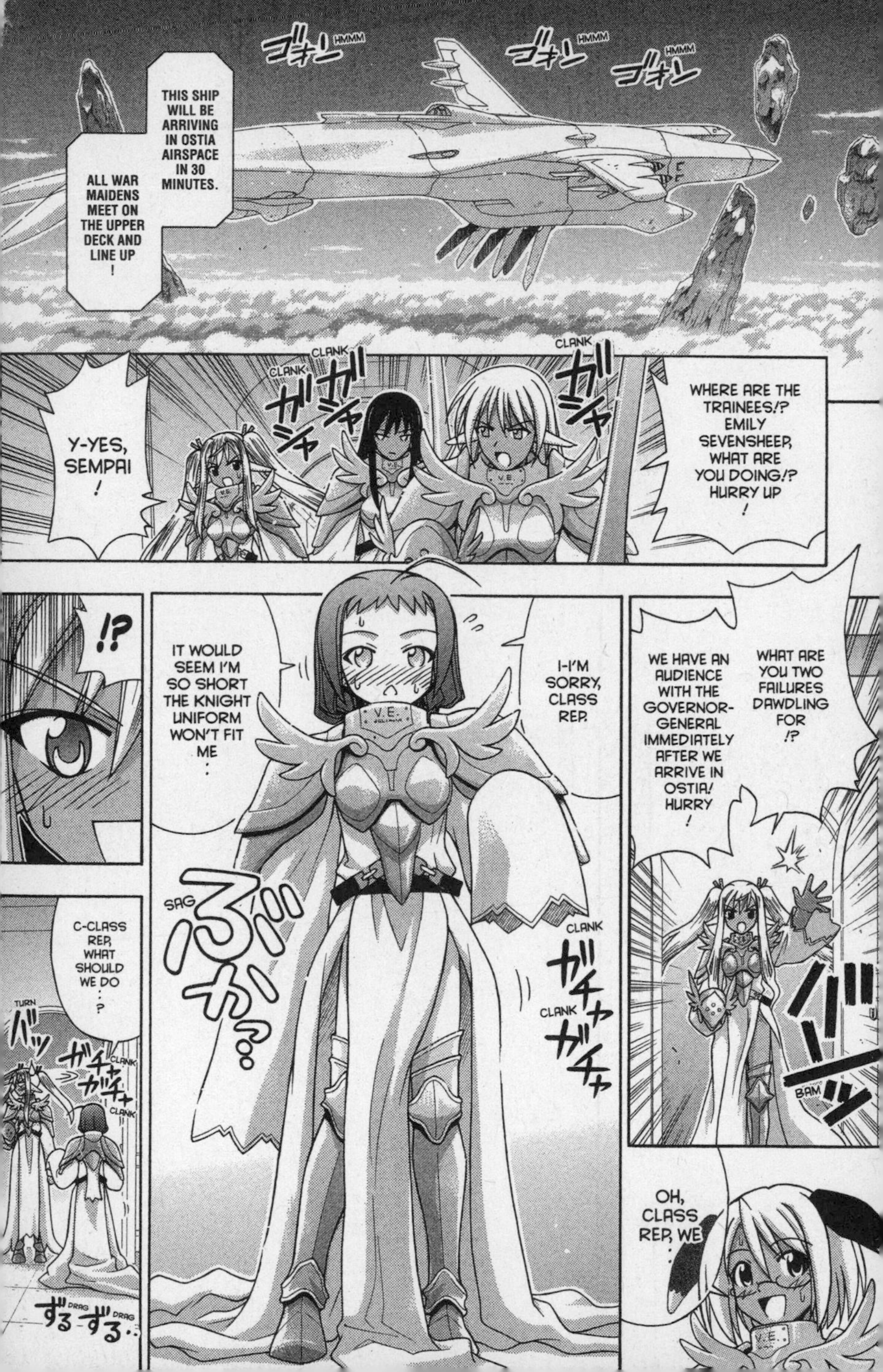
ゴオン HMMM
ゴオン HMMM
ゴオン HMMM
THIS SHIP WILL BE ARRIVING IN OSTIA AIRSPACE IN 30 MINUTES.
ALL WAR MAIDENS MEET ON THE UPPER DECK AND LINE UP!
WHERE ARE THE TRAINEES!? EMILY SEVENSHEEP, WHAT ARE YOU DOING!? HURRY UP!
ガシャ CLANK
ガシャ CLANK
ガシャ CLANK
Y-YES, SEMPAI!
WHAT ARE YOU TWO FAILURES DAWDLING FOR!?
WE HAVE AN AUDIENCE WITH THE GOVERNOR-GENERAL IMMEDIATELY AFTER WE ARRIVE IN OSTIA! HURRY!
バーッ BAM
OH, CLASS REP, WE...
I-I'M SORRY, CLASS REP.
IT WOULD SEEM I'M SO SHORT THE KNIGHT UNIFORM WON'T FIT ME...
ぶかっ SAG
ガチャ CLANK
ガチャ CLANK
!?
C-CLASS REP, WHAT SHOULD WE DO...?
バッ TURN
ガチャ CLANK
ガチャ CLANK
ずる DRAG
ずる DRAG

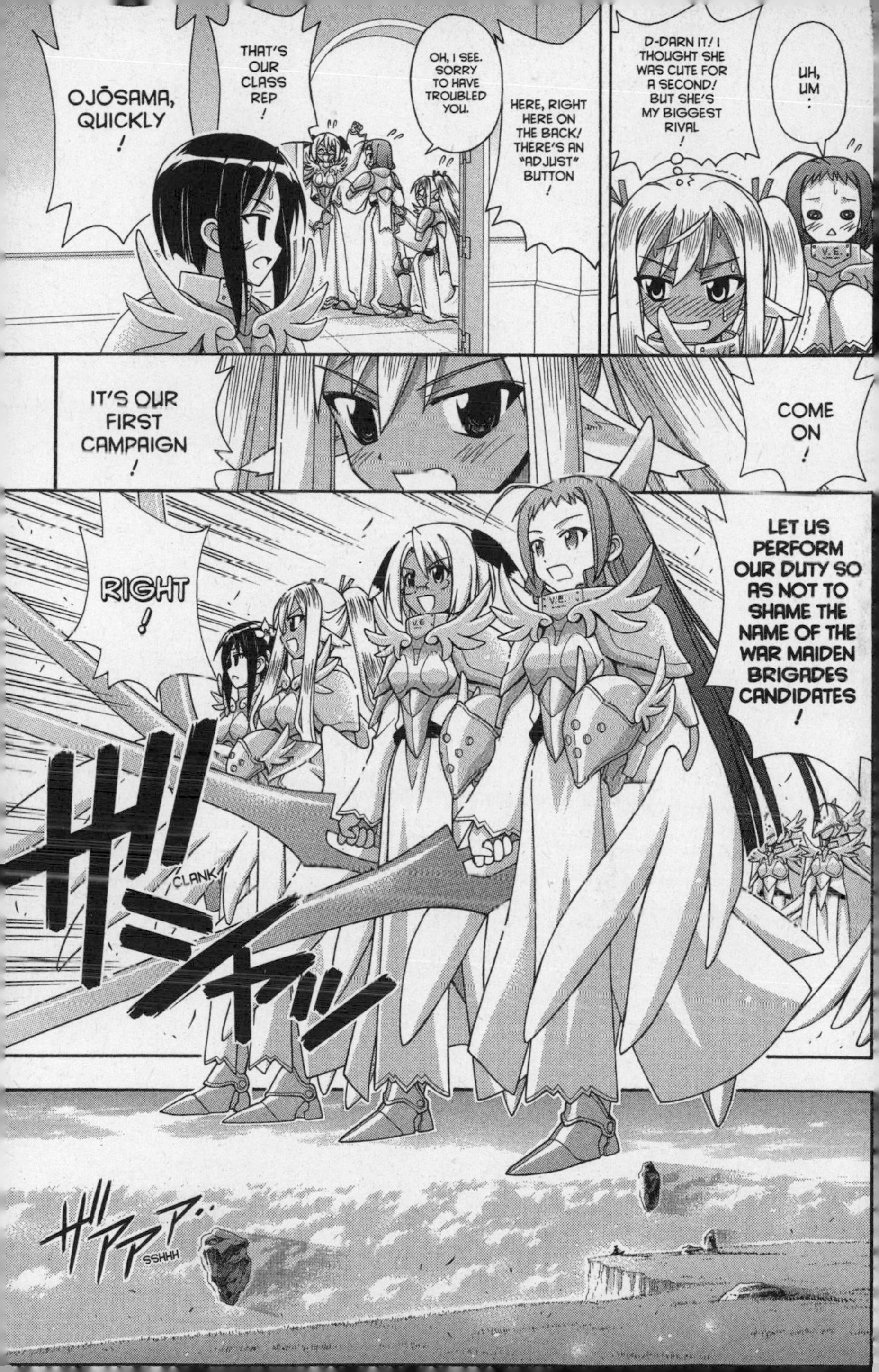
UH, UM :
D-DARN IT! I THOUGHT SHE WAS CUTE FOR A SECOND! BUT SHE'S MY BIGGEST RIVAL !
HERE, RIGHT HERE ON THE BACK! THERE'S AN "ADJUST" BUTTON !
OH, I SEE. SORRY TO HAVE TROUBLED YOU.
THAT'S OUR CLASS REP !
OJŌSAMA, QUICKLY !
COME ON !
IT'S OUR FIRST CAMPAIGN !
LET US PERFORM OUR DUTY SO AS NOT TO SHAME THE NAME OF THE WAR MAIDEN BRIGADES CANDIDATES !
RIGHT !
CLANK
SSHHH

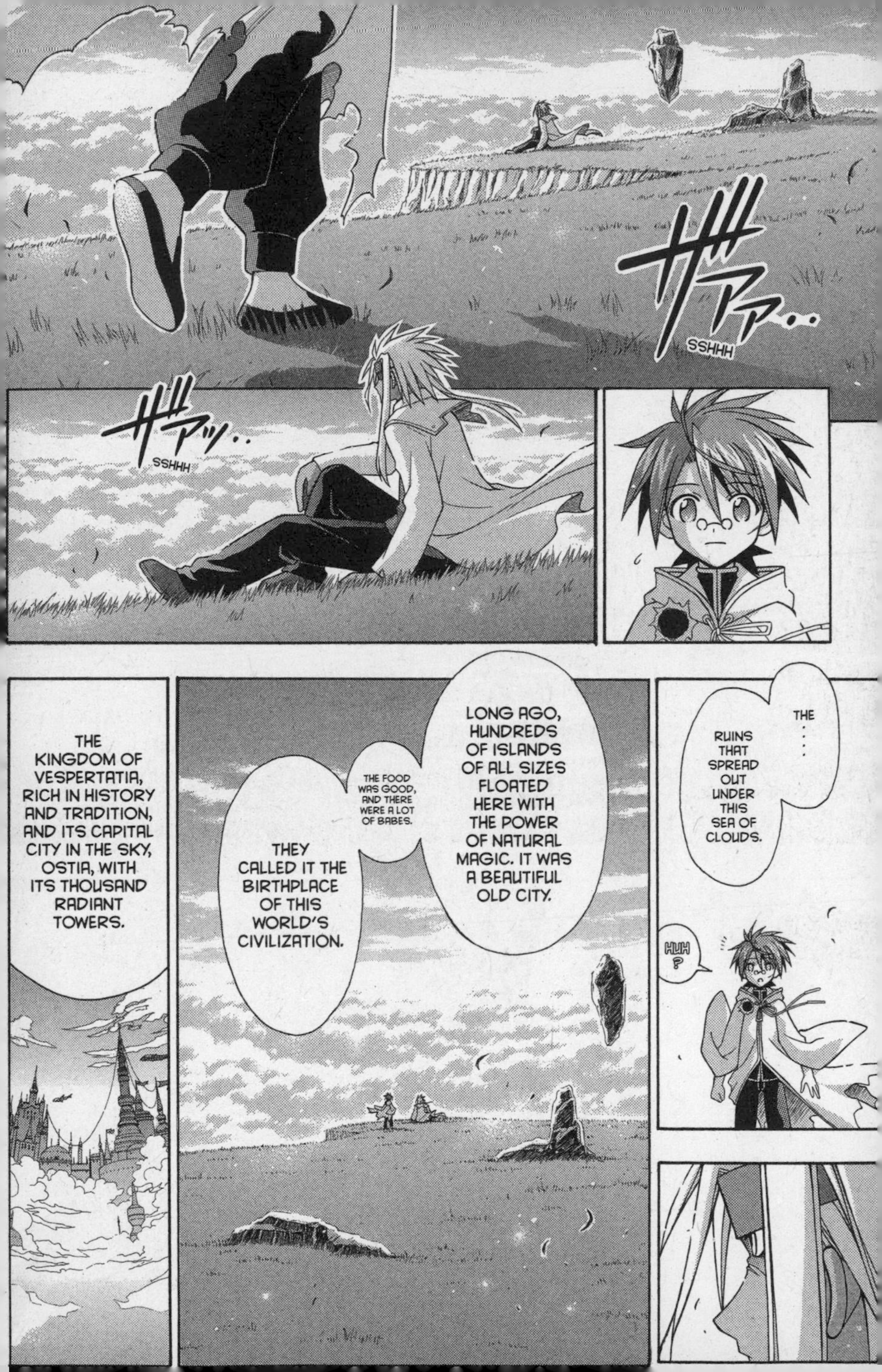
ザァァ..
SSHHH
ザアッ..
SSHHH
THE . . . RUINS THAT SPREAD OUT UNDER THIS SEA OF CLOUDS.
HUH?
LONG AGO, HUNDREDS OF ISLANDS OF ALL SIZES FLOATED HERE WITH THE POWER OF NATURAL MAGIC. IT WAS A BEAUTIFUL OLD CITY.
THE FOOD WAS GOOD, AND THERE WERE A LOT OF BABES.
THEY CALLED IT THE BIRTHPLACE OF THIS WORLD'S CIVILIZATION.
THE KINGDOM OF VESPERTATIA, RICH IN HISTORY AND TRADITION, AND ITS CAPITAL CITY IN THE SKY, OSTIA, WITH ITS THOUSAND RADIANT TOWERS.

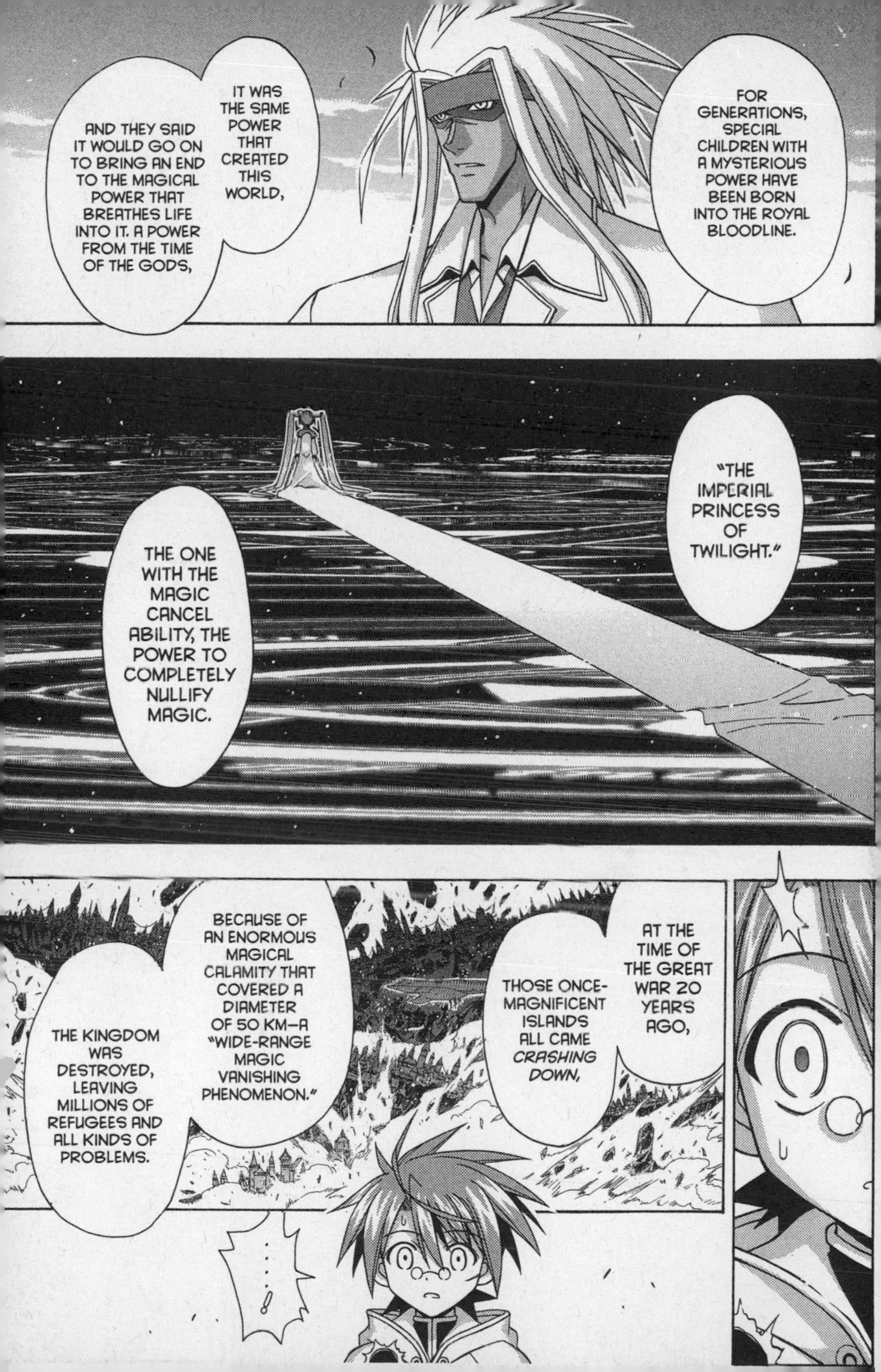
FOR GENERATIONS, SPECIAL CHILDREN WITH A MYSTERIOUS POWER HAVE BEEN BORN INTO THE ROYAL BLOODLINE.
IT WAS THE SAME POWER THAT CREATED THIS WORLD,
AND THEY SAID IT WOULD GO ON TO BRING AN END TO THE MAGICAL POWER THAT BREATHES LIFE INTO IT. A POWER FROM THE TIME OF THE GODS,
"THE IMPERIAL PRINCESS OF TWILIGHT."
THE ONE WITH THE MAGIC CANCEL ABILITY, THE POWER TO COMPLETELY NULLIFY MAGIC.
AT THE TIME OF THE GREAT WAR 20 YEARS AGO,
THOSE ONCE-MAGNIFICENT ISLANDS ALL CAME *CRASHING* DOWN,
BECAUSE OF AN ENORMOUS MAGICAL CALAMITY THAT COVERED A DIAMETER OF 50 KM—A "WIDE-RANGE MAGIC VANISHING PHENOMENON."
THE KINGDOM WAS DESTROYED, LEAVING MILLIONS OF REFUGEES AND ALL KINDS OF PROBLEMS.
...!

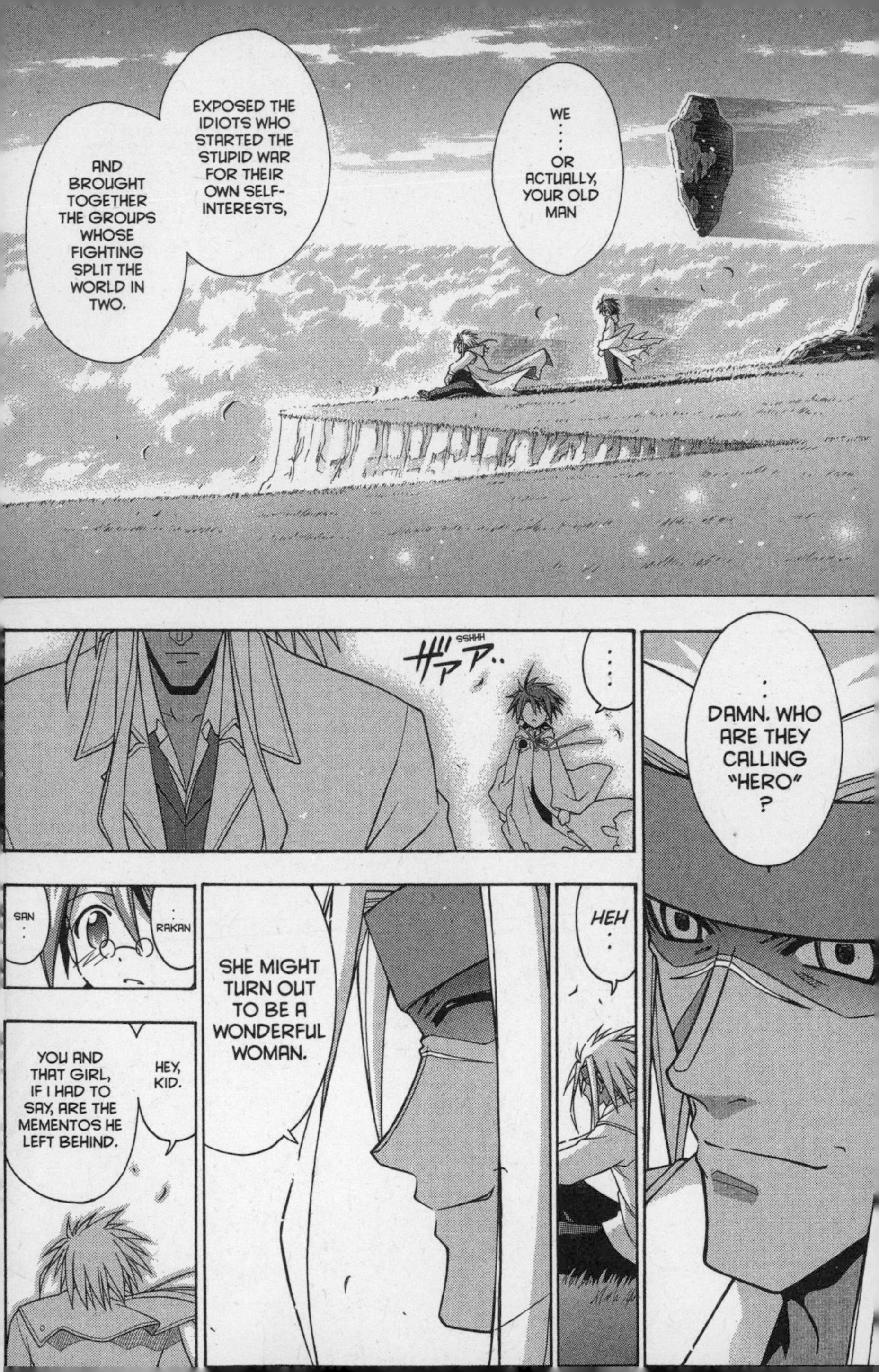
WE ...... OR ACTUALLY, YOUR OLD MAN
EXPOSED THE IDIOTS WHO STARTED THE STUPID WAR FOR THEIR OWN SELF-INTERESTS,
AND BROUGHT TOGETHER THE GROUPS WHOSE FIGHTING SPLIT THE WORLD IN TWO.
...... DAMN. WHO ARE THEY CALLING "HERO"?
ザァァ.. SSHHH
....
HEH ..
SHE MIGHT TURN OUT TO BE A WONDERFUL WOMAN.
.. RAKAN
SAN ..
HEY, KID.
YOU AND THAT GIRL, IF I HAD TO SAY, ARE THE MEMENTOS HE LEFT BEHIND.

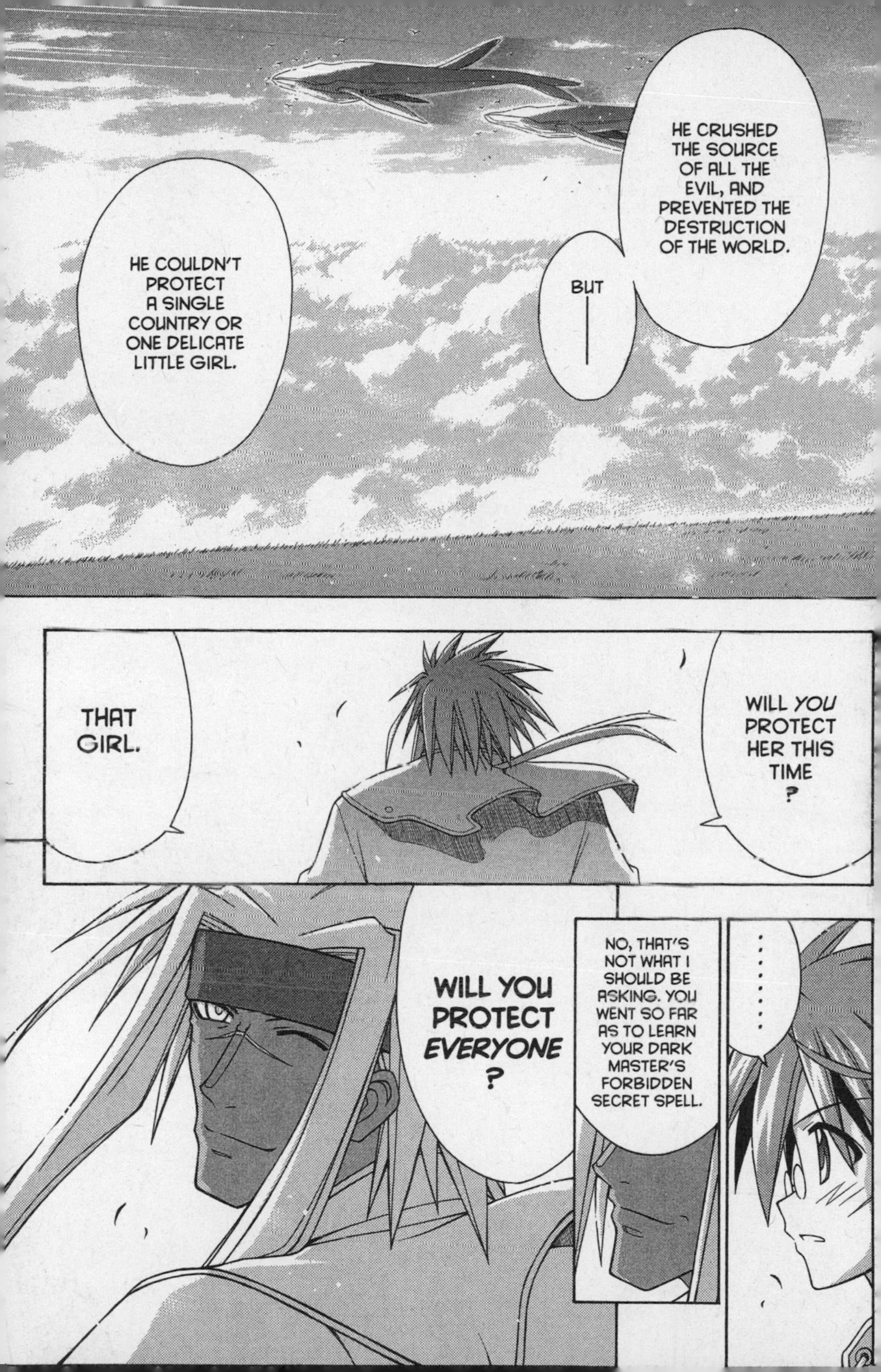
HE CRUSHED THE SOURCE OF ALL THE EVIL, AND PREVENTED THE DESTRUCTION OF THE WORLD.
BUT —
HE COULDN'T PROTECT A SINGLE COUNTRY OR ONE DELICATE LITTLE GIRL.
WILL *YOU* PROTECT HER THIS TIME?
THAT GIRL.
......
NO, THAT'S NOT WHAT I SHOULD BE ASKING. YOU WENT SO FAR AS TO LEARN YOUR DARK MASTER'S FORBIDDEN SECRET SPELL.
WILL YOU PROTECT *EVERYONE*?

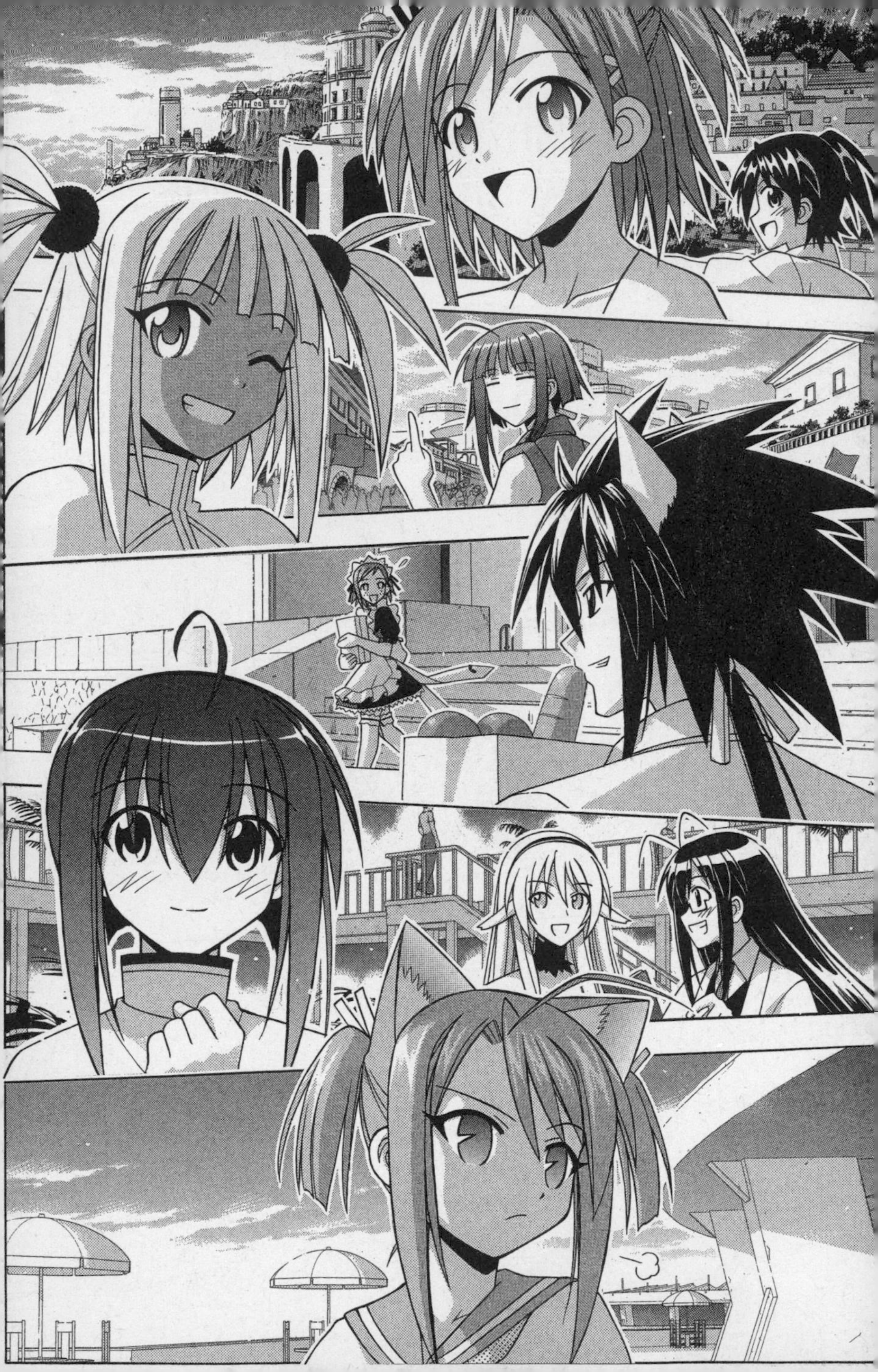

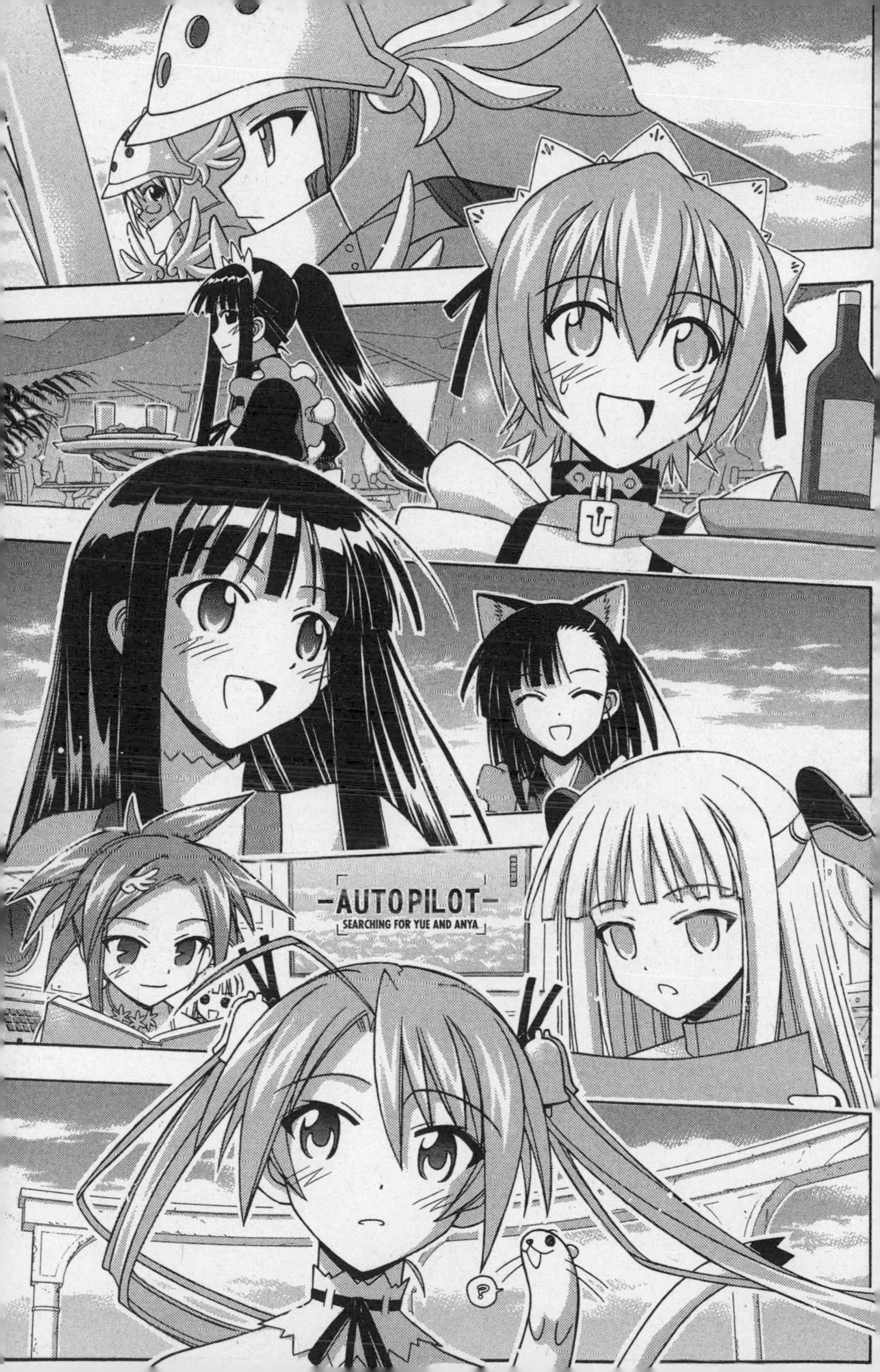

AUTOPILOT
SEARCHING FOR YUE AND ANYA
?

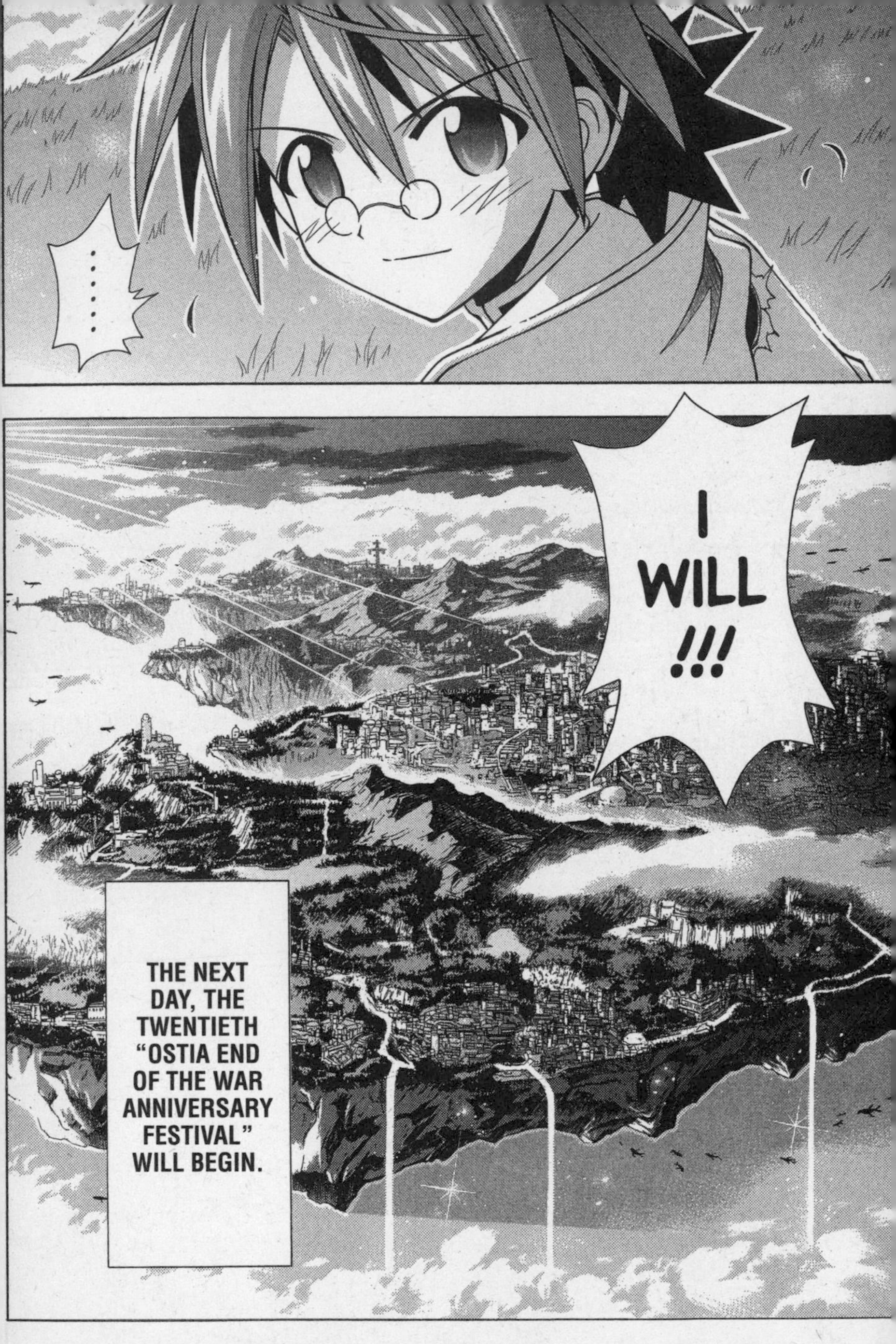
……
I WILL !!!
THE NEXT DAY, THE TWENTIETH "OSTIA END OF THE WAR ANNIVERSARY FESTIVAL" WILL BEGIN.

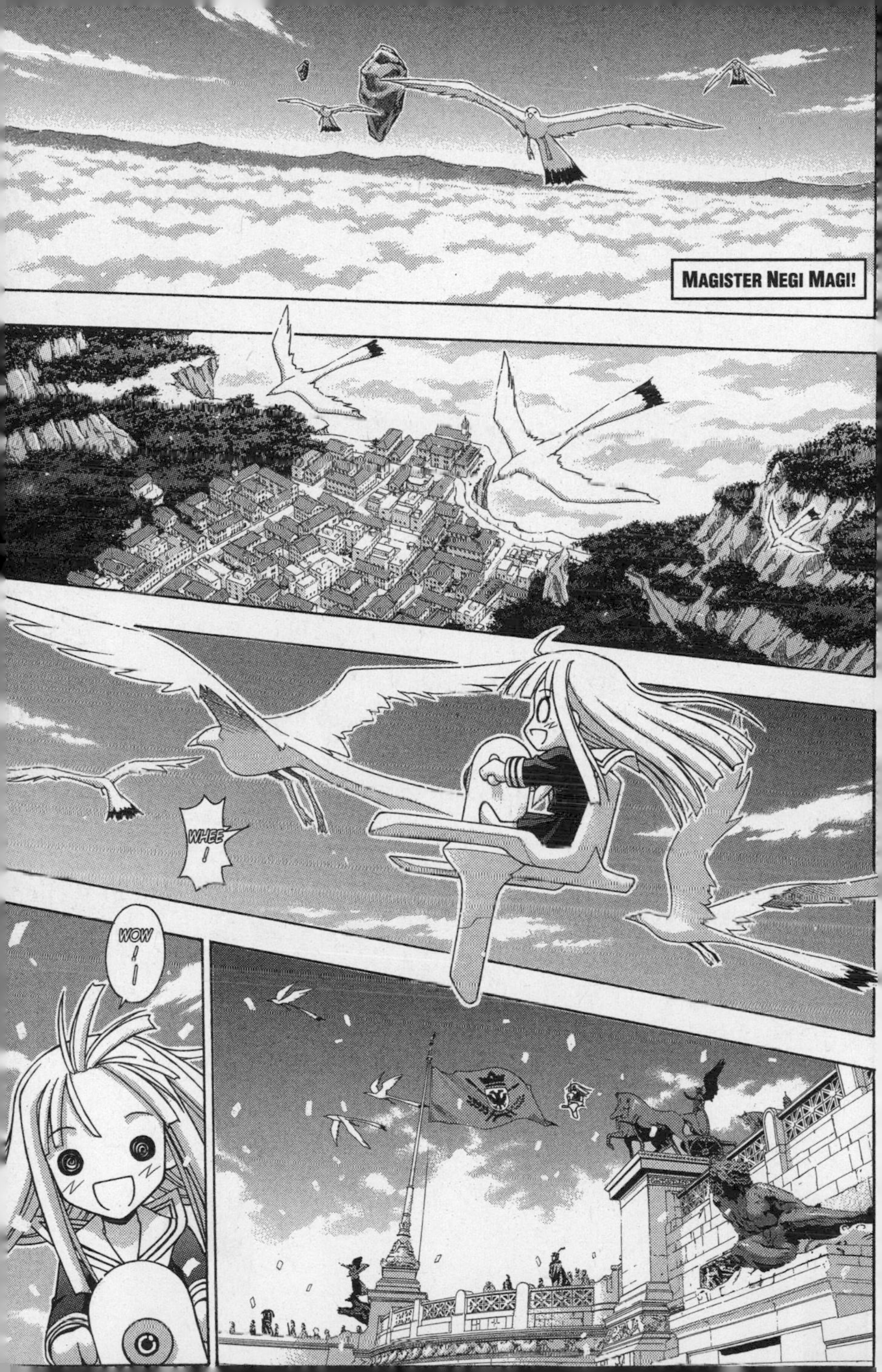
MAGISTER NEGI MAGI!
WHEE!
WOW!!

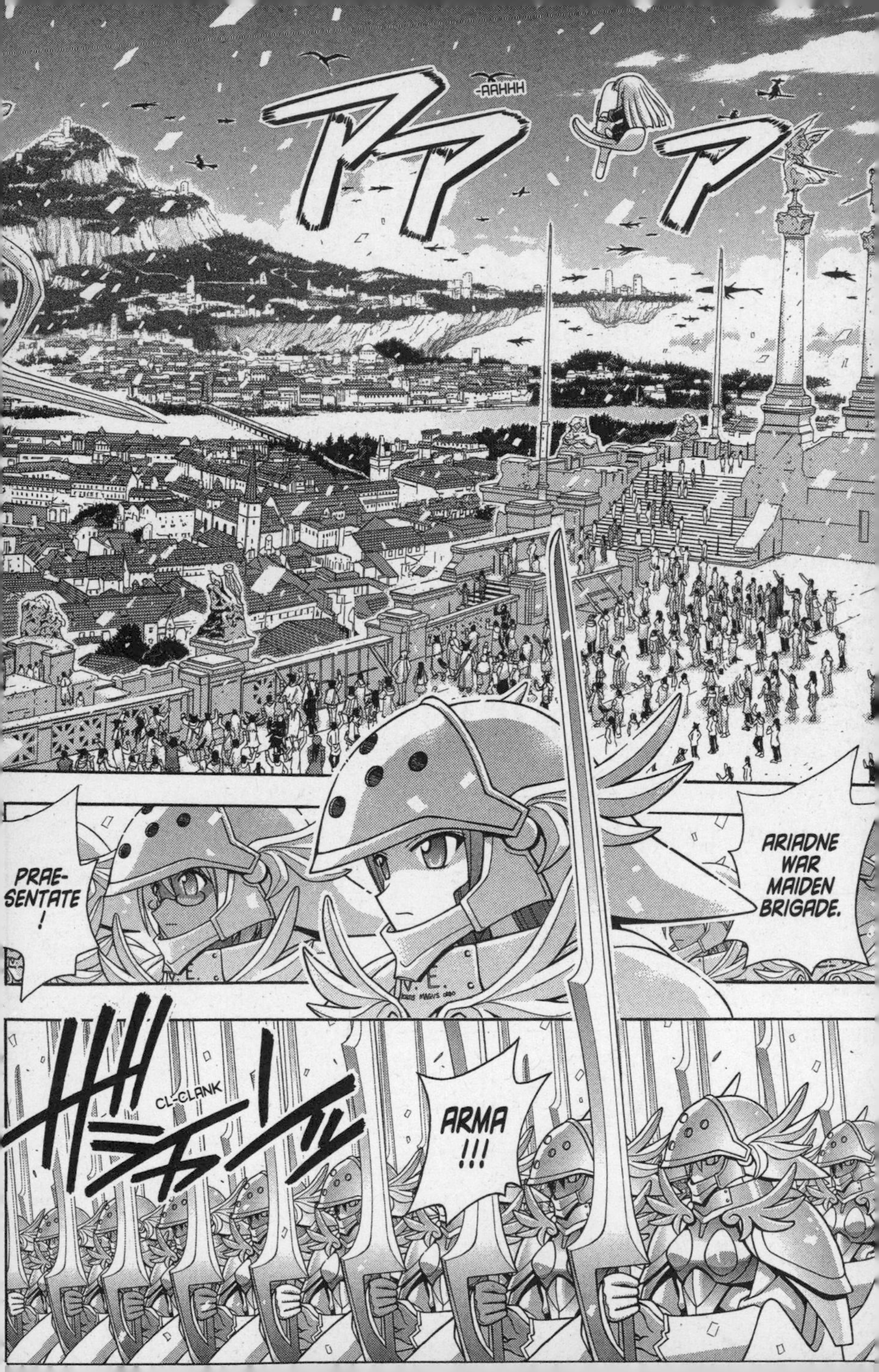

-AAHHH
ARIADNE WAR MAIDEN BRIGADE.
PRAE-SENTATE!
ARMA!!!
CL-CLANK

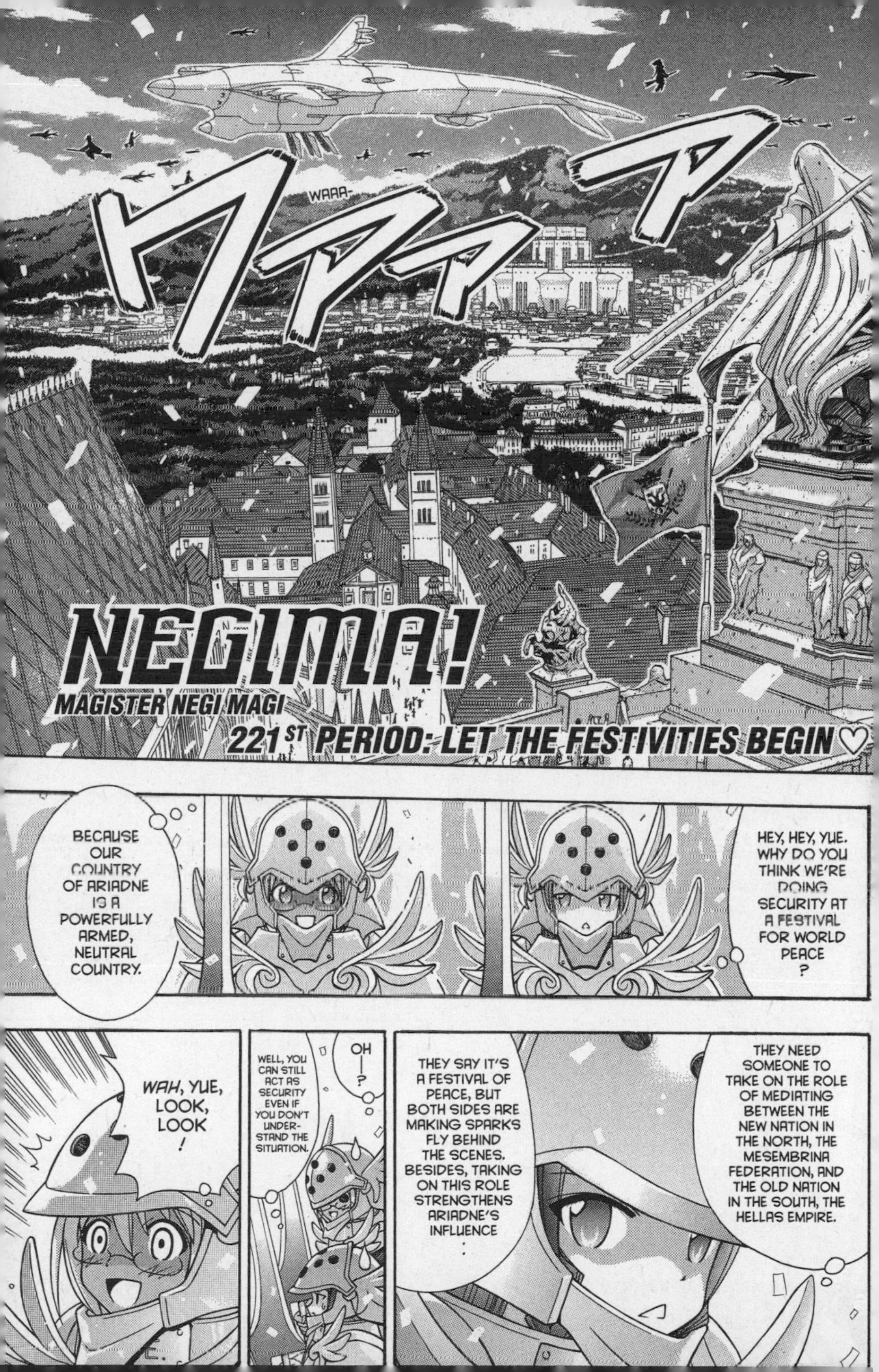
WAAA-
NEGIMA!
MAGISTER NEGI MAGI
221ST PERIOD: LET THE FESTIVITIES BEGIN ♡
HEY, HEY, YUE. WHY DO YOU THINK WE'RE DOING SECURITY AT A FESTIVAL FOR WORLD PEACE?
BECAUSE OUR COUNTRY OF ARIADNE IS A POWERFULLY ARMED, NEUTRAL COUNTRY.
THEY NEED SOMEONE TO TAKE ON THE ROLE OF MEDIATING BETWEEN THE NEW NATION IN THE NORTH, THE MESEMBRINA FEDERATION, AND THE OLD NATION IN THE SOUTH, THE HELLAS EMPIRE.
THEY SAY IT'S A FESTIVAL OF PEACE, BUT BOTH SIDES ARE MAKING SPARKS FLY BEHIND THE SCENES. BESIDES, TAKING ON THIS ROLE STRENGTHENS ARIADNE'S INFLUENCE...
OH—?
WELL, YOU CAN STILL ACT AS SECURITY EVEN IF YOU DON'T UNDERSTAND THE SITUATION.
WAH, YUE, LOOK, LOOK!

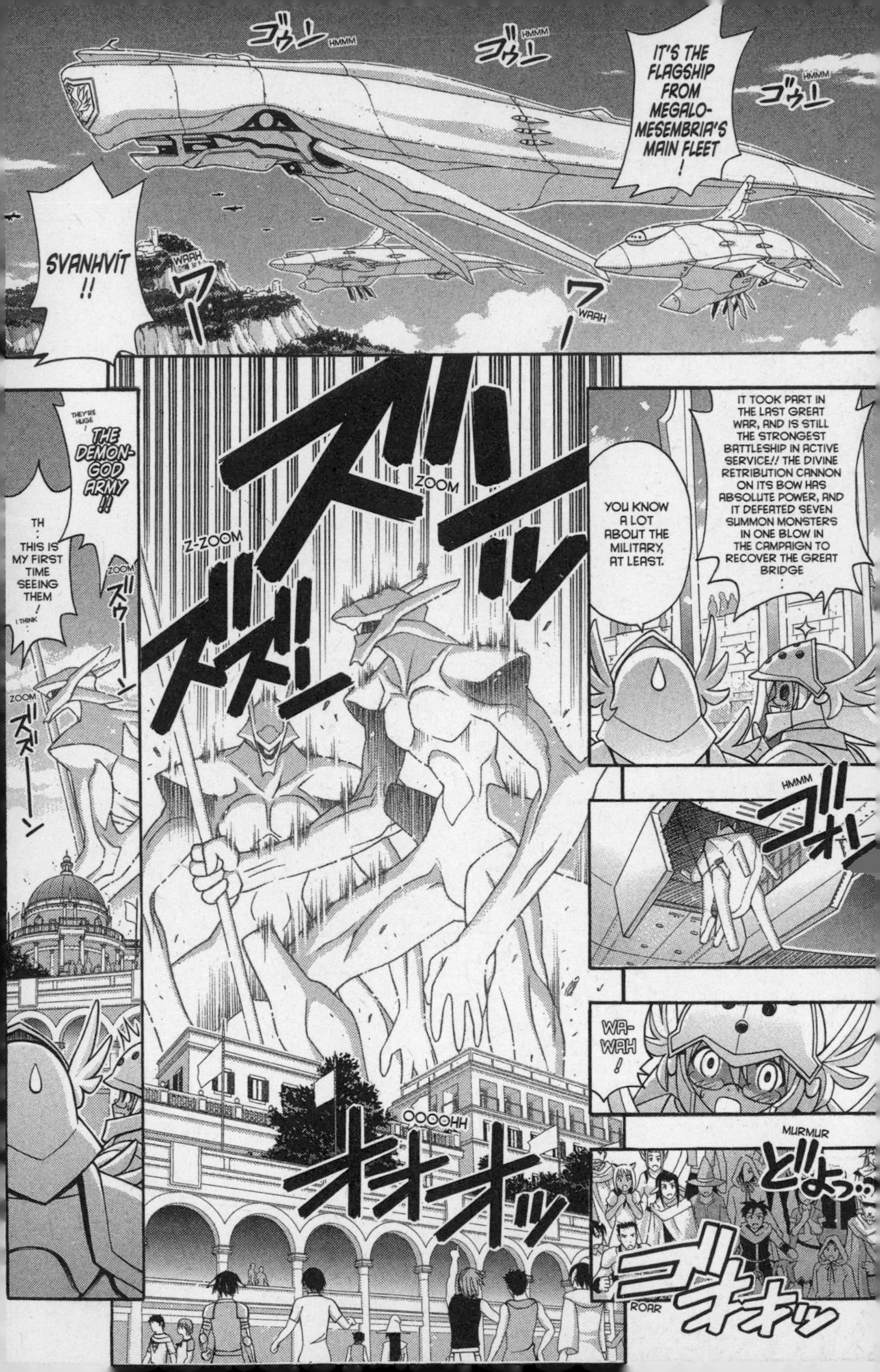
HMMM
HMMM
HMMM
IT'S THE FLAGSHIP FROM MEGALO-MESEMBRIA'S MAIN FLEET!
WAAH
WAAH
SVANHVÍT!!
IT TOOK PART IN THE LAST GREAT WAR, AND IS STILL THE STRONGEST BATTLESHIP IN ACTIVE SERVICE!! THE DIVINE RETRIBUTION CANNON ON ITS BOW HAS ABSOLUTE POWER, AND IT DEFEATED SEVEN SUMMON MONSTERS IN ONE BLOW IN THE CAMPAIGN TO RECOVER THE GREAT BRIDGE...
YOU KNOW A LOT ABOUT THE MILITARY, AT LEAST.
HMMM
WA-WAH!
MURMUR
ROAR
ZOOM
Z-ZOOM
OOOOHH
THEY'RE HUGE!
THE DEMON-GOD ARMY!!
TH... THIS IS MY FIRST TIME SEEING THEM! I THINK
ZOOM
ZOOM

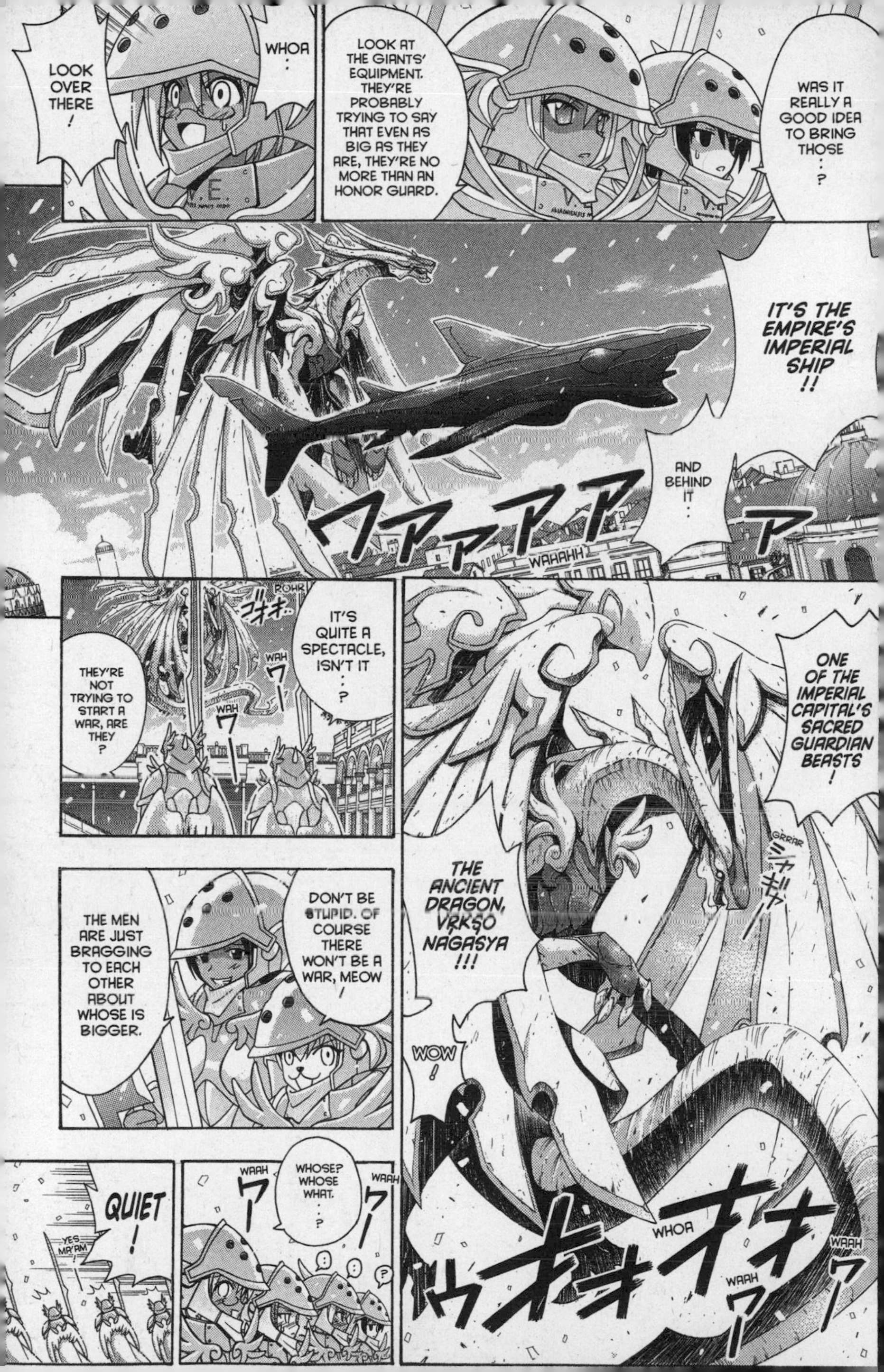
WAS IT REALLY A GOOD IDEA TO BRING THOSE...?
LOOK AT THE GIANTS' EQUIPMENT. THEY'RE PROBABLY TRYING TO SAY THAT EVEN AS BIG AS THEY ARE, THEY'RE NO MORE THAN AN HONOR GUARD.
WHOA...
LOOK OVER THERE!
IT'S THE EMPIRE'S IMPERIAL SHIP!!
AND BEHIND IT...
WAAAHH
ONE OF THE IMPERIAL CAPITAL'S SACRED GUARDIAN BEASTS!
GRRAR
THE ANCIENT DRAGON, VRKSO NAGASYA!!!
WOW!
WHOA
WAAH
WAAH
IT'S QUITE A SPECTACLE, ISN'T IT...?
ROHR
WAH
WAH
THEY'RE NOT TRYING TO START A WAR, ARE THEY?
DON'T BE STUPID. OF COURSE THERE WON'T BE A WAR, MEOW!
THE MEN ARE JUST BRAGGING TO EACH OTHER ABOUT WHOSE IS BIGGER.
WAAH
WHOSE? WHOSE WHAT...?
WAAH
QUIET!
YES MA'AM!

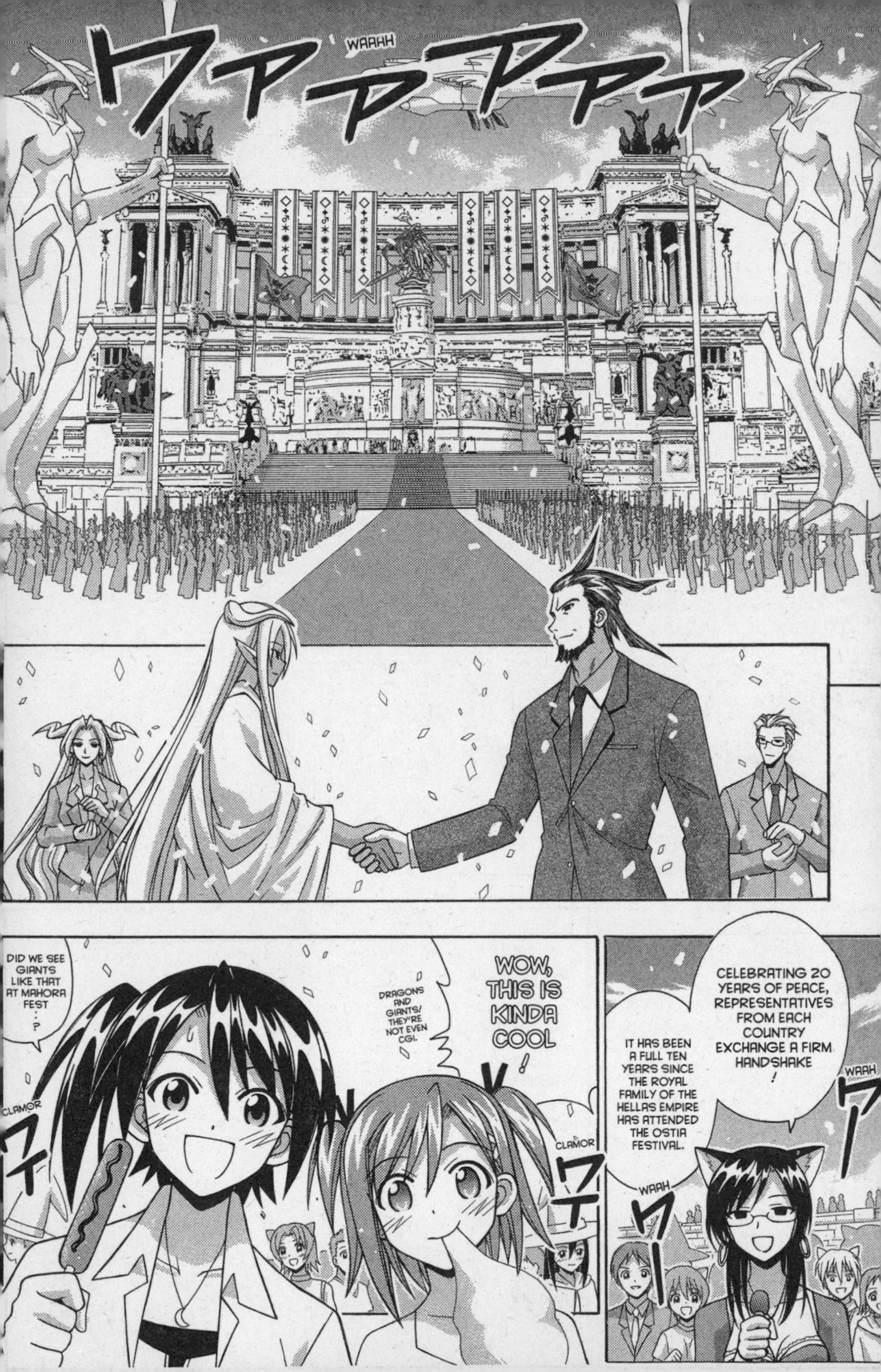

WAAHH
CELEBRATING 20 YEARS OF PEACE, REPRESENTATIVES FROM EACH COUNTRY EXCHANGE A FIRM HANDSHAKE!
WAAH
IT HAS BEEN A FULL TEN YEARS SINCE THE ROYAL FAMILY OF THE HELLAS EMPIRE HAS ATTENDED THE OSTIA FESTIVAL.
WAAH
WOW, THIS IS KINDA COOL!
DRAGONS AND GIANTS! THEY'RE NOT EVEN CGI.
CLAMOR
DID WE SEE GIANTS LIKE THAT AT MAHORA FEST...?
CLAMOR

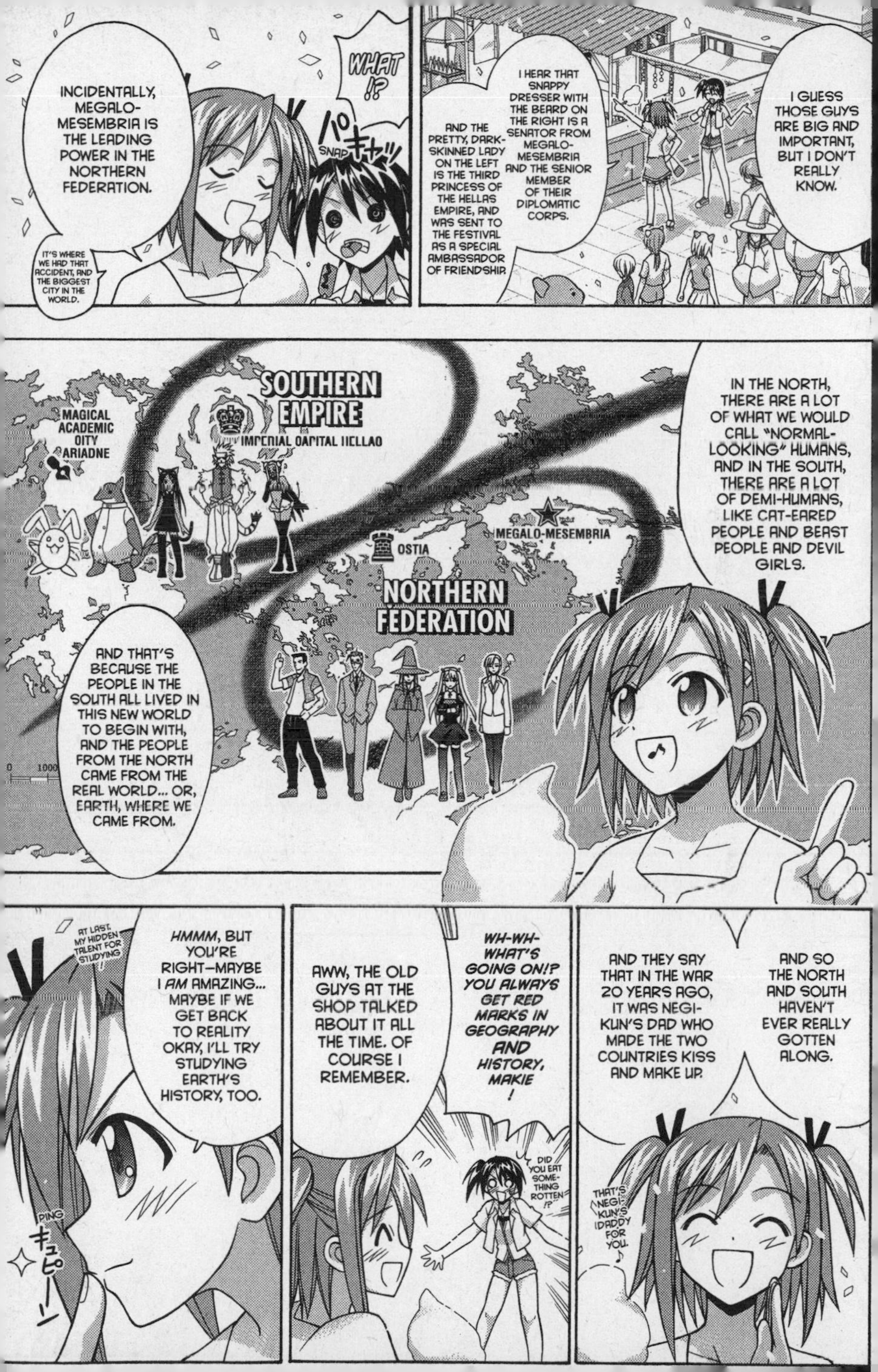
I GUESS THOSE GUYS ARE BIG AND IMPORTANT, BUT I DON'T REALLY KNOW.
I HEAR THAT SNAPPY DRESSER WITH THE BEARD ON THE RIGHT IS A SENATOR FROM MEGALO-MESEMBRIA AND THE SENIOR MEMBER OF THEIR DIPLOMATIC CORPS.
AND THE PRETTY, DARK-SKINNED LADY ON THE LEFT IS THE THIRD PRINCESS OF THE HELLAS EMPIRE, AND WAS SENT TO THE FESTIVAL AS A SPECIAL AMBASSADOR OF FRIENDSHIP.
WHAT!?
SNAP
INCIDENTALLY, MEGALO-MESEMBRIA IS THE LEADING POWER IN THE NORTHERN FEDERATION.
IT'S WHERE WE HAD THAT ACCIDENT, AND THE BIGGEST CITY IN THE WORLD.
IN THE NORTH, THERE ARE A LOT OF WHAT WE WOULD CALL "NORMAL-LOOKING" HUMANS, AND IN THE SOUTH, THERE ARE A LOT OF DEMI-HUMANS, LIKE CAT-EARED PEOPLE AND BEAST PEOPLE AND DEVIL GIRLS.
SOUTHERN EMPIRE
IMPERIAL CAPITAL HELLAS
MAGICAL ACADEMIC CITY ARIADNE
MEGALO-MESEMBRIA
OSTIA
NORTHERN FEDERATION
0
1000
AND THAT'S BECAUSE THE PEOPLE IN THE SOUTH ALL LIVED IN THIS NEW WORLD TO BEGIN WITH, AND THE PEOPLE FROM THE NORTH CAME FROM THE REAL WORLD... OR, EARTH, WHERE WE CAME FROM.
AND SO THE NORTH AND SOUTH HAVEN'T EVER REALLY GOTTEN ALONG.
AND THEY SAY THAT IN THE WAR 20 YEARS AGO, IT WAS NEGI-KUN'S DAD WHO MADE THE TWO COUNTRIES KISS AND MAKE UP.
THAT'S NEGI-KUN'S DADDY FOR YOU. ♪
WH-WH-WHAT'S GOING ON!? YOU ALWAYS GET RED MARKS IN GEOGRAPHY AND HISTORY, MAKIE!
AWW, THE OLD GUYS AT THE SHOP TALKED ABOUT IT ALL THE TIME. OF COURSE I REMEMBER.
DID YOU EAT SOMETHING ROTTEN!?
AT LAST, MY HIDDEN TALENT FOR STUDYING!
HMMM, BUT YOU'RE RIGHT—MAYBE I AM AMAZING... MAYBE IF WE GET BACK TO REALITY OKAY, I'LL TRY STUDYING EARTH'S HISTORY, TOO.
PING

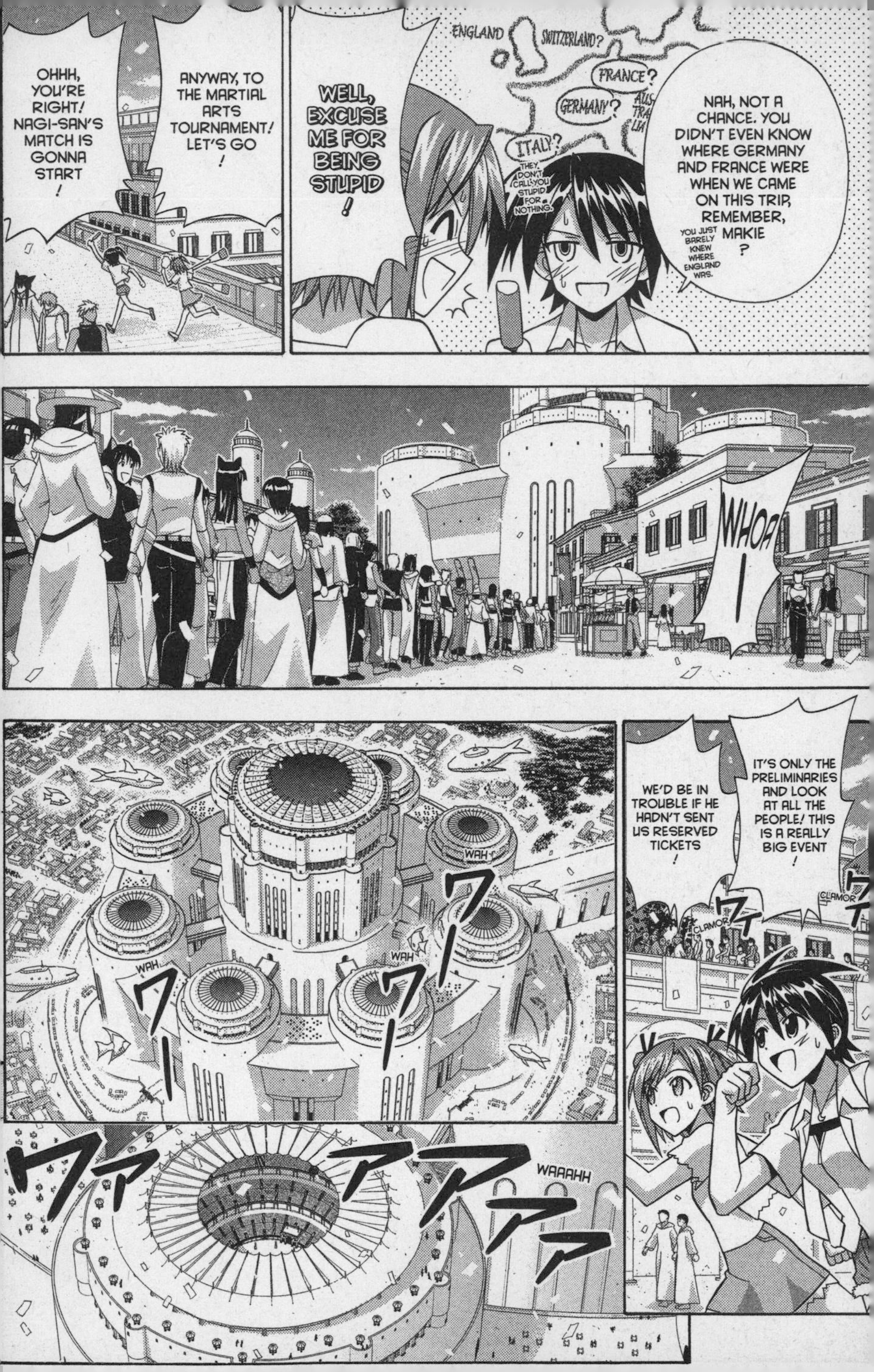
ENGLAND
SWITZERLAND?
FRANCE?
GERMANY?
AUSTRALIA
ITALY?
NAH, NOT A CHANCE. YOU DIDN'T EVEN KNOW WHERE GERMANY AND FRANCE WERE WHEN WE CAME ON THIS TRIP, REMEMBER, MAKIE?
YOU JUST BARELY KNEW WHERE ENGLAND WAS.
THEY DON'T CALL YOU STUPID FOR NOTHING.
WELL, EXCUSE ME FOR BEING STUPID!
ANYWAY, TO THE MARTIAL ARTS TOURNAMENT! LET'S GO!
OHHH, YOU'RE RIGHT! NAGI-SAN'S MATCH IS GONNA START!
WHOA!
IT'S ONLY THE PRELIMINARIES AND LOOK AT ALL THE PEOPLE! THIS IS A REALLY BIG EVENT!
WE'D BE IN TROUBLE IF HE HADN'T SENT US RESERVED TICKETS!
CLAMOR
CLAMOR
WAH
WAH
WAH
WAAAHH

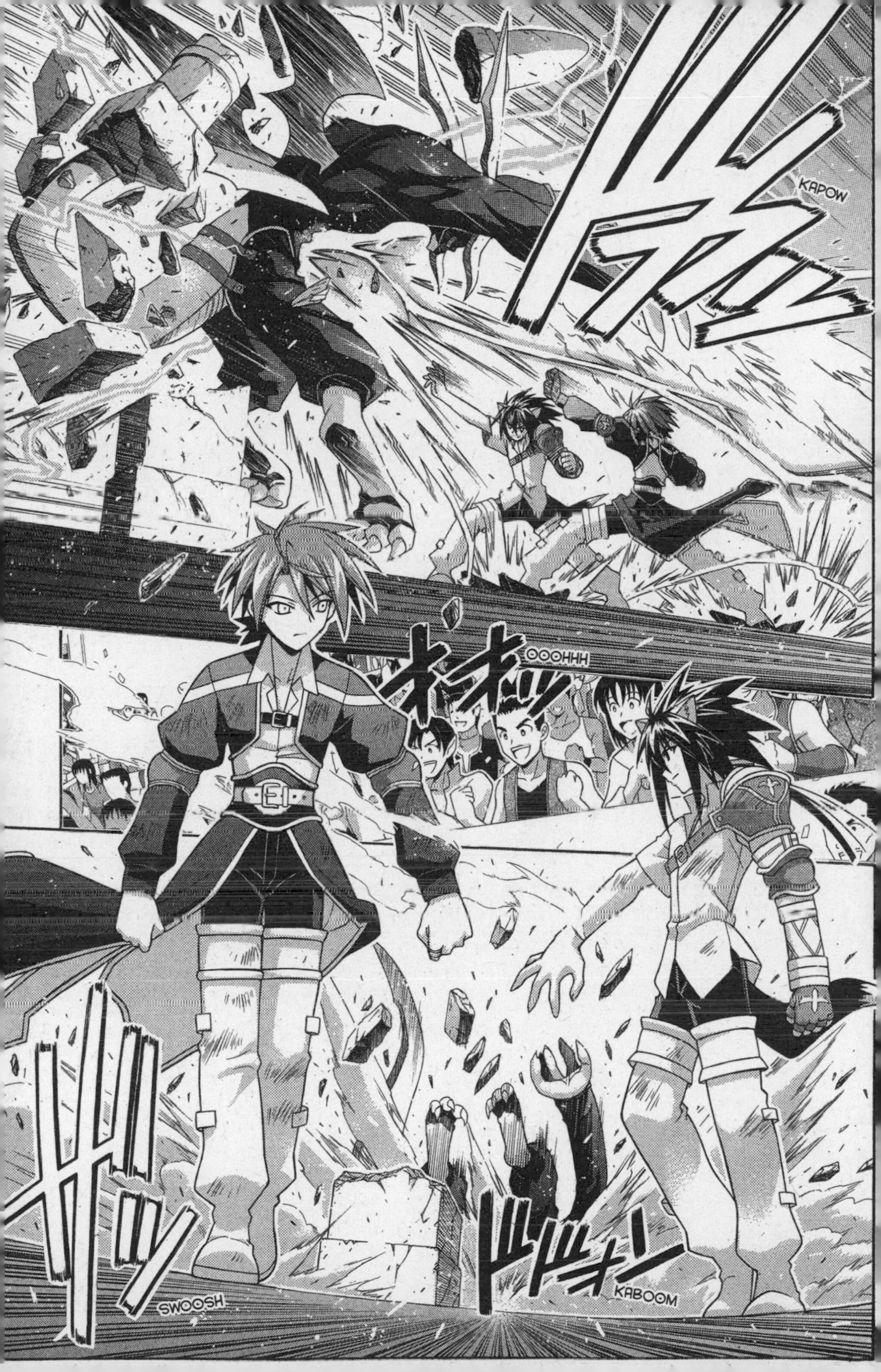
KAPOW
OOOHHH
KABOOM
SWOOSH

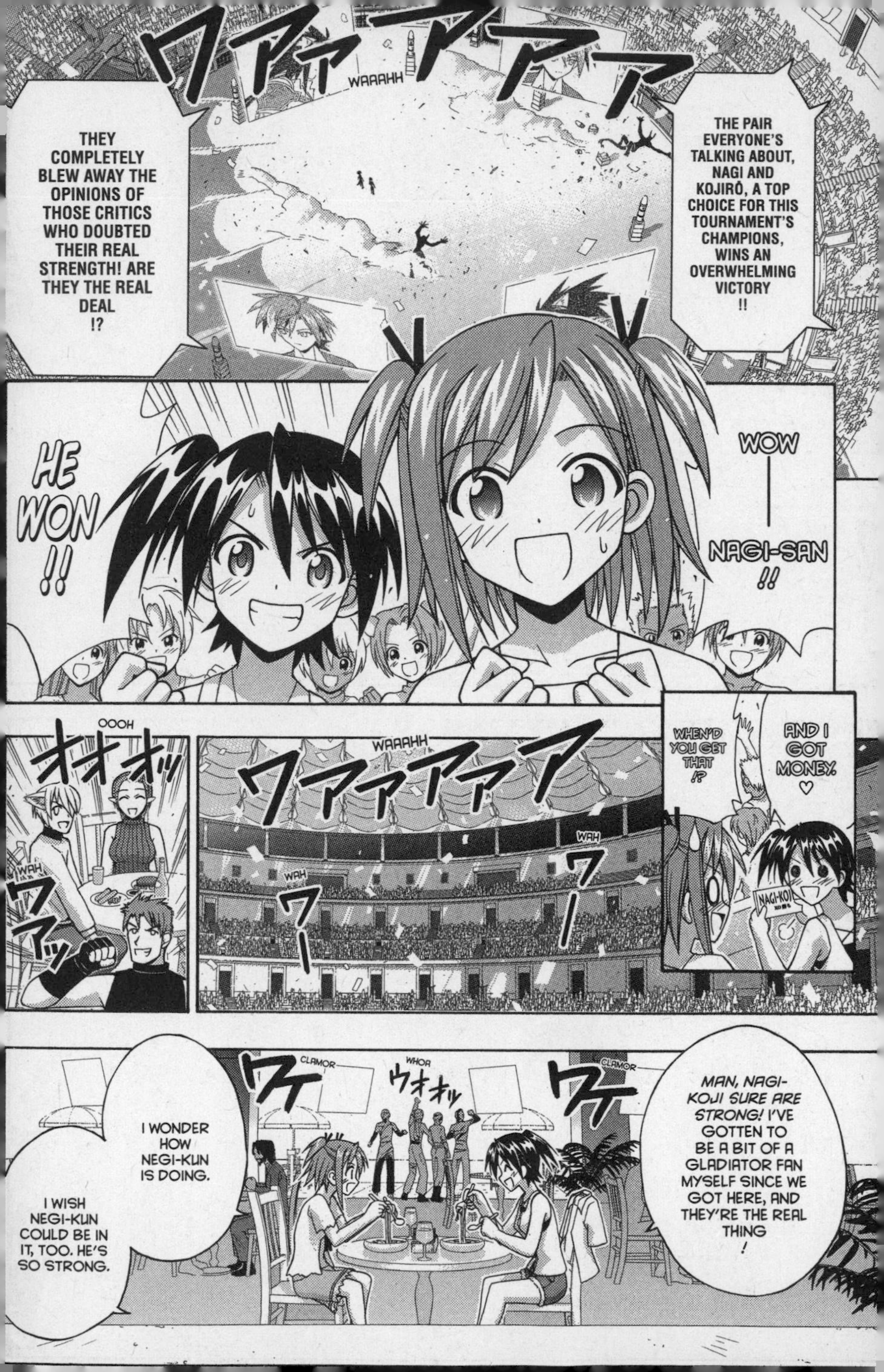
ワァァアアア
WAAAHH
THE PAIR EVERYONE'S TALKING ABOUT, NAGI AND KOJIRÔ, A TOP CHOICE FOR THIS TOURNAMENT'S CHAMPIONS, WINS AN OVERWHELMING VICTORY !!
THEY COMPLETELY BLEW AWAY THE OPINIONS OF THOSE CRITICS WHO DOUBTED THEIR REAL STRENGTH! ARE THEY THE REAL DEAL !?
WOW— NAGI-SAN !!
HE WON !!
AND I GOT MONEY. ♥
WHEN'D YOU GET THAT !?
WAAAHH
ワァァアァア
WAH
ワー
WAH
ワー
OOOH
オオオッ
WAH
ワァッ
CLAMOR
ワイ
WHOA
ウオオッ
CLAMOR
ワイ
MAN, NAGI-KOJI SURE ARE STRONG! I'VE GOTTEN TO BE A BIT OF A GLADIATOR FAN MYSELF SINCE WE GOT HERE, AND THEY'RE THE REAL THING !
I WONDER HOW NEGI-KUN IS DOING.
I WISH NEGI-KUN COULD BE IN IT, TOO. HE'S SO STRONG.

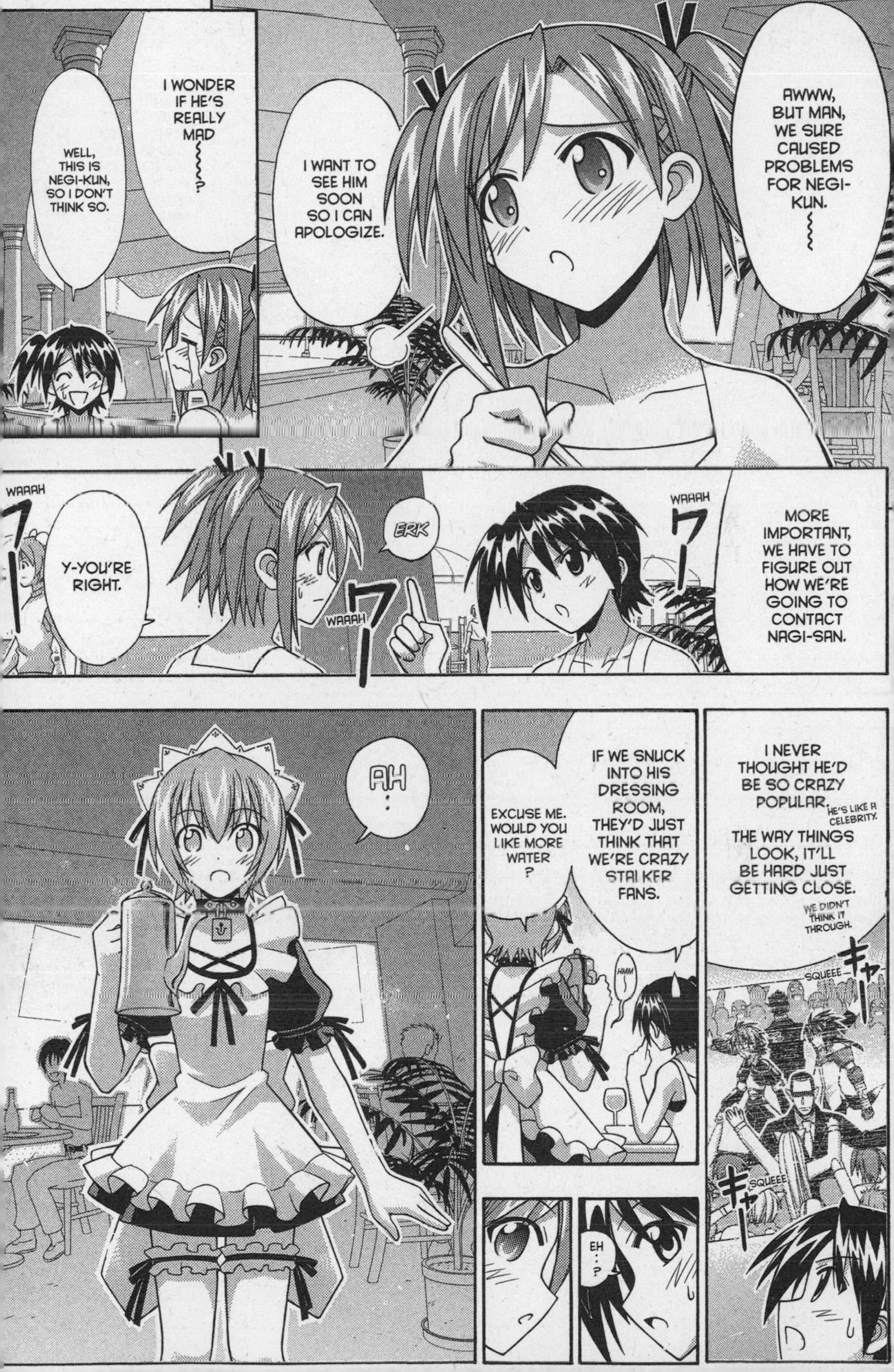
AWWW, BUT MAN, WE SURE CAUSED PROBLEMS FOR NEGI-KUN. ~~~
I WANT TO SEE HIM SOON SO I CAN APOLOGIZE.
I WONDER IF HE'S REALLY MAD ~~~?
WELL, THIS IS NEGI-KUN, SO I DON'T THINK SO.
MORE IMPORTANT, WE HAVE TO FIGURE OUT HOW WE'RE GOING TO CONTACT NAGI-SAN.
WAAAH
ERK
WAAAH
Y-YOU'RE RIGHT.
WAAAH
I NEVER THOUGHT HE'D BE SO CRAZY POPULAR.
HE'S LIKE A CELEBRITY.
THE WAY THINGS LOOK, IT'LL BE HARD JUST GETTING CLOSE.
WE DIDN'T THINK IT THROUGH.
SQUEEE
SQUEEE
IF WE SNUCK INTO HIS DRESSING ROOM, THEY'D JUST THINK THAT WE'RE CRAZY STALKER FANS.
EXCUSE ME. WOULD YOU LIKE MORE WATER?
HMM
EH...?
AH...

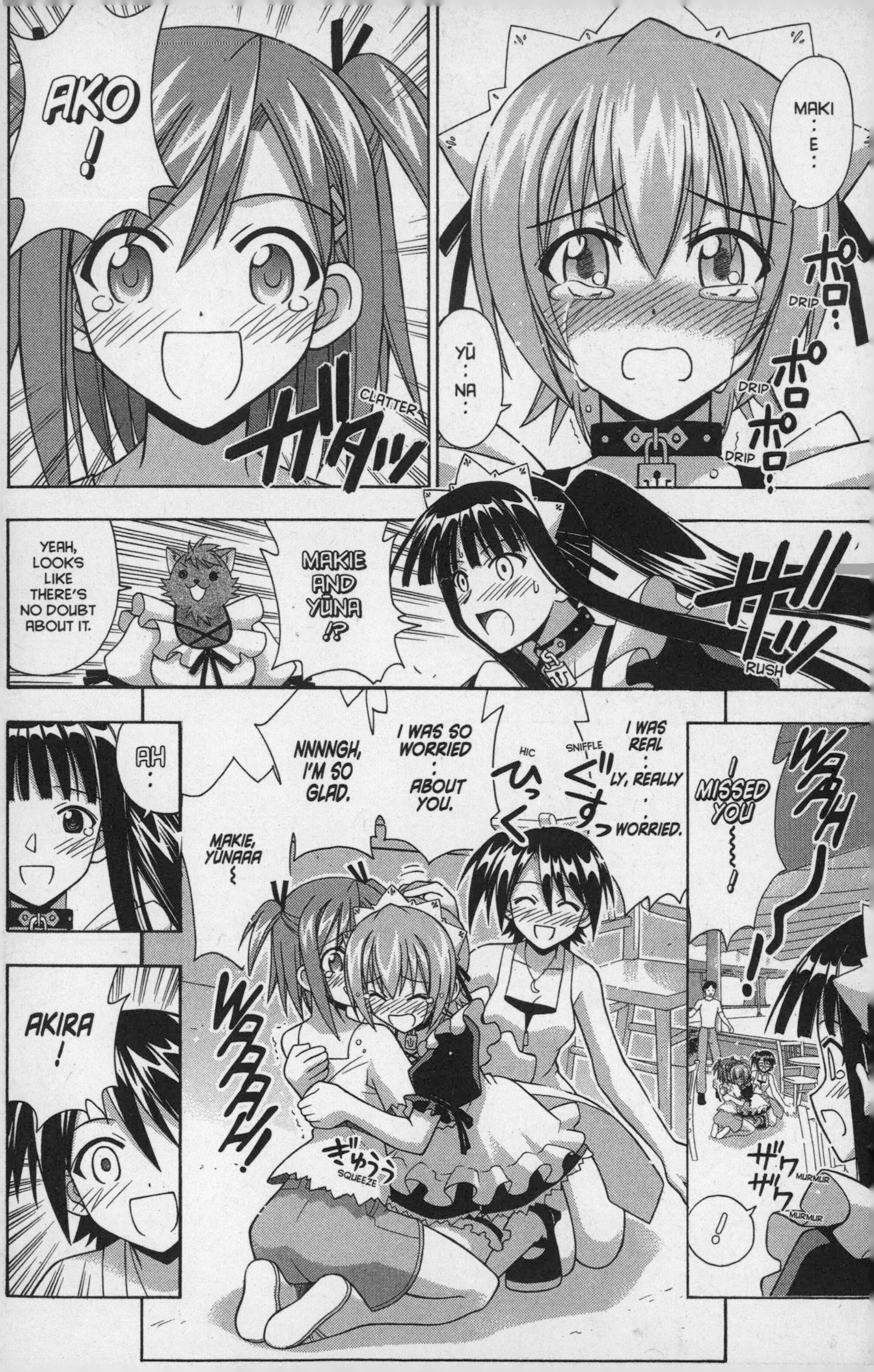
MAKI...E...
YŪ...NA...
DRIP
DRIP
DRIP
AKO!
CLATTER
RUSH
MAKIE AND YŪNA!?
YEAH, LOOKS LIKE THERE'S NO DOUBT ABOUT IT.
WAAH~~!
I MISSED YOU~~!
MURMUR
MURMUR
!
I WAS REAL...LY, REALLY...WORRIED.
SNIFFLE
HIC
I WAS SO WORRIED...ABOUT YOU.
NNNNGH, I'M SO GLAD.
MAKIE, YŪNAAA~
WAAAH!
SQUEEZE
AH...
AKIRA!

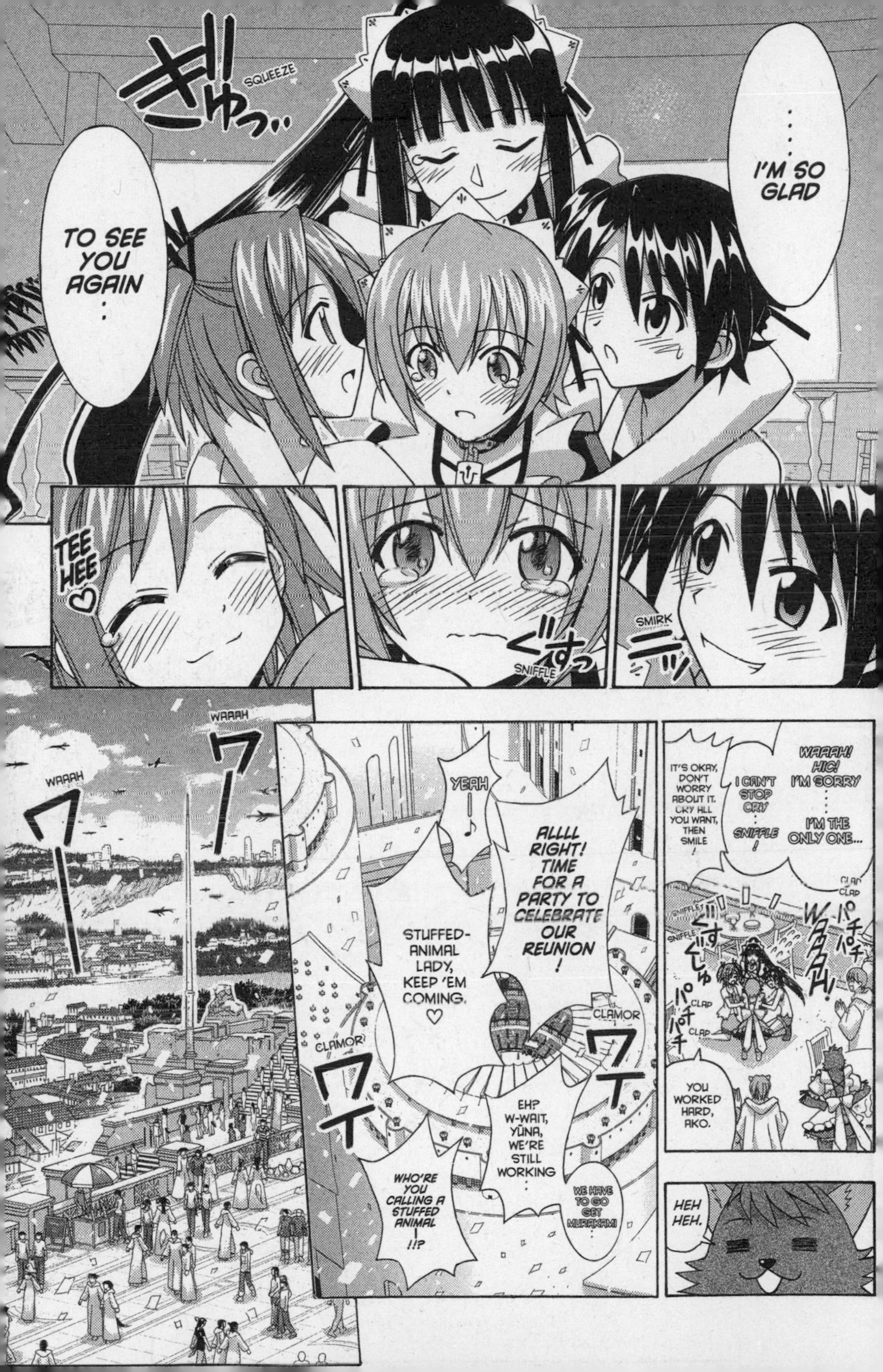

... I'M SO GLAD
SQUEEZE
TO SEE YOU AGAIN ...
SMIRK
SNIFFLE
TEE HEE ♡
WAAAH! HIC! I'M SORRY ... I'M THE ONLY ONE...
I CAN'T STOP CRY... SNIFFLE!
IT'S OKAY, DON'T WORRY ABOUT IT. CRY ALL YOU WANT, THEN SMILE!
CLAP CLAP
SNIFFLE
SNIFFLE
CLAP CLAP
YOU WORKED HARD, AKO.
HEH HEH.
ALLLL RIGHT! TIME FOR A PARTY TO CELEBRATE OUR REUNION!
YEAH!♪
STUFFED-ANIMAL LADY, KEEP 'EM COMING. ♡
CLAMOR
EH? W-WAIT, YŪNA, WE'RE STILL WORKING...
WE HAVE TO GO GET MURAKAMI...
WHO'RE YOU CALLING A STUFFED ANIMAL!!?
CLAMOR
WAAAH
WAAAH

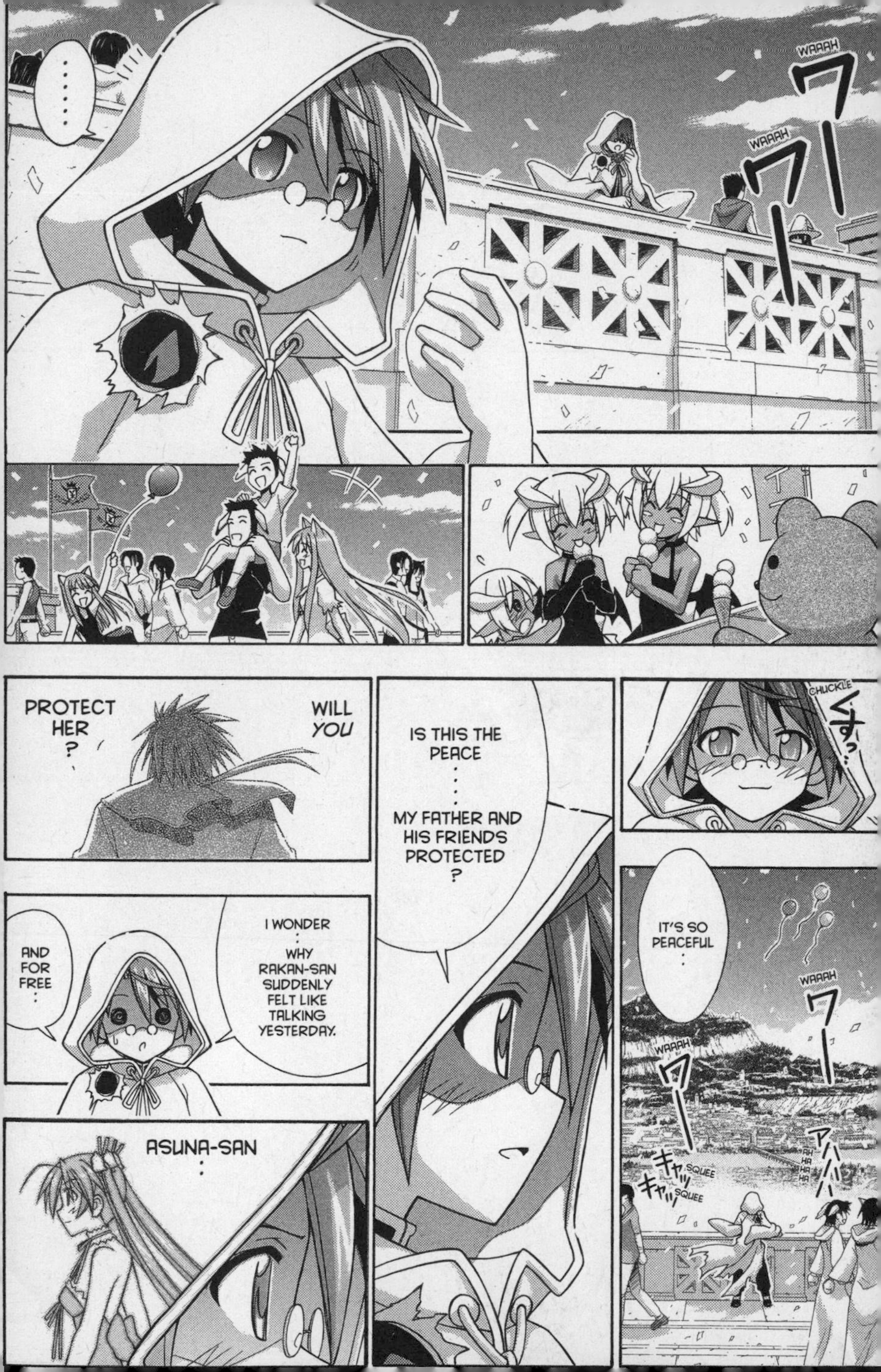
ワー WAAAH
ワー WAAAH
……
くすっ CHUCKLE
IT'S SO PEACEFUL…
ワー WAAAH
ワー WAAAH
アハハハ AH HA HA HA
キャッ SQUEE
キャッ SQUEE
IS THIS THE PEACE… MY FATHER AND HIS FRIENDS PROTECTED?
WILL YOU PROTECT HER?
I WONDER: WHY RAKAN-SAN SUDDENLY FELT LIKE TALKING YESTERDAY.
AND FOR FREE…
ASUNA-SAN…

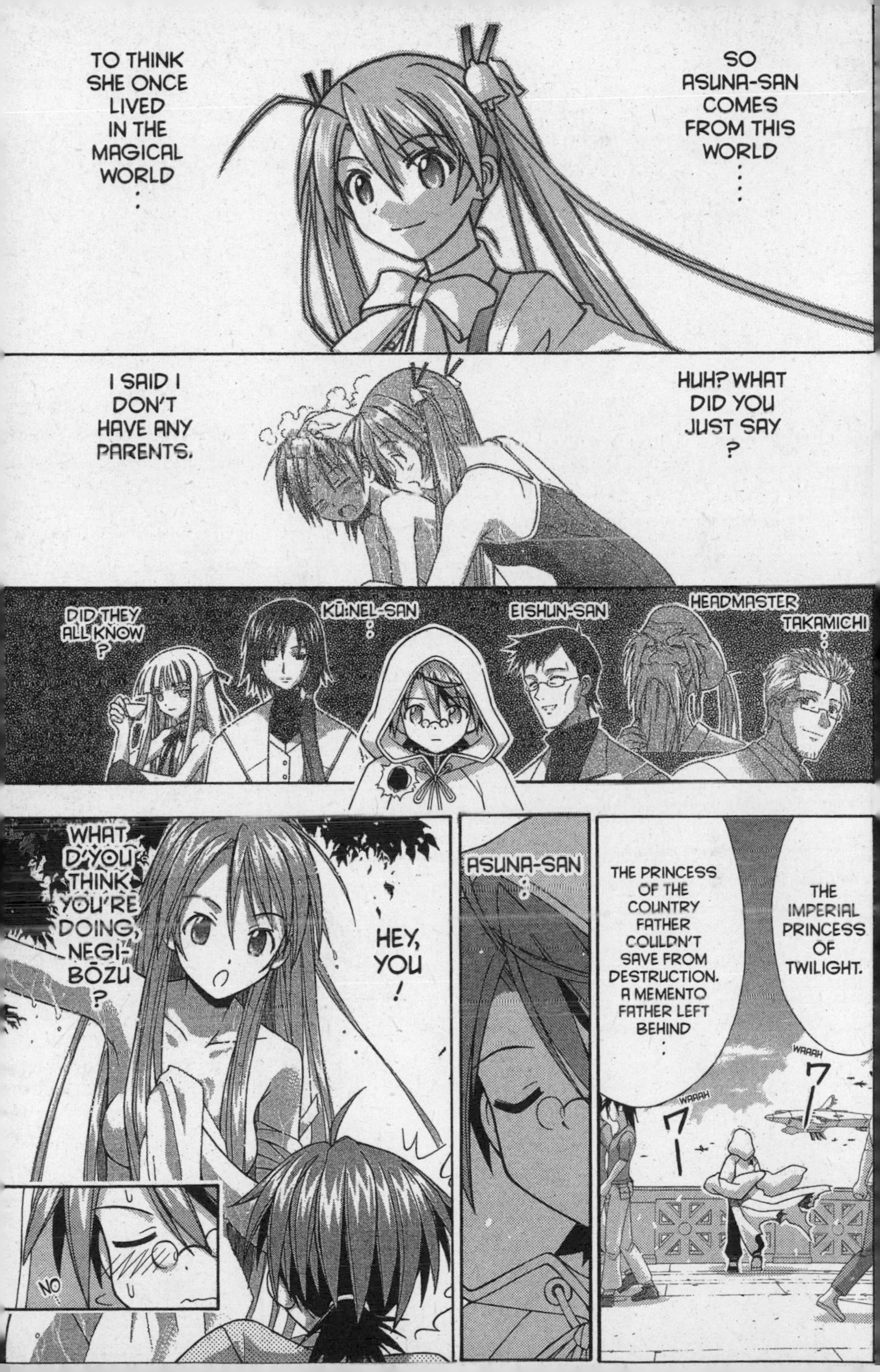
SO ASUNA-SAN COMES FROM THIS WORLD ....?
TO THINK SHE ONCE LIVED IN THE MAGICAL WORLD ...
HUH? WHAT DID YOU JUST SAY?
I SAID I DON'T HAVE ANY PARENTS.
TAKAMICHI ...
HEADMASTER
EISHUN-SAN
KŪNEL-SAN ...
DID THEY ALL KNOW?
THE IMPERIAL PRINCESS OF TWILIGHT.
THE PRINCESS OF THE COUNTRY FATHER COULDN'T SAVE FROM DESTRUCTION. A MEMENTO FATHER LEFT BEHIND ...
WAAAH
WAAAH
ASUNA-SAN ...
HEY, YOU!
WHAT D'YOU THINK YOU'RE DOING, NEGI-BŌZU?
NO

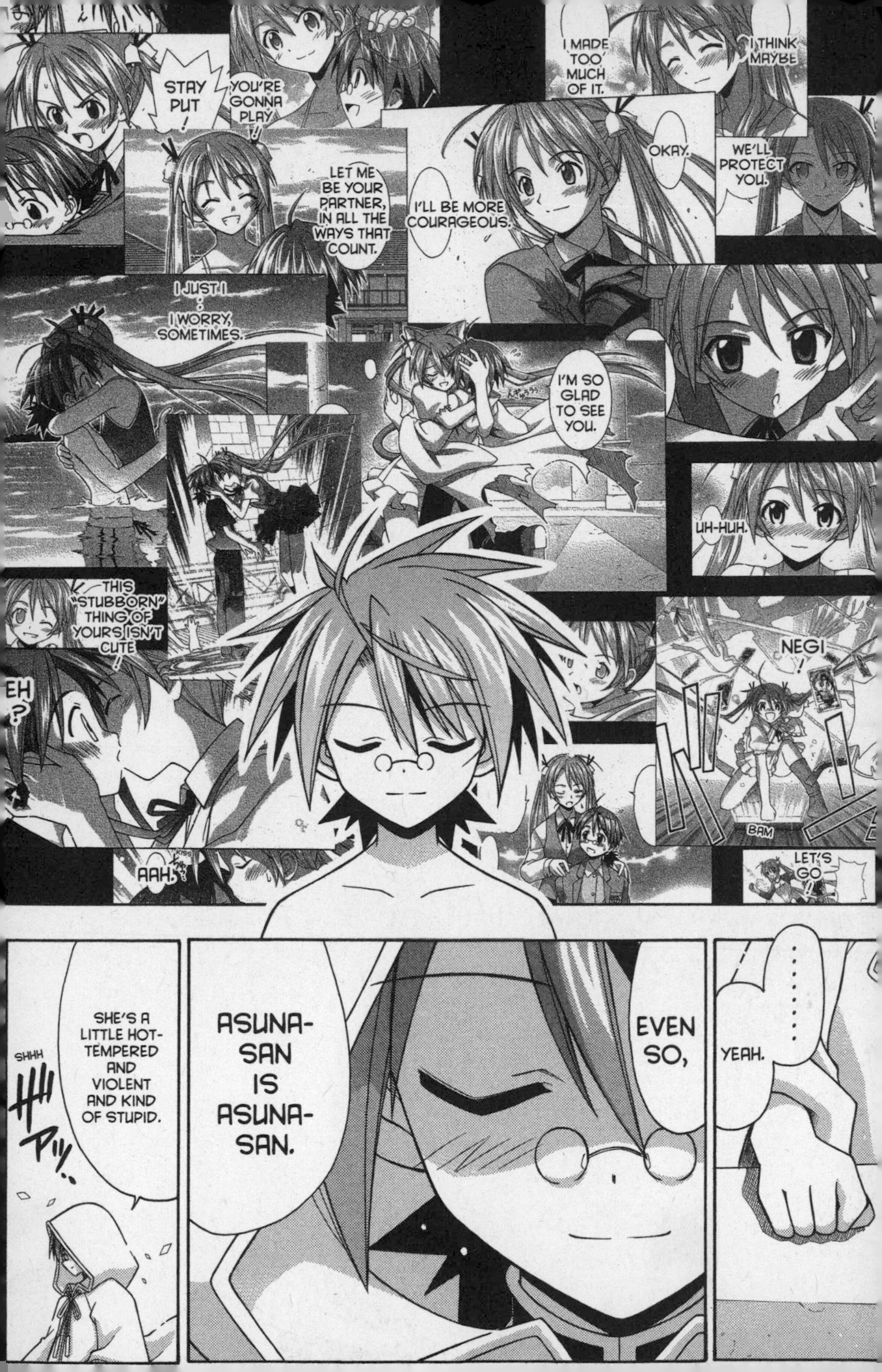

I THINK MAYBE
I MADE TOO MUCH OF IT.
YOU'RE GONNA PLAY!
STAY PUT!
WE'LL PROTECT YOU.
OKAY.
I'LL BE MORE COURAGEOUS.
LET ME BE YOUR PARTNER, IN ALL THE WAYS THAT COUNT.
I'M SO GLAD TO SEE YOU.
I JUST I... I WORRY, SOMETIMES.
UH-HUH.
NEGI!
BAM
THIS "STUBBORN" THING OF YOURS ISN'T CUTE!
EH?
LET'S GO!
KISS
AAH.
......
YEAH.
EVEN SO,
ASUNA-SAN IS ASUNA-SAN.
SHE'S A LITTLE HOT-TEMPERED AND VIOLENT AND KIND OF STUPID.
SHHH

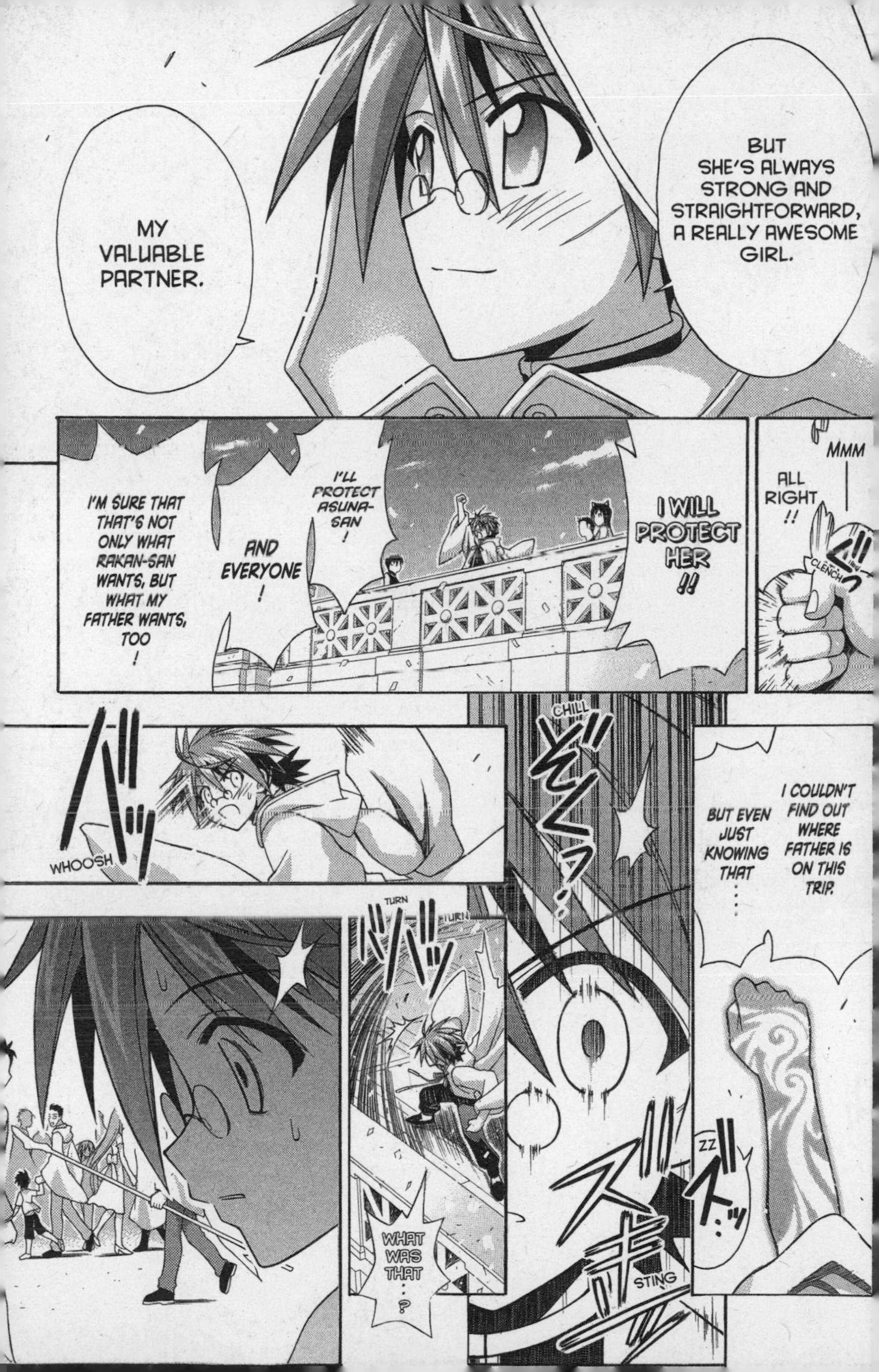
BUT SHE'S ALWAYS STRONG AND STRAIGHTFORWARD, A REALLY AWESOME GIRL.
MY VALUABLE PARTNER.
MMM
ALL RIGHT !!
CLENCH
I WILL PROTECT HER !!
I'LL PROTECT ASUNA-SAN !
AND EVERYONE !
I'M SURE THAT THAT'S NOT ONLY WHAT RAKAN-SAN WANTS, BUT WHAT MY FATHER WANTS, TOO !
I COULDN'T FIND OUT WHERE FATHER IS ON THIS TRIP.
BUT EVEN JUST KNOWING THAT ...
ZZ
STING
CHILL
WHOOSH
TURN
TURN
WHAT WAS THAT ...?

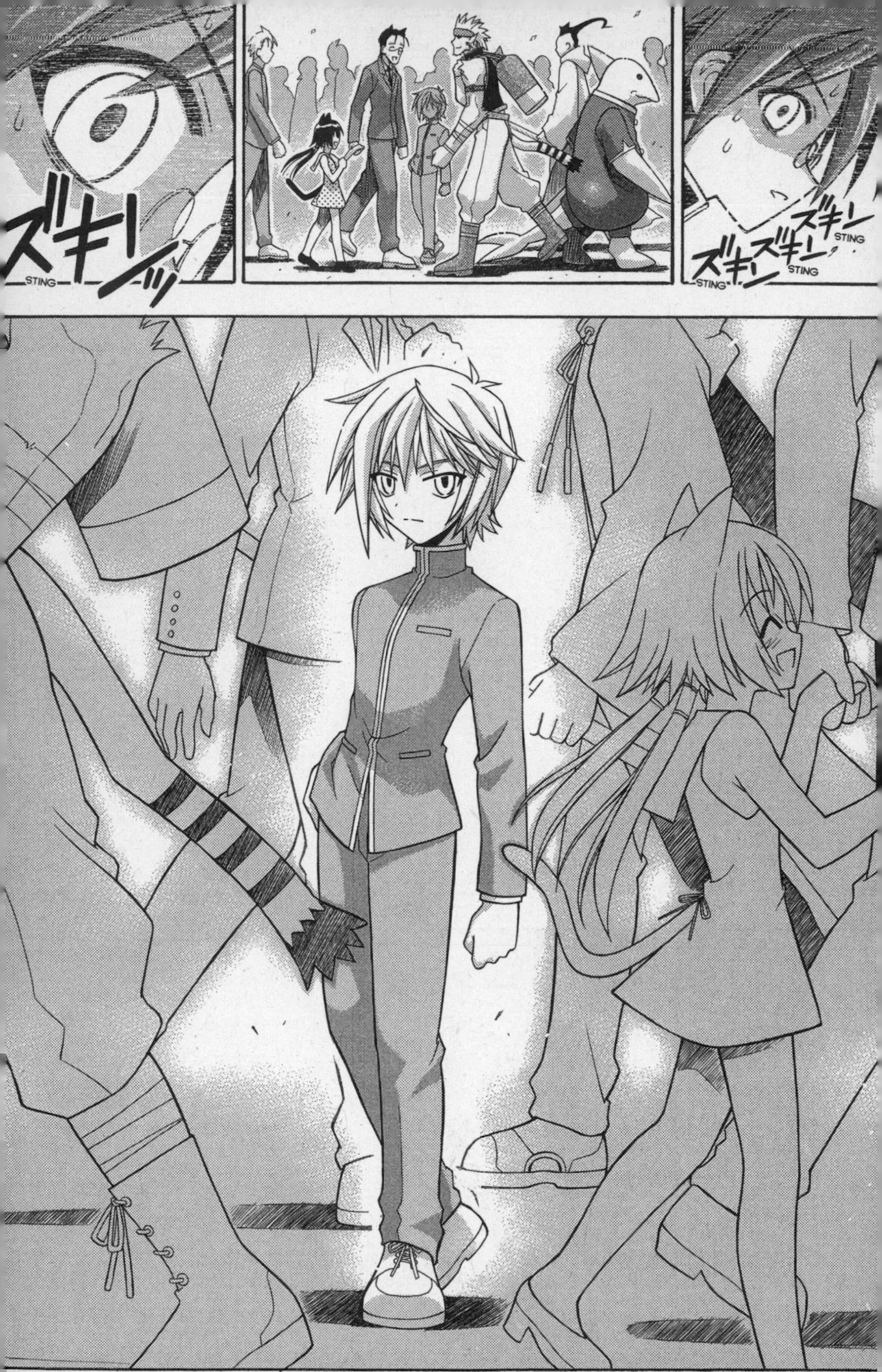
ズキン
STING
ズキン
STING
ズキン
STING
ズキンッ
STING

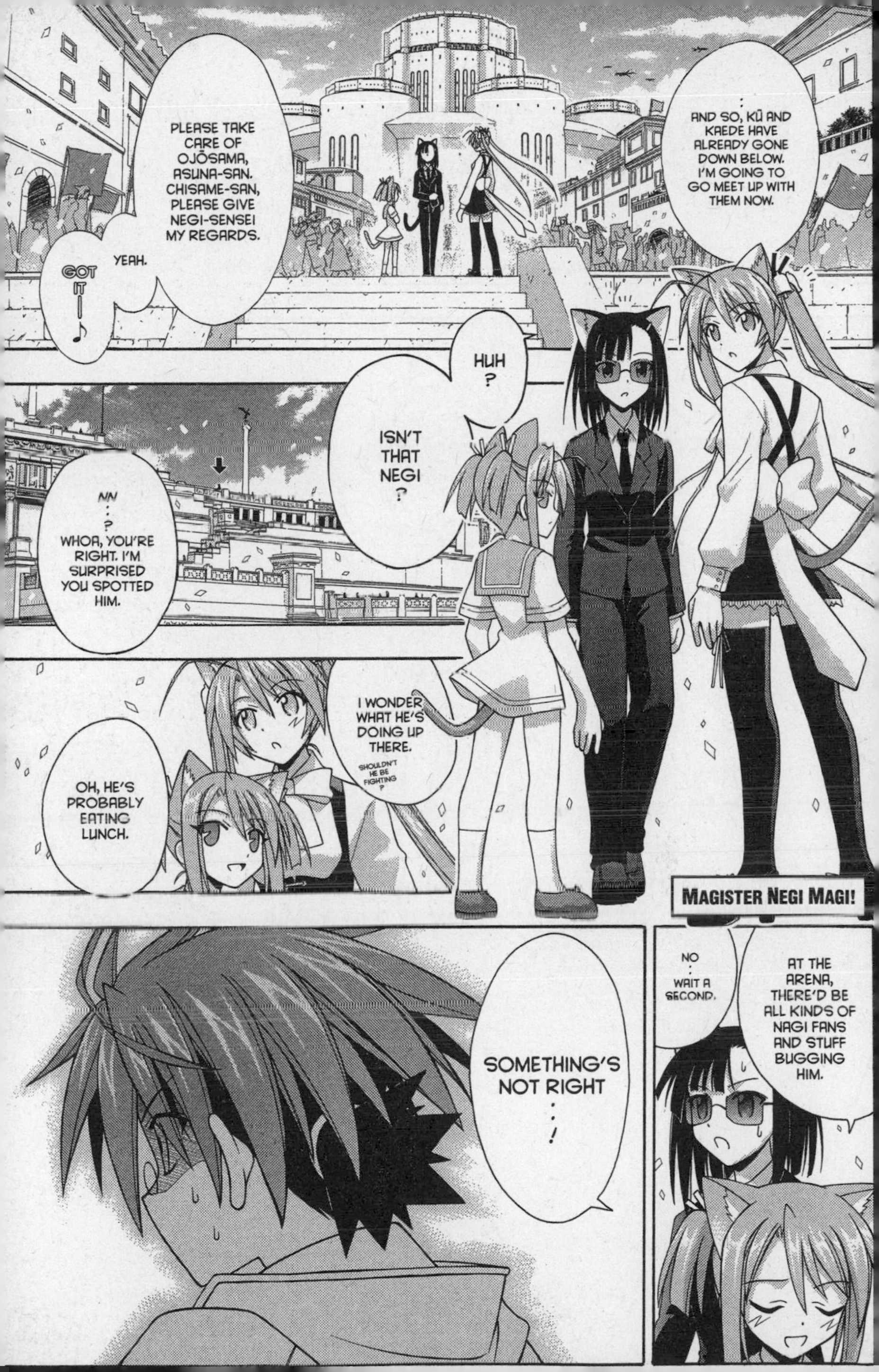

. . AND SO, KŪ AND KAEDE HAVE ALREADY GONE DOWN BELOW. I'M GOING TO GO MEET UP WITH THEM NOW.
PLEASE TAKE CARE OF OJŌSAMA, ASUNA-SAN. CHISAME-SAN, PLEASE GIVE NEGI-SENSEI MY REGARDS.
YEAH.
GOT IT—♪
HUH?
ISN'T THAT NEGI?
NN...? WHOA, YOU'RE RIGHT. I'M SURPRISED YOU SPOTTED HIM.
I WONDER WHAT HE'S DOING UP THERE.
SHOULDN'T HE BE FIGHTING?
OH, HE'S PROBABLY EATING LUNCH.
MAGISTER NEGI MAGI!
AT THE ARENA, THERE'D BE ALL KINDS OF NAGI FANS AND STUFF BUGGING HIM.
NO : WAIT A SECOND.
SOMETHING'S NOT RIGHT . . !

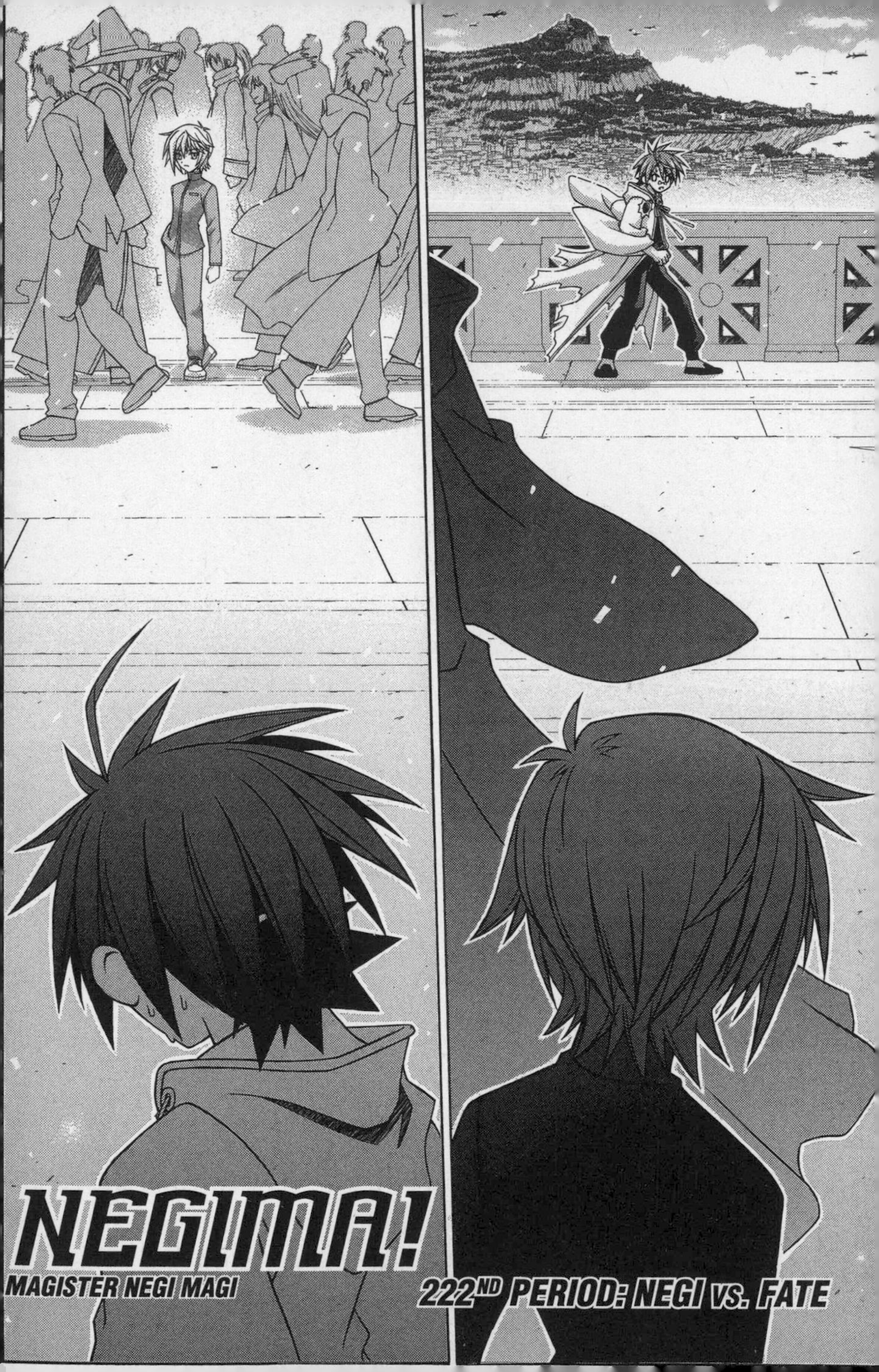
NEGIMA!
MAGISTER NEGI MAGI
222ND PERIOD: NEGI vs. FATE

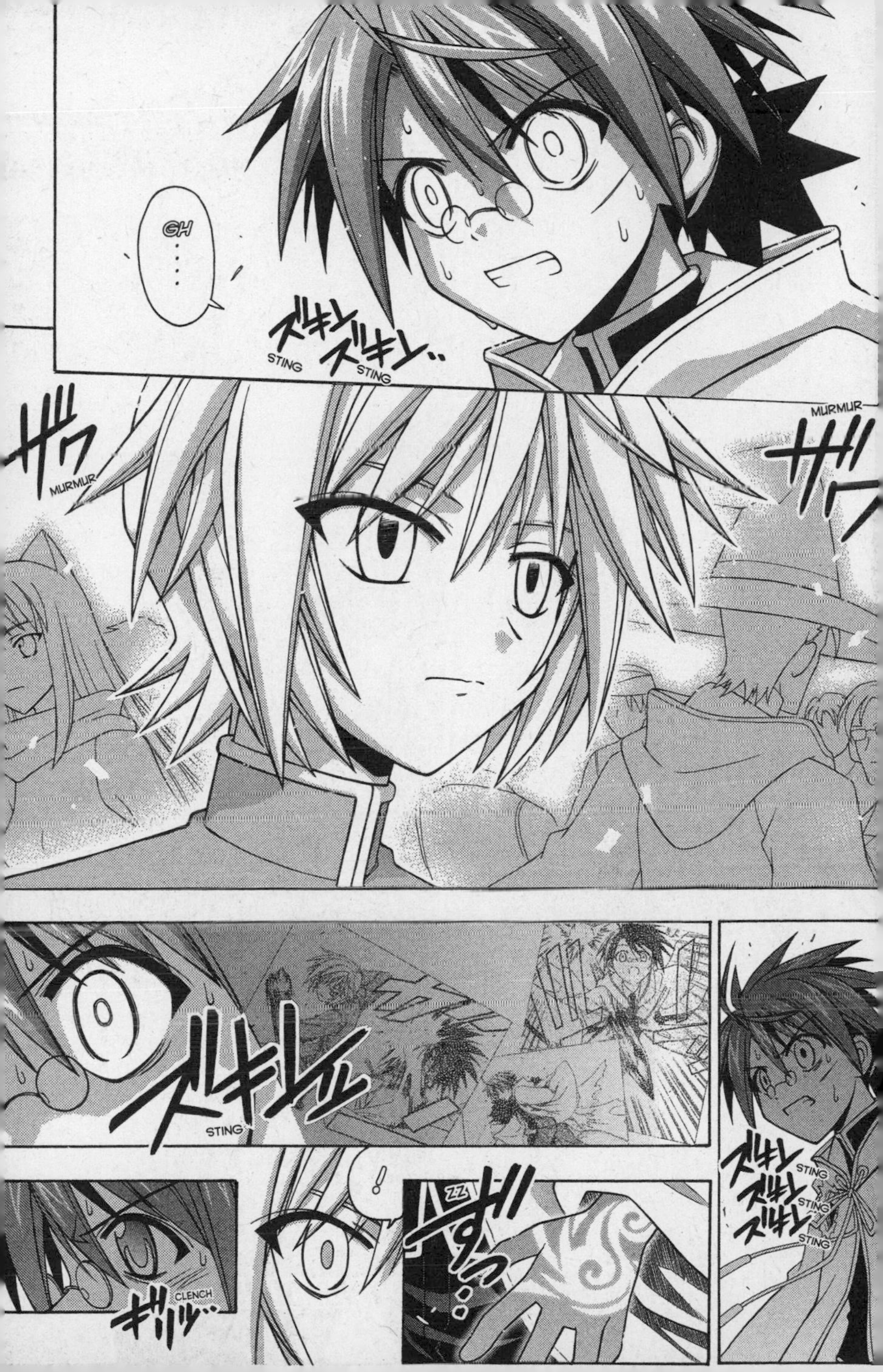

GH ....
STING STING
MURMUR
MURMUR
STING STING STING
STING
ZZ
!
CLENCH

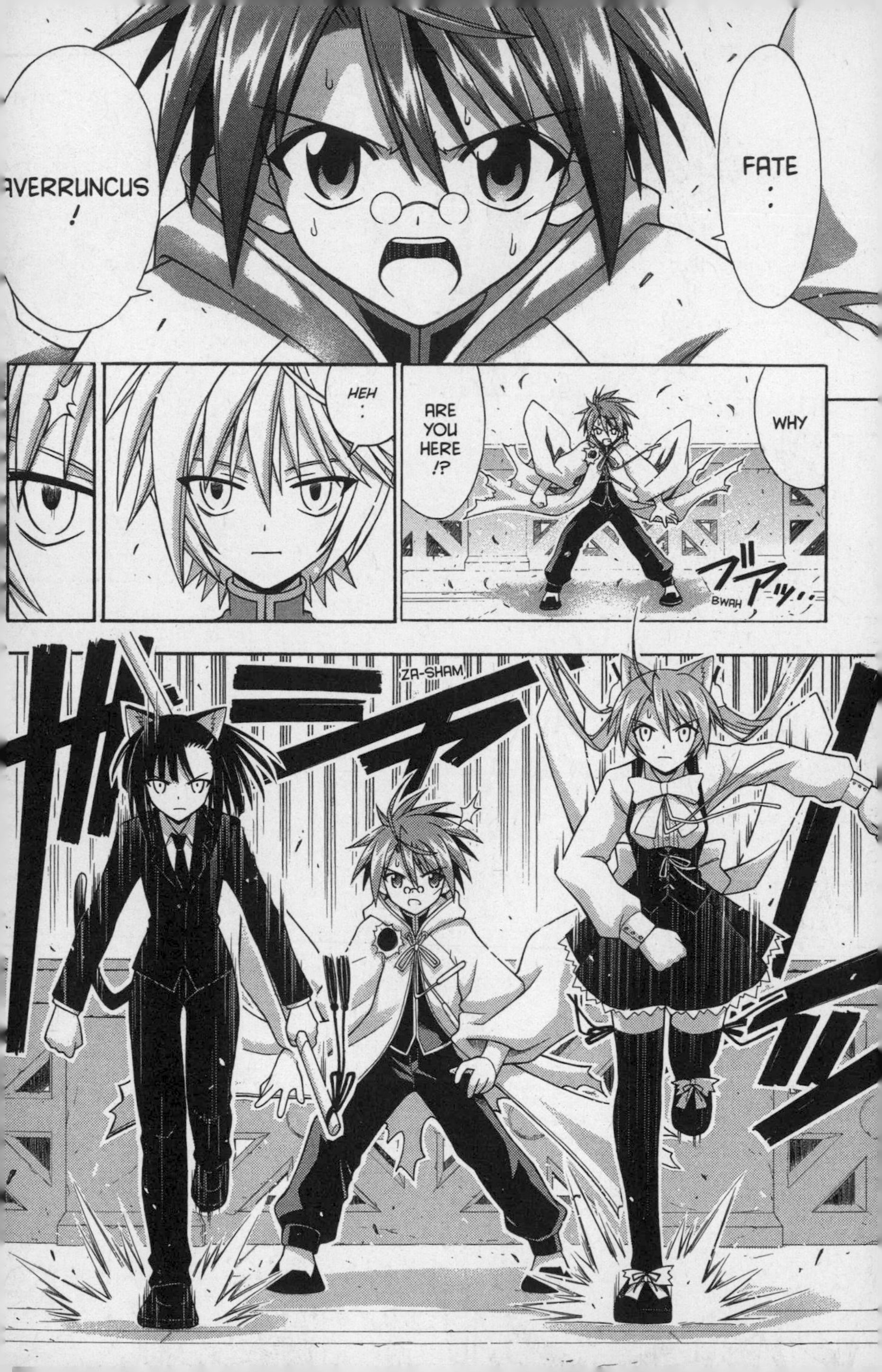
FATE
AVERRUNCUS!
WHY
ARE YOU HERE!?
BWAH
HEH
ZA-SHAM

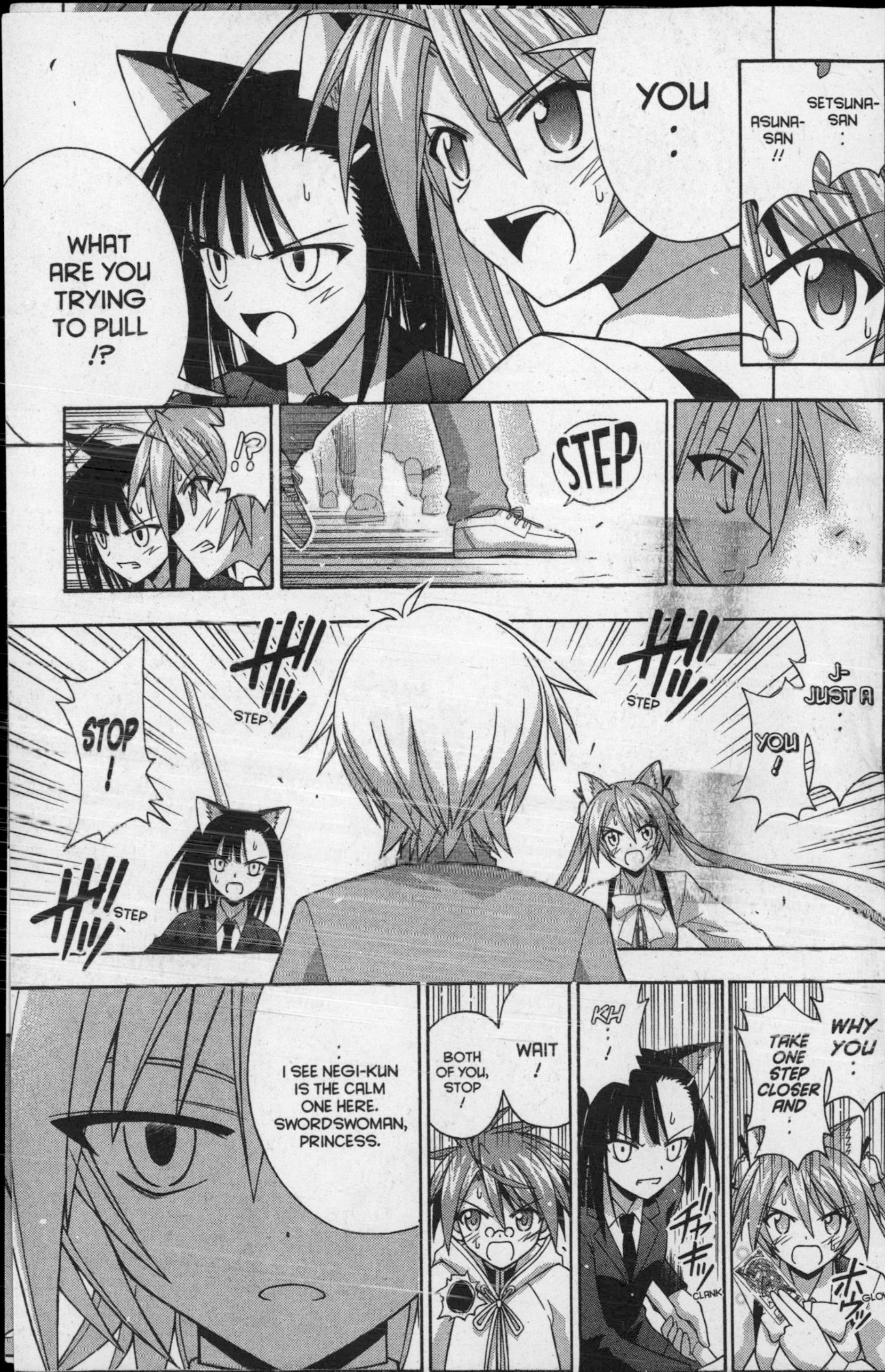
SETSUNA-SAN :
ASUNA-SAN !!
YOU :
WHAT ARE YOU TRYING TO PULL !?
STEP
!?
J- JUST A :
YOU !
STEP
STEP
STOP !
STEP
WHY YOU :
TAKE ONE STEP CLOSER AND :
GLOW
KH : !
CLANK
WAIT !
BOTH OF YOU, STOP !
: I SEE NEGI-KUN IS THE CALM ONE HERE. SWORDSWOMAN, PRINCESS.

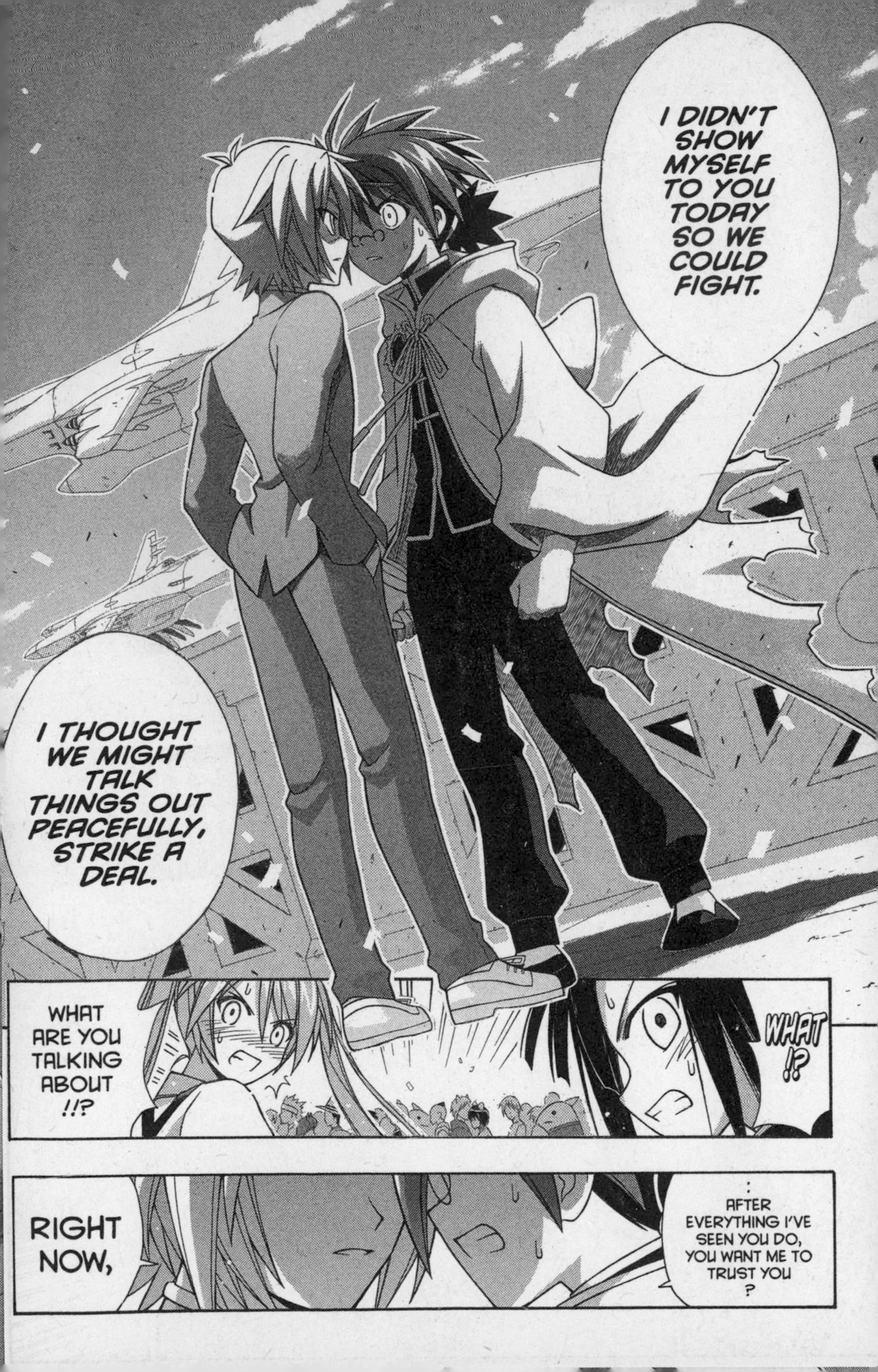
I DIDN'T SHOW MYSELF TO YOU TODAY SO WE COULD FIGHT.
I THOUGHT WE MIGHT TALK THINGS OUT PEACEFULLY, STRIKE A DEAL.
WHAT !?
WHAT ARE YOU TALKING ABOUT !!?
AFTER EVERYTHING I'VE SEEN YOU DO, YOU WANT ME TO TRUST YOU ?
RIGHT NOW,

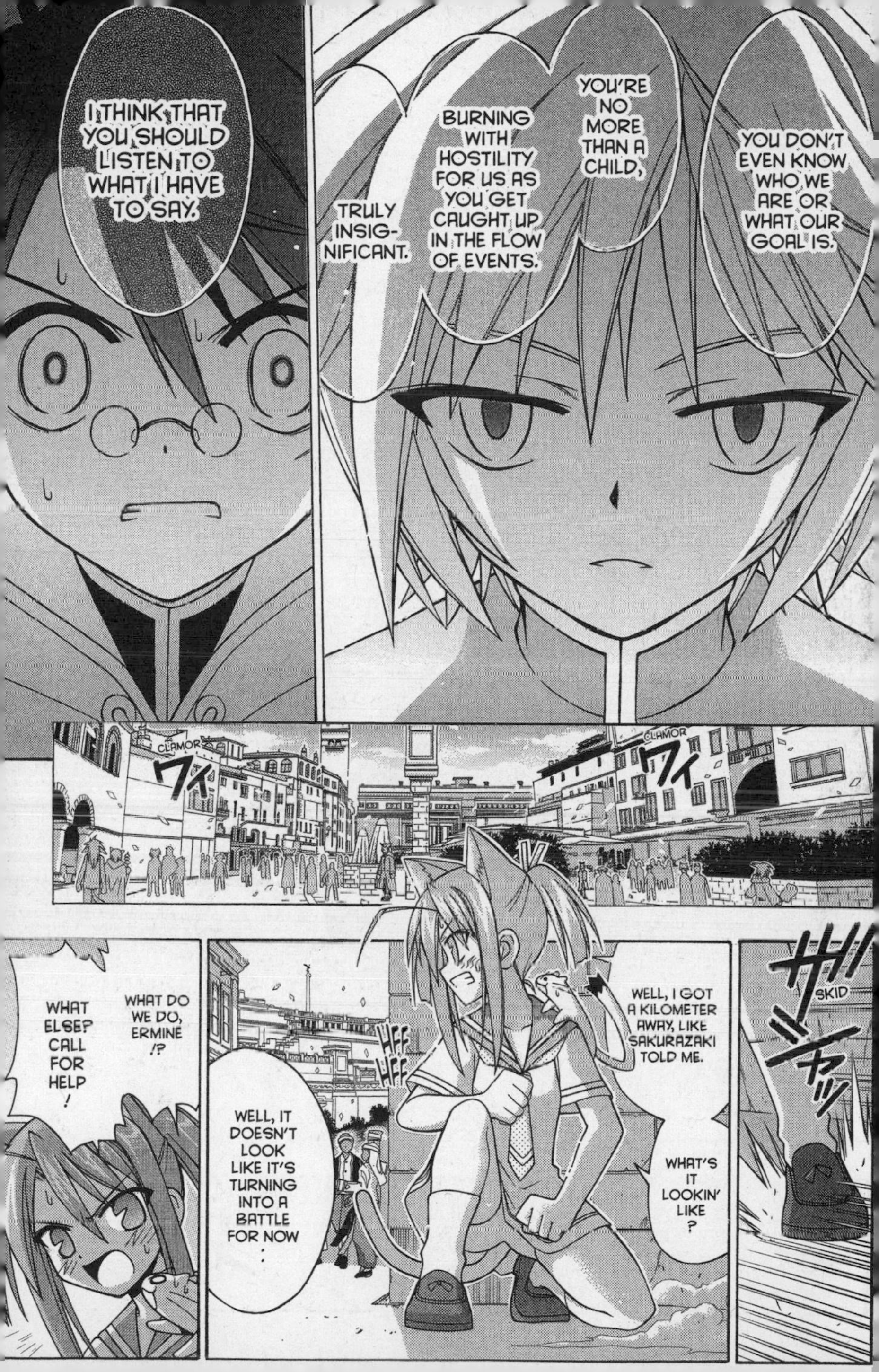
YOU DON'T EVEN KNOW WHO WE ARE OR WHAT OUR GOAL IS.
YOU'RE NO MORE THAN A CHILD,
BURNING WITH HOSTILITY FOR US AS YOU GET CAUGHT UP IN THE FLOW OF EVENTS.
TRULY INSIG-NIFICANT.
I THINK THAT YOU SHOULD LISTEN TO WHAT I HAVE TO SAY.
CLAMOR
CLAMOR
SKID
WELL, I GOT A KILOMETER AWAY, LIKE SAKURAZAKI TOLD ME.
WHAT'S IT LOOKIN' LIKE?
HFF HFF
WELL, IT DOESN'T LOOK LIKE IT'S TURNING INTO A BATTLE FOR NOW...
WHAT DO WE DO, ERMINE!?
WHAT ELSE? CALL FOR HELP!

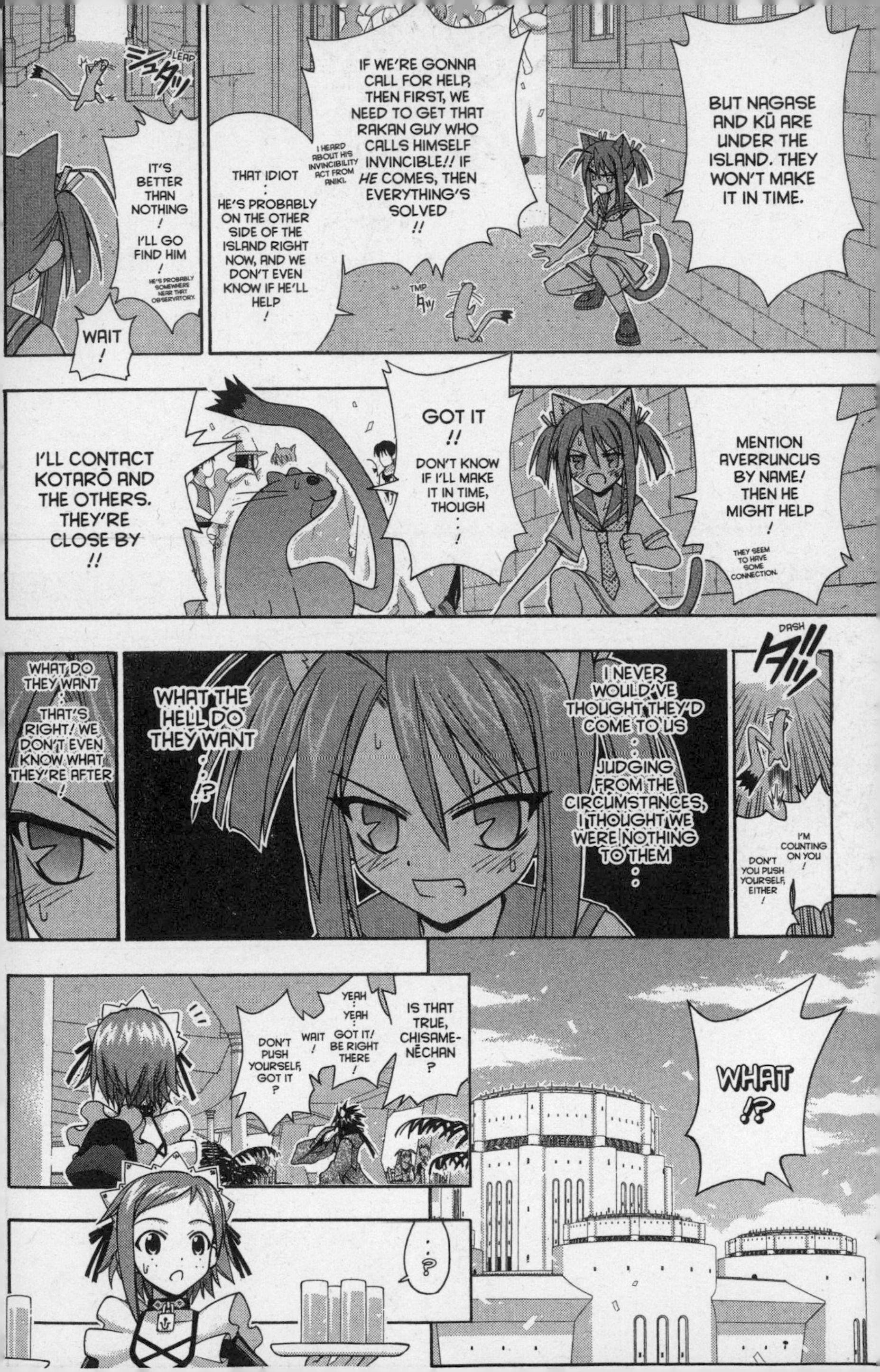
BUT NAGASE AND KŪ ARE UNDER THE ISLAND. THEY WON'T MAKE IT IN TIME.
IF WE'RE GONNA CALL FOR HELP, THEN FIRST, WE NEED TO GET THAT RAKAN GUY WHO CALLS HIMSELF INVINCIBLE!! IF HE COMES, THEN EVERYTHING'S SOLVED!!
I HEARD ABOUT HIS INVINCIBILITY ACT FROM ANIKI.
THAT IDIOT... HE'S PROBABLY ON THE OTHER SIDE OF THE ISLAND RIGHT NOW, AND WE DON'T EVEN KNOW IF HE'LL HELP!
TMP
LEAP
IT'S BETTER THAN NOTHING! I'LL GO FIND HIM!
HE'S PROBABLY SOMEWHERE NEAR THAT OBSERVATORY.
WAIT!
MENTION AVERRUNCUS BY NAME! THEN HE MIGHT HELP!
THEY SEEM TO HAVE SOME CONNECTION.
GOT IT!! DON'T KNOW IF I'LL MAKE IT IN TIME, THOUGH...!
I'LL CONTACT KOTARŌ AND THE OTHERS. THEY'RE CLOSE BY!!
DASH
I'M COUNTING ON YOU!
DON'T YOU PUSH YOURSELF, EITHER!
I NEVER WOULD'VE THOUGHT THEY'D COME TO US... JUDGING FROM THE CIRCUMSTANCES, I THOUGHT WE WERE NOTHING TO THEM...
WHAT THE HELL DO THEY WANT...!?
WHAT DO THEY WANT... THAT'S RIGHT! WE DON'T EVEN KNOW WHAT THEY'RE AFTER!
WHAT!?
IS THAT TRUE, CHISAME-NĒCHAN?
YEAH... YEAH... GOT IT! BE RIGHT THERE!
WAIT!
DON'T PUSH YOURSELF, GOT IT?
...?

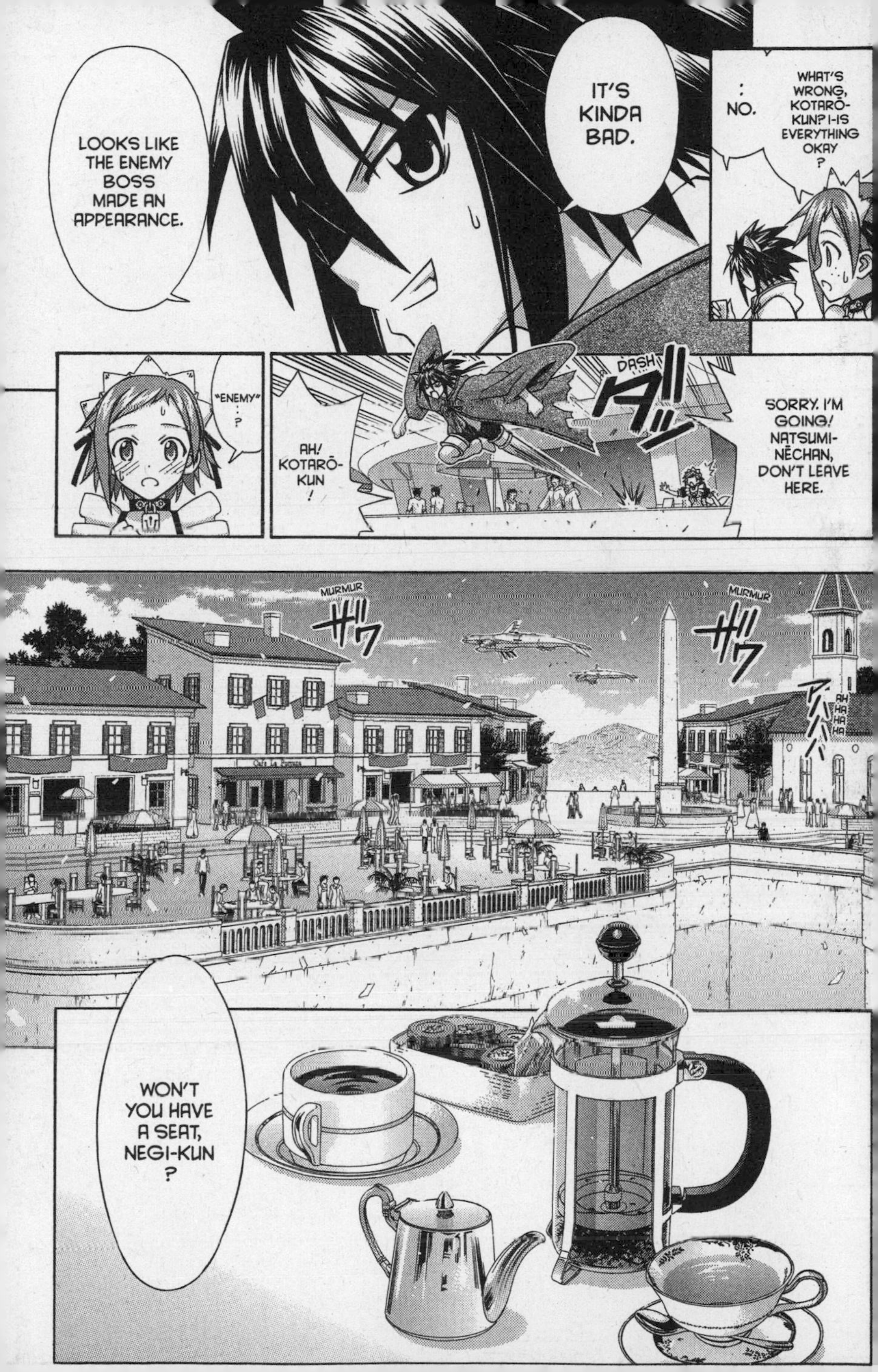
WHAT'S WRONG, KOTARŌ-KUN? I-IS EVERYTHING OKAY?
: NO.
IT'S KINDA BAD.
LOOKS LIKE THE ENEMY BOSS MADE AN APPEARANCE.
SORRY. I'M GOING! NATSUMI-NĒCHAN, DON'T LEAVE HERE.
DASH
AH! KOTARŌ-KUN!
"ENEMY"...?
MURMUR
AH HA HA HA
MURMUR
WON'T YOU HAVE A SEAT, NEGI-KUN?

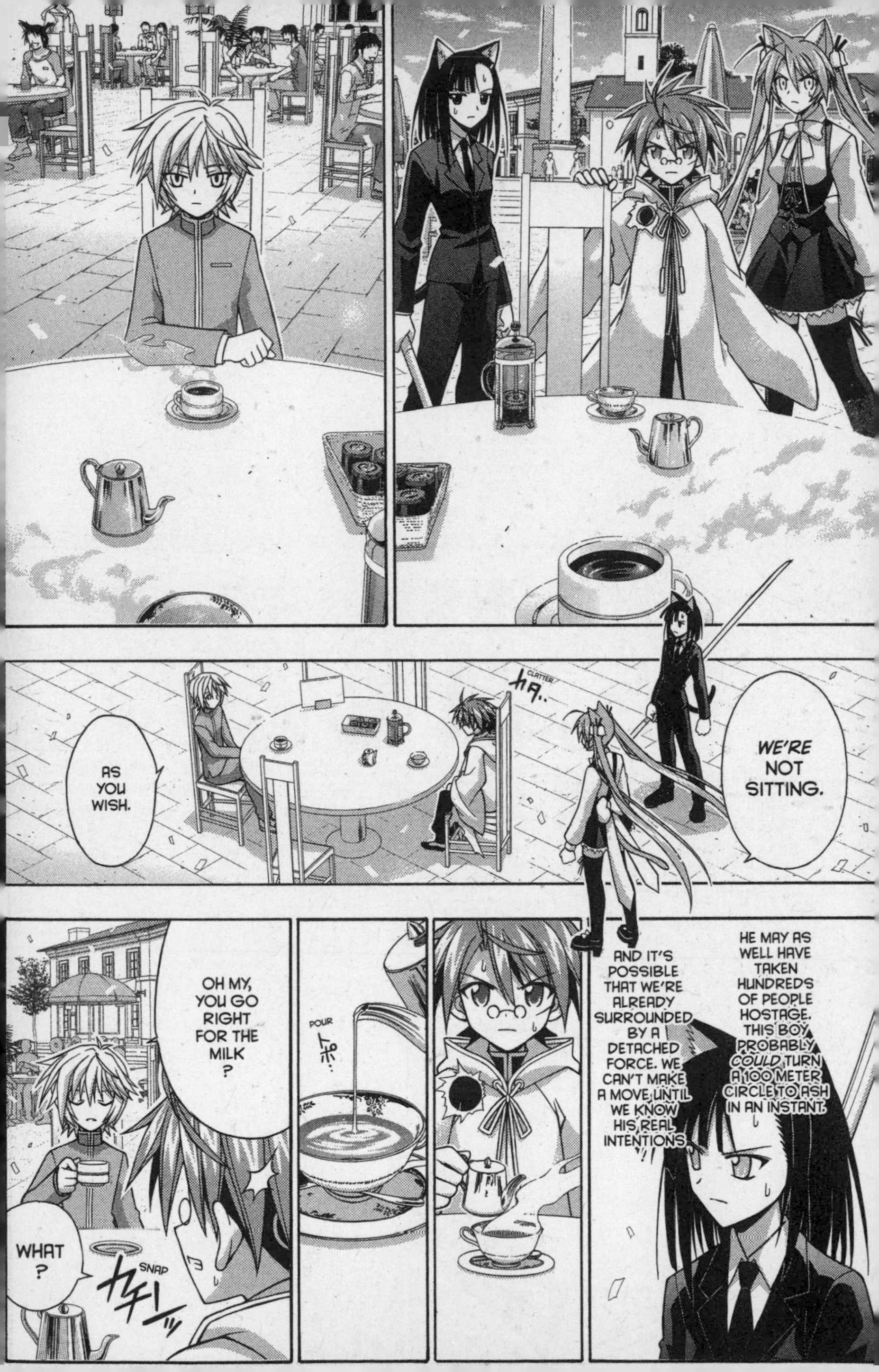

WE'RE NOT SITTING.
CLATTER
AS YOU WISH.
HE MAY AS WELL HAVE TAKEN HUNDREDS OF PEOPLE HOSTAGE. THIS BOY PROBABLY COULD TURN A 100 METER CIRCLE TO ASH IN AN INSTANT.
AND IT'S POSSIBLE THAT WE'RE ALREADY SURROUNDED BY A DETACHED FORCE. WE CAN'T MAKE A MOVE UNTIL WE KNOW HIS REAL INTENTIONS.
POUR
OH MY, YOU GO RIGHT FOR THE MILK?
WHAT?
SNAP

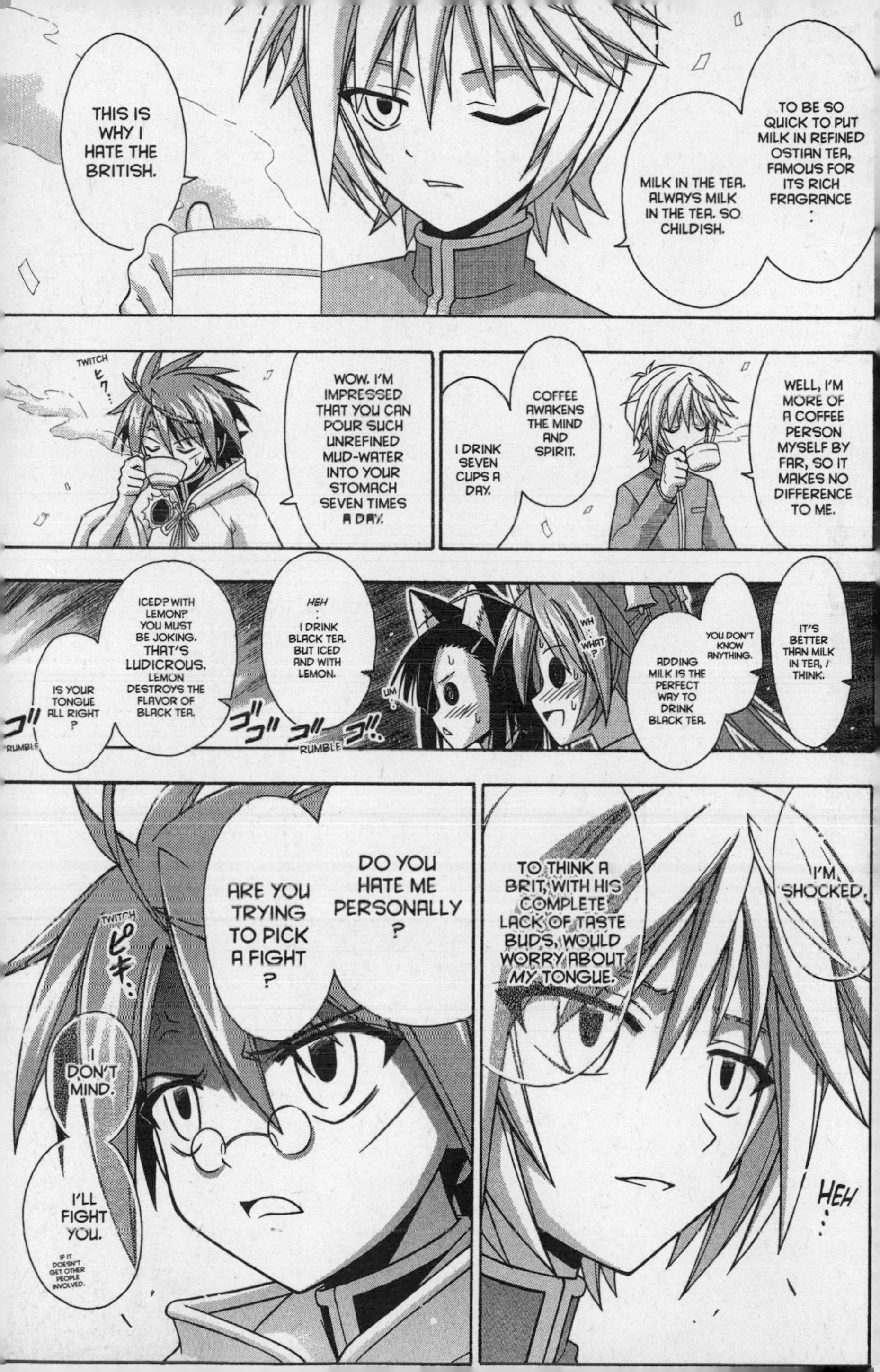
TO BE SO QUICK TO PUT MILK IN REFINED OSTIAN TEA, FAMOUS FOR ITS RICH FRAGRANCE :
MILK IN THE TEA. ALWAYS MILK IN THE TEA. SO CHILDISH.
THIS IS WHY I HATE THE BRITISH.
WELL, I'M MORE OF A COFFEE PERSON MYSELF BY FAR, SO IT MAKES NO DIFFERENCE TO ME.
COFFEE AWAKENS THE MIND AND SPIRIT.
I DRINK SEVEN CUPS A DAY.
WOW. I'M IMPRESSED THAT YOU CAN POUR SUCH UNREFINED MUD-WATER INTO YOUR STOMACH SEVEN TIMES A DAY.
TWITCH ヒク…
IT'S BETTER THAN MILK IN TEA, I THINK.
YOU DON'T KNOW ANYTHING.
ADDING MILK IS THE PERFECT WAY TO DRINK BLACK TEA.
WH- WHAT?
UM
HEH : I DRINK BLACK TEA. BUT ICED AND WITH LEMON.
ICED? WITH LEMON? YOU MUST BE JOKING. THAT'S LUDICROUS. LEMON DESTROYS THE FLAVOR OF BLACK TEA.
IS YOUR TONGUE ALL RIGHT?
ゴゴゴゴ RUMBLE
I'M SHOCKED.
TO THINK A BRIT, WITH HIS COMPLETE LACK OF TASTE BUDS, WOULD WORRY ABOUT MY TONGUE.
HEH :
DO YOU HATE ME PERSONALLY?
ARE YOU TRYING TO PICK A FIGHT?
TWITCH ピキ…
I DON'T MIND.
I'LL FIGHT YOU.
IF IT DOESN'T GET OTHER PEOPLE INVOLVED.

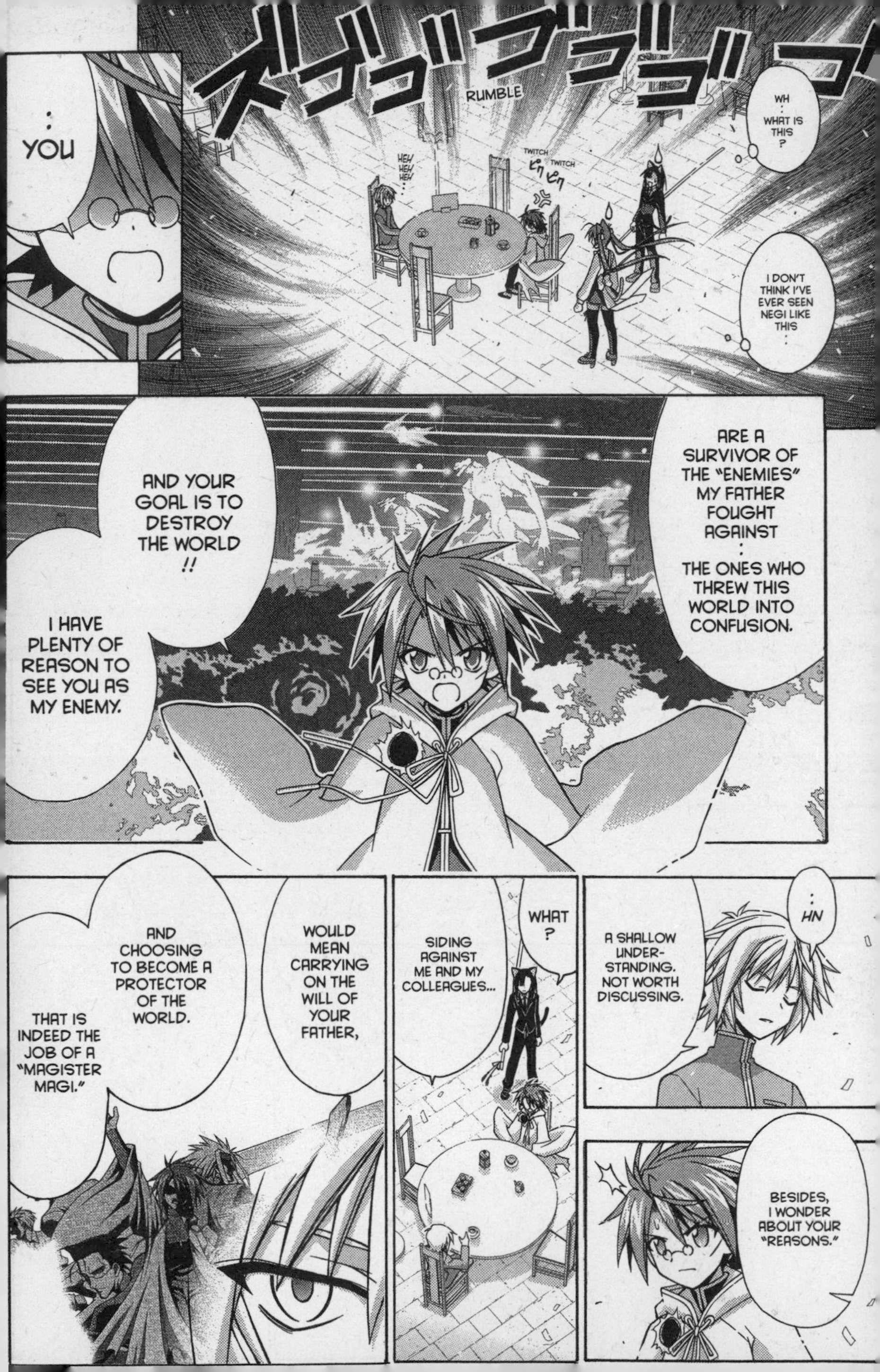
RUMBLE
WH : WHAT IS THIS ?
I DON'T THINK I'VE EVER SEEN NEGI LIKE THIS :
HEH HEH HEH :
TWITCH TWITCH
: YOU
ARE A SURVIVOR OF THE "ENEMIES" MY FATHER FOUGHT AGAINST : THE ONES WHO THREW THIS WORLD INTO CONFUSION.
AND YOUR GOAL IS TO DESTROY THE WORLD !!
I HAVE PLENTY OF REASON TO SEE YOU AS MY ENEMY.
: HN
A SHALLOW UNDER-STANDING. NOT WORTH DISCUSSING.
BESIDES, I WONDER ABOUT YOUR "REASONS."
WHAT ?
SIDING AGAINST ME AND MY COLLEAGUES...
WOULD MEAN CARRYING ON THE WILL OF YOUR FATHER,
AND CHOOSING TO BECOME A PROTECTOR OF THE WORLD.
THAT IS INDEED THE JOB OF A "MAGISTER MAGI."

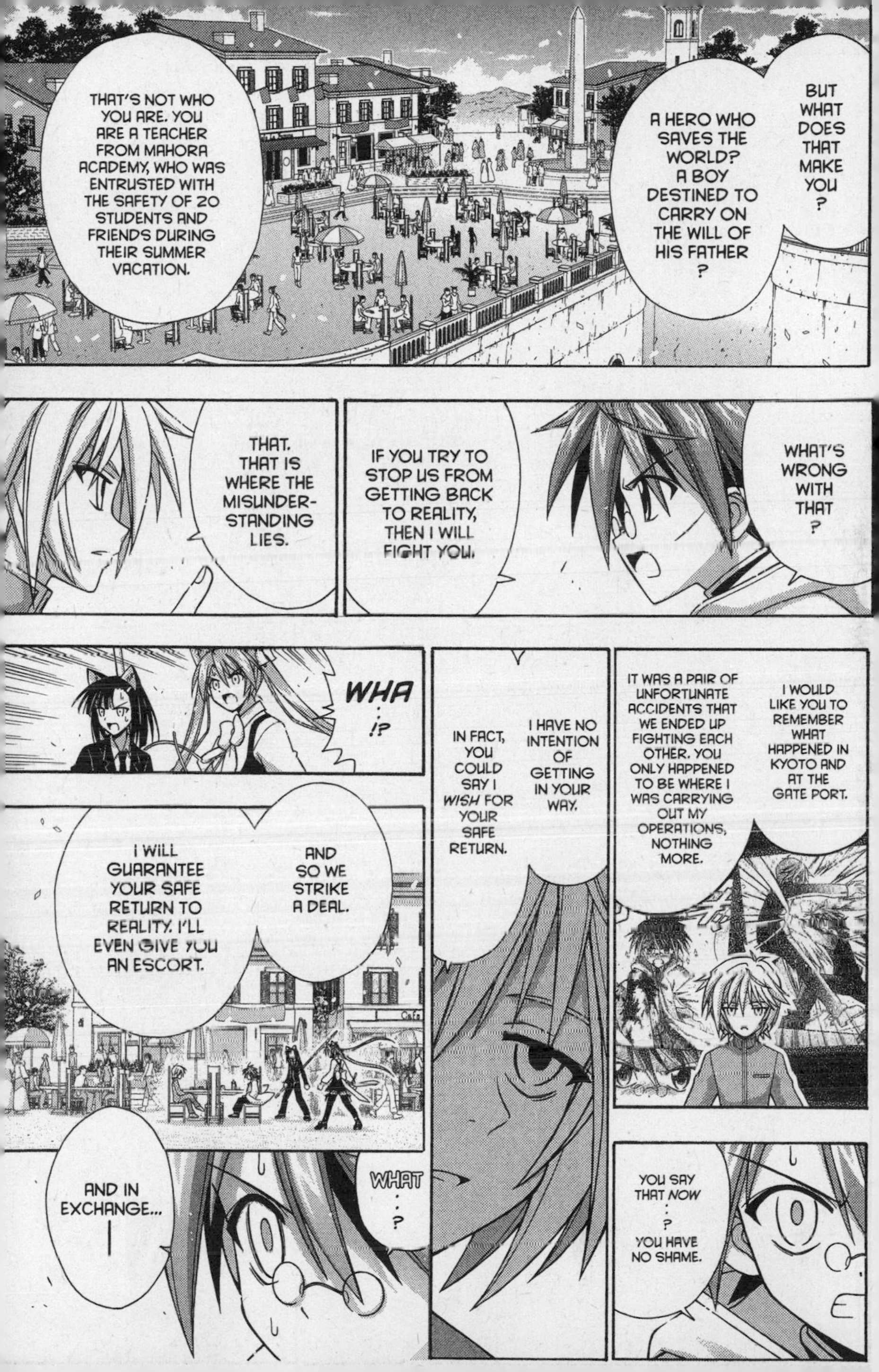
BUT WHAT DOES THAT MAKE YOU?
A HERO WHO SAVES THE WORLD? A BOY DESTINED TO CARRY ON THE WILL OF HIS FATHER?
THAT'S NOT WHO YOU ARE. YOU ARE A TEACHER FROM MAHORA ACADEMY, WHO WAS ENTRUSTED WITH THE SAFETY OF 20 STUDENTS AND FRIENDS DURING THEIR SUMMER VACATION.
WHAT'S WRONG WITH THAT?
IF YOU TRY TO STOP US FROM GETTING BACK TO REALITY, THEN I WILL FIGHT YOU.
THAT. THAT IS WHERE THE MISUNDER-STANDING LIES.
I WOULD LIKE YOU TO REMEMBER WHAT HAPPENED IN KYOTO AND AT THE GATE PORT.
IT WAS A PAIR OF UNFORTUNATE ACCIDENTS THAT WE ENDED UP FIGHTING EACH OTHER. YOU ONLY HAPPENED TO BE WHERE I WAS CARRYING OUT MY OPERATIONS, NOTHING MORE.
YOU SAY THAT *NOW*..? YOU HAVE NO SHAME.
I HAVE NO INTENTION OF GETTING IN YOUR WAY.
IN FACT, YOU COULD SAY I *WISH* FOR YOUR SAFE RETURN.
WHA..!?
AND SO WE STRIKE A DEAL.
I WILL GUARANTEE YOUR SAFE RETURN TO REALITY. I'LL EVEN GIVE YOU AN ESCORT.
WHAT..?
AND IN EXCHANGE...—

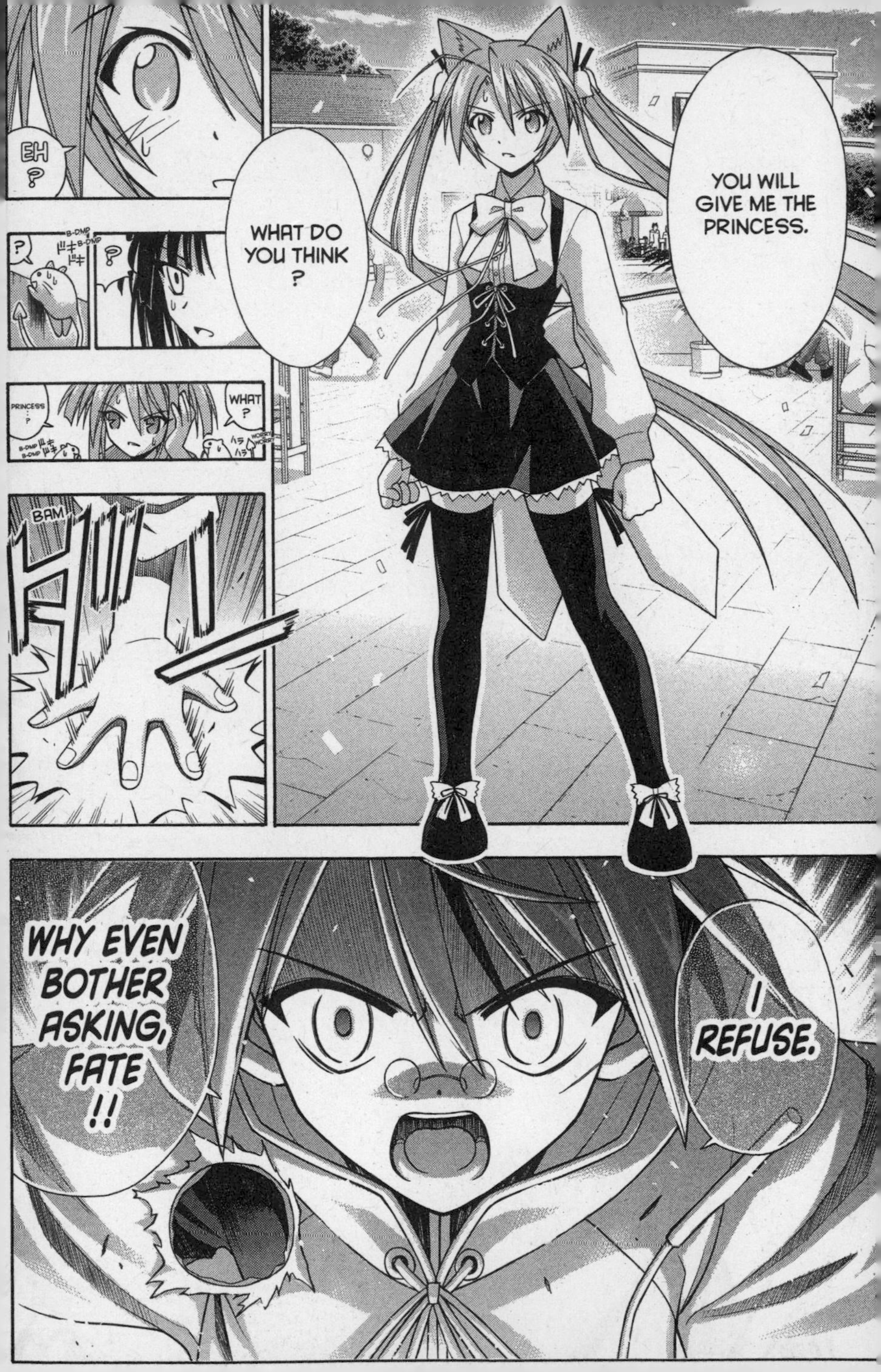
YOU WILL GIVE ME THE PRINCESS.
WHAT DO YOU THINK ?
EH ?
?
B-DMP B-DMP
?
WHAT ?
WORRY WORRY
PRINCESS … ?
B-DMP B-DMP
BAM
I REFUSE.
WHY EVEN BOTHER ASKING, FATE !!

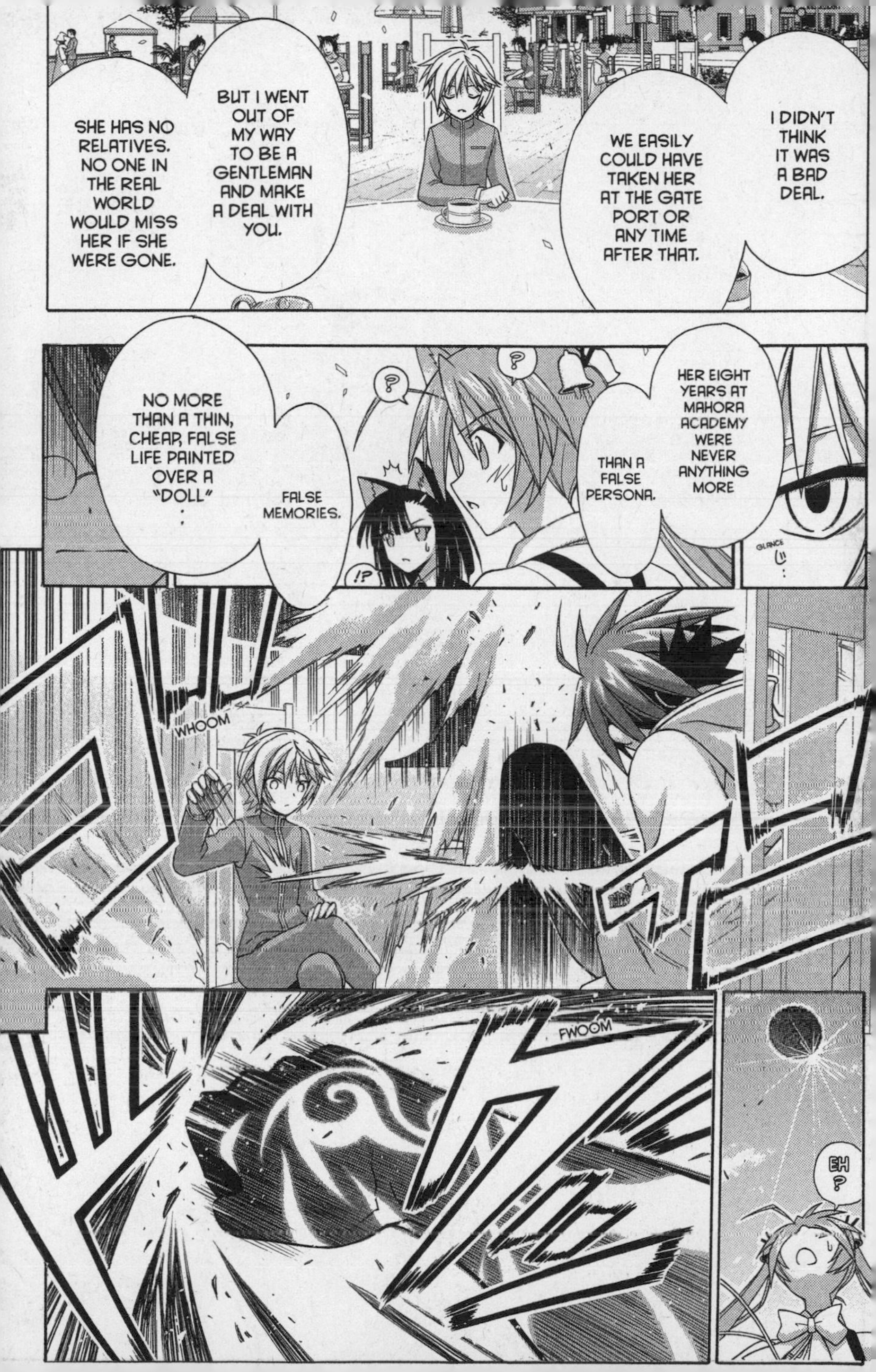
I DIDN'T THINK IT WAS A BAD DEAL.
WE EASILY COULD HAVE TAKEN HER AT THE GATE PORT OR ANY TIME AFTER THAT.
BUT I WENT OUT OF MY WAY TO BE A GENTLEMAN AND MAKE A DEAL WITH YOU.
SHE HAS NO RELATIVES. NO ONE IN THE REAL WORLD WOULD MISS HER IF SHE WERE GONE.
GLANCE
HER EIGHT YEARS AT MAHORA ACADEMY WERE NEVER ANYTHING MORE
THAN A FALSE PERSONA.
?
?
FALSE MEMORIES.
NO MORE THAN A THIN, CHEAP, FALSE LIFE PAINTED OVER A "DOLL"
!?
WHOOM
EH?
FWOOM

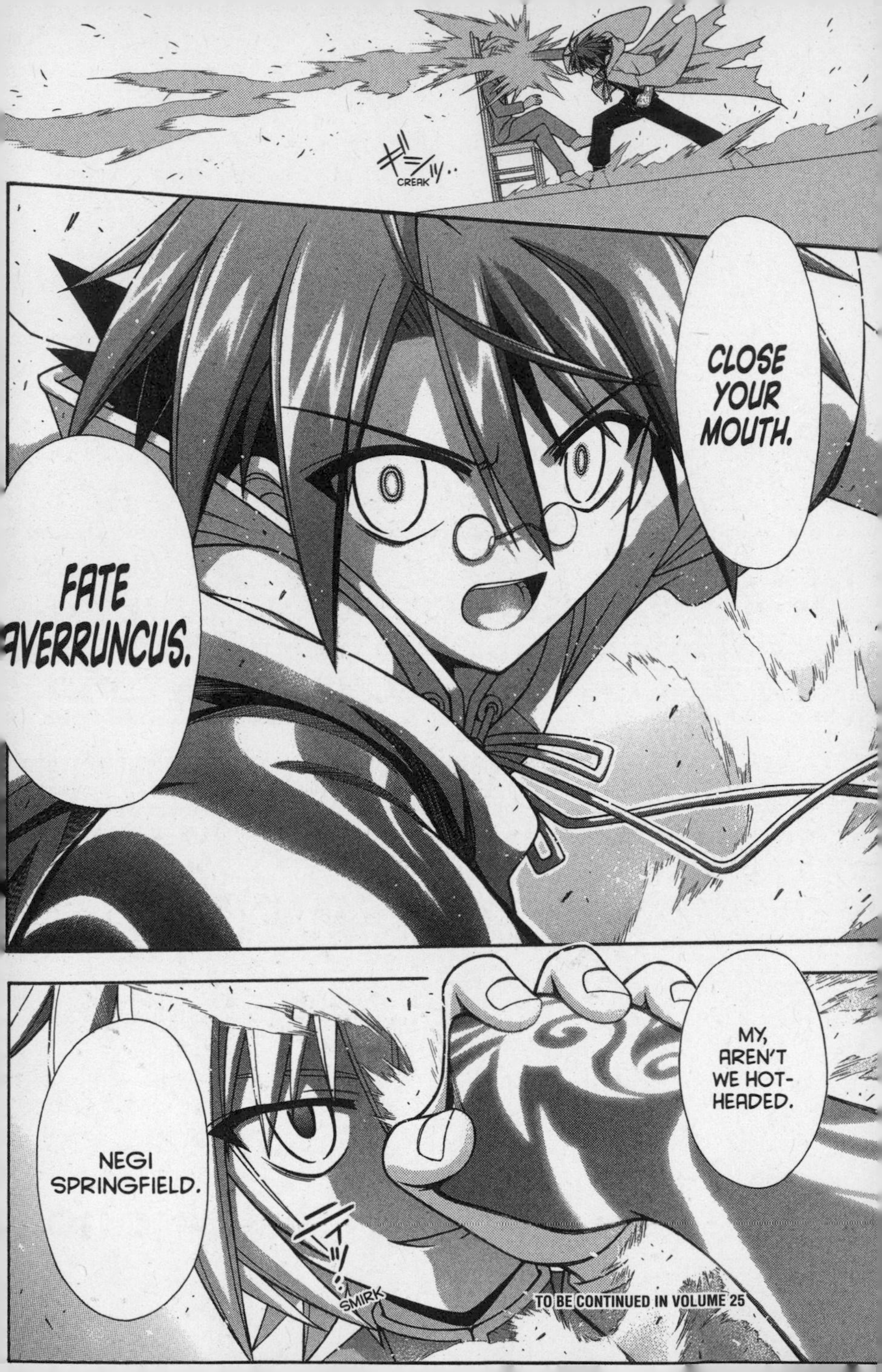
CREAK
CLOSE YOUR MOUTH.
FATE AVERRUNCUS.
MY, AREN'T WE HOT-HEADED.
NEGI SPRINGFIELD.
SMIRK
TO BE CONTINUED IN VOLUME 25

-STAFF-

Ken Akamatsu
Takashi Takemoto
Kenichi Nakamura
Masaki Ohyama
Keiichi Yamashita
Tadashi Maki
Tohru Mitsuhashi
Yuichi Yoshida

Thanks to
Ran Ayanaga

# MAGICAL WORLD MAP & CLASSMATES

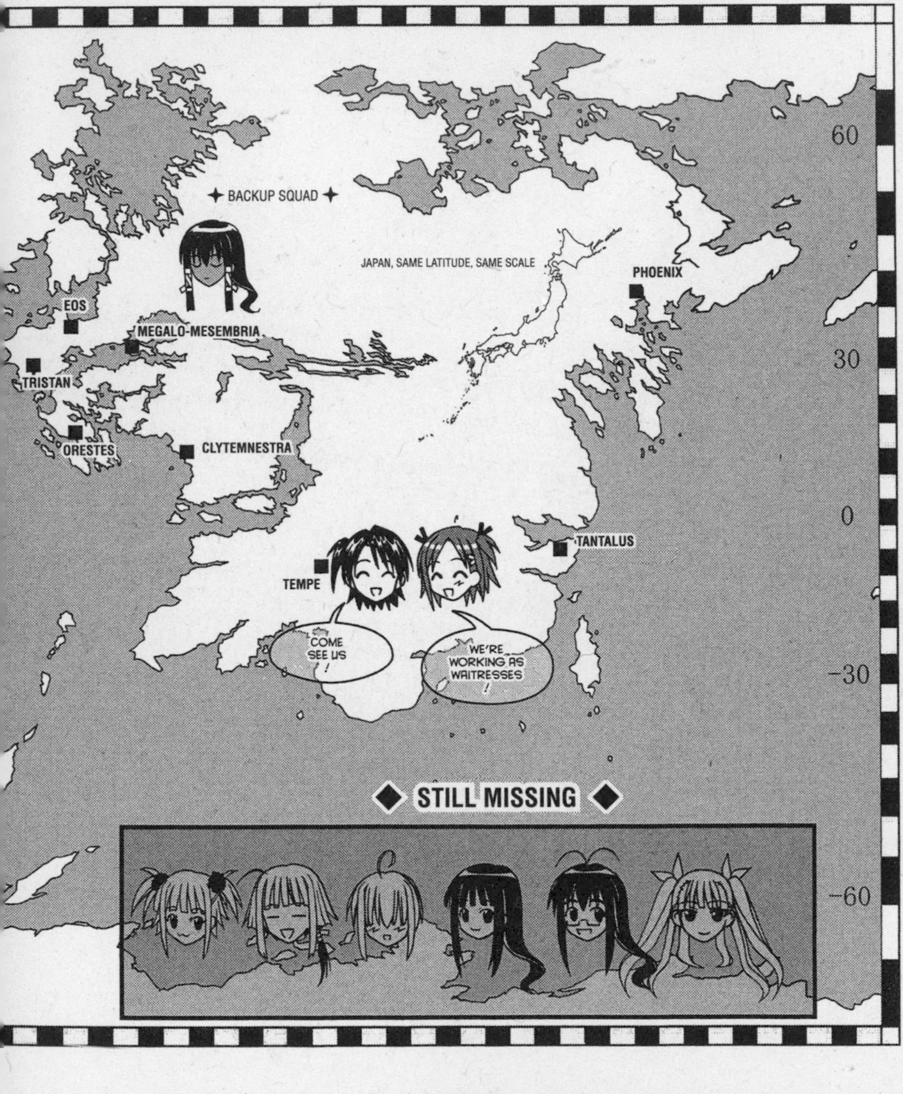
BACKUP SQUAD
JAPAN, SAME LATITUDE, SAME SCALE
PHOENIX
EOS
MEGALO-MESEMBRIA
TRISTAN
ORESTES
CLYTEMNESTRA
TANTALUS
TEMPE
WE'RE WORKING AS WAITRESSES!
COME SEE US!
STILL MISSING
60
30
0
-30
-60

# Tabula Mundi Magici

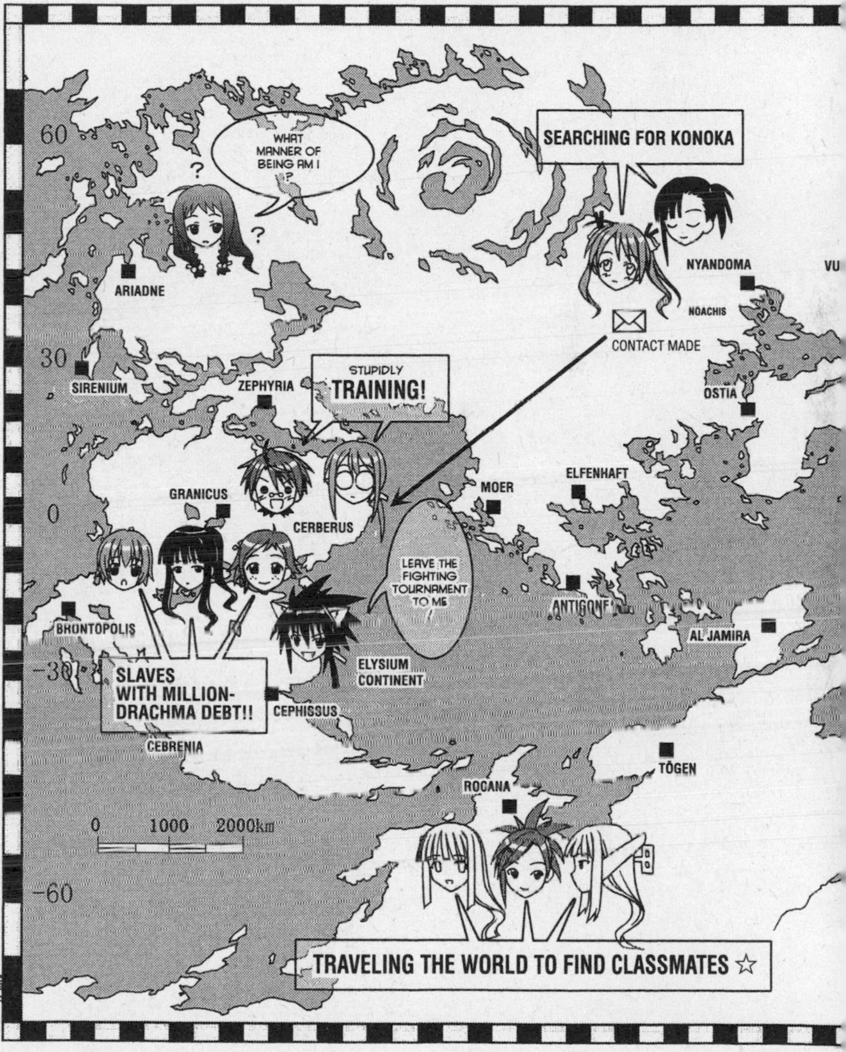

SEARCHING FOR KONOKA
WHAT MANNER OF BEING AM I ?
? ?
60
30
0
-30
-60
NYANDOMA
NOACHIS
ARIADNE
CONTACT MADE
SIRENIUM
ZEPHYRIA
STUPIDLY TRAINING!
OSTIA
ELFENHAFT
MOER
GRANICUS
CERBERUS
LEAVE THE FIGHTING TOURNAMENT TO ME
ANTIGONE
AL JAMIRA
BRONTOPOLIS
SLAVES WITH MILLION-DRACHMA DEBT!!
ELYSIUM CONTINENT
CEPHISSUS
CEBRENIA
TŌGEN
ROCANA
0 1000 2000km
TRAVELING THE WORLD TO FIND CLASSMATES ☆


REMEMBER ME SOMETIMES, TOO!

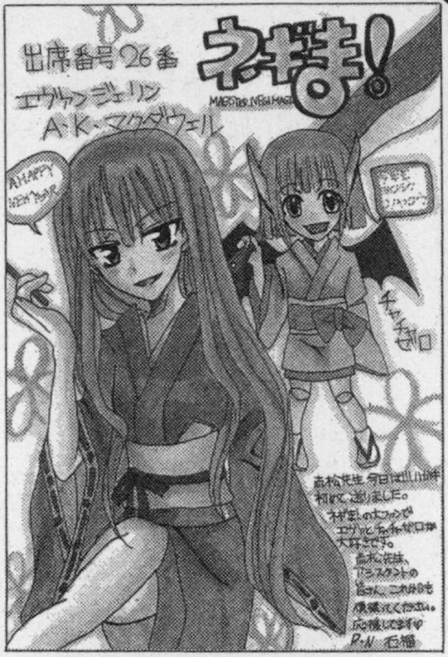
ネギま!

LOOKS GOOD IN JAPANESE CLOTHING, TOO.

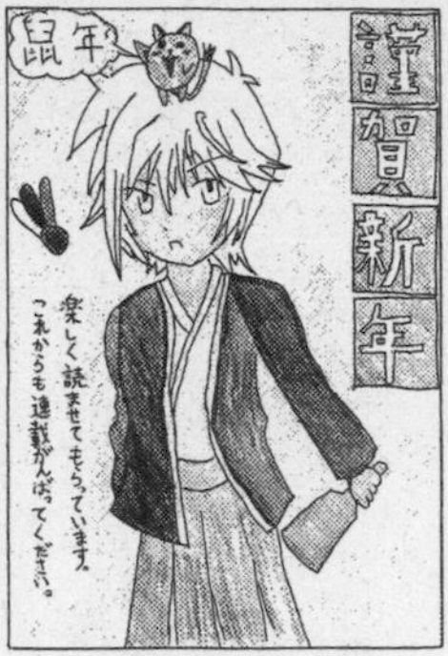

HEARTWARMING FATE

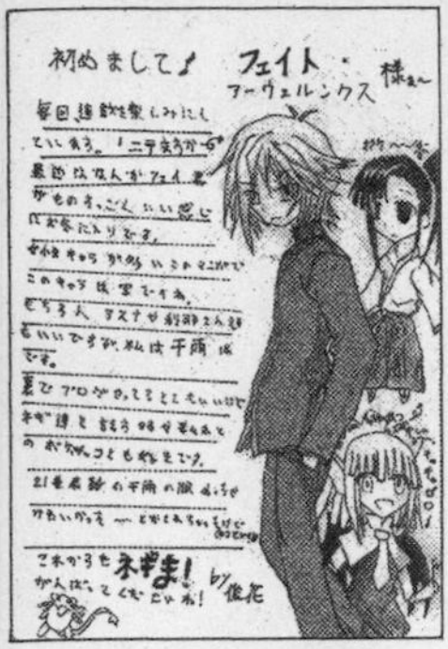

LOOKS POPULAR (LAUGH)

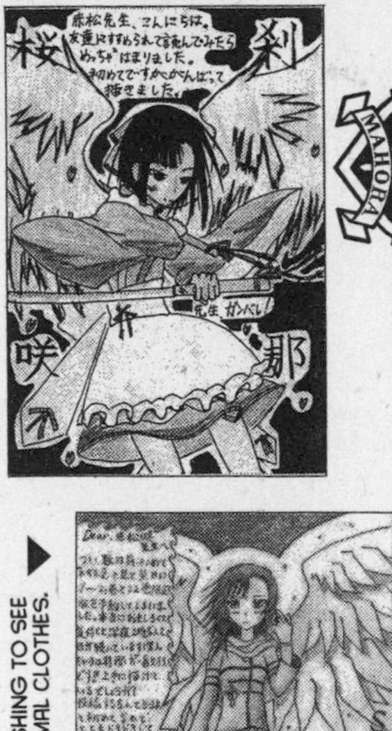

COOL☆

## NEGIMA! FAN ART CORNER

I WRACKED MY BRAINS CHOOSING THESE, TOO (^^; SETSUNA, ASUNA, AND EVA HAVE ALWAYS BEEN POPULAR, BUT NOW I'M STARTING TO FEEL MORE AND MORE LOVE FOR FATE, KOTARŌ, AND ANYA ★ ANYHOW, LET'S GET STARTED (^^)

TEXT BY ASSISTANT MAX

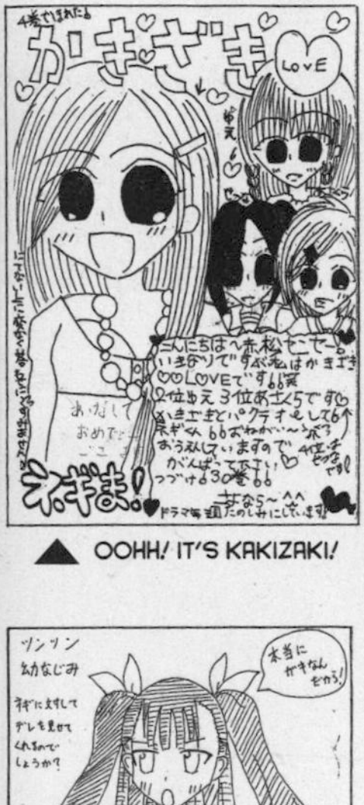

OOHH! IT'S KAKIZAKI!

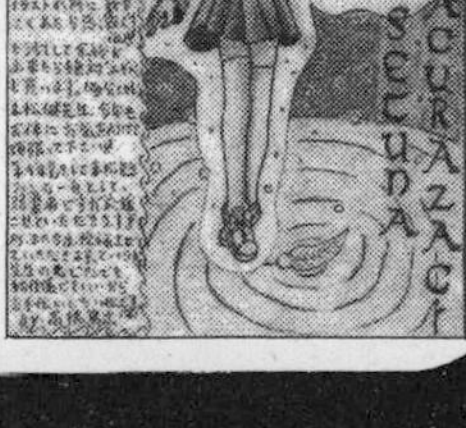

IT'S REFRESHING TO SEE HER IN NORMAL CLOTHES.

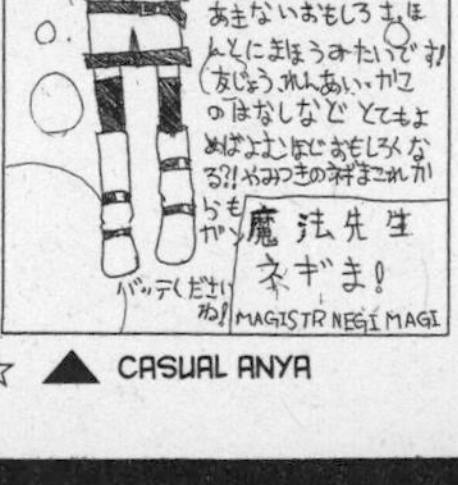

CASUAL ANYA

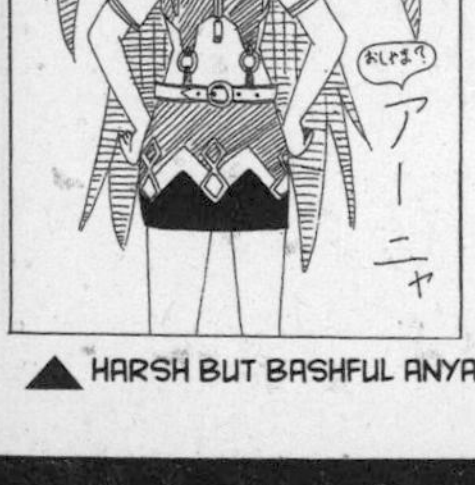

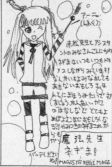

HARSH BUT BASHFUL ANYA☆

NEGI MA!

MAGISTER NEGI MAGI

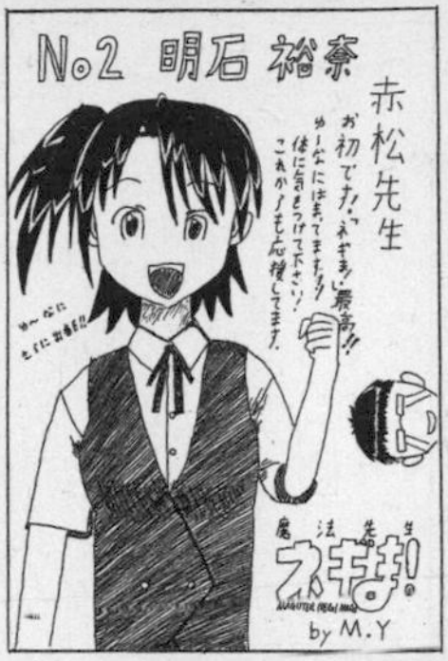

No.2 明石 裕奈
赤松先生
魔法先生
ネギま!
by M.Y

▲ EVER-ENERGETIC YŪNA ☆

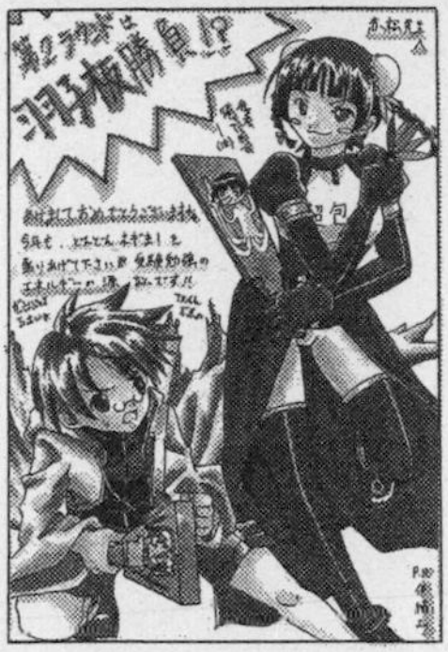
▲ THE PICTURES ON THEIR PADDLES ARE FUN.

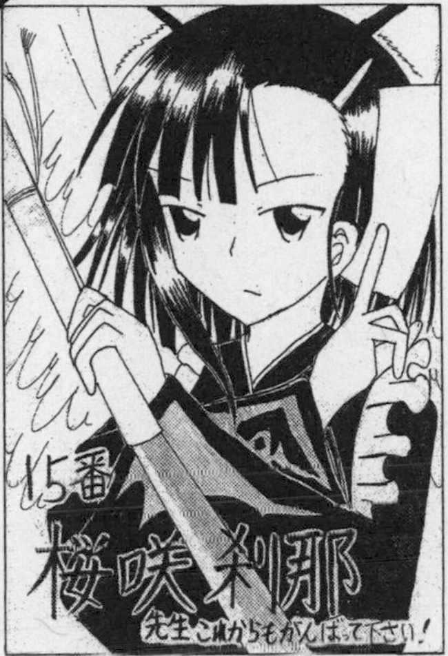

15番
桜咲刹那
先生これからもがんばって下さい!

▲ IT HAS A "FWIP!" FEELING

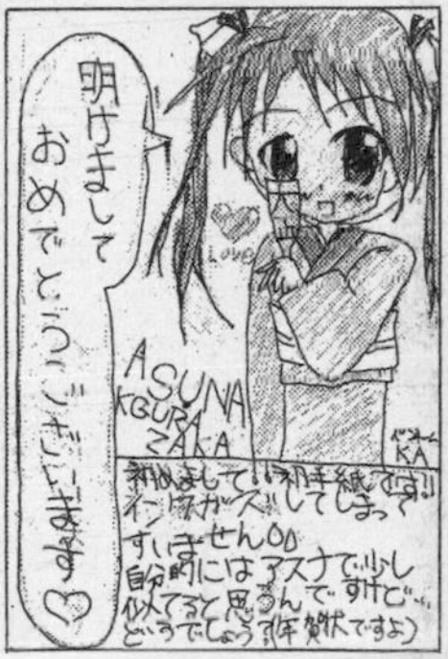

明けましておめでとうございます
ASUNA KGURA ZAKA

▲ IT DOES LOOK LIKE HER(^^)

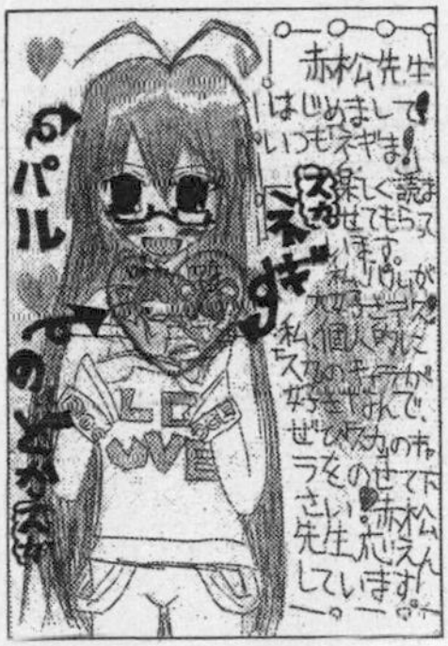

赤松先生
はじめまして
パル

▲ YOU EVEN COLORED HER ANTENNAE ♡

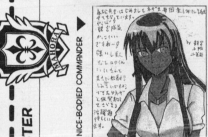

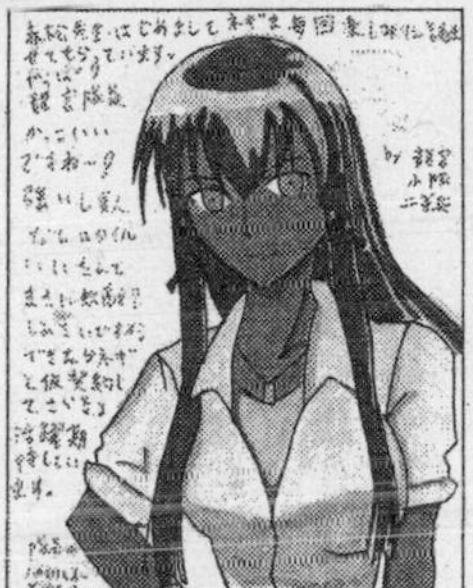
NICE-BODIED COMMANDER ▶

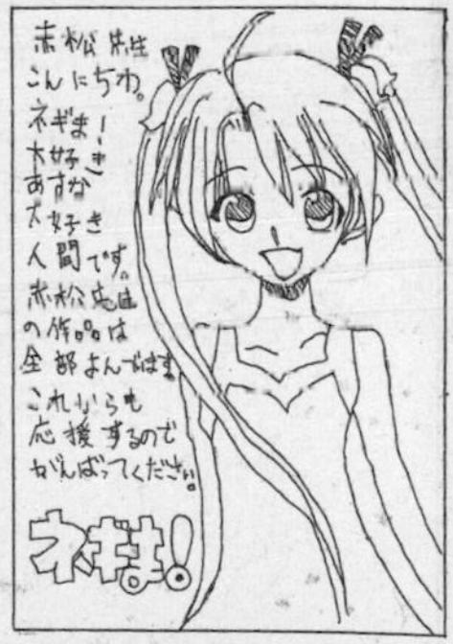

赤松先生
こんにちわ。
ネギま!

▲ YES☆THANK YOU FOR YOUR SUPPORT!

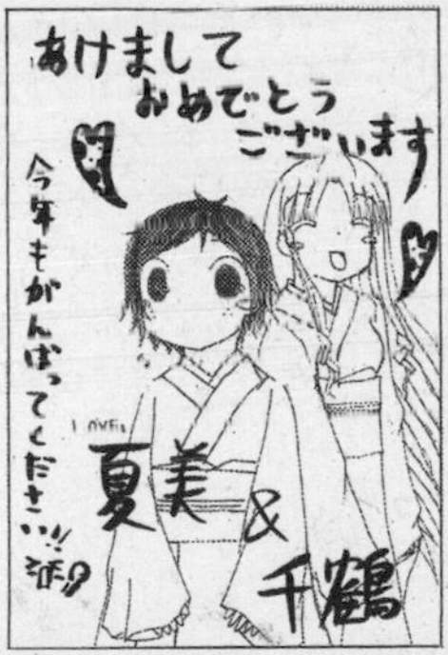

あけまして
おめでとう
ございます
今年もがんばってくださ~い!!
夏美
&
千鶴

▲ THEY WORK WELL TOGETHER, DON'T THEY?

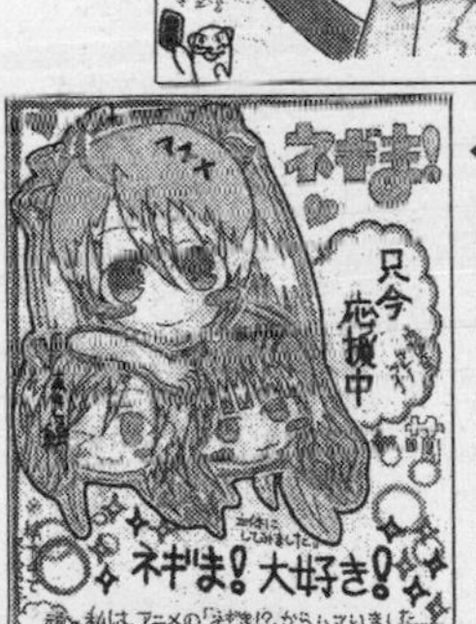

ネギま!
只今
応援中
ネギま! 大好き!

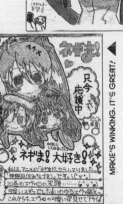

◀ MAKIE'S WINKING. IT'S GREAT!

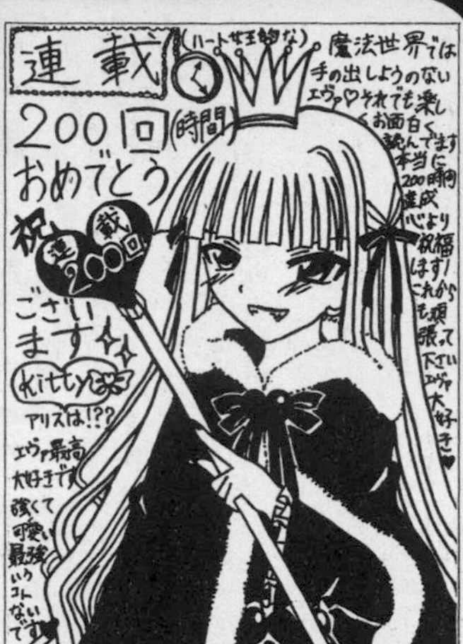
連載200回おめでとうございます
魔法世界では手の出しようのないエヴァ♡それでも楽しく面白く読んでます


THE COSTUME SUITS HER (LAUGH)

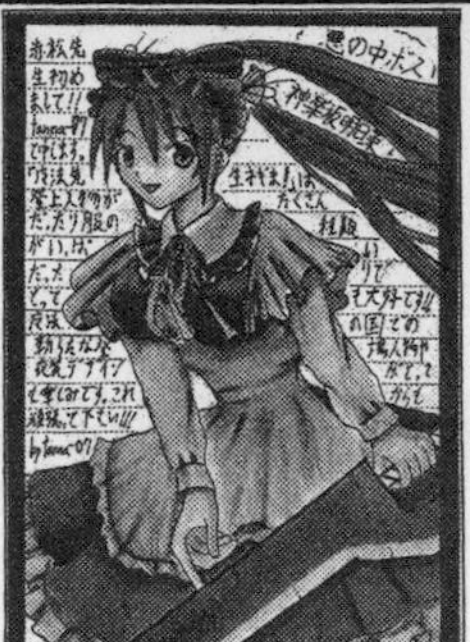

A NICE, RUGGED DESIGN.

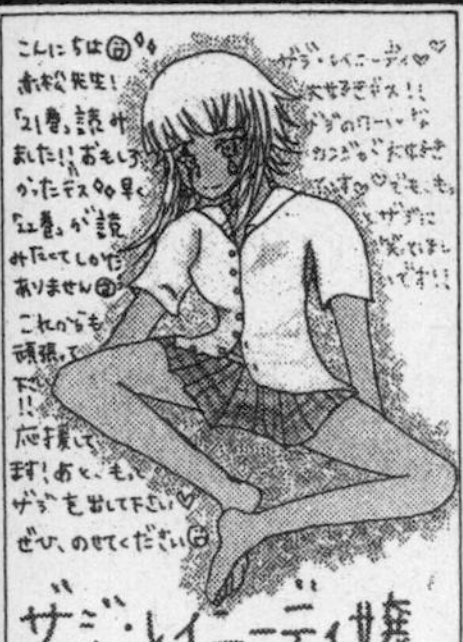
ザジ・レイニーディ嬢

I FEEL ZAZIE'S PRESENCE.

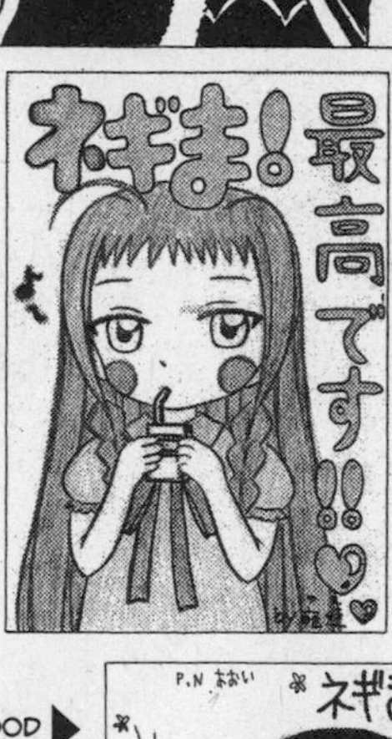
ネギま!最高です!!

WHAT JUICE IS SHE DRINKING? (LAUGH)

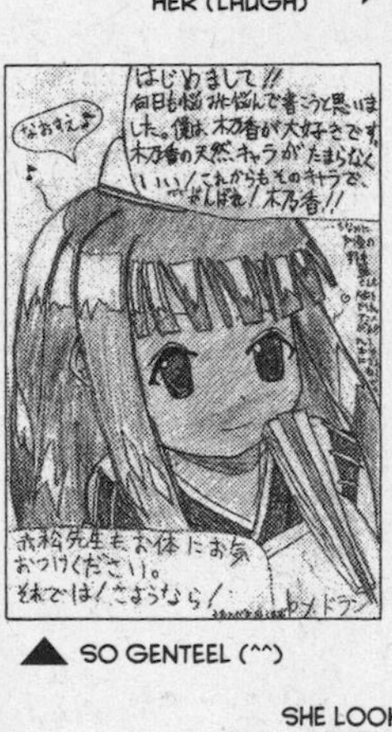
はじめまして!!
それでは!さようなら!


SO GENTEEL (^^)

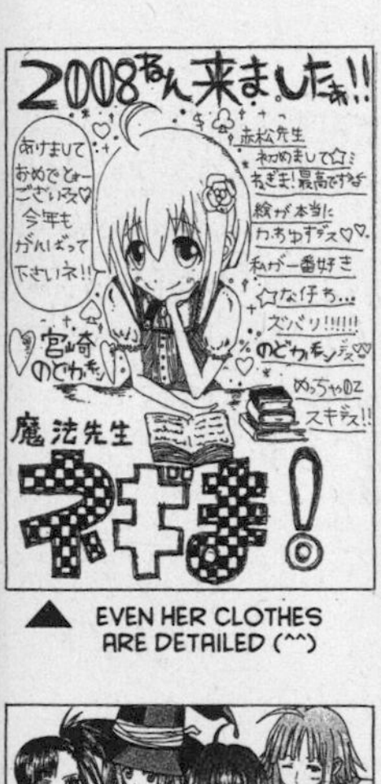
2008ねん来ました!!
魔法先生
ネギま!


EVEN HER CLOTHES ARE DETAILED (^^)

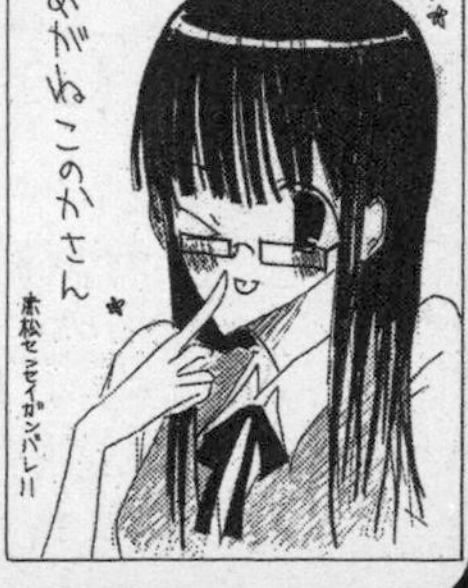
P.N あおい
ネギま!
めがねこのかさん


SHE LOOKS GOOD IN GLASSES.

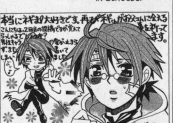

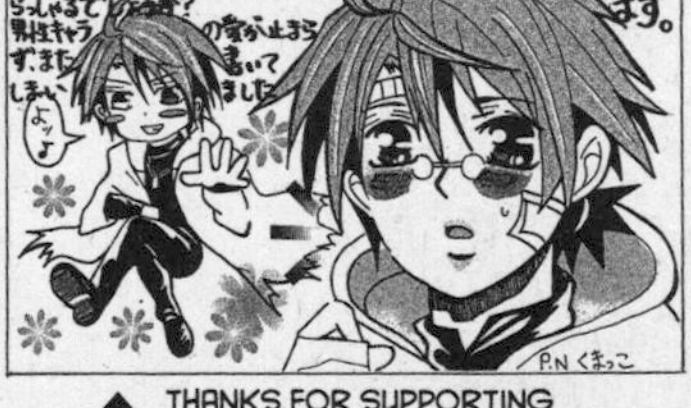
本当にネギま!大好きです。再びネギくんがお父さんに会える事を祈ってます。
P.N くまっこ


THANKS FOR SUPPORTING OUR MALE CHARACTERS!

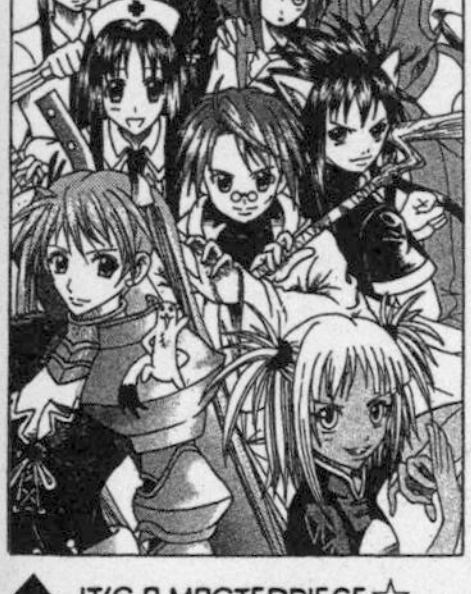

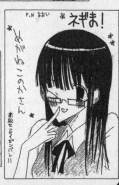

IT'S A MASTERPIECE☆

NEGI MA!

今回の
# FEATURED CHARACTER
## KOTARŌ INUGAMI
## RANKING

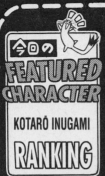

MAGISTER NEGI MAGI

FIRST PLACE

HAPPY NEW YEAR!
毎号楽しく読んでいます。応援しています。

▲ THIS TIME, WE'RE FEATURING KOTARŌ. HE DOES APPEAR IN THE NEW ANIME! TAKAHARA-SAN IS IN FIRST PLACE; HIS USE OF BETA (BLACK) IS VERY GOOD. BLACK IS KOTARŌ'S IMAGE COLOR, AFTER ALL. (^^)

(COMMENTARY: AKAMATSU)

コタロー

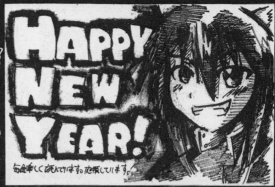

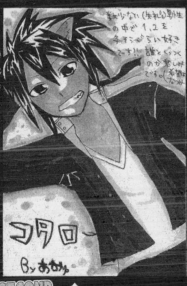

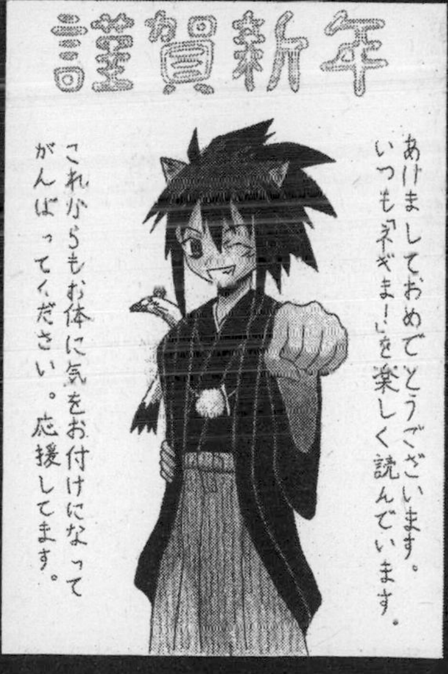

SECOND PLACE

▲ WHO WILL HE END UP WITH, YOU ASK? I GUESS IT HAS TO BE KOTA X NEGI (LAUGH) MAYBE HE'LL SURPRISE US AND END UP WITH KUGIMIYA?

KOTARŌ EVEN LOOKS GOOD IN JAPANESE CLOTHES. NOW THE GIRLS IN 3-A WON'T BE ABLE TO LEAVE HIM ALONE?! (LAUGH) ▼

THIRD PLACE

謹賀新年
あけましておめでとうございます。
いつも「ネギま!」を楽しく読んでいます。
これからもお体に気をお付けになって
がんばってください。応援してます。

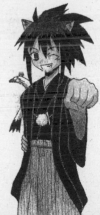

# 3-D BACKGROUNDS EXPLANATION CORNER

IT LOOKS LIKE THIS VOLUME'S MAIN FEATURE
JUST HAS TO BE THIS LARGE STRUCTURE.

## ● GRANICUS ARENAS

SCENE NAME: ARENA    POLYGON COUNT: 503,511

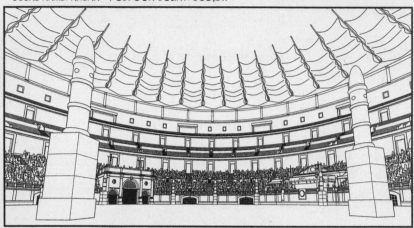

THE GIANT STRUCTURE THAT CAN BE SEEN FROM ANYWHERE IN THE CITY OF GRANICUS IS THIS SET OF ARENAS. OF THE FIVE ARENAS, THE ONE THAT NEGI AND KOTARŌ HAD THEIR MATCHES IN IS THE BIGGEST, BOASTING A DIAMETER OF 60 M, AND THE BUILDING ITSELF HAS A DIAMETER OF 200 M. IT CAN HOLD MORE THAN 50,000 PEOPLE, IS COMPLETE WITH FACILITIES LIKE CAFÉS, AND IS A BIG ENTERTAINMENT CENTER FOR THE CITIZENS.

IT GOES WITHOUT SAYING THAT IT'S MODELED AFTER THE COLISEUM IN ANCIENT ROME; THE SHAPES ARE DIFFERENT IN THAT ONE IS AN ELLIPSE AND ONE IS A CIRCLE, BUT THE ARCHITECTURAL PATTERN IS ALMOST THE SAME.

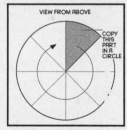

VIEW FROM ABOVE

COPY THIS PART IN A CIRCLE

FOR CYLINDRICAL OBJECTS, I MAKE ONLY ONE PART, COPY, AND ROTATE IT FOR THE REST, SO IT'S EASIER THAN IT LOOKS.

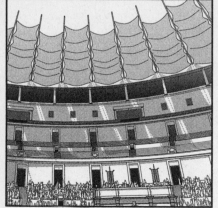

## • THE ARENA'S SHADOWS

THERE ARE CANOPIES SPREAD OVER THE SPECTATOR SEATING IN THE ARENA TO KEEP OUT THE SUN, AND THE SHADOWS THAT THEY CAST OVER THE INSIDE OF THE CYLINDER ARE A LITTLE COMPLICATED, SO IT'S EXTREMELY DIFFICULT TO REPRODUCE THOSE ACCURATELY BY HAND. ONCE I'VE DRAWN UP THE LINES USING THE NORMAL 3-D SOFTWARE, I THEN ESTABLISH A LIGHT SOURCE WITHIN THE 3-D SPACE AND PAINT IN THE SHADOWS AT THE SAME TIME, SO THEY'RE REPRODUCED ACCURATELY.

# LEXICON NEGIMARIUM

[ *Negima!* 196th Period Lexicon Negimarium]

■ **"Sprouting young buds, become a chain and bind my enemy."**
(pullulantes pulli, vinculum facti inimicum captent)
•A spell that uses plant vines as a medium to restrain its target. It's very basic magic, and easier to use by beginners than magic arrows.

■ **"Come, earth, flower spirits, gather with dreaming flowers under the blue sky and create a storm. SPRING TEMPEST"**
(veniant, spiritus terreteres florentes, cum flores somniali sub caelo percurrat una tempestas. VERIS TEMPESTAS FLORENS)
•A tactical hypnosis spell that causes all targets in range to fall unconscious. It is effective as a military spell because it can knock out several targets.

[ *Negima!* 197th Period Lexicon Negimarium]

■ **The Old World**
Mundus Vetus
•Mundus vetus is Latin for "old world." In the Magical World (Mundus Magicus), the world where wizards live with their culture unique to wizards, "Mundus Vetus" is what they call the space where we live with the culture unique to us. With Europe at the center, our world has stripped itself of magic, but since long ago, and even today, we maintain our cultures of sorcery and mythology, so it would not be appropriate to call it the "non-magical world."

As for why the Magical World calls our world the Old World, that is because the relationship between our world and the magical world is the same as the relationship that calls the Americas the "New World," and Asia, Africa, and Europe the "Old World." Also, in keeping with this, people from the Old World are called "veteres."

Furthermore, on page 29, they call Mundus Vetus "the real world," but this is a mistranslation. This is because the Magical World and the Old World are both real worlds, and the Latin for "real world" would be "mundus actualis." That interpretation is an expression of the feeling of distance Asakura, Chisame, and the others still feel toward the Magical World.

[ *Negima!* 198th Period Lexicon Negimarium ]

## ■ One Hundred Shadow Spears
(CENTUM LANCEAE UMBRAE)

• An attack spell of sōei jutsu, the magic that controls manifestations of shadows. It generates an object from the shadows and mounts a physical attack that pierces magic barriers. For more on "shadows" and "sōei jutsu," please refer to the lexicon in the extras at the end of *Negima!* volume 12. [Note—in the volume 12 lexicon, sōei jutsu is listed not as soei jutsu, but as "the ultimate technique of a Shadow Master." In volume 12 itself, Takane calls herself a Shadow User, who uses sōei jutsu.]

## ■ "Executioner's Sword, Imperfect"
(IMPERFECTUS ENSIS EXSEQUENS)

• A spell with high destructive capabilities that mounts a two-stage, phase transition and low-temperature attack by forcing matter to change phase from solid or liquid to gas. For details, see the lexicon in the extras in the back of *Negima!* volume 12. It is a difficult magic to master, and while Evangeline can use it without any problems, Negi has yet to master it fully, and so his is "imperfect."

[ *Negima!* 199th Period Lexicon Negimarium ]

## ■ Chirurgicum

• Chirurgicum is the neuter gender, singular noun form of the Latin adjective "chirurgicus." The neuter gender noun meaning room, "spatium," is omitted. According to *Lewis & Short*, "chirurgicus" translates to "surgical," but it comes the Greek χειρουργία (cheirourgia), "work of the hand," which leads to the Japanese for surgery, "*shujutsu*."

Before modern times, a lot of medicine was performed by high-ranking clergy, so they avoided surgical treatments that would get blood on them, and left these procedures to barbers and bathhouses (it is said that the red, blue, and white barber poles in use by barbershops today signify the arteries, veins, and lymph fluid or bandages in memory of that). But until L. Pasteur (1822–1895), H.H.R. Koch (1843–1910), and others pioneered bacteriology, no one prepared the sanitary environment needed for surgery, and they couldn't utilize its true power as medical treatment.

Nevertheless, for medical magic, sanitation poses little to no problem, so in medical magic, they have developed unique "chirurgia" (work of the hand), which leads to the Japanese "*teate*," for "medical care," literally "put a hand to."

[ *Negima!* 200th Period Lexicon Negimarium ]

## ■ The Hero with a Thousand Faces

O Iros Meta Chilion Prosopon
(ὁ ἥρως μετὰ χίλιων πρόσωπων)

• Jack Rakan is awarded this tool for his use by the power of the pactio with Nagi.

A supreme artifact that can change shape freely to any weapon from stockings to a catapult.

[ *Negima!* 201st Period Lexicon Negimarium ]

## ■ "The Raven's Eye"

Oculus Corvinus

• Kazumi Asakura is awarded this tool for her use by the power of the pactio with Negi, Japanese name: *watarigarasu no hitomi*. It is a spy device that can be remote-controlled from exceedingly long distances. "Oculus" means "eye," or in other words "*hitomi*," which, with different kanji, means "people watcher." "Corvinus" is the adjective form of "corvus," or the common raven (scientific name, "corvus corax"). Because of their great intelligence, ravens are believed to watch the earth as messengers of the gods. For example, in Norse mythology, legend has it that "two ravens sit on his (Odin's) shoulders and whisper in his ears all that they see. The two ravens' names are Huginn and Muninn. When dawn breaks, Odin sends the two ravens out. He does so to let them fly around the entire world. At breakfast time, the two ravens return. Odin hears a multiplicity of tidings from the ravens." (*Snorri's Edda*, part 1, chapter 38), and in the Japanese myth of Emperor Jimmu's Eastern Expedition, it says "Takagi no Ōkami (Takamimusuhi no Kami) no Mikoto spoke, saying...I will send Yatagarasu (raven) from heaven. And the raven will guide you," (Kojiki, middle section) and according to legend, the raven preceded Kamuyamato Iwarebiko no Mikoto (Emperor Jimmu) in his eastward migration and surveyed the way ahead.

■ "Dispel"

DISPULSATIO

• A midlevel spell that students are required to learn at the magic academy. It terminates the paranormal phenomena brought about by magic. The caster's magical power collides with the magical power from the paranormal phenomena, and if the caster's power is greater, it can extinguish the phenomena in question. However, it can easily terminate paranormal phenomena brought into existence by the caster himself. Magic cancel can deploy this "magic erasing magic" voluntarily, constantly, and with maximum output. However, "magic erasing magic" is itself a contradictory magic, so no matter how powerful the wizard, it is impossible to deploy it constantly (with special exceptions).

■ Final pose

• The English social anthropologist J.G. Frazer (1854–1941) said the following: "In many parts of Europe dancing or leaping high in the air are approved homoeopathic modes of making the crops grow high. Thus in Franche-Comté they say that you should dance at the Carnival in order to make the hemp grow tall." (*The Golden Bough*, ch.III, §2) If you were to peruse anthropological texts, you wouldn't have time to count the examples of dance accompanying the use of spells (ibid. ch.V, IX, XI, XII, XX, XXV, XXXIII, XLV, XLVIII, etc.). Dancing fulfills a role in spells that is no less important than singing (incanting). Rakan being so particular about striking a final pose comes from this basic characteristic of spells. It's not unreasonable for Chisame, who is unfamiliar with the culture of spells, to call Rakan a freak for his obsession, but even Negi sees it as "stupidity," which is an indication that Negi himself still has much to learn about magic.


[ *Negima!* 202nd Period Lexicon Negimarium]


■ "Maximum Output"

vis maxima

• A spell that maximizes the effects of such spells as "cantus bellax (song of battle)" and "melodia bellax (melody of battle)." It consumes a great amount of magic power, so it only lasts a very short time.

## ■ Examination in Progress

examinamus

• The present indicative first person plural form of the verb "examinare," which means "to examine." It's what the sprites say when the school nurse at the Academic City Ariadne summons them. They're saying, "We're examining you!"

## ■ Ariadne

[Αριάδνη] Ariadne

• The name of the biggest independent academic city-state in the Magical World. Ariadne is the daughter of Minos, king of Crete, and she is the one who gave the ball of thread to Theseus, the hero who fought the Minotaur, to help him find his way out of the Labyrinth (*Plutarch's Parallel Lives*, Theseus 19:1, etc.). From this story, clues that help people escape from enigmas and dilemmas have come to be called "Ariadne's thread." In keeping with this story, the symbol on the emblem of the Academic City Ariadne is a spindle with thread around it.

The Academic City Ariadne is neutral from all political force and is a free place of learning, governed by the Ariadne Magic Knights (Ariadniensis Magus Ordo).

"Ordo" is translated as "*kishidan*" or "knights," but should really be translated as "order." The Japanese "*kishidan*" and English "knights" could give the wrong impression that it's simply a military group. The famous Knights Templar and Knights of Malta, too, are orders like the Franciscan and Dominican orders of Catholicism. These organizations were orders of knights who participated in the Crusades and organized themselves after the model of other orders. For that reason, the "knights" are not merely armed groups, but are organizations with a set constitution that perform operations such as learning, medical care, and missionary work.

Like the Teutonic Knights and Knights of Malta of old, knightly orders also have their own territory (but it was difficult to distinguish between their territory and the donated land that made up the orders' property). The Ariadne Magic Knights have the Academic City and its surroundings as their territory, and they protect the place of learning from intervention by outside powers. Because of this, the Ariadne Magic Knights have a division responsible for using military force to defend their territory.

■ **"Aviation! Levitation! Fly, Broom!"**

(volatio, levitatio, scopae volent)

•As the words suggest, these are spells for flying on a broom. Flying on a broom without incantations is the basic of the basics, and Negi, Anya, and the other Ariadne Magic Knight trainees *1, etc. don't incant spells unless suddenly accelerating or decelerating.

[ *Negima!* 204th Period Lexicon Negimarium]

■ **"Come, darkness from the abyss, blazing sword!! Great flame of darkness and shadow, of hatred and destruction, of vengeance!! Burn him, burn me, burn all to nothing, Flames of Hell!"**

(Agite, tenebrae abyssi, ensis incendens, et incendium caliginis umbrae inimicitiae destructionis ultionis, incendant et me et eum, sint solum incendentes, INCENDIUM GEHENNAE)

•In Latin, there are many words that mean fire or flame, such as "ignis" (fire), "flamma" (flame), "flagrantia" (blaze), "ardor" (burning heat), "incendium" (big fire), but of them, "incendium" signifies a very large flame. Up to this point, the basic "magic archer" is incanted with "IGNIS," the midlevel "Red Blaze" is incanted with "FLAGRANTIA," and the binding spell "Purple Flame Captor" is incanted with the adjective form of "FLAMMA" (see *Negima!* volume 13, 113th Period; volume 16, 141st Period).

Furthermore, "gehennae" is the singular, genitive case of the Latin used in the Vulgate translation of the New Testament, meaning "hell." This word comes from the Hebrew "gehinom"*2, or the "Valley of Hinnom." This valley was a place in the south of Jerusalem where they burned garbage and the bodies of criminals.

■ **"Stabilize. Seize. Load magic. 'Armament'"**

(stagnet, complexio, supplementum pro armationem.)

•Stops the magical power that was supposed to leave and be released from a spell caster in their hand and absorbs it. "pro" is a preposition meaning "for, in order to," "armationem" is the singular accusative case of the abstract noun that comes from the verb "armare (to arm)."

*1. Order members in training are called novices (novitius). Misora Kasuga isn't a member of the order, but a novice (novitia).

*2. Written in Roman letters instead of Hebrew.

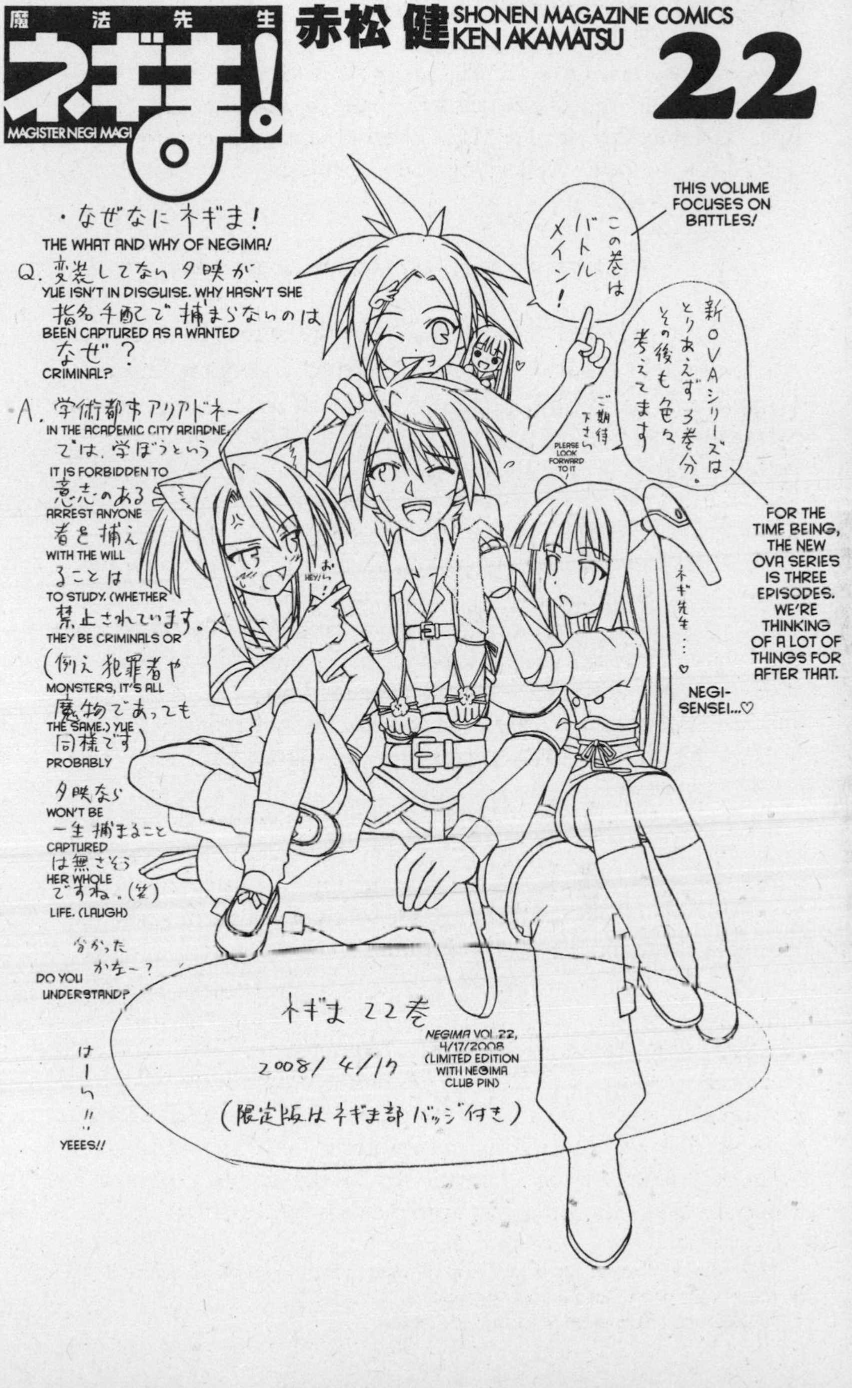
魔法先生
ネギま!
MAGISTER NEGI MAGI
赤松 健
SHONEN MAGAZINE COMICS
KEN AKAMATSU
22
・なぜなにネギま!
THE WHAT AND WHY OF NEGIMA!
Q. 変装してない夕映が、指名手配で捕まらないのはなぜ?
YUE ISN'T IN DISGUISE. WHY HASN'T SHE BEEN CAPTURED AS A WANTED CRIMINAL?
A. 学術都市アリアドネーでは、学ぼうという意志のある者を捕えることは禁止されています。(例え犯罪者や魔物であっても同様です) 夕映なら一生捕まることは無さそうですね。(笑)
IN THE ACADEMIC CITY ARIADNE, IT IS FORBIDDEN TO ARREST ANYONE WITH THE WILL TO STUDY. (WHETHER THEY BE CRIMINALS OR MONSTERS, IT'S ALL THE SAME.) YUE PROBABLY WON'T BE CAPTURED HER WHOLE LIFE. (LAUGH)
分かったかネ〜?
DO YOU UNDERSTAND?
は〜ら!!
YEEES!!
この巻はバトルメイン!
THIS VOLUME FOCUSES ON BATTLES!
新OVAシリーズはとりあえず3巻分。その後も色々考えてます
FOR THE TIME BEING, THE NEW OVA SERIES IS THREE EPISODES. WE'RE THINKING OF A LOT OF THINGS FOR AFTER THAT.
ご期待下さい
PLEASE LOOK FORWARD TO IT
おら!
HEY!
ネギ先生…♡
NEGI-SENSEI...♡
ネギま 22巻
2008/4/17
(限定版はネギま部バッジ付き)
NEGIMA VOL.22, 4/17/2008 (LIMITED EDITION WITH NEGIMA CLUB PIN)

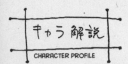

キャラ解説
CHARACTER PROFILE

⑪ 釘宮 円
(11) MADOKA KUGIMIYA

ボーイッシュな釘宮ですが、亜子編での活躍に
BOYISH KUGIMIYA HAD A SUDDEN RISE IN POPULARITY WITH HER INVOLVEMENT
より人気は急上昇! 大人版コタローとの
IN THE AKO EPISODES! HER RELATIONSHIP WITH ADULT-VERSION NEGI HAS
関係も浮上してきて、今後に期待の持てる
COME TO THE SURFACE, AS WELL, SO SHE'S BECOME A CHARACTER YOU CAN
キャラになりましたね。
HAVE HIGH HOPES FOR IN THE FUTURE.

髪型が難しくて、なかなか可愛く描けません。
HER HAIRSTYLE IS DIFFICULT, AND I JUST CAN'T DRAW IT CUTELY.
(…っていうが、ほとんどショート版モトコ?)
(…ER, I GUESS SHE'S LIKE A SHORT-HAIRED MOTOKO?)

チア3人組の中では、色気は少ない方ですが、
OF THE THREE CHEERLEADERS, SHE'S THE LEAST SEXY, BUT I THINK IF I WERE TO
女家にするなら 最適だと思います。(笑)
CHOOSE A BRIDE FROM THEM, SHE WOULD BE THE MOST SUITABLE. (LAUGH)
しっかりしてるから…
BECAUSE SHE'S GOT IT TOGETHER…

アニメ版CVは 出口茉美さん。元気な娘。
THE ACTRESS WHO VOICES HER IN THE ANIME IS MAMI DEGUCHI-SAN.
デビュー当時はまだ10代で、かなり緊張した
SHE'S A CHEERFUL GIRL WHO WAS STILL IN HER TEENS WHEN SHE DEBUTED,
様子でしたが、最近は余裕が出てきたみたい。(^^)
AND SHE LOOKED LIKE SHE WAS PRETTY NERVOUS, BUT IT LOOKS LIKE

ドラマ版は 市川円香さん。
SHE'S MORE CONFIDENT RECENTLY. (^^) IN THE DRAMA, SHE IS PLAYED BY
元リネージュガールで、ネギまでも 水着姿を
MADOKA ICHIKAWA-SAN. SHE USED TO BE A LINEAGE GIRL, AND SHE LETS
披露してくれました! よし、!! ありがとー
US SEE HER IN A SWIMSUIT IN NEGIMA, TOO! ALL RIGHT!! THANK YOU!

赤松
AKAMATSU

# About the Creator

*Negima!* is only Ken Akamatsu's third manga, although he started working in the field in 1994 with *AI Ga Tomaranai* (released in the United States with the title *A.I. Love You*). Like all of Akamatsu's work to date, it was published in Kodansha's *Shonen Magazine*. *AI Ga Tomaranai* ran for five years before concluding in 1999. In 1998, however, Akamatsu began the work that would make him one of the most popular manga artists in Japan: *Love Hina*. *Love Hina* ran for four years, and before its conclusion in 2002, it would cause Akamatsu to be granted the prestigious Manga of the Year award from Kodansha, as well as going on to become one of the bestselling manga in the United States.

## NEGIMA!
### FAN ART CORNER

OH! THE FATE POWER HAS EMERGED. NO, SOME KIND OF VAGUE FORCE IS GRADUALLY MAKING ITS WAY IN (LAUGH). I GOT TO SEE A LOT OF PICTURES THAT WERE OF MULTIPLE CHARACTERS, BUT NOT COUPLES. ANYHOW, LET'S GET STARTED.

TEXT BY MAX

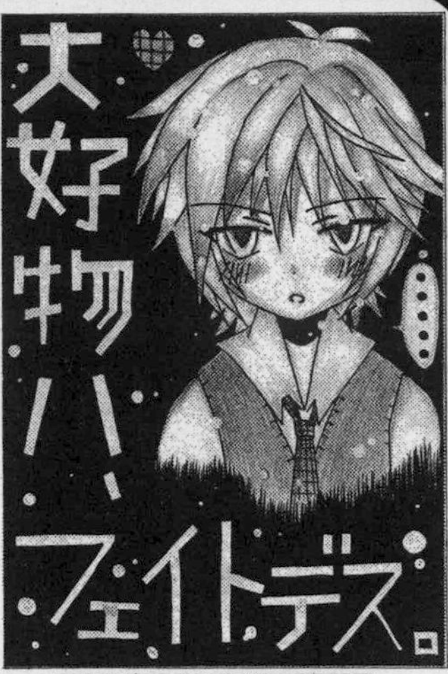
大好物ハ、フェイトデス。

I MIGHT WANT TO PROTECT A FATE LIKE THIS (LAUGH)

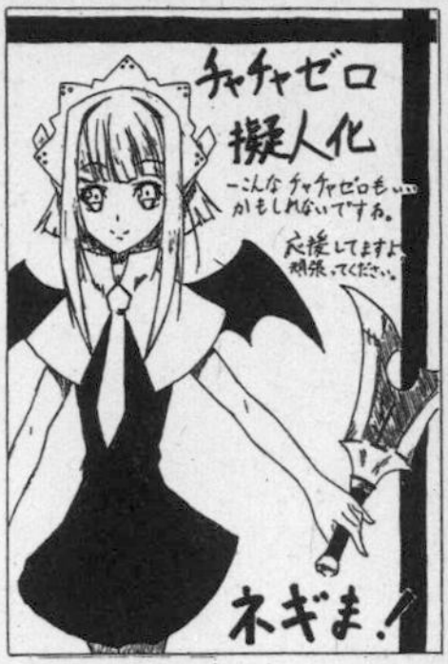
チャチャゼロ擬人化
こんなチャチャゼロもいるかもしれないですね。
応援してますよ。頑張ってください。
ネギま！

A BEAUTIFUL GIRL? (LAUGH)

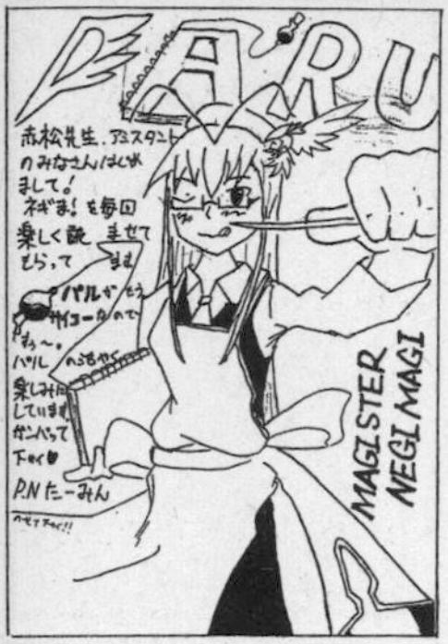
PARU
赤松先生、アシスタントのみなさんはじめまして！
ネギま！を毎回楽しく読ませてもらってます
MAGISTER NEGI MAGI
P.N たーみん

SHE'S READY FOR SOMETHING ☆

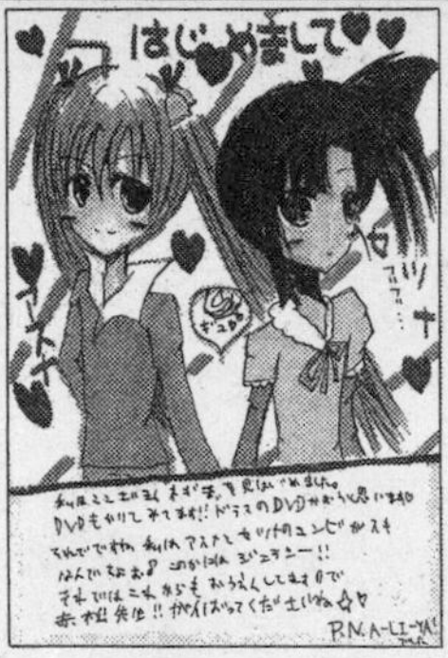
はじめまして

IT KINDA PLUCKS AT YOUR HEARTSTRINGS.

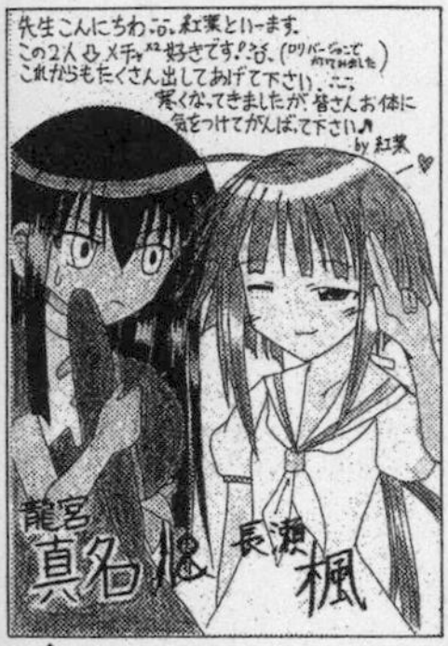
先生こんにちわ。紅葉といいます。
寒くなってきましたが、皆さんお体に気をつけてがんばって下さい♪
by 紅葉
龍宮真名 & 長瀬楓

BATTLE TEAM ☆

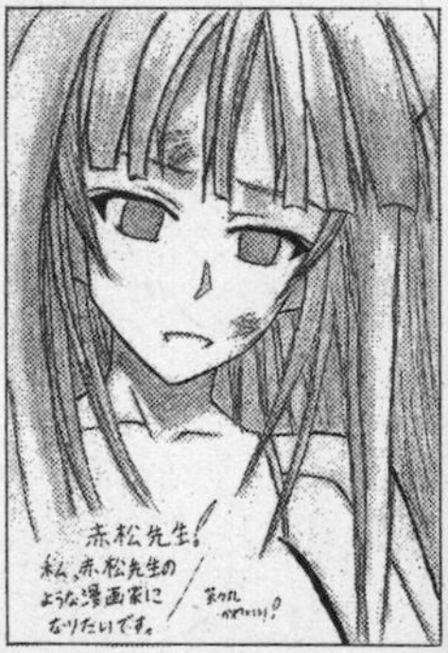
赤松先生！
私、赤松先生のような漫画家になりたいです。

GOOD EYES.

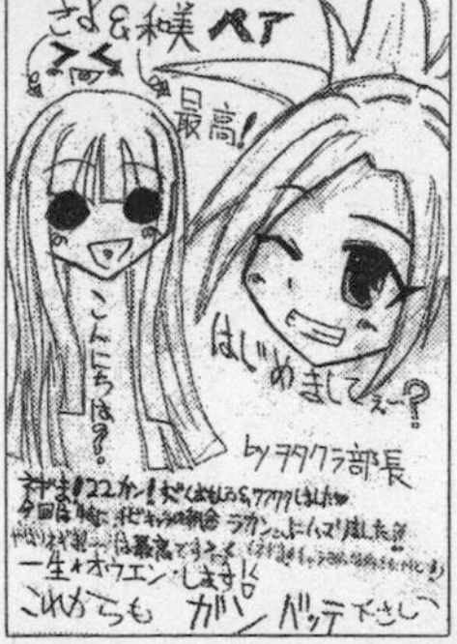
さよ&和美ペア
最高！
こんにちは？
はじめましてぇ～？
by ヲタクラ部長
一生オウエンします
これからもガンバッテ下さい

FRIENDLY PAIR ☆

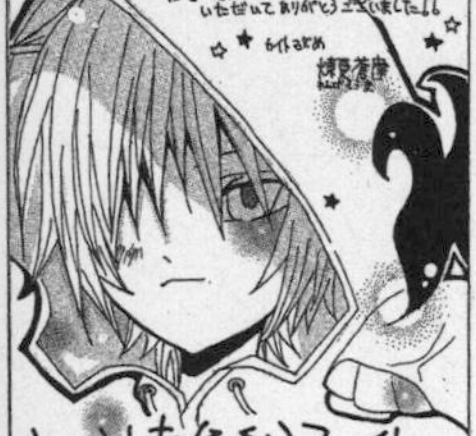
13巻でもイラスト載せていただいてありがとうございました!!
まってました(^ν^*)フェイト君
わーい!! 再登場まってました
また一段とかっこよくなって帰ってきましたね！
ネギパーティーとの関係も気になりますね。
では、これからもがんばって下さい。m(_ _)m ペコ

AND FATE'S HERE.

NEGI MA!

MAGISTER NEGI MAGI

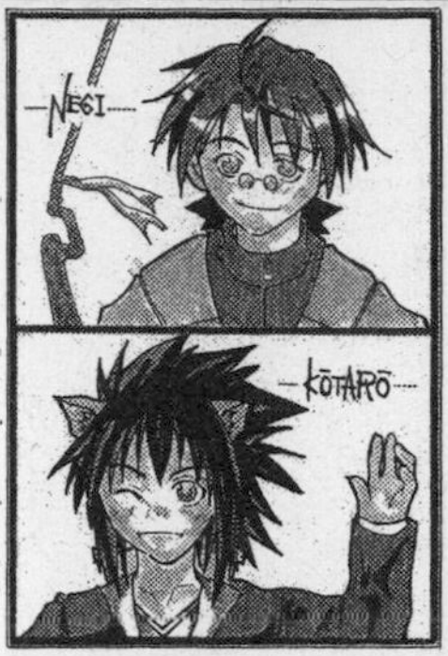
NEGI
KOTARO

▲ KOTA-NEGI★

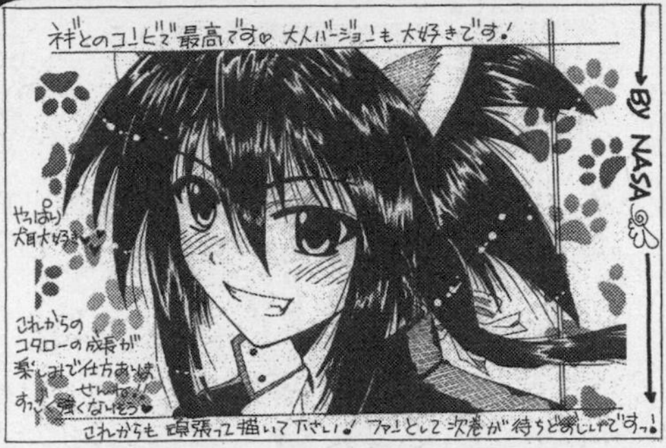
ネギとのコンビで最高です♥ 大人バージョンも大好きです!
BY NASA
やっぱり犬耳大好き♥
これからのコタローの成長が楽しみで仕方ありません!! すっごく強くなりそう♥
これからも頑張って描いて下さい! ファンとして次巻が待ち遠しいです!

▲ THIS...IS TOO CUTE (LAUGH)

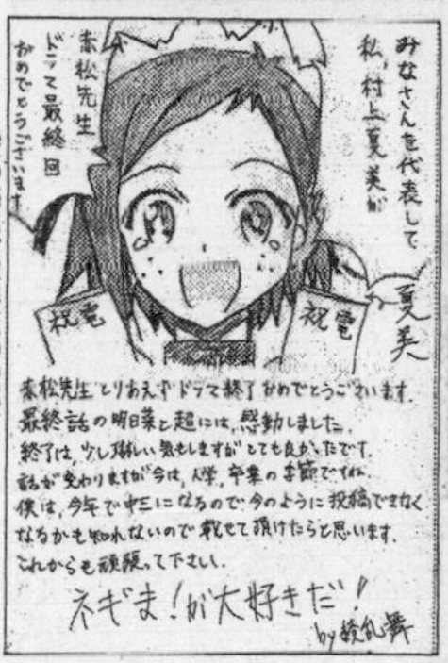
みなさんを代表して私、村上夏美が
赤松先生ドラマ最終回おめでとうございます
祝電
祝電
夏美
ネギま!が大好きだ!

▲ SHE HAS CONGRATULATORY TELEGRAMS (LAUGH)

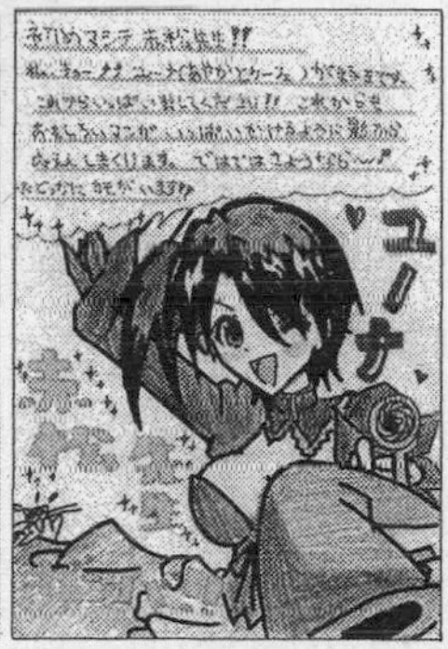
ユーナ

▲ YŪNA SURE IS ENERGETIC.

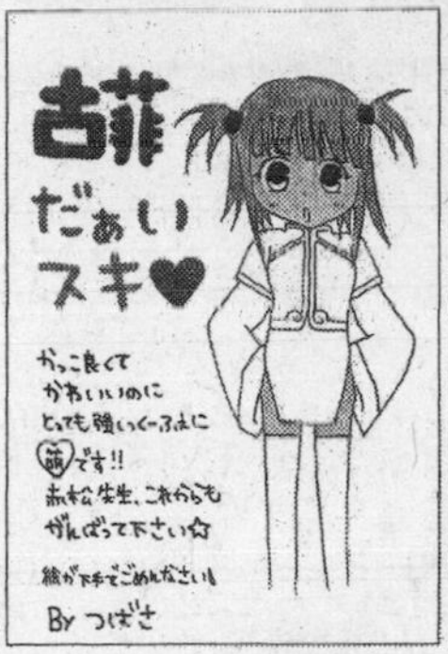
古菲 だぁいスキ♥
かっこ良くてかわいいのにとっても強いくーふぇに萌です!!
赤松先生、これからもがんばって下さい☆
絵が下手でごめんなさい
By つばさ

▲ IT'S LIKE SHE'S SAYING "HAYO?" ("HUH?")

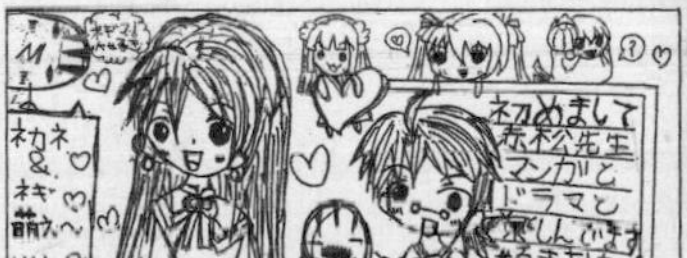
初めまして赤松先生

▲ NEKAWE. THAT'S UNUSUAL.

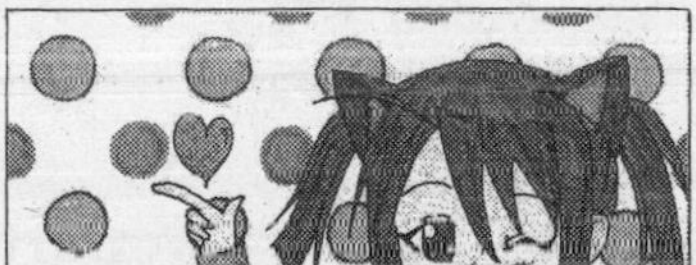
ネギま!

▲ HER TONGUE IS SO CUTE.

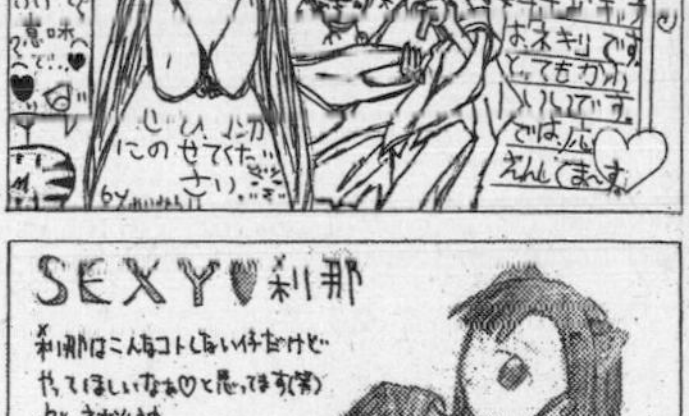
SEXY♥刹那
刹那はこんなコトしない子だけどやってほしいなぁ♥と思ってます(笑)
by ネギ女神

▲ THAT IS SEXY.

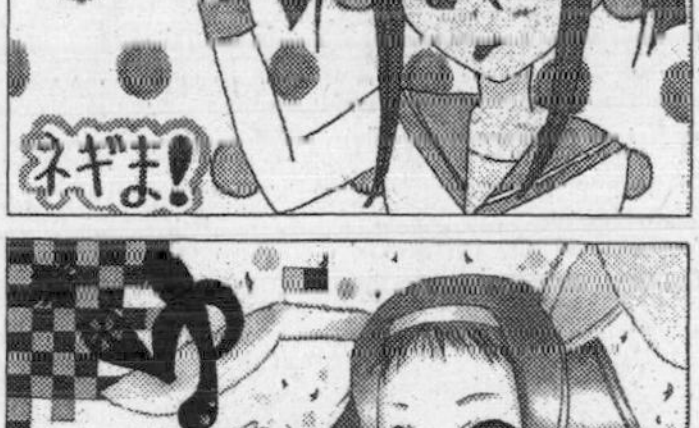

▲ IS THE NEGI (GREEN ONION) TEA ANY GOOD?

## 3-D BACKGROUNDS EXPLANATION CORNER

PRESENTED ALONG WITH THINGS I COULDN'T INTRODUCE IN THE LAST VOLUME.

### • RAKAN'S CASTLE

SCENE NAME: RAKAN'S TOWER POLYGON COUNT: 92,856

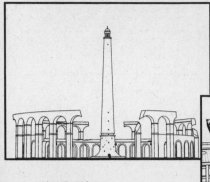

RAKAN'S HOME, STANDING IN THE MIDDLE OF THE DESERT. APPROXIMATELY 320M TALL, WORD IS IT STARTED OUT AS AN ANCIENT RUIN.

THE REASON HE LIVES HERE IS UNKNOWN, BUT IT DOES SEEM LIKE A CONVENIENT PLACE FOR RAKAN, WHO HAS EXTRAORDINARY POWER, TO TRAIN.

• PIER & BED

APPARENTLY HE BROUGHT A BED OUT HERE SO THEY WOULDN'T HAVE TO MOVE NEGI TOO MUCH. THAT'S RAKAN FOR YOU—HE'S REALLY STRONG. (LAUGH)

### • WHALE SHIP

SCENE NAME: WHALE SHIP POLYGON COUNT: 66,114

THE VIEWING DECK ON THE WHALE SHIP ASAKURA AND CHACHAMARU ARE RIDING. IT'S WIDE AND SPACIOUS, AND IT LOOKS LIKE THEY CAN ENJOY A REFINED JOURNEY.

INCIDENTALLY, FOR THE DESIGN I REFERRED TO ORDINARY VIEWING PLATFORMS.

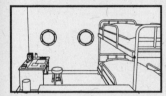

• CABINS

ON THE OTHER HAND, THEIR CABIN IS SIMPLE. IS IT TO SAVE ON TRAVEL EXPENSES?

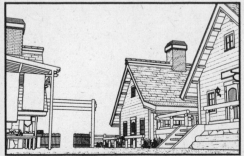

### • RURAL MOUNTAIN VILLAGE

SCENE NAME: VILLAGE
POLYGON COUNT: 503,511

THE MOUNTAIN VILLAGE WHERE ASUNA AND KONOKA WERE REUNITED. IT'S NOT A VERY BIG VILLAGE, BUT IT'S A RELAY POINT FOR TRAVELERS CROSSING THE MOUNTAINS, SO IT GETS A LOT OF VISITORS.

I MADE THE WOOD HOUSES BY REMODELING EVA'S HOUSE. OR WAS THAT OBVIOUS? (LAUGH)

# — ARIADNE MAGIC SCHOOL —

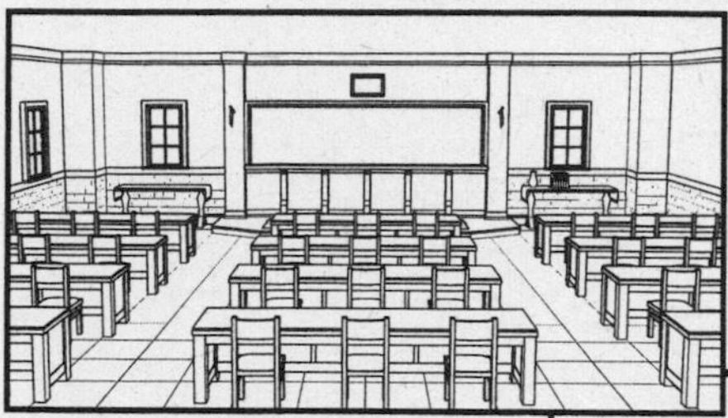

## • CLASSROOM

SCENE NAME: MS CLASSROOM
POLYGON COUNT: 32,900

THE ROOM WHERE YUE, COLLET, AND THE OTHERS LEARN. FITTING OF AN ILLUSTRIOUS SCHOOL OF THE MAGICAL ACADEMIC CITY ARIADNE, YOU CAN FEEL THE HISTORY IN THE WAY IT WAS MADE. BUT ACTUALLY, THE DESKS AND CHAIRS ARE JUST REUSED, SO I HAD A RELATIVELY EASY TIME MAKING IT.

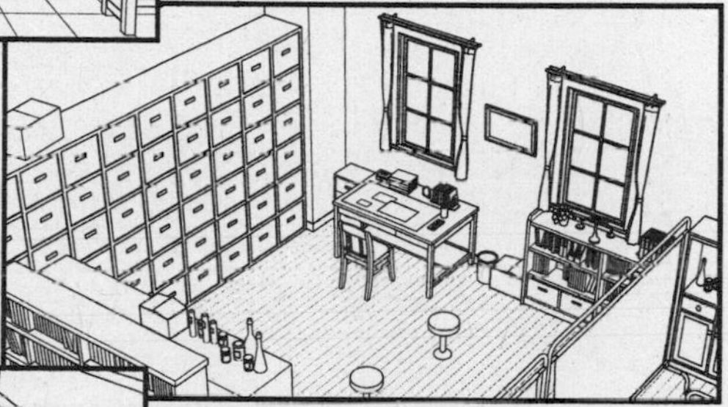

## • NURSE'S OFFICE

SCENE NAME: MS HEALTH ROOM
POLYGON COUNT: 91,914

THE NURSE'S OFFICE THAT APPEARED IN VOLUME 22. THERE ARE ALL KINDS OF MEDICINAL HERBS INSIDE THE LARGE MEDICINE CABINET. THE MEDICINE BOTTLES STAND OUT, TOO.

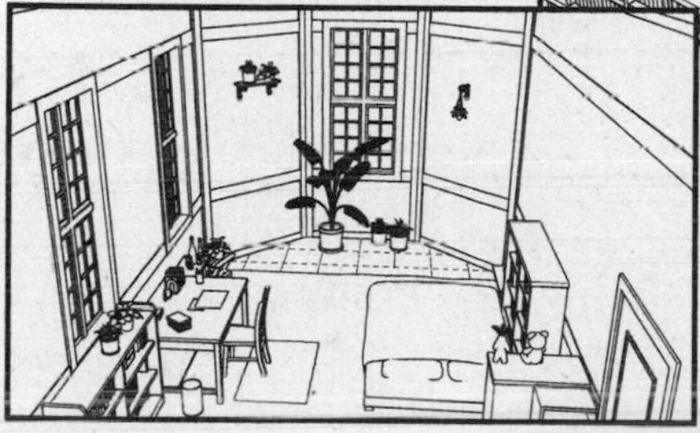

## • COLLET'S ROOM

SCENE NAME: COLLET'S ROOM
POLYGON COUNT: 58,279

COLLET'S ROOM IN THE STUDENT DORMS. THERE ARE A LOT OF POTTED PLANTS, MAYBE BECAUSE SHE'S GROWING THE MEDICINAL HERBS THAT SHE USES IN CLASS.

ALSO, IF YOU LOOK CLOSELY, YOU CAN SEE A WEIRD STUFFED ANIMAL. (LAUGH)

# — OTHER PLACES —

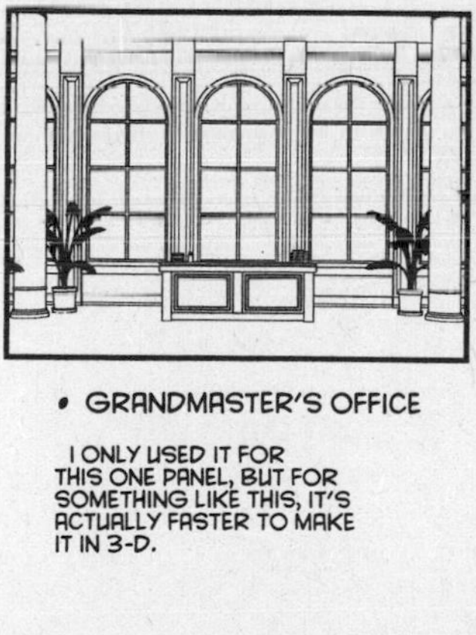

## • GRANDMASTER'S OFFICE

I ONLY USED IT FOR THIS ONE PANEL, BUT FOR SOMETHING LIKE THIS, IT'S ACTUALLY FASTER TO MAKE IT IN 3-D.

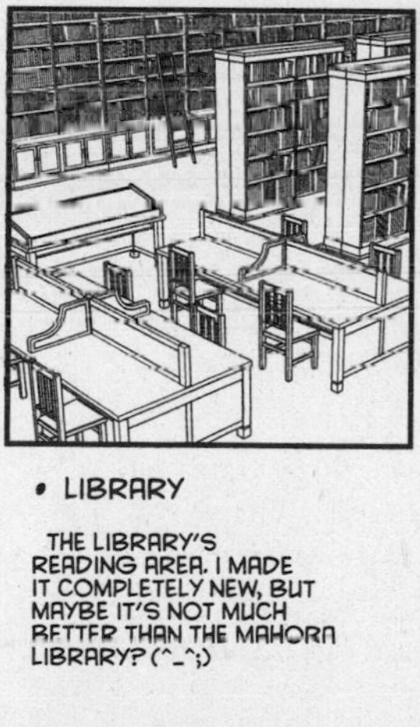

## • LIBRARY

THE LIBRARY'S READING AREA. I MADE IT COMPLETELY NEW, BUT MAYBE IT'S NOT MUCH BETTER THAN THE MAHORA LIBRARY? (^_^;)

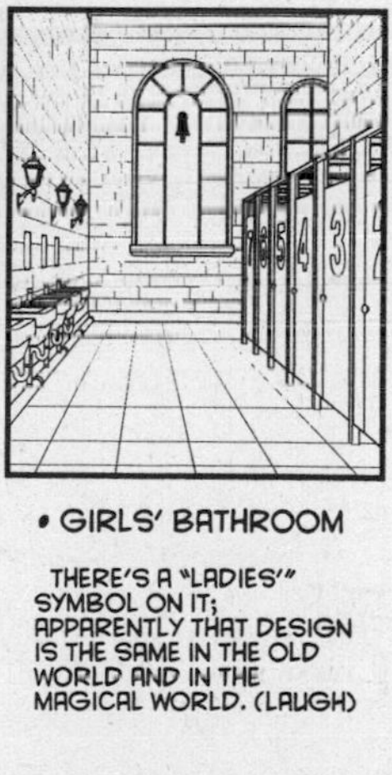

## • GIRLS' BATHROOM

THERE'S A "LADIES'" SYMBOL ON IT; APPARENTLY THAT DESIGN IS THE SAME IN THE OLD WORLD AND IN THE MAGICAL WORLD. (LAUGH)

# LEXICON NEGIMARIUM

[*Negima!* 205th Period Lexicon Negimarium]

## ■ Dark Magic

Magia Erebea

"Magia" is Latin for "magic." "Erebea" is the feminine singular nominative case of the adjective meaning "of Erebos." According to Hesiod, Erebos (Ἔρεβος) is the god of darkness in Greek mythology, the son of one of the original gods, Chaos. The children that Erebos begat with his twin sister Nyx (night) were Aether (shining air)*[1] and Hemera (day), (cf. *Theogony* 123–125), and, being darkness and night, they are the divine beings that precede light. In the words of the German romantic philosopher F. W. J. Schelling (1775–1854), "All birth is birth from darkness to light." (*Investigations of Human Freedom,* SW360; but according to Hesiod, it wasn't that everything was born from Chaos and darkness—the heavens, the oceans, and many others were born from Gaia, who was born at the same time as Chaos.)

Thus, light cannot give birth to darkness, but darkness can give birth to light. Darkness is not in opposition to light. Darkness is a source that holds all things within it, and is tremendously broad-minded. And this broad-mindedness becomes a power that takes in all opposites such as good and evil, superiority and inferiority, self and others, etc. This is because *light* is the basis of opposition and disparity. Schelling says, "Light's advance on the dark aspiration to create something . . . is due to the thoughts that are mingled in chaos becoming distinct . . . and unity being erected" (ibid. SW361). If light is the basis of opposition and disparity, darkness is the basis of nondiscrimination. Therefore, dark magic has the tremendous broad-mindedness to take in all power without discriminating between self and others.

However, things are not that simple. Within darkness, all disparity becomes invisible; the difference between self and others vanishes as well, and the spellcaster loses sight of himself. But magic spells are never anything more than techniques the caster uses to accomplish his willful purposes; their purpose is not to reach some kind of absolute truth. As stated by Schelling's school colleague, G. W. F. Hegel (1770–1830),

---

*[1]: Aether (αθήρ) is the "ether" that we speak of in modern language. In premodern cosmology, it is said to be one of the five elements that makes up things in the heavens. However, going further back and looking at mythological texts, Aether was thought of as the air in the clear sky. The Aether that Hesiod speaks of is one of the twins of light born from the twins of darkness. Because the genealogy of the goddesses goes from night (Nyx) to day (Hemera), the male gods' genealogy would go from darkness to light (however, because the Greek word "aether" does not mean light, but is translated to "*kirameku kūki,*" meaning "bright upper air" in Japanese, it was translated to the single word "*kōki,*" shining air.)

"To pit this single assertion, that 'In the Absolute, all is one,' against the organized whole of determinate and complete knowledge, or of knowledge which at least aims at and demands complete development—to give out its Absolute as the night, in which, as we say, all cows are black—that is the very naivete of emptiness of knowledge." (*Phenomenology of Spirit*, preface). In order to use a technique as a technique, especially within darkness, one must make sure not to lose sight of one's self.

What is needed then is a "confrontation with one's shadow," or "an encounter with one's anima." The battle Negi fights in Phantasmagoria is none other than a "confrontation with his shadow," or "encounter with his anima."

The Swiss psychiatrist C. G. Jung (1875–1961) said the following in regards to encounters with one's self and encounters with one's shadow: "A meeting with one's self first means a meeting with one's shadow. By shadow, I mean none other than a single narrow path, a single gate. . . . What comes after that gate is, unsurprisingly, a limitless, unprecedented uncertainty. There, it is believed there is neither inside nor outside, up nor down, far nor near, self nor other, good nor evil.

That is a world of water, and approximately everything with life there is floating, drifting" *2 (*The Archetypes and the Collective Unconscious*). By encountering one's shadow, one enters into his own soul and, as Hegel points out, enters into an obscure darkness. Jung states the following: "There, I am joined directly and firmly to the world, and it's all too simple to forget who I am in actuality. If I were to characterize this condition, the most appropriate phrase would be 'lost within oneself'" (ibid.). Thus, if one goes through their shadow into darkness, they face the fundamental danger of losing sight of oneself.

What is needed to conquer this danger is an "encounter with one's anima." Those who pass through their shadow selves and search out their souls, (as explained above) enter into a "world of water," but inside this water, people (especially men) meet their anima. "What one who gazes into the water first sees is a form of himself, but soon a living entity surfaces from beneath it. . . . It is a unique kind of water creature. Sometimes a water sprite, or a mermaid caught in a fisherman's net. . . . The water sprite is an early, instinctive stage of the mystical, feminine entity called anima." (ibid.) It is said that the anima's early stage sometimes takes the form of erotic spirits, such as demon girls or vampire women (Lamie). And it is said that "anima appear in the form of goddesses or witches." (ibid.) The Evangeline that Negi encounters in Phantasmagoria in this story is this early stage, this anima. Evangeline first appears in the nude, and we don't even have to point out that she is a vampire and also a witch. And this encounter with an anima results in a certain wisdom. "Indeed the anima is a chaotic life impulse, but on the other hand, in a mysterious sense, it has on hand secret knowledge and concealed wisdom, and is in the most peculiar opposition to one's illogical, spiritual nature. . . . This wisdom aspect appears only to one who confronts his anima. This is an intense labor . . . and can more strongly indicate that something like a secret intention hides behind all cruelty that plays with man's fate. This unpredictable thing, this

---

*2: According to *Archetypes* (Kinokuniya Shoten), take Tode as Tor.

chaotic thing that brings anxiety is precisely what exposes deep meaning. As one becomes aware of this meaning, the anima loses its aggressive personality. The embankments that hold off the flood of chaos gradually build up." (ibid.) When the one who has passed through his shadow and set foot into darkness confronts his anima and touches on that wisdom, he conquers the fundamental danger of losing sight of himself in the darkness and chaos, and obtains a way to use dark magic, or, in other words, the original broad-mindedness that encompasses all opposites.

[*Negima!* 205th Period Lexicon Negimarium]

## ■ Demon's Nursery Rhyme

(Comptina Daemonia)

A magical item that can learn the names of others. In magical culture, it is believed to be extremely dangerous to have one's name known to others (cf. *The Golden Bough,* ch.XXII, §1).

For example, there is an old story from Isawa District in Iwate Prefecture of Japan. A carpenter took on the job of building a bridge over some swift rapids. But the job was too difficult, and he sat near the river, at a loss for what to do. A demon appeared and said he would build the bridge in exchange for the carpenter's eyes. Two days later, the carpenter went to the river, and the bridge was built. The demon appeared and demanded the carpenter's eyes. The carpenter panicked and escaped into the mountains, where he heard a song in the distance: "I hope Oniroku brings the eyes soon" (this song varies depending on tradition; there is a version where it is a nursery rhyme sung by demon children, and a version where it is a lullaby sung to lull demon children to sleep). The next day, the carpenter met the demon, who told him that if he could guess the demon's name, he would not have to give up his eyes. When the carpenter said "Oniroku," the demon was destroyed (Keigo Seki's *Japanese Folktales III,* Iwanami Shoten). The story tells us that even if you are facing a type of demon, if you know their name, you can hold their life in your hands. Furthermore, it also tells us that true names are hidden in nursery rhymes and lullabies. The name "Demon's Nursery Rhyme" means that the item will inform its user of those hidden names.

[*Negima!* 206th Period Lexicon Negimarium]

## ■ 𑖦𑖽

(man)

In Ryōfu Nankoku Sanzō Mandara Sen's translation of *Manjushiri Shosetsu Maka Hannya Haramikkyō,* it says, "Mañjuśrī said, 'I do not see the form of truth in all things. Buddha naturally perceives that all things are emptiness. This is precisely what can prove wisdom.' Buddha said to Mañjuśrī, 'That is correct. Enlightened ones truly perceive and naturally prove the truth of emptiness.'" Mañjuśrī is known as a bodhisattva, one who vows to save all beings before becoming a Buddha, who excelled in wisdom, or prajñā (Sanskrit). Mañjuśrī is his Sanskrit name.

The character "man" is Mañjuśrī's seed syllable (the first syllable of a mantra, in which is contained all meaning), and is said to come from the first character in Mañjuśrī. This seed is written on Kaede's blindfold to share in the good luck of the words of Mañjuśrī, where he says, "I do not see truth in all things, I naturally perceive the truth (that all things are emptiness)," and gain extraordinary perceptive powers.

■ म(ग्न
   (agni)

A word that means "fire," or "god of fire," in Sanskrit (to be more precise, its root and singular noun form is "agnis"). In order to make use of the ninja techniques (or rather Buddhist techniques) that come from explosive fire, Kaede makes a chain of charms with that name written on them in Sanskrit.

■ र्पः म म र्त द र्क ं ं
   (namak samanta vajra nan han)

The mantra said by *Fudō Myō-ō*, Acala the Immovable One, called the "*fudō-ichijishu*." According to a summary of notes on the Mahāvairocana Tantra, "*Dainichikyō Somyōinshō*," "*Fudō Myō-ō* is namely the Great Buddha's embodiment of injunction." That is to say, *Fudō Myō-ō* is believed to be the form Buddha takes to force his sworn enemies into submission (embodiment of injunction), and is the most aggressive of his various personalities. In Esoteric Buddhism, these three embodiments, *Myō-ō* (embodiment of injunction), *Bosatsu* (embodiment of the true way), and *Nyorai* (embodiment of self), unite to complete the mandala circle (cakram), or chakra (Sanskrit). We can assume that Kaede chanted the mantra of the Immovable in order to use Buddhist techniques with high attack power.

[ *Negima!* 207th Period Lexicon Negimarium]

■ **Artemisia Leaves**
   (folium Artemisiae)

According to the ancient Roman military commander Pliny the Elder (AD 23–79), the plant called artemisia is also known as parthenis, ambrosia, botrys, etc. (cf. *Naturalis Historia XXVII*). According to Pliny's work, the name "artemisia" was taken from the queen of Caria in Asia Minor. "The plant that had been called 'parthenis' adopted the name of Maussollos's wife, Artemisia. There are also some who believe the plant gets its name from Artemis Eileithyia. This is because this plant was used especially to heal the afflictions of women....Some call it botrys, and others call it ambrosia, but these grow in Cappadocia." (ibid. XXV)

Pliny also tells of the Magi's view of Artemisia: "It is said that poison, vicious beasts, not even the sun can harm one who carries artemisia on him." (ibid. XXV) From this legend and others (cf. ibid. XXVI), we can assume that the plant artemisia has mysterious power. Further, though not recorded in Pliny, artemisia leaves are well-known for staunching bleeding. However, artemisia leaves are not shaped like trident maple leaves as depicted in this work (those who are interested can observe the wild plants in their neighborhood). Nevertheless, as Pliny points out, artemisia is used for the name of various plants, and many of the plants belonging to the artemisia genus in the aster family are called in Latin "Artemisia...." Perhaps it is because of that that artemisia does not necessarily mean Artemisia vulgaris, common artemisia. Incidentally, artemisia is mugwort.

[ *Negima!* 210th Period Lexicon Negimarium ]

### ■ Read-Aloud Ear
(auris recitans)

A magical item used by those with visual disabilities to read texts. They are marketed in the Magical World. It reads what is in the texts via thought waves, so even those with hearing disabilities can use it.

[ *Negima!* 212th Period Lexicon Negimarium ]

### ■ anétte ti net garnet
Activation key of Collet Farandole, a trainee at the Magical Academic City Ariadne.

### ■ vor so kratika socratica
Activation key of Yue Farandole, a trainee at the Magical Academic City Ariadne.

### ■ Heatwave Disarmament
(CALEFACIENS EXARMATIO)

A magic spell that uses extreme heat to evaporate the enemy's equipment without burning them, thus disarming them. Of course it can't evaporate equipment made of metal, earthenware, or the like, but because its aim is disarmament, it is a complex spell that not only bathes the enemy in heat, but protects the enemy's body by casting heat-resistant magic on them.

### ■ tarot carrot charlotte
Activation key of Emily Sevensheep, a trainee at the Magical Academic City Ariadne.

### ■ Hail of Ice Spears
(JACULATIO GRANDINIS)

An attack spell that causes javelins made of ice to fall like hail. Because the warheads it releases are spears and not arrows, each individual warhead is more powerful than magic arrows made of ice. However, because the basis of the spell is warheads that fall from above, the spell is harder to put into practical use than magic arrows.

# BONUS PAGES 附錄頁

## DISCOVER *NEGIMA!* AGAIN: THE TAIWANESE VERSION!!

IN VOLUME 20, WE INTRODUCED VARIOUS FOREIGN VERSIONS; THIS TIME, WE'VE CREATED A FEATURE FOCUSING ON THE TAIWANESE VERSION. A JAPANESE PERSON WOULD HAVE A PRETTY GOOD UNDERSTANDING OF *NEGIMA!* PRINTED ALL IN KANJI, AND THERE'S NO END TO THE MANY EXQUISITE NEW DISCOVERIES YOU CAN MAKE THROUGH THE KANJI. NOT TO MENTION THE FACT THAT THE TAIWANESE VERSION IS REPUTED TO HAVE A LOT OF CARE PUT INTO ITS TRANSLATION—WE WANT TO INTRODUCE THE *MÓFĂ LĂOSHI (=NEGIMA!)* THAT WE CAN UNDERSTAND EVEN THOUGH WE CAN'T READ IT!

**FIRST, LET'S LOOK AT THE TAIWANESE VERSION OF THE GREETING BETWEEN CLASS REP AND NEGI THAT WE COMPARED IN THE OTHER DIFFERENT LANGUAGES IN VOLUME 20!**

### POINT 1

IN CASES SUCH AS PROPER NOUNS THAT CAN'T BE TRANSLATED AND SPELLS, WHERE THE WAY A WORD SOUNDS IS MORE IMPORTANT THAN THE MEANING, THE CHINESE LANGUAGE VERSIONS USE CHARACTERS TO REPRESENT SOUNDS THAT ARE READ (PRONOUNCED) THE SAME WAY IN JAPANESE. THESE CHARACTERS, "涅吉(BLACK, GOOD LUCK)," ARE READ "NEGI." NAGI IS 納吉(OBTAIN GOOD LUCK); THEY DON'T USE THE KANJI THAT WE PRONOUNCE *NEGI* (葱) IN JAPANESE, WHICH MEANS "GREEN ONION."

### POINT 2

BECAUSE IT'S CHINESE, THEY USE KANJI*. FROM WORDS THAT ARE WRITTEN THE SAME IN JAPANESE (LIKE 昨晚, LAST NIGHT) TO WORDS THAT YOU CAN KIND OF UNDERSTAND (LIKE 班長 (GROUP LEADER: CLASS REP) AND 早安 (EARLY PEACE: GOOD MORNING)), TO THINGS WHERE THE MEANING IN JAPANESE IS DIFFERENT (老師, RŌSHI, MASTER IN JAPANESE, MEANS TEACHER, *LĂOSHI,* IN CHINESE). IF YOU'VE READ THE ORIGINAL *NEGIMA!*, YOU CAN GET THE GIST OF WHAT THEY'RE SAYING.

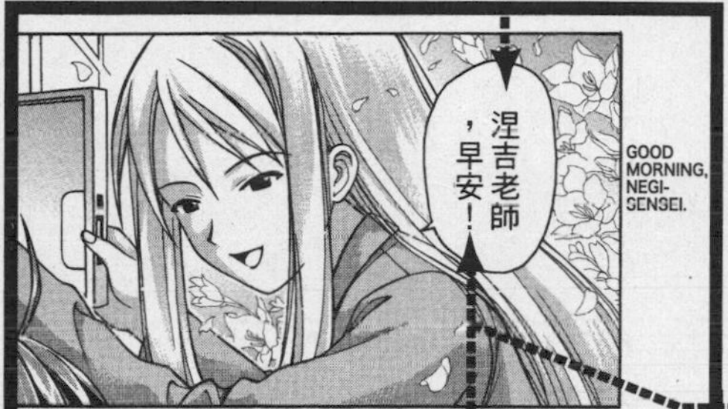
涅吉老師，早安！

GOOD MORNING, NEGI-SENSEI.

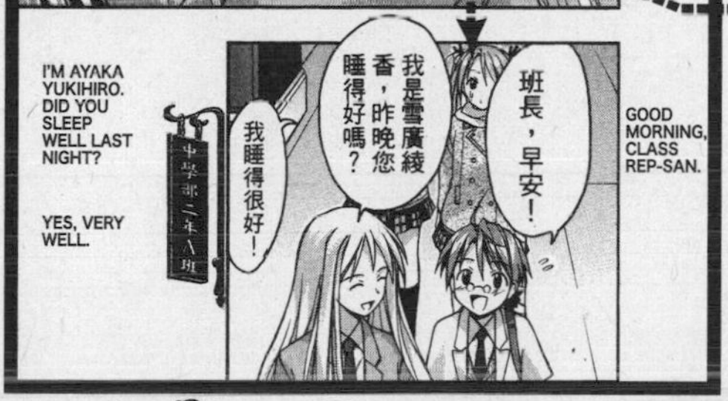
班長，早安！
我是雪廣綾香，昨晚您睡得好嗎？
我睡得很好！

GOOD MORNING, CLASS REP-SAN.

I'M AYAKA YUKIHIRO. DID YOU SLEEP WELL LAST NIGHT?

YES, VERY WELL.

### POINT 3

IN THE JAPANESE VERSION, SOME OF THE JARGON BORROWS ENGLISH WORDS, SUCH AS "ARTIFACT" AND "*NUDE*-BEAM (OR STRIP-BEAM, 'NAKED RAY' IN THE ENGLISH VERSION)." THE TAIWANESE VERSION CHANGES THOSE TO CHINESE CHARACTERS THAT WE CAN READ LIKE, 道具 (*DŌGU,* TOOL) AND 脱衣光線 (*DATSUI KOUSEN,* STRIP-BEAM), MAKING THE JARGON FRESH AND NEW. IN THE BUBBLE IN THE PICTURE BELOW, THE ORIGINAL CALLED THEM THE *NAGI & AKO PAIR,* BORROWING "PAIR" FROM ENGLISH, BUT A "PAIR" IS ALSO A "組 (*KUMI*)" IN JAPANESE...KANJI SURE CAN HOLD A LOT OF INFORMATION.

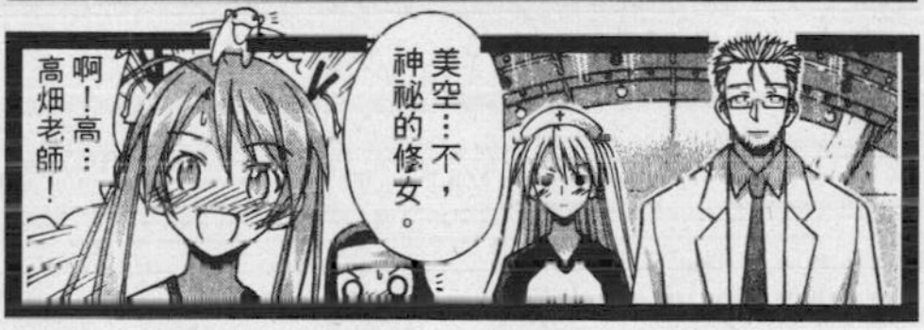
美空…不，神秘的修女。
啊！高…高畑老師！

美空…不、

MISORA-KU... I MEAN

神秘的修女

MYSTERIOUS SISTER-KUN

啊！高…

AH! TA...

高畑老師！

TAKAHATA-SENSEI!

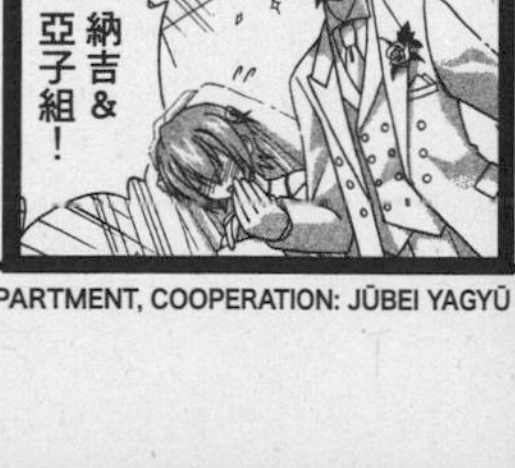
納吉&亞子組！

WORK: SHONEN MAGAZINE EDITORIAL DEPARTMENT, COOPERATION: JŪBEI YAGYŪ

*IN TAIWAN, THEY CALL JAPANESE KANJI "漢字 (HÀNZÌ)," USING THE SAME CHARACTERS WE DO IN JAPAN. THE CHINESE KANJI THAT THEY USE IN TAIWAN ARE CALLED "國字 (GÚOZÌ, NATIVE CHARACTERS)."

INCIDENTALLY, AS FOR TWO CHINESE GIRLS, "CHAO LINGSHEN" IS A NAME THAT SEEMS KIND OF UNLIKELY (AS OF THE PRESENT DAY), BUT APPARENTLY KŪ FEI IS A POSSIBLE NAME. THE SETUP STILL HOLDS.

## BATTLE TERMS & NAMES 戰鬥関係用語&名字集錦

READY? OK! JACULATOR!!!

一、二、三! 攻擊敵人吧

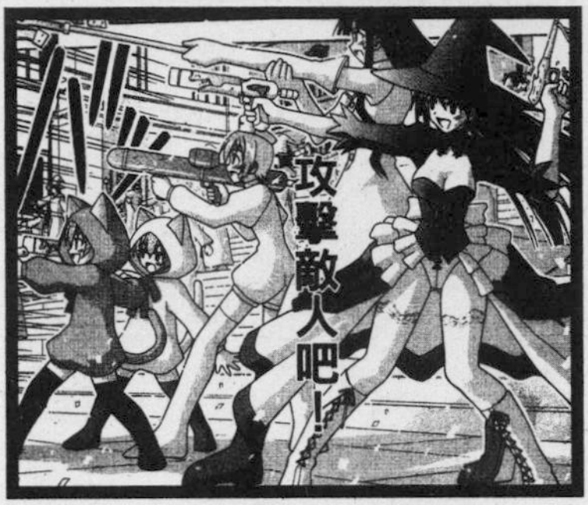
攻擊敵人吧!

佐倉愛衣 = MEI SAKURA

道具 = ARTIFACT

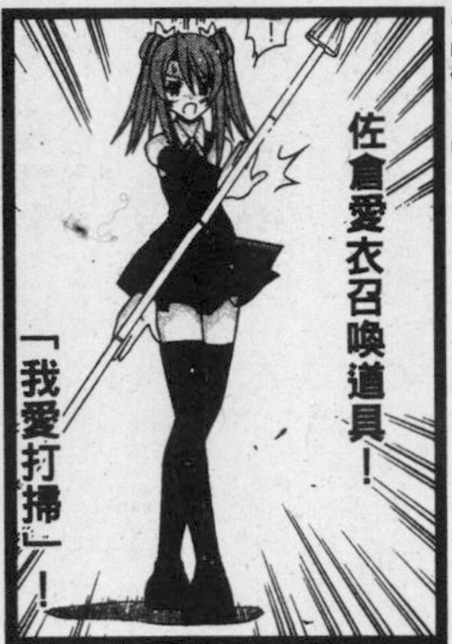
佐倉愛衣召喚道具!
「我愛打掃」!

「我愛打掃」 = I LOVE CLEANING (*favor purgandi*)

雙重愛書狂死光 = (DOUBLE BOOK FREAK DEATH LIGHT) =DOUBLE BIBLIO COLLIDER

愛書狂水之狂想曲 = (BOOK FREAK WATER RHAPSODY) =BIBLIO AQUA RHAPSODY

愛書狂·粉紅鬱金香 BIBLIO PINK TULIP

愛書狂·紅色支配者 BIBLIO ROULIN ROUGE

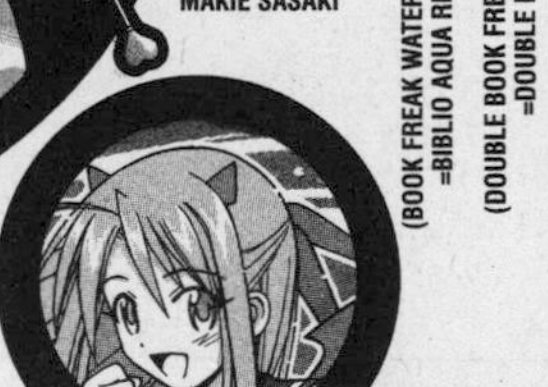
長谷川 千雨
CHISAME HASEGAWA

BIBLIO · SPIRAL SHOOT

愛書狂螺旋奔流

BOOK FREAK SPIRAL CASCADE

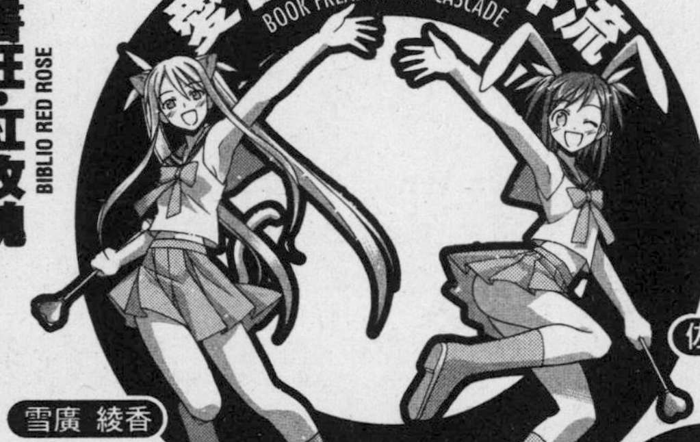
佐佐木時繪
MAKIE SASAKI
雪廣 綾香
AYAKA YUKIHIRO

愛書狂·紅玫瑰 BIBLIO RED ROSE

ETERNAL NEGI FEVER

永恆涅吉狂熱

NEGI BEAM

涅吉光波

NEGI KAISER

涅吉超大光波

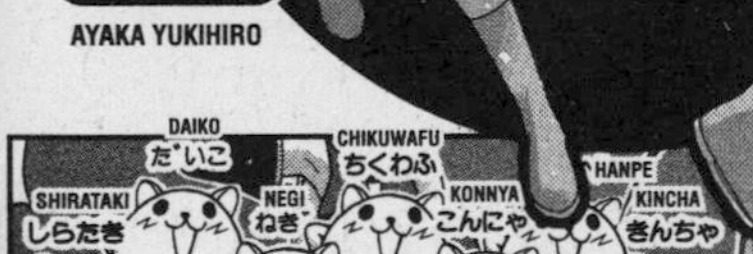
DAIKO
だいこ
CHIKUWAFU
ちくわふ
HANPE
SHIRATAKI
しらたき
NEGI
ねぎ
KONNYA
こんにゃ
KINCHA
きんちゃ

KINCHA = 火熱麻薯(HEATED POTATO)
HANPE = 白嫩魚漿(WHITE YOUNG FISH DRINK)
KONNYA = 超健康蒟(SUPERHEALTHY DEVIL'S TONGUE)
CHIKUWAFU = 美味竹輪(DELICIOUS CHIKUWA)
NEGI = 蔥(GREEN ONION)
DAIKO = 好吃白蘿(DAIKON)
SHIRATAKI = 蒟蒻絲(KONNYAKU THREAD)

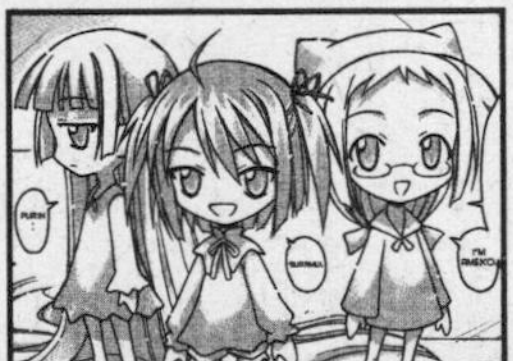

AMEKO = 雨子
SURAMUI = 史萊姆
PURIN = 布丁

AS YOU CAN SEE TO THE LEFT, THE TAIWANESE VERSION IS ACTUALLY PRETTY VARIEGATED, WITH LETTERS OF THE ALPHABET, AND HANDWRITTEN CHARACTERS LEFT IN JAPANESE TO BRING OUT THE AMBIENCE. THEY SAY THAT A LOT OF TAIWANESE READERS CAN READ THE SOUND EFFECTS WITH NO PROBLEM.

モー ファー ラオ スー
# 魔法老師!
MAGISTER NEGI MAGI

*MÓFÂ LÂOSHI!*

魔法老師用語對照翻譯
## "NEGIMA! TERMS" COMPARISON

FINALLY, LET'S GIVE YOU PRONUNCIATIONS AND STUDY CHINESE. TRANSLATING THE TAIWANESE TITLE, "*MÓFÂ LÂOSHI!*" DIRECTLY INTO JAPANESE, IT'S "*MAHŌ SENSEI!*," OR "MAGIC TEACHER!" IN ENGLISH (IN CHINESE, THE KANJI THAT READ *-SENSEI* IN JAPANESE ARE THE EQUIVALENT TO *-SAN* USED FOR MALES). NOW THAT WE KNOW THAT *LÂOSHI* MEANS *SENSEI*, WE CAN USE IT FOR AKAMATSU-SENSEI.

↓

NOW, BECAUSE NEGI'S FULL NAME IS THE SAME IN JAPANESE, CHINESE, AND ENGLISH, LET'S PROVIDE THE NAME OF THE HEROINE. AND WE ALSO PUT CHACHAMARU, BECAUSE HER NAME SOUNDS NICE. (WHEN THEY CALL HER CHACHA-CHAN, IT SOUNDS LIKE TSAA-TSAA.)

### LET'S USE THEIR TAIWANESE NAMES!

赤松 健先生 = KEN AKAMATSU-SENSEI =

**赤松 健老師** CHÌSONG JIÀN-LÂOSHI

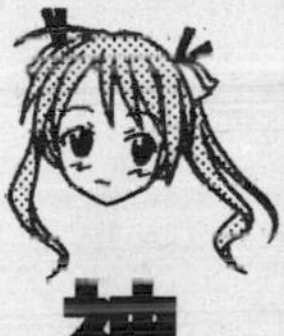

**神楽坂 明日菜** SHÉNLÈBÂN MÍNGRÌCÀI

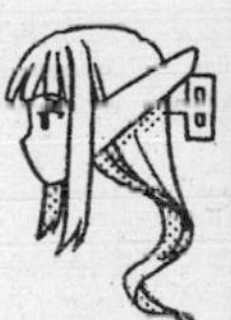

**茶茶丸** CHÁCHÁWÁN

**愛書狂 火焔** (MELODY READING EAR)
火焔 IS ANOTHER WAY OF WRITING 火炎 (*KAEN*, BLAZE). THIS IS A BIBLION MOVE, SO...
↓ BIBLIO FIRE

**朗讀耳**
IN JAPANESE KANJI, THAT BECOMES 朗読耳 (*RŌDOKUMIMI*), ANOTHER WORD FOR THE NAME OF THE ITEM THAT APPEARS IN VOLUME 23.
↓ READ-ALOUD EAR

**火星機器人軍團** (MARS MACHINE-MAN ARMY)
軍團 = 軍団 (*GUNDAN*, ARMY). 火星 IS MARS, THE SAME AS IN JAPANESE.
↓ MARTIAN ROBOT ARMY

**涅吉魔社** (NEGI MAGIC SOCIETY)
THE FIRST TWO CHARACTERS ARE "NEGI." ITS OTHER NAME IS "白色之翼 (WHITE WINGS)."
↓ NEGIMA CLUB

**茶茶零號** (TEA TEA ZERO NUMBER)
號 = 号, *GŌ*, A JAPANESE WORD INDICATING THE NAME OF A SHIP, PLANE, ROBOT, ETC. BUT IN JAPANESE, THE *GŌ* IS TAKEN OFF OF HER NAME...
↓ CHACHAZERO

**年齢詐稱藥** (AGE-FALSIFYING DRUG)
WITHOUT THESE, THE COVER OF VOLUME 22 WOULDN'T WORK.
↓ AGE-MISREPRESENTATION PASTILLES

**小夜仔**
SAYO AISAKA IS 相坂少夜, AND THIS ISN'T A DIRECT TRANSLATION, BUT A LIBERAL TRANSLATION BASED ON THE MEANING... AN ADAPTATION.
↓ SAYO-BŌ

ALSO, KUGIMĪ BECOMES 釘仔.

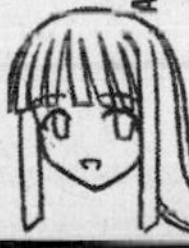

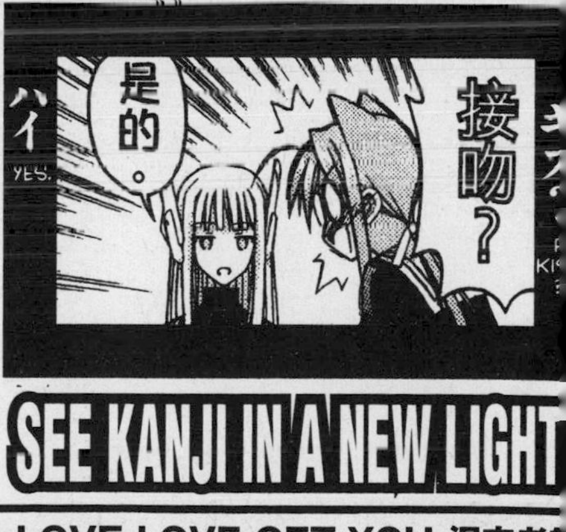
接吻？
KIS
ハイ
YES.
是的。

## SEE KANJI IN A NEW LIGHT

ラブ・ラブ・ゲッチュー・ネギセンセエ＝LOVE.LOVE.GET YOU.涅吉老

魔法先生
# ネギま!
MAGISTER NEGI MAGI

赤松 健
SHONEN MAGAZINE COMICS
KEN AKAMATSU

# 23

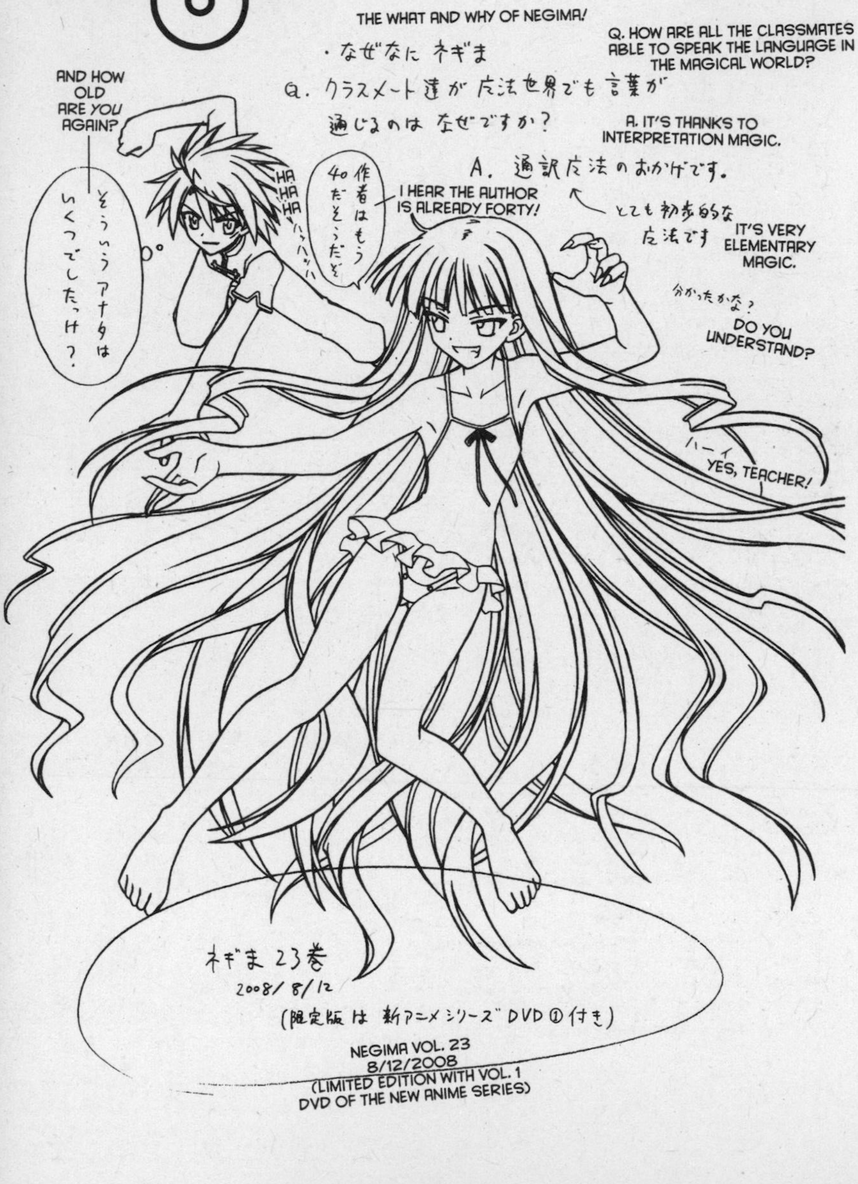
THE WHAT AND WHY OF NEGIMA!
・なぜなに ネギま
Q. クラスメート達が 魔法世界でも 言葉が 通じるのは なぜですか？
Q. HOW ARE ALL THE CLASSMATES ABLE TO SPEAK THE LANGUAGE IN THE MAGICAL WORLD?
A. 通訳魔法のおかげです。
A. IT'S THANKS TO INTERPRETATION MAGIC.
とても初歩的な魔法です
IT'S VERY ELEMENTARY MAGIC.
分かったかな？
DO YOU UNDERSTAND?
ハーイ
YES, TEACHER!
作者はもう40だそうだぞ
I HEAR THE AUTHOR IS ALREADY FORTY!
ハッハッハ
HA HA HA
そういうアナタはいくつでしたっけ？
AND HOW OLD ARE YOU AGAIN?
ネギま 23巻
2008/8/12
(限定版は 新アニメシリーズ DVD ① 付き)
NEGIMA VOL. 23
8/12/2008
(LIMITED EDITION WITH VOL. 1 DVD OF THE NEW ANIME SERIES)

キャラ解説
CHARACTER
PROFILE

⑦ 柿崎美砂
(7) MISA KAKIZAKI

名前は マクロスの キャラから。
I GOT HER NAME FROM A MACROSS CHARACTER.
（漢字ちがいますけど…）
(BUT WITH DIFFERENT KANJI.)

スタイルの良い 4Aの3人組の中でも
OF THE THREE NICE-BODIED CHEERLEADERS,
最も色気というか H.っぽさが
SHE IS THE SEXIEST, OR RATHER,
高い彼女。（笑）
THE HOOCHIEST. (LAUGH)

4巻で
THE EXISTENCE OF
彼氏の存在が確認
HER BOYFRIEND WAS CONFIRMED IN
されましたが、今も
VOLUME FOUR, BUT IT IS UNKNOWN
付き合ってるかどうかは
WHETHER OR NOT SHE IS STILL GOING OUT,
不明です。（もうフッちゃったん
WITH HIM. (I THINK SHE MIGHT HAVE DUMPED HIM
じゃないかな〜）（^^;）
ALREADY...) (^^) OF ALL THE GIRLS IN

3-Aで 一番モテる 女だと思いますよ。
3-A, I THINK SHE'S THE MOST POPULAR.
← 一般人の男に。
AMONG THE AVERAGE GUYS.

アニメ版のCVは 伊藤静さん。
HER VOICE IN THE ANIME IS PROVIDED BY SHIZUKA ITOH-SAN. HER ACTING AND HER
演技も歌も パーフェクトな人で、今 超売れ売れ！
SINGING ARE PERFECT, AND SHE'S A SUPERPOPULAR VOICE ACTRESS THESE DAYS!
「切なくてラビリンス」とか 最高です。（^^）
"SETSUNAKUTE LABYRINTH (HEARTBREAKING LABYRINTH)" IS THE BEST. (^^)

ドラマ版は 大島あすみさん。
IN THE LIVE-ACTION DRAMA, SHE'S PLAYED BY ASUMI ŌSHIMA-SAN. SHE'S IN
キャンギャルだったり モデルだったりと、柿崎と
COMMERCIALS AND DOES MODELING, AND HAS SKILLS LIKE KAKIZAKI. SHE'S
似たようなスキルを持ちます。同じくモテそう〜（笑）
PROBABLY JUST AS POPULAR WITH THE BOYS! (LAUGH)

赤松
AKAMATSU

## NEGIMA!
### FAN ART CORNER

THIS TREND STARTED A LONG TIME AGO, BUT WE'VE BEEN GETTING MORE AND MORE FAN ART SUBMISSIONS FROM ELEMENTARY AND MIDDLE SCHOOL GIRLS☆ THANK YOU VERY MUCH! KEEP SENDING 'EM IN☆

TEXT BY MAX

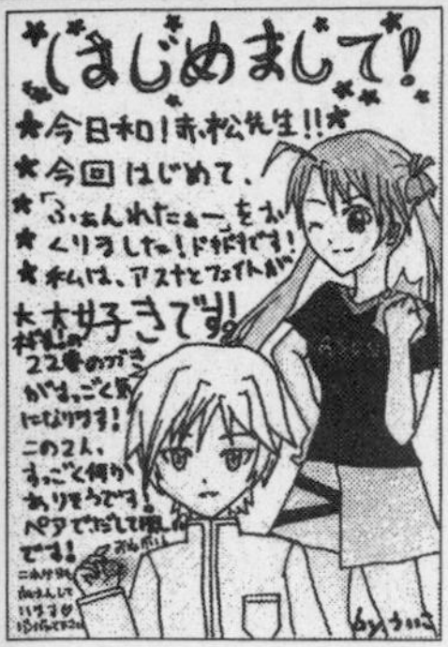
はじめまして!
今日和!赤松先生!!

▲ YOU DON'T SEE THEM TOGETHER OFTEN.

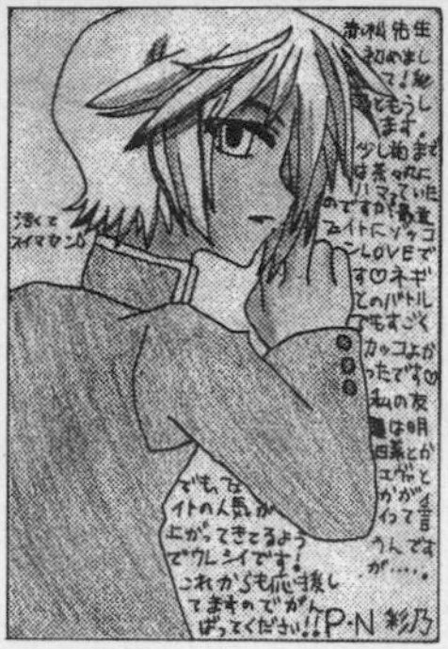

▲ SIDELONG-GLANCING FATE☆

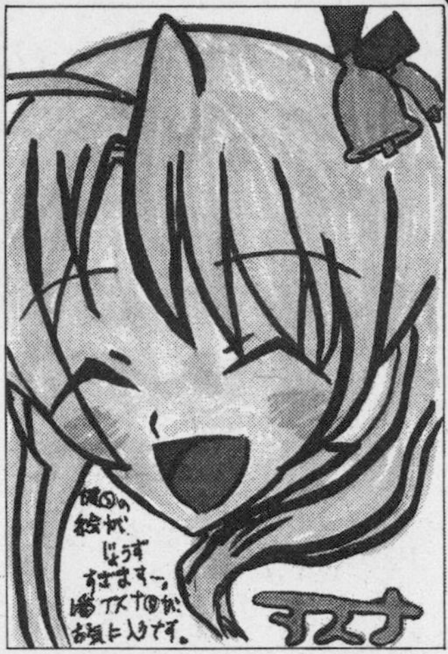

HER FULL-FACED SMILE IS SO BRIGHT. ▶

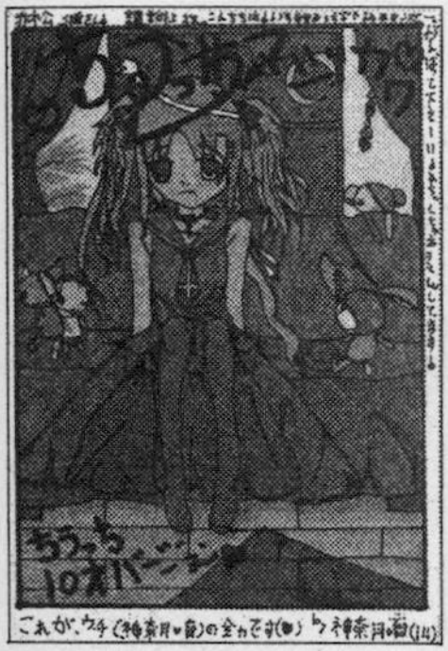

▲ VERY ARTISTIC.

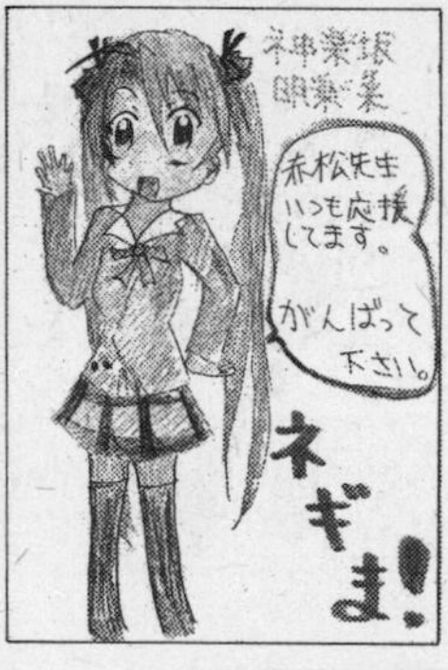
赤松先生
いつも応援してます。
がんばって下さい。
ネギま!

◀ KIND OF BIG-SISTERLY.

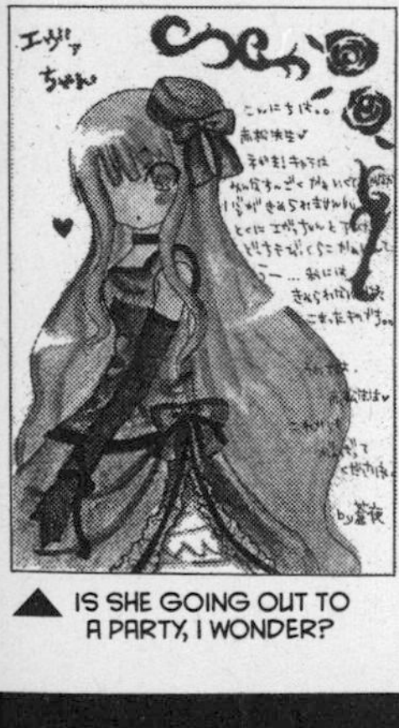

▲ IS SHE GOING OUT TO A PARTY, I WONDER?

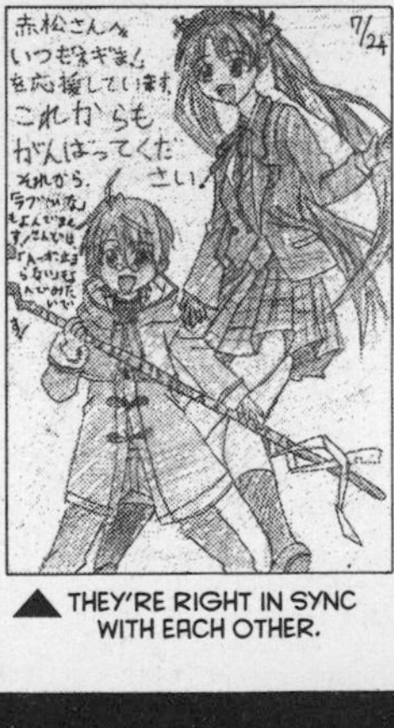

▲ THEY'RE RIGHT IN SYNC WITH EACH OTHER.

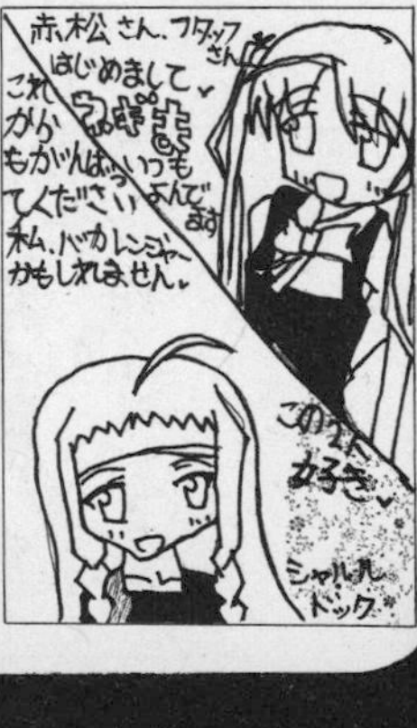

▶ THEY BOTH LOOK SO WELL-BEHAVED.

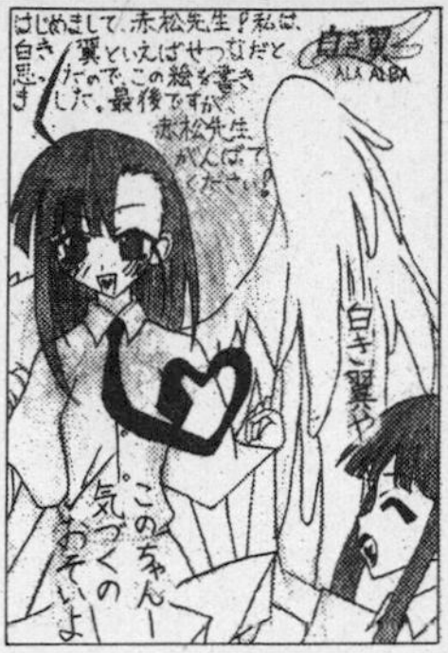
はじめまして、赤松先生!私は、白き翼といえばせっちゃんだと思ったので、この絵を書きました。最後ですが、赤松先生がんばってください。
白き翼
このちゃん気づくのおそいよ

▲ HER NECKTIE MAKES A HEART☆

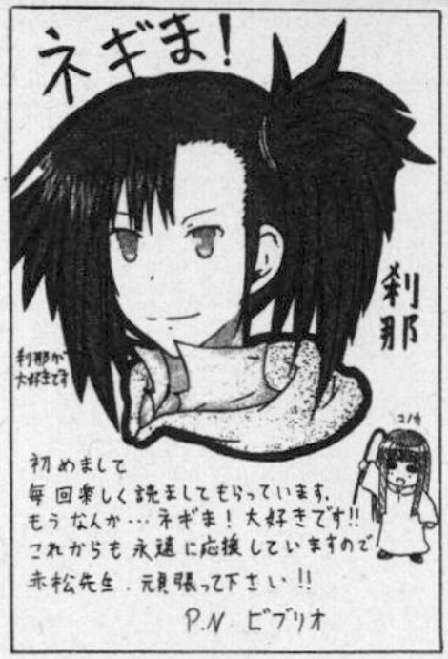
ネギま!
刹那
初めまして
毎回楽しく読ませてもらっています。
もうなんか…ネギま!大好きです!!
これからも永遠に応援していますので
赤松先生、頑張って下さい!!
P.N ビブリオ

▲ SHE'S VERY HANDSOME☆

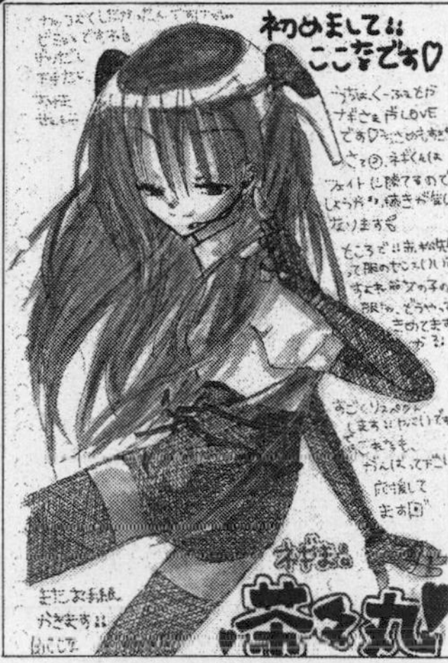
初めまして!! ここなです♡
茶々丸♡

▲ A VERY MATURE CHACHAMARU.

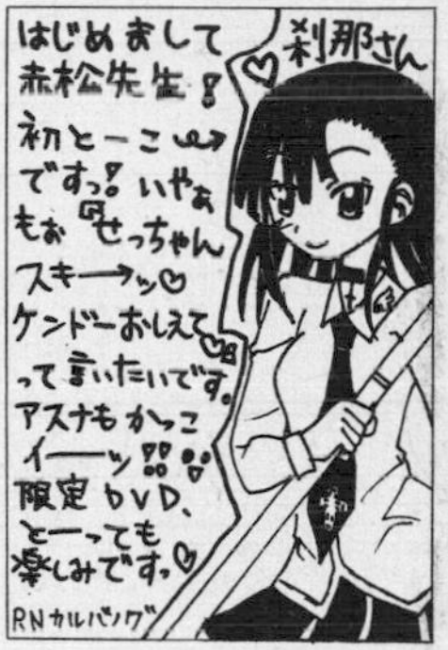
はじめまして
赤松先生!
刹那さん
ですっ!いやぁもぉ『せっちゃんスキー』ッ♡
ケンドーおしえて って言いたいです。
アスナもかっこイーッ!!
限定DVD、とーっても楽しみです。

▲ YOU *WOULD* WANT TO LEARN KENDO FROM HER, WOULDN'T YOU☆

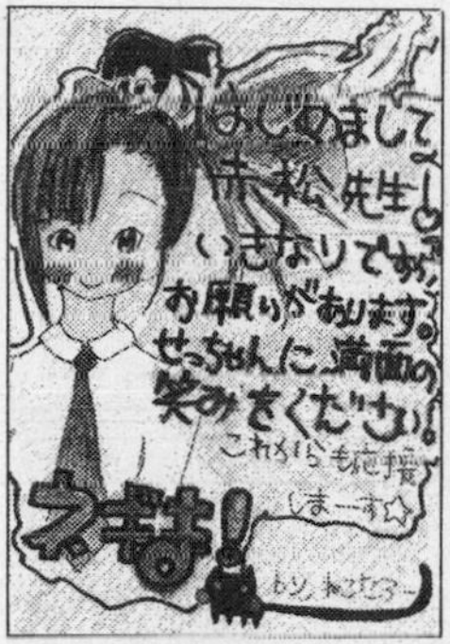
はじめまして赤松先生!
いきなりですが、お願いがあります。
せっちゃんに満面の笑みをください!
これからも応援しまーす☆
ネギま!

▲ A VERY SIMPLE SETSUNA.

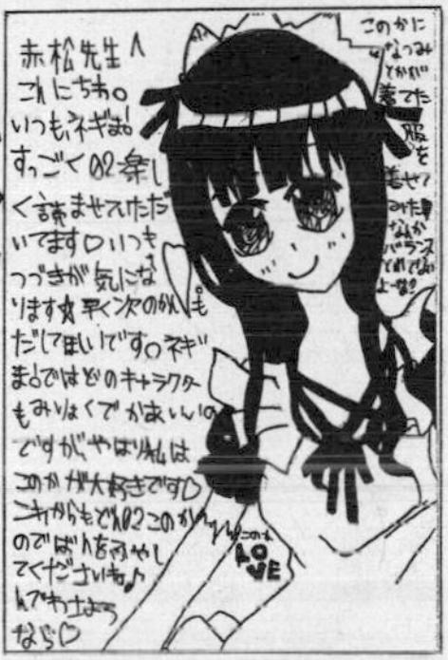
赤松先生へ
こんにちわ。

▲ KONOKA AS A MAID.

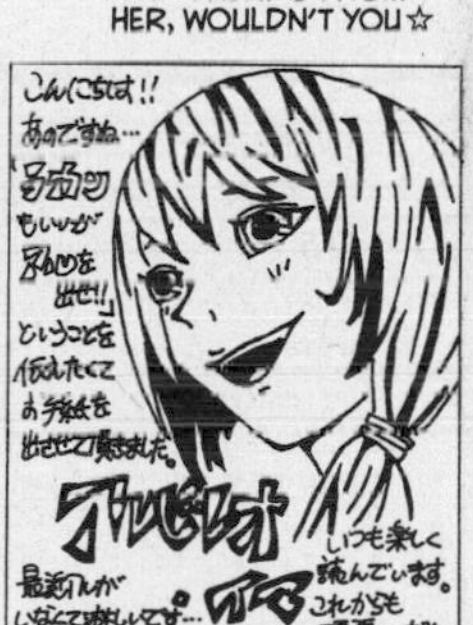
こんにちは!!
アルビレオ

▲ AL LOOKS LIKE HE'S HAVING FUN.

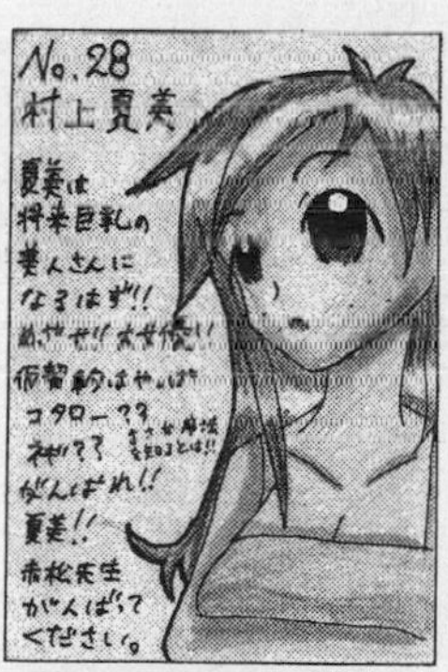
No.28
村上夏美
夏美は将来巨乳の美人さんになるはず!!
赤松先生がんばってください。

▲ A MATURE-LOOKING NATSUMI COULD BE NICE, TOO.

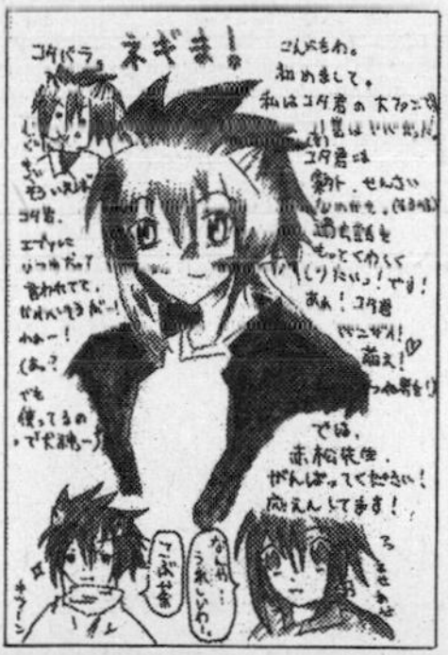
ネギま!
赤松先生、がんばってください!

▲ I SEE YOU'RE REALLY INTO HIM.

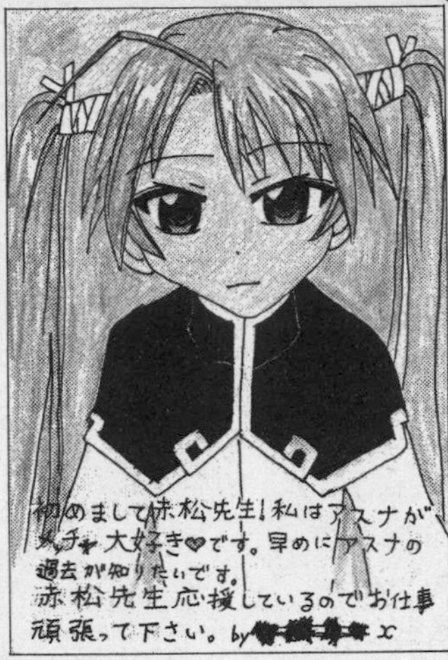
初めまして赤松先生！私はアスナがメチャ大好き♡です。早めにアスナの過去が知りたいです。
赤松先生応援しているのでお仕事頑張って下さい。by [redacted]

▲ THIS IS A NICE ASUNA, TOO.

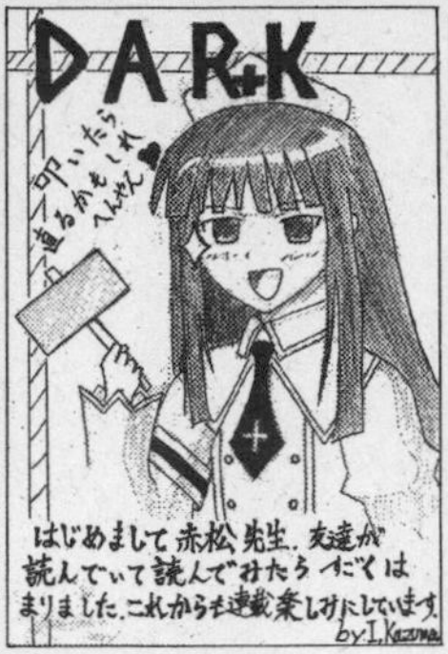
DARK
叩いたら直るかもしれへんやん♥
はじめまして赤松先生。友達が読んでいて読んでみたらはまりました。これからも連載楽しみにしています。
by I.Kazuma

▲ HOW DARK.

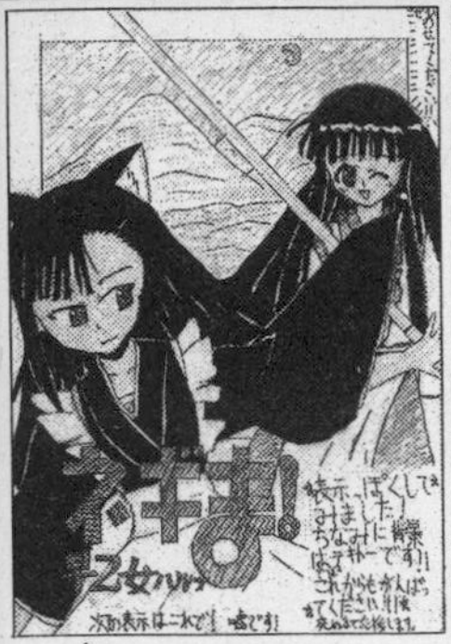
ネギま!

▲ KONO-SETSU...?

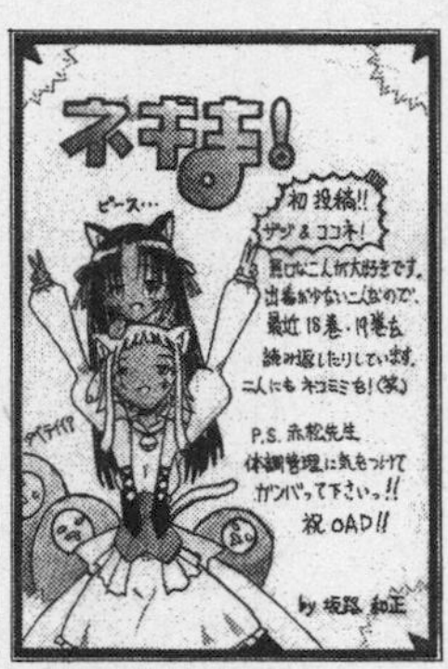
ネギま!
ピース…
初投稿!!
ザジ&ココネ!
P.S. 赤松先生
体調管理に気をつけてガンバって下さいっ!!
祝OAD!!
by 坂路 和正

I MIGHT LIKE THIS DUO. ▶

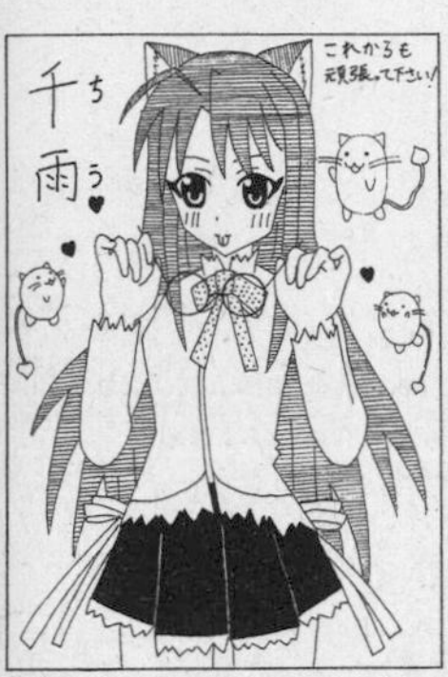
千雨
これからも頑張って下さい!

HER FOLLOWERS ARE WORKING HARD. ▶

▼ LOVE-COMEDY MODE.

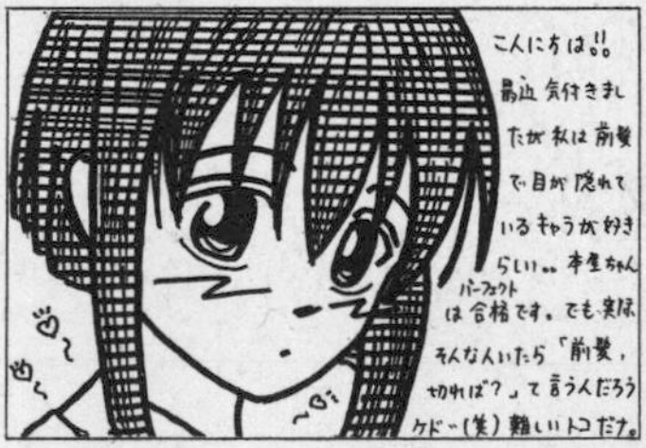
こんにちは!!
最近気付きましたが私は前髪で目が隠れているキャラが好きらしい…。本屋ちゃんパーフェクトは合格です。でも実はそんな人いたら「前髪、切れば？」て言うんだろうケドー(笑)難しいトコだす。

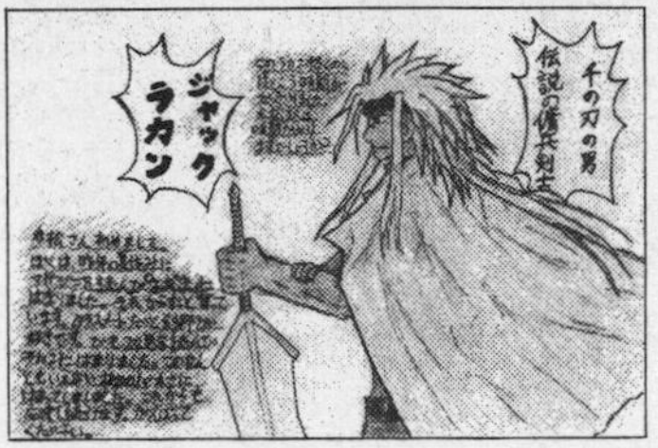
ジャックラカン
千の刃の男
伝説の傭兵剣士

SUCH A MANLY PROFILE. ▶

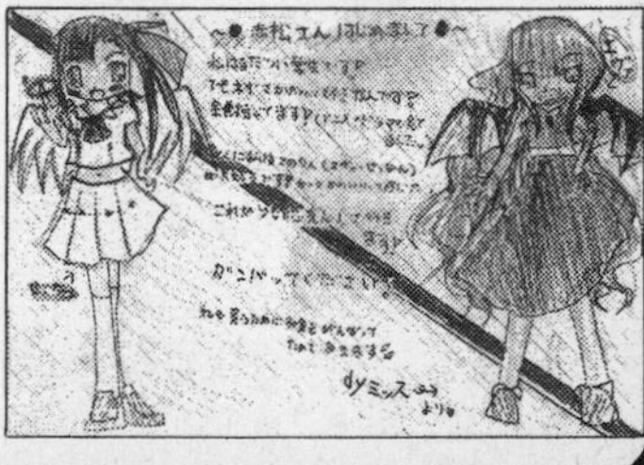
赤松さんはじめまして
がんばって下さい

THE WINGED ONES ☆ ▶

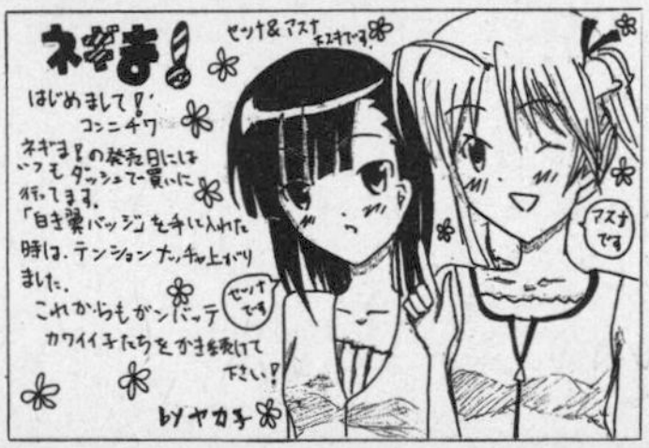
ネギま!
セツナ&アスナ
はじめまして! コンニチワ
ネギま!の発売日にはいつもダッシュで買いに行ってます。「白き翼バッジ」を手に入れた時は、テンションメッチャ上がりました。
これからもがんバッテカワイイ子たちをかき続けて下さい!
アスナです
セツナです
by ヤカチ

THEY LOOK LIKE MODELS. ▶

NEGI MA!

THIS VOLUME'S

# FEATURED CHARACTER

**YUE NAGASE**

## RANKING

FIRST PLACE

THIS IS A CUTE YUE, ISN'T IT!? YOU SAID "MAYBE IF SHE WERE LOLITA STYLE," BUT I GET THE FEELING IT'S NOT MUCH DIFFERENT... (LAUGH)

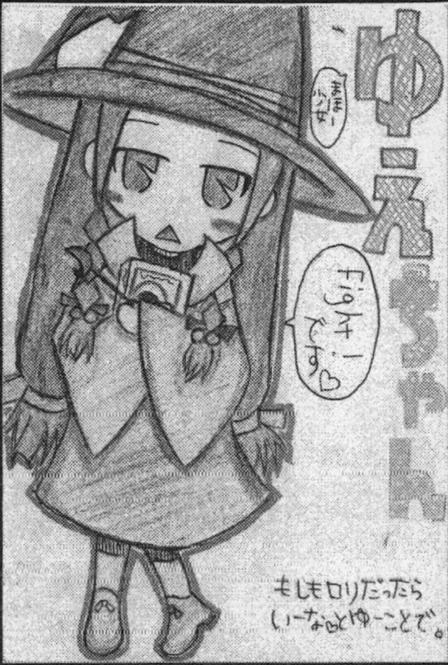
ゆえきちゃん
もしもロリだったらいーなとゆーことで。

SECOND PLACE

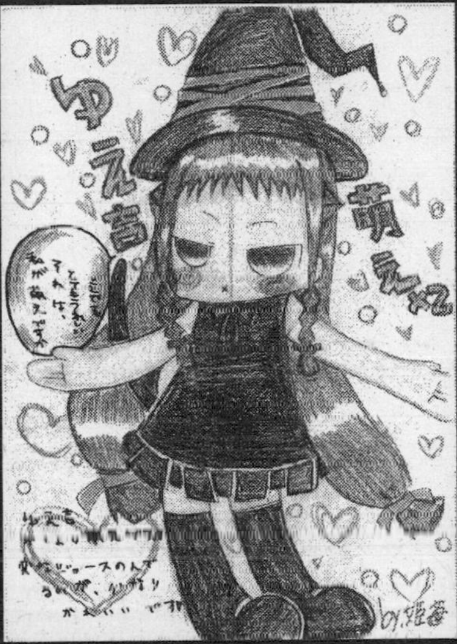

YUECCHI LOOKS LIKE A PLUSHIE. EVEN MORE SO BECAUSE HER MOUTH IS IN AN X SHAPE (LAUGH) YUE IS REALLY POPULAR WITH FEMALE FANS. ♡

MAGISTER NEGI MAGI

THIRD PLACE

YUE AND CHAMO MAKE A GOOD DUO~♡ I HOPE YOU CONTINUE TO CHEER THEM ON!

( AKAMATSU )

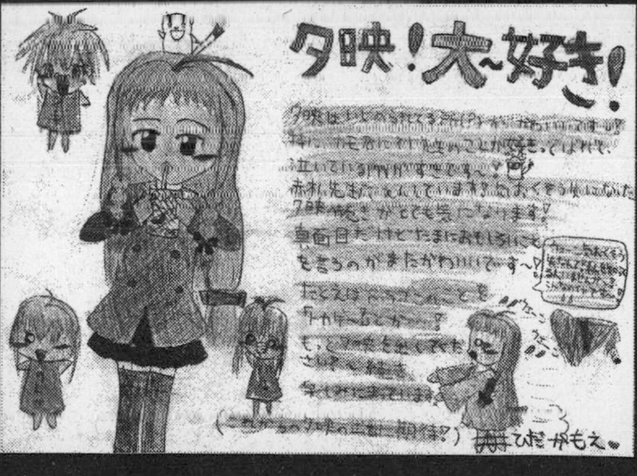
夕映！大～好き！

MAGISTER NEGI MAGI

## 3-D BACKGROUNDS EXPLANATION CORNER

**THE STORY HAS MOVED TO THE FLOATING ISLAND OSTIA!
AND NEW CREATIONS HAVE APPEARED AS BACKGROUNDS.**

### • OSTIA'S BIG ARENA

SCENE NAME: LARGE ARENA POLYGON COUNT: 876,469

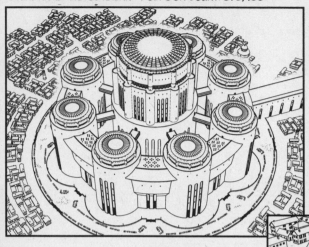

THE BIG ARENA IN OSTIA, WHERE THEY'RE HOLDING THE TOURNAMENT TO COMMEMORATE THE 20TH ANNIVERSARY OF THE END OF THE WAR. MADE UP OF EIGHT SUB-ARENAS COMPARABLE IN SIZE TO GRANICUS' ARENA AND A GIGANTIC MAIN ARENA IN THE CENTER, ITS CIRCUMFERENCE IS APPROXIMATELY TWO KILOMETERS AND... ANYWAY, ITS SIZE IS NOTHING TO BE SNEEZED AT. I PUT CROWDS IN PLACES HERE AND THERE, BUT THEY'RE SO SMALL, YOU CAN HARDLY SEE THEM. (LAUGH)

HOPES GET HIGHER AS YOU WONDER IF NEGI AND FRIENDS CAN REALLY COME OUT VICTORIOUS IN THIS PLACE.

• THE SURROUNDING TOWN.

THE SMALL HOUSES SURROUNDING IT ARE 3-D, TOO, BUT ENLARGED, THEY LOOK LIKE THIS. IT'S PRETTY HALF-HEARTED (LAUGH)

### • OBSERVATORY

SCENE NAME: OBSERVATORY POLYGON COUNT: 10,746

THE OBSERVATORY WHERE NEGI AND ASUNA REUNITED. IT'S IN PART OF THE NATURE PARK LOCATED ON THE EDGE OF OSTIA, AND IT OVERLOOKS A GIANT PANORAMA ABOVE THE SEA OF CLOUDS.

IT'S BUILT WITH THE SAME RING-SHAPED PARTS AS THE GATE PORT IN MEGALO-MESEMBRIA, AND GETS ITS ABILITY TO FLOAT FROM THE SAME PRINCIPLES.

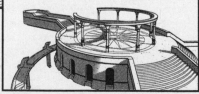

FURTHERMORE, THERE ARE PANELS WHERE I ADDED SHADOWS WITH 3-D TO REPRODUCE THEM REALISTICALLY. THE PICTURE TO THE RIGHT SHOWS THOSE SHADOWS. WE WOULD TREAT THIS PICTURE BY ADDING CLOUD AND SKY TONE BY HAND, THUS COMPLETING THE PANEL.

# LEXICON NEGIMARIUM

[*Negima!* 217th Period Lexicon Negimarium]

## ■ Form of the Dark Night
(Actus Noctis Erebeae)

A way of practicing dark magic. In Latin, it means "gesture of dark night." The translation of "gesture" into "form" refers to the series of actions in which those gestures come together.

## ■ Clairvoyance
(clara visibilitas)

A type of ESP (extrasensory perception); it perceives objects, places, and current events that can't be seen with the naked eye, as if actually witnessing them. Negi's ability to find the location of his wand when he closes his eyes (see *Negima!* volume 3, 21st Period) is another type of this ability.

[*Negima!* 218th Period Lexicon Negimarium]

## ■ Breasts [NOTE: This entry is narrated by Paio Zi, the hunter known for his obsession with breasts.]
(mamma)

German Jewish psychologist E. Neumann (1905–60) said: "Just as do the priestesses, who are put on par with the goddess, the goddess leaves her breasts exposed. Breasts are a symbol of the flow of cultivation, nourishment, and life." (*The Great Mother,* 9.Kap.) In magical cultures, too (especially matriarchal societies), women's breasts—along with the abdomen, buttocks, and genitals—are said to hold extremely sacred meaning, yes? This is because the breasts are the symbol of the fertility that leads to human life. This should be well understood from archaeological artifacts, yes? Neumann said: "Because they are in the central region of the woman's torso, the abdomen and the breasts, often very large breasts, become 'the only realistic thing.' In these statues, the richness of feminine parts is expressed primitively and in a superhuman manner." (ebd.8.Kap.) Thus, women's breasts, especially enormous breasts, are said to have the character of bringing forth and protecting physical life, yes? This is called "a woman's elementary character." This is made evident by the fact that, for example, the Latin word for physical substance, *materia*, comes from the word *mater*, meaning mother, yes?

But a woman's breasts are not only endowed with the "elementary character" of procreation and protection. A woman's breasts, or rather,

her chest area, also has the important element called the "transformative character," yes? "Indeed, many figures emphasize the genitals and breasts, and indicate only the elementary character, only the symbol of procreation and nurturing. However, in other statues, we see that the transformative character and the abdomen, genitals, and buttocks are emphasized, while the chest area is ignored. In these, the contradiction of the feminine parts themselves appears in the contradiction of the paradoxical shapes of the upper and lower halves of the body. The underside of a woman with child is connected to a heterogeny that almost never unifies with it; in other words, the upper body of a young maiden who has not yet become a woman. (...) It becomes clear when viewed from the side that the thin and leaf-like, fleshless physique of the upper body combines with the fully fleshed torso in the form of one statue, and the typical order of the elementary character in the 'lower body' and the transformative character of the 'upper body,' become an example of a pattern of divine physique." (ebd.8.Kap.) According to Neumann, the thin chest seen in ancient female statues symbolizes a woman's "transformative character," yes?[1] This "transformative character" signifies maidenly youth, a more advanced mentality, and, most important, the dynamism to shift toward individual characteristics. (vgl.ebd.3.Kap.)

Indeed, based on this analysis, it seems possible to accurately describe the personalities of the members of "Ala Alba," yes? For example, let's look at Nagase and Sakurazaki. Both of them have wonderful breasts, one with enormous breasts and one with meager breasts, but in Nagase, as indicated by her large breasts, we can see the "woman's elementary character"—a tendency to protect those around her, yes? On the other hand, from someone such as Sakurazaki, we see the "transformative character"—a recklessness that comes from youth. That is exactly why both of them fell so easily into a trap in order to save a hostage, yes?

[ *Negima!* 219th Period Lexicon Negimarium]

## ■ Right Arm Release

(dextra emittam)

"*Dextra*" is a Latin ablative meaning "right hand." An "ablative" indicates a place or a method. "*Emittam*" is in the first-person-singular present-active subjunctive mood. Therefore, this phrase means "may I release from my right hand."

This spell is incanted in order to release delayed magic and the like from the right hand. In the 219th Period, Negi incants the spell to release the magic loaded into his hand through his use of dark magic.

## ■ Lightning Speed

[AGILITAS FULMINIS]

One of the practical uses of dark magic, it takes the magic power from "Thunderous Gale (Jovis Tempestas Fulguriens)" into one's flesh and fuses it with the spirit. In doing so, it gives the caster exceedingly great mobility. But if it fails, not only is there a danger that the gusts and lightning from "Thunderous Gale" will damage the caster's flesh, but there are cases when the wind spirits (spritus) violate the caster's mind (spiritus) and make him go mad.

Why would loading the magic power of "Thunderous Gale" into oneself give the caster such extreme mobility? It is because premodern cultural systems that use spells have a prelogical mentality (mentalité prélogique)[2], so to speak. The French social scientist and anthropologist, L. Lévy-Brühl (1857–1939), states the following: "The mentality of primitive people could be called prelogical just as easily as it could be called mystic." (*How Natives Think,* ch. II, II)[3]

It is believed that the language systems in premodern and prelogical cultures tended to dislike abstract linguistic activity. Therefore, their linguistic activity is made up of extremely specific forms. "The closer the mentality of a societal group comes to prelogical forms, the more power their literal thoughts have. Their language proves that. The typical vocabulary, vocabulary that deals with accurate, general ideas, is almost completely lacking, and their special vocabulary, or in other words, their vocabulary that indicates existences or objects that bring a special, specific image to mind when called by name, is plentiful. (...) [For example] the Tasmanians did not have any words that reproduced abstract ideas. (...) They could not even express properties in abstract ways such as hard, soft, hot, cold, long, short, round, etc. To express "hard," they would say, "*like* a stone;" for "high," they would say, "*big legs*;" and for "round," they would say "*like* a ball" or "*like* the moon." (ibid. ch. IV, V, emphasis added)

As it says here, prelogical languages expressed abstract ideas—whether by simile or by metaphor—through specific things. This, too, is because abstract ideas and specific objects are linked in various ways through a law called the "law of participation (loi de participation)."

Therefore, the spell that produces gales and lightning, "Thunderous Gale," also implies the "rapidity" of a gale and the "swiftness" of lightning, and, as words imbued with the power of a spell, it can also bring about those effects.

### ■ "Ruler of the shadow land, Scathach, grant into my hands thirty thorn-bearing spirit lances. 'Throwing Thunder'"

(locos umbrae regnans, Scathach, in manum meam det jaculum daemonium cum spinis triginta. JACULATIO FULGORIS)

A spell that attacks by releasing electrically charged magical javelins. Because the missiles released are javelins and not arrows, each one of them is stronger than a magic arrow made of lightning, and has greater physical destructive power. However, because they mimic the shape of a javelin, they are easier to dodge than the direct lightning attack "White Lightning (Fulguratio Albicans)."

### ■ "Load"

(supplementum)

A spell that uses dark magic to take magical power into oneself and fuse it with the spirit.

## ■ 𑖤

(ba)

The Sanskrit character for the voiced unaspirated labial sound. It means "baku" or "bind."

[*Negima!* 221st Period Lexicon Negimarium]

## ■ Svanhvít

The flagship of Megalo-Mesembria's international tactical fleet. It was newly made and put in service as a battle cruiser in the middle stages of the Great War. With its long cruising range, its high fire power, and its mobility, it achieves great results in battle. After the previous flagship sustained heavy damage and retired from military service toward the end of the Great War, it was remodeled as the battle mother ship, equipped with a new type of main cannon called the "divine retribution cannon" as well as a crew of Demon-God soldiers, provisions, and maneuvering capabilities, and became the flagship of Megalo-Mesembria's international tactical fleet. In the campaign to retake the Great Bridge, it crushed the Hellas Empire's summon beasts and dealt fatal damage to the enemy's war potential. After the Great War, Megalo-Mesembria's international tactical military underwent a large-scale disarmament, but this flagship is still in service.

"Svanhvít" is the name of a Valkyrie who appears in Völundr's poem supplied in the Elder Edda, and according to the translator of the Reclam edition, A. Klause, it is Old Norse for "a person (woman) who is white like a swan."

## ■ Dragon's Tree

(vṛkṣo nagasya)

A dragon with advanced spiritual character, with much higher intelligence than humans, who lived a long, long time ago. As it is patterned after the gods, like Ryōmen Sukuna no Kami, it will not be destroyed even if its flesh is. It is currently unknown why such a being would be serving as guardian of the Hellas Empire's capital city.

Vṛkṣo nagasya comes from the Sanskrit *vṛkṣas* (tree) and *nagasya* (the singular genitive of naga [snake or dragon]), and according to the law of sandhi (the law of pronunciation change in Sanskrit), the suffix of *vṛkṣas* changes from *-as* to *-o* (when the chapter was published in the magazine, the law was not applied). The name means "dragon's tree."

## ■ Coffee

(قهوه)

There are roughly three legends as to the origin of coffee. One is that the mufti of Aden, Abu 'Abd Allah Muhammad ibn Sa'id (?–1470?) learned of the custom of drinking coffee on his travels (most likely in Ethiopia). Another is that the saint of Mocha and ascetic priest Ali Ibn Umar (?–1418)[4] staved off hunger when he found the coffee bean in the mountains of Yemen. The last is a legend called "The Dancing Goats."

The first person to leave a record of the legend of the dancing goats was the Syrian academic priest Antonius Faustus Naironus Banesius[5], who taught in Rome in the seventeenth century. The following is an excerpt from that record.

> It stands to reason that I should relate evidence concerning a coincidental experience about how this medicine came to be known as *kahve* (in Turkish) or *café* (in Romantic languages). (...) In truth, for example, a common tradition of the Asian people is explained thus: In the Yemen region of Happy Arabia, at the home of monks of a certain monastery, a camel herder, or in another version, a goat herder, had a certain complaint. His complaint was that a few times a week, his herd would stay awake all night and dance furiously, to an abnormal level. The imam at the monastery was moved with curiosity, and when he found the place where the herd came from their pasture, that night, he and his fellows performed a thorough investigation to see where and in what manner the goats, or the camels, danced and ate grass. When they did, the imam came across a certain bush. The camels had been filling their bellies with the fruit from that bush—or rather the juice from it. The imam wanted to test the moral character of this fruit himself. And thus, the imam boiled the fruit in hot water, partook of the drink at night, and experienced a state of wakefulness. It is from this event that the monks determined to use this fruit to stay awake every night. Thus it is said that this handy fruit is more useful for nighttime prayer. (*A Discourse on Coffee: Its Description and Virtues*, 1671)

The root for the Latin referring to this state of wakefulness that can be brought about by taking coffee, *vigilantia* (as well as "to be awake [*vigilare, vigilia*]"), VEG, has sister-relationships with words in Indo-European etymology, such as the Greek *ygieinos*, or "healthy" or the Sanskrit *ugra* (powerful). Thus, according to this legend, the effects of coffee are not only to bring about a simple state of sleeplessness (*exsomnis*), but to bring about a state that includes a strong vitality. This can also be seen in *vigere,* a word akin to *vigilare* (to be awake), which means "to be powerfully lively." This is likely exactly why Naironus believed coffee to be "the best medicine for health." But the drinking of seven cups a day is somewhat questionable.

---

1. When Neumann interpreted the statue of a woman with a thin chest as symbolizing the "transformative character," the historical artifact he referenced was the goddess statue (Venus of Lespugue) excavated in Lespugue in the Haute-Garonne province of France. (But for some reason, in Neumann's original German, it is written as Lespugne.) It is a famous piece, so even if you have no interest in breasts, I recommend looking at it in art history or archaeology photo collections, yes? Those who can use the Internet can do a search on "Venus of Lespugue." But while this goddess statue is damaged, she has large breasts that hang all the way down to her abdomen, yes? Actually, in chapter eight of this same book, Neumann references this goddess statue as a historical example of a woman statue with large breasts. It's just that the breasts on this statue are so large that they hang down to her abdomen and her

chest area becomes flat, yes? Taking all this into account, there is doubt as to whether or not Neumann used appropriate material to support his arguments.

2. "*Shinsei*" is an anthropological term meaning "disposition." To express it in English, the most appropriate word would be "mentality."

3. Lévy-Brühl, in the preface of the Japanese translation of his work, amends his theory by stating that it is not necessarily true that any peoples or societies that are absolutely differentiated from civilization actually exist.

4. It is sometimes written as "Omar," but in Arabic, the O sounds like the U, so it is read "Umar."

5. Also called by Antoine Faust Naironi.

魔法先生ネギま！
MAGISTER NEGI MAGI

赤松 健 SHONEN MAGAZINE COMICS
KEN AKAMATSU

# 24

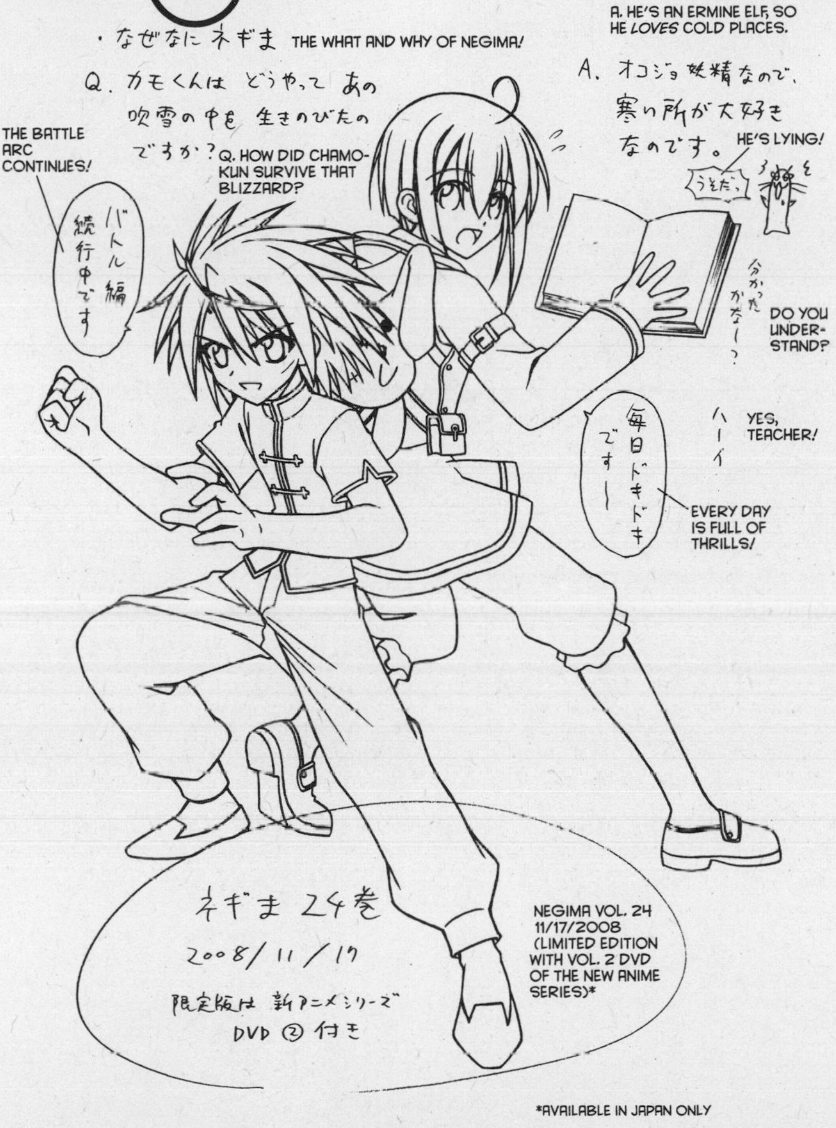

A. HE'S AN ERMINE ELF, SO HE *LOVES* COLD PLACES.
・なぜなにネギま THE WHAT AND WHY OF NEGIMA!
Q. カモくんは どうやって あの 吹雪の中を 生きのびたのですか？
Q. HOW DID CHAMO-KUN SURVIVE THAT BLIZZARD?
A. オコジョ妖精なので、寒い所が大好きなのです。
HE'S LYING!
うそだっ
THE BATTLE ARC CONTINUES!
バトル編続行中です
分かったかなー？
DO YOU UNDER-STAND?
毎日ドキドキです〜
ハーイ
YES, TEACHER!
EVERY DAY IS FULL OF THRILLS!
ネギま 24巻
2008/11/17
限定版は 新アニメシリーズ DVD ② 付き
NEGIMA VOL. 24
11/17/2008
(LIMITED EDITION WITH VOL. 2 DVD OF THE NEW ANIME SERIES)*


*AVAILABLE IN JAPAN ONLY

キャラ解説
CHARACTER
PROFILE

㉒ 鳴滝風香
(22) FŪKA NARUTAKI

双子ちゃんの 元気な方。(笑)
THE HYPER ONE OF THE TWINS. (LAUGH)

いわゆる「ボクっ娘」で、妹より
SHE'S THE SO-CALLED BOKUKKO, AND SHE'S TOUGHER, HAS

強気で ツリ目で ボーイッシュなん
SLANTIER EYES, AND IS MORE BOYISH THAN HER YOUNGER

ですが、オバケがこわかったりする
SISTER, BUT THEY'RE THE SAME IN THAT THEY'RE BOTH

ところは 同じです。かわいーよね♡
SCARED OF GHOSTS AND THINGS. AREN'T THEY CUTE ♡

何か 小学生 みたいですけど、中3です。
SHE LOOKS LIKE AN ELEMENTARY SCHOOL GIRL, BUT SHE'S A

高校生や 大学生になった姿を想像
THIRD-YEAR IN JUNIOR HIGH. I CAN'T IMAGINE WHAT SHE'LL LOOK

できないな・・・(笑)
LIKE WHEN SHE'S IN HIGH SCHOOL OR COLLEGE... (LAUGH)

アニメ版 CVは こやまきみこ さん。
IN THE ANIME, SHE IS VOICED BY KIMIKO KOYAMA-SAN. SHE'S

「陸上防衛隊 まおちゃん」から お世話になってます。
HELPED ME OUT SINCE MAO-CHAN. SHE'S THE AUTHORITY ON

ロリ声の オーソリティです! 歌もうまいよ。
LOLITA VOICES! AND SHE'S A GOOD SINGER.

ドラマ版は 片岡沙耶ちゃん♡
IN THE DRAMA, SHE IS PLAYED BY SAYA KATAOKA-CHAN ♡

撮影当時は 元気少女だったけど、
WHILE FILMING, SHE WAS AN ENERGETIC YOUNG

最近かなり 女らしくなってきた
GIRL, BUT RECENTLY I GET THE FEELING SHE'S BECOME

ような・・・(^^)
MORE OF A WOMAN... (^^)

そのうち グラビア アイドルになっちゃうんじゃ
MAYBE SHE'LL BE A BIKINI MODEL

ないかな?!
SOON?!

赤松
AKAMATSU

# Translation Notes

Japanese is a tricky language for most Westerners, and translation is often more art than science. For your edification and reading pleasure, here are notes on some of the places where we could have gone in a different direction with our translation of the work, or where a Japanese cultural reference is used.

## Volume 22

### That song, page iv

Anyone who has seen the *Negima!* anime would be familiar with its opening theme, "Happy [STAR] Material." This popular theme song is making a comeback for the new original animation DVD (OAD), *Negima ~ Ala Alba ~*.

### Tosaka, page 3

Literally, *tosaka* refers to the crest chicken's have on their heads. Kotarō isn't the only one to call this guy Tosaka, so it's unclear whether he's only calling him by name or insulting his hairstyle by calling him "chickenhead."

### Kanji obsession, page 104

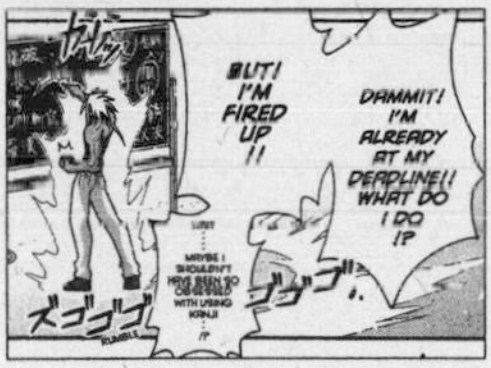
DAMMIT! I'M ALREADY AT MY DEADLINE!! WHAT DO I DO !?
BUT! I'M FIRED UP !!
ズゴゴゴ
RUMBLE

Up until now, Rakan's ideas for attack names have been made entirely of kanji, or Chinese characters, because, as we all know, attack names look that much more awesome when written out in Chinese. Unfortunately, he's having a hard time finding the right Chinese characters to look cool and sound cool at the same time. It probably doesn't help that the kanji that would be pronounced "Negi" means "spring onion."

## Aho, page 112

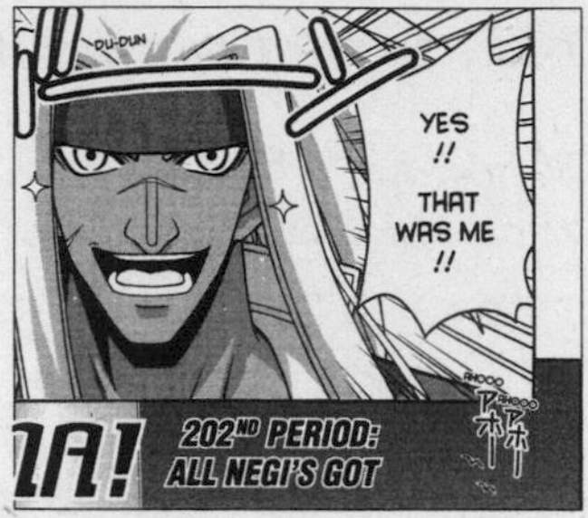
DU-DUN
YES !! THAT WAS ME !!
202ND PERIOD: ALL NEGI'S GOT

The *Negima!* world isn't the only one where the birds have the slightly unusual cry of "aho." They tend to fly by crying it when characters are being especially silly or moronic, as *aho* is Japanese for "moron."

## Shut-in, page 157

In Japan, a shut-in, or *hikikomori,* is someone who has such a hard time dealing with the social pressures of life that they completely refuse to leave their home, and sometimes even refuse to leave their room, for an extended period of time. Negi obviously isn't quite that bad yet, but the way he keeps worrying so much about everything and taking everything onto himself, if he's not careful, Rakan can see where he might end up as one.

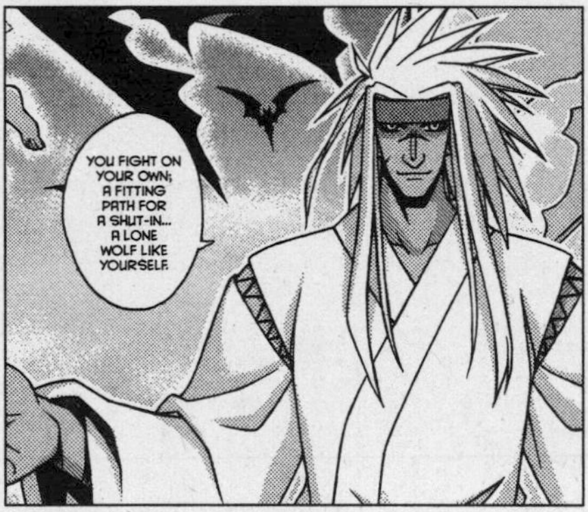
YOU FIGHT ON YOUR OWN; A FITTING PATH FOR A SHUT-IN... A LONE WOLF LIKE YOURSELF.

## Lineage Girl, page 178

When the video game Lineage II came out in Japan, they promoted it by having young idols cosplay as Lineage characters and make appearances at stores and events. Madoka Ichikawa was one of these girls.

## Volume 23

### *Bakusa and bakuenjin*, page 186

*Bakusa* means binding chain. Kaede uses it to restrain the dragon before using *bakuenjin*, which means "exploding flame army."

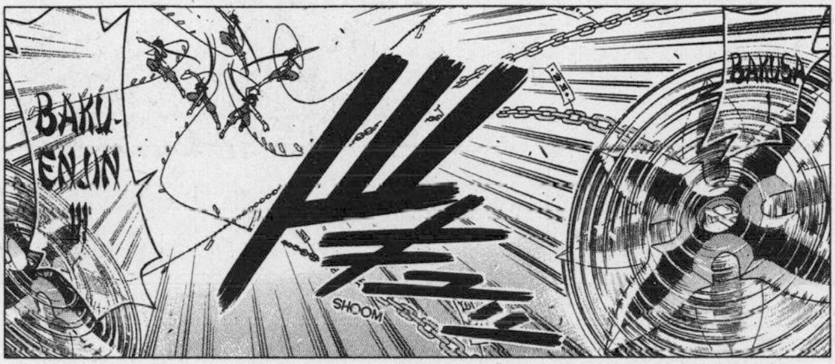
BAKUSA
BAKU-ENJIN !!!
SHOOM

### Negima Club +alpha, page 216

The Greek letter alpha is used to represent an unknown factor. In Japan, when something comes with extras, sometimes they say the name of the thing "+(plus) alpha." In this case, the +alpha refers to the girls who are not in the Negima Club, and Negima Club +alpha means "Negima Club and some others."

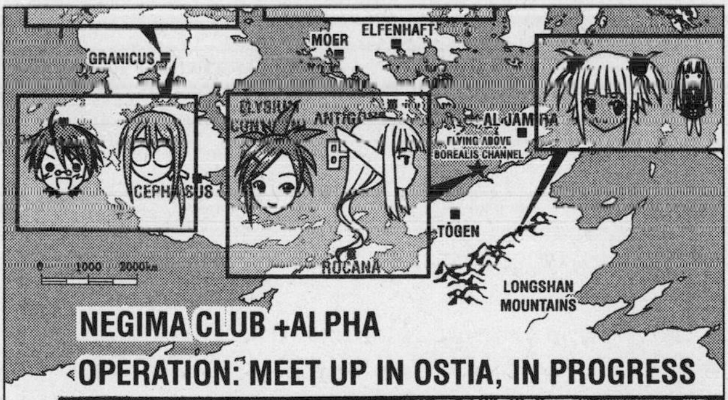
MOER
ELFENHAFT
GRANICUS
AL JAMIRA
FLYING ABOVE BOREALIS CHANNEL
CEPHALSUS
TŌGEN
ROCANA
1000 2000km
LONGSHAN MOUNTAINS
NEGIMA CLUB +ALPHA
OPERATION: MEET UP IN OSTIA, IN PROGRESS

## Chibisuke, page 216

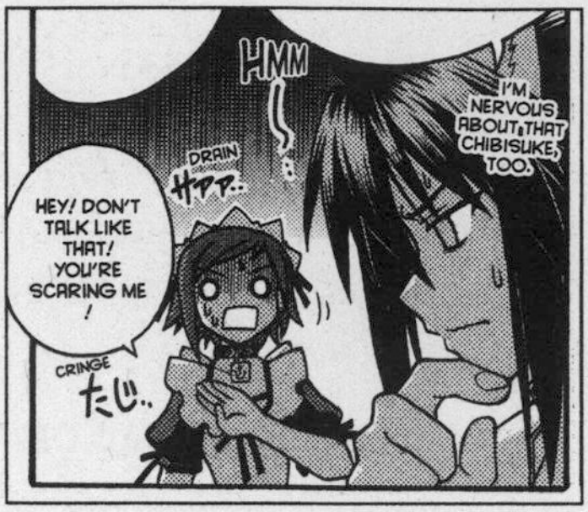
I'M NERVOUS ABOUT THAT CHIBISUKE, TOO.
HMM
DRAIN
HEY! DON'T TALK LIKE THAT! YOU'RE SCARING ME!
CRINGE

Kotarō can't let go of the fact that Yue is very short (maybe it makes him feel better about himself?), so he calls her Chibisuke. *Chibi* roughly means "shorty," and adding *suke* to it makes it a boy's name. Incidentally, Yuekichi, another of Yue's nicknames, is also more masculine.

## Fate-han, page 252

Tsukuyomi, being from the Kansai region of Japan, uses a thick Kansai dialect—so thick that she uses "*han*" instead of "*san*."

## *Annin dofu*, page 256

*Annin dofu* is a kind of dessert made with a jelly made from *annin* (apricot seeds), fruit, and syrup.

## XX-puta, page 321

What Konoka is preventing herself from saying (most likely for copyright reasons) is the name of a certain castle in the sky, featured in a film by Studio Ghibli. We won't tell you what it is, but it starts with L and rhymes with "Raputa."

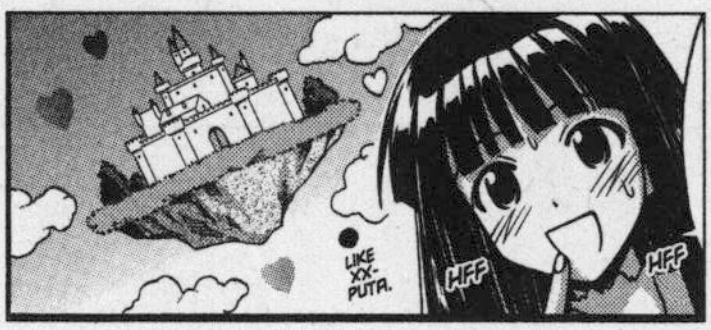
HFF
HFF
LIKE XX-PUTA.

## *Setsunakute* Labyrinth, page 339

This is the title of a song from the third Negima!? PS2 game, sung, as mentioned, by Shizuka Itoh, the voice actress who plays Misa Kakizaki.

## Volume 24

### Nagi-man, page 331

Nagi-man is short for "Nagi *manjū*." A *manjū* is a steamed yeast bun with filling. In this case, they probably have Nagi's face printed on them to commemorate the great war hero.

### Bamboo shoots after rain, page 332

This is a figure of speech in Japan referring to the same thing happening over and over very quickly, like how bamboo shoots grow like crazy after it has rained. We can only imagine how many bounty hunters Setsuna and the others had to fight off.

### World uniforms, page 362

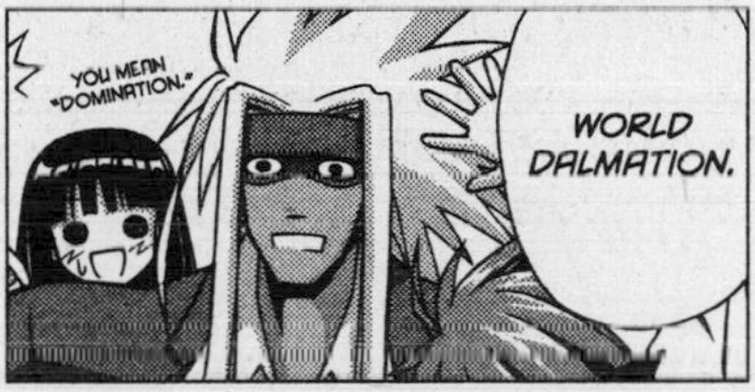
WORLD DALMATION.
YOU MEAN "DOMINATION."

Rakan's mistake isn't quite as random as it may seem at first. In Japanese, the word *seifuku* can mean "domination" (as in world domination) or "uniform" (as in high school uniform), depending on which Chinese characters are used. Rakan uses the characters for "uniforms," though whether he did it on purpose or because he's always thinking about girls in cute outfits remains a mystery.

### Chibi Chiu, page 382

*Chibi* is a Japanese word referring to someone small, and is usually not very flattering. But in this case, because it sounds so nice with Chisame's nickname, Chiu, she wants Negi to use it because it's so cute.

## Alexander Zaitsev, page 405

While this is the name that Chiko☆Tan chose out of shame for his real name, it may be interesting to note that he gets it from a Russian figure-skating champion.

## Kai●-ken, page 432

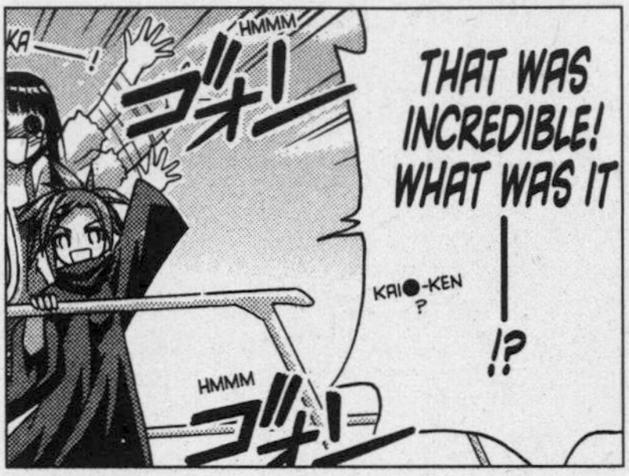
KA—!
HMMM
THAT WAS INCREDIBLE! WHAT WAS IT—!?
KAI●-KEN?
HMMM

Asakura is being censored as she tries to use the copyrighted name Kaio-ken, a technique Dragonball fans will recognize as the one Goku learns from King Kai. Like Negi's technique, it gives the user an enormous boost in strength, but can also damage the user's body.

## Nagi-Koji, page 462

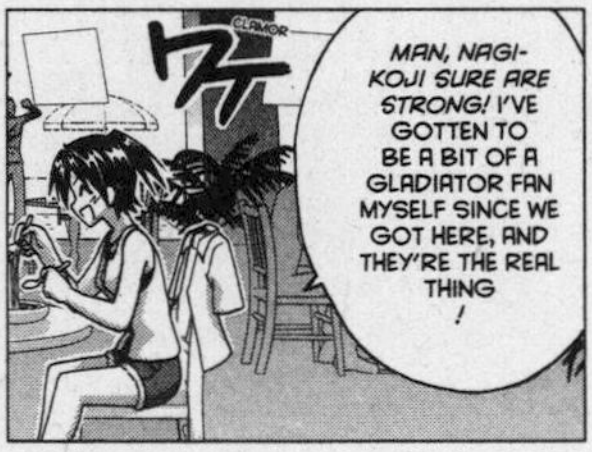
CLAMOR
MAN, NAGI-KOJI SURE ARE STRONG! I'VE GOTTEN TO BE A BIT OF A GLADIATOR FAN MYSELF SINCE WE GOT HERE, AND THEY'RE THE REAL THING!

Maybe because of the way their writing system works in Japan, instead of using initials to shorten things, they'll use the first two syllables of each thing in the phrase. For example, "personal computer" becomes "perso-com (or *pasocon,* for Japanese pronunciation)" instead of PC. In this case, they're using it to refer to pairs of people, like Nagi-Koji for Nagi and Kojirō, or Kono-Setsu for Konoka and Setsuna.

## *Bokukko*, page 502

In Japanese, there are several different ways to say "I," many of which are used mainly by one gender. *Boku* is a first-person pronoun that is usually used by men, but there are some girls who use it, too, like Fūka, and they are called *bokukko,* or "*boku* girls."